WEST ACADEMIC PUBLISHING'S LAW SCHOOL ADVISORY BOARD

JESSE H. CHOPER
Professor of Law and Dean Emeritus
University of California, Berkeley

JOSHUA DRESSLER
Distinguished University Professor Emeritus, Frank R. Strong Chair in Law
Michael E. Moritz College of Law, The Ohio State University

YALE KAMISAR
Professor of Law Emeritus, University of San Diego
Professor of Law Emeritus, University of Michigan

MARY KAY KANE
Professor of Law, Chancellor and Dean Emeritus
University of California, Hastings College of the Law

LARRY D. KRAMER
President, William and Flora Hewlett Foundation

JONATHAN R. MACEY
Professor of Law, Yale Law School

ARTHUR R. MILLER
University Professor, New York University
Formerly Bruce Bromley Professor of Law, Harvard University

GRANT S. NELSON
Professor of Law Emeritus, Pepperdine University
Professor of Law Emeritus, University of California, Los Angeles

A. BENJAMIN SPENCER
Justice Thurgood Marshall Distinguished Professor of Law
University of Virginia School of Law

JAMES J. WHITE
Robert A. Sullivan Professor of Law Emeritus
University of Michigan

SPORTS AND THE LAW
TEXT, CASES, AND PROBLEMS

Sixth Edition

■ ■ ■

Paul C. Weiler
Friendly Professor of Law
Harvard Law School

Gary R. Roberts
Dean Emeritus & Gerald L. Bepko Professor
Indiana University Robert H. McKinney School of Law

Roger I. Abrams
Richardson Professor of Law
Northeastern University

Stephen F. Ross
Professor of Law
Lewis H. Vovakis Distinguished Faculty Scholar
The Pennsylvania State University

Michael C. Harper
Professor of Law and Barreca Labor Relations Scholar
Boston University

Jodi S. Balsam
Associate Professor of Clinical Law
Brooklyn Law School

William W. Berry III
Associate Professor of Law
Frank Montague, Jr. Professor of Legal Studies and Professionalism
The University of Mississippi School of Law

AMERICAN CASEBOOK SERIES®

The publisher is not engaged in rendering legal or other professional advice, and this publication is not a substitute for the advice of an attorney. If you require legal or other expert advice, you should seek the services of a competent attorney or other professional.

American Casebook Series is a trademark registered in the U.S. Patent and Trademark Office.

COPYRIGHT © 1993 WEST PUBLISHING CO.
© 1998, 2004 West, a Thomson Business
© 2011 Thomson Reuters
© 2015 LEG, Inc. d/b/a West Academic
© 2019 LEG, Inc. d/b/a West Academic
    444 Cedar Street, Suite 700
    St. Paul, MN 55101
    1-877-888-1330

West, West Academic Publishing, and West Academic are trademarks of West Publishing Corporation, used under license.

Printed in the United States of America

ISBN: 978-1-64020-235-1

Dedications

* * *

By Steve Ross to Mary Wujek

* * *

By Michael Harper to Marvis Knospe

* * *

By Jodi Balsam to Craig Balsam

* * *

By Will Berry to
Stephanie, Eleanor, William, and Caroline Berry

PREFACE

The sports field has grown to become a multi-billion-dollar industry from its origins in social groups such as the Knickerbocker Club formed in the late 19th Century, which provided sedentary white-collar workers with an opportunity for athletic exercise and gambling, followed by socializing and drinking. The business and law of sports in America has been the subject of this text since Professors Paul Weiler and Gary Roberts published the first edition in 1993. Professors Roger Abrams and Stephen Ross joined the team for the fourth edition in 2011. This sixth edition was prepared by Ross, a leading expert on the operation of sports leagues throughout the world as well as on antitrust law, and three new co-authors, with fresh eyes and perspectives. Professor Michael Harper, a nationally-noted labor law scholar, following Weiler and Abrams, redrafted and updated labor chapters and provided expertise for this edition. Additional new expertise and background comes from Professors Jodi Balsam (intellectual property and sports league in-house counsel) and Will Berry (intercollegiate sports), both of whom redrafted and updated several of the sixth edition's chapters.[*]

Those who have adopted the book for law school courses on the legal issues arising in the business of sports will find that this edition covers all the familiar topics and a few new areas as well. Once again, we have abjured attempting to re-teach basic common law principles reviewed in the first year. Although the day-to-day life of most sports lawyers may principally involve contract negotiation and commercial and tort litigation, the book retains the view that the student of sports law is best served by understanding the business dynamics of sports. This is best communicated in substantial part through the lens of three foundational mainstays of Sports Law—labor law, antitrust law, and intellectual property law, each of which are becoming increasingly relevant to sports at the college level as well. We have expanded our discussion of the basic principles in each field in recognition that not all upper-level students will have studied these topics before venturing into Sports Law. We feel that this course offers an alternative means to introduce student to all three fields. The work also reflects an appreciation that much of sports law is decided not by courts but by private tribunals, with a greater emphasis on labor arbitration and

---

[*] As scholars, the current co-authors come to this effort with well-established views on many of the topics discussed. That said, two of the current co-authors have been compensated by parties on some of the cases, and believe that some readers would want to know this. Jodi Balsam acted for the NFL in litigation from 1994–2002, which includes the *Sullivan* case (Chapter 7) and litigation surrounding intellectual property between the league and the Dallas Cowboys (Chapters 7 and 8), among other matters. Steve Ross consulted with plaintiffs' counsel in the *Laumann* case (Chapter 7).

internal decisionmaking within the unique institution of college sports, the NCAA. NCAA regulation offers an excellent case study in private control of collective endeavor.

The first chapter of the text has been reorganized to emphasize the extraordinary power vested in league commissioners to solve governance problems in club-run leagues, and to address the best interests of sport. Raising the issue of the scope of external law to constrain internal sports league decisions, the edition moves to concentrated coverage of issues in labor law, including instruction in the basic principles that govern all major North American sports where players have selected unions as their exclusive bargaining representative. The casebook then turns to basic principles of antitrust law that govern closely integrated industries requiring cooperation among firms, and then examines the interaction between antitrust and labor law. The antitrust chapters are designed to provide (in Chapter 5) a basic introduction that can suffice for those teaching shorter courses or not emphasizing antitrust, and then detailing labor, product, and collegiate issues separately.

After the antitrust review, the book comprehensively examines the intersection of intellectual property law with the world of sports, and then treats the regulation of sports agents. The next three chapters consider college sports, emphasizing the role of the NCAA as a private regulatory body and the impact of Title IX. The book's last two chapters consider Olympic sports and the legal regulation of health and safety in sports competitions.

The young men of the Knickerbockers discovered that the exploding growth of New York City had squeezed them out of Manhattan. The railroads took the club's playing field for their trains, and thus required the men to find a new home for their game of baseball. They ferried across the Hudson River to the aptly named "Elysian Fields" on the heights of Hoboken, New Jersey. It was there on June 19, 1846, that they played their new game against a rival team made up of former members of the club. With rapid speed, clubs up and down the eastern seaboard and then west across America adopted the rules of the Knickerbockers' game. Football, hockey and basketball followed, as professional team sports became America's secular passion. We have tried in this text to present many of the legal issues generated not only by these professional sports, but also by amateur and other sports as well. We are certain that other issues will arise as sports continue to expand globally. For now, this sixth edition of the book will introduce users to the most salient of the current issues.

STEPHEN F. ROSS
MICHAEL C. HARPER
JODI S. BALSAM
WILLIAM W. BERRY III

September 2018

ACKNOWLEDGMENTS

We first acknowledge our colleagues, Paul Weiler and Gary Roberts, for their inspired decision to take a traditional casebook and turn it into the definitive textbook on the law and the business of sports. Our work has been substantially aided by Roger Abrams' contribution to the fourth and fifth additions. In addition to the insights provided in prior editions, the current co-authors would also like to acknowledge and thank the many colleagues, sports law professors, academics from other disciplines who study sports, practicing sports lawyers, and industry executives—too numerous to name—who over the years have generously shared their own expertise in helping us shape our own perspectives that we were able to apply in crafting revisions to this book.

Each of us benefited from the work of one or more research assistants on the Sixth Edition. At Penn State, Steve Ross would like to thank James Mitsos for timely and helpful work. At Boston University School of Law, Michael Harper would like to thank Kelly Schmidt. At Brooklyn Law School, Jodi Balsam would like to thank Jaron Berman for excellent research assistance. At the University of Mississippi School of Law, Will Berry would like to thank the following students for their research assistance and feedback: Melissa Baker, Rachel Buddrus, Emily Lovelass, McRae Young, and Alayna Murphy.

Summary of Contents

Preface V
Acknowledgments VII
Table of Cases XXV

Chapter 1. Introduction: Commissioner-Led Professional Sports Leagues in North America 1
A. The Legal Status of Professional Sports Leagues 3
B. The History and Legal Authority of the Sports League Commissioner ... 9
C. The Legal Scope of the Commissioner's Authority over Conduct Detrimental to the General Welfare of the Game 14
D. The Commissioner's Function in Protecting the League's Reputation 36

Chapter 2. Labor Law and Collective Bargaining in Professional Sports 71
A. Introduction to National Labor Law 71
B. Application of the Labor Act to Sports 74
C. Union Activity and Employer Retaliation 79
D. Appropriate Bargaining Unit in Sports Leagues 85
E. Union's Exclusive Bargaining Authority 91
F. Duty to Bargain in Good Faith 96
G. Economic Conflict in Sports Labor Relations 106
H. Duty of Fair Representation 115

Chapter 3. Labor Arbitration in Professional Sports 121
A. Contract Interpretation Through Arbitration 123
B. Arbitration of Disciplinary Disputes 127
C. Arbitration of Drug Usage Discipline 141
D. Arbitration as an Exclusive Remedy; § 301 Preemption 148
E. Salary Arbitration 155
F. Judicial Review of Arbitration Awards 165

Chapter 4. Contractual Restraints on Labor Mobility in Professional Sports 185
A. Standards for Enforcement of Contractual Mobility Restraints 185
B. The Reserve System and Its Demise 205
C. Current Restraints—Salary Caps and Taxes 228
D. Baseball's Antitrust Exemption 231

Chapter 5. Basic Principles of Antitrust Law Applied to the Special Nature of the Sports Industry 249
A. Introduction 249

B. General Background to Antitrust Law 250
C. Applying the "Rule of Reason" to Sports League Restraints 256
D. The Nature of a Sports League: Are League Rules the Product of a "Single Entity" or an Agreement Among Competing Club Owners? 274
E. The Problem of Monopoly in Professional Sports 299

Chapter 6. Antitrust Regulation and Business Strategy in Sports Labor Markets 331
A. A Recap of Relevant Learning from Earlier Chapters 331
B. Economic Analysis of Restraints in the Players Market 332
C. Antitrust Analysis of Specific Player Market Restraints 341
D. Labor Exemption from Antitrust 367
E. The Business Dynamics of Regulating Sports Labor Markets 413

Chapter 7. Business Strategy and Antitrust Scrutiny of Internal League Regulation of Inter-Club Competition 419
A. Franchise Ownership Rules 420
B. Admission and Relocation of Sports Franchises 439
C. Television Contracts 469
D. Group Licensing of Merchandise and Related Intellectual Property Rights 510
E. Bargaining Dynamics in Sports League Decision-Making About Commercial Practices 532

Chapter 8. Intellectual Property Law and Sports 539
A. Real-Time Game Accounts and the Right to Broadcast Games 541
B. Copyright in the Game Broadcasts 558
C. Athlete Publicity Rights 574
D. Trademark Rights 608

Chapter 9. Agent Representation of the Athlete 649
A. Legal Relationship Between Sports Agents and Athlete-Clients 651
B. Breakdowns in the Agent-Athlete Relationship 657
C. Agent Representation of Unionized Athletes 677
D. Agent Recruiting of College Athletes 699
E. Government Regulation of Agents 710

Chapter 10. Intercollegiate Sports: The NCAA and Its Member Institutions 719
A. Background 719
B. Procedural Due Process 722
C. Antitrust Limits on the NCAA's Institutional Oversight 734
D. Contracts 743
E. NCAA Infractions 760

Chapter 11. Intercollegiate Sports: The Athlete-University Relationship 787
A. Recruiting and Scholarships 787

B. The Student-Athlete 824
C. Challenging the Student-Athlete Model 880

Chapter 12. Gender Equity in Sports **913**
A. Administrative Development of Title IX 914
B. Resources 917
C. Athletic Program Administration 962
D. Access 969

Chapter 13. International and Olympic Sports **981**
A. Role of International Organizations 983
B. The United States in International Sports 989
C. Recent Cases in International Sport 1014

Chapter 14. Health and Safety Issues in Sports **1049**
A. Injuries from Playing the Game 1049
B. Health and Safety off the Field 1074
C. Disability and the Right to Play 1096

INDEX 1125

TABLE OF CONTENTS

PREFACE V
ACKNOWLEDGMENTS VII
TABLE OF CASES XXV

Chapter 1. Introduction: Commissioner-Led Professional Sports Leagues in North America 1
A. The Legal Status of Professional Sports Leagues 3
   1. A Brief History 3
   2. League Constitutions 4
   3. Sports Leagues as Joint Ventures of Club Owners 5
   4. Comparative Perspectives 5
   5. An Economic Analysis of League Structure 6
   6. Fiduciary Duties and League Governance 7
B. The History and Legal Authority of the Sports League Commissioner ... 9
   Notes and Questions 13
C. The Legal Scope of the Commissioner's Authority over Conduct Detrimental to the General Welfare of the Game 14
   Milwaukee Amer. Ass'n v. Landis 17
   Charles O. Finley v. Bowie Kuhn 21
   Notes and Questions 35
D. The Commissioner's Function in Protecting the League's Reputation 36
   1. Targeting Players for On-Field Injury 38
      In the Matter of New Orleans Saints Pay-for-Performance ("Bountygate") 38
   2. Offensive Personal Behavior and Changing Social Attitudes 49
   3. Gambling 54
      (a) Traditional Aversion to Any Form of Gambling 54
      (b) The Rapid Move Toward Legalized Gambling 56
      (c) Current Legislative Issues Regarding Legalized Sports Gambling 60
         Notes and Questions 63
   4. Drugs of Abuse and Performance Enhancing Drugs 65
   5. Beyond Protection of League Reputation? 66
      (a) Breach of Trust 66
      (b) External Social Policies: Defer to Private Governance, or Subject to Outside Legal Prohibitions? 68

Chapter 2. Labor Law and Collective Bargaining in Professional Sports 71
A. Introduction to National Labor Law 71

xiv   TABLE OF CONTENTS

B.   Application of the Labor Act to Sports 74
       American League of Professional Baseball Clubs & Ass'n of National
           Baseball League Umpires 75
       Notes and Questions 77
C.   Union Activity and Employer Retaliation 79
       Seattle Seahawks v. NFLPA & Sam McCullum 80
       Notes and Questions 84
D.   Appropriate Bargaining Unit in Sports Leagues 85
       North American Soccer League v. NLRB 87
       Notes and Questions 90
E.   Union's Exclusive Bargaining Authority 91
       Morio v. North American Soccer League 91
F.   Duty to Bargain in Good Faith 96
       Silverman v. Major League Baseball Player Relations Committee 101
       Notes and Questions 106
G.   Economic Conflict in Sports Labor Relations 106
       NFL Management Council and NFLPA 107
       Notes and Questions 111
       Notes and Questions 114
H.   Duty of Fair Representation 115
       Peterson v. Kennedy and NFLPA 116
       Notes and Questions 120

Chapter 3. Labor Arbitration in Professional Sports 121
A.   Contract Interpretation Through Arbitration 123
       Alvin Moore & Atlanta Braves 124
       Notes and Questions 126
B.   Arbitration of Disciplinary Disputes 127
       In re Latrell Sprewell 127
       Notes and Questions 138
C.   Arbitration of Drug Usage Discipline 141
       Major League Baseball Players Association and Office of the
           Commissioner of Baseball 143
       Notes and Questions 147
D.   Arbitration as an Exclusive Remedy; § 301 Preemption 148
       Williams v. National Football League 149
       Notes and Questions 154
E.   Salary Arbitration 155
       New Jersey Devils and Scott Gomez 157
       Notes and Questions 164
F.   Judicial Review of Arbitration Awards 165
       Major League Baseball Players Association v. Garvey 166
       Notes and Questions 170
       National Football League Players Ass'n v. National Football League
           (Peterson) 171
       Notes and Questions 182

Chapter 4. Contractual Restraints on Labor Mobility in Professional Sports 185

A. Standards for Enforcement of Contractual Mobility Restraints 185
    Philadelphia Ball Club v. Lajoie 186
    Notes and Questions 190
    Cincinnati Bengals v. Bergey 193
    Notes and Questions 197
    Boston Celtics v. Brian Shaw 200
    Notes and Questions 204
B. The Reserve System and Its Demise 205
    American League Baseball Club of Chicago v. Chase 206
    National & American League Professional Baseball Clubs v. Major League Baseball Players Association 213
    Notes and Questions 219
    Kansas City Royals v. Major League Baseball Players Ass'n 220
    Notes and Questions 224
C. Current Restraints—Salary Caps and Taxes 228
    Notes and Questions 230
D. Baseball's Antitrust Exemption 231
    Flood v. Kuhn 232
    Notes and Questions 242
    Curt Flood Act of 1998 244
    Notes and Questions 245

Chapter 5. Basic Principles of Antitrust Law Applied to the Special Nature of the Sports Industry 249

A. Introduction 249
B. General Background to Antitrust Law 250
    1. The Purposes of the Antitrust Laws 251
    2. The Applicable § 1 Antitrust Standard: *Per Se* or Rule of Reason? 252
C. Applying the "Rule of Reason" to Sports League Restraints 256
    NCAA v. Board of Regents of the Univ. of Oklahoma & Univ. of Georgia Athletic Ass'n 258
    Notes and Questions 272
D. The Nature of a Sports League: Are League Rules the Product of a "Single Entity" or an Agreement Among Competing Club Owners? 274
    1. Single Entity Defense 274
        American Needle, Inc. v. NFL 276
        Notes and Questions 285
    2. Alternative League Structures 294
    3. Non-Antitrust Contexts for Considering the Issue 298
E. The Problem of Monopoly in Professional Sports 299
    1. Antitrust Law and Monopoly Power 302
    2. Monopoly Power and Expansion 307
    3. Monopolizing Conduct and Monopolizing the Supply of Players 310

    Philadelphia World Hockey Club v. Philadelphia Hockey Club 311
  4. Monopolizing Stadiums 316
  5. Television Contracts and Other Monopolistic Practices 320
  6. Monopoly Leveraging 323
    Notes and Questions 325

Chapter 6. Antitrust Regulation and Business Strategy in Sports Labor Markets 331
A. A Recap of Relevant Learning from Earlier Chapters 331
B. Economic Analysis of Restraints in the Players Market 332
  1. Types of Player Restraints 332
  2. Economic Effects of Player Restraints 333
  3. Justifications for Player Restraints 334
  4. Alternatives to Player Restraints 338
  5. Do Player Restraints Achieve Their Desired Pro-Competitive Objective? 339
  6. Are Player Restraints Needed Because of Irrational Club Behavior? 339
    Notes and Questions 340
C. Antitrust Analysis of Specific Player Market Restraints 341
  1. Rookie Draft 341
    Smith v. Pro Football, Inc. 342
    Notes and Questions 353
  2. Veteran Free Agency 355
    Mackey v. NFL (Part 1) 355
    Notes and Questions 362
    Fraser v. Major League Soccer 363
    Notes and Questions 366
D. Labor Exemption from Antitrust 367
  1. History and Background 367
    (a) The Statutory Exemption 368
    (b) The "Non-Statutory" Labor Exemption 369
  2. Judicial Options for the Nonstatutory Labor Exemption 372
  3. Initial Development of the Doctrine in the Lower Courts 373
    (a) The Outer Limits of the Exemption: It Exists but Does Not Protect All Labor-Market Restraints 373
    (b) Application to Restraints Agreed to by the Union but Sought by Management 374
  4. The Supreme Court Speaks 377
    Brown v. Pro Football, Inc. 378
    Notes and Questions 389
  5. Eligibility to Play in Unionized Professional Sports Post-*Brown* 391
    Clarett v. NFL 391
    Notes and Questions 399
  6. Union Responses Post-*Brown* 399
    Brady v. NFL 400

		Notes and Questions 412
E.	The Business Dynamics of Regulating Sports Labor Markets............. 413	
	First Exercise: Constructing Labor Market Rules................................. 414	
	Second Exercise: Negotiating Rules with the Union 415	
	Third Exercise: Individual "Rights" Versus General Welfare............... 416	
	Fourth Exercise: Maneuvering to Advantage in the Future.................. 417	

Chapter 7. Business Strategy and Antitrust Scrutiny of Internal League Regulation of Inter-Club Competition............................. 419

A. Franchise Ownership Rules.. 420
    NASL v. NFL 422
    Notes and Questions 425
    Sullivan v. NFL 426
    Notes and Questions 438
B. Admission and Relocation of Sports Franchises 439
    1. League Refusals to Permit a Club's Relocation............................. 441
       Los Angeles Memorial Coliseum Comm'n v. NFL (Raiders I)....... 442
       NBA v. San Diego Clippers Basketball Club 453
       Notes and Questions 454
    2. League Controls over Entry/Contraction 457
       Mid-South Grizzlies v. NFL 457
       Notes and Questions 461
    3. The Limits of Antitrust: Alternative Non-Antitrust Approaches to Stakeholder Interests in Franchise Movement......................... 463
       (a) Blocking an Undesired Relocation Based on State and Local Government Law or Federal, State, or Local Environmental Laws 463
       (b) Protective Lease Terms 464
       (c) Eminent Domain... 466
       (d) Direct State Legislation 466
       (e) Federal Legislative Reform... 467
          Notes and Questions... 469
C. Television Contracts.. 469
    United States v. NFL 470
    Notes and Questions 474
    1. Collective Selling of Pooled Rights and the Sports Broadcasting Act of 1961... 475
       Notes and Questions 479
    2. League Restrictions on the Sale of Television Rights by Individual Clubs 480
       Chicago Professional Sports Ltd. & WGN v. NBA (Bulls I) 482
       Chicago Professional Sports Ltd. Partnership & WGN v. NBA (Bulls II) 489
       Notes and Questions 492
       Laumann v. NHL... 494
       A Note on Revenue Sharing... 502

3. Vertical Integration of Media Companies and Access to Sports Broadcasting 503
    Comcast Cable Communications, LLC v. Federal Communications Commission 504
    Notes and Questions 508
D. Group Licensing of Merchandise and Related Intellectual Property Rights 510
    Topps Chewing Gum v. Major League Baseball Players Ass'n 513
    Notes and Questions 515
    Major League Baseball Properties, Inc. v. Salvino, Inc. 518
    Notes and Questions 531
E. Bargaining Dynamics in Sports League Decision-Making About Commercial Practices 532
    First Exercise: Revenue Sharing 534
    Second Exercise: Ownership Policies 534
    Third Exercise: Franchise Relocation 535
    Fourth Exercise: New Entry 536
    Fifth Exercise: Internet Baseball 536
    Sixth Exercise: Innovative Club Marketing 537
    A Final Note: Overall Restructuring of the League 537

Chapter 8. Intellectual Property Law and Sports 539
A. Real-Time Game Accounts and the Right to Broadcast Games 541
    1. Common Law Property Rights in Live Game Accounts 542
        Pittsburgh Athletic Co. v. KQV Broadcasting Co. 542
        Notes and Questions 544
    2. Contractual Solutions to Game Broadcast Ownership 546
    3. Advancing Technology and Appropriation of Real-Time Game Accounts 547
        NBA v. Motorola 547
        Notes and Questions 552
    4. Property Rights in Internet Reporting 553
        Morris Communications Corporation v. PGA Tour 554
        Notes and Questions 557
B. Copyright in the Game Broadcasts 558
    1. No Copyright Protection for Ideas or Facts 558
    2. Fair Use of Copyrighted Works 559
        New Boston Television v. Entertainment Sports Programming Network (ESPN) 559
        Notes and Questions 561
    3. Public Performance of Copyrighted Works 563
        American Broadcasting Companies, Inc. v. Aereo, Inc. 565
        Notes and Questions 569
    4. Passive Carrier Exemption to Public Performance 570
    5. Superstations and the Compulsory Licensing-Royalty Scheme 571
        Notes and Questions 574

C. Athlete Publicity Rights 574
   1. Origins of the Right of Publicity 575
   2. Identifiability of the Publicity-Right Owner 577
   3. Scope of the Common Law Right of Publicity 579
   4. First Amendment and the Right of Publicity: Introduction 580
      ETW Corp. v. Jireh Publishing, Inc. 584
      Notes and Questions 588
   5. First-Sale Doctrine 589
      Notes and Questions 591
   6. Game Broadcasts and the Right of Publicity 592
      Notes and Questions 593
   7. First Amendment Defense and Ancillary Entertainment
      Products 595
      C.B.C. Distribution and Marketing, Inc. v. Major League
         Baseball Advanced Media, L.P. 596
      In re NCAA Student-Athlete Name & Likeness Licensing
         Litigation 600
      Notes and Questions 605
D. Trademark Rights 608
   1. Sports Team Names 609
      Indianapolis Colts v. Metropolitan Baltimore Football Club 610
      Notes and Questions 615
   2. Other Sports Phrases and Designations 616
      Notes and Questions 618
   3. Merchandising of Sports Trademarks 619
      Boston Professional Hockey Association v. Dallas Cap and
         Emblem Mfg., Inc. 620
      Notes and Questions 624
   4. Fair Use of a Trademark 626
      WCVB-TV v. Boston Athletic Ass'n 627
      Notes and Questions 631
   5. Trademark Dilution 633
      Notes and Questions 634
   6. Ambush Marketing 635
      Notes and Questions 638
   7. First Amendment Considerations in Trademark 638
      Notes and Questions 640
      Matal v. Tam 641
      Notes and Questions 647

Chapter 9. Agent Representation of the Athlete 649
A. Legal Relationship Between Sports Agents and Athlete-Clients 651
   1. Agency Law Basics 651
   2. Standards for Agent Performance 652
      Zinn v. Parrish 653
      Notes and Questions 656

B. Breakdowns in the Agent-Athlete Relationship 657
    1. Agent Breach of Fiduciary Duties to Athlete-Client 657
        Williams v. CWI, Inc. 658
        Notes and Questions 661
    2. Duty to Act Loyally for Principal's Benefit: Fee Disputes 663
        Brown v. Woolf 663
        Notes and Questions 665
    3. Agent Conflicts of Interest 666
        Detroit Lions and Billy Sims v. Jerry Argovitz 667
        Notes and Questions 671
    4. Disputes Between Sports Agents 672
        Speakers of Sport, Inc. v. ProServ, Inc. 673
        Notes and Questions 676
C. Agent Representation of Unionized Athletes 677
    1. Union Authority to Regulate Agents 678
        Collins v. NBPA & Grantham 679
        Notes and Questions 682
        Barry Rona and Major League Baseball Players Association 684
        Notes and Questions 687
    2. Examples and Impact of Player Association Agent Regulation 688
        NFLPA Regulations Governing Contract Advisors 688
        Notes and Questions 695
    3. Agent as Contract Negotiator in Unionized Sports: Dealing with the CBA Constraints 697
        Notes and Questions 698
D. Agent Recruiting of College Athletes 699
    1. Agent Recruiting Tactics and Enforceability of Representation Agreements 699
        Norby Walters and Lloyd Bloom v. Brent Fullwood 700
        Notes and Questions 703
    2. Enforcing NCAA Amateurism Rules Against Agent Misconduct 705
        United States v. Norby Walters 706
        Notes and Questions 709
E. Government Regulation of Agents 710
    1. State Legislation 710
    2. Federal Legislation 713
    3. Ethics Rules Governing Attorney-Agents 714
        Notes and Questions 717

Chapter 10. Intercollegiate Sports: The NCAA and Its Member Institutions 719
A. Background 719
    Notes and Questions 722
B. Procedural Due Process 722
    NCAA v. Tarkanian 723
    Notes and Questions 729

		Notes and Questions 733
C.	Antitrust Limits on the NCAA's Institutional Oversight...................... 734
	NCAA v. Board of Regents of the Univ. of Oklahoma & Univ. of Georgia Athletic Ass'n.. 734
	Notes and Questions 734
	Law v. NCAA... 737
	Notes and Questions 743
D.	Contracts.. 743
	1.	Coaching Contracts 744
		Vanderbilt University v. DiNardo... 744
		Notes and Questions 752
	2.	Conference Realignment... 754
		ACC v. University of Maryland 754
		Notes and Questions 759
E.	NCAA Infractions 760
	1.	The Death Penalty.. 761
		Southern Methodist University Infractions Report 761
		Notes and Questions 766
		University of Alabama, Tuscaloosa Public Infractions Appeals Committee Report.. 766
		Notes and Questions 770
		University of Miami Public Infractions Report 771
		Notes and Questions 780
	2.	Sanctioning Criminal Conduct 782
		Notes and Questions 785

Chapter 11. Intercollegiate Sports: The Athlete-University Relationship 787

A.	Recruiting and Scholarships... 787
	1. Admissions Standards... 787
	(a) Race Discrimination 787
	Parish v. NCAA.. 788
	Notes and Questions... 792
	Cureton v. NCAA 793
	Notes and Questions... 802
	(b) Sliding Scale and APR... 803
	Notes and Questions... 804
	(c) Disability Law... 804
	Ganden v. NCAA... 805
	Notes and Questions... 811
	2. The University-Athlete Agreement 812
	Taylor v. Wake Forest 813
	Notes and Questions 815
	3. NCAA Recruiting Regulations... 816
	University of Louisville Public Infractions Appeals Committee Report 819
	Notes and Questions 823

B. The Student-Athlete 824
   1. Academic Opportunity 824
      (a) Access to Education 824
          Ross v. Creighton Univ. 824
          Ross v. Creighton Univ. 828
          Notes and Questions 830
          University of North Carolina at Chapel Hill Public
             Infractions Decision 830
          Notes and Questions 836
      (b) Transfer Rules 837
          Deppe v. NCAA 839
          Notes and Questions 845
   2. The Principle of Amateurism and the Scope of Judicial Review ... 846
      (a) Pre-College Sports and Amateurism 846
          Bloom v. NCAA 846
          Notes and Questions 850
          NCAA v. Lasege 851
          Notes and Questions 858
      (b) Pro Contracts and Amateurism 859
          Shelton v. NCAA 859
          Notes and Questions 861
      (c) Drafts and Amateurism 861
          Notes and Questions 862
      (d) Agents and Amateurism 862
          Oliver v. NCAA 863
          Notes and Questions 868
          Banks v. NCAA 869
          Notes and Questions 879
C. Challenging the Student-Athlete Model 880
   1. Labor Challenges 880
      Notes and Questions 881
      Berger v. NCAA 883
      Notes and Questions 888
   2. Antitrust Challenges 889
      O'Bannon v. NCAA 889
      Notes and Questions 904
      In re: NCAA Athletic Grant-in-Aid Cap Antitrust Litigation 905
      Notes and Questions 909

Chapter 12. Gender Equity in Sports 913
A. Administrative Development of Title IX 914
B. Resources 917
   Cohen v. Brown University 918
   Notes and Questions 921
   Kelley v. University of Illinois 922
   Notes and Questions 926
   Cohen v. Brown University 928

      Notes and Questions 939
      Boucher v. Syracuse University 942
      Notes and Questions 948
      Neal v. Board of Trustees of California State Universities 949
      Notes and Questions 951
      Notes and Questions 953
      Biediger v. Quinnipiac University 954
      Notes and Questions 961
C. Athletic Program Administration 962
      Stanley v. University of Southern California 963
      Notes and Questions 966
D. Access 969
      Notes and Questions 972
      Hoover v. Meiklejohn 972
      Notes and Questions 977

Chapter 13. International and Olympic Sports 981
A. Role of International Organizations 983
    1.   The Court of Arbitration for Sport (CAS) 983
    2.   The World Anti-Doping Agency (WADA) 986
         Notes and Questions 988
B. The United States in International Sports 989
    1.   Judicial Review of Sports Governing Bodies 990
         Defrantz v. United States Olympic Committee 990
         Notes and Questions 997
    2.   Athlete Eligibility Standards 998
         Reynolds v. International Amateur Athletic Federation 998
         Notes and Questions 1003
         Lindland v. United States Wrestling Association 1004
         Notes and Questions 1013
C. Recent Cases in International Sport 1014
    1.   Nationalism 1014
         Pechstein v. International Skating Union 1014
         Notes and Questions 1019
    2.   Systematic Doping 1020
         Zubkov v. International Olympic Committee 1021
         Notes and Questions 1032
    3.   Hyperandrogenism 1032
         Chand v. International Ass'n of Athletics Federations 1032
         Notes and Questions 1046

Chapter 14. Health and Safety Issues in Sports 1049
A. Injuries from Playing the Game 1049
    1.   Injury to Athletes—Tort Liability 1049
         Hackbart v. Cincinnati Bengals, Inc. (Hackbart I) 1050
         Hackbart v. Cincinnati Bengals, Inc. (Hackbart II) 1054
         Notes and Questions 1057

	2.	Injury to Athletes—Criminal Liability	1061
		Regina v. McSorley	1064
		Notes and Questions	1066
	3.	Injury to Spectators	1068
		Jane Costa v. The Boston Red Sox Baseball Club	1068
		Notes and Questions	1071
B.	Health and Safety off the Field		1074
	1.	Medical Malpractice	1074
		Krueger v. San Francisco Forty Niners	1076
		Notes and Questions	1081
	2.	League and Team Policies and Practices That Affect Player Health and Safety	1082
		(a) Prescription Drug Abuse Litigation	1082
		(b) Concussion Litigation	1084
		Notes and Questions	1087
	3.	Defective Products and Hazardous Facilities	1089
		Sanchez v. Hillerich & Bradsby Co.	1089
		Notes and Questions	1092
		Bush v. St. Louis Rams	1094
		Notes and Questions	1096
C.	Disability and the Right to Play		1096
	1.	Increased Risk to the Impaired Athlete	1097
		Knapp v. Northwestern University	1098
		Notes and Questions	1104
	2.	Increased Risk to Other Participants	1106
		Montalvo v. Radcliffe	1107
		Notes and Questions	1111
	3.	Modifying the Fundamental Character of the Game	1112
		PGA Tour, Inc. v. Martin	1114
		Notes and Questions	1122
INDEX			1125

TABLE OF CASES

The principal cases are in bold type.

Abbott v. Virginia Beach, 1013
Abdul-Jabbar v. General Motors Corp., 578, 582
Abernathy v. State, 709
ACC v. University of Maryland, 754
Adarand Constructors, Inc. v. Pena, 927
Addyston Pipe & Steel Co., United States v., 250, 256, 287, 439, 447, 518
Agnew v. NCAA, 839, 845, 885
AIAW v. NCAA, 963
Air Line Pilots Ass'n v. O'Neill, 115
Alan Wood Steel Co., 131
Alcan Packaging Co. v. Graphic Commc'n Conference, 176
Alexander v. Choate, 802, 807, 1105
Alexander v. Sandoval, 803
Ali v. Playgirl, 578
Allen Bradley Co. v. IBEW, 370
Allis-Chalmers Corp. v. Lueck, 148, 153
Allison v. Dept. of Corrections, 808
Allison v. Vintage Sports Plaques, 589
Allred v. Capital Area Soccer League, Inc., 1073
Aluminum Co. of Am., United States v., 514
Alvin Moore & Atlanta Braves, 124
American Broadcasting Companies, Inc. v. Aereo, Inc., 565, 569
American Football League v. National Football League, 307
American League Baseball Club of Chicago v. Chase, 206
American League Baseball Club of New York (Yankees) v. Johnson, 15
American League of Professional Baseball Clubs & Ass'n of National Baseball League Umpires, 75
American Med. Ass'n v. United States, 407
American Motor Inns, Inc. v. Holiday Inns, Inc., 898
American Nat'l Can Co. v. United Steelworkers, 177
American Needle, Inc. v. New Orleans La. Saints, 277, 527

American Needle, Inc. v. NFL, 5, 275, 276, 277, 528
American Postal Workers Union v. U.S. Postal Serv., 182
American Ship Building Co. v. NLRB, 106, 108, 383
American Steel Foundries v. Tri-City Cent. Trades Council, 408
American Tobacco Co. v. United States, 380
Anand v. Kapoor, 1060
Anderson v. Akers, 735
Anderson v. Bessemer City, 960
Anderson v. Shipowners' Assn. of Pacific Coast, 385
Andreas, United States v., 251
Andrews, Estate of v. United States, 577
Aspen Highlands Skiing Corp. v. Aspen Skiing Co., 328
Associated Press v. United States, 459
Associated Students, Inc. v. NCAA, 789, 860
Association of Independent Television Stations, Inc. v. College Football Ass'n, 273
AT&T Inc., United States v., 509
Atlanta National League Baseball Club & Ted Turner v. Bowie Kuhn, 27, 28
Atwater v. Nat'l Football League Players Ass'n, 662
Augusta National v. Northwestern Mutual Life Insurance, 617
Averill v. Luttrell, 1058
BAA v. Sullivan, 626
Badgett v. Alabama High School Athletic Assn., 1124
Ballard v. Nat'l Football League Players Ass'n, 1088
Baltimore Orioles, Inc. v. Major League Baseball Players Association, 491, 549, 592
Banks v. NCAA, 843, 869
Barnes v. Gorman, 971
Barnes v. The American Tobacco Co., 946
Bates v. State Bar of Arizona, 725
Bauer v. The Interpublic Group of Companies, Inc., 676
Beasley v. Horrell, 747

Bedford Cut Stone Co. v. Journeymen Stone Cutters' Ass'n of N. Am., 408
Beer Nuts, Inc. v. Clover Club Foods Co., 627
Begley v. Mercer University, 815
Behagen v. Amateur Basketball Ass'n of the United States, 997, 1001
Benejam v. Detroit Tigers, Inc., 1072
Bentley v. Cleveland Browns Football Co., 1075
Berger v. NCAA, 883
Bertuzzi, Regina v., 1066
Bias v. Advantage International, Inc., 656
Bidwill v. Garvey, 111
Biediger v. Quinnipiac Univ., 954, 955
Biediger v. Quinnipiac University, 954
Black v. NFLPA, 683
Blaich v. National Football League, 480
Bloom v. NCAA, 846
Blue Line Publishing, Inc. v. Chicago Blackhawk Hockey Team, 325
Board of Educ. of the City Sch. Dist. of New York v. Harris, 795
Board of Regents v. Roth, 753
Board of Supervisors for Louisiana State Univ. Agric. & Mech. Coll. v. Smack Apparel Co., 615
Bogan v. Hodgkins, 516
Boire v. Greyhound Corp., 86
Bollea v. Gawker Media LLC, 576
Boogaard v. Nat'l Hockey League, 1075
Boston Athletic Ass'n v. Sullivan, 627
Boston Celtics v. Brian Shaw, 200
Boston Professional Hockey Association v. Cheevers, 311
Boston Professional Hockey Association v. Dallas Cap and Emblem Mfg., Inc., 620
Boston Professional Hockey Association v. Reliable Knitting Works, 622
Bouchat v. Baltimore Ravens Football Club, Inc., 625
Boucher v. Syracuse University, 942, 944
Boudreau v. Baughman, 756
Boulahanis v. Board of Regents of Illinois State Univ., 949
Bourque v. Duplechin, 1060
Bowen v. United States Postal Service, 116
Bowman v. McNary, 1060
Boys Market, Inc. v. Retail Clerks Union, Local 770, 122
Brady v. NFL, 400, 411

Bragdon v. Abbott, 1105, 1111
Branco v. Kearny Moto Park, Inc., 1091
Bread Political Action Committee v. FEC, 1013
Brentwood Academy v. Tennessee Secondary Schools Athletic Ass'n, 730, 731
Brisbin v. Washington Sports & Entm't, Ltd., 1074
Broadcast Music Inc. v. Columbia Broadcasting System, Inc., 253, 285, 287, 432, 490, 514
Brotherhood of Maintenance of Way Employees v. Burlington Northern R.R., 1006
Brotherhood of R.R. Trainmen v. Chi. River & Ind. R.R. Co., 406
Brown University, 79
Brown University, United States v., 256
Brown v. Board of Education, 973
Brown v. Elk Grove Unified Sch. Dist., 1123
Brown v. Entm't Merchs. Ass'n, 601
Brown v. Nat'l Football League, 1075
Brown v. Pro Football, Inc., 243, 281, 297, 334, 374, 377, **378,** 394, 410, 435
Brown v. Woolf, 663
Bruce Drug, Inc. v. Hollister, Inc., 898
Bruesewitz v. Wyeth LLC, 408
Brunetti, In re, 647
Bryant v. Colgate Univ., 944
Bryant v. Fox & Chicago Bears, 1076
Bud Rountree v. Boise Baseball, 1072
Buffalo Broadcasting Co. v. ASCAP, 253, 490
Building & Construction Trades Council v. Associated Builders & Contractors, 115
Bureau of Engraving, Inc. v. Graphic Commc'ns Int'l Union, 177
Burkey v. Marshall County Board of Education, 965
Burleson v. Earnest, 651
Burton v. Wilmington Parking Authority, 723
Bush v. St. Louis Rams, 1094
Business Elecs. Corp. v. Sharp Elecs. Corp., 518
Butler v. NCAA, 812
C.B.C. Distribution and Marketing, Inc. v. Major League Baseball Advanced Media, L.P., 596
Cabell v. Markham, 411
Cablevision Consumer Litig., In re, 504

TABLE OF CASES

Cablevision of Michigan v. Sports Palace, 562
Cablevision Sys. Corp. v. Viacom Int'l Inc., 504
Cady v. TAC, 998
Caldwell v. Am. Basketball Ass'n, 395
California Dental Ass'n v. FTC, 516, 528
Cameron Iron Works, 131
Cardinal Mooney High School v. Michigan High School, 857
Cardtoons v. MLB Players Association, 582, 586, 598, 632
Care Heating & Cooling, Inc. v. Am. Standard, Inc., 527
Catalano, Inc. v. Target Sales, Inc., 896
CBS Interactive Inc. v. Nat'l Football League Players Ass'n, Inc., 606
Central New York Basketball v. Barnett, 191, 216
Champion Pro Consulting Grp., Inc. v. Impact Sports Football, LLC, 676
Chand v. International Ass'n of Athletics Federations, 1032
Charles D. Bonanno Linen Service v. NLRB, 86, 379
Charles O. Finley v. Bowie Kuhn, 21, 491
Chevron U.S.A. v. Natural Resources Defense Council, Inc., 923
Chicago National League Ball Club v. Francis Vincent, Jr., 31
Chicago Professional Sports Ltd. & WGN v. NBA (Bulls I), 482, 489, 876
Chicago Professional Sports Ltd. Partnership & WGN v. NBA (Bulls II), 291, 489
Chicago Professional Sports Ltd. Partnership v. NBA, 487, 488, 489
Chuy v. NFLPA, 116
Cincinnati Bengals v. Bergey, 193
Circuit City Stores, Inc. v. Adams, 183
Citizen Publishing Co. v. United States, 327
Clarett v. NFL, 391
Clark v. Arizona Interscholastic Ass'n., 979
Classen v. Izquierdo, 1079
Classic, United States v., 724
Cleburne, Tex., City of v. Cleburne Living Ctr., 1097
Cohane v. NCAA, 733
Cohen v. Brown University, 918, 928, 947, 950
Cole v. NCAA, 849
Collins v. NBPA & Grantham, 679, 682

Columbia Metal Culvert Co. v. Kaiser Aluminum & Chem. Corp., 365
Columbia Univ. in the City, of New York, 103
Comcast Cable Communications, LLC v. Federal Communications Commission, 504
Comedy III Productions, Inc. v. Gary Saderup, Inc., 602
Communities for Equity v. Michigan High School Athletic Ass'n, 979
Compco Corp. v. Day-Brite Lighting, Inc., 623
Concord, Town of v. Boston Edison Co., 427
Coniglio v. Highwood Services, Inc., 324
Connecticut v. Teal, 797, 799
Connell Construction Co. v. Plumbers and Steamfitters, 370, 386
Consolidation Coal Co. v. United Mine Workers, 1006
Continental Can Co. v. Chicago Truck Drivers Pension Fund, 1013
Continental T.V., Inc. v. GTE Sylvania Inc., 254, 435, 485
Cook v. Colgate Univ., 943
Copperweld Corp. v. Independence Tube Corp., 5, 275, 278, 291
Corporation of Gonzaga Univ. v. Pendleton Enterprises, LLC, 632
Cotran v. Rollins Hudig Hall Int'l Inc., 132
Cox v. Roach, 756
Craft v. Commonwealth, Ky., 856
Craig v. Boren, 974
Cramer v. Consolidated Freightways, Inc., 153
Crocker v. Tennessee Secondary School Athletic Ass'n, 856
Cureton v. NCAA, 793, 802
Cuyahoga County Bar Assoc. v. Glenn, 714
Dallas Cowboys Cheerleaders, Inc. v. Pussycat Cinema, Ltd., 632
Dallas Cowboys Football Club, Ltd. v. America's Team Properties, 633
Daniels v. FanDuel, Inc., 607
Daniels v. Seattle Seahawks, 1080
Davis v. Elec. Arts Inc., 606
Deesen v. Professional Golfers' Ass'n, 450
Defrantz v. United States Olympic Committee, 990
DelCostello v. International Bthd. of Teamsters, 117
Denny's Marina, Inc. v. Renfro Prods., Inc., 841

Table of Cases

Dent v. Nat'l Football League, 1082, 1083
DePiano v. Montreal Baseball Club, Ltd., 1075
Deppe v. NCAA, 839
Detroit Football Co. v. Robinson, 193
Detroit Lions and Billy Sims v. Jerry Argovitz, 667
Dewey Ranch Hockey, LLC, In re, 456
Diesel Props. S.r.l. v. Greystone Bus. Credit II LLC, 960
Doe v. McFarlane, 583
Doe v. TCI Cablevision, 583, 597
Doe v. Woodford County Board of Education, 1111
Dow Corning Corp. v. Safety Nat'l Cas. Corp., 181
Dream Team Collectibles, Inc. v. NBA Properties, Inc., 619
Driskill v. Dallas Cowboys Football Club, 324
Dryer v. National Football League, 594
Duplex Printing Press Co. v. Deering, 368
E.I. du Pont de Nemours & Co. (TiO2), 303
E.I. du Pont de Nemours & Co., United States v., 263, 304, 306
Eastern Associated Coal Corp. v. Mine Workers, 169
Eastern Microwave, Inc. v. Doubleday Sports, Inc., 570
Edward C. v. City of Albuquerque, 1073
Edward J. DeBartolo Corp. v. Florida Gulf Coast Bldg. & Constr. Trades Council, 938
EEOC v. Madison Community Unit Sch. Dist. No. 12, 964, 965
Elite Rodeo Ass'n v. Prof'l Rodeo Cowboys Ass'n, 294
Elston v. Talladega County Bd. of Educ., 795
England and Wales Cricket Board Ltd v. Fanatix, 563
Environmental Defense Fund, Inc. v. Wheelabrator Technologies, Inc., 1013
Erin Andrews v. Marriott International Inc., 576
ETW Corp. v. Jireh Publishing, Inc., 584
Evans v. Arizona Cardinals Football Club, LLC, 1084
Federal Baseball Club of Baltimore v. National League of Professional Baseball Clubs, 74, 234

Federation Internationale De Football Ass'n v. Nike, Inc., 637
Feist Publications v. Rural Telephone Service, 559
Ferrari v. National Football League, 79
Ferrell v. Dep't of Transp., 759
Fibreboard Paper Products v. NLRB, 98
First National Maintenance Corp. v. NLRB, 97
Fishman v. Estate of Wirtz, 327, 428, 876
Fitzsimmons, People v., 1067
Fleer v. Topps Chewing Gum & Major League Baseball Players Ass'n, 246, 513
Flood v. Kuhn, 77, 232
Fort Halifax Packing Co. v. Coyne, 383
Fortnightly Corp. v. United Artists Television, 566, 570
Franklin v. Gwinnett County Public Schools, 914
Fraser v. Major League Soccer, L.L.C., 280, 297, 363
Frederick J. Henley, Matter of, 714
Freeman v. San Diego Assn. of Realtors, 280
Freer, People v., 1067
Frontiero v. Richardson, 973
FTC v. Indiana Federation of Dentists, 528, 739
Gaines v. NCAA, 879
Ganden v. NCAA, 805
Garvey v. Roberts, 167
Gatto, United States v., 658, 709
Gauvin v. Clark, 1059
General Motors Corp., United States v., 255, 380
Giles v. Bert Bell/Pete Rozelle NFL Player Ret. Plan, 1075
Gionfriddo v. MLB, 588, 599
Glatt v. Fox Searchlight Pictures, Inc., 884
Golden State Transit Corp. v. City of Los Angeles, 114
Granite Rock Co. v. Int'l Bhd. of Teamsters, 182
Grappone, Inc. v. Subaru of New England, Inc., 435
Great Midwest Mining Corp., 132
Green v. Pro Football, Inc., 1058
Green, Regina v., 1061
Greenhoot, Inc., 89
Gridiron.com, Inc. v. NFLPA, 512, 516, 591
Griggs v. Duke Power Co., 793, 794
Grinnell Corp., United States v., 310, 314

TABLE OF CASES

Grove City College v. Bell, 913
Grove v. Hodges, 188
Groves v. Alabama State Board of Education, 793
Grube v. Bethlehem Area Sch. Dist., 1105
H. A. Artists & Assoc. v. Actors' Equity Ass'n, 369
Hackbart v. Cincinnati Bengals, Inc. (Hackbart I), 1050
Hackbart v. Cincinnati Bengals, Inc. (Hackbart II), 1054
Haddad v. O'Neal, 1074
Haelan Laboratories v. Topps Chewing Gum, 576, 600
Hall St. Assocs., LLC v. Mattel, Inc., 182
Hall v. NCAA, 847
Hall, People v., 1067
Harlem Wizards Entertainment Basketball, Inc. v. NBA Properties, 615
Hart v. Electronic Arts, Inc., 603
Harting v. Dayton Dragons Prof'l Baseball Club, L.L.C., 1073
Hayden v. University of Notre Dame, 1073
Haywood v. National Basketball Ass'n., 78, 239
Hebert v. Los Angeles Raiders, 247
Hecht v. Pro-Football, Inc., 317
Henderson Broadcasting Corp. v. Houston Sports Ass'n, 246
Hennessey v. NCAA, 736, 738
Hernandez v. Childers, 671
Hicks v. PGA Tour, Inc., 589
High Fructose Corn Syrup Antitrust Litig., In re, 251
Hilliard v. Black, 657
Hirsch v. S.C. Johnson & Son, Inc., 578
Hi-Way Billboards, Inc., 381
HMC Management v. New Orleans Basketball Club, 464
Hoffman v. Cargill, Inc., 182
Hoopla Sports and Entertainment, Inc. v. Nike, Inc., 559
Hoover v. Meiklejohn, 972
Horner v. Kentucky High School Athletic Ass'n, 979
Horner v. Mary Inst., 963
Houston Oilers v. Neely, 193
Hubbard Broadcasting, Inc. v. Southern Satellite Systems and TBS, 572
Hurd v. Illinois Bell Telephone Co., 30
Hutcheson, United States v., 369, 405, 407
IHSAA v. Reyes, 857

Illinois High Sch. Ass'n v. GTE Vantage, Inc., 618
Independent Sports & Entm't, LLC v. Fegan, 683
Indianapolis Colts v. Metropolitan Baltimore Football Club, 610
Intercontinental Container Transp. Corp. v. N.Y. Shipping Ass'n, 395
International Bhd. of Elec. Workers, Local Union 824 v. Verizon Fla., LLC, 181
International Bhd. of Teamsters v. United States, 797
International Boxing Club v. United States, 263, 305
International Boxing Club, United States v., 236, 305
International Business Machines Corp. v. United States, 323
International Chem. Workers Union v. Day & Zimmermann, Inc., 180
International News Service v. Associated Press, 543, 544, 628
International Olympic Comm. v. San Francisco Arts & Athletics, 997
International Shoe Co. v. Washington, 1000
Iowa State University v. American Broadcasting Cos., 560
J.I. Case Co. v. NLRB, 91, 375
Jackson v. Birmingham Bd. of Educ., 969
Jackson v. Drake University, 816
Jacobs v. College of William and Mary, 964
Jane Costa v. The Boston Red Sox Baseball Club, 1068
Jason Pierre-Paul v. ESPN, 576
Jenkins v. National Collegiate Athletic Association, 710
Johannesen v. NCAA, 807
John Morrell & Co. v. Local Union 304A of United Food & Commercial Workers, 180
Johnny Blastoff, Inc. v. Los Angeles Rams Football Co., 610
Johnny Carson v. Here's Johnny Portable Toilets, 578
Johnson v. Florida High School Activities Ass'n, Inc., 808
Johnson-Kennedy Radio Corp. v. Chicago Bears Football Club, 546
Jones v. Childers, 657
Jones v. Three Rivers Mgmt. Corp., 1072
Jordan v. Dominick's Finer Foods, 582
Jordan v. Jewel Food Stores, Inc., 582
Joseph E.G. v. E. Irondequoit Cent. Sch. Dist., 1112

Table of Cases

Judge v. Carrai, 1072
Kann v. United States, 706
Kansas City Royals v. Major League Baseball Players Ass'n, 220
Kartell v. Blue Shield of Massachusetts, Inc., 251
Kelley v. University of Illinois, 922
Kentucky High School Athletic Ass'n v. Hopkins Co. Bd. of Educ., Ky. App., 856
KHSAA v. Hopkins County Board of Education, 853
Kimbrough & Co. v. Schmitt, 748
Kish v. Iowa Central Community College, 753
Kivisto v. Nat'l Football League Players Assoc., 695
Kleczek v. Rhode Island Interscholastic League, 978
Klor's, Inc. v. Broadway-Hale Stores, 252, 270
Knapp v. Northwestern University, 1098
Knight v. Jewett, 1059
Krueger v. San Francisco Forty Niners, 1076
Kuehner v. Heckler, 946
Kuketz v. Petronelli, 1123
Laborers Health & Welfare Trust v. Advanced Lightweight Concrete Co., 97
Lafler v. Athletic Board of Control, 977
Laidlaw Corp., 109
Laidlaw Corp. v. NLRB, 109
Larry P. v. Riles, 795
Latrell Sprewell, In re, 127
Laumann v. NHL, 494
Law v. NCAA, 528, 737, 894
Leach v. Texas Tech University, 753
Lemat Corp. v. Barry, 195, 216
Levin v. NBA, 421, 428
Lifteau v. Metropolitan Sports Facilities Comm'n, 465
Lindland v. United States Wrestling Association, 1004, 1005
Lividas v. Bradshaw, 154
Local 58, Int'l Brotherhood of Electrical Workers v. Southeastern Michigan Chapter, Nat'l Electrical Contractors Ass'n, Inc., 103
Local 238 Int'l Bhd. of Teamsters v. Cargill, Inc., 180
Local 825 International Union of Operating Engineers v. NLRB (Harter Equipment), 107
Local Union No. 189, Amalgamated Meat Cutters v. Jewel Tea Co., 370

Lochner v. New York, 385
Lockheed Engineering Sciences Co., 134
Loewe v. Lawlor, 368
Los Angeles Dodgers LLC, In re, 66
Los Angeles Memorial Coliseum Comm'n v. NFL, 271, 283, 288, 437, 442, 450, 456
Los Angeles Rams Football Club v. Cannon, 193
Los Angeles, City of v. Superior Court, 466
Los Angeles, County of v. Davis, 946
Lowe v. California League of Prof. Baseball, 1073
M & H Tire Co. v. Hoosier Racing Tire Corp., 435
Mackey v. NFL, 101, 226, 257, 355, 373, 409
Madison Square Garden, L.P. v. NHL, 516, 518, 532
Magness, In re, 456
Maisonave v. Newark Bears Professional Baseball Club, Inc., 1072
Major League Baseball Players Association and Office of the Commissioner of Baseball, 143
Major League Baseball Players Association v. Garvey, 166, 176
Major League Baseball Properties v. Pacific Trading Cards, 631
Major League Baseball Properties, Inc. v. Salvino, Inc., 284, 518
Major League Baseball Properties, Inc. v. Sed Non Olet Denarius, Ltd., 611, 615
Major League Baseball v. Crist, 246
Maki, Regina v., 1062
Maloney v. T3Media, Inc., 594
Maloney, Regina v., 1062
March Madness Athletic Ass'n v. Netfire, Inc., 619
Marchio v. Letterlough, 190
Marisol A. v. Giuliani, 946
Marshall v. ESPN Inc., 595
Martin v. PGA Tour, Inc., 1113
Maryland Stadium Auth. v. Becker, 609
Massachusetts v. EPA, 403
Mastercard Intern. Inc. v. Sprint Communications Co. L.P., 638
Matal v. Tam, 641
Matuszak v. Houston Oilers, 247
Mayor & City Council of Baltimore v. Baltimore (Colts) Football Club, 466
McCabe v. Nassau County Med. Ctr., 945
McCormack v. NCAA, 843

McCourt v. California Sports, Inc., 374
McFadden v. Grasmick, 1124
McKichan v. St. Louis Hockey Club, L.P., 1058
McNally v. United States, 707
McNeil v. NFL, 360
McSorley, Regina v., 1064
Medcalf v. Trustees of the Univ. of Pennsylvania, 968
Medo Photo Supply Corp. v. NLRB, 93
Mehr v. Féderation Internationale de Football Ass'n, 1087
Melton v. Tippecanoe Cty., 884
Mercer v. Duke University, 971
Metro Broadcasting, Inc. v. Federal Communications Comm'n, 925, 927
Metropolitan Life Insurance Co. v. Massachusetts, 154, 384
Metropolitan Sports Facilities Commission v. Minnesota Twins Partnership, 464
Michels v. United States Olympic Committee, 1009
Microsoft Corp., United States v., 323
Mid-Atlantic Sports Network v. Time Warner Cable Inc., 506
Midler v. Ford Motor Co., 578
Mid-South Grizzlies v. NFL, 281, 428, 457
Miller v. Universal City Studios, 559
Milwaukee Amer. Ass'n v. Landis, 17
Minnesota Citizens Concerned for Life, Inc. v. Swanson, 411
Minnesota Muskies, Inc. v. Hudson, 203
Minnesota Twins Partnership v. State of Minnesota, 246
Miranda v. Selig, 245
Mississippi University for Women v. Hogan, 925
Mitsubishi Motors Corp. v. Soler Chrysler-Plymouth, Inc., 531
Molinas v. NBA, 55
Monahan's Marine, Inc. v. Boston Whaler, Inc., 431
Monroe v. Pape, 724
Monsanto Co. v. Spray-Rite Service Corp., 278
Montalvo v. Radcliffe, 1107
Montana v. San Jose Mercury News, 582, 604
Morio v. North American Soccer League, 91
Morris Communications Corporation v. PGA Tour, 553, 554
Motschenbacher v. R.J. Reynolds Tobacco, 578

Munchak Corp. v. Cunningham, 195, 204
Murphy v. NCAA, 57, 557, 607
Murray v. National Football League, 437
Murray v. West Baton Rouge Parish School Board, 790
N.J.Y.W. v. Fédération Internationale de Natation, 985
NAACP v. Medical Ctr., Inc., 794
Nabozny v. Barnhill, 1059
Nagle v. Feilden, 69
NASL v. NFL, 5, 280, 286, 393, 422, 428
Nassau Sports v. Hampson, 311
Nassau Sports v. Peters, 311
Nathans v. Offerman, 1058
National & American League Professional Baseball Clubs v. Major League Baseball Players Association, 213
National Collegiate Athletic Ass'n v. Kizzang LLC, 608
National Exhibition v. Teleflash, 542
National Football League Mgmt. Council v. National Football Players Ass'n, 182, 183
National Football League Players Ass'n v. National Football League (Peterson), 171
National Football League Players' Concussion Injury Litigation, In re, 1085
National Football League Properties, Inc. v. Consumer Enterprises, Inc., 619
National Football League Properties, Inc. v. New Jersey Giants, Inc., 609
National Football Management Council v. National Football League Players Association, 184
National Hockey League Players' Concussion Injury Litig., In re, 1086
National Hockey League v. Pepsi-Cola Canada Ltd., 637
National Licorice Co. v. NLRB, 93
National Society of Professional Engineers v. United States, 255, 264, 270, 385
Nationwide Mutual Insurance Co. v. Darden, 78, 884
NBA Properties and NFL Properties v. Dahlonega, 630
NBA v. Motorola, 547
NBA v. San Diego Clippers Basketball Club, 453
NBA v. Williams, 390
NCAA Athletic Grant-in-Aid Cap Antitrust Litigation, In re, 905

TABLE OF CASES

NCAA Student-Athlete Concussion Injury Litigation, In re, 1087
NCAA Student-Athlete Name & Likeness Licensing Litigation, In re, 600
NCAA v. Board of Regents of the Univ. of Oklahoma & Univ. of Georgia Athletic Ass'n, 258, 384, 386, 431, 726, **734,** 839, 849, 885, 891, 906
NCAA v. Brinkworth, 847
NCAA v. Lasege, 851
NCAA v. Smith, 802, 843
NCAA v. Tarkanian, 723
Neal v. Board of Trustees of California State Universities, 949
Neeld v. Am. Hockey League, 1105
Neeld v. NHL, 1105
Nemarnik v. Los Angeles Kings Hockey Club, L.P., 1073
New Boston Television v. Entertainment Sports Programming Network (ESPN), 559
New England Patriots Football Club, Inc. v. University of Colorado, 203
New Jersey Devils and Scott Gomez, 157
New Negro Alliance v. Sanitary Grocery Co., 404
New York City Triathlon LLC v. NYC Triathlon Club Inc., 633
New York Football Giants, Inc. v. Los Angeles Chargers Football Club, Inc., 192
New York Times v. Sullivan, 575
New York Typographical Union No. 6 v. Printers League Section of the Assoc. of the Graphic Arts, 102
New York Urban League, Inc. v. New York, 794
New York v. United States, 58
New York Yankees Partnership v. Evil Enterprises, Inc., 616
New York Yankees Partnership v. IET Products and Services, Inc., 634
New York, City of v. New York Jets, 464
Newark Branch, NAACP v. Town of Harrison, New Jersey, 798, 802
Newcombe v. Adolf Coors Co., 578
NFL Management Council and NFLPA, 107
NFL Properties v. Superior Court, 452
NFL Sunday Ticket Antitrust Litig., In re, 478
NFL v. Coors Brewing Co., 630
NFL v. Governor of the State of Delaware, 635
NFL v. iCraveTV, 564
NFL v. Insight Telecommunications Corp., 570
NFL v. McBee & Bruno's, Inc., 563
NFL v. NASL, 288, 448
NFL v. PrimeTime 24 Joint Venture, 564
NFL, United States v., 261, **470,** 475
NLRB v. Acme Industrial Co., 97
NLRB v. Allis-Chalmers Mfg. Co., 375
NLRB v. Bell Aerospace Co., 78
NLRB v. Brown, 381, 388
NLRB v. Catholic Bishop of Chicago, 938
NLRB v. Electrical Workers Local 1229 IBEW, 82
NLRB v. Fleetwood Trailer Co., 109
NLRB v. Great Dane Trailers, 108
NLRB v. Hi-Way Billboards, Inc., 382
NLRB v. Insurance Agents' Int'l Union, 97
NLRB v. Jones & Laughlin Steel Corp., 74
NLRB v. Katz, 92, 97, 397
NLRB v. Kentucky River Community Care, Inc., 78
NLRB v. Mackay Radio and Telegraph, 107
NLRB v. Transportation Management Corp., 81
NLRB v. Truck Drivers, 379, 387
NLRB v. United Insurance Co., 78
NLRB v. Washington Aluminum Co., 405
NLRB v. Wooster Division of Borg-Warner Corp., 98
NLRB v. Wright Line, 81
No Doubt v. Activism Publishing Inc., 603
Norby Walters and Lloyd Bloom v. Brent Fullwood, 700
Norby Walters, United States v., 706
Nordenfelt v. Maxim Nordenfelt Gun & Ammunication Co., 250
Nordstrom v. NLRB, 85
North American Soccer League v. NLRB, 87
Northern Pac. Ry. Co. v. United States, 252
Northwest Wholesale Stationers, Inc. v. Pacific Stationery & Printing Co., 253, 432, 455
Northwestern University, 91
O'Bannon v. NCAA, 734, 885, 888, 889
O'Brien v. Pabst Sales, 576
Oakland Raiders v. NFL, 8, 452

TABLE OF CASES

Oakland, City of v. Oakland Raiders, 466
Oakland-Alameda County Coliseum v. Oakland Raiders, 452
Oaklawn Jockey Club, Inc. v. Kentucky Downs, LLC, 632
Oates v. District of Columbia, 969
Octagon, Inc. v. Richards, 666
Olinger v. United States Golf Association, 1113
Oliver v. NCAA, 863
Order of R.R. Telegraphers v. Chicago & N. W. R. R. Co., 409
Otter Tail Power Co. v. United States, 318
Ovitron Corp. v. General Motors Corp., 316
Pack Concrete, Inc. v. Cunningham, 180
Pagliero v. Wallace China Co., 623
Paramount Famous Lasky Corp. v. United States, 380
Parish v. NCAA, 788, 792, 996
Parrish Chiropractic Ctrs., P.C. v. Progressive Cas. Ins. Co., 847
Partee v. San Diego Chargers Football Co., 246
Payne v. Office of the Comm'r of Baseball, 1072
Payne v. Travenol Labs, Inc., 946
Pebble Beach v. Tour 18 I Ltd., 631
Pechstein v. International Skating Union, 1014
Pederson v. Louisiana State University, 941, 942
Pell, In the Matter of, 133
Pennsylvania v. NCAA, 783
Pepsi-Cola Bottlers Inc., 134
Pereira v. United States, 706
Perrucci v. Gaffey, 946
Peterson v. Kennedy and NFLPA, 116
PGA Tour, Inc. v. Martin, 1114
Philadelphia Ball Club v. Lajoie, 186
Philadelphia World Hockey Club v. Philadelphia Hockey Club, 311, 371
Piazza v. Major League Baseball, 246
Pierce v. Underwood, 1013
Piggie, United States v., 662
Pittsburgh Athletic Co. v. KQV Broadcasting Co., 542
Pittsburgh Steelers, Inc., 402
Players1st Sports Management Group v. National Football League, 682
Plessy v. Ferguson, 976
Post Newsweek v. Travelers, 544

Pottgen v. Missouri State High School Activities Ass'n, 808, 809
Powell v. Nat'l Football League, 102, 410
Prestonettes Inc. v. Coty, 629
Printz v. United States, 58
Production Contractors, Inc. v. WGN Continental Broadcasting Co., 630
Productions, Inc. v. Gary Saderup, Inc., 587
Professional Hockey Corp. v. World Hockey Ass'n, 8, 299
Professional Sports, Ltd. v. Virginia Squires Basketball, 30
Pro-Football, Inc. v. Blackhorse, 641
Quarles v. Oxford Mun. Separate Sch. Dist., 795
Radovich v. National Football League, 77, 238, 289, 388
Regents of the Univ. of Calif. v. American Broadcasting Cos., 273
Regional Rail Reorganization Act Cases, 1013
Reich v. Sea Sprite Boat Co., 1010
Reiter v. Sonotone, 256
Rensing v. Indiana State Univ., 880
Resorts of Pinehurst v. Pinehurst National Corporation, 631
Reynolds v. International Amateur Athletic Federation, 998, 1003
Ricci v. DeStefano, 951
Richard's Lumber & Supply Co. v. U.S. Gypsum Co., 531
Richardson v. Byrd, 946
Right Field Rooftops v. Chicago Cubs Baseball Club, LCC, 246
Riley Stoker Corp., 135
Rizzo v. Children's World Learning Centers, Inc., 1109
Roberts v. Colorado State Bd. of Agriculture, 921
Robertson v. NBA, 415
Robesky v. Qantas Empire Airways Ltd., 118
Robitaille v. Vancouver Hockey Club, 1079
Rodgers v. Georgia Tech Athletic Association, 753
Rogers v. Grimaldi, 604, 639
Rose v. Giamatti, 12
Rosemont Enterprises, Inc. v. Random House, Inc., 560
Ross v. Creighton Univ., 824, 828
Rothery Storage & Van Co. v. Atlas Van Lines, Inc., 256, 280, 432
Rudnick v. Golden West Broadcasters, 1072

Table of Cases

Ryans v. Houston NFL Holdings, L.P., 1096
Saint v. Nebraska School Activities Ass'n, 977
Salerno v. American League, 245
San Francisco Arts & Athletics, Inc. v. U.S. Olympic Comm., 637, 726, 997
San Francisco Seals v. NHL, 441
San Jose, City of v. Office of the Commissioner of Baseball, 245
Sanchez v. Hillerich & Bradsby Co., 1089
Sandison v. Michigan High School Athletic Ass'n, 807, 809
Sanjuan v. Am. Bd. of Psychiatry & Neurology, Inc., 531
SBC Advanced Sols., Inc. v. Commc'ns Workers, Dist. 6, 177
Schacker, People v., 1067
Schmuck v. United States, 706
Schwartz v. Dallas Cowboys, 477
Sea Bay Manor Home for Adults, 103
Sealy, United States v., 255, 279
Sears, Roebuck & Co. v. Stiffel Co., 623
Seattle Seahawks v. NFLPA & Sam McCullum, 80
Seattle Totems Hockey Club, Inc. v. National Hockey League, 428, 460
Secretary of Labor v. Lauritzen, 884
Sharif by Salahuddin v. New York State Educ. Dept., 793
Sharpe v. NFLPA, 116
Shaw v. Boston Am. League Baseball Co., 1070
Shaw v. Dallas Cowboys, 477
Sheet Metal Workers Local Union No. 20 and George Koch Sons, Inc., 103
Shelley, State v., 1067
Shelton v. NCAA, 859
Sherwin v. Indianapolis Colts, Inc., 1075
Shin v. Ahn, 1060
Shubert, United States v., 236
Silver v. New York Stock Exchange, 450, 459
Silverman v. Major League Baseball Player Relations Committee, 101, 106, 395
Simpson v. Union Oil Co. of Cal., 894
Skilling v. United States, 709
Smith v. American General Corporation, 749
Smith v. Houston Oilers, Inc., 1075
Smith v. NCAA, 843
Smith v. Pro Football, Inc., 342, 435
Smith v. State, 756

Socony-Vacuum Oil Co., United States v., 252, 385
Sony Corp. of America v. Universal City Studios, 562, 569
Sorkin, People v., 658
South Dakota v. Wayfair, Inc., 710
South Sydney Rugby League Football Club Ltd v. News Ltd, 461
Spahn v. Julian Messner, Inc., 576
Spark v. Catholic University of America, 995
Speakers of Sport, Inc. v. ProServ, Inc., 673
Spirit Lake Tribe of Indians ex rel. Comm. of Understanding & Respect v. Nat'l Collegiate Athletic Ass'n, 648
SportFuel, Inc. v. Pepsico, Inc. & The Gatorade Co., 632
Sports Blackout Rules, In the Matter of, 476
Sports Ltd. Partnership v. National Basketball Ass'n, 435, 489
St. Louis Convention & Visitors Comm'n v. NFL, 452
Stamatakis Indus., Inc. v. King, 876
Standard Fashion Co. v. Magrane-Houston Co., 508
Standard Oil v. United States, 252
Stanley v. University of Southern California, 963, 966
Star Athletica, LLC v. Varsity Brands, Inc., 625
Steele v. Louisville & Nashville R.R. Co., 115
Steelworkers v. American Mfg. Co., 169
Steinberg Moorad & Dunn Inc. v. Dunn, 677
Stockham Pipe Fittings Co., 133
Stringer v. Minnesota Vikings Football Club, LLC, 1075
Sullivan v. NFL, 281, **426**
Sullivan v. Tagliabue, 437
Swann v. Charlotte-Mecklenburg Bd. of Educ., 928
Tanaka v. Univ. of S. Cal., 895
Taylor v. Wake Forest, 813
TCR Sports Broad. Holding L.L.P. v. FCC, 506
Tennessee Secondary Sch. Ath. Ass'n v. Brentwood Academy, 734
Tennis Channel, Inc. v. Comcast Cable Commc'ns, LLC, 505
Terminal R. R. Ass'n, United States v., 318
Terrell v. Childers, 658
Texas Tech Univ. v. Spiegelberg, 634

Table of Cases

Textile Workers Union v. Lincoln Mills of Alabama, 121
Time Incorporated v. Bernard Geis Assoc., 560
Time, Inc. v. Johnston, 575
Times-Picayune Publishing Co. v. United States, 491
Timken Roller Bearing Co. v. United States, 281
Titan Sports v. Comics World, 582
Tomjanovich v. California Sports, Inc., 1058
Tony & Susan Alamo Found. v. Sec'y of Labor, 884
Toolson v. New York Yankees, 77, 235
Top Rank, Inc. v. Haymon, 294
Topco Associates, Inc., United States v., 241, 252
Topps Chewing Gum v. Major League Baseball Players Ass'n, 513
Total Economic Athletic Management of America v. Pickens, 704
Trade-Mark Cases, 623
Trailways Lines, Inc. v. Trailways, Inc. Joint Council, 179
Trustees of Columbia University, 79
Tuolumne, County of v. Sonora Cmty. Hosp., 897
Turcotte v. Fell, 1058
Turner v. Mandalay Sports Entertainment, LLC, 1073
Turner v. Wells, 575
Twentieth Century Sporting Club v. Transradio Press Service, Inc., 552
Twin City Sportservice Inc. v. Charles O. Finley & Co., 246
Tynes v. Buccaneers Ltd. P'ship, 1096
Tyson v. King, 666
Uhlaender v. Henricksen, 579, 606
United Mine Workers v. Pennington, 370, 388
United Paperworkers Int'l Union v. Misco, Inc., 168, 176, 201, 1008
United States Football League v. National Football League, 276, 311, 320
United States Olympic Comm. v. American Media, Inc., 637
United States Soccer Fed'n, Inc. v. Unites State Nat'l Soccer Team Players Ass'n, 166
United States Steel Corp., United States v., 303
United Steelworkers of America v. American Manufacturing Co., 122
United Steelworkers of America v. Enterprise Wheel & Car Corp., 122, 165, 169, 176, 201, 223, 1008
United Steelworkers of America v. Warrior & Gulf Navigation Co., 122, 177
University Book Store v. Board of Regents of the Univ. of Wisconsin, 615
University of Alabama Bd. of Trustees v. New Life Art, Inc., 639
University of Georgia Athletic Ass'n v. Laite, 624, 627
University of Pittsburgh v. Champion Products Inc., 626
USFL Players Ass'n v. USFL, 204, 298
USFL v. NFL, 319
Vaca v. Sipes, 115
Valley Liquors, Inc. v. Renfield Importers., Ltd., 493, 528
Vande Zande v. Wisc. Dept. of Admin., 808
Vanderbilt University v. DiNardo, 744, 747
Vanskike v. Peters, 884
Ventura v. Titan Sport, Inc., 593
Viacom Int'l, Inc. v. YouTube, Inc., 562
Virgin Atlantic Airways Ltd. v. British Airways PLC, 500
Virginia, United States v., 927
Visa U.S.A., Inc., United States v., 500
VKK Corp. v. NFL, 452
Volvo North America Corp. v. Men's International Professional Tennis Council, 672
W.R. Grace & Co. v. Local Union 759, Int'l Union of United Rubber, Cork, Linoleum & Plastic Workers, 180
Wainwright Securities, Inc. v. Wall Street Transcript Corp., 560
Waldrep v. Texas Employers Insurance Ass'n, 880
Walker, In re Estate of, 701
Walters v. Harmon, 704
Wards Cove Packing Co. v. Atonio, 795
Washington Capitols Basketball Club v. Barry, 195
Washington v. NFL, 286, 478
Wasserman Media Grp., LLC v. Bender, 666
Watson v. Fort Worth Bank and Trust, 794
WCVB-TV v. Boston Athletic Ass'n, 544, **627**
Weinberg v. Chicago Blackhawk Hockey Team, 324
Weinberger v. Rossi, 1013
West Point Mfg. Co. v. Detroit Stamping Co., 623
Weyerhaeuser Co., 382
White v. NFL, 361, 401, 683
White v. Samsung Elec. Am., Inc., 578

Wichard v. Suggs, 666
Williams v. CWI, Inc., 658
Williams v. National Football League, 149, 155, 181
Williams v. School District of Bethlehem, 978
Winfrey v. Simmons Foods, Inc., 182
Wisconsin, State of v. Milwaukee Braves, 247
WNBA Enterprises, LLC, In Re, 609
Wojsko v. State, 758
Wood v. Nat'l Basketball Ass'n, 101, 375, 393
Wright Line, 81
Wright v. Bonds, 676
Wright v. Columbia University, 1105
Wyckoff v. Office of the Commissioner of Baseball, 245
Wynn v. Columbus Municipal Separate School Dist., 969
Zacchini v. Scripps-Howard Broadcasting Co., 545, 580, 593, 597, 598, 601
Zimbauer v. Milwaukee Orthopaedic Grp., Ltd., 1082
Zinn v. Parrish, 653
Zubkov v. International Olympic Committee, 1021
Zumbrun v. University of Southern California, 828

Sports and the Law
Text, Cases, and Problems

Sixth Edition

CHAPTER 1

INTRODUCTION: COMMISSIONER-LED PROFESSIONAL SPORTS LEAGUES IN NORTH AMERICA*

■ ■ ■

Fans come to sports to enjoy the competition. The outcome of each game is uncertain, often not determined until the final whistle or the bottom of the ninth inning. Sports also seem to resonate with basic human qualities. Sports began in pre-historic times as an essential preparation for the hunt for food and the battle against tribal enemies. The ancient Greek Olympics date to 776 BC; wars would be suspended so that young men could travel to competitions where prizes included olive wreaths, trophies and tax-free status for life. Modern professional and amateur sports began in the middle of the nineteenth century and have grown with international passion into a multi-billion-dollar enterprise. Sports can promote social inclusion, drawing diverse residents together. The modern Olympics are a great example of this mix of sport, politics, and money.

The business of every sport is based on contract, specifically the voluntary undertakings by those willing to risk their time, human capital, and financial resources. Those contracts—for example, between entrepreneurs to form a league, between owners and players, and, in the form of collective bargaining agreements, between unions and leagues—give rise to numerous disputes resolved either in court or by arbitrators. It is not surprising that the law would have a role to play when so much money is involved.

Often legal battles are generated by player actions that take place away from the stadium and arena. Back in 1919, the infamous Chicago "Black Sox" lost that year's World Series in exchange for a few thousand dollars in bribes by underworld figures. This event played the major role in producing a century-long governmental prohibition on legalized commercial betting on sports outside Nevada, as well as league bans on players betting on their own teams' games, a rule that still has Pete Rose banned from baseball and its Hall of Fame. Then, just after World War II,

---

* The Casebook Website (http://pennstatelaw.psu.edu/SportsTextWebsite) contains citations to scholarly and other commentary on a variety of topics discussed in this chapter, including: the role of sports to promote social inclusion; history and development of the commissioner's role; gambling scandals in baseball history; contemporary treatment of gambling issues; the Pete Rose scandal; and Commissioner Kuhn's responses to free agency.

Branch Rickey signed Jackie Robinson to play for his Brooklyn Dodgers, finally ending baseball's "gentlemen's agreement" that barred African-American athletes from the Major Leagues.

Many significant changes have required at least some invocation of the formal legal or political process. Attorney General Robert F. Kennedy threatened to sue to force the PGA Tour in 1963 to remove its "Caucasian-only" eligibility rule for golf tournaments. Congress enacted the antitrust laws, labor laws, and anti-discrimination statutes that have had a plenary effect on the sports business; perhaps with no greater transformational effect than Title IX's impact on the growth of women's sports.

The immediate diagnosis of the "Black Sox Scandal" was that a major contributing cause was baseball club owners' inability to police themselves. This led to the view that owners should delegate to an "independent commissioner" the responsibility to decide whether and how to protect the "best interests of the sport" from behavior that threatened the business. Every organization needs a chief executive officer. In the case of sports, someone must establish schedules and league championships, supervise officials, negotiate television and merchandising contracts, and the like. Historically, many viewed the office of the commissioner as the supreme voice about what truly is in the *best* interests (not just the *business* interests) of the game. League constitutions vest the commissioner with power to resolve disputes on that score among players, clubs, and other participants. Commissioners or Presidents also govern individual professional sports like golf and tennis with their tours, and college sports with the NCAA, and Olympic sports with their respective governing bodies. One conspicuous exception is boxing, where a large number of "governing" organizations exist, subject to manipulation by promoters on behalf of particularly popular fighters. This example reinforces the conventional wisdom that any sport that wants to preserve its integrity needs a commissioner.

Although Commissioners have always primarily served ownership, their public image has evolved over time. Baseball, the sport that gave birth in the early 1920s to an independent commissioner whose principal focus was integrity, became the first-ever league to make an owner of one of its teams the commissioner: the Milwaukee Brewers' Allen "Bud" Selig. Selig's appointment signaled a greater emphasis on the role of the Commissioner as a CEO charged with expanding profitability by securing approval of his former fellow owners of initiatives that would grow revenues.

The unique office of sports commissioner raises important questions. Why would owners, who control sports as a private, for-profit business, vest power in a powerful single individual? A commissioner's actions require either legal authority—in the form of delegation in league constitutions or other agreements—or success in obtaining authority from current owners. Given this dynamic, does the public interest warrant external regulation over the power residing in a single person selected by one constituency, the team owners? Understanding the power of the commissioner informs consideration of whether sports warrant special dispensation from external rules applied to other industries, or whether there are special regulations that are warranted because of the unique nature of sport that would not apply to CEOs of other big businesses.

A. THE LEGAL STATUS OF PROFESSIONAL SPORTS LEAGUES

1. A BRIEF HISTORY

The first professional sports league was created in 1876 as the National League of Professional Base Ball Clubs. Organized by William A. Hulbert of the Chicago White Stockings, the NL was created in response to a host of problems with the loose organization known as the National Association that had been organized five years earlier. Clubs were responsible for arranging their own schedule of competition, through agreements often breached; players were unpaid, contracts breached; gambling and match-fixing were rampant. The solution was what we know call a "closed league" controlled by the member clubs. As an economic historian noted:

> Hulbert appealed to the owners, businessmen all, by using some simple economic logic. If the businessmen ran the teams and the players concentrated on playing ball, each party could concentrate on doing what they did best and everyone would be better off. The geographic exclusivity he promised to each club appealed to the owners as well. Exclusivity meant monopoly, and monopoly meant profit. Establishing the NL as the premier professional league, with entry strictly controlled by the monopolists themselves, also appealed to their sense of profits. If the new league was recognized as the premier assemblage of baseball talent then it would be able to attract a greater percentage of the better players, and with no equals to bid them away, it would lower the payroll burden, leaving a larger percentage of the revenues for the owners. Another reason to concentrate the quality of talent at the top was to reduce the number of poor drawing games played against low quality competition in small towns.

Michael Haupert, *William Hulbert and the Birth of the National League*, Baseball Research Journal (spring 2015), *available at* https://sabr.org/research/william-hulbert-and-birth-national-league. A constitution was approved by the eight charter members: the Boston Red Stockings, Hartford Dark Blues, New York Mutuals, Philadelphia Athletics, Cincinnati Red Stockings, Louisville Grays, Chicago White Stockings, and St. Louis Brown Stockings. The constitution provided that the league was to be governed by a board of five owners chosen by lot.

As recounted by Stefan Szymanski and Andrew Zimbalist in *National Pastime: How Americans Play Baseball and the Rest of the World Plays Soccer* (Brookings Inst. Press 2005), this model was emulated by the first sports league in England, the Football League. However, because England had a national sports governing board, the powerful Football Association, who organized the lucrative knock-out FA Cup competition, Football League clubs quickly developed the very different "promotion and relegation" model, leading to what is now known as the European Model of Sport. *See* James A.R. Nafziger, "European and North American models of sports organization," in *Handbook on International Sports Law* (James A.R. Nafziger & Stephen F. Ross, eds. Edward Elgar 2011). Back in North America, the NL model has been largely followed by the other major professional sports and retains much of the form devised by Hulburt and his compatriots nearly a century and a half ago.

2. LEAGUE CONSTITUTIONS

The fundamental structure of the four major North American sports leagues is similar. The Major League Baseball (MLB) Constitution is an agreement among participating clubs (Art. I). It creates the office of a commissioner, and defines the powers delegated to this officer and means for electing and terminating a commissioner (Art. II). Although the text confers broad powers on the Commissioner (including punitive action against owners, employees or players "that is deemed by the Commissioner not to be in the best interests of baseball" (Art. II, § 3), the text also limits authority in specific cases. *See, e.g.,* Art. II, § 4 (limiting application to matters subject to a vote of the owners). The Constitution specifies majority or super-majority votes required for various actions (Art. V, § 2). It specifies (Art. VI) that *all*

> disputes and controversies related in any way to professional baseball between Clubs or between a Club(s) and any Major League Baseball entity(ies) (including in each case, without limitation, their owners, officers, directors, employees and players), other than those whose resolution is expressly provided for by another means in this Constitution, the Major League Rules, the Basic Agreement with the Major League Baseball Players Association, or the collective bargaining agreement with any representative of the Major League umpires, shall be submitted to the Commissioner, as arbitrator, who, after hearing,

shall have the sole and exclusive right to decide such disputes and controversies and whose decision shall be final and unappealable.

The Constitution specifies the teams in the league and the extraordinary circumstances where a team's membership can be terminated (Art. VIII). It also specifies, by state and county, the territories where each club shall operate, while delegating to the Commissioner the designation of broadcast territories (Art. VIII, § 8), and specifying broadcast rights (Art. X § 3).

3. SPORTS LEAGUES AS JOINT VENTURES OF CLUB OWNERS

This brief summary reflects the fundamental nature of North American sports leagues as a contractual relationship among the clubs participating in the competition. The nature of a sports league is a critical issue in determining the appropriate application of the antitrust laws to sport: Chapter 5, Section D discusses the Supreme Court's decision in *American Needle, Inc. v. National Football League,* 560 U.S. 183 (2010). There, the Court observed that each club "is a substantial, independently owned, and independently managed business." *Id.* at 196. Because "the financial performance of each team, while related to that of the others, does not . . . necessarily rise and fall with that of the others," *id.,* citing *North American Soccer League v. NFL,* 670 F.2d 1249, 1252 (2d Cir. 1982), their corporate actions are guided by " 'separate corporate consciousnesses,' and [their] 'objectives are' not 'common.' " 560 U.S. at 196 (citing *Copperweld Corp. v. Indep. Tube Corp.,* 467 U.S. 752, 771 (1984). The Court's analysis makes clear that North American sports leagues are joint ventures, which are functionally distinct from a single enterprise. Although clubs "have common interests in promoting the NFL brand, they are still separate, profit-maximizing entities, and their interests . . . are not necessarily aligned." *Id.* at 196.

The Court's characterization of sports leagues as joint ventures has important implications for how those aggrieved by league policies might seek judicial review. As discussed extensively in Chapters 5–7, parties can use the antitrust laws to allege that these decisions constitute unreasonable restraints of trade in violation of the Sherman Act. As detailed below in Chapter 1, Section B, Part (4), parties can also challenge decisions under the law of private associations.

4. COMPARATIVE PERSPECTIVES

In comparative perspective, another key aspect of North American sports leagues is that their structure is wholly separate from other North American sports institutions. Other than a few specific community-oriented programs, Major League Baseball has little to do with the wholly-separate entities that control Little League, interscholastic and intercollegiate baseball, traveling "pay-for-play" youth teams, and adult recreational competitions often organized by local park and recreation departments. This contrasts with the structure typical in other countries, where a national governing board sits on top of a "pyramid" of governance, with a varying degree of control over commercially-successful major leagues, but also controlling the national team and regulating all aspects of youth and recreational sport. European Commission, *The European Model of Sport*, Consultation Document of DG X (September 1998) 2–3. For example, the clubs in the English Premier League make purely commercial decisions such as broadcast licensing or rules governing sponsorships and marketing, just as clubs in the NFL do. However, rules of the game, on-field regulations, player discipline, and similar matters are determined by the English Football Association (the FA), or federations to which the FA belongs, such as UEFA or FIFA.

5. AN ECONOMIC ANALYSIS OF LEAGUE STRUCTURE

Unusual in business but typical in government, the structure of North American sports leagues requires the approval of multiple stakeholders to respond to changes in a dynamic social and business environment. As with public policy, changes in sports policy are rarely "Pareto efficient" (where everyone is better off and no one is worse off). Thus, proponents of any changes in labor rules, revenue sharing, structure of the playoffs, location of teams, etc., must overcome or assuage stakeholders who are adversely affected by the change, even if the change is good for the sport as a whole.

The insights of two Nobel-prize winning economists are relevant here. Adopting a standard economic model that assumes all parties have perfect information and there are no bargaining costs, Ronald Coase's famous theorem holds that private parties will bargain toward the efficient result regardless of how legal rules allocate rights. A critical corollary to this insight, however, is Coase's view that where imperfect information and significant transaction costs are likely to inhibit efficient bargaining, then the legal system has to consider how best to allocate rights initially. Ronald Coase, *The Problem of Social Costs*, 3 J. Law & Econ. 1 (1960). The extent to which sports leagues feature information asymmetries and bargaining costs that are not overcome by the parties is a critical issue in sports law and business.

If these dynamics significantly inhibit parties from working out efficient results, then the question arises as to why sports leagues would create governance structures that allow stakeholders to veto innovations that are actually good for the sport or league as a whole. These include control by club owners with their own individual interests, and super-majority votes by these owners. Why not vest management of the league in a corporate board of directors and a CEO?

The work of Oliver Williamson provides some answers. (A nice review is in the Prologue to his book, *Mechanisms of Governance* (Oxford Univ. Press 1996).) He explains business structures as techniques to minimize transactions costs. Thus, in a variety of contexts, granting parochial stakeholders a right to veto significant change is a means of securing agreement among the parties and avoiding costly contracting about unforeseen future events: parties can be assured their own interests will be protected as long as they have these veto rights. For example, the legal admission of a new partner to a partnership requires the entire partnership agreement to be redone. The MLB Constitution permits the admission of new clubs with a super-majority vote, without having to deal with this hoary subject in advance.

These insights are useful as we consider a number of issues in sports law:

- When should league owners reserve authority to themselves, and when should they delegate authority to a Commissioner? To what extent can the Commissioner's authority be used to overcome information and bargaining cost problems?

- What vote should be required for important league policies? How can proponents of innovations use economic or legal strategies to overcome a block that can veto the proposals?

- In reviewing legal challenges to sports league decisions, to what extent can judges confidently defer to league choices?

6. FIDUCIARY DUTIES AND LEAGUE GOVERNANCE

As discussed in detail in Chapter 5, Section D, a difference between a North American sports league and an integrated company like McDonald's or General Motors is that publicly-traded corporations are governed by boards of directors with fiduciary duties to the shareholders as a whole. Unlike corporations or partnerships, it does not appear that sports owners, when acting under the league constitution as the governors of the sport, are required to act like directors or partners. The word "fiduciary" does not appear in any of the four major league constitutions. Language in the NFL Constitution suggests that owners may appropriately adopt or reject policies that serve the interests of their club, rather than the league as a whole: Art. II, § 2.1(a) provides that the NFL is organized for the purpose to "promote and foster the primary business of League members, each member being an owner of a professional football club located in the United States." *See also* NHL Const., Art. II, § 2.1 (same). The MLB Constitution seems to assume that owners may act in their own interest, rather than the best interests of baseball, creating limited opportunities for the Commissioner to overrule owners' votes on rules or policies. *See* MLB Const., Art. II, § 4 (allowing Commissioner to override owners' actions on matters requiring a vote of the clubs pursuant to Art. II, § 9 [election of commissioner] or Art. V, § 2 [collective bargaining, schedules, post-season play, playing rules, broadcast rights, expansion or relocation, sale of ownership, divisional play, revenue sharing, exclusion of club from league], but only where the matter "involves the integrity of, or public confidence in, the national game of Baseball."

Claims of breach of fiduciary duty by a fellow owner have been rarely litigated. Indeed, it would appear that under Art. V of the MLB Constitution, such a claim could not be brought in court but would have to be submitted to the Commissioner as arbitrator. In one case involving ongoing disputes between maverick NFL owner Al Davis and the league, *Oakland Raiders v. NFL*, 131 Cal. App. 4th 631 (2005), the court of appeal held the other club owners held no fiduciary duty toward the Raiders regarding league policies. In another case involving a defunct NHL rival, *Professional Hockey Corp. v. World Hockey Ass'n (WHA)*, 143 Cal. App. 3d 410, 191 Cal. Rptr. 773 (1983), a California court held that the representatives of each franchise on the Board of Trustees of the WHA (a corporate entity) had a fiduciary duty to act for the benefit of the league as a whole when making decisions about common league goals.

Under general partnership law, which treats joint ventures as a type of partnership, each partner has a fiduciary duty to place the interests of the venture above his own interests unless the partnership agreement or the other partners allow otherwise. On the other hand, business associations such as limited liability companies (LLCs) typically do not include a requirement that those governing the entity must act in the best interests of the entity as a whole. *See* 1 Larry Ribstein & Robert Keatinge, *Ribstein and Keatinge on Ltd. Liab. Cos.* § 9:12 (2017). In *American Needle*, the Supreme Court cited with approval an insightful analysis, Zenichi Shishido, *Conflicts of Interest and Fiduciary Duties in the Operation of a Joint Venture*, 39 Hastings L. J. 63 (1987). Professor Shishido notes that, unlike for corporate directors, there exists a "duplicity of joint ventures' directors' interests. Almost all the directors of a joint venture are interlocking directors or employees of one of the parent companies; thus, they have interests not only in the joint venture but also in one of the parent companies." *Id.* at 71. Likewise, the well-recognized duty of a controlling shareholder to shareholders of subsidiary companies does not apply in a joint venture setting. He observes that when a conflict arises in the interests of a joint venture and those of "parent companies," officers of both will typically give the interests of the parent (*i.e.* the club, in the sports league context) the higher priority. *Id.* at 73.

Consider the application of this principle to sport leagues. The next section discusses an MLB dispute arising because league executives and most owners believed a realignment placing the Chicago Cubs in the NL West (at a time of two divisions) and the Atlanta Braves in the NL East was superior. The Cubs' ownership objected, reportedly because it feared that adding late-starting west coast games to the Cubs' schedule would detract from the television ratings of the Cubs' games broadcast on the team's corporate sibling, the Chicago superstation WGN. Putting aside the specific powers of the Commissioner in resolving this dispute, should each owner have a judicially enforceable duty to vote in favor of the interests of the league at the expense of its own team's financial rewards? Do owners of clubs in large media markets have a fiduciary duty to vote in favor of sharing their teams' television revenues with teams in smaller markets? Did Baltimore Orioles' owner Peter Angelos breach a duty to fellow owners by blocking the relocation of the failing Montreal Expos to Washington until, after over five years, a complex side deal about broadcast rights was signed? If they are not under such a duty, is that because no such legal duty exists, or because the parties to the Major League Constitution have implicitly waived each owner's duty in certain contexts when they vote on league affairs?

As a comparative note on this issue, the English Premier League's governing documents vest minimal power in their Board of Directors and assign most decisions to the twenty clubs who are "shareholders" in the governing entity. This is done because under English law (as with American law), in most circumstances shareholders do not have a fiduciary duty to adopt policies that maximize the interests of all.

B. THE HISTORY AND LEGAL AUTHORITY OF THE SPORTS LEAGUE COMMISSIONER

The origin and evolution of the unique role of Commissioner of Baseball is detailed by Andrew Zimbalist, *In the Best Interests of Baseball? The Revolutionary Reign of Bud Selig* (Hoboken, N.J.: John Wiley & Sons 2006). In its 1876 Constitution, the National League vested authority in a board of directors of five randomly selected owners, who chose a President from among its ranks. The National Agreement that ended a brief interleague war between the National and American Leagues in 1903 created a National Commission consisting of the presidents of the two leagues and a third member chosen by the other two, subject to renewal annually.

According to Zimbalist, the preservation of regulatory authority in each league president for "conduct detrimental to the general welfare of the game" (see the *Johnson* case in Section B, *infra*), the lack of owner support for the Commission, and the resistance to the leadership of American League President Ban Johnson caused owners to seek structural reform "well before" the Black Sox Scandal broke in 1919. At the same time, when word of the "Black Sox" scandal emerged a full year later, both fans and club owners felt that the source of the problem was the lax disciplinary approach of the National Commission. The owners decided to dismantle the tripartite commission and replace it with a single, powerful commissioner. Their first pick for that position was former President William Howard Taft (an avid baseball fan who was the first chief executive to throw out the first pitch of the baseball season and may also have originated the 7th inning stretch), but he declined. (Taft was rewarded with appointment by President Harding as Chief Justice of the United States six months later). The man actually tagged for that position was Kenesaw Mountain Landis, a 38-year-old federal judge in Chicago who had initially caught the owners' eye with his favorable handling of the Federal League antitrust suit a few years earlier (see Chapter 4). Landis agreed to take this new $50,000 per year (over $600,000 today) position only if the Major League Agreement was rewritten to give the commissioner the sweeping powers described in *Rose v. Giamatti*, which is discussed in the following pages. (Landis originally wanted the title "high commissioner.") *See generally*, David Pietrusza, *Judge and Jury: The Life and Times of Judge Kenesaw Mountain Landis* (South Bend, IN: Diamond Communications, Inc. 1998).

On January 12, 1921, a new National Agreement created the office of Commissioner. Prior to its enactment, Landis spoke to the owners as follows:

> It is my duty to be very frank with you. . . . I got the impression [that you] had a structure outlined which provided for authority to discharge a responsibility and that part of that authority would be control over whatever and whoever had to do with baseball.
>
> Another impression was that there had grown up in baseball certain evils not limited to bad baseball players; that men who controlled ball clubs in the past had been guilty of various offenses and the time had come where somebody would be given the authority, if I may put it brutally, to save you from yourselves. . . .

Quoted in Daniel Ginsburg, *The Fix is In: A History of Baseball Gambling and Game Fixing Scandals* 35 (Jefferson, N.C.: McFarland, 1995). Threatening to refuse the position if, as the latest draft constitution suggested, his powers were limited to crooked ballplayers, the owners granted Landis plenary powers over the entire game.

A case that dramatically raised issues of the integrity of the game and the unique role of a sports league commissioner was the "collision at home plate" between baseball Commissioner Bart Giamatti and baseball superstar Pete Rose. Key legal events are recounted here.

In the early winter of 1989, rumors began to filter into the Commissioner's Office that Rose, then manager of the Cincinnati Reds, had been betting on baseball games, even on games involving his own team. If true, that action would have violated a sixty-year-old Major League Rule that required a one-year suspension for anyone betting on baseball and a lifetime ban for betting on a game involving one's own team. Accordingly, on February 23, newly-elected Commissioner Bart Giamatti, a classics scholar who was the former President of Yale University, hired John Dowd, a Washington lawyer, to investigate this allegation. The Commissioner was acting under the authority granted him by a document known then as the "Major League Agreement" (now renamed the "Constitution"). As it was written then (the current version is available in the Documentary Supplement section of the text's website), Article I, § 2, provided that "the functions of the Commissioner" include:

> (a) To investigate, either upon complaint or upon his own initiative, any act, transaction or practice charged, alleged or suspected to be not in the best interests of the national game of Baseball, with authority to summon persons and to order the production of documents and, in cases of refusal to appear or produce, to impose such penalties as are hereinafter provided;
>
> (b) To determine, after investigation, what preventive, remedial or punitive action is appropriate in the premises, and to take such action either against Major Leagues, Major League Clubs, or individuals, as the case may be.

In early May, after three months of investigating and interviewing some 40 witnesses, including taking sworn statements from Rose and the two key informants against him, Ron Peters and Paul Janszen, Dowd delivered to Giamatti a 225-page report (with seven volumes of evidence and exhibits) that ended with Dowd's judgment that Rose had regularly bet on Reds games (although apparently Rose always bet on his Reds to win). Giamatti immediately sent this report to Rose and his lawyers and scheduled Rose's hearing before him for late June.

On April 18, however, Giamatti had sent a letter to U.S. District Judge Carl Rubin, who was preparing to sentence Ron Peters for federal drug and income tax offenses. Giamatti stated in his letter that Peters had been "candid, forthright and truthful" in providing investigators "critical sworn testimony" about Rose. The Cincinnati-based Judge Rubin, an avowed Reds fan who was highly exercised by what he termed the Commissioner's "vendetta against Pete Rose," sent a copy of the letter to Reuven Katz, Rose's principal lawyer. Armed with this letter, Katz filed suit in state court to enjoin Giamatti from going any further with the disciplinary proceeding. The contention was that Giamatti had prejudged the facts of the case, and thus had denied Rose his right to a proceeding conducted with "due regard for all the principles of natural justice and fair play," as the Commissioner's own disciplinary rules required. Rose won a controversial 10-day restraining order from state court Judge Norbert Nadel, the first time the action of any sports commissioner had been enjoined. (Nadel faced re-election later that year for his judicial office, and the Rose case offered him a unique opportunity to demonstrate to his constituents his adoration of the Reds manager.) Giamatti sought to remove the case to federal district court on diversity of citizenship grounds.

In arguing for removal, the Commissioner's counsel asserted that this case should be heard only by a "national tribunal":

> In the state court in Cincinnati, I need not describe Mr. Rose's standing. He is a local hero, perhaps the first citizen of Cincinnati. And Commissioner Giamatti is viewed suspiciously as a foreigner from New York, trapped in an ivory tower, and accused of bias by Mr. Rose. Your Honor, this is a textbook example of why diversity jurisdiction was created in the Federal Courts and why it exists to this very day.

But that removal could be obtained only if this case were deemed to be a dispute just between Rose, a citizen of Ohio, and Giamatti, a citizen of New York. If the Cincinnati Reds, also a citizen of Ohio in the eyes of the law, were considered a real party to this conflict, then the complete diversity of citizenship required for federal jurisdiction would be lacking. In applying the arcane rules of federal versus state court jurisdiction, the judicial opinion in *Rose v. Giamatti*, 721 F. Supp. 906, 917 (S.D. Ohio, 1989), laid bare "the reality . . . that Major League Baseball is a unique organization . . . [with] extraordinary power invested in the Commissioner."

Rose's argument was quite simple. Rose was the manager of the Reds, under a contract paying him $500,000 a year, a contract whose benefits he was in grave danger of losing because of Giamatti's violation of procedural fairness towards him. Clearly, then, the Reds were an appropriate party in Rose's lawsuit to prevent that from happening.

The commissioner's answer, which the federal court accepted, was that the contract between Rose and the Reds provided that "the Major League and Professional Baseball Agreements and Rules and all amendments thereto hereafter adopted, are hereby made a part of this contract." This feature of Rose's personal employment contract stemmed from the following provision of the Major League Agreement:

> The form of players' contract to be used by the Major Leagues, and all contracts between Major Leagues or Clubs and their officers and employees, shall contain a clause by which the parties agree to submit themselves to the discipline of the Commissioner, and to accept his decisions rendered in accordance with this Agreement.

The commissioner's disciplinary authority was reinforced by the constituent members' further agreement to "be finally and unappealably bound" by all the disciplinary decisions of the commissioner, and to "waive such right of recourse to the courts as would otherwise have existed in their favor." The judge read this network of contractual relationships as establishing a commissioner's office wielding judicial power totally independently of control by either the Reds individually or the 26 clubs collectively. (As the judge observed, the constitution ordained that "neither the Commissioner's powers nor his compensation may be diminished during his term of office.") That meant that only Rose and Giamatti were real parties to this case, which therefore was properly removable to the federal judicial arena.

The district court issued its decision removing the case to federal court on July 31, 1990. Perhaps because he was then facing even more pressing legal problems with the Internal Revenue Service, Rose agreed on August 23 to settle the baseball case on the terms that Rose would withdraw his suit, accept the Commissioner's jurisdiction and penalty, but neither admit nor deny having bet on baseball. As penalty, Giamatti declared Rose permanently ineligible to associate with any major or minor league baseball club. (After a year, however, Rose would be entitled to apply to the commissioner for termination of this lifetime ban.) Eight days later, Giamatti was dead of a heart attack, succeeded in office by his counsel and close friend, Francis "Fay" Vincent. A few months later, Rose went to jail for income tax fraud—in particular, for concealing large cash payments from baseball autograph shows (money that Rose had used to cover his large gambling losses). Rose finally admitted in his best-selling autobiography, *My Prison Without Bars*, what he told Commissioner Selig in late 2002: he had regularly placed bets with bookmakers on his Cincinnati Reds when he was managing as well as playing for them, but always on his team to win. Rose's efforts for reinstatement in baseball's good graces continue, unsuccessfully, to this day.

NOTES AND QUESTIONS

1. *Why Should a Commissioner Decide This Issue?* Why would MLB owners want a Commissioner to decide a case like that of Rose, rather than assign the decision to the ownership of the most concerned club, the Reds? Why would the owners prefer to delegate to a Commissioner rather than to an ad hoc ownership committee?

2. *Legal Basis for Judicial Review?* On what law could Rose base any claim that he was treated unfairly by the Commissioner? Was the Commissioner, or MLB, constrained by the due process clause or any other constitutional provision? Was Rose limited to making common law arguments that would apply to any private association?

3. *The Proper Role of Judges in "Civil Society."* Perhaps the most fundamental issue posed by *Rose v. Giamatti*—the theme that runs through the entire field of sports and the law—is the extent to which public law,

speaking through judges, should overturn decisions made by private leagues, usually speaking through their commissioners. The challenge to the law is captured by this passage from George Will's review of author James Reston's *Collision at Home Plate*:

> Reston does not do justice to how close the *Rose* case came to becoming another case of a familiar political pathology. Yet another functioning American institution—the commissioner's office—almost became a victim of judicial overreaching. Today's courts have an unhealthy itch to supervise and fine-tune virtually every equity judgment in American life. Rose's legal strategy was to find a judge willing to insinuate himself into baseball's disciplinary procedures. If Rose had succeeded, the commissioner's office would have been irreparably damaged. Its core function, which is disciplinary, would permanently have been put in question. Another of civil society's intermediary associations—those that stand between the individual and the state—would have been broken to the saddle of government. A nanny-like judiciary would henceforth have made the commissioner's office negligible—another hitherto private institution permeated by state power.

George Will, *Foul Ball*, N.Y. Rev. of Books, June 27, 1991, at 31, 34. Do you agree with Will? Would you feel the same way had courts sought to intervene regarding the pernicious example of Judge Landis, who strictly maintained apartheid in our National Game?

C. THE LEGAL SCOPE OF THE COMMISSIONER'S AUTHORITY OVER CONDUCT DETRIMENTAL TO THE GENERAL WELFARE OF THE GAME

The source and scope of any judicial scrutiny that could be given to Commissioner Giamatti's treatment of Rose can be traced in the following cases. As you read each of the decisions reproduced in this chapter, look for and reflect upon the answers to the following questions:

1. What is the source of the commissioner's authority to act in the given case? Why is this authority given to the commissioner rather than to an individual club, to an outside arbitrator, or to a public official or judge?

2. What is the scope of the commissioner's power—that is, under the asserted source of authority, in what situations is the commissioner empowered to take action in cases of this type?

3. What procedures should the commissioner follow in deciding on the course of action? What is the source of these procedural requirements?

4. If there are factual doubts or disputes, what standard of proof should the commissioner employ in the given case—

reasonable suspicion, preponderance of the evidence, clear and convincing evidence, or proof beyond a reasonable doubt? Or can he do whatever attracts his fancy?

5. What remedy or penalty may the commissioner employ in the specific case?

6. Finally, and most importantly, what is (and what should be) the jurisdiction of a court (or an arbitrator) to review the commissioner's action, *i.e.*, the commissioner's answers to questions two through five. What legal theories can legitimately be employed to challenge the action? What standard of review will a court use in these legal challenges?

The legal starting point is *American League Baseball Club of New York (Yankees) v. Johnson*, 179 N.Y.S. 498 (N.Y. Sup. Ct. 1919). This litigation occurred near the end of the "National Commission" era in major league governance, during which American League President Byron "Ban" Johnson was acknowledged to be the strongest figure in the game. *See* Eugene X. Murdock, *Ban Johnson: Czar of Baseball* (Westport, CN: Greenwood Press, 1982). Carl Mays, a pitcher for the Boston Red Sox, walked off the field in the middle of a game, and went fishing the next day. While Johnson waited for the Red Sox to take disciplinary action, Sox owner Harry Frazee instead sold Mays to the Yankees (this was a rehearsal for the next such transaction between the two clubs, which involved Babe Ruth). When he learned of the sale, Johnson himself suspended Mays for "deserting his club and breaking contract." Furious at losing Mays' services in the midst of the pennant race, the Yankees sued Johnson, calling him an "unmolested despot." The case was heard by then Judge, later Senator, Robert Wagner of New York.

Judge Wagner's decision began by stating:

> It is undisputed, and, indeed, a matter of common knowledge, that the commercialization of baseball is a highly profitable undertaking, rendering lucrative returns to the member clubs, to their stockholders, and to their employees. Large capital is invested in the enterprise, and the property representative of this capital consists principally of contracts with individual players, together with the reputation of the club for skill and ability in playing the game. Suspension of a player, therefore, not only interferes with his individual contract, but may also interfere with the reputation and collective ability of the club. Inasmuch as the leading clubs of the league and their players are entitled at the end of the season to certain rights and privileges which are unquestionably to be deemed property rights, this interference with an individual player would confuse and possibly destroy the

rights of the respective clubs and their players, for the validity of the games in which Mays participated might be questioned.

Johnson had asserted that the following language of § 20 of the league constitution gave him authority for his action:

> The president, in the performance of his duties, shall have the power to impose fines or penalties, in the way of suspension or otherwise, upon any manager or player who, in his opinion, has been guilty of conduct detrimental to the general welfare of the game.

The Yankees responded, and Judge Wagner agreed, that the wording of § 24 assigned responsibility for these questions to the individual team:

> Each club belonging to this league shall have the right to regulate its own affairs, to establish its own rules, and to discipline, punish, suspend or expel its manager, players or other employees, and these powers shall not be limited to cases of dishonest play or open insubordination, but shall include all questions of carelessness, indifference, or other conduct of the player that may be regarded by the club as prejudicial to its interest, but not in conflict with any provision of the National Agreement or this constitution.

In addition, the league President had the authority to exercise disciplinary authority only "in the performance of his duties," which the judge characterized as follows:

> Under these rules it is the right and duty of the president to regulate the actual playing of the game on the field and to enforce the rules instituted for the governing of the game. Doubtless his powers would extend to the discipline of players for any infringement of these rules upon the field, or for an overt act committed by a player on the field in violation of the rules. Beyond that power, however, it does not seem that the president may proceed, for under the constitution he is given power to discipline only in the performance of his duties, and his duties are only such as are set forth in the constitution and playing rules.

> The offense of which Mays was accused was obviously not one of those embraced within the prohibition of these rules. It was not an overt act committed on the field.

Although that literal reading of the constitution did not square with historical practice, the judge stated:

> On behalf of the defendant, contention is made that many times in the past the defendant Johnson had exercised power similar to that which he claims the right to exercise under the present circumstances, that his jurisdiction to make orders similar to the

one now in dispute has never been questioned, and that the parties to a contract will be bound by the construction which their conduct and acquiescence have placed upon it. Although courts have placed great weight on the construction which parties have put upon contracts existing between them, such considerations must never violate the fundamental concepts of justice. If the original act was unauthorized, repetition does not invest the act with authority. If the construction did not convey power to the president, he cannot prescriptively acquire power by continual usurpation. If the opposite were true he would, in effect, effectuate an amendment of the constitution by usurpation. In his immortal and always useful Farewell Address, Washington said:

> "If in the opinion of the people the distribution or modification of the constitutional powers be in any particular wrong, let it be corrected by an amendment in the way which the Constitution designates, but let there be no change by usurpation."

So in this case there can be no change by usurpation. The structure of precedents must fall, unless laid on the foundation of authority.

Accordingly, Judge Wagner granted a permanent injunction against Mays' suspension. The Yankees' celebratory press release stated that "our fight has not been for Mays alone, but to safeguard the vested property rights of the individual club-owners against the continual encroachments on club rights by the president, who has never been clothed with the powers that he has taken unto himself."

The one reported legal challenge to Commissioner Landis' authority was a skirmish in what was ultimately an unsuccessful effort by the Commissioner to prevent MLB clubs from creating farm systems.*

MILWAUKEE AMER. ASS'N v. LANDIS
49 F.2d 298 (N.D. Ill. 1931)

LINDLEY, DISTRICT JUDGE.

* * *

Under the Major League Agreement the office of commissioner was created, and his functions were defined. . . . He was given jurisdiction to hear and determine finally any disputes between leagues and clubs or to

---

* *See* Zimbalist, *In the Best Interests of Baseball?*, 44–47. The development of farm systems is detailed in a Supplemental Webnote, "Note on Waiver and Option Rules," available on the Casebook's website (http://pennstatelaw.psu.edu/SportsTextWebsite). The note also provides additional background on the disagreement between Commissioner Landis and owners over the development of farm systems.

which a player might be a party, certified to him, and authorized, in case of "conduct detrimental to baseball," to impose punishment and pursue appropriate legal remedies; to determine finally a disagreement over any proposed amendment to the rules; and "to take such other steps as he might deem necessary and proper in the interest and morale of the players and the honor of the game." Optional agreements with players were defined and assignments thereof required to be filed with, and approved by, the commissioner. The parties agreed to abide by the decisions of the latter and the discipline imposed by him under the agreement and severally waived right of recourse to the courts. Similar covenants appear in the Major-Minor agreement, the National Association agreement and the uniform contracts with players.

The Major-Minor League agreement recognizes the office of commissioner and the jurisdiction aforesaid and provides that, in case of any dispute between any Major club and any Minor club, the disputants may certify the dispute to the commissioner for decision, and that his determination shall be final.

The various agreements and rules constituting a complete code for, or charter and by-laws of, organized baseball in America, disclose a clear intent upon the part of the parties to endow the commissioner with all the attributes of a benevolent but absolute despot and all the disciplinary powers of the proverbial *pater familias*.

* * *

The parties endowed the commissioner with wide powers and discretion to hear controversies that might be submitted to him and of his own initiative to observe, investigate and take such action as necessary to secure observance of the provisions of the agreements and rules, promotion of the expressed ideals of, and prevention of conduct detrimental to, baseball. The code is expressly designed and intended to foster keen, clean competition in the sport of baseball, to preserve discipline and a high standard of morale, to produce an equality of conditions necessary to the promotion of keen competition and to protect players against clubs, clubs against players, and clubs against clubs.

* * *

Certain acts are specified as detrimental to baseball, but it is expressly provided that nothing contained in the code shall be construed as exclusively defining or otherwise limiting acts, practices or conduct detrimental to baseball. It is contended that this phrase should be so construed as to include only such conduct as is similar to that expressly mentioned. However, the provisions are so unlimited in character that we can conclude only that the parties did not intend so to limit the meaning of conduct detrimental to baseball, but intended to vest in the commissioner jurisdiction to prevent any conduct destructive of the aims of the code. Apparently it was the intent of the parties to make the commissioner an arbiter, whose decisions made in good faith, upon evidence, upon all questions relating to the purpose of the organization and all conduct detrimental thereto, should be absolutely binding. So great was the parties' confidence in the man selected for the position and so great the trust placed in him that certain of the agreements were to continue only so long as he should remain commissioner.

[Infielder Fred Bennett had been "assigned" several times between the St. Louis Browns and several minor league teams, under terms that did not require the Browns to make Bennett available to other teams through waivers, but presumably gave other teams the ability to purchase Bennett's contract from the minor league club to which he had been "assigned." When Landis learned that all these clubs were secretly controlled by Browns' owner Phil Ball, he refused to approve the assignment to Milwaukee and declared Bennett a free agent.]

Plaintiffs contend that the commissioner has no power to declare a player a free agent. In his answer, the commissioner states that it is his view that, by reason of the alleged breach of the code by plaintiffs and their denial of Bennett's rights, plaintiffs have made it his duty to declare Bennett absolved from any contractual obligations which he may have had with either plaintiff and to declare him a free agent. Obviously declaring Bennett a free agent is a mere declaration of legal effect, that is, the result of finding that the St. Louis Club has forfeited its rights by violating the spirit and intent of the code. Whether there is given to the commissioner the power in so many words to declare Bennett a free agent is immaterial, since the agreements and rules grant to the commissioner jurisdiction to refuse to approve Bennett's assignment by St. Louis to Milwaukee, and to declare him absolved from the burdens of the same and of his contract with St. Louis.

* * *

It is asserted that this wide grant of jurisdiction of the commissioner is an attempt to deprive the court of its jurisdiction and that such a provision as is contained in these agreements, rules, and uniform contract is contrary to public policy. No doubt the decision of any arbiter, umpire, engineer, or similar person endowed with the power to decide may not be exercised in an illegal manner, that is fraudulently, arbitrarily, without legal basis for the same or without any evidence to justify action. The many cases cited upon the power and jurisdiction of such officials are not in serious conflict. An agreement to arbitrate a controverted question and to deprive all courts of jurisdiction, so long as in executory form, is quite commonly held void, but an actual submission to an arbiter or umpire in good faith is proper, and decision under same is binding, unless it is unsupported by evidence, or unless the decision is upon some basis without legal foundation or beyond legal recognition.

Plaintiffs submitted to the defendant as commissioner an optional contract, which under the code could not be effective unless approved by him. After ascertaining the facts, he refused to approve the same. This, if we look at it from the point of arbitration, was an executed agreement for arbitration, and called for more than ministerial action. As we have seen, the commissioner is given almost unlimited discretion in the determination of whether or not a certain state of facts creates a situation detrimental to the national game of baseball. The commissioner rightfully found that the common control of St. Louis and the named Minor Clubs by one person made it possible to create a situation whereby the clear intent of the adopted code that the players under the control of a Major club should not be kept with a Minor club more than two successive seasons without giving other Major clubs the right to claim him was clearly violated, and a result achieved highly detrimental to the national game of baseball. The facts negative any assertion that this decision was made arbitrarily or fraudulently. It was made in pursuance of jurisdiction granted to the commissioner with the expressed desire to achieve certain ends, that is, to keep the game of baseball clean, to promote clean competition, to prevent collusive or fraudulent contracts, to protect players' rights, to furnish them full opportunity to advance in accord with their abilities and to prevent their deprival of such opportunities by subterfuge, covering or other unfair conduct.

Suit dismissed.

―――

The last four decades have witnessed a much more active use of commissioner authority in a fast-changing sports environment. In his autobiography, *Hardball: The Education of a Baseball Commissioner*, at 173–87 and 259–64, former baseball commissioner Bowie Kuhn recounts many such cases: two of the most controversial involved maverick club owners Charlie Finley of the Oakland Athletics and Ted Turner of the Atlanta Braves. (A revealing counterpoint to Kuhn's account of these times and these cases can be found in the memoirs of the leader of the Major League Baseball Players Association when it won free agency for its members. Marvin Miller, *A Whole Different Ball Game: The Sport and Business of Baseball* (New York: Birch Lane Press, 1991).) Both of these cases grew out of an arbitration ruling reproduced in Chapter 4: the 1975 arbitration decision in the *Andy Messersmith/Dave McNally* grievance that eviscerated the "reserve clause" that had tied baseball players for life to their original team, and gave players the freedom to move to a new team upon expiration of their current contracts.

Among the most concerned was Athletics' owner Charles Finley. Despite an ill-advised move from Kansas City to Oakland, where the Athletics had to compete with the San Francisco Giants for support in the Bay Area, Finley had successfully used the draft system (instituted by baseball in 1965) to build the most powerful team in the game in the early 1970s: five straight divisional titles and three straight World Series championships. Unfortunately, Finley tended to treat his players like "plantation hands" (as Kuhn observed), including such stars as Reggie Jackson, Vida Blue, and Jim "Catfish" Hunter. With free agency pending, the A's appeared to risk the loss of its players. Still, Finley had a few aces up his sleeve. Because of MLB rules barring "tampering" with players currently under contract with other teams until they became free agents, Finley not only enjoyed the exclusive right to the baseball services of stars like Jackson and Blue but also the exclusive right to negotiate a new contract with them. Thus, Finley articulated the following strategy: he would sell off his current player assets, the veteran stars of his three-time World Series Champion A's, and invest the proceeds in development via the farm system of future assets—young stars who could not command high salaries through free agency. There was only one roadblock to his plan—Commissioner Kuhn.

CHARLES O. FINLEY V. BOWIE KUHN
569 F.2d 527 (7th Cir. 1978)

SPRECHER, CIRCUIT JUDGE.

[Just before baseball's trading deadline of June 15, 1976, Finley and the Athletics sold the contract rights to the services of Joe Rudi and Rollie Fingers to the Boston Red Sox for $2 million and of Vida Blue to the New York Yankees for $1.5 million. (To put this in perspective, the average salary in 1976 was $51,000 and the new owners of the expansion Toronto Blue Jays paid $7 million for the franchise.) Rudi and Fingers were to become free agents upon the expiration of their contracts at the end of the 1976 season. Just before the Athletics' transaction with the Yankees, Blue signed a three-year contract extension, the benefit of which was transferred to the Yankees in this sale. The day after a quickly scheduled hearing on June 17, Commissioner Kuhn disapproved the assignments of the contracts of Rudi, Fingers, and Blue to the Red Sox and Yankees "as inconsistent with the best interests of baseball, the integrity of the game and the maintenance of public confidence in it." The Commissioner expressed his concern for (1) the debilitation of the Oakland club, (2) the loss of competitive balance in professional baseball through the buying of success by the wealthier clubs, and (3) "the present unsettled circumstances of baseball's reserve system." A week later, Finley brought this suit challenging Kuhn's authority to take such action.]

II

Basic to the underlying suit brought by Oakland and to this appeal is whether the Commissioner of baseball is vested by contract with the authority to disapprove player assignments which he finds to be "not in the best interests of baseball." In assessing the measure and extent of the Commissioner's power and authority, consideration must be given to the circumstances attending the creation of the office of Commissioner, the language employed by the parties in drafting their contractual understanding, changes and amendments adopted from time to time, and the interpretation given by the parties to their contractual language throughout the period of its existence.

* * *

[After recounting the story we read earlier about how the "Black Sox Scandal" had "proved the catalyst" for creating a commissioner position with full authority over baseball, the judge continued.]

* * *

The Major Leagues and their constituent clubs severally agreed to be bound by the decisions of the Commissioner and by the discipline imposed by him. They further agreed to "waive such right of recourse to the courts as would otherwise have existed in their favor." Major League Agreement, Art. VII, Sec. 2.

Upon Judge Landis' death in 1944, the Major League Agreement was amended in two respects to limit the Commissioner's authority. First, the parties deleted the provision by which they had agreed to waive their right of recourse to the courts to challenge actions of the Commissioner. Second the parties added the following language to Article I, 3:

> No Major League Rule or other joint action of the two Major Leagues, and no action or procedure taken in compliance with any such Major League Rule or joint action of the two Major Leagues shall be considered or construed to be detrimental to Baseball.

The district court found that this addition had the effect of precluding the Commissioner from finding an act that complied with the Major League Rules to be detrimental to the best interests of baseball.

The two 1944 amendments to the Major League Agreement remained in effect during the terms of the next two Commissioners, A.B. "Happy" Chandler and Ford Frick. Upon Frick's retirement in 1964 and in accordance with his recommendation, the parties adopted three amendments to the Major League Agreement: (1) the language added in 1944 preventing the Commissioner from finding any act or practice "taken in compliance" with a Major League Rule to be "detrimental to baseball" was removed; (2) the provision deleted in 1944 waiving any rights of recourse to the courts to challenge a Commissioner's decision was restored; and (3) in places where the language "detrimental to the best interests of the national game of baseball" or "detrimental to baseball" appeared those words were changed to "not in the best interests of the national game of Baseball" or "not in the best interests of Baseball."

* * *

III

Despite the Commissioner's broad authority to prevent any act, transaction or practice not in the best interests of baseball, Oakland has attacked the Commissioner's disapproval of the Rudi-Fingers-Blue transactions on a variety of theories which seem to express a similar thrust in differing language.

The complaint alleged that the "action of Kuhn was arbitrary, capricious, unreasonable, discriminatory, directly contrary to historical precedent, baseball tradition, and prior rulings and actions of the Commissioner." In pre-trial answers to interrogatories, Oakland acknowledged that the Commissioner could set aside a proposed assignment of a player's contract "in an appropriate case of violation of (Major League) Rules or immoral or unethical conduct."

* * *

The plaintiff has argued that it is a fundamental rule of law that the decisions of the head of a private association must be procedurally fair. Plaintiff then argued that it was "procedurally unfair" for the Commissioner to fail to warn the plaintiff that he would "disapprove large cash assignments of star players even if they complied with the Major League Rules."

In the first place it must be recalled that prior to the assignments involved here drastic changes had commenced to occur in the reserve system and in the creation of free agents. In his opinion disapproving the Rudi, Fingers and Blue assignments, the Commissioner said that "while I am of course aware that there have been cash sales of player contracts in the past, there has been no instance in my judgment which had the potential for harm to our game as do these assignments, particularly in the present unsettled circumstances of baseball's reserve system and in the highly competitive circumstances we find in today's sports and entertainment world."

Absent the radical changes in the reserve system, the Commissioner's action would have postponed Oakland's realization of value for these players. Given those changes, the relative fortunes of all major league clubs became subject to a host of intangible speculations. No one could predict then or now with certainty that Oakland would fare better or worse relative to other clubs through the vagaries of the revised reserve system occurring entirely apart from any action by the Commissioner.

In the second place, baseball cannot be analogized to any other business or even to any other sport or entertainment. Baseball's relation to the federal antitrust laws has been characterized by the Supreme Court as an "exception," an "anomaly" and an "aberration." Baseball's management through a commissioner is equally an exception, anomaly and aberration. . . . In no other sport or business is there quite the same system, created for quite the same reasons and with quite the same underlying policies. Standards such as the best interests of baseball, the interests of the morale of the players and the honor of the game, or "sportsmanship which accepts the umpire's decision without complaint," are not necessarily familiar to courts and obviously require some expertise in their application. While it is true that professional baseball selected as its first Commissioner a federal judge, it intended only him and not the judiciary as a whole to be its umpire and governor.

As we have seen in Part II, the Commissioner was vested with broad authority and that authority was not to be limited in its exercise to situations where Major League Rules or moral turpitude was involved. When professional baseball intended to place limitations upon the Commissioner's powers, it knew how to do so. In fact, it did so during the 20-year period from 1944 to 1964.

The district court found and concluded that the Rudi-Fingers-Blue transactions were not, as Oakland had alleged in its complaint, "directly contrary to historical precedent, baseball tradition, and prior rulings." During his almost 25 years as Commissioner, Judge Landis found many acts, transactions and practices to be detrimental to the best interests of baseball in situations where neither moral turpitude nor a Major League Rule violation was involved, and he disapproved several player assignments.

On numerous occasions since he became Commissioner of baseball in February 1969, Kuhn has exercised broad authority under the best interests clause of the Major League Agreement. Many of the actions taken by him have been in response to acts, transactions or practices that involved neither the violation of a Major League Rule nor any gambling, game-throwing or other conduct associated with moral turpitude. Moreover, on several occasions Commissioner Kuhn has taken broad preventive or remedial action with respect to assignments of player contracts.

On several occasions Charles O. Finley, the principal owner of the plaintiff corporation and the general manager of the Oakland baseball club, has himself espoused that the Commissioner has the authority to exercise broad powers pursuant to the best interests clause, even where there is no violation of the Major League Rules and no moral turpitude is involved.

Twenty-one of the 25 parties to the current Major League Agreement who appeared as witnesses in the district court testified that they intended and they presently understand that the Commissioner of baseball can review and disapprove an assignment of a player contract which he finds to be not in the best interests of baseball, even if the assignment does not violate the Major League Rules and does not involve moral turpitude.

* * *

We conclude that the evidence fully supports, and we agree with, the district court's finding that "[t]he history of the adoption of the Major League Agreement in 1921 and the operation of baseball for more than 50 years under it [strongly indicate] that the Commissioner has the authority to determine whether any act, transaction or practice is 'not in the best interests of baseball,' and upon such determination, to take whatever preventive or remedial action he deems appropriate, whether or not the act, transaction or practice complies with the Major League Rules or involves moral turpitude." Any other conclusion would involve the courts in not only interpreting often complex rules of baseball to determine if they were violated but also, as noted in the Landis case, the "intent of the [baseball] code," an even more complicated and subjective task.

The Rudi-Fingers-Blue transactions had been negotiated on June 14 and 15, 1976. On June 16, the Commissioner sent a teletype to the Oakland, Boston and New York clubs and to the Players' Association expressing his "concern for possible consequences to the integrity of baseball and public confidence in the game" and setting a hearing for June 17. Present at the hearing were 17 persons representing those notified. At the outset of the hearing the Commissioner stated that he was concerned that the assignments would be harmful to the competitive capacity of Oakland; that they reflected an effort by Boston and New York to purchase star players and "bypass the usual methods of player development and acquisition which have been traditionally used in professional baseball"; and that the question to be resolved was whether the transactions "are consistent with the best interests of baseball's integrity and maintenance of public confidence in the game." He warned that it was possible that he might determine that the assignments not be approved. . . .

[In his decision] the Commissioner recognized "that there have been cash sales of player contracts in the past," but concluded that "these transactions were unparalleled in the history of the game" because there was "never anything on this scale or falling at this time of the year, or which threatened so seriously to unbalance the competitive balance of baseball." The district court concluded that the attempted assignments of

Rudi, Fingers and Blue "were at a time and under circumstances making them unique in the history of baseball."

We conclude that the evidence fully supports, and we agree with, the district court's finding and conclusion that the Commissioner "acted in good faith, after investigation, consultation and deliberation, in a manner which he determined to be in the best interests of baseball" and that "[w]hether he was right or wrong is beyond the competence and the jurisdiction of this court to decide."[44]

* * *

V

Following the bench trial, the district court reached its decision in favor of the Commissioner without considering the impact of Article VII, 2 of the Major League Agreement, wherein the major league baseball clubs agreed to be bound by the Commissioner's decisions and discipline and to waive recourse to the courts.

* * *

Oakland has urged us to apply the substantive law dealing with the "policies and rules of a private association" to the Major League Agreement and actions taken thereunder. Illinois has developed a considerable body of law dealing with the activities of private voluntary organizations and we agree that the validity and effect of the waiver of recourse clause should initially be tested under these decisions.

Even in the absence of a waiver of recourse provision in an association charter, "[i]t is generally held that courts . . . will not intervene in questions involving the enforcement of bylaws and matters of discipline in voluntary associations."

* * *

Viewed in light of these decisions, the waiver of recourse clause contested here seems to add little if anything to the common law nonreviewability of private association actions. This clause can be upheld as coinciding with the common law standard disallowing court interference. We view its inclusion in the Major League Agreement merely as a manifestation of the intent of the contracting parties to insulate from review decisions made by the Commissioner concerning the subject matter of actions taken in accordance with his grant of powers.

---

[44] It is beyond the province of this court to consider the wisdom of the Commissioner's reasons for disapproving the assignments of Rudi, Blue and Fingers. There is insufficient evidence, however, to support plaintiff's allegation that the Commissioner's action was arbitrary or capricious, or motivated by malice, ill will or anything other than the Commissioner's good faith judgment that these attempted assignments were not in the best interests of baseball. The great majority of persons involved in baseball who testified on this point shared Commissioner Kuhn's view.

* * *

Even if the waiver of recourse clause is divorced from its setting in the charter of a private, voluntary association and even if its relationship with the arbitration clause in the agreement is ignored, we think that it is valid under the circumstances here involved. Oakland claims that such clauses are invalid as against public policy. This is true, however, only under circumstances where the waiver of rights is not voluntary, knowing or intelligent, or was not freely negotiated by parties occupying equal bargaining positions. The trend of cases in many states and in the federal courts supports the conclusion of the district court under the circumstances presented here that "informed parties, freely contracting, may waive their recourse to the court."

Although the waiver of recourse clause is generally valid for the reasons discussed above, we do not believe that it forecloses access to the courts under all circumstances. Thus, the general rule of nonreviewability which governs the actions of private associations is subject to exceptions 1) where the rules, regulations or judgments of the association are in contravention to the laws of the land or in disregard of the charter or bylaws of the association, or 2) where the association has failed to follow the basic rudiments of due process of law. Similar exceptions exist for avoiding the requirements of arbitration under the United States Arbitration Act. We therefore hold that, absent the applicability of one of these narrow exceptions, the waiver of recourse clause contained in the Major League Agreement is valid and binding on the parties and the courts.

* * *

Suit dismissed.

The court in *Finley v. Kuhn* endorsed a broad authority of the commissioner to nullify club transactions. Another decision, *Atlanta National League Baseball Club & Ted Turner v. Bowie Kuhn*, 432 F. Supp. 1213 (N.D. Ga. 1977), was issued between the dates of the district and appellate court rulings in *Finley v. Kuhn*. *Turner* dealt with the commissioner's authority to discipline owners and employees of the member teams, and thus raised many issues similar to those posed later in Pete Rose's case.

In July 1976, following the events described in the *Finley* case above, Major League Baseball and its Players Association negotiated a new collective agreement with an elaborate free agency system. Players with six years of service in the Major Leagues could declare their intention to become free agents before the end of October. In early November, a draft would be conducted for those "declared" free agents, under which up to twelve teams could elect to bid for any one player. Before the draft, though, only his prior club had the right to negotiate with that player.

In August 1976, Commissioner Kuhn issued a series of directives to owners that warned them against any dealings with potential free agents prior to the "reentry draft." In September 1976, the Commissioner found that the Atlanta Braves' General Manager had made improper contact with Gary Matthews of the San Francisco Giants. For this "tampering" offense the Commissioner fined the Braves $5,000 and took away the club's first pick in the winter amateur draft. Subsequently, at a cocktail party in October 1976, Braves' owner Ted Turner told Giants' owner Bob Lurie that the Braves would go as high as necessary to get Matthews. Members of the media present at this exchange published the story.

The free agent draft was conducted on November 4, and the Braves succeeded in signing Matthews on November 17. Subsequently, on December 30, Commissioner Kuhn upheld Lurie's complaint against Turner. Kuhn decided, however, not to disapprove Matthews' contract with the Braves. Instead, the Commissioner suspended Turner from baseball for one year, and deprived Atlanta of its first-round pick in the next summer's amateur draft. Turner and the Braves went to court to try to overturn Kuhn's ruling.

District Judge B. Avant Edenfield acknowledged the traditional broad authority of the Commissioner to "punish" baseball people "for acts considered not in the best interests" of the game. Complicating this situation, though, was the fact that the Major League Agreement among the owners had to be read in tandem with the new labor agreement between the owners and the Players Association—the document that had created both free agency and a reentry draft for players like Matthews. "The two agreements must now be read together as forming the framework for the government of Major League baseball," which meant that the powers of the Commissioner had to be interpreted "so as to avoid infringing upon the rights secured by the parties to the collective bargaining agreement." *Atlanta National League Baseball Club, Inc. v. Kuhn*, 432 F. Supp. 1213, 1221 (N.D. Ga.1977).

Even with this caveat, the judge concluded ("with some misgivings") that the Commissioner had the authority to issue and enforce directives that barred any owner from "dealing" with another team's players before the draft. With respect to the penalties for the Braves breaching that directive, the judge also found it strange that Kuhn had allowed the Braves to sign and keep Matthews, but forbade Turner, the owner, to operate his Braves team.

> ... [T]he casual observer might call this an Indian massacre in reverse. In their encounter with the Commissioner, the Braves took "nary" a scalp, but lived to see their owner dangling from the

> lodgepole of the Commissioner, apparently only as a warning to others.

432 F. Supp. at 1222. Ultimately, though, the court did not judge this to be an "abuse of commissioner discretion."

> In Article VII, § 2, of the Major League Agreement the clubs explicitly agreed to be bound by the discipline imposed by the Commissioner and obviously intended to give him a certain amount of leeway to choose the appropriate sanction. Judicial review of every sanction imposed by the Commissioner would produce an unworkable system that the Major League Agreement endeavors to prevent. Here, Turner was warned of the suspension, he asked for the suspension, the contract specifically authorized it, and he got it.

Id. at 1223.

The judge, however, concluded that he had the authority to rule that Commissioner Kuhn went beyond the scope of his authority by taking away from the Braves their first pick in the next June rookie draft. The court's rationale was that such a draft penalty was not one of the specific commissioner sanctions then mentioned in Article II, § 3, of the Major League Agreement [the clause has since been broadened, as noted in the new text found in the Documentary Supplement section of the text website]. Although Kuhn's counsel had emphasized the phrasing in § 3 to the effect that "punitive actions by the Commissioner . . . *may involve* any one or more of the following. . ." (emphasis added), Judge Edenfield concluded that the textual language

> seems to imply that the list of sanctions in § 3 is exclusive, and basic rules of contract construction support this conclusion. Prior to the original Major League Agreement, there were no presumed powers vested in a Commissioner. The 1921 agreement created the office of the Commissioner and defined his powers out of whole cloth. In such a situation, the maxim "Expressio unius est exclusio alterius" is particularly applicable. Moreover, in light of the fact that this contract purports to authorize the imposition of a penalty or forfeiture, it must be strictly construed.

Id. at 1225. Nor was the court persuaded by the fact that Kuhn's predecessors had regularly imposed disciplinary sanctions that were not listed in § 3, without anyone having gone off to court to seek relief.

> That the Commissioner's authority in those cases went unchallenged does not persuade this court of the Commissioner's unlimited punitive powers in light of contractual language and established rules of construction to the contrary. If the Commissioner is to have the unlimited punitive authority as he

says is needed to deal with new and changing situations, the agreement should be changed to expressly grant the Commissioner that power. The deprivation of a draft choice was first and foremost a punitive sanction, and a sanction that is not specifically enumerated under § 3. Accordingly, the court concludes that the Commissioner was without the authority to impose that sanction, and its imposition is therefore void.

Id. at 1226.

Kuhn argued that even if the judge believed he had exceeded his authority, judicial review was foreclosed because he was acting as an arbitrator of a dispute between the Braves and the Giants. The court rejected the claim, reasoning that Kuhn had solicited clubs to alert his office to tampering violations, rather than passively adjudicating an inter-team dispute:

> In this respect, and bearing in mind that it was the Commissioner's own directive that he was claiming to enforce, the instant case is similar to *Professional Sports, Ltd. v. Virginia Squires Basketball*, 373 F. Supp. 946, 950 (W.D. Tex. 1974), wherein the court found an agreement to be bound by the Commissioner of Basketball's arbitration decision inapplicable where the dispute was one generated by the Commissioner himself. *See Hurd v. Illinois Bell Telephone Co.*, 136 F. Supp. 125, 155 (N.D. Ill. 1955):
>
>> The judicial mind is so strongly against the propriety of allowing one of the parties, or its especial representative, to be judge or arbitrator in its own case, that even a strained interpretation will be resorted to if necessary to avoid that result.
>
> That the Commissioner did not act as an arbitrator herein is supported by the sanctions imposed. Typically, in an arbitration dispute the arbitrator adjudicates the rights as between two parties and accords relief to one of them. Here, the Commissioner was not deciding Lurie's rights vis a vis Turner, and granting relief to Lurie; rather, a punishment was imposed which would primarily affect only Turner and the Atlanta Club.
>
> The court is inclined to view the Commissioner's authority as deriving not from the arbitration clause of the Major League Agreement, but from Article I, § 2, where he is given the power to "INVESTIGATE, either upon complaint or upon his own initiative, any act ... alleged or suspected to be not in the best interests of the national game of Baseball," and "TO DETERMINE, after investigation, what ... punitive action is appropriate ...." (Emphasis in original.)

Id. at 1219.

A more important restriction on the scope of the Commissioner's powers surfaced in 1992, in a dispute arising out of the National League's expansion to include the Colorado Rockies and the Florida Marlins. This sparked an effort by several owners to review the overall two-division alignment, with the vast majority of clubs favoring a shift of the Chicago Cubs and St. Louis Cardinals to the West and Cincinnati Reds and Atlanta Braves to the East. This move would ease travel times, enhance geographic rivalries, and keep more away-game telecasts in prime time viewing in the home markets. The Cubs, however, were strongly opposed. The stated reason for their opposition was the loss of long-standing rivalries with teams such as the New York Mets. The unstated, but widely assumed, reason was that under the National League's unbalanced divisional schedule, the Cubs would play many more games in western time zones, which would impair the television ratings of the Cubs' corporate sibling within the Chicago Tribune empire—the superstation WGN. The Cubs (supported by the New York Mets) exercised their right under the National League constitution to veto their transfer to another division, and thereby blocked the overall proposal.

A number of National League clubs decided to pursue the matter further and asked Commissioner Fay Vincent to order realignment through his "best interests of baseball" authority under Article I, § 2 of the Major League Agreement (MLA). The Cubs (now supported by National League President Bill White) argued to the Commissioner that his authority in this case was limited to and by Article VII of the MLA, which empowers the Commissioner to decide:

> all disputes and controversies related in any way to professional baseball between clubs . . . *other than those whose resolution is expressly provided for by another means in this Agreement* . . . in the constitution of either Major League or the Basic Agreement between the Major Leagues and the Major League Baseball Players Association. (emphasis added).

When Vincent invoked his "best interests" powers and ordered that the Cubs (and the Cardinals) be shifted to the National League's Western Division, the Cubs went to federal district court in Chicago to secure an injunction blocking this move. In an unreported decision, *Chicago National League Ball Club v. Francis Vincent, Jr.*, 1992 WL 179208 (N.D. Ill. 1992), Judge Suzanne B. Conlon concluded that the Commissioner's general authority under Article I was limited by the specific language in Article VII that "no member club may be transferred to a different division without its consent." The judge was not prepared to allow the Commissioner to "unilaterally amend the National League Constitution simply because he finds that a constitutional provision or procedure is 'not in the best interests of baseball.'"

> Under Illinois rules for construing contracts, it is clear that the broad authority granted the Commissioner by Article I of the Major League Agreement is not as boundless as he suggests. Giving the language of Article I its common sense and ordinary meaning, the Commissioner's authority to investigate "acts," "transactions" and "practices" and to determine and take "preventive, remedial or punitive action" does not encompass restructuring the divisions of the National League. There has been no conduct for the Commissioner to investigate, punish or remedy under Article I. The veto exercised by the Chicago Cubs as a matter of contractual right merely resulted in the maintenance of long-standing divisional assignments reflected in the National League Constitution.

Echoing the views of the district court in *Turner*, Judge Conlon was not impressed by the long history of untrammeled commissioner authority in baseball.

> The Commissioner also cites two prior actions to support his position: Commissioner Kuhn's 1976 reversal of the National League's rejection of an expansion plan and Commissioner Ueberroth's 1985 approval of a new minority owner of the Texas Rangers. In both of these actions, the Commissioner overrode voting requirements of a league constitution. The Commissioner contends that these actions constitute "strong precedent" for his realignment decision. These incidents did not arise under comparable factual circumstances and implicated different constitutional provisions. More importantly, the fact that these actions did not result in a court challenge is neither probative nor persuasive evidence that the Commissioner in fact acted within his authority on those occasions.

Thus, the Court granted an injunction to keep the Cubs in the East, though when both leagues divided themselves into three rather than just two divisions, Chicago's baseball teams played in the central divisions of their respective circuits.

Chicago Cubs was just one of a series of controversial decisions made in 1992 by Commissioner Vincent that gradually alienated a growing number of owners, leading to a vote of no confidence and Vincent's eventual resignation (despite his protests that the Commissioner should not be subject to dismissal by the owners). The owners appointed Milwaukee Brewers' owner Allen "Bud" Selig as Chairman of the Major League Baseball Executive Committee, and placed him in charge of the game's day-to-day affairs. The owners stated publicly that no successor to Vincent would be installed as Commissioner until they had secured a new and more favorable labor agreement from the players' union.

In 1994, as a sidelight to their labor negotiations with the players, the baseball owners created an *ad hoc* Restructuring Committee to study how to alter and improve the office of commissioner. The Committee's recommendations, approved by the owners, included a number of significant revisions to the Major League Agreement.

First, the owners added a clause to Article I, § 2(a), which specified that the future commissioner would be the chair of the Player Relations Committee. This would officially make the commissioner a direct participant and partisan for the owners in the collective bargaining process, a sharp departure from the "neutral" role that previous commissioners had always claimed for themselves in player-club relations. To make sure the commissioner would not intervene unilaterally in labor matters—as Bowie Kuhn did in 1976 by ending the owners' spring training lockout of the players, and as Peter Ueberroth did in the summer of 1985 by ordering the clubs to make their financial records available to the Players Association—a new § 5 was added to Article 1:

> Sec. 5. [T]he powers of the Commissioner to act in the best interests of Baseball shall be inapplicable to any matter relating to a subject of collective bargaining between the Clubs and the Major League Baseball Players Association.

Undoubtedly with an eye on the *Chicago Cubs* case, a new § 4 was also added to Article 1 to clarify another limitation on the commissioner's power to act "in the best interests of Baseball."

> Sec. 4. Notwithstanding the provisions of Section 2, above, the Commissioner shall take no action in the best interests of Baseball that (i) requires the Clubs to take, or to refrain from taking, joint League action (by vote, agreement, or otherwise) on any of the matters requiring a vote of the Clubs at a Joint Major League Meeting that are set forth in Article I, Section 9 or in Article V, Section 2(b) or (c), or (ii) requires the member Clubs of either League to take, or to refrain from taking, League action (by vote, agreement, or otherwise) on any matter to be voted upon by Member Clubs of the League pursuant to their League Constitution; *provided, however*, that nothing in this Section 4 shall limit the Commissioner's authority to act on any matter that involves the integrity of, or public confidence in, the national game of Baseball.

Article VII, § 1, which empowers the commissioner to arbitrate all disputes between clubs or club personnel, had this concluding sentence added to it:

The procedure set forth in this Section is separate from and shall not alter or affect either the procedure set forth in Article V governing the role of the Commissioner at Joint Meetings of the two Major Leagues *or the Commissioner's powers to act in the best interests of Baseball under Article I*. [Emphasis added.]

Despite the disagreement between the owners and Vincent over whether the owners had the power to remove him from office during his term, no effort was made to amend the Major League Agreement to clarify this ambiguity. In January 2000, Major League Baseball owners decided to make yet another major change in the Commissioner's authority, ending the 80-year-old division of authority between the Commissioner and the American and National League Presidents by terminating the latter two positions. The Commissioner's office would now address matters previously handled by the league presidents (*e.g.*, disciplining players for on-field misconduct, and hiring, assigning, and supervising umpires). The Commissioner's power to impose fines was increased from up to $250,000 to $2 million for team offenses, and to $50,000 for player (or other individual) offenses.

Perhaps most important of all, the owners expanded the powers of the Commissioner to act "in the best interests of Baseball" to include financial as well as moral issues. As the new version of Section 4 states:

> ... nothing in this Section 4 shall limit the Commissioner's authority to act on any matter that involves the integrity of, or public confidence in, the national game of baseball. Integrity shall include without limitation, as determined by the Commissioner, the ability of, and the public perception that, players and clubs perform and compete at all times to the best of their abilities. Public confidence shall include without limitation the public perception, as determined by the Commissioner, that there is an appropriate level of long-term competitive balance among Clubs.

The basic structure of league governance in the other major team sports has long been similar, though not identical, to baseball's structure. For example, the National Football League's constitution gives the commissioner disciplinary authority to protect the "integrity of the sport." The National Basketball Association (under § 35 of its constitution), like the National Hockey League (under § 17 of its by-laws), gives its commissioner the authority to expel, suspend, or fine any club official, employee, or player for conduct "detrimental or prejudicial to the Association" (in the NHL, conduct "dishonorable, prejudicial to, or against the welfare of the League"). In both leagues, though, such chief executive decisions can be appealed to the Board of Governors, which consists of all the owners or their designated representatives.

NOTES AND QUESTIONS

1. *Compare* Finley *and* Turner. Review the *Finley* and *Turner* decisions to identify the precise basis of judicial review under the common law of private associations. Did the courts apply the same level of judicial scrutiny to Commissioner Vincent's determination that the Cubs' veto of divisional realignment was contrary to the best interests of baseball and Commissioner Kuhn's similar determination regarding cash sales of star players? Why did the district court in *Finley* express its agreement with Kuhn's conclusion that these cash sales were distinguishable from others that prior commissioners had approved? Why did the Seventh Circuit expressly reject Charlie Finley's claim that Kuhn's decision was malicious?

2. *Waiver of Recourse?* Would the standard of review articulated in *Finley v. Kuhn* have been any different if the "waiver of legal recourse" clause had not been included in the Major League Agreement?

3. *Private Association Law.* From what legal foothold can judges scrutinize and overturn any aspect of the decisions made by a private association such as a sports league? Should courts be more or less ready to review the decisions of a baseball commissioner than those of a union official, for example? (A classic article on the general common law in this area is Zechariah Chafee, Jr., *The Internal Affairs of Associations Not for Profit*, 43 Harv. L. Rev. 993 (1930).) Does your answer depend upon whether the person challenging the commissioner is an owner, a manager, or a player? On whether the commissioner's decision infringes on specially favored public policies? For example, suppose a team executive is disciplined for speaking out against the commissioner's drug policy or the league's poor record in hiring minorities as managers, coaches, or in front office positions?

4. *Revisiting* Chicago Cubs. Return now to the *Chicago Cubs* case, and consider how that case might have been resolved on an appeal to the Seventh Circuit, particularly in light of the circuit precedent in *Finley v. Kuhn*. Which of the two arguably relevant provisions of the Major League Agreement (MLA) should take precedence—Article I, regarding the "best interests" of baseball, or Article VII, regarding "disputes and controversies" in baseball? Suppose the case were to have arisen under the 1995 revisions, with both the new § 4 in Article 1 and the new sentence at the end of Article VII, § 1: would these make any difference in the legal outcome?

5. *Effect of Possible MLA Amendments.* At the 1994 Senate hearings concerning a bill to remove baseball's antitrust exemption (addressed in Chapter 4), Ohio Senator Howard Metzenbaum claimed that the cumulative effect of the pending amendments to the Major League Agreement would be to weaken the authority and power of the commissioner to protect the interests of fans and communities in baseball. Bud Selig, testifying as acting Commissioner, responded that these amendments were redefining the office in a manner that not only retained the historic authority of the commissioner's office, but, in key respects, strengthened it. Which of these views is correct—or is the answer somewhere in-between?

6. *Revisiting* Finley *on the Merits*. Ignoring for the moment the appropriate scope of judicial scrutiny of commissioner decisions, consider the merits of Commissioner Kuhn's ruling in the *Finley* case. Is there anything wrong with one owner selling a player's services to another? The world of baseball is very different in the late-2010s than it was in the mid-1970s. It is now quite common each summer to see teams out of the pennant race transfer star players to top contenders, sometimes for young talent (often to be selected and named later), and occasionally just to move a high salary player off a payroll when game attendance is dropping. While baseball still has a version of the *Kuhn* doctrine that bars explicit *sales* of players for excessive (though now much larger) sums, and the NFL expressly bars the *sale* of players for cash, this is not true of all sports. A 1989 blockbuster hockey deal sent Wayne Gretzky from the Edmonton Oilers to the Los Angeles Kings for $15 million plus players, a deal replicated in 1992 by the Quebec Nordiques who sent Eric Lindros to the Philadelphia Flyers for $15 million and players. Would it have been in the best interests of hockey for then-NHL President John Ziegler to have disallowed either of these transactions just because of the huge sums of money involved?

D. THE COMMISSIONER'S FUNCTION IN PROTECTING THE LEAGUE'S REPUTATION

As noted above, the MLB Constitution vests the Commissioner of Baseball with authority to prevent acts "deemed by the Commissioner not to be in the best interests of Baseball." Art. II, § 3. The relevant provision of the NFL Constitution, Art. VIII, § 8.13, authorizes the Commissioner to take action against those involved with the NFL who are "guilty of conduct detrimental to the welfare of the League or professional football." (Likewise, § 8.6 gives the Commissioner the power to take action against outsiders "in the best interests of either the League or professional football."). The chapter highlighted above how owners have recognized that someone other than themselves must exercise authority over challenges to the "best interests" of sport with regard to gambling and game-fixing, player misconduct, evasion of the spirit of labor market rules, tampering with players under contract to other clubs, and selfish exercise of business prerogatives.

One might define the "best interests of the sport" as the long-term interests of those who make the rules. In this case, legal recognition simply follows contract law. Thus, the power of a sports league (through a commissioner or collectively through the owners) to take actions against those acting in a manner detrimental to "best interests" would be construed to effectuate the parties' intent.

An alternative way to consider the "best interests of the sport" is to recognize the legal and political contexts in which sports operate. Those who do not get to make the rules—including fans, players (subject to contractual limits on owners in collective bargaining agreements), taxpayers, and groups marginalized or excluded from the sport, may turn to legislatures to impose their own conception of "the best interests of the sport" externally, through law. Even those who do make the rules (professional club owners, major colleges and universities) may find it very costly to reach agreement on rules in the best interest of the sport, when dynamic responses to changed circumstances result in winners and losers. These stakeholders may also turn to the law to impose external restraints.

The interaction between private law and external restraints is illustrated by the dynamics of the negotiated drug policy in baseball. MLB and the MLBPA had negotiated a new drug policy in 2002 that, for the first time, called for steroid testing. However, the discovery of a virtually undetectable designer steroid, tetrahydrogesytinone (THG) in 2003 led to calls for changes in MLB policies. A syringe containing THG, and purported to be manufactured by Bay Area Laboratory Co-Operative (BALCO), was anonymously delivered to the United States Anti-Doping Agency (USADA). On September 3, 2003, federal and local agents raided BALCO's San Francisco offices and found that BALCO had been distributing THG to prominent players including Barry Bonds, Jason Giambi, and Gary Sheffield. In light of this scandal, Senator John McCain and the United States Senate Committee on Commerce, Science, and Technology held hearings on performance-enhancing drugs. Joseph M. Saka, *Comment: Back to the Game: How Congress can Help Sports Leagues Shift the Focus from Steroids to Sports*, 23 J. Contemp. Health L. & Pol'y 341, 351 (2007).

Legislators proposed a number of bills that would regulate performance-enhancing drugs in all professional sports by setting standards and penalties for the leagues and require more frequent and random drug testing, more severe penalties for positive tests, and additional substances on the banned substances list. Senator McCain gave the league an ultimatum: either the MLB and MLBPA agree to a tougher drug policy, or Congress would pass legislation setting the standards for the league using the Commerce Clause of the Constitution. *Id.* at 355. The external pressure was effective, and in November 2005, MLB and the MLBPA came to a new drug-testing agreement. Under this agreement, a player's first testing offense would result in a 50-game suspension, their second offense would result in a 100-game ban, and their third offense would result in a lifetime suspension. Additionally, many stimulants were banned for the 2006 season. *A Timeline of MLB's Drug-Testing Rules*, USA Today, March 28, 2014.

External restraints including labor, antitrust, and anti-discrimination law, are discussed in following chapters. This section's focus is on the Commissioner's function to protect the league's reputation, both for commercial objectives and to limit external interference. Consider whether the specific examples are legitimate objects of concern for a commissioner, whether others should be included, and whether the reputation-protecting function of a Commissioner's power should be the sole basis for use of "best interests" powers. Consider also whether these powers are adequate to protect the interests of the sport and the public, or whether further external regulation is needed.

1. TARGETING PLAYERS FOR ON-FIELD INJURY

The authority to discipline misconduct by players or other employees who have organized unions is significantly limited by the terms and conditions of employment negotiated in collective bargaining agreements. However, in limited cases league commissioners retain authority regarding certain kinds of player misconduct, and commissioner discipline remains subject only to league constitutions with regard to owners and non-union employees (such as front office executives and coaches). The scope of the commissioner's authority is illustrated in the following decision, where NFL Commissioner Roger Goodell delegated the final authority to his predecessor, Paul Tagliabue.

IN THE MATTER OF NEW ORLEANS SAINTS PAY-FOR-PERFORMANCE ("BOUNTYGATE")

Final Decision on Appeal (December 11, 2012)

PAUL TAGLIABUE, HEARING OFFICER

INTRODUCTION AND SUMMARY

The matter before me involves appeals by four present or former New Orleans Saints' players who are challenging findings of misconduct and disciplinary actions taken by Commissioner Roger Goodell on October 9, 2012. The players are Anthony Hargrove, Scott Fujita, Will Smith and Jonathan Vilma. The imposed discipline was the result of the National Football League's (the "NFL") investigation of allegations concerning a pay-for-performance program (the "Program") conducted by the Saints during the 2009 through 2011 seasons to reward particular plays by Saints' defensive players that ultimately incentivized rendering opposing players unable to play, and allegations concerning a specific bounty being placed on Brett Favre to injure him during the NFC Championship game against the Minnesota Vikings in January 2010.

The present appeals are a small piece of a much larger picture. Senior Saints' coaches conceived, encouraged and directed the Program. While it included performance rewards for recovering fumbles, interceptions and the like, it also came to include higher cash incentives to "cart-off" or "knockout" an opposing player. The Program eventually led to allegations of a bounty being placed on Favre. Making matters far more serious—as well as challenging for Commissioner Goodell and League investigators—Saints' coaches and managers led a deliberate, unprecedented and effective effort to obstruct the NFL's investigation into the Program and the alleged bounty. Commissioner Goodell found and properly characterized the Program, any bounty and the obstruction to be organizational misconduct by the New Orleans Saints. The Commissioner determined the misconduct to be "particularly unusual and egregious," "totally unacceptable" and to constitute "conduct detrimental" to the game of professional football and the NFL and to be a violation of the NFL Constitution and Bylaws. Commissioner Goodell fined the Saints $500,000; forfeited the team's second-round draft selections in 2012 and 2013; suspended the Saints' head coach Sean Payton for the entire 2012 NFL season; suspended Saints' general manager Mickey Loomis for eight games and fined him $500,000; suspended Saints' assistant head coach Joe Vitt for six games and fined him $100,000; and suspended the now former Saints' defensive coordinator Gregg Williams indefinitely. These suspensions thus deprived the Saints of vitally important coaching and leadership talent, and they represented a severe competitive penalty for the Saints' team, its fans and indirectly for the New Orleans / Gulf Coast region. Commissioner Goodell's findings and the resulting suspensions of these Saints' personnel are final and no longer subject to appeal.

Unlike the Saints' broad organizational misconduct, the player appeals involve sharply focused issues of alleged individual player misconduct in several different aspects of the Saints' Program. The challenges involving the four players to Commissioner Goodell's October 9, 2012 decisions can fairly be summarized as follows:

Anthony Hargrove: Commissioner Goodell found that Hargrove falsely answered questions put to him by an NFL investigator during the initial investigation of Saints' misconduct in March 2010. That investigation was obstructed in multiple ways by the Saints' head coach, senior coaches and other team officials, including their instructing Hargrove to answer questions falsely, though it remains unclear what exactly Hargrove was asked by investigators regarding the Program. Hargrove was suspended seven games, for which he was credited with having served five games, leaving a suspension of two games.

Scott Fujita: Commissioner Goodell found that Fujita offered his own incentive program to reward big plays, not including rewards for cart-offs and knockouts, and that he failed to report the existence of the Program. Two dozen other Saints' defensive players were aware of the Program, many participated in it and all were present at defensive team meetings that are central to the events under review here. Fujita was suspended for one game.

Will Smith: Commissioner Goodell found that Smith endorsed, agreed to and financially contributed to the Program. Many other Saints' defensive players participated in the Program similar to Smith without suspension. He was suspended for four games.

Jonathan Vilma: Commissioner Goodell found that Vilma endorsed, agreed to and financially contributed to the Program and offered a $10,000 bounty reward to any Saints' player who could knock Vikings' quarterback Brett Favre out of the Saints-Vikings NFC Championship game in January 2010. The evidence as to whether Vilma made such an offer is sharply disputed, but other key points are undisputed: the Saints' coaches conducted, directed and choreographed all defensive team meetings; in the same defensive team meeting where Vilma allegedly offered a bounty, the Saints' defensive coordinator, Gregg Williams, admits that he offered a $5,000 bounty reward of his own to knock Favre out of the game; and Williams admitted that he was the responsible team official who unfortunately let the team meeting get out of control. The NFL assessed fines totaling $30,000 against certain Saints' players after the Vikings game, none of which included any player here, and no Saints' player was suspended for conduct on the field. Vilma was suspended for the entire 2012 NFL season.

I affirm Commissioner Goodell's factual findings as to the four players. I conclude that Hargrove, Smith and Vilma—but not Fujita—engaged in "conduct detrimental to the integrity of, and public confidence in, the game of professional football." However, for the reasons set forth in this decision, I now vacate all discipline to be imposed upon these players.

Although I vacate all suspensions, I fully considered but ultimately rejected reducing the suspensions to fines of varying degrees for Hargrove, Smith and Vilma. My affirmation of Commissioner Goodell's findings could certainly justify the issuance of fines. However, as explained in my discussion below, this entire case has been contaminated by the coaches and others in the Saints' organization. Moreover, the League has not previously suspended or fined players for some of the activities in which these players participated and has in the recent past imposed only minimal fines on NFL Clubs—not players—of a mere $25,000 or less.

. . .

[Discussion of Tagliabue's appointment under the collective bargaining agreement omitted. This issue is discussed in Chapter 3, Section B. However, he announced he was giving "appropriate deference to Commissioner Goodell's reasonable findings" and was "reviewing the discipline for consistency of treatment, uniformity of standards for parties similarly situated and patent unfairness or selectivity." In reaching his decision, Tagliabue applied the standard whether the misconduct was "detrimental to the integrity of, or public confidence in, the game of professional football." This language comes from Art. 46 of the NFL-NFLPA collective bargaining agreement. It slightly contrasts with the authority the Commissioner possesses under the NFL Constitution to discipline conduct "detrimental to the welfare of the League or of professional football."]

There are vital reasons why all NFL-NFLPA Collective Bargaining Agreements since the 1970s have consistently given the Commissioner the exclusive and broad authority to decide what constitutes conduct detrimental. The integrity of and public confidence in the game of professional football are essential to the playing of the game itself and are critical to public interest in NFL football and to public respect for all those participating in NFL football—owners, coaches, players, officials and executives. Equally important, the matters that can affect such integrity and public confidence evolve and change over time depending on both developments within and external to the League, and the parties to the CBAs have agreed not to operate with a static or frozen definition of conduct detrimental. . . .

FRAMEWORK FOR CONSIDERING PLAYER DISCIPLINE

Before turning to the specific issues before me, it is important to establish an understanding of how the NFL has approached important turning points related to the culture and safety of the game. In this context, it is critical to recognize that player safety in the NFL is the responsibility of everyone involved in the League. Strict enforcement of safety rules and policies serves the interests of all players and teams and is essential to the integrity of and public confidence in the game. But safety concerns have evolved—and will continue to evolve—significantly over the years.

. . . A fundamental principle of the game of professional football is that strict enforcement of playing rules with respect to player safety is essential for the League, the teams and all players. The NFL, its teams and its players have long recognized that overly aggressive playing tactics often create unacceptable retaliation cycles that encourage impermissible violence on the playing field. . . . Neither a competitive advantage nor any other justification warrants the encouragement of overly aggressive tactics or the cycle of retaliation that often ensues. Any such tactics are detrimental to the integrity of the game of professional football. . . .

. . .

The evidence before me reflects the realities of NFL team workplaces: sometimes prohibitions and policies that seem clear in the team front office or the League office become blurred in team meeting rooms and on practice fields. Techniques or programs intended to prepare teams to win sometimes ignore or contradict League rules and policies. Teams mimic each other. Coaches, staff and players move from team to team, carrying their techniques and programs with them. Sometimes techniques and programs are misdescribed or become modified or mismanaged. Shortcuts turn out to be dead ends.

As Commissioner Goodell has suggested, part of the player safety and injury challenge in the NFL may be an issue of culture. Presumably, this could mean, at least in part, that there is a pervasive, entrenched and undesirable acceptance of overly aggressive play—including financial rewards, intimidation tactics and "trash talk" to encourage aggressive play. Such a culture could include dismissive attitudes about player injury risks and player safety. Commissioner Goodell clearly recognizes that the responsibility for player safety in the NFL starts at the top, with the Commissioner and the entire League office. . . .

In this context, confronted with the events here, Commissioner Goodell correctly set out aggressively to address them. But when an effort to change a culture rests heavily on prohibitions, and discipline and sanctions that are seen as selective, ad hoc or inconsistent, then people in all industries are prone to react negatively—whether they be construction workers, police officers or football players. They will push back and challenge the discipline as unwarranted. As reflected in the record in the present appeals, they will deny, hide behind a code of silence, destroy evidence and obstruct. In other words, rightly or wrongly, a sharp change in sanctions or discipline can often be seen as arbitrary and as an impediment rather than an instrument of change. This is what we see on the record here.

For whatever reasons—entrenched pay-for-performance practices thought to be common in the NFL, bad judgment by coaches or lack of clarity in the rules or their enforcement—the Saints' coaches here resented the League's investigative/enforcement efforts and improperly resisted and blocked them. As Coach Williams put it, the strategy was to "deny, deny, deny" (New Orleans Saints Article 46 Appeal Proceedings Hr'g Tr. 1105:5–11), possibly in part to avoid tarnishing what everyone saw as an incredibly important and well-earned Saints Super Bowl victory.

As NFL counsel stated at the opening of the hearings here, the "code of locker-room silence is, indeed, strong" in the League. (Hr'g Tr. 167:4–6.) NFL counsel thus noted Jonathan Vilma's statement to the Commissioner in a September meeting, "What we say in-house is kept in-house." (Hr'g Tr. 142:2–3.) And NFL counsel continued, comparing this culture to the "blue wall of silence in another context [that] also makes investigating and proving police corruption quite difficult." (Hr'g Tr. 168:7–10.)

Regardless of what caused the Saints' coaches so strongly to resent and obstruct the League's investigation, it is critical to focus on and get to the root of these questions because clearly a League policy of "strict compliance and strict enforcement" based on well-grounded concern for player safety has not yielded a constructive outcome here. Often one way of avoiding or minimizing the severe reaction of parties subject to discipline—such as Saints' coaches and players in this matter—and the unconscionable obstruction led by non-player personnel is to eliminate the motivation to deny. This can be done by creating a tailored type of safe haven for individuals to respond to inquiries or provide information about the destructive culture and help change it—without risk of sanction for a specified period of time. Common examples include whistleblower programs with defined and limited immunities; specified immunities for informants or witnesses in various contexts; and the use of company-managed investigative or fact-gathering panels to identify clearly the character and causes of negative cultures. Such systems are antidotes to the code of silence or culture that condones or encourages illegal or improper conduct despite organization rules and policies against such conduct.

There is an important example in the NFL's own history of using a short-term exemption from discipline as a means of swiftly facilitating an intensified effort to change a negative culture to enhance the safety and health of NFL players. I find persuasive and instructive the lessons to be drawn from a safety-related disciplinary program instituted in the 1980s by then NFL Commissioner, Pete Rozelle. [Here, Tagliabue recounted a year-long amnesty program Rozelle instituted for steroids in the late 1980s.]

. . .

FINDINGS AND FINAL DETERMINATION REGARDING THE FOUR PLAYERS

In challenging the discipline, all four players rely upon Commissioner Goodell's findings of wrongdoing by the Saints in each of the three respects noted above. But the players urge that there is an insufficient basis—both evidentiary and legally—for the imposition of discipline on them, asserting multiple grounds for finding the discipline to be unwarranted. Among other arguments, they contend that these players are victims of inconsistent treatment compared to how the League has disciplined—or declined to discipline—other players; that it was the Saints' coaches and other officials who created and directed the challenged activities in which the players are alleged to have participated; and that there is no evidence of any intent by any of the players to injure any opposing players—and that such intent is an essential element of any finding of culpability.

. . .

[*Anthony Hargrove*] Commissioner Goodell charged Hargove with providing false information regarding a bounty on Brett Favre or a "pay for performance bounty program," which is presumably the Program. Although I affirm Commissioner Goodell's general finding that Hargrove contributed to the obstruction of the investigation by providing denials as instructed by his coaches, a number of factors complicate and mitigate the propriety of his remaining two-game suspension. The context of previous

NFL punishment for obstruction suggests that a seven-game suspension is unprecedented and unwarranted here. In December 2010, the NFL fined Brett Favre $50,000—but did not suspend him—for obstruction of a League sexual harassment investigation. Although not entirely comparable to the present matter, this illustrates the NFL's practice of fining, not suspending players, for serious violations of this type. There is no evidence of a record of past suspensions based purely on obstructing a League investigation. In my forty years of association with the NFL, I am aware of many instances of denials in disciplinary proceedings that proved to be false, but I cannot recall any suspension for such fabrication. This is not to mitigate in any way the severity of obstruction of an investigation with substantial issues as unique as those involved here.

As a further complication, it is unclear exactly what NFL investigators asked Hargrove regarding the Program or any other alleged program and, thus, unclear whether he lied about the Program or the fact that it included cart-offs and knockouts. There is evidence in the appeals record that NFL investigators may not have asked Hargrove whether the Saints employed any particular program. The investigators focused on the alleged bounty placed on Brett Favre prior to the NFC Championship game in January 2010, which was the impetus for questioning Hargrove, who allegedly told a Vikings player of the Favre bounty. If Hargrove denied only the existence of the alleged bounty on Favre, he is no more guilty of conduct detrimental than the numerous Saints' defensive team members from the 2009–2010 season who have provided sworn statements or testimony to the same effect and who have not been suspended or otherwise disciplined.

Finally, given the comprehensive, overt and ongoing nature of the obstruction by coaches and their direct instructions to Hargrove to lie, combined with their control over his football career, it is clear that Hargrove was under tremendous pressure to follow the chain of command in order to keep his job.

I have concluded that there is not sufficient evidence to demonstrate in these unique circumstances that Anthony Hargrove's alleged misconduct is deserving of a suspension. I therefore vacate the suspension imposed on Hargrove.

[*Scott Fujita and Will Smith*] The basis of the discipline issued to Fujita and Smith centers on their participation in the Program or, in Fujita's case, creating his own performance pool.

[Tagliabue recounted the NFL's decades-long prohibitions of pay-for-performance programs and non-contract bonuses for many decades. These practices were specifically part of the negotiations around a collectively bargained salary cap beginning in 1994. Although players were aware of the bar on bonuses in collective bargaining agreements, he concluded that neither "the League nor the NFLPA appears to have developed a fully articulated, concrete set of guidelines or prohibitions related to performance pools that take into account the current realities of signing bonuses, reporting bonuses, performance bonuses and other incentive arrangements often included in NFL player contracts." Specifically, he found that "the NFL in its policies sends a mixed message by allowing 'kangaroo courts' where players are fined for mental lapses and other onfield mistakes but prohibiting any distributions to players via those courts. Most important, no matter what the League rules and policies are or have been, if many teams in the League allow pay-for-performance programs to operate in the locker room, as seems to be the case, and, in the main, the League has tolerated this behavior without punishment of players, then many players may not have a clear understanding that such behavior is prohibited or where the lines are between permissible and impermissible conduct."]

In the testimony before me, current NFL executive Troy Vincent, a former outstanding player with the Philadelphia Eagles, confirmed that during his time with the Eagles the defensive backs had created a performance pool that simply covered three types of plays—interceptions, fumble recoveries and touchdowns—none of which rewarded the purposeful injury of an opponent. Indeed, Vincent testified that the pool conducted within the Eagles in his career covered both regular season games as well as team practices. Obviously, such a program cannot reasonably be viewed as having been created or managed to injure players.

Other programs on other teams involving greater sums of money were discussed at the appeals hearings. For example, Vincent's former teammate, Reggie White, while an outstanding player for the Green Bay Packers, can be seen on an ESPN video on Super Bowl Sunday in January 1997 describing the payouts to players for big plays. When asked about White's description of the Packers' program, Vincent confirmed that it was considerably broader in scope and funding than any program with which he was familiar. The evidence before me—specifically, the video of the ESPN program—contains a statement attributable to an NFL spokesman, who reportedly (and evidently reliably) told ESPN: "What does the NFL have to say about this incentive program that players insist is not a bounty. A league spokesman said the Smash4Cash program is within the rules as long as players use their own monies; the amounts are not exorbitant, and the payments are not for illegal hits."

. . .

The record includes PowerPoint slide presentations made by the Saints' coaching staff to Saints' players following the Saints' victories in 2009 season playoff games against the Arizona Cardinals (with quarterback Kurt Warner) and the Minnesota Vikings (with quarterback Brett Favre). Several of these presentations are very graphic and suggest that the aim of the Saints' defense was to injure these quarterbacks. For example, one slide set following the game against the Cardinals includes a photo of Kurt Warner lying on the ground with a caption: "SO WE WILL JUST DESTROY EACH QUARTERBACK LEAVING EACH TEAM WITHOUT A FIELD GENERAL! ONE DOWN TWO QB's TO GO!" (Record on Appeal, Ex. 80 at 3.)

. . .

NFL players on average have short careers; their careers can end suddenly through injury or declining skills; players want to be good, cohesive members of the team, or unit, not complainers or dissenters; and players accept that they work for coaches, in "programs" conceived by coaches. These are programs for which coordinators and assistant coaches are often specially selected and hired to execute. Here we have a classic example: Head Coach Payton hired Defensive Coordinator Williams with directions to make the Saints' defense "nasty."

In such circumstances, players may not have much choice but to "go along," to comply with coaching demands or directions that they may question or resent. They may know—or believe—that from the coaches' perspective, "it's my way or the highway." Coaching legends such as George Halas and Vince Lombardi are not glorified or remembered because they offered players "freedom of choice."

. . .

[Tagliabue rejected the NFL counsel's argument that it was not important that Fujita did not offer money for hits on opponents such as cart-offs or knockouts. In the past, the NFL had disciplined clubs, but not players, for pay-for-performance bonuses.] Accordingly, the NFL's decision to suspend a player here for participating in a program for which the League typically fines a club certainly raises significant issues regarding inconsistent treatment between players and teams.

. . .

The Commissioner found that Smith's assertion that rewards for cart-offs or knockouts in the Program were offered only when an opposing player was disabled for a play or two because he had the wind knocked out of him, and not if he sustained some other type of injury, was not credible. I affirm Commissioner Goodell's judgment that rewarding players for these categories incentivizes injury of opposing players to a degree that is detrimental to the integrity of and public confidence in the game.

Within the Saints' defensive unit, Smith was one of approximately two dozen Saints' defensive players who participated in the Program. Although Commissioner Goodell found Smith's role as a defensive leader to be a basis, at least in part, for singling Smith out for discipline, this is inappropriate when most or all of the Saints' defensive unit committed the same or similar acts as those underpinning the discipline of Smith.

In addition, I am not aware of previous League discipline that similarly rested on whether or not a player was a team leader. It may indeed be very constructive, in this and other contexts, to expect team captains, other team leaders, or even players with years of seniority to meet higher standards of responsibility for team conduct, and to take such status into account in imposing fines and other discipline. This is a concept that would require in-depth discussion with coaches and players. (I can foresee many different, legitimate points of view.) But, in any event, this is not an issue for me to decide. On the present record, selective prosecution of allegations of misconduct and enforcement of discipline relative to Smith cannot be sustained. Whatever the reason for such selective enforcement, it does not satisfy basic requirements for consistent treatment of player employees similarly situated. Therefore, I vacate the suspension of Will Smith.

[*Jonathan Vilma*] [Tagliabue reviewed the credibility of four key witnesses and conflicting evidence (including one coach who changed his testimony several times. He concluded that "there is an insufficient basis to reject Commissioner Goodell's findings on the offer of the Favre bounty."]

. . .

It is essential to recognize that Vilma is being most severely disciplined for "talk" or speech at a team meeting on the evening before the Saints-Vikings game. He is not being punished for his performance on the field and, indeed, none of the discipline of any player here relates to on-field conduct. No Saints' player was suspended for on-field play by the League after the game in question. If the League wishes to suspend a player for pre-game talk including "offers" to incentivize misconduct, it must start by imposing enhanced discipline for illegal hits that involve the kind of player misconduct that it desires to interdict. The relationship of the discipline for the off-field "talk" and actual on-field conduct must be carefully calibrated and reasonably apportioned. This is a standard grounded in common sense and fairness. It rests also on the competence of NFL officiating and the obligation and ability of the League to closely observe playing field misconduct, record it and review for illegal hits or other related misconduct.

. . .

If one were to punish certain off-field talk in locker rooms, meeting rooms, hotel rooms or elsewhere without applying a rigorous standard that separated real threats or "bounties" from rhetoric and exaggeration, it would open a field of inquiry that would lead nowhere. More specifically, there is no question that Coach Williams and other coaches orchestrated the Program to incentivize cart-offs and knockouts; carefully choreographed defensive team meetings, including presenting graphic slide presentations showing injuries to opposing players; ensured that any player who would speak at team meetings was adequately prepared or supported; and generally created an atmosphere in the 2009 season and playoffs that suggested to Saints' players that offering a $10,000 bounty to injure an opposing player was permissible behavior. . . .

Adding to the complexity, there is little evidence of the tone of any talk about a bounty before the Vikings game. Was any bounty pledged serious? Was it inspirational only? Was it typical "trash talk" that occurs regularly before and during games? The parties presented no clear answers. No witness could confirm whether Vilma had any money in his hands as he spoke; no evidence was presented that $10,000 was available to him for purposes of paying a bounty or otherwise. There was no evidence that Vilma or anyone else paid any money to any player for any bounty-related hit on an opposing player in the Vikings game.

I neither excuse nor condone the alleged offer of a bounty on Favre, whether offered by any player, coach, other Saints' employee or third party. Such conduct has no place in the game of professional football. I cannot, however, uphold a multi-game suspension where there is no evidence that a player's speech prior to a game was actually a factor causing misconduct on the playing field and that such misconduct was severe enough in itself to warrant a player suspension or a very substantial fine. Nor can I find justified a suspension where Williams and other Saints' personnel so carefully crafted an environment that would encourage and allow a player to make such an ill-advised and imprudent offer. I therefore vacate the suspension of Jonathan Vilma.

CONCLUSIONS AND ORDER

For the reasons set forth in this Final Decision on Appeal, I affirm the factual findings of Commissioner Goodell; I conclude that Hargrove, Smith, and Vilma engaged in "conduct detrimental to the integrity of, and public confidence in, the game of professional football"; and I vacate all player discipline.

/s/ Paul Tagliabue

The proceedings against the Saints were extraordinary because of the focus on off-field planning for excessive, unduly risky contact on the field. League commissioners traditionally retain the power to discipline players for on-field misconduct.

As a comparative matter, the North American reliance on the originally-independent Office of the Commissioner to impose discipline contrasts with the approach in the rest of the world. Perhaps because competitions in soccer, rugby, cricket, and other sports are often international in character, a single individual (necessarily identified with one country) would not be trusted to independently resolve disputes. Thus, challenges to discipline have almost always been before respected current or former judges, represented by leading trial advocates. For example, during the World Rugby Cup, disciplinary issues that are not resolved during a match are dealt with in a process similar to arbitration. Each game is watched by a citing commissioner, who looks for any misconduct that should be brought in front of the disciplinary panel. The disciplinary panel consists of ten appointed judicial officers who are typically experts in rugby and law. The accused player (often with their team lawyer) appears before a judicial officer with any relevant witnesses and the tournament's "designated disciplinary officer" to determine whether to uphold the citing complaint made by the citing commissioner. This decision may be appealed to a panel, which is comprised of three appeal officers (chosen from a pool of four). Daniel Saoul, *Avoiding the legal scrum: Arbitration in the Rugby World Cup,* LexisNexis Dispute Resolution, Oct. 22, 2015. Similarly, the Cherwell Cricket League of the United Kingdom performs its disciplinary hearings before a disciplinary panel appointed by the League Chairman, which consists of no less than three panelists. Cricket players are also entitled to an appeal, which takes place in front of three different appointed panelists who did not sit at the initial hearing. Cherwell Cricket League Disciplinary Regulations § 5 (2018).

2. OFFENSIVE PERSONAL BEHAVIOR AND CHANGING SOCIAL ATTITUDES

Despite the broad wording of the Commissioner's authority, poor stewardship of a franchise has not been grounds for intervention to discipline or remove an owner. Consider former Los Angeles Clippers owner Donald Sterling. He exemplified the worst ownership in sports, notorious for putting profits over success, making inappropriate comments about players, and operating a franchise characterized by obscurity and irrelevance, Joshua S.E. Lee and Jaimie K. McFarlin, *Sports Scandals from the Top-Down: Comparative Analysis of Management, Owner, and Athletic Discipline in the NFL & NBA,* 23 Jeffrey S. Moorad Sports L.J. 69, 86 (2016). But he did not face official rebuke until a public scandal emerged from a tabloid website's exposé of a heated argument with his mistress that she had secretly recorded. During the argument, Sterling made derogatory and racist comments about African Americans and other minorities, generally demanding she not socialize in public with black men and singling out the legendary Magic Johnson. Sponsors withdrew support and Clippers players joined others in publicly protesting his continued ownership. Four days after these recordings were made public, Commissioner Adam Silver banned Sterling for life and fined him $2.5 million. Silver also announced he would recommend that the Board of

Governors (the other owners) invoke the powers reserved to them in the NBA Constitution to strip Sterling of his ownership. After threats and preliminary litigation, Sterling agreed to sell the Clippers to Microsoft magnate Steve Ballmer for over $2 billion.

Silver, who had recently succeeded David Stern as NBA Commissioner, announced his decision in a widely viewed press conference. He stated:

> Shortly after the release of an audio recording this past Saturday morning of a conversation that allegedly included Clippers owner Donald Sterling, the NBA commenced an investigation, which among other things, included an interview of Mr. Sterling. That investigation is now complete. The central findings of the investigation are that the man whose voice is heard on the recording and on a second recording from the same conversation that was released on Sunday is Mr. Sterling and that the hateful opinions voiced by that man are those of Mr. Sterling.
>
> The views expressed by Mr. Sterling are deeply offensive and harmful; that they came from an NBA owner only heightens the damage and my personal outrage. Sentiments of this kind are contrary to the principles of inclusion and respect that form the foundation of our diverse, multicultural and multiethnic league.
>
> I am personally distraught that the views expressed by Mr. Sterling came from within an institution that has historically taken such a leadership role in matters of race relations and caused current and former players, coaches, fans and partners of the NBA to question their very association with the league.
>
> To them, and pioneers of the game like Earl Lloyd, Chuck Cooper, Sweetwater Clifton, the great Bill Russell, and particularly Magic Johnson, I apologize. Accordingly, effective immediately, I am banning Mr. Sterling for life from any association with the Clippers organization or the NBA. Mr. Sterling may not attend any NBA games or practices. He may not be present at any Clippers facility, and he may not participate in any business or player personnel decisions involving the team. He will also be barred from attending NBA Board of Governors meetings or participating in any other league activity. I am also fining Mr. Sterling $2.5 million, the maximum amount allowed under the NBA constitution. These funds will be donated to organizations dedicated to anti-discrimination and tolerance efforts that will be jointly selected by the NBA and its Players Association.
>
> As for Mr. Sterling's ownership interest in the Clippers, I will urge the Board of Governors to exercise its authority to force a

sale of the team and will do everything in my power to ensure that that happens. This has been a painful moment for all members of the NBA family. I appreciate the support and understanding of our players during this process, and I am particularly grateful for the leadership shown by Coach Doc Rivers, Union President Chris Paul and Mayor Kevin Johnson of Sacramento, who has been acting as the players' representative in this matter.

We stand together in condemning Mr. Sterling's views. They simply have no place in the NBA.

Transcript available at https://www.usatoday.com/story/sports/nba/2014/04/29/adam-silver-commissioner-opening-statement-donald-sterling/8467947/.

Silver intriguingly disclosed that in meting out punishment, he did not take into account Sterling's past behavior, which also included multiple claims that as a property owner he had engaged in racial discrimination. However, he explicitly stated that the Board of Governors would "take into account a lifetime of behavior" in determining "his overall fitness to be an owner in the NBA."

The Clippers sale mooted a number of interesting issues regarding Sterling's expulsion from the league. The relevant constitutional provision, Art. 13, sets forth ten specific grounds for expulsion. Do you agree with Commissioner Silver that one or more of these grounds were met?

(a) Willfully violate any of the provisions of the Constitution and By-Laws, resolutions, or agreements of the Association.

(b) Transfer or attempt to transfer a Membership or an interest in a Member without complying with the provisions of Article 5.

(c) Fail to pay any dues or other indebtedness owing to the Association within thirty (30) days after Written Notice from the Commissioner of default in such payment.

(d) Fail or refuse to fulfill its contractual obligations to the Association, its Members, Players, or any other third party in such a way as to affect the Association or its Members adversely.

[subsections (e), (f), and (g) all involve gambling]

(h) Disband its Team during the Season, dissolve its business, or cease its operation.

(i) Willfully fail to present its Team at the time and place it is scheduled to play in an Exhibition, Regular Season, or Playoff Game.

(j) Willfully misrepresent any material fact contained in its application for Membership in the Association.

In 2010, a 20-year-old college student in Milledgeville, Georgia, accused Pittsburgh Steelers' QB Ben Roethlisberger of sexual assault. Due to insufficient evidence, the local prosecutor did not file criminal charges, but Commissioner Robert Goodell suspended Roethlisberger for the first six games of the season, and refused to allow him to participate in any offseason activities until he underwent a "comprehensive behavioral evaluation by professionals." Although the case did not result in a criminal conviction, Goodell cited his reason for the suspension as "[players] are held to a higher standard as an NFL player, and there is nothing about [Roethlisberger's] conduct in Milledgeville that can remotely be described as admirable, responsible, or consistent with either the values of the league or the expectations of our fans." Roethlisberger admitted taking a 20-year old woman into the men's bathroom at a bar, and engaging in sex. Roethlisberger did not contest the ruling.

On January 14, 2010, authorities formally charged Gilbert Arenas, a guard for the Washington Wizards, with felony gun possession after bringing an unlicensed firearm outside his home into the Wizard's locker room. Arenas claims it was a joke aimed at his teammate, Javaris Crittenton. The two had an argument over a gambling debt when Arenas brought an unloaded firearm to the locker room. Crittenton then brought his own firearm into the same facility. National Basketball Association Commissioner David Stern decided to suspend Arenas without pay because his behavior showed "[he is] not currently fit to take the court." In response to his suspension, Arenas made shooting gestures with his hands. Stern thought his actions showed a blatant disregard for the situation. He therefore suspended Arenas indefinitely. Arenas entered into a plea agreement with the prosecution, agreeing to plead guilty. On March 26, 2010, Arenas was sentenced to two years' probation and 30 days in a halfway house, avoiding any jail time. Arenas continued to play for the Washington Wizards. Team president Ernie Grunfeld decided not to void his contract, believing Arenas had changed.

When can a commissioner appropriately impose discipline for criminal misconduct? Should suspension occur, for example, as soon as a sports figure is charged with a crime? Only after a formal indictment? Only after conviction? Once a player is convicted of a serious crime, should the Commissioner impose a lifetime ban? Should re-entry be based on rehabilitation? As this casebook goes to press, many of these questions are raised in the case of a star college player who pled guilty as a teenager in a juvenile court proceeding sexually abusing his young niece. S.L. Price, *Prospect and Pariah*, Sports Illustrated, May 21, 2018, at 30.

Sports "shape and stabilize social and even political identities around the globe . . . [they] mobilize collective emotions and often channel societal conflicts." Andrei S. Markovits and Lars Rensmann, *Gaming the World: How Sports are Reshaping Global Politics and Culture* (Princeton Univ. Press 2010), at 3. More critically, a leading sociologist claims: "we find [in sport] the basic elements and expressions of bureaucratization, commercialization, racism, sexism, homophobia, greed, exploitation of the powerless, alienation, and the ethnocentrism found in the larger society." D. Stanley Eitzen, *Sport and Contemporary Society* (Boulder, Colo.: Paradigm 2009), at 10–11. As society affects sports, sports affect society. Markovits and Rensmann assert that "professional team sports are not just a crucial part of (global) popular culture but also significant agents of cultural change and global communication." *Id.* at 26. Specific to the topic of social justice, they claim that

> Global players on the field, who draw admiration from locals but also from across the world, are both representatives and facilitators of more inclusive cultural self-understandings in today's diverse societies. . . . Sports' universalistic focus on individual merit rather than exclusive cultural difference corresponds with, and helps generate, the rise of . . . egalitarian and inclusive sets of beliefs. . . .

Id. at 30.

The focus of this section is on how these societal concerns affect our perception of the "best interest of sport," and the institutional and legal response to these concerns. Unlawful discrimination is the topic of Chapter 12. Here, we focus on a case study of sports' response to changing social attitudes toward the LGBTQ community.

Little or no overt or official discrimination has been directed against gay and lesbian athletes by sports organizations (although there is evidence that once outed gay and lesbian athletes have often been ostracized and badly tormented by their heterosexual colleagues and coaches), and recent events show strong official support for LGBT athletes. Illustrative of changing attitudes is the story behind the organization "You Can Play" (youcanplayproject.org), an advocacy group with the slogans "If you can play, you can play" and "Gay athletes. Straight allies. Teaming up for respect." Its co-founder is Patrick Burke, now NHL Director of Player Safety, an attorney and former Philadelphia Flyers' scout. Burke joined with others to form the project in memory of his brother Brendan, who was a high school hockey player and college hockey manager before publicly revealing his homosexuality. Brendan had chosen also to pursue a law career potentially to advocate for gays and lesbians when he was tragically killed in an auto accident. With support from his father, longtime NHL executive Brian Burke, You Can Play has since evolved with Patrick Burke ceding organizational leadership to former collegiate athlete Wade Davis, an openly gay man.

Sports have been at the vanguard of rapidly changing social attitudes toward discrimination on the basis of sexual orientation. Leagues have all adopted new policies designed to strengthen existing policies against harassment and discrimination based on sexual orientation. MLB and the NFL have both worked with the New York Attorney General to adopt a "workplace code of conduct" that has been distributed to all teams and players barring any form of discrimination against gay players. Veteran NBA player Jason Collins came out as a gay man to much public attention and official NBA support, and was thereafter employed by the Brooklyn Nets with rapidly decreasing attention to his sexuality and increased attention to the Nets' playoff run. Michael Sam became the first openly gay player to be drafted in 2014, by the St. Louis Rams, after his selection as SEC defensive player of the year from Missouri, although he was cut from the squad during the final roster cutdown after the Rams' final pre-season game. In the front office, Golden State Warriors President Rick Welts came out in 2011, and this year was elected to the Pro Basketball Hall of Fame.

Because of the paucity of openly gay men in North American professional sport, there are no recent reports of commissioner discipline to enforce anti-gay discrimination. However, the related problem of homophobic slurs directed at straight men has received attention. The NFL commissioned an outside law firm's investigation into Miami Dolphins workplace conduct, available at http://63bba9dfdf9675bf3f10-68be460ce4 3dd2a60dd64ca5eca4ae1d.r37.cf1.rackcdn.com/PaulWeissReport.pdf, and lineman Richie Incognito was suspended for racist and homophobic bullying of teammate Jonathan Martin. (In a sad coda, in 2017 Martin was in the news again for attempting suicide.)

3. GAMBLING

(a) Traditional Aversion to Any Form of Gambling

The Black Sox and Pete Rose scandals demonstrate sports leagues' overriding concern with how gambling can affect sports reputation. In today's globalized sports environment, this remains true, with many observers attributing the challenges of building Chinese sports leagues to widespread perception of corruption in domestic sports. Besides these two scandals, commissioners have acted forcefully over the decades: Commissioner Landis required Philadelphia Phillies' owner William Cox to sell his team in 1942 Landis discovered Cox had placed about a dozen small bets on the Phillies to win. In 1963, NFL Commissioner Pete Rozelle suspended for a year All-Pros Paul Hornung of the Green Bay Packers and Alex Karras of the Detroit Lions for betting on their own teams to win. On the other hand, in 1986, Tulane's star center John "Hot Rod" Williams was indicted for allegedly taking money and drugs from gamblers in exchange for "point shaving" in a 1985 game against Memphis State. NBA Commissioner David Stern permitted the Cleveland Cavaliers to draft and pay Williams, but not to play him pending trial, in which Williams was ultimately acquitted by a New Orleans jury. Based on the acquittal, Stern took no action against Williams, who went on to a successful and lucrative NBA career with Cleveland and Phoenix.

Baseball's sensitivity to gambling is reflected in disciplinary action against players and managers merely for associating with gambling, even when no personal betting was involved. For example, Landis' successor, Albert "Happy" Chandler, suspended Dodgers' manager Leo Durocher for the 1947 season just for associating with gamblers, and Commissioner Bowie Kuhn suspended New York Yankees' owner George Steinbrenner from the baseball (though not the financial) affairs of the Yankees for paying a gambler, Howard Spira, to produce unsavory information about his own player, Dave Winfield. Indeed, in 1979 Bowie Kuhn went so far as to ban Willie Mays and Mickey Mantle from any official connections with professional baseball because they took public relations jobs with Atlantic City gambling casinos, a decision rescinded by his successor, Peter Ueberroth, in 1985.

The only judicial ruling about the legality of this severe treatment for gambling came in an antitrust suit filed by an ex-NBA player, who charged that his lifetime expulsion constituted an illegal antitrust conspiracy of all teams in the league to boycott his services, *Molinas v. NBA,* 190 F. Supp. 241 (S.D.N.Y. 1961). Jack Molinas graduated from Columbia University in 1953 and was drafted by the NBA's Fort Wayne Pistons. In January 1954, he admitted that he had regularly bet on the Pistons to win certain games—depending on the relative point spread between the two teams. In just a few months he had accumulated a net betting profit of around $400. However, as soon as the NBA Commissioner Maurice Podoloff learned of this practice, he suspended Molinas indefinitely for violating both Section 79 of the league's constitution and Clause 15 of his contract, both prohibiting any such gambling. Over the next several years, Podoloff rejected several Molinas requests for reinstatement, saying that he was such a "cancer to the league" that he must never be allowed to reenter it. In the meantime, Molinas attended Brooklyn Law School and was admitted to the New York State Bar. He then filed an antitrust suit against the league for enacting and enforcing such a rule prohibiting someone playing for a team that still wanted him.

Judge Irving Kaufman rejected the claim. He concluded that rules or jointly-maintained contract clauses providing for the suspension of those who place wagers on games in which they are participating "seems not only reasonable, but necessary for the survival of the league." He rejected the claim that the conduct was not immoral because he bet only on his own team to win:

> The vice inherent in the plaintiff's conduct is that each time he either placed a bet or refused to place a bet, this operated inevitably to inform bookmakers of an insider's opinion as to the adequacy or inadequacy of the point-spread or his team's ability to win. Thus, for example, when he chose to place a bet, this would indicate to the bookmakers that a member of the Fort Wayne team believed that his team would exceed its expected performance. Similarly, when he chose not to bet, bookmakers thus would be informed of his opinion that the Pistons would not perform according to expectations. It is certainly reasonable for the league and Mr. Podoloff to conclude that this conduct could not be tolerated and must, therefore, be eliminated. The reasonableness of the league's action is apparent in view of the fact that, at that time, the confidence of the public in basketball had been shattered, due to a series of gambling incidents. Thus, it was absolutely necessary for the sport to exhume gambling from its midst for all times in order to survive.

The *Molinas* decision had an ironic aftermath. While the litigation was underway, Molinas was actually the ringleader in a nationwide point-shaving scheme in college basketball.

Chapters 5–7 of this book detail the application of the Sherman Antitrust Act's ban on "contracts, combinations, or conspiracies in restraint of trade." As applied to commissioner discipline, we simply note here that the antitrust "rule of reason" upon which the court relied in *Molinas* no longer turns on a court's intuitive judgment of whether a particular practice seems sensible and equitable, but rather on economic analysis of whether the challenged practice is, on balance, procompetitive or anticompetitive. This, in turn, requires a judgment about whether the practice enhances or diminishes "consumer welfare" (whatever that term means). If one focuses on that economic question, was the court correct in its conclusion that suspending Molinas was "reasonable?"

(b) The Rapid Move Toward Legalized Gambling

The legality of sports gambling remains in considerable flux. The Wire Act of 1961, 18 U.S.C. § 1084(a), criminalizes the use of wire communications to place bets on sporting events, to transmit information to facilitate the placing of bets, or to send or receive funds resulting from bets. However, § 1084(b) provides that the Act does not "prevent the transmission in interstate or foreign commerce of information for use in news reporting of sporting events or contests, or for the transmission of information assisting in the placing of bets or wagers on a sporting event or contest from a State or foreign country where betting on that sporting event or contest is legal into a State or foreign country in which such betting is legal."

Times change. Taking the lead among sport league commissioners was the NBA's Adam Silver, who wrote an op-ed article in 2014 calling for sports gambling to be legalized and regulated. Adam Silver, *Legalize and Regulate Sports Betting*, New York Times (Nov. 13, 2014). The State of New Jersey was most active, enacting legislation to legalize sports gambling in Atlantic City casinos. Lower federal courts held that New Jersey's proposals ran afoul of federal legislation, the Professional and Amateur Sports Protection Act (PASPA). PASPA included two principal prohibitions. First, 28 U.S.C. § 3702(1) prohibited governmental entities from licensing or authorizing by law lotteries, sweepstakes, or gambling on amateur or professional sports. Second, 28 U.S.C. § 3702(2) barred both governmental entities and private individuals from sponsoring, operating, advertising or promoting the same. These courts granted relief to the petitioners—the NCAA and major professional sports leagues—who remained concerned about the reputational harm their sports would suffer were gambling to be legalized.

In *Murphy v. NCAA,* 138 S. Ct. 1461 (2018), the Supreme Court struck down PASPA on constitutional grounds, concluding that § 3702(1) had unconstitutionally "commandeer[ed]" states to enforce federal law in violation of the Tenth Amendment. The decision is principally about constitutional federalism rather than sports law, but reveals important background and perceptions about how sports leagues, legislators, and regulators should approach the issue.

Justice Alito's majority opinion began by observing that "Americans have never been of one mind about gambling, and attitudes have swung back and forth. By the end of the 19th century, gambling was largely banned throughout the country, but beginning in the 1920s and 1930s, laws prohibiting gambling were gradually loosened." Justice Alito traced widespread bans on gambling before and after the turn of the 20th Century, and the gradual loosening of state controls at the end of the century. Legalized gambling increased significantly with passage of the federal Indian Gaming Regulatory Act in 1988, 25 U.S.C. § 2701 *et seq.*, permitting casinos on Indian land throughout the country.

Justice Alito noted the strong opposition to sports gambling. He cited claims from PASPA's legislative history and by the Act's proponents (the lead sponsor was Senator Bill Bradley, a former college and professional basketball star with Princeton and the New York Knicks) that it is particularly addictive and especially attractive to young people with a strong interest in sports, and in the past gamblers corrupted and seriously damaged the reputation of professional and amateur sports. Apprehensive about the potential effects of sports gambling, professional sports leagues and the National Collegiate Athletic Association (NCAA) long opposed legalization. *See* Professional and Amateur Sports Protection, S. Rep. No. 102–248, p. 8 (1991); Hearing before the Subcommittee on Patents, Copyrights and Trademarks of the Senate Committee on the Judiciary, 102d Cong., 1st Sess., 21, 39, 46–47, 59–60, 227 (1991) (S. Hrg. 102-499).

In response to the PASPA complaint filed by the major professional sports leagues and the NCAA in federal court against the New Jersey law, the State argued, among other things, that PASPA unconstitutionally infringed the State's sovereign authority to end its sports gambling ban. In making this argument, the State relied primarily on what has been dubbed the "anticommandeering" principle. To briefly summarize this constitutional doctrine, set forth largely in *New York* v. *United States*, 505 U.S. 144 (1992), and *Printz* v. *United States*, 521 U.S. 898 (1997), Art. I, § 8 of the Constitution authorizes Congress to directly regulate citizens, but not sovereign states. The Court's rationale is that this doctrine preserves a "healthy balance of power between the States and the Federal Government," reduces "the risk of tyranny and abuse from either front," promotes political accountability, by making clear that a mandate comes from Congress and prevents Congress from shifting the costs of regulation to the States.

Significantly, the majority acknowledged that Congress has the power to bar state or private entities from actually sponsoring sports betting, and that it did so in § 3702(2) of PASPA. However, the Court also held this provision to be invalid, because the Court concluded that Congress would not have enacted the provision independently of the invalid ban on state authorization in § 3702(1). The Court observed that the 1992 law was designed to bar both state-run sports lotteries and legalized casino sports bookmaking. The majority concluded that Congress would not have wanted to prevent states from running sports lotteries, while giving legislatures the freedom to authorize sports gambling in privately owned casinos:

> The present cases illustrate exactly how Congress must have intended § 3702(1) and § 3702(2) to work. If a State attempted to authorize particular private entities to engage in sports gambling, the State could be sued under § 3702(1), and the private entity could be sued at the same time under § 3702(2). The two sets of provisions were meant to be deployed in tandem to stop what PASPA aimed to prevent: state legalization of sports gambling. But if, as we now hold, Congress lacks the authority to prohibit a State from legalizing sports gambling, the prohibition of private conduct under § 3702(2) ceases to implement any coherent federal policy.

> Under § 3702(2), private conduct violates federal law only if it is permitted by state law. That strange rule is exactly the opposite

of the general federal approach to gambling. Under 18 U. S. C. § 1955, operating a gambling business violates federal law only if that conduct is illegal under state or local law. Similarly, 18 U. S. C. § 1953, which criminalizes the interstate transmission of wagering paraphernalia, and 18 U. S. C. § 1084, which outlaws the interstate transmission of information that assists in the placing of a bet on a sporting event, apply only if the underlying gambling is illegal under state law. *See also* 18 U. S. C. § 1952 (making it illegal to travel in interstate commerce to further a gambling business that is illegal under applicable state law).

These provisions implement a coherent federal policy: They respect the policy choices of the people of each State on the controversial issue of gambling. By contrast, if § 3702(2) is severed from § 3702(1), it implements a perverse policy that undermines whatever policy is favored by the people of a State. If the people of a State support the legalization of sports gambling, federal law would make the activity illegal. But if a State outlaws sports gambling, that activity would be lawful under § 3702(2). We do not think that Congress ever contemplated that such a weird result would come to pass.

138 S. Ct. at 1483.

The Court concluded by observing:

The legalization of sports gambling is a controversial subject. Supporters argue that legalization will produce revenue for the States and critically weaken illegal sports betting operations, which are often run by organized crime. Opponents contend that legalizing sports gambling will hook the young on gambling, encourage people of modest means to squander their savings and earnings, and corrupt professional and college sports.

The legalization of sports gambling requires an important policy choice, but the choice is not ours to make. Congress can regulate sports gambling directly, but if it elects not to do so, each State is free to act on its own.

Id. at 1484–85.

Justice Ginsburg (joined by Justices Sotomayor and Breyer) dissented. She complained that the majority had deployed "a wrecking ball" to destroy PASPA, when Congress clearly had the constitutional authority to stop private parties from operating sports gambling schemes even if state law authorized them to do so. Citing precedents that require judges to engage "in a salvage rather than a demolition operation" when a statute is unconstitutional, she concluded that Congress would have wanted the constitutionally-valid prohibition on gambling to remain.

Sports league commissioners, of course, have no jurisdiction over casinos, state gaming regulators, and individual bettors who have no affiliation with sports. Thus, legislatures must inevitably deal with various proposals concerning the scope of legalized sports better, as they are doing as this casebook goes to print. The key issues that legislation must address include:

(1) The type of sports betting that can occur, and who (regulators, bookmakers, sports leagues) can approve or veto specific wagers;

(2) Procedures for identifying suspicious betting patterns and notifying relevant stakeholders;

(3) Confidential information that can be shared among law enforcers, gambling regulators, bookmakers, and leagues;

(4) Who shares in the profits from sports wagering: taxes for federal, state, and local governments, and fees for cooperation from sports leagues; and

(5) Whether players have a right to a share of the proceeds directly (this question is considered with regard to publicity rights in Chapter 8).

(c) Current Legislative Issues Regarding Legalized Sports Gambling

Two jurisdictions that currently feature legalized sports gambling offer models for federal and state legislatures to consider.

Nevada. Currently, Nevada uses the same licensing and enforcement agents to regulate both casinos and sports books. Keith Miller & Anthony Cabot, *Regulatory Models for Sports Wagering: The Debate Between State vs. Federal Oversight*, 8 UNLV Gaming L.J. 153, 164 (2018). All bookmaking establishments must receive a license from state gaming authorities. Nev. Rev. Stat. § 463.0129(1)(d)(e) (2017). Nevada will not issue a license to any establishment until they present satisfactory evidence that they are financially capable of paying off all current obligations. Nev. Gaming Comm. § 3.050 (2017). In addition to financial requirements, the Nevada Gaming Commission (NGC) also requires all licensees to be of good character, display adequate business competence and maintain a reputation that will not adversely affect the publicity of the Nevada gambling industry as a whole. *Id.* § 3.090(1). The Gaming Commission also regulates the location of gambling establishments.

Nevada has taken the stance that gaming regulators also act as consultants to the licensees. Public policy seeks a cooperative, working relationship with licensees. Regulators not only enforce gaming regulations, but also help licensees find solutions and plan ahead. Licensees are able to use regulators as a resource, and will thus be better able to avoid possible infractions. Regulators will be able to counsel licensees in the best courses of action, and therefore will be less likely to expend resources on disciplining licensees. Nicole Laudwig, Note, *Gaming Regulatory Systems: How Emerging Jurisdictions Can Use the Three Major Players as a Guide in Creating a Tailored System for Themselves*, 3 UNLV Gaming L.J. 277, 292 (2012). Bookmakers are required to file reports on suspicious wagers. Nev. Gaming Comm. § 22.121. When analysts can't discern a reason for the suspicious activity, they make the sports property aware of the suspicious activity. Bill King, *Gaming Industry, leagues differ on integrity guards,* https://www.bizjournals.com/losangeles/news/2018/04/19/gaming-industry-leagues-differ-on-integrity-guards.html (last visited 6/11/18). If a sports league has reservations of suspicious activity, it can ask for an investigation through the state's gaming control board, which is guaranteed access to all information about every bet and who placed it. Bookmakers rely on preserving the integrity of games to make money, and are typically more than willing to report any suspicious activity to the board. That said, once the NGC licenses a bookmaker, it is up to the bookmaker to decide which sporting events to offer the public for wagering. The bookmakers typically report any suspicious activity to the Nevada Gaming Control Board, which is the investigative, licensing, and enforcement agency in Nevada. They act in a prosecutorial capacity, with the NGC functioning as an adjudicator. Both the Board and the NGC have discretion to determine if the event should be considered a risk to the integrity of gaming and the protection of the public.

Competition organizers' consent is not required unless the team's home field is in Nevada or it is a professional team participating in an event played in Nevada. Nev. Gaming Comm. § 22.120(1)(d). As long as the licensed bookmakers follow the specifications laid out in regulation § 22.060, there are no other means of limiting a bookmaker's offering a bet on a particular type of play, as long as the particular type of play can be recorded or proven to have or have not occurred. Licensed sports pools may accept wagers on specific sporting events regarding who will win and whether the total points scored in a specified event will be higher or lower than a number specified for the event. The other contingencies that sports pools may accept wagers on are outcomes of bets that are recorded: (1) in general newspapers; (2) in public records maintained by the league that the event involves; or (3) by employees of the book that are televised live at the book and records contain the time and event of the particular occurrence that was bet on. Nev. Gaming Comm. § 22.060. House rules for wagers must be submitted to the NGC chair for approval. Nev. Gaming Comm. § 22.150.

Under these provisions, Nevada bookmakers accept "prop bets" (known elsewhere as "spot bets") on statistically discrete events beyond the outcome of the game. Common examples of prop bets are: which team will score first, how many balls or strikes will a pitcher throw in a game, the duration of the national anthem sung before a game, number of strikeouts a pitcher will have in a game, which player will score the first touchdown in a game, etc.

Australia. Sports wagering in Australia largely takes place under the auspices of the Gambling and Racing Legislation Amendment (Sports Betting) Act 2007 of the State of Victoria. The Act's Division 3, Section 4 delegates to the Victorian Commission for Gambling and Liquor Regulation the authority to grant sporting events, sports controlling bodies, and sports betting agencies the right of sports betting. The Commission considers such factors as: (1) whether the event is an unmanageable integrity risk; (2) whether the event is administered by an organization capable of enforcing rules regarding integrity; (3) whether betting on the event is offensive or against the public interest; (4) whether the event is an unreasonable expansion of the scope of gambling in Victoria; and (5) any other matter the Commission deems relevant. The Commission also reserves the right to revoke approval at any time for reasonable cause, as determined by the Commission.

Gambling is permitted on application of a "sports controlling body," typically a sports league. The Commission considers such factors as: (1) whether the applicant has control of the event or administers the event; (2) whether the applicant has adequate rules in place to ensure integrity; (3) whether the applicant complies with international codes relating to integrity in sport; (4) whether the applicant has resources and authority to monitor integrity systems; (5) "whether the applicant has clear policies on the provision of information that may be relevant to the betting market;" (6) whether the applicant has a clear process for reporting the results of the event and hearing appeals relating to the results; (7) whether the applicant has a clear policy of sharing information with sports betting providers in order to investigate suspicious betting activity; (8) whether the applicant is the most appropriate body to be approved as the controlling body for the event; (9) whether approval supports the public interest; and (10) any other objections filed and any other relevant matter the Commission deems appropriate.

To be considered a sports betting provider, a company must meet three prerequisites. First, the sports betting provider must have an agreement with the sports controlling body in charge of the sporting event, unless the event is wholly outside of Victoria. Second, the agreement must promote integrity by providing for information sharing. And third, the agreement must also stipulate whether the sports betting agency will pay a fee to the sports controlling body and specify the amount of the fee. If the sports betting provider is unable to reach an agreement with a sports controlling body, the provider may apply to the Commission for the right to service bets.

NOTES AND QUESTIONS

1. *On the Merits.* Do you agree with Justice Alito that Congress in 1992 would not have wanted to retain the ban on state or private sponsorship of sports betting, had it known it was constitutionally barred from prohibiting state authorization of gambling?

2. *State-by-State?* Justice Alito suggests that Americans' diverse and changing views on sports gambling meant that the issue should be decided on a state-by-state basis. Do you agree? Consider, from a comparative perspective, the Australian view that integrity is enhanced when gambling is legal and regulated with full cooperation between sports leagues, law enforcement, gaming regulators, and bookmakers. *See* Stephen F. Ross, James Gorman III, & Ryan Mentzer, *Reform of Sports Gambling in the United States: Lessons from Down Under,* 5 Ariz. St. Sports & Ent. L. J. 7 (2015). The Australian perspective is that corruption is far higher in countries where betting is illegal and thus unregulated. Stephen F. Ross & Adrian Anderson, "Strong regulation could inject integrity into sports gambling," *Sports Bus. J.* Feb. 16, 2015, *available at* https://www.sportsbusinessdaily.com/Journal/Issues/2015/02/16/Opinion/Ross-Anderson.aspx.

(a) Perception of a major scandal threatened one of the fasting growing sports leagues, the Indian Premier League of cricket. In 2013, three Rajasthan Royals players and assorted illegal bookmakers were disciplined for "spot fixing." Under the scheme, the corrupt players signaled to bookies at the beginning of an over (loosely like a baseball inning, consisting of six balls bowled to the batsman by the same bowler) that they would concede a certain number of runs. When a Bollywood actor was also arrested, he further implicated a senior official of the Chennai Super Kings, who is also the son-in-law of N. Srinivasan, the chairman of the Board of Control of Cricket in India. Commenting on the scandal, an Indian newspaper opined:

> Legalising betting is another essential step towards cleaning up cricket. While players from other countries have been implicated in fixing, it is an uncomfortable fact that South Asia is the nexus of the entire enterprise. Not coincidentally, betting happens to be illegal in India but legal in a number of other cricket-playing nations like England and Australia. It should come as no surprise that driving betting underground in the country that is the hub of the sport's economic activity will have a vitiating effect on the entire game. The current crop of guilty players may have been dealt with—but unless these larger factors are addressed, it won't be the last one.

"Far from a clean sweep," DNA, Sept. 16, 2013, available at http://www.dnaindia.com/analysis/editorial-dna-edit-far-from-a-clean-sweep-1889418.

(b) Like in most American states, legalized gambling in Singapore is strictly limited to certain casinos and sports gambling is not lawful. Yet Europol revealed in February 2013 that criminals based in Singapore had orchestrated a global match-fixing corruption conspiracy that had recently rigged as many as 680 soccer matches across the world.

(c) Massive corruption in Chinese football (soccer) was exposed in the summer of 2012, when two former Chinese Football Administrative Center directors were both sentenced to 10 years of imprisonment for taking bribes. Four prominent players in China's only trip to the World Cup in 2002 were also punished to varying degrees for taking payments to shave points or throw matches. Since then, as many as two dozen former football officials, players, coaches and referees have been sentenced to prison and fined various amounts as the Chinese government demonstrated what it referred to as a bold attempt to clean up the corruption-plagued sport.

3. *Effect on Actors Like Donaghy?* Ross, Gorman & Mentzer, *supra* at 14, detail how a legalized gambling regime that dries up the market for illegal wagers would likely have inhibited improper gambling such as the scandal involving NBA referee Timothy Donaghy. Donaghy used his access to non-public information, including the identity of officiating crews for upcoming games, the interactions between certain referees and team personnel and players, and the physical condition of certain players. In 2007, after the FBI learned of the referee's involvement through its investigation of illegal gambling interests, Donaghy pled guilty to two criminal counts alleging conspiracy to commit wire fraud and served eleven months in federal prison.

4. *Gambling and the Best Interests of Sport.* Should it have made a difference that the Commissioner found that Pete Rose always bet on his own Reds team to win? What should baseball have done to Albert Belle, who in a 1997 deposition in a lawsuit admitted that he had lost tens of thousands of dollars betting with bookies on football or basketball (though never baseball) games, something that is a misdemeanor under Ohio state law? Or to the Philadelphia Phillies' Len Dykstra, who one year apparently lost $100,000 playing in a privately-organized and illegal poker game during the off-season? Or the NBA's Michael Jordan who, while playing for the Chicago Bulls, created a huge controversy when (with his father) he traveled down from Madison Square Garden after a playoff game with the New York Knicks to gamble at a (legal) casino in Atlantic City? What exactly is it about gambling that makes this behavior (or just associating with it) "detrimental to the best interests of the sport"? Jeffrey Standen, in *The Beauty of Bets: Wagers as Compensation for Professional Athletes*, 42 Willamette L. Rev. 639 (2006), argues that allowing betting by athletes would be in the best interest of sports.

5. *The Australian Example.* In Australia, major tennis tournaments are sponsored by Betfair Australia, a gambling house. This continues despite recent allegations of match fixing in international tennis, in particular directed

at Russian Nikolay Davydenko, who was ranked fourth on the ATP Tour, based on suspicious betting patterns in a 2007 match against Martin Vassallo Arguello. As the match in Poland progressed, more bets were placed on Davydenko to lose, even after he won the first set. Davydenko was ultimately cleared of involvement.

Do you think sports should allow gambling sponsorships? A number of clubs in the English Premier League sport kits with gambling sponsors. Gambling houses are actually quite good at spotting weird betting patterns that will not be discovered by underground betting. Consider the views of Australian sports officials, in the context of a country where sports betting is significant and legal. Former Australian Football League executive Adrian Anderson notes that Victoria (home to Melbourne and nine AFL clubs) has tough laws that give sports leagues a say in types of bets permitted (corruption tends to occur initially on obscure bets that have little outcome on the match). Anderson emphasizes another provision requiring licensed bookmakers to provide access to their betting records as an essential tool in anti-corruption efforts. He also criticizes Australian federal provisions barring confidential information sharing between law enforcement agencies and sports leagues. "Enough of talk, it's time government walked the walk on corruption," *The Australian,* July 27, 2013.

There are commercial as well as integrity concerns regarding legalized gambling. Australian bookmakers routinely enter agreements with sports leagues for the right to provide "wagering services." Victorian state law requires them to do so, and the power of states to require sporting bodies to condition use of information regarding sporting events for gambling purposes on the payment of fees was upheld in *Betfair Pty Ltd v. Racing New South Wales* (HCA unreported, 2012 HCA 12). The potential is sufficiently lucrative that the Australian Competition and Consumer Commission recently blocked an effort by bookmakers to collectively bargain with the National Rugby League, concluding that this would give them excessive economic power. *Australian Wagering Council Ltd—Collective Bargaining Notification Draft Objection Notice* (Feb. 26, 2014), *available at* http://registers.accc.gov.au/content/index.phtml/itemId/1139980/fromItemId/815577/display/acccDecision.

4. DRUGS OF ABUSE AND PERFORMANCE ENHANCING DRUGS

Another significant aspect of the Commissioner's duties to protect the league's reputation concerns the use of drugs of abuse or performance enhancing drugs by players. Because the law surrounding these important issues cannot be divorced from relevant labor law and provisions of collective bargaining agreements, our discussion of this topic is deferred until Chapter 3, Section 3.

5. BEYOND PROTECTION OF LEAGUE REPUTATION?

The sports league constitutions studied in this chapter grant Commissioners broad power to act in the league's "best interests." Courts have broadly construed this power, with great deference to the Commissioner's judgment. The specific topics covered in this Section related to matters that patently affect the league's reputation among avid fans, casual viewers, sponsors, and others who provide revenue to America's commercialized sports leagues.

As a descriptive matter, the modern sports league commissioner has become the Chief Executive Officer of a major commercial operation, who ultimately reports to club owners who have invested millions (and occasionally billions) in their franchises. Many would view skeptically the claim that these commissioners would act to protect some broader concept of a league's "best interests" beyond those necessary to preserve reputation. The question for public policy, and ultimately law, is how we can best achieve what *society* believes to be in sports' "best interests" if they diverge from the interests of owners as a collective.

(a) Breach of Trust

In a landmark decision, MLB Commissioner Bud Selig suggested that the best interests of an individual owner may be contrary to the best interests of baseball. A settlement of litigation claims, briefly noted in a preliminary opinion in *In re Los Angeles Dodgers LLC*, 457 B.R. 308 (Bank. D. Del. 2011), precluded an important judicial decision concerning the scope of the Commissioner's best interest powers. The issue was whether the Commissioner could intervene to protect a club's long-term economic prospects from what the Commissioner believes to be improvident business decisions by the current owner. Consider whether this decision expands the "best interests" power, or fits more comfortably within the framework of reputation-protection that the other examples in this chapter have discussed.

The dispute arose when Los Angeles Dodgers' owner Frank McCourt, who had acquired the storied team from News Corporation in a leveraged transaction, found himself facing personal financial difficulties (largely due to a messy and very expensive divorce proceeding). McCourt sought to alleviate this problem by entering into a new long-term media rights deal with Fox, totaling $1.7 billion over 17 years, which including an up-front cash payment of $385 million to McCourt. Under Art. VIII, § 4(f) of the MLB Constitution, this contract required the approval of the Commissioner. Selig rejected the contract as contrary to the best interests of baseball. He concluded that McCourt was harming the Dodgers' future for a quick fix of his personal financial issues, that the agreement precluded long-term maximization of media rights, and took great exception to the diversion of most of the $385 million for McCourt's personal use. Selig also expressed concern that future ownership would be locked into a below-market deal. The letter concluded:

> As the Dodgers' control owner, you have the duty to manage the Club "for its own sake, in a sound fiscal manner, and not for the benefit of another business," and a contractual commitment to operate the Dodgers "with the intention of being profitable and with respect to all operations and control in the best interests of the Los Angeles Dodgers and Major League Baseball." Instead, you have run the Club consistently for your own benefit and that of your family members, and your lifestyle, with little or no regard for the distinction between the Club's finances and your own.

Letter from Bud Selig, Comm'r, Major League Baseball, to Frank McCourt, Owner, L.A. Dodgers Baseball Club 7–8 (June 20, 2011), *quoted in* Frank J. Mallaro, Jr., Note, *Permeating the Good Old Boys Club: Why Holding the Commissioner of Baseball to a Fiduciary Duty of Loyalty is in the "Best Interests of the Game,"* 7 Brook J. Corp. Fin. & Com. L. 475, 485 (2013).

Without an influx of cash from a new television deal, the Dodgers could not meet payroll obligations. Rather than cede control of the team to Major League Baseball, McCourt filed for Chapter 11 bankruptcy, even though such a step directly violates the Major League Agreement and can result in an owner being stripped of his ownership rights. (Article VIII § 4(ii)(*l*) of the Major League Agreement states, "the rights, privileges and other property rights of a Major League Club hereunder and under any other Baseball-related agreement may be terminated . . . if the Club in question shall . . . file a voluntary petition in bankruptcy." Article II § 3(c) of the Major League Agreement grants the Commissioner the right to suspend or remove any owner of a Major League Club.) After legal skirmishing, the bankruptcy litigation was settled. McCourt finally succumbed to financial and legal pressures, and agreed with Major League Baseball that the Dodgers would be sold at auction. The team was subsequently sold in a complicated transaction to a group led by Guggenheim Partners, and including long-time baseball executive Stan Kasten and local basketball star Earvin "Magic" Johnson, for $2.2 billion. The new owners were able to obtain a 25-year media deal with Fox' rival, Time Warner Cable, valued at over $7 billion.

Are there social reasons to recognize a special trust in sports that goes beyond the "branding" inherent in other commercial products and services whose providers seek to preserve reputation? Consider the following:

> The relationship between a sports fan and a team owner or a league is not the same as between . . . the buyer of computer software and its supplier . . . in sports, no one *wants* market retribution to be swift. We hope that Los Angelenos and others

who grew up as Dodger fans with Vin Scully's Hall of Fame broadcast will remain loyal despite management travails that have impeded recent performance. We honor members of Red Sox Nation who lived and died with years of ineptitude, which some believe was supernaturally imposed. With sports, the customer is not buying something that depends largely on the current behavior of the owner, but is rather buying into a tradition.... The 'trust' that fans place in their favorite teams is what makes sports the special entertainment and civil institution that it is.

Stephen F. Ross & Stefan Szymanski, *Fans of the World, Unite! A (Capitalist) Manifesto for Sports Consumers*, at 6–7. Do you agree? If so, when owners act commercially to breach this trust, is that contrary to the best interests of sport?

(b) External Social Policies: Defer to Private Governance, or Subject to Outside Legal Prohibitions?

Virtually all the organized team sports played and watched around the world originated in countries that were once ruled by King George III. This is probably not a coincidence: the English common law permitted individuals to form associations for any purpose not specifically barred by the law, which facilitated the formation of private sporting clubs. In contrast, continental European countries historically banned private associations unless expressly authorized by government, which directed sports into activities like French cycling or German gymnasiums with more demonstrable use for military purposes. Team sports evolved from 18th-century English clubs. Gentlemen organized clubs around sporting competitions, with the incidental benefit of physical exercise and the primary purpose of facilitating drinking, gambling, and socializing. Sporting clubs similarly developed in 19th-century America. Other than the public interest in allowing individuals the freedom to choose their leisure activities, competitive sports originated in private organizations for private amusement. *See* Stefan Szymanski, *A Theory of the Evolution of Modern Sport*, 35 J. Sports Hist. 1 (2006).

A 1966 landmark English legal decision acknowledged how sport had evolved into a part of society about which the public had a vital interest. Participation in English horse racing was limited to jockeys and trainers who had licenses from a private organization, the Jockey Club. The leaders of this private club chose not to admit women, so a skilled trainer could not practice her trade. The Court of Appeal held that this was an unreasonable agreement in restraint of trade and void. Lord Denning, an eminent jurist, explicitly distinguished private dining clubs from sporting organizations that assumed a monopoly regulatory position: "But we are not considering a social club, we are considering an association which exercises a virtual monopoly in an important field of human activity." *Nagle v. Feilden,* [1966] 2 QB 633 (C.A.).

In assessing the reasonableness of sporting rules challenged in court, judges continue to exhibit significant deference to the judgment of private sporting organizations. Consider the following observations by another British judge:

> I think that the courts must be slow to allow any implied obligation to be fair to be used as a means of bringing before the Courts for review honest decisions of bodies exercising jurisdiction over sporting and other activities which those bodies are far better fitted to judge than the Courts. This is so even where those bodies are concerned with the means of livelihood of those who take part in those activities. Concepts of natural justice and the duty to be fair must not be allowed to discredit themselves by making unreasonable requirements and imposing undue burdens, bodies such as the board which promote a public interest by seeking to maintain a high stance in a field of activity which otherwise might easily become degraded or corrupt ought not to be hampered in their work without good cause. Such bodies should not be tempted or coerced into granting licences that otherwise they would refuse by reason of the Courts having imposed on them procedure for refusal which facilitates litigation against them.... The individual must indeed be protected against impropriety; but any claim of this or anything more must be balanced against what the public interest requires.

McInnes v. Onslow-Fane, [1978] 1 W.L.R. 1520, 1535 (Ch.).

These English cases foreshadow the important external limits that society now places on sport. Sports "hold a singular position among leisure time activities and have an unparalleled impact on the everyday lives of billions of people." Andrei S. Markovits and Lars Rensmann, *Gaming the World: How Sports are Reshaping Global Politics and Culture* (Princeton Univ. Press 2010), at 1. This subject is part of a vast literature in the fields of sport philosophy, ethics and sociology of sport, and how sport and culture have interacted throughout time is a major feature in the sports history literature.

CHAPTER 2

LABOR LAW AND COLLECTIVE BARGAINING IN PROFESSIONAL SPORTS*

■ ■ ■

A. INTRODUCTION TO NATIONAL LABOR LAW

A basic understanding of national labor law is necessary to comprehend the operation of professional sports leagues in America. Although professional sports in America are regulated by antitrust law as well as labor law, the Supreme Court has bestowed preeminence on the principles of national labor policy. As explained in Chapter 6, what would otherwise be treated as antitrust violations—such as unreasonable restraints on the market for players' services—can be insulated from regulation by a collective bargaining relationship between a league and a union that represents the league's athletes.

In the nineteenth century—long before the advent of sports unions—state courts considered unions to be illegal conspiracies subject to criminal prosecution whenever they withdrew the services of their members in support of demands for increased wages and improved labor conditions. As the organization of craft and some industrial workers continued into the twentieth century, courts continued to serve management's interests by granting employers injunctive relief against union-related concerted activity.

Unions eventually received support from the federal legislative branch. Congress granted unions relief from judicial injunctive interference in labor disputes—first in the Clayton Act of 1914 and then more broadly in the Norris-LaGuardia Act of 1932. In 1935, moreover, as the nation suffered from the continuing Depression, Congress provided affirmative governmental protection to the efforts of employees to bargain collectively with their employers. The Wagner Act of 1935—entitled the National Labor Relations Act (NLRA or Labor Act)—protected from employer interference the rights of employees to self-organize, to demand to bargain collectively, and to engage in concerted activities. The Labor Act established a federal agency—the National Labor Relations Board (NLRB or Labor Board)—charged with securing employee rights and with conducting secret ballot elections in which employees could vote to form or

---

* For commentary and other materials on labor law topics relevant to this chapter, please see the Casebook Website (http://pennstatelaw.psu.edu/SportsTextWebsite).

not to form a union. Congress expected the Labor Act to both foster industrial peace and to improve employee wages. Congress hoped that the processes of collective bargaining would result in stable terms of employment that reflected the relative economic power of the parties involved in the negotiations, rather than solutions imposed by government.

The Taft-Hartley Act substantially amended the Labor Act in 1947. Taft-Hartley added protections from union as well as employer restraint and the rights of employees to refrain from as well as to engage in concerted activities, including collective bargaining. In the Landrum-Griffin Act of 1959, Congress both amended the Labor Act further to close some loopholes and also addressed issues of internal union democracy in a separate statute. Since 1959, however, the statutory framework of federal labor policy has not been significantly altered.

Employees, unions, or employers that believe that an employer or a union has committed a violation of the Labor Act can file an unfair labor practice charge with a regional office of the Labor Board. Board attorneys investigate the charge. If found to have merit, the General Counsel of the Labor Board may issue a complaint that is tried before an administrative law judge (ALJ). ALJ decisions are reviewed by the Labor Board, which is empowered by the Labor Act to issue orders with equitable remedies, including the reinstatement of wrongfully discharged employees with back pay. The Labor Board also can direct an employer to bargain in good faith with a union. These orders must be enforced in a federal Circuit Court of Appeals. A party aggrieved by a Labor Board order also can appeal to a Circuit Court of Appeals for review. Courts of Appeals, however, give some deference to the Labor Board's judgment.

Unions of professional sports teams' athletes generally have been the beneficiaries of the Labor Act and the interpretive case law elaborated by the Labor Board and the courts. The Labor Board and the courts have been able to adapt labor law principles to sports unions and the distinctive work situations their members face. The seeds of modern collective action by professional athletes were sown in the 1950s after the enactment of the NLRA with the formation of player organizations in all four team sports. In each sport, organizers deliberately named these bodies associations rather than unions, because the latter term was considered appropriate only for the teams' concession vendors or maintenance crews, not for elite athletes. Not until the mid-1960s did players begin to realize that, for all their status in the outside world, if they were to induce owners to change the structure of the players' market, they would have to engage in full-fledged collective bargaining and concerted activity under professional union leadership.

Collective bargaining in the sports industry has proved contentious. Sports unions first had to convince club owners that they were actually real unions and not simply fraternities of sporting athletes who were satisfied simply to have the opportunity to play their chosen sport. The genuine sports unions that evolved in the 1960s in the four major team sports had to overcome the fact that on average their membership would turn over every four years because of the short careers of their members. Sports unions had to employ economic weapons and withhold the services of their members to firmly establish their legitimacy with the owners. The owners, in turn, have resorted to locking out the athletes in an effort to prove that highly paid and short-career sports workers could not maintain the solidarity needed to withstand the owners' demands. Many of these battles have focused on the system used to determine the compensation of athletes and the systems that bind an athlete to a particular club.

By the current day, for each major professional team sports league, through work stoppages, peaceful collective bargaining, and labor arbitration, unionism has transformed the rules for dealings between individual teams and players. In particular, veteran free agency has become the rule, but with different forms of salary constraints imposed on the amount that a team can offer its players. Ultimately, as professional league teams flourished more and more economically, the players began to earn their fair share of the profits.

Major League Baseball experienced decades of particularly contentious labor relations. Led by Marvin Miller, the MLB Players Association (MLBPA) approached collective bargaining with the same zeal as the United Steelworkers union, where Miller had earlier served as chief economist. Baseball club owners, who generally had experienced labor relations only in non-unionized industries, found the collective bargaining process to be inhospitable. Miller and his successor Donald Fehr had to repeatedly prove to the owners each time a collective bargaining agreement (CBA) expired that the players were genuine unionists. The result was eight successive work stoppages—either union strikes or management-directed lockouts.

In 2002, however, negotiations in baseball achieved a stable relationship between owners and players. In large measure this was the result of the work of two experienced labor law experts—the late Michael Weiner, the successor to Donald Fehr as the Executive Director of the MLBPA, and Rob Manfred, now Commissioner of Major League Baseball. The two forged a productive relationship that until the time of this edition has helped keep baseball free from the work stoppages that continued to afflict professional football, basketball, and hockey in the twenty-first century.

In the late 1960s, when real unionism first came to the sports world, the average salaries in baseball, hockey, basketball, and football ranged from $19,000 to $25,000. By 2018, average player salaries ranged from $2.1

million in football to almost $6 million in basketball. Compared with the average American worker, baseball players earned 3.5 times more in salaries in 1967, while by 2018 they were making 92 times more. This huge player salary spiral has been accompanied by comparable leaps in fan attendance, television and merchandising deals, league expansion, and team franchise values. Sports unions and sports management have both flourished financially over recent decades.

The focus of this chapter and the two chapters to follow is on how federal labor law, private labor negotiations, and the use of labor arbitration have addressed employment conflicts in professional sports. Over the last eight decades, the NLRB and the courts have developed an elaborate labor law jurisprudence. The more than five decades of active union representation in professional sports has produced decisions that illustrate the important doctrinal spheres in contemporary labor law.

B. APPLICATION OF THE LABOR ACT TO SPORTS

Congress enacted the Labor Act pursuant to its power to regulate interstate commerce. The Labor Act was a key feature of President Franklin Delano Roosevelt's New Deal, based in part on the premise that unionization and collective bargaining would enhance worker's buying power and help drive the nation out of the Depression, as well as secure industrial peace. It was not at all clear, however, that the Supreme Court would find this legislative strategy constitutional. The Court had a narrow perspective on the reach of interstate commerce. In fact, the Supreme Court in 1922 had ruled in *Federal Baseball Club of Baltimore v. National League of Professional Baseball Clubs*, 259 U.S. 200 (1922), that baseball was too localized a form of business enterprise to be subject to federal antitrust law. Nevertheless, a closely divided Supreme Court, in *NLRB v. Jones & Laughlin Steel Corp.*, 301 U.S. 1 (1937), broadened that perspective and upheld the constitutional validity of the Labor Act.

Although the *Jones & Laughlin* decision did not apply the Labor Act to professional sports, it did seem to provide the Labor Board with the authority to address the issue. The Labor Board decision that ultimately did so and thereby gave professional athletes rights under the Labor Act was rendered in response to a union representation petition filed by American League umpires.

AMERICAN LEAGUE OF PROFESSIONAL BASEBALL CLUBS & ASS'N OF NATIONAL BASEBALL LEAGUE UMPIRES
180 N.L.R.B. 190 (1969)

* * *

[The Labor Board first considered whether baseball sufficiently involved interstate commerce so that the NLRA could apply.] The Board's jurisdiction under the Act is based upon the commerce clause of the Constitution, and is coextensive with the reach of that clause... [Notwithstanding *Federal Baseball*], since professional football and boxing have been held to be in interstate commerce and thus subject to the antitrust laws, it can no longer be seriously contended that the Court still considers baseball alone to be outside of interstate commerce. Congressional deliberations regarding the relationship of baseball and other professional team sports to the antitrust laws likewise reflect a Congressional assumption that such sports are subject to regulation under the commerce clause. It is, incidentally, noteworthy that these deliberations reveal Congressional concern for the rights of employees such as players to bargain collectively and engage in concerted activities. Additionally, legal scholars have agreed, and neither the parties nor those participating as *amici* dispute, that professional sports are in or affect interstate commerce, and as such are subject to the Board's jurisdiction. Therefore, on the basis of the above, we find that professional baseball is an industry in or affecting commerce, and as such is subject to Board jurisdiction under the Act.

* * *

Section 14(c)(1) of the National Labor Relations Act, as amended, permits the Board to decline jurisdiction over labor disputes involving any "class or category of employers, where, in the opinion of the Board, the effect of such labor dispute on commerce is not sufficiently substantial to warrant the exercise of its jurisdiction. . . ." The Employer and other employers contend that because of baseball's internal self-regulation, a labor dispute involving the American League of Professional Baseball Clubs is not likely to have any substantial effect on interstate commerce; and that application of the National Labor Relations Act to this Employer is contrary to national labor policy because Congress has sanctioned baseball's internal self-regulation. The Employer also contends that effective and uniform regulation of baseball's labor relations problems is not possible through Board processes because of the sport's international aspects.

* * *

We have carefully considered the positions of the parties, and the *amicus* briefs, and we find that it will best effectuate the mandates of the

Act, as well as national labor policy, to assert jurisdiction over this Employer. We reach this decision for the following reasons.

Baseball's system for internal self-regulation of disputes involving umpires is made up of the Uniform Umpires Contract, the Major League Agreement, and the Major League Rules, which provide, among other things, for final resolution of disputes through arbitration by the Commissioner. The system appears to have been designed almost entirely by employers and owners, and the final arbiter of internal disputes does not appear to be a neutral third party freely chosen by both sides, but rather an individual appointed solely by the member club owners themselves. We do not believe that such a system is likely either to prevent labor disputes from arising in the future, or, having once arisen, to resolve them in a manner susceptible or conducive to voluntary compliance by all parties involved. Moreover, it is patently contrary to the letter and spirit of the Act for the Board to defer its undoubted jurisdiction to decide unfair labor practices to a disputes settlement system established unilaterally by an employer or group of employers. Finally, although the instant case involves only umpires employed by the League, professional baseball clubs employ, in addition to players, clubhouse attendants, bat boys, watchmen, scouts, ticket sellers, ushers, gatemen, trainers, janitors, office clericals, batting practice pitchers, stilemen, publicity, and advertising men, grounds keepers and maintenance men. As to these other categories, there is no "self-regulation" at all. This consideration is of all the more consequence for those employees in professional baseball whose interests are likely to call the Board's processes into play, the great majority are in the latter-named classifications.

We can find, neither in the statute nor in its legislative history, any expression of a Congressional intent that disputes between employers and employees in this industry should be removed from the scheme of the National Labor Relations Act.

* * *

[W]e are not here confronted with the sort of small, primarily intrastate employer over which the Board declines jurisdiction because of failure to meet its prevailing monetary standards. Moreover, it is apparent that the Employer, whose operations are so clearly national in scope, ought not have its labor relations problems subject to diverse state laws.

The Employer's final contention, that Board processes are unsuited to regulate effectively baseball's international aspects, clearly lacks merit, as many if not most of the industries subject to the Act have similar international features.

* * *

MEMBER JENKINS, dissenting:

[Member Jenkins would have declined to assert jurisdiction over baseball, reasoning that Congress' silence on whether the Labor Act covered baseball meant that the agency should not assert jurisdiction. In 1935 when it enacted the Wagner Act, Congress knew that the Supreme Court had held that baseball did not affect interstate commerce. Even if the Board had discretion to assert or decline jurisdiction, it should not do so because "[t]here is no showing that this industry is wracked with the kinds of labor disputes which are likely to constitute a burden on commerce." Any disputes that might arise could be addressed by the internal commissioner system.]

NOTES AND QUESTIONS

1. *Effect on Interstate Commerce.* This decision may not seem earth-shaking, but it is the first case where a court or an agency ruled that baseball affects interstate commerce. Impact on interstate commerce is the constitutional nexus for both the Labor Act and the antitrust laws examined in subsequent chapters. How would you determine whether a sport affects interstate commerce? What kind of evidence would you consider?

2. *Self-Regulation of Labor Disputes?* What is your reaction to the contrasting observations by the NLRB members about the relevance of baseball's system of internal self-regulation? Does Member Jenkins realistically assume a Commissioner who is neutral between owners and employees?

3. *Reliance Interest.* Should the Board in 1969 have weighed more heavily the reliance of the American League and its member clubs on the Supreme Court's 1922 decision in *Federal Baseball* before asserting jurisdiction under the Labor Act? The Supreme Court had reaffirmed the Sherman Act's non-coverage of baseball in *Toolson v. New York Yankees*, 346 U.S. 356 (1953), and again did so in *Flood v. Kuhn*, 407 U.S. 258 (1972). The latter decision is presented in Chapter 4 below. Consider whether the clubs' reliance interest might be stronger for non-coverage by antitrust law than for non-coverage by labor law.

The Board's assertion of jurisdiction over other more recently developed professional leagues in other sports is less controversial, because the Supreme Court had never held that these leagues did not operate in interstate commerce for purposes of antitrust law or any other laws. Indeed, in *Radovich v. National Football League*, 352 U.S. 445 (1957), the Court refused to extend *Federal Baseball* and applied the Clayton Act to professional football. *See also Haywood v. National Basketball Assn.*, 401 U.S. 1204 (1971) (Douglas, J., acting as Circuit Justice).

On the other hand, the determination that Congress has Commerce Clause authority to regulate professional sports leagues did not mean that the Labor Act protects all the employees of these leagues or all professional athletes. The Labor Act, as amended in 1947, expressly excludes from the definition of protected employees, "any individual having the status of an independent contractor, or any individual employed as a supervisor." 29 U.S.C. § 152(3).

The latter term "supervisor" in turn is defined broadly to include "any individual having authority, in the interest of the employer, to hire, transfer, suspend, lay off, recall, promote, discharge, assign, reward, or discipline other employees, or responsibly direct them, or to adjust their grievances, or effectively to recommend such action, if . . . such authority . . . requires the use of independent judgment." 29 U.S.C. § 152 (11). The Supreme Court has required the Board to interpret this exclusion expansively, *see, e.g., NLRB v. Kentucky River Community Care, Inc.*, 532 U.S. 706 (2001), and to continue to maintain an implied exclusion of "managerial employees" who "formulate and effectuate management policies by expressing and making operative the decision of their employers." *See NLRB v. Bell Aerospace Co.*, 416 U.S. 267 (1974). These exclusions would seem to preclude the protection not only of club presidents and general managers, but also of managers and coaches. Why do they not also preclude the coverage of umpires and referees?

Even athletes in many professional sports, such as tennis and golf, are denied the Labor Act's protection by the Act's exclusion of independent contractors. The Taft-Hartley Congress added this exclusion to require the Board to observe the common law distinction of independent contractors from employees. *See NLRB v. United Insurance Co.*, 390 U.S. 254 (1968). The Supreme Court subsequently has clarified that for purposes of federal statutes this common law distinction should follow the multifactor "right-to-control" test adopted by the Restatements of Agency. *See, e.g., Nationwide Mutual Insurance Co. v. Darden*, 503 U.S. 318 (1992). As reformulated in § 1.01 of the Restatement of Employment Law, this multifactor test determines whether the workers can perform their work in their own independent business interest.

Tennis and golf professionals operate independent businesses employing their own coaches and "teams." These athletes, rather than their tours, determine in which tournaments they will compete and when, where and how they will practice and compete. Similarly, boxers, race car drivers, horse jockeys, and mixed martial arts fighters generally are treated as independent contractors. A sports owner's use of an independent contractor designation is not determinative of workers' actual status, however. The designation of NFL cheerleaders as independent contractors by the clubs that closely control their work, for instance, seems open to challenge. *See, e.g., Ferrari v. National Football League,* 61 N.Y.S.3d 421 (2017) (certifying class to determine whether cheerleaders designated as contractors are really employees).

The managerial exclusion is not the only implied departure from the common law definition of employee that the Board has recognized to restrict its jurisdiction. Most importantly for college athletes, the Board has held that Congress did not intend to treat graduate students discharging compensated teaching or research responsibilities as employees when their relationship with their universities is "primarily educational." *Brown University,* 342 N.L.R.B. 483 (2004). Whether or not the President Obama-appointed Board's reversal of the *Brown* decision in *Trustees of Columbia University,* 364 N.L.R.B. No. 90 (2016) is confirmed by subsequent Boards, the Labor Board would have to determine that college athletes in at least revenue producing sports were employees under the Labor Act before it could protect their efforts to form a union. Furthermore, athletes at public universities could not be protected because the Labor Act's definition of employer excludes states and their subdivisions. For further discussion of college athlete unionization, as well as the treatment of compensation of college athletes, see Chapter 11 *infra.*

C. UNION ACTIVITY AND EMPLOYER RETALIATION

Employees covered by the NLRA gain federal administrative protection against employer retaliation for supporting a union. For most workers, this legal protection can be most important in the early days of union organization confronting employers determined to stay union-free. In professional sports, however, players had organized their associations and secured collective bargaining agreements even before they could be sure that the Labor Board would assert jurisdictional coverage. In addition, as explained below in Chapter 6, sports clubs and leagues are unusual employers because they need and want a union for their players in order to secure and retain the benefit of the implied labor exemption to the antitrust laws

The rights of employees secured by the Labor Act, however, extend beyond initial union organization to encompass any concerted activity for employee mutual aid or protection, whether or not union related. These employee rights also encompass actions in support of the union in its bargaining efforts—for example, engaging in strikes and rallying fellow employees in favor of the union and against the employer during a strike. Section 8(a)(1) of the Labor Act makes it an unfair labor practice for the employer to "interfere with, restrain, or coerce" employees engaged in any such "concerted activities," and § 8(a)(3) forbids "discrimination in regard to hire or tenure of employment to encourage or discourage membership in any labor organization."

While these employee rights and employer obligations are firmly embedded in labor jurisprudence, they are inevitably murky in application. Even a determined anti-union employer, recognizing the presence of the Labor Act in the background, is likely to be careful to direct such retaliation only against employees whose work history provides some colorable basis for discharge or other punitive action. As a result, unfair labor practice charges based on § 8 involve difficult and time-consuming examinations of both the employer's true motivation for its actions and the employee's record of performance.

This difficulty may be exacerbated in professional sports. Unlike most other workers, athletes can have no expectation of keeping their positions just because they are doing a reasonably competent job. Veteran players continuously face the threat of release and replacement by rookie challengers. The standard NFL player contract, for example, has provided:

> *Skill, Performance and Conduct.* Player understands that he is competing with other players for a position on Club's roster within the applicable player limits. If at any time, in the sole judgment of Club, Player's skill or performance has been unsatisfactory as compared with that of other players competing for positions on Club's roster, or if Player has engaged in personal conduct reasonably judged by Club to adversely affect or reflect on Club, then Club may terminate this contract. In addition, during the period any salary cap is legally in effect, this contract may be terminated if, in Club's opinion, Player is anticipated to make less of a contribution to Club's ability to compete on the playing field than another player or players whom Club intends to sign or attempts to sign, or another player or players who is or are already on Club's roster, and for whom Club needs room.

Deciding whether a club's exercise of managerial judgment about a player's relative skill was contaminated by animus against his union activities may pose a severe test for the Labor Board. This problem becomes magnified when union representatives are respected veterans who may have passed their peak performance years but still have relatively large salaries.

SEATTLE SEAHAWKS V. NFLPA & SAM MCCULLUM
292 N.L.R.B. 899 (1989)

[From 1976 through 1981, Sam McCullum was a starting wide receiver for the Seattle Seahawks. In 1981, McCullum was selected by his teammates to be their union player representative. McCullum's prominent role in union activities in the following bargaining year (leading up to the

SEC. C   UNION ACTIVITY AND EMPLOYER RETALIATION

lengthy players' strike during the 1982 season) produced severe tensions with Seahawks' coach Jack Patera. In particular, Patera was upset by McCullum's orchestration of the "solidarity handshake" by his teammates with members of the opposing team at the beginning of their first pre-season game. Nevertheless, McCullum started all of the August 1982 pre-season games for the Seahawks. In a trade made at the end of training camp, however, the Seahawks obtained from the Baltimore Colts another wide receiver, Roger Carr, and McCullum was cut from the team's final roster. An unfair labor practice charge was then filed by McCullum and the NFLPA.

The evidence at trial before an administrative law judge (ALJ) showed that the Seahawks' Director of Football Operations, Mike McCormick, and its General Manager, John Thompson, had been trying for months to trade for Carr on favorable terms. Also, Jerry Rhome, the offensive coordinator, had been closely involved in deciding which of the team's four wide receivers should be let go to make room for Carr. However, the ALJ found that both of these team decisions were influenced by the Seahawks'—and especially Patera's—anti-union sentiments directed at McCullum. In this decision, a divided NLRB grapples with the Seahawks' appeal from the ALJ's ruling.

In *Wright Line*, 251 N.L.R.B. 1083 (1980), *enf'd*, 662 F.2d 899 (1st Cir. 1981), the NLRB clarified its test for determining when an employer has committed an unfair labor practice by firing an employee. Rather than simply determining whether antiunion motivation was a "cause" of the firing, the Board required the NLRB General Counsel to show only that union activities were a "motivating factor" in the employer's decision to terminate, but then allowed the employer to defend by showing that the employee would have been fired even if he had not engaged in union activities. The Supreme Court accepted this process and its ultimate "but for" test in *NLRB v. Transportation Management Corp.*, 462 U.S. 393, 400–03 (1983). The Seahawks first challenged the ALJ's ruling on the ground that it misapplied the *Wright Line* test by finding no more than that McCullum's union activities were "in part" a factor in his release.]

It is incontestable that the judge, notwithstanding his occasional use of the term "in part" to describe the extent of the Respondent's unlawful motivation, found that antiunion considerations were a motivating factor in the decision that produced McCullum's release, and that he fully considered the Respondent's *Wright Line* defense. We therefore find that his analysis fully comports with the *Wright Line* standard.

The Respondent has also excepted to the judge's implicit finding that certain remarks that Sam McCullum made in his role as the team's player representative at a February 19, 1982 press conference and that produced negative reactions from both the team's general manager, John Thompson, and its head coach, Jack Patera, are in fact protected under § 7 of the Act. In particular, the Respondent argues that McCullum's expression of his view that team doctors, whom he saw as identified with management, released injured players for games too soon, when the players were not fully recovered, constituted "disloyal" disparagement of the employer, which, pursuant to the theory of *NLRB v. Electrical Workers Local 1229 IBEW (Jefferson Standard)*, 346 U.S. 464 (1953), is not protected activity under § 7. The Respondent also argues, as to the "solidarity handshake" episode, that any hostility would naturally be against the Union—as the author of this activity throughout the league—rather than against McCullum. We disagree with both contentions.

In *Jefferson Standard*, the Supreme Court held that a union's public attacks on the quality of the employer's product were not protected under § 7 when they had no connection with the employee's working conditions or any current labor controversy. It seems indisputable, however, that the relative haste with which injured players are returned to the football field is a matter that directly affects the players' working conditions. Although McCullum's views may have been exaggerated or not soundly based, that does not withdraw the protection of the Act from them. Indeed, employees and employers frequently differ greatly in their views whether the employees are properly treated.

We do not mean to suggest, of course, that it was unlawful for either Thompson or Patera to take issue with McCullum's statements. The fact remains, however, that McCullum established himself at this press conference as a fairly aggressive union spokesman. McCullum's role as player representative was highlighted again when he and two other players approached Patera in August to apprise him of the players' intention to support the Union's "solidarity handshake" plan by engaging in such a handshake with the opposing team in the upcoming August 13 game with St. Louis. Although it was another player who mentioned the "union solidarity" symbolism of the handshake, it was McCullum who—after Patera had expressed his opposition—said that the players might go ahead and do it anyway. We agree with the judge that Patera's prediction of the subsequent fines ('I'll fine you as much as I can') and the heavy fines that the Respondent sought to impose reveal animus toward union activity for which, at this point, McCullum was the obvious focus on the team.

* * *

Finally, we address two of the Respondent's arguments concerning alleged inconsistencies between the judge's factual findings and the record evidence. . . .

First, the Respondent argues that a finding that it was seeking to obtain Carr in order to rid itself of McCullum is inconsistent with the evidence that the Respondent had declined to accept Baltimore's offer of

Carr in late spring for a first round draft choice, that it had declined another Baltimore offer in August for a "high" draft choice, and that the Respondent had even toughened its position by insisting on September 2 that it would give up only a fourth round draft choice for Carr. We do not see that conduct as inconsistent with the judge's motivation finding for the reasons essentially given by the judge.

An employer may harbor an unlawful intent to rid itself of a troublesome employee but still wish to do so on the most advantageous terms possible. Furthermore, the testimony of the Respondent's own witnesses shows that they reasonably believed that Baltimore wanted to be rid at all costs of the injury-prone Carr.

* * *

It is undeniable that Rhome was responsible for rating the wide receivers throughout training camp and the pre-season games and that Patera would reasonably take seriously his judgment, after the Carr trade, that McCullum should be released rather than Steve Largent, Byron Walker, or Paul Johns. But it is clear from Rhome's testimony that he was not consulted about the desirability of having Carr, as opposed to McCullum, at the point in the season that Carr was finally acquired. Thus, Rhome testified that he could not rate Carr because he had not seen him play very recently. Rhome obviously approached the evaluation process with the realization that Carr was not for cutting. As he testified, "You can't just eliminate Roger Carr because you just got through trading for him." Hence, having Carr as one of the wide receivers going into the new season was essentially imposed on Rhome by the trade. He made no considered judgment that an injury-prone player who had not participated in any training camp that summer and did not know Seattle's system of offensive plays would be more valuable than McCullum.

Although Carr's name was first mentioned by McCormick when he joined the Respondent's organization in March and the initial decision to make inquiries about Carr occurred after a conversation among McCormick, Patera, and Thompson about the matter, Patera made the initial call, while subsequent negotiations with Baltimore were carried out first by McCormick and later by Thompson. But Patera's role was crucial. As Thompson testified, Patera was the one to decide who would make the team. Given the time at which Carr was finally acquired—just before the opening of the season—it was clear that, as Rhome recognized, acquiring him meant bringing him onto the team. Nothing in the record suggests that efforts to acquire players would have been made without continuing consultation with the head coach. Thus, it had to be up to Patera whether negotiations to acquire Carr would continue just before the start of the season, when cuts were to be made. . . .

Given the reports that Rhome says he made to Patera about the progress of players Walker and Johns in the training camp and pre-season games, the continued pursuit of Carr is suspect. McCullum was rated a very good wide receiver in many respects—allegedly all except for the ability to go deep and catch "the bomb." But this was an area in which Johns and Walker were now rated highly, so the need to obtain Carr for that particular skill was diminishing rapidly according to the Respondent's own witnesses.

The Respondent simply has not shown that the acquisition of Roger Carr on September 3 would have occurred even in the absence of the animus of the Respondent's management—more notably, but not solely, the animus of Patera—against McCullum as an outspoken representative of union sentiment on the team. The animus against the Union's solidarity had been powerfully expressed, but thwarted in August, when the Respondent imposed fines for the 'solidarity handshake' that greatly exceeded those imposed by any other NFL team and then was forced to rescind the fines. The opportunity for the Respondent to rid itself of the most visible team symbol of that solidarity was finally seized upon in September through the acquisition of Carr.

Charges upheld.

NOTES AND QUESTIONS

1. *Seahawks' Motivation?* Why do you think the Seahawks released Sam McCullum? After his release, McCullum played for the Minnesota Vikings for two seasons after which he retired from professional football, but continued to stay active in the NFL Players Association.

2. *Difficulty of Proving Discriminatory Motive.* Could the Seahawks have avoided easily the NLRB's finding of anti-union discrimination against McCullum by a more careful sequencing of their decisionmaking? How hard do you think it is generally for the NLRB's General Counsel to prove that personnel decisions have an anti-union motivation? Is it likely to be harder or easier for professional athletes? Does this depend somewhat on whether the player is a star or rather a marginal performer? On whether the athlete's contract is guaranteed and whether the club is operating under a salary cap?

3. *Best Union Representatives?* Does this case have implications for an average player deciding on whom to elect as his club's union representative? Should he vote for a younger star player who is unlikely to be released but also less likely to be sympathetic to the union's goals on behalf of journeymen players, or for an older journeymen player who is more susceptible to being cut by the team but more committed to union activities? Consider also which type of player is more likely to be critical to the success of any union organized work stoppage.

4. *Adequate Remedies?* The remedies available under the NLRA are only equitable; they do not include legal damages. Is the prospect of being ordered to provide reinstatement and back pay to discharged union activists likely to deter the normal employer who fears the impact of unionization on its labor costs? Is it more likely to deter owners of professional sports teams who have similar concerns? What if reinstatement would result in a club violating a league salary cap? Is reinstatement in any event an adequate remedy without an immediate preliminary injunction? (The Board has the discretion, but not the resources or the political will, to seek injunctions in the usual discriminatory discharge case).

5. *Effect of Delay?* Consider also the not atypical delay in securing a final remedy in the *McCullum* case. The NLRB rendered its decision in 1989, and the D.C. Circuit eventually upheld the Board's unfair labor practice finding and $250,000 back pay award in *Nordstrom v. NLRB*, 984 F.2d 479 (D.C. Cir. 1993). That final legal ruling in this case took place *eleven years* after the Seahawks released McCullum for the reasons detailed above. What is the likely effect of such administrative-judicial delay on the protection of worker rights of self-organization against employer retaliation? Is delay more or less significant in securing the policies of the Labor Act in the sports context?

6. *Alternative Remedy Through Arbitration. McCullum* does not reflect the typical manner by which athletes represented by sports unions challenge allegedly unfair personnel decisions. As explained in the next chapter, arbitration systems framed in collective bargaining agreements generally can offer a better form of protection than that provided by the regulatory processes of the NLRB.

D. APPROPRIATE BARGAINING UNIT IN SPORTS LEAGUES

The various major professional sports leagues in the late 1960s voluntarily recognized their comparatively weak players associations on the basis of the associations' demonstration of majority support. Absent an employer's voluntary recognition, a union may petition the NLRB to conduct a secret ballot election if it can demonstrate substantial allegiance (a 30-percent "showing of interest") among the employees "in a unit appropriate" for collective bargaining. If the union receives a majority of the votes cast, the Board then certifies the union as the exclusive bargaining agent for all the employees in the unit (§ 9(c)(1)). But before any such election can be conducted, the Board must define the scope of the relevant employee constituency—that is, whether the union seeks to represent a "unit appropriate for the purposes of collective bargaining" under § 9(b) of the Labor Act.

The NLRB and the courts have developed an elaborate jurisprudence for determining whether the employees within a proposed grouping share a sufficient "community of interest" to become a recognized "bargaining unit." The Labor Board determines whether a unit proposed by a union is <u>an</u> appropriate bargaining unit, not whether it is the best unit or the only appropriate unit. Unions sculpt units based on whether they believe they can prevail in an election. In some instances, for example, a union may petition for a representation election in a single plant where it has support among the employees and not in all the company's plants at one time. As long as the single plant unit is an appropriate grouping of employees, the Labor Board will proceed to conduct the election.

Section 9(b) of the Labor Act authorizes the Board to choose an "employer unit, craft unit, plant unit, or subdivision thereof." It does not authorize multiemployer units. Thus, labor law has permitted bargaining in multiemployer units only where each employer and the union all consent. Nonetheless, multiemployer bargaining became and remains a common feature of the industrial relations landscape, particularly in industries, such as trucking or construction, in which there are hosts of small firms dealing with a few large unions, such as the Teamsters or the Carpenters. Both employers and unions in these industries found they have a complementary long-term interest in bargaining that avoids labor cost competition between employers. Both the Board and the Supreme Court have fashioned doctrine to support consensual multiemployer bargaining by prohibiting any party from unilaterally withdrawing from a multiemployer unit during a particular round of bargaining just because negotiations have not gone as that party hoped. Thus, in *Charles D. Bonanno Linen Service v. NLRB*, 454 U.S. 404 (1982), the Supreme Court held that even a negotiating impasse did not warrant an employer leaving the larger multiemployer unit.

The Board, with approval from the Supreme Court, also has determined that some employees are jointly employed by more than one employer where the employees' working conditions and benefits are controlled in part by both. The Board designates some joint employer units as appropriate even without the consent of the employers. *See, e.g., Boire v. Greyhound Corp.*, 376 U.S. 473 (1964).

When a sports league recognizes a sports union as the representative of the players employed by all clubs in a single bargaining unit, it accordingly accepts a combination of multiemployer and joint employer bargaining. It should not be difficult to understand why the leagues and unions have preferred league-wide rather than individual-club bargaining. Consider, for instance, the many sports labor issues that need to be resolved consistently for all clubs in a league. But what if a league for some reason does not consent to this multiemployer, joint employer bargaining framework? Can this framework be required by the Board? Consider the following case.

North American Soccer League v. NLRB
613 F.2d 1379 (5th Cir. 1980)

RONEY, CIRCUIT JUDGE.

[In 1977, the National Football League Players Association (NFLPA) financed and staffed a new North American Soccer League Players Association (NASLPA), which then organized players from the 19 NASL clubs (two of which were Canadian teams) and petitioned the NLRB for certification of a single, league-wide bargaining unit. The division of authority between soccer clubs and their league (under its commissioner) was essentially the same as in other team sports. In the case of player relations, individual teams selected, compensated, traded, and released their players. However, league rules regarding rookie drafts, waivers, free agency, and the like governed such individual team player dealings, and all players were required to sign a standard NASL contract that accepted the ultimate disciplinary authority of the commissioner.

Given these facts, the Labor Board accepted the position of the Player Association that a single league-wide unit was an (though not the only) appropriate bargaining unit in an employment relationship in which the League and individual clubs were "joint employers" of the players, because both exercised a significant degree of control over their respective personnel policies. The Board majority decided, though, not to exercise jurisdiction over the two Canadian owned and based clubs, the Toronto Metros and the Vancouver Whitecaps, notwithstanding the dissent's observation that these two teams played nearly half their games in the United States and shared in both gate receipts and television revenues from this country. The League and its member clubs appealed the Board's certification of a single unit encompassing all of the players on American teams.]

* * *

Joint Employers.

Whether there is a joint employer relationship is "essentially a factual issue," and the Board's finding must be affirmed if supported by substantial evidence on the record as a whole.

The existence of a joint employer relationship depends on the control which one employer exercises, or potentially exercises, over the labor relations policy of the other. In this case, the record supports the Board's finding that the League exercises a significant degree of control over essential aspects of the clubs' labor relations, including but not limited to the selection, retention, and termination of the players, the terms of individual player contracts, dispute resolution and player discipline. Furthermore, each club granted the NASL authority over not only its own labor relations but also, on its behalf, authority over the labor relations of the other member clubs. The evidence is set forth in detail in the Board's decision and need be only briefly recounted here.

The League's purpose is to promote the game of soccer through its supervision of competition among member clubs. Club activities are governed by the League constitution, and the regulations promulgated thereunder by a majority vote of the clubs. The commissioner, selected and compensated by the clubs, is the League's chief executive officer. A board of directors composed of one representative of each club assists him in managing the League.

The League's control over the clubs' labor relations begins with restrictions on the means by which players are acquired. An annual college draft is conducted by the commissioner pursuant to the regulations, and each club obtains exclusive negotiating rights to the players it selects. On the other hand, as the Board recognized, the League exercises less control over the acquisition of "free agent" players and players "on loan" from soccer clubs abroad.

The regulations govern interclub player trades and empower the commissioner to void trades not deemed to be in the best interest of the League. Termination of player contracts is conducted through a waiver system in accordance with procedures specified in the regulations.

The League also exercises considerable control over the contractual relationships between the clubs and their players. Before being permitted to participate in a North American Soccer League game, each player must sign a standard player contract adopted by the League. The contract governs the player's relationship with his club, requiring his compliance with club rules and the League constitution and regulations. Compensation is negotiated between the player and his club, and special provisions may be added to the contract. Significantly, however, the club must seek the permission of the commissioner before signing a contract which alters any terms of the standard contract.

Every player contract must be submitted to the commissioner, who is empowered to disapprove a contract deemed not in the best interest of the League. The commissioner's disapproval invalidates the contract. Disputes between a club and a player must be submitted to the commissioner for final and binding arbitration.

Control over player discipline is divided between the League and the clubs. The clubs enforce compliance with club rules relating to practices and also determine when a player will participate in a game. The League, through the commissioner, has broad power to discipline players for misconduct either on or off the playing field. Sanctions range from fines to suspension to termination of the player's contract.

SEC. D APPROPRIATE BARGAINING UNIT IN SPORTS LEAGUES

Although we recognize that minor differences in the underlying facts might justify different findings on the joint employer issue, the record in this case supports the Board's factual finding of a joint employer relationship among the League and its constituent clubs.

Having argued against inclusion of the Canadian clubs in the NLRB proceeding, petitioners contend on appeal that their exclusion renders the Board's joint employer finding, encompassing 21 clubs, inconsistent with the existence of a 24-club League. The jurisdictional determination is not before us on appeal, however, and the Board's decision not to exercise jurisdiction over the Canadian clubs does not undermine the evidentiary base of its joint employer finding.

Even assuming the League and the clubs are joint employers, they contend that *Greenhoot, Inc.*, 205 N.L.R.B. 250 (1973), requires a finding of a separate joint employer relationship between the League and each of its clubs, and does not permit all the clubs to be lumped together with the League as joint employers. In *Greenhoot*, a building management company was found to be a joint employer separately with each building owner as to maintenance employees in the buildings covered by its contracts. The present case is clearly distinguishable, because here each soccer club exercises through its proportionate role in League management some control over the labor relations of other clubs. In *Greenhoot*, building owners did not exercise any control through the management company over the activities of other owners.

Appropriate Unit.

The joint employer relationship among the League and its member clubs having been established, the next issue is whether the leaguewide unit of players designated by the Board is appropriate. Here the Board's responsibility and the standard of review in this Court are important.

The Board is not required to choose the most appropriate bargaining unit, only to select a unit appropriate under the circumstances. The determination will not be set aside "unless the Board's discretion has been exercised 'in an arbitrary or capricious manner.'"

Notwithstanding the substantial financial autonomy of the clubs, the Board found they form, through the League, an integrated group with common labor problems and a high degree of centralized control over labor relations. In these circumstances the Board's designation of a leaguewide bargaining unit as appropriate is reasonable, not arbitrary or capricious.

In making its decision, the Board expressly incorporated the reasons underlying its finding of a joint employer relationship. The Board emphasized in particular both the individual clubs' decision to form a League for the purpose of jointly controlling many of their activities, and the commissioner's power to disapprove contracts and exercise control over disciplinary matters. Under our "exceedingly narrow" standard of review, no arguments presented by petitioners require denial of enforcement of the bargaining order.

Thus the facts successfully refute any notion that because the teams compete on the field and in hiring, only team units are appropriate for collective bargaining purposes. Once a player is hired, his working conditions are significantly controlled by the League. Collective bargaining at that source of control would be the only way to effectively change by agreement many critical conditions of employment.

Order enforced.

NOTES AND QUESTIONS

1. *Why Not Require Clubs' Consent?* Note the *NASL* court's discussion of the Board's *Greenhoot* decision. The holding of this case, that competitive joint employers cannot be placed in the same multiemployer bargaining unit without each employer's consent, remains good law. Did the *NASL* court convincingly distinguish *Greenhoot*?

2. *Only Appropriate Unit?* Is a league-wide unit not only *an* appropriate unit for a professional sports league; is it also the *only* appropriate unit? Could the Board accept the request of a sports union for a single club and league, joint employer unit? Could it accept a request for a single club, single employer unit? Would a sports union have any reason for requesting less than a league-wide bargaining unit?

In seeking to end the 2012 NHL lockout, the players sought to invoke the jurisdiction of Canadian regulators over individual hockey teams. One effort was rejected when the Alberta Board exercised its discretion to decline to intervene because it found jurisdictional questions to be "ambiguous." Prominent labor expert Professor William Gould opined in similar proceedings in Quebec (unresolved due to the dispute's settlement) that collective bargaining has to be conducted on a league-wide basis to meet the interests of the parties, as well as of the public. Do you agree? Just as the United Steelworks are free to choose whether to engage in multi-employer bargaining with steel companies or to bargain individually, should the MLBPA be able to announce that the next round of bargaining will only be with individual clubs? Reconsider this question after studying the labor exemption to antitrust regulation treated in Chapter 6 below.

3. *College Athlete Bargaining Units?* The Board has not treated as employees subject to its jurisdiction college athletes, even in revenue producing sports. Assume, however, that labor law did treat these athletes as employees with the right to form unions and to bargain collectively. Would a single university unit be appropriate, notwithstanding significant regulation of collegiate athletics by the National Collegiate Athletics Association (NCAA)

and various athletic conferences? Is it relevant that most universities with revenue producing sports programs, at least in football, are public universities beyond the Board's jurisdiction? *See Northwestern University,* 362 N.L.R.B. No. 167 (2015) (without deciding question of employee status, unanimous, full-Board opinion declines to assert jurisdiction over Northwestern football players seeking a unit for a single team that is regulated by NCAA and by a Big Ten conference otherwise consisting of public universities.) For further discussion, see Chapter 11 below.

E. UNION'S EXCLUSIVE BARGAINING AUTHORITY

If a majority of the employees choose to be represented for purposes of collective bargaining by a union, the union becomes the "exclusive representative of all the employees in the unit for purposes of collective bargaining" (§ 9(a) of the Labor Act). The Supreme Court, in its crucial decision in *J.I. Case Co. v. NLRB,* 321 U.S. 332 (1944), found a congressional intent underlying this provision to make the collective agreement prevail over any individually negotiated employment conditions:

> It is equally clear since the collective trade agreement is to serve the purpose contemplated by the Act, the individual contract cannot be effective as a waiver of any benefit to which the employee otherwise would be entitled under the trade agreement. The very purpose of providing by statute for the collective agreement is to supersede the terms of separate agreements of employees with terms which reflect the strength and bargaining power and serve the welfare of the group. Its benefits and advantages are open to every employee of the represented unit, whatever the type or terms of his pre-existing contract of employment.

321 U.S. at 338.

MORIO V. NORTH AMERICAN SOCCER LEAGUE
501 F. Supp. 633 (S.D.N.Y. 1980)

MOTLEY, DISTRICT JUDGE.

[Following the NLRB's certification of the NASL Players Association as bargaining agent for NASL soccer players, the League sought (unsuccessfully) to challenge the Board's league-wide unit determination in court. While its appeal was pending, the League refused to bargain collectively with the union, and its clubs continued to negotiate new contracts with individual players. League authorities unilaterally instituted a number of changes in the general working conditions that were embodied in these contracts: the summer season was extended by two weeks; a new winter season was created; roster sizes were reduced from 30 to 26 players; and players were required to use the footwear selected by their club (absent consent by the latter). The Players Association filed unfair labor practice charges with the NLRB, alleging that this NASL conduct violated the union's exclusive bargaining authority under the NLRA; the Labor Board issued a complaint against the League and the Labor Board's General Counsel went to federal district court to secure a § 10(j) interim injunction against such negotiation of new individual contracts (by then covering 97% of league players).]

* * *

The unilateral changes which Respondents [the League and its clubs] admit have occurred since September 1, 1978, in the terms and conditions of employment, may violate the employer's obligations to bargain with the exclusive bargaining representative of the players. The duty to bargain carries with it the obligation on the part of the employer not to undercut the Union by entering into individual contracts with the employees. In *NLRB v. Katz*, 369 U.S. 736 (1962), the Supreme Court noted: "A refusal to negotiate in fact as to any subject which is within § 8(d) and about which the Union seeks to negotiate violates § 8(a)(5)."

[The judge first rejected the NASL owners' claim that they could legally refuse to negotiate at all with the players' union for the three years they had spent challenging its certification election. She then turned to the] Respondents' most vigorous opposition, [which] comes in response to Petitioner's application for an order requiring Respondents to render voidable, at the option of the Union, all individual player contracts, whether entered into before or after the Union's certification on September 1, 1978. Respondents' claim that such power in the hands of the Union, a non-party to this action, would result in chaos in the industry and subject Respondents to severe economic loss and hardship since these individual contracts are the only real property of Respondents.

It should be noted, at the outset, that the relief requested by Petitioner is not a request to have all individual contracts declared null and void. It should be emphasized that Petitioner is not requesting that the "exclusive rights" provision of the individual contracts, which bind the players to their respective teams for a certain time, be rendered voidable. Moreover, the Board seeks an order requiring Respondents to maintain the present terms and conditions in effect until Respondents negotiate with the Union—except, of course, for the unilateral changes—unless and until an agreement or a good faith impasse is reached through bargaining with the Union. Petitioner does not, however, seek to rescind that unilateral provision which provided for the present summer schedule. The Board has consciously limited its request for relief to prevent any unnecessary disruption of Respondents' business. The Board is seeking to render voidable only those unilateral acts taken by the Respondents, enumerated above, which Respondents admit have in fact occurred.

These unilateral changes appear to modify all existing individual contracts entered into before September 1, 1978, in derogation of the Union's right to act as the exclusive bargaining agent of all employees in the unit.

The court finds that Petitioner is entitled to the temporary injunctive relief which it seeks with respect to all of the individual contracts. The individual contracts entered into since September 1, 1978, are apparently in violation of the duty of the Respondents to bargain with the exclusive bargaining representative of the players. The Act requires Respondents to bargain collectively with the Union. The obligation is exclusive. This duty to bargain with the exclusive representative carries with it the negative duty not to bargain with individual employees. *Medo Photo Supply Corp. v. NLRB,* 321 U.S. 678 (1944).

* * *

In *National Licorice Co. v. NLRB,* 309 U.S. 350 (1940), the Supreme Court held that the Board has the authority, even in the absence of the employees as parties to the proceeding, to order an employer not to enforce individual contracts with its employees which were found to have been in violation of the NLRA. Petitioner is seeking temporary relief to this effect as to those individual contracts entered into before September 1, 1978, as well as relief with respect to those contracts entered into prior to September 1, 1978. The evidence discloses that Petitioner has reasonable cause to believe that Respondents have used, and will continue to use, the individual contracts entered into prior to September 1, 1978, to forestall collective bargaining.

[The court concluded that the Labor Board and the NASL Players Association were entitled to require NASL to "render voidable" the particular contract provisions that the union objected to—relief that "has been carefully tailored to avoid chaos in (the League's) industry and to avoid any economic hardship to (League members)."]

Injunction granted.

A union vested with exclusive bargaining authority under § 9(a) is entitled to eliminate all individual bargaining, even bargaining to secure better terms than the collectively negotiated minimum. Indeed, individual bargaining is unthinkable in most unionized industries. But collective bargaining in sports, as in the entertainment industry generally, has followed a different path, under which the labor agreement sets out guaranteed benefits and a minimum salary scale and then usually permits each player (or each movie star) to negotiate whatever extra remuneration the market will bear. Such individual freedom of contract operates at the sufferance of, and within parameters set by, the collective bargaining agreement—with the performer's agent serving, in a sense, as delegate for the union. Why do sports unions handle salary negotiations this way? How might this feature affect the solidarity of the union members during collective bargaining negotiations or a work stoppage? How might it affect the political dynamics within the union and its leadership?

This free-market orientation first became pronounced in baseball after the free agency system was established in 1976. Not only were baseball salaries dramatically higher by the 2010s than they were four decades earlier, but also the salary range was much wider; for example, in 2018 salaries ranged from the minimum set forth in the parties' Basic Agreement, $545,000, to Mike Trout's $34,083,333 salary. Nor are these figures just isolated extremes. In 1967, when Marvin Miller was appointed Executive Director of the MLBPA and set out to turn the organization into a true union, the average baseball salary was $19,000 a year and the median salary was $17,000; in 1976, just before free agency became operative, the average salary was $52,000, the median $40,000; but by the opening of the 2018 season, the median salary was only about a third of the average salary. Thus, the outcome of sports collective bargaining is sharply different from what one finds in most unionized sectors, where the salary scale tends to tilt towards the average career veteran rather than the exceptional star.

On one occasion, a sports union sought to act like a mainstream labor union. During the 1982 negotiations in football, the NFL Players Association (NFLPA) under Ed Garvey unsuccessfully tried to establish a fixed-salary scale weighted toward seniority and specific accomplishments. Garvey would have restructured the existing salary pattern that turns more on playing position (for example, quarterback as opposed to offensive lineman) or original draft position (for example, early in the first round rather than in a later round). Though unsuccessful, the NFLPA certainly had the legal authority to negotiate such constraints on individual salary negotiations, as the Supreme Court explained in *J.I. Case*, supra:

> But it is urged that some employees may lose by the collective agreement, that an individual workman may sometimes have, or be capable of getting, better terms than those obtainable by the group and that his freedom of contract must be respected on that account. We are not called upon to say that under no circumstances can an individual enforce an agreement more advantageous than a collective agreement, but we find the mere possibility that such agreements might be made no ground for holding generally that individual contracts may survive or

surmount collective ones. The practice and philosophy of collective bargaining looks with suspicion on such individual advantages. Of course, where there is great variation in circumstances of employment or capacity of employees, it is possible for the collective bargain to prescribe only minimum rates or maximum hours or expressly to leave certain areas open to individual bargaining. But except as so provided, advantages to individuals may prove as disruptive of industrial peace as disadvantages. They are a fruitful way of interfering with organization and choice of representatives; increased compensation, if individually deserved, is often earned at the cost of breaking down some other standard thought to be for the welfare of the group, and always creates the suspicion of being paid at the long range expense of the group as a whole. Such discriminations not infrequently amount to unfair labor practices. The workman is free, if he values his own bargaining position more than that of the group, to vote against representation; but the majority rules, and if it collectivizes the employment bargain, individual advantages or favors will generally in practice go in as a contribution to the collective result. We cannot except individual contracts generally from the operation of collective ones because some may be more individually advantageous.

321 U.S. at 338–39.

After rejecting the effort of the NFLPA to institute a salary scale in the 1982 negotiations, the NFL five years later proposed a salary scale of its own, this time targeting rookies. The NFLPA (in return for somewhat relaxed veteran free agency) ultimately agreed to establish a separate salary pool for each team's annual crop of rookies. Each team was to divide up this amount in individual negotiations with its various draft picks. In 1995, though, the sports unions in both hockey and basketball used their exclusive bargaining authority rights to define a specific salary range that would be permitted for each pick in each round of the draft. Then, in 1998, the National Basketball Players Association (NBPA) became the first major sports union to agree to a cap, not just a floor, on individual player salaries—one that immediately limited such hoop greats as Tim Duncan and Kobe Bryant to $9 million in the year when they became free agents, rather than the $21 million a year deal that their counterpart Kevin Garnett had secured by signing his free agency contract just before the prior CBA had expired. Why might the NBPA have agreed to such a cap?

On one occasion, a sports union exercised its exclusive representative status to prevent a player from giving up any of his contract salary. In 2003, the Texas Rangers and Boston Red Sox negotiated a deal to trade Alex Rodriguez for Manny Ramirez. In order to limit its exposure under MLB's payroll tax, the Red Sox insisted that Rodriguez reduce his salary by a total of $29 million over the remaining seven years of his contract. Rodriguez (and his agent, Scott Boras) agreed. Undoubtedly, Rodriguez also felt that he could more than make up that reduction in salary by the increased value of his endorsement rights playing in Boston for a pennant contender.

The MLBPA, however, rejected the new player contract. Its contention was that the collective bargaining agreement did not permit individual players and clubs to agree to salary reductions; rather, it barred any salary reduction in a guaranteed contract unless the union was satisfied that the terms "actually or potentially provide additional benefits to the player." The MLBPA officials said they would let Rodriguez take a total seven year pay cut of $12 million (rather than the proposed $29 million) if the team would add to his contract a provision that allowed him to use the Red Sox name and logo in selling his personal publicity rights. While the team owners were fully prepared to agree to that latter term, they would not accept the additional $17 million financial cost (and potential salary tax). MLB Commissioner Bud Selig ultimately rejected the contract to avoid a union grievance and a subsequent arbitration. Did the MLBPA best represent its membership by not allowing Alex Rodriguez to accept a reduction in his salary in order to facilitate his trade from the Rangers to the Red Sox? Suppose that rather than this Rodriguez-Red Sox deal, another player who had been paid $1.5 million annually under a multi-year contract largely to sit on his team's bench, told the union that he wanted to be traded to another lower-paying team where he could be the starting shortstop if he would agree to reduce his salary to $1.2 million a year? What should the MLBPA do, if anything?

F. DUTY TO BARGAIN IN GOOD FAITH

The Board's certification or an employer's recognition of a union as an exclusive bargaining agent imposes duties on both the employer and the union to bargain "collectively" with each other. Section 8(d) of the NLRA defines that obligation as follows:

> [T]o bargain collectively is . . . to meet at reasonable times and confer in good faith with respect to wages, hours, and other terms of employment, . . . but such obligation does not compel either party to agree to a proposal or require the making of a concession.

The principal focus of this duty is procedural, rather than substantive. As long as a party does not engage in *surface* bargaining, that is, go through the motions with no real intent to try to arrive at a settlement, the party is perfectly free to engage in *hard* bargaining and to not make concessions from its negotiating position. The statutory policy of free collective bargaining presumes that the ultimate way to break a deadlock at the bargaining table is through the economic pressure of a strike or a lockout or perhaps mere insistence, not through unfair labor practices or a petition of some sort in which one party tries to persuade the Labor Board that its position is more reasonable than the other side's. As the Supreme Court observed in *NLRB v. Insurance Agents' Int'l Union*, 361 U.S. 477 (1960):

> It must be realized that collective bargaining under a system where the Government does not attempt to control the results of negotiations, cannot be equated with an academic collective search for truth—or even with what might be thought to be the ideal of one. The parties . . . still proceed from contrary and to an extent antagonistic viewpoints and concepts of self-interest. The system has not reached the ideal of the philosophic notion that perfect understanding among people would lead to perfect agreement among them on values. The presence of economic weapons in reserve, and their actual exercise on occasion by the parties, is part and parcel of the system that the Wagner and Taft-Hartley Acts have recognized.

361 U.S. at 488–89. There is no better illustration of the Court's appraisal of collective bargaining than the sports world's experience with bargaining over free agency and salary caps during the last forty years.

While the law has adopted a hands-off attitude about the *content* of the collective bargain, it has been more interventionist in prescribing standards of *behavior* in the bargaining process. Perhaps the two most important doctrines are (i) an obligation of the employer (and, on occasion, the union) to supply all relevant information that is "needed by the bargaining representative for the proper performance of its duties," *see NLRB v. Acme Industrial Co.*, 385 U.S. 432, 435–36 (1967), and (ii) the obligation to refrain from unilateral changes in employment conditions, whether to the employees' benefit or detriment, at least until "impasse" has been reached in bargaining, *see NLRB v. Katz*, 369 U.S. 736, 743, 745 (1962). The assumption of the Supreme Court is that "freezing the status quo ante after a collective agreement has expired promotes industrial peace by fostering a noncoercive atmosphere that is conducive to serious negotiations on a new contract." *See Laborers Health & Welfare Trust v. Advanced Lightweight Concrete Co.*, 484 U.S. 539, 544 n. 6 (1988). Both doctrines require determining whether the issue in dispute falls within the phrase "terms and conditions of employment" under § 8(d); if the issue does not concern a term or condition, there is no obligation to provide information or to refrain from unilateral action.

The Board and the courts for several decades thus have made difficult substantive judgments about the meaning of the "terms and conditions" phrase, what is defined as the scope of "mandatory" bargaining. The important Supreme Court decision in *First National Maintenance Corp. v. NLRB*, 452 U.S. 666, 673 (1981), held that key management decisions "about the scope and direction of the enterprise," such as closings of facilities, are not mandatory subjects of bargaining, regardless of their direct impact on employee lives. The Court majority echoed the sentiment in Justice Stewart's concurring opinion in *Fibreboard Paper Products v. NLRB*, 379 U.S. 203, 223, 226 (1964), that § 8(d) does not detract from the prerogative of private business management under "the traditional principles of free enterprise" to make decisions that "lie at the core of entrepreneurial control." On the other hand, management's prerogative not to bargain about its entrepreneurial *decision*, for example, to close down a facility, does not relieve the employer of its duty to bargain with the union about the *effects* of that action on its employees. *See generally* Michael C. Harper, *Leveling the Road from* Borg-Warner *to First National Maintenance: the Scope of Mandatory Bargaining*, 68 Va. L. Rev. 1447 (1982).

Bargaining about topics that are not *mandatory* is not *illegal*. Indeed, purely voluntary negotiation about *permissive* topics takes place regularly in different bargaining relationships, and each party can induce bargaining on a permissive topic by being more or less reasonable on a mandatory topic. But the line drawn between mandatory and permissive subjects is significant not only because the employer has no duty to discuss the latter topics (nor to supply information and to remain inactive about them), but also because the union is not entitled to insist—in particular, to the point of a strike—on bargaining about them. *See NLRB v. Wooster Division of Borg-Warner Corp.*, 356 U.S. 342 (1958).

Consider whether the following range of sports issues should be judged to be mandatory subjects for bargaining by owners with players.

(i) Enlarging the regular schedule or playoffs, adopting interleague or international play, or realigning teams among the leagues and their divisions.

(ii) Adding in the NL, or eliminating in the AL, the designated hitter in baseball.

(iii) Instituting (or eliminating) overtime to break ties in hockey or football.

(iv) Deciding to install artificial turf in football or baseball parks.

(v) Using instant replay (here, consider whether mandatory bargaining required with either the players or the umpires association).

(vi) Imposing time limits between pitches or between innings.

(vii) Setting new rules regarding hand checking by defensive players in basketball.

(viii) Altering the league's no gambling policies.

(ix) Requiring players to stand at attention before fans during the playing of the national anthem.

(x) Shifting some of a team's home games to a new location (*e.g.*, the Tampa Bar Rays playing several "home" games in Puerto Rico), as compared to full relocation of the team, or expansion into new cities or countries.

(xi) Eliminating one or more teams in a league.

(xii) Appointing or discharging the commissioner.

The distinction between mandatory and permissive subjects proved determinative in the litigation that brought an end to the 1994–95 baseball strike. As noted above, the Labor Act requires management, even after the expiration of the collective bargaining agreement, to maintain the status quo on mandatory topics of bargaining until negotiations reach a genuine impasse. At that point management can implement the final offer it made to the union. On the other hand, if a bargaining topic is deemed a permissive subject of bargaining, management can unilaterally institute a change without violating the statute, and upon the expiration of the collective bargaining agreement, without violating the collective agreement.

In the early 1990s, baseball owners seemingly decided to reassert greater control over player salaries by enfeebling the MLBPA sufficiently to allow management to eliminate free agency and salary arbitration and install the kind of salary cap that was imposed by the other professional sports leagues. At this time, for purposes of determining salaries under the existing collective bargaining agreement, baseball players not under contract fell into three basic categories. Those in their first three seasons were limited to offers from their own team with a floor set by the CBA's guaranteed minimum amount; those players with three to six years of Major League service could have a neutral arbitrator assess and choose between their final salary proposal and the team's proposal; those with six or more years of Major League service were entitled to free agency bidding by any major league team.

The owners' first step toward overturning this system was to ensure that the commissioner would not attempt to intervene in collective bargaining as a neutral mediator. (Previously, commissioners had invoked their "best interest of baseball" powers to override owner tactics and preclude lockouts.) The owners fired Commissioner Fay Vincent and installed one of their number, Alan "Bud" Selig, the owner of the Milwaukee Brewers, as the acting commissioner. The owners then orchestrated a plan to negotiate with the MLBPA to the point of "impasse" when they would unilaterally install their new labor relations system and return the game to management predominance. In response to management's proposed changes, the MLBPA called a strike in August 1994, but management would not budge from its plan and Selig cancelled the World Series.

An essential part of the owners' plan was to hire "replacement" players who would maintain baseball until the union buckled. They contacted minor leaguers and recently retired players in preparation for spring training the following March. In mid-December 1994, the MLBPA made a new proposal to impose a significant "tax" on owners based on their total team salaries. The tax would deter (although not prohibit) individual clubs from spending freely on free agents because of the increased price of doing so.

This proposal did not satisfy the owners—it was not part of their strategy—and they declared that an "impasse" had been reached in bargaining. Baseball management then implemented its prior position on a salary cap and restricted free agency. The MLBPA responded by filing an unfair labor practice charge with the Labor Board claiming bad faith bargaining because of the unilateral change in terms and conditions of employment in the absence of a genuine impasse. Management restored the previous status quo after the Labor Board General Counsel made a tentative decision that the owners had violated the Labor Act and that a formal complaint should be issued. The General Counsel then held the Board's unfair labor practice proceedings in abeyance.

Just three days later, though, the owners informed the MLBPA that there would be no more negotiations between individual teams and players for new contracts. Instead, all player contracts for the upcoming season would have to be worked out between the owners' Player Relations Committee (PRC) and the MLBPA. In those negotiations, salary arbitration would not be available to any player, and the prior contractual ban against concerted action by owners or players would be revoked. The Association immediately filed new unfair labor practice charges against these three owner moves. President Clinton called both sides to the White House in an unsuccessful effort to secure a settlement.

In mid-March 1995, while the teams were conducting spring training with replacement squads (without a single crossover from major league strike rosters), the General Counsel of the NLRB issued a formal complaint against the owners' latest unilateral actions. The Labor Board voted 3–2 to authorize the General Counsel to seek a preliminary injunction in district court barring the owners' action. The owners did not try to defend this unilateral action on the basis that an impasse had been reached on these matters. Instead, the PRC's claim was that their three unilateral changes involved *permissive*, not *mandatory*, topics and thus their changes were not constrained by the duty to bargain in good faith. Following is the opinion by future Supreme Court Justice, and avid baseball fan, Sonia Sotomayor, hearing her first labor case on the federal district court.

SILVERMAN V. MAJOR LEAGUE BASEBALL PLAYER RELATIONS COMMITTEE
880 F. Supp. 246 (S.D.N.Y. 1995)

SOTOMAYOR, DISTRICT JUDGE.

* * *

Collective bargaining in the context of professional sports presents issues different from most other contexts. On the one hand, the talent of an individual athlete can provide him with extraordinary bargaining power, but on the other hand, a player may sell his talent only to a circumscribed group of owners, who have something akin to monopoly power in the sport at issue. These circumstances in professional sports have given rise to the development of the reserve/free agency system, which, perhaps not surprisingly, is quite different from other models of collective bargaining in less specialized and unique industries.

To look for guidance, then, in deciding whether the Board had reasonable cause for making its determination that the provisions changed by the Owners were mandatory, I find most helpful precedent that involves professional sports. *Accord, Wood v. Nat'l Basketball Ass'n*, 809 F.2d 954, 961 (2d Cir. 1987) (collective bargaining between athletes and their leagues "raises numerous problems with little or no precedent in standard industrial relations"). And in the sports context, courts have overwhelmingly held that the constituent parts of reserve/free agency systems are mandatory, not permissive, subjects of bargaining.

For example, this Circuit held in *Wood* that the agreement between professional basketball players and team owners "is a unique bundle of compromises," and matters such as salary caps, minimum individual salaries, fringe benefits, minimum aggregate team salaries, guaranteed revenue-sharing, and first refusal provisions are all mandatory subjects of bargaining, as "each of them is intimately related to 'wages, hours, and other terms and conditions of employment.'" *Id.* at 961–62. Likewise, in *Mackey v. Nat'l Football League*, 543 F.2d 606, 615 (8th Cir. 1976), cert. dismissed, 434 U.S. 801 (1977), the Eighth Circuit held that the Rozelle Rule, even though it does not on its face deal with wages, hours, and other terms and conditions of employment, is a mandatory subject of bargaining because it "operates to restrict a player's ability to move from one team to another and depresses player salaries." *See also, Powell v. Nat'l Football League,* 930 F.2d 1293, 1298–99 (8th Cir. 1989) (agreements establishing first refusal and compensation system are mandatory subjects).

* * *

Maintaining the reserve/free agency systems in the interim between collective bargaining agreements does not alter the rights of Owners to have the PRC represent them for purposes of negotiating a successor agreement or to continue to oppose the inclusion of the systems in any successor agreement. The Owners can, if they successfully bargain, end the free agency and salary arbitration systems, exclude the anti-collusion provision, and create an entirely new system. What they cannot do is alter particular individual's wages until the system is changed by agreement or until the parties negotiate to impasse. That is the nub of all wage negotiations which are inherently mandatory subjects of bargaining. It must be remembered that many employers are forced to continue sometimes onerous and debilitating wage obligations until the collective bargaining process runs its course, just as many employees may earn less than they would in a system that more closely duplicates the free market. Having freely entered into the free agency and reserve systems in their Basic Agreement, the Owners are bound to that system until they bargain in good faith to an impasse.

In view of the abundant case law in the professional sports context that has found that constituent parts of the reserve/free agency system are mandatory subjects of collective bargaining, I find that the Board had substantial reasonable cause to conclude, and a substantial likelihood of success ultimately in establishing, that the unilateral changes made by the Owners to the free agency system before impasse violated the rule against changes to mandatory subjects of bargaining. In summary, the Board has clearly met its injunctive remedy standard in demonstrating that the Owners committed an unfair labor practice by their unilateral abrogation of Article XX(F) and the free agency system.

For substantially similar reasons, I find that salary arbitration for reserve players is also a mandatory part of the collective bargaining process between the Players and the Owners. The Owners argue that their salary arbitration system is indistinguishable from interest arbitration clauses, which are generally classified as permissive subjects of bargaining. Thus, the Owners contend, they have no statutory obligation to preserve salary arbitration until the formation of a new collective bargaining agreement.

The Second Circuit has recognized two basic types of arbitration in the labor context: interest arbitration and rights arbitration. *New York Typographical Union No. 6 v. Printers League Section of the Assoc. of the Graphic Arts,* 919 F.2d 3, 3 n. 2 (2d Cir. 1990). Interest arbitration "concerns disputes over terms of new or renewal contracts." *Id.*; *see also*

Local 58, Int'l Brotherhood of Electrical Workers v. Southeastern Michigan Chapter, Nat'l Electrical Contractors Ass'n, Inc., 43 F.3d 1026, 1030 (6th Cir. 1995) (interest arbitrator acts as legislator in fashioning new contractual obligations, rather than as judicial officer who concentrates on construing terms of existing agreement). Rights arbitration, in contrast, is for disputes "over the interpretation or application of a contract." *Printers League*, 919 F.2d at 3 n.2. Because interest arbitration clauses involve "a mechanism for resolving disputes which may arise as to the terms of future contracts," as opposed to existing terms and conditions of employment, they are a non-mandatory topic of bargaining. *Sheet Metal Workers Local Union No. 20 and George Koch Sons, Inc.*, 306 NLRB 834 (1992).

I agree with the Board's conclusion that the salary arbitration clause at issue here is not a traditional interest arbitration clause. The distinction blurred by the Owners' argument is that new future contractual obligations are not being created by the salary arbitrator. By the time a player and owner go to salary arbitration, a UPC [Uniform Player Contract], created by the terms of the Basic Agreement, has already been entered into by the parties. The only item missing from the executed contract is a dollar amount. The Owners cannot escape the plain and unambiguous language of Article VI(F)(6), which provides:

> Form of submission: The Player and the Club shall each submit to the arbitrator and exchange with each other in advance of the hearing single salary figures for the coming season (which need not be figures offered during the prior negotiations). At the hearing, the Player and the Club shall deliver to the arbitrator a Uniform Player's Contract executed in duplicate, complete except for the salary figure to be inserted in paragraph 2. Upon submission of the salary issue to arbitration by either Player or Club, the Player shall be regarded as a signed Player. . . .

Basic Agreement, Article VI(F)(g) (emphasis added); *see also id.* at Article VI(F)(5) (within 24 hours of hearing arbitrator shall insert salary figure awarded in the duplicate UPC's delivered to him or her). Before the arbitrator rules, there is no question that the player will provide his services to the club for a specified period of time and that the club will pay for those services. The arbitrator's only task is, literally, to fill in the blank where the salary figure goes.

Even if the salary arbitration clause contained in the Basic Agreement is an interest arbitration clause, however, I also agree with the Board's reasoning in *Sea Bay Manor Home for Adults*, 253 NLRB 739 (1980) and *Columbia Univ. in the City of New York*, 298 NLRB 941 (1990) that interest arbitration clauses can survive the expiration of collective bargaining agreements where the clauses

[are] so intertwined with and inseparable from the mandatory terms and conditions for the contract currently being negotiated as to take on the characteristics of the mandatory subjects themselves.

The essence of the reasoning in *Sea Bay* and *Columbia Univ.* is that in some industries the result of collective bargaining is not to stop talking in the future about a dispute but a recognition that the best continuing process for the parties to establish wages is in arbitration. In these situations, a salary arbitration is a current term of employment. That is the situation in baseball. Salary arbitration is the collectively bargained wage in the parties' Agreement, and the Board's view of it as such is not clearly or otherwise erroneous. For the foregoing reasons, the Board has sustained its burden of proving that the Owners committed unfair labor practices both by eliminating Article XX(F) of the free agency system and the salary arbitration provisions of the Basic Agreement.

* * *

[The court then turned to the question of whether an interim injunction was warranted for this violation of the Labor Act. One key value that seemed to require such immediate legal action was the public's interest in more productive and peaceful collective bargaining in baseball.]

... This strike has captivated the public's attention, given the popularity of the sport as well as the protracted nature and well-documented bitterness of the strike. Thus, this strike is about more than just whether the Players and Owners will resolve their differences. It is also about how the principles embodied by federal labor law operate. In a very real and immediate way, this strike has placed the entire concept of collective bargaining on trial. It is critical, therefore, that the Board ensure that the spirit and letter of federal labor law be scrupulously followed. If the Board is unable to enforce the NLRA, public confidence in the collective bargaining process will be permanently and severely undermined.... Issuing the injunction before Opening Day is important to ensure that the symbolic value of that day is not tainted by an unfair labor practice and the NLRB's inability to take effective steps against its perpetuation.

* * *

[The private interests of players was also a sufficient ground for injunctive relief. In particular, the judge was not persuaded by the owners' argument that monetary damages for lost pay would be sufficient to rectify any losses suffered by affected players. For example, with respect to the obstacles erected to free agent movement,]

... [s]alary is just one factor a free agent considers when seeking and accepting offers. A free agent may wish to join a team because of personal reasons such as family considerations, or because of promises of more playing time. Likewise, a free agent may select a team that pays less money but whose coaching staff and team roster make it a World Series contender.... The protections of the NLRA extend to non-monetary bargaining topics that are "terms and conditions of employment." ... In professional baseball, whether to leave a team, where to go and why are of "deep concern" to the affected players and the loss of those choices in the terms and conditions of employment cannot be adequately recompensed by money.

* * *

[While salary arbitration seemed to be concerned purely with money (as the decision had asserted earlier), the judge believed it would be impossible to reconstruct later what would have been the appropriate arbitration verdicts. One key reason was that the systems of free agency and salary arbitration were "inextricably intertwined," such that illegal alteration of one such feature in the baseball players' market would inevitably change the product of the other.]

Similarly, to the extent the salary arbitration system is intimately intertwined with the choice for both owners and players between free agency or arbitration, it is nearly impossible to reconstruct retrospectively the factors that would have influenced each side's decision at the time of election. Hence, even though it is easier later to reconstruct the actual process of salary arbitration and more precisely determine a lost wage from that process, monetary damages are insufficient to recompense for the harm caused in eliminating the salary arbitration process as a choice in the integrated reserve/free agency systems.

* * *

Thus, a poisoning of the free agency bargaining process will also affect the wage negotiations of reserve and salary arbitration players. Conversely, the loss of salary arbitration in the reserve system skews the choice of free agency rights. The unusual wage structure in this monopoly industry makes it extraordinarily difficult if not nearly impossible to reconstruct past market conditions for purposes of retroactive damage calculations.

[Since monetary damages would be too difficult to ascertain after the fact, injunctive relief was needed before the harm was done.]

Injunction granted.

Judge Sotomayor rendered her decision on Friday, March 31, just before opening day of the 1995 season. The injunction transformed the situation on the field: this time the two sides agreed to "Play Ball!" The players voted on Saturday to end their strike and return to work, and the owners voted on Sunday to cancel the opening game scheduled for that night with replacements (generally referred to by unionists as "scabs"). Instead, the beginning of the regular season was postponed until April 26, and the next three weeks were devoted to signing and training the regular players. Later that fall, the Second Circuit (in an opinion authored by Judge Winter) affirmed Judge Sotomayor's decision. *See Silverman v. MLBPRC*, 67 F.3d 1054 (2d Cir. 1995). There were no further work stoppages during the 1995 and 1996 seasons, and in December 1996, the two sides finally reached a settlement of their three-year labor dispute.

NOTES AND QUESTIONS

1. *Mandatory Subjects?* Do you agree with Judge Sotomayor's judgment that the freedom of individual clubs to sign players not under contract was a mandatory topic of bargaining? With her similar judgment regarding salary arbitration for individual players, as contrasted with interest arbitration for future collective agreements? With her similar judgment about the clubs' and players' earlier undertaking not to act "in concert" in individual salary negotiations?

2. *Proper Doctrinal Compromise?* As a matter of general labor law policy, why should there be a bar on unilateral changes in working conditions, even when proposed at the bargaining table, until after an impasse has been reached in negotiations? Alternatively, why should the law allow unilateral changes even after impasse, rather than require the parties to reach a compromise? Should lockouts (and strikes) also be prohibited before impasse?

G. ECONOMIC CONFLICT IN SPORTS LABOR RELATIONS

Under federal labor law, the principal means for breaking deadlocks at the bargaining table are the economic pressures of strikes or lockouts, not the legal pressures of an unfair labor practice charge. Section 7 of the original Labor Act protects employees' right "to engage in concerted activities for the purpose of collective bargaining"—which of course includes engaging in strikes. After thirty years of doctrinal evolution, the Supreme Court read the Act to afford employers a reciprocal economic weapon—a lockout of their employees to force the union to compromise at the bargaining table. *See American Ship Building Co. v. NLRB*, 380 U.S. 300 (1965). From the fans' perspective, both the leagues and the players unions have been only too ready to exercise these prerogatives to achieve their goals in negotiations.

While each side enjoys the legal right to stop work and thereby attempt to alter the balance of power in negotiations, the other side may respond. In particular, since a pronouncement in dicta in the Supreme Court's decision in *NLRB v. Mackay Radio and Telegraph*, 304 U.S. 333 (1938), employers free of associated unfair labor practices have been free to attempt to continue operating during an economic strike by hiring replacement workers who are promised that strikers will not bump them out of their jobs when the strike ends. For a period in the late twentieth century, the issue of "permanent" status for strike replacements was a prominent political issue. The use of permanent replacements has never been an issue for professional athletes in the major sports leagues, however. Do you understand why?

The collapse of the NFLPA strike in 1987 after the NFL's three-week use of replacement players shows that a professional sports league's ability to recruit and use *temporary* replacements who have no guarantees of job security nonetheless may be a sufficient counter weapon. An employer can hire such temporary replacements even when it is the *employer* that initiates the work stoppage through a lockout. *See Local 825 International Union of Operating Engineers v. NLRB (Harter Equipment)*, 829 F.2d 458 (3d Cir. 1987).

National labor law, as explained above, does not find inconsistent with good faith bargaining employers' and unions' use of disruptive economic weapons to secure a contract settlement on their preferred terms. Nevertheless, the Board does find certain employer responses to protected strike activity to constitute impermissible retaliation against the exercise of statutory rights. An interesting exploration of where a line between such retaliation and legitimate self-defense should be located is this decision by the Labor Board involving the troubled bargaining relationship in football in the 1980s.

NFL MANAGEMENT COUNCIL AND NFLPA
309 N.L.R.B. 78 (1992)

[After its experience with the lengthy players strike in 1982, the NFL Management Council (NFLMC) decided that if the NFLPA went on strike during the 1987 contract negotiations, the league would continue its regular schedule using replacement players. The Council Executive Committee (CEC) and its Executive Director, Jack Donlan, asked CEC official (and former NFL quarterback) Eddie LeBaron, to coordinate this effort under which the clubs would rely mainly on players who were at their training camps in August that year but who had failed to make the regular roster. The NFL players did go on strike after the third game of the 1987 season. After canceling the following week's games, the NFL clubs were able to present replacement games in each of the next two weeks. The fact that these games were played induced a considerable number of striking players to cross their union teammates' picket line and return to work. The pressures felt by the general union membership forced the Association to call off the strike and send all the players back to work on Thursday, October 15th. Pursuant to the league's labor policy, however, all the clubs refused to use any of their striking veterans for that weekend's games, because these players had not reported by 1:00 p.m. on Wednesday. At the same time, the clubs used replacement players who signed as late as 4:00 p.m. on Saturday, October 17th for that Sunday's games (or by 4:00 p.m. Monday for the Monday night game). The NFLPA then filed unfair labor charges with the Labor Board on the ground that this NFL policy discriminated against those players who had exercised their statutory right to strike, and thus deprived strikers of one-sixteenth of their annual salaries for the sixteen-game season.]

* * *

The Supreme Court has recognized that "there are some practices which are inherently so prejudicial to union interests and so devoid of significant economic justification . . . that the employer's conduct carries with it an inference of unlawful intent so compelling that it is justifiable to disbelieve the employer's protestations of innocent purpose." *American Ship Building Co. v. NLRB*, 380 U.S. 300 (1965). If an employer's conduct falls within this category, "the Board can find an unfair labor practice even if the employer introduces evidence that the conduct was motivated by business considerations." *NLRB v. Great Dane Trailers*, 388 U.S. 26, 34 (1967).

On the other hand, if the impact on employee rights of the discriminatory conduct is:

> comparatively slight, an antiunion motivation must be proved to sustain the charge if the employer has come forward with evidence of legitimate and substantial business justifications for the conduct. Thus, in either situation, once it has been proved that the employer engaged in discriminatory conduct which could have adversely affected employee rights to some extent, the burden is upon the employer to establish that it was motivated by legitimate objectives since proof of motivation is most accessible to him.

Id. at 34.

Applying these principles to this case, we find as an initial matter that the Wednesday deadline rule clearly constitutes discriminatory conduct which adversely affects employee rights. On its face, the rule discriminates against strikers by applying different, and more stringent, standards for eligibility to participate in NFL games (and to be paid for such participation). Moreover, the rule also adversely affects one of the most significant rights protected by the Act—the right to strike. The Board and the courts, applying the principles of *Great Dane*, have long recognized that the right to strike includes the right to full and complete reinstatement upon unconditional application to return. *NLRB v. Fleetwood Trailer Co.*, 389 U.S. 375, 380–381 (1967); *see also Laidlaw Corp.*, 171 NLRB 1366, 1368–1369 (1968), *enf'd.*, 414 F.2d 99 (7th Cir. 1969), cert. denied 397 U.S. 920 (1970).

As in *Laidlaw*, the Respondents—in reliance on their Wednesday reporting deadline—offered the striking employees who reported for work on October 15 "less than the rights accorded by full reinstatement" (*i.e.*, the right to participate in the games scheduled for October 18–19 and to be paid for those games). Thus, the Wednesday deadline adversely affected the striking employees in the exercise of their right to strike or to cease participating in the strike, by prohibiting the full and complete reinstatement, for the October 18–19 games, of those employees who chose to return to work after the Respondents' deadline had passed.

* * *

The Respondents assert that the Wednesday deadline was justified by the Clubs' need for sufficient time to prepare returning players for game conditions. In this regard, the Respondents presented evidence that the strikers' physical condition would be expected to deteriorate as the strike progressed. In addition, NFL Management Council official Eddie LeBaron testified that players could not maintain their "football condition" without participating in practices involving physical contact. The Respondents also assert that they particularly did not wish to risk injuries to so-called franchise players.

The Respondents also assert that the rule is justified by their goal of ensuring that each Club operates from the same competitive position. Thus, the Wednesday deadline would give each Club the same amount of preparation time with returning players, prevent situations in which a replacement squad was "mismatched" against a squad composed of veterans who had reported late in the week, and ensure that Clubs could prepare for specific players during the Wednesday and Thursday practices when game plans were typically practiced.

Finally, the Respondents assert that the Wednesday deadline was justified in light of substantial administrative difficulties allegedly posed if strikers returned at a late date in the week . . .

In evaluating the Respondents' justifications, we initially note the unprecedented nature of the Wednesday deadline and the absence of any evidence that the Respondents have imposed a deadline of this type on employees outside of a strike setting. In particular, the record shows that players who withheld their services in pursuit of individual goals (*i.e.*, players holding out for a more lucrative contract) are not subject to comparable restraints on their status on their return. Rather, such players are eligible to play immediately so long as they are included in the Club's active roster. If the Club determines that the player is not in shape to play, he may be placed on an Exempt list, as noted above. However, there is no automatic disqualification from participation in NFL games, or from being paid for a game while on the Exempt list, as was the case with the striking employees in 1987. This is so whether or not the individual is considered a "franchise player." Likewise, after the 1982 strike, players were immediately restored to their prestrike status—including players who did not report or practice until the Thursday prior to the next weekend's games. . . .

It is undisputed that the Wednesday deadline was only applicable to striking players. The Respondents could and did sign nonstrikers to contracts subsequent to the date the strikers were declared ineligible; the nonstrikers were eligible to play in and were paid for the October 18–19 games. . . .

Under these circumstances, we find that the Respondents have not established legitimate and substantial justifications for the deadline rule. While it may be true that some striking employees' physical conditioning declined during the strike, the same considerations were present in the case of holdouts and of replacement players. Likewise, safety concerns did not preclude the immediate reinstatement of the striking players in 1982, even though they had been out for 57 days, while the 1987 strike lasted only 25 days. . . .

We also find that the Respondents' asserted competitiveness concerns are unpersuasive. Although the Respondents were entitled to ensure that all clubs operated under the same rules, adopting a deadline which discriminated against strikers was unnecessary to the achievement of this goal. The Respondents' argument that Clubs needed the practice time provided by the Wednesday deadline to prepare the strikers to play (and, for the purpose of those practices, needed to know who would be playing for its opponent) is contradicted by their willingness to allow nonstrikers with substantially less preparation time to play in those games. Moreover, the Respondents' claim that late-returning strikers would have a disproportionate impact on the game unless Clubs had an opportunity to prepare their players to face them would seem to contradict their prior claim that these same players were so out of shape that it would be unsafe to play them. Again, in the case of returning holdouts, replacement players, and the players returning from the 1982 strike, competitiveness concerns did not dictate the imposition of an eligibility deadline like the Wednesday deadline at issue here. We find that such concerns did not justify that deadline in 1987 either.

In addition, we find that the logistical and administrative burden of reinstating the strikers does not justify the rule either. In this regard, the Respondents' arguments are premised entirely on the burden of reinstating the entire 1100 player complement, even though the rule on its face would apply to a single striker who elected to return to work. The Respondents provide no justification for the application of the rule in these circumstances.[24] We also note that the Respondents maintained a substantial complement of replacement players well after the strikers had been fully reinstated. Accordingly, we find that any administrative burden associated with maintaining two separate squads for the games on October 18–19 is not a legitimate and substantial justification for the Wednesday deadline.

* * *

Complaint upheld.

The NLRB directed NFL teams to compensate each striking player for the salary lost (plus interest) as a result of this unfair labor practice— estimated to total $30 million for 1,100 players. In that same first week in October 1992, a jury in an antitrust suit found the NFL liable for $30 million in trebled damages for having imposed a $1,000-a-week cap on salaries payable to 235 development squad players. Just a few months earlier, the NFL had lost its final appeal of another $30 million judgment for disputed contributions (and interest) payable to the players' pension fund. *See Bidwill v. Garvey*, 943 F.2d 498 (4th Cir. 1991). As part of a class action settlement of broader free agency-salary cap issues in January 1993, the NFL agreed to pay the players the bulk of the sums awarded by the Board and the jury in the *NFLMC* and *Bidwill* cases, respectively. The development squad antitrust case eventually made its way to the Supreme Court, with consequences considered in Chapter 6.

NOTES AND QUESTIONS

1. *Treatment of "Injured Reserve" Players?* In the portion of the *NFL Management Council* decision excerpted above, the Board ruled that players who were on the active roster when the strike began were entitled to be paid for the "deadline games" played after the strike ended, despite the League's contention that they would not be ready to play that weekend. Therefore,

---

[24] Indeed, we note that the deadline rule was anomalous in other respects as well. Thus, as the judge noted, it was applied to preclude even specialty players such as kickers from participation in the games, notwithstanding the lack of any evidence that the Respondents' asserted justifications applied in their case. Likewise, the rule was applied to players on injured reserve throughout the strike even though those players would not have been eligible in any event and the only effect of the Wednesday deadline was to prevent them from receiving compensation to which they would otherwise have been entitled as injured players. The Wednesday deadline was also applied to players whose next scheduled game was on Monday, October 19 even though they had as much time to prepare for a Sunday game. The Respondents admit that safety or logistical reasons could not justify the application of the rule to these individuals.

players who were on "injured reserve" when the strike began and ended—and who were paid their normal salaries before the strike—were even more clearly entitled to payment for the "deadline games," since there was no issue about their readiness to play. But should these players also have been entitled to be paid for games cancelled or played during the strike? Does the answer to this question depend on whether injured reserve players also were on strike? If so, how would you determine whether an injured player was on strike? If you were a Players Association official, would you encourage injured players to "report" for work during a strike or to maintain "solidarity" with the striking players?

2. *What if a Common Reporting Deadline?* How could the NFL Management Council have avoided the unfair labor practice charge? Could it have simply required all players—strikers and replacements as well—to report by the same deadline, whether Wednesday or some other day of the week? What would the Labor Board have decided if those were the facts?

3. *Work Stoppage Strategy in Sports.* Consider the broader industrial relations factors that influence the protagonists in deciding how to exercise their statutory rights in a sports labor dispute.

   a. Why did the baseball players choose to strike in August 1994 (in late-season), and the hockey owners choose to lock out in October 1995 (at the start of their season)? Why have all work stoppages in professional sports leagues since 1994 been lockouts during the off-season or at the start of the season? Does your answer suggest that there may never be another player strike?

   b. Why did NBA Commissioner David Stern on July 1, 1998, the day after an NBA collective agreement expired (immediately after the end of the playoffs), announce that all the basketball players were instantly locked out of their current contracts, not just during the season that fall?

   c. Why were replacement players used during the 1987 football strike but not used in either the 1994 hockey lockout or the 1998 hockey and basketball work stoppages? Further, why were replacement players planned for baseball in the spring of 1995 before litigation aborted those plans?

   d. Why is it that football stars like Tony Dorsett, Joe Montana, and Lawrence Taylor chose to cross the players' picket line to play in replacement games in October 1987, but baseball stars like Ken Griffey, Jr., Frank Thomas, and Greg Maddux made it clear they would not do that in April 1995? (Indeed, Cal Ripken announced that he would give up his chance to break Lou Gehrig's historic consecutive games streak, rather than break his commitment to his Association teammates.) Are the explanations to be found in the structures or the cultures of the respective sports?

4. *Service Time Versus Pay During Strike.* Why did the MLBPA make it an absolute condition to settling their three-year dispute with baseball owners in December 1996 that the latter agree to count as player "service time" the period lost because of the strike late in the 1994 season and early in 1995? Is there any difference between earning pay during a strike (which the players

union did not insist upon) and earning service credit for eligibility for salary arbitration and free agency?

Unlike the NFL (but like the NHL and the NBA), Major League Baseball is a North American league with franchises in Toronto and previously in Montreal. The fact that a league does most of its business in the United States does not insulate it from Canadian law governing that part of its operations (just as U.S. law governs Japanese auto manufacturers for their American operations). Canadian labor law is largely within the legislative authority of provinces, such as Ontario and Quebec. Unlike the constitutional situation in the United States, the fact that a manufacturer may have plants in different provinces does not put its labor relations within the Canadian national government's authority.

The major practical significance of this constitutional situation is that the labor laws of several provinces (though not yet the Canada Labor Code) have barred use of *temporary*, as well as *permanent*, replacements in legal strikes and lockouts. That is why the Toronto Blue Jays (whose home is in Ontario) could not have used replacements for their striking players in 1995 in games played in the SkyDome (although the Montreal Expos could have because the MLBPA was not certified in Quebec). As events transpired following the *Silverman* ruling in the spring of 1995, Ontario's replacement ban never did figure directly in the League's bargaining dispute and eventual settlement with the MLBPA.

The Ontario law did, however, come into play at the end of April 1995, because the owners had begun their season with replacements for the umpires they had locked out that winter. Thus, the Umpires Association filed an unfair labor practice complaint with the Ontario Labor Board. This complaint posed the intriguing legal questions whether the umpires were employed just by the American League (based in New York) and not jointly by the Blue Jays, and even if so, whether Ontario law barred use of replacements for U.S. employees performing their regular duties in Ontario. (The flip side of that issue was whether the Blue Jays could legally use replacements for the regular players they employed in Ontario to play games outside Ontario, as the Jays did during spring training in Florida in 1995.) A panel of the Ontario Board delivered an expedited ruling in favor of the Umpires Association and barred future use of replacements in the SkyDome. The issue was rendered moot by settlement of the bargaining dispute just a few days later, but many attributed the difficulties caused by this Ontario law as being a major factor in forcing MLB to make critical concessions. This issue of Canadian labor law is potentially important for the future of North American labor relations in professional baseball, hockey, and basketball.

NOTES AND QUESTIONS

1. *How Should Labor Law Treat Replacements?* American labor law continues to permit permanent replacements based on the principal argument that employers need the permanent replacement option to be able to recruit competent workers to keep operating during a strike, and, as a result, maintain a fair balance of bargaining power in their labor disputes. In Canada, the argument in favor of banning even temporary replacements is that blocking the employer from continuing to operate while legally striking (or locked-out) employees are out of work is necessary to maintain a fair balance of bargaining power in the same disputes. How would you appraise those competing positions about the role of law in labor disputes, based on the planned effort to use replacements in baseball in 1995 and their actual use in football during the 1987 NFL strike?

2. *Union Treatment of Replacements During Strike.* Employees not only have a legal right to strike; they also have a right *not* to strike, free of retaliation from their union. The latter legal rule, however, does not preclude nonthreatening verbal expressions of displeasure by members of sports (and other labor) unions against "scabs" or replacements, during and after the strike.

3. *Disparate Treatment of League Reprisals Against Dissident Owners?* A similar issue can confront owners involved in multi-employer bargaining disputes. In baseball, for example, Peter Angelos, who had represented unions in his law practice, decided not to allow his Baltimore Orioles to play games with replacements, partly because of his concern for Cal Ripken's historic pursuit of Lou Gehrig's record for consecutive games played. Suggestions were made that Angelos and the Orioles might be penalized—indeed, might have the franchise put into trusteeship—for violating the decision made by the rest of the owners. The Labor Act, which grants affirmative rights just to employees, not employers (or unions), does not prohibit such league reprisals against owner-employers, as it prohibits certain union reprisals, including fines, against player-employees who cross their teammates' picket lines, at least after resigning from the union. Is it players or owners who benefit the most from such disparate protection of dissidents in labor-management conflicts?

4. *Preemption of Regulatory but Not Proprietary State Action.* In the spring of 1995, both the City of Baltimore and the State of Maryland enacted legislation that barred use of replacement players in Camden Yards (in order to head off any overruling of Angelos's decision by his fellow baseball owners). A number of Supreme Court decisions have made it clear that the employer's right to use replacements under federal labor law preempts any state laws to the contrary. *See, e.g., Golden State Transit Corp. v. City of Los Angeles*, 475 U.S. 608 (1986). The Maryland legislators said, though, that they were acting not in a regulatory, but in a proprietary, capacity to protect the state's and

city's investment in its Camden Yards stadium. This distinction was based on the Supreme Court's allowance of state efforts to achieve labor peace on its own construction projects, see *Building & Construction Trades Council v. Associated Builders & Contractors*, 507 U.S. 218 (1993). Do you think the distinction should make a difference in the legal result in this case? Suppose, alternatively, that a city like San Francisco had taken the position in 1995 that the use of replacements by the Giants violated the terms of its lease for its public stadium, requiring the club "to field a team of major league baseball players in accordance with major league rules." Is that state action preempted?

5. *Third Party Contracts.* What are the obligations of teams using replacements to their season ticket-holders, broadcast stations, and concessionaires with whom the teams contract to deliver "major league baseball?" Are the owners permitted to deem any games played in their facilities to be "major league," whatever the quality of replacement players (or umpires)?

H. DUTY OF FAIR REPRESENTATION

During the same term that the Supreme Court delineated the scope of a union's statutorily conferred authority as exclusive bargaining representative in its *J.I. Case* decision, supra page 91, the Court in *Steele v. Louisville & Nashville R.R. Co.*, 323 U.S. 192 (1944), held that any such statutory authority must implicitly create a duty of fair representation (DFR) owed by the union to individual employees. *Steele* was a Railway Labor Act case involving egregious union race discrimination. But the Court soon held that the Labor Act imposed the same duty by virtue of the exclusive bargaining authority it conferred. In *Vaca v. Sipes*, 386 U.S. 171 (1967), the Court first articulated its most authoritative description of this duty, stressing its limited scope: "[A] breach of the statutory duty of fair representation occurs only when a union's conduct toward a member of the collective bargaining unit is arbitrary, discriminatory, or in bad faith." This same standard applies for union negotiation of collective bargaining agreements as well as for union implementation of agreements. *See, e.g., Air Line Pilots Ass'n v. O'Neill*, 499 U.S. 65 (1991) (when applying the "arbitrary, discriminatory, or bad faith" standard to collective bargaining, courts must offer unions latitude "within a wide range of reasonableness.")

The *Vaca* decision involved an employee's effort to sue his employer for violation of a collective bargaining agreement between the employer and the employee's union. The Court held that the employee could not do so where the employee's claim was subject to an arbitration process that the union, without violating its DFR, had chosen not to invoke. An employee like the plaintiff in *Vaca* thus must first demonstrate that his union has violated its DFR before recovering from the employer for violating the collective bargaining agreement. *Vaca* expresses the national labor policy that the resolution of disputes that arise in the unionized workplace should be resolved by procedures set forth in a collective bargaining agreement, including arbitration. Access to these procedures is negotiated by and is typically under the control of a union. The DFR requires union decision makers to be fair and principled in using this control, but it does not require them to invoke arbitration regardless of the merits of grievances or the extent of union resources.

Suppose, for instance, that a player files a grievance alleging that his release violated a "no cut" guarantee in his contract, and the MLBPA agrees with the club and the league that the contract language will not bear that interpretation and drops the grievance rather than take it to arbitration. The player would have to sue in court both the association and the club, establish first that the union's judgment in dropping the grievance was "arbitrary, discriminatory, or in bad faith," and then try to sustain the merits of his contract claim against the team (in court, not in arbitration). If the player succeeded on both counts, the club would be responsible for the damage done by the contract violation and the union for the additional costs attributable to use of this more complex procedure, such as legal fees incurred in the lawsuit and additional salary losses incurred because it took longer to obtain a ruling in litigation than in arbitration. *See Bowen v. United States Postal Service*, 459 U.S. 212 (1983). For sports cases illustrating this process, *see, e.g., Chuy v. NFLPA*, 495 F. Supp. 137 (E.D. Pa. 1980), and *Sharpe v. NFLPA*, 941 F. Supp. 8 (D.D.C. 1996).

PETERSON V. KENNEDY AND NFLPA
771 F.2d 1244 (9th Cir. 1985)

REINHARDT, CIRCUIT JUDGE.

[James Peterson of the Tampa Bay Buccaneers signed one-year contracts for each of the 1976, 1977, and 1978 football seasons. Besides the standard injury protection clause that provided for payment of that year's salary in case of an injury occurring during any one season, Peterson's contract contained a special clause that entitled him to his salary for the 1977 and 1978 seasons if he were unable to play because of a football-related injury in a previous year. Peterson injured his knee early in the 1976 season and missed the entire year because of surgery. When Peterson reported to training camp in the summer of 1977, he was cut from the team after one week of drills. This was done pursuant to the standard player contract provision that allows the club to terminate the contract if a player's performance appears "unsatisfactory" compared to other players competing for positions on the squad.

In August 1977, after allegedly talking with Harold Kennedy, a NFLPA staff member, Peterson's agent filed a grievance under the "injury grievance procedure" in the NFL-NFLPA collective agreement in order to recover the salary due for the 1977 and 1978 seasons. The parties disputed whether the NFLPA had been informed at the outset of the special "injury protection" clause in Peterson's contract. However, when Richard Berthelson, the NFLPA General Counsel, learned of that clause in 1978, he sought to channel the grievance into the "non-injury" grievance procedure. Unfortunately, because the switch took place after the sixty days permitted for filing non-injury grievances, the contract arbitrator found the non-injury grievance to be time-barred. Meanwhile, the arbitrator ruled against Peterson's claim under the injury grievance procedure, on the ground that this particular procedure was used only to collect salary payments owed for the year during which the injury occurred.

Having lost both sides of his contract claim against the Buccaneers, Peterson sued the NFLPA for breach of the labor law duty of fair representation—in particular, by erroneously advising him to file an injury grievance and then failing to rectify this error while there still was time to do so. Although the jury found in favor of Peterson's legal claim, the trial judge granted the NFLPA's motion for judgment notwithstanding the verdict (JNOV). The principal ground was that the union's conduct amounted to no more than negligence, and negligence could not constitute unfair representation under the NLRA. Peterson appealed that ruling.]

* * *

The district court concluded that the evidence presented was legally insufficient to sustain the jury's verdict that the union breached its duty of fair representation. We agree. After reviewing all of the evidence in the light most favorable to Peterson, we conclude that the union did not breach its duty of fair representation; the record is devoid of evidence that the union acted in an arbitrary, discriminatory, or bad faith manner.

The duty of fair representation is a judicially established rule imposed on labor organizations because of their status as the exclusive bargaining representative for all of the employees in a given bargaining unit. The Supreme Court [in *DelCostello v. International Bthd. of Teamsters*, 462 U.S. 151 (1983)] recently explained the basis and scope of the duty:

> The duty of fair representation exists because it is the policy of the National Labor Relations Act to allow a single labor organization to represent collectively the interests of all employees within a unit, thereby depriving individuals in the unit of the ability to bargain individually or to select a minority union as their representative. In such a system, if individual employees are not to be deprived of all effective means of protecting their own interests, it must be the duty of the representative organization to "serve the interests of all members without hostility or discrimination toward any, to exercise its discretion with complete good faith and honesty, and to avoid arbitrary conduct."

462 U.S. at 164, n. 14.

A union breaches its duty of fair representation only when its conduct toward a member of the collective bargaining unit is "arbitrary, discriminatory, or in bad faith." The duty is designed to ensure that unions represent fairly the interests of all of their members without exercising hostility or bad faith toward any. It stands "as a bulwark to prevent arbitrary union conduct against individuals stripped of traditional forms of redress by the provisions of federal labor law."

The Supreme Court has long recognized that unions must retain wide discretion to act in what they perceive to be their members' best interests. To that end, we have "stressed the importance of preserving union discretion by narrowly construing the unfair representation doctrine." We have emphasized that, because a union balances many collective and individual interests in deciding whether and to what extent it will pursue a particular grievance, courts should "accord substantial deference" to a union's decisions regarding such matters.

A union's representation of its members "need not be error free." We have concluded repeatedly that mere negligent conduct on the part of a union does not constitute a breach of the union's duty of fair representation.

* * *

Whether in a particular case a union's conduct is "negligent", and therefore non-actionable, or so egregious as to be "arbitrary", and hence sufficient to give rise to a breach of duty claim, is a question that is not always easily answered. A union acts "arbitrarily" when it simply ignores a meritorious grievance or handles it in a perfunctory manner, for example, by failing to conduct a "minimal investigation" of a grievance that is brought to its attention. We have said that a union's conduct is "arbitrary" if it is "without rational basis," or is "egregious, unfair and unrelated to legitimate union interests." In *Robesky v. Qantas Empire Airways Ltd.*, 573 F.2d 1082, 1089–90 (9th Cir. 1978), we held that a union's unintentional mistake is "arbitrary" if it reflects a "reckless disregard" for the rights of the individual employee, but not if it represents only "simply negligence violating the tort standard of due care."

There are some significant general principles that emerge from our previous decisions. In all cases in which we found a breach of the duty of fair representation based on a union's arbitrary conduct, it is clear that the union failed to perform a procedural or ministerial act, that the act in question did not require the exercise of judgment and that there was no rational and proper basis for the union's conduct.

* * *

We have never held that a union has acted in an arbitrary manner where the challenged conduct involved the union's judgment as to how best to handle a grievance. To the contrary, we have held consistently that unions are not liable for good faith, non-discriminatory errors of judgment made in the processing of grievances. We have said that a union's conduct may not be deemed arbitrary simply because of an error in evaluating the merits of a grievance, in interpreting particular provisions of a collective bargaining agreement, or in presenting the grievance at an arbitration hearing. In short, we do not attempt to second-guess a union's judgment when a good faith, non-discriminatory judgment has in fact been made. It is for the union, not the courts, to decide whether and in what manner a particular grievance should be pursued. We reaffirm that principle here.

Sound policy reasons militate against imposing liability on unions for errors of judgment made while representing their members in the collective bargaining process. [We have] recognized that holding unions liable for such errors would serve ultimately to "defeat the employees' collective bargaining interest in having a strong and effective union." If unions were subject to liability for "judgment calls," it would necessarily undermine their discretion to act on behalf of their members and ultimately weaken their effectiveness. In the long run, the cost of recognizing such liability would be borne not by the unions but by their memberships. Not only would the direct costs of adverse judgments be passed on to the members in the form of increased dues, but, more importantly, unions would become increasingly reluctant to provide guidance to their members in collective bargaining disputes. Such a result would be inconsistent with our oft-repeated commitment to construe narrowly the scope of the duty of fair representation in order to preserve the unions' discretion to decide how best to balance the collective and individual interests that they represent.

* * *

Whether liability for a loss occasioned by ordinary negligence of the union might be spread more equitably among the membership as a whole, rather than be borne by the individual member who is harmed, is no longer an open question.

In applying the foregoing principles to the case at hand, we conclude, as a matter of law that Peterson failed to establish that the NFLPA breached its duty of fair representation. . . . The alleged error was one of judgment. Viewing the evidence in the light most favorable to Peterson, the most that can be said is that the union provided him with incorrect advice and did not alter its judgment until it was too late to rectify the error. In this case, deciding whether to file an injury or a non-injury grievance was not a purely mechanical function; the union attorneys were required to construe the scope and meaning of the injury and non-injury grievance provisions of the collective bargaining agreement and to determine which of the two grievance procedures was more appropriate. As we have indicated earlier, the answer was not as simple as a literal reading of the two contract sections might indicate.

* * *

Although the union's representatives may have erred in initially advising Peterson to file an injury grievance and in failing to recognize its mistake in time to file a non-injury grievance in its stead, we are unwilling to subject unions to liability for such errors in judgment. Accordingly, we affirm the district court's conclusion that the evidence presented was insufficient, as a matter of law, to support the jury's verdict against the union.

Appeal denied.

NOTES AND QUESTIONS

1. *Ministerial Versus Discretionary.* Do you understand the distinction between "ministerial" and "discretionary" actions made by the court in *Peterson v. Kennedy*? Of what relevance is it to the standard for a union's duty of fair representation? How did it apply to the facts of that case?

2. *Union's Dual Constituency.* A union serving as exclusive representative of a bargaining unit has a duty to represent each employee serving in a job within the unit, regardless of the degree of support the employee gives the union. A union thus has dual overlapping constituencies: its active members and the employees it represents. What then should be a sports union's duty toward players who have crossed over picket lines to replace striking players? Can the union negotiate lower employer contributions to a pension fund for such replacement players? Can it negotiate to provide no credit for free agency for the time the replacements played during a strike? Why is it also not a violation of the union's duty to exclude replacements from membership in the union and hence eligibility to collect a share of licensing fees?

3. *Non-Allowance of Rodriguez Trade.* Consider again the MLBPA's refusal to allow the trade of Alex Rodriguez to the Red Sox in 2004, as described above on page 96. Was that refusal a violation of the union's duty of fair representation? Why or why not?

CHAPTER 3

LABOR ARBITRATION IN PROFESSIONAL SPORTS*

■ ■ ■

The use of negotiated private arbitration to resolve disputes over the interpretation and application of collective bargaining agreements spread with the proliferation of unionized work places after the passage of the Labor Act in 1935. Union leaders favored arbitration before bilaterally selected neutrals in part because of the leaders' lingering suspicion of a judiciary that had been hostile to collective worker action for over a century. These leaders also recognized that private arbitration can provide a cheaper and certainly quicker forum for resolving disputes than can courts, advantages especially important to unions with limited relative resources. Furthermore, management has been attracted to arbitration as an alternative to work stoppages over unresolved grievances during the term of collective agreements; indeed, labor relations professionals soon came to view management agreements to submit grievances to final and binding arbitration as a "quid pro quo" for a union agreement not to strike over such grievances.

Before the rise of unions in professional sports, moreover, the Supreme Court used a grant of jurisdiction provided by the Labor Management Relations Act (LMRA) in 1947 to assert law favorable to the adoption and enforcement of arbitration provisions in collective bargaining agreements. Section 301 of the LMRA grants federal courts jurisdiction over "[s]uits for violation of contracts between an employer and a labor organization . . . without respect to the amount in controversy or without regard to the citizenship of the parties." In *Textile Workers Union v. Lincoln Mills of Alabama,* 353 U.S. 448 (1957), the Court provided a constitutional basis for this grant of jurisdiction—"arising under" Article III jurisdiction—by holding that the provision must intend federal courts to fashion substantive law to govern collective agreements "from the policy of our national labor laws." The *Lincoln Mills* Court then fashioned the first principle of this new law: notwithstanding any contrary state contract law, or the anti-injunction commands of the Norris-LaGuardia Act, CBA agreements to arbitrate can be specifically enforced through injunctions,

---

* For commentary and other materials on labor arbitration relevant to topics in this chapter, please see the course web site (http://pennstatelaw.psu.edu/SportsTextWebsite).

not only through damages. Doing so, the Court suggested, encourages the peaceful resolution of labor disputes in accord with national labor policy.

Three years later in a trilogy of cases involving the United Steelworkers, the Court provided further support for arbitration under labor agreements. One of the cases, *United Steelworkers of America v. Enterprise Wheel & Car Corp.*, 363 U.S. 593 (1960), held that courts should not review the merits of an arbitration award and is treated more fully in the last section of this chapter. The other two cases involved standards for the enforcement of agreements to arbitrate. In *United Steelworkers of America v. American Manufacturing Co.*, 363 U.S. 564 (1960), the Court held that a court should enforce a CBA provision to arbitrate a grievance even if the court considered the grievance "frivolous" or "patently baseless." "Whether the moving party is right or wrong is a question of contract interpretation for the arbitrator" not the court. In *United Steelworkers of America v. Warrior & Gulf Navigation Co.*, 363 U.S. 574 (1960), the Court recognized that courts must decide whether the parties to a collective agreement intended a particular dispute to be subject to the jurisdiction of the arbitrator, but it held that they should do so with a strong presumption in favor of arbitration: "[a]n order to arbitrate the particular grievance should not be denied unless it may be said with positive assurance that the arbitration clause is not susceptible of an interpretation that covers the asserted dispute. Doubts should be resolved in favor of coverage." Ten years after the *Steelworkers Trilogy*, in *Boys Market, Inc. v. Retail Clerks Union, Local 770*, 398 U.S. 235 (1970), the Court gave management further encouragement to agree to final and binding arbitration by holding that the Norris-LaGuardia Act does not preclude the specific enforcement of union commitments not to strike over grievances that are subject to resolution by neutral arbitrators.

Today labor arbitration continues to be a central part of successful collective bargaining in the unionized work place. Although collective bargaining agreements cover less than 7% of the private sector workforce, the CBAs that do exist almost always contain arbitration clauses to resolve disputes over interpretation and application.

The industry of professional sports illustrates the importance of arbitration to successful collective bargaining. From their first collective agreements the players associations and league managements have utilized negotiated labor arbitration systems. In baseball, the owners and union have traditionally selected a single independent neutral to chair a panel of three persons charged with deciding unsettled disputes. The union selects one member of the panel, as does management. The neutral runs the hearing and, in fact, makes the determination, which is joined by one member of the panel or the other. In the NFL, NBA, and NHL, the two sides have selected a single person who becomes the sole arbitrator. In all the leagues, the parties normally choose experienced and respected arbitrators to serve as their permanent umpires. They are typically elected members of the honorary association of labor neutrals, the National Academy of Arbitrators. The arbitrators hear all disputes that the CBA assigns to independent arbitration until they are dismissed in accordance with the agreement's procedures. In the case of collective bargaining agreements adapted from antitrust class action case settlements, the district court that approved the settlement retained jurisdiction to hear disputes involving terms derived from those settlements, and in the process appointed a special master, who typically has not been an experienced arbitrator, to hear and make recommendations in individual cases.

A. CONTRACT INTERPRETATION THROUGH ARBITRATION

Collective bargaining agreements in some ways are similar to legislative enactments. Like legislators with different political priorities seeking acceptable compromises, parties negotiating collective agreements often agree only on general principles that require interpretation before being applied in particular cases. Sometimes the parties have a different understanding of the principles, but do not want to upset an agreement by pressing their point of view. Sometimes the parties do not anticipate the particular cases that require further interpretation. In any case, the parties anticipate that clarification can be offered in arbitration during the course of the agreement, and that renegotiation is available before signing the next agreement. The arbitration process, like the judicial process for legislation, thus can be an integral part of the development of a collective bargaining relationship.

The most important example from the sports industry of how arbitral interpretation of a collective agreement can prompt refinement of the agreement and affect future labor relations is treated in Chapter 4 on player mobility restraints. That example, the *Messersmith-McNally* decision, excerpted at page 213 infra, changed assumptions about the meaning of a clause in baseball players' individual contracts, and effectively forced Major League Baseball to bargain with the MLBPA about rules to govern free agency in baseball. The result of this bargaining was a collective agreement that not only specified when a player could become a free agent and what compensation (in the form of draft picks) was owed to the former team, but also created a draft procedure whereby a specified number of teams could secure the right to bid for the free agents the teams wanted to pursue. That last feature of the free agency system was dispensed with in the 1981 baseball agreement, but not before an arbitrator interpreted its meaning and scope in a decision that illustrates how arbitral interpretations can be a central part of the collective bargaining process.

ALVIN MOORE & ATLANTA BRAVES
MLB-MLBPA Arb. 77-18 (1977)

PORTER, ARBITRATOR.

[In April 1977, Alvin Moore signed a one-year contract with the Atlanta Braves. That contract contained a clause that said that if Moore told the Braves he was "not satisfied with his playing time by June 15, 1977," the Braves had to trade him to another team (approved by Moore). If such a trade had not been consummated before the end of the season, Moore would "become a free agent if he so desires." National League President Feeney disapproved of this "special covenant" as "inconsistent with the Reserve System Article of the new Basic Agreement." The Players Association filed a grievance on Moore's behalf, based on the Article II Recognition clause in the MLB Agreement, which permitted players to negotiate not just individual salaries above the prescribed league minimum, but also "Special Covenants . . . which actually or potentially provide additional benefits to the Player." The issue for the arbitrator was whether this provision in the Moore/Braves contract met the test.]

According to the Association, there are only three valid reasons for a League President to disapprove a special covenant. He may do so: (1) if the covenant does not meet the test of Article II in that it does not "actually or potentially provide additional benefits to the Player;" (2) if the covenant violates an applicable law or is specifically prohibited by a Major League rule which is not inconsistent with the Basic Agreement (*e.g.*, if the covenant provides for the giving of a bonus for playing, pitching or batting skill or a bonus contingent on the Club's standing, types of bonuses specifically prohibited by Major League Rule 3[a]); or (3) if the covenant purports to bind some third party whom the Club and the Player have no authority to bind (*e.g.*, a covenant stating that, regardless of what a Player does on the field, an Umpire cannot eject him from a game or the League President or the Commissioner cannot discipline him). . . .

The Clubs reply that the Moore covenant strikes at the very heart of the reserve system which the parties negotiated following the Arbitration Panel's Decision No. 29, the so-called *"Messersmith-McNally"* case. In the wake of the *Messersmith-McNally* case, all players were theoretically free to play out their contracts and become free agents after an additional renewal year. Confronted by the impending collapse of the reserve system, the Clubs observe, the parties, for the first time, jointly negotiated a new reserve system and incorporated the new system in Article XVII of the 1976–1979 Basic Agreement. In the Clubs' view, Article II of the Basic Agreement does not provide authority for an individual Club and Player to negotiate what, in their opinion, is an entirely new reserve system, merely because such a system would provide a benefit to the Player. . . .

The Clubs concede that, in practice, the League Presidents have approved particular covenants which differ from and hence are arguably "inconsistent" with the provisions of the Basic Agreement. In their view, however, the inconsistencies in these approved covenants involved interests of the individual Clubs and Player alone—e.g., covenants guaranteeing a player's salary for one or more years, covenants waiving a Club's rights regarding commercial endorsements, medical examinations, etc. They did not involve covenants, such as the Moore covenant, wherein the Club and the Player sought to waive the interests of others—in this case the 25 other Clubs' interest in maintaining the kind of competitive balance among the various Clubs which the Reserve System of Article XVII was and is designed to provide.

The Moore covenant is said by the Clubs to contravene the scheme of Article XVII in three main respects. First, it grants to Moore, who presently has less than one year of Major League service, a conditional right to demand a trade, should he "not be satisfied with his playing time by June 15, 1977. . . ."

Second, if a trade is not consummated by the end of the 1977 season, the Moore covenant renders Moore eligible to become a free agent, if he so desires, despite the fact that he will then have only a little more than a year's Major League service. . . .

Third, the Moore covenant does not expressly make him subject to the [free agent] re-entry procedure, with its quota and compensation provisions. . . .

The objective of this re-entry procedure, the Clubs contend, is to provide for an even and equitable distribution of players among all the Clubs and prevent a few of the richer Clubs from buying up a disproportionate share of the available free agent talent. To permit the Atlanta Club and Player Moore to by-pass the re-entry procedure would defeat this objective and allow the Atlanta Club to waive the rights which the other 25 Clubs have in maintaining the competitive balance which the re-entry procedure is designed to foster, the Clubs conclude. They ask, accordingly, that league President Feeney's disapproval of the Moore covenant be sustained by the Panel.

* * *

In the Chairman's judgment, both parties have advanced sound positions in support of their respective claims, but each has pushed his position to an unsound extreme. For reasons to be given more fully below, the Chairman is convinced the Moore covenant can be interpreted in a way which does not impinge upon the legitimate interests of the other Clubs and could and should have been approved on that basis. No reason appears why the Atlanta Club may not accord to Moore conditional rights to demand a trade and to become a free agent under Article XVII, B(2), despite the fact that he does not have the requisite years of Major League service to claim these rights unilaterally. The 5- and 6-year service requirements for Players seeking to exercise such rights unilaterally under Article XVII, D and B(2), respectively, are for the individual Club's benefit; and no persuasive evidence or argument has been presented to show why the benefit of long-term title and reservation rights to Moore's contract may not be waived by his club. But if Atlanta may waive the length of service requirements designed for its benefit, it may not waive the reentry procedure designed for the benefit of all 26 Clubs. . . .

Negotiations between individual Clubs and Players are not. . . conducted in a vacuum. To the contrary, and at the risk of belaboring the obvious, individual Player-Club negotiations are conducted not only within the framework of applicable law but within the framework of organized professional baseball and the attendant rules, agreements and regulations by which the sport or industry is governed and by which the Association on behalf of the Players and the Clubs comprising the two Major Leagues have agreed to be bound. Within the latter framework are innumerable matters affecting the interests and rights of all the Clubs and Players, such as the number of Player contracts to which each Club may have title and reservation rights, the number of Players each Club may retain on its active roster, the length of the intra or interleague trading periods, etc. Variations in any one of these provisions might give a Player "additional benefits" but are beyond the Club's power to make. . . .

To the extent the Association seeks to push its "additional benefit" argument to the point where the Moore covenant is to be interpreted as exempting Moore from the free agent quota system and other aspects of the reentry procedure designed to protect the interests of all 26 Clubs, the Chairman believes it presses its argument too far.

* * *

Grievance upheld in part.

NOTES AND QUESTIONS

1. *Arbitrator's Role?* Which clauses in the 1976 collective agreement did arbitrator Porter interpret in this decision? Did these clauses directly answer the questions posed to and answered by the arbitrator? If not, how exactly were the clauses relevant to his decision? Why did the arbitrator decide one of the questions favorably to MLB and the other favorably to the MLBPA? Was the arbitrator simply offering the parties a compromise that would make his continuing employment palatable to each, or did his opinion offer a coherent and consistent interpretation of the collective agreement?

2. *Further Application.* In 1978, an arbitrator invalidated an individual contract signed under the 1976 agreement because it specified that, at its termination, the player would become a free agent without compensation, that is, the contracting team waived its right to whatever draft pick it would receive from a new team signing the player. What do you suppose was the arbitrator's reasoning?

B. ARBITRATION OF DISCIPLINARY DISPUTES

The grievances presented to neutral arbitration authorized under collective agreements most often involve challenges to the discharge or discipline of employees covered by the agreement. Even such cases may facilitate further collective bargaining and a refinement of the collective agreement. Consider the following decision.

IN RE LATRELL SPREWELL
NBA-NBPA Arb. (1998)

JOHN FEERICK, ARBITRATOR

Facts

The Grievant entered the NBA as a player for the Warriors in 1992 as a result of the draft. From that time until his suspension on December 1, 1997, he played for the Warriors under four different head coaches, each with their own style of coaching. Although he was fined from time to time and participated, according to the record, in two physical altercations with other players,* he never was suspended from a practice or a game until the 1995/96 season. He worked hard, played hard, and achieved All-Star status. He also was the Warriors' best player and its captain by appointment of the Team.

Head Coach Peter Carlesimo joined the Warriors in June 1997, after several successful seasons with the Portland Blazers and a successful college coaching career at Seton Hall. It appears from the record that the Grievant and Head Coach had a reasonably good pre-season in terms of their relationship, though some cracks began to develop as the season opened in late October and early November 1997. During the month of November the relationship between the two deteriorated with the player wanting to be traded and the Team wanting to trade him so it might build its future in a different direction.

The record reveals that the Grievant engaged in some acts of defiance in November and felt singled out, not listened to, and blamed to some extent for the Team's lack of success. Coaches and players testified in the hearings before me that the Head Coach was not abusive toward the

---

* In neither altercation was he disciplined, in one the other player was disciplined.

Grievant. There also was testimony that the Head Coach was in the Grievant's "ear" on a fairly regular basis in order to motivate him to achieve an even higher level of excellence. [Warriors Assistant Coach Mark] Grabow testified that he "felt that P.J.'s prodding of players was equally distributed among all the players but because Spree was his star and he needed Spree's offense and defensive energy, he needed Spree to be his guy and for us to be successful." In response to my question as to whether or not more was asked of the Grievant, he added, "[t]hen perhaps he did, but I never looked at it as he was picking on him or anything like that." In reply to a follow-up question by counsel, he said, "[h]e needed him more than any other player for us to be successful."

Testimony was also given that screaming and profanity in general were not an infrequent occurrence, and there was testimony that the Grievant and Donyell Marshall seemed to be singled out more than the other players. By the end of November a great deal of frustration had set in as a result, it appears, of the Team's failure to win more than one of its first 14 games. [Warriors Assistant Coach Bob] Staak testified: "Everybody on the team was unhappy. It was no fun at that point in time."

As of December 1, 1997, trade discussions involving the Grievant were being actively pursued by the Warriors with one or more other teams. Trading the Grievant, however, was not easy because it involved finding a team with salary cap room or with a player or players the Warriors would wish to add to its roster. The salary cap was not an insignificant issue inasmuch as the Grievant earned a high salary and, at best, only a few teams had much room left in their cap at that point in the season.

On December 1, 1997, the Warriors engaged in a regular, closed door practice, preparing for its next game scheduled for December 3 against Cleveland. The coaches participated in different ways with the players as the Head Coach moved from one practice court to another. One of the drills that day was a three-man, two-ball exercise in which one player rebounds, another receives a pass from the rebounder and throws the ball to the third person, who takes a shot at the basket. The object of the drill is to have the shooter take as many shots as possible within a 55-second period. When the Head Coach reached the court on which the Grievant was playing with Grabow and [point guard Muggsy] Bogues, he told the Grievant to put more speed on the ball when making a pass. The practice was proceeding in a normal manner and the Head Coach spoke in a low tone and then raised his voice a bit louder, saying the words a second time. The Grievant proceeded to slam the ball down and express a number of expletives reasonably approximating "get out of my face, get the f— out of here and leave me the f— alone." The Head Coach responded: "you're the f— out of here." Thereupon, Grievant immediately either walked to or lunged at the Head Coach, placing his two hands around his neck. With his arms fully extended, the Grievant moved the Coach backwards saying, "I will kill you." Apparently no one else heard him use these words except the Head Coach, who did not believe he intended to kill him although he thought he was trying to inflict serious bodily harm. The Grievant, upset and angry, said that he used the words figuratively, as he (and others) testified, in the same manner that they are used from time to time in the sport in fight situations.

Almost as soon as the Grievant had placed his two hands around the Head Coach's neck, Grabow intervened in an effort separate the two, as others came to the area to help. Between seven and ten seconds elapsed during which the Grievant had his hands around the Coach's neck. The Head Coach remained calm and offered no resistance except toward the end when he raised his arms, palms down, toward his shoulders at about which point the Grievant's hands came free of his neck. The Head Coach testified that his breathing became more difficult toward the end of the seven to ten second period. Grievant testified that he was applying some pressure but did not intend any serious harm.

The testimony is not entirely clear as to how the Grievant came to remove his hands from the Head Coach's' neck. In response to questions concerning getting the Grievant off the Coach, Grabow said: "I was trying to get Spree off him, like the three of us were waltzing around the floor a little bit, but then I felt Tom Abdenour, our trainer, come over my shoulder and we finally got Spree's hands off of Coach and Tommy just kind of escorted Spree toward the locker room." The testimony suggests that Grievant may have removed his own hands.

After the Grievant and Head Coach were separated, Tom Abdenour took the Grievant to the door leading from the playing facility to the locker room and shower. At that point, they were joined by [Warriors assistant coach Rod] Higgins and [player Bimbo] Coles. As Grievant and Abdenour moved toward the door Grievant angrily said a number of expletives, including "trade me, get me out of here, I will kill you." The Head Coach responded with words to the effect of "I am here." In leaving the facility, Grievant slammed the door hard and knocked over the water cooler immediately inside the door. As Coles was walking through the door with Grievant to talk to him, someone told him to come back in to continue the practice. No one, it appears, joined the Grievant in the locker-room area.

With respect to the period during which he was in the locker room, between ten and 20 minutes, the Grievant testified that he reflected on all the negative things that had gone on between him and the Head Coach up to that point, including what had just happened in practice. He said: "For through that whole incident, from the time I went into the shower and put on sweats and flip-flops, I am moving fast. I never sat down and reflected on what happened or anything. I walked back out there at a fast pace."

Grievant returned to the practice facility after showering and changing. In his testimony he said that he had not calmed down at all and remained angry. Coach Grabow, apparently the first to see him upon his return, heard the Grievant say "you better get my ass out of here, get me the f— out of here." Grabow said, "he didn't say anything at that point that was threatening to anyone." He said that the Grievant was walking with "a purpose" and he (Grabow) uttered "someone grab him." [Assistant Coach Bob] Staak and then Coach Higgins tried unsuccessfully to arrest the Grievant's fast movement around the baseline toward the basket under which the Head Coach was standing as a full-court drill was in progress. Grabow, as well as [Assistant Coach Paul] Westhead, testified that the Grievant became more enraged as people grabbed him. Staak said that, in entering, there was no question that Grievant's "intent was to get closer to P.J.," adding that he was extremely mad. When Staak said, "Spree, it is bad enough. You don't want to do this," he said that Grievant's response was "get the f— out of my way, don't touch me." Others testified that upon seeing him after his return, Grievant appeared mad, enraged, angry and upset, though it was not clear at all when they saw him in relation to when Grabow first observed him.

At some point Grievant and Head Coach came within a foot or two or each other. Coach Grabow testified that as people grabbed the Grievant it "became a chaotic scene," with coaches and players being drawn closer to each other as if a melee were taking place. The testimony is quite confused at the point when Grievant and the Head Coach were within reach of each other. What is clear is that efforts were being made by those present to prevent them from having any contact. The Grievant testified that he sought to free himself from those grabbing him by kicking his feet and flailing his arms. He said it was possible that in doing so, he may have hit the Head Coach in a flailing motion. Other testimony was given that there was a moment in time when the Grievant either freed himself from the clutch of others, or at least his arms, and directed a punch at the Coach which grazed the side of his right cheek. I find that, as a melee was occurring, Grievant did direct an overhand punch which landed on the Coach in the area near his right shoulder but the testimony does not establish whether it was directed or the result of a flailing motion. Almost immediately Grievant was moved away from the Head Coach and the Head Coach was moved away as well. From that point until he left the playing facility, the Grievant was firmly in the clutch of Coach Higgins and players Ferrell and Coles. As he was leaving, Grievant uttered words similar to those he used after the first incident, including "I will kill you."

Upon leaving the playing facility, Grievant went to [Warrior General Manager Garry] St. Jean's office and said he wanted to be traded using various expletives. The General Manger, who at that point was speaking to the Grievant's agent, handed the Grievant the telephone. The Grievant shouted into it "get me out of here today, get me the f— out of here." He then strongly placed the phone on St. Jean's desk and walked out. St. Jean testified as to his concern for Grievant because of "his emotional state." . . .

[The opinion next describes the twin investigations by the Warriors and the league. Although the Warriors initially pursued the idea of trading Sprewell, by December 3 they decided that the best course was to terminate his contract. Commissioner Stern then decided to suspend Sprewell for one year.]

Legal Framework

I turn to the principles of the law that have guided my deliberations and consideration of this matter.

First, I begin by emphasizing that violence in the work place is not tolerated in the field of labor and employment law. The subject has been dealt with strongly by arbitrators, leading to severe discipline including termination where an assault is made on a supervisor or manager. I note as well that the idea of fairness runs throughout the field of labor and employment law, finding expression in contracts, arbitration decisions, court decisions, statutes and constitutions. Some of the elements of fairness are expressed by a number of arbitral principles. Arbitrators apply progressive discipline, take account of mitigating factors, and look to see whether discipline is consistent with prior penalties for comparable acts. Variations in penalties are appropriate depending on the circumstances and context surrounding the act in question. As the arbitrator noted in the seminal decision *Alan Wood Steel Co.*, 21 LA 843, 849 (Short, 1954), where "the nature of the offense is the same, but other circumstances vary, variations in the discipline imposed must nevertheless be reasonably appropriate to the variations in the 'other circumstances.' Stated otherwise, an essentially proportionate relationship must be maintained." Moreover, previous lax discipline on the part of an employer will not require similar treatment of subsequent misconduct where clear notice is given that such behavior would warrant greater discipline.

Another aspect of fairness is the notion of industrial due process. It is, however, a less exacting standard than its constitutional counterpart. As the arbitrator noted in *Cameron Iron Works*, 73 LA 878 (Marlett, 1979): "[E]mployers and unions meet in bargaining on approximately equal terms, and their contracts speak of 'just cause' rather than 'due process.' The distinction is significant. The essential question for an arbitrator is not whether disciplinary action was totally free from procedural error, but rather whether the process was fundamentally fair." An employee subject to discipline is entitled to notice of the charges, an opportunity to be heard and an adequate and fair investigation. Indeed, the California Supreme Court recently emphasized that, while employers had wide discretion in the area of employment termination, an employer's factual determination must be a "reasoned conclusion supported by substantial evidence gathered through an adequate investigation that includes notice of the claimed misconduct and a chance for the employee to respond." *Cotran v. Rollins Hudig Hall Int'l Inc.*, 17 Cal. 4th 93, 948 P.2d 412 (1998).

Sometimes notice to an employee is obviated where it is clear that the conduct would not be tolerated. Adolph M. Koven & Susan L. Smith, *Just Cause: The Seven Tests* 31, 59–161 (rev. by Donald F. Farwell, 2nd ed. 1992). Interviewing a grievant also may not be required, unless provided for by contract, although the presence or absence of such an opportunity may be relevant to a just cause termination. As for an adequate and fair investigation, the authors of a leading treatise on arbitration declare: "[E]xcept in the most obvious and heinous of situations, management must conduct a fair and impartial investigation of the incident." Elkouri & Elkouri, *How Arbitration Works* 919 (Marlin M. Volz & Edward P. Goggins eds. 5th ed. 1997) (quoting *Great Midwest Mining Corp.* 82 LA 52, 55 (Milrut, 1984)).

* * *

Against this background, I turn to the arguments made by the parties, most particularly as follows: (1) whether the standard of review of the Commissioner's one-year suspension is just cause or arbitrary and capricious; (2) whether a just cause standard of review is applicable to the termination of Grievant's Player Contract by the Warriors; (3) whether the CBA allows discipline to be imposed jointly by the Commissioner and Warriors with respect to the same conduct; (4) whether the actions taken by the Commissioner and Warriors violate double jeopardy principles of labor law; and (5) whether the actions taken by the Commissioner and Warriors are appropriate.

(1) Whether the Standard of Review of the Commissioner's One-year Suspension Is Just Cause or Arbitrary and Capricious.

The parties disagree on whether just cause or an arbitrary and capricious standard is applicable in reviewing the Commissioner's one-year suspension of the Grievant. To determine which is applicable, one must interpret the CBA. Two of the relevant provisions of the CBA are as follows:

> The parties recognize that a player may be subjected to disciplinary action for just cause by his Team or the Commissioner (or his designee). Therefore, in Grievances regarding discipline, the issue to be resolved shall be whether there has been just cause for the penalty imposed. CBA Art. XXXI, Section 14(c)

> In any Grievance that involves an action taken by the Commissioner (or his designee) concerning (I) the preservation of the integrity of, or the maintenance of public confidence in, the game of basketball, and (ii) a fine and/or suspension that results

in a financial impact to the player of more than $25,000, the Grievance Arbitrator shall apply an arbitrary and capricious standard of review. CBA, AR. XXXI, Section 5(c).

Also relevant is Article 35 of the NBA Constitution entitled "Misconduct," which governs all players and is referenced in Paragraph 5 of the Uniform Player Contract. * * *

It is difficult to fashion a bright-line rule for determining conduct that implicates the integrity of our public confidence in the game of basketball. I find that such conduct would include, as in this proceeding, a well-publicized violent subversion of the most fundamental authority relationship in the game, that between player and coach. An attack on a head coach puts in jeopardy the entire structure and organization of a team, affecting its morale and the sport at large. The witnesses who testified said that they have never seen an incident before of a player attacking a head coach. Westhead put it tellingly: "I was kind of emotionally very, very concerned, concerned because this is not something that is good for a team. There was such stillness going on that it kind of cut right to the [heart] of the team, you know, player/coach, coach/player."

With respect to a review based on an arbitrary and capricious standard, the New York Court of Appeals has stated, in an administrative agency context, that it chiefly relates to whether a particular action should have been taken or is justified and whether the action is without foundation in fact. *In the Matter of Pell*, 34 N.Y. 2d 222, 231, 313 N.E. 2d 321 (1974). Under this standard, courts consider whether a determination is based on a consideration of the relevant factors and whether a clear error of judgment has been committed.

Arbitrators have followed a similar application of arbitrary and capricious. In *United Paper Workers and Rayonier, Inc.*, 1996 WL 865274, the arbitrator said that, "so long as the discharge bears a reasonable relation to the facts and surrounding circumstances, it must stand." Arbitrator Whitley P. McCoy stated that, "where an employee has violated a rule or engaged in conduct meriting disciplinary action, it is primarily the function of management to decide upon the proper penalty. If management acts in good faith upon a fair investigation and fixes a penalty not inconsistent with that imposed in other like cases, an arbitrator should not disturb it. The only circumstances under which a penalty imposed by management can be rightfully set aside are those where discrimination, unfairness, or capricious and arbitrary action are proved—in other words, where there has been abuse of discretion." *Stockham Pipe Fittings Co.*, 1 L.A. 160, 162 (1945). *See also* Elkouri and Elkouri, *supra* at 910, and Owen Fairweather, *Practice and Procedure in Labor Arbitration*, 245 (2d 1981) (great deference is owed to the employer).

Interestingly, counsel for NBPA and Grievant, in their closing oral arguments, almost said as much by expressing the view that deference should be given to the Commissioner's action under even a just cause standard. Although the arbitrary and capricious standard is applicable to this proceeding, I find that it should be read together with the just cause standard of Article XXXI, Section 14(c), which provides that "in grievances regarding discipline, the issue to be resolved shall be whether there has been just cause for the penalty imposed." (emphasis mine). As counsel for the NBA have noted in their post-hearing brief, some arbitrators have linked arbitrary and capricious with just cause. *See Lockheed Engineering Sciences Co.*, 101 L.A. 1161, 1163 (Neas, 1993); *Pepsi-Cola Bottlers Inc.*, 87 L.A. 83 (Morgan, 1986).

(2) Whether a Just Cause Standard of Review Is Applicable to the Termination of Grievant's Player Contract by the Warriors

The record establishes beyond dispute that the termination of Grievant's contract was issued as additional punishment for the incidents of December 1. The letter sent to Grievant on December 1, entitled "Notice of Suspension," expressed a specific form of discipline (a suspension of a minimum of ten games) and held out the possibility of further discipline, including an increased suspension and possible termination. Subsequently, the Warriors made a decision to terminate Grievant's contract, so as not to reward him, as Baggett testified would have been the case if he were traded. The record is beyond dispute that the termination was done to punish Grievant for what he had done on December 1. Since the disciplinary nature of this action is plain, a just cause standard of review under Section 14(c) of Article XXXI of the CBA is applicable.

As for the standard of just cause, one distinguished arbitrator has stated:

> It is ordinarily the function of an Arbitrator in interpreting a contract provision which requires "sufficient cause" as a condition precedent to discharge not only to determine whether the employee involved is guilty of wrong-doing and, if so, to confirm the employer's right to discipline where its exercise is essential to the objective of efficiency, but also to safeguard the interest of the discharged employee by making reasonably sure that the causes for discharge were just and equitable and such as would appeal to reasonable and fair-minded persons as warranting discharge. To be sure, no standards exist to aid an Arbitrator in finding a conclusive answer to such a question and, therefore, perhaps the best he can do is to decide what reasonable man, mindful of the habits and customs of industrial life and of the standards of justice and fair dealing prevalent in the community, ought to have done under similar circumstances and in that light to decide whether

the conduct of the discharged employee was defensible and the disciplinary penalty just. *Riley Stoker Corp.*, 7 L.A. 764, 767 (Platt and Lavery, 1947).

In a proceeding involving just cause, the burden of proof is with the employer and I have determined to apply a clear and convincing standard regarding material issues of dispute given the nature of the conduct and the discipline involved in this proceeding.

* * *

(5) Whether Actions Taken by the Commissioner and Warriors Are Appropriate

I finally turn to the issue of whether the applicable standards have been satisfied with respect to the discipline imposed by the Commissioner and the Team. [The arbitrator found that the NBA's investigation "was done in good faith and was fair and adequate under the exigencies of the well-publicized situation with which it was then confronted" and that Stern was not required to meet with Sprewell personally, because the relevant sections of the NBA constitution did not require a hearing. Thus, he found "that the NBA complied with the standard of industrial due process." The Warriors' investigation, however, was complicated by the simultaneous league investigation. Reliance on a telephone conversation between league investigators and Sprewell was insufficient prior to contract termination, but became irrelevant because the league effectively pre-empted the club.]

When I consider the two disciplinary actions alongside each other with respect to the same conduct and against the background of just cause, I note the following:

There has never been a case of contract termination in the history of the NBA for a physical assault or a one-year suspension for such conduct or, it appears from the record, in the sports of baseball and football. In the case of the NFL, joint action by a team and the League is prohibited as a matter of contract. Although there is no specific contract provision in the NBA, as I have found, the evidence indicates that there is no history of both the League and a team imposing discipline for the same violent conduct, on or off the court.... This speaks to the issue of fairness, as I see it. The major cases of violence in the NBA that were brought to my attention all involved discipline by the NBA itself and not a team.... In the instant matter, the two disciplines together are unprecedented, as well as the severity of each, with respect to an act of violence. Given the magnitude of the Warriors' earlier discipline of the Grievant on December 1 and the NBA having become the dominant in the investigatory process after that, I am unable to sustain the termination of the Grievant's contract as meeting a standard of just cause.... I also find that the conduct in question was born of anger and passion and did not constitute an act of moral turpitude which is at the core of the Team's action.

* * *

My review of the Commissioner's discipline, however, proved to be exceedingly difficult, since he is entitled to great deference as the spokesperson for the sport of basketball in the National Basketball Association and is accountable for the integrity of the League. That is his duty and it would be wrong for me to substitute my judgment for his in terms of discipline. Such is not the role of a grievance arbitrator. In approaching my responsibility in the instant matter, I considered whether I should apply to the Commissioner's decision a level of review that asked and answered whether the NBA conducted a fair and adequate investigation and rendered a fair and reasonable judgment based on what was before it as a result of that investigation. Applying such a standard, I would sustain the decision of a one-year suspension of the Grievant. On the other hand, all the parties spent nine days in hearings before me, as the Grievance Arbitrator under the CBA, producing 21 witnesses for examination and much documentary evidence. In the end, they asked that I establish the facts and determine whether the penalties were appropriate. Having done so, they are entitled to the judgment of the Grievance Arbitrator as to what has been established by the evidence.

I have already indicated my findings with respect to the established facts. I now add my finding that the conduct of the Grievant on December 1, 1997, which was grievous in nature, was not the result of premeditation and deliberation. I do not find that the Grievant cooled down or cooled off during the 10 to 20 minute time period between the first incident and the second incident on December 1, 1997. I do not consider the time spent by him in the locker room to have been a sufficient and adequate cooling off period under all the circumstances. The record establishes that the anger, if not rage, that erupted in the first incident fed on itself during the period he spent alone in the locker room between the incidents, continuing the fury of the first and connecting the two incidents and making them actually one. . . . The record in this long and protracted proceeding establishes, and I so find, that the Grievant never cooled off or reflected in the broad sense of that term. This finding, of course, does not justify his misconduct but is a factor to be considered in rendering a fair and just determination.

* * *

I note the Commissioner's testimony before me that if he had information indicating that the second incident on December 1 was not premeditated, he would have imposed a lesser penalty. Indeed, with respect to the incidents in question he had before him from his deputy the question of a suspension limited to the 1997/98 season. While the violence inflicted by the Grievant on his Head Coach is to be condemned, the form of the condemnation in terms of discipline must be tempered by principles of fairness, as the Commissioner recognized at the hearings. Confidence in the game of basketball is dependent not only on appropriated punishment for misconduct but also on the fairness of proceedings where that punishment is reviewed. After a great deal of reflection and consideration, I have determined to uphold the discipline imposed by the NBA, but to limit it to the 1997/98 season. In justice and fairness the Grievant should be allowed to start the 1998/99 season with this tragic event behind him instead of having it extend into the next season. In reaching this judgment, I note that a suspension for the 1997/98 season involves the loss of 68 games and $6.4 million. It is many times the aggregate suspensions imposed on other players for acts of physical violence, exceeding the total of all suspensions imposed on all players for physical altercations during the 1995/96 and 1996/97 seasons combined, and all suspensions imposed for acts of altercations during the 1992/93, 1993/94, and 1994/95 seasons combined.

I find that a penalty of 68 games is commensurate with the severity of the misconduct, addresses the wrong done to the Head Coach, the Grievant's Team, and the NBA and conveys a message that violence in the NBA will be dealt with severely, but always with due regard to principles of fairness. I also find that based on other NBA disciplinary actions with respect to violence in the sport, both on and off the court, a greater penalty would be unreasonable and disproportionate to the circumstances involved in this proceeding. As for a penalty of $6.4 million against a history of lesser penalties for misconduct not involving a Coach, I find it justified by virtue of the singularity of the misconduct and the emphasis placed on combating violence by both the NBA and NBPA. A suspension of practically an entire season is one of great severity, to be sure, but appropriate given the fact that physical altercations with a head coach strike at the very core of a structure that provides stability for a team and an organized sport.

Having concluded, I should note that the Grievant, on December 1, 1997, acted out of anger and passion, not a premeditated state, and despite some earlier acts of defiance by him with respect to his coach, he has had an honorable career in the NBA. He has worked hard and played hard, has won All-Star status on a number of occasions; carried the captaincy of his Team by its appointment through December 1, 1997; and won the Team's Most Inspirational Player Award during one of his playing seasons. At the hearings before me, he conducted himself in a calm and restrained manner, even at moments that would have challenged the most even-tempered of individuals. The severity of the discipline, the commentary that has accompanied this matter, and the experience undergone by the Grievant may well equip him in the future years of his life to be an example of a person who can overcome adversity and be a role model. As Commissioner Stern noted at the conclusion of the testimonial portion of the hearings:

"[Grievant] is a gifted athlete who has done well in the NBA. . . . We want Mr. Sprewell in the NBA. We expect him to be in the NBA during the '98/'99 season."

NOTES AND QUESTIONS

1. *Usual Just Cause Standard.* Most collective bargaining agreements state that discipline can be imposed on members of the bargaining unit only for "just cause." Pursuant to this standard, arbitrators determine both whether the employer had cause to impose any discipline and also whether the particular level of discipline imposed was justified, although some agreements expressly negate the latter arbitral authority. Does Arbitrator Feerick in the *Sprewell* case purport to evaluate both the league's as well as the team's discipline under a "just cause" standard, or does he claim, for his review of the league's discipline, to adopt a much more deferential "arbitrary or capricious" standard, borrowed from the review of administrative law decisions? If the latter, does Feerick actually apply a more deferential standard, or does he revert to determining whether Commissioner Stern had just cause to suspend Sprewell for the 1998–1999 season as well as for the remainder of the 1997–1998 season?

2. *Just Cause Factors.* In determining whether an employer had just cause for imposing particular discipline for particular conduct, arbitrators consider a range of factors, including whether the grievant had adequate notice of possible punishment, the grievant's past contributions to the enterprise and past disciplinary record, comparisons with the employer's treatment of other employees who engaged in similar conduct, other arbitral decisions under the same and additional similar collective agreements, whether the grievant had been subjected to multiple punishments for the same conduct, and a range of possible mitigating factors. Which of these considerations did Feerick find relevant in the *Sprewell* case?

3. *Comparative Punishments.* Were you persuaded by Feerick's comparisons with the lesser punishments imposed on other players for "physical altercations" during previous seasons in the 90s? Might the league have had good reason to distinguish those altercations?

4. *Arbitrator's Authority to Weigh Evidence.* Of what relevance was arbitrator Feerick's finding of fact, based on testimony at the hearing, that Sprewell's second attack on the coach was an expression of his original anger, rather than coolly premeditated? Note that the arbitrator cites the testimony of Commissioner Stern that he would have imposed a lesser penalty had he information that the second attack was not premeditated. Was it appropriate for the arbitrator to weigh that testimony heavily?

5. *Judicial Review?* Consider whether the league should be able to have this decision vacated on appeal, and then reconsider this question after reading the last section of this chapter on judicial review.

Recognition that the parties can modify in the next collective bargaining session any precedent established by an arbitration decision may be relevant to how closely courts should review arbitration decisions like that in *Sprewell*. Indeed, in the wake of the *Sprewell* decision, the NBA collective bargaining agreement now contains a clause, Article 6, § 10, that states that the NBA and a team shall not discipline a player for the same conduct, and that a league penalty will preclude or supersede disciplinary action by any team for the same conduct. However, this same section excepts conduct of an "egregious" nature so "lacking in justification" as to warrant a double penalty of both termination of the team's contract and suspension by the league.

Another controversial NBA arbitration decision provides a further example of how arbitration is an extension of the collective bargaining process. In November 2004, near the end of an NBA basketball game at the palace in Auburn Hills, Michigan between the Detroit Pistons and the Indiana Pacers, a typical on-court altercation between players escalated into a brawl between visiting players and Detroit fans in the stands. The melee resulted in suspensions for numerous players. The NBPA grieved the suspensions, but the NBA claimed that the grievance arbitrator had no jurisdiction because the NBA's collective bargaining agreement then provided that the Commissioner's discipline for "on court" conduct was exclusive and could not be appealed. The arbitrator nonetheless ruled that he did have jurisdiction because the incident was in the stands and thus "obviously not on the playing court." Following the proceeding, the NBA and the players union revised the CBA to provide a fuller definition of "on the playing court" and exclusive jurisdiction for the Commissioner to impose fines of up to $50,000 and/or suspensions of up to 12 games for conduct "on the playing court." In exchange, the union obtained for its members the right to appeal to the grievance arbitrator if the discipline exceeds the Commissioner limits, even for conduct on the playing court. The new agreement also provided, however, that in such cases, as well as in cases involving the integrity of the game of basketball, the arbitrator can overturn the Commissioner's discipline only upon finding that the decision was "arbitrary and capricious," not just lacking in "just cause."

The other professional leagues also have detailed and somewhat complicated provisions dealing with the players' rights to obtain arbitral review of discipline. Each league's provisions are special to the league and each differs from those typical in collective bargaining agreements outside sports. All the agreements, like that of the NBA, distinguish discipline for conduct more directly associated with the playing of the game. For instance, MLB's agreement does not provide for arbitration before a neutral for discipline imposed for "conduct on the playing field or in the ballpark." While players cannot appeal such discipline beyond the Commissioner's office, the discipline does not result in any sacrifice of salary because suspensions for on the field conduct are not without pay. Suspensions or other discipline for off the field conduct, including the violation of external law, may result in the loss of salary and may be appealed to an impartial arbitrator under a "just cause" standard. The agreement also states that if the Commissioner determines the league's actions involved "the preservation of the integrity of, or the maintenance of public confidence in, the game of baseball," the Commissioner's final decision "shall have the same effect as a Grievance decision of the Arbitration Panel." This authority was originally intended to cover disciplinary action for gambling, and has not been used more broadly. The agreement further provides that the union has the right to reopen the agreement if the authority is used in ways the union deems "unsatisfactory."

The NFL's collective agreement empowers the Commissioner or his designee, and not a neutral arbitrator, to decide appeals of disciplinary fines or suspensions for conduct on the playing field other than for unnecessary roughness or unsportsmanlike conduct, or "for conduct detrimental to the integrity of, or public confidence in, the game of professional football." NFL Commissioner Roger Goodell, however, has used his unilateral authority on occasion to appoint a hearing officer with authority to act as an arbitrator. For instance, in 2012 Goodell appointed his predecessor as commissioner, Paul Tagliabue, to review the league's discipline of four New Orleans Saints players for participating in a conspiracy organized by Saints' coaches to reward players with "bounty" payments for disabling targeted players, like star quarterback Brett Favre, on other teams. Tagliabue, invoking the authority of an independent arbitrator, vacated all discipline against the players, basically because they were not the initial instigators of the conspiracy and their involvement was not sufficiently distinct from other players not disciplined. (For additional discussion of this "bounty-gate" case, see Chapter 1, Section D, Part 1.)

In 2014, Commissioner Goodell took the further step of obtaining the agreement of the NFLPA before appointing an independent retired federal judge, Barbara Jones, to review his suspension of Baltimore Ravens' running back Ray Rice based on Rice's admitted physical assault of his fiancée. Initially, the league treated the assault as a minor infraction, suspending him only for two games. However, a national furor developed after a celebrity news website released a video showing Rice punching his fiancée in an elevator, knocking her out. Commissioner Goodell subsequently suspended Rice indefinitely and the Ravens terminated his contract.

The NFLPA appealed the Rice suspension, claiming that since the Commissioner had initially imposed a two-game suspension, the subsequent indefinite suspension constituted unfair "double jeopardy." The Commissioner continued to claim publicly that he had not known about the severity of Rice's assault of his fiancée until the tape was made public. Goodell agreed with the NFLPA that in this instance, because he would have to testify as to his knowledge at the time of his initial suspension of Rice, an independent outside person should serve as the reviewing hearing officer. In her opinion after the hearing, Judge Jones, claiming the authority of an arbitrator, detailed the evidence concerning the investigatory meeting between Goodell and Rice, and concluded that Rice had adequately informed Commissioner before the first suspension of the severity of his assault. Judge Jones also found that, at the time the initial suspension was imposed, the NFL had known about the existence of the tape made in the elevator. Jones therefore vacated the Commissioner's indefinite suspension of Rice. Notably, she stated that she did so under a more deferential "arbitrary or capricious" standard, rather than under a "just cause" standard, because Article 46 does not include a "just cause" provision, unlike another article in the NFL collective agreement covering club discipline.

Other controversial uses of Commissioner Goodell's authority under Article 46 are considered in the last section of this chapter on judicial review of arbitration awards.

C. ARBITRATION OF DRUG USAGE DISCIPLINE

The professional sports leagues, like most American employers, treat drug abuse as a significant problem. Discipline for drug abuse, and associated grievance arbitrations, since the emergence of sports unions, initially addressed the use of illegal recreational drugs, like cocaine and marijuana. In the past two decades, however, the focus has expanded to eliminating, or at least controlling, an increased use of drugs, like anabolic steroids or human growth hormones, taken to enhance athletic performance or accelerate the recovery from injury.

Athletes have used performance-enhancing substances on the American sports scene since the nineteenth century. Players ingested anything (including lethal concoctions) that might enhance their stamina and power. In fact, in 1889, future Hall-of-Fame pitcher James "Pud" Galvin took testosterone shots. *See* Roger I. Abrams, *The Dark Side of the Diamond: Gambling, Violence, Drugs and Alcoholism in the National Pastime* 103–09 (Rounder Books, 2007). Amphetamines ("greenies") were ubiquitous in locker rooms and dugouts through much of the twentieth century. Use of performance enhancing drugs, however, seemed to increase significantly with the enhanced financial incentives now offered to professional athletes and the greater sophistication of pharmaceuticals. The general public became hostile to athletes using any drugs to increase stamina and power, in part because most of these drugs could be harmful, and the use by some athletes motivated others, including impressionable youths, to take the same risks. Some of the public hostility toward such drugs also derived from the desire of fans, perhaps especially baseball fans, to compare through statistics the "natural" ability of athletes, including athletes who played in different eras. For these fans, regardless of the rules imposed by leagues, improving performance through pharmaceuticals, rather than through a better diet or conditioning, was "cheating."

Fan hostility toward the drugs resulted in Congressional pressure, and the leagues began negotiating drug polices with the sports unions (*see* Chapter 1, Section D). Today each league prohibits the use of a range of performance-enhancing drugs, imposes a schedule of penalties—including long suspensions—when a prohibited drug's presence is discovered in scheduled or non-scheduled drug tests, and provides procedures, including arbitration, through which players can challenge any penalties. MLB, the NFL, and the NBA all have especially detailed agreements with their unions. Major League Baseball, for instance, has negotiated a 120-page supplementary Joint Drug Agreement (JDA) with the MLBPA that specifies prohibited drugs, considers exemptions for the treatment of certain mental health issues, sets clear severe penalties, provides treatment plans for drug abuse, and sets special arbitration provisions. The JDA also includes forty-six pages covering the protocols for urine and blood tests. The NFL now covers these topics in two lengthy supplementary agreements with the NFLPA, one on "Substances of Abuse" and the other on "Anabolic Steroids and Related Substances," while the NBA's collective agreement covers most of the topics in 38 pages of its collective bargaining agreement.

MLB's JDA, like the NFL and NBA agreements, requires MLB to prove only a player's use of a prohibited drug; it does not require the league to prove the player's intent or even negligence. The JDA, like the NFL agreements and the NBA collective agreement, at least formally affords players an affirmative defense of unintentional and non-negligent use. All the agreements, however, state that the player cannot demonstrate a defense by merely denying intentional use. The NFL agreements further state that a player "cannot satisfy his burden" merely by demonstrating "that he was given the substance by a Player, doctor or trainer" or "that he took a mislabeled or contaminated product."

Most league penalties for violation of drug prohibitions have been based on positive drug test results, so the only possible issues in challenges would be whether adequate testing protocols were observed and whether the player could carry the very difficult burden of proving a defense of unintentional and non-negligent use. Consider the following decision, however.

Major League Baseball Players Association and Office of the Commissioner of Baseball

132 Lab. Arb. Rep. (BNA) 1397 (2014)

Fredric Horowitz, Arbitrator

[Alex Rodriguez, a 38-year-old infielder with the New York Yankees, had not previously been suspended by MLB for a violation of its drug agreement with the Players Association. Anthony Bosch, who operated a clinic named Biogenesis in Miami, testified by the Arbitrator that he provided Rodriquez with performance-enhancing substances (PES) over a multi-year period, including lozenges containing testosterone, testosterone creams, injections of human growth hormone and other substances all banned under the drug agreement. Bosch designed a detailed protocol for Rodriguez indicating the days and times when he should use the banned substances.

Throughout the baseball season, Rodriguez and Bosch communicated with each other directly by telephone, text messages, and BlackBerry messages related to the doses and timing of administration of the protocol, as well as the payments for Bosch's services. After stories about Rodriguez's use of banned substances appeared in the Miami New Times, MLB investigated Rodriguez using a variety of methods to obtain information. On August 5, 2013, Commissioner Bud Selig issued Rodriguez a notice imposing a substantial suspension, and the MLBPA grieved on his behalf.]

MLB contends that Rodriguez was disciplined for just cause. MLB maintains Rodriguez committed multiple violations of the JDA [Joint Drug Agreement] over the course of three seasons by the continuous use and possession of a variety of PES [performance-enhancing substances]. MLB asserts the multiple efforts by Rodriguez to obstruct MLB's investigation of his violations of the JDA violated the Basic Agreement. MLB argues adverse inferences be drawn from Rodriguez's failure to testify under oath in this proceeding or present other witnesses to refute the evidence of his misconduct. MLB contends the penalty in this case is appropriate and justified in light of the scope and gravity of the misconduct by Rodriguez . . .

Rodriguez contends MLB has failed to meet its burden of proving the alleged misconduct by clear and convincing evidence. Rodriguez argues MLB did not show he possessed and used PES and that the testimony by Bosch, his notebooks, and the BBMs [BlackBerry messages] are inherently unreliable, must be stricken, and can be afforded no weight. Rodriguez contends that science establishes he did not use PES. Rodriguez also asserts MLB failed to establish he obstructed MLB's investigation of Biogenesis and Bosch. Rodriguez further maintains that all of the evidence presented by MLB is irrevocably tainted by investigatory misconduct and coercion of witnesses, including Bosch.

OPINION OF THE PANEL CHAIRMAN

This is an appeal by Alexander Rodriguez of a 211-game suspension which covered the remainder of the 2013 season and the 2014 season and was issued by MLB for alleged violations of the Basic Agreement [BA] and Joint Drug Agreement [JDA]. The Basic Agreement and JDA contain a grievance procedure which allows a Player who chooses to contest the validity of a suspension to have the matter decided by a neutral arbitrator. These collectively bargained agreements require MLB to have just cause to impose a suspension on any Player. This means that MLB carries the burden of establishing just cause in arbitration by demonstrating that some or all of the alleged offenses occurred, and, if so, that its imposed penalty is appropriate. The sole question presented by the parties for decision by this Panel is whether MLB had just cause to suspend Rodriguez for the remainder of the 2013 season and the 2014 season (211 games)....

MLB contends Rodriguez repeatedly violated the JDA over a three-year period by use and possession of multiple banned substances. MLB asserts Rodriguez then aggravated his offenses by obstructing MLB's investigation in violation of the BA. MLB defends the 211-game suspension as appropriate given the nature, extent, and severity of his offenses. In defense of these allegations, Rodriguez through counsel flatly denies any use or possession of PES during the period in question. Rodriguez and the MLBPA assert no credible evidence has been presented by MLB which establishes any violation of the BA or JDA. Alternately, Rodriguez and the MLBPA argue MLB is prevented from imposing any penalty because of egregious misconduct during the course of its investigation. The MLBPA and Rodriguez further contend the 211-game penalty cannot be justified when compared to suspensions received by other Players for drug or PES violations.

A review of all the evidence and argument presented by all parties in this proceeding clearly and convincingly establishes Rodriguez committed multiple violations of the JDA and BA warranting a substantial disciplinary penalty. It follows that the suspension imposed by MLB, as reduced by this Panel, will be sustained.

JDA Violations

The evidence confirms that Rodriguez used and/or possessed three discrete PES banned by Section 2.B. of the JDA during the three-year period in question: testosterone, IGF-1, and hGH. Direct evidence of those violations was supplied by the testimony of Anthony Bosch and corroborated with excerpts from Bosch's personal composition notebooks, BBMs exchanged between Bosch and Rodriguez, and reasonable inferences drawn from the entire record of evidence.

In this case, the testimony under oath from Bosch about JDA violations by Rodriguez was direct, credible, and squarely corroborated by excerpts from several of the hundreds of pages of his personal composition notebooks that were stolen in late December 2012 or early January 2013. The original notebooks have not been located or produced. Rodriguez asserts the copies in evidence are unreliable because the originals were stolen, the copies introduced were not in order, there is no way to know if the copies are complete, the time and date of many entries are unclear, and the notebooks were never kept in a secure location while in Bosch's possession. Despite these concerns, Bosch verified the entries relied upon herein were in fact his notes made contemporaneously with the events he described. No direct evidence was presented to demonstrate the excerpts he identified from the copies of his notebooks that implicated Rodriguez had been forged or fabricated. Bosch had many clients to whom he prescribed many substances, banned or otherwise. As a practical matter, he needed to keep track of clients, protocols, and payments. Bosch elected to use those composition notebooks to record this information by hand for his own use and reference. The protocols, visits, and cash payments pertaining to Rodriguez he wrote in the excerpts he identified in this proceeding confirm and corroborate the JDA violations he has described.

Similar support for his testimony is found in the evidence of BBMs [BlackBerry messages exchanged] between Rodriguez and Bosch. Those messages corroborate the JDA violations described by Bosch as well as illustrate the course and nature of their dealings. The BBMs by and to Rodriguez address doses, timing, and administration of PES to Rodriguez, as well as payment for drugs and services. The BBMs also reflect the deliberate efforts taken by Bosch and Rodriguez to conceal their activities and to avoid a positive MLB drug test. . . . Rodriguez complains the case as presented by MLB lacks specificity concerning the precise dates and times, dosages, and frequency of the alleged violations. Rodriguez decries the absence of documentation concerning the sources of PES obtained by Bosch or introduction of samples which confirm the substances Bosch claimed he used were indeed ones banned by the JDA. Yet these and other deficiencies in MLB's case cited by Rodriguez do not eviscerate credible testimony from Bosch about his activities in supplying and administering PES to Rodriguez over a three-year period or the BBMs and composition notebook pages that confirm the violations occurred. The only reasonable inference to be drawn from the weight of the evidence is that Rodriguez violated the JDA as alleged.

The claim by Rodriguez that science exonerates him in this case is not supported by any evidence in this record. It is recognized Rodriguez passed eleven drug tests administered by MLB from 2010 through 2012. The assertion that Rodriguez would have failed those tests had he consumed those PES as alleged is not persuasive. As advanced as MLB's program has become, no drug testing program will catch every Player. In this case, the blood testing required to detect hGH or IGF-1 had not yet been implemented in the JDA and therefore was not administered during the 2010, 2011, and 2012 seasons. With respect to testosterone, the record establishes that during the period in question it was possible for an individual to pass a drug test despite having recently used the substance, depending on variables such as the route of administration (*i.e.*, transdermal, sublingual, or intramuscular), dosage, concentration, the baseline value of the individual's natural testosterone to epitestosterone ratio ("T/E"), and how soon after use the individual's urine sample is collected. Bosch testified that he considered several of these variables when developing Rodriguez's protocols, and the BBM communications between Bosch and Rodriguez show multiple exchanges where Bosch instructed Rodriguez to use testosterone at such times, and in such forms and doses, as would prevent Rodriguez from testing positive. For these reasons, the absence of a positive test during the three years in question, in and of itself, does not and cannot overcome the unrebutted direct evidence in this record of possession and use. In any event, a positive drug test is not required to establish a violation of the JDA for use or possession of a PES.

Obstruction

MLB charges Rodriguez with violating Article XII(B) of the BA by attempting to cover-up his JDA violations through a course of conduct since January 2013 intended to obstruct and frustrate MLB's investigation of Biogenesis and Bosch. MLB accuses Rodriguez and his representatives of purchasing and then destroying the original Bosch composition notebooks, as well as deactivating and destroying his own BlackBerry to prevent MLB from learning their contents. . . . MLB alleges that Rodriguez's press release on January 29, 2013, falsely denying any relationship with Bosch, and Rodriguez's role in facilitating Bosch's own false public denial later that day, which included a commitment by Rodriguez to pay Bosch $25,000 for attorneys fees, also violated the BA. MLB further asserts that Rodriguez's attempt on May 31, 2013, to get Bosch to sign a false affidavit and the offer to pay Bosch to leave the country rather than testify in this proceeding constitute additional examples of improper conduct in violation of the BA meriting a severe disciplinary response. For his part, Rodriguez denies through counsel having possessed or destroyed Bosch's original composition notebooks, any improper attempts to influence the testimony of Medina or Bosch, or that the evidence supports any of these charges.

Deliberate efforts to obstruct an MLB investigation under the JDA, or to cover-up misconduct by a Player who is subject to such an investigation, if established, may subject a Player to additional disciplinary sanctions under Article XII(B) of the Basic Agreement. In this case, the evidence considered in its entirety supports a minimum of two such violations. Rodriguez, having himself publicly denied being treated or advised by

Bosch—a denial which he knew to be false—played an active role in inducing Bosch to issue his own public denial on January 29, 2013, which Rodriguez also knew to be false. Rodriguez also attempted to induce Bosch to sign a sworn statement on May 31, 2013, attesting that Bosch never supplied Rodriguez with PES and had no personal knowledge that Rodriguez had ever used them, statements that Rodriguez also knew to be false. These actions, viewed in the context of the record as a whole, were clearly designed to cover up Rodriguez's relationship with Bosch and the fact that Rodriguez had received PES from Bosch, to inhibit MLB's efforts to investigate Rodriguez's use and possession of PES, and to avoid punishment under the JDA. The remaining allegations of obstruction, while troubling, need not be addressed because they would not affect the ultimate determination regarding the appropriate penalty in this matter.

* * *

Penalty

[The Arbitrator reduces the suspension to the entire 2014 season and postseason based on prior baseball arbitration awards.]

Conclusion

Based on the entire record from the arbitration, MLB has demonstrated with clear and convincing evidence there is just cause to suspend Rodriguez for the 2014 season and 2014 postseason for having violated the JDA by the use and/or possession of testosterone, IGF-1, and hGH over the course of three years, and for the two attempts to obstruct MLB's investigation described above, which violated Article Xll(B) of the Basic Agreement. While this length of suspension may be unprecedented for a MLB Player, so is the misconduct he committed. The suspension imposed by MLB as modified herein is hereby sustained.

NOTES AND QUESTIONS

1. *A Rare Public Arbitration.* The Alex Rodriguez case may have been the most public labor arbitration proceeding ever conducted. Even though the proceeding itself was private and participants for the most part maintained the pledge of confidentiality that is required by the Joint Drug Agreement, attorneys for the grievant made statements to the media before the proceeding and Rodriquez appeared on sports talk radio after he walked out of the hearing, proclaimed his total innocence of the charges against him and vowed to appeal.

2. *Burden of Proof.* Arbitrators normally require employers to carry the burden of proving that an employee engaged in conduct warranting an imposed discipline. On whom did the arbitrator place the burden of proof in this case? Under what standard of proof? Given Rodriguez's passage of all drug tests, did the evidence against him depend totally on the credibility of Bosch?

3. *Player's Lawyer's Tactics.* Note that Rodriguez, unlike almost all employees in disciplinary arbitrations, declined to testify. The absence of his testimony made it easier for the arbitrator to credit the testimony of Bosch, despite Bosch's involvement in criminal activity and his public misrepresentation of himself as a medical doctor. Why did Rodriguez's lawyer not have him testify? Rodriguez subsequently admitted use, apologized to Yankee fans, returned to play in 2015, reached several significant milestones, including 3000 hits and 2000 RBIs, and then continued to work for the Yankees after his retirement. Do you think Rodriguez was well served by his aggressive lawyers and other advisors before and during the arbitration?

4. *MLB Business Strategy.* Major League Baseball expended significant resources investigating the Biogenesis operation and then pressuring Bosch to cooperate in developing cases against not only Rodriguez, but many other ballplayers, thirteen of whom also received suspensions for their involvement with Biogenesis. Was it a wise business decision for the MLB to work to taint its own product? If players evade detection by a strong drug testing program like that of MLB and do not openly use drugs, how is MLB harmed by non-public, covert use?

5. *Should All Performing Enhancing Drugs Be Prohibited?* Assume that a particular performance enhancing drug has been approved by the Food and Drug Administration as both safe and effective. Is there any good reason why athletes' ingestion of that drug should be banned by a sports league or other regulatory authority? Same answer for safe and effective drugs that accelerate recovery time from injuries, or that reduce fatigue?

D. ARBITRATION AS AN EXCLUSIVE REMEDY; § 301 PREEMPTION

The Court's decision in *Lincoln Mills, see* page 121 *supra,* to read § 301 of the LMRA to confer federal substantive law control over collective bargaining agreements ensured that the interpretation of such agreements would not vary between states. Although state courts have concurrent jurisdiction over suits to enforce collective agreements, they must apply the federal law fashioned by the Supreme Court. Not surprisingly, the Court also has held that the states cannot circumvent the authority of federal § 301 law by using an interpretation of a collective agreement as a basis for the imposition of some state law. *See, e.g., Allis-Chalmers Corp. v. Lueck,* 471 U.S. 202, 211–12 (1985) (action on Wisconsin tort claim that company failed to implement collectively bargained disability insurance in good faith must be brought under collective agreement through grievance arbitration system). The Court in *Lueck* stressed that a further reason "to pre-empt this kind of derivative tort claim is that only that result preserves the central role of arbitration." This § 301 "preemption" of state law has been asserted in many challenges to state statutes as well as to state common law torts, including some laws relevant to drug testing and discipline.

Consider the following important challenge to the NFL drug testing and discipline system.

WILLIAMS V. NATIONAL FOOTBALL LEAGUE
582 F.3d 863 (8th Cir. 2009)

SHEPHERD, J.

[The NFL and the NFLPA's 2006 collective bargaining agreement (CBA) incorporated the Policy on Anabolic Steroids and Related Substances (Policy). The Policy banned NFL players from using a number of prohibited substances, including " 'blocking' or 'masking' agents" such as "diuretics or water pills, which have been used in the past by some players to reach an assigned weight." It adopted a rule of strict liability under which "[p]layers are responsible for what is in their bodies," and explained that "a positive test result will not be excused because a player was unaware he was taking a Prohibited Substance." In 2006, several NFL players tested positive for bumetanide, a prescription diuretic and masking agent that is banned under the Policy. The NFL determined that StarCaps, a dietary supplement, contained bumetanide, although the product's label did not disclose it as an ingredient. It prohibited players from endorsing any products manufactured by Balanced Health Products, the maker of StarCaps, but did not ban StarCaps as a Prohibited Substance under the Policy or inform the players of its findings, although it knew the product contained bumetanide.

In July and August 2008, players in the NFL submitted to random testing for steroids and other substances in accordance with the Policy. Five players—Kevin Williams and Pat Williams of the Minnesota Vikings, and Charles Grant, Deuce McAllister, and Will Smith of the New Orleans Saints—tested positive for bumetanide after using StarCaps. In late September and early October 2008, all of the players were advised by letter that their positive results were a violation of the Policy, and they were suspended without pay for four games. All five players appealed their suspensions, and their appeals were heard by Jeffrey Pash, Vice President and General Counsel of the NFL, who was designated by the commissioner as the hearing officer under the Policy. Pash upheld the suspensions under the Policy's rule of strict liability.

The players filed suit in Minnesota state court. The NFL removed the action to federal court. The players sought to have Pash's decisions vacated. In addition, they raised a violation of Minnesota's Drug and Alcohol Testing in the Workplace Act (DATWA), Minnesota's Consumable Products Act (CPA) and a variety of common law tort claims. The district court granted a preliminary injunction, which allowed the players to continue playing football while their suit proceeded. The trial court denied the players' motion for summary judgment, concluding that their common law claims were preempted by section 301 of the federal Labor Management Relations Act (LMRA), the Pash arbitration awards did not fail to draw their essence from the CBA, Mr. Pash was not a biased arbitrator, and he acted within the scope of his discretion under the Policy. The court also ruled that the NFL did not have a duty to warn the players about StarCaps, even though it knew it contained a banned substance. However, the district court concluded that the players' claims under the Minnesota statutes were not preempted by section 301 of the Labor Management Relations Act. Both parties appealed portions of the district court's order.] We affirm in all respects. . .

II.

We review the preemption issues de novo.

A.

We first consider the [state law] DATWA claim. The NFL asserts that the DATWA claim is preempted because: (1) the claim turns on analysis of the Policy in order to determine whether it "meets or exceeds" DATWA's requirements, (2) the claim requires interpretation of the Policy in order to determine whether the NFL qualifies as an employer under DATWA such that the statute's protections extend to the Players, and (3) uniform interpretation of the CBA/Policy is necessary to preserve the integrity of the NFL's business as a national organization.

We begin our analysis by reviewing the section 301 preemption doctrine. Section 301 applies to "[s]uits for violation of contracts between an employer and a labor organization," or, in other words, suits for breaches of CBAs. The Supreme Court has held that federal law exclusively governs suits for breach of a CBA, and that "the pre-emptive force of [section] 301 extends beyond state-law contract actions." Section 301 preempts state-law claims that are "substantially dependent upon analysis" of a CBA, because "the application of state law. . . might lead to inconsistent results since there could be as many state-law principles as there are States." Rather, "federal labor-law principles-necessarily uniform throughout the nation-must be employed to resolve the dispute." However, the Court has established that section 301 does not preempt state law claims merely because the parties involved are subject to a CBA and the events underlying the claim occurred on the job.

In applying the section 301 preemption doctrine, we begin with "the claim itself,", and apply a two-step approach in order to determine if the claim is sufficiently "independent" to survive section 301 preemption. First, a "state-law claim is preempted if it is 'based on' [a]. . . provision of the CBA[,]" meaning that "[t]he CBA provision at issue" actually sets forth the right upon which the claim is based. Second, section 301 preemption applies where a state-law claim "is 'dependent upon an analysis' of the relevant CBA," meaning that the plaintiff's state-law claim requires interpretation of a provision of the CBA.

DATWA governs drug and alcohol testing in the Minnesota workplace by imposing "minimum standards and requirements for employee protection" with regard to an employer's drug and alcohol testing policy. DATWA lists minimum informational requirements for the contents of drug policies. DATWA sets forth the criteria that a testing laboratory must meet in order for an employer to use its services.

DATWA also requires that an employer provide an employee, who tests positive for drug use, with "written notice of the right to explain the positive test [,]" an opportunity "to explain that result," and the ability to "request a confirmatory retest of the original sample at the employee's or job applicant's own expense . . ." DATWA precludes an employer from "discharg[ing][or] disciplin[ing] . . . an employee on the basis of a positive result . . . that has not been verified by a confirmatory test." Specifically, with respect to first-time offenders, an employer cannot discharge such an employee unless the employee is first given the opportunity to participate in treatment and refuses to participate or fails to successfully complete the program.

DATWA expressly addresses CBAs. Subdivision two of section 181.955 mandates that DATWA applies to all CBAs in effect after passage of the law in 1987. However, subdivision one of section 181.955 provides that DATWA "shall not be construed to limit the parties to a collective bargaining agreement from bargaining and agreeing with respect to a drug and alcohol testing policy that meets or exceeds, and does not otherwise conflict with, the minimum standards and requirements for employee protection. . . ."

We note that it is unclear which specific violations of DATWA that the Players are alleging, other than the failure to use certified laboratories. The amended complaint does not flesh out the claim but generally states that the "[d]efendants have violated the Players' substantive and procedural rights under the Minnesota Drug and Alcohol Testing in the Workplace Act." The district court, in discussing the DATWA claim, noted that "[a]mong other things, DATWA provides that an employee may not be disciplined on the basis of an initial positive test and requires the employer to allow the employee the right to explain a positive test[,]" and that "[t]he NFL concedes that its steroid testing procedures do not comply with the letter of Minnesota law, but argues that the differences are negligible and do not require the Court to invalidate the Williamses' positive tests for bumetanide."

First, the NFL contends that, because the Players were tested pursuant to a collectively bargained-for drug policy, DATWA liability hinges on whether the Policy affords protections that are equivalent to or greater than DATWA's mandatory protections. The NFL asserts that DATWA creates two paths to compliance such that an employer may conduct its drug testing either: (1) in compliance with DATWA or (2) pursuant to a CBA providing employees with equivalent or greater protections than DATWA. The NFL argues that this will necessarily require a court to construe the terms of the Policy in order to determine whether its protections for players "meets or exceeds" DATWA's protections such that any DATWA claim alleged by the Players is preempted by section 301. Thus, the NFL is essentially arguing that an employee has no DATWA claim if he or she is a party to a CBA that is at least as protective of the employee as DATWA. We disagree.

DATWA does not state that an employee who is a party to such a CBA cannot bring a claim under DATWA. Rather, where there is a CBA that is at least as protective of employees as DATWA, the number of possible claims an employee has against his or her employer will be affected. Where the employer complies with DATWA but not with its CBA that provides greater protection, the employee could only have a claim for breach of contract. Where the employer does not comply either with DATWA or its CBA that provides equivalent or greater protection than DATWA, the employee could potentially have two claims, a claim for breach of contract and a DATWA claim.

Here, a court would have no need to consult the Policy in order to resolve the Players' DATWA claim. Rather, it would compare the facts and the procedure that the NFL actually followed with respect to its drug testing of the Players with DATWA's requirements for determining if the Players are entitled to prevail. Such a claim is not preempted.

* * *

Second, the NFL contends that, because DATWA provides employees with a cause of action against their employers, interpretation of the CBA/Policy is required in order to determine if the NFL qualifies as an employer under DATWA. Section 301 preempts a state law claim if its "resolution . . . *depends upon the meaning* of a collective-bargaining agreement." "[T]he Supreme Court has distinguished those which require interpretation or construction of the CBA from those which only require reference to it." "An otherwise independent claim will not be preempted if the CBA need only be consulted during its adjudication." In sum, section 301 does not preempt every employment dispute, and it does not preempt all other disputes concerning CBA provisions. "Rather, the crucial inquiry is whether 'resolution of a state-law claim depends upon the meaning of a [CBA].'"

The NFL does not point to a specific provision of either the CBA or the Policy which must be interpreted. . . . Finally, the NFL argues that denying preemption and subjecting the Policy to divergent state regulations would render the uniform enforcement of its drug testing policy, on which it relies as a national organization for the integrity of its business, nearly impossible. The Ninth Circuit, sitting en banc, has rejected a similar argument. *See Cramer v. Consolidated Freightways, Inc.*, 255 F.3d 683, 695 n.9 (9th Cir. 2001) (en banc). In *Cramer,* the employer, a large trucking company, "argue[d] that the terms of CBAs affecting employees in multiple states should supersede inconsistent state laws." The Ninth Circuit observed, "This contention overreaches, however, because the LMRA certainly did not give employers and unions the power to displace any state regulatory law they found inconvenient." We think this is the proper result. . . in light of the Supreme Court's observation that:

> [T]here [is not] any suggestion that Congress, in adopting § 301, wished to give the substantive provisions of private agreements the force of federal law, ousting any inconsistent state regulation. Such a rule of law would delegate to unions and unionized employers the power to exempt themselves from whatever state labor standards they disfavored. *Clearly, § 301 does not grant the parties to a [CBA] the ability to contract for what is illegal under state law.* In extending the pre-emptive effect of § 301 beyond suits for breach of contract, it would be inconsistent with congressional intent under that section to preempt state rules that proscribe conduct, or establish rights and obligations, independent of a labor contract.

[*Allis-Chalmers Corp. v. Lueck,*] 471 U.S. 202, 211–12 (1985) (footnote omitted) (emphasis added). Therefore, the NFL's national uniformity argument fails.

In sum, the Players' DATWA claim is predicated on Minnesota law, not the CBA or the Policy, and the claim is not dependent upon an interpretation of the CBA or the Policy. Thus, the Players' DATWA claim is not preempted by section 301.

[The court similarly concludes that the Players' claim under the Minnesota Consumable Products Act is not preempted, but that the Players' common law claims for breach of fiduciary duty, aiding and abetting a breach of fiduciary duty, violations of public policy, fraud, constructive fraud, negligent misrepresentation, negligence, gross negligence, intentional infliction of emotional distress, and vicarious liability are preempted by section 301.]

[Finally, the Court dismisses objection to Pash's awards.] Thus, it is clear that the arbitrator did not "ignore" the provisions of either the 2006 or 2008 Policies when he issued the awards . . . [The NFL was under no clear public policy obligation to inform the Players that StarCaps contained bumetanide. The Union waived any objection to Mr. Pash serving as the arbitrator and his action did not demonstrate "evident partiality."]

Therefore, we decline to vacate the awards on this basis. In sum, we reject each of the Union's arguments for vacating the awards. Accordingly, we affirm the district court's order confirming the awards... For the foregoing reasons, we affirm the judgment of the district court in all respects.

NOTES AND QUESTIONS

1. *Why No § 301 Preemption?* Do you understand why the court in *Williams* held that the plaintiffs' claims under Minnesota's DATWA statute were not preempted by § 301 federal law? Were the players' DATWA claims in any way dependent upon the players' coverage by a collective bargaining agreement? Did adjudication of the DATWA claims in any way require consideration of the NFL's collective bargaining agreement, even as a possible affirmative defense? If not, what would preemption preserve for federal law or for an arbitrator assigned responsibility for interpretation of the agreement? *See generally* Michael C. Harper, *Limiting Section 301 Preemption: Three Cheers for the Trilogy, Only One for Lingle and Lueck*, 66 Chicago-Kent Law Review 685 (1990).

2. *Complicating Collective Bargaining?* Even if the decision correctly applies § 301 preemption law, does allowing individual states to impose regulations like those in DATWA on employers subject to multistate collective bargaining agreements, like those in professional sports, not at least complicate collective bargaining? Does the NFL now have to be careful to fashion a drug testing and disciplinary policy that complies with the law of all other states in which it offers football? Does this mean that a uniform national drug testing regime is impossible, or does state law like DATWA impose only minimum procedures that can be exceeded in private contracts?

3. *A Special Rule for Sports Leagues?* The Court has held that federal labor law does not preclude states from requiring employers within their jurisdiction to offer the same minimum benefits to employees covered by collective agreements as those the employers are required to offer to non-unionized employees. *See, e.g., Metropolitan Life Insurance Co. v. Massachusetts*, 471 U.S. 724 (1985) (allowing Massachusetts to mandate mental health coverage in general health insurance policies, including those negotiated in collective agreements). Indeed, the Court has held that federal labor law prevents a state from discriminating against employees covered by collective agreements by exempting these employees from protections mandated for non-union employees. *See, e.g., Lividas v. Bradshaw*, 512 U.S. 107 (1994) (California's penalties for non-payment of wages must be available to employees covered by collective agreements). Could lobbyists for the NFL and the other professional leagues nonetheless make a strong argument to Congress for preemptive federal regulation of drug testing and discipline in professional sports?

4. *Resolution of the* Williams *Case.* The state law challenge to the National Football League ultimately was unsuccessful in the Minnesota courts because bumetanide was not included in DATWA's list of covered drugs. *See Williams v. National Football League*, 794 N.W.2d 391 (Minn. App. 2011).

E. SALARY ARBITRATION

When most sports fans think of arbitration, they imagine not *grievance*, but *salary*, arbitration. Salary arbitration, as practiced in MLB and the NHL, is distinct because it does not purport to interpret or enforce contract rights already established by the collective bargaining agreement. It instead establishes a key term in the individual player's contract, how much the player will be paid the coming season (or in hockey possibly the next two seasons), based on criteria set forth in the collective bargaining agreement. Salary arbitration, similar to grievance arbitration, involves private presentations of the contending positions of the club and the player before a neutral arbitrator, or in baseball a panel of three arbitrators. Under baseball's procedure the player's case in salary arbitration may be presented by his personal agent, although the players association also has someone present to assist the player's agent and to make sure the interests of the entire bargaining unit are protected.

Salary arbitration first emerged in hockey in the early 1970s. By contrast with football or basketball, hockey resembled baseball (at least prior to the advent of free agency) in its assumption that the player contract was perpetually renewable. That posed the question of how to fix the salary figure in each year's unilaterally renewed contract. Traditionally, that prerogative had been reserved to the owners. With the emergence of independent players associations in the late 1960s, the perceived unfairness and anti-competitiveness of this practice led to the utilization of salary arbitration—in hockey in 1970 and in baseball in 1973. The hockey and baseball systems of salary arbitration also eliminated holdouts by eligible employees. The adoption of negotiated systems of free agency in both sports did not result in the elimination of salary arbitration in either, as both systems continued to include salary arbitration for some players.

The procedures operate quite differently in the two sports. Hockey utilizes a more conventional arbitration model in which hearings are conducted after briefing before a single arbitrator during the summer in Toronto. The arbitrator issues a written decision that includes a statement of the reasons for the decision within forty-eight hours of the close of the proceedings. The arbitrator is allowed to write a contract for whatever salary and other clauses the arbitrator deems appropriate. After the arbitrator issues the award, however, a club can "walk away" from an award. Article 12 of the 2012–2022 collective bargaining agreement provides:

If a Club has elected to arbitrate a one-year SPC, and the award issued is for $3,500,000 or more per annum, then the Club may, within forty-eight (48) hours after the award of the Salary Arbitrator is issued . . . notify the Player or his Certified Agent, if any, the NHLPA and the NHL in writing . . . that it does not intend to tender to the Player [a contract] based on the award as determined by the Salary Arbitrator. Upon receipt of that notice, the Player shall automatically be deemed to be an Unrestricted Free Agent. . . [A] Club may exercise the walk-away rights . . . not more than one (1) time in a League Year in which the Club has only one (1) salary arbitration award, one (1) time in a League Year in which the Club has two (2) salary arbitration awards, two (2) times in any League Year in which the Club has three (3) salary arbitration awards, two (2) times in any League Year in which the Club has four (4) salary arbitration awards, three (3) times in any League Year in which the Club has five (5) salary arbitration awards and so on.

A hockey player's eligibility for salary arbitration depends upon two variables: his age when he first signed a standard player contract and his years of experience in the League. For example, a player who signed at age 21 becomes eligible after three years of experience, but a player who signed at a younger age is eligible only after four years of experience.

In baseball, each salary arbitration is conducted before a three-person panel of arbitrators during a three-week period in February, and each panel simply gives the final verdict without any supporting decision within 24 hours of the end of the hearing. In contrast to hockey arbitrators, baseball arbitrators cannot strike a compromise or draft any contract that they deem appropriate; the arbitrators can only select one of the two figures proposed—the club's offer or the player's demand.

Baseball's "last best offer" system of arbitration is designed to encourage settlement agreements without a hearing by increasing the risk to both sides of non-settlement. The design generally has been successful. Typically 80–90 percent of all cases submitted to arbitration have been resolved privately without the intervention of the panel of three neutrals. In fact, in 2013, although dozens of players were eligible for salary arbitration, all cases were settled and no hearings were held. In 2018, however, perhaps because of rancor generated by slower signings of free agents, twenty-two cases were submitted to a hearing, with the players prevailing in twelve. This was the most since 1990, when players prevailed in fourteen out of twenty-four cases.

There are many advantages to settling a dispute short of arbitration. First, the arbitration hearing itself imposes a cost on the parties. It tends to strain the relationship between the player and his club. The result in salary arbitration is a simple one-year contract. If the parties settle instead of litigating, they can agree to a multi-year deal and be creative in designing a compensation package, including bonuses, for example, or a no-trade clause. Finally, a settlement can build the parties' relationship rather than rupture it. Both parties win to some degree. In salary arbitration, there is always one winner and one loser.

The final-offer baseball salary arbitration process has evolved since the mid-1970s, and salaries awarded have increased considerably. Even players who lose in arbitration usually leave as multi-millionaires. Many players eligible to file for salary arbitration threaten to use the process to leverage higher pay levels. To avoid salary arbitration, some clubs have offered their junior star performers multi-year contracts at premium rates. If the clubs and their players cannot settle their salary differences through negotiations, baseball's salary arbitration provides a quick, informal, and, most importantly, final resolution of the salary dispute. There are no appeals from arbitrators' decisions, and the ballplayers report to spring training under signed one-year contracts.

Not all baseball players are eligible for salary arbitration. The current collective agreement provides that all players with at least three years, but fewer than six years, of major league service are eligible for salary arbitration. A player with at least two years, but less than three years, of major league service is eligible for salary arbitration if "he has accumulated at least 86 days of service during the immediately prior season" and "he ranks in the top twenty-two percent" of the players in the two-year service group in terms of major league service. The eligibility of these "super-two's," as the parties call them, is obviously the result of a compromise reached during collective bargaining negotiations between owners and the players association.

Because baseball salary arbitration never results in supporting opinions, it is not possible to examine the arbitrators' reasoning. The opinion of hockey arbitrators, by contrast, can be lengthy. Reading these opinions offers a revealing look at what player agents and team executives have to do by way of salary comparisons and appraisals, not just for purposes of arbitration, but also for negotiation. The following decision was issued by Richard Bloch, an experienced Washington-based sports neutral.

NEW JERSEY DEVILS AND SCOTT GOMEZ
NHL-NHLPA Arb. (2006)

Before RICHARD I. BLOCH, ESQ.

Facts

Scott Gomez is a 26 year old centerman for the New Jersey Devils. He has played six seasons in the NHL, all with the New Jersey club. At the end of his rookie season, 1999–00, the Player won the Calder Memorial Trophy for the outstanding rookie, was selected to the NHL all rookie team and played in the NHL All-Star game. The Player was also a member of the 2006 US Olympic Hockey Team. Gomez became a restricted Group II Free Agent with his prior contract ended on July 1, 2006. At that time, he requested arbitration for the purpose of determining his 2006–07 compensation. In accordance with the CBA, this arbitration award is to be for one year. The Club has offered Gomez $3.5 million for the 2006–07 season. The Player seeks $6.5 million.

In August of 2004, Mr. Gomez and the Club arbitrated the Player's compensation for the 2004–05 season. In his decision, Arbitrator Michel Picher echoed the Club's assessment of Mr. Gomez as a "gifted playmaker," but one whose goal production was, at the time, "relatively modest":

> . . . He has never again achieved the high of 19 goals scored in his rookie year and he has averaged 14 goals per season while playing on a highly successful Club and seeing fairly extensive powerplay action.

The arbitrator concluded Scott Gomez is "extremely good at what he does well, which is to make offensive plays and, consequently, to register a high number of assists.

In certain respects, the essence of Mr. Gomez's skill set has not changed. He remains primarily an offensive forward who cannot reasonably be described as a two-way player. The statistics, which amply bear out that assessment, need not be repeated here; the premise is not in dispute. In one significant respect, however, his performance during the 2005–06 season, with a career high 33 goals, 51 assists and 84 points suggest a certain balancing of his offensive capabilities. Even accounting for rule changes that, in the immediate past season, led to a dramatic league-wide scoring increase—goals were up by almost 18%—Gomez's offensive performance was nothing less than stellar. The Club seeks to temper the impact of his achievements by noting he has been part of a very successful team, playing on lines with the likes of Patrick Elias and Brian Gointa, for example. This contention, particularly in this case, hardly advances the resolution of this case: Good players generally play better together, and whatever the alchemy responsible for the product, the fact is Mr. Gomez and his team have been to three Stanley Cup finals during his tenure and won two of them. The Devils Club is appropriately characterized as a disciplined defensive bunch, complete with specialists who are utilized as role players: Scott Gomez has shown in the most recent season that he is increasingly stepping up to his role has a very talented offensive specialist. The evidence also supports the claim that he is among the very best 5-on-5 players in the League.

* * *

Most of the proposed comparable players have signed multi-year contacts. Such agreements often, but not always, represent a premium situation, the Club paying more for longer term personnel stability. A team wishing to ensure continued availability of a young rising star, for example, may well pay more, particularly if the player forfeits free agency rights in the process. But it is also true that a player may, for a variety of reasons, conclude that long-term security, even at a reduced annual salary, is prudent on his part. As one of the seasoned advocates has noted, "The only thing one can know is that one cannot know." And that, in the final analysis, is the point. Whether one infers a premium paid by the Club or, contrarily, an "under-market" concession by the Player, the multi-year agreement is problematical for comparison purposes. The task is made no easier when one attempts to parse the meaning of "level" agreements (repeated iterations of a single salary) as contrasted with those that are "stepped." There are simply too many dynamics, financial, psychological, tactical, and otherwise, that enter the bargaining process to reduce this aspect of comparative analysis to anything approaching science. This does not require rejection of all such agreements as *per se* inapplicable. They may, in a given case, serve to inform. It means that one must exercise extreme caution before relying on them to draw pat conclusions on comparability.

One begins with several players who cannot reasonably be viewed as comparable. Martin St. Louis is a winger with the Tampa Bay Lightening. Originally joining the NHL with Calgary, he was claimed by Tampa Bay on waivers and has played with that Club since the 2000–01 season. He won the Hart Trophy in 2003–04, at the same time winning the Art Ross Trophy as the League's leading scorer and the Pearson Trophy, awarded by the NHLPA as the MVP. Prior to the 05–06 season, he signed a 6 year contract with the Tampa Bay Club that paid him $6.5 million in '05/'06 and will pay him $6.0, $6.0, $5.0, $4.0, and $4.0 in the outlying years of the contract term. The Player notes that St. Louis was 30 years old at signing and that St. Louis' career path is distinct from that of Gomez, leading the Player to conclude his contract is not instructive. The Arbitrator agrees.

Brad Richards, a 26-year old center with the Tampa Bay Club, entered the League prior to the 2000–01 season and, therefore, played fewer games than Gomez. However he has more goals (107 to 103) and a higher point per game average (.90 to .82). He has scored more than 20 goals in each of his NHL seasons except one and is properly regarded as an all-situational player who garners substantially more time on ice than does Gomez and has been used extensively both on the power play and in short-handed situations. Moreover, four of the five years involved in this multi-year contract ($7.8 million per year) are Unrestricted Free Agent years. Richards won the Conn Smythe Trophy as the MVP in the 2004 playoffs and was the recipient of the Lady Byng Trophy. In the overall, the Richards comparison is unenlightening.

Steve Sullivan is a veteran forward with the Nashville Predators. Originally drafted in 1994 by the Devils, he was traded to the Toronto Maple Leafs in 1996 and subsequently claimed on waivers by the Chicago Blackhawks in 1999. He was traded to Nashville during the 2003–04 season. Following that season, a very good one for Sullivan, he signed a four-year contract for the 2005 through 2009 seasons that paid $3.2M each year. Offensive production statistics favor Gomez, as do career accomplishments. On a career through platform year comparison, while Sullivan has more total goals and points (but not assists) than Gomez—he began his NHL 4 seasons before Gomez—Gomez has more points per game (.82 to .75). On a platform year comparison, Gomez has 33 goals to Sullivan's 24 and a point/game average of 1.02 to Sullivan's .91. Gomez has been to 3 Stanley Cup Finals, as indicated earlier.

In this case, circumstances surrounding the negotiation of the long-term agreement are revealing, if not the four-year agreement itself; one cannot ignore the fact that Sullivan's contract was consummated when he was 31. The promise and the performance of the 26-year old Gomez are clearly distinguishable.

Milan Hejduk is a 30-year old right winger who plays for the Colorado Avalanche. Hejduk is an accomplished player, outpacing Gomez substantially as a goal-scorer—on a career through platform year comparison (both players have participated in essentially the same number games) he had 197 goals to Gomez's 103 and .89 points per game, compared to Gomez's .82.

Name	Career	PY	GP	G	A	Pts	Pts/G	+/−	PIMs/G	ESPts	ESPts/G
Gomez, Scott	1999–00	2005–06	476	103	287	390	0.82	52	0.67	271	0.57
Hejduk, Milan	1998–99	2003–04	470	197	219	416	0.89	125	0.33	264	0.56

On a platform year comparison, Gomez fairs better, scoring 1.02 points per game to Hejduk's .91. Other statistics are closely aligned: Hejduk scored 35 goals to Gomez's 33, both players were utilized essentially the same amount of time during the games and their performance in terms of even strength production was similar, although Gomez was used more on the power play. Like Gomez, Hejduk also has substantial playoff experience. He also has a Stanley Cup ring, Olympic team membership and two All-Star games under his belt. He is, as the Club argues, one of the premier players in the League. His offensive output has been substantial and consistent, including a 50 goal season, in 02–03, a 41 goal season in 00–01 and two 30+ goal seasons. He has received numerous votes for All-Star, as well as for the Hart, Lady Byng and Selke trophies, the latter recognition being a reflection of his defensive capabilities, as well.

At age 28, following the '03–'04 season, Hejduk signed a five-year contract providing for payment of $3.7, $3.8 and $4.0 million dollars for the final three years. The Player says the contact is undervalued—Hejduk having taken a lower long-term contract in exchange for security, it is suggested. While this may be so, particularly considering the forfeiture of four UFA years, this is the type of speculation that tends to outstrip the capabilities of this very expedited fact finding process. In all, the age, length and terms of this contract make it difficult to rely upon as a benchmark.

Alex Tanguay and Scott Gomez are in many respects very comparable players. Tanguay is a 26-year old winger with the Calgary Flames. Following the 05–06 season, when he was traded by the Avalanche to the Flames, Tanguay signed a three-year contract that paid $5.0, $5.375 and $5.375 million. The two players have similar career statistics. Both entered the League in the 1999–00 season and Tanguay finished just behind Gomez in rookie scoring; both were finalists for the Calder Trophy that Gomez won. On a career through platform year comparison, the games played are reasonably close, with Tanguay holding a slight edge on a points per game basis of .89 as contrasted with Gomez's .82. Tanguay has scored more goals (137 to 103; Gomez leads in assists 287–263.) The platform year comparison is also close, with Gomez scoring a few more goals and Tanguay leading on a point per game basis.

Name	PY	GP	G	A	Pts	Pts/G	+/–	PIMs/G	ESPts	Min/G	ESPts/G	PPMin/G
Gomez, Scott	2005–06	82	33	51	84	1.02	8	42	51	18.77	13.54	5.07
Tanguay, Alex	2005–06	71	29	49	78	1.10	8	46	49	18.35	13.14	4.99

Their records in the playoffs are virtually identical.

Name	GP	G	A	Pts	Pts/G	+/–	PIMs	PIMs/G	Min/G
Gomez, Scott	86	17	34	51	0.59	8	36	0.42	15.15
Tanguay, Alex	83	18	32	50	0.60	3	28	0.34	16.58

Name	PY	GP	G	A	Pts	Pts/G	+/–	PIMs	Min/G
Gomez, Scott	2005–06	9	5	4	9	1.00	–1	6	18.11
Tanguay, Alex	2005–06	9	2	4	6	0.67	1	12	18.11

The Player argues that Tanguay benefits from having played on a line with a Hall of Fame center for his entire career (Joe Sakic and Peter Forsberg). "This," says the Player, "has no doubt freed up Tanguay from a significant amount of offensive attention, and enabled him to rack up points at a more frequent pace. He also has played on a team that has always scored a lot of goals. The argument has a family ring. Commenting on Gomez's playmaking abilities, the Club argues that "equipped with this skill, he has been lined-up with a variety of talented, all-round players who have both exploited his talent and, at the same time, compensated for his deficiencies. In 2002–03 and 2003–04 Gomez was paired primarily with Patrik Elias, the Club's leading scorer for five straight seasons . . . and an NHL All-Star. In 2005–06, Gomez was paired with the Club's leading scorer, Brian Gionta, for the entire season, and Patrik Elias in the second half of the season as well." These claims, one concludes, ultimately canceled themselves out. Once more, it is not surprise that good players play well when paired with good players. The Player again claims that Tanguay's multi-year contract is "low," that "for whatever reason, [Tanguay] agreed to a deal that was below market . . ." As proof, the Player directs the Arbitrator's attention to the contracts of Messrs. Gaborik, Hossa, Lecavalier, and Richards.

Marian Gaborik is a 24-year old winder with the Minnesota Wild. He joined the Wild as their first choice in the 2000 entry draft and has led that club in scoring 4 out of 5 NHL seasons. He has three 30+ goal seasons and the evidence supports the Club's claim that he played a major role in helping the team advance to the semi-finals in 2002–03. And, he was the high scorer for the team in those playoffs, with 17 points in 18 games, ranking third in the League that year in playoff scoring. After a slow season in 03–04, he had a strong year in 05–06, scoring 38 goals and 28 assists for a total of 66 points, averaging in 65 games, 1.01 points per game. After that season, he and the Club agreed on a three-year contract paying $5.0, $6.5 and $7.5 million dollars. In the course of this contract, Gaborik forfeited 2 years of unrestricted free agency. That, according to the Club, makes Gaborik's situation "completely different, and his contract not useful for comparison purposes, unless substantially discounted." There are, as indicated above, reasons to recognize a certain premium being paid for long-term contracts. At the same time, the performance statistics for Gaborik and Gomez are revealing. On a career through platform year basis, Gaborik has scored more goals (134 to 103) and has done so in substantially fewer games (360 as contrasted with Gomez's 476). But Gomez has more than twice the assists—287 to 140 and leads in the points per game comparison .82 to .76. Gaborik is used substantially more on short-handed situations, showing his defensive prowess. But overall time on ice (Gomez is used somewhat more in even strengths situations) is close on both a platform year and a career to platform year basis.

										Time on Ice Per Game			
Name	PY	GP	G	A	Pts	Pts/Gm	PIM	PIM/G	+/-	Total	Even	PP	SH
Gomez	2006	82	33	51	84	1.02	42	0.51	8	18.78	13.54	5.07	0.17
Gaborik	2006	65	38	28	66	1.02	64	0.99	6	18.43	12.75	5.06	0.63

										Time on Ice Per Game			
Name	PY	GP	G	A	Pts	Pts/Gm	PIM	PIM/G	+/-	Total	Even	PP	SH
Gomez	2006	476	103	287	390	0.82	320	0.67	52	16.63	13.39	3.13	0.10
Gaborik	2006	360	134	140	274	0.76	196	0.54	22	17.22	12.89	3.90	0.44

Gomez, unlike Gaborik, has substantially more playoff experience and has received some voting recognition for Byng and Selke trophies.

Marion Hossa is a 27-year old right wing with the Atlanta Thrashers. Hossa entered the NHL with the Ottawa Senators in 1997 and played with them through the 2003–04 season. Prior to the 05–06 season, Hossa was traded to Atlanta and the Thrashers signed him to a three-year contract prior to the 05–06 season that paid $5.0, $6.0 and $7.0. The platform year statistics are almost identical although the Club notes, with some justification, one concludes, that Hossa's platform year scoring was achieved in 2003–04, when scoring was considerably lower than in the most recent season.[5]

										Time on Ice Per Game			
Name	PY	GP	G	A	Pts	Pts/Gm	PIM	PIM/G	+/-	Total	Even	PP	SH
Gomez	2006	82	33	51	84	1.02	42	0.51	8	18.78	13.54	5.07	0.17
Hossa	2004	81	36	46	82	1.01	46	0.57	4	18.62	13.17	4.05	1.41

										Time on Ice Per Game			
Name	PY	GP	G	A	Pts	Pts/Gm	PIM	PIM/G	+/-	Total	Even	PP	SH
Gomez	2006	476	103	287	390	0.82	320	0.67	52	16.63	13.39	3.13	0.10
Hossa	2004	467	188	202	390	0.84	243	0.52	64	17.59	13.49	3.32	0.78

On a career basis, however, Hossa substantially outpaces Gomez as a consistent offensive force. In five of his six full seasons, for example, he has scored between 29 and 45 goals, for a total of 188 to Gomez's 103. Hossa is more of a two-way player and has received substantial League recognition that well surpasses Gomez, including a total of 134 All-Star Votes to

---

[5] A note here is in order with respect to the new rules and "goal inflation". To be sure, there should be some recognition that goal production during the 05–06 season, with revised rules designed to enhance just that, was up. But the arbitrator rejects an arithmetic approach that would somehow apply a fixed numerical adjustment factor to any such statistics. There are simply too many variables to allow for that kind of mechanical application. It suffices to note that scoring was easier after the rule changes.

Gomez's 12 on a career to platform basis. He is properly compensated higher than Gomez.

In summary, both parties in this case have presented a range of reasonably comparable players whose compensation varies, for the reasons noted above. The conclusion here, based on a careful review of each of these players and their situations results in the conclusion that Scott Gomez should receive $5 million for the 2006–07 season and shall be entitled to participate in team bonus plan.

NOTES AND QUESTIONS

1. *Standard for Salary Arbitration?* What exactly is arbitrator Bloch trying to determine through his comparative analysis? A "fair" salary? What Gomez would receive if he were an unrestricted free agent? Is there a difference? Should the age of Gomez compared to other players be relevant? Should his participation in the playoffs?

2. *Are Compromises Appropriate in Hockey System?* How does arbitrator Bloch's award compare to the salary levels proposed by the team and the player? Does it seem that the award was in part influenced by the arbitrator's desire to avoid fully displacing either side? If so, is this necessarily inconsistent with the intent of the system? On the other hand, would compromising in every case render the hockey system ineffective?

3. *Why Not Adopt Last Best Offer?* Baseball's last-best-offer arbitration has historically resulted in a higher level of settlement than has hockey's more traditional system. Why might the NHL nonetheless have declined to adopt baseball's system?

4. *Baseball Criteria.* Although baseball's collective bargaining agreement expressly provides that there shall be no arbitration opinion, it does specify the criteria the arbitrators are to use.

Article VI, Section E(10) of the Basic Agreement provides:

(A) The criteria will be the quality of the Player's contribution to his Club during the past season (including but not limited to his overall performance, special qualities of leadership and public appeal), the length and consistency of his career contribution, the record of the Player's past compensation, comparative baseball salaries . . . , the existence of any physical or mental defects on the part of the Player, and the recent performance record of the Club including but not limited to its League standing and attendance as an indication of public acceptance . . .

(B) Evidence of the following shall not be admissible:

(i) The financial position of the Player and the Club;

(ii) Press comments, testimonials or similar material bearing on the performance of either the Player or the Club, except that recognized annual Player awards for playing excellence shall not be excluded;

(iii) Offers made by either Player or Club prior to arbitration;

(iv) The cost to the parties of their representatives, attorneys, etc.;

(v) Salaries in other sports or occupations.

The provision does not weigh these factors, however. The parties direct their arbitrators to assign "such weight to the evidence as shall appear appropriate under the circumstances."

Does the provision direct a different weighing than that taken by arbitrator Bloch in the *Gomez* case? Aside from his compromise between the parties' proposals, could Bloch's analysis in that case have been rendered under this provision?

F. JUDICIAL REVIEW OF ARBITRATION AWARDS

As stated in the introduction to this chapter, the third case in the Supreme Court's *Steelworkers* trilogy, *United Steelworkers of America v. Enterprise Wheel & Car Corp.*, 363 U.S. 593 (1960), concerned judicial enforcement of arbitral awards after they are issued. The Court held in this case that, just as a court should enforce an agreement to arbitrate regardless of its view of the strength of the merits of a grievance, so should it enforce an arbitration award regardless of its view of the merits of the arbitrator's ultimate decision. The Court stated, "[i]t is the arbitrator's construction which was bargained for, and so far as the arbitrator's decision concerns construction of the contract, the courts have no business overruling him because their interpretation of the contract is different from his." *Id.* at 599. Courts may refuse to enforce or to vacate only awards that an arbitrator manifestly based not on an attempt to implement the party's agreement, but instead based in "essence" on some other consideration, such as external law or the arbitrator's view of what the agreement should have said, *i.e.*, "his own brand of industrial justice." The Court thus directed lower courts to review arbitral decisions only to determine whether the arbitrator was attempting to construe or apply the contract, not whether the arbitrator did so correctly, or even what the court deferentially might view as reasonably or minimally competently.

Not surprisingly, some lower court judges, perhaps themselves anxious to express their "own brand of industrial justice," have resisted this restraint on their authority to review arbitral decisions. Some judges have charged arbitrators with expressing their "own brand of industrial justice" whenever the arbitrators' interpretation of an agreement varies from that of the judges. This has been particularly true when the judges find the contract language to be "clear and unambiguous," despite the arbitrator's claim of ambiguity. For a recent example from the sports world, see *United States Soccer Fed'n, Inc. v. Unites State Nat'l Soccer Team Players Ass'n*, 838 F.3d 826 (7th Cir. 2016) (arbitrator cannot resort to consideration of past practice to interpret "clear and unambiguous" specified obligations of employer under agreement).

Other judges have misinterpreted language in the *Enterprise Wheel & Car* decision that an arbitral "award is legitimate only so long as it draws its essence from the collective bargaining agreement" to mean that the award must be consistent with the "essence" of the agreement, rather than the award must be primarily based on the agreement. In response, in a series of decisions in the half century after the Trilogy, the Court has had to confirm the teaching of *Enterprise Wheel & Car*. One of the clearest of these confirmations involved an important incident in the history of labor relations in Major League Baseball.

MAJOR LEAGUE BASEBALL PLAYERS ASSOCIATION V. GARVEY
532 U.S. 504 (2001)

PER CURIAM.

The Court of Appeals for the Ninth Circuit here rejected an arbitrator's factual findings and then resolved the merits of the parties' dispute instead of remanding the case for further arbitration proceedings. Because the court's determination conflicts with our cases limiting review of an arbitrator's award entered pursuant to an agreement between an employer and a labor organization and prescribing the appropriate remedy where vacation of the award is warranted, we grant the petition for a writ of certiorari and reverse. The motions for leave to file briefs *amicus curiae* of the National Academy of Arbitrators and the Office of the Commissioner of Baseball are granted.

In the late 1980's, petitioner Major League Baseball Players Association (Association) filed grievances against the Major League Baseball Clubs (Clubs), claiming the Clubs had colluded in the market for free-agent services after the 1985, 1986 and 1987 baseball seasons, in violation of the industry's collective-bargaining agreement. A free agent is a player who may contract with any Club, rather than one whose right to contract is restricted to a particular Club. In a series of decisions, arbitrators found collusion by the Clubs and damage to the players. The Association and Clubs subsequently entered into a Global Settlement Agreement (Agreement), pursuant to which the Clubs established a $280 million fund to be distributed to injured players. The Association also designed a "Framework" to evaluate the individual player's claims, and, applying that Framework, recommended distribution plans for claims relating to a particular season or seasons.

The Framework provided that players could seek an arbitrator's review of the distribution plan. The arbitrator would determine "only whether the approved Framework and the criteria set forth therein have been properly applied in the proposed Distribution Plan." *Garvey v. Roberts,* 203 F.3d 580, 583 (CA9 2000) (Garvey I). The Framework set forth factors to be considered in evaluating players' claims, as well as specific requirements for lost contract-extension claims. Such claims were cognizable " 'only in those cases where evidence exists that a specific offer of an extension was made by a club prior to collusion only to thereafter be withdrawn when the collusion scheme was initiated.' " *Id.* at 584.

Respondent Steve Garvey, a retired, highly regarded first baseman, submitted a claim for damages of approximately $3 million. He alleged that his contract with the San Diego Padres was not extended to the 1988 and 1989 seasons due to collusion. The Association rejected Garvey's claim in February 1996, because he presented no evidence that the Padres actually offered to extend his contract. Garvey objected, and an arbitration hearing was held. He testified that the Padres offered to extend his contract for the 1988 and 1989 seasons and then withdrew the offer after they began colluding with other teams. He presented a June 1996 letter from Ballard Smith, Padres' President and CEO from 1979 to 1987, stating that, before the end of the 1985 season, Smith offered to extend Garvey's contract through the 1989 season, but that the Padres refused to negotiate with Garvey thereafter due to collusion.

The arbitrator denied Garvey's claim, after seeking additional documentation from the parties. In his award, he explained that " 'there exists . . . substantial doubt as to the credibility of the statements in the Smith letter.' " *Id.* at 586. He noted the "stark contradictions" between the 1996 letter and Smith's testimony in the earlier arbitration proceedings regarding collusion, where Smith, like other owners, denied collusion and stated that the Padres simply were not interested in extending Garvey's contract. *Ibid.* The arbitrator determined that, due to these contradictions, he " 'must reject [Smith's] more recent assertion that Garvey did not receive [a contract] extension' " due to collusion, and found that Garvey had not shown a specific offer of extension. *Ibid.* He concluded that:

> " 'the shadow cast over the credibility of the Smith testimony coupled with the absence of any other corroboration of the claim submitted by Garvey compels a finding that the Padres declined to extend his contract not because of the constraints of the collusion effort of the clubs but rather as a baseball judgment founded upon [Garvey's] age and recent injury history.' " *Ibid.*

Garvey moved in Federal District Court to vacate the arbitrator's award, alleging that the arbitrator violated the Framework by denying his claim. The District Court denied the motion. The Court of Appeals for the Ninth Circuit reversed by a divided vote. The court acknowledged that judicial review of an arbitrator's decision in a labor dispute is extremely limited. But it held that review of the merits of the arbitrator's award was warranted in this case, because the arbitrator " 'dispensed his own brand of industrial justice.' " *Id.* at 589. The court recognized that Smith's prior testimony with respect to collusion conflicted with the statements in his 1996 letter. But in the court's view, the arbitrator's refusal to credit Smith's letter was "inexplicable" and "bordered on the irrational," because a panel of arbitrators, chaired by the arbitrator involved here, had previously concluded that the owners' prior testimony was false. *Id.* at 590. The court rejected the arbitrator's reliance on the absence of other corroborating evidence, attributing that fact to Smith and Garvey's direct negotiations. The court also found that the record provided "strong support" for the truthfulness of Smith's 1996 letter. *Id.* at 591–592. The Court of Appeals reversed and remanded with directions to vacate the award.

The District Court then remanded the case to the arbitration panel for further hearings, and Garvey appealed. The Court of Appeals, again by a divided vote, explained that *Garvey I* established that "the conclusion that Smith made Garvey an offer and subsequently withdrew it because of the collusion scheme was the only conclusion that the arbitrator could draw from the record in the proceedings." [. . . T]he Court clarified that *Garvey I* "left only one possible result—the result our holding contemplated—an award in Garvey's favor." The Court of Appeals reversed the District Court and directed that it remand the case to the arbitration panel with instructions to enter an award for Garvey in the amount he claimed.

The parties do not dispute that this case arises under § 301 of the Labor Management Relations Act, 1947, 61 Stat. 156, 29 U.S.C. § 185(a), as the controversy involves an assertion of rights under an agreement between an employer and a labor organization. Although Garvey's specific allegation is that the arbitrator violated the Framework for resolving players' claims for damages, that Framework was designed to facilitate payments to remedy the Clubs' breach of the collective-bargaining agreement. Garvey's right to be made whole is founded on that agreement.

Judicial review of a labor-arbitration decision pursuant to such an agreement is very limited. Courts are not authorized to review the arbitrator's decision on the merits despite allegations that the decision rests on factual errors or misinterprets the parties' agreement. *Paperworkers v. Misco, Inc.*, 484 U.S. 29, 36 (1987). We recently reiterated that if an " 'arbitrator is even arguably construing or applying the contract and acting within the scope of his authority,' the fact that 'a court is convinced he committed serious error does not suffice to overturn his decision.'" *Eastern Associated Coal Corp. v. Mine Workers,* 531 U.S. 57, 62 (2000) (quoting *Misco, supra,* at 38). It is only when the arbitrator strays from interpretation and application of the agreement and effectively "dispenses his own brand of industrial justice" that his decision may be unenforceable. *Steelworkers v. Enterprise Wheel & Car Corp.,* 363 U.S. 593, 597 (1960). When an arbitrator resolves disputes regarding the application of a contract, and no dishonesty is alleged, the arbitrator's "improvident, even silly, factfinding" does not provide a basis for a reviewing court to refuse to enforce the award. *Misco,* 484 U.S. at 39.

In discussing the courts' limited role in reviewing the merits of arbitration awards, we have stated that "'courts . . . have no business weighing the merits of the grievance [or] considering whether there is equity in a particular claim.'" *Id.* at 37 (quoting *Steelworkers v. American Mfg. Co.,* 363 U.S. 564 (1960)). When the judiciary does so, "it usurps a function which . . . is entrusted to the arbitration tribunal." *Id.* at 569; *see also Enterprise Wheel & Car Corp., supra,* at 599 ("It is the arbitrator's construction [of the agreement] which was bargained for . . . ").

Consistent with this limited role, we said in *Misco* that "even in the very rare instances when an arbitrator's procedural aberrations rise to the level of affirmative misconduct, as a rule the court must not foreclose further proceedings by settling the merits according to its own judgment of the appropriate result." 484 U.S. at 40–41, n. 10. That step, we explained, "would improperly substitute a judicial determination for the arbitrator's decision that the parties bargained for" in their agreement. *Ibid.* Instead, the court should "simply vacate the award, thus leaving open the possibility of further proceedings if they are permitted under the terms of the agreement." *Ibid.*

To be sure, the Court of Appeals here recited these principles, but its application of them is nothing short of baffling. The substance of the Court's discussion reveals that it overturned the arbitrator's decision because it disagreed with the arbitrator's factual findings, particularly those with respect to credibility. The Court of Appeals, it appears, would have credited Smith's 1996 letter, and found the arbitrator's refusal to do so at worst "irrational" and at best "bizarre." *Garvey I,* 203 F.3d at 590–591. But even "serious error" on the arbitrator's part does not justify overturning his decision, where, as here, he is construing a contract and acting within the scope of his authority. *Misco, supra,* at 38.

In *Garvey II,* the court clarified that *Garvey I* both rejected the arbitrator's findings and went further, resolving the merits of the parties' dispute based on the court's assessment of the record before the arbitrator. For that reason, the court found further arbitration proceedings inappropriate. But again, established law ordinarily precludes a court from resolving the merits of the parties' dispute on the basis of its own factual determinations, no matter how erroneous the arbitrator's decision. *Misco, supra,* at 40, n. 10; see also *American Mfg. Co.,* 363 U.S. at 568. Even when the arbitrator's award may properly be vacated, the appropriate remedy is to remand the case for further arbitration proceedings. *Misco, supra,* at 40, n. 10. The dissent suggests that the remedy described in *Misco* is limited to cases where the arbitrator's errors are procedural. *Post,* at 1 (opinion of STEVENS, J.) *Misco* did involve procedural issues, but our discussion regarding the appropriate remedy was not so limited. If a remand is appropriate *even* when the arbitrator's award has been set aside for "procedural aberrations" that constitute "affirmative misconduct," it follows that a remand ordinarily will be appropriate when the arbitrator simply made factual findings that the reviewing court perceives as "irrational." The Court of Appeals usurped the arbitrator's role by resolving the dispute and barring further proceedings, a result at odds with this governing law.

The fact that an earlier panel of arbitrators rejected the owners' testimony as a whole does not compel the conclusion that the panel found Smith's specific statements with respect to Garvey to be false. The arbitrator's explanation for his decision indicates that he simply found Smith an unreliable witness and that, in the absence of corroborating evidence, he could only conclude that Garvey failed to show that the Padres had offered to extend his contract. The arbitrator's analysis may have been unpersuasive to the Court of Appeals, but his decision hardly qualifies as serious error, let alone irrational or inexplicable error. And, as we have said, any such error would not justify the actions taken by the court.

For the foregoing reasons, the Court of Appeals erred in reversing the order of the District Court denying the motion to vacate the arbitrator's award, and it erred further in directing that judgment be entered in Garvey's favor. The judgment of the Court of Appeals is reversed, and the case is remanded for further proceedings consistent with this opinion.

JUSTICE GINSBURG, concurring in part and concurring in the judgment (omitted)

JUSTICE STEVENS, dissenting (omitted).

NOTES AND QUESTIONS

1. *Meaning of "Own Brand of Industrial Justice"?* On what did the Ninth Circuit Court of Appeals base its conclusion that the arbitrator dispensed "his own brand of industrial justice?" Did the Court of Appeals do anything other than substitute its credibility judgment for that of the arbitrator? What evidence might "manifest" an arbitrator's "infidelity" to his

or her "obligation" to enforce the parties' agreement rather than some independent view of what is just?

2. *Effect of Vacatur of Arbitration Award?* Note the Court's iteration of its earlier directive in the *Misco* case that where a court appropriately determines that it cannot enforce an arbitration award, even because of an arbitrator's "affirmative misconduct," the appropriate response is not to decide the case itself, but rather simply to vacate the award and remand the case, perhaps for further arbitration. An arbitrator's lack of contractual authority to issue an award against a party to a collective agreement thus does not empower a court to issue a different award. Does this mean that any action challenged by the grievance before the arbitrator, such as some disciplinary penalty, must stand, at least until challenged in a subsequent arbitration? Consider the following case.

Early in the 2014 football season a Texas grand jury indicted Adrian Peterson, the then star running back of the Minnesota Vikings, for felony injury to a child, his four-year old son. Peterson had hit his son with a tree branch as punishment. The punishment reportedly inflicted "cuts and bruises to the child's back, buttocks, ankles, legs, and scrotum, along with defensive wounds to the child's hands." Peterson subsequently stated that he would "never eliminate whooping my kids . . . because I know how being spanked has helped me in my life." After the grand jury's charge was entered, Peterson took a paid leave from the team pending adjudication of his criminal case. As explained below, however, the NFL took further action.

NATIONAL FOOTBALL LEAGUE PLAYERS ASS'N v. NATIONAL FOOTBALL LEAGUE (PETERSON)
831 F.3d 985 (8th Cir. 2016)

COLLOTON, CIRCUIT JUDGE.

During the 2014 football season, National Football League Commissioner Roger Goodell suspended Minnesota Vikings running back Adrian Peterson indefinitely for "conduct detrimental to . . . the game of professional football," and fined Peterson a sum equivalent to six games' pay. Peterson's suspension stemmed from his plea of *nolo contendere* in November 2014 to a charge of misdemeanor reckless assault on one of his children. Peterson appealed his discipline to an arbitrator, who affirmed the suspension and fine.

Peterson petitioned the district court to vacate the arbitration decision. The court granted the petition, and the League appeals. After the district court ruled, the Commissioner reinstated Peterson. He has resumed playing professional football, and this appeal does not involve his eligibility to play. The remaining dispute concerns whether the League may collect the fine imposed by the Commissioner and upheld by the arbitrator. We conclude that the parties bargained to be bound by the decision of the arbitrator, and the arbitrator acted within his authority, so we reverse the district court's judgment vacating the arbitration decision.

I.

The NFL Players Association is the exclusive collective bargaining representative for present and future players in the National Football League. Collective Bargaining Agreement (2011) [hereinafter "CBA"]. . . . Article 46 of the Agreement authorizes the Commissioner to impose discipline for "conduct detrimental to the integrity of, or public confidence in, the game of professional football." *Id.* art. 46, § 1(a). The standard NFL player contract further acknowledges that the Commissioner has the power "to fine Player in a reasonable amount; *to suspend Player for a period certain or indefinitely*; and/or to terminate this contract." . . . The Agreement does not define "conduct detrimental" or prescribe maximum or presumptive punishments for such conduct.

The Agreement establishes an exclusive arbitration process for resolving disputes over player discipline. Any player sanctioned under Article 46 for conduct detrimental to the game has the right to appeal to the Commissioner. *Id.* art. 46, §§ 1(a), 2(a). The Commissioner may hear the appeal himself, or he may designate one or more persons to serve as hearing officers. *Id.* § 2(a).

Pursuant to Article 46, the Commissioner has promulgated a Personal Conduct Policy that applies to all players. The Policy specifies behavior that may be considered "conduct detrimental," explains the types of penalties violators may receive, and describes the procedures for imposing and appealing Commissioner discipline. Players are advised that "[d]iscipline may take the form of fines, suspension, or banishment from the League," and that violators might also be required to undergo clinical evaluation or mental health treatment.

The Personal Conduct Policy effective June 1, 2013, listed various forms of off-the-field conduct, including domestic violence, that could subject a player to discipline for conduct detrimental. The Policy does not establish maximum or presumptive punishments; rather, it provides that discipline will depend on "the nature of the incident, the actual or threatened risk to the participant and others, any prior or additional misconduct . . . , and other relevant factors." An identical policy was reissued on June 1, 2014.

On August 28, 2014, Commissioner Goodell sent a letter to all NFL owners to "communicate our position and strengthen our policies on domestic violence and sexual assault." An attached memorandum to all NFL personnel explained that violations of the Personal Conduct Policy involving domestic violence would be subject to "enhanced discipline." These communications followed criticism of the League's handling of a highly publicized incident of domestic violence involving Baltimore Ravens running back Ray Rice. In July 2014, the Commissioner suspended Rice without pay for the first two games of the 2014 season and fined Rice an additional week's salary after Rice was charged with assaulting his then-fiancée. The NFL and Goodell were sharply criticized in many quarters for treating Rice too leniently.

The August 2014 communications outlined measures to "reinforce and enhance" the League's approach to domestic violence. Specifically, the memorandum announced that a first domestic violence offense would be subject to a suspension of six weeks without pay, and that more severe discipline would be imposed if aggravating circumstances were present. Goodell's letter to the owners said that the enhanced discipline was "consistent with [the League's] Personal Conduct Policy."

Adrian Peterson entered the NFL in 2007 and has spent his entire career with the Minnesota Vikings. On September 11, 2014—two weeks after Goodell issued the August 2014 communications—a Texas grand jury indicted Peterson for felony injury to a child. The indictment alleged that in May 2014, Peterson hit his four-year-old son with a tree branch as a form of corporal punishment. . . .

On November 4, 2014, Peterson pleaded *nolo contendere* to a reduced charge of reckless assault, a class A misdemeanor. Two weeks later, Goodell suspended Peterson indefinitely (for a minimum of the six games remaining in the 2014 season), fined him six-weeks' salary, and required him to meet with a League-appointed psychiatrist. Goodell relied on the "baseline discipline" of a six-game suspension that was announced in the August 2014 memorandum. Goodell also identified several aggravating circumstances that merited the lengthy suspension: the age and vulnerability of the child, the emotional and psychological trauma inflicted on a young child, and Peterson's lack of remorse and suggestion that he would not refrain from engaging in similar conduct in the future. Goodell told Peterson that he would periodically review Peterson's progress towards reinstatement, with the first review to occur in April 2015.

The Players Association appealed on Peterson's behalf under the procedures of the Collective Bargaining Agreement. The Commissioner designated Harold Henderson to hear Peterson's appeal. Henderson is the president of the Player Care Foundation, a League-affiliated charity. He previously served for sixteen years as the League's vice president for labor relations and chairman of the NFL Management Council Executive Committee. The Association asked Henderson to recuse himself from the hearing due to his close ties to League officials and his role in shaping the League's disciplinary policies. Henderson denied the request, noting that the Association had not objected to his designation as arbitrator in dozens of past disciplinary appeals.

The Players Association's primary argument before Arbitrator Henderson was that custom and practice under the Personal Conduct Policy in effect at the time of Peterson's misconduct limited the Commissioner's disciplinary authority to a maximum two-game suspension for a first-time domestic violence offense. The Association argued that Goodell was required to apply the policies in force on the date of the misconduct, and asked the arbitrator to reduce Peterson's punishment to a two-game suspension and a fine equivalent to two-weeks' salary. The Association also challenged the process by which Peterson's discipline was determined and the conditions placed on his reinstatement, accusing the League of "making up the process and punishment as it goes." The Personal Conduct Policy issued June 1, 2013, was in effect on the date of Peterson's offense, and an identical policy was reissued on June 1, 2014, so references to either version address the policy in place at the time of the misconduct.

The arbitrator affirmed Peterson's discipline, finding that it was "fair and consistent." He concluded that the August 2014 communications did not constitute a change of the Personal Conduct Policy, but rather "reinforce[d] that policy with initiatives to explain and enhance it." He observed that the Personal Conduct Policy, which had not been rescinded, authorized suspensions and provided that "[t]he specifics of the disciplinary response will be based on the nature of the incident" and other relevant factors. The arbitrator explained that the Commissioner has "broad discretion" under Article 46 of the Agreement and the Personal Conduct Policy, and concluded that the August 2014 pronouncements "simply reflect his current thinking on domestic violence and other incidents involving physical force."

The arbitrator quoted from a prior arbitration decision in 2010 concerning the suspension of a Miami Dolphins player:

> The Commissioner has considerable discretion in assessing discipline. If he should determine that the current level of discipline imposed for certain types of conduct has not been effective in deterring such conduct, it is within his authority to increase discipline in such cases. He is not forever bound to historical precedent.

In the *Dolphins Player* case, the player argued that a one-game suspension for domestic violence was inconsistent with prior cases in which the League had imposed only fines for first-time domestic violence offenses. The arbitrator there observed, however, that "domestic violence is an area where discipline has been increased, and a suspension for a first offense is now the norm rather than the exception. [The Commissioner] should not be handcuffed by prior cases." In Peterson's case, the arbitrator reasoned that just as the Commissioner was permitted to begin suspending, rather than fining, players for first-time offenses in 2010, he had "broad discretion" to increase the magnitude of suspensions and fines in 2014 if he concluded that past sanctions had been an insufficient deterrent.

The arbitrator also rejected the Players Association's contention that the Commissioner's discipline of Peterson was inconsistent with an arbitrator's decision in the Ray Rice case. Although the Commissioner initially suspended Rice for two games, he later changed the punishment to an indefinite suspension after a website published video footage of Rice's assault. An arbitrator vacated the indefinite suspension, finding that the second suspension was an arbitrary repunishment for misconduct that already had been punished. The *Rice* arbitrator opined, however, that "[i]f this were a matter where the *first discipline imposed* was an indefinite suspension, an arbitrator would be hard pressed to find that the Commissioner had abused his discretion." Arbitrator Henderson thus concluded that the Commissioner's indefinite suspension of Peterson was not inconsistent with the reasoning in *Rice*.

The arbitrator then stated that it was unnecessary to find whether the June 2014 policy and the August 2014 communications were "a single policy or two, or which one was applied, because the result is the same in either instance." He explained that the Commissioner's discipline of Peterson fit both the Personal Conduct Policy and the August 2014 communications. The arbitrator acknowledged that Peterson's discipline was more severe than in most prior domestic violence cases, but found that the "severe beating of a four year old child" was "arguably one of the most egregious cases of domestic violence in this Commissioner's tenure." He said that "[t]here is no comparing this brutal incident to the typical violence against another adult."

The arbitrator rejected the Players Association's argument that Peterson lacked fair notice of the potential punishment. He found no evidence that Peterson knew what level of discipline had been imposed in prior domestic violence cases or that he relied in any way on an understanding about potential disciplinary measures. The arbitrator distinguished a case involving a "fine for missing the last few minutes of a Thursday practice" and other cases cited by the Association, finding no reason to believe that "Peterson might not have inflicted those injuries on his young son if he had known he could be suspended six weeks rather than two." The arbitrator saw no lack of basic fairness in the Commissioner's approach. Accordingly, the arbitrator denied the grievance and affirmed the Commissioner's discipline of Peterson.

The Players Association petitioned the district court to vacate the arbitration award. The Association argued that the case involved "the rare Arbitration Award that must be set aside" and sought to vacate the award on four grounds, alleging: (1) the Commissioner retroactively punished Peterson, in violation of the Collective Bargaining Agreement; (2) the arbitrator exceeded his authority by hypothesizing whether the Commissioner could have disciplined Peterson in the same manner prior to the August 2014 memorandum; (3) the arbitrator was evidently partial; and (4) the award violated the principle of fundamental fairness.

The district court accepted the Association's first two arguments and granted the petition. First, the court ruled that the Commissioner retroactively applied a new disciplinary standard to Peterson, in violation of the Collective Bargaining Agreement as interpreted by past arbitration awards. The district court concluded that the August 2014 communications effected a "New Policy" that "cannot be applied retroactively, notwithstanding the Commissioner's broad discretion in meting out punishment under the CBA." The district court found "no valid basis" for the arbitrator's distinction of the award in *Rice* and faulted the arbitrator for failing to "explain why the well-recognized bar against retroactivity did not apply to Peterson." The district court also ruled that the arbitrator "exceeded his authority by adjudicating the hypothetical question of whether Peterson's discipline could be sustained under the previous Policy." The court concluded that the arbitrator's authority was limited to deciding the question presented by the Players Association—namely, " 'the pure legal issue' of whether the New Policy could be applied retroactively."

The League appeals the district court's order. After the district court ruled, the Commissioner reinstated Peterson to play football, and this appeal concerns only the monetary sanction imposed by the Commissioner and upheld by the arbitrator. We review the district court's decision *de novo*. *Alcan Packaging Co. v. Graphic Commc'n Conference*, 729 F.3d 839, 841 (8th Cir. 2013).

II.

In an arbitration case like this one, the role of the courts is very limited. *Major League Baseball Players Ass'n v. Garvey*, 532 U.S. 504, 509 (2001) (per curiam). This case arises under the Labor Management Relations Act of 1947, in which Congress evinced a preference "for private settlement of labor disputes without the intervention of government." *United Paperworkers Int'l Union v. Misco, Inc.*, 484 U.S. 29, 37 (1987). We thus do not apply our own view of what would be appropriate player discipline, and we do not review whether the arbitrator "correctly" construed the Collective Bargaining Agreement when he reviewed the Commissioner's decision. "It is the arbitrator's construction which was bargained for; and so far as the arbitrator's decision concerns construction of the contract, the courts have no business overruling him because their interpretation of the contract is different from his." *United Steelworkers v. Enter. Wheel & Car Corp.*, 363 U.S. 593, 599 (1960). So long as the arbitrator "is even arguably construing or applying the contract and acting within the scope of his authority," the arbitral decision must stand. *Misco*, 484 U.S. at 38. Vacatur of an arbitration award is appropriate only when the decision does not "draw [ ] its essence from the collective bargaining agreement," and the arbitrator instead has "dispense[d] his own brand of industrial justice." *Enter. Wheel*, 363 U.S. at 597.

The gravamen of the Players Association's petition is that the arbitrator ignored "law of the shop" that forbids the retroactive application of a new disciplinary policy to Peterson. The Association maintains that industrial common law developed under the Personal Conduct Policy before Peterson's misconduct constrained the League to impose no more than a two-game suspension for a first-time domestic violence infraction. The Association argues that the Commissioner relied on a "new policy" set forth in the August 2014 communications to impose a more severe penalty on Peterson, and that the arbitrator ignored the law of the shop when he upheld the discipline. The district court, relying primarily on the *Rice* arbitration, ruled that the arbitrator "simply disregarded the law of the shop."

To be sure, "the industrial common law—the practices of the industry and the shop—is equally a part of the collective bargaining agreement although not expressed in it." *United Steel Workers v. Warrior & Gulf Nav. Co.*, 363 U.S. 574, 581–82 (1960). We have said, therefore, that "[t]he essence of the CBA is derived not only from its express provisions, but also from the industrial common law." *Bureau of Engraving, Inc. v. Graphic Commc'ns Int'l Union*, 164 F.3d 427, 429 (8th Cir. 1999). At the same time, however, "an arbitrator's error in failing to give precedential or preclusive effect to a previous arbitration award is not alone sufficient to vacate an arbitration award." *SBC Advanced Sols., Inc. v. Commc'ns Workers, Dist. 6*, 794 F.3d 1020, 1030 (8th Cir. 2015); *see Am. Nat'l Can Co. v. United Steelworkers*, 120 F.3d 886, 892–93 (8th Cir. 1997). An arbitrator acts within his authority as long as he is arguably construing or applying the contract, even if a court disagrees with the arbitrator's construction or application. *Misco*, 484 U.S. at 38. The same holds true for the law of the shop: as long as the arbitrator is arguably construing or applying arbitral precedents, a court's disagreement with the arbitrator's application of precedent is not sufficient grounds to vacate an arbitration decision. *See Am. Nat'l Can*, 120 F.3d at 892–93.

The district court concluded that the arbitrator ignored the law of the shop set forth in the *Rice* decision—namely, that the "new policy" arising from the August 2014 communications cannot be applied retroactively. But the arbitrator addressed *Rice* head-on. He explained that *Rice* involved *second* discipline imposed on a player for conduct that was already subject to a suspension and fine, whereas Peterson's sanction was the *first* discipline imposed. The arbitrator also quoted language from the *Rice* decision that plainly supports upholding the Commissioner's decision on Peterson: "If this were a matter where the first discipline imposed was an indefinite suspension, an arbitrator would be hard pressed to find that the Commissioner had abused his discretion."

The district court disagreed with the arbitrator's decision and found "no valid basis to distinguish this case from the *Rice* matter." In resolving a motion to vacate an arbitration award, however, the question for the courts is not whether the arbitrator's distinction is persuasive enough to withstand ordinary judicial review. An erroneous interpretation of a contract, including the law of the shop, is not a sufficient basis for disregarding the conclusion of the decisionmaker chosen by the parties. *Misco*, 484 U.S. at 38; *Alcan Packaging*, 729 F.3d at 843. The dispositive question is whether the arbitrator was at least arguably construing or applying the contract, including the law of the shop. The arbitrator here undoubtedly construed the *Rice* decision in reaching his decision. Disagreement with his conclusion is not a valid ground on which to vacate the decision

Aside from the *Rice* decision, the Players Association contends that the arbitrator ignored other arbitral precedents that establish a prohibition on retroactive punishment. The arbitrator, however, disagreed with the Association's premise that the Commissioner applied a "new" policy that called for discipline that was unavailable under the "old" policy. He concluded instead that the August 2014 communications "do not constitute a change" of the preexisting Personal Conduct Policy, because the communications did not effect a change in the Commissioner's disciplinary power.

The arbitrator relied on the Collective Bargaining Agreement and the law of the shop to reach this conclusion. The Agreement gives the Commissioner discretion to impose fines and suspensions for conduct detrimental to the game. The Personal Conduct Policy allows for fines and suspensions based on the nature of the incident and other relevant factors; it does not establish maximum punishments. Citing the 2010 *Dolphins Player* decision, the arbitrator reasoned that the Commissioner "is not forever bound to historical precedent," and that "[i]f he should determine that the current level of discipline imposed for certain types of conduct has not been effective in deterring such conduct, it is within his authority to increase discipline in such cases." As applied to Peterson's case, therefore, the arbitrator thought the terms of the Agreement, the law of the shop, and the Personal Conduct Policy gave the Commissioner discretion to impose a six-game suspension and fine if he concluded that shorter suspensions in prior cases had been inadequate. The arbitrator's decision on this point was grounded in a construction and application of the terms of the Agreement and a specific arbitral precedent. It is therefore not subject to second-guessing by the courts.

* * *

Article 46 and the Personal Conduct Policy by their terms place no limit on the Commissioner's authority to suspend players. In his August 2014 letter to NFL owners, Goodell described the attached memorandum and the six-game suspension for first-time domestic violence offenses as "*consistent with* our Personal Conduct Policy." App. 29 (emphasis added). And, as we have explained, the law of the shop included arbitral precedent stating that the Commissioner is not forever bound to historical precedent if prior discipline under the Personal Conduct Policy provided insufficient deterrence. In other words, the League might change its discipline without changing its policy.

The parties have delegated to the arbitrator the job of reconciling conflicting evidence. The arbitrator, having been presented with the Commissioner's statements, concluded that the August 2014 communications did not constitute a change of the Personal Conduct Policy. He necessarily found, therefore, that Goodell's statements were not admissions to the contrary. Courts are not permitted to review the merits of an arbitration decision even when a party claims that the decision rests on factual errors. *See Garvey*, 532 U.S. at 509; *Misco*, 484 U.S. at 39.

The Players Association further argues that the arbitrator ignored four arbitral decisions requiring advance notice to a player of the consequences of a violation. The arbitrator mentioned these decisions and found them distinguishable. A close reading of the prior decisions shows why. . . .

In any event, the question for a reviewing court is not whether the arbitrator's distinctions were correct, but whether the arbitrator was arguably construing and applying the contract and the law of the shop. The arbitrator applied the law of the shop: he relied on the *Dolphins Player* case concerning the Commissioner's authority to adjust disciplinary sanctions for domestic violence and concluded that precedents favored by the Players Association were distinguishable. *Dicta* from *Trailways Lines, Inc. v. Trailways, Inc. Joint Council*, 807 F.2d 1416, 1425 (8th Cir. 1986), concerning an arbitrator who ignored arbitral precedent without explanation or simply because he disagreed with it, are therefore inapposite. We see no basis for setting aside the decision under a federal court's limited scope of review.

The Players Association also argues that the arbitrator ignored an "admission" by Commissioner Goodell, when testifying in the *Rice* case, that he could not apply retroactively the "new" policy of imposing a six-game suspension for first-time domestic violence offenses. . . .

The arbitrator obviously did not agree with the Association that Goodell's testimony in *Rice* was an admission that he could not apply a six-game suspension to Peterson. The meaning of Goodell's statement is a question of fact. Given the context of the *Rice* testimony, the arbitrator reasonably concluded that Goodell did not testify to one belief on November 5, 2014, and then act to the contrary two weeks later when he disciplined Peterson. In any case, a federal court may not set aside an arbitrator's decision based on "improvident, even silly, factfinding," so the Association's reliance on Goodell's testimony does not carry the day. *Garvey*, 532 U.S. at 509, 532 U.S. at 509 (quoting *Misco*, 484 U.S. at 39).

III.

* * *

[T]he Players Association contends that the arbitrator exceeded his authority by altering the issues presented for decision. It argues that the arbitrator was limited to adjudicating " 'the pure legal issue' of whether the New Policy could be applied retroactively." The district court agreed, concluding that the arbitrator "strayed beyond the issues submitted by the NLFPA."

It is true that "[w]hen *two parties submit* an issue to arbitration, it confers authority upon the arbitrator to decide *that* issue." *Local 238 Int'l Bhd. of Teamsters v. Cargill, Inc.*, 66 F.3d 988, 990–91 (8th Cir. 1995) (per curiam) (first emphasis added). But the parties here did not stipulate to the issues for arbitration. The scope of the arbitrator's authority, therefore, was itself a question delegated to the arbitrator. *W.R. Grace & Co. v. Local Union 759, Int'l Union of United Rubber, Cork, Linoleum & Plastic Workers*, 461 U.S. 757, 765 (1983). "It is appropriate for the arbitrator to decide just what the issue was that was submitted to it and argued by the parties." *Int'l Chem. Workers Union v. Day & Zimmermann, Inc.*, 791 F.2d 366, 369 (5th Cir. 1986) (quotation omitted). And "an arbitrator's interpretation of the scope of the issue submitted to him is entitled to the same deference accorded his interpretation of the collective bargaining agreement." *John Morrell & Co. v. Local Union 304A of United Food & Commercial Workers*, 913 F.2d 544, 560 (8th Cir. 1990) (quoting *Pack Concrete, Inc. v. Cunningham*, 866 F.2d 283, 285 (9th Cir. 1989)).

The Players Association seeks to limit the issue for arbitration to a question advanced in its opening statement before the arbitrator: "[W]hat we have is the pure legal issue as to whether . . . it is fair and consistent for the League to retroactively apply the new policy to the May conduct." App. 72. But it is not the exclusive prerogative of the party seeking arbitration to define the issue for arbitration. *See John Morrell & Co.*, 913 F.2d at 560–61. The League framed the issue more broadly: "[I]s the discipline appropriate?" The League maintained that the Commissioner has the authority to "impose levels of discipline that are higher than what has been imposed in past cases depending on the circumstances before him," and that Peterson's discipline was authorized by the Personal Conduct Policy.

The arbitrator at least arguably acted within the scope of the issues submitted to him, so his decision must be upheld. *See W.R. Grace & Co.*, 461 U.S. at 764–65; *Int'l Bhd. of Elec. Workers, Local Union 824 v. Verizon Fla., LLC*, 803 F.3d 1241, 1246–47 (11th Cir. 2015); *cf. John Morrell & Co.*, 913 F.2d at 561 (vacating award where arbitrator was not "even arguably" acting within the scope of the issue submitted). The Players Association's framing of the issue assumed a premise that was contested by the League— namely, that the August 2014 communications constituted a new policy authorizing discipline that was not allowed under the preexisting policy. The arbitrator was not required to accept the Association's disputed premise; he properly asserted authority to resolve whether the premise was correct. The Association itself, moreover, raised arguments that required consideration of what discipline was permitted under the June 2014 Personal Conduct Policy. The Association urged the arbitrator to reduce Peterson's punishment to the maximum allowable at the time of Peterson's offense, and argued that "any punishment must be assessed and imposed consistent with the Policy and practices prior to August 28." These contentions required the arbitrator to examine what level of discipline was authorized before the August 2014 communications. The arbitrator thus did not exceed his authority by considering whether the August 2014 communications constituted a change to the Personal Conduct Policy and whether Peterson's discipline was consistent with the preexisting policy.

IV.

* * *

The Association [also] asserts that Arbitrator Henderson was "evidently partial," because he demonstrated "such a degree of partiality that a reasonable person could assume that the arbitrator had improper motives." *Dow Corning Corp. v. Safety Nat'l Cas. Corp*, 335 F.3d 742, 750 (8th Cir. 2003) (quotation omitted). In *Williams v. National Football League*, 582 F.3d 863 (8th Cir. 2009), an NFL player raised a virtually identical challenge to the League's general counsel serving as an arbitrator in a dispute arising under the previous collective bargaining agreement. We held that the Association had "waived its objection to [the general counsel] serving as arbitrator by agreeing in the CBA that the Commissioner's designee . . . could serve as arbitrator." *Id.* at 885–86. Allowing the Commissioner or the Commissioner's designee to hear challenges to the Commissioner's decisions may present an actual or apparent conflict of interest for the arbitrator. But the parties bargained for this procedure, and the Association consented to it. *See* CBA art. 46 § 2(a). It was foreseeable that arbitration under the Agreement sometimes would involve challenges to the credibility of testimony from Goodell or other League employees. When parties to a contract elect to resolve disputes through arbitration, a grievant "can ask no more impartiality than inheres in the method they have chosen." *Winfrey v. Simmons Foods, Inc.*, 495 F.3d 549, 551 (8th Cir. 2007) (quotation omitted). The Association's challenge to Henderson's service as arbitrator is thus foreclosed by *Williams*, and a remand is unnecessary. *Accord Nat'l Football League Mgmt. Council v. Nat'l Football Players Ass'n*, 820 F.3d 527, 548 (2d Cir. 2016).

The Association's remaining contention is that the arbitration was "fundamentally unfair." Fundamental fairness is a not a basis for vacatur identified in the Labor Management Relations Act or the Federal Arbitration Act. The latter statute informs our analysis in labor arbitration cases. *See Granite Rock Co. v. Int'l Bhd. of Teamsters*, 561 U.S. 287, 298 n.6 (2010); *Am. Postal Workers Union v. U.S. Postal Serv.*, 754 F.3d 109, 112 n.4 (2d Cir. 2014). Even assuming for the sake of analysis that there could be grounds for vacatur that are not specified in the statutes, *cf. Hall St. Assocs., LLC v. Mattel, Inc.*, 552 U.S. 576, 589 (2008), "our narrow construction of extra-statutory review militates against" adopting a "fundamental fairness" standard. *Hoffman v. Cargill, Inc.*, 236 F.3d 458, 462 (8th Cir. 2001). *Hoffman* did not "categorically reject the possibility of such a standard," but said that it could apply only "to arbitration schemes so deeply flawed as to preclude the possibility of a fair outcome." *Id.* at 462–63.

The Players Association does not identify any structural unfairness in the Article 46 arbitration process for which it bargained. The Association's fundamental fairness argument is little more than a recapitulation of its retroactivity argument against the merits of the arbitrator's decision. We have never suggested that when an award draws its essence from the collective bargaining agreement, a dissatisfied party nonetheless may achieve vacatur of the arbitrator's decision by showing that the result is "fundamentally unfair." The Association's fairness argument does not fit within the narrow window left open for consideration in *Hoffman*, and we therefore conclude that the contention is without merit.

For the foregoing reasons, the judgment of the district court is reversed, and the case is remanded with directions to dismiss the petition.

NOTES AND QUESTIONS

1. *Basis for Reviewing Arbitrator Under § 301 Precedent?* Did the union have any basis to argue that arbitrator Henderson based his decision on his own view of "industrial justice" or fairness rather than on the discretion that he determined the agreement afforded Commissioner Goodell? If not, could the district court's decision to vacate Henderson's affirmation of Goodell's

punishment have been consistent with the Court's clear directive in *Enterprise Wheel & Car Corp.*, *Misco*, and *Garvey*? Was it the arbitrator or the district judge that attempted to impose personal views on what is fair or just, regardless of the extent to which the agreement limited managerial discretion?

2. *Effect of District Court's Vacatur?* What should have been the effect of the district court's vacation of Henderson's decision on the appeal of the punishment imposed by Commissioner Goodell? Based on the Supreme Court's decisions in *Misco* and *Garvey*, the judge had authority only to vacate the arbitral decision, not to vacate any punishment. Article 46 affords players a right to appeal, but does not stay any punishment during the appeal. Did the district judge have any authority to enjoin punishment pending another arbitration hearing and decision? He in fact only remanded "for further proceedings before the arbitrator as permitted by the CBA."

3. *Federal Arbitration Act.* Note the Eighth Circuit's citation of the Federal Arbitration Act (FAA) when addressing the union's argument that the arbitration was "fundamentally unfair." The 1925-enacted FAA renders "enforceable" an agreement to arbitrate in any contract involving interstate commerce. When the Supreme Court rendered its decisions in *Lincoln Mills* and the *Trilogy*, the parties and the Justices apparently assumed that § 301 of the LMRA would have to be the basis for enforcement of agreements to arbitrate because § 1 of the FAA exempted "contracts of employment" like collective bargaining agreements. However, the Supreme Court subsequently invigorated the FAA, and in *Circuit City Stores, Inc. v. Adams*, 532 U.S. 105 (2001), held that this exemption covered employment contracts only of workers directly engaged in foreign or interstate commerce, such as railroad workers or truckers. This means that the FAA provides another basis for the enforcement of agreements to arbitrate in professional sports. Section 10 of the FAA also seems to provide further procedural grounds for vacating awards, including "evident partiality or corruption" or "refusing to hear evidence pertinent and material," but it does not provide for any judicial substantive review.

4. *The Tom Brady/Deflate-Gate Case.* For another appellate court's reversal of a district court review of an Article 46 hearing, see *NFL Management Council v. NFLPA*, 820 F.3d 527 (2d Cir. 2016) (Brady), cited in the Peterson case. There, the district court refused the NFL's request to confirm Commissioner Goodell's decision as the collectively bargained reviewer of the four-game suspension of New England Patriots quarterback Tom Brady for his involvement in the team's partial deflation of footballs he used in a playoff game. The district court instead vacated Arbitrator Goodell's decision and also Brady's four-game suspension. The district court did not explain how its vacation of the suspension was consistent with *Misco* and *Garvey*, or with Article 46 of the collective agreement. The Second Circuit reversed the district court and, like the Eighth Circuit in Peterson, adhered to the *Enterprise Wheel & Car* standard for limited judicial review and refused to allow the district judge to impose his own standards of "fundamental fairness" or "adequate notice."

The Second Circuit in Brady also considered the union's arguments under the review standards in the FAA. The court held that Goodell's Article 46-authorized review of Brady's punishment did not suffer from "evident partiality" because the parties to a collective agreement "can ask for no more partiality than inheres in the method they have chosen." 820 F.3d at 548. The court also held that the FAA does not restrict broad arbitral control over the admission of evidence unless that control is exercised to deny "fundamental fairness."

5. *Fundamental Fairness as a Review Standard?* The Second Circuit's interpretation of the FAA in the Brady case to allow vacatur of an arbitral award for the denial of "fundamental fairness" raises the question of whether courts can apply this standard to the review of any labor arbitration award. In another review of an Article 46 arbitration award, a district court in the Second Circuit refused to read the Brady case to expand this standard for judicial review of labor arbitration awards because doing so would be inconsistent with the jurisprudence developed by the Supreme Court under § 301 of the LMRA. *National Football Management Council v. National Football League Players Association*, 296 F. Supp. 3d 614 (S.D.N.Y. 2017) (Elliott). This decision denied a motion to vacate arbitrator Harold Henderson's acceptance of Commissioner Goodell's six-game suspension of star Dallas Cowboy running back Ezekiel Elliott for the violent physical abuse of his ex-girlfriend. The district court alternatively held that Henderson did not deny "fundamental fairness" by refusing to compel the Commissioner or the ex-girlfriend accuser to testify. The Second Circuit then declined to stay on appeal the district court's ruling, effectively defeating the NFLPA's efforts to enjoin the suspension. Do you agree that adoption of a "fundamental fairness" standard would undermine the finality and functionality of the arbitration process promised by the Court's § 301 decisions, including the *Trilogy*? Is the standard even implicit in the FAA grounds for vacatur quoted in note 3 above?

6. *Do Unilaterally Appointed Arbitrators Deserve the Same Deference?* Might the departure of the district judges in the Peterson and Brady cases from the review standard established in *Enterprise Wheel & Car* be in part explained by the judges' discomfort with arbitrators that are not chosen by both sides? Should the *Trilogy* apply only when arbitrators are chosen through a bilateral arbitration process? Or would the involvement of courts in judicial review of arbitrations conducted under management-empowering provisions like Article 46 lead only to an alternative loosening of substantive constraints on management discretion?

For an argument that decisions by the Commissioner under Article 46 should not be reviewed as arbitration decisions, but rather as decisions governing a private association subject to the common law arbitrariness review applied in the *Finley v. Kuhn* decision in Chapter 1, Section C, see Stephen Ross and Roy Eisenhardt, *Clear Statement Rules and the Integrity of Labor Arbitration*, 10 Arbitration Law Review 1 (2018).

CHAPTER 4

CONTRACTUAL RESTRAINTS ON LABOR MOBILITY IN PROFESSIONAL SPORTS*

■ ■ ■

Disputes about player movement from one team to another have been the central preoccupation of sports litigation since the 1870s. From the 1880s to the 1960s, the principal focus of court adjudication in professional sports was on contract law that defined the relationship between individual player and club. Teams regularly sought to enforce, and players to elude, restrictions that limited players to negotiating contracts with a single team. As suggested in the two prior chapters, these restrictions have been loosened through collective bargaining and the arbitration system it supports. By the early 1970s, moreover, unions representing players in professional sports leagues other than MLB helped launch successful federal antitrust litigation against player restraints. By the beginning of the 1980s, the players associations in each of the four major team sports—baseball, football, basketball, and hockey—had negotiated in their collective agreements new rules that specified whether and when a player could become a "free agent" and be entitled to move to any other team within that league that made him a better contract offer.

Contract law nonetheless remains relevant to current labor markets in professional sports for several reasons. First, it provides the background law that is modified by collective bargaining. Second, it continues to govern player movement between sports leagues. And third, it applies to working relationships not governed by collective agreements, including those of independent contractors, like tennis or golfing professionals, or coaches or other managerial employees of professional teams.

A. STANDARDS FOR ENFORCEMENT OF CONTRACTUAL MOBILITY RESTRAINTS

From the earliest days of American team sports, employers imposed contract terms on talented young athletes who wanted to play. Owners colluded to set limits on what they would pay their players. The contracts also contained provisions granting management the right to terminate the

---

* For commentary and other materials relevant to the topics in this chapter, check the Casebook Website (http://pennstatelaw.psu.edu/SportsTextWebsite).

contract upon fairly short notice and a promise by the player only to play for that particular club and no other club.

The earliest challenges to these restraints on player mobility came not from sports unions, but from player attempts to move to clubs that did not honor the restraints because of their membership in rival leagues. For instance, in their fourth year of operation in 1879, the baseball club owners of the National League created a "reserve system" because of the owners' concern with players moving from one club to another, sometimes in the middle of a season, for modest increases in salary. This management device worked well for the owners within the National League, but the device was challenged when Ban Johnson and eight entrepreneurs created the rival American League in 1901. The American League business strategy was to induce the marquee players of the National League to jump to the Americans. Fans followed their favorites to the new league. Among the finest stars of the American League was Napoleon Lajoie, a future Hall of Fame second baseman. Lajoie had anchored the Philadelphia Phillies' infield for five seasons. His $2,400 annual salary payable under his Phillies' contract was the ceiling imposed on players' salaries by agreement of the owners of the National League. To avoid this ceiling, Lajoie moved crosstown to play in the fledgling American League for the Athletics club owned and managed by Connie Mack. The Phillies brought suit against Napolean Lajoie, and his case was the first important sports law case decided by American courts.

PHILADELPHIA BALL CLUB V. LAJOIE
202 Pa. 210, 51 A. 973 (1902)

POTTER, JUSTICE.

The defendant in this case contracted to serve the plaintiff as a baseball player for a stipulated time. During that period he was not to play for any other club. He violated his agreement, however, during the term of his engagement, and, in disregard of his contract, arranged to play for another and a rival organization. The plaintiff, by means of this bill, sought to restrain him during the period covered by the contract. The court below refused an injunction.

* * *

The learned judge who filed the opinion in the court below, with great industry and painstaking care, collected and reviewed the English and American decisions bearing upon the question involved, and makes apparent the wide divergence of opinion which has prevailed. We think, however, that in refusing relief unless the defendant's services were shown to be of such a character as to render it impossible to replace him he has taken extreme ground. It seems to us that a more just and equitable rule is laid down in *Pom. Spec. Perf.* p. 31, where the principle is thus declared: "Where one person agrees to render personal services to another, which require and presuppose a special knowledge, skill, and ability in the employee, so that in case of a default the same service could not easily be obtained from others, although the affirmative specific performance of the contract is beyond the power of the court, its performance will be negatively enforced by enjoining its breach.... The damages for breach of such contract cannot be estimated with any certainty, and the employer cannot, by means of any damages, purchase the same service in the labor market." ... [W]hen, owing to special features, the contract involves peculiar convenience or advantage, or where the loss would be a matter of uncertainty, then the breach may be deemed to cause irreparable injury.

* * *

The court below finds from the testimony that "the defendant is an expert baseball player in any position; that he has a great reputation as a second baseman; that his place would be hard to fill with as good a player; that his withdrawal from the team would weaken it, as would the withdrawal of any good player, and would probably make a difference in the size of the audiences attending the game." We think that, in thus stating it, he puts it very mildly, and that the evidence would warrant a stronger finding as to the ability of the defendant as an expert ball player. He has been for several years in the service of the plaintiff club, and has been re-engaged from season to season at a constantly increasing salary. He has become thoroughly familiar with the action and methods of the other players in the club, and his own work is peculiarly meritorious as an integral part of the teamwork which is so essential. In addition to these features which render his services of peculiar and special value to the plaintiff, and not easily replaced, Lajoie is well known, and has great reputation among the patrons of the sport, for his ability in the position which he filled, and was thus a most attractive drawing card for the public. He may not be the sun in the baseball firmament, but he is certainly a bright particular star. We feel, therefore, that the evidence in this case justifies the conclusion that the services of the defendant are of such a unique character, and display such a special knowledge, skill, and ability, as renders them of peculiar value to the plaintiff, and so difficult of substitution that their loss will produce "irreparable injury," in the legal significance of that term, to the plaintiff. The action of the defendant in violating his contract is a breach of good faith, for which there would be no adequate redress at law, and the case, therefore, properly calls for the aid of equity in negatively enforcing the performance of the contract by enjoining against its breach.

[The court then turned to the lower court's argument that the contract lacked "mutuality of remedy," because while Lajoie was bound to "perpetually renewable" obligations, the team could release him (without pay) with just ten days' notice. The appeals court first quoted paragraphs in the contract whereby the "consideration" for Lajoie's salary was deemed to be not just performance of services, but also his "concession of the options of release and renewal," and acceptance of equitable relief against performing services for anybody else. The court then continued.]

* * *

We have, then, at the outset, the fact that the paragraphs now criticized and relied upon in defense were deliberately accepted by the defendant, and that such acceptance was made part of the inducement for the plaintiff to enter into the contract. We have the further fact that the contract has been partially executed by services rendered, and payment made therefore, so that the situation is not now the same as when the contract was wholly executory. The relation between the parties has been so far changed as to give to the plaintiff an equity, arising out of the part performance, to insist upon the completion of the agreement according to its terms by the defendant. This equity may be distinguished from the original right under the contract itself, and it might well be questioned whether the court would not be justified in giving effect to it by injunction, without regard to the mutuality or nonmutuality in the original contract. The plaintiff has so far performed its part of the contract in entire good faith, in every detail, and it would therefore be inequitable to permit the defendant to withdraw from the agreement at this late day.

The term "mutuality" or "lack of mutuality" does not always convey a clear and definite meaning. As was said in *Grove v. Hodges*, 55 Pa. 516:

> The legal principle that contracts must be mutual does not mean that in every case each party must have the same remedy for a breach by the other.

In the contract now before us the defendant agreed to furnish his skilled professional services to the plaintiff for a period which might be extended over three years by proper notice given before the close of each current year. Upon the other hand, the plaintiff retained the right to terminate the contract upon 10 days' notice and the payment of salary for that time and the expenses of defendant in getting to his home. But the fact of this concession to the plaintiff is distinctly pointed out as part of the consideration for the large salary paid to the defendant, and is emphasized as such; and owing to the peculiar nature of the services demanded by the business, and the high degree of efficiency which must be maintained, the stipulation is not unreasonable. Particularly is this true when it is remembered that the plaintiff has played for years under substantially the same regulations.

We are not persuaded that the terms of this contract manifest any lack of mutuality in remedy. Each party has the possibility of enforcing all the rights stipulated for in the agreement. It is true that the terms make it possible for the plaintiff to put an end to the contract in a space of time much less than the period during which the defendant has agreed to supply his personal services; but mere difference in the rights stipulated for does not destroy mutuality of remedy. Freedom of contract covers a wide range of obligation and duty as between the parties, and it may not be impaired, so long as the bounds of reasonableness and fairness are not transgressed.... We cannot agree that mutuality of remedy requires that each party should have precisely the same remedy, either in form, effect, or extent. In a fair and reasonable contract, it ought to be sufficient that each party has the possibility of compelling the performance of the promises which were mutually agreed upon.

* * *

The court cannot compel the defendant to play for the plaintiff, but it can restrain him from playing for another club in violation of his agreement. No reason is given why this should not be done, except that presented by the argument, that the right given to the plaintiff to terminate the contract upon 10 days' notice destroys the mutuality of the remedy. But to this it may be answered that, as already stated, the defendant has the possibility of enforcing all the rights for which he stipulated in the agreement, which is all that he can reasonably ask. Furthermore, owing to the peculiar nature and circumstances of the business, the reservation upon the part of the plaintiff to terminate upon short notice does not make the whole contract inequitable.

* * *

Upon a careful consideration of the whole case, we are of the opinion that the provisions of the contract are reasonable, and that the consideration is fully adequate. The evidence shows no indications of any attempt at overreaching or unfairness. Substantial justice between the parties requires that the court should restrain the defendant from playing for any other club during the term of his contract with the plaintiff.

Injunction granted.

The Lajoie litigation offered the National League its greatest victory against the rival American circuit, but it would prove short-lived. Most other courts refused to grant negative injunctions and clubs of the American League flourished at the box office. Ultimately, the economic battle was settled by negotiation and not litigation or economic warfare.

Napoleon Lajoie was, as the court stated, a "bright particular star." Over his 21-year career Lajoie had 3,251 hits and a .339 batting average.

He was the first second baseman voted into the Hall of Fame, part of the eleven Immortals, with Babe Ruth and Ty Cobb.

Despite their judicial victory, the Phillies failed to retrieve their star second baseman. The Philadelphia Athletics simply traded Lajoie to their Cleveland counterparts, and the Ohio courts refused the Phillies demand to give the Pennsylvania injunction "full faith and credit." Shortly thereafter, the National and American Leagues settled their war with the 1903 Major League Agreement that established the foundation for organized baseball. Lajoie stayed with the Cleveland franchise, which was renamed the "Naps" in his honor.

NOTES AND QUESTIONS

1. *Negative Not Affirmative Injunction.* Note that the court does not approve an affirmative injunction that would have forced Lajoie to play for the Nationals, but only a negative injunction against him playing for the Americans.

2. *Any Bargaining Leverage?* How could Lajoie have obtained better contract terms from the Phillies?

3. *Adequate Mutuality?* Do you agree with the conclusion in *Lajoie* that there was mutuality in the terms of this player contract? Does mutuality mean that two parties have reached an agreement, or should it mean more than that? Should courts have broad discretion to decide whether there is sufficient mutuality or fairness to make it equitable to enforce a contract? For all contracts, or only for personal service contracts?

4. *Unique Player?* Was Lajoie sufficiently "unique?" Weren't there other athletes who could play second base for the Phillies? (There were seven other second basemen in the National League and eight in the new American League—and many minor leagues operating all over the country in 1901.) What does the court mean when it says: "He may not be the sun in the baseball firmament, but he is certainly a bright particular star?" After he jumped to the Athletics in 1901, Lajoie led the American League in runs (145), hits (232), doubles (48), home runs (12), total bases (350), runs batted in (125), batting average (.426), on base percentage (.483), and slugging percentage (.643). Not a bad year! *Total Baseball*'s sabermetric ratings show Lajoie leading the AL in the all-important statistical category of Runs Created (179). Lajoie's Total Player Rating of 8.9 more than doubled the AL runner-up.

5. *Time to Change American Law? Lajoie* still seems to command strong support among modern American judges. *See, e.g., Marchio v. Letterlough*, 237 F. Supp. 2d 580 (E.D. Pa. 2002) (citing decisions supporting negative injunctions upon finding services are unique or extraordinary). By contrast, based on a concern that workers generally have inferior bargaining power compared to employers, many European jurisdictions explicitly permit workers

to terminate contracts with minimal penalties. *See* Frank Hendrickx, "Employment Relationships at National Level: Belgium," in *Regulating Employment Relationships in Professional Football* 39, 47–48 (Michele Colucci and Frank Hendrickx eds., 2014). Furthermore, there is a school of academics and worker-rights advocates who argue against the "commodification" of labor and therefore suggest workers should not be able to contract away their right to choose for whom to work. For a summary of the literature and application of the argument to Australian sports, see Matt Nichol, *The Commodification of Labour in the Australian Football League: What is the Impact of Free Agency?*, 31 Australian Journal of Labour Law 73 (2018). Do you agree that players should not be subject to negative injunctions that effectively force them to 'play out their contract' with an employer for whom they no longer wish to work? How might this affect initial salaries paid players for multi-year contracts?

The *Lajoie* case was actually one of the few cases in which a baseball team ever secured an injunction against its own player, but it was an important victory nonetheless. Lajoie was the American League's finest catch when it raided the rosters of the 25-year-old National League. (The only comparable player who did not jump to the American League was Honus Wagner, who stayed with his hometown Pittsburgh Pirates.) The possibility that courts might stop players from jumping to the new league raised by the Lajoie case made it critical that the two circuits reach a rapprochement, which they did in 1903. Even more important than judicial involvement were the economic realities of the time. The new American League was prospering in those cities where one of their clubs went head-to-head with a National League rival. The Nationals gave in and Ban Johnson, president of the American League, became baseball's strongman for almost two decades, until the Black Sox scandal compelled baseball's sixteen owners to find an even more dictatorial commander-in-chief, Kenesaw Mountain Landis, baseball's first commissioner (*see* Chapter 1, Section B).

A series of cases in the twentieth century arose in other professional team sports when rival leagues battled over the rights to contract with important players. By the 1950s, courts had largely overcome their reluctance (notwithstanding *Lajoie*) to issue injunctions against athletes. The courts' attention shifted from the supposed inequity of the contract toward the player (its lack of mutuality) to the team's need to retain especially talented athletes. In *Central NY Basketball, Inc. v. Barnett*, 181 N.E.2d 506 (Ohio Ct. Comm. Pleas 1961), the same type of Ohio court that had refused to enforce the negative injunction against Lajoie in 1902, granted a negative injunction to the Syracuse Nationals of the NBA barring

Dick Barnett from playing for another basketball team so as to pressure their stellar guard to fulfill his contract promise: "Professional players in the major baseball, football, and basketball leagues have unusual talents and skills or they would not be so employed. Such players, the defendant Barnett included, are not easily replaced." 181 N.E.2d 517.

Courts applied the equitable doctrine of "unclean hands" in two notable injunction cases involving the rivalry between the National Football League and the American Football League. In *New York Football Giants, Inc. v. Los Angeles Chargers Football Club, Inc. (Flowers)*, 291 F.2d 471 (5th Cir. 1961), the NFL's New York Giants signed Charlie Flowers, a star player for the University of Mississippi football team, to a pro football contract in December 1959 while he was still in college. If they had publicized the contract signing at that time, Flowers would have lost his NCAA eligibility to play in the New Year's Day Sugar Bowl against Mississippi's traditional rival, Louisiana State. Accordingly, Giants owner Wellington Mara acceded to Flower's request to keep the contract (and signing bonus) secret until January 2, 1960; thus, the team did not submit the contract to NFL Commissioner Pete Rozelle for his approval.

Later in December, the Los Angeles Chargers of the new American Football League offered Flowers more money to play for them. Flowers notified the Giants that he was withdrawing from their contract and returning their uncashed bonus checks. Flowers signed with the Chargers on January 1, immediately after the Sugar Bowl, and the Giants went to court seeking an injunction to nullify Flowers' contract with the Chargers and bar him from playing for the AFL team. In court, the Giants were met with "the age old but sometimes overlooked doctrine that 'he who comes into equity must come with clean hands.'"

> Here the plaintiff's [Giants'] whole difficulty arises because it admittedly took from Flowers what it claims to be a binding contract, but which it agreed with Flowers it would, in effect, represent was not in existence in order to deceive others who had a very material and important interest in the subject matter. If there had been a straightforward execution of the document, followed by its filing with the Commissioner, none of the legal problems now presented to this court to untangle would exist. We think no party had the right thus to create problems by its devious and deceitful conduct and then approach a court of equity with a plea that the pretended status which it has foisted on the public be ignored and its rights be declared as if it had acted in good faith throughout.
>
> When it became apparent from uncontradicted testimony of Mara that this deceit was practiced in order to bring into being

the "contract" sued upon, the trial court should have dismissed the suit without more on the basis of the "clean hands" doctrine.

Id. at 474.

The commercial war between the NFL and the AFL in the early 1960s produced numerous cases of players trying to renege on secret pre-college-bowl game contracts (and bonus payments) with a team in one league in order to sign with a team in the other league. While *Flowers* reflected the standard approach to this kind of case, the Tenth Circuit in *Houston Oilers v. Neely*, 361 F.2d 36 (1966), granted an injunction despite similar misconduct by the AFL Oilers in violation of NCAA rules. In addition to the *Neely* and *Flowers* cases, see *Detroit Football Co. v. Robinson*, 186 F. Supp. 933 (E.D. La.1960), and *Los Angeles Rams Football Club v. Cannon*, 185 F. Supp. 717 (S.D. Cal. 1960), where the district courts found agreements not approved by the football league commissioner to be merely revocable offers. Interestingly, in every one of these cases the court ended up siding with the AFL team and against the NFL team. Is that just a coincidence, or did it reflect a judicial desire to assist the upstart football league against the established league that had far greater market power? The *Neely* court made a great deal out of the fact that Ralph Neely was intelligent and sophisticated. He knew what he was doing when he helped hide the contract from his college and the NCAA. Should this be a factor on which a case should turn? What if the deception were proposed by the club, and not by the player? What if the player was relatively naive and uninformed and thus more likely to be led astray by the professional team?

The next case brings the story up to the 1970s and the competition launched against the NFL by the World Football League (WFL). In the course of his opinion, the judge describes comparable litigation involving basketball stars Rick Barry and Billy Cunningham, who were courted by both the NBA and the American Basketball Association (ABA), a competitor that emerged in the late 1960s. The interesting legal question is whether it is consistent with a player's contractual obligations to his present team to sign a contract to play for another team in the future.

CINCINNATI BENGALS V. BERGEY
453 F. Supp. 129 (S.D. Ohio 1974)

PORTER, DISTRICT JUDGE.

[Bill Bergey, a star linebacker for the Cincinnati Bengals of the NFL, earned slightly less than $40,000 per year under a non-guaranteed contract for 1974 that gave the Bengals an option on his services for 1975. In April 1974, Bergey signed a no-cut, three-year contract with the Virginia Ambassadors of the newly formed WFL, which agreed to pay Bergey

$125,000 per year plus a $150,000 signing bonus. This WFL contract was designed to begin with the 1976 football season, but would be accelerated forward if the Bengals released Bergey for any reason. Bergey was one of several Bengal stars pursued by the WFL (including starting linemen such as Bob Trumpy, Bob Johnson, and Rufus Mayes), as part of a WFL effort to stockpile a large number of NFL players for the new league. The threat of competition from the WFL moved NFL teams to sharply elevate their salary levels—the Bengals offered Bergey a new five-year contract for a total of $400,000. Unsuccessful in that bidding war, the Bengals sued Bergey, the Ambassadors, and the WFL, on the grounds that Bergey's future service agreement with the WFL team undermined and interfered with the Bengals' rights under its existing contract with Bergey.

Extensive testimony was offered about the special character of football as a sport and as a business enterprise, particularly from Bengals' founder and head coach, Paul Brown, and its assistant coach, Bill Walsh. The judge concluded that, notwithstanding the special emotional demands of football, Bergey's signing of a "futures" contract with another team would not reduce his effectiveness with the Bengals during his existing contract. However, the judge felt there likely would be an adverse impact if several other Bengals' stars were to follow Bergey's lead, because "a football team is a sort of delicate mechanism, the success of whose operation is dependent upon the coordination of various cohesive units."

On the other side of the ledger, though, was the harmful effect on the WFL if its teams were barred from signing NFL contract players for promotion of this new venture. The court noted that "starting a new franchise and a new league is a risky business." It then continued . . .]

* * *

Increased television coverage of professional football games has produced a sophisticated audience. The costs of fielding a competitive team are much higher today than in 1960 [when the American Football League first played]. The cost of acquiring players of exceptional ability has contributed significantly to the substantial increase in ticket prices (though these price increases have not been proportionately as great as the increase in costs). The higher ticket prices mean that sports fans expect major league entertainment for their sports dollar. Faced with the stiff competition for the sports dollar by the NFL, as well as other professional sports organizations, the WFL seeks to ensure its future by signing established NFL players to give the new league "credibility" in the eyes of the public. The signing of professional players is also necessary to overcome the doubts of college players as to the future of the league. . . . Mr. Putnam stated that the signing of name players to future contracts is "essential" to the WFL's success, since the league's financial future is dependent in great part on the earliest possible public acceptance of the WFL as a marketer of "major league" professional football.

[Turning to the legal issues, the court considered two earlier precedents involving Rick Barry and Billy Cunningham, who had been the subject of a similar tug of war between the National Basketball Association and the American Basketball Association in the late 1960s.

Barry's case was extremely entangled. While under contract with the NBA's San Francisco Warriors for 1967–1968, Barry signed a three-year deal with the ABA's Oakland Oaks. Barry was enjoined from jumping to the Oaks for the 1967–1968 season (*see Lemat Corp. v. Barry*, 80 Cal. Rptr. 240 (Cal. App. 1969)), but he did play for Oakland in 1968–69. However, when the Oaks were bought by the Washington Capitols, Barry, who wanted to remain in the Bay area, signed a five-year contract with the Warriors. When the Capitols sought injunctive relief against the NBA team, Barry's argument was that the Oakland contract had been tainted from the outset because of the conflict with his earlier agreement with the Warriors. The Ninth Circuit rejected this argument in *Washington Capitols Basketball Club v. Barry*, 419 F.2d 472 (9th Cir.1969). There was no actionable wrong in an athlete (like any other employee) signing a new contract during the period of his existing contract, as long as "performance and consideration" under the new contract were to begin after the expiration of the existing agreement, and there was no "encouragement" to terminate the latter contract early.

A similar ruling was rendered in *Munchak Corp. v. Cunningham*, 457 F.2d 721 (4th Cir.1972), in which the court refused to nullify Cunningham's contract to play for the Carolina Cougars in the 1971–1972 season, even though the three-year agreement had been signed in August 1969 when Cunningham was under contract to the Philadelphia 76ers. The judge in the *Bergey* case then addressed and rejected the Bengals' argument that judicial precedents from basketball should not govern the assertedly different world of professional football.]

* * *

When *Barry* and *Cunningham* are applied to the case at bar, the Court can only conclude that neither the WFL nor Bergey committed a tortious or otherwise unlawful act in entering into negotiations for and reaching agreement upon a contract for Bergey's personal services to commence after the expiration of his contract with the Bengals. In the language of Cunningham, there are no more obligations to be protected by either party to the Bengals contract after May 1, 1976.

Plaintiff argues that the acceleration clause of Bergey's WFL contract induces Bergey to seek his release prior to his NFL contract's expiration. We reject this argument, however, because we accept as true Bergey's testimony that he has no intention of seeking an early release. And, notwithstanding plaintiff's interpretation of *Barry*, we do not read the Ninth Circuit's opinion in that case as granting to Barry the right to breach his contract. Bergey will be liable should he breach his contract while its terms are still in effect.

* * *

In short, we conclude that *Barry* and *Cunningham* support the proposition that it is not illegal for either the player or the sports organization, at the time when the player is under a valid contract to one team, to negotiate and enter into a contract with a different, competing, team and league, under the terms of which the player agrees to render his services at the expiration of his current contract.

* * *

Harm To Public Interest

* * *

Next, we flesh out the bare bones conclusion that plaintiff has failed to show an absence of harm to the public interest if an injunction is granted herein. As we view it, the "public interest" within the meaning of that phrase as it is used here is the policy such as that behind the antitrust laws to encourage to the fullest extent practicable free and open competition in the marketplace. Restraints on competition are not favored.

* * *

The Court would be blind if it did not recognize that there is a public interest of another sort. This is the concern among fans over the actual and prospective loss of key members of a team of which they are devoted followers and the effect this may have on that team's "chances." It is clear that the Court cannot take such "public interest" into consideration. The only public interest that can properly be taken into account is the policy of the law to encourage free competition in the marketplace. Hence, the denial of an injunction is not a case of the Court's turning its back on the fans and the owners of the plaintiff's franchise, as the plaintiff improperly suggested in final argument that it might be.

Harm to WFL and Plaintiff

* * *

The conclusion that plaintiff has not made a clear showing of irreparable injury to itself is a difficult one to make. One reason it is, is that there is nothing to go on because this case is unique. As pointed out by Coach Brown, in all his forty years: "I've never had one like this, where I had a football player playing for me who is also under contract to somebody else." For another, while it may be too late to close the barn door as far as Bergey and Chomyszak are concerned, the threatened damage from the loss of Bob Johnson, et al., may not occur, and will not occur, if the Bengals match any offer they get from a WFL team. The Bengals argue that the fact that in order to match WFL offers they may have to tear up existing contracts and pay more for present services is evidence of irreparable injury.

We recognize that it will cost the Bengals something to bid for the future services of its players to preserve the continuity of the team's performance when present contracts expire. We do not, however, follow the argument that that is evidence of irreparable injury. Prior to the emergence of the World Football League, the teams in the National Football League could rest in relative assurance that the services of their players presently under short term contracts would remain available beyond the termination dates should the clubs desire to offer players further contracts. The absence of a competitor league justified that self-assurance, for the NFL, until now, has been "the only game in town." With the rise of the WFL, the NFL can no longer rely upon the absence of a competitor for protection of its claims to the future services of players, for which the established teams have neither bargained nor paid consideration.

It is not the players' present services for which the clubs will have to pay more, for those are protected by contracts which can presumably be enforced in the usual manner. It is only when the NFL chooses (and such decision is likely) to join the competition for the later services of its players that it will incur these higher costs. In our best judgment, such higher costs will be attributable to competition and not unfair competition.

* * *

Injunction denied.

NOTES AND QUESTIONS

1. *Injunction Against Futures Contract?* Might there be circumstances where a team could get a negative injunction or court order nullifying a futures contract?

2. *Effect of Multiple Contracts?* What if several starters on the team signed with another team? Might that changed circumstance warrant judicial intervention?

3. *Alternative Remedy?* What if a player under a futures contract with another team started to play very poorly or faked an injury or started publicly trashing the current team or league? What would be the appropriate remedy?

4. *Intraleague Anti-Tampering Policies.* North American professional sports leagues currently have anti-tampering rules—incorporated by reference in collective bargaining agreements—that prohibit teams from negotiating with or even soliciting the services of any player while he is under contract with another team. These rules effectively give clubs *two* intraleague exclusive rights for the duration of a player's contract: the right to the player's services in the sport, and the right to negotiate any potential extension of the contract. The policies also cover coaches and high-level front office employees, like general managers and team presidents.

Litigation about player contracts vividly displays the conflict between two visions of contract and its enforcement. One view pictures contracts as personal promises that create moral obligations and entitlements and are worthy of as much legal teeth as the law can sensibly provide. From this perspective, while judges might reasonably be cautious about issuing a specific order forcing a player to play for the team to which he is under contract, they should not hesitate to enjoin him from playing for another team, which because of financial pressures would then usually soon yield the first result.

An alternative conception of contract sees it as an economic instrument the law should enforce only to the extent such judicial intervention produces an efficient allocation of society's resources. Under this theory, a player should be entitled to break an initial commitment to one team as long as he is willing to pay that team for its financial losses suffered through loss of his services. The assumption is that such contract breaches will be committed only when it is socially efficient to do so—in other words, when someone else finds the player's services more valuable and thus worth enough extra money to leave the player better off after compensation damages are paid to the original team.

The cases we have read leave no doubt that in terms of bottom line results, if not underlying rationale, the courts and arbitrators (including commissioners) have embraced the first view about player contracts, enforcing the value of promise keeping. But is this judicial verdict socially desirable? Consider these specific questions about sports cases:

1. Is society (at least the sports community) better off with the athlete playing for the original team or the new team? How do you decide?

2. Is it possible to calculate the actual damages inflicted on a team if a player defects? By analogy, how would you go about calculating the tort damages payable to a team that lost a star player because of physical injuries due to someone else's fault?

3. Suppose that a court issues an injunction that forbids a player to move to another team. Is the player likely to stay and perform effectively

for his original team? If not, has litigation been futile for that team? Or has the club nonetheless gained something of tangible value from the judicial order? The Coase theorem posits that the law's initial allocation of the right to an asset does not dictate its ultimate destination, so long as some voluntary transactions are permitted, are feasible regarding disposition of the asset, both parties have reasonably complete access to relevant information, and bargaining costs are not significant. What does this theorem imply for the way these legal doctrines play themselves out in sports over the longer run? Specifically, if bargaining is permitted, is the issuance of an injunction likely to impede efficient movement of players, or to ensure that the original employer is fully compensated for their own expected losses?

4. An alternative way of characterizing the issue is the following: whereas limiting the team's remedy to damages treats the contract as simply a liability rule, giving the club injunctive relief means that the contract has, in effect, conferred on the team a property right in the player's services. In the sports world, the latter term is not merely a rhetorical label. A standard feature of the player contract in every sport has been a right of the team to sell or trade the player's services to another team by assigning his contract for cash or other players' contracts. Owners have used that right to sell even the greatest players in the game—the Boston Red Sox sold Babe Ruth to the New York Yankees in 1919, and the Edmonton Oilers sold Wayne Gretzky to the Los Angeles Kings in 1988. As long ago as *Lajoie*, however, courts have observed that players are paid more than generously for giving the teams that prerogative. Is this judicial sentiment apt? Is it even accurate?

Most interleague competition for player services disappeared from the four major U.S. professional sports leagues by the 1990s because existing leagues had either merged with their rivals or crushed them in the economic contest. Players could find teams willing to employ them in the face of a contractual restraint only by departing for a foreign league or for another sport. The next case presents an international player contract dispute in the contemporary context of a collective agreement negotiated by a players' union and interpreted by a labor arbitrator. Brian Shaw was drafted by the Boston Celtics in 1988 and signed a one-year contract. The next year after the Celtics offered Shaw a modest increase in salary, Shaw signed a two-year contract with an Italian basketball team, Il Messaggero Roma, paying him $800,000 in the first year and $900,000 in the second. That contract also gave Shaw the option to opt out of the second year if he wanted to return to the NBA.

In January of 1990, Celtics executives flew to Rome and signed Shaw to a five-year deal—with a $450,000 bonus and an average salary of slightly over $1 million a year. Shaw undertook to terminate his Il Messaggero contract during the designated window period. At that time, Shaw was without an agent, although he signed the contract in front of the United States consul in Rome. Later that spring, Shaw retained an agent, who told his client that the Celtics' contract did not reflect Shaw's potential market value and that he should not leave Il Messaggero that year. (If Shaw had played another year in Rome, he would have been a free agent and able to negotiate with any NBA club and not just the Celtics.) The Celtics took the dispute to the permanent arbitrator under the NBA Players Association collective bargaining agreement, whose terms were incorporated by reference in Shaw's (and all other players') individual contracts. The arbitrator ruled that Shaw had to deliver the registered termination letter to Il Messaggero, and a federal district judge issued an order of enforcement. Shaw appealed.

BOSTON CELTICS V. BRIAN SHAW
908 F.2d 1041 (1st Cir. 1990)

BREYER, CIRCUIT JUDGE.

* * *

II. The Legal Merits

Shaw makes two basic categories of argument in his effort to show that the district court lacked the legal power to enter its order. First, he says that the arbitration award was itself unlawful. Second, he says that regardless of the lawfulness of the award, the district court followed improper procedures. We shall address these arguments in turn and explain why we find each not persuasive.

A. *The Arbitrator's Decision*

Shaw says that the district court should not have enforced the arbitrator's award because that award was itself unlawful, for any of five separate reasons.

1. The termination promise. Shaw argues that the arbitrator could not reasonably find that he broke a contractual promise to the Celtics because, he says, the Celtics had previously agreed with the Players Association that contracts with individual players such as Shaw would not contain promises of the sort here at issue, namely, a promise to cancel a contract to play with a different team. Shaw says that this previous agreement between the Celtics and the Players Association renders his promise to terminate Il Messaggero "null and void." To support this argument, he points to Article I, § 2 of the Collective Bargaining Agreement, which Shaw and the Celtics, through cross-reference, made part of their individual agreement. Section 2 says, "Any amendment to a Uniform Player Contract [of the type Shaw and the Celtics used], other

than those permitted by this [Collective Bargaining] Agreement, shall be null and void." The Agreement permits amendments (a) "in . . . respect to the compensation . . . to be paid the player," (b) "in respect to specialized compensation arrangements," (c) in respect to a "compensation payment schedule," and (d) in respect to "protect[ion]" of compensation in the event of contract termination. Shaw says that his promise to cancel the Il Messaggero agreement was an amendment to the Uniform Players Contract that does not concern compensation, specialized compensation, compensation schedules, or compensation protection; therefore, it is "null and void."

Shaw's argument, while logical, fails to show that the arbitrator's contrary finding is unlawful. The reasons it fails are fairly straightforward. First, the argument concerns the proper interpretation of a contract negotiated pursuant to a collective bargaining agreement. Second, federal labor law gives arbitrators, not judges, the power to interpret such contracts. The Supreme Court, noting the strong federal policy favoring the voluntary settlement of labor disputes, has written that a labor arbitration award is valid so long as it "draws its essence" from the labor contract. *See United Steelworkers v. Enterprise Wheel & Car Corp.*, 363 U.S. 593, 597 (1960). An award "draws its essence" from the contract so long as the "arbitrator is even arguably construing or applying the contract and acting within the scope of his authority." *United Paperworkers Int'l v. Misco*, 484 U.S. 29, 38 (1987).

* * *

Third, one can find "plausible arguments" favoring the arbitrator's construction. Shaw's "rescission" promise defines the beginning of the compensation relationship. It also plausibly determines, at the very least, whether Shaw's compensation will begin at $1.1 million (and continue for three years) or whether it will begin at $1.2 million (and continue for only two years). More importantly, and also quite plausibly, Shaw's overall compensation might have been much different had he declined to promise to play for the Celtics in 1990–91, thereby forcing the Celtics, perhaps, to obtain the services of a replacement for that year. The NBA Commissioner, who reviews all player contracts, found that the term was related to "compensation," as did the arbitrator. We cannot say that their findings lack any "plausible" basis.

* * *

In sum, we find the arbitration award lawful; and, in doing so, it has not been necessary for us to consider the Celtics' additional argument that Shaw bears an especially heavy legal burden in this case because the Players Association does not support him.

B. The District Court Proceedings

[The court then turned to the question whether the district court's injunction ordering Shaw to rescind "forthwith" his contract with Il Messaggero and barring him from playing basketball for anyone but the Celtics satisfied the standards for preliminary injunctive relief.]

* * *

To begin with, the Celtics have shown a clear likelihood of success on the merits.... The Celtics also have demonstrated irreparable harm. Without speedy relief, they will likely lose the services of a star athlete next year, *see Wright & Miller* § 2948, at 439 & n. 34 (1972) (collecting cases that have found irreparable harm "in the loss by an athletic team of the services of a star athlete"), and, unless they know fairly soon whether Shaw will, or will not play for them, they will find it difficult to plan intelligently for next season. Indeed, in his contract Shaw expressly:

> represents and agrees that he has extraordinary and unique skill and ability as a basketball player ... and that any breach by the Player of this contract will cause irreparable injury to the Club.

Further, the court could reasonably find that the "balance of harms" favors the Celtics. Of course, a preliminary injunction, if ultimately shown wrong on the merits, could cause Shaw harm. He might lose the chance to play in the country, and for the team, that he prefers. On the other hand, this harm is somewhat offset by the fact that ultimate success on the merits—*i.e.,* a finding that Shaw was not obligated to terminate Il Messaggero after all—would likely result in the following scenario: Shaw might still be able to sign with Il Messaggero and, if not, he would always have the Celtics contract of over $5 million to fall back upon. At the same time, the court's failure to issue the injunction, if the merits ultimately favored the Celtics, could cause them serious harm of the sort just mentioned (*i.e.,* significantly increased difficulty in planning their team for next season). Given the very small likelihood that Shaw would ultimately prevail on the merits, and the "comparative" harms at stake, the district court could properly decide that the overall "balance" favored the Celtics, not Shaw.

Finally, the court could properly find that issuing a preliminary injunction would not harm the public interest. Indeed, as we have pointed out, the public interest favors court action that "effectuate[s]" the parties' intent to resolve their disputes informally through arbitration. Where the dispute involves a professional basketball player's obligation to play for a particular team, one could reasonably consider expeditious, informal and effective dispute-resolution methods to be essential, and, if so, the public interest favoring court action to "effectuate" those methods of dispute-resolution would seem at least as strong as it is in respect to work-related disputes typically arising under collective bargaining agreements. *See New England Patriots Football Club, Inc. v. University of Colorado*, 592 F.2d 1196, 1200 (1st Cir.1979) (collecting cases in which professional sports players were enjoined from playing for rival teams). Shaw, while conceding that the public also has an interest in seeing that contracts between consenting adults are honored, points to a general policy disfavoring enforcement of personal service contracts. That latter policy, however, typically prevents a court from ordering an individual to perform a personal service; it does not prevent a court from ordering an individual to rescind a contract for services and to refrain from performing a service for others.

Shaw makes an additional argument. He notes that courts will not provide equitable relief such as an injunction to a party with "unclean hands," and he argues that the Celtics' hands are not clean. To support this argument, he has submitted an affidavit saying, in effect, that he signed the contract in a weak moment. His trip to Italy had made him "homesick;" he was "depressed" by what he viewed as undeserved and "negative criticism" in the Italian press; he was not represented by an agent; the Celtics had been urging him to sign up; he read the contract only for about 20 minutes while he was driving around Rome with a Celtics official; and no one ever explained to him that if he did not sign and played with Il Messaggero for another year, he would become a "free agent," able to bargain thereafter with any American team, perhaps for an even greater salary than the Celtics were willing to pay him.

Other evidence in the record, however, which Shaw does not deny, shows that he is a college graduate; that he has played under contract with the Celtics before; that the contract is a standard form contract except for a few, fairly simple, rather clear, additions; that he had bargained with the Celtics for an offer that increased from $3.4 million (in December) to $5.4 million (less than one month later); that he looked over the contract before signing it; that he told the American consul in Rome (as he signed it) that he had read and understood it; and that he did not complain about the contract until he told the Celtics in June that he would not honor it.

Given this state of the record, the district court could easily, and properly, conclude that the Celtics' hands were not "unclean." The one case Shaw cites in support of his position, *Minnesota Muskies, Inc. v. Hudson*, 294 F. Supp. 979, 981 (M.D.N.C.1969), is not on point. The player in Muskies had a contract with Team A that permitted Team A, not the player, to renew the contract for additional years. Team B lured the player away from Team A even though it knew that Team A intended to exercise its contractual right to keep the player. The court held that this contractual interference amounted to "unclean hands" and refused Team B's request for an injunction preventing the player from returning to Team A. Here, in contrast, Il Messaggero has no contractual right to retain Shaw; whether or not the contract is renewed or rescinded is entirely up to Shaw, not Il Messaggero. Under those circumstances, we cannot find anything improper, "unclean," or unfair about the Celtics' convincing Shaw (indeed, paying Shaw) to exercise his contractual right in their favor. *Cf.* Restatement (Second) of Torts § 768 (1979).

* * *

Injunction upheld.

NOTES AND QUESTIONS

1. *Effect of Arbitration Decision?* Unlike in *Lajoie* and *Bergey*, in *Shaw* there was an earlier adjudication of the issues by a labor arbitrator jointly appointed by the NBA and its Players Association under their collective agreement. Should this fact make a court more willing to order equitable relief against a player seeking to stay in another league?

2. *Assignment Clause.* In the middle of the 1991–1992 season, the Celtics traded an injured Shaw to the Miami Heat for the latter's equally disenchanted point guard, Sherman Douglas. Such trades are made possible by the assignment clause in the standard player contract that gives the team, the player's employer, the right to assign the personal services contract to another team in the same league. Though unthinkable in most other employment contexts, this provision is standard in athlete's contracts unless the player can negotiate a "no-trade" clause, or the collective bargaining agreement gives a veteran player some control over being traded. Should this feature of the contract influence a court's decision about whether to force the player to play for the team with which he originally signed? For the team to which he was traded?

More generally, is this assignment clause fair and reasonable, or should it be void as against public policy? Would your answer hinge on whether the players union had agreed to the inclusion of such a clause in the standard contract? (It did.) For what reasons do club owners want such a clause? What would be the long-term effect on player-club relations if such clauses were not enforced by the courts? Does this provision, along with that requiring commissioner approval before the contract can become valid, essentially mean that the player is as much under contract to the league as to the club? Should the league, then, also be liable for any breach of contract (*i.e.*, failure to pay) by the club? *See USFL Players Ass'n v. USFL*, 650 F. Supp. 12 (D. Or.1986) (league and clubs were not single employer, so that league could not be held liable for wages owed by member club).

3. *Meaning of No-Trade Clause.* In *Munchak Corp. v. Cunningham*, 457 F.2d 721 (4th Cir. 1972), Billy Cunningham negotiated a "no-trade" clause in his basketball contract with the ABA's Carolina Cougars. Subsequently, the Cougars were sold and all of the team's player contracts were assigned to the

new owner. Cunningham sought to avoid being held to his contract by arguing that this assignment made it void. The Fourth Circuit rejected his argument and held that a standard "no assignment" clause merely meant that the player could not be traded to a different club, not that he could not be traded to a different owner of the same club. Is this a fair interpretation of general "no-trade" language? Would your answer be different if the team was sold to a new owner who immediately relocated the franchise to a different city and changed the name of the team?

B. THE RESERVE SYSTEM AND ITS DEMISE

As noted above, in 1879, the eight club owners of baseball's National League formulated the first reserve system in professional sports. The reserve system created a restricted market in which the players could sell their services. Each player could only negotiate with one club, creating a monopsony in economic terms. Previous to the establishment of the reserve system, players "revolved" from one club to another, sometimes in the middle of a season, seeking better pay. Under the reserve system, pay levels dropped dramatically as cartel rules controlled the movement of players.

To ease reading of the following *Chase* opinion, consider this capsule summary of the reserve system:

1. Each team in a league was entitled to list a certain number of players with whom it had a contract relationship and to which the team claimed exclusive rights.

2. All other teams in the league agreed to respect the reserve lists of their fellow league members and not to "tamper" with another team's players by inducing them to move.

3. All teams in the league agreed to sign players only to a single standard form contract. A key provision in that contract was that when its term expired, the team retained an option to renew the contract for another season with the same provisions as before—including this perpetually renewable option clause—except for salary. In case of disagreement over salary, the team had the prerogative to set the salary for the upcoming year.

4. A further feature of the reserve system was the draft, whereby major league teams agreed to select (in reverse order of finish in the previous season) from among minor league players talented enough to play in the major leagues. The modern rookie draft was actually first developed in football in 1936, emulated in basketball in the late 1940s, and adopted by baseball and hockey only in the mid-1960s. The players selected were reserved to the drafting club even before they signed the first standard form contract.

AMERICAN LEAGUE BASEBALL CLUB OF CHICAGO V. CHASE
86 Misc. 441, 149 N.Y.S. 6 (1914)

BISSELL, JUDGE.

[Hal Chase played first base for the Chicago White Sox in the American League. In March 1914 he signed a one-year contract with the Sox for the upcoming season. However, on June 15, 1914, Chase gave the White Sox notice that he was terminating the contract, and on June 20, he jumped to the Buffalo team in the new Federal Baseball League. The White Sox filed suit for breach of contract and sought an immediate injunction barring Chase from playing for Buffalo.

The court quoted from a number of provisions in Major League Baseball's National Agreement, the Rules of the National Commission, and the terms of the standard player agreement. This combination of baseball rules gave each team an "absolute right and title" to players it had "selected" (or drafted), required all players to enter into the standard contract prescribed by the National Commission and incorporated in this contract a term that gave the team the option to renew each player's contract (if the team so chose) on the same terms as in the previous year, but also gave the team the right to terminate a player's contract on ten days' notice (the provision that had generated the "mutuality" issue in the earlier *Lajoie* case).]

* * *

It appears that originally the defendant was a "selected" player; but whether he was a selected player at the time he entered the service of the plaintiff is immaterial. Had he come from the vacant lots of the cities, or the fields of the country, or from the college campus, and therefore been "a free agent" at the time he made his entry into "organized baseball," the result would have been the same. If a sale or trade is to be made by one major league club to another, section 3 of article VI governs, and "The right and title of a major league club to its players shall be absolute."

If a sale or trade is to be made by a major league club to a minor league club, section 9 of article VI governs, and the sale or trade is not absolute until waivers have been obtained from the other major league clubs. Thus a player in the highest league, without the exercise of any individual choice, may be required to take service with a club of a lower league where smaller salaries are paid, and where both the aggregate of the salary list and the salary of each individual player is subject to strict limitation under the terms of the National Agreement. No opportunity is afforded the player to solicit employment upon his own account. No right is afforded to enable him to resist an unjust limitation upon his power to earn. No consideration is afforded either himself or his family with respect to choosing a home. In short, he is placed where he must, at all times while playing in "organized baseball," consider that his home is only the place in which his services are for the time being controlled.

The baseball player, even though about to be discharged, is still a thing of value to the club owner. The termination of the obligations by the club owner pursuant to the 10-day provision is not accomplished by him without securing some return. If the player goes to another major league club, it is either in exchange for some other more desired player or players, or for the waiver price; and the same is true if the discharged player is sent to a league of lower grade.

It seems that the promotion of the ball player is also hedged about with such limitations as to make the property in him absolute whether he will accept terms or not, and to make those terms when arrived at only liberal enough to prevent the player from seeking other means of earning his livelihood.

* * *

"Organized baseball" as conducted under the terms of the National Agreement further seeks to enforce and perpetuate its title to and control of its players as follows:

Section 1, Article VI, of the National Agreement provides:

All parties to this agreement pledge themselves to recognize the right of reservation and respect contracts between players and clubs under its protection. No club operating under this agreement shall at any time negotiate for the purchase or lease of the property of another club without first securing the consent of such club.

Section 2 of Article VI is as follows:

Any club or league which harbors a player who refuses to observe his contract with a club member of any party to this agreement, or to abide by its reservation, shall be considered an outlaw organization, and its claim to contractual and territorial rights ignored.

Thus the baseball player is made a chattel; the title of the club to the player . . . is made absolute.

Section 2 of Article VI recognizes the property of the club in the player as existing under two conditions: First, under a contract; and, second, under reserve without a contract.

* * *

If the player has ideas of his own, which fail to accord with those of the club, the National Agreement enables the club to enforce its own terms, leaving the player the option to enter some other trade, calling, or profession, if he is not satisfied.

The scheme of the National Agreement to perpetuate control over a player by means of contracts apparently legal is interesting and pertinent. Each term contract, as appears by Section 1 of Article VIII, must contain a reserve clause or option to renew, and this article of the National Agreement is further enforced by Section A, Rule 17, of the National Commission, which is as follows:

> A nonreserve clause in the contract of a major league player without the approval of the commission or of a minor league player without the approval of the National Board shall not be valid.

So that each new contract of the player must contain a reserve clause, and so by a series of contracts, "organized baseball" is able to perpetuate its control over the services of the player. But if, upon the other hand, a contract is at any time unobtainable, or even in fact not in good faith sought to be obtained, as the club owner might offer an immoderately low salary, then the provisions for reservation and the respecting thereof, apply and safeguard the "absolute title" of the club.

But why should a player enter into a contract when his liberty of conduct and of contract is thus curtailed? The answer is that he has no recourse. He must either take the contract under the provisions of the National Agreement, whose organization controls practically all of the good ball players of the country, or resort to some other occupation.

[The court then quoted several provisions of the National Agreement and Rules promulgated by the National Commission, which prohibited teams from using players who had not signed formal playing contracts that contained the renewable option clause.]

* * *

This somewhat extended analysis shows to what extent the contract between the plaintiff and the defendant presents reciprocal and mutual, enforceable obligations. The plaintiff can terminate the contract at any time on 10 days' notice. The defendant is bound to many obligations under the remarkable provisions of the National Agreement. The Player's Contract executed in accordance with its terms, binds him, not only for the playing season of six months from April 14th to October 14th, but also for another season, if the plaintiff chooses to exercise its option, and if it insists upon the requirement of an option clause in each succeeding contract, the defendant can be held for a term of years. His only alternative is to abandon his vocation. Can it fairly be claimed that there is mutuality in such a contract? The absolute lack of mutuality, both of obligation and of remedy, in this contract, would prevent a court of equity from making it the basis of equitable relief by injunction or otherwise. The negative covenant, under such circumstances, is without a consideration to support it, and is unenforceable by injunction.

[The court then addressed the question of whether this contractual regime in baseball violated federal antitrust law.]

The novel argument is presented with much earnestness by the learned counsel for the defendant that the combination formed by the operation of the National Agreement and the rules and regulations of the National Commission thereunder, with which the defendant is connected through his contract with the plaintiff, is in direct violation of an act to protect trade and commerce against unlawful restraints and monopolies, in force July 2, 1890, and popularly known as the Sherman Antitrust Law. It is apparent from the analysis already set forth of the agreement and rules forming the combination of the baseball business, referred to as "organized baseball," that a monopoly of baseball as a business has been ingeniously devised and created in so far as a monopoly can be created among free men; but I cannot agree to the proposition that the business of baseball for profit is interstate trade or commerce, and therefore subject to the provisions of the Sherman Act. An examination of the cases cited by the defendant confirms rather than changes my conclusion.

* * *

Baseball is an amusement, a sport, a game that comes clearly within the civil and criminal law of the state, and it is not a commodity or an article of merchandise subject to the regulation of Congress on the theory that it is interstate commerce.

[The court then turned to the question of what was the appropriate treatment under the common law of player contracts entered into within this baseball structure.]

Another question to be determined upon this motion is whether so-called "organized baseball," operating under the provisions of the National Agreement and the Rules and Contracts subsidiary thereto, is an illegal combination or monopoly in contravention of the common law. The affidavits read on the hearing of this motion show that a combination of 40 leagues, major and minor, has been formed under the terms of the National Agreement, controlling for profit the services of 10,000 players of professional baseball, practically all of the good or skillful players in the country. The analysis of the National Agreement and the Rules of the Commission, controlling the services of these skilled laborers, and providing for their purchase, sale, exchange, draft, reduction, discharge, and blacklisting, would seem to establish a species of quasi peonage unlawfully controlling and interfering with the personal freedom of the men employed. It appears that there is only one league of any importance operating independently of the National Commission, and that is the newly organized Federal League which comprises eight clubs in eight cities. "Organized baseball" is now as complete a monopoly of the baseball business for profit as any monopoly can be made. It is in contravention of the common law, in that it invades the right to labor as a property right, in that it invades the right to contract as a property right, and in that it is a combination to restrain and control the exercise of a profession or calling.

* * *

If a baseball player like the defendant, who has made baseball playing his profession and means of earning a livelihood, desires to be employed at the work for which he is qualified and is entitled to earn his best compensation, he must submit to dominion over his personal freedom and the control of his services by sale, transfer, or exchange, without his consent, or abandon his vocation and seek employment at some other kind of labor. While the services of these baseball players are ostensibly secured by voluntary contracts, a study of the system as hereinabove set forth, and as practiced under the plan of the National Agreement, reveals the involuntary character of the servitude which is imposed upon players by the strength of the combination controlling the labor of practically all of the players in the country. This is so great as to make it necessary for the player either to take the contract prescribed by the commission or abandon baseball as a profession and seek some other mode of earning a livelihood. There is no difference in principle between the system of servitude built up by the operation of this National Agreement, which as has been shown, provides for the purchase, sale, barter, and exchange of the services of baseball players—skilled laborers—without their consent, and the system of peonage brought into the United States from Mexico and thereafter existing for a time within the territory of New Mexico. The quasi peonage of baseball players under the operations of this plan and agreement is contrary to the spirit of American institutions, and is contrary to the spirit of the Constitution of the United States. . . .

The system created by "organized baseball" in recent years presents the question of the establishment of a scheme by which the personal freedom, the right to contract for their labor wherever they will, of 10,000 skilled laborers, is placed under the dominion of a benevolent despotism through the operation of the monopoly established by the National Agreement. This case does not present the simple question of a laborer who has entered into a fair contract for his personal services.

While the question of the dissolution of this combination on the ground of its illegality is not before this court for decision, it has nevertheless been thought necessary for the purpose of ascertaining whether or not this plaintiff comes into a court of equity with clean hands to inquire into the organization and operations of the combination to which the plaintiff is a party. A court of equity, insisting that "he who comes into equity must come with clean hands," will not lend its aid to promote an unconscionable transaction of the character which the plaintiff is endeavoring to maintain and strengthen by its application for this injunction. The court will not assist in enforcing an agreement which is a part of a general plan having for its object the maintenance of a monopoly, interference with the personal liberty of a citizen, and the control of his free right to labor wherever and for whom he pleases, and will not extend its aid to further the purposes and practices of an unlawful combination, by restraining the defendant from working for any one but the plaintiff.

Injunction vacated.

———

Chase casts in a different light the contracts signed by Nap Lajoie a decade earlier, or even by Dick Barnett fifty years later. One question is whether the league arrangements justify the court's refusal to enforce individual contracts through injunctions. While over the years most courts have answered "no," a more important question is whether even a hands-off approach by courts to player contracts would be a sufficient response to the problems players have with these league arrangements.

In *Chase*, the player tried to use antitrust policy as a *shield* against a contract injunction sought by the American League Club that had reserved his services. That tactic was sufficient for Chase's purposes because another club in the rival Federal League had been prepared to bid handsomely for his services. Nonetheless, since the demise of the Federal League just a year later, Major League Baseball has faced no such competition in its players market, and other professional leagues have encountered rivals only intermittently. Whether or not a judge enforces the restrictive terms in a contract between a player and his team, if the other teams in the league have agreed not to "tamper" with the services of their respective players except under strictly defined rules and conditions (an agreement enforced by the commissioner), there will be no effective market for the players' services and the players will have to accept any salary offered by the clubs to which they are "reserved." That is why players have tried to use antitrust law as a *sword* against such an intraleague arrangement, as examined in Chapter 6.

For a reason that is highlighted at the end of this chapter, baseball players were never successful in using antitrust as such a sword. They were, however, able to use collective bargaining to slay the reserve system. Under the second baseball collective bargaining agreement, a neutral arbitrator, Peter Seitz, replaced Commissioner Bowie Kuhn as interpreter of both the baseball labor agreement and the player contract. Seitz was a universally respected neutral under collective bargaining agreements throughout the American economy. His work as the baseball neutral had a profound effect on the sport. Arbitrator Seitz was presented with a case that required him to construe the meaning and scope of the key components of the reserve system based on the provisions of the uniform player's contract that was negotiated by MLB and the MLBPA as part of their collective bargaining agreement.

In 1974, Jim "Catfish" Hunter had a 25–13 record with the Oakland A's, his fourth year as a 20-game winner. He had signed a two-year contract with club owner Charlie Finley for a $100,000 annual salary. Half of the salary each year would be paid to him directly; $50,000 would be paid to a deferment plan of Hunter's choice, which allowed him to avoid immediate tax liability. Apparently, Finley belatedly discovered that under Hunter's deferred compensation scheme the club could not deduct the annual $50,000 annuity payment as a business expense in the current year, and that Finley would lose control over the funds. Finley then simply refused to make the payments as he had promised. Hunter made repeated requests, but the deferred payments were not made. Hunter filed a grievance claiming he could terminate the contract for non-payment.

Section 7(a) of Hunter's Uniform Player Contract explained the implication of Finley's action. It read: "The Player may terminate this contract . . . if the Club shall default in the payments to the Player." Arbitrator Peter Seitz ruled this provision was "pellucidly clear." The contract was not ambiguous. Since Hunter no longer had a valid contract with the A's, he was a free agent and could entertain offers from any other club.

On December 31, 1974, Hunter accepted a Yankees' offer for the then unprecedented salary package of a $1 million signing bonus, and $150,000 a year for five years, life insurance benefits worth $1 million and a substantial amount of deferred compensation. Hunter's case demonstrated both the extent to which the reserve system suppressed player salaries and, for the first time, the formidable power of labor arbitration in the sports business. The decision heralded an enormous shift in power within the baseball enterprise brought about by collective bargaining. The *Hunter* case also foreshadowed the role arbitrator Peter Seitz would play the following year when the MLBPA launched a full-frontal attack on baseball's venerable reserve system. Catfish Hunter's case was, after all, a unique situation—an obstinate owner materially breached a contract freeing his star player and no other owner was upset with the decision because it involved the prodigal owner of baseball, Charlie Finley.

The following year, the Players Association submitted to the labor agreement umpire Seitz the most critical issue in the business of sports, whether a player is bound to his club in perpetuity or whether he is allowed to sell his services to any club he wishes upon the expiration of his contract term plus one option year with his current team. The status quo was the perpetual reserve system, but the MLBPA's grievance claimed that the system was not embodied in the parties' collective bargaining agreement.

NATIONAL & AMERICAN LEAGUE PROFESSIONAL BASEBALL CLUBS V. MAJOR LEAGUE BASEBALL PLAYERS ASSOCIATION

(Messersmith and McNally Grievances)
66 Lab. Arb. Rep. (BNA) 101 (1976)

SEITZ, ARBITRATOR.

[Andy Messersmith of the Los Angeles Dodgers and Dave McNally of the Montreal Expos had both refused to sign new player contracts at the end of the 1974 season; instead, they played the 1975 season under the terms of § 10(c) of the Uniform Player's Contract, which gave their clubs the right to renew for one year the old contract "on the same terms" (except for salary, the amount of which had recently been subjected to binding arbitration in cases of dispute). The question posed to the arbitrator was whether the contract as renewed by the club contained this option clause as well. If it did, the club could include the player indefinitely on its reserve list through use of this perpetually renewable option. If, on the other hand, the reserve option clause was spent after its first use, the two players had now become free agents. In addition to that merits issue of contract interpretation, the arbitrator faced a preliminary question whether he even had jurisdiction to entertain this issue, because of the presence of the following curious provision in the collective agreement:

> Except as adjusted or modified hereby, *this agreement does not deal with the reserve system*. The Parties have different views as to the legality and as to the merits of such system as presently constituted. This agreement shall in no way prejudice the position or legal rights of the parties or of any player regarding the reserve system. During the term of this agreement neither of the parties will resort to any form of concerted action with respect to the issue of the reserve system, and there shall be no obligation to negotiate with respect to the reserve system. (Emphasis supplied.)

In the first half of his decision, Seitz wrestled with the meaning of this apparent exclusion of the reserve clause from the collective bargaining agreement upon which his authority rested. Eventually, he concluded that he did have jurisdiction to resolve grievances about the meaning of different provisions in the collective bargaining agreement and the standard player contract. Although the parties agreed to a clause that stated that their agreement did not deal with the reserve system, a number of the provisions of the agreement served as critical features of the reserve system. Seitz's decision on "arbitrability" will be examined below in the Eighth Circuit Court of Appeals decision that affirmed Seitz's conclusion.

Here, we present the arbitrator's analysis of the scope of the reserve clause in baseball.

The arbitrator first reviewed the origins and development of the reserve clause.]

* * *

The Reserve System of the leagues is nowhere defined in a sentence or a paragraph. Reference is commonly and frequently made in the press and by the news media to a "Reserve Clause;" but there is no such single clause encompassing the subject matter. It seems fair to say, on the basis of what has been presented, that the "Reserve System" refers to a complex and a congeries of rules of the leagues (and provisions in the collective Basic Agreement and the Uniform Players Contract) related to the objective of retaining exclusive control over the service of their players in the interest of preserving discipline, preventing the enticement of players, maintaining financial stability and promoting a balance or a relative parity of competitive skills as among clubs. Such "exclusive control," it is said, is exercised by a Club placing the name of a player on its "reserve list" which is distributed to the other clubs in both leagues. A player on such a list, assert the leagues, cannot "play for or negotiate with any other club until his contract has been assigned or he has been released" (Rule 4-A(a) and may not be the subject of "tampering" as described in Rule 3(g).

This system of reservation of exclusive control is historic in baseball and is traceable to the early days of the organized sport in the 19th century. Over the years, the scheme and structure of provisions designed to establish and maintain that control has been changed in expression. The leagues assert that the system was designed, initially, to combat the institutional chaos that resulted when players under contract with one club defected to another. In an effort to deal with the problem, it is represented, various versions of reserve clauses had been adopted.

The problems facing the National League in the closing years of the 19th century, however, in respect of defecting players, were not limited to the circumstances of a player defecting to another club in the league. Other leagues came into being from time to time and disappeared. The League, in 1899, in an effort to prevent defection of players to other leagues, placed in the individual player's contract a "renewal clause," so called. This clause, according to the leagues, was the legal basis for clubs applying to the courts of equity to enjoin players from "jumping" to a rival league. As Club Exhibit 16 evidences, contract renewal clauses, over time, differed in their provisions; but all gave an option to a Club to renew its contracts with players for stated periods.

[The current version of the renewal clause in MLB's Uniform Player's Contract was developed in 1947. If the Club had tendered a contract to the player by February 1 and the parties had not agreed to new contract terms by March 1, the Club had the prerogative under § 10(a) (via written notice to the player within the next ten days) "to renew the contract for the period of one year on the same terms." The only exception was salary, which the club could fix at an amount not less than 75% of the prior year's salary. However, for the following reasons arbitrator Seitz rejected the club's argument that this renewal provision incorporated the option clause among all the other terms incorporated in the renewed contract. That meant that Messersmith and McNally were no longer under contract to the Dodgers and Expos, respectively, when their 1975 option year had expired.]

It deserves emphasis that this decision strikes no blow emancipating players from claimed serfdom or involuntary servitude such as was alleged in the *Flood* Case. It does not condemn the Reserve System presently in force on constitutional or moral grounds. It does not counsel or require that the System be changed to suit the predilections or preferences of an arbitrator acting as a Philosopher-King intent upon imposing his own personal brand of industrial justice on the parties. To go beyond this would be an act of quasi judicial arrogance! . . . [T]he scope and effect of a reserve system is for the Parties to determine, not the Panel. As stated, the Panel's role is restricted to an interpretation and application of the agreement of the parties.

* * *

No one challenges the right of a Club to renew a Player's contract with or without his consent, under § 10(a), "for the period of one [renewal] year." I read the record, however, as containing a contention by the leagues that when a Club renews a Player's contract for the renewal year, the contract in force during that year contains the "right of renewal" clause as one of its terms, entitling the Club to renew the contract in successive years, to perpetuity, perhaps, so long as the Player is alive and the Club has duly discharged all conditions required of it. This is challenged by the Players Association whose position it is that the contractual relationship between the Club and the Player terminates at the end of the first renewal year. Thus, it claims that there was no longer any contractual bond between Messersmith and the Los Angeles Club on September 29, 1975.

The leagues' argument is based on the language in § 10(a) of the Player's Contract that the Club "may renew this contract for the period of one year *on the same terms;*" and that among those "terms" is the right to further contract renewal.

In the law of contract construction, as I know it, there is nothing to prevent parties from agreeing to successive renewals of the terms of their bargain (even to what had been described as "perpetuity"), provided the contract expresses that intention with explicit clarity and the right of subsequent renewals does not have to be implied. . . .

There is nothing in § 10(a) which, explicitly, expresses agreement that the Players Contract can be renewed for any period beyond the first renewal year. The point the leagues present must be based upon the implication or assumption, that if the renewed contract is "on the same terms" as the contract for the preceding year (with the exception of the amount of compensation) the right to additional renewals must have been an integral part of the renewed contract. I find great difficulties, in so implying or assuming, in respect of a contract providing for the rendition of personal services in which one would expect a more explicit expression of intention. There are numerous provisions and terms in the Uniform Players Contract that are renewed in the renewal year when a Club exercises its renewal rights under § 10(a). Provision of the right to make subsequent and successive renewals is in an entirely different category, however, than the numerous terms in the Players Contract which deal with working conditions and duties which the Club and the Player owe to each other. That right, critically, concerns and involves the continued existence of the contract itself as expressing the mutual undertakings of the parties and the bargain which they struck. All of the other "terms" of the Player-Club relationship stand or fall according to whether the contract, as such, is renewed.

[The arbitrator then discussed two basketball cases—*Lemat Corp. v. Barry*, 275 Cal. App. 2d 671, 80 Cal. Rptr. 240 (1969) and *Central New York Basketball v. Barnett*, 181 N.E.2d 506 (Ohio C.P. Ct.1961), both involving similar renewal clauses. In *Barnett*, the club had argued and the court agreed, that the option clause in basketball's standard player contract was for one renewal year only, not in perpetuity, and *Barry* followed *Barnett*.]

* * *

In this connection it is also pertinent to observe that the "no tampering rule" (which, in baseball, is contained in Major League Rule 3(g)), has its equivalent, in NBA basketball, in § 35 of the NBA constitution. The prohibition there, however, applies to any player "who is under contract to any other member of the Association." (Emphasis supplied.) Thus, in the "reserve system" of the NBA basketball league, the player must have been under contract to be reserved; but in this case, the leagues argue that even if the contract be construed to have expired, the player may be reserved.

In these circumstances I find that § 10(a) falls short of reserving to a Club the right to renew a contract at the end of the renewal year. Accordingly, I find that Messersmith was not under contract when his renewal year came to an end.

[The clubs advanced a second argument for their position on the merits. Under Major League Rule 4-A(a), each club was to transmit to the commissioner, by November 20th, "a list not exceeding forty (40) active and eligible players whom the clubs desire to reserve for the ensuing season . . .

and thereafter no player on any list shall be eligible to play for and negotiate with any other club until his contract has been assigned or he has been released." Rule 4-A(a) was supplemented and reinforced by Rule 3(g), which provided that "to preserve discipline and competition and to prevent the enticement of players . . . there shall be no negotiations or dealings respecting employment, either present or prospective, between any player . . . and any club other than the club with which he is under contract . . . or by which he is reserved . . ."]

We now turn to the Major League Rules, as to which it has already been stated that, by virtue of § 9(a) of the Uniform Players Contract and Article XIII of the Basic Agreement, they are a part of the agreements of the parties if not inconsistent with the provisions of the Basic Agreement and the Players Contract.

The parties are in sharp conflict on this. The leagues claim that there is exclusive reservation of a player's services under Rule 4-A(a) regardless of the continued existence of any contractual relationship between the Club and the Player. Thus, Counsel for the National League asserted that:

> The club may continue the pattern of career long control over the player and that this pattern of career long control is not essentially dependent upon the renewal clause (Section 10-A) at all.

The Players Association, on the other hand, asserts that in the absence of a nexus or linkage of contract between the Player and the Club, there can be no exclusive reservation of the right to his future services.

* * *

These provisions and others in the very Rules which, allegedly, establish the kind of reservation of services for which the leagues contend, all subsume the existence of a contractual relation. The leagues would have it that it is only when there is a release or assignment that a contract must have been in existence; but even if there were no contract in existence (the players' contract having expired) a Club, by placing the name of a player on a list, can reserve exclusive rights to his services from year to year for an unstated and indefinite period in the future. I find this unpersuasive. It is like the claims of some nations that persons once its citizens, wherever they live and regardless of the passage of time, the swearing of other allegiances and other circumstances, are still its own nationals and subject to the obligations that citizenship in the nation imposes. This "status" theory is incompatible with the doctrine or policy of freedom of contract in the economic and political society in which we live and of which the professional sport of baseball ("the national game") is a part.

* * *

Finally, on this point, it is evident that traditionally, the leagues have regarded the existence of a contract as a basis for the reservation of players. In Club's Exhibit No. 15 there is set forth the Cincinnati Peace Compact of the National and American Leagues, signed January 10, 1903—probably the most important step in the evolution and development of the present Reserve System. In that document it provided:

> Second—A *reserve* rule shall be recognized, by which each and every club may reserve players *under contract*, and that a uniform contract for the use of each league shall be adopted. (Emphasis supplied.)

* * *

[Finally, Arbitrator Seitz addressed the League's concern that the absence of a lifetime reserve system would devastate baseball.]

I am not unmindful of the testimony of the Commissioner of Baseball and the Presidents of the National and American League given at the hearings as to the importance of maintaining the integrity of the Reserve System. It was represented to me that any decision of the Arbitration Panel sustaining the Messersmith and McNally grievances would have dire results, wreak great harm to the Reserve System and do serious damage to the sport of baseball.

Thus, for example, it was stated that a decision favoring these grievants would encourage many other players to elect to become free agents at the end of the renewal years; that this would encourage clubs with the largest monetary resources to engage free agents, thus unsettling the competitive balance between clubs, so essential to the sport; that it would increase enormously the already high costs of training and seasoning young players to achieve the level of skills required in professional baseball and such investments would be sacrificed if they became free agents at the end of a renewal year; that driven by the compulsion to win, owners of franchises would over extend themselves financially and improvident bidding for players in an economic climate in which, today, some clubs are strained, financially; that investors will be discouraged from putting money in franchises in which several of the star players on the club team will become free agents at the end of a renewal year and no continuing control over the players' services can be exercised; and that even the integrity of the sport may be placed in hazard under certain circumstances.

I do not purport to appraise these apprehensions. They are all based on speculations as to what may ensue. Some of the fears may be imaginary or exaggerated; but some may be reasonable, realistic and sound. After all, they were voiced by distinguished baseball officials with long experience in the sport and a background for judgment in such matters much superior to my own. However, as stated above, at length, it is not for the Panel (and especially the writer) to determine what, if anything, is good or bad about the reserve system. The Panel's sole duty is to interpret and apply the agreements and undertakings of the parties. If any of the expressed apprehensions and fears are soundly based, I am confident that the dislocations and damage to the reserve system can be avoided or minimized through good faith collective bargaining between the parties. There are numerous expedients available and arrangements that can be made that will soften the blow—if this decision, indeed, should be regarded as a blow. This decision is not the end of the line by any means. The parties, jointly, are free to agree to disregard it and compose their differences as to the reserve system in any way they see fit.

* * *

Grievance upheld.

NOTES AND QUESTIONS

1. *Evaluation of Policy or Interpretation?* Early in his opinion, Arbitrator Seitz emphatically stated that his role was not to evaluate the merits of baseball's reserve system, but merely to interpret the meaning of its constituent provisions. Look closely at the passages in which the arbitrator considers and selects from the alternative interpretations advanced by the Players Association and the League about the proper interpretation of the option clause in the player's contract and the reserve clause in the major league rules. Is there such a sharp distinction between evaluation and interpretation of these legal documents?

2. *A Convincing Interpretation?* Was Arbitrator Seitz correct in his reading of the collective bargaining agreement? Remember that the owners had originally designed the Reserve System in the nineteenth century to keep players from "revolving" from club to club in the nascent National League. Why would they construct a player control system that would last only for two years and would not accomplish this goal of institutional stability?

3. *Effect of Past Practice?* The parties had negotiated over the extent and reach of the Reserve System, but they could not reach an agreement. Instead, they agreed to disagree. Do you think anyone who had been at those negotiations would have been surprised by the arbitrator's conclusion that the parties had mutually agreed on a "one-year-only" option? Shouldn't their "non-agreement" on any significant change have perpetuated their hundred-year-old understanding that the Reserve System was, in fact, perpetual?

4. *Arbitrator as Bargaining Catalyst?* Could Seitz have ruled for the Players Association because he knew that this was the only way to get the parties to the bargaining table where they would be forced to address the Reserve System issue? Had the owners prevailed, would the Reserve System

have remained in its historic form for a substantially longer period? If this was Seitz's strategy, is this a proper role for an arbitrator?

The Kansas City Royals, representing Major League Baseball, appealed the federal district court decision upholding Arbitrator Seitz's ruling. A young, local lawyer from Kansas City named Donald Fehr represented the union, the beginning of his career with the baseball labor organization.

KANSAS CITY ROYALS V. MAJOR LEAGUE BASEBALL PLAYERS ASS'N
532 F.2d 615 (8th Cir. 1976)

HEANEY, CIRCUIT JUDGE.

[The Players Association and the Owners had entered into two collective bargaining agreements (prior to the 1973 agreement at issue in the *Messersmith* arbitration) that dealt with the arbitrability of issues involving the reserve system. The 1968 Basic Agreement established the arbitration procedure for grievances, designated the Commissioner as arbitrator, and specifically excluded two types of disputes (neither relating to the reserve system) from arbitration. With respect to the reserve system, the agreement provided that:

> The parties shall review jointly . . . possible alternatives to the reserve clause as now constituted. . . .
>
> The joint review of the reserve clause shall be completed prior to the termination date of this Agreement. . . .
>
> [I]t is mutually agreed that the Clubs shall not be obligated to bargain or seek agreement with the Players Association on [the reserve clause] during the term of this Agreement.

The 1970 Basic Agreement replaced the Commissioner as arbitrator with an independent three-judge panel (such as the one used in *Messersmith*), and added two more specific exclusions from arbitration (again neither involved the reserve system). During the negotiation of this agreement, Curt Flood filed a suit (ultimately decided in the Supreme Court opinion discussed in Chapter 2 challenging the reserve system under federal antitrust laws. In the face of this pending litigation, and unable to reach agreement on modifications to the reserve system, the parties inserted the following provision in Article XIV of the Basic Agreement:

> Regardless of any provision herein to the contrary, this Agreement does not deal with the reserve system. The parties have differing views as to the legality and as to the merits of such system as presently constituted. This Agreement shall in no way

prejudice the position or legal rights of the Parties or of any Player regarding the reserve system.

It is agreed that until the final and unappealable adjudication (or voluntary discontinuance) of Flood v. Kuhn now pending in the federal district court of the Southern District of New York, neither of the Parties will resort to any form of concerted action with respect to the issue of the reserve system, and there shall be no obligation to negotiate with respect to the reserve system. Upon the final and unappealable adjudication (or voluntary discontinuance) of Flood v. Kuhn either Party shall have the right to reopen the negotiations on the issue of the reserve system. . . .

A lawyer for the National League claimed that Players Association leader Marvin Miller said during the negotiations that the reserve system "is going to be outside the Agreement. It will not be subject to the Agreement, but we will acquiesce in the continuance of the enforcement of the rules as house rules and we will not grieve over those house rules." Miller denied making the statement.

During the term of the 1970 agreement, players filed grievances involving one or more of the provisions that comprise the reserve system. The owners did not challenge the arbitrator's jurisdiction to rule on these grievances because, they later explained, they felt that the grievances did not concern the "core" or "heart" of the reserve system.

During the negotiation of the 1973 Basic Agreement, the parties agreed to two modifications of the reserve system: the "five and ten" rule (a player with ten years of big league experience, the last five years with the same team, could veto a trade to any other team), and, much more significantly, the arbitration of salary disputes. However, the parties failed to reach agreement on other modifications to the reserve system proposed by the Players Association. Therefore, Article XIV of the 1970 agreement became Article XV of the 1973 agreement, except that the reference to the *Flood* litigation was removed and the phrase "except as adjusted or modified hereby"—which both parties recognized to be ambiguous—was inserted before "this Agreement does not deal with the reserve system." (The owners wanted some recognition of the agreed upon changes in the reserve system as a safeguard against Miller's efforts to get Congress to repeal baseball's antitrust exemption, which had been upheld by the Supreme Court in the *Flood* case.) In addition, the owners agreed in a letter to Miller that "[n]otwithstanding [Article XV], it is hereby understood and agreed that the Clubs will not during the term of the Agreement make any unilateral changes in the Reserve System which would affect player obligations or benefits."]

* * *

We cannot say, on the basis of the evidence discussed above, that the record evinces the most forceful evidence of a purpose to exclude the grievances here involved from arbitration.

(a) The 1968 agreement clearly permitted the arbitration of grievances relating to the reserve system. It, therefore, cannot be said that the Club Owners never consented to the arbitration of such grievances. The Club Owners might have argued that they agreed to arbitrate such grievances because the Commissioner of Baseball was designated as the arbitrator, and that he, recognizing the importance of the reserve system to baseball, would interpret the disputed provisions to allow perpetual control by a Club Owner over its players. That argument, however, was not advanced before either the arbitration panel, the District Court or this Court. Moreover, the argument would not be particularly flattering to any Commissioner of Baseball.[19]

(b) Article XIV, the predecessor to Article XV, was suggested by the Players Association for rather specific purposes and the Club Owners clearly did what they could to preserve their right to argue that the reserve system remained a part of the collective bargaining agreement. Indeed, if the Club Owners' counterproposals with respect to Article XIV had been accepted, the reserve system would clearly have remained subject to arbitration.

Article XV was clearly designed to accomplish the same purposes as Article XIV. If in accomplishing these purposes the players had clearly agreed to exclude disputes arising out of the operation of the reserve system from arbitration, the Messersmith-McNally grievances would not be arbitrable. For the reasons discussed in this opinion, however, no such agreement can be found.

(c) From 1970 to 1973, a number of grievances concerning the reserve system were submitted to arbitration. The Club Owners raised no jurisdictional objections. While this fact alone is not of controlling significance, because the grievances submitted did not go to what the Club Owners regard as the "core" or "heart" of the reserve system, the submission of grievances relating to the reserve system is certainly a fact that detracts from the Club Owners' contention that the parties clearly understood Article XIV to mean that grievances relating to the reserve system would not be subject to arbitration.

---

[19] Mr. Bowie Kuhn, the present Commissioner of Baseball, testified, in substance, that he felt that Article X of the 1973 agreement gave him the power to withdraw a grievance from arbitration if he felt that the grievance involved the "preservation of the integrity of, or the maintenance of public confidence in, the game of baseball." He testified further that he did not withdraw these grievances from arbitration because he didn't want to do anything to adversely affect the collective bargaining process: he respected the reputation of Mr. Seitz, the impartial arbitrator, and he respected the arbitration process.

(d) The fact that Marvin Miller may have given assurances, during the 1970 negotiations, that the players would not grieve over house rules cannot be viewed as the most forceful evidence of a purpose to exclude the Messersmith-McNally grievances from arbitration. First, there is some dispute in the record as to whether Miller made such a statement. Second, assuming he did, the term "house rules" is ambiguous. Third, and we think most important, the weight of the evidence, when viewed as a whole, does not support the conclusion that Article XV was intended to preclude arbitration of any grievances otherwise arbitrable.

(e) The essence of the Club Owners' arguments on the question of arbitrability was perhaps best articulated in the testimony of Larry McPhail, President of the American League, in which he stated: "Isn't it fair to say that our strong feelings on the importance of the core of the reserve system would indicate that we wouldn't permit the reserve system to be within the jurisdiction of the arbitration procedure?" The weaknesses in this argument have been previously discussed in paragraphs (a), (b) and (c) above. We add only that what a reasonable party might be expected to do cannot take precedence over what the parties actually provided for in their collective bargaining agreement.

The Club Owners contend that even if the arbitration panel had jurisdiction, the award must be vacated. They argue that the award exceeded the scope of the panel's authority by "fundamentally altering and destroying the Reserve System as it historically existed and had been acquiesced in by the Association."

As we have previously noted, our review of the merits of an arbitration panel's award is limited. The award must be sustained so long as it "draws its essence from the collective bargaining agreement." *United Steelworkers of America v. Enterprise Wheel & Car Corp.*, 363 U.S. 593, 597 (1960).

The nub of the Club Owners' argument is that both they and the Players Association understood the reserve system to enable a club to perpetually control a player, that this understanding was reflected in the 1973 agreement, and that the arbitration panel was without authority to alter the agreed upon operation of the reserve system.

We cannot agree that the 1973 collective bargaining agreement embodied an understanding by the parties that the reserve system enabled a club to perpetually control a player. First, the agreement contained no express provision to that effect. Second, while there is evidence that the reserve system operated in such a manner in recent years, the record discloses that various Players Association representatives viewed the system as allowing a player to become a free agent by playing under a renewed contract for one year.

Moreover, it can be argued that the arbitration panel's award did not "alter" the reserve system. To the extent that the reserve system did enable a club to perpetually control a player, it was not necessarily by virtue of successive invocations of the renewal clause, or application of the reserve list and no tampering rules in the absence of a contractual obligation. Other provisions operate to deter a player from "playing out his option," as is evidenced by the fact that few players have done so. On this basis, it may be said that the arbitration panel's decision did not change the reserve system, but merely interpreted various elements thereof under circumstances which had not previously arisen.

The 1973 agreement empowered the arbitration panel to "interpret, apply or determine compliance with the provisions of agreements" between the players and the clubs. We find that the arbitration panel did nothing more than to interpret certain provisions of the Uniform Player's Contract and the Major League Rules. We cannot say that those provisions are not susceptible of the construction given them by the panel. Accordingly, the award must be sustained.

Conclusion

We hold that the arbitration panel had jurisdiction to hear and decide the Messersmith-McNally grievances, that the panel's award drew its essence from the collective bargaining agreement, and that the relief fashioned by the District Court was appropriate. Accordingly, the award of the arbitration panel must be sustained, and the District Court's judgment affirmed. In so holding, we intimate no views on the merits of the reserve system. We note, however, that Club Owners and the Players Association's representatives agree that some form of a reserve system is needed if the integrity of the game is to be preserved and if public confidence in baseball is to be maintained. The disagreement lies over the degree of control necessary if these goals are to be achieved. Certainly, the parties are in a better position to negotiate their differences than to have them decided in a series of arbitrations and court decisions. We commend them to that process and suggest that the time for obfuscation has passed and that the time for plain talk and clear language has arrived. Baseball fans everywhere expect nothing less.

* * *

Appeal dismissed.

Notes and Questions

1. *Final Verdict?* Having read both the arbitral and judicial opinions, what do you think was the proper construction of baseball's collective agreement as it relates to the reserve system? To what extent are your views influenced by your sentiments about the equities of the issue? If you feel that Arbitrator Seitz's reading may have been somewhat dubious, does this affect

your evaluation of the *Enterprise Wheel & Car* standard for judicial review of arbitral construction of labor agreements (*see* pages 165–166) supra? Or does this case support the national labor police that parties to labor agreements should accept the decision maker and the process for which they have contracted?

2. *Arbitrator Selection Strategy.* Recall that the parties mutually select their arbitrator and that either party can terminate the appointment if displeased with any one ruling. Such dismissal befell Tom Roberts, the baseball arbitrator in 1986, following his decision striking down the drug testing covenants in individual player contracts. The same fate overtook Peter Seitz following his *Messersmith* decision. The baseball owners actually almost dismissed Seitz before the *Messersmith* hearing because of Seitz' decision in the Jim "Catfish" Hunter case a year earlier. Indeed, Commissioner Bowie Kuhn, in his autobiography, *Hardball*, relates that the club owners rejected Kuhn's recommendation to replace Seitz. The Player Relations Committee felt that Seitz, having ruled for the Players Association in *Hunter*, would likely lean toward the owners in *Messersmith,* with that case's quite different contract footing and more momentous implications.

3. *Lasting Impact or Easy Renegotiation?* Even though a party may guess wrongly how its current arbitrator will rule, a second key difference between contract arbitration and statutory administration is that the parties can renegotiate the contractual language that an outside arbitrator may have misconstrued, a step the parties certainly cannot take with respect to an administrative interpretation of a statute without a significant Congressional detour. In fact, the baseball agreement expired around the time the *Messersmith* decision was rendered, and the agreement was renegotiated long before any more players reached free agent status. According to the Coase theorem, Seitz's interpretation of the reserve clause, right or wrong, was largely irrelevant to the real world outcome of those negotiations. Do you agree?

4. *Avoiding Mandatory Bargaining?* In order to re-establish its reserve system after *Messersmith*, did Major League Baseball need to have the consent of the Players Association? There were two contractual features of the traditional system, the perennially renewable option clause in the player contract and the anti-tampering clause in the league rules. Could baseball have simply amended its own rules to address this problem? With what risks under labor law? In industrial relations? In public relations?

The legal implication of the final-and-binding *Messersmith* ruling was that any baseball player could become a free agent simply by playing out his option year without signing a new contract. As the *Messersmith* decision was being rendered and judicially reviewed in the winter of 1975–76, the baseball collective bargaining agreement (referred to in baseball as the "Basic Agreement") was itself expiring and being renegotiated.

Naturally enough, free agency became the central issue in these negotiations. After a 17-day owner lockout of the players during spring training—a work stoppage that was unilaterally ended by Commissioner Bowie Kuhn in the "best interests of the sport"—the Players Association and the owners' Player Relations Committee reached a new collective bargaining agreement in the summer of 1976.

The new contract modified free agency considerably. During his first two years in the league, a player had to accept his club's unilateral contract offers or not play, and for years three through six, the player was still contractually bound to his initial club but had the right to final-offer arbitration to establish the appropriate amount of salary. Free agency began only after six years of Major League service. The owners saw this as a significant victory. Seitz had set the players free and then the players negotiated away their rights. In fact, the Players Association understood economics better than baseball management. Had all Major League players flooded the free agent market each year, the surplus of talent would have driven down salaries. Instead, limiting free agency to players with six or more years of Major League service drove prices up, in turn affecting the salaries of all players and the salary arbitration awards that three through six-year players received.

Messersmith and its baseball progeny stand in stark contrast to what happened in football. As explained in Chapter 6, shortly after the arbitral ruling in the *Messersmith* grievance, federal appeals courts held that the NFL's restraints on competition for players violated federal antitrust laws. *See, e.g., Mackey v. NFL*, 543 F.2d 606 (8th Cir. 1976). Like their counterparts in basketball and hockey, though, the NFL Players Association subsequently agreed in collective bargaining to alternative restraints on free agency.

The post-*Mackey* regime in football allowed a player to become a free agent after five years of service. This right was largely illusory, however, in the absence of a competing football league because the collective agreement gave the incumbent team a right of first refusal over any offer made by another club to one of the team's free agent players. If the incumbent team chose not to match the offer, it was awarded specified draft picks of the new team determined by the transferring player's new salary, which was intended to compensate for the value of the player being lost. Unlike baseball, then, football did not establish any time at which a veteran player would enjoy unrestricted free agency. Experience soon made it clear that there would be little or no competitive bidding for players under this system, and as a result the NFLPA sought to emulate their baseball counterpart's success through labor arbitration.

The case of *NFL Players Association and NFL Management Council* (Dutton) (Arbitration 1980) involved John Dutton, an All-Pro defensive lineman with the Baltimore Colts. Dutton completed his contract in 1978, received no offers from other teams as a free agent, and thus played the next "option" season with the Colts for 110% of his prior year's salary, as provided for in § 17 of Article XV (Right of First Refusal/Compensation) of the NFL labor agreement. At the expiration of the 1979 season, Dutton again sought free agent offers, but received none, even though he was one of the leading defensive ends in the league. The reason was that the NFL Management Council interpreted the prior club's right to elect first refusal or draft pick compensation as applying perpetually to any free agent, even one coming off an option year contract, not just one whose previous negotiated contract had just expired. Thus Dutton and the NFLPA sought a ruling from the football arbitrator similar to *Messersmith*—that these obstacles to free agency applied only after the expiration of the contract signed by the player, not after the year of automatic contract renewal via the collective agreement (*i.e.*, that these restraints do not exist in perpetuity).

Arbitrator Burt Luskin observed that the evidence before him indicated that, during the several months of labor negotiations in the winter and spring of 1977, neither side had ever explicitly raised or addressed the *Messersmith* question, though that decision and its impact on baseball had occurred the prior year. The football players' argument was that, absent express contract language or clear negotiating history, the general wording of § 17 must not be interpreted as creating a perpetually renewable option for the teams (though with option year salaries going up, not down, as had been the case in baseball). Arbitrator Luskin rejected this argument after he had situated § 17 within the broader array of provisions in Article XV. Section 1 seemed to subject all "veteran free agents" to this regime, not just those who "play out the options in their contracts," and § 18 created an Extreme Personal Hardship exception that denied the prior club a right of first refusal to keep the player on that team, but still granted the club a right of compensation. Given these and several other clues in related contract provisions, the arbitrator concluded that he could not "infer from the absence of affirmative or negative language that the parties reached an agreement or understanding that would serve to confer total free agent status to a veteran player who had completed a year of service pursuant to a § 17(b) contract...."

Thus, Andy Messersmith was able to win free agency for his baseball counterparts, but John Dutton failed in his effort in football. While there were some textual variations in the language of the collective agreements in the two sports, differences in the negotiating scenarios that produced the language (and perhaps also in the arbitrators' philosophical inclinations) might also account for the opposite outcomes. The stark contrast between baseball's and football's labor markets after *Messersmith* and *Dutton* drove home to both players and owners (in basketball and hockey as well) what a difference a labor agreement could make. Not until the early 2000s (and following fierce legal and labor relations conflicts) did the governing rules begin to converge across the professional sports leagues.

C. CURRENT RESTRAINTS—SALARY CAPS AND TAXES

From the early 1970s to the early 1990s, collective bargaining and antitrust litigation in professional team sports were primarily targeted at securing a freer labor market for the players. By the mid-1990s, however, the focus of player-owner conflict had shifted. Owners were now prepared to accept (perhaps even embrace) free movement of players from one team to another. They insisted, though, on creation of league-wide constraints on the amount of money that individual teams could spend to induce such player movement—via salary caps or salary taxes.

This concept of free player movement with salary constraints was first proposed in the 1982 negotiations by NFLPA Executive Director Ed Garvey. Garvey's idea was that 55% of league revenues should be allocated to player compensation. The bulk of this money would be paid in fixed salary rates determined by position and seniority. The rest would be paid in bonuses for personal and team performance, as measured by statistical factors developed and administered by the NFLPA. The NFL owners, under Commissioner Pete Rozelle, rejected this salary sharing idea as "socialism in disguise," and an unacceptable inroad upon each team's property rights in a capitalist market.

Just a year later, basketball instituted a revised version of salary capping and sharing came into existence in basketball. By contrast with football, the NBA was in a sorry state in the early 1980s. Two-thirds of its teams were losing money every year, and a few (especially the Cleveland Cavaliers) were both spending and losing so much that the league office considered taking control of them. Thus, NBPA founder and leader Larry Fleisher, Commissioner Larry O'Brien, and O'Brien's chief counsel and soon to be successor, David Stern, developed a league salary formula designed to accommodate the interests of both sides. Ten years later, new football leadership (NFLPA Executive Director Gene Upshaw and Commissioner Paul Tagliabue) agreed to their own version of the salary cap after two decades of football suits and strikes over free agency. Then, in 1997 the baseball negotiators fashioned a "soft" salary tax system to settle their three-year labor battle, one they revised and strengthened in their peaceful 2002, 2006, 2011, and 2016 labor negotiations. In the aftermath of the NHL lockout of its players in 2004, the parties agreed on a salary cap system, individual salary restrictions and new free agency rules.

Sec. C   CURRENT RESTRAINTS—SALARY CAPS AND TAXES   229

Salary cap and tax provisions take up dozens of densely written pages in the NBA, NFL, NHL and MLB collective agreements. In the capped leagues—the NBA, NFL and NHL—each year the league office and the players association add up the gross revenue received by all clubs from defined sources—not just gate receipts and television revenues, but also merchandising sales, luxury box and club seat rentals, and the like. An agreed-to percentage of that revenue is assigned for player compensation. Part of that compensation fund is reserved for payment of the player retirement, disability, and other benefit funds. The remainder is then divided by the number of clubs in the league to establish the cap on each team's total player compensation.

In all three leagues, this system imposes not just a ceiling on the amount that teams may pay their players, but also a floor on the amount that each team must pay in salaries. This combination of a cap and a floor means that the NBA, NHL and NFL labor agreements actually function to give players a guaranteed share in aggregate league revenues. The leagues also have developed a variety of revenue-sharing devices to ensure that each team can and does meet the specified salary floor.

There is, however, a crucial difference between the NFL, NHL and NBA versions of the salary cap. The NBA's cap is a "soft" cap because it is qualified by several complicated exceptions. Most importantly, the scheme largely exempts the amount that clubs can spend to sign their current players to new contracts. This feature has always been known as the "Larry Bird" exception, because it was inserted in the 1983 NBA collective agreement to enable the Celtics to re-sign Larry Bird for the salary they knew he was seeking without having to release or trade Bird's star teammates. The sole aim of the NBA cap, then, was to prevent the Celtics (or the Knicks and Lakers) from using large salary offers to lure players away from the Cavaliers and other smaller market teams. But because the Larry Bird exception did allow teams to spend a much larger percentage of their revenue on player salaries than was consistent with the intent of the cap system, the collective agreement also creates a tax on the amount a team's payroll exceeds a threshold that is set significantly above the cap amount, thus making the NBA system a hybrid between the NFL's/NHL's hard payroll caps and MLB's payroll "luxury tax" regime. The NBA was also the first league to negotiate individual salary caps that limited the amount individual players may earn, not just a salary cap for an entire club that can be allocated among a team's players.

The NFL owners and players, and later the NHL owners and players, eventually agreed to a "hard" cap, one that forced teams to release some of their higher paid players when their overall salary budget exceeded the collectively bargained limit. The NFLPA also negotiated a graduated minimum salary for the players as well as a rookie player payroll cap that assigned to each team a maximum amount that it could pay to all of its first-year players, with the amount varying depending on how many rookies the team drafted and how high they were taken in the draft. The agreement also set forth a series of basic minima for NFL players that increase for each year of service in the league.

Baseball's negotiations in 2002 threatened to be a reprise of the strife of the mid-1990s, but the productive work of Michael Weiner for the MLBPA and Rob Manfred for MLB resulted in a last-minute settlement imposing a tax on the amount of a team's payroll that exceeded a certain pre-established threshold, with the percentage of the excess that is taxed increasing as a team goes over the threshold in successive years. The luxury tax has not operated as an effective salary cap because it has been set at a level substantially above the payroll of most teams. The tax seems intended to dampen the spending of only certain large market franchises, such as the Yankees, Dodgers, and Red Sox. Over the years, most MLB teams have never exceeded the limit and thus have never paid what is now called the "competitive balance" tax. For many years, only the Yankees consistently exceeded the threshold, though more recently several other clubs, including the Red Sox, Dodgers, and Nationals, also have paid substantial taxes.

Baseball's 2016 agreement raised the penalties for exceeding the threshold, which ranges as high as $210 million for the final contract year of 2021. Teams are taxed 20% of their excess payroll for a first breach of the threshold, 30% for a second breach, and 50% for a third. An additional surcharge of 12% is imposed on any excess between $20 million and $40 million; and for any excess above $40 million, a further surcharge of over 40% is imposed. Furthermore, luxury tax offenders who sign a top free agent may sacrifice their second and fifth picks in the league's primary player draft. These increased penalties may have contributed to a relatively slow-moving free agent market in the 2017–2018 off-season. In 2018, even the ownership of the Yankees pushed payroll under the cap, as well as under the payrolls of several other teams, including more than $40 million dollars below that of their tax-paying rivals, the Red Sox.

NOTES AND QUESTIONS

1. *Hard Cap, Soft Cap, or Tax?* What are the pros and cons of the NBA's softer cap (with its Larry Bird exception and excessive payroll tax) versus the NFL's and NHL's harder versions? Of any cap versus MLB's past or current tax system? From the broader perspective of instruments for social control of private behavior, what are the virtues and limitations of regulatory standards as compared to tax incentives?

2. *Specific Caps or Revenue Sharing Formula?* Is it better to have the parties negotiate specific amounts for their salary ceilings (as they did in

baseball), or to develop a salary-sharing formula based on a numerical percentage of overall league revenues? An obvious virtue of the formula approach is that it automatically adjusts to changes in league revenues over the longer run. Calculating revenues for purposes of applying the formula may still remain contentious, however.

3. *How to Define Revenue?* An even bigger labor issue is which revenue sources should be shared with the players. For instance, should the NBA owners continue to agree to include their upward spiraling merchandising earnings in the revenue base? The simple answer (and the one the players obviously favor) is to count all owner earnings having anything to do with the sport except for franchise value appreciation. In football, though, this poses a potentially significant problem because of the lucrative stadium deals enjoyed by some but not all teams that can generate substantial revenues from luxury box suites, club seating, seat licenses, parking, and concessions. If these unshared team revenues lift the amount that teams can (and must) pay in salaries, a significant problem is posed for other teams that have not been able to extract such deals from their community's taxpayers or are situated in a market without a critical mass of moneyed local fans and businesses.

4. *What Percentage to Assign to Players?* Even when the two sides do reach an understanding about which revenues and how much revenues are to be counted, they must answer the most difficult question: the percentage to be assigned to the players. Relevant considerations may differ from sport to sport. For example, football and basketball do not face the substantial expenditures made by baseball and hockey to run farm systems that develop talent for their games. Furthermore, football teams have as many as 50 players under contract and substantial medical expenses compared to only about 15 players under contract on NBA teams that also have far fewer medical expenses per player.

D. BASEBALL'S ANTITRUST EXEMPTION

History explains why baseball players, unlike their counterparts in the other professional team sports, could not use antitrust law as well as labor law to replace the old system of almost total owner control of their labor market with the current negotiated and balanced system. The National and American Leagues emerged before the broadening of the interpretation of interstate commerce as the basis for both Congressional power and the congruent limit on the reach of antitrust law, which requires "trade or commerce among the several States." As a result, only the baseball owners could claim a reliance on the earlier more narrow interpretation of interstate commerce. The following famous (or infamous) application of the principle of *stare decisis* reflects the strength of that claim.

FLOOD V. KUHN
407 U.S. 258 (1972)

JUSTICE BLACKMUN delivered the opinion of the Court.

[Curt Flood was an All-Star center fielder for the St. Louis Cardinals throughout the 1960s, helping lead his team to the World Series in 1964, 1967, and 1968. Flood's salary rose from $4,000 in his initial 1956 contract to $90,000 in 1969. In October 1969, Flood was stunned to learn that, at the age of 31, he had been traded to the Philadelphia Phillies. Although the Phillies offered him a pay raise to $100,000, Flood rejected the trade, declared himself a free agent, and filed suit to establish these rights under federal and state antitrust law (as well as under the Thirteenth Amendment's bar on "involuntary servitude"). After the lower courts had rejected his core antitrust claim based on the judicially-fashioned exemption for baseball, the Supreme Court accepted the case to take yet another look at this issue.]

* * *

For the third time in 50 years the Court is asked specifically to rule that professional baseball's reserve system is within the reach of the federal antitrust laws.[1] Collateral issues of state law and of federal labor policy are also advanced.

I
THE GAME

It is a century and a quarter since the New York Nine defeated the Knickerbockers 23 to 1 on Hoboken's Elysian Fields June 19, 1846, with Alexander Jay Cartwright as the instigator and the umpire. The teams were amateur, but the contest marked a significant date in baseball's beginnings. That early game led ultimately to the development of professional baseball and its tightly organized structure.

The Cincinnati Red Stockings came into existence in 1869 upon an outpouring of local pride. With only one Cincinnatian on the payroll, this professional team traveled over 11,000 miles that summer, winning 56 games and tying one. Shortly thereafter, on St. Patrick's Day in 1871, the National Association of Professional Baseball Players was founded and the professional league was born.

The ensuing colorful days are well known. The ardent follower and the student of baseball know of General Abner Doubleday; the formation of the National League in 1876; Chicago's supremacy in the first year's

---

[1] The reserve system, publicly introduced into baseball contracts in 1887, centers in the uniformity of player contracts; the confinement of the player to the club that has him under the contract; the assignability of the player's contract; and the ability of the club annually to renew the contract unilaterally, subject to a stated salary minimum. . . .

competition under the leadership of Al Spalding and with Cap Anson at third base; the formation of the American Association and then of the Union Association in the 1880s; the introduction of Sunday baseball; interleague warfare with cut-rate admission prices and player raiding; the development of the reserve "clause"; the emergence in 1885 of the Brotherhood of Professional Ball Players, and in 1890 of the Players League; the appearance of the American League, or "junior circuit," in 1901, rising from the minor Western Association; the first World Series in 1903, disruption in 1904, and the Series' resumption in 1905; the short-lived Federal League on the majors' scene during World War I years; the troublesome and discouraging episode of the 1919 Series; the home run ball; the shifting of franchises; the expansion of the leagues; the installation in 1965 of the major league draft of potential new players; and the formation of the Major League Baseball Players Association in 1966.

Then there are the many names, celebrated for one reason or another, that have sparked the diamond and its environs and that have provided tinder for recaptured thrills, for reminiscence and comparisons, and for conversation and anticipation in-season and off-season: Ty Cobb, Babe Ruth, Tris Speaker, Walter Johnson, Henry Chadwick, Eddie Collins, Lou Gehrig, Grover Cleveland Alexander, Rogers Hornsby, Harry Hooper, Goose Goslin, Jackie Robinson, Honus Wagner, Joe McCarthy, John McGraw, Deacon Phillippe, Rube Marquard, Christy Mathewson, Tommy Leach, Big Ed Delahanty, Davy Jones, Germany Schaefer, King Kelly, Big Dan Brouthers, Wahoo Sam Crawford, Wee Willie Keeler, Big Ed Walsh, Jimmy Austin, Fred Snodgrass, Satchel Paige, Hugh Jennings, Fred Merkle, Iron Man McGinnity, Three-Finger Brown, Harry and Stan Coveleski, Connie Mack, Al Bridwell, Red Ruffing, Amos Rusie, Cy Young, Smokey Joe Wood, Chief Meyers, Chief Bender, Bill Klem, Hans Lobert, Johnny Evers, Joe Tinker, Roy Campanella, Miller Huggins, Rube Bressler, Dazzy Vance, Edd Roush, Bill Wambsganss, Clark Griffith, Branch Rickey, Frank Chance, Cap Anson, Nap Lajoie, Sad Sam Jones, Bob O'Farrell, Lefty O'Doul, Bobby Veach, Willie Kamm, Heinie Groh, Lloyd and Paul Waner, Stuffy McInnis, Charles Comiskey, Roger Bresnahan, Bill Dickey, Zack Wheat, George Sisler, Charlie Gehringer, Eppa Rixey, Harry Heilmann, Fred Clarke, Dizzy Dean, Hank Greenberg, Pie Traynor, Rube Waddell, Bill Terry, Carl Hubbell, Old Hoss Radbourne, Moe Berg, Rabbit Maranville, Jimmie Foxx, Lefty Grove. The list seems endless.

And one recalls the appropriate reference to the "World Serious," attributed to Ring Lardner, Sr.; Ernest L. Thayer's "Casey at the Bat";[4] the

---

[4] Millions have known and enjoyed baseball. One writer knowledgeable in the field of sports almost assumed that everyone did until, one day, he discovered otherwise:

I knew a cove who'd never heard of Washington and Lee, Caesar and Napoleon from the ancient jamboree, But, bli'me, there are queerer things than anything like that, For here's a cove who never heard of 'Casey at the Bat'!

ring of "Tinker to Evers to Chance";[5] and all the other happenings, habits, and superstitions about and around baseball that made it the "national pastime" or, depending upon the point of view, "the great American tragedy."

* * *

IV
THE LEGAL BACKGROUND

A. *Federal Baseball Club v. National League*, 259 U.S. 200 (1922), was a suit for treble damages instituted by a member of the Federal League (Baltimore) against the National and American Leagues and others. The plaintiff obtained a verdict in the trial court, but the Court of Appeals reversed. The main brief filed by the plaintiff with this Court discloses that it was strenuously argued, among other things, that the business in which the defendants were engaged was interstate commerce; that the interstate relationship among the several clubs, located as they were in different States, was predominant; that organized baseball represented an investment of colossal wealth; that it was an engagement in moneymaking; that gate receipts were divided by agreement between the home club and the visiting club; and that the business of baseball was to be distinguished from the mere playing of the game as a sport for physical exercise and diversion.

Mr. Justice Holmes, in speaking succinctly for a unanimous Court, said:

> The business is giving exhibitions of baseball, which are purely state affairs. . . . But the fact that in order to give the exhibitions the Leagues must induce free persons to cross state lines and must arrange and pay for their doing so is not enough to change the character of the business. . . . [T]he transport is a mere incident, not the essential thing. That to which it is incident, the exhibition, although made for money would not be called trade or commerce in the commonly accepted use of those words. As it is put by the

---

Ten million never heard of Keats, or Shelley, Burns or Poe; But they know "the air was shattered by the force of Casey's blow" They never heard of Shakespeare, nor of Dickens, like as not, But they know the somber drama from old Mudville's haunted lot.

He never heard of Casey! Am I dreaming? Is it true? Is fame but windblown ashes when the summer day is through? Does greatness fade so quickly and is grandeur doomed to die. That bloomed in early morning, ere the dusk rides down the sky?

"He Never Heard of Casey," Grantland Rice, The Sportlight, New York Herald Tribune, June 1, 1926, p. 23.

[5] "These are the saddest of possible words, 'Tinker to Evers to Chance.' Trio of bear cubs, and fleeter than birds, 'Tinker to Evers to Chance.'

Ruthlessly pricking our gonfalon bubble, Making a Giant hit into a double—Words that are weighty with nothing but trouble: 'Tinker to Evers to Chance.'"

Franklin Pierce Adams, *Baseball's Sad Lexicon*.

defendant, personal effort, not related to production, is not a subject of commerce. That which in its consummation is not commerce does not become commerce among the States because the transportation that we have mentioned takes place. To repeat the illustrations given by the Court below, a firm of lawyers sending out a member to argue a case, or the Chautauqua lecture bureau sending out lecturers, does not engage in such commerce because the lawyer or lecturer goes to another State.

If we are right the plaintiff's business is to be described in the same way and the restrictions by contract that prevented the plaintiff from getting players to break their bargains and the other conduct charged against the defendants were not an interference with commerce among the States.[10]

* * *

B. In the years that followed, baseball continued to be subject to intermittent antitrust attack. The courts, however, rejected these challenges on the authority of *Federal Baseball*. In some cases stress was laid, although unsuccessfully, on new factors such as the development of radio and television with their substantial additional revenues to baseball. For the most part, however, the Holmes opinion was generally and necessarily accepted as controlling authority. And in the 1952 Report of the Subcommittee on *Study of Monopoly Power*, of the House Committee on the Judiciary, H.R. Rep. No. 2002, 82d Cong., 2d Sess., 229, it was said, in conclusion:

> On the other hand the overwhelming preponderance of the evidence established baseball's need for some sort of reserve clause. Baseball's history shows that chaotic conditions prevailed when there was no reserve clause. Experience points to no feasible substitute to protect the integrity of the game or to guarantee a comparatively even competitive struggle. The evidence adduced at the hearings would clearly not justify the enactment of legislation flatly condemning the reserve clause.

C. The Court granted certiorari, in the *Toolson*, *Kowalski*, and *Corbett* cases, and, by a short per curiam (Warren, C.J., and Black, Frankfurter, Douglas, Jackson, Clark, and Minton, JJ.), affirmed the judgments of the respective courts of appeals in those three cases. *Toolson v. New York Yankees, Inc.*, 346 U.S. 356 (1953). *Federal Baseball* was cited as holding "that the business of providing public baseball games for profit

---

[10] "What really saved baseball, legally at least, for the next half century was the protective canopy spread over it by the United States Supreme Court's decision in the Baltimore Federal League antitrust suit against Organized Baseball in 1922. . . . It should be noted that, contrary to what many believe, Holmes did call baseball a business; time and again those who have not troubled to read the text of the decision have claimed incorrectly that the court said baseball was a sport and not a business." 2 H. Seymour, *Baseball* 420 (1971).

between clubs of professional baseball players was not within the scope of the federal antitrust laws," and:

> Congress has had the ruling under consideration but has not seen fit to bring such business under these laws by legislation having prospective effect. The business has thus been left for thirty years to develop, on the understanding that it was not subject to existing antitrust legislation. The present cases ask us to overrule the prior decision and, with retrospective effect, hold the legislation applicable. We think that if there are evils in this field which now warrant application to it of the antitrust laws it should be by legislation. Without re-examination of the underlying issues, the judgments below are affirmed on the authority of *Federal Baseball Club of Baltimore v. National League of Professional Baseball Clubs*, supra, so far as that decision determines that Congress had no intention of including the business of baseball within the scope of the federal antitrust laws.

This quotation reveals four reasons for the Court's affirmance of *Toolson* and its companion cases: (a) Congressional awareness for three decades of the Court's ruling in *Federal Baseball*, coupled with congressional inaction. (b) The fact that baseball was left alone to develop for that period upon the understanding that the reserve system was not subject to existing federal antitrust laws. (c) A reluctance to overrule *Federal Baseball* with consequent retroactive effect. (d) A professed desire that any needed remedy be provided by legislation rather than by court decree. The emphasis in *Toolson* was on the determination, attributed even to *Federal Baseball*, that Congress had no intention to include baseball within the reach of the federal antitrust laws.

[Justice Blackmun then described and quoted from *United States v. Shubert*, 348 U.S. 222 (1955), in which the Court refused to extend professional baseball's antitrust immunity to a nationwide theatre company. Chief Justice Warren's opinion stresses that the result in *Toolson* was based on *Federal Baseball* and stare decisis and concluded that "[i]f the *Toolson* holding is to be expanded—or contracted—the appropriate remedy lies with Congress."]

* * *

E. *United States v. International Boxing Club*, 348 U.S. 236 (1955), was a companion to *Shubert* and was decided the same day. This was a civil antitrust action against defendants engaged in the business of promoting professional championship boxing contests. Here again the District Court had dismissed the complaint in reliance upon *Federal Baseball* and *Toolson*. The Chief Justice observed that "if it were not for *Federal Baseball* and *Toolson*, we think that it would be too clear for dispute that the Government's allegations bring the defendants within the scope of the Act."

He pointed out that the defendants relied on the two baseball cases but also would have been content with a more restrictive interpretation of them than the *Shubert* defendants, for the boxing defendants argued that the cases immunized only businesses that involve exhibitions of an athletic nature. The Court accepted neither argument. It again noted that "*Toolson* neither overruled *Federal Baseball* nor necessarily reaffirmed all that was said in *Federal Baseball*." It stated:

> The controlling consideration in *Federal Baseball* and *Hart* was, instead, a very practical one—the degree of interstate activity involved in the particular business under review. It follows that *stare decisis* cannot help the defendants here; for, contrary to their argument, *Federal Baseball* did not hold that all businesses based on professional sports were outside the scope of the antitrust laws. The issue confronting us is, therefore, not whether a previously granted exemption should continue, but whether an exemption should be granted in the first instance. And that issue is for Congress to resolve, not this Court.

The Court noted the presence then in Congress of various bills forbidding the application of the antitrust laws to "organized professional sports enterprises"; the holding of extensive hearings on some of these; subcommittee opposition; a postponement recommendation as to baseball; and the fact that "Congress thus left intact the then-existing coverage of the antitrust laws."

Mr. Justice Frankfurter, joined by Mr. Justice Minton, dissented. "It would baffle the subtlest ingenuity," he said, "to find a single differentiating factor between other sporting exhibitions . . . and baseball insofar as the conduct of the sport is relevant to the criteria or considerations by which the Sherman Law becomes applicable to a trade or commerce." He went on:

> The Court decided as it did in the *Toolson* case as an application of the doctrine of *stare decisis*. That doctrine is not, to be sure, an imprisonment of reason. But neither is it a whimsy. It can hardly be that this Court gave a preferred position to baseball because it is the great American sport. . . . If *stare decisis* be one aspect of law, as it is, to disregard it in identical situations is mere caprice.
>
> Congress, on the other hand, may yield to sentiment and be capricious, subject only to due process. . . .
>
> Between them, this case and *Shubert* illustrate that nice but rational distinctions are inevitable in adjudication. I agree with the Court's opinion in *Shubert* for precisely the reason that constrains me to dissent in this case.

Mr. Justice Minton also separately dissented on the ground that boxing is not trade or commerce. He added the comment that "Congress has not attempted" to control baseball and boxing. The two dissenting Justices, thus, did not call for the overruling of *Federal Baseball* and *Toolson*; they merely felt that boxing should be under the same umbrella of freedom as was baseball and, as Mr. Justice Frankfurter said, they could not exempt baseball "to the exclusion of every other sport different not one legal jot or tittle from it."

F. The parade marched on. *Radovich v. National Football League*, 352 U.S. 445 (1957), was a civil Clayton Act case testing the application of the antitrust laws to professional football. The District Court dismissed. The Ninth Circuit affirmed in part on the basis of *Federal Baseball* and *Toolson*. The court did not hesitate to "confess that the strength of the pull" of the baseball cases and of *International Boxing* "is about equal," but then observed that "[f]ootball is a team sport" and boxing an individual one.

This Court reversed with an opinion by Mr. Justice Clark. He said that the Court made its ruling in *Toolson* "because it was concluded that more harm would be done in overruling *Federal Baseball* than in upholding a ruling which at best was of dubious validity." He noted that Congress had not acted. He then said:

> All this, combined with the flood of litigation that would follow its repudiation, the harassment that would ensue, and the retroactive effect of such a decision, led the Court to the practical result that it should sustain the unequivocal line of authority reaching over many years.
>
> [S]ince *Toolson* and *Federal Baseball* are still cited as controlling authority in antitrust actions involving other fields of business, we now specifically limit the rule there established to the facts there involved, *i.e.*, the business of organized professional baseball. As long as the Congress continues to acquiesce we should adhere to—but not extend—the interpretation of the Act made in those cases. . . .
>
> If this ruling is unrealistic, inconsistent, or illogical, it is sufficient to answer, aside from the distinctions between the businesses, that were we considering the question of baseball for the first time upon a clean slate we would have no doubts. But *Federal Baseball* held the business of baseball outside the scope of the Act. No other business claiming the coverage of those cases has such an adjudication. We therefore, conclude that the orderly way to eliminate error or discrimination, if any there be, is by legislation and not by court decision. Congressional processes are more accommodative, affording the whole industry hearings and an opportunity to assist in the formulation of new legislation. The

resulting product is therefore more likely to protect the industry and the public alike. The whole scope of congressional action would be known long in advance and effective dates for the legislation could be set in the future without the injustices of retroactivity and surprise which might follow court action.

* * *

G. Finally, in *Haywood v. National Basketball Assn.*, 401 U.S. 1204 (1971), Mr. Justice Douglas, in his capacity as Circuit Justice, reinstated a District Court's injunction pendente lite in favor of a professional basketball player and said, "Basketball . . . does not enjoy exemption from the antitrust laws."

H. This series of decisions understandably spawned extensive commentary, some of it mildly critical and much of it not; nearly all of it looked to Congress for any remedy that might be deemed essential.

I. Legislative proposals have been numerous and persistent. Since *Toolson* more than 50 bills have been introduced in Congress relative to the applicability or nonapplicability of the antitrust laws to baseball. A few of these passed one house or the other. Those that did would have expanded, not restricted, the reserve system's exemption to other professional league sports. And the Act of Sept. 30, 1961, Pub. L. 87–331, 75 Stat. 732, and the merger addition thereto effected by the Act of Nov. 8, 1966, Pub. L. 89–800, § 6(b), 80 Stat. 1515, 15 U.S.C. §§ 1291–1295, were also expansive rather than restrictive as to antitrust exemption.

V

In view of all this, it seems appropriate now to say that:

1. Professional baseball is a business and it is engaged in interstate commerce.

2. With its reserve system enjoying exemption from the federal antitrust laws, baseball is, in a very distinct sense, an exception and an anomaly. *Federal Baseball* and *Toolson* have become an aberration confined to baseball.

3. Even though others might regard this as "unrealistic, inconsistent, or illogical," the aberration is an established one, and one that has been recognized not only in *Federal Baseball* and *Toolson*, but in *Shubert, International Boxing,* and *Radovich*, as well, a total of five consecutive cases in this Court. It is an aberration that has been with us now for half a century, one heretofore deemed fully entitled to the benefit of *stare decisis*, and one that has survived the Court's expanding concept of interstate commerce. It rests on a recognition and an acceptance of baseball's unique characteristics and needs.

4. Other professional sports operating interstate—football, boxing, basketball, and, presumably, hockey and golf—are not so exempt.

5. The advent of radio and television, with their consequent increased coverage and additional revenues, has not occasioned an overruling of *Federal Baseball* and *Toolson*.

6. The Court has emphasized that since 1922, baseball, with full and continuing congressional awareness, has been allowed to develop and to expand unhindered by federal legislative action. Remedial legislation has been introduced repeatedly in Congress but none has ever been enacted. The Court, accordingly, has concluded that Congress as yet has had no intention to subject baseball's reserve system to the reach of the antitrust statutes. This, obviously, has been deemed to be something other than mere congressional silence and passivity.

7. The Court has expressed concern about the confusion and the retroactivity problems that inevitably would result with a judicial overturning of *Federal Baseball*. It has voiced a preference that if any change is to be made, it come by legislative action that, by its nature, is only prospective in operation.

8. The Court noted in *Radovich* that the slate with respect to baseball is not clean. Indeed, it has not been clean for half a century.

This emphasis and this concern are still with us. We continue to be loath, 50 years after *Federal Baseball* and almost two decades after *Toolson*, to overturn those cases judicially when Congress, by its positive inaction, has allowed those decisions to stand for so long and, far beyond mere inference and implication, has clearly evinced a desire not to disapprove them legislatively.

Accordingly, we adhere once again to *Federal Baseball* and *Toolson* and to their application to professional baseball. We adhere also to *International Boxing* and *Radovich* and to their respective applications to professional boxing and professional football. If there is any inconsistency or illogic in all this, it is an inconsistency and illogic of long standing that is to be remedied by the Congress and not by this Court. If we were to act otherwise, we would be withdrawing from the conclusion as to congressional intent made in *Toolson* and from the concerns as to retrospectivity therein expressed. Under these circumstances, there is merit in consistency even though some might claim that beneath that consistency is a layer of inconsistency.

The petitioner's argument as to the application of state antitrust laws deserves a word. Judge Cooper rejected the state law claims because state antitrust regulation would conflict with federal policy and because national "uniformity [is required] in any regulation of baseball and its reserved system." The Court of Appeals, in affirming, stated, "[A]s the burden on interstate commerce outweighs the states' interests in regulating baseball's reserve system, the Commerce Clause precludes the application here of state antitrust law." As applied to organized baseball, and in the light of this Court's observations and holding in *Federal Baseball*, in *Toolson*, in *Shubert*, in *International Boxing*, and in *Radovich*, and despite baseball's allegedly inconsistent position taken in the past with respect to the application of state law, these statements adequately dispose of the state law claims.

* * *

[W]hat the Court said in *Federal Baseball* in 1922 and what it said in *Toolson* in 1953, we say again here in 1972: the remedy, if any is indicated, is for congressional, and not judicial, action.

The judgment of the Court of Appeals is affirmed.

JUSTICE MARSHALL, with whom JUSTICE BRENNAN concurs, dissenting.

* * *

To non-athletes it might appear that petitioner was virtually enslaved by the owners of major league baseball clubs who bartered among themselves for his services. But, athletes know that it was not servitude that bound petitioner to the club owners; it was the reserve system. The essence of that system is that a player is bound to the club with which he first signs a contract for the rest of his playing days. He cannot escape from the club except by retiring, and he cannot prevent the club from assigning his contract to any other club.

* * *

We have only recently had occasion to comment that:

Antitrust laws in general, and the Sherman Act in particular, are the Magna Charta of free enterprise. They are as important to the preservation of economic freedom and our free-enterprise system as the Bill of Rights is to the protection of our fundamental personal freedoms. . . . Implicit in such freedom is the notion that it cannot be foreclosed with respect to one sector of the economy because certain private citizens or groups believe that such foreclosure might promote greater competition in a more important sector of the economy. (*United States v. Topco Associates, Inc.*, 405 U.S. 596, 610 (1972).)

The importance of the antitrust laws to every citizen must not be minimized. They are as important to baseball players as they are to football players, lawyers, doctors, or members of any other class of workers. Baseball players cannot be denied the benefits of competition merely because club owners view other economic interests as being more important, unless Congress says so.

Has Congress acquiesced in our decisions in *Federal Baseball Club* and *Toolson*? I think not. Had the Court been consistent and treated all sports in the same way baseball was treated, Congress might have become concerned enough to take action. But, the Court was inconsistent, and baseball was isolated and distinguished from all other sports. In *Toolson* the Court refused to act because Congress had been silent. But the Court may have read too much into this legislative inaction.

Americans love baseball as they love all sports. Perhaps we become so enamored of athletics that we assume that they are foremost in the minds of legislators as well as fans. We must not forget, however, that there are only some 600 major league baseball players. Whatever muscle they might have been able to muster by combining forces with other athletes has been greatly impaired by the manner in which this Court has isolated them. It is this Court that has made them impotent, and this Court should correct its error.

We do not lightly overrule our prior constructions of federal statutes, but when our errors deny substantial federal rights, like the right to compete freely and effectively to the best of one's ability as guaranteed by the antitrust laws, we must admit our error and correct it. We have done so before and we should do so again here.

* * *

To the extent that there is concern over any reliance interests that club owners may assert, they can be satisfied by making our decision prospective only. Baseball should be covered by the antitrust laws beginning with this case and henceforth, unless Congress decides otherwise.

Accordingly, I would overrule *Federal Baseball Club* and *Toolson* and reverse the decision of the Court of Appeals.

* * *

[Justice Marshall went on to explain that if the Court were to hold baseball subject to antitrust as a general matter, this did not mean that Flood's claim was necessarily actionable. In particular, baseball would still be entitled to offer as a defense the fact that the terms of Flood's player contract were mandatory subjects of collective bargaining between Major League Baseball and its Players Association, and thus arguably protected by the labor exemption from antitrust liability.]

NOTES AND QUESTIONS

1. *Holmes and Stare Decisis.* Justice Oliver Wendell Holmes, Jr., who wrote the Supreme Court's opinion in *Federal Baseball*, had earlier made the

following observations about *stare decisis* in his famous lecture on "The Path of the Law":

> It is revolting to have no better reason for a rule of law than that it was laid down in the time of Henry IV. It is still more revolting if the grounds upon which it was laid down have vanished long since, and that rule simply persists from blind imitation of the past.

How would (should) Justice Holmes have reacted to Justice Blackmun's adherence in *Flood* to Holmes' decision in *Federal Baseball* given that *Flood* rejected every one of the premises upon which *Federal Baseball* was founded?

2. *Reliance for What?* Is there any reason other than the baseball owners' reliance on their antitrust exemption for the Court to continue to honor the out dated *Federal Baseball* decision? What exactly had the owners done in reliance on that decision? Was it simply the earlier purchase of their teams? Is concern about reevaluation of assets usually a sufficient argument against otherwise sensible legal change, even for change that is judicial in origin? Or might one argue that professional baseball's structure, including its minor league system, depended upon the antitrust exemption?

3. *Union Strategy?* Can you explain why Flood would pursue his suit knowing that the Supreme Court had twice ruled that baseball did not affect interstate commerce and thus was not covered by the federal antitrust laws? The most significant business development in the sport following the *Toolson* case was the establishment of the Major League Baseball Players Association which fully funded Flood's effort. Might that explain Flood's willingness to pursue this matter?

4. *Same Result if a Discrimination Case?* How would the *Toolson* Court in 1953 (or the *Flood* Court in 1972) have reacted if, instead of allowing Jackie Robinson to play, baseball had tried to protect its Jim Crow segregation policies from federal antitrust scrutiny? Keep in mind that the Court had greatly expanded the scope of Congress' "trade and commerce" power in the later stages of the New Deal, but Congress did not enact the Civil Rights Act barring employment discrimination until 1964.

The *Flood* decision was a significant loss both for baseball players and their union and for Curt Flood. Even so, Peter Seitz's arbitration decision interpreting the reserve clause was issued only four years later in 1976, and the players union has prevented the reserve system challenged by Flood from returning. Furthermore, in 1996 the Supreme Court broadly applied another immunity from the antitrust laws, based on the existence of a collective bargaining relationship, to professional sports, in a decision considered in Chapter 6, *Brown v. Pro Football, Inc.*, 518 U.S. 231 (1996). Perhaps finding reassurance in the *Brown* decision and under renewed pressure from members of Congress threatening to eliminate the antitrust exemption because of the loss of the 1994 World Series, baseball owners finally agreed to passage of legislation to contract their exemption, at least for the major league players market where they accepted the continuation of entrenched collective bargaining. Indeed, the 1996 collective agreement included a final provision that both sides "jointly request and cooperate in lobbying Congress to pass a law clarifying that Major League Baseball players are covered under the antitrust laws . . . along with a provision that makes it clear that the passage of that bill does not change the application of the antitrust laws in any other context or with respect to any other person or entity . . . ." The legislation, aptly named the Curt Flood Act of 1998, passed two years later, less than two years after Curt Flood's untimely death at the age of 59.

CURT FLOOD ACT OF 1998
15 U.S.C. § 26b

(a) Major league baseball subject to antitrust laws

Subject to subsections (b) through (d), the conduct, acts, practices, or agreements of persons in the business of organized professional major league baseball directly relating to or affecting employment of major league baseball players to play baseball at the major league level are subject to the antitrust laws to the same extent such conduct, acts, practices, or agreements would be subject to the antitrust laws if engaged in by persons in any other professional sports business affecting interstate commerce.

(b) Limitation of section

No court shall rely on the enactment of this section as a basis for changing the application of the antitrust laws to any conduct, acts, practices, or agreements other than those set forth in subsection (a). This section does not create, permit or imply a cause of action by which to challenge under the antitrust laws, or otherwise apply the antitrust laws to, any conduct, acts, practices, or agreements that do not directly relate to or affect employment of major league baseball players to play baseball at the major league level, including but not limited to

(1) any conduct, acts, practices, or agreements of persons engaging in, conducting or participating in the business of organized professional baseball relating to or affecting employment to play baseball at the minor league level, any organized professional baseball amateur or first-year player draft, or any reserve clause as applied to minor league players;

(2) the agreement between organized professional major league baseball teams and the teams of the National Association of Professional Baseball Leagues, commonly known as the "Professional Baseball Agreement", the relationship between organized professional major league baseball and organized professional minor league baseball, or any other matter relating to organized professional baseball's minor leagues;

(3) any conduct, acts, practices, or agreements of persons engaging in, conducting or participating in the business of organized professional baseball relating to or affecting franchise expansion, location or relocation, franchise ownership issues, including ownership transfers, the relationship between the Office of the Commissioner and franchise owners, the marketing or sales of the entertainment product of organized professional baseball and the licensing of intellectual property rights owned or held by organized professional baseball teams individually or collectively;

(4) any conduct, acts, practices, or agreements protected by Public Law 87-331 (15 U.S.C. § 1291 et seq.) (commonly known as the "Sports Broadcasting Act of 1961");

(5) the relationship between persons in the business of organized professional baseball and umpires or other individuals who are employed in the business of organized professional baseball by such persons; or

(6) any conduct, acts, practices, or agreements of persons not in the business of organized professional major league baseball.

(c) Standing to sue

Only a major league baseball player has standing to sue under this section. . . .

NOTES AND QUESTIONS

1. *Effect of Curt Flood Act?* Does this statute provide baseball more secure antitrust immunity in markets other than the major league players' labor market than that which existed before its passage? Does it at least support an argument that Congress assumed that baseball's preexisting antitrust immunity extends to markets other than the major league players' labor market, including those expressly mentioned, such as the minor league players' labor market, and the franchise expansion, location, and ownership markets? If the latter, does it weaken any argument that the *stare decisis* basis for the *Flood* decision should not extend beyond the players' market at issue in *Federal Baseball, Toolson*, and *Flood*?

2. *How Broad an Exemption?* Given the *Flood* decision and the Curt Flood Act, how broadly should courts now apply baseball's antitrust exemption? Is it at least clear that it applies to other labor markets of baseball employees? *See, e.g., Miranda v. Selig*, 860 F.3d 1237 (9th Cir. 2017) (exemption extends to minor league players market); *Wyckoff v. Office of the Commissioner of Baseball*, 795 Fed. Appx. 26 (2d Cir. 2017) (exemption extends to baseball scouts market); *Salerno v. American League*, 429 F.2d 1003 (2d Cir.1970)) (exemption extends to umpires labor market). How about the relocation of franchises? *See City of San Jose v. Office of the Commissioner of*

Baseball, 776 F.3d 686 (9th Cir. 2015) (exemption extends). The contraction of franchises? *See Major League Baseball v. Crist*, 331 F.3d 1177 (11th Cir. 2003) (exemption extends). The sale of franchises? *Compare Minnesota Twins Partnership v. State of Minnesota*, 592 N.W.2d 847 (Minn. 1999), *with Piazza v. Major League Baseball*, 8311 F. Supp. 420 (E.D. Pa. 1993). For a recent case applying the exemption to protect the Cubs' efforts to control the views into Wrigley Field, see *Right Field Rooftops v. Chicago Cubs Baseball Club, LCC*, 870 F.3d 682 (7th Cir. 2017)

Finally, should the exemption extend to baseball's dealings with other industries? Some pre-Flood Act cases refused to extend the exemption to baseball's dealings with concessionaires, *see Twin City Sportservice Inc. v. Charles O. Finley & Co. (Oakland Athletics)*, 365 F. Supp. 235 (N.D. Cal.1972), *rev'd on other grounds*, 512 F.2d 1264 (9th Cir.1975)); with broadcast outlets, *see Henderson Broadcasting Corp. v. Houston Sports Ass'n (Houston Astros)*, 541 F. Supp. 263 (S.D.Tex.1982); and with merchandisers, *see Fleer v. Topps Chewing Gum & Major League Baseball Players Ass'n*, 658 F.2d 139 (3d Cir. 1981). Are at least these cases still good law after the Flood Act?

3. *MLB Control over Minors.* As suggested by § (b)(1) of the Curt Flood Act, MLB and its controlling owners seem particularly concerned about any regulation of their control of minor league baseball. That concern became salient again when minor league ball players brought suit in 2014 to collect overtime pay for working more than forty hours per week. The minor leaguers would have been owed that pay under the federal Fair Labor Standards Act (FLSA) if baseball owners had not properly applied an FLSA exemption for amusement or recreational employees. The baseball owners did not have to wait for the courts to resolve the issue, however, because their lobbyists were able to insert a more specific exemption of baseball players from overtime pay regulation in the one paragraph "Save America's Pastime Act," included in the 2,232-page 2018 Omnibus Budget Act, with one Congressional sponsor and without any committee hearing or other legislative history.

The *Flood* decision did more than maintain baseball's exemption from federal antitrust law. It also established an immunity for baseball from *state* antitrust law. Moreover, this immunity from state antitrust law is based on the "dormant Commerce Clause" principle of federal constitutional law that applies just as much to other sports leagues and organizations.

For instance, Dennis Partee, the San Diego Chargers' kicker faced this obstacle when he sought to strike down the NFL's version of the reserve system under California antitrust law. In *Partee v. San Diego Chargers Football Co.*, 34 Cal.3d 378, 194 Cal. Rptr. 367, 668 P.2d 674 (1983), a divided Supreme Court of California highlighted a key feature of dormant Commerce Clause jurisprudence. State business regulation is judged to have imposed an unreasonable burden on interstate commerce where it governs "those phases of the national commerce which, because of the need for national uniformity, demand their regulation, if any, be prescribed by a single authority." *Id.* at 677. In the majority's view, professional football clearly met that standard:

> Professional football is a nationwide business structured essentially the same as baseball. Professional football's teams are dependent upon the league playing schedule for competitive play, just as in baseball. The necessity of a nationwide league structure for the benefit of both teams and players for effective competition is evident as is the need for a nationally uniform set of rules governing the league structure. Fragmentation of the league structure on the basis of state lines would adversely affect the success of the competitive business enterprise, and differing state antitrust decisions if applied to the enterprise would likely compel all member teams to comply with the laws of the strictest state.
>
> We are satisfied that national uniformity required in regulation of baseball and its reserve system is likewise required in the player-team-league relationships challenged by Partee and that the burden on interstate commerce outweighs the state interests in applying state antitrust laws to those relationships.

668 P.2d at 678–79.

Another California court concluded that the same Commerce Clause principle precluded quarterback Bobby Hebert from using California's Labor Code (which makes it illegal for any business to deprive a person of the opportunity to earn his livelihood) to move freely from the New Orleans Saints to the Los Angeles Raiders. *See Hebert v. Los Angeles Raiders*, 234 Cal. App. 3d 36, 285 Cal. Rptr. 449 (Ct. App.), *review granted and opinion superseded*, 2 Cal. Rptr. 2d 489, 820 P.2d 999 (1991). Earlier decisions to the same effect are *Matuszak v. Houston Oilers*, 515 S.W.2d 725 (Tex. Ct. Civ. App. 1974) (refusing to apply Texas antitrust law to NFL restraints on player movement), and *State of Wisconsin v. Milwaukee Braves*, 31 Wis.2d 699, 144 N.W.2d 1 (1966) (refusing to apply Wisconsin antitrust law to block the move of the Braves from Milwaukee to Atlanta).

CHAPTER 5

BASIC PRINCIPLES OF ANTITRUST LAW APPLIED TO THE SPECIAL NATURE OF THE SPORTS INDUSTRY*

■ ■ ■

A. INTRODUCTION

For some sports lawyers, the constraints and strategic opportunities created by the antitrust laws form a critical part of their practice. Many, however, take the "rules of the game" as they are; perhaps daunted by the complexity of antitrust doctrine, they may engage in "willful blindness" about the interplay between antitrust and sports, leaving it to special counsel to assist on antitrust issues where necessary. Antitrust analysis is worthy of introductory consideration for all sports lawyers, and serious consideration for any sophisticated ones. Although antitrust liability may play a small role in many sports law practices, the disputes considered here provide some of the best case studies to understand the business of sports, and how this accords with economic understandings. Moreover, the potential to use antitrust litigation as a shield or a sword is a vital strategic tool for any good sports lawyer.

This chapter provides a basic summary of important antitrust principles. It considers a leading Supreme Court case that illustrates the basic structure of sports leagues and how this impacts antitrust analysis, then provides an overview of the leading Supreme Court doctrinal articulation of the "Rule of Reason" that applies to most sports antitrust litigation. For those interested in more extended treatment, the chapter concludes with consideration of how best to reconcile the tendency of sports leagues to be monopolies (or monopsonies) with situations where antitrust doctrine may not deal adequately with the resulting problems. Chapters 6 and 7 apply antitrust law to labor markets and to intra-league rules, respectively. These chapters have a two-fold focus: both to convey antitrust *doctrine*, and to review important *topics* in sports business to allow an

---

* The Casebook Website (http://pennstatelaw.psu.edu/SportsTextWebsite) contains citations to scholarly and other commentary on a variety of topics discussed in this chapter, including the overall goals of antitrust law; the impact of *Board of Regents*; special economic features of sports leagues; sports leagues as single entities; monopoly structure of sports; a history of rival sports leagues; and the essential facilities doctrine.

analysis of how business strategy is and can be affected by antitrust doctrine.

The two landmark cases featured in this chapter—*NCAA v. Board of Regents* and *American Needle v. NFL*—are perhaps less important to the typical sports lawyer for their doctrinal significance to antitrust law, than to provide an important framework to understand how the sports business works. As we will see, *Board of Regents* requires consideration of (1) how league rules will affect the price, output, and quality of sports entertainment services and whether those rules are responsive to consumer preferences; (2) what are the real reasons that leagues adopt rules, and which of these reasons are legitimate; and (3) whether leagues have alternative means of achieving their goals. These concerns link together with *American Needle*'s observations about the ways in which league rules might be motivated by the individual self-interest of league members, rather than the overall interests of the league. When sports executives and lawyers consider league rules, antitrust inquiry is both relevant to legality under the Sherman Act and useful to provide strategic business insight to all stakeholders—and their effective counsel.

B. GENERAL BACKGROUND TO ANTITRUST LAW

Congress enacted the Sherman Act in 1890 as the first federal competition law. For sports lawyers, the two most relevant provisions are § 1, which prohibits "[e]very contract, combination in the form of trust or otherwise, or conspiracy, in restraint of trade or commerce among the several States, or with foreign nations," and § 2, which prohibits "monopolization." Congress supplemented this legislation in 1914 by enacting the Clayton Act; the provisions most relevant to sports lawyers are § 4, which permits anyone damaged "in their business or property" to sue antitrust violators for treble damages and attorneys' fees, and § 6 (considered in Chapter 6) relating to labor.

What do these broadly worded statutes mean? Before topping his career with service as Chief Justice and President, then-Judge William Howard Taft opined that §§ 1 and 2 were meant to make criminal and tortious those acts that had been void under the common law restraint of trade doctrine. *United States v. Addyston Pipe & Steel Co.*, 85 Fed. 271, 278–79 (6th Cir. 1898), *aff'd*, 175 U.S. 211 (1899). The common law is evolutionary, but a landmark British case still provides a useful benchmark. *Nordenfelt v. Maxim Nordenfelt Gun & Ammunication Co.*, [1894] A.C. 535, 565 (H.L.), sets forth the broad notion of reasonableness with regard to restraints of trade, which must be considered "in reference to the interests of the parties concerned and reasonable in reference to the interests of the public, so framed and so guarded as to afford adequate protection to the party in whose favour it is imposed, while at the same time it is in no way injurious to the public."

1. THE PURPOSES OF THE ANTITRUST LAWS

Although controversial within antitrust circles, for our purposes it is probably sufficient to observe that the immediate target of antitrust law, at least since the mid-1970s, is excessive market power, whether in the hands of a single firm (like the Standard Oil or American Tobacco monopolies a century ago) or a group of firms who jointly acquire such market power through anticompetitive agreements.

Normally when one thinks of market power and its adverse effects, one does so in the context of a firm operating in a product market—selling its goods or services to consumers. Market power exists when consumers have few if any alternatives to the seller's product, thus enabling the seller to dictate terms based on profit maximization rather than competitive pressure. Economists have identified two general consequences of such market power. Consider the cartel fixing prices on beverage sweeteners. *See In re High Fructose Corn Syrup Antitrust Litig.*, 295 F.3d 651 (7th Cir. 2002); *United States v. Andreas*, 216 F.3d 645 (7th Cir. 2000). First, customers who purchase sweetened beverages have to pay higher prices (or obtain lower quality products); many of us who fancy or are even addicted to soft drinks pay the higher amount and keep on drinking, which results in a "wealth transfer" from customers to producers. Second, some folks cannot afford the higher prices, or choose not to pay, so that the overall amount of the good or service produced will drop. This inflicts a "deadweight loss" upon the economy as a whole as total consumer utility declines, because some factors of production (labor, materials, capital, land, or equipment) that would be most efficient at making the sweetened beverages are either left unemployed or are diverted into producing other goods and services for which they are less well-suited. (Antitrust professors argue about whether wealth transfers are an appropriate basis of concern, but the cases we discuss in these three chapters do not turn on these disputes.)

Just as the power of a single seller or a cartel of conspiring rival sellers can cause *monopoly* power, a single buyer or cartel of conspiring rival buyers can cause *monopsony* power with similar anticompetitive effects. Antitrust commentators are more divided on whether the "wealth transfer" effect of lower prices for goods and services ought to be considered symmetrically with monopoly power. For example, in *Kartell v. Blue Shield of Massachusetts, Inc.*, 749 F.2d 922 (1st Cir. 1984), the First Circuit dismissed an antitrust claim filed by doctors against Blue Shield, the dominant provider of health insurance in Massachusetts, which required all doctors who performed services for Blue Shield insureds to accept its fee schedule as full payment for the service, and not charge the patient any more. As then-Judge Stephen Breyer observed,

> ... the prices at issue here are low prices, not high prices. Of course, a buyer, as well as a seller, can possess significant market power; and courts have held that agreements to fix prices—whether maximum or minimum—are unlawful. Nonetheless, the Congress that enacted the Sherman Act saw it as a way of protecting consumers against prices that were too high, not too low. And the relevant economic conditions may be very different when low prices, rather than high prices, are at issue. These facts suggest that courts at least should be cautious—reluctant to condemn too speedily—an arrangement that, on its face, appears to bring low price benefits to the consumer.

749 F.2d at 930–31. *Kartell*, then, implies that at least some monopsony power—because it may improve the situation of at least some consumers in the marketplace—may not warrant the same kind of close antitrust scrutiny as does monopoly power, which always threatens the interests of all its consumers. At the same time, the court does not suggest that these agreements are necessarily lawful.

2. THE APPLICABLE § 1 ANTITRUST STANDARD: *PER SE* OR RULE OF REASON?

The Supreme Court has made it clear that not all restraints of trade are illegal; rather, only those judged to be unreasonable violate § 1. *See Standard Oil v. United States*, 221 U.S. 1 (1911). Some early sports law decisions were influenced by an earlier antitrust doctrinal trend where courts tended to find various business arrangements unreasonable *per se*: that is, it was sufficient to show that the defendants had engaged in practices such as price fixing (*United States v. Socony-Vacuum Oil Co.*, 310 U.S. 150 (1940)); market allocation (*United States v. Topco Assocs.*, 405 U.S. 596 (1972)); or group boycotts (*Klor's, Inc. v. Broadway-Hale Stores*, 359 U.S. 207 (1959)), to condemn the agreement without any further analysis. In *Northern Pac. Ry. Co. v. United States*, 356 U.S. 1, 5 (1958), the Court observed that "there are certain agreements or practices which because of their pernicious effect on competition and lack of any redeeming virtue are conclusively presumed to be unreasonable and therefore illegal without elaborate inquiry as to the precise harm they have caused or the business excuse for their use."

Because these categories were vaguely defined, earlier § 1 jurisprudence allowed courts to condemn forms of conduct that the judges disapproved of for social, political, or economic reasons. Beginning in the mid-1970s, the Supreme Court sharply altered its antitrust stance by either expressly overruling or drastically limiting application of the various *per se* categories. The following summarizes a few such decisions—the ones most relevant for analyzing sports law cases.

In *Broadcast Music Inc. v. Columbia Broadcasting System, Inc.*, 441 U.S. 1 (1979), the Supreme Court narrowed the *per se* approach to price fixing by rejecting a claim that an organization that held nonexclusive copyright licenses for the musical compositions of hundreds of composers automatically violated the antitrust laws when it charged commercial broadcasters a set price for the right to play all of its licensed music to commercial broadcasters. The Court reasoned that, even though the composers literally fixed the price for their "blanket license," it achieved major cost savings for purchasers, who otherwise would have had to traverse the globe to obtain individual licenses from the composer of every musical piece they wished to broadcast. They explained further:

> This substantial lowering of costs, which is of course potentially beneficial to both sellers and buyers, differentiates the blanket license from individual use licenses. The blanket license is composed of the individual compositions plus the aggregating service. Here, the whole is truly greater than the sum of its parts; it is, to some extent, a different product. The blanket license has certain unique characteristics: it allows the licensee immediate use of covered compositions, without the delay of prior individual negotiations, and great flexibility in the choice of musical material. . . . Thus, to the extent the blanket license is a different product, ASCAP is not really a joint sales agency offering the individual goods of many sellers, but is a separate seller offering its blanket license, of which the individual compositions are raw material. ASCAP, in short, made a market in which individual composers are inherently unable to compete fully effectively.

441 U.S. at 21–22. As a result, the Court directed a Rule of Reason analysis of the agreement among competing copyright holders. On remand, the lower court concluded that this blanket, but non-exclusive, license satisfied the Rule of Reason standard. *Buffalo Broadcasting Co. v. ASCAP*, 744 F.2d 917 (2d Cir. 1984) (finding terms reasonable because potential purchasers could obtain desired copyright licenses from individual holders as well as from joint licensing organizations.)

Next, the Supreme Court limited the *per se* condemnation of "group boycotts" in *Northwest Wholesale Stationers, Inc. v. Pacific Stationery & Printing Co.*, 472 U.S. 284 (1985). It held that a wholesale purchasing cooperative formed by a group of small stationery retailers was not guilty of a *per se* violation when it expelled one of its members for operating a wholesale stationery supply business in competition with the cooperative. The Court observed that the cooperative created purchasing efficiencies for its members, which in turn produced lower prices for consumers, and that enforcement of the rule against members who competed against the cooperative was arguably important for the cooperative to be able to provide these economic advantages. Refining prior precedents, the Court suggested that *per se* condemnation of group boycotts applied only to agreements where firms sought to disadvantage *competitors* by persuading or coercing suppliers or customers "to deny relationships the competitors need in the competitive struggle" and where the challenged practice was "not justified by plausible argument that they were intended to enhance overall efficiency and make markets more competitive." The Court concluded that "[u]nless the cooperative possesses market power or exclusive access to an element essential to effective competition, the conclusion that expulsion [for violating the rule] is virtually always likely to have an anticompetitive effect is unwarranted." Under this reasoning, restrictive labor practices harming players, rather than rival clubs or leagues, would not be labeled as *per se* illegal group boycotts.

In *Continental T.V., Inc. v. GTE Sylvania Inc.*, 433 U.S. 36 (1977), the Supreme Court expressly overturned the *per se* rule against a television manufacturer placing vertical territorial restrictions on its distributors. The Court reasoned that such restrictions on distributors might improve the firm's overall marketing strategy and make the company more efficient and competitive vis-a-vis its rivals, and such competition among producers would ultimately produce lower prices and higher quality for consumers. The Court noted that while vertical restraints may reduce competition among sellers of one manufacturer's brand (intrabrand competition), they might also stimulate greater competition among sellers of different manufacturers' brands (interbrand competition):

> Vertical restrictions reduce intrabrand competition by limiting the number of sellers of a particular product competing for the business of a given group of buyers. Location restrictions have this effect because of practical constraints on the effective marketing area of retail outlets. Although intrabrand competition may be reduced, the ability of retailers to exploit the resulting market may be limited both by the ability of consumers to travel to other franchised locations and, perhaps more importantly, to purchase the competing products of other manufacturers. . . .

> Vertical restrictions promote interbrand competition by allowing the manufacturer to achieve certain efficiencies in the distribution of his products. . . . Economists have identified a number of ways in which manufacturers can use such restrictions to compete more effectively against other manufacturers. For example, [manufacturers] can use the restrictions in order to induce competent and aggressive retailers to make the kind of investment on capital and labor that is often required in the distribution of products unknown to the consumer, [or] to induce retailers to engage in promotional activities or to provide service and repair facilities necessary to the efficient marketing of their products. . . . The availability and quality of such services affect a

manufacturer's goodwill and the competitiveness of his product. Because of market imperfections such as the so-called "free rider" effect, these services might not be provided by retailers in a purely competitive situation, despite the fact that each retailer's benefit would be greater if all provided the services than if none did.

433 U.S. at 54–55.

In conducting Rule of Reason review, courts remain more skeptical of "horizontal" restraints agreed to by rivals, while the *Sylvania* case demonstrates increasing judicial benevolence toward "vertical" restraints imposed on "downstream" firms (such as retailers or franchisees) by "upstream" companies (like manufacturers or franchisors). In contrast to the Supreme Court's more benign view of limits on Sylvania retailers, *United States v. Sealy*, 388 U.S. 350 (1967), which was decided ten years earlier during the closing years of the Supreme Court's populist antitrust era, held that a scheme to limit retail sales of mattresses was *per se* illegal because the "manufacturer" (Sealy) was really controlled by the retailers themselves. In *United States v. General Motors*, 384 U.S. 127 (1966), the Court condemned as *per se* illegal an agreement among GM dealers not to sell Chevrolets to unauthorized discount retailers, but Justice Fortas' opinion explicitly distinguished the challenged scheme from a plan where GM had "by unilateral action" determined that its cars should not be sold to discounters. (The insights from these cases are relied upon by Justice Stevens in the *American Needle* excerpt discussed in Section D, *infra*.)

National Society of Professional Engineers v. United States, 435 U.S. 679 (1978), clarified permissible factors to be considered during a Rule of Reason review. The Justice Department had charged the Society governing civil engineers with a *per se* violation of § 1 for adopting a rule that prohibited engineers from quoting a price in their project bids. The Society defended its price ban as necessary to protect the public from unsafe structures that engineers might design if they became too cost conscious in order to win bids and jobs. The Court rejected this argument as "nothing less than a frontal assault on the basic policy of the Sherman Act."

> The Sherman Act reflects a legislative judgment that ultimately competition will produce not only lower prices, but also better goods and services.... The assumption that competition is the best method of allocating resources in a free market recognizes that all elements of a bargain—quality, service, safety, and durability—and not just the immediate cost, are favorably affected by the free opportunity to select among alternative offers. Even assuming occasional exceptions to the presumed consequences of competition, the statutory policy precludes inquiry into the question whether competition is good or bad.

Id. at 695–96.

The antitrust Rule of Reason therefore requires judges and juries to balance only an agreement's effects on economic competition. Courts must weigh the injury to the consumer stemming from any increase in defendants' market power due to the arrangement (allocative inefficiency) against any benefits to the consumer that occur because defendants can make and sell their product(s) at a lower price, or make more and higher quality products at the same price (productive efficiency). This suggests that sports leagues or sports governing bodies cannot justify restrictive commercial practices on non-economic grounds, although occasionally courts will suggest that some non-economic grounds may be relevant if the objectives are salutary and not motivated by the defendants' economic self-interest. *See United States v. Brown Univ.*, 3 F.3d 658 (3d Cir. 1993) (stating that it was relevant in considering whether an agreement among Ivy League colleges to standardize the size of scholarship offers to needy students violated section 1 to consider whether the agreement "promoted the social ideal of equality of educational access and opportunity").

A challenge in applying these precedents to sports leagues arises because, akin to comparing apples and oranges, restrictive practices that leagues adopt as the purchasers of services (such as from players) are justified by sports leagues as improving the quality of the overall product for the benefit of consumers. Economists differ sharply over both the market power and the efficiency effects of any particular business arrangement, so this balancing exercise can be problematic for judges, let alone lay juries. Judge Robert Bork noted this problem in *Rothery Storage & Van Co. v. Atlas Van Lines, Inc.*, 792 F.2d 210 (D.C. Cir. 1986), in an important non-sports antitrust opinion which resurrected the "ancillary restraints" doctrine that had first been formulated by then-Chief Judge Taft in *United States v. Addyston Pipe & Steel Co.*, 85 Fed. 271 (6th Cir. 1898), *aff'd*, 175 U.S. 211 (1899). This venerable doctrine held that restraints are reasonable if "ancillary" to a lawful agreement among the parties, and reasonably necessary to protect the parties' "legitimate" interests. Though the Supreme Court has not yet explicitly endorsed this concept, we will see it figure in several sports law opinions reproduced in this and the following chapters. In general, the more recent cases suggest that, because the Sherman Act is a "consumer welfare prescription," *Reiter v. Sonotone*, 442 U.S. 330 (1979), leagues have the freedom to adopt restraints on competition for player services that can be justified as reasonably necessary to produce a sporting competition that maximizes fan appeal.

C. APPLYING THE "RULE OF REASON" TO SPORTS LEAGUE RESTRAINTS

Two important judicial decisions teach us when and how the Rule of Reason applies to sports league restraints. The first, explored in more detail in Chapter 6, is *Mackey v. NFL*, 543 F.2d 606 (8th Cir. 1976). This was an antitrust challenge by veteran NFL players to the "Rozelle Rule" that limited the ability of NFL clubs to compete for their services, by requiring a club signing a player previously employed by another NFL club to provide substantial "compensation" that would be determined by the NFL commissioner. The Eighth Circuit employed a three-step test in finding that the NFL rule was an unreasonable restraint of trade in violation of § 1.

First, the court found that the agreement had a **significant anticompetitive effect**. The court found that the rule:

> acts as a substantial deterrent to players playing out their options and becoming free agents; that it significantly decreases players' bargaining power in contract negotiations; that players are thus denied the right to sell their services in a free and open market; that as a result, the salaries paid by each club are lower than if competitive bidding were allowed to prevail; and that absent the Rozelle Rule, there would be increased movement in interstate commerce of players from one club to another.

Id. at 620.

Second, the court considered "whether the restraint imposed is **justified by legitimate business purposes**." *Id.* (We consider the specific justifications offered by the NFL—harm to competitive balance, protecting the clubs' investment in scouting expenses and player development costs, and the need for player continuity on the same team, in Chapter 6.)

Third, the court examined whether the restraint "is **no more restrictive than necessary**." In this regard, the court looked both at other alternatives, and whether the scope of the restraint was broader than necessary to achieve the NFL's stated goals.

The three-part framework utilized by *Mackey* was applied and more fully expanded by the Supreme Court in its landmark exposition of how the rule of reason applies to sports, as well as multiple other industries. The Court's observations about specific issues surrounding intercollegiate sports are considered in detail in Chapter 11.

NCAA v. BOARD OF REGENTS OF THE UNIV. OF OKLAHOMA & UNIV. OF GEORGIA ATHLETIC ASS'N
468 U.S. 85 (1984)

JUSTICE STEVENS for the Court.

* * *

History of the NCAA Television Plan

In 1938, the University of Pennsylvania televised one of its home games.[3] From 1940 through the 1950 season all of Pennsylvania's home games were televised. That was the beginning of the relationship between television and college football.

On January 11, 1951, a three-person "Television Committee," appointed during the preceding year, delivered a report to the NCAA's annual convention in Dallas. Based on preliminary surveys, the committee had concluded that "television does have an adverse effect on college football attendance and unless brought under some control threatens to seriously harm the nation's overall athletic and physical system." The report emphasized that "the television problem is truly a national one and requires collective action by the colleges."

[In 1951 the NCAA adopted a television plan that permitted only one game per week to be broadcast in each area, and limited each school to two television appearances per season. The University of Pennsylvania at first insisted on televising all its home games, but after the NCAA declared it a member in bad standing and the four schools scheduled to play at Pennsylvania that year threatened to cancel the games, the school agreed to follow the NCAA plan.

Studies in each of the next five years indicated that television had an adverse effect on attendance. The NCAA continued to formulate a television policy for all its members. From the mid-1960s to the late 1970s, ABC held the exclusive network right to broadcast college football games. In 1981, the NCAA negotiated four-year agreements with both ABC and CBS, under which each network could broadcast 14 games per season in return for an annual $33 million apiece. In addition, the NCAA granted Turner Broadcasting System (TBS) exclusive cable rights for a limited number of games, for $9 million a year.

The "appearance requirements and limitations" followed the same pattern as before. Under the new contracts, over a two-year cycle each network had to carry games showing at least 82 NCAA members, with six being the maximum number for any one college team (and only four on national coverage). The NCAA's rules, as reflected in the network

---

[3] According to the NCAA football television committee's 1981 briefing book: "As far as is known, there were [then] six television sets in Philadelphia: and all were tuned to the game."

contracts, also barred any individual member from selling its own team's broadcast rights.

However, the [College Football Association (CFA)] members were unhappy with these restraints, and they negotiated a different contract with NBC that gave these "big-time" college football powers both more appearances and more money. The NCAA threatened any team that allowed its game to be broadcast on NBC with sanctions, not only against their football program, but against all of their sports. Thus, the Universities of Oklahoma and Georgia filed suit in an Oklahoma federal district court, and secured an injunction against any effort by the NCAA to interfere with CFA's dealings with NBC. The Supreme Court agreed to hear the NCAA's appeal.]

* * *

II

There can be no doubt that the challenged practices of the NCAA constitute a "restraint of trade" in the sense that they limit members' freedom to negotiate and enter into their own television contracts. In that sense, however, every contract is a restraint of trade, and as we have repeatedly recognized, the Sherman Act was intended to prohibit only unreasonable restraints of trade.

It is also undeniable that these practices share characteristics of restraints we have previously held unreasonable. The NCAA is an association of schools which compete against each other to attract television revenues, not to mention fans and athletes. As the District Court found, the policies of the NCAA with respect to television rights are ultimately controlled by the vote of member institutions. By participating in an association which prevents member institutions from competing against each other on the basis of price or kind of television rights that can be offered to broadcasters, the NCAA member institutions have created a horizontal restraint—an agreement among competitors on the way in which they will compete with one another. A restraint of this type has often been held to be unreasonable as a matter of law. Because it places a ceiling on the number of games member institutions may televise, the horizontal agreement places an artificial limit on the quantity of televised football that is available to broadcasters and consumers. By restraining the quantity of television rights available for sale, the challenged practices create a limitation on output; our cases have held that such limitations are unreasonable restraints of trade. Moreover, the District Court found that the minimum aggregate price in fact operates to preclude any price negotiation between broadcasters and institutions, thereby constituting horizontal price fixing, perhaps the paradigm of an unreasonable restraint of trade.

Horizontal price fixing and output limitation are ordinarily condemned as a matter of law under an "illegal per se" approach because the probability that these practices are anticompetitive is so high; a per se rule is applied when "the practice facially appears to be one that would always or almost always tend to restrict competition and decrease output." In such circumstances a restraint is presumed unreasonable without inquiry into the particular market context in which it is found. Nevertheless, we have decided that it would be inappropriate to apply a per se rule to this case. This decision is not based on a lack of judicial experience with this type of arrangement, on the fact that the NCAA is organized as a nonprofit entity, or on our respect for the NCAA's historic role in the preservation and encouragement of intercollegiate amateur athletics. Rather, what is critical is that this case involves an industry in which horizontal restraints on competition are essential if the product is to be available at all.

As Judge Bork has noted: "[S]ome activities can only be carried out jointly. Perhaps the leading example is league sports. When a league of professional lacrosse teams is formed, it would be pointless to declare their cooperation illegal on the ground that there are no other professional lacrosse teams." R. Bork, *The Antitrust Paradox* 278 (1978). What the NCAA and its member institutions market in this case is competition itself—contests between competing institutions. Of course, this would be completely ineffective if there were no rules on which the competitors agreed to create and define the competition to be marketed. A myriad of rules affecting such matters as the size of the field, the number of players on a team, and the extent to which physical violence is to be encouraged or proscribed, all must be agreed upon, and all restrain the manner in which institutions compete. Moreover, the NCAA seeks to market a particular brand of football—college football. The identification of this "product" with an academic tradition differentiates college football from and makes it more popular than professional sports to which it might otherwise be comparable, such as, for example, minor league baseball. In order to preserve the character and quality of the "product," athletes must not be paid, must be required to attend class, and the like. And the integrity of the "product" cannot be preserved except by mutual agreement; if an institution adopted such restrictions unilaterally, its effectiveness as a competitor on the playing field might soon be destroyed. Thus, the NCAA plays a vital role in enabling college football to preserve its character, and as a result enables a product to be marketed which might otherwise be unavailable. In performing this role, its actions widen consumer choice—not only the choices available to sports fans but also those available to athletes—and hence can be viewed as procompetitive. . . .

Respondents concede that the great majority of the NCAA's regulations enhance competition among member institutions. Thus, despite the fact that this case involves restraints on the ability of member institutions to compete in terms of price and output, a fair evaluation of their competitive character requires consideration of the NCAA's justifications for the restraints.

Our analysis of this case under the Rule of Reason, of course, does not change the ultimate focus of our inquiry.... Under the Sherman Act the criterion to be used in judging the validity of a restraint on trade is its impact on competition.

III

Because it restrains price and output, the NCAA's television plan has a significant potential for anticompetitive effects.[28] The findings of the District Court indicate that this potential has been realized. The District Court found that if member institutions were free to sell television rights, many more games would be shown on television, and that the NCAA's output restriction has the effect of raising the price the networks pay for television rights. Moreover, the court found that by fixing a price for television rights to all games, the NCAA creates a price structure that is unresponsive to viewer demand and unrelated to the prices that would prevail in a competitive market. And, of course, since as a practical matter all member institutions need NCAA approval, members have no real choice but to adhere to the NCAA's television controls.

The anticompetitive consequences of this arrangement are apparent. Individual competitors lose their freedom to compete. Price is higher and output lower than they would otherwise be, and both are unresponsive to consumer preference.[33] This latter point is perhaps the most significant, since "Congress designed the Sherman Act as a 'consumer welfare prescription.'" A restraint that has the effect of reducing the importance of consumer preference in setting price and output is not consistent with this

---

[28] In this connection, it is not without significance that Congress felt the need to grant professional sports an exemption from the antitrust laws for joint marketing of television rights. *See* 15 U.S.C. § 1291–1295. The legislative history of this exemption demonstrates Congress' recognition that agreements among league members to sell television rights in a cooperative fashion could run afoul of the Sherman Act, and in particular reflects its awareness of the decision in *United States v. National Football League*, 116 F. Supp. 319 (E.D.Pa.1953), which held that an agreement between the teams of the National Football League that each team would not permit stations within 75 miles of the home city of another team to telecast its games on a day when that team was playing at home violated § 1 of the Sherman Act.

[33] The District Court provided a vivid example of this system in practice:

A clear example of the failure of the rights fees paid to respond to market forces occurred in the fall of 1981. On one weekend of that year, Oklahoma was scheduled to play a football game with the University of Southern California. Both Oklahoma and USC have long had outstanding football programs, and indeed, both teams were ranked among the top five teams in the country by the wire service polls. ABC chose to televise the game along with several others on a regional basis. A game between two schools which are not well-known for their football programs, Citadel and Appalachian State, was carried on four of ABC's local affiliated stations. The USC-Oklahoma contest was carried on over 200 stations. Yet, incredibly, all four of these teams received exactly the same amount of money for the right to televise their games.

fundamental goal of antitrust law.[34] Restrictions on price and output are the paradigmatic examples of restraints of trade that the Sherman Act was intended to prohibit. At the same time, the television plan eliminates competitors from the market, since only those broadcasters able to bid on television rights covering the entire NCAA can compete. Thus, as the District Court found, many telecasts that would occur in a competitive market are foreclosed by the NCAA's plan.

Petitioner argues, however, that its television plan can have no significant anticompetitive effect since the record indicates that it has no market power—no ability to alter the interaction of supply and demand in the market. We must reject this argument for two reasons, one legal, one factual.

As a matter of law, the absence of proof of market power does not justify a naked restriction on price or output. To the contrary, when there is an agreement not to compete in terms of price or output, "no elaborate industry analysis is required to demonstrate the anticompetitive character of such an agreement." Petitioner does not quarrel with the District Court's finding that price and output are not responsive to demand. Thus the plan is inconsistent with the Sherman Act's command that price and supply be responsive to consumer preference. We have never required proof of market power in such a case. This naked restraint on price and output requires some competitive justification even in the absence of a detailed market analysis. As a factual matter, it is evident that petitioner does possess market power. The District Court employed the correct test for determining whether college football broadcasts constitute a separate market—whether there are other products that are reasonably substitutable for televised NCAA football games. Petitioner's argument that it cannot obtain supracompetitive prices from broadcasters since advertisers, and hence broadcasters, can switch from college football to other types of programming simply ignores the findings of the District Court. It found that intercollegiate football telecasts generate an audience uniquely attractive to advertisers and that competitors are unable to offer programming that can attract a similar audience. These findings amply support its conclusion that the NCAA possesses market power. Indeed, the District Court's subsidiary finding that advertisers will pay a premium price per viewer to reach audiences watching college football because of their demographic characteristics is vivid evidence of the uniqueness of this product. Moreover, the District Court's market analysis is firmly supported

---

[34] As the District Court observed:

Perhaps the most pernicious aspect is that under the controls, the market is not responsive to viewer preference. Every witness who testified on the matter confirmed that the consumers, the viewers of college football television, receive absolutely no benefit from the controls. Many games for which there is a large viewer demand are kept from the viewers, and many games for which there is little if any demand are nonetheless televised.

by our decision in *International Boxing Club v. United States*, 358 U.S. 242 (1959), that championship boxing events are uniquely attractive to fans and hence constitute a market separate from that for non-championship events. Thus, respondents have demonstrated that there is a separate market for telecasts of college football which "rest[s] on generic qualities differentiating" viewers. It inexorably follows that if college football broadcasts be defined as a separate market—and we are convinced they are—then the NCAA's complete control over those broadcasts provides a solid basis for the District Court's conclusion that the NCAA possesses market power with respect to those broadcasts. "When a product is controlled by one interest, without substitutes available in the market, there is monopoly power." *United States v. E.I. du Pont de Nemours & Co.*, 351 U.S. 377, 394 (1956).

Thus, the NCAA television plan on its face constitutes a restraint upon the operation of a free market, and the findings of the District Court establish that it has operated to raise price and reduce output. Under the Rule of Reason, these hallmarks of anticompetitive behavior place upon petitioner a heavy burden of establishing an affirmative defense which competitively justifies this apparent deviation from the operations of a free market.

IV

[P]etitioner argues that its television plan constitutes a cooperative "joint venture" which assists in the marketing of broadcast rights and hence is procompetitive. . . .

The District Court did not find that the NCAA's television plan produced any procompetitive efficiencies which enhanced the competitiveness of college football television rights; to the contrary it concluded that NCAA football could be marketed just as effectively without the television plan. There is therefore no predicate in the findings for petitioner's efficiency justification. Indeed, petitioner's argument is refuted by the District Court's finding concerning price and output. If the NCAA's television plan produced procompetitive efficiencies, the plan would increase output and reduce the price of televised games. The District Court's contrary findings accordingly undermine petitioner's position. In light of these findings, it cannot be said that "the agreement on price is necessary to market the product at all." . . . Here production has been limited, not enhanced. No individual school is free to televise its own games without restraint. The NCAA's efficiency justification is not supported by the record.

Neither is the NCAA's television plan necessary to enable the NCAA to penetrate the market through an attractive package sale. Since broadcasting rights to college football constitute a unique product for which there is no ready substitute, there is no need for collective action in order to enable the product to compete against its nonexistent competitors. This is borne out by the District Court's finding that the NCAA's television reduces the volume of television rights sold.

V

Throughout the history of its regulation of intercollegiate football telecasts, the NCAA has indicated its concern with protecting live attendance. This concern, it should be noted, is not with protecting live attendance at games which are shown on television; that type of interest is not at issue in this case. Rather, the concern is that fan interest in a televised game may adversely affect ticket sales for games that will not appear on television.[56]

Although studies in the 1950s provided some support for the thesis that live attendance would suffer if unlimited television were permitted, the District Court found that there was no evidence to support that theory in today's market. . . .

There is, however, a more fundamental reason for rejecting this defense. The NCAA's argument that its television plan is necessary to protect live attendance is not based on a desire to maintain the integrity of college football as a distinct and attractive product, but rather on a fear that the product will not prove sufficiently attractive to draw live attendance when faced with competition from televised games. At bottom the NCAA's position is that ticket sales for most college games are unable to compete in a free market. The television plan protects ticket sales by limiting output—just as any monopolist increases revenues by reducing output. By seeking to insulate live ticket sales from the full spectrum of competition because of its assumption that the product itself is insufficiently attractive to consumers, petitioner forwards a justification that is inconsistent with the basic policy of the Sherman Act. "[T]he Rule of Reason does not support a defense based on the assumption that competition itself is unreasonable." *National Society of Professional Engineers v. United States*, 435 U.S. 679, 696 (1978).

VI

Petitioner argues that the interest in maintaining a competitive balance among amateur athletic teams is legitimate and important and that it justifies the regulations challenged in this case. We agree with the first part of the argument but not the second.

---

[56] The NCAA's plan is not even arguably related to a desire to protect live attendance by ensuring that a game is not televised in the area where it is to be played. No cooperative action is necessary for that kind of "blackout." The home team can always refuse to sell the right to telecast its game to stations in the immediate area. The NCAA does not now and never has justified its television plan by an interest in assisting schools in "blacking out" their home games in the areas in which they are played.

Our decision not to apply a per se rule to this case rests in large part on our recognition that a certain degree of cooperation is necessary if the type of competition that petitioner and its member institutions seek to market is to be preserved. It is reasonable to assume that most of the regulatory controls of the NCAA are justifiable means of fostering competition among amateur athletic teams and therefore procompetitive because they enhance public interest in intercollegiate athletics. The specific restraints on football telecasts that are challenged in this case do not, however, fit into the same mold as do rules defining the conditions of the contest, the eligibility of participants, or the manner in which members of a joint enterprise shall share the responsibilities and the benefits of the total venture.

The NCAA does not claim that its television plan has equalized or is intended to equalize competition within any one league.[62] The plan is nationwide in scope and there is no single league or tournament in which all college football teams complete. There is no evidence of any intent to equalize the strength of teams in Division I-A with those in Division II or Division III, and not even a colorable basis for giving colleges that have no football program at all a voice in the management of the revenues generated by the football programs at other schools.[63] The interest in maintaining a competitive balance that is asserted by the NCAA as a justification for regulating all television of intercollegiate football is not related to any neutral standard or to any readily identifiable group of competitors.

The television plan is not even arguably tailored to serve such an interest. It does not regulate the amount of money that any college may spend on its football program, nor the way in which the colleges may use the revenues that are generated by their football programs, whether

---

[62] It seems unlikely, for example, that there would have been a greater disparity between the football prowess of Ohio State University and that of Northwestern University in recent years without the NCAA's television plan. The District Court found that in fact the NCAA has been strikingly unsuccessful if it has indeed attempted to prevent the emergence of a "power elite" in intercollegiate football. Moreover, the District Court's finding that there would be more local and regional telecasts without the NCAA controls means that Northwestern could well have generated more television income in a free market than was obtained under the NCAA regime.

[63] Indeed, the District Court found that the basic reason the television plan has endured is that the NCAA is in effect controlled by schools that are not restrained by the plan:

> The plaintiffs and other CFA members attempted to persuade the majority of NCAA members that NCAA had gone far beyond its legitimate role in football television. Not surprisingly, none of the CFA proposals were adopted. Instead the membership uniformly adopted the proposals of the NCAA administration which "legitimized" NCAA's exercises of power. The result was not surprising in light of the makeup of the voting membership. Of approximately 800 voting members of the NCAA, 500 or so are in Divisions II and III and are not subjected to NCAA television controls. Of the 275 Division I members, only 187 play football, and only 135 were members of Division I-A at the time of the January Convention. Division I-A was made up of the most prominent football-playing schools, and those schools account for most of the football games shown on network television. Therefore, of some 850 voting members, less than 150 suffer any direct restriction on their right to sell football games to television.

derived from the sale of television rights, the sale of tickets, or the sale of concessions or program advertising. The plan simply imposes a restriction on one source of revenue that is more important to some colleges than to others. There is no evidence that this restriction produces any greater measure of equality throughout the NCAA than would a restriction on alumni donations, tuition rates, or any other revenue producing activity. At the same time, as the District Court found, the NCAA imposes a variety of other restrictions designed to preserve amateurism which are much better tailored to the goal of competitive balance than is the television plan, and which are "clearly sufficient" to preserve competitive balance to the extent it is within the NCAA's power to do so. And much more than speculation supported the District Court's findings on this score. No other NCAA sport employs a similar plan, and in particular the court found that in the most closely analogous sport, college basketball, competitive balance has been maintained without resort to a restrictive television plan.

Perhaps the most important reason for rejecting the argument that the interest in competitive balance is served by the television plan is the District Court's unambiguous and well supported finding that many more games would be televised in a free market than under the NCAA plan. The hypothesis that legitimates the maintenance of competitive balance as a procompetitive justification under the Rule of Reason is that equal competition will maximize consumer demand for the product. The finding that consumption will materially increase if the controls are removed is a compelling demonstration that they do not in fact serve any such legitimate purpose.[68]

VII

The NCAA plays a critical role in the maintenance of a revered tradition of amateurism in college sports. There can be no question but that it needs ample latitude to play that role, or that the preservation of the student-athlete in higher education adds richness and diversity to intercollegiate athletics and is entirely consistent with the goals of the Sherman Act. But consistent with the Sherman Act, the role of the NCAA must be to preserve a tradition that might otherwise die; rules that restrict output are hardly consistent with this role. Today we hold only that the record supports the District Court's conclusion that by curtailing output and blunting the ability of member institutions to respond to consumer preference, the NCAA has restricted rather than enhanced the place of intercollegiate athletics in the Nation's life. Accordingly, the judgment of the Court of Appeals is

---

[68] This is true not only for television viewers, but also for athletes. The District Court's finding that the television exposure of all schools would increase in the absence of the NCAA's television plan means that smaller institutions appealing to essentially local or regional markets would get more exposure if the plan is enjoined, enhancing their ability to compete for student athletes.

Affirmed.

JUSTICE WHITE with whom JUSTICE REHNQUIST joins, dissenting.

* * *

I

"While it would be fanciful to suggest that colleges are not concerned about the profitability of their ventures, it is clear that other, noncommercial goals play a central role in their sports programs." J. Weistart & C. Lowell, *The Law of Sports* § 5.12 (1979). The NCAA's member institutions have designed their competitive athletic programs "to be a vital part of the educational system." Deviations from this goal, produced by a persistent and perhaps inevitable desire to "win at all costs," have in the past led, and continue to lead, to a wide range of competitive excesses that prove harmful to students and institutions alike. . . .

The NCAA, in short, "exist[s] primarily to enhance the contribution made by amateur athletic competition to the process of higher education as distinguished from realizing maximum return on it as an entertainment commodity." In pursuing this goal, the organization and its members seek to provide a public good—a viable system of amateur athletics—that most likely could not be provided in a perfectly competitive market. "Without regulation, the desire of member institutions to remain athletically competitive would lead them to engage in activities that deny amateurism to the public. No single institution could confidently enforce its own standards since it could not trust its competitors to do the same." Note, *Antitrust and Nonprofit Entities*, 94 Harv. L. Rev. 802, 817–18 (1981). The history of intercollegiate athletics prior to the advent of the NCAA provides ample support for this conclusion. By mitigating what appears to be a clear failure of the free market to serve the ends and goals of higher education, the NCAA ensures the continued availability of a unique and valuable product, the very existence of which might well be threatened by unbridled competition in the economic sphere.

In pursuit of its fundamental goal and others related to it, the NCAA imposes numerous controls on intercollegiate athletic competition among its members, many of which "are similar to those which are summarily condemned when undertaken in a more traditional business setting." J. Weistart & C. Lowell, *supra*, at § 5.12.b. Thus, the NCAA has promulgated and enforced rules limiting both the compensation of student-athletes, and the number of coaches a school may hire for its football and basketball programs; it also has prohibited athletes who formerly have been compensated for playing from participating in intercollegiate competition, restricted the number of athletic scholarships its members may award, and established minimum academic standards for recipients of those scholarships; and it has pervasively regulated the recruitment process, student eligibility, practice schedules, squad size, the number of games played, and many other aspects of intercollegiate athletics. One clear effect of most, if not all, of these regulations is to prevent institutions with competitively and economically successful programs from taking advantage of their success by expanding their programs, improving the quality of the product they offer, and increasing their sports revenues. Yet each of these regulations represents a desirable and legitimate attempt "to keep university athletics from becoming professionalized to the extent that profit making objectives would overshadow educational objectives." Significantly, neither the Court of Appeals nor this Court questions the validity of these regulations under the Rule of Reason.

Notwithstanding the contrary conclusion of the District Court, and the majority, I do not believe that the restraint under consideration in this case—the NCAA's television plan—differs fundamentally for antitrust purposes from the other seemingly anticompetitive aspects of the organization's broader program of self-regulation. The television plan, like many of the NCAA's actions, furthers several complementary ends. Specifically, the plan is designed "to reduce, insofar as possible, the adverse effects of live television . . . upon football game attendance and, in turn, upon the athletic and related educational programs dependent upon the proceeds therefrom; to spread football television participation among as many colleges as practicable; to reflect properly the image of universities as educational institutions; to promote college football through the use of television, to advance the overall interests of intercollegiate athletics, and to provide college football television to the public to the extent compatible with these other objectives." More generally, in my view, the television plan reflects the NCAA's fundamental policy of preserving amateurism and integrating athletics and education. Nor does the District Court's finding that the plan is intended to maximize television revenues, warrant any implication that the NCAA and its member institutions pursue this goal without regard to the organization's stated policies.

* * *

[I]t is essential at this point to emphasize that neither the Court of Appeals nor this Court purports to hold that the NCAA may not (1) require its members who televise their games to pool and share the compensation received among themselves, with other schools, and with the NCAA; (2) limit the number of times any member may arrange to have its games shown on television; or (3) enforce reasonable blackout rules to avoid head-to-head competition for television audiences. As I shall demonstrate, the Court wisely and correctly does not condemn such regulations. What the Court does affirm is the Court of Appeals' judgment that the NCAA may not limit the number of games that are broadcast on television and that it may not contract for an overall price that has the effect of setting the price for individual game broadcast rights. I disagree with the Court in these respects.

* * *

III

Even if I were convinced that the District Court did not err in failing to look to total viewership, as opposed to the number of televised games, when measuring output and anticompetitive effect and in failing fully to consider whether the NCAA possesses power to fix the package price, as opposed to the distribution of that package price among participating teams, I would nevertheless hold that the television plan passes muster under the Rule of Reason. The NCAA argues strenuously that the plan and the network contracts "are part of a joint venture among many of the nation's universities to create a product—high-quality college football— and offer that product in a way attractive to both fans in the stadiums and viewers on [television]. The cooperation in producing the product makes it more competitive against other [television] (and live) attractions." The Court recognizes that, "[i]f the NCAA faced 'interbrand' competition from available substitutes, then certain forms of collective action might be appropriate in order to enhance its ability to compete." It rejects the NCAA's proffered procompetitive justification, however, on the ground that college football is a unique product for which there are no available substitutes and "there is no need for collective action in order to enable the product to compete against its nonexistent competitors." This proposition is singularly unpersuasive.

It is one thing to say that "NCAA football is a unique product," that "intercollegiate football telecasts generate an audience uniquely attractive to advertisers and that competitors are unable to offer programming that can attract a similar audience." It is quite another, in my view, to say that maintenance or enhancement of the quality of NCAA football telecasts is unnecessary to enable those telecasts to compete effectively against other forms of entertainment. The NCAA has no monopoly power when competing against other types of entertainment. Should the quality of the NCAA's product "deteriorate to any perceptible degree or should the cost of 'using' its product rise, some fans undoubtedly would turn to another form of entertainment.... Because of the broad possibilities for alternative forms of entertainment," the NCAA "properly belongs in the broader 'entertainment' market rather than in ... [a] narrower marke[t]" like sports or football.

The NCAA has suggested a number of plausible ways in which its television plan might enhance the ability of college football telecasts to compete against other forms of entertainment. Although the District Court did conclude that the plan is "not necessary for effective marketing of the product," its finding was directed only at the question whether college football telecasts would continue in the absence of the plan. It made no explicit findings concerning the effect of the plan on viewership and thus did not reject the factual premise of the NCAA's argument that the plan might enhance competition by increasing the market penetration of NCAA football. The District Court's finding that network coverage of NCAA football would likely decrease if the plan were struck down, in fact, strongly suggests the validity of the NCAA's position. On the record now before the Court, therefore, I am not prepared to conclude that the restraints imposed by the NCAA's television plan are "such as may suppress or even destroy competition" rather than "such as merely regulat[e] and perhaps thereby promot[e] competition."

IV

Finally, I return to the point with which I began—the essentially noneconomic nature of the NCAA's program of self-regulation. Like Judge Barrett, who dissented in the Court of Appeals, I believe that the lower courts "erred by subjugating the NCAA's educational goals (and, coincidentally, those which Oklahoma and Georgia insist must be maintained in any event) to the purely competitive commercialism of [an] 'every school for itself' approach to television contract bargaining." Although the NCAA does not enjoy blanket immunity from the antitrust laws, it is important to remember that the Sherman Act "is aimed primarily at combinations having commercial objectives and is applied only to a very limited extent to organizations . . . which normally have other objectives." *Klor's Inc. v. Broadway-Hale Stores, Inc.*, 359 U.S. 207, 213, n.7 (1959).

The fact that a restraint operates on nonprofit educational institutions as distinguished from business entities is as "relevant in determining whether that particular restraint violates the Sherman Act" as is the fact that a restraint affects a profession rather than a business. The legitimate noneconomic goals of colleges and universities should not be ignored in analyzing restraints imposed by associations of such institutions on their members, and these noneconomic goals "may require that a particular practice, which could properly be viewed as a violation of the Sherman Act in another context, be treated differently." The Court of Appeals, like the District Court, flatly refused to consider what it termed "noneconomic" justifications advanced by the NCAA in support of the television plan. It was of the view that our decision in *National Society of Professional Engineers v. United States*, 435 U.S. 679 (1978), precludes reliance on noneconomic factors in assessing the reasonableness of the television plan. This view was mistaken, and I note that the Court does not in so many words repeat this error.

Professional Engineers did make clear that antitrust analysis usually turns on "competitive conditions" and "economic conceptions." Ordinarily, "the inquiry mandated by the Rule of Reason is whether the challenged agreement is one that promotes competition or one that suppresses competition." The purpose of antitrust analysis, the Court emphasized, "is to form a judgment about the competitive significance of the restraint; it is not to decide whether a policy favoring competition is in the public interest, or in the interest of the members of an industry." Broadly read, these statements suggest that noneconomic values like the promotion of amateurism and fundamental educational objectives could not save the television plan from condemnation under the Sherman Act. But these statements were made in response to "public interest" justifications proffered in defense of a ban on competitive bidding imposed by practitioners engaged in standard, profit-motivated commercial activities. The primarily noneconomic values pursued by educational institutions differ fundamentally from the "overriding commercial purpose of [the] day-to-day activities" of engineers, lawyers, doctors, and businessmen, and neither *Professional Engineers* nor any other decision of this Court suggests that associations of nonprofit educational institutions must defend their self-regulatory restraints solely in terms of their competitive impact, without regard for the legitimate noneconomic values they promote.

When these values are factored into the balance, the NCAA's television plan seems eminently reasonable. Most fundamentally, the plan fosters the goal of amateurism by spreading revenues among various schools and reducing the financial incentives toward professionalism. As the Court observes, the NCAA imposes a variety of restrictions perhaps better suited than the television plan for the preservation of amateurism. Although the NCAA does attempt vigorously to enforce these restrictions, the vast potential for abuse suggests that measures, like the television plan, designed to limit the rewards of professionalism are fully consistent with, and essential to the attainment of, the NCAA's objectives. . . . The collateral consequences of the spreading of regional and national appearances among a number of schools are many: the television plan, like the ban on compensating student-athletes, may well encourage students to choose their schools, at least in part, on the basis of educational quality by reducing the perceived economic element of the choice; it helps ensure the economic viability of athletic programs at a wide variety of schools with weaker football teams; and it "promot[es] competitive football among many and varied amateur teams nationwide." These important contributions, I believe, are sufficient to offset any minimal anticompetitive effects of the television plan.

Another formulation of the Rule of Reason was the focus on substantive antitrust analysis in another case considered in detail in Chapter 7, *Los Angeles Memorial Coliseum Comm'n v. NFL*, 726 F.2d 1381

(9th Cir. 1984). There, the court considered the traditional doctrine of ancillary restraints that Judge Taft, in his landmark *Addyston Pipe* decision, had borrowed from the common law of restraints of trade. Under this doctrine, some agreements that restrain competition may be valid if they are "subordinate and collateral to another legitimate transaction and necessary to make that transaction effective." *Id.* at 1395 (quoting Robert Bork, *The Rule of Reason and the Per Se Concept: Price Fixing and Market Division*, 74 Yale L.J. 775, 797–798 (1965) and citing *Addyston Pipe*, 85 F. at 281–82. This formulation may simply be a restatement of the second and third inquiries under the Rule of Reason set forth in *Mackey, supra*.

The *NCAA* decision is an example of what has been called a "quick look" review under the Rule of Reason. Because of the obvious restriction in the number of games shown on television, the court considered and then rejected the defendants' business justification. In contrast, a "full rule of reason review" would require the plaintiff to establish that the challenged restraint actually resulted in higher prices, lower output, or output unresponsive to consumer preference in a properly defined relevant market. The Court cited settled antitrust doctrine in suggesting, in this regard, that the principal focus should be on whether other products which consumers view as substitutes are available in the marketplace.

NOTES AND QUESTIONS

1. *Are NCAA Rules Procompetitive?* The Court does not directly deal with the widespread view that alternative social values should trump market competition in the area of college sports. Sticking with precedents interpreting the Sherman Act to mandate competition as the overriding public policy for interstate commerce, the majority suggests that many NCAA rules are actually procompetitive. The Court reasons that these rules contribute to the creation of a unique product that would not otherwise be available—amateur athletics. From the perspective of consumer demand, is college football different from NFL football? Does college tennis differ from professional tennis? Are you persuaded by the Court's arguments that the NCAA's television rules did not significantly contribute to the preservation of amateur athletics?

2. *Conference Television Contracts.* After this decision, the CFA (as well as the Pac-Ten and Big Ten conferences) entered into network contracts that gave exclusive network rights to broadcast members' football games and thus prevented individual schools from negotiating their own television deals. (Almost every college basketball conference has negotiated similar television packages.) If, as the Court holds, any agreement among different colleges that has the effect (indeed, the express purpose) of reducing output and raising prices violates the Rule of Reason, would the CFA's contracts be any more legal

than the NCAA's? *See Regents of the Univ. of Calif. v. American Broadcasting Cos.,* 747 F.2d 511 (9th Cir. 1984) (generally approving contracts but enjoining provision barring CFA members from allowing games with non-members to be televised elsewhere); and *Association of Independent Television Stations, Inc. v. College Football Ass'n,* 637 F. Supp. 1289 (W.D. Okla. 1986) (summary judgment for plaintiff rejected, *inter alia,* because of factual disputes of market power of CFA).

3. *Market Definition.* The *Board of Regents* ruling involved the use of antitrust law to eliminate restrictive agreements that affected the supply and price of a product offered to consumers, the principal constituency of antitrust policy. A key step in Rule of Reason analysis is defining the market in which the defendant's product competes. Study the majority opinion closely. Does the Court indicate or suggest whether any one league's games should be considered as just one of the many sports and entertainment products that compete for consumer patronage, either at the live gate or on the television screen? As will be clear in later cases applying *Board of Regents,* absent a facial showing of anticompetitive effect sufficient to warrant a "quick look," courts often require either a large market share in properly defined market, or clear evidence of an actual effect on prices or output.

Justice White noted in his *NCAA* dissent that the antitrust victory won by these CFA members might come back to haunt the CFA in its own dealings with the television networks. In the immediate aftermath of the *Board of Regents* ruling, the price of network television packages dropped sharply, after having risen from $1.1 million in 1952, to $5 million per year in the early 1960s, to $75 million per year in the early 1980s. Although there were nearly three times as many college football games on television in 1984 as in 1983 (under a CFA contract with ABC, a Big Ten/Pac Ten contract with CBS, and a host of deals between individual schools and cable networks or television sports distributors), the price per game was cut from just under $1 million to $250,000 (and total game attendance rose marginally). Not until 1990 was the CFA able to negotiate a $70 million per year deal with ABC and ESPN, in addition to a Big Ten/Pac Ten package (which by then had been awarded to ABC). Toward the end of those negotiations, Notre Dame broke away and signed a separate 5-year, $35 million deal with NBC for the rights to telecast its home games, to the great displeasure of its fellow CFA members. As we compare the pre-1984 landscape (approximately five games per week on television, with strict limits on the number of appearances for each club) to today, we see that virtually all major college football games are televised. The major conferences typically have agreements with national networks for premier games, and have created special conference networks for the remainder; these networks also provide conference-oriented features as well as broadcasts of other sports.

D. THE NATURE OF A SPORTS LEAGUE: ARE LEAGUE RULES THE PRODUCT OF A "SINGLE ENTITY" OR AN AGREEMENT AMONG COMPETING CLUB OWNERS?

Chapter 1 provided a glimpse of the distinctive structure of the sports league. In each of the four historically "major" North American team sports, the dominant league rests upon an elaborate contractual agreement among the member teams—its "constitution." Each owner holds both a franchise that the team runs in its (usually) exclusive territory and a vote in the governance of the league. Through its governing bodies, the club owners in turn develop by-laws and rules that define the rights and obligations of all participants in the enterprise—in particular, the division of revenues from gate receipts, television contracts, and marketing of the league and team names. At the apex of this structure is a commissioner who wields broad authority, subject always to the ultimate collective power of club owners, to determine and enforce "the best interests of the sport," including adjudication of disputes between league participants.

As we saw in Chapter 1, when objections are launched against the commissioner's formulation of the league's "best interests," courts have generally displayed a deferential attitude toward decisions reached through internal league councils. Courts show much less deference, however, when attacks are launched against the underlying validity of the league contract—particularly challenges under antitrust law. Three different types of non-government challengers may surface against league practices. One group consists of third parties attempting to deal with the existing league, such as players, fans, stadiums, aspiring club owners, and television networks. The second group includes team owners who may oppose a rule or policy of their league. The third type of challenger is a new league trying to develop and maintain itself as a viable competitor to the established league. Whenever these parties are adversely affected by league policies or practices, they can strategically utilize the antitrust laws to advance their goals, principally by challenges brought under § 1 of the Sherman Act, which bars any "contract, combination, or conspiracy . . . in restraint of trade," and § 2, which condemns anyone who "monopolize[s] or attempt[s] to monopolize" a market.

1. SINGLE ENTITY DEFENSE

In this setting, a crucial legal issue that underlies all § 1 sports litigation within both the product and the labor markets is: Does a sports league consist of a collection of distinct and economically competitive clubs who have come together to cooperate in some aspects of otherwise autonomous businesses—akin to the joint venture created by MGM Hotels and GVC Holdings, an online gambling operator, to take advantage of legalized sports gambling? Or is a sports league more aptly treated as a single integrated entity, analogous to a national law firm with partners based in several cities, which is thus incapable of *conspiracy* in restraint of trade when it establishes its internal operating rules and structure?

The basic premises of the "single entity defense" are that (i) the league members jointly create the athletic product offered in the broader sports and entertainment market, and those members are inherently incapable of producing anything of value independently of their league; and (ii) while each team *competes athletically* on the field in order to produce an attractive league product, they *cooperate economically* as partners within a joint venture through which they jointly create and own the business assets of the league.

The doctrinal framework for that question was set forth by the Supreme Court in *Copperweld Corp. v. Independence Tube Corp.*, 467 U.S. 752, 771–72 (1984). That case held a parent corporation incapable of conspiring for purposes of § 1 with its wholly-owned subsidiary, because "a parent and a wholly owned subsidiary *always* have a 'unity of purpose or a common design'" and because "the parent may assert full control at any moment if the subsidiary fails to act in the parent's best interests." The court suggested that single entity status turns on whether the defendants "represent a sudden joining of two independent sources of economic power" or instead derive their strength from a single source of economic power. *Id.* at 771, 774.

The Supreme Court largely resolved this issue in its recent decision in *American Needle, Inc. v. NFL*, 560 U.S. 183 (2010), with a determination that policies established by the NFL and the other club-run major leagues constitute horizontal agreements by the club owners and not the unilateral decision of a single entity, the league itself. How the law characterizes sports leagues remains both important and controversial, however, for a number of reasons.

First, sports leagues and those who defend their practices continue to express skepticism that legal treatment of sports league policies should turn on challenges by private parties before generalist judges and juries. *See, e.g.,* Gary Roberts, *The Single Entity Status of Sports Leagues Under Section 1 of the Sherman Act: An Alternative View*, 60 Tulane L. Rev. 562 (1986). Leagues continue to seek creative ways to avoid Rule of Reason inquiry of their practices. Your own analysis of this question may depend in part how well you believe courts have analyzed the issues presented in Chapters 5–7. Second, cases requiring a judicial determination as to the structure of sports leagues are relevant to whether the club-run structure of sports leagues, which are evaluated in this section, may itself be anticompetitive and contrary to the public interest. Stephen F. Ross and Stefan Szymanski, *Fans of the World, Unite! A (Capitalist) Manifesto for*

Sports Consumers (Stanford Univ. Press 2008). Third, understanding the economic significance of the potential differences between club-run leagues and sporting competitions organized by unitary entities is important for any student of North American sports leagues. Fourth, focusing on the specific ways in which rules adopted by club owners in their own interests can diverge from the best interests of the league provides sports executives and their counsel with strategic opportunities to block, or evade, owner self-interest. Fifth, questions remain about how league decisions concerning assets controlled by the league itself, rather than member clubs (most notably intellectual property) should be evaluated after *American Needle*. And finally, regardless of how we label or characterize sports leagues, Justice Stevens in the final paragraphs in the *American Needle* opinion cautions that the unique structure and product of the NFL requires that the Rule of Reason be applied cautiously and that "depending on the concerted activity in question, the Rule of Reason may not require a detailed analysis; it can 'sometimes be applied in the twinkling of an eye.'" *Id.* at 2216–17.

AMERICAN NEEDLE, INC. V. NFL
560 U.S. 183 (2010)

STEVENS, J., delivered the opinion for a unanimous Court.

"Every contract, combination in the form of a trust or otherwise, or, conspiracy, in restraint of trade" is made illegal by *§ 1* of the Sherman Act, ch. 647, 26 Stat. 209, as amended, *15 U.S.C. § 1*. The question whether an arrangement is a contract, combination, or conspiracy is different from and antecedent to the question whether it unreasonably restrains trade. This case raises that antecedent question about the business of the 32 teams in the National Football League (NFL) and a corporate entity that they formed to manage their intellectual property. We conclude that the NFL's licensing activities constitute concerted action that is not categorically beyond the coverage of *§ 1*. The legality of that concerted action must be judged under the Rule of Reason.

I

Originally organized in 1920, the NFL is an unincorporated association that now includes 32 separately owned professional football teams.[1] Each team has its own name, colors, and logo, and owns related intellectual property. Like each of the other teams in the league, the New Orleans Saints and the Indianapolis Colts, for example, have their own

---

[1] The NFL was founded in Canton, Ohio as the "American Professional Football Association." *United States Football League v. National Football League*, 842 F.2d 1335, 1343 (CA2 1988). It took its current name in 1922. *Ibid.* Forty-one franchises failed in the first forty-one years of the League's existence. *Ibid.*

distinctive names, colors, and marks that are well known to millions of sports fans.

Prior to 1963, the teams made their own arrangements for licensing their intellectual property and marketing trademarked items such as caps and jerseys. In 1963, the teams formed National Football League Properties (NFLP) to develop, license, and market their intellectual property. Most, but not all, of the substantial revenues generated by NFLP have either been given to charity or shared equally among the teams. However, the teams are able to and have at times sought to withdraw from this arrangement.

Between 1963 and 2000, NFLP granted nonexclusive licenses to a number of vendors, permitting them to manufacture and sell apparel bearing team insignias. Petitioner, American Needle, Inc., was one of those licensees. In December 2000, the teams voted to authorize NFLP to grant exclusive licenses, and NFLP granted Reebok International Ltd. an exclusive 10-year license to manufacture and sell trademarked headwear for all 32 teams. It thereafter declined to renew American Needle's nonexclusive license.

American Needle filed this action in the Northern District of Illinois, alleging that the agreements between the NFL, its teams, NFLP, and Reebok violated §§ *1* and *2* of the Sherman Act. In their answer to the complaint, the defendants averred that the teams, NFL, and NFLP were incapable of conspiring within the meaning of § *1* "because they are a single economic enterprise, at least with respect to the conduct challenged." After limited discovery, the District Court granted summary judgment on the question "whether, with regard to the facet of their operations respecting exploitation of intellectual property rights, the NFL and its 32 teams are, in the jargon of antitrust law, acting as a single entity." *American Needle, Inc. v. New Orleans La. Saints*, 496 F. Supp. 2d 941, 943 (2007). The court concluded "that in that facet of their operations they have so integrated their operations that they should be deemed a single entity rather than joint ventures cooperating for a common purpose." *Ibid.*

The Court of Appeals for the Seventh Circuit affirmed. The panel observed that "in some contexts, a league seems more aptly described as a single entity immune from antitrust scrutiny, while in others a league appears to be a joint venture between independently owned teams that is subject to review under § *1*." 538 F.3d 736, 741 (2008). Relying on Circuit precedent, the court limited its inquiry to the particular conduct at issue, licensing of teams' intellectual property. The panel agreed with petitioner that "when making a single-entity determination, courts must examine whether the conduct in question deprives the marketplace of the independent sources of economic control that competition assumes." *Id.*, at 742. The court, however, discounted the significance of potential competition among the teams regarding the use of their intellectual property because the teams "can function only as one source of economic power when collectively producing NFL football." *Id.*, at 743. The court noted that football itself can only be carried out jointly. *See ibid.* ("Asserting that a single football team could produce a football game . . . is a Zen riddle: Who wins when a football team plays itself"). Moreover, "NFL teams share a vital economic interest in collectively promoting NFL football . . . [to] compet[e] with other forms of entertainment." *Ibid.* "It thus follows," the court found, "that only one source of economic power controls the promotion of NFL football," and "it makes little sense to assert that each individual team has the authority, if not the responsibility, to promote the jointly produced NFL football." *Ibid.* Recognizing that NFL teams have "license[d] their intellectual property collectively" since 1963, the court held that § 1 did not apply. *Id.*, at 744.

We granted certiorari.

II

As the case comes to us, we have only a narrow issue to decide: whether the NFL respondents are capable of engaging in a "contract, combination . . . , or conspiracy" as defined by § 1 of the Sherman Act, *15 U.S.C. § 1*, or, as we have sometimes phrased it, whether the alleged activity by the NFL respondents "must be viewed as that of a single enterprise for purposes of § 1." *Copperweld Corp. v. Independence Tube Corp.*, 467 U.S. 752, 771 (1984).

* * *

The meaning of the term "contract, combination . . . or conspiracy" is informed by the " 'basic distinction' " in the Sherman Act " 'between concerted and independent action' " that distinguishes § 1 of the Sherman Act from § 2. *Copperweld*, 467 U.S., at 767 (quoting *Monsanto Co. v. Spray-Rite Service Corp.*, 465 U.S. 752, 761 (1984)). Section 1 applies only to concerted action that restrains trade. *Section 2*, by contrast, covers both concerted and independent action, but only if that action "monopolize[s]," *15 U.S.C. § 2*, or "threatens actual monopolization," *Copperweld*, 467 U.S., at 767, a category that is narrower than restraint of trade. Monopoly power may be equally harmful whether it is the product of joint action or individual action.

Congress used this distinction between concerted and independent action to deter anticompetitive conduct and compensate its victims, without chilling vigorous competition through ordinary business operations. The distinction also avoids judicial scrutiny of routine, internal business decisions.

* * *

III

We have long held that concerted action under *§ 1* does not turn simply on whether the parties involved are legally distinct entities. Instead, we have eschewed such formalistic distinctions in favor of a functional consideration of how the parties involved in the alleged anticompetitive conduct actually operate.

As a result, we have repeatedly found instances in which members of a legally single entity violated § 1 when the entity was controlled by a group of competitors and served, in essence, as a vehicle for ongoing concerted activity. In *United States v. Sealy, Inc.*, 388 U.S. 350 (1967), for example, a group of mattress manufacturers operated and controlled Sealy, Inc., a company that licensed the Sealy trademark to the manufacturers, and dictated that each operate within a specific geographic area. *Id.*, at 352–353. The Government alleged that the licensees and Sealy were conspiring in violation of § 1, and we agreed. *Id.*, at 352–354. We explained that "[w]e seek the central substance of the situation" and therefore "we are moved by the identity of the persons who act, rather than the label of their hats." *Id.*, at 353. We thus held that Sealy was not a "separate entity, but . . . an instrumentality of the individual manufacturers." *Id.*, at 356.
* * *

Conversely, there is not necessarily concerted action simply because more than one legally distinct entity is involved. Although, under a now-defunct doctrine known as the "intraenterprise conspiracy doctrine," we once treated cooperation between legally separate entities as necessarily covered by § 1, we now embark on a more functional analysis.

[The court retraced the defunct doctrine, culminating in *Copperweld*'s rejection of earlier precedents and holding that an agreement between a corporation and a wholly-owned subsidiary was not subject to § 1. Here, the court read *Copperweld* as focused on the fact that both parties were controlled by a single center of decisionmaking and they control a single aggregation of economic power.]

IV

As *Copperweld* exemplifies, "substance, not form, should determine whether a[n] . . . entity is capable of conspiring under *§ 1*." 467 U.S., at 773, n. 21. This inquiry is sometimes described as asking whether the alleged conspirators are a single entity. That is perhaps a misdescription, however, because the question is not whether the defendant is a legally single entity or has a single name; nor is the question whether the parties involved "seem" like one firm or multiple firms in any metaphysical sense. The key is whether the alleged "contract, combination . . ., or conspiracy" is concerted action—that is, whether it joins together separate decisionmakers. The relevant inquiry, therefore, is whether there is a "contract, combination . . . or conspiracy" amongst "separate economic actors pursuing separate economic interests," *id.*, at 769, such that the agreement "deprives the marketplace of independent centers of decisionmaking," *ibid.*, and therefore of "diversity of entrepreneurial interests," *Fraser v. Major League Soccer, L.L.C.*, 284 F.3d 47, 57 (CA1 2002) (Boudin, C. J.), and thus of actual or potential competition, *see Freeman v. San Diego Assn. of Realtors*, 322 F.3d 1133, 1148–1149 (CA9 2003) (Kozinski, J.); *Rothery Storage & Van Co. v. Atlas Van Lines, Inc.*, 792 F.2d 210, 214–215 (CADC 1986) (Bork, J.); *see also* Areeda & Hovenkamp ¶ 1462b, at 193–194 (noting that the "central evil addressed by Sherman Act § 1" is the "elimin[ation of] competition that would otherwise exist").

Thus, while the president and a vice president of a firm could (and regularly do) act in combination, their joint action generally is not the sort of "combination" that § 1 is intended to cover. Such agreements might be described as "really unilateral behavior flowing from decisions of a single enterprise." Copperweld, 467 U.S., at 767. Nor, for this reason, does § 1 cover "internally coordinated conduct of a corporation and one of its unincorporated divisions," *id.*, at 770, because "[a] division within a corporate structure pursues the common interests of the whole," *ibid.*, and therefore "coordination between a corporation and its division does not represent a sudden joining of two independent sources of economic power previously pursuing separate interests," *id.*, at 770–771. Nor, for the same reasons, is "the coordinated activity of a parent and its wholly owned subsidiary" covered. *See id.*, at 771. They "have a complete unity of interest" and thus "[w]ith or without a formal 'agreement,' the subsidiary acts for the benefit of the parent, its sole shareholder." *Ibid.*

Because the inquiry is one of competitive reality, it is not determinative that two parties to an alleged *§ 1* violation are legally distinct entities. Nor, however, is it determinative that two legally distinct entities have organized themselves under a single umbrella or into a structured joint venture. The question is whether the agreement joins together "independent centers of decisionmaking." *Id.*, at 769. If it does, the entities are capable of conspiring under *§ 1*, and the court must decide whether the restraint of trade is an unreasonable and therefore illegal one.

V

The NFL teams do not possess either the unitary decisionmaking quality or the single aggregation of economic power characteristic of independent action. Each of the teams is a substantial, independently owned, and independently managed business. "[T]heir general corporate actions are guided or determined" by "separate corporate consciousnesses," and "[t]heir objectives are" not "common." Copperweld, 467 U.S., at 771; *see also North American Soccer League v. NFL*, 670 F.2d 1249, 1252 (CA2 1982) (discussing ways that "the financial performance of each team, while related to that of the others, does not . . . necessarily rise and fall with that of the others"). The teams compete with one another, not only on the playing field, but to attract fans, for gate receipts and for contracts with managerial and playing personnel. *See Brown v. Pro Football, Inc.*, 518 U.S. 231, 249 (1996); *Sullivan v. NFL*, 34 F.3d 1091, 1098 (CA1 1994); *Mid-South Grizzlies v. NFL*, 720 F.2d 772, 787 (CA3 1983); cf. *NCAA*, 468 U.S., at 99.

Directly relevant to this case, the teams compete in the market for intellectual property. To a firm making hats, the Saints and the Colts are two potentially competing suppliers of valuable trademarks. When each NFL team licenses its intellectual property, it is not pursuing the "common interests of the whole" league but is instead pursuing interests of each "corporation itself," *Copperweld*, 467 U.S., at 770; teams are acting as "separate economic actors pursuing separate economic interests," and each team therefore is a potential "independent cente[r] of decisionmaking," *id.*, at 769. Decisions by NFL teams to license their separately owned trademarks collectively and to only one vendor are decisions that "depriv[e] the marketplace of independent centers of decisionmaking," *ibid.*, and therefore of actual or potential competition. *See NCAA*, 468 U.S. at 109, n. 39 (observing a possible § 1 violation if two separately owned companies sold their separate products through a "single selling agent"); *cf.* Areeda & Hovenkamp ¶ 1478a, at 318 ("Obviously, the most significant competitive threats arise when joint venture participants are actual or potential competitors").

In defense, respondents argue that by forming NFLP, they have formed a single entity, akin to a merger, and market their NFL brands through a single outlet. But it is not dispositive that the teams have organized and own a legally separate entity that centralizes the management of their intellectual property. An ongoing § 1 violation cannot evade § 1 scrutiny simply by giving the ongoing violation a name and label. "Perhaps every agreement and combination in restraint of trade could be so labeled." *Timken Roller Bearing Co. v. United States*, 341 U.S. 593, 598 (1951).

The NFL respondents may be similar in some sense to a single enterprise that owns several pieces of intellectual property and licenses them jointly, but they are not similar in the relevant functional sense. Although NFL teams have common interests such as promoting the NFL brand, they are still separate, profit-maximizing entities, and their interests in licensing team trademarks are not necessarily aligned. *See generally* Hovenkamp, *Exclusive Joint Ventures and Antitrust Policy*, 1995 Colum. Bus. L. Rev. 1, 52–61 (1995); Shishido, *Conflicts of Interest and Fiduciary Duties in the Operation of a Joint Venture*, 39 Hastings L.J. 63, 69–81 (1987). Common interests in the NFL brand "*partially* unit[e] the economic interests of the parent firms," Broadley, *Joint Ventures and*

Antitrust Policy, 95 Harv. L. Rev. 1521, 1526 (1982) (emphasis added), but the teams still have distinct, potentially competing interests.

It may be, as respondents argue, that NFLP "has served as the 'single driver' of the teams" "promotional vehicle," " 'pursu[ing] the common interests of the whole.'" Brief for NFL Respondents 28 (quoting Copperweld, 467 U.S., at 770–771; brackets in original). But illegal restraints often are in the common interests of the parties to the restraint, at the expense of those who are not parties. It is true, as respondents describe, that they have for some time marketed their trademarks jointly. But a history of concerted activity does not immunize conduct from *§ 1* scrutiny. "Absence of actual competition may simply be a manifestation of the anticompetitive agreement itself." *Freeman*, 322 F.3d at 1149.

Respondents argue that nonetheless, as the Court of Appeals held, they constitute a single entity because without their cooperation, there would be no NFL football. It is true that "the clubs that make up a professional sports league are not completely independent economic competitors, as they depend upon a degree of cooperation for economic survival." *Brown*, 518 U.S., at 248. But the Court of Appeals' reasoning is unpersuasive.

The justification for cooperation is not relevant to whether that cooperation is concerted or independent action. A "contract, combination . . . or conspiracy," § 1, that is necessary or useful to a joint venture is still a "contract, combination . . . or conspiracy" if it "deprives the marketplace of independent centers of decisionmaking," *Copperweld*, 467 U.S., at 769. See NCAA, 468 U.S., at 113 ("[J]oint ventures have no immunity from antitrust laws"). Any joint venture involves multiple sources of economic power cooperating to produce a product. And for many such ventures, the participation of others is necessary. But that does not mean that necessity of cooperation transforms concerted action into independent action; a nut and a bolt can only operate together, but an agreement between nut and bolt manufacturers is still subject to § 1 analysis. Nor does it mean that once a group of firms agree to produce a joint product, cooperation amongst those firms must be treated as independent conduct. The mere fact that the teams operate jointly in some sense does not mean that they are immune.[7]

---

[7] In any event, it simply is not apparent that the alleged conduct was necessary at all. Although two teams are needed to play a football game, not all aspects of elaborate interleague cooperation are necessary to produce a game. Moreover, even if leaguewide agreements are necessary to produce football, it does not follow that concerted activity in marketing intellectual property is necessary to produce football.

The Court of Appeals carved out a zone of antitrust immunity for conduct arguably related to league operations by reasoning that coordinated team trademark sales are necessary to produce "NFL football," a single NFL brand that competes against other forms of entertainment. But defining the product as "NFL football" puts the cart before the horse: Of course the NFL produces NFL football; but that does not mean that cooperation amongst NFL teams is immune from *§ 1* scrutiny. Members of any cartel could insist that their cooperation is necessary to produce the "cartel product" and compete with other products.

The question whether NFLP decisions can constitute concerted activity covered by § 1 is closer than whether decisions made directly by the 32 teams are covered by § 1. This is so both because NFLP is a separate corporation with its own management and because the record indicates that most of the revenues generated by NFLP are shared by the teams on an equal basis. Nevertheless we think it clear that for the same reasons the 32 teams' conduct is covered by § 1, NFLP's actions also are subject to § 1, at least with regards to its marketing of property owned by the separate teams. NFLP's licensing decisions are made by the 32 potential competitors, and each of them actually owns its share of the jointly managed assets. *Cf. Sealy*, 388 U.S., at 352–354. Apart from their agreement to cooperate in exploiting those assets, including their decisions as the NFLP, there would be nothing to prevent each of the teams from making its own market decisions relating to purchases of apparel and headwear, to the sale of such items, and to the granting of licenses to use its trademarks.

We generally treat agreements within a single firm as independent action on the presumption that the components of the firm will act to maximize the firm's profits. But in rare cases, that presumption does not hold. Agreements made within a firm can constitute concerted action covered by *§ 1* when the parties to the agreement act on interests separate from those of the firm itself, and the intrafirm agreements may simply be a formalistic shell for ongoing concerted action. See, e.g., *Topco Associates, Inc.*, 405 U.S., at 609; *Sealy*, 388 U.S., at 352–354.

For that reason, decisions by the NFLP regarding the teams' separately owned intellectual property constitute concerted action. Thirty-two teams operating independently through the vehicle of the NFLP are not like the components of a single firm that act to maximize the firm's profits. The teams remain separately controlled, potential competitors with economic interests that are distinct from NFLP's financial well-being. See generally Hovenkamp, 1995 Colum. Bus. L. Rev., at 52–61. Unlike typical decisions by corporate shareholders, NFLP licensing decisions effectively require the assent of more than a mere majority of shareholders. And each team's decision reflects not only an interest in NFLP's profits but also an interest in the team's individual profits. See generally Shusido, 39 Hastings L.J., at 69–71. The 32 teams capture individual economic benefits separate and apart from NFLP profits as a result of the decisions they make for the NFLP. NFLP's decisions thus affect each team's profits from licensing its own intellectual property. "Although the business interests of" the teams "will *often* coincide with those of the" NFLP "as an entity in itself, that commonality of interest exists in every cartel." *Los Angeles Memorial Coliseum Comm'n v. NFL*, 726 F.2d 1381, 1389 (CA9 1984) (emphasis added). In making the relevant licensing decisions, NFLP is therefore "an instrumentality" of the teams. *Sealy*, 388 U.S., at 352–354; *see also Topco Associates, Inc.*, 405 U.S., at 609.

If the fact that potential competitors shared in profits or losses from a venture meant that the venture was immune from § 1, then any cartel "could evade the antitrust law simply by creating a 'joint venture' to serve as the exclusive seller of their competing products." *Major League Baseball Properties, Inc. v. Salvino, Inc.*, 542 F.3d 290, 335 (CA2 2008) (Sotomayor, J., concurring in judgment). "So long as no agreement," other than one made by the cartelists sitting on the board of the joint venture, "explicitly listed the prices to be charged, the companies could act as monopolies through the 'joint venture.'" *Ibid*. (Indeed, a joint venture with a single management structure is generally a better way to operate a cartel because it decreases the risks of a party to an illegal agreement defecting from that agreement). However, competitors "cannot simply get around" antitrust liability by acting "through a third-party intermediary or 'joint venture'." *Id.* at 336.[9]

VI

Football teams that need to cooperate are not trapped by antitrust law. "[T]he special characteristics of this industry may provide a justification" for many kinds of agreements. *Brown*, 518 U.S., at 252 (STEVENS, J., dissenting). The fact that NFL teams share an interest in making the entire league successful and profitable, and that they must cooperate in the production and scheduling of games, provides a perfectly sensible justification for making a host of collective decisions. But the conduct at issue in this case is still concerted activity under the Sherman Act that is subject to § 1 analysis.

When "restraints on competition are essential if the product is to be available at all," *per se* rules of illegality are inapplicable, and instead the restraint must be judged according to the flexible Rule of Reason. *NCAA*, 468 U.S., at 101; *see id.*, at 117 ("Our decision not to apply a *per se* rule to this case rests in large part on our recognition that a certain degree of cooperation is necessary if the type of competition that petitioner and its

---

[9] For the purposes of resolving this case, there is no need to pass upon the Government's position that entities are incapable of conspiring under § 1 if they "have effectively merged the relevant aspect of their operations, thereby eliminating actual and potential competition . . . in that operational sphere" and "the challenged restraint [does] not significantly affect actual or potential competition . . . outside their merged operations." Brief for United States as *Amicus Curiae* 17. The Government urges that the choices "to offer only a blanket license" and "to have only a single headwear licensee" might not constitute concerted action under its test. *Id.* at 32. However, because the teams still own their own trademarks and are free to market those trademarks as they see fit, even those two choices were agreements amongst potential competitors and would constitute concerted action under the Government's own standard. At any point, the teams could decide to license their own trademarks. It is significant, moreover, that the teams here control NFLP. The two choices that the Government might treat as independent action, although nominally made by NFLP, are for all functional purposes choices made by the 32 entities with potentially competing interests.

member institutions seek to market is to be preserved"); *see also Dagher*, 547 U.S., at 6. In such instances, the agreement is likely to survive the Rule of Reason. *See Broadcast Music, Inc. v. Columbia Broadcasting System, Inc.*, 441 U.S. 1, 23 (1979) ("Joint ventures and other cooperative arrangements are also not usually unlawful . . . where the agreement . . . is necessary to market the product at all"). And depending upon the concerted activity in question, the Rule of Reason may not require a detailed analysis; it "can sometimes be applied in the twinkling of an eye." *NCAA*, 468 U.S., at 109, n. 39.

Other features of the NFL may also save agreements amongst the teams. We have recognized, for example, "that the interest in maintaining a competitive balance" among "athletic teams is legitimate and important," *NCAA*, 468 U.S., at 117. While that same interest applies to the teams in the NFL, it does not justify treating them as a single entity for *§ 1* purposes when it comes to the marketing of the teams' individually owned intellectual property. It is, however, unquestionably an interest that may well justify a variety of collective decisions made by the teams. What role it properly plays in applying the Rule of Reason to the allegations in this case is a matter to be considered on remand.

* * *

Accordingly, the judgment of the Court of Appeals is reversed, and the case is remanded for further proceedings consistent with this opinion.

It is so ordered.

NOTES AND QUESTIONS

1. *Distinguishing* Copperweld. The Court rejected the NFL's argument that decisions by a sports league like the NFL are akin to decisions by a parent corporation vis-a-vis a subsidiary (the holding of *Copperweld*). Precisely what is it about the NFL's structure that resulted in this distinction? If the NFL were so inclined, what could it do to restructure the league in order to meet the requirements for single entity status set forth in *American Needle*?

2. *League Intellectual Property. American Needle* involved collective decisions concerning intellectual property that the member clubs each independently initially owned and developed. What about intellectual property that has always been owned and developed by the league as a whole (for example, licensing decisions concerning the NFL's famous shield)? Should it be relevant whether there is any potential conflict between the owners' interests in maximizing return on league properties and their own club interests? If the NFL owners grant a license for the shield exclusively to Anheuser-Busch for beer marketing purposes, should it matter whether or not some owners would prefer to allow clubs to use the shield for club beer sponsors?

In *Washington v. NFL*, 880 F. Supp. 2d 1004 (D. Minn. 2012), the district court dismissed an antitrust challenge to the NFL's refusal to either compensate players for their name, image, and likeness rights in game films used to promote the league, or to allow players to use the film for games in which they played. Invoking the single entity theory, the *Washington* court viewed *American Needle* as limited to its facts: "that teams in the NFL could not be treated as a single entity under the Sherman Act 'when it comes to the marketing of the teams' individually owned intellectual property.' " *Id.* at 1006, *citing* 560 U.S. at 204. The district court reasoned that, unlike team logos and colors, "historical football game footage, something that the individual teams do not separately own, and never have separately owned," is something that clubs "must cooperate to produce and sell . . . ; no one entity can do it alone." *Id.* As explained in Chapter 8, Section A, however, the common law grants the home team the right to broadcast games, which presumably would include recording of game footage for historical use. The clubs' agreement to grant all game footage to NFL Films may be lawful, but after *American Needle* it constitutes an agreement for purposes of § 1.

3. *Precise Antitrust Concerns That Warrant § 1 Scrutiny of Sports League Decisions.* In allowing the North American Soccer League to proceed with an antitrust challenge to a threatened NFL rule barring football owners from also owning soccer clubs, the Second Circuit reversed the trial court's embrace of the single entity defense, reasoning that the single entity defense was a "loophole" that would

> permit league members to escape antitrust responsibility for any restraint entered into by them that would benefit their league or enhance their ability to compete even though the benefit would be outweighed by its anticompetitive effects. Moreover, the restraint might be one adopted more for the protection of individual league members from competition than to help the league. . . . The sound and more just procedure is to judge the legality of such restraints according to well-recognized standards of our antitrust laws rather than permit their exemption on the ground that since they in some measure strengthen the league competitively as a "single economic entity," the combination's anticompetitive effects must be disregarded.

NASL v. NFL, 670 F.2d 1249, 1257 (2d Cir. 1982).

Is it a legitimate concern under Sherman Act § 1 that the NFL might adopt policies that "would benefit their league or enhance their ability to compete even though the benefit would be outweighed by its anticompetitive effects?" The court also suggested that the policy "might be one adopted more for the protection of individual league members from competition than to help the league," noting that the policy was the result of pressure from Minnesota Vikings' owner Max Winter and Philadelphia Eagles' owner Leonard Tose, whose clubs were facing substantial competition from NASL teams in their home cities. Do you agree that the last concern should have influenced the court?

4. *Are Rival Clubs Economic as Well as Sporting Competitors?* Justice Rehnquist dissented from the denial of certiorari in *NASL v. NFL*. He argued:

> The NFL owners are joint venturers who produce a product, professional football, which competes with other sports and other forms of entertainment in the entertainment market. Although individual NFL teams compete with one another on the playing field, they rarely compete in the marketplace. The NFL negotiates its television contracts, for example, in a single block. The revenues from broadcast rights are pooled. Indeed, the only interteam competition occurs when two teams are located in one major city, such as New York or Los Angeles. These teams compete with one another for home game attendance and local broadcast revenues. In all other respects, the league competes as a unit against other forms of entertainment.
>
> This arrangement, like the arrangement in *Broadcast Music, Inc. v. Columbia Broadcasting System, Inc.*, 441 U.S. 1 (1979), is largely a matter of necessity. If the teams were entirely independent, there could be no consistency of staffing, rules, equipment, or training. All of these are at least arguably necessary to permit the league to create an appealing product in the entertainment market. Thus, NFL football is a different product from what the NFL teams could offer independently, and the NFL, like ASCAP, is "not really a joint sales agency offering the individual goods of many sellers, but is a separate seller offering its [product], of which the individual [teams] are raw material. [The NFL], in short, made a market in which individual [teams] are inherently unable to compete fully effectively."
>
> The cross-ownership rule, then, is a covenant by joint venturers who produce a single product not to compete with one another. The rule governing such agreements was set out over 80 years ago by Judge (later Chief Justice) Taft: A covenant not to compete is valid if "it is merely ancillary to the main purpose of a lawful contract, and necessary to protect the covenantee in the enjoyment of the legitimate fruits of the contract, or to protect him from the dangers of an unjust use of those fruits by the other party." *United States v. Addyston Pipe and Steel Co.*, 85 F. 271, 281 (6th Cir. 1898), *aff'd as modified*, 175 U.S. 211 (1899).
>
> The cross-ownership rule seems to me to meet this test. Its purposes are to minimize disputes among the owners and to prevent some owners from using the benefits of their association with the joint venture to compete against it. Participation in the league gives the owner the benefit of detailed knowledge about market conditions for professional sports, the strength and weaknesses of the other teams in the league, and the methods his co-venturers use to compete in the marketplace. It is only reasonable that the owners would seek to

prevent their fellows from giving these significant assets, which are in some respects analogous to trade secrets, to their competitors.

. . .

. . . it seems to me that the cross-ownership rule was narrowly drawn to vindicate the legitimate interests described above. The owners are limited only in areas where the special knowledge and skills provided by their co-owners can be expected to be of significant value. They are not prohibited from competing with the NFL in areas of the entertainment market other than professional sports. An owner may invest in television movies, rock concerts, plays, or anything else that suits his fancy.

NFL v. NASL, 459 U.S. 1074, 1077–80 (1982).

Prior to *American Needle*, a major single-entity precedent arose from the antitrust litigation filed by the Los Angeles Memorial Coliseum Commission, and later joined by Oakland Raiders' owner Al Davis, against the NFL for their refusal to allow the Raiders' relocation to the Los Angeles Coliseum, after the Los Angeles Rams moved to suburban Anaheim. The substantive antitrust issues are discussed below in Chapter 7. In *Los Angeles Memorial Coliseum Comm'n v. NFL (Raiders I)*, 726 F.2d 1381 (9th Cir. 1984), a divided court of appeals rejected the NFL's single entity argument that it was a single entity and thus the agreement among club owners not to allow the Raiders to relocate was not reviewable under § 1 of the Sherman Act. The majority emphasized that the NFL Constitution stated that the league's purpose was to "promote and foster the primary business of" the individual clubs. *Id.* at 1389. Judge Spencer Williams wrote an extensive dissent, arguing among other points, that:

> The NFL cannot truly be separated from its member clubs, which are simultaneously franchisees and franchisors. The Raiders did not, and do not now, seek to compete with the other clubs in any sense other than in their win/loss standings; they do not challenge the plethora of other ancillary regulations attendant to the league structure, including the draft, regulation and scheduling of meetings between teams, and the system of pooled and shared revenues among the clubs because they wish to remain within its beneficial ambit.
>
> . . .
>
> In the case of the member clubs, this "downstream output" is professional football, and the organ of regulation is the unincorporated, not-for-profit, association commonly known as the NFL. There is virtually no practical distinction between the League, administered by the appointed Commissioner, per se and the member clubs; the NFL represents to all clubs, including the Raiders, the least costly and most efficient manner of reaching day-to-day decisions regarding the production of their main, and collectively produced, product.

Although the NFL determines matters of scheduling, resolving player disciplinary matters and inter-club disputes as well as other routine matters, critical league decisions, such as the matter of franchise location, are submitted to an Executive Committee comprised of a representative of each club. There can be no instance of the Executive Committee acting in other than the collective interests of the member clubs, since by definition, that body's decisions are the consensus of NFL members. There is no distinct interest of the NFL, since it exists solely to coordinate the members' participation in the joint production of professional football.

Id. at 1405–06. Do you agree with Justice Rehnquist and Judge Williams that clubs do not compete in the marketplace?

5. *The Need to Justify Restraints Under the Rule of Reason.* Is Justice Rehnquist's reasoning that the league is a single entity immune from all § 1 challenges, or rather because, in his judgment, the cross-ownership restriction was ancillary to the main agreement among owners to produce NFL football, and necessary to protect their legitimate interests in that main agreement? Is this approach consistent with *American Needle*'s rejection of the *per se* legality that would result from recognition of the single entity defense? A major difference between the single entity defense and the ancillary restraints defense cited by Justice Rehnquist highlights one of the key issues relating to the antitrust characterization of sports leagues: whether sports leagues should have to demonstrate that their internal rules are appropriately tailored to protect objectively legitimate interests. If a sports league is found to be a single entity, could those who believe they are unjustifiably harmed by league policies still challenge those policies in court?

6. *What's the Harm in Subjecting Sports Leagues to the Rule of Reason?* In his *Raiders I* dissent, Judge Williams also argued that "extreme caution is warranted in defining precisely what competitive units exist in the marketplace. It is equally as important to permit collaboration and concerted action among branches of a single economic entity in the marketplace with impunity from the Sherman Act § 1, as it is to police conspiracies between economic competitive entities." 726 F. 2d at 1403–04. Do you agree with Judge Williams's concern that subjecting internal NFL rules to § 1's Rule of Reason effectively prevents enforcement of collective decisions over the dissent of one club member? That without the ability to engage in unfettered collaboration, the NFL will be unable (or unwilling out of fear of an unpredictable adverse antitrust ruling) to control free-riding or take advantage of economies of scale?

7. *Legislative Support for Sports Leagues Avoidance of Rule of Reason Scrutiny.* Chapter 4 traced the origins of the antitrust exemption that the Supreme Court created for baseball. After the Supreme Court had declared it would not extend the exemption to other sports in *Radovich v. NFL*, 352 U.S. 445 (1957), Congress turned its attention in earnest to the question. The House Judiciary Committee reported legislation that would explicitly apply the antitrust laws to all sports, but created an exemption for agreements that were

"reasonably necessary" to (1) the equalization of competitive playing teams, (2) the right to operate in exclusive geographic territories, (3) the preservation of public confidence in the integrity of sports contests, and (4) the regulation of broadcasting rights. H. Rep. 1720, 85th Cong. 2d Sess. (1958). On the House floor, dissenting members of the Judiciary Committee proposed a substitute amendment that would grant an absolute exemption for any rules "relating to" the player draft, the reserve clause, exclusive territories, and actions taken to preserve confidence in the honesty of sports. The amendment's supporters argued that "the present bill would force organized professional team sports to run a gauntlet of legal proceedings to save themselves from complete ruin." *Id.* at 10. They claimed that the bill was "an open invitation to every disgruntled player to litigate the fine points of the game in courts throughout the land." *Id.* at 11. The committee chair, Rep. Emanuel Celler of New York, complained that in his many years in Congress, "I have never seen more pressure exerted upon Members than during the last week, pressure directed from the headquarters of the high commissioner of baseball and his counsel." 104 Cong. Rec. 12075 (1958). However, one of the amendment's proponents responded: "Can anyone say with conviction that there is reason for foisting upon the already overburdened courts of this land an ill-suited role as arbiters of disputes within the sports family?" *Id.* at 12085 (remarks of Rep. Keating). The amendment passed the House by a voice vote, although the bill later died in the Senate.

For a debate on this issue, compare Stephen F. Ross, *Antitrust, Professional Sports, and the Public Interest*, 4 J. Sports Econ. 318 (2003) (concluding that antitrust decisions have served the public interest), with Gary R. Roberts, *The Case for Baseball's Special Antitrust Immunity*, 4 J. Sports. Econ. 302 (concluding that the Sherman Act's broad prohibitions are poor bases for evaluating sports league agreements). As you read further materials, do you think the majority that prevailed in the House of Representatives in 1958 was correct?

8. *Is Revenue Sharing Relevant to the Single Entity Question?* To what extent are the actual interests of clubs within a league unified or disparate? Inherently ordained or voluntarily negotiated? Does the degree of unity depend on the league's tradition, culture, and leadership? Compare, for example, baseball under Judge Landis in the 1920s and 1930s with baseball under Bud Selig in the 1990s. Does it depend on the degree of revenue sharing among the clubs in the league? Should the NFL, which divides about 90% of its revenues according to league-determined formulas, be deemed a different "entity" than the NHL, where less than 10% of revenues are shared? *See* Scott E. Atkinson, Linda R. Stanley & John Tschirhart, *Revenue Sharing as an Incentive in an Agency. Problem: An Example from the National Football League*, 19 Rand J. Econ. 27 (1988).

9. *Are Decisions by NFL Owners Analogous to Decisions by the Board of Directors of General Motors?* Do member clubs of a sports league compete with each other like independent oil companies or auto manufacturers, or like divisions of a single corporation (like General Motors with its various largely autonomous divisions) in which each division's economic rewards are based on

SEC. D THE NATURE OF A SPORTS LEAGUE 291

its varying performance? Is it relevant whether the internal disputes are resolved by those with a fiduciary duty to the league as a whole?

These questions were extensively debated by the Seventh Circuit in a pre-*American Needle* decision involving a dispute between the Chicago Bulls, who wished to broadcast games featuring their dynastic team including Michael Jordan on WGN, a local Chicago station that could maximize the Bulls' local ratings. WGN was also a "superstation" carried into homes of cable and satellite customers across the country. The NBA sought to limit the number of games shown outside of Chicago. Litigation ensued, with the majority suggesting that in the specific context of game broadcasts, the single entity defense applied. *Chicago Professional Sports Ltd. Partnership & WGN v. NBA*, 95 F.3d 593 (7th Cir. 1996) (Bulls II). (The substantive antitrust challenge to restrictions on club broadcast rights is discussed below in Chapter 7.)

For the majority, Judge Frank Easterbrook opined that decisions by the owners comprising the NBA Board of Governors were analogous to those of a corporate board of directors:

> Separate ownership of the clubs promotes local boosterism, which increases interest; each ownership group also has a powerful incentive to field a better team, which makes the contests more exciting and thus more attractive. These functions of independent team ownership do not imply that the league is a cartel, however, any more than separate ownership of hamburger joints (again useful as an incentive device, *see* Benjamin Klein & Lester F. Saft, *The Law and Economics of Franchise Tying Contracts*, 28 J.L. & Econ. 345 (1985)) implies that McDonald's is a cartel. Whether the best analogy is to a system of franchises (no one expects a McDonald's outlet to compete with other members of the system by offering pizza) or to a corporate holding company structure (on which see *Copperweld Corp. v. Independence Tube Corp.*, 467 U.S. 752 (1984)) does not matter from this perspective. The point is that antitrust law permits, indeed encourages, cooperation inside a business organization the better to facilitate competition between that organization and other producers. To say that participants in an organization may cooperate is to say that they may control what they make and how they sell it: the producers of Star Trek may decide to release two episodes a week and grant exclusive licenses to show them, even though this reduces the number of times episodes appear on TV in a given market, just as the NBA's superstation rule does.

Id. at 597–98.

The majority scolded the district court for rejecting the corporate analogy, based on the lower court's "quite narrow" reading of *Copperweld* as applying only because the parent and subsidiary have a 'complete unity of interest' " (quoting from 467 U.S. at 771):

> As a proposition of law, it would be silly. Even a single firm contains many competing interests. One division may make inputs for another's finished goods. The first division might want to sell its products directly to the market, to maximize income (and thus the salary and bonus of the division's managers); the second division might want to get its inputs from the first at a low transfer price, which would maximize the second division's paper profits. Conflicts are endemic in any multi-stage firm, such as General Motors or IBM, *see* Robert G. Eccles, "Transfer Pricing as a Problem of Agency," in *Principals and Agents: The Structure of Business* 151 (Pratt & Zeckhauser eds. 1985), but they do not imply that these large firms must justify all of their acts under the Rule of Reason. Or consider a partnership for the practice of law (or accounting): some lawyers would be better off with a lockstep compensation agreement under which all partners with the same seniority have the same income, but others would prosper under an "eat what you kill" system that rewards bringing new business to the firm. Partnerships have dissolved as a result of these conflicts. Yet these wrangles—every bit as violent as the dispute among the NBA's teams about how to generate and divide broadcast revenues—do not demonstrate that law firms are cartels, or subject to scrutiny under the Rule of Reason their decisions about where to open offices or which clients to serve.

95 F.3d at 598.

Judge Richard Cudahy dissented from the majority's single entity analysis. He focused on whether "individual teams have some chance of economic gain at the expense of the league." *Id.* at 602. He noted that joint ventures, as opposed to single firms, warrant antitrust scrutiny

> for at least two reasons—(1) the venture could possess market power with respect to the jointly produced product (essentially act like a single firm with monopoly power) or (2) the fact that the venturers remain competitors in other arenas might either distort the way the joint product is managed or allow the venturers to use the joint product as a smokescreen behind which to cut deals to reduce competition in the other arenas.
>
> . . .
>
> There is potential for inefficient decisionmaking regarding the joint product of "league basketball" even when the individual teams engage in no economic activity outside of the league. This potential arises because the structure of the league is such that all "owners" of the league must be "owners" of individual teams and decisions are made by a vote of the teams. This means that the league will not necessarily make efficient decisions about the number of teams fielded or, more generally, the competitive balance among teams. Thus, the fact that several teams are required to make a league does

not necessarily imply that the current makeup of the league is the most desirable or "efficient" one.

Id. at 602–03. Specifically, Judge Cudahy noted that because broadcast revenues are distributed unequally to clubs (each club receives more for their own locally-licensed games), a conflicting economic interest between league and clubs existed.

10. *Relevance of the League's Structure of Governance. American Needle* focused on the decision-making structure of NFL Properties, a separately incorporated for-profit corporation; all major decisions are made by the 32 club owners who were equal shareholders in the corporation. Justice Stevens emphasized that "each team's decision reflects not only an interest in NFLP's profits but also an interest in the team's individual profits." Judge Cudahy, in his *Bulls II* opinion, articulated this point in more detail:

> The analogy, within the context of an ordinary firm, is to allow the salespeople to vote on the bonuses each is to get. Each salesperson has some incentive, of course, to promote the overall efficiency of the firm on which his or her salary, or perhaps the value of his or her firm stock, depends and therefore to award the larger bonuses to the most productive salespersons. However, in this scenario each salesperson has two ways of maximizing personal wealth—increasing the overall efficiency of the firm and redistributing income within the firm. The result of the vote might not be to distribute bonuses in the most efficient fashion. The potential for this type of inefficiency is particularly great when, as with the NBA, the league is "the only game in town" so that a team does not have the option of going elsewhere if it is not receiving revenues commensurate with its contribution to the overall league product. In any event, a group of team owners who do not share all revenues from all games might well make decisions that do not maximize the profit of the league as a whole.

Id. at 604–05.

a. Do you agree that Rule 4.3, barring the Raiders from relocating to Los Angeles, is no more of a restraint that an intra-corporate directive regulating the location of a branch of a multi-outlet business? In thinking about this, consider the economic incentives of those individuals who decide where the Raiders might be located, and whether they are the same as the incentives of those individuals who decide where a branch of a multi-outlet company might be located.

b. How would this affect antitrust scrutiny of Major League Baseball Advanced Media, a formally separate business entity that is controlled by a Board of Directors including a representative of the Commissioner's office and a number of owners? Is it relevant that these owners are charged, in adopting MLBAM rules, with a fiduciary duty to all "shareholders" (the rest of the owners)?

11. *When to Apply the Rule of Reason After* American Needle? In the last two paragraphs of the *American Needle* opinion, Justice Stevens noted that where "restraints on competition are essential if the product is to be available at all," per se rules of illegality are inappropriate, and the Rule of Reason analysis must take into account the unique nature of the sports league product. Citing back to the *Board of Regents* decision, Justice Stevens notes "that the interest in maintaining a competitive balance" among "athletic teams is legitimate and important." He concluded that this is "unquestionably an interest that may well justify a variety of collective decisions made by the teams." 560 U.S. at 203–04. What Justice Stevens does not say, however, is how to factor these unique characteristics into the Rule of Reason analysis, leaving that instead for the lower courts to work out. Does the three-part Rule of Reason test (balancing anti- and pro-competitive effects and factoring in whether there are less restrictive alternatives) need to be modified to take into account the peculiar aspects of the sports league structure and product?

12. *Judicial Recognition of Single-Entity Sports Defendants*. Some sports industry actors have successfully asserted that their decisions reflect those of a single economic entity and not an agreement among stakeholders. *See, e.g., Top Rank, Inc. v. Haymon*, 2015-2 Trade Reg. Rep. (CCH) ¶ 79,332 (C.D. Cal. Sept 17, 2015) (investors and boxing promoters were a "single enterprise" with "a complete unity of economic interest in the venture's success"); *Elite Rodeo Ass'n v. Prof'l Rodeo Cowboys Ass'n*, 159 F. Supp. 3d 738 (N.D. Tex. 2016) (defendant's board of directors had a single interest where only a small number of board members had any conflicting interests).

2. ALTERNATIVE LEAGUE STRUCTURES

Sports fans might think that leagues can be run only collectively by member teams, because that is how the first league in the world (baseball's National League) was organized in 1876. But oldest doesn't necessarily mean best and certainly doesn't mean only. As noted in Stephen F. Ross and Stefan Szymanski, *Fans of the World, Unite! A (Capitalist) Manifesto for Sports Consumers* 70–71 (Stanford Univ. Press, 2008):

> The concept that an independent competition organizer [may be] more efficient has not been dreamed up by us in the pristine confines of ivory-tower academia. In developing . . . NASCAR, impresario Bill France Sr. recognized, according to one observer, that to achieve success, "it would require a central racing organization whose authority outranked all drivers, car owners, and track owners." Indeed, from the early chaotic conditions of independently-owned race tracks setting different rules with no league competition, NASCAR developed into a national sport in large part because an independent entrepreneur was able to identify the best locations for racing, establish complex rules designed to produce close races with cars perceived to be similar

to those driven by fans, and determine the appropriate economic rewards that would attract the best drivers, engineers and crews.

Over the years, a variety of other leagues have used different structures, in some cases to achieve efficiencies, while others seemed primarily designed with the goal of insulating the league against antitrust liability. The American Basketball League, a women's professional league that eventually lost out to the WNBA, organized itself as a pure single limited liability company that owned all of the teams and employed everyone involved from franchise executives to coaches to players. The WNBA itself was structured differently, operated by a Board of Directors of four owners with WNBA teams, four owners with no WNBA clubs, and the Commissioner's designee.

Consider the following international example from the sport of cricket, discussed in Ian Preston, Stephen F. Ross and Stefan Szymanski, *Seizing the Moment: A Blueprint for Reform of World Cricket* in *The Comparative Economics of Sport* (Stefan Szymanski, ed. Palgrave MacMillan 2010). For decades, the only significant form of professional cricket featured contests between representative teams from different countries. (Imagine baseball without MLB and only the World Baseball Classic and other similar tournaments!) A proposal for a new international club competition, where privately owned franchises featuring the best players from around the world would compete, was blocked by the International Cricket Council (ICC), ostensibly because it was contrary to the self-interest of the national governing boards that controlled the ICC. Likewise, a proposal for a new club competition located in England was blocked by the English Cricket Board (ECB), ostensibly because it harmed the interest of county cricket clubs that were heavily subsidized to sponsor "minor league" cricket competitions between English players that attract few fans. However, when a rival organization threatened to start such a club competition in India, the Board of Control for Cricket in India (BCCI) acted quickly to overcome the sort of objections prevailing at the highest levels of international and English cricket, setting up the new Indian Premier League (IPL). This illustrates an aspect of monopoly power that is often overlooked: the effect of transactions costs when business initiatives that do not face vigorous competition require collaboration.

Faced with a credible threat from a rival league, BCCI Vice President Lalit Modi was able to persuade his colleagues to proceed quickly to authorize a new cricket league structured more like NASCAR than the NFL. The BCCI appointed a five-member Board of Directors that controls the new IPL, rather than being controlled by the franchises. The league initially awarded eight franchises based on a competitive bidding process, subject to terms devised by BCCI. Contracts for franchises in a league with a relatively short season (14 games plus a playoff, over a two-month period) attracted lucrative bids, the largest one for US$117m for the Mumbai franchise. Most significantly, these highly attractive franchises were offered on terms that most North American club owners claim to be intolerable: (i) open bidding for prized locations; (ii) participation subject to rules set by someone else; (iii) clubs guaranteed a fixed and decreasing percentage of league-wide revenues based on a revenue sharing formula devised by independent board; (iv) an initial salary cap for the first year subject to change by the BCCI-controlled Board, not the club owners.

Major League Soccer (MLS) was created to take advantage of the huge American interest in soccer generated by the hosting of the 1994 FIFA World Cup. Its creator, Alan Rothenberg, a notable Los Angeles attorney, had been a co-owner of the Los Angeles Aztecs in the North American Soccer League, president of the NBA's Los Angeles Clippers, and then leader of the host organization for the 1994 FIFA World Cup. Based on that legal and industry experience, Rothenberg originally designed MLS in a fashion that the league hoped would satisfy the "single entity" test that excludes any scrutiny under § 1 of the Sherman Act. Rather than have each team owned by separate persons, MLS was established as a Delaware limited-liability company that would itself own and operate all the teams around the country.

Whatever its legal promise, this design encountered a major practical problem. There were few, if any, wealthy sports fans prepared to put up the initial $5 million investment, plus take on the additional risk of significant start-up costs, just to be faceless investors in a league venture whose visible figures would all be in the MLS head office.

Thus, in order to attract the money to begin Major League Soccer in 1996, the league had to significantly alter its structure. MLS still was the formal owner of all its franchises. However, for most teams, the league sold a separate special class of stock to each of its "investor-operators" who received almost full operating control over the teams in their areas. In essentially the same way as he does with his NFL New England Patriots, Robert Kraft, the "investor-operator" of the MLS New England Revolution, decides who will run the front office; who will be the coach; who will be the team's players; where the games will be played; and what prices will be charged for tickets, local broadcasts, merchandise, and the like. The revenues that come from these local sources are split 50–50 between the individual "investor-operator" and the league, while all revenues generated from national television and merchandising deals go to MLS (which uses this money to pay each team's player salaries as well as league expenses, and then distributes any profits or dividends to the MLS shareholders). The special stock owned by Kraft and other investor-operated franchisees, with their rights in particular teams, can be sold to outside buyers, which allows these stock owners to reap all the capital gain (or loss) that flows out of their team's performance on the field as well as off it. MLS, like other sports leagues, is now run by those who have a substantial economic investment in "their" club, more than their investment in the league.

The one key feature of Rothenberg's original design that remains in place is the relationship of the league to players. Once a team decides which players it would like to have, the league negotiates and pays the contract with each player as his employer—subject to the league's reserve and team salary cap constraints. These restraints on the players' market became the subject of the lengthy *Fraser* class action antitrust suit treated in Chapter 6.

The MLS players opted not to form a labor union that would be precluded from challenging labor restraints after *Brown v. Pro Football, Inc.*, 518 U.S. 231 (1996) (also discussed in Chapter 6). This enabled the MLS players to allege that the centralized method of setting the salaries of all MLS players violated various provisions of the antitrust laws, including § 1. In *Fraser v. Major League Soccer*, 284 F.3d 47 (2d Cir. 2002), discussed more fully in Chapter 6, the appellate court rejected the claim by holding that the players had failed to establish the first prong of the Rule of Reason discussed above, a showing of anticompetitive effect, because of other reasonable substitute employers for players' services. The court did discuss, though did not resolve, the single entity issue that the district judge had relied on to dismiss the plaintiffs' § 1 claim.

Initially, Chief Judge Michael Boudin (formerly the Deputy Assistant Attorney General in the Justice Department's Antitrust Division) observed that if "ordinary investors decided to set up a company that would own and manage all of the teams in a league," then company labor rules would be considered a decision of a single entity and not an agreement among separate parties subject to § 1. *Id.* at 56.

Yet the court held that the formal integration of operations into a single business entity was not conclusive. Chief Judge Boudin proceeded to identify ways in which Major League Soccer's structure differed from the structure of a single entity:

> First, there is a diversity of entrepreneurial interests that goes well beyond the ordinary company. MLS and its operator/investors have separate contractual relationships giving the operator/investors rights that take them part way along the path to ordinary sports team owners: they do some independent hiring and make out-of-pocket investments in their own teams; they retain a large portion of the revenues from the activities of their teams; and each has limited sale rights in its own team that relate to specific assets and not just shares in the common enterprise. One might well ask why the formal difference in corporate structure should warrant treating MLS differently than the

National Football League or other traditionally structured sports leagues.

. . .

Second, in this case the analogy to a single entity is weakened, and the resemblance to a collaborative venture strengthened, by the fact that the operator/investors are not mere servants of MLS; effectively, they control it, having the majority of votes on the managing board. The problem is especially serious where, as here, the stockholders are themselves potential competitors with MLS and with each other. Here, it is MLS that has two roles: one as an entrepreneur with its own assets and revenues; the other (arguably) as a nominally vertical device for producing horizontal coordination, *i.e.,* limiting competition among operator/investors.

From the standpoint of antitrust policy, this prospect of horizontal coordination among the operator/investors through a common entity is a distinct concern. Whatever efficiencies may be thought likely where a single entrepreneur makes decisions for a corporate entity (or set of connected entities), the presumption is relaxed—and may in some contexts be reversed—where separate entrepreneurial interests can collaborate; the fixing of above market prices by sellers is the paradigm. This does not make MLS a mere front for price fixing, but it does distinguish *Copperweld* by introducing a further danger and a further argument for testing it under section 1's rule of reason.

Id. at 57–58.

3. NON-ANTITRUST CONTEXTS FOR CONSIDERING THE ISSUE

Whether a sports league is best viewed as a joint venture of independent clubs, a single entity comprised of separately managed divisions, or something in between, has arisen in other contexts. For example, recall from Chapter 3 that the National Labor Relations Board treated the North American Soccer League as a "joint employer" that was required to negotiate with a single bargaining unit of all players represented by its Players' Association (a decision upheld by the Fifth Circuit). A few years later, the USFL Players' Association brought suit against that league to collect the unpaid salaries of players for the defunct Portland Breakers' franchise. In ruling against the Players Association, the judge emphasized the difference between *joint* and *single* employer status, and held that a sports league did not exhibit the integrated operation under common ownership and management that warranted "single employer" treatment. See *USFLPA v. USFL,* 650 F. Supp. 12 (D. Or. 1986).

Bankruptcies in recent years by the NHL's Pittsburgh Penguins, Buffalo Sabres, Ottawa Senators, and Phoenix Coyotes also raise the question of whether creditors of a team should have recourse against the entire league for some or all of the team's debts. Having seen in earlier chapters the league policies that establish uniform player contracts, entry-level drafts, waiver and trade rules, and restrictions on veteran free agency and salary caps, do you agree that players left unpaid by one franchise should have no recourse against the league as a whole? Is this relevant to whether a league is a single entity for antitrust purposes?

In another case, *Professional Hockey Corp. v. World Hockey Ass'n* (WHA), 143 Cal. App. 3d 410, 191 Cal. Rptr. 773 (1983), a California court held that the representatives of each franchise on the Board of Trustees of the WHA (a corporate entity) had a fiduciary duty to act for the benefit of the league as a whole when making decisions about common league goals—in this case whether or not to approve a new league owner whose financial strength or weakness could affect the league-wide venture. The court explicitly rejected the argument that, for example, merely because the San Diego Chargers were involved in fierce athletic competition with the Los Angeles Raiders, this meant that Gene Klein, then owner of the Chargers, owed no duty of "obedience, diligence, and loyalty" to his bitter rival, Raiders' owner Al Davis.

In the *World Hockey Association* case, the court did not have to decide how far the fiduciary duty of corporate directors extends, because the judge found no factual basis for any breach of such a duty. However, under general partnership law, which treats joint ventures as a type of partnership, each partner has a fiduciary duty to place the interests of the venture above his own interests unless the partnership agreement or the other partners allow otherwise.

E. THE PROBLEM OF MONOPOLY IN PROFESSIONAL SPORTS

In appraising the legal policies that legislatures and courts fashion for professional sports, of paramount importance is the fact that each established sport is dominated by only one major professional league. This "monopoly" state, in turn, is the principal source of many of the conflicts that arise between the league and its constituents, and of the difficult problems that these disputes pose for traditional legal doctrines.

Previous chapters have described how player salaries and franchise values have soared during the last several decades. Underlying both trends has been a remarkable rise in the total revenues flowing into professional sports, from fans attending the games, from broadcasters (and now digital distributors of content) paying huge rights fees, and from product manufacturers paying for the rights to use team names and emblems. In

1950, for example, Major League Baseball's revenues from all sources barely totaled $30 million. By 2009, baseball's revenues surpassed $6.6 billion annually, and Forbes magazine's annual review reported that MLB's 2017 revenue exceeded $10 billion for the first time. The same kind of financial bonanza has been experienced in football, starting in the late 1950s, and in basketball and hockey, especially since the early 1980s. This section considers whether the total size of the pie is due in part to the fact that there is almost always only one major league in each sport selling this product to an enthusiastic fandom—and if so, what is the law's responsibility for that state of affairs.

Chapters 6 and 7 consider a number of cases challenging rules that allegedly restrain trade in various markets relating to professional sports. Consider what the effect would be on many of the economic issues facing professional sports if two, three, or even four leagues presented viable alternatives for those who claimed to be injured by league rules.

Players—What if other baseball leagues were bidding for Curt Flood when he had to decide whether to sign a contract that permitted the Cardinals to trade him to the Phillies without his consent? What would be the economic and legal effect of challenges to the NFL, NHL, or NBA salary caps if there were rival leagues in each sport?

Television—Suppose several professional basketball leagues were seeking exposure and revenue from television networks and superstations. Would the NBA want to limit superstation coverage of one of its most popular teams? If it had done so, would the availability of other leagues and games have ameliorated the impact of the NBA's policy on television viewers who wanted to watch professional basketball?

Franchises—Suppose that the American Football League had continued as a rival to the National Football League, perhaps accompanied by one or more of the other leagues that have sought to challenge the NFL's dominance. Would there still have been only one professional football team in the Los Angeles area in the late 1970s, so that the city of Anaheim was forced to offer Rams' owner Carroll Rosenbloom 95 acres of prime real estate to induce him to move his team from the Coliseum? Or more starkly, would the NFL have left Los Angeles, the nation's second largest metropolitan area, without any team as it did for over 20 years beginning in 1995 when the Rams and Raiders left for St. Louis and Oakland? In these situations, would not the AFL have moved aggressively to occupy such a lucrative market, and would not that have encouraged the NFL to try to fill that void first? Similarly, following the demise of the WFL in the mid-1970s, would not another hypothetical league have eagerly sought to adopt the Memphis Grizzlies to establish a presence in the "football-mad" South?

Products—Although league resistance to innovations that may improve the quality of the sport only rarely generates antitrust litigation by product suppliers, such innovation has an important value for consumer welfare. The competitive pressures generated by a challenger league create an incentive for innovations that enhance enjoyment of the sport. Perhaps the best example is the American Basketball Association, whose heritage for professional basketball includes not only the *Oscar Robertson* case and veteran free agency, but also the three-point shot and the slam dunk.

Fans—What is the reason why, in 2018, the average cost of going to a Major League Baseball game, according to Team Marketing Report, was $32.44, and the average premium ticket cost $114.50? These averages mask, of course, wide variation: an average ticket price to get into the new Yankee Stadium was $47.62 with an average premium price ticket at $346.53. In contrast, an average ticket price to escape the desert heat to watch an Arizona Diamondbacks game in their air-conditioned stadium was $19.65.

The assumption of some is that the best guarantee that such arrangements will enhance rather than harm social welfare is the force of market competition faced by such businesses. Courts have, however, been unwilling to embrace that position fully in sports cases. The undeniable lesson from history is that interleague competition in a single sport is very much the exception, not the rule, and even when it occurs it is usually short-lived.

For example, while organized baseball regularly faced rival leagues during its first fifty years of existence, no new league has played games since the demise of the Federal League in 1915 (that league's principal legacy being the 1922 Supreme Court decision that produced baseball's antitrust immunity). Similarly, once the National Hockey League (formed in 1917) established its dominance in that sport in the 1920s, only one competitor has come on the scene. The World Hockey Association disappeared after only six seasons, with a 1979 agreement under which the NHL absorbed four WHA teams—the Edmonton Oilers, Winnipeg Jets, Hartford Whalers, and Quebec Nordiques—while the other WHA teams folded. Likewise, the National Basketball Association (formed in 1949) faced a short-lived American Basketball League for only one season, and then struggled against the American Basketball Association for nine seasons (1967–1976) before a peace treaty brought four ABA teams—the New Jersey Nets, Denver Nuggets, Indiana Pacers, and San Antonio Spurs—into the NBA, with the other ABA teams folding.

The National Football League (formed in 1920) has faced by far the most vigorous interleague competition. The most serious challenges came from the All-American Football Conference, which lasted from 1946 to 1949, when the NFL absorbed three AAFC teams—the Cleveland Browns,

San Francisco 49ers, and Baltimore Colts—and then from the American Football League, whose growing impact from 1960 through 1966 led the NFL to merge with the AFL and take in all nine AFL teams (with the blessing of an express antitrust exemption granted by Congress). This larger, more powerful NFL, with its annual Super Bowl championship, had little trouble in fending off subsequent challenges from the World Football League in the mid-1970s and the United States Football League in the mid-1980s. At the present time in football, as in all the other men's professional team sports, the established league faces no visible prospect of serious competition.

While the above factual record is clear, the explanation for it is not. Does the historic tendency toward monopoly indicate that this is the "natural" state for professional sports, or does it reveal a failure to implement the legal policy against monopolization? This is the underlying question posed in the cases and materials in this section.

1. ANTITRUST LAW AND MONOPOLY POWER

The principal source of law in this area is § 2 of the Sherman Act, which prohibits firms from "monopolizing [or attempting to monopolize] trade and commerce," supplemented by § 7 of the Clayton Act which forbids mergers that may tend substantially to "lessen competition or tend to create a monopoly." A monopolization charge consists of two elements: the possession of monopoly market power, and the use of unacceptable means to acquire, entrench or maintain that market power. An "attempt to monopolize" claim requires a showing that the defendant has a dangerous probability of acquiring monopoly market power and has acted with the specific intent to achieve monopoly status. In both types of § 2 claims, there are essentially two elements: the first requires substantial market power of some degree; and the second, improper conduct that creates, entrenches, or enlarges that market power. To facilitate discussion, we focus upon the monopolization offense.

The first legal issue, which also has key significance for business strategy, is to apply the concept of monopoly power to the sports marketplace. From an economic point of view, monopoly is not to be equated with "bigness" as such. Companies as huge as General Motors have learned, to their chagrin, that mere size is no guarantee against the forces of market competition. *A firm has a measure of monopoly power only if it has the ability to lower the quantity or quality of its product and in turn to raise prices significantly above marginal production costs without experiencing a decrease in profits* (perhaps not even in sales). The immediate source of such market power is "inelasticity of demand": when so few consumers will substantially reduce their purchases of the firm's products in response to higher prices or lower product quality that the firm can get away with these anti-consumer practices. A long-run source is "inelasticity of supply": despite the presence of monopoly profits, barriers to entry obstruct the emergence of new competitors that would give consumers an alternative source of supply.

In practice, however, it is difficult to detect and measure monopoly power in the precise economic sense of the term, and even more difficult to demonstrate such market reality in the artificial setting of a courtroom. Consequently, courts have adopted a surrogate test for monopoly power: does the firm have a large majority of the total production (or sales) in the *relevant market*, which is defined by both a product type and a geographical area within which the products in question are viable alternatives for most buyers (or sellers)—*e.g.*, television rights to football games in the northeastern United States, tickets to sporting events in southern California, or professional football players in the United States? (Many have suggested that this is an exercise that seems as much theological as scientific.) Once the plaintiff demonstrates a sufficiently large market share (usually somewhere over 70%), the burden shifts to the defendant to show that it does not actually have the power to raise prices above or reduce output below their competitive levels without a sharp decline in sales and thus profits. Few defendants can meet the burden of proving this negative—the absence of market power—when they are found to have a huge share of some relevant market.

In thinking about § 2's ban on monopolization, it is important to remember that the two elements of a violation—monopoly market power and improper conduct—are wholly separate. A firm with monopoly power might not use that power in an improper way to maintain its monopoly. For instance, using monopoly profits to invest in newer more efficient plants probably would not constitute monopolization. *E. I. du Pont de Nemours & Co. (TiO$_2$)*, 96 F.T.C. 653 (1980). On the other hand, evidence that an industry leader had to hold elaborate dinners to persuade rivals to fix prices, while likely a criminal violation of § 1, demonstrated that the misbehaving executive's firm did not have monopoly power. *United States v. United States Steel Corp.*, 251 U.S. 417, 442 (1920). Furthermore, the conduct constituting the monopolizing act does not have to involve directly the market being monopolized.

The key task in the legal determination of monopoly power, is establishing the precise scope of the market that the defendant is alleged to dominate. Defining the relevant product market is not as easy a task as it might appear. What initially looks like an insulated enclave for a particular firm if the market is viewed narrowly often can be a strongly competitive environment when one takes account of the entire array of choices available to participants in the broader marketplace.

The National Football League, for example, has regularly argued (though without much success) that professional football faces market competition from college football, as well as from professional baseball, basketball, and other sports, and that all sports face competition from movies, concerts, theater, and other forms of entertainment. The major judicial precedent in this regard is *United States v. E.I. du Pont de Nemours & Co.* (the "Cellophane" case), 351 U.S. 377 (1956). This case involved a § 2 complaint against du Pont, which produced 75% of the country's cellophane; cellophane, however, constituted just 20% of all "flexible packaging materials." The following passages indicate how the Supreme Court analyzes such market definition issues:

> Market delimitation is necessary under du Pont's theory to determine whether an alleged monopolist violates § 2. The ultimate consideration in such a determination is whether the defendants control the price and competition in the market for such part of trade or commerce as they are charged with monopolizing. Every manufacturer is the sole producer of the particular commodity it makes but its control in the above sense of the relevant market depends upon the availability of alternative commodities for buyers: *i.e.*, whether there is a cross-elasticity of demand between cellophane and the other wrappings. This interchangeability is largely gauged by the purchase of competing products for similar uses, considering the price, characteristics and adaptability of the competing commodities.

* * *

> If a large number of buyers and sellers deal freely in a standardized product, such as salt or wheat, we have complete or pure competition. Patents, on the other hand, furnish the most familiar type of classic monopoly. As the producers of a standardized product bring about significant differentiations of quality, design, or packaging in the product that permit differences of use, competition becomes to a greater or less degree incomplete and the producer's power over price and competition greater over his article and its use, according to the differentiation he is able to create and maintain. A retail seller may have in one sense a monopoly on certain trade because of location, as an isolated country store or filling station, or because no one else makes a product of just the quality or attractiveness of his product, as for example in cigarettes. Thus one can theorize that we have monopolistic competition in every nonstandardized commodity with each manufacturer having power over the price and production of his own product. However, this power that, let us say, automobile or soft-drink manufacturers have over their trademarked products is not the power that makes an illegal monopoly. Illegal power must be appraised in terms of the competitive market for the product.

Determination of the competitive market for commodities depends on how different from one another are the offered commodities in character or use, how far buyers will go to substitute one commodity for another. For example, one can think of building materials as in commodity competition, but one could hardly say that brick competed with steel or wood or cement or stone in the meaning of the Sherman Act litigation; the products are too different. This is the interindustry competition emphasized by some economists. On the other hand, there are certain differences in the formulae for soft drinks, but one can hardly say that each one is an illegal monopoly.

* * *

What is called for is an appraisal of the "cross-elasticity" of demand in the trade. The varying circumstances of each case determine the result. In considering what is the relevant market for determining the control of price and competition, no more definite rule can be declared than that commodities reasonably interchangeable by consumers for the same purposes make up that "part of the trade or commerce," monopolization of which may be illegal.

351 U.S. at 380–81.

Shortly after *du Pont (Cellophane)*, the Supreme Court rendered its second decision in the litigation involving *International Boxing Club v. United States* (at 358 U.S. 242 (1959)). In its initial decision in these proceedings, at 348 U.S. 236 (1955), the Supreme Court ruled for the first time that a sport was subject to antitrust law (thereby beginning the progression of cases whereby the immunity won earlier by baseball would be confined to that sport by *Flood v. Kuhn*). This second decision dealt with the merits of an antitrust complaint concerning boxing. James Norris, owner of Detroit's Olympia Arena and hockey Red Wings, and Willard Wirtz, owner of Chicago's Stadium and Black Hawks, allegedly had formed the International Boxing Club (IBC) to try to dominate professional boxing. IBC used Joe Louis and Sugar Ray Robinson as the levers to win exclusive control of the champions and contenders in boxing's heavyweight, middleweight and welterweight divisions, and bought Madison Square Garden to secure control of all the major sites for big time fights. The Justice Department charged IBC with monopolizing and restraining trade in *championship* boxing, and the district court found violations of both §§ 1 and 2 of the Sherman Act. The following is the key passage from the Supreme Court's analysis of the merits of IBC's appeal:

Appellants launch a vigorous attack on the finding that the relevant market was the promotion of *championship* boxing contests in contrast to *all* professional boxing events. They rely primarily on *United States v. du Pont & Co.*, 351 U.S. 377 (1956).... The appellants argue that the "physical identity of the products here would seem necessarily to put them in one and the same market." They say that any boxing contest, whether championship or not, always includes one ring, two boxers and one referee, fighting under the same rules before a greater or lesser number of spectators either present at ringside or through the facilities of television, radio, or moving pictures.

We do not feel that this conclusion follows. As was also said in *du Pont, supra*, at 404:

> The 'market' ... will vary with the part of commerce under consideration. The tests are constant. That market is composed of products that have reasonable interchangeability for the purposes for which they are produced—price, use and qualities considered.

With this in mind, the lower court in the instant case found that there exists a "separate, identifiable market" for championship boxing contests. This general finding is supported by detailed findings to the effect that the average revenue from all sources for appellants' championship bouts was $154,000 compared to $40,000 for their nonchampionship programs; that television rights to one championship fight brought $100,000, in contrast to $45,000 for a nontitle fight seven months later between the same two fighters; that the average "Nielsen" ratings over a two-and-one-half-year period were 74.9% for appellants' championship contests, and 57.7% for their nonchampionship programs (reflecting a difference of several million viewers between the two types of fights); that although the revenues from movie rights for six of appellants' championship bouts totaled over $600,000, no full-length motion picture rights were sold for a nonchampionship contest; and that spectators pay "substantially more" for tickets to championship fights than for nontitle fights. In addition, numerous representatives of the broadcasting, motion picture and advertising industries testified to the general effect that a "particular and special demand exists among radio broadcasting and telecasting [and motion picture] companies for the rights to broadcast and telecast [and make and distribute films of] championship contests in contradistinction to similar rights to non-championship contests."

In view of these findings, we cannot say that the lower court was "clearly erroneous" in concluding that nonchampionship fights are not "reasonably interchangeable for the same purpose" as championship contests.... [C]hampionship boxing is the "cream" of the boxing business, and, as has been shown above, is a sufficiently separate part of the trade or commerce to constitute the relevant market for Sherman Act purposes.

358 U.S. at 249–52.

2. MONOPOLY POWER AND EXPANSION

Another early sports monopolization case raising monopoly power and monopoly conduct issues was *American Football League v. National Football League*, 323 F.2d 124 (4th Cir. 1963), which wrestled with the geographic contours of the sports market, as the court considered a complaint by the fledgling AFL that the NFL had adopted tactics designed to stifle its potential rival from the outset. The AFL charged that the NFL had offered expansion franchises to the cities of Dallas and Minneapolis in order to frustrate the AFL's plan to move into these two prime football sites. A trial judge dismissed the antitrust suit, and the AFL appealed.

In 1959, the NFL operated with twelve teams located in eleven cities. There were two teams in Chicago and one each in Cleveland, New York, Philadelphia, Pittsburgh, Washington, Baltimore, Detroit, Los Angeles, San Francisco, and Green Bay, Wisconsin. The NFL had begun discussing expansion as early as 1956, and in 1960, it awarded two additional franchises, one in Dallas and one in Minneapolis-St. Paul. The Dallas team was to begin play in 1960 and the Minneapolis-St. Paul team in 1961. In 1961, one of the Chicago teams, the Cardinals, moved to St. Louis.

One of the applicants for the NFL's Dallas franchise was Lamar Hunt, who decided to form a new league instead. By the end of 1959, he had organized the AFL, which began with a full schedule of games in 1960. Affiliated with it were eight teams located in eight cities: Boston, Buffalo, Houston, New York, Dallas, Denver, Los Angeles, and Oakland. Significantly, the NFL had eliminated Houston as a viable candidate for a franchise because of the unavailability of an adequate stadium. Instead, the NFL had lured away the prospective owners of the AFL Minneapolis-St. Paul franchise, who forfeited the $25,000 franchise fee already paid to AFL founder Lamar Hunt and joined the NFL as the Minnesota Vikings. Hunt and new AFL commissioner Joe Foss then searched for a new eighth team and found a willing ownership group in Oakland whose team became the Raiders. After the 1960 season, the Los Angeles AFL team moved to San Diego and the Dallas Texans, which won the first AFL championship, moved to Kansas City, as the Chiefs.

In identifying the relevant market for the AFL's antitrust claims, the district court recognized that the two leagues and their member teams competed with each other in several ways, and that the relevant market with respect to one aspect of their competition would not necessarily be the relevant market with respect to another. Since each league recruited players and coaches throughout the nation, the judge concluded that the relevant market with respect to their competition in recruiting was nationwide. He necessarily found that their competition for nationwide television coverage, with a blackout only of the area in which the televised game was played, was nationwide. As for the competition for spectators, he found the relevant market to be those thirty-one metropolitan areas in the United States having a population of more than 700,000 people according to the 1960 census, based upon testimony that a metropolitan area of that size might be expected to support a major league professional football team.

In considering whether the NFL had monopolized the market, the appeals court noted that, in addition to those cities in which the AFL had franchises, AFL founder and Kansas City Chiefs' owner Lamar Hunt testified that there was substantial interest in a franchise in Vancouver, Seattle, Kansas City, Louisville, Cincinnati, Philadelphia, Jacksonville, Miami, Atlanta, St. Louis, and Milwaukee. The court rejected the AFL's claim that the market was those 17 cities where the NFL had or was seriously considering franchises.

> . . . location of the franchise is only a selection of a desirable site in a much broader, geographically unlimited market. It is not unlike the choice a chain store company makes when it selects a particular corner lot as the location of a new store. It preempts that lot when it acquires it for that purpose, but, as long as there are other desirable locations for similar stores in a much broader area, it cannot be said to have monopolized the area, or, in a legal sense, the lot or its immediate vicinity.
>
> . . .
>
> Though there may be in the nation no more than some thirty desirable sites for the location of professional football teams, those sites, scattered throughout the United States, do not constitute the relevant market. The relevant market is nationwide, though the fact that there are a limited number of desirable sites for team locations bears upon at the question of National's power to monopolize the national market.

Id. at 130. For this reason, the Fourth Circuit found that the trial court's conclusion that the NFL did not have the power to monopolize the relevant market "appears plainly correct."

> In 1959, it occupied eleven of the thirty-one apparently desirable sites for team locations, but its occupancy of some of them as New York and San Francisco-Oakland was not exclusive, for those metropolitan areas were capable of supporting more than one team. Twenty of the thirty-one potentially desirable sites were entirely open to American. Indeed, the fact that the American League was successfully launched, could stage a full schedule of

games in 1960, has competed very successfully for outstanding players, and has obtained advantageous contracts for national television coverage strongly supports the District Court's finding that National did not have the power to prevent, or impede, the formation of the new league. Indeed, at the close of the 1960 season, representatives of the American League declared that the League's success was unprecedented.

Id. at 130–31.

Finally, the court rejected the AFL's complaint that the NFL, the first upon the scene, had occupied the more desirable of the thirty-one potential sites for team locations. Some locations were not exclusive, and being the first to enter a market with room for only one firm does not violate the Sherman Act, the court reasoned: "When one has acquired a natural monopoly by means which are neither exclusionary, unfair, nor predatory, he is not disempowered to defend his position fairly." *Id.* at 131.

The AFL's argument that the NFL had unlawfully expanded was, of course, impaired by the new league's very success. Perhaps a better example was Major League Baseball's response to an upstart Continental League, designed by legendary baseball executive Branch Rickey in the late 1950s. With an anchor team in New York City to fill the void created by the Dodgers and Giants relocation to the west coast, Rickey's new league included franchises in Dallas-Ft. Worth, Houston, Atlanta, Buffalo, Toronto, Minneapolis, and Denver. A critical blow to the league's viability was the decision of the National and American Leagues to add the Los Angeles Angels, Minnesota Twins, New York Mets, and Houston Astros to their leagues. For a detailed description of the league and its antitrust and legislative fights, see Michael Shapiro, *Bottom of the Ninth* (New York: Times Books 2009).

The fact that no major professional sports league has ever had to face serious competition for more than a few years (in the U.S. or any other country in any sport) may be the strongest argument that such leagues are natural monopolies. Others have argued, however, that more nefarious reasons explain the inability of upstart leagues to survive. In some cases, already dominant leagues use their power to prevent the new entry, *i.e.*, to create "barriers to entry" (indeed, this was the heart of the claim by the Federal Baseball League in the lawsuit on which Judge Kenesaw Mountain Landis refused to rule; the eventual settlement of that suit, to the satisfaction of all Federal League owners but the Terrapins' Ned Hanlon, resulted in the lawsuit by the Federal Baseball League Club of Baltimore against organized baseball that eventually led to the judicial creation of the baseball exemption we explored in Chapters 2 and 4). In other cases, the perception that the Justice Department or Congress would eventually allow rival leagues to merge led both the upstart and dominant league to behave in ways that inevitably led to that result, rather than adopting strategies calculating to compete with each other over the long-term.

3. MONOPOLIZING CONDUCT AND MONOPOLIZING THE SUPPLY OF PLAYERS

The mere existence of monopoly power in the relevant market, however defined, is not sufficient to establish a violation of § 2 of the Sherman Act. As the Supreme Court put it in *United States v. Grinnell Corp.*, 384 U.S. 563, 570–71 (1966), a § 2 violation also requires "the willful acquisition or maintenance of that power as distinguished from growth or development as a consequence of a superior product, business acumen, or historic accident." Over the last century, courts have developed a sizable jurisprudence regarding how to distinguish legitimate from illegitimate sources of monopoly power.

From the point of view of antitrust policy, the question is not whether a monopolistic firm has exploited its power by raising prices or lowering output to maximize its profits. While this practice harms consumers in the short run (and may be subject to government regulation on that account), the presence of monopoly profits in a particular market often serves as an inducement to other firms to enter the market if they can, which in the long run creates a competitive environment for the benefit of consumers. Indeed, the prospect of new entry may discourage the established firm from fully exploiting its monopoly power in the first place. The true evil aimed at by American antitrust law, then, is action by the monopolist that excludes others from entering or remaining in the market and providing competitive balance. (This is quite different than in Europe, where Art. 102 of the European Union's Treaty makes it a violation for a firm to "abuse a dominant position," not merely to acquire or maintain it.)

Nonetheless, not all exclusionary practices warrant legal prohibition. Superior efficiency itself can effectively deter would-be competitors. But if the size or competence of an established firm allows it to develop high quality products sold at low prices that cannot be matched by its rivals, it hardly enhances consumer welfare for a judge to penalize the firm for being so efficient in its effort to satisfy its customers. The challenge in this area of antitrust law is to distinguish between those exclusionary practices by the dominant firm that benefit consumers, and hence are legally tolerable, and exclusionary practices that are improper or unfair, and thus warrant legal prohibition.

In this regard, the fairly standard monopolization claim of "predatory pricing" (as in the government's successful prosecution of Standard Oil for slicing prices below sustainable levels and then charging monopoly profits after its rivals were driven out of business) can be applied to sports leagues if they engage in "predatory spending." As discussed in Stephen F. Ross,

Monopoly Sports Leagues, 73 Minn. L. Rev. 643, 728–733 (1989), this occurs where an established league facing a new rival league increases spending on players to unsustainable levels, in hopes that its deeper pockets can outlast the new league and allow it to return to levels where it can pay players lower than competitive salaries because it is the only league in town. *See, e.g., USFL v. NFL*, 842 F.2d 1335, 1349 (2d Cir. 1987) (jury found that NFL adopted strategy of "spending the USFL dollar" as well as adding additional roster spaces that NFL owners, pre-merger, considered unnecessary, in order to deprive USFL of player talent).

Controlling entry into the labor market tends to be less effective in football and basketball, because every year the intercollegiate "farm clubs" in these sports "graduate" a new class of athletes of demonstrated quality and considerable renown. Perhaps this is one of the reasons why the NFL and NBA never included provisions in their player contracts that perpetually bound players to the team and prevented them from signing with teams *in a different league* (if one existed) when the contract expired. By contrast, in baseball and hockey, the intercollegiate game is much less prominent; thus the major leagues have created or supported their own farm systems to develop player talent for parent clubs. Since a network of contract restrictions bound every young player from the time he entered the minor leagues to the time he retired from the big leagues, it was crucial to the success of new leagues aspiring to big-time status to break that stranglehold. The appropriate legal vehicle was § 2 of the Sherman Act; the following decision is the principal example of its use in this context.

PHILADELPHIA WORLD HOCKEY CLUB v. PHILADELPHIA HOCKEY CLUB

351 F. Supp. 462 (E.D. Pa. 1972)

HIGGINBOTHAM, DISTRICT JUDGE.

[This decision concerned an antitrust suit filed by the fledgling World Hockey Association (WHA) against its established rival, the National Hockey League (NHL). The WHA's primary objective was to secure a federal court injunction barring the NHL and its clubs from seeking state court injunctions to prevent more than 60 NHL players who had signed WHA contracts from moving to the WHA in apparent violation of their NHL standard player contracts. *See Boston Professional Hockey Ass'n v. Cheevers*, 348 F. Supp. 261 (D. Mass. 1972), *rev'd on other grounds*, 472 F.2d 127 (1st Cir. 1972), and *Nassau Sports v. Hampson*, 355 F. Supp. 733 (D. Minn. 1972) (both denying the negative injunction); *contra Nassau Sports v. Peters*, 352 F. Supp. 870 (E.D.N.Y. 1972) (granting the injunction). The trial judge provided an elaborate description of the structure of professional hockey, relations between the NHL and amateur and minor professional hockey leagues, the reserve system and the standard player contract, expansion of the NHL in the late 1960s, and the emergence of the WHA in the early 1970s. Specifically, Judge Higginbotham (a former Federal Trade Commissioner) described how, at the time, almost all major league hockey players came from amateur teams governed by the Canadian Amateur Hockey Association (CAHA). Since 1967, an umbrella NHL-CAHA agreement expected NHL clubs to contribute over $1 million per year for amateur player development. At the same time, the NHL began to conduct an annual draft of 150 or so of the approximately 7,000 amateur players turning 20 years of age. Specified payments were made to CAHA club members for each player drafted, and again for each of the 45 or so players who signed an NHL contract. Almost all newly drafted players began professional hockey in one of three minor hockey leagues—the American, Western, and Central Hockey Leagues—all of whose teams were either directly sponsored by, or had an affiliation or player loan arrangement with an NHL club.]

[While the WHA planned to recruit a significant number of players from the minor professional leagues, the judge concluded that in order to succeed the WHA also needed access to players who had developed the ability to excel in the NHL. The major obstacle to the WHA's recruiting of NHL players was the NHL standard player contract. Under Clause 17 of that contract, the club was entitled to renew the contract for one year upon its expiration on the same terms as before, with the exception of the salary amount, which was set anew each year. (This was essentially the same approach that the MLB player contract followed until the *Messersmith-McNally* arbitration decision in 1976 excerpted in Chapter 4.) Since one of the terms in the existing contract was Clause 17 itself, the player contract was perpetually renewable. Similar terms were included in the standard contracts in the AHL, the WHL, and the CHL constitutions.]

The similarities of phraseology and basic incorporation of Clause 17 in the Standard Player's Contract of the AHL, CHL, WHL, and NHL is the result of a common agreement, mutual understanding, and conspiracy by the NHL and its affiliated minor leagues to maintain a monopolistic position so strong that the NHL precludes effective competition by the entry of another major professional hockey league. Through the totality of many interlocking arrangements, including the Joint Affiliation Agreement, the Pro-Amateur Agreement, and Clause 17 in the Standard Player's Contract, the NHL perpetuates a conspiracy and combination with the intent to monopolize and which monopolizes major league professional hockey. These concerted efforts were done not solely to maintain a high level of professional competition among the NHL teams, but rather the major reason was the desire to preclude others from ever having immediate access to the reservoir of players who could become part of another major professional hockey league which could be a material and viable competitor to the NHL. In the words of Mr. Clarence Campbell, President of the NHL, part of the NHL's purpose was to make certain that the NHL would always be ". . . the only major professional hockey league operating from coast-to-coast in the United States or Canada."

* * *

In August 1971, the NHL learned of the imminent formation of the WHA. In reaction, the NHL took two major steps. One was to authorize further expansion into Atlanta and Long Island, at $6 million per franchise. Long Island was crucial because the WHA had been actively negotiating for a franchise lease in the newly-constructed Nassau Coliseum, the only site available for a hockey team in the New York metropolitan area (other than Madison Square Garden, which had an exclusive hockey lease with the NHL Rangers). When the NHL awarded a franchise to Roy Boe (who also paid $4 million in territorial indemnity to the Rangers), the Nassau Coliseum signed a lease with the NHL's New York Islanders.

The NHL's other step was to form a Legal Committee that, through the Washington law firm of Covington and Burling, coordinated vigorous enforcement of the reserve clause through injunction proceedings against NHL players seeking to move to the WHA for much higher salaries.

The WHA's response was to launch this antitrust suit against the NHL. . . .

[At the heart of the WHA's case was § 2 of the Sherman Act, which prohibited monopolization. Although NHL teams had always had a perpetually renewable option clause in their Standard Player's Contract, Judge Higginbotham viewed this arrangement, which had been fashioned by NHL owners with monopoly power, to be a clearcut violation of § 2. He held] that in the circumstances of this case, the three-year restraint following the expiration of a current contract (considering this factor along with the other numerous interlocking agreements the NHL has fashioned and shaped over the years to monopolize a hockey player's professional career) is unreasonable, and in violation of § 2 of the Sherman Act.

Finally, apart from the collective bargaining negotiations relative to the arbitration of salary, there have been no modifications of Clause 17 of the Standard Player's Contract which have altered or eliminated the basic perpetual option which the NHL has over any hockey player once he has first signed a Standard Player's Contract.

B. *Monopoly Power.*

* * *

Here, through the use, inter alia, of (1) Standard Players' Contracts, including the "reserve clause" in paragraph 17 of that contract, (2) the agreements between the NHL and three of the major semi-professional leagues, and (3) the agreements between the professional and semi-professional leagues and the amateur leagues, it is clear that the NHL overwhelmingly controls the supply of players who are capable and available for play in a new league where the level of internal competitions fairly approaches the levels currently existing in the NHL. In an attempt to minimize the NHL's extraordinary degree of control over the players, the NHL asserts that there are many other available players who will shortly be able to play major league professional hockey. However, the relevant market place is the market place of today, not the market place of 1980 or even the market place of 1975. A monopolist may not today excuse his present predatory practices because someday in the future his total domination of the market place may be lessened.

The NHL's monopoly power is their power to control overwhelmingly the supply of hockey players who are today available for play in any major professional league. It is that total control by the NHL which I hold is proscribed by § 2 of the Sherman Act. One who builds the most modern steel mill cannot operate without an adequate supply of iron ore. The 50,000 amateur hockey players allegedly available to the WHA are the "iron ore" from which viable competition can be built. If the WHA is to compete effectively for attendance and television rights with commensurate payments, the WHA must have a "show" which is equal or nearly equal to that of the NHL today. Since the WHA is a newcomer, the quality of play need not instantly equal that of the NHL, but there must be a prospect that the product will be nearly equal in a relatively short period of time.

Of course, I recognize that the NHL has neither prevented the birth of the infant WHA nor has the NHL caused the WHA to sustain a premature demise, but monopoly power may be restrained before its full wrath is felt.

C. *Willfulness & Intent.*

The mere possession of monopoly power in the relevant market does not alone constitute a violation of § 2 of the Sherman Act, 15 U.S.C. § 2. There must also be "(2) the willful acquisition or maintenance of that power as distinguished from growth or development as a consequence of a superior product, business acumen, or historic accident." *United States v. Grinnell*, 384 U.S. 563, 570–71 (1966).

The activities of the NHL go beyond mere possession of monopoly power in the relevant market to breach these aforementioned prohibitions articulated in *United States v. Grinnell.*

The NHL has willfully acquired and maintained its monopoly power through the use of the many agreements. . . . Its continuing and overriding goal is to maintain a monopoly over the supply of major league professional hockey players.

The NHL employs devices such as reserve clauses, Standard Player Contracts, an NHL semi-professional league Joint-Affiliation Agreement, and control over the amateurs through the Pro-Am Agreement in which the amateurs agreed to recognize the NHL as the "sole and exclusive governing body of professional hockey." If the NHL reserve clause were valid for those players whose contracts terminated in September, 1972, then the NHL would have the power, directly or indirectly, to prevent any player under "contract" to the NHL or one of its affiliated minor professional leagues from playing with any other team or league outside the NHL System.

Upon reading the self-serving tributes for its expenditure of millions of dollars to develop amateur and minor league hockey, one might infer that the millions were spent solely for the honor and glory of amateur and minor league hockey. The NHL's motives were not quite so noble; these expenditures to develop the amateur and minor professional leagues were essential to maintain the NHL's monopolistic position.

In *American Football League v. National Football League,* the Court noted:

> In 1959 the NFL had most of the ablest players under contract. However, colleges graduate annually large numbers of talented players, and, because after the season starts professional football rosters are usually limited to around 35 players, many good players are released each year after the training season and are available to be signed by clubs in any league. Moreover, NFL players become free agents after a period of years.

In contrast to the above picture of relative openness and availability of players in professional football, the NHL has a system which controls access to all professional and semi-professional players for at least three years. As my discussion, *supra*, concerning the reserve clause conclusively demonstrates, if the operation of the NHL's current reserve clause is not restrained, the NHL's control over the players is absolute for at least three years after the expiration of any current contract. Further, the value of the minor league professional hockey players as a source of supply to the major leagues is not the equivalent of college-level players in football. Moreover, the minor league professional hockey players are likewise bound by standard player contracts which contain reserve clauses materially identical to the NHL standard player contract. Finally, the general practice is that if a minor professional league player does not make the NHL team, nevertheless he is still bound by his former minor professional league contract and is thus not free to sign with another club or any other league. These differences between the football and hockey reserve systems are crucial.

Secondary evidence of the NHL's intent to maintain its control over professional hockey is its continuing policy of expansion tied to the increasing demand for hockey in the United States and also in Canada. Of course, if even this burgeoning interest in hockey in North America could nonetheless support only one supplier, then this court would be bound to conclude that the NHL enjoys a "natural monopoly." In *Ovitron Corp. v. General Motors Corp.*, 295 F. Supp. 373, 378 (S.D.N.Y. 1969), the Court noted "the natural monopolist is entitled to compete vigorously and fairly in a struggle for a market which cannot support more than one supplier."

* * *

Keeping in mind both the many agreements employed by the National Hockey League and its continuing expansion, it is apparent that the National Hockey League's intent is and was the willful acquisition and maintenance of a position as the only major professional hockey league in the United States and Canada.

* * *

The expansion of the NHL during the WHA's formative period and the creation of the WHA itself are both responses to an increased market for the sport and thus increased economic attractiveness for those entering as well as those already in the field.

Here, I do not rely solely on the expansion of the NHL to show that it had the intent to monopolize; for the President of the NHL, Clarence Campbell, has explained his league's intent as a determined drive to assure that the NHL is 'the only major professional hockey league operating from coast to coast in the United States or Canada.'

Expansion of the NHL was one factor indicative of the wrongful intent of the older league to totally monopolize hockey and remain the only major professional hockey league operating with the United States, but expansion was only one of the several threads spun in the monopolistic fabric of the NHL to blanket players from entry to another league.

Injunction granted.

4. MONOPOLIZING STADIUMS

Expansion into desirable cities targeted by a new league is a favorite tactic of established leagues, not only in hockey (*see Philadelphia World Hockey Club*) and in football (*see AFL v. NFL*), but also in baseball. However effective these preemptive steps may be in opposing the new sporting venture, judges understandably feel qualms about erecting absolute bars against such league action. Such a rule would forever deny fans in "have-not" cities the opportunity to secure a team in the established major league. Even if an upstart league came along, at best these fans would acquire a team in the less attractive league that would still be the city's only team in that sport. Standard antitrust analysis would suggest that the ideal would be two or more major league teams in each sport playing in the same city, at least if the population is not so small that it effectively constitutes a natural monopoly market. Fans would then have a choice of which team to patronize and clubs would face pressure to be more efficient managers and to charge lower ticket prices. In some cases, there may be a major obstacle to accomplishing that goal—the limited number of stadiums and arenas available for play. Such sports facilities are typically provided by the municipality at a heavily subsidized price; sometimes the city even gives the team valuable land upon which to build a privately-owned facility, such as the land the Dodgers secured in Chavez Ravine when the team was induced to move from Brooklyn to Los Angeles. Cash-strapped local governments would be far less eager to subsidize two facilities.

Another legal theory that rival leagues might pursue is to invoke the "essential facilities" doctrine, explained in the sports context in *Hecht v. Pro-Football, Inc.*, 570 F.2d 982 (D.C. Cir. 1977). The case involved the unsuccessful effort by a department store magnate to bring an AFL team to Washington, D.C., in 1965 to compete against the NFL's Washington Redskins. When the AFL instead opted to expand into Miami (the Dolphins), Hecht alleged that this was due to his inability to secure a lease to play in RFK Stadium. Although RFK's landlord, the federal government's Interior Department, was willing to offer a lease, Pro Football, Inc. (the corporate owner of the NFL club) invoked a provision in their own 30-year lease making them the exclusive football tenant. A jury ruled in favor of the defendant, and Hecht appealed.

First, the court of appeals reversed the trial judge's conclusion that the relevant geographic market was national.

> In this case Hecht sought to enter the market for professional football in Washington, D.C. He argues that the Redskins frustrated his entry by denying him use of RFK stadium, access to which was a condition precedent to his submitting a successful franchise application. Given this posture of the case, it seems evident that the relevant geographical market is the D.C. metropolitan area: it is here that "the seller operates;" it is here alone that the Redskins' customers (primarily, their ticket purchasers) can "practicably turn" for the supply of professional football. Hecht sought to compete for these customers by obtaining a franchise of his own, and it can scarcely be doubted that "the area of effective competition" between him and the Redskins would be the nation's capital.

Id. at 980.

Next, the court rejected the trial judge's argument that, to prevail without proof of specific unfair practices, Hecht had to demonstrate that the Washington metropolitan area could support two professional football teams. The appellate court agreed that, if the defendants had a "natural monopoly"—that is to say it was the only firm in the market because the market was not large enough to support two firms, "such a monopoly does not violate the antitrust laws unless it was acquired or maintained by exclusionary, unfair, or predatory means." *Id.* at 991. However, it reversed the instruction that Hecht bore the burden of proving that the Redskins did not have a natural monopoly; rather, it was the defendant's obligation to prove the claim. Otherwise, Circuit Judge Malcolm Wilkey reasoned,

> a defendant is entitled to remain free of competition unless the plaintiff can prove, not only that he would be a viable competitor, but also that he and defendant both would survive. This result would be ironic indeed: we cannot say that it is in the public interest to have the incumbent as its sole theatre, or its sole newspaper, or its sole football team, merely because the incumbent got there first. Assuming that there is no identity of performance, the public has an obvious interest in competition, "even though that competition be an elimination bout." "It has been the law for centuries," Justice Holmes once wrote, "that a man may set up a business in a small country town, too small to support more than one, although thereby he expects and intends to ruin some one already there, and succeeds in his intent." The newcomer and the incumbent may both succeed, or either or both may fail; this is what competition is all about.

Id. at 991–92.

Finally, the appeals court reversed the trial judge's refusal to instruct the jury to consider a claim that the defendant had beached obligations owed by monopolists under the "essential facility doctrine." This doctrine states that "where facilities cannot practicably be duplicated by would-be competitors, those in possession of them must allow them to be shared on fair terms. It is illegal restraint of trade to foreclose the scarce facility." *Id.* at 992. Derived from the Supreme Court's 1912 decision in *United States v. Terminal R. R. Ass'n,* 224 U.S. 383 (1912) (a group of railroads controlling all switching facilities in St. Louis, where topography precluded other routes to the city, required to admit other railroads to their group on equal terms) and reaffirmed in *Otter Tail Power Co. v. United States,* 410 U.S. 366, 377–78 (1973) (power company controlling wholesale transmission lines had to allow its lines to be used by rival retail power companies), the court observed that to be "essential" a facility need not be indispensable; it is sufficient if duplication of the facility would be economically infeasible and if denial of its use inflicts a severe handicap on potential market entrants. The court emphasized that "this principle must be carefully delimited: the antitrust laws do not require that an essential facility be shared if such sharing would be impractical or would inhibit the defendant's ability to serve its customers adequately." *Id.* at 992–93. Judge Wilkey concluded:

> In this case Hecht presented evidence that RFK stadium is the only stadium in the D.C. metropolitan area that is suitable for the exhibition of professional football games. He also presented evidence that proper agreements regarding locker facilities, practice sessions, choice of playing dates, and so forth would have made sharing of the stadium practical and convenient. Accordingly, Hecht requested an instruction that if the jury found (1) that use of RFK stadium was essential to the operation of a professional football team in Washington; (2) that such stadium facilities could not practicably be duplicated by potential competitors; (3) that another team could use RFK stadium in the Redskins' absence without interfering with the Redskins' use; and (4) that the restrictive covenant in the lease prevented equitable sharing of the stadium by potential competitors, then the jury must find the restrictive covenant to constitute a contract in unreasonable restraint of trade, in violation of Sherman Act §§ 1 and 2. This instruction was substantially correct and failure to give it was prejudicial error.

Id. at 993.

Unfortunately for Hecht, despite the above ruling, he still had evidentiary problems. The two main defenses upon which the defendant would have relied during retrial were that the University of Maryland's Byrd Stadium (just outside Washington in College Park) was a suitable alternative that Hecht could have used, and that Hecht was not in fact injured because the AFL would have never given him a franchise in the first place. Because of this, Hecht finally agreed to settle the case in 1979, about nine years after it had been filed, for $200,000.

In *USFL v. NFL*, 634 F. Supp. 1155, 1176–80 (S.D.N.Y.1986), the district judge granted summary judgment to the defendant NFL against a feature of the USFL's wide-ranging antitrust claim—the allegation that NFL teams had hampered efforts by potential USFL franchises to play in stadiums where NFL teams had leases. Most of the alleged offenders were NFL teams that leased municipally-owned stadiums. The judge held that any NFL team's effort to persuade the public stadium authority not to grant a lease to a USFL rival, or at least a lease on unfavorable terms, was insulated from antitrust scrutiny by the *Noerr-Pennington* doctrine. That doctrine, based on a pair of Supreme Court decisions bearing these names, holds that a private actor's effort to persuade a public body to exercise its prerogative favorably to the petitioner's position cannot violate the

Sherman Act even if done for an anticompetitive purpose. The USFL did not appeal this feature of the trial judge's ruling, which held that such First Amendment immunity to antitrust regulation applied to municipal decisions made in a commercial or a proprietary (as well as in a regulatory) capacity.

5. TELEVISION CONTRACTS AND OTHER MONOPOLISTIC PRACTICES

The last essential ingredient for a viable sports major league is a reasonably lucrative television contract. This source of guaranteed revenue is needed not so much to pay the new league's stadium rentals and administrative expenses, as to pay the players for whose services the new league is bidding against its entrenched rival. This was one of the key issues before the appellate court in a lengthy lawsuit filed by another new league, the United States Football League, against the established NFL in the 1980s. In *USFL v. NFL,* 842 F.2d 1335 (2d Cir. 1988), the court of appeals rejected the USFL's appeal from a judgment awarding it just $1 in damages after it went out of business following three seasons.

The USFL began as a spring football league in March 1983, bolstered by television contracts with ABC and ESPN. At the urging of Donald Trump, owner of the New Jersey Generals, the USFL made an effort to move to a fall schedule in 1986, supposedly the more natural time for fans to watch football. However, the League was unable to secure a network television contract and it folded. Blaming the NFL (which had contracts with all three major TV networks—NBC and CBS for Sunday games and ABC on Monday nights) for its failure, the USFL sued, but the jury rejected the USFL's principal allegation—that the NFL had denied the USFL access to the essential resource of network television.

Judge Ralph Winter, affirming, noted that the USFL had begun play with teams in major TV markets, which resulted in multimillion dollar network and cable television contracts with ABC and ESPN. However, over its short life, the USFL demonstrated little stability, with numerous and frequent changes in franchise location and ownership.

Regarding monopolizing television contracts, Judge Winter observed that the NFL's 1982–86 contracts were nonexclusive and did not forbid a network from televising another football league's games at any time when it was not broadcasting NFL games, and when the NFL's network contracts expired in 1986, the networks were free to contract with a competing league's games for all time slots. Indeed, because the NFL was forbidden by its network contracts to televise games on cable, cable television contracts were open to a competing league, although such contracts were less lucrative than network contracts.

The court described the challenges facing the upstart league:

> The USFL's first year of play, 1983, was a mixed success. The league received extensive media exposure when it signed Heisman Trophy winner Herschel Walker to a three-year, $3,250,000 contract. The Nielsen television rating for the first week of games was 14.2, a figure comparable to NFL ratings. As the season went on, however, the USFL's television ratings declined; average television ratings for the year were 6.23 on ABC and 3.28 on ESPN. Average attendance for the year was approximately 25,000. Nevertheless, these figures were consistent with the league's and networks' preseason projections.
>
> On the financial side, the picture was not as bright. The USFL lost a total of almost $40 million, or an average of $3.3 million per team. The league had projected losses of only about $2 million per year for each team over the first three years. The unanticipated financial losses were chiefly the result of the failure to stay within the original salary guidelines. Indeed, in a November 1983 letter to other owners, Tad Taube of the Oakland team warned that: "If we are not successful in establishing player [salary] caps I can guarantee you that there will not be a USFL within three years, irrespective of improved revenue [from] television. . . . We have sighted the enemy and they are us!"
>
> The USFL's second year was marked by change. Four teams shifted locations. For example, the owner of the Chicago franchise exchanged that franchise for the Phoenix franchise, taking his winning Chicago coach and players while the original Phoenix team moved to Chicago under a new owner. The league, over the objection of some owners, expanded from twelve teams to eighteen. Five of the original owners left the league. Some of the new owners, notably Donald Trump of the New Jersey Generals, believed that the USFL ought to play in the fall. Thereafter, the issue of when to play became divisive, and several owners came to believe that Trump was trying to bring about a merger with the NFL that would include only some USFL teams.

Id. at 1351.

Moreover, Judge Winter recited extensive evidence that, rather than trying to establish itself as a long-term competitor with the NFL, the USFL followed Trump's merger strategy, which ultimately caused the USFL's downfall. The merger strategy, the NFL argued, involved escalating financial competition for players as a means of putting pressure on NFL expenses, playing in the fall to impair NFL television revenues, shifting USFL franchises out of cities where NFL teams played into cities thought to be logical expansion (through merger) cities for the NFL, and, finally, bringing this antitrust suit. *Id.* at 1351–52.

The jury did find the NFL guilty of monopolization in violation of § 2 in a number of ways, including an effort to co-opt potential USFL owners such as Donald Trump or franchise locations such as Oakland (a strategy sketched in a presentation to NFL executives by Harvard Business School Professor Michael Porter, called "Conquering the USFL"). However, the jury rejected the USFL argument that the NFL had monopolized access to television in the fall, a key predicate to the USFL's damages claim.

The court affirmed this finding, reasoning that the jury could have found that the USFL was free to sell its rights to all three networks at the expiration of the NFL's contracts, that ABC (which at the time only showed Monday Night Football) was free to show USFL games on the weekend, that the NFL did not seek exclusionary terms, and that even if the NFL had monopolized the television market, this was not the cause of the plaintiffs' demise.

The court emphasized precedent that a "firm with lawful monopoly power has no general duty to help its competitors, whether by holding a price umbrella over their heads or by otherwise pulling its competitive punches." *Id.* at 1360. It upheld the jury instruction as follows:

> A monopoly achieved or maintained as a result of . . . legitimate good business practices is not unlawful. A monopolist has the same right to compete as any other company. Under the antitrust laws, a monopolist is encouraged to compete vigorously with its competitors and to remain responsive to the needs and demands of its customers. At the same time, a monopolist cannot use its lawfully acquired power to maintain its monopoly. In addition, there is nothing in the antitrust laws that requires a monopolist to act against its own self interest so long as the monopolist does not at the same time exercise its power to maintain that power. Thus, a monopolist is under no duty affirmatively to help or aid its competitors and is free to set as its legitimate goal the maximization of its own profits so long as it does not exercise its power to maintain that power.

Id. at 1361.

Having upheld the one-dollar damage award (that was automatically trebled to three dollars), the court also rejected the USFL's request to use these antitrust findings as a basis for sweeping injunctive relief—restructuring the NFL into two leagues, each limited to a single network contract.

> What the USFL seeks is essentially a judicial restructuring of major-league professional football to allow it to enter. Because of

the explicit congressional authorization in 1966 for the NFL-AFL merger and single-league operation, the USFL does not attack the league structure directly. Instead, the USFL asks us to prevent networks from broadcasting, and fans from watching, NFL games in the hope that they will turn to the USFL. Absent a showing of an unlawful barrier to entry, however, new sports leagues must be prepared to make the investment of time, effort and money that develops interest and fan loyalty and results in an attractive product for the media. The jury in the present case obviously found that patient development of a loyal following among fans and an adherence to an original plan that offered long-run gains were lacking in the USFL. Instead, the USFL quickly changed to a strategy of competition with the NFL in the fall, hoping thereby to force a merger of a few USFL teams into the NFL. That led to a movement of USFL teams out of large television markets and a resultant reduction in value of USFL games to television. As USFL owner and negotiator Einhorn predicted, abandoning major television markets precluded the possibility of obtaining a network contract. The USFL hoped, however, that if a merger did not occur, a jury verdict in the instant litigation followed by a decree effectively forcing a network to televise its product would save the day. Instead, the jury found that the failure of the USFL was not the result of the NFL's television contracts but of its own decision to seek entry into the NFL on the cheap.

Id. at 1380.

6. MONOPOLY LEVERAGING

Section 2 of the Sherman Act forbids those who may have lawfully obtained monopoly power in one market to leverage that power in anticompetitive ways in order to obtain monopoly power in a second market. A modern example is *United States v. Microsoft Corp.*, 253 F.3d 34 (D.C. Cir. 2001), where the courts found that Microsoft had illegally used its monopoly in the market for computer operating systems (Windows) to eliminate a rival internet browser (Netscape).

This theory may also play out in § 1 cases, where a firm with market power is accused of leveraging its power to force consumers seeking to acquire a product or service with no reasonable substitutes to acquire another product or service from them. Both §§ 1 and 2 are informed by more narrowly-drafted provisions § 3 of the Clayton Act, that prohibit sellers or lessors of goods and commodities to condition their sale or lease on the understanding that the purchaser or lessee not use goods sold by a competitor, where the effect may be to substantially lessen competition. An early example of this sort of arrangement was *International Business Machines Corp. v. United States*, 298 U.S. 13 (1936), where the Court found illegal IBM's practice of tying leased machines to the purchase of unpatented punchcards (originally required for computers to read data).

On the other hand, the theory is not available where the practice, although potentially exploitive of consumers, does not affect commerce in other markets. Thus, courts have rejected challenges to the widespread NFL practice that conditions the sale of regular season tickets on the purchase of exhibition pre-season tickets. *See, e.g., Coniglio v. Highwood Services, Inc.*, 495 F.2d 1286, 1291–92 (2d Cir. 1974); *Driskill v. Dallas Cowboys Football Club*, 498 F.2d 321, 323 (5th Cir. 1974).

Another judicial ruling addressing the problem of a team using its control over a facility to secure control in a sports market, though this time in the merchandising side of the business, is *Weinberg v. Chicago Blackhawk Hockey Team*, 274 Ill. App. 3d 637, 653 N.E.2d 1322 (1995). (Although the case arose under the Illinois Antitrust Act, Illinois state courts have interpreted this statute as being substantively identical to the Sherman Act.) The Blackhawks refused to grant the plaintiff media credentials and stadium access to generate content for his unofficial game program, *The Blue Line*, which he sold outside Chicago Stadium in competition with the Blackhawks' own program, *Face Off*.

First, the court described the particular offense of "monopoly leveraging", as requiring proof:

> (1) that defendant has monopoly power in one market, (2) that defendant used this power to exact a competitive advantage for itself in a second market, (3) that the competitive advantage was not won on competitive merits, but rather stemmed from a coercive use of the monopoly power in the first market, (4) that the defendant acted with the intent to gain the unwarranted advantage in the second market and (5) the anti-competitive conduct resulted in a lessening of competition.

274 Ill. App. 3d, at 640.

The court found that the plaintiffs' complaint adequately contained allegations of fact supporting a finding of all the necessary elements.

> As to the first element, the Blackhawks unquestionably have monopoly power in National Hockey League hockey in Chicago. We note that a professional sports team, like the Blackhawks, is an absolutely unique entity providing the public with an absolutely unique product. The second element, concerning the use of monopoly power to gain an advantage in a second market, is established by the allegations relating to the Blackhawks' refusal to grant plaintiffs media credentials and press access to prevent *The Blue Line* from competing with *Face Off*. The same allegations satisfy the third element. The advantage *Face Off* has

acquired was achieved not through pro-competitive efficiencies, but rather through denying plaintiffs access to the Blackhawks' games. The fourth element, intent, is supplied by the quote from the assistant director of public relations wherein he stated: "I don't think we want to set aside credentials for a publication that is conceivably competing . . . ."

The only remaining element under the monopoly leveraging theory is whether plaintiffs have sufficiently alleged that the Blackhawks' course of conduct has had an anti-competitive effect. . . . The complaint clearly states that the Blackhawks have effectively excluded *The Blue Line* from the immediate and intimate access to the games and players to which the Blackhawks' own publication enjoys and to which one would reasonably expect any game day program to have. From the very existence of media credentials, press boxes, press rooms and press conferences, we can reasonably infer that a publication without access to these credentials, locations and events is less competitive than it would otherwise be. Through the course of conduct alleged in the complaint, plaintiffs are unable to obtain the quality of photographs, reports and interviews, including answers to plaintiffs' own questions which they would otherwise have. Denying such access necessarily makes *The Blue Line* less competitive.

Id. at 640–41.

On remand, the trial court granted summary judgment for the Blackhawks, and this time both the court of appeals and the state supreme court affirmed, on the ground that selling programs outside of one hockey arena did not constitute "a substantial part of trade or commerce" of the State of Illinois and thus the relevant market was too small to warrant application of the state's antitrust law. *Blue Line Publishing, Inc. v. Chicago Blackhawk Hockey Team*, 201 Ill. 2d 561, 786 N.E.2d 180, *aff'g* 329 Ill. App. 3d 859, 263 Ill. Dec. 895, 769 N.E.2d 97 (2002).

NOTES AND QUESTIONS

1. *Starting a New League.* If you were an upstart league alleging that an established league was trying to prevent you from becoming a viable competitor, in what market would you allege that the established league clearly held monopoly (or monopsony) market power that it most wanted to maintain? In what market are the competitive effects of a second league most immediately apparent and dramatic? What do established leagues fear most from new leagues?

2. *Revisiting Market Definition.* In light of the *du Pont* and *International Boxing* line of analysis, how much weight should be given to the NFL's argument that its teams compete in a broad entertainment market for the patronage of fans attending games, watching television, or purchasing merchandise? Would you answer be different if the league were the WNBA or the National Lacrosse League? In any case, would such a market be a national, regional, or local market?

3. *Is Expansion Good or Bad? Philadelphia Hockey* referred to the NHL's expansion initiative, taken at the same time that the WHA was trying to establish itself, as further evidence of its intent to monopolize. Thinking back to the *AFL* case, can expansion that fills the public's growing demand for more franchises be an illegal erection of barriers to a new league's entry, by depriving any new entrant of the most attractive areas in which to locate profitable teams? From a policy standpoint, should Congress put more pressure on existing leagues to expand into areas where there is great demand, or should it act to limit the size of existing leagues in order to preserve attractive virgin markets for potential new leagues? Since all of the major leagues today have approximately 30 teams, are there enough attractive markets available for a new league to have any hope of surviving in these sports? (And does your answer to this question depend to some extent on the degree of revenue sharing that exists within the league?) Does this make the existing major leagues illegal monopolists for having expanded into so many cities, or natural monopolists in a market where no new league could possibly survive? Remember that the 1966 NFL-AFL merger into a single league of 26 teams was given an express congressional exemption. Was that good antitrust and/or sports policy?

4. *Can Rival Leagues Really Compete?* Does the failure of the American Basketball League, which started operations a half-year before the WNBA, support the view that there is a naturally dominant league in each sport or, given the WNBA's access to the NBA's resources and connections, new leagues fail when they have to face the power of established leagues? Or merely that start up leagues will always need deep-pocketed investors willing and able to cover inevitable large losses for several years before it can hope to become an established product in the minds of sports fans?

5. *Predatory Spending.* Facilitated by the *Philadelphia Hockey* decision, the WHA's entry on the hockey scene resulted in a fierce bidding war for players that sent average salaries soaring and team balance sheets into the red. The same scenario took place in football and basketball, whose established leagues faced the challenge of new competitors without a perpetually renewable option in their standard player contracts. Why were teams willing to spend huge sums of money on players, irrespective of the effect on their balance sheets? Does this practice make good business sense for teams in the new league? For teams in the established league? Is there—or should there be—a legal barrier to such spending, especially by the established league?

Consider the analogy of illegal "predatory pricing" by a dominant firm faced by a new rival—*i.e.*, deliberately pricing a product below cost to force weaker firms out of the market. Should there be a similar bar to "predatory salary-paying"? If so, how would a court determine when a salary had escalated above the player's legitimate competitive market value (*i.e.*, his marginal revenue product) and become an illegitimate predatory wage level? (Recall the "natural monopoly" market hypothesis described earlier.) Why does an established league such as the NFL, the NBA, and the NHL always choose to compete by paying higher salaries to its players, rather than by charging lower prices to its fans? The explanation is crucial to understanding the peculiar features of monopoly in sports.

6. *Challenging League Mergers.* The culmination of the legal and financial struggle between the NHL and the WHA was a 1979 agreement under which four WHA clubs moved into the NHL and the other WHA owners received monetary compensation to fold their teams. The NHL Players Association agreed not to challenge the legality of this arrangement under the Sherman Act in return for a collective agreement containing significant modifications of labor market restrictions. An almost identical scenario occurred in basketball at about that same time. Is resolution in a collective bargaining process sufficient to allay public policy concerns about interleague mergers? If not, who should challenge such arrangements? In what circumstances, if any, should sports mergers be allowed to occur?

Should the law allow an established league to merge with all or some of the clubs in an upstart league? Under what circumstances would you permit such a merger? What is the likely alternative if such a merger is not permitted? Why did the NFL not try to merge with or buy-off the USFL? For a non-sports look at the so-called "failing company" exception to otherwise unlawful mergers, *see Citizen Publishing Co. v. United States*, 394 U.S. 131 (1969). *See also* 4A P. Areeda, H. Hovenkamp, & J. Solow, *Antitrust Law* ¶¶ 951–54 (rev. ed. 1998).

7. *Exclusive Lease Arrangements.* If you were counsel for an NFL team negotiating a lease with a local stadium authority, would you seek an exclusivity clause of the type the Redskins had, in light of *Hecht*? Even if it turned out that § 2 prevented the team from enforcing that provision, might it still have some value to the NFL team in the event a team in a new league sought to obtain a lease?

8. *What Is an "Essential" Facility?* In *Fishman v. Estate of Wirtz*, 807 F.2d 520 (7th Cir. 1986) (with Judge Easterbrook dissenting at length), the court found that Chicago Stadium was an "essential facility" for the NBA Chicago Bulls, which could not lawfully be withheld from Fishman, a prospective buyer of the Bulls, by the Wirtz family (owners of the Stadium and the NHL Chicago Black Hawks) in their competition to purchase the Bulls. As the *Hecht* test requires, this is a fact-based determination based on the availability of alternative sites. Does it matter that Bulls' revenues warranted

bids in the $3–4 million range, compared to current franchise values in the billions?

9. *Relevance of Stadium Access Today.* In today's marketplace, effective competition may require each club to own (or at least have total control over) its own stadium to take advantage of the many revenue streams clubs have created since *Hecht* was litigated. For example, suppose the Washington Redskins were required under the *Hecht* precedent to permit a team in the New American Football League to play at FedEx field. While this would give the rival league a venue, the stadium owner (the Redskins) would still collect all the revenue from parking, concessions, suite ownership (which often gives the owner access to all stadium events), etc.

10. *Break up the NFL?* The jury found only $1 (trebled to $3) in USFL damages because it believed that irrespective of the NFL's illegal monopolizing behavior, the USFL's business strategy and conduct was such that it would have failed anyway. However, if the purpose of private antitrust actions is to encourage private enforcement, and the NFL was found to be an illegal monopoly, why was the court unwilling to grant the USFL's requested injunction that would have forced the NFL to divide into two independent leagues? Is the court's reasoning persuasive? Would consumer welfare and competition have been benefited by granting the requested relief?

Whatever your diagnosis of the causes of the current sports monopoly, would it be desirable or feasible for Congress or an antitrust court to break up the established leagues, all of whose current divisions enjoy "big league" status in the popular mind? Each such division would be made an independent entity headed by its own commissioner: no agreements would be permitted with the other new leagues for allocation of players or franchises, or for the sale of television rights and marketing licenses. If that policy course were to be followed, should the several new leagues be entitled to (or required to) cooperate in staging a single championship playoff? In effect, should the Super Bowl or the World Series be deemed an "essential facility" that must be made accessible to each league in order to preserve a competitive sports marketplace (by analogy to the appeals court ruling in *Aspen Highlands Skiing Corp. v. Aspen Skiing Co.*, 738 F.2d 1509 (10th Cir. 1984), *aff'd on other grounds*, 472 U.S. 585 (1985))?

Among the different constituencies observed in earlier chapters—owners, players, players associations, agents, municipalities, television networks, and fans—who would win and who would lose from such a dramatically different structure to the sports world? Why? What do you think would be the likely long run result of breaking up a league into two equal parts? Would the two leagues continue to stay equal, or would one of the leagues be likely to continue to build on its perceived superiority? Would it be necessary for the Antitrust Division or the FTC to vigorously monitor league spending, to assure that neither league used any temporary advantage or perceived superiority to spend in a predatory manner to exclude its rival? If the inevitable result of multiple leagues is dominance, does this suggest a different kind of natural monopoly in sports leagues?

11. *Consequence of a Single League in Each Sport.* If each major league is judged to be a natural monopoly that it is neither desirable nor feasible to break up, should Congress deal with the economic problems created in the sports world in the manner that natural monopolies have historically been treated? A federal regulatory commission could be established to determine (or at least approve) how many franchises there would be, where they would be located, who would be allowed to own them, what television rights could be sold to whom and for how much, for how much and to whom trademarks and logos could be licensed, the length of the season, and many other important decisions that a monopolist would otherwise make against the best interests of the public. What are the pros and cons of having sports governed by such an agency?

CHAPTER 6

ANTITRUST REGULATION AND BUSINESS STRATEGY IN SPORTS LABOR MARKETS*

■ ■ ■

A. A RECAP OF RELEVANT LEARNING FROM EARLIER CHAPTERS

Chapter 4 explains how Congress chose to partially address *Flood* and baseball's special antitrust exemption in the Curt Flood Act of 1998, and how the Major League Baseball Players Association had already demonstrated that it did not need congressional help to dismantle Baseball's reserve system. The Supreme Court confirmed in *Flood* that all other sports were subject to antitrust law, which launched a burst of antitrust litigation against restrictive practices across the spectrum of professional sports and major intercollegiate sports. Chapter 5 explored the general contours of the Rule of Reason used to evaluate antitrust challenges under § 1 of the Sherman Act. Specifically, the chapter

- identified two major purposes of the antitrust law as an efficient allocation of resources and the prevention of exploitation of victims by those with economic power;
- reviewed precedents holding that the "Rule of Reason" will apply to most sports league restraints;
- studied the landmark *Board of Regents* case defining an unreasonable (and thus illegal) trade restraint as one that raises price, reduces the quantity or quality of output, or renders output unresponsive to consumer preference;
- reviewed the *American Needle* decision suggesting that where owners of clubs in a sports league have distinct economic interests, a league "rule" may constitute an agreement subject to evaluation under the Rule of Reason rather than the decision of a single economic entity;

---

* The Casebook Website (http://pennstatelaw.psu.edu/SportsTextWebsite) contains citations to scholarly and other commentary on a variety of topics discussed in this chapter, including the "invariance principle" in sports economics, legal analysis of player restraints under antitrust law; economic analysis of player restraints; draft eligibility; the labor exemption; commentary on *Brown v. Pro-Football*; and the effect on the labor exemption of union disclaimer/decertification.

- distilled a 3-part test for the Rule of Reason including an analysis of (1) actual anticompetitive effect; (2) legitimate business justifications (*i.e.*, efficiencies or procompetitive benefits), and (3) less restrictive alternatives.

This chapter recounts the key legal and industry consequences of antitrust litigation and its impact on the player labor market. It also introduces the business dynamics of collective bargaining between employers with multiple and different interests and players whose union owes them a duty of fair representation.

B. ECONOMIC ANALYSIS OF RESTRAINTS IN THE PLAYERS MARKET

The landmark *Board of Regents* decision excerpted in Chapter 5 focused the attention of judges and litigants on the actual anticompetitive effect of challenged restraints. With regard to challenges in the players market, the questions include whether the restraint had the effect of misallocating resources in the player labor market, and whether some actual marketplace benefits for consumers could justify the restraint. Answering these questions requires understanding the fundamental economics of player restraints.

1. TYPES OF PLAYER RESTRAINTS

In most professional sports leagues around the world, participating clubs compete among themselves to sign players, subject to rules imposed by the league or agreed to among themselves. These rules often significantly restrain this intraleague competition for players. The labor restraints sometimes include a *reserve list*, whereby clubs will not bid for reserved players at the expiration of a contract; the player must either re-sign with his prior employer or seek employment outside the league. Some leagues use a *restricted list*, so that any club desiring a player's services agrees to provide compensation to the former employer, or to allow the former employer to match the best offer. Common among North American and Australian leagues is a *player draft*, whereby amateurs or veterans not under contract can only negotiate with the team that selects them; teams usually select in reverse order of finish from the prior season unless they trade a selection to or acquire one from another team.

In recent years, many leagues have adopted *club salary (or payroll) caps*, which prevent a club from competing for players when total player payroll exceeds a specified amount, or a more modest version of this restraint, a *luxury tax* on payrolls that exceed a certain amount, thereby making it more expensive for high-payroll teams to compete for the services of players. Some leagues also employ *individual player salary caps* that limit the amount a player can receive based on years of service within the league or his previous salary. (They often also ensure that a negotiated percentage of total league revenue is shared with players in salary, guaranteeing that players share in the league's prosperity.)

Other common practices also can significantly affect a club's ability to compete for player services. *Debt limits,* by which clubs agree not to spend more than a certain percentage of their own revenue on players, can take profligate or poorly managed clubs out of the bidding for players. North American leagues also employ *roster limits* and *waiver rules.* In combination, these provisions limit the total number of major league-quality players that any team can employ; and the existing contracts for players in excess of that number must be offered for assignment, for a modest fixed fee, to other teams (that may select in reverse order of their current position in the standings).

European football leagues have adopted *"financial fair play"* regulations that limit club spending on operations to the actual revenues derived from the sport. The rules are designed to prevent both improvident spending by clubs that lack adequate resources, as well as to bar cash infusions from wealthy owners. Some North American leagues also ban another practice that may not seem at first blush to affect player restraints—significant cash sales, the primary means by which players are exchanged in European football. If significant cash sales are banned, clubs seeking a star player must either sign one of the few "free agents" (a player whose contract has expired, and who is not subject to any of the aforementioned restrictive rules) or arrange a trade with another club.

2. ECONOMIC EFFECTS OF PLAYER RESTRAINTS

The more restrictive of the aforementioned rules are prevalent where clubs adhering to restraints do not face significant competition from others for the services of players. For example, the NFL allows clubs to reserve players with less than four years of service (most players), has an annual draft for all rookie players, places a cap on the payroll for player personnel, and puts a specific limit on the salaries payable to the pool of rookie players.

Restraints are less prevalent where players have credible options to play elsewhere. For example, Serie A (the top Italian soccer league) seriously considered imposing a salary cap but decided against such a rule, because it was clear that the top players would simply leave Serie A and play for clubs in other European soccer leagues. Soccer, however, is the only major league sport played in the United States where serious inter-league competition exists for the world's best players. The revenue disparities between American baseball, basketball, and hockey leagues and those in other countries where these sports are played are so great that the option to play elsewhere is not a viable substitute for most players, especially the stars, and American football is only played professionally in North America.

The most obvious and immediate effect of the imposition of player restraints by clubs with monopsony power is lower salaries for players. This restraint thus represents a significant transfer of wealth from players to clubs. If the salary restraint is too severe, it may discourage some athletes from working hard to become professionals, affect players' decisions on when to end their careers, and potentially hurt the quality of the sport. (This point was made by Judge Patricia Wald in her dissenting opinion in *Brown v. Pro-Football*, 50 F.3d 1041, 1060–61 (D.C. Cir. 1995), *aff'd*, 518 U.S. 231 (1996).) Professional athletes' next-best occupation usually pays so much below the salary they can command in their best sport, however, that restraints probably do not significantly affect the supply of players.

Another important concern is that restraints often result in the inefficient allocation of players among teams. In general, the optimal allocation of players among teams in a league will be to allow the market to place the players with the teams that value them the most. Contrary to conventional wisdom, some scholarship suggests that player restraints often *harm* competitive balance, by making it more difficult for underperforming teams to improve quickly. *See, e.g.,* Stephen F. Ross, *The Misunderstood Alliance Between Sports Fans, Players, and the Antitrust Laws*, 1997 U. Ill. L. Rev. 519 [hereafter *Misunderstood Alliance*].

3. JUSTIFICATIONS FOR PLAYER RESTRAINTS

Defenders of sports league practices limiting competition for players have offered myriad justifications, many of which would not be accepted as procompetitive in other industries. This section focuses on the economic underpinnings of these proffered justifications.

Economists generally reject the claim that *high salaries drive up ticket prices,* especially in the short- or medium-run. Suppose a club plays in a 50,000-seat stadium. Perhaps the club could sell out each game by charging $5/ticket. Assuming an average of $5/person profit from parking, concessions, etc., this would bring in revenue of $500,000/game. The club could also charge $995/ticket. If it could attract 500 purchasers, it could bring in about $500,000/game in revenue. But perhaps with a $20 ticket, the club could attract 35,000 fans, or revenue of $875,000/game. This illustrates that there is some profit-maximizing price for the tickets: once that level is reached, the club cannot raise prices further to pay for a higher payroll. Economists recognize one exception to the rule that higher payrolls do not affect ticket prices, but this rule counts against, rather than in favor of, player restraints. If, because of an unrestrained market for player services, a club spends more to bring in better players, then demand for seats should increase, as should price. *See* Andrew Zimbalist, "Economics 100: Higher Ticket Prices Not Caused by Payroll," *Sports Bus. J.,* July 10, 2000, at p. 46.

In the real world, things may well be more complex. The economic analysis assumes that the team owner is trying to maximize revenue; owners with non-profit or other strategic motivations might charge below-market ticket prices but then alter pricing if compelled to increase significantly payroll costs. Moreover, because ticket pricing for discretionary consumer goods like sporting events is often partially a function of public perception, an owner might be able to get away with a larger ticket price increase by blaming player salaries.

Another justification that has occasionally been asserted is the need for player restraints to *allow clubs in smaller towns to remain viable.* Owners, politicians, commentators, or ordinary fans might favor player restraints for this purpose for at least three conceptually distinct reasons. One is a business decision that the league's overall output (live attendance, television audience, merchandise sales, sponsorships, etc.) will be increased if there are many teams in many towns, even if those towns are not economically capable of supporting a profitable team that pays competitive salaries to players. Another reason to ensure that clubs remain viable in smaller towns is to preclude any possibility of entry from a rival league: even if the dominant league is established in larger towns, competition with a new league could drive up salaries significantly. Finally, there are cultural reasons to favor having clubs in major national sports located in small towns across the continent.

Smaller towns might maintain a major league club in a variety of ways, even when free market forces preclude viability. Clubs in highly profitable markets could share revenue, or national or sub-national governments could provide operating subsidies. Scholars of law and economics have observed that player restraints effectively amount to a "subsidy" to small towns and their clubs from the players, whose salaries are being reduced to achieve this goal. *See* Michael J. Trebilcock, *The Common Law of Restraint of Trade* (Toronto: Carswell, 1986), at 227–28. If a community determines that having a major sports team is important to the local culture, the community as a whole should provide the subsidy; if the society at large wants to preserve and enhance cultural life in mid-sized cities, then it can provide a national subsidy. To the extent that progressive citizens believe that the burden of this subsidy should fall upon those who can more easily shoulder it, then perhaps special taxes should be imposed on affluent professional athletes, as well as affluent investment brokers, movie moguls, and any others in the top income bracket.

Yet another justification for player restraints is the club's interest in recouping its *investment in training and developing players.* Of course, this problem is not unique to sports. In many industries, employers train younger workers who potentially could leave for a better offer after receiving training. Nor can the NFL and NBA invoke this claim, as they are the beneficiaries of millions of dollars of free training for their athletes by NCAA schools. Some economists have suggested that restraints of trade are unnecessary to training recoupment, because clubs that provide training to young athletes can sign them to individually-negotiated, multi-year contracts that allow adequate recoupment. Trebilcock, *supra,* at 228. Indeed, this practice is common in international soccer, where elite players rarely become "free agents" playing out their contracts: if a club perceives it will be unable to re-sign a player, the player's contract is sold prior to expiration to a wealthier club for a substantial transfer fee. At the same time, FIFA regulations permit smaller clubs to obtain compensation for training services for young players who do play out their contract.

The principal economic argument in favor of player restraints is that they *help promote competitive balance.* Logically, the argument relies on three distinct propositions:

(1) fans prefer a more balanced competition;

(2) absent player restraints, the competition will be less balanced than fans prefer;

(3) player restraints actually result in improved competitive balance.

As a matter of theory and anecdotal evidence, it seems apparent that neither total imbalance nor perfect parity in any given season maximizes a sport's fan appeal. Interest seems to decline if one or a few teams dominate every year, with no one else having a remote possibility of winning a championship in the foreseeable future. For example, the All-American Football Conference in the 1940s–50s folded in large part because of complete dominance by the Cleveland Browns. On the other hand, fans seem to like the notion of dynasties being challenged. Hence, the English Premier League has shown unprecedented popularity at the same time Manchester United and now Manchester City have shown unprecedented dominance, and the NBA flourished during the era of the Chicago Bulls' dynasty and the current dominance of the Golden State Warriors.

At the same time, theory suggests that (except for football, where so few games are played and largely viewed on television) a league where Pittsburgh and New York won the exact same number of games and championships would not maximize appeal, in light of the much greater number of fans of New York teams than Pittsburgh teams. Many economic studies have considered this question empirically (summarized in Stefan Szymanski, *The Economic Design of Sporting Contests* 41 J. Econ. Lit. 1137 (2003)). The results are decidedly mixed, with many studies showing that more balanced competitions are not any more attractive to fans than imbalanced ones. MLB asked a panel of outside consultants to study the issue, resulting in the so-called "Blue Ribbon Report" that recommended ensuring that "every well-run club has a regularly recurring hope of reaching postseason play" (or "RRRPP"), rather than seeking to achieve rough parity. Richard C. Levin, George J. Mitchell, Paul A. Volcker, & George F. Will, *The Report of the Independent Members of the Commissioner's Blue Ribbon Panel on Baseball Economics* (July 2000), *available at* http://www.mlb.com/mlb/downloads/blue_ribbon.pdf.

Assuming that fans do indeed prefer a particular range of competitive balance, the next question is why free markets will not produce the degree of competitive balance that fans prefer. Indeed, the Blue Ribbon Report found that baseball was reasonably balanced during the free agency period 1976–92. Economic theory suggests that markets should promote the competitive balance fans prefer, assuming, however, that all of the teams have roughly similar revenue-generating potential. All else equal (which, of course, it never is), a star player is going to be more valuable to an *inferior* team, because the marginal contribution of that player will be greater for the weaker team.

According to the Blue Ribbon Report, however, after 1992 the payroll disparity between the high- and low-payroll teams became so significant that many teams no longer had an RRRPP. When the economic value of a win is much greater for Club A than for Club B, Club A presumably will spend more for the player, even if the player is more valuable on the field to Club B. To illustrate, some data suggests that each additional win (within the range of their actual success) produced about $2.4 million in revenue for the Yankees, and about $400,000 for the Pirates. Thus, if a player is predicted to add 2 wins ($4.8m additional revenue) to the Yankees and 6 wins ($2.4m additional revenue) for the Pirates, the Yankees are likely to win the bidding for his services. In the short-run, this advances consumer preferences, as, all else equal, more fans prefer to see the Yankees than the Pirates win. But suppose the result is that fans in many smaller cities lose any hope of an RRRPP, and stop attending games? This is a real harm, but is not considered by the Yankees in making its bid. The Yankees are only concerned with how much they earn, not the effect on others. This is what provides the economic justification for some form of player restraints.

MLB owners adopted (and secured MLBPA agreement to) a variety of revenue sharing and luxury tax policies in response to the Blue Ribbon Report. The result has been a reduction of the disparity in payrolls from the top quartile of teams to the bottom quartile from 3.5:1 in 1999 to 2.4:1 in 2017, when 5 of the 10 playoff teams were below median in terms of payroll. One of those teams, the Arizona Diamondbacks, was in Quartile IV. These below-median clubs won a total of 14 playoff games and one, the

Houston Astros, won the World Series with a payroll in the third-lowest quartile.

The foregoing, however, is economic theory, not real life. In real life, for free markets persistently to create imbalance, the clubs bidding the most actually have to succeed at buying the best players. If clubs' ability to predict the success of veteran free agents is poor—in statistical terms, if there is a weak correlation between player pay and team performance—then the beneficial influence of player restraints on competitive balance is diminished. Empirical studies summarized by Professor Szymanski, *supra*, have shown that clubs in North America do a much poorer job of matching pay with performance than do European soccer clubs. Indeed, although the labor market for hockey resulted in most teams losing money prior to 2004, over the prior three seasons 12 different teams participated in the Stanley Cup semi-finals.

4. ALTERNATIVES TO PLAYER RESTRAINTS

One frequently mentioned alternative to player restraints is revenue sharing. Designing a reasonable revenue sharing scheme, however, is not easy. If all clubs shared all revenue, the result would be to remove any incentive for each club to succeed. If clubs share a portion of local revenue, the result could actually harm balance. Suppose that teams shared 1/3 of their revenue from live gate and concessions with the visiting team, and that higher attendance yields $3m/win in large markets (like Los Angeles and New York) and $900,000/win in small markets (like Milwaukee or Kansas City). If a player is expected to produce three additional wins for each club, then the Brewers, Royals and other small market clubs will be able to claim a 1/3 share of the $9m additional gate received by the large market club, but would only keep a 2/3 share of the additional $1.8m if the player signs with their own club. See Stefan Szymanski, *Professional team sports are only a game: The Walrasian fixed supply conjecture model, Contest-Nash equilibrium and the invariance principle*, 5 J. Sports. Econ. 111 (2004). Thus, Professor Andrew Zimbalist has suggested a formula that provides revenues to teams based on weak market *potential*, which they would continue to receive regardless of their actual performance. Using this formula would provide weak market teams with additional revenues regardless of whether the wealthier teams perform better or worse, and would provide better incentives for clubs to participate in the labor market in a manner that will facilitate the level of competitive balance that fans prefer. See Andrew Zimbalist, *May the Best Team Win: Baseball Economics and Public Policy* 103–07 (Washington: Brookings Inst. Press, 2003).

5. DO PLAYER RESTRAINTS ACHIEVE THEIR DESIRED PRO-COMPETITIVE OBJECTIVE?

Even if (1) fans prefer some level of competitive balance, and (2) free markets will not necessarily produce the level of competitive balance fans prefer, the next economic question is whether the particular restraint chosen by a league has the desired effect of promoting competitive balance.

An oft-cited economic argument against player restraints is that they are unlikely to affect the allocation of players among teams, since the large-market teams will simply find another way of getting highly-valued players (economists call this claim the "invariance principle"). This is clearly true in European soccer, where an active market in the cash sale of players exists. Suppose a player is worth £4.8 million to Manchester United and £2 million to West Bromwich Albion. If the player is a free agent, he will receive up to £4.8 million and sign with Man U. If the player is reserved for life to West Bromwich and must play for a salary of £100,000, Man U would be willing to pay West Brom up to £4.7m to acquire his services. The only effect of the reserve rule is who gets the money.

This argument has less salience in North America because in practice all the major leagues prohibit or strictly limit the assignment of player contracts in return for large amounts of cash. Thus, for a player to be transferred, a trade must be arranged. The resulting bargaining difficulties can result in players remaining on one club even if more valuable to another. And, if players are more valuable to inferior teams, the result of player restraints and a ban on cash sales is a more rigid labor market, and good teams staying good, bad teams staying bad, and competitive balance getting worse.

6. ARE PLAYER RESTRAINTS NEEDED BECAUSE OF IRRATIONAL CLUB BEHAVIOR?

In an intriguing article, two leading American sports practitioners assert that sports club owners are uniquely unable to act as economically rational profit-maximizers. As a result, absent some meaningful labor market restraints, "in their relentless desire to win games," owners will "commit economic suicide." The authors' argument is succinctly put:

> The need and desire to win, the pressure from coaches, fans, and the media to be successful on the court, field, or ice, will often cloud and distort even the most astute business judgment. In order to win games, a team must sign talented players, and to sign talented players, a team may conclude it has no choice other than to meet financial demands that are *not realistic in relation to the revenues that team is able to generate.*

One seemingly simple answer to this is just to say no to a player's financial demands. But experience teaches that those who just say no usually are not able to field the most competitive teams. In the era of free agency, if a team is not prepared to pay whatever happens to be the going rate, the better players will go elsewhere, where some other owner is willing to meet their demands, *heedless of the financial consequences* to that team or the league.

Jeffrey A. Mishkin & Shepard Goldfein, *Professional Sports Leagues Need Fiscal Responsibility* N.Y.L.J., Aug. 7, 2000, at 12. Player restraints that are designed to ensure that payroll designs are economically rational, then, may also make economic sense.

NOTES AND QUESTIONS

1. Do player restraints significantly restrain trade?

2. *Are Player Restraints Pretext for Lowering Payroll?* Are there any reasons to justify player restraints? In NASCAR rules are set by an independent third party. NASCAR has adopted thousands of engineering rules designed to promote competitive balance, but absolutely no restraints on competition in the labor market for talented drivers, crew chiefs, crews, or engineers. Is that relevant to your answer?

3. *Competitive Balance.* Player restraints are often justified to promote competitive balance; what does competitive balance mean and why is it desirable? Once you have defined a measure of competitive balance in a particular league, compare the current level of balance with the expected amount of balance if:

   a. there are no restraints on the ability of a player to receive competing salary offers whenever the player's current contract expires;

   b. players are bound for life to their initial employer, but cash sales between clubs are permitted;

   c. players are bound for life to their initial employer, but cash sales between clubs are forbidden;

   d. clubs adopt one or more different schemes to share revenue:

   i. high-revenue teams are "taxed" and money redistributed to low-revenue teams

   ii. teams from large media markets are taxed and money redistributed to teams in small media markets

   iii. home teams share 1/3 of live gate with visiting team

   iv. all live gate revenue shared

v. all broadcast rights revenue shared

vi. broadcast rights shared in part in equal shares, in part based on number of games the club appears on national broadcast, and in part based on actual order of finish in the competition

e. teams are subject to a fairly rigid salary cap

4. *Are Clubs Rational?* Why would clubs accept player payrolls that they did not expect to recoup in increased revenues? What sort of player restraints can prevent or deter economic irrationality?

C. ANTITRUST ANALYSIS OF SPECIFIC PLAYER MARKET RESTRAINTS

We now turn to the key substantive issues raised in antitrust litigation by players against restraints imposed on the labor market by leagues. The major cases have taken place in football, and treat three specific player restraints involving the rookie draft, developmental squads, and restraints on veteran free agency.

1. ROOKIE DRAFT

The draft of college players originated in football in the late 1930s and later spread to other professional sports. While there are variations across the sports, the basic structure of the draft is simple. Proceeding in reverse order of finish from the prior season, each team selects a player from the pool of new players available that year, unless it trades away or acquires a draft pick in a deal with another team. (The NBA and the NHL conduct a lottery for drafting positions among the teams that miss the playoffs, but this is still heavily weighted towards the clubs with the worst records that season.) The consequence is that a player can either negotiate a contract to play with the team that selected him, or not play in the league at all (unless he can force a trade to another team, as star rookie quarterbacks John Elway and Eli Manning famously did). Reciprocally, each team is only allowed to negotiate with those players it has drafted, so if a star draft pick is not signed, the team will not be able to approach another rookie player at the same position. Thus, both sides have significant incentive to reach a deal. Nonetheless, the impact of not reaching a deal is usually going to be more severe for the player, especially when the player can turn to no other league to play his sport. In a case involving football, one player lodged an antitrust suit when he was unhappy with the contract offer he was able to secure from the team that drafted him.

SMITH V. PRO FOOTBALL, INC.
593 F.2d 1173 (D.C. Cir. 1978)

WILKEY, CIRCUIT JUDGE.

[James "Yazoo" Smith, an All-American defensive back at the University of Oregon, was selected by the Washington Redskins as the twelfth pick in the first round of the 1968 draft. He signed a one-year contract for a total of $50,000—$22,000 in salary and $28,000 in bonuses. Smith suffered a career-ending neck injury in the last game of the 1968 regular season, and the Redskins paid him an additional $19,800 (the amount he would have received had he played out the option year of his contract).

Two years later, Smith filed a lawsuit that, among other things, attacked the legality of the rookie draft under antitrust law. Smith contended that, but for the draft, he would have secured a more lucrative contract that would have better protected him from the financial consequences of his injury. The district court ruled that the NFL's draft violated federal antitrust law and had cost Smith $92,000—the amount the judge calculated as the difference between what Smith would have received in a "free market" without a draft, and what he actually received. These financial losses were automatically trebled to a $276,000 damage award.]

I. Background

[As noted above, the NFL uses a reverse-order-of-finish draft. In 1968 there were 16 succeeding rounds, the same order of selection being followed in each round. Each of the 26 teams had one choice per round unless they had traded their choice in that round to another team (a fairly common practice).]

The NFL draft, like similar procedures in other professional sports, is designed to promote "competitive balance." By dispersing newly arriving player talent equally among all NFL teams, with preferences to the weaker clubs, the draft aims to produce teams that are as evenly-matched on the playing field as possible. Evenly-matched teams make for closer games, tighter pennant races, and better player morale, thus maximizing fan interest, broadcast revenues, and overall health of the sport.

The draft is effectuated through the NFL's "no-tampering" rule. Under this rule as it existed in 1968, no team was permitted to negotiate prior to the draft with any player eligible to be drafted, and no team could negotiate with (or sign) any player selected by another team in the draft. The net result of these restrictions was that the right to negotiate with any given player was exclusively held by one team at any given time. If a college player could not reach a satisfactory agreement with the team holding the rights to his services, he could not play in the NFL.

* * *

The NFL player draft differs from the classic group boycott in two significant respects. First, the NFL clubs which have "combined" to implement the draft are not *competitors* in any economic sense. The clubs operate basically as a joint venture in producing an entertainment product—football games and telecasts. No NFL club can produce this product without agreements and joint action with every other team. To this end, the League not only determines franchise locations, playing schedules, and broadcast terms, but also ensures that the clubs receive equal shares of telecast and ticket revenues. These economic joint venturers "compete" on the playing field, to be sure, but here as well cooperation is essential if the entertainment product is to attain a high quality: only if the teams are "competitively balanced" will spectator interest be maintained at a high pitch. No NFL team, in short, is interested in driving another team out of business, whether in the counting-house or on the football field, for if the League fails, no one team can survive.

The draft differs from the classic group boycott, secondly, in that the NFL clubs have not combined *to exclude competitors or potential competitors* from their level of the market. Smith was never seeking to "compete" with the NFL clubs, and their refusal to deal with him has resulted in no decrease in the competition for providing football entertainment to the public. The draft, indeed, is designed not to insulate the NFL from competition, but to improve the entertainment product by enhancing its teams' competitive equality.

In view of these differences, we conclude that the NFL player draft cannot properly be described as a group boycott, at least not the type of group boycott that traditionally has elicited invocation of a *per se* rule. The "group boycott" designation, we believe, is properly restricted to concerted attempts by competitors to exclude horizontal competitors; it should not be applied, and has never been applied by the Supreme Court, to concerted refusals that are not designed to drive out competitors but to achieve some other goal.

[The court further explained why, even if not in the precise category of a *per se* illegal group boycott, the draft did not meet the general standards for *per se* condemnation from *Northern Pacific Railway*: a pernicious effect of competition and lack of any redeeming virtue.] Some form of player selection system may serve to regulate and thereby promote competition in what would otherwise be a chaotic bidding market for the services of college players. The Redskins, moreover, presented considerable evidence at trial that the draft was designed to preserve, and that it made some contribution to preserving, playing-field equality among the NFL-teams with various attendant benefits. The draft, finally, like the vertical restraints challenged in *Continental T.V.*, is "widely used" in our economy and has both judicial and scholarly support for its economic usefulness. [The Court therefore found that the Rule of Reason should apply.]

B. Rule of Reason

Under the rule of reason, a restraint must be evaluated to determine whether it is significantly anticompetitive in purpose or effect.... If, on analysis, the restraint is found to have legitimate business purposes whose realization serves to promote competition, the "anticompetitive evils" of the challenged practice must be carefully balanced against its "procompetitive virtues" to ascertain whether the former outweigh the latter. A restraint is unreasonable if it has the "net effect" of substantially impeding competition.

* * *

The draft that has been challenged here is undeniably anticompetitive both in its purpose and in its effect. The defendants have conceded that the draft "restricts competition among the NFL clubs for the services of graduating college players" and, indeed, that the draft "is designed to limit competition" and "to be a 'purposive' restraint" on the player-service market. The fact that the draft assertedly was designed to promote the teams' playing-field equality rather than to inflate their profit margins may prevent the draft's purpose from being described, in subjective terms, as nefarious. But this fact does not prevent its purpose from being described, in objective terms, as anticompetitive, for suppressing competition is the Telos, the very essence of the restraint.

The trial judge was likewise correct in finding that the draft was significantly anticompetitive in its *effect*. The draft inescapably forces each seller of football services to deal with one, and only one buyer, robbing the seller, as in any monopolistic market, of any real bargaining power. The draft, as the District Court found, "leaves no room whatever for competition among the teams for the services of college players, and utterly strips them of any measure of control over the marketing of their talents." The predictable effect of the draft, as the evidence established and as the District Court found, was to lower the salary levels of the best college players. There can be no doubt that the effect of the draft as it existed in 1968 was to "suppress or even destroy competition" in the market for players' services.

The justification asserted for the draft is that it has the legitimate business purpose of promoting "competitive balance" and playing-field equality among the teams, producing better entertainment for the public, higher salaries for the players, and increased financial security for the clubs. The NFL has endeavored to summarize this justification by saying that the draft ultimately has a "procompetitive" effect, yet this shorthand entails no small risk of confusion. The draft is "procompetitive," if at all, in a very different sense from that in which it is anticompetitive. The draft is anticompetitive in its effect on the market for players' services, because it virtually eliminates economic competition among buyers for the services of sellers. The draft is allegedly "procompetitive" in its effect on the playing field; but the NFL teams are not economic competitors on the playing field, and the draft, while it may heighten athletic competition and thus improve the entertainment product offered to the public, does not increase competition in the economic sense of encouraging others to enter the market and to offer the product at lower cost. Because the draft's "anticompetitive" and "procompetitive" effects are not comparable, it is impossible to "net them out" in the usual rule-of-reason balancing. The draft's "anticompetitive evils," in other words, cannot be balanced against its "procompetitive virtues," and the draft be upheld if the latter outweigh the former. In strict economic terms, the draft's demonstrated procompetitive effects are nil.

The defendants' justification for the draft reduces in fine to an assertion that competition in the market for entering players' services would not serve the best interests of the public, the clubs, or the players themselves. This is precisely the type of argument that the Supreme Court only recently has declared to be unavailing. In *National Society of Professional Engineers v. United States,* the Court held that a professional society's ban on competitive bidding violated § 1 of the Sherman Act. In so holding the Court rejected a defense that unbridled competitive bidding would lead to deceptively low bids and inferior work "with consequent risk to public safety and health," terming this justification "nothing less than a frontal assault on the basic policy of the Sherman Act." . . . The purpose of antitrust analysis, the Court concluded, "is to form a judgment about the competitive significance of the restraint; it is not to decide whether a policy favoring competition is in the public interest, or in the interest of the members of an industry. Subject to exceptions defined by statute, that policy decision has been made by Congress."

Confining our inquiry, as we must, to the draft's impact on competitive conditions, we conclude that the draft as it existed in 1968 was an unreasonable restraint of trade. The draft was concededly anticompetitive in purpose. It was severely anticompetitive in effect. It was not shown to have any significant offsetting procompetitive impact in the economic sense. Balancing the draft's anticompetitive evils against its procompetitive virtues, the outcome is plain. The NFL's defenses, premised on the assertion that competition for players' services would harm both the football industry and society, are unavailing; there is nothing of procompetitive virtue to balance, because "the Rule of Reason does not support a defense based on the assumption that competition itself is unreasonable."

We recognize . . . that professional football "may differ significantly from other business services, and, accordingly [that] the nature of the competition" for player talent may vary from an absolute "free market" norm. Given the joint-venture status of the NFL clubs, we do not foreclose the possibility that some type of player selection system might be defended as serving "to regulate and promote . . . competition" in the market for players' services. But we are faced here, as the Supreme Court was faced in *Professional Engineers*, with what amounts to a "total ban" on competition, and we agree with the District Court that this level of restraint cannot be justified. The trial judge concluded, with pardonable exaggeration, that the draft system at issue was "absolutely the most restrictive one imaginable." Even though the draft was justified primarily by the need to disperse the best players, it applied to all graduating seniors, including average players who were, in a sense, fungible commodities. It permitted college players to negotiate with only one team. If a player could not contract with that team, he *could not play at all.*

Without intimating any view as to the legality of the following procedures, we note that there exist significantly less anticompetitive alternatives to the draft system which has been challenged here. The trial judge found that the evidence supported the viability of a player selection system that would permit "more than one team to draft each player, while restricting the number of players any one team might sign." A less anticompetitive draft might permit a college player to negotiate with the team of his choice if the team that drafted him failed to make him an acceptable offer. The NFL could also conduct a second draft each year for players who were unable to reach agreement with the team that selected them the first time. Most obviously, perhaps, the District Court found that the evidence supported the feasibility of a draft that would run for fewer rounds, applying only to the most talented players and enabling their "average" brethren to negotiate in a "free market." The least restrictive alternative of all, of course, would be for the NFL to eliminate the draft entirely and employ revenue-sharing to equalize the teams' financial resources, a method of preserving "competitive balance" nicely in harmony with the league's self-proclaimed "joint-venture" status.

We are not required in this case to design a draft that would pass muster under the antitrust laws. We would suggest, however, that under the Supreme Court's decision in *Professional Engineers*, no draft can be justified merely by showing that it is a relatively less anticompetitive means of attaining sundry benefits for the football industry and society. Rather, a player draft can survive scrutiny under the rule of reason only if it is demonstrated to have positive, economically procompetitive benefits that offset its anticompetitive effects, or, at the least, if it is demonstrated to accomplish legitimate business purposes and to have a net anticompetitive effect that is insubstantial. Because the NFL draft as it existed in 1968 had severe anticompetitive effects and no demonstrated procompetitive virtues, we hold that it unreasonably restrained trade in violation of § 1 of The Sherman Act.

* * *

MacKinnon, Circuit Judge, dissenting.

* * *

The Nature of the Business.

* * *

Professional sports teams are in some respects traditional economic units seeking to sell a product to the public. But economic competition between teams is not and cannot be the sole determinant of their behavior. Professional sports leagues are uniquely organized economic entities; the ultimate success of the league depends on the economic cooperation rather than the economic competition of its members. The product being offered to the public is more than an isolated exhibition, it is a series of connected exhibitions that culminate in the annual grand finale contest between the two teams with the best records in the League, which have demonstrated their prowess in organized, rigidly scheduled League competition. The product being offered the public is the "league sport," and the value of this product at the stadium gate and to the television networks depends on the competitive balance of the teams in the league. Spectators and television viewers are not interested in lopsided games or contests between weak teams.

In many respects, the business of professional football as carried on by the NFL resembles a "natural monopoly." The structure of the League as a single entity outside the antitrust laws was also specifically authorized in 1966 by Act of Congress. As defined by two authorities, a natural monopoly is a monopoly resulting from economies of scale, a relationship between the size of the market and the size of the most efficient firm such that one firm of efficient size can produce all or more than the market can take at a remunerative price, and can continually expand its capacity at less cost than that of a new firm entering the business. In this situation, competition may exist for a time but only until bankruptcy or merger leaves the field to one firm; in a meaningful sense, competition here is self-destructive. At the present time, the NFL, as an organized association of various teams (or firms), has a statutorily recognized monopoly over production of the "league sport" of major professional football. Anyone who wishes to watch a major professional football game must watch an NFL game, played under NFL rules with NFL teams and players. History suggests that it is easier for the NFL to expand the number of teams than it is for another league to form and operate successfully. Competition may exist for a time, as the experiences of the American Football League and the World Football League demonstrate, but in the long run such competition is destructive and many teams fail, even as they did within the NFL in its free market formative years.

The History and Effect of the Draft.

[Here Judge MacKinnon detailed a number of features of life in the NFL in the mid-1930s at the time the draft was adopted. (Note that George MacKinnon was an All-American center for the University of Minnesota Golden Gophers in the 1920s.) There were just nine teams with squads of 22 to 26 players. Though a free market existed for players coming out of college, a career in professional football was not that attractive to many players as they graduated from college. Many opted to go on to graduate or professional school, to go into business, or to begin college or high school football coaching. These alternatives were attractive as compared to the NFL, where salaries were modest, careers were short, and there was always a possibility of a permanently disabling injury. In 1936, the NFL instituted the draft after the last-place Cincinnati team had dropped out of the league. Initially covering 30 rounds, the draft had been cut to 17 rounds by the time that Smith challenged its legality under antitrust law four decades later.]

* * *

In my view, there are compelling reasons why the draft has continued so long without serious challenge. In effect a player draft is *natural for league sports*. Competitive equality among the component teams is an inherent requirement for meaningful sports competition and the survival of a conference or league high school, college, or professional and all of its members. Close rivalries are the backbone of any successful sport. When the NFL established the draft, its objective was to give each team the same fair *opportunity to* be competitive; it sought to achieve a competitive balance among all the League's teams, that is, to "try to equalize the teams." The intended result was to create a situation where each League game would become a closer contest, where spectator interest in the game and the players themselves would be increased, where the interesting individual contests would create an interesting League championship race, and where ultimately the teams and their players would benefit from the greater income resulting from the increased fan interest.

* * *

All major sports, in recognition of the need for competitive balance, have drafts. Hockey and basketball have drafts, and baseball instituted a draft when it became clear from the long domination of the New York Yankees that the farm system was not producing competitive balance.

Since the first college football player draft was held in 1936, the results sought to be accomplished have clearly been achieved. Some argue that this has been caused by other factors, but the preponderance of the factual testimony and record evidence supports a conclusion that the college player draft was the key factor which produced the competitive balance of the teams, which in turn brought about the exciting games and interesting championship races and increased public interest in the sport, which ultimately led to the huge gate receipts and large television contracts that are presently producing enormous benefits for the players themselves. There was no showing to the contrary in the 2,000 page record. The majority argue that it is television that produces the interest and the revenues but the balanced teams produced by the draft came first and caused the close contests which attracted the public and eventually television.

Since 1935, the number of teams has increased from nine to today's League of 28 teams, and the number of players per team has also been increased substantially. Instead of the small squads of around 26 players in the early days of the sport, the modern team's roster once swelled to 47 and was later reduced to 43 players. This has increased the total number of active players in the League as a whole to slightly over 1,200. Gate receipts have increased tremendously due to the increased popular interest in the game. Also important are the television revenues, which constitute a large part of each team's annual income. The NFL television contracts between the League and the television networks have distributed hundreds of millions of dollars to all teams in the League; and current news reports indicate that the payments are to be substantially increased. The lucrative television contract, made possible by an *exemption* from the antitrust laws enacted by Congress, is negotiated for all teams by the League Commissioner. These moneys are distributed *equally* to each team in the League without regard to the size of the team's local television market. In 1968 the revenues from television accounted for approximately 30% of the total revenue of the Redskins and this was approximately the same percentage as the average for all NFL teams in that year. Team revenue from gate receipts, television contracts, and other sources has increased tremendously since 1935, and the NFL teams and their players are the direct recipients of the benefits of the increased national interest in NFL games. College players, 22 years old, coming out of college in 1976 and playing in the NFL were making $20,000 to $150,000 their first year.

* * *

Due to the increased benefits afforded professional football players, the competition for graduating college football players that previously existed from lucrative coaching positions and numerous other business and professional opportunities has been successfully met, if not altogether eliminated as a practical matter. The increasing popularity of pro football and its attractiveness to graduating college players assures those interested in the success of the game, such as television and radio broadcasters and networks, stadium owners, team owners, and players already playing in the NFL, that the best college football players year after year will continue to join the professional ranks and assure the quality and attractiveness of their games. In fact, a great many players now go to college for the sole purpose of establishing a playing record which will result in their being drafted by one of the professional teams; a first-round draft choice in the professional league is viewed by many as the substantial equivalent of *summa cum laude* and first-round draft choices are generally paid much higher starting salaries.

* * *

From my analysis, the testimony of record overwhelmingly supports the conclusion that the growth of football between 1935 and 1968 was largely due to the competitive balance that the League achieved during those years and to the creation of a quality product, the "league sport." This competitive balance, and the consequential tremendous growth in public interest, which has inured greatly to the benefit of the players themselves, is in large part a result of the college player draft. . . . The draft created the competitive balance, that created the public interest, that led other cities to organize teams, that led to national expansion of the league, that enlarged the total gate receipts, that led to the large revenue-producing television contracts.

[The dissent then addressed the majority's argument that a less restrictive draft system should have been devised by the NFL.]

A pure draft takes all of the college players that are coming into the market with the teams with the poorest records having preference in the order of their won and lost records. The draft as it existed in 1968 was a pure draft, and it is submitted that the draft should be that extensive if the opportunity for maximum competitive balance is to be assured. If the draft only lasts two rounds, as the trial court here suggested, the rest of the players are left for the free market and the preponderance of those players, or at least the preponderance of the better players in that group, would go to teams with special attractions and the teams owned by super-wealthy millionaires who desire very greatly to own a winning team. Not even a complete sharing of team revenues could overcome the unfair advantage posed by wealthy owners and collateral attractions of a few cities. Large cities such as New York, Chicago, Los Angeles, and Washington offer special advantages for publicity, endorsements, and lucrative off-field jobs in business. Cities with better weather are more attractive to some players, and teams with better prospects of winning in a particular season furnish a certain attraction for some players. Larger cities with larger stadiums realize more income and hence are somewhat able to offer larger salaries than teams with smaller cities and stadiums. So are teams owned by wealthy sportsmen who place a premium on winning and are willing to support their desires with almost unlimited financial resources. The draft has substantially reduced the ability of these owners to dominate the league.

Given these factors that would permit a few teams to corner the "developing players" that in a great many instances eventually surpass developed players, drafted in the earlier rounds, it is necessary to have a draft that reaches the *maximum number of potential players who are absolutely necessary to preserve competitive balance.* When the draft does not reach that many players, the few stronger teams with the natural advantages will be able to corner the best remaining prospects who become free agents. The testimony indicated that a few "super wealthy" owners with a very deep pocketbook could obtain a very substantial advantage if there were a substantial pool of free market players.

* * *

The Rule of Reason and the College Player Draft.

* * *

[T]he important consideration is the effect of the draft. The majority concludes that the draft strips the players of "any real bargaining power," lowers their salaries, and suppresses if not destroys competition for their services. I disagree. The majority opinion and the trial court only looked at the draft from the players' side and only at a portion of that. As for bargaining power, the operation of the draft also restrains the team from dealing with other players (even though there are exceptions, discussed below). This is particularly true when a team drafts for a position, as the Redskins did in drafting Smith as their first-round choice in 1968. The Redskins drafted Smith in the first round to fill a need at the "free safety position." In using their first-round draft choice to select a player for that particular position, they practically put all of their eggs in one basket for that year. In selecting Smith, they passed over or did not reach, all other players of nearly equal ability for that position. After the Redskins had exercised their first draft selection, these other players would be chosen by other teams with later picks, and would thus not be available in later rounds. Even if another player was later available, it would be a waste of a valuable draft choice for the Redskins to use any subsequent choice to draft for that same position, since the position needed only one player and the team had other needs to fill as well. That is the way the 1968 player draft went for the Redskins. After they had drafted Smith first to fill that position, the team practically had to sign him if they wanted to fill what they considered was a vital team vacancy. These circumstances gave Smith very substantial bargaining leverage, as his professional negotiating agent frequently reminded the Redskins. Also, a first-round draft choice commands considerable publicity in the locality, and the team is under very considerable pressure from its fans to sign the player and thereby put the first-round pick in a uniform. Smith was the beneficiary, as a first-round choice, of such public pressure.

While in a free market a player could negotiate with several teams, a team could also negotiate with several players of nearly equal ability and play one off against the others. If Smith had negotiated with the Redskins in a free market, the Redskins could also have simultaneously negotiated with the next-best prospect for free safety as well and the availability of the other player might have served to reduce the salary offers to Smith. Then if Smith and the Redskins could not come to terms, the Redskins could always opt for one of the other prospects they considered to be close to Smith in ability, well realizing, as experience has many times proven, that the ultimate development and performance of the second or third choice might eventually eclipse that of their first favored choice. Drafting college players is not an exact science.

* * *

Simply because the draft is essential to the vitality of the business does not mean that players entering the League, as opposed to veterans already playing in the League, have no interest in the existence of a draft. It would be error to suggest otherwise because without a draft a less stable League with fewer franchises and lower salaries would result. Incoming players receive salaries and bonuses far in excess of what they could command in a free market of teams in a league that did not have the competitive balance which a player draft produces. The vitality of the League, which is admittedly dependent in large measure on the balanced team competition produced by the draft, has attracted so great a public interest that the public in most localities, as referred to above, has subsidized the teams by the erection of huge stadiums without full contribution to their cost by the teams that use them. This fact has enabled salaries paid to draftees to be higher than what they would be in a free market with the attendant destructive competition, unequal competitive balance, and resulting shaky franchises. It cannot be said that rookie players have no interest in the existence of the college player draft.

In short, in my opinion, the evidentiary record here supports the conclusion that the draft also has a favorable effect on the bargaining position of players, which to a considerable extent nets out the adverse effect it has in limiting the players' right to negotiate with other teams. And this bargaining equivalency vitiates the assertion that players' salaries are depressed on account of the draft.

NOTES AND QUESTIONS

1. *Consistent Reasoning?* Is the *Smith* majority's analysis in the first part of the opinion, which defends the competitive virtues of the draft against a charge of *per se* illegality, fully compatible with its analysis in the second part of the opinion, which condemns the anticompetitive effect of the draft under the Rule of Reason?

2. *Causes of NFL Success.* In several very long footnotes, the *Smith* majority and dissent debated a number of the factual underpinnings to their respective arguments:

   a. Was it the player draft, instituted in 1935, or network television, which emerged in the late 1950s, or some linkage between the two, that was the true source of pro football's economic success?

   b. How much competitive balance can really be contributed by the rookie draft (or restraints on veteran free agency), given the team dynasties associated with legendary head coaches? To improve competitive balance, should sports leagues place similar limits on the ability of winning teams to hire top coaches and front office executives from other clubs?

   c. Is the true secret of evenly balanced athletic competition the sharing of revenues among owners, not just from network and cable television and trademark licensing, but also from gate receipts and other revenue sources? What effect might such league "socialism" have on teams' ability and incentive to pay their players higher salaries? How would your answer be different if the league had, as the NFL does today, a "hard" team salary cap (and floor)? Indeed, is there any competitive balance need for a draft at all if the league has a team salary cap as in the NFL or NBA today, or a rookie pool salary cap as in the NFL and NHL today?

3. *Legitimacy of Competitive Balance as a Justification.* The *Smith* majority seems to state that it is irrelevant for Rule of Reason analysis that a league practice such as the draft enhances competitive balance within the league. As demonstrated in the *Bd. of Regents v. NCAA* decision in Chapter 5, that position has not stood the test of time. Indeed, if a league cannot defend the legality of restrictive internal practices on the grounds that they improve the quality of the product offered to its fans, how could a less restrictive draft (or any conduct-standardizing rule) pass muster, as the *Smith* majority intimates it could in the latter part of its decision?

4. *Do Restraints Help Small-Market Clubs?* The principal argument for the draft is that it is necessary to preserve balanced athletic competition against the threat posed by big market teams. But is there any guarantee that the draft will have that effect, at least as long as teams can sell their top picks to other clubs? Consider, for example, the significance of the Quebec Nordiques dealing Eric Lindros to the Philadelphia Flyers in 1992, for $15 million and five players. (The Nordiques franchise had been purchased in 1989 for $15 million, though it became far more valuable in the late-1990s as the Stanley Cup champion Colorado Avalanche.) In addition, is it possible that the draft

also obstructs achievement of competitive balance? Does not the football draft guarantee the Super Bowl winner the exclusive right to valued players, which may obstruct the ability of weaker teams to make rapid improvements in their relative strength? Can you think of ways to restructure the draft to enhance its contribution to equality on the playing field (as well as its ability to pass the Rule of Reason test)?

5. *Are Draftees Exploited?* Opponents of the draft assert that it permits exploitation of new players, who are left with no choice but to accept a "take it or leave it" offer by the drafting team, the only team with which they are permitted to deal. Yet in sports like football or basketball, top rookie draft picks sign multiyear contracts worth tens of millions of dollars, suggesting that they must have significant bargaining leverage as well. For example, in 1992 Shaquille O'Neal received a $40 million, 7-year deal from the Orlando Magic. Even in a less wealthy sport such as hockey, Eric Lindros signed that same year a $21-million, 6-year contract with the Philadelphia Flyers.

In more recent collective bargaining agreements, this issue has been mooted because unions have agreed to sharp limits on salaries given to rookies in the context of overall schemes that ensure a fixed percentage of revenues will go to club payroll, thus increasing pay to veterans.

6. *Less Restrictive Alternatives.* The previous questions suggest the possibility of "more reasonable" or "less restrictive" alternatives to the current "restraint of trade" flowing from the draft. How do you define a "less restrictive alternative" (LRA)? Does the LRA have to achieve the exact same level of benefit, or can it achieve almost the same benefit to the league with far less adverse effects on players? Is the suggested LRA something that necessarily is an alternative to the restraint, or could it be supplementary, in which case how would the degree to which it might enhance the already procompetitive effects factor into the analysis?

For example, if a court believes that professional football with the existing draft is more procompetitive (more attractive to fans) than football without a draft, does the possibility of a less restrictive draft (one that has less anticompetitive impact on the players market) make the existing system illegal? How can a judge determine which version of the draft is more or less restrictive for players? For example, compare a three-round draft with players tied to the drafting team for two years to a six-round draft with players tied to the team for just one year. How does one compare the incremental gains to players from relaxing the draft's prohibition against teams bidding for rookies to the incremental losses to fans from a reduction in competitive athletic balance within the league (on the assumption that the draft does contribute at least some measure of competitive equality)? Alternatively, could a plaintiff advocate that greater revenue sharing within the league would accomplish the same competitive balance benefits as effectively as the draft? Should a jury then be able to find a violation if it decides that increased sharing of some unspecified revenues would also promote competitive balance? Does the process of antitrust litigation about these issues give the league sufficient guidance in designing its system for allocating new players to the teams? Does the threat of litigation give the league the incentive to explore more optimal solutions along both dimensions of this issue? And whatever restraint the league decides to adopt, isn't there always going to be some alternative that someone can imagine that is less restrictive?

2. VETERAN FREE AGENCY

Recall from Chapter 4 that none of the opinions in *Flood v. Kuhn* reached the merits of Curt Flood's claim that baseball's reserve clause was an unreasonable restraint of trade. Unlike baseball, the NFL never had a reserve clause; rather, at the expiration of a player's contract the practice evolved by the 1960s that he was free to sign with another team after playing out one "option year" at a 10% increase in salary. However, there was one major condition: the new team was required to provide what the commissioner judged to be "fair and equitable" compensation (by way of players, draft choices, or both) to the team that had lost the player off its roster. If the two teams could not agree on what the free agent compensation would be, the commissioner (then Pete Rozelle) would determine it, and his decision was final and unappealable. The players objected to the "Rozelle Rule" because, unless there was an upstart league competing for players at the time, this requirement meant that football players had no greater opportunity to obtain competing offers for their services than baseball players.

MACKEY V. NFL (PART 1)
543 F.2d 606 (8th Cir. 1976)

LAY, CIRCUIT JUDGE.

* * *

HISTORY.

* * *

[The Rozelle Rule], unchanged in form, is currently embodied in § 12.1(H) of the NFL Constitution. The ostensible purposes of the rule are to maintain competitive balance among the NFL teams and protect the clubs' investment in scouting, selecting and developing players.

During the period from 1963 through 1974, 176 players played out their options. Of that number, 34 signed with other teams. In three of those cases, the former club waived compensation. In 27 cases, the clubs involved mutually agreed upon compensation. Commissioner Rozelle awarded compensation in the four remaining cases.*

[The Court first determined that the Rozelle Rule was not protected by the labor exemption. This is summarized in Section C of this chapter.]

We turn, then, to the question of whether the Rozelle Rule, as implemented, violates § 1 of the Sherman Act, which declares illegal "every contract, combination . . . or conspiracy, in restraint of trade or commerce among the several States." The district court found the Rozelle Rule to be a *per se* violation of the Act. Alternatively, the court held the Rule to be violative of the Rule of Reason standard.

* * *

PER SE VIOLATION.

* * *

There is substantial evidence in the record to support the district court's findings as to the effects of the Rozelle Rule. We think, however, that this case presents unusual circumstances rendering it inappropriate

---

* [The district court detailed these four cases:
- In 1967, Pat Fischer played out the option year with the St. Louis Cardinals and was signed by the Washington Redskins. Commissioner Rozelle awarded the Cardinals a second round draft choice in the 1969 draft and a third round draft choice in the 1970 draft.
- In 1967, Pro Bowl tight end David Parks played out the option with the San Francisco 49ers and became a free agent, subsequently signing with the New Orleans Saints. There had been no agreement on compensation between the two clubs. Commissioner Rozelle awarded as compensation from the New Orleans Saints to the San Francisco 49ers the Saints' first round draft choice in the earlier 1968 draft, and the Saints' first round draft choice in the upcoming 1969 draft. The then-superior 49ers club used the two picks awarded by Rozelle to select two future Pro Bowl starters, center Forrest Blue and tight end Ted Kwalik.
- In 1971 the New England Patriots neglected to timely exercise their option over Phil Olsen's services for the upcoming 1972 season. Commissioner Rozelle declared Olsen a free agent and no longer a member of the New England Patriots team. Olsen then signed with the Los Angeles Rams. Commissioner Rozelle awarded to the New England Patriots the Los Angeles Rams' first round draft choice in the 1972 draft and stated that additional compensation would be awarded to the Patriots from the Rams at the conclusion of the 1971 season. He also directed the Rams to pay to the Patriots the sum of $35,000 constituting Olsen's initial signing bonus and other expenses. In January 1972 Commissioner Rozelle awarded additional compensation to the New England Patriots: the Rams' third round draft choice which they had previously acquired from the Washington Redskins.
- Dick Gordon played out the option with the Chicago Bears during the 1971 season and became a free agent. Although a number of clubs thereafter expressed interest in obtaining Gordon's services, no club was able to work out a compensation agreement with the Chicago Bears. Because of this fact, no club would sign Gordon due to the unknown compensation that would be awarded should it do so. The situation was at an impasse well into the 1972 regular season. Finally, Commissioner Rozelle announced in advance of any signing what the compensation to the Chicago Bears would be: a first round draft choice for the draft following the 1973 football season. Immediately thereafter the Los Angeles Rams signed Gordon to a contract.]

to declare the Rozelle Rule illegal per se without undertaking an inquiry into the purported justifications for the Rule.

[T]he line of cases which has given rise to *per se* illegality for the type of agreements involved here generally concerned agreements between business competitors in the traditional sense. Here, however, as the owners and Commissioner urge, the NFL assumes some of the characteristics of a joint venture in that each member club has a stake in the success of the other teams. No one club is interested in driving another team out of business, since if the League fails, no one team can survive. Although businessmen cannot wholly evade the antitrust laws by characterizing their operation as a joint venture, we conclude that the unique nature of the business of professional football renders it inappropriate to mechanically apply *per se* illegality rules here, fashioned in a different context. This is particularly true where, as here, the alleged restraint does not completely eliminate competition for players' services.

* * *

RULE OF REASON.

The focus of an inquiry under the Rule of Reason is whether the restraint imposed is justified by legitimate business purposes, and is no more restrictive than necessary.

In defining the restraint on competition for players' services, the district court found that the Rozelle Rule significantly deters clubs from negotiating with and signing free agents; that it acts as a substantial deterrent to players playing out their options and becoming free agents; that it significantly decreases players' bargaining power in contract negotiations; that players are thus denied the right to sell their services in a free and open market; that as a result, the salaries paid by each club are lower than if competitive bidding were allowed to prevail; and that absent the Rozelle Rule, there would be increased movement in interstate commerce of players from one club to another.

We find substantial evidence in the record to support these findings. Witnesses for both sides testified that there would be increased player movement absent the Rozelle Rule. Two economists testified that elimination of the Rozelle Rule would lead to a substantial increase in player salaries. Carroll Rosenbloom, owner of the Los Angeles Rams, indicated that the Rams would have signed quite a few of the star players from other teams who had played out their options, absent the Rozelle Rule. [The court then cited evidence identifying two free agent players who probably would have signed with and moved to new teams but for the Rozelle Rule's deterrent effect on the potential new teams.]

In support of their contention that the restraints effected by the Rozelle Rule are not unreasonable, the defendants asserted a number of justifications. First, they argued that without the Rozelle Rule, star players would flock to cities having natural advantages such as larger economic bases, winning teams, warmer climates, and greater media opportunities; that competitive balance throughout the League would thus be destroyed; and that the destruction of competitive balance would ultimately lead to diminished spectator interest, franchise failures, and perhaps the demise of the NFL, at least as it operates today. Second, the defendants contended that the Rozelle Rule is necessary to protect the clubs' investment in scouting expenses and player developments costs. Third, they asserted that players must work together for a substantial period of time in order to function effectively as a team; that elimination of the Rozelle Rule would lead to increased player movement and a concomitant reduction in player continuity; and that the quality of play in the NFL would thus suffer, leading to reduced spectator interest, and financial detriment both to the clubs and the players. Conflicting evidence was adduced at trial by both sides with respect to the validity of these asserted justifications.

The district court held the defendants' asserted justifications unavailing. As to the clubs' investment in player development costs, Judge Larson found that these expenses are similar to those incurred by other businesses, and that there is no right to compensation for this type of investment. With respect to player continuity, the court found that elimination of the Rozelle Rule would affect all teams equally in that regard; that it would not lead to a reduction in the quality of play; and that even assuming that it would, that fact would not justify the Rozelle Rule's anticompetitive effects. As to competitive balance and the consequences which would flow from abolition of the Rozelle Rule, Judge Larson found that the existence of the Rozelle Rule has had no material effect on competitive balance in the NFL. Even assuming that the Rule did foster competitive balance, the court found that there were other legal means available to achieve that end: *e.g.*, the competition committee, multiple year contracts, and special incentives. The court further concluded that elimination of the Rozelle Rule would have no significant disruptive effects, either immediate or long term, on professional football. In conclusion the court held that the Rozelle Rule was unreasonable in that it was overly broad, unlimited in duration, unaccompanied by procedural safeguards, and employed in conjunction with other anticompetitive practices such as the draft, Standard Player Contract, option clause, and the no-tampering rules.

We agree that the asserted need to recoup player development costs cannot justify the restraints of the Rozelle Rule. That expense is an ordinary cost of doing business and is not peculiar to professional football. Moreover, because of its unlimited duration, the Rozelle Rule is far more restrictive than necessary to fulfill that need.

We agree, in view of the evidence adduced at trial with respect to existing players turnover by way of trades, retirements and new players entering the League, that the club owners' arguments respecting player continuity cannot justify the Rozelle Rule. We concur in the district court's conclusion that the possibility of resulting decline in the quality of play would not justify the Rozelle Rule. We do recognize, as did the district court, that the NFL has a strong and unique interest in maintaining competitive balance among its teams. The key issue is thus whether the Rozelle Rule is essential to the maintenance of competitive balance, and is no more restrictive than necessary. The district court answered both of these questions in the negative.

We need not decide whether a system of inter-team compensation for free agents moving to other teams is essential to the maintenance of competitive balance in the NFL. Even if it is, we agree with the district court's conclusion that the Rozelle Rule is significantly more restrictive than necessary to serve any legitimate purposes it might have in this regard. First, little concern was manifested at trial over the free movement of average or below average players. Only the movement of the better players was urged as being detrimental to football. Yet the Rozelle Rule applies to every NFL player regardless of his status or ability. Second, the Rozelle Rule is unlimited in duration. It operates as a perpetual restriction on a player's ability to sell his services in an open market throughout his career. Third, the enforcement of the Rozelle Rule is unaccompanied by procedural safeguards. A player has no input into the process by which fair compensation is determined. Moreover, the player may be unaware of the precise compensation demanded by his former team, and that other teams might be interested in him but for the degree of compensation sought.

* * *

In sum, we hold that the Rozelle Rule, as enforced, unreasonably restrains trade in violation of § 1 of the Sherman Act.

From the 1978 *Smith* decision until the 1993 antitrust settlement discussed below, the NFL's rookie draft remained virtually the same other than a reduction to 12 rounds. Nonetheless, this period witnessed constant innovation and experimentation with different modes of free agency in all leagues. Collective bargaining with the players' associations produced almost all those variations. But after a bargaining impasse in 1988, NFL owners unilaterally introduced one new practice—Plan B, a less restrictive alternative to the Rozelle Rule found illegal in *Mackey*. Plan B entitled each team each year to protect 37 players on its reserve list. Protected players, whether or not their contract had expired, could move to other NFL teams only if their current team chose not to match new offers received, and then the new team had to pay compensation to the player's current team (in the form of draft picks whose number and round varied with the size of the new salary offer). By contrast, all unprotected players (even those still under contract) could try to negotiate a better deal with another club that paid no compensation to the team that lost the player (though just during the months of February and March). If a player did not receive a better offer from another club, he could return to his existing team under whatever contract he enjoyed or was able to negotiate with the latter. In the four years of Plan B, many veteran players (although no stars) moved to other clubs for sizable signing bonuses and salary increases.

In 1989, eight players, backed by the NFLPA, challenged the NFL's Plan B restrictions on each team's 37 protected players. (As we will see in the next section, the players were able to avoid application of the labor exemption defense after the district judge held that the NFLPA had successfully renounced its status as a union bargaining agent.) The merits of the antitrust issues were tried during the summer of 1992, and the jury found that Plan B violated the Rule of Reason. *McNeil v. NFL,* Civ. No. 4-90-476, 1992 WL 315292, at 1 (D. Minn. Sept. 10, 1992). In responding to a series of special interrogatories, the jury found (1) that Plan B harmed players by diminishing competition among NFL clubs for their services, (2) that nonetheless the system contributed significantly to competitive balance among NFL teams, but (3) that the system was unreasonable because it was more restrictive than necessary for that purpose.

On point (2), the players claimed that sports leagues did not need competitive balance to survive, asserting that too much parity would harm fan interest and that college football was enormously popular despite metrics suggesting it is severely imbalanced. The plaintiffs also argued that player movement restrictions harm, rather than create, competitive balance, noting that 13 different teams had won a World Series since free agency was introduced in baseball while at the same time only 7 of 28 NFL teams had won the Super Bowl, and that weaker teams are unable to improve by signing better players. The jury apparently was persuaded by the NFL's arguments that competitive balance was important to a league's attractiveness to fans, that the NFL was well-balanced, and that the NFL's best players would avoid moving to losing teams or cold-weather cities or small market teams where endorsement opportunities were far more limited. On point (3), the plaintiffs argued that a variety of other factors could address the NFL's concerns with free agency if the challenged restrictions were removed, including revenue sharing, imbalanced scheduling, investment in superior management and coaching, and qualitative ways in which players are treated.

A contentious issue in *McNeil* concerned less restrictive alternatives. Although it is well settled that a challenged agreement is unreasonable under the Rule of Reason if it is more restrictive than necessary to achieve the defendants' legitimate business purposes, Judge David Doty did not require the plaintiffs to identify the alternatives, but instead instructed the jury to place the burden on the NFL to show that no less restrictive alternatives were available. The jury found that the NFL had failed to meet this burden.

The jury found that only four of the eight plaintiffs actually suffered damages—totaling $1.6 million. Once Judge Doty rendered a final judgment with an injunctive order, the NFL appealed the verdict on several grounds, including the important issue of who had the burden of proof regarding alternatives. The case was settled by the players and owners before the Eighth Circuit issued an opinion.*

The settlement, which was part of an overall resolution of the long-standing legal and labor-relations conflict between the NFL and NFLPA, emerged from the burst of litigation that followed the *McNeil* verdict. The NFL paid $195 million to the players it had restricted under Plan B and several other NFL policies that had generated lawsuits. In *White v. NFL*, 836 F. Supp. 1458 (D. Minn. 1993), Judge Doty reviewed the settlement of the class action under Fed. R. Civ. P. 23(b) and found it to be "fair, reasonable and adequate" for the affected class. In so doing, the judge overruled objections by veteran players who disapproved of the salary cap, recent college graduates who disapproved of the special rookie salary cap provisions, and Eagles owner Norman Braman, who disapproved of the settlement provision that allowed the NFLPA to control group licenses (licenses for more than five players) of player publicity rights. After the settlement, the union recertified and both sides compromised their legal and public relations positions to generate the framework for a new collective agreement, which they have extended repeatedly, through the 2020 season, with largely the same structural characteristics.

The basic architecture of the post-1993 regime as it applies to free agency remains in place. Veteran players are unrestricted free agents when their contracts expire at any time after five full years of service. Each club, however, can protect one free agent by designating him as its "franchise" player, who is then guaranteed a salary of either the average of the highest five players in the league at his position or 120% of his prior year's salary (whichever is higher). In addition, each club can designate two "transition" players among its free agents. For these, the club has a right to match any offer the player receives from another team. If no such offer is received, the club must pay the player the average of the ten highest paid players in the league at his position or 120% of his prior year's salary. Players with two

---

* The substantive arguments summarized above come from insightful papers delivered after the jury verdict by two of the leading litigators at the 1993 Sports Lawyers Association annual conference. *See* Jeffrey L. Kessler, "A Look at the *McNeil* Litigation and its Results," and Jeffrey Pash, "Free Agency Litigation in the National Football League." These papers are available on the Casebook Website (http://pennstatelaw.psu.edu/SportsTextWebsite).

to five years of service are restricted free agents when their contracts expire, subject to the club's right of first refusal and right to receive draft choice compensation from any new club with which the player signs (as under the old agreement).

In exchange for this system of veteran free agency, the NFLPA agreed to continue the rookie draft, though with the number of rounds reduced from twelve to seven. Most important, the NFLPA accepted a team salary cap, officially triggered by the league's overall player costs reaching 67% of total Defined Gross Revenues (DGR) in any one season (which has happened each year). The owners agreed that clubs must spend a designated percentage of DGR on player costs each season (the percentage has varied over time). In the first year of free agency in 1993, average salaries shot up to $650,000 from $488,000 in 1992. Thus, the cap, divided by the number of teams, immediately took effect for 1994, and has remained so since then, except for an uncapped year in 2010 that was the final year of the then collective agreement. As long as the cap is in effect, veteran free agents become unrestricted after four years of service instead of five. The end of this chapter reviews the bargaining dynamics that led the parties to negotiate this result.

NOTES AND QUESTIONS

1. *Allocation of Players.* Essentially the same questions posed earlier about the rookie draft can also be asked about the system that requires clubs who sign veteran free agents to compensate the players' former teams. Does this arrangement really contribute to stronger competition on the field, or does it inhibit the ability of weaker teams to catch up to their stronger rivals, or does it do some of both? What lessons can be drawn from baseball's experience before and after 1976, when free agency rights were given to six-year veterans? Or from comparing the level of competitiveness in baseball with that in football over the next fifteen years, with football experiencing a more restrictive scheme between 1977–94 and a less restrictive scheme (constrained by a salary cap) since then?

2. *Effect on Player Salaries.* Do limits on competition really produce unacceptable exploitation of players by the teams? Keep in mind that salaries paid by NFL clubs still soared over the same fifteen-year period. What is more important from either an economic or equity standpoint—the *average* or the *median* salary in a sport? The average player *salary* or the average club *payroll*? The proportion of either salary figure to average club *revenues*?

3. *Proving Less Restrictive Alternatives.* Who should bear the burden of proof as to whether a challenged player restraint is overbroad? Do you believe that the NFL could achieve a desired degree of competitive balance without the Plan B restraints challenged in *McNeil*? Would any plan you can conceive

of to promote competitive balance predictably survive a less restrictive alternative analysis?

As detailed in Chapter 5, MLS varies from the structure of most major North American sports leagues. In practice, the principal impact of this MLS variation from the NFL structure is felt in the players market. The league, not the individual clubs, employs and pays all players (but only the players) on each team. Players negotiate contracts and their salaries only with a department in the MLS office. Once MLS signs player contracts, it distributes the players among the clubs. The league does this first through a "rookie" draft, after which the team has the freedom to retain, release, or trade the player to another team, depending on how the investor-operator and his staff views the player's performance and the club's needs.

The asserted objective of this MLS structure for its players market is to avoid the fate of the North American Soccer League (NASL), in which "competition among teams . . . drove up acquisition costs of the players," thus generating "destructive, economically irrational spending" that eventually led to the dissolution of that league in the early 1980s. Complaint at 14, *Fraser v. Major League Soccer*, No. 97-10342 (D. Mass filed Feb. 13, 1997). Under MLS rules, each player must sign a Standard Player Agreement which gives the league the unilateral right to renew it for varying terms based on the player's age and length of contract after the negotiated contract term expires. Teams are limited to players whose total salary levels do not exceed the league's salary cap. The Standard Player Agreement assigns to the league the exclusive right to license on a group basis the player's name and image for merchandising purposes. In other leagues, player unions are largely financed by group licensing revenues.

FRASER V. MAJOR LEAGUE SOCCER
284 F.3d 47 (1st Cir. 2002)

BOUDIN, CHIEF JUDGE.

* * *

I. BACKGROUND FACTS

Despite professional soccer's popularity abroad, the sport has achieved only limited success in this country. Several minor leagues have operated here (four such leagues exist today), but before the formation of MLS, only one other U.S. professional league—the North American Soccer League ("NASL")—had ever obtained Division I, or top-tier, status. Launched in 1968, the NASL achieved some success before folding in 1985; MLS attributes the NASL's demise in part to wide disparities in the financial resources of the league's independently owned teams and a lack of centralized control.

* * *

At issue in this case is MLS's control over player employment. MLS has the "sole responsibility for negotiating and entering into agreements with, and for compensating, Players." In a nutshell, MLS recruits the players, negotiates their salaries, pays them from league funds, and, to a large extent, determines where each of them will play. For example, to balance talent among teams, it decides, with the non-binding input of team operators, where certain of the league's "marquee" players will play.

II. SHERMAN ACT SECTION 1

[As excerpted in Chapter 5, the appellate court reviewed the district court's summary dismissal of the plaintiffs' § 1 claim on the grounds that MLS was a single entity. It declined to definitively rule on the issue, affirming the dismissal on other grounds.]

... [E]ven if we assume that section 1 applies, it is clear to us that the venture cannot be condemned by *per se* rules and presents at best a debatable case under the rule of reason. More significantly, as structured by plaintiffs themselves, this case would have been lost at trial based on the jury's rejection of plaintiffs' own market definition.

* * *

The possibility that a less integrated and restrictive salary regime might make some individual salaries even higher is hardly conclusive. Without the restrictions, MLS might not exist or, if it did, might have larger initial losses and a shorter life. This would hardly enhance competition.... As in any other non-per se case, players would have to show that MLS exercised significant market power in a properly defined market, that the practices in question adversely affected competition in that market and that on balance the adverse effects on competition outweighed the competitive benefits.

Here, the jury said that neither the United States nor Division I delimited the relevant market—findings that imply that MLS faced significant competition for player services both from outside the United States and from non-Division I teams. That inference at a minimum creates uncertainty as to whether the jury could have found market power under section 1. However, the peculiar assemblage of evidence, including MLS-authored materials suggesting that it expected to exercise some control over player salaries, makes it impossible to rule out abstractly the possibility of a jury finding of MLS market power in a broader market.

[The court acknowledged that there theoretically "may be a broader market which plaintiffs might show (without contradicting the jury findings) in which unrestricted salary competition between the MLS operator/investors might result in somewhat higher player salaries." However, the court noted that the plaintiffs had alleged that the relevant market was "competition for Division I soccer players in the United States."]

Proof of such a market was the consistent theme of plaintiffs' *section 2* trial evidence. To be sure, had the *section 1* claim been put to trial, the plaintiffs could have sought to amend their complaint to allege a different market, but there is no obvious reason to think that they would have done so. The United States/Division I theory alleged in the complaint was the most favorable for each of their claims and the easiest to define; and the focus on a single market theory would have allowed the plaintiffs to focus their proof on a single market definition. Plaintiffs did have some incentive to allege a broader market under sections 1 and 7,[9] but that incentive existed when they filed their complaint as well.

* * *

We [ ] have every reason to think that if the *section 1* claim had not been dismissed on summary judgment it would have been presented at trial with the same market analysis alleged in the complaint. It follows that had the district court allowed the *section 1* claim, it too would have been defeated by the jury's finding that the market alleged in the complaint had not been proved. Accordingly, any error in dismissing the claim based on a single entity theory was harmless so long as the jury verdict stands. . . .

III. SHERMAN ACT SECTION 2

At trial, players alleged three possible violations of *section 2*: that MLS monopolized the market for Division I professional soccer in the U.S.; that it attempted to monopolize that market; and that it conspired with the [United States Soccer Federation] to monopolize the same market. The jury found that players had failed to establish the relevant market as alleged; it reached no other issue in the case. The court thereafter entered judgment for the defendants on all three section 2 claims.

[The court then proceeded to uphold the jury verdict on the section 2 claims by rejecting a plethora of arguments by the players claiming that the jury instructions were faulty and that evidence was either improperly allowed or excluded. It then concluded that the jury's finding was supported by substantial evidence.]

---

[9] Whereas section 2 requires monopoly power or a prospect of it, significant market power is enough to trigger section 1's rule of reason approach; similarly, something less than monopoly power is required to condemn mergers under section 7's "substantially lessen competition" test. *Columbia Metal Culvert Co. v. Kaiser Aluminum & Chem. Corp.*, 579 F.2d 20, 27 n.11 (3d Cir. 1978).

IV. CLAYTON ACT SECTION 7

In their final argument, players say that the district court erred in dismissing their claim that the formation of MLS violated section 7 of the Clayton Act. Count IV of the complaint alleged that, "[i]f not for this combination of assets and purchase of stock, MLS Member Teams would compete with each other for players, like teams in all other major professional sports leagues in the United States." Section 7 prohibits, with certain commerce-related conditions, stock or asset acquisitions whose effect "may be substantially to lessen competition, or to tend to create a monopoly." 15 U.S.C § 18.

The district court granted summary judgment to the defendants on the ground that "[t]here can be no § 7 liability because the formation of MLS did not involve the acquisition or merger of existing business enterprises, but rather the formation of an entirely new entity which itself represented the creation of an entirely new market." *Fraser*, 97 F. Supp. 2d at 140. . . .

* * *

It might be argued that [this ruling] present[s] issues that a jury ought to consider; but there is one final objection that the jury did effectively consider. Even advocates of a broader reading of section 7 concede that striking down a combination that does not threaten present competition could be justified, in the hope of obtaining more competition in the future, only in already concentrated markets. . . .

Thus, even on the broader reading of section 7 and allowing room for conjectures about future effects, it would have been necessary for players to prove that MLS operates within a relevant economic market that is presently concentrated. In their section 7 count, the players alleged the same relevant United States/Division I market as in their section 1 and section 2 counts. For reasons already discussed in connection with the section 1 claim, the jury's rejection of this relevant market would also have doomed the section 7 claim based on enhancing future competition if it too had been presented.

Affirmed.

NOTES AND QUESTIONS

1. *Market Power Under Different Antitrust Provisions.* The amount of market power that must be shown in order to establish a § 2 violation is more than that required to establish a § 1 or Clayton Act § 7 merger violation. Judge Boudin acknowledged as much in footnote 9 of *Fraser*. Given the jury's finding that the relevant market was worldwide, and its finding, implicit in its verdict for MLS on the § 2 claims, that MLS lacked monopoly market power and a

likelihood of ever acquiring it, did this result necessarily dispose of the § 1 and Clayton Act § 7 claims as well?

2. *Broader Implications.* What lesson does the *Fraser* decision hold for players in other start-up leagues who might want to challenge league player restraints under antitrust law? Would cases brought against those leagues by their players be likely to come out the same way, or are there material distinctions?

D. LABOR EXEMPTION FROM ANTITRUST

1. HISTORY AND BACKGROUND

When Major League Soccer and Arena Football League players began to consider how to improve their bargaining power, they initially decided not to form themselves into a labor union to engage in collective bargaining with their respective leagues. Instead, the players' initial strategy was to initiate collective antitrust litigation against the league. Arena League owners were so hostile to this tactic that they sought to force players to join a union, going so far as to threaten a lockout if the players did *not* organize! Arena league Commissioner David Baker and the team owners had publicly urged the players to form a labor union and to engage in collective bargaining, a management position that is now almost unheard-of in any other American industry. Simultaneously, a rival group of AFL players that many suspected were being supported by the league formed for the purpose of collecting enough players' signatures to force a union certification election. Thus, when the AFLPA filed its antitrust suit instead, the owners voted to cancel the upcoming 2000 season, as they had threatened to do. The initial players group then filed an unfair labor practices charge with the National Labor Relations Board (NLRB) claiming that the owners had violated § 8 (a)(1) of the NLRA by coercing players in the exercise of their right not to have a union. Before the NLRB could resolve the complaint, the parties settled on terms that disposed of the antitrust litigation and established a collective agreement between players and the league.

The likely explanation for this superficially bizarre management tactic is the subject of this section. The application of the antitrust laws to labor markets raises a number of important questions, concerning the extent to which antitrust policy should be subordinate to a separate federal labor laws designed to foster and protect labor organizations and collective bargaining. This question took on real urgency in the sports world in the 1970s, because almost all the important antitrust litigation about free agency restraints was either launched or backed by the player unions that had emerged by the late 1960s in all four major professional sports.

A fundamental tension exists between antitrust law, which bars any "contract, combination, or conspiracy in restraint of trade," and labor law, which facilitates collective action among employees in dealing with their employers. Indeed, for the first two decades of its existence, judges used the Sherman Act more often against trade unions than against business corporations. *See, e.g., Loewe v. Lawlor,* 208 U.S. 274 (1908) (applying the Sherman Act to unions and their national consumer boycott against a non-union hat manufacturer).

(a) The Statutory Exemption

Concerned about this threat to their very existence, let alone their effectiveness, unions belonging to the American Federation of Labor persuaded new Democratic President Woodrow Wilson (and his chief advisor on antitrust and labor issues, Louis Brandeis) to include in the 1914 Clayton Act amendments to the Sherman Act a new § 6 which declared:

> That the labor of a human being is not a commodity or article of commerce. Nothing contained in the anti-trust law shall be construed to forbid the existence and operation of labor ... organizations, instituted for the purposes of mutual help ... or to forbid or restrain individual members of such organizations from lawfully carrying out the legitimate objects thereof; nor shall such organizations, or the members thereof, be held or construed to be illegal combinations or conspiracies in restraint of trade, under the anti-trust laws.

Samuel Gompers, founder and president of the AFL, celebrated this new section as the "Magna Carta of labor!" To buttress its legal force, Clayton Act § 20 went on to state that in disputes between employers and employees about terms and conditions of employment, collective action undertaken by employees through strikes, picketing, and boycotts, should not "be considered or held to be violations of any law of the United States."

Despite the apparent breadth of this legislative directive, the Supreme Court held in *Duplex Printing Press Co. v. Deering*, 254 U.S. 443 (1921), that the Clayton Act protected unions and their members from antitrust liability and federal court injunctions only when the union members were pursuing the "normal and legitimate objects" of a union, not when they "engage in an actual combination or conspiracy in restraint of trade." In *Duplex*, the Court held that a secondary boycott of the only major non-union printing press manufacturer in the country was outside the scope of Clayton Act protection and therefore could be enjoined under § 1 of the Sherman Act. Dissenting, Justice Brandeis argued that the injunction granted by the majority deprived unions of forms of collective action that Congress had expressly sought to legalize. *Id.* at 486.

During the Great Depression and the New Deal of the 1930s, labor was in a political position to secure the protection it thought it had won two decades earlier. Labor's first victory was the Norris-LaGuardia Act of 1932 (drafted by *Professor* Felix Frankfurter). This Act clarified that regardless of whether a labor dispute went beyond the normal bounds of conflict between an employer and its immediate employees, federal courts could not enjoin strikes, pickets, and other forms of employee self-help. Although the language of the Norris-LaGuardia Act expressly barred only federal *injunctive* remedies in "labor disputes," nine years later *Justice* Felix Frankfurter authored the Supreme Court's decision in *United States v. Hutcheson*, 312 U.S. 219 (1941), involving a criminal antitrust prosecution, which read the Act as having tacitly overruled *Duplex* and restored the Clayton Act's intended protection of labor disputes from substantive antitrust liability:

> So long as a union acts in its self-interest and does not combine with non-labor groups, the licit and the illicit under Section 20 [of the Clayton Act] are not to be distinguished by any [judicial] judgment regarding the wisdom or unwisdom, the rightness or wrongness, the selfishness or unselfishness of the end of which the particular union activities are the means.

312 U.S. at 232.

Hutcheson's interpretation of the statutory exemption limited its scope by conditioning it on the union not combining with a "non-labor group," presumably because such a combination might be used to restrain a product market to benefit that group. Subsequent decisions applying the statutory exemption thus have asked whether a union had combined with a group that might be interested in such restraint, or whether the union only had acted with those who could affect the labor market it attempted to control. *See, e.g., H. A. Artists & Assoc. v. Actors' Equity Ass'n*, 451 US. 804 (1981) (theatrical agents, though independent contractors, are part of a labor group as they perform functions that outside of special context would be performed by the union).

(b) The "Non-Statutory" Labor Exemption

This construction of the statutory exemption did not cover collective bargaining agreements that unions sign with employers, however. Such agreements constitute a combination with a non-labor group. *Hutcheson* thus created an anomaly. It made little sense to allow a union to strike to get a collective bargaining agreement from the employer, but then to subject the agreement itself to antitrust liability. This result seems even more anomalous from the perspective of the 1935 National Labor Relations Act (NLRA). As discussed in Chapter 2, this law (1) created an affirmative right of employees to organize themselves into unions, (2) recognized the employees' chosen union as the *exclusive* bargaining agent for the employees, and then (3) imposed on the employer a duty to bargain in good faith with the union in an effort to reach a collective bargaining agreement.

In the 1947 Taft-Hartley amendments to the NLRA, the duty to bargain in good faith was also imposed on unions. Furthermore, both in practice and under the law, such bargaining is often conducted on a wide-ranging multi-employer basis. As a result, collective bargaining agreements often bind, either legally or practically, some individual workers and employers who do not necessarily favor its terms.

The Supreme Court thus recognized the need for a "nonstatutory" (*i.e.*, implicit or implied) labor exemption for collectively bargained agreements in some cases. It has not, however, granted collective bargaining agreements the same blanket antitrust exemption that it has extended to union concerted action short of agreements with non-labor groups. This is because the Court also has understood that unions and employers may find it in their mutual interest to agree upon restrictive practices that control markets other than the labor market. In three key decisions, *Allen Bradley Co. v. IBEW*, 325 U.S. 797 (1945), *United Mine Workers v. Pennington*, 381 U.S. 657 (1965), and *Connell Construction Co. v. Plumbers and Steamfitters*, 421 U.S. 616 (1975), the Supreme Court struggled to formulate a legal test to be applied when the antitrust legality of a collective agreement is challenged. In all three cases, the Court held the nonstatutory exemption inapplicable, and allowed the antitrust claim to proceed.

In each, the Court found that the alleged restraint had a significant effect in the employers' product market, and that the plaintiffs were business competitors of the employers who were not members of the multiemployer unit that had signed the collective bargaining agreement. For example, in *Pennington* the United Mine Workers had not only agreed with large mining companies to specified wages, hours, and working condition for the large companies' workers, but had promised that they would not agree to lower wages with smaller mining rivals.

A divided Court reached a different result in a case decided the same day as *Pennington*, *Local Union No. 189, Amalgamated Meat Cutters v. Jewel Tea Co.*, 381 U.S. 676 (1965), shielding from antitrust scrutiny provisions in a collective agreement that restricted a product market. Jewel Tea challenged a collective bargaining agreement arising out of multi-employment bargaining in which it had participated, along with myriad other employers of butchers, with the Meat Cutters Union. The union had insisted on inserting in its collective agreement with the Chicago grocery stores a provision that barred the sale of fresh meat at nighttime, in order to protect the unionized butchers from employer pressures to work in the evenings, and to protect the jobs of butchers working for small stores that did not stay open in the evening (in contrast with the Jewel supermarkets). A divided Supreme Court held that this contract term was protected from antitrust challenge by the labor exemption.

Three justices, in an opinion by Justice Douglas, would have found the bargain to be illegal under the antitrust laws, holding that antitrust concerns always trumped labor concerns. Three justices, in an opinion by Justice Goldberg, would have found any agreement between union and management on terms about which the parties were required to bargain under the NLRA always to be exempt from antitrust scrutiny. (Justice Goldberg, formerly counsel to the Steelworkers' Union and President Kennedy's Secretary of Labor, detailed the historical use of antitrust laws to harm unions and workers.) Justice White's decisive opinion (for himself and two other Justices) took a middle ground. This oft-cited passage explains the plurality's view on the scope of the exemption:

> Thus the issue in this case is whether the marketing-hours restriction, like wages, and unlike prices, is so intimately related to wages, hours and working conditions [mandatory subjects of collective bargaining under the NLRA] that the union's successful attempt to obtain that provision through bona fide, arms' length bargaining in pursuit of their own labor union policies, and not at the behest of or in combination with non-labor groups, falls within the protection of the National Labor Policy and is therefore exempt from the Sherman Act.

381 U.S. at 689–90.

This same scenario has also arisen in the sports context, when the operation of a collectively bargained lifetime reserve clause denies a new league access to the available supply of top-flight athletes whom the new league needs to survive as a serious competitor to the established league (*see Philadelphia World Hockey Club v. Philadelphia Hockey Club*, 351 F. Supp. 462 (E.D. Pa. 1972)). As discussed in Chapter 5, the court found that the agreement unlawfully monopolized major league professional hockey in violation of § 2 of the Sherman Act. Before reaching the merits, however, Judge Leon Higgenbotham first held that the labor exemption was not applicable. His review of the cases discussed above led him to conclude that "those cases all involved situations where the union had been sued for its active, conspiratorial role in restraining competition of a product market, and the union, not the employer, sought to invoke the labor exemptions." *Id.* at 498. Moreover, "the cases cited above pertained to issues which furthered the interests of the union members and on which there had been extensive collective bargaining. *Id.* at 498–99. Finally:

> even if, arguendo, there had been substantial arm's-length collective bargaining by the National Hockey League and the Players' Association to revise the perpetual option provision of the reserve clause, those negotiations would not shield the National Hockey League from liability in a suit by outside competitors who

sought access to players under the control of the National Hockey League.

* * *

I reject the argument that an employer (National Hockey League) can conspire with or take advantage of a union to restrain competition and seriously impair the business dealings and transactions of competitors. To grant the National Hockey League an exemption in this proceeding would undermine and thwart the policies which have evolved over the years in disposing of labor-management and anti-trust disputes. I cannot compatibly reconcile the National Hockey League's monopolistic actions here with the labor exemptions from the Sherman Act. The NHL can do no more than could the employers and union in *Allen Bradley, supra*. Even if the National Hockey League was primarily concerned about the welfare of its players, its purported good intentions would be insufficient to insulate its actions. . . .

351 F. Supp. at 500.

2. JUDICIAL OPTIONS FOR THE NONSTATUTORY LABOR EXEMPTION

With respect to situations involving collective employer restraints whose direct impact is felt only inside, not also outside, the employment relationship, the following alternative formulations of the nonstatutory labor exemption have each been advanced by at least one judge or scholar.

Option 1: There should be no non-statutory exemption from antitrust at all—unions and employers should have no right to do through their agreement what would otherwise be illegal by statute.

Option 2: There should be exemption only for provisions that have been inserted in the agreement at the behest of the union for the benefit of the employees—the historic purpose of the labor exemption is to help workers, not employers.

Option 3: The exemption should protect all, but only, the terms within an existing collective agreement—the essential condition for relief from antitrust must be actual consent to the practice by the employees through their union.

Option 4: The exemption should protect all employment practices that exist in an employee unit represented by a union—since the employees now have the right under labor law to force the employer to negotiate about the practice, they should not also enjoy the right to litigate about the practice under antitrust law.

Option 5: There should be no antitrust liability at all for restraints in employment—as § 6 of the Clayton Act stated, "the labor of a human being is not a commodity or article of commerce" for purposes of antitrust law.

Consider the pros and cons of these options as we trace the history of the labor exemption in sports until its final resolution by the Supreme Court.

3. INITIAL DEVELOPMENT OF THE DOCTRINE IN THE LOWER COURTS

(a) The Outer Limits of the Exemption: It Exists but Does Not Protect All Labor-Market Restraints

In *Mackey v. NFL*, 543 F.2d 606 (8th Cir. 1976), whose factual underpinnings and substantive antitrust treatment were presented earlier in this chapter in Section C, Part 2, the Eighth Circuit rejected Options 1 and 5. The NFL relied on the text of Clayton Act § 6—"[t]he labor of a human being is not a commodity or article of commerce"—to argue that labor restraints are beyond the scope of the antitrust laws.

The Eighth Circuit rejected the NFL's argument:

> On the surface, the language relied on by defendants lends merit to the defense. However, we cannot overlook the context in which the language arose. Section 6 of the Clayton Act was enacted for the benefit of unions to exempt certain of their activities from the antitrust laws after courts had applied the Sherman Act to legitimate labor activities. . . .
>
> In other cases concerning professional sports, courts have not hesitated to apply the Sherman Act to club owner imposed restraints on competition for players' services. . . . In other contexts, courts have subjected similar employer imposed restraints to the scrutiny of the antitrust laws. We hold that restraints on competition within the market for players' services fall within the ambit of the Sherman Act.

543 F.2d at 617–18.

At the other extreme, the Eighth Circuit also rejected the players' attempt to narrow *Jewel Tea* to lawsuits where the union was a defendant:

> We must disagree. Since the basis of the nonstatutory exemption is the national policy favoring collective bargaining, and since the exemption extends to agreements, the benefits of the exemption logically extend to both parties to the agreement. Accordingly, under appropriate circumstances, we find that a non-labor group may avail itself of the labor exemption.

Id. at 612.

The court ultimately rejected the application of the labor exemption to the challenged Rozelle Rule based on its own reading of *Jewel Tea* that required the challenged position to be "the product of bona fide arm's-length bargaining." *Id.* at 614. This test was rejected by the Supreme Court in *Brown v. Pro Football, Inc.,* 518 U.S. 231 (1996), discussed below.

(b) Application to Restraints Agreed to by the Union but Sought by Management

During the late 1970s, nascent player unions agreed to collective bargains that marginally improved wages, hours, and working conditions for players but incorporated highly restrictive rules regarding competition for player services. Individuals challenging these rules offered Option 2 above: that the labor exemption should only, as in *Jewel Tea,* protect anti-competitive agreements inserted in a collective bargaining agreement at the behest of workers. In *McCourt v. California Sports, Inc.,* 600 F.2d 1193 (6th Cir. 1979), the Sixth Circuit rejected this argument. The court found the non-statutory labor exemption protected the system embedded in NHL By-law 9A, incorporated in the 1976 collective agreement with the NHLPA, that required that an "equalization payment" similar to the Rozelle Rule at issue in *Mackey,* although the determination was to be made by a neutral arbitrator, rather than the commissioner. The district court had held that the challenged provision had not been negotiated in *bona fide,* arms-length bargaining. On appeal, the Sixth Circuit reversed.

> Contrary to the trial judge's conclusion, the very facts relied upon by him in his opinion illustrate a classic case of collective bargaining in which the reserve system was a central issue. It is apparent from those very findings that the NHLPA used every form of negotiating pressure it could muster. It developed an alternate reserve system and secured tentative agreement from the owner and player representatives, only to have the proposal rejected by the players. It refused to attend a proposed meeting with the owners to discuss the reserve system further. It threatened to strike. It threatened to commence an antitrust suit and to recommend that the players not attend training camp.
>
> For its part, the NHL, while not budging in its insistence upon By-Law Section 9A, at least in the absence of any satisfactory counter proposal by the players, yielded significantly on other issues. . . .
>
> . . .
>
> From the express findings of the trial court, fully supported by the record, it is apparent that the inclusion of the reserve system in the collective bargaining agreement was the product of

good faith, arm's-length bargaining, and that what the trial court saw as a failure to negotiate was in fact simply a failure to succeed, after the most intensive negotiations, in keeping an unwanted provision out of the contract. This failure was a part of and not apart from the collective bargaining process, a process which achieved its ultimate objective of an agreement accepted by the parties.

600 F.2d at 1202–03.

The Second Circuit in *Wood v. NBA*, 809 F.2d 954 (2d Cir. 1987), further articulated the rationale for why anticompetitive labor market terms should be exempt if included in a collective bargaining agreement, even if the term was not sought by workers. The NBA's collective bargain with its players contained a salary cap: a negotiated maximum (and a minimum) salary budget that can be spent by any team in signing new players—whether veteran free agents from other teams or rookie draft selections. Any team that was over the salary cap was permitted to offer a new player just the minimum $75,000 salary in a one-year contract.

Leon Wood was the 1984 first-round draft pick of the Philadelphia 76ers (who were then over the cap). Thus, Wood filed an antitrust suit against this feature of the cap. The trial judge dismissed the suit on the basis of the labor exemption, and the Second Circuit affirmed. Judge Ralph Winter emphasized the fundamental principle of federal labor policy (in § 9(a) of the NLRA) that "employees may eliminate competition among themselves through a governmentally supervised majority vote selecting an exclusive bargaining representative."

> Federal labor policy thus allows employees to seek the best deal for the greatest number by the exercise of collective rather than individual bargaining power. Once an exclusive representative has been selected, the individual employee is forbidden by federal law from negotiating directly with the employer absent the representative's consent, *NLRB v. Allis-Chalmers Mfg. Co.*, 388 U.S. 175, 180 (1967), even though that employee may actually receive less compensation under the collective bargain than he or she would through individual negotiations. *J.I. Case Co. v. NLRB,* 321 U.S. 332, 338–39 (1944).
>
> The gravamen of Wood's complaint, namely that the NBA-NBPA collective agreement is illegal because it prevents him from achieving his full free market value, is therefore at odds with, and destructive of, federal labor policy. It is true that the diversity of talent and specialization among professional athletes and the widespread exposure and discussions of their "work" in the media make the differences in value among them as "workers" more visible than the differences in efficiency and in value among

industrial workers. High public visibility, however, is no reason to ignore federal legislation that explicitly prevents employees, whether in or out of a bargaining unit, from seeking a better deal where that deal is inconsistent with the terms of a collective agreement.

809 F.2d at 959. Wood's counsel objected to the fact that this new basketball system assigned new players coming into the league to work for particular clubs they might not like, for salaries that were set at artificially low levels. Judge Winter pointed out that this collectively-bargained regime, while it might generate lower salaries for some players than their individual talent seemed to justify, had many analogies in the wage systems, hiring halls, seniority clauses, bars on outside contracts, and other standard fare in labor agreements.

> ... Wood's assertion that he would be paid more in the absence of the draft and salary cap also implies that others would receive less if he were successful. It can hardly be denied that the NBA teams would be more resistant to benefits guaranteed to all, such as pensions, minimum salaries, and medical and insurance benefits. In fact, the salary cap challenged by Wood is one part of a complex formula including minimum team salaries and guaranteed revenue sharing.

809 F.2d at 961. Finally, Judge Winter emphasized the incompatibility of Wood's antitrust position with that feature of national labor policy that "attaches prime importance to freedom of contract between the parties to a collective agreement."

> Freedom of contract is an important cornerstone of national labor policy for two reasons. First, it allows an employer and a union to agree upon those arrangements that best suit their particular interests. Courts cannot hope to fashion contract terms more efficient than those arrived at by the parties who are to be governed by them. Second, freedom of contract furthers the goal of labor peace. To the extent that courts prohibit particular solutions for particular problems, they reduce the number and quality of compromises available to unions and employers for resolving their differences.
>
> Freedom of contract is particularly important in the context of collective bargaining between professional athletes and their leagues. Such bargaining relationships raise numerous problems with little or no precedent in standard industrial relations. As a result, leagues and player unions may reach seemingly unfamiliar or strange agreements. If courts were to intrude and to outlaw such solutions, leagues and their player unions would have to arrange their affairs in a less efficient way. It would also increase

the chances of strikes by reducing the number and quality of possible compromises.

The issues of free agency and entry draft are at the center of collective bargaining in much of the professional sports industry. It is to be expected that the parties will arrive at unique solutions to these problems in the different sports both because sports generally differ from the industrial model and because each sport has its own peculiar economic imperatives. The NBA/NBPA agreement is just such a unique bundle of compromises. The draft and the salary cap reflect the interests of the employers in stabilizing salary costs and spreading talent among the various teams. Minimum individual salaries, fringe benefits, minimum aggregate team salaries, and guaranteed revenue sharing reflect the interests of the union in enhancing standard benefits applicable to all players. The free agency/first refusal provisions in turn allow individual players to exercise a degree of individual bargaining power. Were a court to intervene and strike down the draft and salary cap, the entire agreement would unravel. This would force the NBA and NBPA to search for other avenues of compromise that would be less satisfactory to them than the agreement struck down. It would also measurably increase the chances of a strike. We decline to take that step.

809 F.2d at 961–62.

4. THE SUPREME COURT SPEAKS

In 1989, NFL owners agreed to establish six-player developmental squads for each team at a league-mandated salary level of $1,000 a week. These squads were to be made up of first or second year players who had not made the regular 47-man roster, but whose teams wanted to keep them for practices and possible replacement of injured or poorly-performing regulars. The system was designed to eliminate the practice of teams "stashing" players who had not made the regular roster on their injured reserve list. This league initiative was not the subject of collective bargaining (let alone agreement) prior to 1989. The NFLPA applauded the creation of these squads, but insisted that developmental players' salaries be individually negotiated in the same manner as regular players' salaries. The Association filed an antitrust suit when the NFL proceeded to implement its fixed salary scale of $1,000 per week, which was not just a cap, but a huge cut in the average salary paid to this category of player (*i.e.*, to new players previously "stashed" on injured reserve), a figure that dropped from as much as $60,000 per year in 1988 to $16,000 in 1989.

In *Brown v. Pro-Football, Inc.*, 782 F. Supp. 125 (D.D.C. 1991), the district court rejected the NFL's labor exemption defense to this action, concluding that the labor exemption expired immediately upon expiration of a collective bargaining agreement (in effect Option 3 above). At trial, the jury found this salary arrangement violated the Sherman Act and awarded $10 million in damages, which was trebled to a $30 million award plus legal costs. On appeal, a divided panel of the D.C. Circuit reversed, 50 F.3d 1041 (D.C. Cir. 1995). The majority opinion held that the non-statutory labor exemption protected a league from all antitrust suits brought by or on behalf of their players' union with respect to conduct engaged in during the collective bargaining process, as long as the bargaining relationship with the union exists. NFL sought certiorari, which the Supreme Court granted.

BROWN V. PRO FOOTBALL, INC.
518 U.S. 231 (1996)

JUSTICE BREYER delivered the opinion of the Court.

[The court began by framing the specific question posed by this case as whether "club owners who had bargained to an impasse with the players union about a wage issue, and had then agreed among themselves (but not with the union) to implement the terms of their own last best bargaining offer" should have their agreement shielded by federal labor laws from antitrust attack. After sketching the history of the "implicit ('nonstatutory')" labor exemption, Justice Breyer stated that its point was to limit] . . . an antitrust court's authority to determine, in the area of industrial conflict, what is or is not a "reasonable" practice. It thereby substitutes legislative and administrative labor-related determinations for judicial antitrust-related determinations as to the appropriate legal limits of industrial conflict.

As a matter of logic, it would be difficult, if not impossible, to require groups of employers and employees to bargain together, but at the same time to forbid them to make among themselves or with each other any of the competition-restricting agreements potentially necessary to make the process work or its results mutually acceptable. Thus, the implicit exemption recognizes that, to give effect to federal labor laws and policies and to allow meaningful collective bargaining to take place, some restraints on competition imposed through the bargaining process must be shielded from antitrust sanctions. . . .

The petitioners and their supporters concede, as they must, the legal existence of the exemption we have described. They also concede that, where its application is necessary to make the statutorily authorized collective-bargaining process work as Congress intended, the exemption must apply both to employers and to employees. Nor does the dissent take issue with these basic principles. Consequently, the question before us is one of determining the exemption's scope: Does it apply to an agreement among several employers bargaining together to implement after impasse the terms of their last best good-faith wage offer? We assume that such conduct, as practiced in this case, is unobjectionable as a matter of labor law and policy. On that assumption, we conclude that the exemption applies.

Labor law itself regulates directly, and considerably, the kind of behavior here at issue—the post-impasse imposition of a proposed employment term concerning a mandatory subject of bargaining. Both the [National Labor Relations] Board and the courts have held that, after impasse, labor law permits employers unilaterally to implement changes in preexisting conditions, but only insofar as the new terms meet carefully circumscribed conditions. For example, the new terms must be "reasonably comprehended" within the employer's pre-impasse proposals (typically the last rejected proposals), lest by imposing more or less favorable terms, the employer unfairly undermined the union's status. The collective-bargaining proceeding itself must be free of any unfair labor practice, such as an employer's failure to have bargained in good faith. These regulations reflect the fact that impasse and an accompanying implementation of proposals constitute an integral part of the bargaining process.

Although the caselaw we have cited focuses upon bargaining by a single employer, no one here has argued that labor law does, or should, treat multiemployer bargaining differently in this respect. Indeed, Board and court decisions suggest that the joint implementation of proposed terms after impasse is a familiar practice in the context of multiemployer bargaining. We proceed on that assumption.

Multiemployer bargaining itself is a well-established, important, pervasive method of collective bargaining, offering advantages to both management and labor. *See* Appendix (multiemployer bargaining accounts for more than 40% of major collective-bargaining agreements, and is used in such industries as construction, transportation, retail trade, clothing manufacture, and real estate, as well as professional sports); *NLRB v. Truck Drivers*, 353 U.S. 87, 95 (1957) (*Buffalo Linen*) (Congress saw multiemployer bargaining as "a vital factor in the effectuation of the national policy of promoting labor peace through strengthened collective bargaining"); *Charles D. Bonanno Linen Service, Inc. v. NLRB*, 454 U.S. 404, 409 n.3 (1982) (*Bonanno Linen*) (multiemployer bargaining benefits both management and labor, by saving bargaining resources, by encouraging development of industry-wide worker benefits programs that smaller employers could not otherwise afford, and by inhibiting employer competition at the workers' expense). The upshot is that the practice at issue here plays a significant role in a collective-bargaining process that itself comprises an important part of the Nation's industrial relations system.

In these circumstances, to subject the practice to antitrust law is to require antitrust courts to answer a host of important practical questions about how collective bargaining over wages, hours and working conditions is to proceed—the very result that the implicit labor exemption seeks to avoid. And it is to place in jeopardy some of the potentially beneficial labor-related effects that multiemployer bargaining can achieve. That is because unlike labor law, which sometimes welcomes anticompetitive agreements conducive to industrial harmony, antitrust law forbids all agreements among competitors (such as competing employers) that unreasonably lessen competition among or between them in virtually any respect whatsoever. *See, e.g., Paramount Famous Lasky Corp. v. United States*, 282 U.S. 30 (1930) (agreement to insert arbitration provisions in motion picture licensing contracts). Antitrust law also sometimes permits judges or juries to premise antitrust liability upon little more than uniform behavior among competitors, preceded by conversations implying that later uniformity might prove desirable, *see, e.g., United States v. General Motors Corp.*, 384 U.S. 127, 142–143 (1966), or accompanied by other conduct that in context suggests that each competitor failed to make an independent decision, *see, e.g., American Tobacco Co. v. United States*, 328 U.S. 781, 809–810 (1946).

If the antitrust laws apply, what are employers to do once impasse is reached? If all impose terms similar to their last joint offer, they invite an antitrust action premised upon identical behavior (along with prior or accompanying conversations) as tending to show a common understanding or agreement. If any, or all, of them individually impose terms that differ significantly from that offer, they invite an unfair labor practice charge. Indeed, how can employers safely discuss their offers together even before a bargaining impasse occurs? A pre-impasse discussion about, say, the practical advantages or disadvantages of a particular proposal, invites a later antitrust claim that they agreed to limit the kinds of action each would later take should an impasse occur. The same is true of post-impasse discussions aimed at renewed negotiations with the union. Nor would adherence to the terms of an expired collective-bargaining agreement eliminate a potentially plausible antitrust claim charging that they had "conspired" or tacitly "agreed" to do so, particularly if maintaining the status quo were not in the immediate economic self-interest of some. All this is to say that to permit antitrust liability here threatens to introduce instability and uncertainty into the collective-bargaining process, for antitrust law often forbids or discourages the kinds of joint discussions and behavior that the collective-bargaining process invites or requires.

We do not see any obvious answer to this problem. We recognize, as the Government suggests, that, in principle, antitrust courts might themselves try to evaluate particular kinds of employer understandings, finding them "reasonable" (hence lawful) where justified by collective-bargaining necessity. But any such evaluation means a web of detailed rules spun by many different nonexpert antitrust judges and juries, not a set of labor rules enforced by a single expert administrative body, namely the Labor Board. The labor laws give the Board, not antitrust courts, primary responsibility for policing the collective-bargaining process. And one of their objectives was to take from antitrust courts the authority to determine, through application of the antitrust laws, what is socially or economically desirable collective-bargaining policy. . . . ; *see also Jewel Tea*, 381 U.S. at 716–719 (opinion of Goldberg, J.).

III

Both petitioners and their supporters advance several suggestions for drawing the exemption boundary line short of this case. We shall explain why we find them unsatisfactory.

A

Petitioners claim that the implicit exemption applies only to labor-management agreements—a limitation that they deduce from caselaw language, *see, e.g., Connell*, 421 U.S. at 622 (exemption for "some union-employer agreements"), and from a proposed principle—that the exemption must rest upon labor-management consent. The language, however, reflects only the fact that the cases previously before the Court involved collective-bargaining agreements; the language does not reflect the exemption's rationale.

Nor do we see how an exemption limited by petitioners' principle of labor-management consent could work. One cannot mean the principle literally—that the exemption applies only to understandings embodied in a collective-bargaining agreement—for the collective-bargaining process may take place before the making of any agreement or after an agreement has expired. Yet a multiemployer bargaining process itself necessarily involves many procedural and substantive understandings among participating employers as well as with the union. Petitioners cannot rescue their principle by claiming that the exemption applies only insofar as both labor and management consent to those understandings. Often labor will not (and should not) consent to certain common bargaining positions that employers intend to maintain. Similarly, labor need not consent to certain tactics that this Court has approved as part of the multiemployer bargaining process, such as unit-wide lockouts and the use of temporary replacements. *See NLRB v. Brown*, 380 U.S. 278, 284 (1965); *Buffalo Linen*, 353 U.S. at 97.

Petitioners cannot save their consent principle by weakening it, as by requiring union consent only to the multiemployer bargaining process itself. This general consent is automatically present whenever multiemployer bargaining takes place. *See Hi-Way Billboards, Inc.*, 206 N.L.R.B. 22 (1973) (multiemployer unit "based on consent" and "established by an unequivocal agreement by the parties"), *enf. denied on other grounds*, 500 F.2d 181 (5th Cir. 1974); *Weyerhaeuser Co.*, 166 N.L.R.B. 299, 299–300 (1967). As so weakened, the principle cannot help decide which related practices are, or are not, subject to antitrust immunity.

B

The Solicitor General argues that the exemption should terminate at the point of impasse. After impasse, he says, "employers no longer have a duty under the labor laws to maintain the status quo," and "are free as a matter of labor law to negotiate individual arrangements on an interim basis with the union."

Employers, however, are not completely free at impasse to act independently. The multiemployer bargaining unit ordinarily remains intact; individual employers cannot withdraw. The duty to bargain survives; employers must stand ready to resume collective bargaining. And individual employers can negotiate individual interim agreements with the union only insofar as those agreements are consistent with "the duty to abide by the results of group bargaining." Regardless, the absence of a legal "duty" to act jointly is not determinative. This Court has implied antitrust immunities that extend beyond statutorily required joint action to joint action that a statute "expressly or impliedly allows or assumes must also be immune."

More importantly, the simple "impasse" line would not solve the basic problem we have described above. Labor law permits employers, after impasse, to engage in considerable joint behavior, including joint lockouts and replacement hiring. *See, e.g., Brown*, supra, at 289 (hiring of temporary replacement workers after lockout was "reasonably adapted to the achievement of a legitimate end—preserving the integrity of the multiemployer bargaining unit"). Indeed, as a general matter, labor law often limits employers to four options at impasse: (1) maintain the status quo, (2) implement their last offer, (3) lock out their workers (and either shut down or hire temporary replacements), or (4) negotiate separate interim agreements with the union. What is to happen if the parties cannot reach an interim agreement? The other alternatives are limited. Uniform employer conduct is likely. Uniformity—at least when accompanied by discussion of the matter—invites antitrust attack. And such attack would ask antitrust courts to decide the lawfulness of activities intimately related to the bargaining process.

The problem is aggravated by the fact that "impasse" is often temporary; it may differ from bargaining only in degree; it may be manipulated by the parties for bargaining purposes; and it may occur several times during the course of a single labor dispute, since the bargaining process is not over when the first impasse is reached. How are employers to discuss future bargaining positions during a temporary impasse? Consider, too, the adverse consequences that flow from failing to guess how an antitrust court would later draw the impasse line. Employers who erroneously concluded that impasse had not been reached would risk antitrust liability were they collectively to maintain the status quo, while employers who erroneously concluded that impasse had occurred would risk unfair labor practice charges for prematurely suspending multiemployer negotiations.

The Solicitor General responds with suggestions for softening an "impasse" rule by extending the exemption after impasse "for such time as would be reasonable in the circumstances" for employers to consult with counsel, confirm that impasse has occurred, and adjust their business operations; by reestablishing the exemption once there is a "resumption of good-faith bargaining"; and by looking to antitrust law's "rule of reason" to shield—"in some circumstances"—such joint actions as the unit-wide lockout or the concerted maintenance of previously-established joint benefit or retirement plans. But even as so modified, the impasse-related rule creates an exemption that can evaporate in the middle of the bargaining process, leaving later antitrust courts free to second-guess the parties' bargaining decisions and consequently forcing them to choose their collective-bargaining responses in light of what they predict or fear that antitrust courts, not labor law administrators, will eventually decide.

C

Petitioners and their supporters argue in the alternative for a rule that would exempt post-impasse agreement about bargaining "tactics," but not post-impasse agreement about substantive "terms," from the reach of antitrust. They recognize, however, that both the Board and the courts have said that employers can, and often do, employ the imposition of "terms" as a bargaining "tactic." *See, e.g., American Ship Building Co. v. NLRB*, 380 U.S. 300, 316 (1965). This concession as to joint "tactical" implementation would turn the presence of an antitrust exemption upon a determination of the employers' primary purpose or motive. But to ask antitrust courts, insulated from the bargaining process, to investigate an employer group's subjective motive is to ask them to conduct an inquiry often more amorphous than those we have previously discussed. And, in our view, a labor/antitrust line drawn on such a basis would too often raise the same related (previously discussed) problems. *See Jewel Tea*, 381 U.S. at 716 (opinion of Goldberg, J.) (expressing concern about antitrust judges "roaming at large" through the bargaining process).

D

The petitioners make several other arguments. They point, for example, to cases holding applicable, in collective-bargaining contexts, general "backdrop" statutes, such as a state statute requiring a plant-closing employer to make employee severance payments, *Fort Halifax*

Packing Co. v. Coyne, 482 U.S. 1 (1987), and a state statute mandating certain minimum health benefits, *Metropolitan Life Ins. Co. v. Massachusetts*, 471 U.S. 724 (1985). Those statutes, however, " 'neither encouraged nor discouraged the collective-bargaining processes that are the subject of the [federal labor laws].' " *Fort Halifax*, supra, at 21 (quoting *Metropolitan Life*, supra, at 755). Neither did those statutes come accompanied with antitrust's labor-related history.

Petitioners also say that irrespective of how the labor exemption applies elsewhere to multiemployer collective bargaining, professional sports is "special." We can understand how professional sports may be special in terms of, say, interest, excitement, or concern. But we do not understand how they are special in respect to labor law's antitrust exemption. We concede that the clubs that make up a professional sports league are not completely independent economic competitors, as they depend upon a degree of cooperation for economic survival. *National Collegiate Athletic Assn. v. Board of Regents of Univ. of Okla.*, 468 U.S. 85, 101–102 (1984). In the present context, however, that circumstance makes the league more like a single bargaining employer, which analogy seems irrelevant to the legal issue before us.

We also concede that football players often have special individual talents, and, unlike many unionized workers, they often negotiate their pay individually with their employers. But this characteristic seems simply a feature, like so many others, that might give employees (or employers) more (or less) bargaining power, that might lead some (or all) of them to favor a particular kind of bargaining, or that might lead to certain demands at the bargaining table. We do not see how it could make a critical legal difference in determining the underlying framework in which bargaining is to take place. *See generally* Jacobs & Winter, *Antitrust Principles and Collective Bargaining by Athletes: Of Superstars in Peonage*, 81 Yale L.J. 1 (1971). Indeed, it would be odd to fashion an antitrust exemption that gave additional advantages to professional football players (by virtue of their superior bargaining power) that transport workers, coal miners, or meat packers would not enjoy.

. . . Ultimately, we cannot find a satisfactory basis for distinguishing football players from other organized workers. We therefore conclude that all must abide by the same legal rules.

* * *

For these reasons, we hold that the implicit ("nonstatutory") antitrust exemption applies to the employer conduct at issue here. That conduct took place during and immediately after a collective-bargaining negotiation. It grew out of, and was directly related to, the lawful operation of the bargaining process. It involved a matter that the parties were required to negotiate collectively. And it concerned only the parties to the collective-bargaining relationship.

Our holding is not intended to insulate from antitrust review every joint imposition of terms by employers, for an agreement among employers could be sufficiently distant in time and in circumstances from the collective-bargaining process that a rule permitting antitrust intervention would not significantly interfere with that process. *See, e.g.*, 50 F.3d at 1057 (suggesting that exemption lasts until collapse of the collective-bargaining relationship, as evidenced by decertification of the union); *El Cerrito Mill & Lumber Co.*, 316 N.L.R.B. at 1006–1007 (suggesting that "extremely long" impasse, accompanied by "instability" or "defunctness" of multiemployer unit, might justify union withdrawal from group bargaining). We need not decide in this case whether, or where, within these extreme outer boundaries to draw that line. Nor would it be appropriate for us to do so without the detailed views of the Board, to whose "specialized judgment" Congress "intended to leave" many of the "inevitable questions concerning multiemployer bargaining bound to arise in the future."

The judgment of the Court of Appeals is affirmed.

JUSTICE STEVENS, dissenting.

In his classic dissent in *Lochner v. New York*, 198 U.S. 45, 75 (1905), Justice Holmes reminded us that our disagreement with the economic theory embodied in legislation should not affect our judgment about its constitutionality. It is equally important, of course, to be faithful to the economic theory underlying broad statutory mandates when we are construing their impact on areas of the economy not specifically addressed by their texts. The unique features of this case lead me to conclude that the Court has reached a decision that conflicts with the basic purpose of both the antitrust laws and the national labor policy expressed in a series of congressional enactments.

I

The basic premise underlying the Sherman Act is the assumption that free competition among business entities will produce the best price levels. *National Soc. of Professional Engineers v. United States*, 435 U.S. 679, 695 (1978). Collusion among competitors, it is believed, may produce prices that harm consumers. *United States v. Socony-Vacuum Oil Co.*, 310 U.S. 150, 226, n. 59 (1940). Similarly, the Court has held, a market-wide agreement among employers setting wages at levels that would not prevail in a free market may violate the Sherman Act. *Anderson v. Shipowners' Assn. of Pacific Coast*, 272 U.S. 359 (1926).

The jury's verdict in this case has determined that the market-wide agreement among these employers fixed the salaries of the replacement players at a dramatically lower level than would obtain in a free market. While the special characteristics of this industry may provide a justification for the agreement under the rule of reason, *see National Collegiate Athletic Assn. v. Board of Regents of Univ. of Okla.*, 468 U.S. 85, 100–104 (1984), at this stage of the proceeding our analysis of the exemption issue must accept the premise that the agreement is unlawful unless it is exempt.

The basic premise underlying our national labor policy is that unregulated competition among employees and applicants for employment produces wage levels that are lower than they should be. Whether or not the premise is true in fact, it is surely the basis for the statutes that encourage and protect the collective-bargaining process, including the express statutory exemptions from the antitrust laws that Congress enacted in order to protect union activities. Those statutes were enacted to enable collective action by union members to achieve wage levels that are higher than would be available in a free market.

The statutory labor exemption protects the right of workers to act collectively to seek better wages, but does not "exempt concerted action or agreements between unions and nonlabor parties." *Connell Constr. Co. v. Plumbers*, 421 U.S. 616, 621–622 (1975). It is the judicially crafted, nonstatutory labor exemption that serves to accommodate the conflicting policies of the antitrust and labor statutes in the context of action between employers and unions.

The limited judicial exemption complements its statutory counterpart by ensuring that unions which engage in collective bargaining to enhance employees' wages may enjoy the benefits of the resulting agreements. The purpose of the labor laws would be frustrated if it were illegal for employers to enter into industry-wide agreements providing supracompetitive wages for employees. For that reason, we have explained that "a proper accommodation between the congressional policy favoring collective bargaining under the NLRA and the congressional policy favoring free competition in business markets requires that some union-employer agreements be accorded a limited nonstatutory exemption from antitrust sanctions."

Consistent with basic labor law policies, I agree with the Court that the judicially crafted labor exemption must also cover some collective action that employers take in response to a collective bargaining agent's demands for higher wages. Immunizing such action from antitrust scrutiny may facilitate collective bargaining over labor demands. So, too, may immunizing concerted employer action designed to maintain the integrity of the multi-employer bargaining unit, such as lockouts that are imposed in response to "a union strike tactic which threatens the destruction of the employers' interest in bargaining on a group basis." *NLRB v. Truck Drivers*, 353 U.S. 87 (1957).

In my view, however, neither the policies underlying the two separate statutory schemes, nor the narrower focus on the purpose of the nonstatutory exemption, provides a justification for exempting from antitrust scrutiny collective action initiated by employers to depress wages below the level that would be produced in a free market. Nor do those policies support a rule that would allow employers to suppress wages by implementing noncompetitive agreements among themselves on matters that have not previously been the subject of either an agreement with labor or even a demand by labor for inclusion in the bargaining process. That, however, is what is at stake in this litigation.

II

In light of the accommodation that has been struck between antitrust and labor law policy, it would be most ironic to extend an exemption crafted to protect collective action by employees to protect employers acting jointly to deny employees the opportunity to negotiate their salaries individually in a competitive market. Perhaps aware of the irony, the Court chooses to analyze this case as though it represented a typical impasse in an unexceptional multiemployer bargaining process. In so doing, it glosses over [several] unique features of the case that are critical to the inquiry into whether the policies of the labor laws require extension of the nonstatutory labor exemption to this atypical case.

First, in this market, unlike any other area of labor law implicated in the cases cited by the Court, player salaries are individually negotiated. The practice of individually negotiating player salaries prevailed even prior to collective bargaining. The players did not challenge the prevailing practice because, unlike employees in most industries, they want their compensation to be determined by the forces of the free market rather than by the process of collective bargaining. Thus, although the majority professes an inability to understand anything special about professional sports that should affect the framework of labor negotiations, in this business it is the employers, not the employees, who seek to impose a noncompetitive uniform wage on a segment of the market and to put an end to competitive wage negotiations.

Second, respondents concede that the employers imposed the wage restraint to force owners to comply with league-wide rules that limit the number of players that may serve on a team, not to facilitate a stalled bargaining process, or to revisit any issue previously subjected to bargaining. The employers could have confronted the culprits directly by stepping up enforcement of roster limits. They instead chose to address the problem by unilaterally forbidding players from individually competing in the labor market.

* * *

Given these features of the case, I do not see why the employers should be entitled to a judicially crafted exemption from antitrust liability. We have explained that the "the nonstatutory exemption has its source in the strong labor policy favoring the association of employees to eliminate competition over wages and working conditions." *Connell Constr. Co.*, 421 U.S. at 622. I know of no similarly strong labor policy that favors the association of employers to eliminate a competitive method of negotiating wages that predates collective bargaining and that labor would prefer to preserve.

Even if some collective action by employers may justify an exemption because it is necessary to maintain the "integrity of the multiemployer bargaining unit," *NLRB v. Brown*, 380 U.S. 278, 289 (1965), no such justification exists here. The employers imposed a fixed wage even though there was no dispute over the pre-existing principle that player salaries should be individually negotiated. They sought only to prevent certain owners from evading roster limits and thereby gaining an unfair advantage. Because "the employer's interest is a competitive interest rather than an interest in regulating its own labor relations," *Mine Workers v. Pennington*, 381 U.S. 657, 667 (1965), there would seem to be no more reason to exempt this concerted, anticompetitive employer action from the antitrust laws than the action held unlawful in *Radovich v. National Football League*, 352 U.S. 445 (1957).

The point of identifying the unique features of this case is not, as the Court suggests, to make the case that professional football players, alone among workers, should be entitled to enforce the antitrust laws against anti-competitive collective employer action. Other employees, no less than well-paid athletes, are entitled to the protections of the antitrust laws when their employers unite to undertake anticompetitive action that causes them direct harm and alters the state of employer-employee relations that existed prior to unionization. Here that alteration occurred because the wage terms that the employers unilaterally imposed directly conflict with a pre-existing principle of agreement between the bargaining parties. In other contexts, the alteration may take other similarly anticompetitive and unjustifiable forms.

* * *

Accordingly, I respectfully dissent.

The Court thus adopted Option 4. Justice Stevens used the latter part of his dissent to document that the principal precedent cited by the majority was the earlier opinion written by Justice Goldberg in *Jewel Tea*.

As Justice Stevens pointed out, *Jewel Tea* was one of the two major labor exemption decisions rendered by the Court on the same day in 1965, the other being *Pennington*. Both cases involved antitrust suits filed by employers against unions and the wage or hours provisions the latter had secured in collective agreements, with the unions' defense being the labor exemption. As discussed in Part 1(b) of this Section, the Court's opinions in the two decisions expressed three different positions about the appropriate relationship between antitrust and labor law, each position embraced by three separate groups of Justices. It was the three-member opinion by Justice White group whose votes and opinion were decisive in both cases, not Justice Goldberg's view that labor law should always prevail. Indeed, Justice Stevens went on to document Justice Goldberg's subsequent change of heart in the brief he filed with the Court in the early 1970s, on behalf of his client Curt Flood. What Justice Stevens was too polite to note in his dissent is that during the term when Justice Goldberg was unsuccessful in persuading a majority of his views in *Jewel Tea,* among his law clerks was Stephen Breyer.

NOTES AND QUESTIONS

1. *Antitrust-Labor Balance?* In *Pennington,* the Supreme Court refused application of the labor exemption after finding that the union-management bargain harmed the management's rival coal producers and contractors. It concluded that the antitrust values of competition in the product market outweighed the labor law values of collective bargaining. In *Jewel Tea,* where labor relations concerns were judged stronger, the Court held that the labor exemption precluded use of antitrust law to strike down even a restraint whose immediate impact (though not its purpose) was on the product market: banning sales of meat after 6:00 p.m. is a classic example of distorting output in a manner unresponsive to consumer preference. In the *Brown* case, the petitioners argued that there was a strong antitrust interest in precluding employer collusion to eliminate a competitive labor market for development squad players, and a minimal (actually a negative) labor law interest in forcing all the NFL players either to go on strike or to decertify their union in order to allow the development squad players to use antitrust law to remove the large salary cut that the owners had collectively imposed on them. How did the Court's opinion respond to that argument?

2. *Drawing a Line at Impasse?* All parties involved in the case recognized significant industrial relations problems in exposing to antitrust scrutiny multi-employer bargaining associations whose *raison d'etre* was to coordinate and constrain individual employer dealings with their employees. Since unionized employees often benefit from the multiemployer bargaining process as much as do employers, everyone agreed that there had to be some measure of labor exemption for such collective employer action. The position of

the Solicitor General was that employer associations such as the NFL were fully insulated from antitrust suits *before* bargaining reached an impasse, but that they lost the exemption once it was clear that impasse had been reached. (Even after that point the NFL owners would be entitled to defend their actions under all relevant antitrust doctrines.) The Court's opinion focused on this doctrinal proposal and rejected it. What are your views on this score? Which approach would foster collective bargaining?

3. *Scope of* Brown's *Holding?* Consider the last two paragraphs in the majority opinion in *Brown*. What limits do they suggest might be placed on the Court's holding? Does it apply only to employer, and union, bargaining tactics that are not unfair labor practices? Only to tactics that concern mandatory topics of bargaining? What temporal limits are suggested? Might union decertification necessarily negate the exemption?

4. *Is Multiemployer Bargaining in Sports Distinguishable?* Why does Justice Stevens argue in dissent that a union's bargaining to encourage individual negotiation of player salary makes a league's unilateral imposition of a set salary different than the imposition of a wage level by a typical multiemployer consortium? Is it relevant to the scope of the exemption that in sports bargaining, it is the employers, rather than the union, that tries to avoid "the forces of the free market?" Does the majority adequately respond to Justice Stevens on this point? For an argument in support of Justice Stevens, see Michael C. Harper, *Multiemployer Bargaining, Antitrust Law, and Team Sports: The Contingent Choice of a Broad Exemption*, 38 Wm & Mary L. Rev. 1663 (1997).

Consider a hypothetical raised by Judge Winter in *NBA v. Williams*, 45 F.3d 684 (2d Cir. 1995), another pre-*Brown* decision applying the labor exemption: an association employing union printers, whose collective bargaining agreement with the printers union had expired, unilaterally implements its offer of a five percent wage increase rather than the ten percent increase sought by the union. In *Brown*, the players agreed with Judge Winter that such post-impasse collective action by the employers' association was immune from antitrust challenge, because the union in that industry had consented to the principle of standardized wages in place of competition among employers and individual employees; the only thing it had not agreed to was the specific standardized wage level. The players argued, however, that a key difference in the sports world is that players' unions seek to preserve or expand, not to eliminate, a competitive labor market for the setting of salaries. The players noted that sports actually resembles the entertainment, not the printers', labor market. Just as in sports, entertainment performers negotiate (through their agents) individual contract terms above the collectively-established minimum floors. If the Court had recognized this distinction, how would the exemption apply to unilateral action by NFL owners to lengthen the playing season, reduce existing pension or disability benefits, expand the commissioner's disciplinary authority, or revise the rookie draft, current restraints on free agency, and the specifics of the existing salary cap?

5. ELIGIBILITY TO PLAY IN UNIONIZED PROFESSIONAL SPORTS POST-*BROWN**

CLARETT V. NFL
369 F.3d 124 (2d Cir. 2004)

SOTOMAYOR, CIRCUIT JUDGE.

Defendant-appellant National Football League ("NFL" or "the League") appeals from a judgment of the United States District Court for the Southern District of New York (Scheindlin, J.) ordering plaintiff-appellee Maurice Clarett ("Clarett") eligible to enter this year's NFL draft on the ground that the NFL's eligibility rules requiring Clarett to wait at least three full football seasons after his high school graduation before entering the draft violate antitrust laws. In reaching its conclusion, the district court held, *inter alia,* that the eligibility rules are not immune from antitrust scrutiny under the non-statutory labor exemption.[1]

We disagree and reverse.

BACKGROUND

* * *

[The court noted that the litigation arises in the context of an ongoing collective bargaining agreement between the NFL and its players, negotiated between the NFL Management Council ("NFLMC"), which is the NFL member clubs' multi-employer bargaining unit, and the NFL Players Association ("NFLPA"), the NFL players' exclusive bargaining representative.] Despite the collective bargaining agreement's comprehensiveness with respect to, *inter alia,* the manner in which the NFL clubs select rookies through the draft and the scheme by which rookie compensation is determined, the eligibility rules for the draft do not appear in the agreement.

* * *

[The court observed that three provisions of the collective bargaining agreement refer to the NFL Constitution and Bylaws, where the draft eligibility rules appear.] First, in Article III, Section 1 (Scope of Agreement), the collective bargaining agreement states:

---

* This Part focuses on eligibility rules for professional sports, all of which are now subject to collective bargaining agreements with players unions. Earlier cases discuss how antitrust laws would apply to eligibility rules if the labor exemption were not applicable. These can be found on the Casebook Website (http://pennstatelaw.psu.edu/SportsTextWebsite).

[1] Because we find that the eligibility rules are immune from antitrust scrutiny under the non-statutory labor exemption, we do not express an opinion on the district court's legal conclusions that Clarett alleged a sufficient antitrust injury to state a claim or that the eligibility rules constitute an unreasonable restraint of trade in violation of the antitrust laws.

> This Agreement represents the complete understanding of the parties as to all subjects covered herein, and there will be no change in the terms and conditions of this Agreement without mutual consent.... [T]he NFLPA and the Management Council waive any rights to bargain with one another concerning any subject covered or not covered in this Agreement for the duration of this Agreement, *including the provisions of the NFL Constitution and Bylaws;* provided, however, that if any proposed change in the NFL Constitution and Bylaws during the term of this Agreement could significantly affect the terms and conditions of employment of NFL players, then the [NFLMC] will give the NFLPA notice of and negotiate the proposed change in good faith.

(emphasis added). Second, Article IV, Section 2 (No Suit) provides generally that "neither [the NFLPA] nor any of its members" will sue or support a suit "relating to the presently existing provisions of the Constitution and Bylaws of the NFL as they are currently operative and administered." Third, Article IX, Section 1 (Non-Injury Grievance) makes "[a]ny dispute ... involving the interpretation of, application of, or compliance with, ... any applicable provision of the NFL Constitution and Bylaws pertaining to terms and conditions of employment of NFL players" subject to the grievance procedures afforded under the collective bargaining agreement.

Before the collective bargaining agreement became effective, a copy of the Constitution and Bylaws, as amended in 1992, was provided by the NFL to the NFLPA along with a letter, dated May 6, 1993, that "confirm[ed] that the attached documents are the presently existing provisions of the Constitution and Bylaws of the NFL referenced in Article IV, Section 2, of the Collective Bargaining Agreement." The May 6 letter was signed by representatives of the NFL and the NFLPA. The only other evidence presented to the district court by the NFL concerning the negotiation of the collective bargaining agreement were the two declarations of Peter Ruocco, Senior Vice President of Labor Relations at the NFLMC. In the second declaration, Ruocco attests that "[d]uring the course of collective bargaining that led to the [collective bargaining agreement], the [challenged] eligibility rule itself was the subject of collective bargaining."

* * *

DISCUSSION

Clarett argues that the NFL clubs are horizontal competitors for the labor of professional football players and thus may not agree that a player will be hired only after three full football seasons have elapsed following that player's high school graduation. That characterization, however, neglects that the labor market for NFL players is organized around a collective bargaining relationship that is provided for and promoted by federal labor law, and that the NFL clubs, as a multi-employer bargaining unit, can act jointly in setting the terms and conditions of players' employment and the rules of the sport without risking antitrust liability. For those reasons, the NFL argues that federal labor law favoring and governing the collective bargaining process precludes the application of the antitrust laws to its eligibility rules. We agree. . . .

I.

[The court first traced the history of the nonstatutory labor exemption in several Supreme Court decisions, particularly *Allen Bradley* (1945), *Pennington* (1965), *Jewel Tea* (1965), and *Connell Construction* (1975). Judge Sotomayor, as she then was, rejected Clarett's arguments that the challenged eligibility rule was not exempt. She explained her view of why the Eighth Circuit's decision in *Mackey* requiring a bona fide arms' length agreement did not properly define the limits of the non-statutory exemption.]

. . . Moreover, we disagree with the Eighth Circuit's assumption in *Mackey* that the Supreme Court's decisions in *Connell, Jewel Tea, Pennington,* and *Allen Bradley* dictate the appropriate boundaries of the non-statutory exemption for cases in which the only alleged anticompetitive effect of the challenged restraint is on a labor market organized around a collective bargaining relationship. Indeed, we have previously recognized that these decisions are of limited assistance in determining whether an athlete can challenge restraints on the market for professional sports players imposed through a collective bargaining process, because all "involved injuries to *employers* who asserted that they were being excluded from competition in the product market." *Wood v. Nat'l Basketball Ass'n,* 809 F.2d 954, 963 (2d Cir. 1987) (emphasis in original).

Clarett does not contend that the NFL's draft eligibility rules work to the disadvantage of the NFL's competitors in the market for professional football or in some manner protect the NFL's dominance in that market. *Compare N. Am. Soccer League v. Nat'l Football League,* 670 F.2d 1249 (2d Cir. 1982). He challenges the eligibility rules only on the ground that they are an unreasonable restraint upon the market for players' services. *See Clarett,* 306 F. Supp. 2d at 399. Thus, we need not decide here whether the *Mackey* factors aptly characterize the limits of the exemption in cases in which employers use agreements with their unions to disadvantage their competitors in the product or business market, because our cases have counseled a decidedly different approach where, as here, the plaintiff complains of a restraint upon a unionized labor market characterized by a collective bargaining relationship with a multi-employer bargaining unit. Moreover, as the discussion below makes clear, the suggestion that the

Mackey factors provide the proper guideposts in this case simply does not comport with the Supreme Court's most recent treatment of the nonstatutory labor exemption in *Brown v. Pro Football, Inc.*, 518 U.S. 231 (1996).

II.

* * *

B.

* * *

. . . Our prior cases highlight a number of consequences resulting from the advent of this collective bargaining relationship that are relevant to Clarett's litigation. For one, prospective players no longer have the right to negotiate directly with the NFL teams over the terms and conditions of their employment. That responsibility is instead committed to the NFL and the players union to accomplish through the collective bargaining process, and throughout that process the NFL and the players union are to have the freedom to craft creative solutions to their differences in light of the economic imperatives of their industry. Furthermore, the NFL teams are permitted to engage in joint conduct with respect to the terms and conditions of players' employment as a multi-employer bargaining unit without risking antitrust liability. The arguments Clarett advances in support of his antitrust claim, however, run counter to each of these basic principles of federal labor law.

Because the NFL players have unionized and have selected the NFLPA as its exclusive bargaining representative, labor law prohibits Clarett from negotiating directly the terms and conditions of his employment with any NFL club [citation omitted], and an NFL club would commit an unfair labor practice were it to bargain with Clarett individually without the union's consent [citation omitted]. The terms and conditions of Clarett's employment are instead committed to the collective bargaining table and are reserved to the NFL and the players union's selected representative to negotiate. [Citation omitted.]

The players union's representative possesses "powers comparable to those possessed by a legislative body both to create and restrict the rights of those whom it represents." [Citations omitted.] In seeking the best deal for NFL players overall, the representative has the ability to advantage certain categories of players over others, subject of course to the representative's duty of fair representation. [Citation omitted.] The union representative may, for example, favor veteran players over rookies [citation omitted], and can seek to preserve jobs for current players to the detriment of new employees and the exclusion of outsiders [citations omitted]. This authority and exclusive responsibility is vested in the players' representative "once a mandatory collective bargaining relationship is established and continues throughout the relationship." *Caldwell* [*v. Am. Basketball Ass'n*, 66 F.3d 523, 528 (2d Cir. 1995)] For the duration of that relationship, federal labor law then establishes a " 'soup-to-nuts array' of rules, tribunals and remedies to govern [the collective bargaining] process." *Id.* at 529 (quoting *Williams*, 45 F.3d at 693).

Clarett's argument that antitrust law should permit him to circumvent this scheme established by federal labor law starts with the contention that the eligibility rules do not constitute a mandatory subject of collective bargaining and thus cannot fall within the protection of the non-statutory exemption. Contrary to the district court, however, we find that the eligibility rules are mandatory bargaining subjects. Though tailored to the unique circumstance of a professional sports league, the eligibility rules for the draft represent a quite literal condition for initial employment and for that reason alone might constitute a mandatory bargaining subject. *See Caldwell*, 66 F.3d at 529 (describing the mandatory bargaining subject "pertinent" to that case as "the circumstances under which an employer may . . . refuse to hire an employee"); R. Gorman, *Labor Law* at 504 ("In accordance with the literal language of the Labor Act, the parties must bargain about the requirements or 'conditions' of initial employment."). But moreover, the eligibility rules constitute a mandatory bargaining subject because they have tangible effects on the wages and working conditions of current NFL players. Because the unusual economic imperatives of professional sports raise "numerous problems with little or no precedent in standard industrial relations," *Wood*, 809 F.2d at 961, we have recognized that many of the arrangements in professional sports that, at first glance, might not appear to deal with wages or working conditions are indeed mandatory bargaining subjects, *see Silverman v. Major League Baseball Player Relations Comm., Inc.*, 67 F.3d 1054, 1061 (2d Cir. 1995). . . . The eligibility rules in other words cannot be viewed in isolation, because their elimination might well alter certain assumptions underlying the collective bargaining agreement between the NFL and its players union.

Furthermore, by reducing competition in the market for entering players, the eligibility rules also affect the job security of veteran players. *See Fibreboard*, 379 U.S. at 210–15 (recognizing union members' "vital concern" in preserving jobs for union members); *see also Intercontinental Container Transp. Corp. v. N.Y. Shipping Ass'n*, 426 F.2d 884, 887–88 (2d Cir. 1970) ("[T]he preservation of jobs is within the area of proper union concern[, and u]nion activity having as its object the preservation of jobs for union members is not violative of the anti-trust laws." (internal citations omitted)). Because the size of NFL teams is capped, the eligibility rules diminish a veteran player's risk of being replaced by either a drafted rookie or a player who enters the draft and, though not drafted, is then hired as a rookie free agent. *See* Michael S. Jacobs & Ralph K. Winter, Jr.,

Antitrust Principles and Collective Bargaining by Athletes: Of Superstars in Peonage, 81 Yale L.J. 1, 16 (1971) (recognizing that entry of new players through draft "has an enormous effect on those already in the unit and the collective agreement which governs them"). Consequently, as was true in *Silverman,* we find that to regard the NFL's eligibility rules as merely permissive bargaining subjects "would ignore the reality of collective bargaining in sports." *Silverman,* 67 F.3d at 1061–62.

Clarett, however, argues that the eligibility rules are an impermissible bargaining subject because they affect players outside of the union. But simply because the eligibility rules work a hardship on prospective rather than current employees does not render them impermissible. *See Wood,* 809 F.2d at 960. The eligibility rules in this respect are not dissimilar to union demands for hiring hall arrangements that have long been recognized as mandatory subjects of bargaining. [Citation omitted.] In such hiring hall arrangements, the criteria for employment are set by the rules of the hiring hall rather than the employer alone. Nevertheless, such an arrangement constitutes a permissible, mandatory subject of bargaining despite the fact that it concerns prospective rather than current employees. *Wood,* 809 F.2d at 960.

As a permissible, mandatory subject of bargaining, the conditions under which a prospective player, like Clarett, will be considered for employment as an NFL player are for the union representative and the NFL to determine. Clarett, however, stresses that the eligibility rules are arbitrary and that requiring him to wait another football season has nothing to do with whether he is in fact qualified for professional play. But Clarett is in this respect no different from the typical worker who is confident that he or she has the skills to fill a job vacancy but does not possess the qualifications or meet the requisite criteria that have been set. In the context of this collective bargaining relationship, the NFL and its players union can agree that an employee will not be hired or considered for employment for nearly any reason whatsoever so long as they do not violate federal laws such as those prohibiting unfair labor practices, or discrimination. [Citation omitted.] Any challenge to those criteria must "be founded on labor rather than antitrust law." *Caldwell,* 66 F.3d at 530.

Even accepting that an individual club could refuse to consider him for employment because he is less than three full seasons out of high school, Clarett contends that the NFL clubs invited antitrust liability when they agreed amongst themselves to impose that same criteria on every prospective player. As a consequence of the NFL's unique position in the professional football market, of course, such joint action deprives Clarett of the opportunity to pursue, at least for the time being, the kind of high-paying, high-profile career he desires. In the context of collective bargaining, however, federal labor policy permits the NFL teams to act collectively as a multi-employer bargaining unit in structuring the rules of play and setting the criteria for player employment. Such concerted action is encouraged as a matter of labor policy and tolerated as a matter of antitrust law, *see Williams*, 45 F.3d at 593, despite the fact that it "plainly involve[s] horizontal competitors for labor acting in concert to set and to implement terms of employment," *Caldwell*, 66 F.3d at 529. Multi-employer bargaining in professional sports, moreover, offers the added advantage of allowing the teams to agree with one another and, as required, bargain with the union over the host of uniform rules needed for the successful operation of the league, such as the "[n]umber of games, length of season, playoff structures, and roster size and composition." *Williams*, 45 F.3d at 689. The fact that the challenged rules govern eligibility for the NFL draft, thereby excluding some potential employees from consideration, does not render the NFL's adherence to its eligibility rules as a multi-employer bargaining unit suspect.

The threat to the operation of federal labor law posed by Clarett's antitrust claims is in no way diminished by Clarett's contention that the rules were not bargained over during the negotiations that preceded the current collective bargaining agreement. The eligibility rules, along with the host of other NFL rules and policies affecting the terms and conditions of NFL players included in the NFL's Constitution and Bylaws, were well known to the union, and a copy of the Constitution and Bylaws was presented to the union during negotiations. Given that the eligibility rules are a mandatory bargaining subject for the reasons set out above, the union or the NFL could have forced the other to the bargaining table if either felt that a change was warranted. *See* NLRB v. Katz, 369 U.S. 736, 743 (1962). Indeed, according to the declaration from the NFLMC's Vice President for Labor Relations, Peter Ruocco, this is exactly what the NFL did.

. . . In the collective bargaining agreement, the union agreed to waive any challenge to the Constitution and Bylaws and thereby acquiesced in the continuing operation of the eligibility rules contained therein—at least for the duration of the agreement. The terms of that waiver not only keep the eligibility rules in effect for the length of the agreement but also leave the NFL in control of any changes to the eligibility rules on the condition that any significant change potentially affecting the terms and conditions of players' employment would be preceded by notice to the union and an opportunity to bargain. The value of such a clause to the NFL is obvious, as control over any changes to the eligibility rules is left in the hands of management at least until the expiration of the collective bargaining agreement. Although it is entirely possible that the players union might not have agreed entirely with the eligibility rules, the union representative might not have regarded any difference of opinion with respect to the eligibility rules as sufficient to warrant the expenditure of precious time at the bargaining table in light of other important issues.

Clarett would have us hold that by reaching this arrangement rather than fixing the eligibility rules in the text of the collective bargaining agreement or in failing to wrangle over the eligibility rules at the bargaining table, the NFL left itself open to antitrust liability. Such a holding, however, would completely contradict prior decisions recognizing that the labor law policies that warrant withholding antitrust scrutiny are not limited to protecting only terms contained in collective bargaining agreements. *See Brown*, 518 U.S. at 243–44; *Caldwell*, 66 F.3d at 528–29 & n. 1. The reach of those policies, rather, extends as far as is necessary to ensure the successful operation of the collective bargaining *process* and to safeguard the "unique bundle of compromises" reached by the NFL and the players union as a means of settling their differences.[19] *Wood*, 809 F.2d at 961. It would disregard those policies completely to hold that some "particular *quid pro quo* must be proven to avoid antitrust liability," *id.* at 962 n. 5, or to allow Clarett to undo what we assume the NFL and its players union regarded as the most appropriate or expedient means of settling their differences, *id.* at 961. We have cautioned before that "[t]o the extent that courts prohibit particular solutions for particular problems, they reduce the number and quality of compromises available to unions and employers for resolving their differences." *Id.* Clarett would have us disregard our own good advice.

The disruptions to federal labor policy that would be occasioned by Clarett's antitrust suit, moreover, would not vindicate any of the antitrust policies that the Supreme Court has said may warrant the withholding of the non-statutory exemption. This is simply not a case in which the NFL is alleged to have conspired with its players union to drive its competitors out of the market for professional football. *See Pennington*, 381 U.S. at 665. Nor does Clarett contend that the NFL uses the eligibility rules as an unlawful means of maintaining its dominant position in that market. *See Allen Bradley Co.*, 325 U.S. at 809 ("The primary objective of all the Antitrust legislation has been to preserve business competition and to proscribe business monopoly."). This lawsuit reflects simply a prospective employee's disagreement with the criteria, established by the employer and the labor union, that he must meet in order to be considered for employment. Any remedies for such a claim are the province of labor law. Allowing Clarett to proceed with his antitrust suit would subvert "principles that have been familiar to, and accepted by, the nation's workers for all of the NLRA's [sixty years] in every industry except professional sports." *Caldwell*, 66 F.3d at 530. We, however, follow the Supreme Court's lead in declining to "fashion an antitrust exemption [so as to give] additional advantages to

---

[19] We therefore need not determine whether as a matter of law the Constitution and Bylaws that contained the eligibility rules were incorporated by reference into the current collective bargaining agreement.

professional football players . . . that transport workers, coal miners, or meat packers would not enjoy." *Brown*, 518 U.S. at 249.

NOTES AND QUESTIONS

1. *Further Rejection of* Mackey. In *Mackey*, the Eighth Circuit concluded that the Rozelle Rule was not the product of genuine collective bargaining and thus would not enjoy antitrust immunity. By comparison, Judge Sotomayor explains that immunity does not require that the union achieve a good deal or even that it formally bargained over a management proposal. Which approach do you think is preferable? Which approach is consistent with the Court's opinion in *Brown*?

2. *Scope of* Clarett *Holding*. Does Judge Sotomayer's analysis depend on finding that the union affirmatively agreed to the eligibility rule? Should it? What do you think would be the impact on deadline-driven, last minute collective bargaining over matters like salary levels if a league to avoid antitrust suits had to ensure union acknowledgement of its agreement with all the league's employment practices?

3. *A Viable Antitrust Claim?* Did Clarett, in any event, have any viable antitrust claim against the NFL, even in the absence of the labor exemption? Does the eligibility requirement operate like a monopsonist's restraint on the labor market, suppressing wages by limiting demand, or does it instead suppress supply and thereby inflate the wages of players?

Instead, assume, perhaps wrongly, that Clarett had standing to assert that the league's eligibility rule helps monopolize the product market. Does the rule do so, or did it provide an opportunity for a new league of competitors in that market?

4. *Procompetitive Purpose of the Eligibility Rule?* If the rule does not have an anticompetitive purpose, why did the NFL adopt it? To please the NFLPA by limiting labor supply, as unions historically have wanted? Or might the rule have a procompetitive purpose of ensuring a higher quality product by avoiding teams feeling compelled to draft players before they are ready to play? Would it serve the competitive balance objective of the draft if a 19-year old quarterback were drafted by a dominant team and apprenticed behind an elite veteran nearing retirement? Might teams feel compelled to draft "prospects" before rival teams do so unless the "collective action" problem is solved by a rule like the NFL's?

6. UNION RESPONSES POST-*BROWN*

During an 18-month period from the summer of 2011 until January 2013, the sports unions and the sports leagues in all four major team sports were engaged in collective bargaining and—in three out of the four sports— the use of economic weapons. The most important of those disputes involving America's most popular sport, football, featured the Players Association's use of a "doomsday" strategy. Having unsuccessfully challenged anticompetitive labor restraints through industrial action during their failed 1987 strike, and through litigating *Brown*, the NFLPA developed another strategy: it arranged for its members to disclaim the union's authority to collectively negotiate on their behalf, and then proceeded with antitrust litigation. Without a collective bargaining arrangement, the players anticipated that cooperation among football clubs would not be exempt from the antitrust laws, and many of the agreements among clubs ratified previously in collective bargaining would be unlawful.

The history of this strategy is explained in the *Brady* excerpt below. The NFL responded to this tactic in turn by, following due notice to union officials, locking out all players immediately following the CBA's expiration. The players tried to preempt the league's strategy by terminating the union's status as their collective bargaining agent hours before the expiration of the agreement, and then filing an antitrust challenge to the lockout. As discussed in the excerpt below, the trial judge granted an injunction against the lockout that was reversed by the court of appeals.

BRADY V. NFL
644 F.3d 661 (8th Cir. 2011)

COLLOTON, CIRCUIT JUDGE

* * *

The League proceeded with its planned lockout on March 12, 2011. The Players moved for a preliminary injunction in the district court, urging the court to enjoin the lockout as an unlawful group boycott that was causing irreparable harm to the Players. The district court granted a preliminary injunction, and the League appealed. We conclude that the injunction did not conform to the provisions of the Norris-LaGuardia Act, 29 U.S.C. § 101 *et seq.*, and we therefore vacate the district court's order.

A.

Some historical background will place this case in context. [The court recounted the judicial application of the antitrust laws to the NFL, the NLRB's application of labor laws and recognition of the NFLPA as the exclusive bargaining representative of all NFL players, and the history of collective bargaining in the NFL. It noted the contentious history included strikes and litigation, as well as a response to continued application of the labor exemption that resulted in the NFLPA executive committee's decision to abandon the organization's collective bargaining rights in an effort to end the NFL's nonstatutory labor exemption from the antitrust laws. This decision resulted in a verdict in the *McNeil* case discussed in Section C, Part 2 above, awarding substantial damages. The appeal of that case and other issues was resolved when the parties settled ongoing litigation in *White v. NFL*, 822 F. Supp. 1389 (D. Minn. 1993).]

. . . Many disputes between the League and the players were resolved when the parties entered into a class action settlement agreement in *White*. . . . The NFLPA subsequently collected authorization cards from NFL players re-designating the organization as the players' exclusive collective bargaining representative, and the NFL voluntarily recognized the NFLPA as the players' union on March 29, 1993. The district court approved the parties' Stipulation and Settlement Agreement ("SSA") in April 1993, and the NFL and the NFLPA entered into a new CBA shortly thereafter. The NFL and the NFLPA agreed to amend various portions of the SSA to conform to the provisions of the new CBA, and the district court approved the requested amendments. The court entered a consent decree incorporating the terms of the amended SSA on August 20, 1993.

[The court then described *Brown*'s holding and quoted its discussion of when the labor exemption might end.]

* * *

B.

. . . Although the NFL and the NFLPA engaged in more than two years of negotiations toward a new CBA, the League and the players were unable to reach an agreement. The League filed an unfair labor practice charge with the NLRB in February 2011, asserting that the union failed to confer in good faith. The Players say that the charge is meritless. [The NFL claimed that the union was engaged in what it termed "surface bargaining," a tactic designed to avoid reaching an agreement before the collective bargaining agreement expired so that it could disclaim its representative status and allow its members to pursue antitrust litigation and injunctive relief against the League to try to block the NFL's expected lockout. The union responded that the players sought "a fair, new and long-term deal" and it had "offered proposals and solutions on every issue" the owners had raised. The Labor Board would never rule on whether the NFLPA's strategy constituted bad faith bargaining.]

As the deadline approached, a substantial majority of NFL players voted to end the NFLPA's status as their collective bargaining representative. . . .

The League filed an amended unfair labor practice charge on March 11, alleging that the NFLPA's disclaimer was a "sham" and that the combination of a disclaimer by the union and subsequent antitrust litigation was "a ploy and an unlawful subversion of the collective bargaining process." The Players dispute the charge, citing an advice memorandum of an associate general counsel of the NLRB in *Pittsburgh Steelers, Inc.*, No. 6-CA-23143, 1991 WL 144468 (NLRB G.C. June 26, 1991). The memorandum concluded that the NLFPA's 1989 disclaimer was valid, and that it was "irrelevant" whether the disclaimer was motivated by "litigation strategy," so long as the disclaimer was "otherwise unequivocal and adhered to." *Id.* at *2 & n.8.

The Players, funded by the NFLPA, commenced this action on the same day as the disclaimer, March 11, 2011....

* * *

On April 25, 2011, the district court granted the Players' motion to enjoin the lockout, rejecting the League's assertions that the court lacked jurisdiction to enter the injunction, that the court should defer to the primary jurisdiction of the NLRB, and that the League is in any event immune from antitrust liability under the nonstatutory labor exemption. The court concluded that the Norris-LaGuardia Act ("NLGA" or "Act"), 29 U.S.C. § 101 *et seq.*, which restricts the power of federal courts to issue injunctions in cases "involving or growing out of a labor dispute," *id.* § 1, was inapplicable, because the term "labor dispute" connotes a dispute between an employer and a union, and the Act therefore does not apply "absent the present existence of a union." ...

The district court also declined to stay the action pending the NLRB's resolution of the League's pending unfair labor practice charges. The court determined that a stay would not be appropriate because the delay could cause significant hardship for the plaintiffs, and because "[t]he Board has articulated the standard under which disclaimers must be evaluated in a clear and consistent fashion, and application of that established standard requires no particular specialized expertise." Finally, the district court concluded that the nonstatutory labor exemption does not protect the League from antitrust liability related to the lockout. In the court's view, the exemption applies only to agreements concerning "mandatory subjects of collective bargaining," such as wages, hours, and other terms and conditions of employment, and an employer's imposition of a lockout is not exempted because "[a] lockout is not a substantive term or condition of employment." The court distinguished the Supreme Court's decision in *Brown* on the basis that the parties here "have left the collective bargaining framework entirely."

* * *

II.

We consider first the League's contention that the Norris-LaGuardia Act deprived the district court of jurisdiction to enter the injunction. [The recounted the history of the Act, summarized above.]

The language of the Act, however, extends well beyond the specific issues decided in [the anti-union cases that led to the Act's enactment.] The impetus for the NLGA was dissatisfaction with injunctions entered against workers in labor disputes, but the statute also requires that an injunction against an employer participating in a labor dispute must conform to the Act. [Citations omitted.] This case requires us to decide whether, and if so how, the Act applies to the district court's injunction against the League.

To determine whether the NLGA forbids or places conditions on the issuance of an injunction here, we begin with the text of the statute. *Section 1* provides that "[n]o court of the United States . . . shall have jurisdiction to issue any . . . temporary or permanent injunction in a case involving or growing out of a labor dispute, except in strict conformity with the provisions of this chapter." 29 U.S.C. § 101. As noted, the district court concluded that the Act is inapplicable to this action, because the case is not one "involving or growing out of a labor dispute."

Section 13(c) of the Act states that "[t]he term 'labor dispute' includes *any controversy concerning terms or conditions of employment*, or concerning the association or representation of persons in negotiating, fixing, maintaining, changing, or seeking to arrange terms or conditions of employment, regardless of whether or not the disputants stand in the proximate relation of employer and employee." 29 U.S.C. § 113(c) (emphasis added). This lawsuit is a controversy concerning terms or conditions of employment. The Players seek broad relief that would affect the terms or conditions of employment for the entire industry of professional football. In particular, they urge the court to declare unlawful and to enjoin several features of the relationship between the League and the players, including the limit on compensation that can be paid to rookies, the salary cap, the "franchise player" designation, and the "transition player" designation, all of which the Players assert are anticompetitive restrictions that violate § 1 of the Sherman Act. . . .

We are not convinced by the Players' contention that because § 13(c) uses the term "includes," rather than "means," to introduce the substance of a "labor dispute," Congress did not fully define the term. They urge that § 13(c) merely expanded in one respect (to disputes outside the employer-employee relationship) a preexisting definition of "labor dispute"—a definition that was not codified and that, according to the Players, extended only to disputes involving organized labor. Whatever might be the significance of the verb "include" when used in other contexts, *cf. Massachusetts v. EPA*, 549 U.S. 497 (2007) (Scalia, J., dissenting), Congress stated in § 13 of the NLGA that "labor dispute" is "defined in this section," 29 U.S.C. § 113(a), and the Supreme Court consistently has described § 13(c) as a "definition" of "labor dispute." [citations omitted]. Not only has the Supreme Court repeatedly characterized § 13(c) as a definition, but contrary to the suggestion that an established meaning should be used to narrow the text, the Court has observed that "the statutory definition itself is extremely broad," *Jacksonville Bulk Terminals, Inc.*, 457 U.S. at 712, and explained that "Congress made the definition broad because it wanted it to be broad." Order of R.R. Telegraphers, 362 U.S. at 335–36.

The Act also states expressly that "[a] case shall be held to involve or grow out of a labor dispute when the case involves persons who are engaged in the same industry, trade, craft, or occupation." 29 U.S.C. § 113(a). This case, of course, involves persons engaged in the "same industry," namely, professional football. The statute continues that such a case "shall be held to involve or grow out of a labor dispute" when "such dispute is . . . between one or more employers or associations of employers and one or more employees or associations of employees." *Id.* This dispute is between one or more employers or associations of employers (the League and the NFL teams) and one or more employees (the Players under contract). By the plain terms of the Act, this case "shall be held to involve or grow out of a labor dispute."

The district court reached a contrary conclusion by departing from the text of § 13(a). The court thought the phrase "one or more employees or associations of employees" did not encompass the Players in this dispute, because "one or more employees" means "individual *unionized* employee or employees." We see no warrant for adding a requirement of unionization to the text.

A similar argument did not persuade the Supreme Court in *New Negro Alliance v. Sanitary Grocery Co.*, 303 U.S. 552 (1938). There, a company sought an injunction against the New Negro Alliance, which the Supreme Court described as "a corporation composed of colored persons, organized for the mutual improvement of its members and the promotion of civic, educational, benevolent, and charitable enterprises." *Id.* at 555. The Alliance allegedly had conspired to picket and boycott one of the company's grocery stores to pressure the store to employ African-American clerks. *Id.* at 555–56. The company claimed, among other things, that the Alliance's acts were "unlawful, [and] constitute[d] a conspiracy in restraint of trade." *Id.* at 558–59. . . .

The Supreme Court reversed. Although no labor organization was involved in the dispute, and the company argued that "a recognized labor union or unions or individual members thereof were involved" in all but one of the "labor dispute" precedents cited by the Alliance, Brief for Respondent at 24, the Court ruled that the definitions in the Act "plainly embrace the controversy which gave rise to the instant suit and classify it as one arising out of a dispute defined as a labor dispute." *New Negro Alliance*, 303 U.S. at 560. The Court observed that § 13(a) provides that a case shall be held to involve or grow out of a labor dispute "when the case involves any conflicting or competing interests in a 'labor dispute' . . . of 'persons participating or interested' therein," and ruled that the Alliance and its individual members were "persons interested in the dispute." *Id.* (internal quotation omitted). If § 13(a) were limited to controversies involving unions or unionized employees, then the Court could not have reached this conclusion.

Further confirmation that the present existence of a union is not required for a "labor dispute" comes from *NLRB v. Washington Aluminum Co.*, 370 U.S. 9 (1962). There, a group of seven employees who were "wholly unorganized" and had "no bargaining representative" or "representative of any kind to present their grievances to their employer" staged a walkout to protest cold working conditions in a machine shop. *Id.* at 14–15. Although the employees were not part of a union, the Supreme Court held that the walkout "did grow out of a 'labor dispute' within the plain meaning of the definition of that term in § 2(9) of the [National Labor Relations] Act." *Id.* at 15. The definition of "labor dispute" in the National Labor Relations Act is "virtually identical" to the definition of "labor dispute" in the NLGA, and the two provisions "have been construed consistently with one another" by the Supreme Court. *Jacksonville Bulk Terminals, Inc.*, 457 U.S. at 711 n.11; *accord* United States v. Hutcheson, 312 U.S. 219, 234 n.4 (1941).

* * *

The text of the Norris-LaGuardia Act and the cases interpreting the term "labor dispute" do not require the present existence of a union to establish a labor dispute. Whatever the precise limits of the phrase "involving or growing out of a labor dispute," this case does not press the outer boundary. The League and the players' union were parties to a collective bargaining agreement for almost eighteen years prior to March 2011. They were engaged in collective bargaining over terms and conditions of employment for approximately two years through March 11, 2011. At that point, the parties were involved in a classic "labor dispute" by the Players' own definition. Then, on a single day, just hours before the CBA's expiration, the union discontinued collective bargaining and disclaimed its status, and the Players filed this action seeking relief concerning industry-wide terms and conditions of employment. Whatever the effect of the union's disclaimer on the League's immunity from antitrust liability, the labor dispute did not suddenly disappear just because the Players elected to pursue the dispute through antitrust litigation rather than collective bargaining.

III.

[This part, an important question of labor law but unnecessary for resolution of sports law issues given Part II, discusses and rejects the Players' claim that § 4 of the Act does not apply at all to employer lockouts.

One general interpretive rationale, which would seemingly apply to Part II as well, deserves inclusion in this excerpt:]

Aside from the text and structure of § 4, the Players argue that the policy of the NLGA and the legislative history support their position that § 4(a) offers no protection to employers. To be sure, the policy stated in § 2 is that the individual unorganized worker should be free from the interference, restraint, or coercion of employers in the designation of representatives, self-organization, or other concerted activities. But it does not follow that a prohibition on injunctions against employer lockouts is contrary to the policy of the Act. The Supreme Court has observed that while the Act was designed to protect workingmen, the broader purpose was "to prevent the injunctions of the federal courts from *upsetting the natural interplay of the competing economic forces of labor and capital.*" *Bhd. of R.R. Trainmen v. Chi. River & Ind. R.R. Co.*, 353 U.S. 30, 40 (1957) (emphasis added). An employer's lockout is part of this interplay; it is not the equivalent of a judicial injunction that interferes with the ability of workers to exercise organized economic power.

The Court elsewhere explained that "powerful judicial dissents," such as that of Justice Brandeis in *Duplex Printing*, urged that labor disputes were an "area of economic conflict that had best be left to economic forces and the pressure of public opinion and not subjected to the judgment of courts." *Hutcheson*, 312 U.S. at 231. In support of that view, the Brandeis dissent cited this excerpt from the 1915 Report of the Committee on Industrial Relations:

> [T]here are apparently, only two lines of action possible: First to restrict the rights and powers of employers to correspond in substance to the powers and rights now allowed to trade unions, and second, to remove all restriction which now prevent the freedom of action of both parties to industrial disputes, retaining only the ordinary civil and criminal restraints for the preservation of life, property and the public peace. The first method has been tried and failed absolutely. * * * *The only method therefore seems to be the removal of all restrictions upon both parties, thus legalizing the strike, the lockout, the boycott, the blacklist, the bringing in of strike-breakers, and peaceful picketing.*

Duplex Printing, 254 U.S. at 486 n.7 (Brandeis, J., dissenting) (emphasis added); *see also* 75 Cong. Rec. 5478 (1932) (remarks of Rep. LaGuardia) ("If the courts had administered even justice to both employers and employees, there would be no need of considering a bill of this kind now."); *id.* at 4915 (remarks of Sen. Wagner) ("The policy and purpose which give meaning to the present legislation is its implicit declaration that the Government shall occupy a neutral position, lending its extraordinary power neither to those who would have labor unorganized nor to those who would organize it and limiting its action to the preservation of order and the restraint of fraud."). A one-way interpretation of § 4(a)—prohibiting injunctions against strikes but not against lockouts—would be in tension with the purposes of the Norris-LaGuardia Act to allow free play of economic forces and "to withdraw federal courts from a type of controversy for which many believed they were ill-suited and from participation in which, it was feared, judicial prestige might suffer." *Marine Cooks & Stewards*, 362 U.S. at 369 n.7. We are not convinced that the policy of the Act counsels against our textual analysis of § 4(a). *Cf. Am. Med. Ass'n v. United States*, 317 U.S. 519, 535 (1943) ("It is not our province to define the purpose of Congress apart from what it has said in its enactments, and if [a party's] activities fall within the classes defined by the [Clayton and Norris-LaGuardia] acts, we are bound to accord [the party] . . . the benefit of the legislative provisions.").

* * *

B.

[Discussion of another technical point regarding the Norris-LaGuardia Act concerning the refusal to deal with free agents and rookies omitted.]

IV.

Given our conclusion that the preliminary injunction did not conform to the provisions of the Norris-LaGuardia Act, we need not reach the other points raised by the League on appeal. In particular, we express no view on whether the League's nonstatutory labor exemption from the antitrust laws continues after the union's disclaimer. The parties agree that the Act's restrictions on equitable relief are not necessarily coextensive with the substantive rules of antitrust law, and we reach our decision on that understanding.

The district court's order of April 25, 2011, granting a preliminary injunction is vacated, and the case is remanded for further proceedings.

BYE, CIRCUIT JUDGE, dissenting.

In 1914, after twenty years of judicial interference in labor conflicts on the side of the employers, Congress stepped in to protect organized labor by passing sections 6 and 20 of the Clayton Act. Section 20 of the Act generally prohibited the issuance of injunctions in cases involving or growing out of labor disputes. *See* 29 U.S.C. § 52. It soon became apparent, however, that what was supposed to be the "charter of liberty of labor," Felix Frankfurter & Nathan Greene, *The Labor Injunction* 164 (1930) (remarks of William Howard Taft), fell short of the promise. The *Lochner*-era judges adopted a narrow interpretation of the Act, restricting it to "trade union activities directed against an employer by his own employees." *United States v. Hutcheson*, 312 U.S. 219, 230 (1941). "[T]o protect the rights of labor in the same manner the Congress intended when it enacted the Clayton Act," *id.* at 236, Congress passed the Norris-LaGuardia Act, under which "the allowable area of union activity was not to be restricted . . . to an immediate employer-employee relation." *Id.* at 231. Through its holding in this case today, the majority reaffirms the wisdom of the old French saying used by Felix Frankfurter and Nathan Greene when describing judicial reluctance to enforce § 20 of the Clayton Act: "the more things are legislatively changed, the more they remain the same judicially." Felix Frankfurter & Nathan Greene, *The Labor Injunction* 176 (1930). Despite the repeated efforts of the legislative branch to come to the rescue of organized labor, today's opinion puts the power of the Act in the service of employers, to be used against non-unionized employees who can no longer avail themselves of protections of labor laws. Because I cannot countenance such interpretation of the Act, I must and hereby dissent.

I.

A. "Labor Dispute"

First, I have to disagree with the majority's reading of the term "labor dispute." As the majority recounts, "[t]he underlying aim of the Norris-LaGuardia Act was to restore the broad purpose which Congress thought it had formulated in the Clayton Act but which was frustrated, so Congress believed, by unduly restrictive judicial construction." *United States v. Hutcheson*, 312 U.S. at 235–36. The unequivocal goal of the new legislation was to overturn the Supreme Court's decisions in *Duplex Printing* and *Bedford Cut Stone*, which had restricted § 20 of the Clayton Act to labor union activities directed against employees' immediate employers. . . .

However, in passing the NLGA, Congress never intended to change the well-accepted calculus of the Clayton Act as the legislation for the benefit of organized labor. The Clayton Act was always understood as an attempt to assist the organized labor movement at the time its progress was impeded by judicial misuse of injunctions. *See, e.g., Hutcheson*, 312 U.S. at 229–30 (explaining § 20 of the Clayton Act "withdrew from the general interdict of the Sherman Law specifically enumerated practices of labor unions by prohibiting injunctions against them"); *Bedford Cut Stone Co. v. Journeymen Stone Cutters' Ass'n of N. Am.*, 274 U.S. 37, 56 (1927) (separate opinion by Stone, J.) (describing the Clayton Act as being concerned with "organized labor"); *Am. Steel Foundries v. Tri-City Cent. Trades Council*, 257 U.S. 184, 208–09 (1921) ("Labor unions are recognized by the Clayton Act as legal when instituted for mutual help and lawfully carrying out their legitimate objects."); *see also* Frankfurter & Green, *The Labor Injunction*, at 130–31, 139 (describing the Clayton Act's preoccupation with organized labor). It is this well-entrenched understanding of the term "labor dispute" as centered on the struggle between employers and organized labor that informs interpretation of the same definition under the NLGA. *See Bruesewitz v. Wyeth LLC*, 131 S. Ct. 1068, 1082 (2011) ("When 'all (or nearly all) of the' relevant judicial decisions have given a term or concept a consistent judicial gloss, we presume Congress intended the term or concept to have that meaning when it incorporated it into a later-enacted statute.") (citation omitted).

Like the Clayton Act, the NLGA has been consistently cited in connection with protection of unions' rights. [Citations omitted]. This interpretation is in part dictated by § 2 of the Act, which "explicitly formulated the 'public policy of the United States' in regard to the industrial conflict." *Hutcheson*, 312 U.S. at 231. Such public policy expressed concern with the plight of the "individual unorganized worker," whom Congress deemed "helpless to exercise actual liberty of contract and to protect his freedom of labor, and thereby to obtain acceptable terms and conditions of employment" when confronted with "corporate and other forms of ownership association" assumed by employers. 29 U.S.C. § 102. Commenting on the judicial respect § 2 deserves, the Supreme Court explained that "[t]here are few pieces of legislation where the congressional hearings, committee reports, and the language in the legislation itself more clearly point to the necessity for giving an Act a construction that will protect the congressional policy the Act adopted." *See Order of R.R. Telegraphers v. Chicago & N. W. R.R. Co.*, 362 U.S. 330, 335 (1960). In the NLGA's case, the congressional policy was about helping the unions.

* * *

B. "Involving or Growing Out"

Second, I must take issue with the majority's conclusion as to this case not representing the outer boundary of the phrase "involving or growing out of a labor dispute." Like the nonstatutory labor exemption, statutory exemption from antitrust liability, which rests in part on the Norris-LaGuardia Act, *Connell Construction Co.*, 421 U.S. at 621–22, lies at the intersection between labor and antitrust laws. . . . *Mackey v. NFL*, 543 F.2d 606, 613 (8th Cir. 1976) (availability of the labor exemption "turns upon whether the relevant federal labor policy is deserving of preeminence over federal antitrust policy under the circumstances of the particular case"). "While the Norris-LaGuardia Act's bar of federal-court labor injunctions is not explicitly phrased as an exemption from the antitrust laws, it has been interpreted broadly as a statement of congressional policy that the courts must not use the antitrust laws as a vehicle to interfere in labor disputes." *H.A. Artists & Associates, Inc.*, 451 U.S. at 714. The scope of the two exemptions differs somewhat—"the statutory exemption allows unions to accomplish some restraints by acting unilaterally, [whereas] the nonstatutory exemption offers no similar protection when a union and a nonlabor party agree to restrain competition in a business market," *see Connell Construction Co.*, 421 U.S. at 622,—but there is no place for the application of either at the time labor laws no longer govern and labor policy is no longer implicated.

The Supreme Court recognized as much when it explained that nonstatutory immunity from antitrust review is no longer necessary when "an agreement among employers [is] sufficiently distant in time and in circumstances from the collective-bargaining process that a rule permitting antitrust intervention would not significantly interfere with that process." *Brown*, 518 U.S. at 250. As an example of such endpoint, the Court cited "collapse of the collective-bargaining relationship, as evidenced by decertification of the union." *Id.* (quoting Brown v. Pro Football, Inc., 50 F.3d 1041, 1057 (D.C. Cir. 1995)). With the players having voted to end the NFLPA's status as their collective bargaining representative and the NFLPA likewise having disclaimed its status as the players' representative, this case has reached that endpoint.

Indeed, the League itself anticipated dissolution of antitrust remedy fetters upon disclaimer of union representation, as is evident from its concessions in previous cases. *See Powell v. NFL*, 930 F.2d 1293, 1303 n.12 (8th Cir. 1989) (describing the League's concession that "the Sherman Act could be found applicable, depending on the circumstances, . . . if the affected employees ceased to be represented by a certified union"); *see also* Appellees Special Add. at 370 (transcript of the League's Supreme Court argument in *Brown v. Pro Football, Inc.*, where the League conceded antitrust immunities would not apply when "employees ultimately elect, in good faith, . . . to give up their rights under the labor laws"). The League's view was consistent with those of the courts, who saw disassociation from the union as the point beyond which labor laws yield to the antitrust regime. *Brown*, 50 F.3d at 1057 ("If employees wish to seek the protections of the Sherman Act, they may forego unionization or even decertify their unions. We note that the NFL players took exactly this latter step after the Eighth Circuit's *Powell* decision."); *Powell*, 930 F.2d at 1305 (Heaney, J., dissenting) (criticizing the majority opinion for continuing the labor exemption for too long—in effect, "until the bargaining relationship is terminated either by a NLRB decertification proceeding or by abandonment of bargaining rights by the union"). This realization as to the players' membership in a union acting as a shield against the possibility of antitrust charges is the reason why, in the 1993 *White* settlement, the League insisted the NFLPA be reconstituted as the players' representative and the collective bargaining relationship between the parties be reestablished.

At some point in the "arising out of" spectrum, the antitrust immunities stemming from statutory and nonstatutory labor exemptions must come to an end and give way to antitrust remedies. Such point does not come a year from the union disclaimer, nor one business cycle from it, as suggested by the League's counsel. Rather, such point comes at the moment of the union disclaimer.

II.

[Dissent re majority's conclusion that § 4(a) protects employers omitted. The dissent emphasized portions of the legislative history that Congress intended the Act to stop anti-union injunctions. He noted that the Norris-LaGuardia Act was explicitly intended to overrule judicial decisions that Congress felt had improperly weakened § 20 of the Clayton Act, intended to exempt collective action by workers organizing unions from antitrust liability. That section has not been construed to symmetrically exempt employer groups from antitrust liability. The dissent concluded]:

Viewing the legislative history of § 4(a) in its entirety, Congress did not intend to protect employers under the provision. *See De Arroyo*, 425 F.2d at 291 ("Our understanding of the legislative history behind section 4(a) leads us to conclude that that section was not intended as a protection for employers."). Moreover, the purpose delineated in § 2 further bolsters this conclusion. *See Baseball Players and the Antitrust Laws*, 53 Colum. L. Rev. 242, 249 n.71 (1953) ("Given the purpose of the Norris-LaGuardia Act it is improbable that an association of employers which deprives an 'individual unorganized worker' of his 'freedom of labor' comes within its protection."). Interpreting the text of § 4(a) in light of the legislative history and express policy of the NLGA, I would conclude § 4(a) does not protect employers.

In the end, I find illustrative the wise words of Judge Learned Hand:

> Of course it is true that the words used, even in their literal sense, are the primary, and ordinarily the most reliable, source of interpreting the meaning of any writing: be it a statute, a contract, or anything else. But it is one of the surest indexes of a mature and developed jurisprudence not to make a fortress out of the dictionary; but to remember that statutes always have some purpose or object to accomplish, whose sympathetic and imaginative discovery is the surest guide to their meaning.

Cabell v. Markham, 148 F.2d 737, 739 (2d Cir. 1945). In this case, "the fact remains that Congress passed the Norris-LaGuardia Act to forestall judicial attempts to narrow labor's statutory protection." *Bhd. of Maint. of Way Emps.*, 481 U.S. at 443. This is exactly what the majority has done. As a consequence, I am compelled to and must dissent.[9]

---

[9] Although the majority confines its analysis to the NLGA, I remain strongly convinced the other traditional injunction factors favor the Players. *See Minn. Citizens Concerned for Life, Inc. v. Swanson*, 640 F.3d 304, 310 (8th Cir. 2011) (setting forth the factors a court must consider). For the reasons set forth in my prior dissent, *see Brady v. NFL*, 640 F.3d 785, 794–96 (8th Cir. 2011) (Bye, J., dissenting), which have only intensified given the current juncture, I would affirm the district court.

NOTES AND QUESTIONS

1. *A Distortion of the Norris-LaGuardia Act?* Do you find it strange that the court uses a statute enacted by Congress in the mid-1930s with the immediate objective of freeing unions from judicial interference to bolster management in its labor battle with a labor organization? Remember that the federal courts took the same side in the first decade of the Sherman Act by holding repeatedly that a statute designed to attack combinations of capital was easily contorted to apply to organizations in the nascent labor movement. Does *Brady* suggest that unions and workers should conclude that self-help and private alternative dispute resolution are better tools for achieving institutional goals than is antitrust litigation?

2. *An Even Broader Interpretation of the Labor Exemption.* For an argument that the literal language of § 6 takes all labor market restraints outside the scope of federal antitrust law, see Gary Roberts, *Reconciling Federal Labor and Antitrust Policy: The Special Case of Sports League Labor Market Restraints*, 75 Geo. L.J. 19, 26–58 (1986), and *Brown v. Pro Football, Inc.: The Supreme Court Gets It Right For The Wrong Reasons*, 42 The Antitrust Bulletin 595, 618–24 (Fall 1997). If Roberts' arguments were accepted, even non-union players, and other workers, would never be able to seek antitrust protection from their employers' restrictive labor market practices. Do you agree that this could have been Congress' intent when passing the Clayton Act in response to labor's lobbying?

3. *Were Damages Available?* What if the players had not sought an injunction of the lockout, but had sought only the treble damages available under antitrust law? Had settlement not ensued, how should a court have ruled on the application of *Brown*?

4. *Disclaimer or Decertification as an Option.* Aside from the reach of the labor exemption, another problem with the strategy of disclaiming collective bargaining and suing the owners is that even if the owners were found to have violated the antitrust laws by locking out the players, there would be no union available to resolve the underlying labor dispute. The individual players could not claim to represent the bargaining unit. In fact, although the NFL Players Association announced it was defunct, it stood ready to resume collective bargaining once the owners' lockout was enjoined. Neither the courts nor the Labor Board ruled on the legality of this strategy. After management ultimately prevailed in court, the NFL recognized the NFLPA's status as the players' collective bargaining representative on July 30, 2011, and the parties proceeded to negotiate terms for a new collective bargaining agreement. The agreement became effective after ratification by the players on August 4, 2011.

5. *Disclaimer Versus Decertification?* Under labor law, a union can disclaim when 50% of members show they do not want to be represented by a union; a union is decertified following an election among workers in the bargaining unit, following a petition signed by 30% of the members. However, once a union has been decertified, there cannot be a new election to certify a

union for 12 months. *See* 29 U.S.C. § 159. Some observers have suggested that a complete decertification, which would bar the union from representing players for over a year and involves more procedural requirements, is the appropriate point for terminating protection of the labor exemption. Another option would be to bar unions from withdrawing from multi-employer bargaining and cutting deals with individual employers during a particular "bargaining cycle." Are either of these workable and desirable standards?

E. THE BUSINESS DYNAMICS OF REGULATING SPORTS LABOR MARKETS

The doctrinal questions about when and how the Sherman Act applies to professional sports leagues' labor restraints also generate important and more broadly applicable insights into the underlying business dynamics involved. Such insights may affect a public policy evaluation of the correctness of judicial interpretations, allow lawyers who counsel "in the shadow" of these rules and collective agreements to better understand them, and create potential opportunities for third-party stakeholders to interact strategically with owners and players' unions to achieve their own goals.

Foundational concepts in studying bargaining dynamics

Launching an antitrust lawsuit against a sports league's labor rules presumes that success will actually change things: that the landscape will be different if the plaintiff wins than if the plaintiff loses. Ronald Coase argued that the established rules do not matter in a world of perfect information and zero transaction costs. The proper inference from the existence of all the material in Sections B and C of this chapter is that the process of adopting and negotiating over labor market rules is an endeavor featuring significant differences in information as well as costly bargaining.

Less abstractly, keep in mind that labor restraints in North American professional sports leagues are initially the product of agreements among the member clubs, and then the result of collective bargaining between the clubs and players unions during which both sides have a duty to bargain in good faith. Recall from Chapter 2 that union executives representing players owe a Duty of Fair Representation to all members of the union, and that ultimately any agreement must be approved by the membership or their elected representatives. Recall from Chapter 5's discussion of the *American Needle* case that professional sports leagues are governed by their member clubs, whose interests relate to the overall profitability of the league as well as to specific profits for their own club. Consider these dynamics in the following exercises, which can either be thought experiments, group projects, or topics for class discussion.

A third key concept to consider is that these considerations don't take place in a vacuum. Sports leagues have histories and contexts, and any change from the status quo will make some stakeholders better off and others worse off. Consider how parties strategically interact to make it easier or more difficult to implement changes in the status quo.

First Exercise: Constructing Labor Market Rules

Consider the Rozelle Rule that was successfully challenged in the *Mackey* litigation. Prior to 1947, the NFL had a reserve clause similar to the baseball rule that was unsuccessfully challenged in *Flood v. Kuhn*. In that year, however, owners adopted an "option system" that allowed a club to renew a player's contract for an additional year, but only one year, at 90% of his prior year's salary. However, it appeared that no player had taken advantage of this option to secure a large raise from a rival club. As described in Lionel S. Sobel, *Professional Sports and the Law* 109 (New York: Law Arts Publishers 1977), playing out an option "is a risky thing for a professional athlete to do." Such a strategy would mean that

> a player must accept at least a 10% cut in pay, which in reality could amount to a much greater cut from what the player could have earned had he been willing to sign a new contract. . . . The player must face the risk he might be injured while playing out the option. And he must do all this without knowing in advance what salary any other team might be willing to pay him . . .

Prior to the 1963 season, however, star receiver R. C. Owens (purportedly the originator of the "alley oop catch") played out his option with the San Francisco 49ers and signed with the Baltimore Colts. Thereafter, Commissioner Pete Rozelle announced a new rule that he would award players or draft picks of the acquiring club to the former club "as the Commissioner in his sole discretion deems fair and equitable."

1. Why did the owners substitute an option system for a reserve clause in 1947? (Hint: review the defenses to an injunction if a player wanted to switch to a rival league raised in Chapter 4 and note that the NFL was in a "war" with the All-American Football Conference at that time.)

2. Why was the 1963 change imposed by Commissioner Rozelle rather than adopted by league owners?

3. Would Baltimore Colts' owner Carroll Rosenbloom have supported the Rozelle Rule?

4. After the 1963 season, the Los Angeles Rams had a 3-year record of 10–31. Would they have been in favor of the Rozelle Rule's continuance? If not, do you think it likely they could have prevailed on fellow owners to overturn the rule?

5. Why wasn't anyone worried that the NFL would be hurt as players who could not receive rival bids from other NFL clubs would seek employment elsewhere? (Consider the *Fraser v. MLS* case earlier in the chapter.)

Second Exercise: Negotiating Rules with the Union

Consider the situation facing the NBA in the early 1980s. After a costly "war" with the rival American Basketball Association in the 1970s, a planned merger was preliminarily enjoined in a suit brought by NBA players. (The litigation history is recounted in *Robertson v. NBA*, 72 F.R.D. 64 (S.D.N.Y. 1976).) Following extensive pre-trial proceedings and voluminous discovery, the players and the NBA reached a settlement in 1976 that included extensive free agency subject to a "right of first refusal" by the player's current employer.

Despite the end to inter-league rivalry, the league was struggling in part due to continued imprudent spending by some clubs, poor consumer perception because of well-publicized instances of drug abuse, and other factors. Famously, weeknight NBA finals games were broadcast after the late-night news on tape delay.

The strategy successfully implemented by David Stern as Executive Vice President and later Commissioner of the NBA, and upheld against antitrust challenge in *Wood, supra,* resulted in continued free agency for veteran players but subject to a salary cap on overall team payroll, pegged at a fixed percentage of basketball revenue earned by the clubs. The cap contained several exceptions, the most important of which (the "Larry Bird exception") allowed teams to re-sign their own players regardless of the cap.

1. Prior to the attempted merger with the ABA, the NBA owners were able to resist their players' demands for free agency; once they sought to merge, they conceded partial free agency to get a settlement of the players' litigation; by 1982, the owners were proposing a salary cap. Why couldn't the NBA owners just adhere to strict limits on competition for players that prevailed in the NFL until 1994?

2. Why would the owners of the Boston Celtics, New York Knicks, and Los Angeles Lakers agree to a salary cap (albeit a "soft" one with the Larry Bird exception)?

3. In the two prior seasons before the 1982 agreement, the Cleveland Cavaliers' record was 43–121. Why would the Cavaliers have wanted a salary cap to limit their ability to spend on new players?

4. Why would a majority of owners agree to give the Celtics such an advantage in re-signing Larry Bird?

5. Why were the owners able to get player agreement for a salary cap in 1982, when the players insisted on uncapped free agency subject only to a right of first refusal in 1976?

6. Why would the NBPA agree to a scheme where top rookies were paid minimal terms if drafted by teams with no cap room?

Third Exercise: Individual "Rights" Versus General Welfare

The NBA's "one and done" rule—barring clubs from signing players until they are both 19 years of age and one year removed from high school—remains controversial in many quarters (and, by the time you study this, may soon be amended by agreement of the owners and the players' association). Legally, the Second Circuit's decision in *Clarett* would seem to shield the rule from antitrust challenge. Consider a proposed change to raise the minimum age for participating in the NBA to 20, and assume that the effect will be that some players will remain in college for two years, while other players will opt to move from high school to the NBA's wholly-owned Developmental League (D-League).

1. Given that all rookies have to go into the draft, and are subject to the salary cap, why would NBA clubs want to limit their ability to sign the next Kevin Garnett/Lebron James?

2. Some NBA clubs currently have D-League affiliate teams, while others do not; should this affect an owner's position on changing the rule?

3. Would the National Basketball Players Association support raising the age limit? If not, would they demand huge or modest concessions from the owners in order to amend the collective bargaining agreement in this manner?

4. How would the small number of teenagers who might be immediately drafted into the NBA absent the rule voice their objections to a higher age limit?

5. Which other stakeholders might oppose increasing the minimum age?

6. What would the following stakeholders think about the proposal:

    a. college basketball coaches and athletic directors?

    b. entrepreneurs who own D-League franchises with affiliate relationships with a "parent" NBA club?

    c. CBS Sports (which currently holds the broadcast rights to D-League games)?

7. What actions can third-party stakeholders take in order to influence the NBA-NBPA negotiations?

Fourth Exercise: Maneuvering to Advantage in the Future

Following the 2010–11 NBA season, the league's collective bargaining agreement with its players expired. When negotiations did not result in an agreement, the league locked out the players through December; at that time the parties agreed to a new bargain. The key features include maintenance of the salary cap regime from prior agreements, albeit with a lower percentage of revenues going to players. Meanwhile, the union's executive director from the 2011 negotiations, Billy Hunter, has been replaced by Michele Roberts, the first female sports union leader.

1. Why did the NBA owners lock out the players, instead of negotiating to impasse and then imposing their own rules?

2. Assuming that the owners are not inclined either to increase revenues or to loosen the salary cap restrictions on player compensation, should the NBPA decertify as a union upon expiration of the agreement (in contrast to a disclaimer used by the NFLPA, a decertification prevents workers from forming a new union for 12 months)?

    a. Would such a decertification clearly constitute an end to the owners' immunity from antitrust suit under the labor exemption?

    b. Would such a decertification lead a court to conclude that an ensuing lockout was not a "labor dispute" for purposes of the Norris-LaGuardia Act?

    c. Would a lockout constitute a violation of § 1 of the Sherman Act?

    d. Would the current salary cap restrictions constitute a violation of § 1?

3. If the NBPA decertified, should the NBA:

    a. Continue operations and litigate any antitrust challenges?

    b. File a claim with the National Labor Relations Board alleging that the decertification is a form of bad faith bargaining?

    c. Implement a lock out until the players either agree to a new collective bargaining agreement or settle any class action litigation?

    d. Seek to implement a new set of rules that strengthen their likelihood of success in antitrust litigation?

CHAPTER 7

BUSINESS STRATEGY AND ANTITRUST SCRUTINY OF INTERNAL LEAGUE REGULATION OF INTER-CLUB COMPETITION

■ ■ ■

This chapter concludes our study of antitrust and business strategy with a detailed examination of how the law treats the relationship between clubs and their league. The significance of this inquiry can be seen in the economic trends in sports over the last few decades. Despite spiraling player costs, baseball and football franchises that sold for approximately $7 million in 1967 were selling—at least for large market teams like those in Los Angeles—for billions of dollars thirty-five years later. The same has been true for hockey and basketball. The NHL charged $2 million for an expansion franchise in 1967 and $80 million in 1997, and Microsoft's Steve Ballmer agreed to pay $2 billion for the NBA's Los Angeles Clippers in 2014.

Franchise values continue to increase because league revenues from all sources (*i.e.*, ticket sales, luxury boxes and club seats, ancillary stadium revenues, television, merchandise licensing, and internet rights) continue to rise. This upward trend was displayed even more dramatically in the use of taxpayer dollars to build new stadiums and arenas. The concept of a "new" stadium was short-lived, as many stadiums built in the 1960s and 1970s were replaced in the 1990s, when taxpayers contributed more than $10 billion of the $15 billion total spent to replace many of those "ancient" facilities with far more luxurious sites in which to watch the games.

The cycle repeated in this century, with Atlanta as the "poster child" for this phenomenon: the NFL Falcons moved to Mercedes-Benz Stadium in 2017 after 25 years in the Georgia Dome and the MLB Braves moved to Suntrust Park after only 20 years in Turner Field. State and local governments have also been generous with taxpayer money to fund soccer-only stadiums for MLS teams: since 2003, 13 soccer-specific facilities have been constructed. The smaller size of soccer stadiums, however, provides a business model for some owners to incorporate real estate development opportunities in their facilities plans and thereby reduce public subsidy. *See generally* Kristen Leigh Painter, *When building MLS stadiums, formulas are all over the map,* Minneapolis Star-Tribune (May 19, 2015), available at http://www.startribune.com/april-23-when-building-mls-stadiums-formulas-are-all-over-the-map/301011471/.

Recognizing these financial trends is important for two reasons. First, although a more favorable legal environment has enabled players to secure a larger share of the game's revenues—player salaries have gone up somewhat more than franchise prices—the lion's share of salary increases is attributable to increases in the game's revenues that also enlarge ownership profits (or for some teams reduce ownership losses). Sports over the past few decades serve as an apt illustration of what the eminent British economist Alfred Marshall called the first "law" of labor economics: the employer's demand for labor is derived from the consumer's demand for the goods and services produced by that labor.

The second reason to be conscious of the explosion in team values is the law's importance to this economic trend. This chapter explores the legal structure of sports ownership within a league, and how this structure influences franchise values and the amount of revenue teams and leagues extract from fans who attend the games, broadcasters and advertisers that televise the games, merchandisers that draw upon the team's names and logos that are seen in the games, and communities that subsidize the facilities in which the games are played. The focus of this chapter is both on antitrust doctrine (for lawyers primarily concerned about doctrine) and on the key topics that consume the attention of sports executives, topics on which legal restraints largely come from antitrust.

A. FRANCHISE OWNERSHIP RULES

It takes more than financial wherewithal to purchase an interest in a major league sports team. All leagues have rules about who may own their clubs, and these rules may differ depending on whether the transaction is for a minority or controlling interest. The rules invite litigation when the result is the rejection of a prospective owner. The parties inevitably frame the issue differently. To the league, the question is whether the rejected applicant should be their partner in their joint effort to compete with other forms of entertainment. Others may perceive the rejection as an agreement by owners to exclude a new rival who may be more effective in competing with them.

An early illustration was litigation arising out of the NBA's rejection of the application by Irving Levin and Harold Lipton to purchase the Boston Celtics from Ballantine Brewery in 1972. Levin alleged that they were rejected because of their personal and business associations with Sam Schulman, the maverick owner of the Seattle SuperSonics, who was allegedly a "troublemaker." The NBA denied this, claiming that its conflict-of-interest rules precluded approval: Levin and Schulman were both employees of the same corporation and Levin owned a minority interest in the Sonics. Federal district judge Richard Owen did not venture into the merits of the contrary views asserted by the parties about the nature and legitimacy of the grounds for rejection. Instead, he summarily dismissed the claim on the ground that this case presented no antitrust concerns:

> While it is true that the antitrust laws apply to a professional athletic league, and that joint action by members of a league can have antitrust implications, this is not such a case. Here the plaintiffs wanted to join with those unwilling to accept them, not to compete with them, but to be partners in the operation of a sports league for plaintiffs' profit. Further, no matter which reason one credits for the rejection, it was not an anti-competitive reason. Finally, regardless of the financial impact of this rejection upon the plaintiffs, if any, the exclusion of the plaintiffs from membership in the league did not have an anticompetitive effect nor an effect upon the public interest. The Celtics continue as an operating club, and indeed are this year's champion.
>
> The law is well established that it is competition, and not individual competitors, that is protected by the antitrust laws. . . .
>
> It is also clear that where the action the plaintiffs attack, the rejection from co-partnership, has neither anticompetitive intent nor effect, that conduct is not violative of the antitrust laws. . . .

Levin v. NBA, 385 F. Supp. 149, 152 (S.D.N.Y. 1974).

League advocates can read *Levin* broadly to support the claim that league membership is akin to joining a law or accounting firm partnership, an issue about which competition law has little to say. Challengers can read *Levin* more narrowly, emphasizing that the court found no claim that the NBA's rejection of Levin as an owner was "an anti-competitive reason."

In some cases, the parties agree on the "reason" but disagree as to whether it is anticompetitive. All of the major U.S. sports leagues have rules against the same owner controlling multiple teams. European soccer varies this approach because of its somewhat unusual structure, where clubs primarily compete in domestic leagues but some also compete in two competitions sponsored by UEFA, the European governing body. UEFA adopted a rule in 1998 that bars a single person or entity from owning a majority interest in two different teams that participate in the same European-wide competition, on the theory that such common ownership would compromise the appearance of honest competition. The English National Investment Company (ENIC), which owned a majority interest in soccer teams in several different national leagues, owned teams in both Greece and The Czech Republic who qualified for the UEFA Cup competition in 1998. Because of the newly adopted rule, the Greek team was disqualified from participating. An interim order (*i.e.,* a preliminary injunction) of the Court of Arbitration for Sport (CAS) allowed both teams to participate in the UEFA Cup. Meanwhile, the case proceeded to a trial in March 1999 (at which co-authors Paul C. Weiler and Gary R. Roberts appeared as expert witnesses on opposite sides). In July 1999, the CAS rendered an opinion upholding the UEFA ban on multiple ownership, deciding that the rule did not violate European or Swiss competition law. Subsequently, in 2003, the European Commission (the executive body of the European Union) issued an opinion that the UEFA rule was consistent with Art. 81 of the Treaty of Rome (the analogue to Sherman Act § 1). Compare MLS, which for a time operated with several investors controlling multiple teams, a process that ended in 2015 when AEG divested the Houston Dynamo, retaining LA Galaxy.

North American sports leagues have a variety of ownership rules, largely dealing with a proposed owner's finances and character. The major source of antitrust litigation about specific sports ownership rules in the United States concerns two NFL policies not explicitly adopted by other leagues, restricting owners' ability to control clubs in *other* leagues, and an unwritten policy against any NFL franchise being owned by publicly-traded corporations. (The Green Bay Packers, which has always been a not-for-profit corporation owned by citizens of Green Bay, Wisconsin, under a special statute passed by the Wisconsin legislature, is a grandfathered exception to this league policy.) The NFL enforces these rules by requiring three-quarters of the clubs to approve any change in ownership of a team.

Cross-ownership is quite common elsewhere: *e.g.*, Atlanta's baseball Braves and basketball Hawks (as well as the NHL 1999 expansion Thrashers) were until late 2003 all owned by the same corporate entity; Chicago's baseball White Sox and basketball Bulls are owned by Jerry Reinsdorf; New York's basketball Knicks and hockey Rangers belong to Cablevision. Two cases excerpted below analyze the antitrust validity of the NFL restraint under the Rule of Reason. Note the separate theories of competitive harm. In *NASL v. NFL*, the claim was that the NFL's rule harms competition in the broader market for professional sports by limiting the ability of the NASL to compete against the NFL. In *Sullivan v. NFL*, the claim was that the NFL rule harms competition in the narrow market for professional football, by limiting the ability of teams funded by outside stockholder investment to compete against clubs owned by individuals.

NASL v. NFL
670 F.2d 1249 (2d Cir. 1982)

MANSFIELD, CIRCUIT JUDGE.

[The North American Soccer league challenged the NFL's cross-ownership ban, seeking to allow two NFL owners to be able to maintain their investment in NASL franchises. Chapter 5 discussed the court's treatment of the single entity issue with regard to this dispute.]

Because of the economic interdependence of major league team owners and the requirement that any sale be approved by a majority of the league members, an owner may in practice sell his franchise only to a relatively narrow group of eligible purchasers, not to any financier. The potential investor must measure up to a profile having certain characteristics. Moreover, on the supply side of the sports capital market the number of investors willing to purchase an interest in a franchise is sharply limited by the high risk, the need for active involvement in management, the significant exposure to publicity that may turn out to be negative, and the dependence on the drawing power and financial success of the other members of the league. The record thus reveals a market which, while not limited to existing or potential major sports team owners, is relatively limited in scope and is only a small fraction of the total capital funds market. The evidence further reveals that in this sports capital and skill market, owners of major professional sports teams constitute a significant portion. Indeed the existence of such a submarket and the importance of the function of existing team owners as sources of capital in that market are implicitly recognized by the defendants' proven intent in adopting the cross-ownership ban. If they believed, as NFL now argues, that all sources of capital were fungible substitutes for investment in NASL sports teams and that the ban would not significantly foreclose the supply of sports capital, they would hardly have gone to the trouble of adopting it.

Unless the ban has procompetitive effects outweighing its clear restraint on competition, therefore, it is prohibited by § 1 of the Sherman Act. That law does not require proof of the precise boundaries of the sports capital market or the exact percentage foreclosed; it is sufficient to establish, as was done here, the general outlines of a separate submarket of the capital market and that the foreclosed portion of it was likely to be significant.

NFL argues that the anticompetitive effects of the ban would be outweighed by various procompetitive effects. First it contends that the ban assures it of the undivided loyalty of its team owners in competing effectively against the NASL in the sale of tickets and broadcasting rights, and that cross-ownership might lead NFL cross-owners to soften their demands in favor of their NASL team interests. We do not question the importance of obtaining the loyalty of partners in promoting a common business venture, even if this may have some anticompetitive effect. But in the undisputed circumstances here the enormous financial success of the NFL league despite long-existing cross-ownership by some members of NASL teams demonstrates that there is no market necessity or threat of disloyalty by cross-owners which would justify the ban. Moreover, the NFL was required to come forward with proof that any legitimate purposes could not be achieved through less restrictive means. This it has failed to do. The NFL, for instance, has shown no reason why it could not remedy any conflict of interest arising out of NFL-NASL competition for broadcast rights by removing cross-owners from its broadcast rights negotiating committee.

For the same reasons we reject NFL's argument that the ban is necessary to prevent disclosure by NFL cross-owners of confidential information to NASL competitors. No evidence of the type of information characterized as "confidential" is supplied. Nor is there any showing that the NFL could not be protected against unauthorized disclosure by less restrictive means. Indeed, despite the existence of NFL cross-owners for some years there is no evidence that they have abused confidentiality or that the NFL has found it necessary to adopt confidentiality rules or sanctions. Similarly, there is no evidence that cross-ownership has subjected the personnel and resources of NFL cross-owners to conflicting or excessive demands. On the contrary, successful NFL team owners have been involved in ownership and operation of other outside businesses despite their equal potential for demands on the owners' time and resources. Moreover, a ban on cross-ownership would not insure that NFL team owners would devote any greater level of their resources to team operations than they otherwise would.

Reversed.

Notwithstanding its legal victory, the NASL suffered a fatal financial defeat in the sports marketplace in the early 1980s and was forced to fold. When the new Major League Soccer (MLS) began play in 1996, two key investors were the NFL Chiefs' Lamar Hunt, with his Kansas City Wizards and Columbus Crew, and the NFL Patriots' Robert Kraft, with his New England Revolution. This time, the NFL membership adopted a resolution that expressly carved out exceptions for owners whose franchises in another league are either in the same city as their NFL team, or in a city that did not have any NFL team in its market. Thus, the NFL now precludes its owners from owning teams in a competing league only if those other teams are in cities where somebody else's NFL team is located. (Under this exception, Paul Allen owns the NBA Portland Trailblazers and the NFL Seattle Seahawks.)

An interesting twist on this new NFL policy arose in 2003 when Malcolm Glazer, owner of the Tampa Bay Buccaneers, began serious efforts to purchase the Los Angeles Dodgers, which Fox's News Corp. had put up for sale. There was no NFL team in Los Angeles, so Glazer would not have violated the new policy, and Commissioner Tagliabue and many NFL owners were anxious to see a team located in the nation's second largest TV market as soon as possible. Were Glazer to have purchased the Dodgers and an NFL team then moved to L.A., however, Glazer would have found himself suddenly in violation. To avoid this, the NFL insisted that a contingency plan acceptable to the league be in place before the league would give Glazer assurance that it would not force him to sell the Bucs or the Dodgers should the NFL return to L.A. The delay that ensued resulted in the Dodgers being sold to Boston real estate developer Frank McCourt for $430 million before Glazer could work out suitable arrangements with the NFL. If Glazer were to have sued the NFL, claiming that the prospective enforcement of its policy kept him from acquiring the Dodgers and violated § 1, what should the result be? What damages or other remedy could Glazer obtain?

NOTES AND QUESTIONS

1. *League Motivations for Ownership Policies.* What lessons do the exceptions to the NFL's cross-ownership ban teach us about the underlying reasons for this league restraint? What variables does *NASL* allow a court to consider in determining whether application of a cross-ownership restriction is lawful under the rule of reason? Are these distinctions sensible as a matter of antitrust policy?

Is the NFL's rule primarily designed to protect the entire league's effort to compete against the NASL, or to protect individual clubs from local competition against strangers? Do you think McDonald's might bar its franchisees from operating Taco Bell franchises? If so, do you think McDonald's would create an exception for those who owned McDonald's and Taco Bell restaurants in the same neighborhood?

2. *Section 2 Versus Section 1.* In *NASL*, the court found that the NFL's cross-ownership ban injured competition by weakening the ability of the NASL to be a viable entity, presumably one that would compete with the NFL in some relevant market. Would this be a problem normally more suited for analysis and resolution under § 2's proscription on attempts to monopolize or under § 1's ban on agreements in restraint of trade?

3. *Is NASL's Doctrine Limited to New Leagues?* What anticompetitive effects would flow from the NFL enforcing its ban on cross-ownership to prevent an NFL owner from owning a MLB or NBA team? The apparent concern in *NASL v. NFL* was that not allowing NFL owners to invest in the NASL would make the NASL less able to compete effectively. Is that a problem if the "other" league in which NFL owners cannot own a team is MLB or the NBA? Is the holding of *NASL* effectively limited to bans on NFL owners holding interests in teams in a financially struggling league that competes with the NFL?

4. *Cross-Ownership in Minor Leagues in Other Sports.* Does the NFL's current iteration of the cross-ownership ban apply to NFL owners who have

ownership interests in *minor* league teams in other sports? Arguably, the language of the previously unpublished resolution applied only to ownership of other major league teams. However, in 1993, New Orleans Saints owner Tom Benson's efforts to relocate a Class AA Southern League baseball club was approved by NFL Commissioner Paul Tagliabue only upon condition that it play in New Orleans (a deal consistent with the exception later formalized in 1997). Does any underlying policy for the cross-ownership ban justify extending the ban to minor league teams? Is consumer welfare (*i.e.*, price, product quantity or quality, or consumer choice) in any way damaged because someone other than Tom Benson owned the minor league baseball team for which there was no shortage of interested buyers?

5. *Business Strategy in Ownership Policy.* Abstracting from the external legal questions, what are the pros and cons of a ban on cross-ownership from the point of view of the league itself? Unlike the NFL, the other three major sports leagues have welcomed owners from other leagues and sports. If you were the commissioner of a sports league, what policy would you advocate on this score, and why? Is the public interest enhanced or diminished by a ban or limitation on sports cross-ownership?

6. *Distinguishing Between Restrictions on Current and Prospective Owners.* Would the Second Circuit have ruled differently if Joe Robbie, instead of being a current owner told to divest his NASL interests, had been a prospective owner, rejected like Irving Levin in his bid to purchase a team? Standard partnership law expressly prohibits joint venture partners from assigning their partnership interests to anyone without the unanimous consent of the other venturers, unless the partnership agreement provides otherwise. Should this basic principle of partnership law (reinforced by § 502 of the new Uniform Partnership Act) be a sufficient justification under federal antitrust law for the NFL's restrictions on who can own a league franchise?

7. *Anti-Competitive Theories for Rejecting a Prospective Owner.* Suppose an owner of a large-market MLB club was anxious to sell and a willing buyer came forward who had extraordinary wealth and a strong interest in spending on players, coaches, and executive talent to build a championship team. If the other league owners rejected this applicant, would that violate the antitrust laws?

SULLIVAN V. NFL
34 F.3d 1091 (1st Cir. 1994)

TORRUELLA, CIRCUIT JUDGE.

[In 1987, New England Patriots owner Billy Sullivan sought to alleviate his financial distress by putting up 49% of the team in a public stock offering. The Sullivan family's financial troubles were attributable in large part to Michael Jackson's "Victory Tour" which inflicted huge losses on Billy's son, Charles "Chuck" Sullivan, the Tour's underwriter and owner of Foxboro Stadium in which the Patriots played. The idea for a Patriots' minority-share stock offering came from the remarkable success enjoyed by the Boston Celtics when that team fashioned a similar limited partnership venture in 1986. However, allegedly because the NFL rule precluded public ownership, Sullivan decided in October 1988 to sell the Patriots (for $84 million) to a limited partnership largely owned by Victor Kiam. Then, when Kiam sold the Patriots to James Orthwein in 1992 for approximately $110 million, Sullivan sued the NFL for damages under the Sherman Act, claiming that absent the NFL's policy against public ownership he would have been able to retain the controlling interest in a rapidly-appreciating football asset, instead of having to sell it at a depressed price to private buyers. After a trial in December 1993, the jury awarded Sullivan $38 million in damages, which the trial judge remitted to $17 million, before trebling. The NFL appealed.]

III. Issues Allegedly Requiring Judgment for the NFL

A. *Lack of Antitrust Injury*

To establish an antitrust violation under § 1 of the Sherman Act, Sullivan must prove that the NFL's public ownership policy is "in restraint of trade." Under antitrust law's "rule of reason," the NFL's policy is in restraint of trade if the anticompetitive effects of the policy outweigh the policy's legitimate business justifications. Anticompetitive effects, more commonly referred to as "injury to competition" or "harm to the competitive process," are usually measured by a reduction in output and an increase in prices in the relevant market. Injury to competition has also been described more generally in terms of decreased efficiency in the marketplace which negatively impacts consumers. Thus, an action harms the competitive process "when it obstructs the achievement of competition's basic goals— lower prices, better products, and more efficient production methods." *Town of Concord v. Boston Edison Co.*, 915 F.2d 17, 22 (1st Cir. 1990).

The jury determined in this case, via a special verdict form, that the relevant market is the "nationwide market for the sale and purchase of ownership interests in the National Football League member clubs, in general, and in the New England Patriots, in particular." The jury went on to find that the NFL's policy had an "actual harmful effect" on competition in this market.

The NFL argues on appeal that Sullivan has not established the existence of any injury to competition, and thus has not established a restraint of trade that can be attributed to the NFL's ownership policy. The league's attack is two-fold, asserting (1) that NFL clubs do not compete with each other for the sale of ownership interests in their teams so there exists no competition to be injured in the first place; and (2) Sullivan did not present sufficient evidence of injury to competition from which a reasonable jury could conclude that the NFL's policy restrains trade. Although we agree with the NFL that conceptualizing the harm to competition in this case is rather difficult, precedent and deference to the jury verdict ultimately require us to reject the NFL's challenge to the finding of injury to competition.

Critically, the NFL does not challenge on appeal the jury's initial finding of the relevant market and no corresponding challenge was raised at trial.... The NFL nevertheless maintains that NFL teams do not compete against each other for the sale of their ownership interests, even if we accept that a market exists for such ownership interests.

1. No Competition Subject to Injury as Matter of Law

The NFL correctly points out that member clubs must cooperate in a variety of ways, and may do so lawfully, in order to make the football league a success. On the other hand, it is well established that NFL clubs also compete with each other, both on and off the field, for things like fan support, players, coaches, ticket sales, local broadcast revenues, and the sale of team paraphernalia. The question of whether competition exists between NFL teams for sale of their ownership interests, such that the NFL's ownership policy injures this competition, is ultimately a question of fact. The NFL would have us find, however, that, as a matter of law, NFL teams do not compete against each other for the sale of their ownership interests. We decline to make such a finding.

The NFL relies on a series of cases which allegedly stand for the "well established" rule that a professional sports league's restrictions on who may join the league or acquire an interest in a member club do not give rise to a claim under the antitrust laws. *Seattle Totems Hockey Club, Inc. v. National Hockey League*, 783 F.2d 1347 (9th Cir. 1986); *Fishman v. Estate of Wirtz*, 807 F.2d 520 (7th Cir. 1986); *Mid-South Grizzlies v. National Football League*, 720 F.2d 772, at 772 (3d Cir. 1983); *Levin v. National Basketball Ass'n*, 385 F. Supp. 149 (S.D.N.Y. 1974). These cases, all involving a professional sport's league's refusal to approve individual transfers of team ownership or the creation of new teams, do not stand for the broad proposition that no NFL ownership policy can injure competition. *See, e.g., North American Soccer League v. National Football League*, 670 F.2d 1249, 1259–61 (2d Cir. 1982) (finding that the NFL's policy against cross-ownership of NFL teams and franchises in competing sports leagues, which also effectively barred certain owners who owned other sports franchises from purchasing NFL teams, injured competition between the NFL and competing sports leagues and thus violated § 1 of the Sherman Act).

None of the cases cited by the NFL considered the particular relevant market that was found by the jury in this case or a league policy against public ownership. *Seattle Totems* and *Mid-South Grizzlies* considered potential inter-league competition when a sports league rejected plaintiffs' applications for new league franchises. Those decisions found no injury to competition because the plaintiffs were not competing with the defendant sports leagues, but rather were seeking to join those leagues. *Mid-South Grizzlies* left open the possibility that potential intra-league competition between NFL football clubs could be harmed by the NFL's action, but found that the plaintiff in that case had not presented sufficient evidence of harm to such competition.

The *Fishman* and *Levin* cases concerned the National Basketball Association's ("NBA") rejection of plaintiffs' attempts to buy an existing team. Those cases also based their finding that there was no injury to competition on the fact that the plaintiffs were seeking to join with, rather than compete against, the NBA. Neither case considered whether competition between teams for investment capital was injured.

The important distinction to make between the cases cited by the NFL and the present case is that here Sullivan alleges that the NFL's policy against public ownership generally restricts competition between clubs for the sale of their ownership interests, whereas in the aforementioned cases, a league's refusal to approve a given sale transaction or a new team merely prevented particular outsiders from joining the league, but did not limit competition between the teams themselves. To put it another way, the NFL's public ownership policy allegedly does not merely prevent the replacement of one club owner with another—an action having little evident effect on competition—it compromises the entire process by which competition for club ownership occurs.

* * *

2. Insufficient Evidence of Harm to Competition

The NFL contends that Sullivan did not present sufficient evidence concerning: (1) the existence of competition between NFL clubs for the sale of ownership interests, or (2) a decrease in output, an increase in prices, a detrimental effect on efficiency or other incidents of harm to competition in the relevant market, from which a reasonable jury could conclude that the NFL's policy injured competition. Although we agree that the evidence of all these factors is rather thin, we disagree that the evidence is too thin to support a jury verdict in Sullivan's favor.

With respect to evidence of the existence of competition for the sale of ownership interests, one of Sullivan's experts, Professor Roger Noll, testified that "one of the ways in which the NFL exercises monopoly power in the market for the franchises and ownership is by excluding certain people from owning all or part—any type part of an NFL franchise." Dr. Noll explained that this "enables a group of owners, in this case, you only need eight owners, to exclude from the League and from competing with them, people who might be more effective competitors than they are." The record also contains statements from several NFL owners which could reasonably be interpreted as expressions of concern about their ability to compete with other teams in the market for investment capital in general, and for the sale of ownership interests in particular. For example, Arthur Rooney II of the Pittsburgh Steelers stated in a letter that he did not "believe that the individually or family owned teams will be able to compete with the consolidated groups." Ralph Wilson of the Buffalo Bills stated that big corporations should not own teams because it gives them an "unfair competitive advantage" over other teams since corporations will funnel money into the team and make it "more competitive" than the other franchises. Former NFL Commissioner Pete Rozelle admitted that similar sentiments had been expressed by NFL members.

Although it is not precisely clear that the "competition" about which Noll, Rooney, and Wilson were discussing is the same competition at issue here—that is competition for the sale of ownership interests—a jury could reasonably interpret these statements as expressing a belief that the competition exists between teams for the sale of ownership interests. The statements of the two NFL owners imply that greater access to capital for all teams will put increased pressure on some teams to compete with others for that capital, and all the statements reveal that the ownership rules, particularly the rule against public ownership, are the main obstacle preventing such access. The fact that ownership by "consolidated groups" is not necessarily the same as public ownership does not affect the conclusion that teams face competitive pressure in selling their ownership interests generally to whoever might buy them. We also note that evidence of actual, present competition is not necessary as long as the evidence shows that the potential for competition exists. It would be difficult indeed to provide direct evidence of competition when the NFL effectively prohibits it.

* * *

The NFL is correct that, in one sense, the overall pool of potential output is fixed because there are only 28 NFL teams and, although their value may fluctuate, the quantity of their ownership interests cannot. However, the NFL's public ownership policy completely wipes out a certain type of ownership interest—public ownership of stock. By restricting output in one form of ownership, the NFL is thereby reducing the output of ownership interests overall. In other words, the NFL is literally restricting the output of a product—a share in an NFL team.

There was considerable testimony concerning the price effects of the NFL policy. Both of Sullivan's experts testified that the policy depressed the price of ownership interests in NFL teams because NFL franchises would normally command a premium on the public market relative to their value in the private market, which is all that the league currently permits. Professor Noll testified that fan loyalty would push up the price of ownership interests if sales to the public were allowed. Even former Commissioner Pete Rozelle acknowledged that "it was pointed out, with justification, it has been over the years, that [the ownership policy] does restrict your market and, very likely, the price you could get for one of our franchises if you wanted to sell it, because you are eliminating a very broad market.... And they have said that there is a depression on the price they could get for their franchise."

The NFL points out that the alleged effect of its ownership policy is to reduce prices of NFL team ownership interests, rather than to raise prices which is normally the measure of an injury to competition. *E.g., Town of Concord*, 915 F.2d at 22. We acknowledge that it is not clear whether, absent some sort of dumping or predatory pricing, *see, e.g., Monahan's Marine, Inc. v. Boston Whaler, Inc.*, 866 F.2d 525, 527 (1st Cir. 1989), a decrease in prices can indicate injury to competition in a relevant market. The Supreme Court has emphasized, however, that overall consumer preferences in setting output and prices is more important than higher prices and lower output, per se, in determining whether there has been an injury to competition. *NCAA v. Board of Regents*, 468 U.S. 85, 107 (1984). In this case, regardless of the exact price effects of the NFL's policy, the overall market effects of the policy are plainly unresponsive to consumer demand for ownership interests in NFL teams. Dr. Noll testified that fans are interested in buying shares in NFL teams and that the NFL's policy deprives fans of this product. Moreover, evidence was presented concerning the public offering of the Boston Celtics professional basketball team which demonstrated, according to some of the testimony, fan interest in buying ownership of professional sports teams. Thus, a jury could conclude that the NFL's policy injured competition by making the relevant market "unresponsive to consumer preference."[3]

As for overall efficiency of production in the relevant market[4] Sullivan's experts testified that the NFL's policy hindered efficiency gains, and that allowing public ownership would make for better football teams. Professor Noll stated that the NFL's public ownership policy prevented

---

[3] The NFL maintains that price and output are not affected because its ownership policy does not limit the number of games or teams, does not raise ticket prices or the prices of game telecasts and does not affect the normal consumer of the NFL's product in any other way. Such facts might be relevant to an inquiry of whether the NFL's policy harms overall efficiency, see infra note [4], but it is not relevant to whether the policy affects output and prices in the relevant market for ownership interests. Just because consumers of "NFL football" are not affected by output controls and price increases does not mean that consumers of a product in the relevant market are not so affected. In this case, two types of consumers are denied products by the NFL policy: consumers who want to buy stock of the Patriots or other teams, and consumers like Sullivan who want to "purchase" investment capital in the market for public financing.

[4] Although the product at issue in the relevant market is "ownership interests," efficiency in production of that product can be measured by the value of the ownership interest. That is, an improved product produced more efficiently will be reflected in the value of the output in question (regardless of the price). In this case, the value of the product depends on the success of the Patriots' football team, the overall efficiency of its operations, and the success of the NFL in general.

individuals who might be "more efficient and much better at running a professional football team" from owning teams. Dr. Noll also stated that publicly owned NFL teams would be better managed, and produce higher quality entertainment for the fans. Noll testified that the ownership rule excluded certain types of management structures which would likely be more efficient in running the teams, resulting in higher franchise values. One NFL owner, Lamar Hunt, acknowledged that increased access to capital can improve a team's operations and performance. A memorandum prepared by an NFL staff member stated that changes to the NFL's public ownership policy could contribute to each NFL team's own financial strength and viability, which in turn would benefit the entire NFL because the league has a strong interest in having strong, viable teams.

The NFL presented a large amount of evidence to the contrary and now claims on appeal that Sullivan's position was based on nothing more than sheer speculation. We have reviewed the record, however, and we cannot say that the evidence was so overwhelming that no reasonable jury could find against the NFL and in favor of Sullivan. We therefore refuse to enter judgment in favor of the NFL as a matter of law.

B. Ancillary Benefits

The NFL next argues that even if its public ownership policy injures competition in a relevant market, it should be upheld as ancillary to the legitimate joint activity that is "NFL football" and thus not violative of the Sherman Act. We take no issue with the proposition that certain joint ventures enable separate business entities to combine their skills and resources in pursuit of a common goal that cannot be effectively pursued by the venturers acting alone. *See, e.g., Broadcast Music, Inc. v. Columbia Broadcasting System, Inc.*, 441 U.S. 1 (1979). We also do not dispute that a "restraint" that is ancillary to the functioning of such a joint activity—*i.e.* one that is required to make the joint activity more efficient—does not necessarily violate the antitrust laws. *Broadcast Music*, 441 U.S. at 23–25; *Rothery Storage & Van Co. v. Atlas Van Lines, Inc.*, 253 U.S. App. D.C. 142, 792 F.2d 210, at 223–24 (D.C. Cir. 1986); *see also Northwest Wholesale Stationers, Inc. v. Pacific Stationery & Printing Co.*, 472 U.S. 284, 295–96 (1985). We further accept, for purposes of this appeal, that rules controlling who may join a joint venture can be ancillary to a legitimate joint activity and that the NFL's own policy against public ownership constitutes one example of such an ancillary rule. Finally, we accept the NFL's claim that its public ownership policy contributes to the ability of the NFL to function as an effective sports league, and that the NFL's functioning would be impaired if publicly owned teams were permitted, because the short-term dividend interests of a club's shareholder would often conflict with the long-term interests of the league as a whole. That is, the policy avoids a detrimental conflict of interests between team shareholders and the league.

We disagree, however, that these factors are sufficient to establish as a matter of law that the NFL's ownership policy does not unreasonably restrain trade in violation of § 1 of the Sherman Act. The holdings in *Broadcast Music, Rothery Storage,* and *Northwest Stationers,* do not throw the "rule of reason" out the window merely because one establishes that a given practice among joint venture participants is ancillary to legitimate and efficient activity—the injury to competition must still be weighed against the purported benefits under the rule of reason. . . .

One basic tenet of the rule of reason is that a given restriction is not reasonable, that is, its benefits cannot outweigh its harm to competition, if a reasonable, less restrictive alternative to the policy exists that would provide the same benefits as the current restraint. The record contains evidence of a clearly less restrictive alternative to the NFL's ownership policy that would yield the same benefits as the current policy. Sullivan points to one proposal to amend the current ownership policy by allowing for the sale of minority, nonvoting shares of team stock to the public with restrictions on the size of the holdings by any one individual. Dividend payments, if any, would be within the firm control of the NFL majority owner. Under such a policy, it would be reasonable for a jury to conclude that private control of member clubs is maintained, conflicts of interest are avoided, and all the other "benefits" of the NFL's joint venture arrangement are preserved while at the same time teams would have access to the market for public investment capital through the sale of ownership interests.

C. Causation of Injury in Fact

[The court here addressed and rejected the NFL's claim that Sullivan's case should have been dismissed because there was no evidence to support a finding that the NFL's policy against public ownership in fact had caused economic injury to Sullivan. The court noted that "[a]lthough the evidence of causation is not overwhelming, it is nevertheless sufficient to support the verdict." With regard to the NFL's argument that Sullivan never asked for a vote, and thus the League never actually voted on whether he could sell 49% of the team through a public offering, the court concluded that the jury had sufficient evidence to find that the parties believed that a formal vote would have been futile, and thus the NFL owners' prior practice had effectively denied Sullivan permission to issue public stock in the Patriots. With respect to the NFL's second argument, that its evidence showed that a public offering of minority shares would not have raised the $70 million necessary to keep Sullivan from having to sell the team, the court stated: "[a]lthough we share the NFL's skepticism that Sullivan would have succeeded in his public offering if the NFL had allowed him to try it, we cannot say that, as a matter of law, the evidence was so overwhelming that no reasonable jury could find that the NFL's policy harmed Sullivan by preventing him from doing something he would otherwise have been able to do."]

The NFL's arguments concerning the application of § 1 of the Sherman Act to the facts of this case raise a substantial challenge to the jury verdict and are certainly weighty enough to give us pause. Upon careful consideration of the issues, however, we find Sullivan's theory of the case to be a plausible one and ultimately find the evidence sufficient to support it. For the foregoing reasons, therefore, we see no justification, as a matter of law, for ringing the death knell on this litigation.

IV. Trial Errors

Having reviewed those issues which would have warranted a judgment in favor of the NFL, had we decided any of those issues in the NFL's favor, we now turn to the NFL's claim that it is entitled to a new trial because of allegedly erroneous jury instructions and other trial errors.

* * *

D. Balancing Procompetitive and Anticompetitive Effects in the Relevant Market

As we noted above, the rule of reason analysis requires a weighing of the injury and the benefits to competition attributable to a practice that allegedly violates the antitrust laws. The district court instructed the jury on its verdict form to balance the injury to competition in the relevant market with the benefits to competition in that same relevant market. The NFL protested, claiming that all procompetitive effects of its policy, even those in a market different from that in which the alleged restraint operated, should be considered. The NFL's case was premised on the claim that its policy against public ownership was an important part of the effective functioning of the league as a joint venture. Although it was not readily apparent that this beneficial effect applied to the market for ownership interests in NFL teams, the relevant market found by the jury, the NFL argued that its justification should necessarily be weighed by the jury under the rule of reason analysis. Sullivan responded, and the district court agreed, that a jury cannot be asked to compare what are essentially apples and oranges, and that it is impossible to conduct a balancing of alleged anticompetitive and procompetitive effects of a challenged practice in every definable market.

The issue of defining the proper scope of a rule of reason analysis is a deceptive body of water, containing unforeseen currents and turbulence lying just below the surface of an otherwise calm and peaceful ocean. The waters are muddied by the Supreme Court's decision in *NCAA*—one of the more extensive examples of the Court performing a rule of reason analysis—where the Court considered the value of certain procompetitive effects that existed outside of the relevant market in which the restraint operated. NCAA, 468 U.S. at 115–20 (considering the NCAA's interest in protecting live attendance at untelevised games and the NCAA's "legitimate and important" interest in maintaining competitive balance between amateur athletic teams as a justification for a restraint that operated in a completely different market, the market for the telecasting of collegiate football games). Other courts have demonstrated similar confusion. *See, e.g., L.A. Coliseum,* 726 F.2d at 1381, 1392, 1397, 1399 (stating that the "relevant market provides the basis on which to balance competitive harms and benefits of the restraint at issue" but then considering a wide variety of alleged benefits, and then directing the finder of fact to "balance the gain to interbrand competition against the loss of intrabrand competition", where the two types of competition operated in different markets).

To our knowledge, no authority has squarely addressed this issue. On the one hand, several courts have expressed concern over the use of wide ranging interests to justify an otherwise anticompetitive practice, and others have found particular justifications to be incomparable and not in correlation with the alleged restraint of trade. *Smith v. Pro Football, Inc.,* 593 F.2d 1173, 1186 (D.C. Cir. 1978); *Brown v. Pro Football, Inc.,* 812 F. Supp. 237, 238 (D.D.C. 1992); *Chicago Pro. Sports Ltd. Partnership v. National Basketball Ass'n,* 754 F. Supp. 1336, 1358 (N.D. Ill. 1991). We agree that the ultimate question under the rule of reason is whether a challenged practice promotes or suppresses competition. Thus, it seems improper to validate a practice that is decidedly in restraint of trade simply because the practice produces some unrelated benefits to competition in another market.

On the other hand, several courts, including this Circuit, have found it appropriate in some cases to balance the anticompetitive effects on competition in one market with certain procompetitive benefits in other markets. *See, e.g., NCAA,* 468 U.S. at 115–20; *Grappone, Inc. v. Subaru of New England, Inc.,* 858 F.2d 792, 799 (1st Cir. 1988); *M & H Tire Co. v. Hoosier Racing Tire Corp.,* 733 F.2d 973, 986 (1st Cir. 1984); *L.A. Coliseum,* 726 F.2d at 1381, 1392, 1397, 1399. Moreover, the district court's argument that it would be impossible to compare the procompetitive effects of the NFL's policy in the interbrand market of competition between the NFL and other forms of entertainment, with the anticompetitive effects of the intrabrand market of competition between NFL teams for the sale of their ownership interests, is arguably refuted by the Supreme Court's holding in *Continental T.V., Inc. v. GTE Sylvania Inc.,* 433 U.S. 36 (1977). *Continental T.V.* explicitly recognized that positive effects on interbrand competition can justify anticompetitive effects on intrabrand competition. Although *Continental T.V.* can reasonably be interpreted as referring only to interbrand and intrabrand components of the same relevant market, there is also some indication that interbrand and intrabrand competition necessarily refer to distinct, yet related, markets. *Continental T.V.*, 433 U.S. at 52 n.19 ("The degree of intrabrand competition is wholly independent of the level of interbrand competition."). Arguably, the market put forward by the NFL—that is the market for NFL football in competition with other forms of entertainment—is closely related to the relevant market found by the jury such that the procompetitive benefits in one can be compared to the anticompetitive harms in the other. Clearly this question can only be answered upon a much more in-depth inquiry that we need not, nor find it appropriate to, embark upon at this time.

Finally, we note that although balancing harms and benefits in different markets may be unwieldy and confusing, such is the case with a number of balancing tests that a court or jury is expected to apply all the time.

* * *

Although the issue of the proper scope of the rule of reason analysis is more appropriately resolved in a case where it is dispositive and more fully briefed, we can draw at least one general conclusion from the case law at this point: courts should generally give a measure of latitude to antitrust defendants in their efforts to explain the procompetitive justifications for their policies and practices; however, courts should also maintain some vigilance by excluding justifications that are so unrelated to the challenged practice that they amount to a collateral attempt to salvage a practice that is decidedly in restraint of trade.

In any event, we need not enter these dangerous waters to resolve the instant dispute. The NFL wanted the jury to consider its proffered justifications for the public ownership policy—namely that the policy enhanced the NFL's ability to effectively produce and present a popular entertainment product unimpaired by the conflicting interests that public ownership would cause. These procompetitive justifications should have been considered by the jury, even under Sullivan's theory of the proper scope of the rule of reason analysis. [However], to the extent the NFL's policy strengthens and improves the league, resulting in increased competition in the market for ownership interests in NFL clubs through, for example, more valuable teams, the jury may consider the NFL's justifications as relevant factors in its rule of reason analysis. The danger of the proffered instructions on the verdict form is that they may have mislead the jury into thinking that it was precluded from considering the NFL's justifications for its ownership policy. Therefore, the relevant market language on the verdict form should be removed, or else the jury should be informed that evidence of benefits to competition in the relevant market can include evidence of benefits flowing indirectly from the public ownership policy that ultimately have a beneficial impact on competition in the relevant market itself.

[The court also found several other trial court errors that required reversal of the jury verdict; for example, the fact that the trial judge had erroneously refused to give the jury an instruction about the NFL's "equal involvement" defense, by which the league claimed that Sullivan was barred from challenging its public ownership ban because of his "complete, voluntary, and substantially equal participation" in the formulation and enforcement of the ban over his years as an NFL owner. For all of these reasons, the decision below was reversed and remanded.]

The second trial on Sullivan's claim was held during the fall of 1995 and ended in a hung jury. Before a third trial could begin, the parties settled with the help of court-ordered mediation: the NFL paid Sullivan $11 million to drop his suit. The league's ban on public ownership remains unchanged. Meanwhile, Billy's son, Chuck Sullivan, had also filed suit against the League. Chuck Sullivan contended that when the NFL denied his father the right to do a public stock offering for the Patriots, this severely damaged the economic value of the Patriots' home field, then renamed Sullivan Stadium, owned by Chuck's Stadium Management Corporation (SMC). The fact the Sullivan family had less funds available meant it could not improve the stadium facility, lease, and revenue stream. In turn, that put SMC into bankruptcy and forced a sale of the stadium to Robert Kraft at a "bargain basement" price of $25 million. (Happily for New England football fans, Kraft's ownership of the re-renamed Foxboro Stadium, which had a Patriot's lease until the year 2002, gave him the leverage to block a move of the Patriots to St. Louis by its 1993 owner, James Orthwein, and then to buy the team for himself for $160 million.)

However, the First Circuit, in *Sullivan v. Tagliabue,* 25 F.3d 43 (1st Cir. 1994), held that Chuck Sullivan had not suffered the kind of direct injury from the NFL's "no corporate ownership" rule that antitrust is designed to prevent, and thus he had no standing to sue. The Circuit distinguished not only the situation of Chuck's father Billy, the Patriot's owner, but also *Los Angeles Memorial Coliseum v. NFL,* 791 F.2d 1356 (9th Cir. 1986), in which the L.A. Coliseum (as well as the Raiders' owner) was able successfully to sue the NFL for blocking the Raiders' move from Oakland to Los Angeles. What are the distinguishing features of the financial injuries suffered by Sullivan Stadium and the L.A. Coliseum as a result of these NFL rules? Do these distinctions warrant the difference in legal result? If not, which result is more in line with antitrust doctrine? *See also Murray v. National Football League,* 1996–2 Trade Cases (CCH) ¶ 71,479 (E.D. Pa.1996) (denying NFL motion to dismiss claim that owner of option to buy Patriots kept him from purchasing team).

NOTES AND QUESTIONS

1. *In Which Market Was There an Anticompetitive Effect?* The only market in which the court found evidence of an anticompetitive effect was the "nationwide market for the sale and purchase of ownership interests in NFL member clubs." By restricting the number of potential buyers for interests in franchises, the court acknowledged that the effect of the ban was to lower the price NFL owners could get for their teams. Is there an antitrust concern (*i.e.*, an injury to consumer welfare) if joint venture partners impose a limitation on who can be partners, when the impact of the rule may be to *depress* the value of their own franchise interest? Do you agree with the court that a jury could reasonably find that NFL team owners compete against each other for the sale of their franchises? Why would owners agree to a scheme to lower the value of their franchises? Suppose Warren Buffet invested in the NFL, with a special stock that entitled him to 5% of all NFL revenues; would he think the cross-ownership rule was good or bad for his investment?

2. *Consumers' Interest in Stock Purchases and the Antitrust Laws.* The court indicated that the anticompetitive effect of the ban was that it deprived consumers of the ability to buy shares of NFL teams, and that the rule caused the league to be "unresponsive to consumer demand for ownership interests in NFL teams." Are equity interests in a business a consumer good for which antitrust law requires the business to maintain a competitive market? How would restrictions on the sale of equity interests in any partnership, joint venture, close corporation, or limited liability company (which are pervasive in our economy) fare under the Rule of Reason inquiry recognized in *Sullivan*? Is there something distinctive about the Patriots as compared to other business ventures in Boston?

3. *Market Definition.* Is there anything distinctive about the market for NFL franchises, or is this simply a subset of the larger capital market in which investors buy and sell ownership rights in sports franchises generally—indeed, in any part of the business world (*e.g.*, the sale of McDonald's franchises)? Is that question relevant to a court's judgment about the competitive impact of the NFL's policy against public ownership?

4. *Disconnect Between Plaintiff's Theory and Plaintiff's Expert.* Sullivan's expert witness, noted sports economist Roger Noll, opined that the ban on public ownership harmed football fans by depriving them of competition between clubs that might be more efficient or aggressively competitive. Sullivan, however, seemed to want to sell stock to the public so that he could continue personally to own and control the Patriots notwithstanding financial losses caused by family mismanagement. Is this disconnect something that should affect the court's judgment in an antitrust case?

5. *The Real Motivation Behind the NFL Policy.* Do you think that the reason for the NFL's ban on public ownership was, as Professor Noll testified, to prevent more efficient competitors from owning rival teams? Would a limit on minority investors serve legitimate interests, such as a desire for each club to have a single accountable public "face?" Or avoiding the nuisance of

compliance with financial, disclosure and other regulations imposed on public traded companies or the often cumbersome process by which corporate entities make decisions? Do you agree with the testimony in *Sullivan* that corporate entities would be unduly focused on short-term, immediate shareholder-profit-maximizing thinking of corporate entities?

6. *Ongoing Impact of Ancillary Restraints Doctrine.* The relationship between the ancillary restraints doctrine and the Rule of Reason reflects a continuing imprecision in antitrust doctrine, dating back to then-Circuit Judge William Howard Taft's decision in *United States v. Addyson Pipe & Steel Co.*, 85 F. 271 (6th Cir. 1898), *aff'd*, 175 U.S. 211 (1899). The *Sullivan* court's view that a restraint ancillary to a legitimate underlying agreement is still unlawful if there were a less restrictive alternative would appear consistent with *Addyston Pipe*. For a contrary view, *see* Gabriel A. Feldman, *The Misuse of the Less Restrictive Alternative Inquiry in Rule of Reason Analysis*, 58 Am. U. L. Rev. 561 (2009).

It is not clear, however, that an agreement that was both ancillary to the NFL's legitimate purpose and reasonably necessary to achieve that purpose would still be struck down because of some general balancing: there are no sports cases where we know this has occurred. With respect to its substantive reasonability, the court agreed that the league's policy against public ownership "contributes to the ability of the NFL to function as an effective sports league," and that "the policy avoids a detrimental conflict of interest between team shareholders and the league." What precisely is the positive contribution of this rule? Consider the experience in other leagues which all have publicly-owned teams—*e.g.*, baseball's Chicago Cubs, basketball's New York Knicks, hockey's Boston Bruins, indeed, even football's (not-for-profit corporation) Green Bay Packers. Are the league's fans, players, or other owners better or worse off because such public ownership has been permitted?

7. *Balancing Procompetitive Effects in One Market Against Harm in Another.* Another crucial issue in *Sullivan* was whether defendants can rely on procompetitive effects felt in a different market to offset anticompetitive harms in the relevant market. Does this seem like a difficult question? (Remember the same issue arose in the *Yazoo Smith* case in Chapter 6.) If the only procompetitive effects a jury could consider are those in the same market as the anticompetitive effects, how would that affect the Rule of Reason analysis in the player restraint cases we considered in Chapter 6? In the *NASL* case we looked at earlier in this chapter? Keep in mind the question of what procompetitive effects a jury is allowed to consider as you assess the Rule of Reason issues in franchise relocation and television restriction cases later in this chapter, and the cases involving NCAA rules in Chapter 11.

B. ADMISSION AND RELOCATION OF SPORTS FRANCHISES

Before a competitive sports league can commence operations, someone must decide five critical questions: (1) how many clubs will participate; (2)

which clubs will participate; (3) how many games will be played; (4) when will the games be played; and (5) where will the games be played (*i.e.*, where will each clubs' home field be located). In North America, existing club owners make each of these determinations, which, has been to date subject to limited external oversight, primarily in the form of the precedent established in the *Raiders* case excerpted below.

Not surprisingly, North American sports league clubs have adopted a policy that guarantees each club a permanent spot in the league (subject to extraordinary termination provisions). Because leagues tend to expand more slowly than the economy grows, civic leaders and local businesses in locations without franchises have sought to induce existing clubs to relocate. This surge in actual or potential franchise relocation has forced cities and states seeking to obtain or retain major league franchises to spend huge amounts of money on sports facilities. For example, Miami built a $65 million arena in the mid-1980s to house both the NBA Heat and NHL Panthers. However, by the late 1990s, each of those teams had secured a new $150 million facility just for itself.

"Franchise free agency" (the idea that an owner can sell the location of his team's home games to the highest bidder) has proven to be very lucrative not just for the wealthy owners of the teams, but also for the players who can utilize their own free agency rights to extract more sizeable salary contracts from the teams that now can afford to pay even more to try to win a championship. It has not been so beneficial to the taxpayers who must foot the bill for the new stadium deals—and almost always through some version of a sales tax or a tax on visitors renting hotel rooms or cars, rather than from higher income or capital gains taxes collected from the well-to-do who watch the games from the most luxurious seats.

Teams controlled by owners who have made a sizable financial investment to acquire their club are not likely to relocate unless the move is in the team's financial interest, but the effect of relocation on the league as a whole can be less clear. NHL Commissioner Gary Bettman and a majority of owners have pursued a long-term strategy of securing broader exposure in southern and western markets that were without teams, including franchise expansions as well as relocations of franchises from Winnipeg and Quebec City to Phoenix and Denver (although the Atlanta Flames returned to Manitoba as the Winnipeg Jets). Similar relocations in baseball are largely seen as enhancing the game's growth and popularity, for example, when the Giants and Dodgers moved from New York to California, and when the second team in eastern cities relocated as with the Boston (now Atlanta) Braves and Philadelphia (now Oakland) Athletics. The same applies to basketball, with the Minneapolis Lakers and Buffalo Braves (now Clippers) moving to California, and the Rochester Royals' westward journey through Cincinnati and Kansas City to become the Sacramento Kings. The major exception to that rule was football, where Commissioner Rozelle and the owners in the 1970s and 80s judged that few, if any, of these individual owner relocation decisions were in the best interests of the league as a whole (which found itself with no team from 1995–2017 in Los Angeles, the second largest market in the country). At the same time, even NFL leaders have been clear since the *Raiders* case in the early 1980s about their willingness to support relocations when, in their judgment, local taxpayers were being insufficiently supportive of stadium subsidies.

The internal rules and practices of each league require consent of a super-majority of club owners to create a new franchise, and even to accept the new owner of an existing franchise. Once part of the league, the franchise enjoys an exclusive right (a shared-right in the largest markets) to operate a team in that geographic area. However, any attempt by an owner to move the club to a new location (whether or not occupied by another team) is also supposed to gain league-wide consent. There are a host of social, economic, and legal factors that have contributed to franchise free agency and taxpayer subsidies. The principal legal constraint on league policies is the antitrust doctrine discussed below.

1. LEAGUE REFUSALS TO PERMIT A CLUB'S RELOCATION

An early legal challenge to traditional league prerogatives came in *San Francisco Seals v. NHL*, 379 F. Supp. 966 (C.D. Cal. 1974). One of the six NHL expansion franchises created in 1967, the Seals enjoyed little success in the San Francisco Bay area. In 1969, the team sought to move to what then was still-vacant territory in Vancouver, British Columbia. The League's Board of Governors (comprised of one representative from each team) refused to approve the move, and the Seals sued under § 1 of the Sherman Act. The trial court summarily rejected this claim in a brief decision with the following key passage:

> What then is the relevant market? I find that the relevant product market with which we are here concerned is the production of professional hockey games before live audiences, and that the relevant geographical market is the United States and Canada.
>
> Now let us examine plaintiff's relationship with the defendants within the relevant market. Plaintiff, of course, wishes to participate in this market, but not in competition with the defendants. It expects to maintain its league membership and to accept and enjoy all of the exclusive territorial benefits which the National Hockey League affords. As a member team, it will continue cooperating with the defendants in pursuit of its main

purpose, *i.e.*, producing sporting events of uniformly high quality appropriately scheduled as to both time and location so as to assure all members of the league the best financial return. In this respect, the plaintiff and defendants are acting together as one single business enterprise, competing against other similarly organized professional leagues.

Id. at 969–70.

LOS ANGELES MEMORIAL COLISEUM COMM'N v. NFL (RAIDERS I)
726 F.2d 1381 (9th Cir. 1984)

ANDERSON, CIRCUIT JUDGE.

[This case was precipitated by the 1978 decision of Carroll Rosenbloom, owner of the Los Angeles Rams, to move his team's home games from the Los Angeles Coliseum to Anaheim, attracted by a lucrative lease arrangement offered by that city. At the same time, Al Davis had reached a stalemate in efforts to negotiate the terms for renewal of the Raiders' lease with the Oakland Coliseum. Conversations thus began between Davis and L.A. Coliseum officials about a possible Raiders' move to the Coliseum. At the time, NFL Rule 4.1 had defined "home territory" as extending for a 75-mile radius from the boundaries of the team's home city as designated in the NFL Constitution. Thus, Los Angeles was still the home city of the Rams playing in Anaheim. Rule 4.3 then provided that any team proposing to move into another's home territory needed unanimous approval from all other teams. Other relocations required only a three-quarters vote. Concerned about the vulnerability of these rules to legal challenge, the NFL owners amended the rules in late 1978: amended Rule 4.3 applied the three-quarters formula to all relocations regardless of the new site, thus removing the possibility of a veto by an incumbent club. On March 1, 1980, Davis signed a "memorandum of agreement" to move the Raiders to the L.A. Coliseum. On March 10, 1980, the NFL took a vote on the proposed move (over Davis' objections). The result was 22–0 against, with five teams (including the Rams) abstaining and the Raiders not participating.

Shortly thereafter, the Raiders joined an amended suit filed in 1978 by the Coliseum against the NFL initially claiming that the League violated section 1 by not putting an expansion team in the Coliseum when the Rams left. Over the objections of the NFL (and the Oakland Coliseum, which intervened as a party), Los Angeles was retained as the venue for the jury trial. After a three-month jury trial in 1981 on liability alone, a trial that focused largely on the single entity defense, Judge Harry Pregerson, who had just become a Ninth Circuit judge but had retained this one case as the trial judge, granted a directed verdict for plaintiffs on this issue and thus removed it from jury consideration. Nonetheless, the jury could not reach a rule of reason verdict and a mistrial was declared. A lengthy liability retrial in 1982 resulted in a verdict that found that the NFL's action was an unreasonable restraint of trade. An injunction was entered barring the league from blocking the Raiders' relocation, and the NFL immediately appealed. The excerpt below provides the appellate court's application of the rule of reason to the NFL's refusal to approve the relocation.]

In a quite general sense, the case presents the competing considerations of whether a group of businessmen can enforce an agreement with one of their co-contractors to the detriment of that co-contractor's right to do business where he pleases. More specifically, this lawsuit requires us to engage in the difficult task of analyzing the negative and positive effects of a business practice in an industry which does not readily fit into the antitrust context. Section 1 of the Sherman Act was designed to prevent agreements among competitors which eliminate or reduce competition and thereby harm consumers. Yet, as we discussed in the context of the single entity issue, the NFL teams are not true competitors, nor can they be.

The NFL's structure has both horizontal and vertical attributes. On the one hand, it can be viewed simply as an organization of 28 competitors, an example of a simple horizontal arrangement. On the other, and to the extent the NFL can be considered an entity separate from the team owners, a vertical relationship is disclosed. In this sense the owners are distributors of the NFL product, each with its own territorial division. In this context it is clear that the owners have a legitimate interest in protecting the integrity of the League itself. Collective action in areas such as League divisions, scheduling and rules must be allowed, as should other activity that aids in producing the most marketable product attainable. Nevertheless, legitimate collective action should not be construed to allow the owners to extract excess profits. In such a situation the owners would be acting as a classic cartel. Agreements among competitors, *i.e.*, cartels, to fix prices or divide market territories are presumed illegal under § 1 because they give competitors the ability to charge unreasonable and arbitrary prices instead of setting prices by virtue of free market forces.

On its face, Rule 4.3 divides markets among the 28 teams, a practice presumed illegal, but, as we have noted, the unique structure of the NFL precludes application of the per se rule. Instead, we must examine Rule 4.3 to determine whether it reasonably serves the legitimate collective concerns of the owners or instead permits them to reap excess profits at the expense of the consuming public.

1. Relevant Market

[The court then turned to the NFL's argument that the trial judgment should be reversed on the grounds that there had been no adverse impact on the relevant market, defined in both "product" and "geographic" terms. In the court's view, the scope of the market turned on what range of products had the ability to take significant amounts of business away from the others. This required judgments about the "reasonable interchangeability" of the products for similar uses and the "cross-elasticity of demand" for one product based on price changes in the other, which in turn depended on the "economically significant" geographic area of effective competition in which these products were traded. For their case, the Raiders claimed that the relevant market consisted just of NFL football (the product) in greater Los Angeles (the geographic area). The L.A. Coliseum claimed that its market consisted of stadiums offering facilities to NFL teams across the United States. The NFL's position was that the relevant product markets consisted of all entertainment and stadium uses across the entire country.]

* * *

That NFL football has limited substitutes from a consumer standpoint is seen from evidence that the Oakland Coliseum sold out for 10 consecutive years despite having some of the highest ticket prices in the League. A similar conclusion can be drawn from the extraordinary number of television viewers—over 100 million people—that watched the 1982 Super Bowl, the ultimate NFL product. NFL football's importance to the television networks is evidenced by the approximately $2 billion they agreed to pay the League for the right to televise the games from 1982–1986. This contract reflects the networks' anticipation that the high number of television viewers who had watched NFL football in the past would continue to do so in the future.

To some extent, the NFL itself narrowly defined the relevant market by emphasizing that NFL football is a unique product which can be produced only through the joint efforts of the 28 teams. Don Shula, coach of the Miami Dolphins, underscored this point when he stated that NFL football has a different set of fans than college football.

The evidence from which the jury could have found a narrow pro football product market was balanced, however, with other evidence which tended to show the NFL competes in the first instance with other professional sports, especially those with seasons that overlap with the NFL's. On a broader level, witnesses such as Pete Rozelle and Georgia Frontierre (owner of the L.A. Rams) testified that NFL football competes with other television offerings for network business, as well as other local entertainment for attendance at the games.

In terms of the relevant geographic market, witnesses testified, in particular Al Davis, that NFL teams compete with one another off the field for fan support in those areas where teams operate in close proximity such as New York City-New Jersey, Washington, D.C.-Baltimore, and formerly San Francisco-Oakland. Davis, of course, had firsthand knowledge of this when his team was located in Oakland. Also, the San Francisco Forty-Niners and the New York Giants were paid $18 million because of the potential for harm from competing with the Oakland Raiders and the New York Jets, respectively, once those teams joined the NFL as a result of the merger with the American Football League. Al Davis also testified at length regarding the potential for competition for fan support between the Raiders and the Los Angeles Rams once his team relocated in Los Angeles.

Testimony also adequately described the parameters of the stadia market. On one level, stadia do compete with one another for the tenancy of NFL teams. Such competition is shown by the Rams' move to Anaheim. Carroll Rosenbloom was offered what he considered to be a more lucrative situation at the Big A Stadium, so he left the L.A. Coliseum. In turn, the L.A. Coliseum sought to lure existing NFL teams to Los Angeles. Competition between the L.A. Coliseum and the Oakland Coliseum for the tenancy of the Raiders resulted.

* * *

The NFL claims that it is places, not particular stadia, that compete for NFL teams. This is true to a point because the NFL grants franchises to locales (generally a city and a 75 mile radius extending from its boundary). It is the individual stadia, however, which are most directly impacted by the restrictions on team movement. A stadium is a distinct economic entity and a territory is not.

It is also undoubtedly true, as the NFL contends, that stadia attempt to contract with a variety of forms of entertainment for exhibition in their facilities. In the case of the L.A. Coliseum, this includes college football, concerts, motorcycle races and the like. An NFL football team, however, is an especially desirable tenant. The L.A. Coliseum, for example, had received the highest rent from the Rams when they played there. We find that this evidence taken as whole provided the jury with an adequate basis on which to judge the reasonableness of Rule 4.3 both as it affected competition among NFL teams and among stadia.

We conclude with one additional observation. In the context of this case in particular, we believe that market evidence, while important, should not become an end in itself. Here the exceptional nature of the industry makes precise market definition especially difficult. To a large extent the market is determined by how one defines the entity: Is the NFL a single entity or partnership which creates a product that competes with other entertainment products for the consumer (*e.g.*, television and fans) dollar? Or is it 28 individual entities which compete with one another both on and off the field for the support of the consumers of the more narrow football product? Of course, the NFL has attributes of both examples and a variety of evidence was presented on both views. In fact, because of the exceptional structure of the League, it was not necessary for the jury to accept absolutely either the NFL's or the plaintiff's market definitions. Instead, the critical question is whether the jury could have determined that Rule 4.3 reasonably served the NFL's interest in producing and promoting its product, *i.e.*, competing in the entertainment market, or whether Rule 4.3 harmed competition among the 28 teams to such an extent that any benefits to the League as a whole were outweighed. As we find below, there was ample evidence for the jury to reach the latter conclusion.

2. The History and Purpose of Rule 4.3

The NFL has awarded franchises exclusive territories since the 1930s. In the early days of professional football, numerous franchises failed and many changed location in the hope of achieving economic success. League members saw exclusive territories as a means to aid stability, ensuring the owner who was attempting to establish an NFL team in a particular city that another would not move into the same area, potentially ruining them both.

Rule 4.3 is the result of that concern. Prior to its amendment in 1978, it required unanimous League approval for a move into another team's home territory. That, of course, gave each owner an exclusive territory and he could vote against a move into his territory solely because he was afraid the competition might reduce his revenue. Notably, however, the League constitution required only three-quarters approval for all other moves. The 1978 amendment removed the double-standard, and currently three-quarters approval is required for all moves.

That the purpose of Rule 4.3 was to restrain competition among the 28 teams may seem obvious and it is not surprising the NFL admitted as much at trial. It instead argues that Rule 4.3 serves a variety of legitimate League needs, including ensuring franchise stability. We must keep in mind, however, that the Supreme Court has long rejected the notion that "ruinous competition" can be a defense to a restraint of trade. Conversely, anticompetitive purpose alone is not enough to condemn Rule 4.3. The rule must actually harm competition, and that harm must be evaluated in light of the procompetitive benefits the rule might foster.

3. Ancillary Restraints and the Reasonableness of Rule 4.3

The NFL's primary argument is that it is entitled to judgment notwithstanding the verdict because under the facts and the law, Rule 4.3 is reasonable under the doctrine of ancillary restraints. The NFL's argument is inventive and perhaps it will breathe new life into this little used area of antitrust law, but we reject it for the following reasons.

The common-law ancillary restraint doctrine was, in effect, incorporated into Sherman Act § 1 analysis by Justice Taft in *United States v. Addyston Pipe & Steel Co.*, 85 F. 271 (6th Cir. 1898), aff'd as modified, 175 U.S. 211 (1899). Most often discussed in the area of covenants not to compete, the doctrine teaches that some agreements which restrain competition may be valid if they are "subordinate and collateral to another legitimate transaction and necessary to make that transaction effective."

Generally, the effect of a finding of ancillary is to "remove the per se label from restraints otherwise falling within that category." R. Bork, *Ancillary Restraints and the Sherman Act*, 15 Antitrust L.J. 211, 212 (1959). We assume, with no reason to doubt, that the agreement creating the NFL is valid and the territorial divisions therein are ancillary to its main purpose of producing NFL football. The ancillary restraint must then be tested under the rule of reason, the relevance of ancillary being it "increases the probability that the restraint will be found reasonable." As we have already noted, the rule of reason inquiry requires us to consider the harms and benefits to competition caused by the restraint and whether the putative benefits can be achieved by less restrictive means.

The competitive harms of Rule 4.3 are plain. Exclusive territories insulate each team from competition within the NFL market, in essence allowing them to set monopoly prices to the detriment of the consuming public. The rule also effectively foreclosed free competition among stadia such as the Los Angeles Coliseum that wish to secure NFL tenants. The harm from Rule 4.3 is especially acute in this case because it prevents a move by a team into another existing team's market. If the transfer is upheld, direct competition between the Rams and Raiders would presumably ensue to the benefit of all who consume the NFL product in the Los Angeles area.

The NFL argues, however, that territorial allocations are inherent in an agreement among joint venturers to produce a product. This inherent nature, the NFL asserts, flows from the need to protect each joint venturer in the "legitimate fruits of the contract, or to protect him from the dangers of an unjust use of those fruits by the other party." We agree that the nature of NFL football requires some territorial restrictions in order both to encourage participation in the venture and to secure each venturer the legitimate fruits of that participation.

Rule 4.3 aids the League, the NFL claims, in determining its overall geographical scope, regional balance and coverage of major and minor markets. Exclusive territories aid new franchises in achieving financial stability, which protects the large initial investment an owner must make to start up a football team. Stability arguably helps ensure no one team has an undue advantage on the field. Territories foster fan loyalty which in turn promotes traditional rivalries between teams, each contributing to attendance at games and television viewing.

Joint marketing decisions are surely legitimate because of the importance of television. Title 15, U.S.C. § 1291 grants the NFL an exemption from antitrust liability, if any, that might arise out of its collective negotiation of television rights with the networks. To effectuate this right, the League must be allowed to have some control over the placement of teams to ensure NFL football is popular in a diverse group of markets.

Last, there is some legitimacy to the NFL's argument that it has an interest in preventing transfers from areas before local governments, which have made a substantial investment in stadia and other facilities, can recover their expenditures. In such a situation, local confidence in the NFL is eroded, possibly resulting in a decline in interest. All these factors considered, we nevertheless are not persuaded the jury should have concluded that Rule 4.3 is a reasonable restraint of trade. The same goals can be achieved in a variety of ways which are less harmful to competition.

As noted by Justice Rehnquist, a factor in determining the reasonableness of an ancillary restraint is the "possibility of less restrictive alternatives" which could serve the same purpose. *See* Justice Rehnquist's dissent from the denial of certiorari in *North American Soccer League*, 459 U.S. 1074 (1982). This is a pertinent factor in all rule of reason cases. Here, the district court correctly instructed the jury to take into account the existence of less restrictive alternatives when determining the reasonableness of Rule 4.3's territorial restraint. Because there was substantial evidence going to the existence of such alternatives, we find that the jury could have reasonably concluded that the NFL should have designed its "ancillary restraint" in a manner that served its needs but did not so foreclose competition.

The NFL argues that the requirement of Rule 4.3 that three-quarters of the owners approve a franchise move is reasonable because it deters unwise team transfers. While the rule does indeed protect an owner's investment in a football franchise, no standards or durational limits are incorporated into the voting requirement to make sure that concern is satisfied. Nor are factors such as fan loyalty and team rivalries necessarily considered.

The NFL claims that its marketing and other objectives are indirectly accounted for in the voting process because the team owners vote to maximize their profits. Since the owners are guided by the desire to increase profits, they will necessarily make reasonable decisions, the NFL asserts, on such issues of whether the new location can support two teams, whether marketing needs will be adversely affected, etc. Under the present

Rule 4.3, however, an owner need muster only seven friendly votes to prevent three-quarters approval for the sole reason of preventing another team from entering its market, regardless of whether the market could sustain two franchises. A basic premise of the Sherman Act is that regulation of private profit is best left to the marketplace rather than private agreement. The present case is in fact a good example of how the market itself will deter unwise moves, since a team will not lightly give up an established base of support to confront another team in its home market.

The NFL's professed interest in ensuring that cities and other local governments secure a return on their investment in stadia is undercut in two ways. First, the local governments ought to be able to protect their investment through the leases they negotiate with the teams for the use of their stadia. Second, the NFL's interest on this point may not be as important as it would have us believe because the League has in the past allowed teams to threaten a transfer to another location in order to give the team leverage in lease negotiations.

Finally, the NFL made no showing that the transfer of the Raiders to Los Angeles would have any harmful effect on the League. Los Angeles is a market large enough for the successful operation of two teams, there would be no scheduling difficulties, facilities at the L.A. Coliseum are more than adequate, and no loss of future television revenue was foreseen. Also, the NFL offered no evidence that its interest in maintaining regional balance would be adversely affected by a move of a northern California team to southern California.

It is true, as the NFL claims, that the antitrust laws are primarily concerned with the promotion of interbrand competition. To the extent the NFL is a product which competes with other forms of entertainment, including other sports, its rules governing territorial division can be said to promote interbrand competition. Under this analysis, the territorial allocations most directly suppress intrabrand, that is, NFL team versus NFL team, competition. A more direct impact on intrabrand competition does not mean, however, the restraint is reasonable. The finder of fact must still balance the gain to interbrand competition against the loss of intrabrand competition. Here, the jury could have found that the rules restricting team movement do not sufficiently promote interbrand competition to justify the negative impact on intrabrand competition.

To withstand antitrust scrutiny, restrictions on team movement should be more closely tailored to serve the needs inherent in producing the NFL "product" and competing with other forms of entertainment. An express recognition and consideration of those objective factors espoused by the NFL as important, such as population, economic projections, facilities, regional balance, etc., would be well advised. Fan loyalty and location continuity could also be considered. Al Davis in fact testified that in 1978 he proposed that the League adopt a set of objective guidelines to govern team relocation rather than continuing to utilize a subjective voting procedure.

Some sort of procedural mechanism to ensure consideration of all the above factors may also be necessary, including an opportunity for the team proposing the move to present its case. *See Silver v. New York Stock Exchange*, 373 U.S. 341 (1963) (without procedural safeguards, the collective act of the Exchange in disconnecting the wire service to a broker constituted a boycott, per se illegal under § 1); *cf. Deesen v. Professional Golfers' Ass'n*, 358 F.2d 165 (9th Cir. 1966) (where PGA had reasonable rules governing eligibility of players for tournaments, there was not a § 1 violation). In the present case, for example, testimony indicated that some owners, as well as Commissioner Rozelle, dislike Al Davis and consider him a maverick. Their vote against the Raiders' move could have been motivated by animosity rather than business judgment.

Substantial evidence existed for the jury to find the restraint imposed by Rule 4.3 was not reasonably necessary to the production and sale of the NFL product. Therefore, the NFL is not entitled to judgment notwithstanding the verdict.

Affirmed.

[The appeals court majority concluded that the jury's verdict about the unreasonableness of this restraint—the opinion labeled this a "paradigm fact question"—was based on adequate evidence in the record.]

The *Raiders I* decision concerned only the NFL's antitrust liability for rejecting the Raiders' proposed move to Los Angeles. Following a second trial on the damages question, the jury awarded the Raiders $11.55 million for profits lost due to the two-year delay in their move south. The NFL appealed this sizable damage award (trebled under the Sherman Act to over $34 million) on various grounds, including that the benefits the Raiders realized by taking from the NFL the opportunity to create an expansion franchise in Los Angeles should be deducted from the team's lost profits. This produced the *Raiders II* decision, *Los Angeles Memorial Coliseum Comm'n v. NFL*, 791 F.2d 1356 (9th Cir. 1986). The court of appeals there endorsed the basic premise of the NFL's argument that the NFL as a whole owned the right to expand into the Los Angeles area, a valuable right foreclosed by the Raiders' relocation. Considering the difference between the value of this right and the value to the NFL of expanding into Oakland (as the NFL has expanded to Houston, Baltimore, and Cleveland after teams in those cities relocated), the uncontradicted testimony at trial showed the Los Angeles market to be a significantly more lucrative franchise opportunity. Indeed, the Raiders' managing general partner, Al Davis, testified that the Raiders increased their value by some $25 million by moving to Los Angeles. Thus, this "windfall benefit" had to be offset against the damages awarded to the Raiders for the two-year delay in their move to Los Angeles. The court continued:

> Application of this offset rule is consistent with, and indeed, virtually compelled by, this court's *Raiders I* opinion. In analyzing the "unique" nature of professional athletic leagues vis-a-vis the antitrust laws, this panel expressly acknowledged that "the nature of NFL football requires some territorial restrictions in order both to encourage participation in the venture *and to secure each venturer the legitimate fruits of that participation*." Here, the league owners collectively possessed the value that had accumulated in the Los Angeles expansion opportunity. This value, as indicated above, was created at least in part through the NFL's development, over the years, of a popular spectator sport with a national following. Although this panel upheld the liability jury's conclusion that Rule 4.3 as it was applied to the Raiders' move was an unreasonable restraint of trade, the opinion noted several less onerous forms of territorial restrictions that could pass muster under the rule of reason. Among these were standards restricting team movement that expressly recognized certain objective factors such as population, economic projections and the like, that the league could legitimately consider in deciding whether to permit a team to move. If such restrictions, applied in a non-arbitrary manner, would be reasonable under the Sherman Act, then *a fortiori*, a rule requiring merely an objectively-determined payment to league members as compensation for the right to take a valuable, jointly-owned franchise opportunity out of the league's hands, would also be a reasonable restriction.

791 F.2d at 1373.

A wave of relocations and inter-city bidding for NFL teams in the mid-1990s generated several § 1 lawsuits against the league's revised Rule 4.3, which had been amended after *Raiders I* to include several "objective" factors the owners must consider when voting on a proposed relocation. Al Davis and his Raiders continued to use the precedent to challenge a variety of league rules with which they disagreed, although none of the lawsuits yielded important sports law precedents. Another challenge was dismissed on the ground that the owner had signed a valid waiver of right to sue when he obtained the league's approval to sell the club. *VKK Corp. v. NFL*, 55 F. Supp. 2d 196 & 229 (S.D.N.Y. 1999), *aff'd*, 244 F.3d 114 (2d Cir. 2001).*

St. Louis also sued the NFL in the aftermath of the Rams move to their city, alleging that the league violated § 1 and tortiously interfered with the city's contract with the Rams by charging the Rams a $30 million relocation fee, which the team required St. Louis to subsidize. The league, which had not charged the Raiders such a fee, based it in part on anticipated reduced TV ratings and correspondingly lower broadcast rights fees. In 1997, after a lengthy trial, the trial judge granted a directed verdict for the NFL based on a lack of evidence of any conspiracy to keep other clubs from competing with the Rams for a potential St. Louis relocation opportunity. The Eighth Circuit affirmed the judgment. *St. Louis Convention & Visitors Comm'n v. NFL*, 154 F.3d 851 (8th Cir. 1998).

Raiders II was significant not just in sharply reducing the size of the NFL's damage liability to the Raiders, but also in offering somewhat greater support for league restraints on unilateral team movements. The latter effect became apparent soon afterwards in litigation involving the National Basketball Association and the San Diego Clippers. The Clippers decided to move their operations from San Diego to the Los Angeles Sports Arena (which was also owned by the Los Angeles Memorial Coliseum Commission), where the Clippers would compete for fans with the Los Angeles Lakers who were playing across town. After *Raiders I*, but before *Raiders II*, the NBA decided not to risk trebled damages by refusing to schedule Clippers' games in Los Angeles. Instead, the league sued the Clippers in San Diego, seeking a judicial declaration that the league could lawfully prohibit this relocation. After the district court had summarily dismissed the league's suit, the Ninth Circuit provided yet another interpretation of its holdings in *Raiders I* and *Raiders II*.

---

* These two cases are discussed because of their significance for antitrust doctrine related to the relocation of sports league franchises. They are the tip of the iceberg, however, regarding lawsuits between the litigious Raiders owner and the NFL. Additional litigation included: *Oakland Raiders v. NFL*, 93 Cal. App. 4th 572 (2001) (affirming dismissal of a host of state law claims challenging NFL's decision to require clubs to participate in a league-owned European league); *Oakland Raiders v. NFL*, 41 Cal. 4th 624 (2007) (affirming trial verdict and judgment in favor of NFL against claims that the NFL was liable to the Raiders for the expansion opportunity given back to the league when the Raiders relocated back to Oakland from Los Angeles, and that the NFL failed to provide sufficient support for a new stadium in Los Angeles); *NFL Properties v. Superior Court*, 65 Cal. App. 4th 100 (Cal. Ct. App. 1998) (reversing discovery order in litigation challenging operation of venture controlling intellectual property rights of NFL clubs, noting that Raiders were shareholders in NFL Properties); *Oakland-Alameda County Coliseum v. Oakland Raiders*, 197 Cal. App. 3d 1049 (1988) (affirming summary judgment for unpaid rent).

NBA v. SAN DIEGO CLIPPERS BASKETBALL CLUB
815 F.2d 562 (9th Cir. 1987)

FERGUSON, CIRCUIT JUDGE.

* * *

The antitrust issues are directly controlled by the two *Raiders* opinions, although the district judge had the benefit only of *Raiders I* when he rendered judgment. Collectively, the *Raiders* opinions held that rule of reason analysis governed a professional sports league's efforts to restrict franchise movement. More narrowly, however, *Raiders I* merely held that a reasonable jury could have found that the NFL's application of its franchise movement rule was an unreasonable restraint of trade. *Raiders II* confirmed that the jury's liability verdict affirmed in *Raiders I* "held Rule 4.3 [the franchise movement rule] invalid only as it was applied to the Raiders' proposed move to Los Angeles." The Clippers' and the Coliseum's efforts to characterize *Raiders I* as presenting guidelines for franchise movement rules are thus unavailing. Neither the jury's verdict in *Raiders*, nor the court's affirmance of that verdict, held that a franchise movement rule, in and of itself, was invalid under the antitrust laws . . . [T]he panel set down no absolute rule for sports leagues. Instead, it examined the facts before it and concluded that the jury's conclusion that the NFL violated the antitrust laws was supported by the record.

Yet the Clippers argue, as they must to support summary judgment, that the "NBA three-quarters rule . . . is illegal under *Raiders I*"—i.e., either that the NBA rule is void as a matter of law under *Raiders I*, or that the NBA has not adduced genuine issues of fact to allow the rule to stand. The Clippers assert that the rule "is illegal as applied . . . [but that under *Raiders I*], a professional sports league's club relocation rule must at least be 'closely tailored' and incorporate objective standards and criteria such as population, economic projections, playing facilities, regional balance, and television revenues." . . . The Clippers' confusion, and that of a number of commentators, may derive from the *Raiders I* panel's painstaking efforts to guide sports leagues toward procedures that might, in all cases, withstand antitrust analysis. The objective factors and procedures recounted by the Clippers are "well advised," and might be sufficient to demonstrate procompetitive purposes that would save the restriction from the rule of reason. They are not, however, necessary conditions to the legality of franchise relocation rules.

. . . As we have demonstrated, antitrust analysis under *Raiders I* indicates that the question of what restraints are reasonable is one of fact. We believe that numerous issues of fact remain.

The NBA asserts a number of genuine issues of fact: (1) the purpose of the restraint as demonstrated by the NBA's use of a variety of criteria in evaluating franchise movement, (2) the market created by professional basketball, which the NBA alleges is substantially different from that of professional football, and (3) the actual effect the NBA's limitations on movements might have on trade. The NBA's assertions, if further documented at trial, create an entirely different factual setting than that of the Raiders and the NFL. Further, as the NBA correctly notes, the antitrust issue here is vastly different than that in the *Raiders* cases: the issue here is "whether the mere requirement that a team seek [NBA] Board of Governor approval before it seizes a new franchise location violates the Sherman Act." The NBA here did not attempt to forbid the move. It scheduled the Clippers in the Sports Arena, and when faced with continued assertions of potential antitrust liability, brought this suit for declaratory relief. Given the *Raiders I* rejection of per se analysis for franchise movement rules of sports leagues, and the existence of genuine issues of fact regarding the reasonableness of the restraint, the judgment against the NBA must be reversed.

Summary judgment reversed.

After this decision, the NBA and the Clippers settled their litigation, with the Clippers agreeing to make a substantial payment to the league for the right to remain in Los Angeles.

NOTES AND QUESTIONS

1. *Balancing Competitive Effects.* How was the jury in the *Raiders* case supposed to balance effects on both interbrand and intrabrand competition? As for intrabrand competition, would the Raiders' presence in Los Angeles affect the competitive behavior of either the Rams or the Raiders? If so, would the Raiders absence from the San Francisco area affect the 49ers' competitive behavior in the opposite manner? What does interbrand competition mean in this context? Does a "monopolist" (assuming *arguendo* that the NFL has monopoly market power in one or more markets) that increases its efficiency enhance interbrand competition by making a higher quality or less expensive product, or does it diminish interbrand competition by raising barriers to entry? In the *Raiders* case, how would you have balanced the intrabrand competitive effects in Los Angeles and San Francisco and the interbrand effects in the larger entertainment market? Can *Raiders* be read narrowly as an extraordinary case where the jury rejected *all* of the NFL's asserted procompetitive arguments for enhanced interbrand competition?

How would you balance the intrabrand and interbrand competitive effects in the proposed moves to St. Louis where there was no other NFL team? Does it matter that the Patriots would have moved there from a Greater Boston market with no other NFL team, but the Rams moved there from a Los Angeles market that at the time had a second team (the Raiders) playing there? In making these determinations, should juries undertake *de novo* evaluation of the competitive effects, or should they give some deference to the judgment of the league owners?

2. *Less Restrictive Alternatives and "Due Process."* The *Raiders I* majority noted that one factor in determining reasonableness was whether less restrictive alternatives existed that could serve the same purpose. This analysis follows from the ancillary restraints doctrine of the *Addyston Pipe* case cited by the majority, limiting competitor agreements to those reasonably necessary to protect each party's "legitimate" interests. As applied to franchise relocation in sports, what does this mean? How would a jury use such an instruction in its deliberations? After the case was concluded, the NFL amended Rule 4.3 to include a list of "objective factors" that club owners should consider in deciding whether to approve a franchise relocation—for example, market size, stadium adequacy, and attendance. Had this language been in the rule prior to the teams' 22–0 vote against the Raiders move, would the rule or its application in the *Raiders* case have been less restrictive? Given that the court majority perceived that the jury's conclusion was that NFL owners voted against the Raiders' relocation despite no objective harm to the league, in order to protect the Rams from competition, would this realistically have changed any votes in the *Raiders* case?

Subsequently, the Supreme Court ruled in a non-sports case that (contrary to suggestions in the *Silver* case cited in *Raiders I*) fair procedures would not shield anticompetitive agreements from antitrust liability, while unfair procedures would not condemn collective decisions that had no anticompetitive effect. *Northwest Wholesale Stationers, Inc. v. Pacific Stationery & Printing Co.*, 472 U.S. 284 (1985). However, adherence to established procedures may be relevant to protect a league from accusations that its adverse decisions were arbitrary, capricious, or malicious, under the law governing private associations considered in Chapter 1.

3. *Applying the Ancillary Restraints Doctrine.* The *Raiders I* majority rejected the NFL's claim that Rule 4.3 was inherently reasonable as a restraint ancillary to a larger lawful contract. The court stated that classification of a restraint as ancillary means only that the restraint is not *per se* illegal. How should a restraint's ancillary nature be considered in subsequent rule of reason analysis? What instructions should a trial court give to a jury?

4. *Relocation Fees and Jury Deference to League Judgments.* *Raiders II* indicated that it would have been reasonable and thus legal if, instead of blocking the Raiders' move to Los Angeles, the league had merely levied a charge against the Raiders for the difference in the value of the Los Angeles and Oakland markets. How would such values be calculated? Could the Raiders refuse to pay the amount determined by the league, and then sue for treble damages under § 1, claiming that the amount charged was in fact greater than it should have been? If so, would a jury reviewing the amount of

the charge substitute its own judgment of the correct amount, or should it be instructed to give some deference to the league's determination?

5. *Relocation of Bankrupt Clubs.* How should the validity of league refusals to permit relocation be affected when the franchise at issue has declared bankruptcy? This issue arose in the context of the future of the NHL's Phoenix Coyotes. Between the relocation of the original Winnipeg Jets in 1996 and 2009, the Coyotes accumulated losses of $315 million. Seeking a way out, owner Jerry Moyes filed a voluntary petition for bankruptcy under Chapter 11 of the Bankruptcy Code (which permits corporate reorganization, rather than the liquidation of all assets). He then filed a motion authorizing the sale of the club to PSE Sports & Entertainment, LP (PSE), a firm controlled by Canadian businessman James Balsillie for $212.5 million in cash. The bid would have provided unsecured creditors with about 63 cents on the dollar, but was contingent on Balsillie's relocation of the franchise from Arizona to Hamilton, Ontario. Subsequent proceedings led to an alternative bid of $140 million by a new corporation owned by the remaining NHL owners for the purpose of keeping the Coyotes in Arizona.

The NHL argued that the Balsillie bid should be rejected because the NHL's Constitution reserves to the owners the right to approve any change in franchise ownership, and that they had properly acted to refuse to approve Balsillie as an NHL owner. PSE argued that the NHL's claim that Balsillie was not an appropriate owner was pretextual; it argued that the owners were really restraining trade by refusing the relocation in order to protect the nearby Toronto Maple Leafs and Buffalo Sabres from competition. PSE sought to invoke § 363(f) of the Bankruptcy Code, which allows the court to approve a sale of property free and clear of any restrictions. If this argument had been accepted by the bankruptcy judge, it would have excused PSE from the need to obtain NHL approval of Balsillie as an owner or to comply with the NHL Constitution's detailed rules governing approval of franchise relocations. But this provision allows such sales only when there is "adequate protection" for other interests in the property being sold.

The judge agreed with the NHL that Balsillie's offer to pay a relocation fee, per *Raiders II,* was not sufficient. *In re Dewey Ranch Hockey, LLC,* 414 B.R. 577 (Bankr. D. Ariz. 2009) (*Coyotes II*). He held that the "very nature of professional sports requires some territorial restrictions in order both to encourage participation in the venture and to secure to each venturer the legitimate fruits of that participation. *See Los Angeles Memorial Coliseum Com'n v. NFL,* 726 F.2d 1381, 1396 (9th Cir. 1984)." 414 B.R. at 591. The court relied on a bankruptcy precedent, *In re Magness,* 972 F.2d 689 (6th Cir. 1992), where the court prohibited a bankruptcy trustee from selling a golf and country club membership, where such sale would move the sale of that membership ahead of those on the country club's waiting list.

In ruling for the NHL, the bankruptcy judge refused to rule on the Sherman Act's limits on league relocation decisions. If, following the rejection of his bid, Balsillie had filed a Sherman Act suit against the NHL, would he likely have been able to prove to a jury that the refusal was an unreasonable restraint of trade? Would it matter under U.S. antitrust law that the market that was arguably restrained was located in Canada while the city losing the team would have been in the U.S.? In light of *Raiders II* and *Rams*, would the NHL be justified in conditioning relocation on payment of a substantial fee? How should it compute such a fee? What standard should a judge use in reviewing the legality of the fee? Should the bankruptcy judge decline to rule on Balsillie's claim that the league's refusal was unlawful?

6. *Counseling Leagues After* Raiders/Clippers. What are the broader guidelines that emerge from *Raiders* and from *Clippers* for the benefit of leagues and teams that naturally want to know *before* antitrust litigation whether a team's proposed move from one city to another can either be made or be blocked? What kind of legal liability does the league—or the club—face if it guesses incorrectly about the state and application of the law?

7. *Comparing Relocation Dynamics in NFL and MLB.* A number of owners have moved from larger to smaller markets because of more favorable stadium deals. Why is this more prevalent in the NFL, featuring 8 home games and centralized and shared television revenues, than in MLB, featuring 81 home games and largely local broadcast rights sales? Should the NFL's history be a concern of antitrust law, which is supposed to ensure that price (including tax subsidies to owners as the "price" of relocation) and output are responsive to consumer preference?

2. LEAGUE CONTROLS OVER ENTRY/CONTRACTION

Three owners from the defunct World Football League took the best players from their former WFL teams and sought to persuade a federal appellate court that they were entitled to admission to the National Football League—not as purchasers of an existing team, but as creators of a new team. These owners brought with their application not just a city, a stadium, and a fan base, but also a team of players looking for a league in which to play.

MID-SOUTH GRIZZLIES V. NFL
720 F.2d 772 (3d Cir. 1983)

GIBBONS, CIRCUIT JUDGE.

[The Memphis Southmen were one of the few successful franchises in the World Football League, which opened in 1974 and closed midway through the 1975 season. The team then reorganized with players from two other WFL teams (the Philadelphia Bell and the Southern California Sun), named itself the Grizzlies, and applied for a franchise in the National Football League. The Grizzlies claimed that they were an established football enterprise operating in a city, Memphis, which had demonstrated strong popular demand for professional football, and was not included in the 75-mile "home territory" of any existing NFL franchise. The NFL rejected the Grizzlies' application; the reasons given were recent expansion to Seattle and Tampa, the scheduling need for an even number of teams, and an uncertain labor relationship with the NFLPA (the *Mackey* suit was still being litigated). The Grizzlies then filed an antitrust suit in Philadelphia. The suit relied not only on the Sherman Act, but also upon 15 U.S.C.A. § 1291 (Public Law 87–331), which gave professional sports leagues a limited antitrust exemption to pool and sell their television rights, and upon Public Law 89–800, which in 1966 amended § 1291 to permit the merger of the National and American Football Leagues "if such agreement increases rather than decreases the number of professional football clubs." The trial judge granted the NFL's motion for summary dismissal, and the Grizzlies appealed. The circuit court rejected the Grizzlies' claim that the additional monopoly power conferred on an expanded NFL by that special legislation imposed on the league an affirmative obligation, in effect, to share that power with franchise-seekers such as the Grizzlies. The court then turned to the question whether the NFL's rejection of the Grizzlies' application constituted a violation of the basic Sherman Act.]

* * *

As to the acquisition of dominant position and monopoly power, the facts are undisputed. Long before the Grizzlies and the World Football League came into existence, Congress authorized the merger of the two major football leagues extant in 1966, and granted to the merged league the power to pool television revenues. That congressional decision conferred on the NFL the market power which it holds in the market for professional football. Congress could not have been unaware that necessary effect of the television revenue sharing scheme which it approved for the NFL would be that all members of that league would be strengthened in their ability to bid for the best available playing and coaching personnel, to the potential disadvantage of new entrants.

* * *

As to competition with NFL members in the professional football market, including the market for sale of television rights, the exclusion was patently pro-competitive, since it left the Memphis area, with a large stadium and a significant metropolitan area population, available as a site for another league's franchise, and it left the Grizzlies' organization as a potential competitor in such a league. If there was any injury to competition, actual or potential, therefore, it must have been to intra-league competition.

The NFL defendants' position is that the summary judgment record establishes conclusively the absence of competition, actual or potential, among league members. Rather, they urge, the league is a single entity, a joint venture in the presentation of the professional football spectacle.

For the most part the congressionally authorized arrangements under which the NFL functions eliminate competition among the league members. Indeed it is undisputed that on average more than 70% of each member club's revenue is shared revenue derived from sources other than operations at its home location. The Grizzlies do not challenge the legality of the NFL's revenue sharing arrangements, and seek to participate in them. The Grizzlies emphasize that there nevertheless remains a not insignificant amount of intra-league non-athletic competition. We need not, in order to affirm the summary judgment, accept entirely the NFL's position that there is no intra-league competition. Conceivably within certain geographic submarkets two league members compete with one another for ticket buyers, for local broadcast revenue, and for sale of the concession items like food and beverages and team paraphernalia. Thus rejection of a franchise application in the New York metropolitan area, for example, might require a different antitrust analysis than is suggested by this record. But the Grizzlies were obliged, when faced with the NFL denial of the existence of competition among NFL members and a potential franchisee at Memphis, to show some more than minimal level of potential competition, in the product markets in which league members might compete. They made no such showing. The record establishes that the NFL franchise nearest to Memphis is at St. Louis, Mo., over 280 miles away. There is no record evidence that professional football teams located in Memphis and in St. Louis would compete for the same ticket purchasers, for the same local broadcast outlets, in the sale of team paraphernalia, or in any other manner.

The Grizzlies contend on appeal, although they did not so contend in the trial court, that league members compete in what they call the "raw material market" for players and coaching personnel. Entirely apart from the propriety of considering a legal theory not presented in the trial court, there are major defects in this Grizzlies' argument. First, the Grizzlies exclusion from the league in no way restrained them from competing for players by forming a competitive league. Second, they fail to explain how, if their exclusion from the league reduced competition for team personnel, that reduction caused an injury to the Grizzlies' business or property.

One final Grizzlies' argument in support of their § 1 Sherman Act claim bears mentioning. Relying on the essential facilities doctrine developed in cases such as *Silver v. New York Stock Exchange*, 373 U.S. 341 (1963) and *Associated Press v. United States*, 326 U.S. 1 (1945), they urge that because the NFL is a practical monopoly it had an obligation to admit members on fair, reasonable, and equal terms, absent some procompetitive justification for their exclusion. This Grizzlies argument suffers from the same defect as the others. The essential facilities doctrine is predicated on the assumption that admission of the excluded applicant would result in additional competition, in an economic rather than athletic sense. The Grizzlies have simply failed to show how competition in any arguably relevant market would be improved if they were given a share of the NFL's monopoly power.

Since on the record before us the Grizzlies have shown no actual or potential injury to competition resulting from the rejection of their application for an NFL franchise, they cannot succeed on their § 1 Sherman Act claim.

Affirmed.

―――

A similar antitrust suit to force expansion in hockey was summarily dismissed in *Seattle Totems v. National Hockey League*, 783 F.2d 1347 (9th Cir. 1986).

―――

The flip side of expansion is contraction, a concept largely unimagined in the major professional sports leagues in modern times—until 2001. The day after the World Series ended, Commissioner Bud Selig announced a decision by his fellow owners to dissolve two of the 30 teams before the 2002 season began. (An antitrust challenge was rejected by the Minnesota Supreme Court because of the baseball exemption, discussed in Chapter 4.)

Some interesting insights on the issue, however, might be gleaned from a similar case on the other side of the world. The Australian Rugby League had embarked by 1995 on an ambitious expansion program that included 20 teams. When media magnates Kerry Packer and Rupert Murdoch battled over television rights, Murdoch set up his own rival Superleague. In addition to battling the ARL for the services of top players, Murdoch secured agreements with 8 of the ARL clubs to switch leagues. After a financially destructive 2-year "war," the parties entered into an agreement merging the ARL and Superleague into a new competition, the National Rugby League. Murdoch insisted, despite strong resistance from the ARL, on shrinking the NRL to 14 teams over three years. Through insolvency and mergers between traditional rivals, the NRL shrunk to 15 teams in 2000. At that time, the league's board, comprised of three officials designated by Murdoch and three designated by the old ARL, kicked the South Sydney Rabbitohs out of the competition. Souths sued under Australian competition (*i.e.*, antitrust) law, lost in the trial court, and prevailed in the appellate tribunal. At this point, the NRL gave in and agreed to re-admit South Sydney to the competition, but continued to pursue the litigation appeal.

Although the actual litigation turned on a technical point of Australian competition law not present in Sherman Act jurisprudence, Australian courts used an important concept regarding the relevant markets where competition was allegedly being restrained that has relevance for American antitrust doctrine. As the Court described the issue, sports leagues provide "competition organizing services" for clubs: "the supply of the services of organising and running top level rugby league competitions to ... [a] rugby league club willing and able to provide a team to participate competitively in a top level rugby league competition." In turn, clubs provide "team services" to leagues: clubs provide the actual teams to participate in competitions to be organized by those providing "competition organizing services." *South Sydney Rugby League Football Club Ltd v. News Ltd* (2003) 200 ALR 157.

We tend not to appreciate this distinction in North America, because in team sports the commercial entity that provides competition organizing services is a joint venture of the clubs providing the team services (except in auto racing where NASCAR and the IndyCar League provide the organizing service and the individual racing teams provide the racers). In economic terms, there is a "vertical integration" between the providers of what are, analytically, two distinct services.

NOTES AND QUESTIONS

1. *Admission to Monopoly Leagues.* As long as there is only one major league in each sport, should a league be required to admit any qualified applicant? How would a judgment be made as to whether an applicant was "qualified" and under what criteria?

2. *Impact of* Grizzlies *on Other Relocations.* The court concluded in *Grizzlies* that the NFL's refusal to add this new team to the league did not affect market competition because no other NFL teams were located near Memphis, a situation that differed in this respect from the league's earlier effort to block the Raiders relocation to Los Angeles where a second NFL team was proximately located. What does the reasoning of *Raiders* and *Grizzlies* imply about the legal right of the Baltimore Colts to move (in the mid-1980s) to Indianapolis? What about the Los Angeles Rams to St. Louis (in the mid-1990s) at a time when the Raiders were still based in Los Angeles, and the St. Louis Rams' decision to move back to Los Angeles in 2017, when the Raiders had returned to Oakland?

3. Grizzlies' *Rejection of Inter-Club Competition.* In any event, the Grizzlies also argued that NFL teams competed economically with one another in broader national markets—*e.g.*, for players, coaches, and other personnel. How did the court deal with this argument? Is the court's response persuasive?

4. *Antitrust Claims from Contraction.* Could those aggrieved by a team's elimination bring a plausible antitrust claim? Based on the *Raiders, Clippers,* and *Grizzlies* cases, what competition might arguably be restrained? Would your answer be different if the team being eliminated were playing in a one or two-team market? Or in a market in which it was the only major league sports team in any sport?

5. *How to Evaluate Antitrust Claims for Rejected Entry.* As a practical matter, the way new golfers and tennis players gain access to their respective tours differs from the manner team sports leagues add new expansion franchises. Generally, new golfers and tennis players are accepted for tournaments when they prove more competitive at the game than the people they replace. In contrast, new league franchises are added when owners of the existing teams agree that expansion to a particular area is in the league's best economic or political interests, and then only upon payment of huge expansion fees. How would the judge decide that a particular area was the best place for NFL expansion, and how would the judge calculate the appropriate franchise fee? Could the court be guided by how clubs now decide these issues?

6. *Promotion and Relegation in the Rest of the World.* For most professional sports in the rest of the western world, admission into the "major league" is determined in an entirely different way, known as "promotion and relegation." Unlike North American leagues, the major leagues sit on top of a hierarchy of lower-tier leagues, with the best teams in lower leagues being promoted to the next higher tier league at the end of each season, and the worst teams in higher leagues being relegated. These lower-tier leagues are not farm teams, although often individual players are "loaned" to lower-tier leagues for training and play much as minor leagues exist in North America. To minimize economic dislocation, most leagues arrange for "parachute payments," often 50% of television rights, if a team falls to a lower division. Rarely do top teams get relegated, but when they do, it doesn't last long as they easily dominate the lower league and get promoted within a season.

Is promotion and relegation a better way to determine entry into the major leagues? Suppose, in contrast, the current PGA tour golfers all voted to leave the PGA and form the Elite Golfers Association, where they promised to play only each other or anyone whose rights to participate were purchased from an existing member. For an economic analysis of this proposal, *see* Stephen F. Ross and Stefan Szymanski, *Fans of the World, Unite! A (Capitalist) Manifesto for Sports Consumers* (Stanford Univ. Press 2008). These authors sketch a legal argument on why the existing "closed league" model in the United States could be considered a violation of the Sherman Act in *Open Competition in League Sports*, 2002 Wis. L. Rev. 625.

3. THE LIMITS OF ANTITRUST: ALTERNATIVE NON-ANTITRUST APPROACHES TO STAKEHOLDER INTERESTS IN FRANCHISE MOVEMENT

Reconsider the lessons learned to this point regarding the number and location of major league sports franchises. Under governance principles discussed in Chapter 1, these decisions are made collectively by the other franchise owners collectively. Under the discussion of monopoly power in Chapter 5, for a variety of reasons the usual antitrust policy of competition—in the form of rival leagues within each sport—is not available to ensure that communities that could economically support viable businesses can patronize them. Under the doctrines established in *Raiders* and *Grizzlies*, the antitrust laws only intervene to protect stakeholder interests when the league has prevented a relocation to protect existing club owners from local competition.

The result is predictable under competition policy: more communities would like to support a major league franchise than there are such franchises, and as a result there is fierce financial bidding for a scarce number of sports franchises. The result of these bidding wars is that many teams, whether or not they move, are regularly favored with large public subsidies. This leverage by clubs over communities anxious to keep or acquire a professional franchise is a textbook example of exercising enormous market power, perhaps even monopoly power (lawfully acquired or not), to drive the "price" of franchises up by artificially restricting supply in the face of growing demand. With little support for a National Sports Commission to regulate this exploitation, stakeholders turn to a number of other strategies to achieve a goal that would be easily achieved in other industries where consumers and taxpayers have competitive alternatives.

These strategies are summarized in this section, for two reasons. First, they are relevant areas of law about which sports lawyers should be familiar. Second, they shape a normative evaluation about the efficacy of antitrust to protect consumers and taxpayers from monopoly power.

(a) Blocking an Undesired Relocation Based on State and Local Government Law or Federal, State, or Local Environmental Laws

Often, citizens who oppose efforts to relocate a franchise to their community resort to a variety of legal challenges based on statutes governing the operation of state or local government or judicial review of local government decisions, or based on federal, state, or local environmental laws. The former vary by state, and the latter are worthy of the entire course of Environmental Law. None have unique sports law content, and so are not discussed further in this casebook.

(b) Protective Lease Terms

Communities can try to protect themselves against departures of their "home" teams by favorable terms in leases between municipally-owned stadiums and major league clubs. Some courts have found that the city-lessor's damages from a team's breach of contract are not irreparable, and that monetary damages are sufficient. Others have granted equitable relief based on the unique and irreplaceable value of the franchise. *Compare City of New York v. New York Jets,* 394 N.Y.S.2d 799 (1977), with *HMC Management v. New Orleans Basketball Club,* 375 So.2d 700 (La. App. 1979).

Seattle's retention of the NFL Seahawks may largely be credited to a lease provision that expressly gave King County, WA, the right to obtain specific performance. As a result, when owner Kenneth Behring threatened to move the club to Los Angeles in 1996, King County sued and ultimately persuaded Behring to agree to sell the team for $200 million to Microsoft magnate Paul Allen, who promised to keep the Seahawks in Seattle (in return for a $325 million taxpayer subsidy for a new retractable-dome, football-only stadium). The Seahawks initially defended the County's suit by arguing that the lease was voidable because the County had allowed the Kingdome to deteriorate to where it no longer met adequate earthquake standards. (This "concern" led Behring to say he wanted to move to Los Angeles.) What would a team have to show in order to establish that a stadium had so deteriorated that the lease was voidable?

After the 2001 season, MLB threatened to contract the Minnesota Twins, offering a generous buyout to the Twins' owner. However, after a Minnesota state court judge enjoined contraction based on his interpretation of the Twins' lease, the MLBPA also objected, and in the 2002 collective bargaining agreement the owners agreed to postpone contraction indefinitely. The injunction was not based on antitrust but rather on state contract and tort law. The trial judge had found that sports leases are unique, because the "welfare, recreation, prestige, prosperity, trade, and commerce of the people of the community are at stake." This argument was similar to the one that that Twins' owner Carl Pohlad had made to try to persuade the community to build a luxurious new stadium for his Twins. In *Metropolitan Sports Facilities Commission v. Minnesota Twins Partnership,* 638 N.W.2d 214 (2002), the court of appeals affirmed. Chief Judge Toussaint first synopsized the trial judge's reasons for finding irreparable harm to not only the stadium authority, but also the state and its citizens—particularly, the fans—if the Twins were to play no 2002 home games at the Metrodome. The trial judge:

> (1) cited the role of baseball as a tradition and as a national pastime, the history of the Twins in Minnesota for some 40 years, including two World Series championships, the role of Twins

legends who have bettered the community by their volunteer work with children, and the availability of Twins games as affordable family entertainment; (2) noted that private buildings had been condemned to build the Metrodome; (3) found that the welfare, recreation, prestige, prosperity, trade, and commerce of the people of the community are at stake; and (4) ruled that the vital public trust outweighs any private interest.

638 N.W.2d at 221.

After then citing the legal and economic reasons why specific performance could occasionally be available as a form of equitable relief in certain exceptional commercial-lease cases, Judge Toussaint noted the state Supreme Court's decision in *Lifteau v. Metropolitan Sports Facilities Comm'n,* 270 N.W.2d 749 (Minn. 1978), which had accepted Baseball's position that "the use of public funds for construction of the Metrodome . . . constituted a public purpose for which public expenditures may legally be undertaken."

> The public interest in Major League Baseball franchises in general has been recognized by others. In discussing possible effects of the potential loss of baseball's antitrust exemption, Chairman Selig stated that it could irreparably injure [fans] by leading to the removal of live professional baseball from communities that have hosted major league and minor league teams for decades. Similarly, based on his own unsuccessful efforts to stop the relocation of the Milwaukee Braves, Selig told Congress that he believed that the professional sports league and Major League Baseball should vigilantly enforce strong policies prohibiting clubs from abandoning local communities which have supported them. [Citation to Hearings omitted] He further stated that franchise relocation should be prohibited except in the most dire circumstances where the local community has, over a sustained period, demonstrated that it cannot or will not support the franchise.

638 N.W.2d of 224–25.

The Twins lease may not be typical of lease arrangements. Team owners typically possess strong leverage in lease negotiations due to the league's monopoly over the sport and the undersupply of major league franchises. The threat of relocation leads to a strong effort on the part of the city to cede favorable terms at the expense of taxpayers. Matthew J. Mitten & Bruce W. Burton, *Professional Sports Franchise Relocations From Private Law Public Law Perspectives: Balancing Marketplace Competition, League Autonomy, and the Need for Level Playing Field,* 56 Maryland Leve. 57, 70–71 (1997). For example, the City of Cleveland ultimately failed in its efforts to hold the Browns to the three years remaining on its lease of Municipal Stadium, in part because the Browns' lease was not with the City, but rather with a management corporation owned by Browns' owner Art Modell, which two decades earlier had entered into its own deal with the City to operate the stadium.

(c) Eminent Domain

After the Ninth Circuit upheld the antitrust challenge against the NFL's refusal to permit the Raiders from relocating to Los Angeles, the City of Oakland tried to use its power of eminent domain to purchase the club forcibly for fair market value, and then resell the club to a suitable buyer who promised to keep the club in its current location. Initially, the California Supreme Court ruled in favor of the City: it reversed the lower court's dismissal of proceedings and held that the property to be taken—the bundle of contract rights to operate a club in the NFL—were legitimate targets for the eminent domain power, and that preserving a major league football team in a city was a "public use." *City of Oakland v. Oakland Raiders,* 646 P.2d 835 (Cal. 1982). On the last point, the Court cited with approval its prior decision in *City of Los Angeles v. Superior Court,* 333 P.2d 745 (Cal. 1959), upholding the use of eminent domain for the eventual use by the Los Angeles Dodgers. However, further merits proceedings resulted in defeat for the city: the court of appeals subsequently held that the use of eminent domain power to prevent a relocation within a nationwide sports league constituted an unconstitutional interference with interstate commerce. *City of Oakland II,* 220 Cal. Rptr. 153 (Ct. App. 1st Dist. 1985).

The actual use of the strategy, even if legal, is logistically problematic. In *Mayor & City Council of Baltimore v. Baltimore (Colts) Football Club,* 624 F. Supp. 278 (D. Md. 1985), the court ruled that the ordinance did not apply when, prior to the enactment of the local ordinance to acquire the Colts forcibly, owner Robert Irsay hastily arranged for all personal property of the club to be placed in moving vans and shipped to their new home in Indianapolis. Furthermore, it is conceptually problematic to think about a government "seizing" an intangible asset like the right to play games in a sports league. Even had Baltimore taken physical possession of the Colts' uniforms, blocking sleds and office equipment, the team's greatest asset is its franchise in the NFL. While the California courts have indicated that this is a legitimate target for eminent domain, how would a city "seize" that if the league scheduled the team's games in the new location?

(d) Direct State Legislation

Following the move of the Cleveland Browns to Baltimore in 1996, the Ohio state legislature enacted Ohio Revised Code § 9.67, titled "Restrictions on owner of professional sports team." Colloquially named the "Art Modell Law" after the Browns' owner who relocated the original franchise to Baltimore as the Ravens, it prohibits owners who use tax-supported facilities and accept financial assistance from the state from moving to another city without six months' notice and an opportunity being given to individuals who live in the area to purchase the team.

As the casebook goes to press, MLS Columbus Crew owner Anthony Precourt has challenged this law's inhibition on his plan to move the team to Austin, Texas. Both Ohio and Columbus officials have sought an injunction to bar the move unless the terms of the Art Modell Law are satisfied. They note that taxpayers provided approximately $5 million to improve team parking facilities, and a special tax agreement with the city of Columbus to forego $1.3 million in tax revenue. Scott Andresen, *With Lawsuit, Columbus Seeks To Keep Crew From Leaving Like Art Modell's Browns*, Forbes (May 9, 2018). MLS counsel claim that the law unconstitutionally interferes with interstate commerce.

(e) Federal Legislative Reform

In order to strengthen leagues' ability to keep teams in place, politicians introduced numerous versions of antitrust reform in Congress in the mid-1990s. The prospects for actual enactment were never very promising: for every community (and politician) that loses a team, another gains one. Legislation removing antitrust scrutiny from league decisions to block a proposed regulation is only effective in preventing "bad" relocations that would actually be blocked by the league. However, as the post-*Raiders* experience has made clear, many actual or threatened moves that result in huge public subsidies are done with the full support of commissioners and fellow owners.

These and other substantive legal proposals raise an underlying institutional question. Who should make the judgment about where particular sports teams should be located? The individual owner who is most involved in and affected by the fate of his team? The league's owners, collectively deciding how the move affects the interests of all teams and owners? Or some combination of courts and lawmakers seeking to protect the interests of the affected communities? One point of view is that the people in Brooklyn, for example, should have had a "moral" right to keep their Dodgers, and the people in Cleveland their Browns. Alternatively, if the objective is to protect the broader public welfare, the ideal free-market test asks which city's fans are willing to pay the most either to gain or to keep the free-agent franchise.

Ironically, the NFL's internal revenue sharing system, one that was supposedly designed to protect smaller market teams from the competitive pressures of the bigger market teams in the players market, has actually generated movement from larger to smaller communities in the franchise market.

Although Congress considered legislation to reform the franchise relocation process, in part motivated by concerns about taxpayer subsidies, it did not exercise its authority to regulate interstate Congress to employ an extremely important tool used by the European Union to regulate trade among its member states. Article 107(1) of the EU Treaty provides:

> Save as otherwise provided in the Treaties, any aid granted by a Member State or through State resources in any form whatsoever which distorts or threatens to distort competition by favouring certain undertakings or the production of certain goods shall, in so far as it affects trade between Member States, be incompatible with the internal market.

Thus, in Europe, stadium subsidies are only permitted under limited conditions. Some general principles were laid down in a letter from the European Commission's Directorate-General for Competition to Germany regarding State funding for the Hanover football stadium. Aid for the construction of stadiums or other sports infrastructure could be argued not to constitute aid, provided it fulfills the following criteria: (1) the type of infrastructure involved is generally unlikely to be provided by the market because it is not economically viable; (2) it is not apt to selectively favour a specific undertaking: in other words, the site provides facilities for different types of activities and users and is rented out to undertakings at adequate market based compensation; (3) it is a facility needed to provide a service that is considered as being part of the typical responsibility of the public authority to the general public.

As a European White Paper explained:

> Since professional sport clubs are engaged in economic activities, there is no compelling argument why they should be exempted from the State aid rules.

> The need to ensure competitive equality between players, clubs and competitions as well as the necessity to ensure uncertainty of results can in fact be guaranteed most effectively by the application of State aid rules, which are meant to establish a level playing field and ensure that States or municipalities that are most willing or able to grant subsidies to their clubs will not disrupt fair competition.

EU Commission staff working document, The EU and Sport: Background and Context, available at http://eur-lex.europa.eu/legal-content/EN/TXT/HTML/?uri=CELEX:52007SC0935&from=EN.

NOTES AND QUESTIONS

1. *Are Stadium Leases Different than Other Commercial Leases?* Is it persuasive that a stadium lease with a major league sports team is substantively different from other types of commercial leases because the consideration provided by the team is not rent to the landlord but rather entertainment for the public? If so, is the only reasonable remedy for a breach an injunction for specific performance? Would the result be different if the team is required to pay rent under the lease or any other financial terms? Would the result be different if the stadium is privately owned but was constructed with significant public subsidies?

2. *Intra-Metropolitan Relocations.* Would the rationale used by the Minnesota court in the *Twins* lease litigation apply equally in cases where a team was not attempting to go out of business, but simply to relocate to another community? If so, does this case (and the likelihood of local judges in other states threatened with the loss of their team adopting the same view) provide a vehicle for making relocations almost impossible if the stadium lease has not expired? How does this ruling affect the ability of teams to use the threat of leaving to extract huge public subsidies?

3. *State Aids.* Should Congress follow the European approach and simply ban tax subsidies? Would such a bar on state and local governments be constitutional? Would applying or enforcing it be feasible?

C. TELEVISION CONTRACTS

The primary source of soaring sports revenues has been an increasing fan appetite for watching games at home on television or on their computers and hand-held devices. A crucial condition has been the legality of teams joining together to sell a single package of broadcasting and marketing rights to the highest bidder. Consider whether such legal arrangements are in the best interests of fans of the sport and consumers of products advertised during game broadcasts or emblazoned with team logos. League-wide controls upon the sale of television rights has been the principal setting for this legal debate about the compatibility of league licensing packages and rules with antitrust law's commitment to a competitive consumer market.

The new television medium posed a special threat to the fundamental principle of territorial exclusivity embodied in league constitutions, a principle that insulated franchise owners from intrusion by other clubs into their home markets. Broadcasts of games involving the more successful teams (such as the New York Yankees in baseball and the Cleveland Browns in football) could be beamed into any part of the country. Thus, the earliest league television policy sought to limit the breadth of broadcasts of games played by any one team. This policy generated the first antitrust challenge encountered by leagues in their internal dealings—in fact, the one and only antitrust suit filed by the Justice Department against professional sports.

UNITED STATES v. NFL
116 F. Supp. 319 (E.D. Pa. 1953)

GRIM, DISTRICT JUDGE.

[The NFL's initial stance was to permit each individual team to contract for the telecasting (and radio broadcasting) of games in which that team was participating. However, the League's by-laws contained a blanket prohibition against teams broadcasting their games into the home territories of other teams. The Justice Department charged that this league policy constituted an agreement in restraint of trade in violation of § 1 of the Sherman Antitrust Act.]

I.

Is the provision which prevents the telecasting of outside games into the home territories of other teams on days when the other teams are playing at home illegal?

There can be little doubt that this provision constitutes a contract in restraint of trade. The market for the public exhibition of football no longer is limited to the spectators who attend the games. Since the advent of television and radio, the visual and aural projections of football games can be marketed anywhere in the world where there are television or radio facilities to transmit and receive them. When a football team agrees to restrict the projection of its games in the home areas of other teams, it thereby cuts itself off from this part of its potential market. Since the clubs of the National Football League have agreed at certain times not to project their games into the home territories of other clubs, they have given that part of their market at those certain times exclusively to other teams. In return, each of them has been given the right to market its own games without competition in its own home area under the same circumstances. The purpose and effect of this is to restrict outside competition on the part of other teams in the home area of each club. This, therefore, is a clear case of allocating marketing territories among competitors, which is a practice generally held illegal under the anti-trust laws.

An allocation of marketing territories for the purpose of restricting competition, however, is not always illegal.... The principal question in the present case is whether the particular restraints imposed by Article X are reasonable or unreasonable.

Professional football is a unique type of business. Like other professional sports which are organized on a league basis, it has problems which no other business has. The ordinary business makes every effort to sell as much of its product or services as it can. In the course of doing this it may and often does put many of its competitors out of business. The ordinary businessman is not troubled by the knowledge that he is doing so well that his competitors are being driven out of business.

Professional teams in a league, however, must not compete too well with each other, in a business way. On the playing field, of course, they must compete as hard as they can all the time. But it is not necessary and indeed it is unwise for all the teams to compete as hard as they can against each other in a business way. If all the teams should compete as hard as they can in a business way, the stronger teams would be likely to drive the weaker ones into financial failure. If this should happen not only would the weaker teams fail, but eventually the whole league, both the weaker and the stronger teams, would fail, because without a league no team can operate profitably.

It is particularly true in the National Football League that the teams should not compete too strongly with each other in a business way. The evidence shows that in the National Football League less than half the clubs over a period of years are likely to be financially successful. There are always teams in the League which are close to financial failure. Under these circumstances it is both wise and essential that rules be passed to help the weaker clubs in their competition with the stronger ones and to keep the League in fairly even balance.

The winning teams usually are the wealthier ones and unless restricted by artificial rules the rich get richer and the poor get poorer (as Commissioner Bell put it). Winning teams draw larger numbers of spectators to their games than do losing teams and from the larger gate receipts they make greater profits than do losing teams. With this greater wealth they can spend more money to obtain new players, they can pay higher salaries, and they can have better spirit among their players than can the weaker teams. With these better and happier players they will continue to win most of their games while the weaker teams will continue to lose most of their games. The weaker teams share in the prosperity of the stronger teams to a certain extent, since as visiting teams they share in the gate receipts of the stronger teams. But in time even the most enthusiastic fans of strong home teams will cease to be attracted to home games with increasingly weaker visiting teams. Thus, the net effects of allowing unrestricted business competition among the clubs are likely to be, first, the creation of greater and greater inequalities in the strength of the teams; second, the weaker teams being driven out of business; and, third, the destruction of the entire League.

In order to try to keep its teams at approximately equal strength and to protect weaker teams from stronger teams, a league theoretically might use a number of devices. It might (1) limit the bonus price which could be paid to new players, (2) give the weaker teams a prior right over stronger teams to draft new players, (3) prohibit the sale of players after a certain day in the playing season, (4) limit the number of players on each team, (5) limit the total amount of salaries which a team can pay, (6) give the lowest team in the league the right to draft a player from the highest team, when and if the highest team has won a certain number (three for instance) of consecutive championships, and (7) reasonably restrict the projection of games by radio or television into the home territories of other teams.

It is easy to see that the first six devices would make it easier for weaker teams to compete with stronger ones. The usefulness of the seventh device, however, in the protection of the weaker teams may not be so obvious, particularly since it prevents the weaker teams from televising into the home territories of the stronger teams as much as it prevents the stronger teams from telecasting into the home territories of the weaker ones. The evidence indicates that television audiences and sponsors have so little interest in games between weak teams that it is very difficult to obtain sponsors for outside telecasts of such games. Consequently, the weaker teams lose practically nothing by this television restriction. But they benefit greatly from it in that the restriction adds to their home game attendance by preventing potential spectators from staying at home to watch on television exciting outside head-on games between strong teams. The competitive position of the weaker teams is improved by this increase in home attendance, while the competitive position of the stronger teams is weakened somewhat by their inability to sell to sponsors the right to televise their desirable head-on games into the home territories of the weaker teams when the weaker teams are playing at home.

A large part of defendants' evidence was directed to the question of whether the televising of a team's own home games in that team's home territory has an adverse effect on attendance at these home games. The evidence on this point, particularly the evidence relating to the great decrease in home attendance of the Los Angeles Rams during the 1950 season when all its home games were televised at home, shows quite clearly that the telecasting of a home game into a home territory while the home game is being played has an adverse effect on the attendance at the game. This clearly indicates by implication that the telecast of an outside game, particularly a head-on game, also adversely affects attendance at a home game.

* * *

The greatest part of the defendant clubs' income is derived from the sale of tickets to games. Reasonable protection of home game attendance is essential to the very existence of the individual clubs, without which there can be no League and no professional football as we know it today.

This is not a case of one industry fighting the competition of another, as for instance coal fighting the competition of oil, or railroads fighting the competition of trucks, or moving pictures fighting the competition of television. Football provides a magnificent spectacle for television programs and television provides an excellent outlet and market for football. They both can use and indeed need each other. By working together intelligently each will be an important adjunct to the other. The objective of the clubs in agreeing to a television blackout of the home territory (except for the remote possibility of a home game telecast) during the day a home game is played is not to restrain competition among the individual clubs in the sale of television rights or competition among television stations and networks and advertisers and advertising agencies in the purchase of such rights. This particular restriction promotes competition more than it restrains it in that its immediate effect is to protect the weak teams and its ultimate effect is to preserve the League itself. By thus preserving professional football this restriction makes possible competition in the sale and purchase of television rights in situations in which the restriction does not apply.

The purposes of the Sherman Act certainly will not be served by prohibiting the defendant clubs, particularly the weaker clubs, from protecting their home gate receipts from the disastrous financial effects of invading telecasts of outside games. The member clubs of the National Football League, like those of any professional athletic league, can exist only as long as the league exists. The League is truly a unique business enterprise, which is entitled to protect its very existence by agreeing to reasonable restrictions on its member clubs. The first type of restriction imposed by Article X is a reasonable one and a legal restraint of trade.

II.

Is the restriction on telecasting outside games in home territories when the home teams are playing away games and telecasting them in their home territories illegal?

The reasonableness of this particular restriction must also be tested by its effect on the attendance and gate receipts of a team's home games. It is obvious that on a day when the home team is playing an away game there is no gate attendance to be harmed back in its home area and the prohibition of outside telecasts within its home area cannot serve to protect gate attendance at the away game, which is played in the opponent's home territory.

Several of defendants' witnesses attempted to justify the restriction with the opinion that it is necessary in this situation to protect the home team's "good will" by which they meant that the restriction is necessary to protect the home team from loss in gate receipts at subsequent home games. However, there is not one shred of evidence, not one specific example based on actual experience, to support this opinion which, more accurately stated, is nothing more than conjecture.

It is probably true, though not proved by the evidence, that the simultaneous telecasting of an outside game and an away game in the home area of the team playing away would result in a division of the television audience between the two games. Obviously the existence or the prospect of such competition would make the television rights to the home club's away games less attractive to sponsors and consequently less profitable to the club. But this does not concern attendance at football games. Indeed, the testimony of defendants' witnesses consistently indicates that the primary reason for the restrictions in this situation actually is to enable the clubs in the home territories to sell monopoly rights to purchasers of television rights to away games.

The record in this case contains no factual justification for Article X's suppression of competing telecasts of League games when, for example, the Philadelphia Eagles' away game is being televised in its home territory. Defendants' speculation or conjecture that without such restriction gate attendance would decline a week or two later at the Eagles' home game has little probative value. Article X's restriction on this type of competition is an unreasonable and illegal restraint of trade.

Charge upheld in part.

NOTES AND QUESTIONS

1. *Gate Protection Versus Radio Rights Protection.* In effect, Judge Grim ruled that it was lawful for the NFL to eliminate competition between member clubs when one was selling tickets to its live home games and another was selling a competing NFL game via television, but it was unlawful for the league to eliminate competition between two teams both of which were selling competing NFL games via television (or radio). What was the basis for this distinction? From an antitrust policy or rule of reason standpoint, does this distinction make sense?

2. *Presaging the Modern Rule of Reason.* Note that Judge Grim's decision presages the more nuanced and sophisticated Rule of Reason analysis courts would develop two decades later. In his discussion, Judge Grim reasons that the blackout to protect live gate was necessary to improve the weaker teams at the expense of the stronger teams. Is that an essential element in a competitive balance defense?

3. *Harm to Live Gate.* Do you agree that telecasting games of rival teams in the same league harms live gate in today's entertainment world?

1. COLLECTIVE SELLING OF POOLED RIGHTS AND THE SPORTS BROADCASTING ACT OF 1961

As is clear from *United States v. NFL*, the principal concern of the league as well as the district court was the perceived impact of television on the home team's game attendance, rather than on the financial value of potential television viewership and contracts. As a result, the precise decree entered in the case prohibited the National Football League and its clubs from adopting any rules or entering into any television contracts that restricted the area in which any team's games would be broadcast, except into a team's home territory on the day it was playing a home game.

In 1960, the American Football League (AFL) started up operations and immediately negotiated a league-wide television contract with ABC. At this time, each NFL club was still selling its television rights separately. The new NFL Commissioner, Pete Rozelle, believed that if the AFL was going to operate with the advantage of a league-wide television package, the NFL had to do the same. Such a contract, under which all clubs would share revenues equally, was becoming more important to the NFL because teams in the large markets were starting to obtain much greater revenues for their television rights than were teams in smaller cities. The resulting disparity in income, coupled with competition for players from the AFL, threatened the ability of small-market clubs to field good teams. Thus, Rozelle promptly negotiated a league-wide television contract with CBS. The NFL then petitioned Judge Grim to approve the new CBS contract.

Naturally, a provision of the NFL-CBS contract barred individual teams from selling television rights for their games to competing broadcasters. Judge Grim therefore held that the contract violated the terms of his 1953 antitrust decree. 196 F. Supp. 445 (E.D. Pa. 1961). The NFL went to the Congress and persuaded it to pass the Sports Broadcasting Act (SBA). Section 1 of the SBA, 15 U.S.C. § 1291, states that:

> The antitrust laws ... shall not apply to any joint agreement by or among persons engaging in or conducting the organized professional team sports of football, baseball, basketball, or hockey, by which any league of clubs ... sells or otherwise transfers all or any part of the rights of such league's member clubs in the sponsored telecasting of the games of football, baseball, basketball, or hockey as the case may be, engaged in or conducted by such clubs. ...

Section 1292 made it clear, though, that the antitrust immunity conferred by § 1291 was only available to league-wide television contracts that limited "black-outs" of NFL games to those "home territories" in which a member club was playing a home game on the day of the blackout. At the time, the motivation of blackout rules was to protect home gate receipts and enhance the financial stability of the leagues by assuring equal distribution of broadcast revenues. *See* H. Rep. No. 87–1178, at 2–3.

These statutory prohibitions were supplemented by regulations issued by the FCC from 1971–2014. Initially designed to protect local free-to-air stations from out-of-market cable competition, the rules required a blackout unless a team failed to sell a certain percentage of its tickets. *Amendment of Part 76 of the Commission's Rules and Regulations Relative to Cable Television Systems and the Carriage of Sports Programs on Cable Television Systems*, Report and Order, 54 FCC 2d 265, 285, ¶ 62. *See also* 47 C.F.R. § 76.111(a). In an order dated September 30, 2014, the FCC eliminated the sports blackout rules, finding they were no longer needed since television revenues had replaced ticket sales as the NFL's primary source of revenue. *In the Matter of Sports Blackout Rules*, FCC 14–141 at 10, ¶ 14 (2014).

Technological advances have generated a judicial exploration of the nature and limits of the Sports Broadcasting Act (SBA). They have also raised issues as to the application of § 1 to league contracts when the SBA does not protect them from rule of reason scrutiny. Evolving from a league playing only on Sunday afternoons, the NFL now features nationally-televised games on Thursday, Sunday, and Monday nights, and even late season Saturday games after college football's season ends. The long-time tradition remains that on Sunday afternoons, fans get to watch one or two games targeted by the networks at their particular region.

At one time, however, fans would not be able to watch a Sunday afternoon game if it was not televised in their local market. Beginning in the mid-1990s, the NFL entered into an agreement with a satellite broadcast distributor, DirecTV, to offer fans a new "NFL Sunday Ticket" package that lets them bring in through their satellite TV dish all of the games from around the country at a single subscription fee of $139 a season (now around $200). This would permit, for example, fans of the New England Patriots who had moved to New Orleans, or of the New Orleans Saints who had moved to Boston, to watch their favored team play every week whether or not the game was televised on a local cable or over-the-air channel.

The only offer available was a package for all out-of-market NFL games. A group of fans filed a class-action antitrust suit against the NFL, claiming a "restraint of trade" in the use of this new technological product. In particular, they asserted that fans who want to use their satellite dishes to secure just their favorite team's games should be able to strike such deals with the teams directly. Presumably this would be at a much lower price than the league-wide package, not just because of the smaller number of games, but because all 30 NFL franchises would be competing against each other in a readily accessible national satellite market.

The NFL's first defense was that the Sports Broadcasting Act precluded an antitrust claim because these telecasts involved SBA-protected "sponsored telecasting of the game of football." The league's reasoning was that even though the Sunday Ticket was clearly a "pay-per-season" arrangement, the telecasts themselves were created for over-the-air broadcasts and the Sunday Ticket merely distributed the "residual rights" in those clearly SBA-protected broadcasts via a satellite. However, in *Shaw v. Dallas Cowboys,* 172 F.3d 299, 301–02 (3d Cir. 1999), the Third Circuit rejected that defense.

> The NFL's underlying rights are in the games themselves and, more specifically, they include the right to sell the images of those games for broadcast through various media. The broadcast rights sold to sponsored telecasters do not subsume the separate broadcast rights sold to a non-sponsored medium. Each transaction is a sale of a part of the NFL's underlying right in the images of the games, but only the former is exempt from antitrust scrutiny ... [T]he NFL obtained in the 1961 Act an expressly limited exception to "the normal prohibition on monopolistic behavior;" one which permitted it to sell pooled rights to sponsored telecasters and which expressly did not apply to subscription television. The NFL got what it lobbied for: it cannot now expect the federal courts to transform "narrow, discrete, special-interest" legislation [quoting the district judge] into a far broader exemption.

Though this class action case was settled in early 2001, the district judge found the settlement not to be acceptable in *Schwartz v. Dallas Cowboys,* 157 F. Supp. 2d 561 (E.D. Pa. 2001). The court held that of the approximately $13.5 million being paid by the NFL to settle the case, the $7.5 million for the satellite fan plaintiffs was too small relative to that for the lawyers' fees ($3.7 million) and for administrative costs ($2.3 million). Thus, the parties revised the settlement to provide an additional one million dollars to the plaintiffs, with $600,000 of that coming out of the legal fees and $400,000 from the costs. Also, the parties revised the deal so that the NFL was protected only from legal challenges to the past and current DirecTV regime, not from challenges to any future satellite television schemes or to any of its television, cable, or Internet arrangements. The core settlement term that remained unchanged, and was not disapproved of by the judge, was the NFL's agreement to offer a new Single Sunday Ticket package—making games available by the week instead of only by the year so that for $30 a fan could receive any game on a given Sunday (as an alternative to the $159 full-season subscription). However, the package still did not offer the option of securing just one game involving a particular team at some fraction of the full Single Sunday package. With these changes, the judge upheld the revised settlement and the NFL implemented the modified satellite TV service for the 2001 season. No judicial determination issued as to whether the Sunday Ticket plan, as originally conceived or after the settlement, violates antitrust law.

Class action plaintiffs also were unsuccessful in challenging the exclusive Sunday Ticket plan in *In re NFL Sunday Ticket Antitrust Litig.,* 2017-1 Trade Cas. (CCH) ¶ 80,045 (C.D. Cal. June 30, 2017). The court first examined the "vertical" agreement whereby the NFL exclusively licensed DirecTV to provide out-of-market games. It interpreted *NCAA v. Board of Regents* as focusing on restrictions on the ability to broadcast a game. In this case, "there is no limit on output, *i.e.*, no requirement that certain games not be broadcast at all; on the contrary, all NFL Sunday afternoon games are broadcast—there are merely limitations placed on where these games are broadcast and on who may broadcast them." *Id.* Responding to plaintiffs' alternative measure of viewership, the court observed: "while viewers would have had access to no more than three NFL Sunday afternoon games broadcast in any given broadcasting market, through Sunday Ticket, viewers may now access as many as thirteen games being played on Sunday afternoons—games which, before Sunday Ticket, would have gone unseen outside of the local broadcast market. Thus, Sunday Ticket has also increased the availability—or viewership—of out-of-market games." *Id.*

Turning to the "horizontal" agreement whereby NFL clubs pooled their efforts to license out-of-market games, the court initially rejected the NFL's claim that the Sports Broadcasting Act exempted this pooling. Applying the doctrine of narrow construction of antitrust exemptions, it relied on precedents that "SBA applies only to 'network broadcast television and does not apply to non-exempt channels of distribution such as cable television, pay-per-view, and satellite television networks.'" *Id.* However, the court found that the pooling agreement did not violate the Sherman Act. Relying on *Washington v. National Football League,* 880 F. Supp. 2d 1004, 1005–07 (D. Minn. 2012), the court found that because "multiple entities must act collectively to broadcast the games in order for the games to be broadcast at all," therefore the pooling was not a horizontal agreement.

However, on the merits, the court rejected the antitrust challenge. The court reasoned that consumers can watch free broadcasts on CBS and Fox, so Sunday Ticket lacks market power

> because consumers may choose to view these free games as alternatives to paid-for out-of-market games, thereby driving market prices down naturally. If, on the other hand, the out-of-market games available only on Sunday Ticket are not

competitive with the other free over-the-air NFL game broadcasts because consumers desire to view only certain specific out-of-market games—for example, a consumer wants to watch only the Denver Broncos game every week—then Plaintiffs have failed to establish how selling the rights to all out-of-market games on the open market would prevent artificial price inflation.

Id. The court observed that if an avid Denver fan only wished to watch the Broncos each week, selling rights on the open market would not provide the consumer with any more options.

What is your judgment on that score? What are the procompetitive and anticompetitive effects, and how would you balance them?

NOTES AND QUESTIONS

1. *Cable Networks and the Sports Broadcasting Act.* Are league contracts with cable networks covered by the SBA? By its terms, § 1291 extends antitrust immunity to a league's sale of pooled-rights for "sponsored telecasting of games." The major sports cable networks such as ESPN, TNT, and Fox Sports are funded partially by subscriber's fees and partially by advertising revenues. In addition, the transmission by cable from event to television screen fits within the term "telecasting." The legislative history of the SBA, however, casts doubt on whether Congress intended to grant antitrust immunity to any league contracts other than those with the "free" over-the-air television networks. When the SBA was enacted in 1961, its chief proponent, NFL Commissioner Pete Rozelle, told Congress that "[T]his bill covers only the free telecasting of professional sports contests, and does not cover pay TV." *Telecasting of Professional Sports Contests: Hearings on H.R. 8757 Before the Subcomm. on Antitrust (Subcomm. No. 5) of the House Comm. on the Judiciary*, 87th Cong., 1st Sess. 36 (1961). In 1982, then-NFL counsel (and later Commissioner) Paul Tagliabue reiterated to a Senate Committee that "the words 'sponsored telecasting' were intended to exclude pay and cable. This is clear from the legislative history and from the committee reports. So, that statute does not authorize us to pool and sell to pay and cable." *Professional Sports Antitrust Immunity: Hearings on S. 2784 and S. 2821 Before the Senate Comm. on the Judiciary*, 97th Cong., 2d Sess. 41 (1982).

In light of these comments before and after enactment of the SBA, how should a court interpret the Act with respect to NFL television contracts with ESPN? With reference to the NHL's 1988–92 contract with SportsChannel America? With respect to any attempts to put the Super Bowl, or the NBA playoffs, or regular season games, on pay-per-view television?

2. *Cable Contracts and the Rule of Reason.* If the SBA does not provide antitrust immunity for league contracts with cable networks, do these contracts, under a rule of reason analysis, violate § 1 of the Sherman Act?

3. *Playoff Games.* Does an NFL restriction on the telecasting of a playoff game or the Super Bowl violate § 1 under the reasoning of *United States v. NFL*? If such restrictions are a violation, does the SBA exempt them? *See Blaich v. National Football League*, 212 F. Supp. 319 (S.D.N.Y. 1962) (No, and no).

4. *Does the SBA Have Any Implications for League Revenue Sharing?* Article 10.3 of the NFL Constitution provides that all member clubs share equally in the league's television revenues. It was a major political accomplishment of new Commissioner Pete Rozelle in 1961 to persuade the Mara family (owner of the New York Giants), George Halas (Chicago Bears), and Dan Reeves (Los Angeles Rams) to agree to this policy, which transferred significant dollar revenues from their clubs to those in smaller media markets. Similar suggestions over the years in other major sports leagues have been quickly killed by large market owners. Even though the legislative history makes it clear that one important rationale for the SBA was to allow NFL teams to share television revenues, does the SBA's language exempt the sharing of network television revenues? If not exempt, would such network revenue sharing, or the sharing of any other type of revenue (such as local radio and television revenues, gate receipts, luxury box rental fees, parking and concessions revenues, and trademark licensing fees), violate § 1?

5. *The SBA and Other Sports.* Section 1291 protects league pooled-rights contracts only in the "team sports of football, baseball, basketball, or hockey." If Major League Soccer were to negotiate a league-wide contract with CBS similar to the NFL's original contract in 1961, would the SBA protect it? Could MLS claim that it is "football," since that is what soccer is called in the rest of the world? Would the WNBA be protected? How about the Arena Football League or the Inline Skate Hockey League? Is there any reason why any of these leagues should not have the same protection for their TV contracts as the NFL or NBA?

2. LEAGUE RESTRICTIONS ON THE SALE OF TELEVISION RIGHTS BY INDIVIDUAL CLUBS

In most professional sports leagues (other than the NFL), individual member clubs negotiate broadcast contracts for the majority of their games, with only a small minority of games televised pursuant to nationwide pooled-rights contracts. Local television rights sales now account for a significant portion of each club's revenue and constitute the principal source of wide disparity in income among MLB, NBA, and NHL clubs. By way of illustration, the 2014 rights deals ranged from a $3.6 billion 20-year deal between the Lakers and Time Warner Cable to a $109 million 10-year deal between the Charlotte Bobcats and Fox Sports Carolinas.

In the 1980s, emerging satellite technology created local "superstations" whose programs could be shown nationwide, exacerbating revenue disparities among teams. A club whose local games are broadcast nationwide via a superstation is better off: it will share the higher broadcast revenues gleaned from advertising fees and cable subscription payments from viewers outside of the local market. However, the games are joint products of two clubs, and the broadcasts have the potential to affect adversely the overall value of rights to national contracts, as well as the value of each club's local broadcast rights. MLB clubs agreed to a scheme for sharing local revenues and requiring member clubs to contribute 42% of superstation revenue to that pot.

The NBA took another approach, beginning in 1991 when the NBA voted to reduce from 25 to 20 the number of games that it would allow individual teams to sell to "superstations"—local over-the-air stations whose signals are transmitted and shown on cable outlets throughout the country. The team most directly affected was the Chicago Bulls, which for the 1991-92 season had already sold to WGN the broadcast rights in 25 games. WGN and the Bulls brought launched a six-year litigation battle against the NBA's enforcement of the new rule, alleging that it was a horizontal agreement among the teams to limit competition among themselves in a way that restricted output in violation of § 1 of the Sherman Act.

The NBA had two basic reasons for wanting to reduce, and eventually to eliminate, superstation broadcasts of games sold by individual teams. First, because these broadcasts are shown on cable in the markets of most other NBA teams, weaker teams in smaller markets allegedly suffered revenue losses from having to compete against these superstation telecasts. These losses came in the form of both reduced ticket sales for their home games and reduced fees for the rights to televise all of their games in their local market. This competitive impact of superstation telecasts was particularly acute during the early and mid-1990s because of the tremendous popularity of then perennial NBA champion Bulls, led by Michael Jordan and Scottie Pippen. In fact, because WGN was available to about 30% of American homes, Bulls' games were viewed in an average of 650,000 homes. This was almost double the Chicago-only audience for the non-superstation Bulls' broadcasts on Chicago SportsChannel, and only slightly less than TNT's usual national cable audience of 750,000 homes under its league contract, although far less than NBC's 4.7 million viewers on regular-season Sunday afternoons.

The second concern was the impact on the NBA's league-wide network contracts with NBC and TNT, totaling roughly $180 million in the 1991-92 season. The value of these contracts was allegedly reduced when games televised by NBC and TNT had to compete across the country in the same time slots against superstation broadcasts of the Bulls, Nets, and/or Hawks—particularly against the popular games of the Bulls shown on WGN. The revenues generated by the league's television contracts, which all NBA teams share equally, were a crucial component (as much as 50%) of the lower-revenue teams' income. Thus, the league felt it needed to protect the value of these network contracts by limiting superstation broadcasts. As a result, NBA policies on superstation broadcasts became increasingly restrictive, culminating in 1990 with the Board of Governors' adopt of a rule—opposed only by the Bulls and the New Jersey Nets—that reduced the maximum number of superstation games to 20.

CHICAGO PROFESSIONAL SPORTS LTD. & WGN v. NBA (BULLS I)
961 F.2d 667 (7th Cir. 1992)

EASTERBROOK, CIRCUIT JUDGE.

* * *

[T]he Sports Broadcasting Act applies only when the league has "transferred" a right to "sponsored telecasting." Neither the NBA's contract with NBC nor its contract with Turner Network Television transfers to the network a right to limit the broadcasting of other contests. Both contracts and, so far as we can tell, the league's articles and bylaws, reserve to the individual clubs the full copyright interest in all games that the league has not sold to the networks. As the "league of clubs" has not transferred to the networks either the right to show, or the right to black out, any additional games, the Sports Broadcasting Act does not protect its 20-game rule.

The NBA protests that such an approach is arbitrary. What if the league had assumed control of all broadcast rights and licensed only 20 of the Bulls' games to WGN? That would have been a "transfer" by a "league of clubs." What could be the point of forbidding a different mechanism (the rule limiting to 20 the number of games teams may sell to superstations) that leads to the same result? Other mechanisms to achieve similar outcomes abound. The league might have put a cap of 20 superstation games in its contracts with NBC and Turner, or it might have followed the path of professional baseball and allowed unlimited broadcasting over superstations while claiming a portion of the revenues for distribution among the clubs. (Sharing of revenues occurs in all team sports, although less so in the NBA than other leagues.)

Whether there are ways to achieve the NBA's objective is not the question. Laws often treat similar things differently. One has only to think of tax law, where small differences in the form of a business reorganization have large consequences for taxation. Substance then follows form. Antitrust law is no exception: agreements among business rivals to fix prices are unlawful per se, although a merger of the same firms, even more effective in eliminating competition among them, might be approved with little ado. Such distinctions are not invariably formal. The combined business entity might achieve efficiencies unavailable to the cartelists. But then the line in the Sports Broadcasting Act is not entirely formal either. Perhaps the reason the NBA has not commandeered all of the telecasting rights and sold limited numbers of games to superstations is that it cannot obtain the approval of the clubs to do this—for a change in the allocation of rights is apt to affect the allocation of revenues, making the bargaining problem difficult with 27 clubs. A league's difficulty in rearranging its affairs to obtain the protection of the Sports Broadcasting Act is one source of protection for competition.

What the NBA might have done, it did not do. The Sports Broadcasting Act is special interest legislation, a single-industry exception to a law designed for the protection of the public. When special interests claim that they have obtained favors from Congress, a court should ask to see the bill of sale. Special interest laws do not have "spirits," and it is inappropriate to extend them to achieve more of the objective the lobbyists wanted. What the industry obtained, the courts enforce; what it did not obtain from the legislature—even if similar to something within the exception—a court should not bestow . . .

III

[The appellate panel, assuming for the sake of this case that the NBA was a joint venture governed by the rule of reason, next assessed the league's market power.]

As the NBA points out, sports is a small fraction of all entertainment on TV, and basketball a small fraction of sports televising. Viewers of basketball games do not have qualities uniquely attractive to advertisers—and if they do, the advertisers can reach them via other sports programs and many other programs too. NBC advertises basketball games during sitcoms and other programs, implying that the market in viewers extends well beyond weekend sports programming. Higher prices, the hallmark of a reduction in output, are missing: advertisers pay no more per thousand viewers of NBA basketball than they do for other sports audiences, and substantially less than they pay per thousand viewers of other entertainment. During 1990 the cost per thousand viewers (CPM) of a regular-season NBA network game was $8.17. NCAA football fetched $11.50, and viewers of prime-time programs were substantially more expensive. The CPM for "L.A. Law" was $19.34, the CPM for "Coach" $13.40. The NBA hardly has cornered the market on the viewers advertisers want to reach.

According to the NBA, this means that its rules do not injure viewers or advertisers, and it makes more sense to understand them as ways to compete against other suppliers of entertainment programming, all of which—right down to the smallest producers of syndicated programs—find it in their interest to sell exclusive rights to a small number of episodes.

The NBA contends that until it tried to adopt a rational structure for television it had a much smaller audience than it does now. During 1980 and 1981 CBS carried the final game of the championship series by delayed broadcast! In 1982 only five NBA games appeared on network TV. A "restraint" that in the end expands output, serves the interests of consumers and should be applauded rather than condemned. Rules keeping some popular games off superstations may help weaker teams attract the support of their local audiences, something that (like the sharing of revenues) in the longer run promotes exciting, competitive games. Teams in smaller markets depend more on live gate to finance operations that will compete with the Bulls, Lakers, and Knicks on the court. Rivalry makes for a more attractive product, which then attracts a larger audience—the very expansion of output that the antitrust laws foster.

A market defined by TV viewers is not the only way to look at things. The district court in *NCAA* defined a market of games shown. If "basketball games" are the product, then the NBA's plan cuts output by definition even if more persons watch the fewer (and more attractive) games shown on TV. The NCAA tried to persuade the Supreme Court that the plaintiffs should be required to establish power in a viewership market. The Court replied:

> We must reject this argument for two reasons, one legal, one factual. As a matter of law, the absence of proof of market power does not justify a naked restriction on price or output.... This naked restraint on price and output requires some competitive justification even in the absence of a detailed market analysis.

468 U.S. at 109–10. Although this passage is not entirely clear, we understand it as holding that any agreement to reduce output measured by the number of televised games requires some justification—some explanation connecting the practice to consumers' benefits—before the court attempts an analysis of market power. Unless there are sound justifications, the court condemns the practice without ado, using the "quick look" version of the Rule of Reason advocated by Professor Areeda and by the Solicitor General's brief in *NCAA*.

The district court proceeded in this fashion, examining the league's justifications; finding each wanting, the judge enjoined the 20-game rule without defining a market. In this court, the league's lead-off justification is that the telecasting rule prevents the clubs from "misappropriating" a "property" right that belongs to the NBA: the right to exploit its symbols and success. The district court properly rejected this argument on two grounds. First, it mischaracterizes the NBA's articles and bylaws, which leave with the teams the intellectual property in their games. The NBA could acquire a property interest in all broadcasting rights but has not done so. The 20-game rule does not transfer any broadcasting rights to the league; instead it shortens the list of stations to which clubs may sell rights the teams concededly possess. Second, it has nothing to do with antitrust law. We want to know the effects of the TV policy on consumers' welfare, not whether the league possesses sufficient contractual rights that it has become the "owner" of the copyright. *See Continental T.V., Inc. v. GTE Sylvania Inc.*, 433 U.S. 36, 52–53 & n.21 (1977) (rejecting an argument that legality of restraints under the antitrust laws depends on the characterization of a transaction in the law of property). A cartel could not insulate its agreement from the Sherman Act by giving certain producers contractual rights to sell to specified customers. Agreements limiting to whom, and how much, a firm may sell are the defining characteristics of cartels and may not be invoked as justifications of a cutback in output. That the NBA's cutback is only five games per year is irrelevant; long ago the Court rejected the invitation to inquire into the "reasonableness" of price and output decisions. Competition in markets, not judges, sets price and output. A court applying the Rule of Reason asks whether a practice produces net benefits for consumers; it is no answer to say that a loss is "reasonably small." (What is more, if five superstation games is tiny in relation to the volume of telecasting, the benefits from the limitation are correspondingly small.)

[The court then addressed the NBA's argument that the reduction to 20 games that might be broadcast on superstations was justified as a restraint on "free riders."]

It costs money to make a product attractive against other contenders for consumers' favor. Firms that take advantage of costly efforts without paying for them, that reap where they have not sown, reduce the payoff that the firms making the investment receive. This makes investments in design and distribution of products less attractive, to the ultimate detriment of consumers. Control of free-riding is accordingly an accepted justification for cooperation.

Three forms of free-riding characterize the Bulls' telecasting, according to the NBA. First, the contracts with NBC and TNT require these networks to advertise NBA basketball on other shows; the Bulls and WGN receive the benefit of this promotion without paying the cost. Second, the NBA has revenue-sharing devices and a draft to prop up the weaker teams. The Bulls took advantage of these while they were weak (and through the draft obtained their current stars) but, according to the league, are siphoning viewers (and thus revenues) to their own telecasts, thus diminishing the pot available for distribution to today's weaker teams. Third, the Bulls and WGN are taking a free ride on the benefits of the cooperative efforts during the 1980s to build up professional basketball as a rival to baseball and football—efforts that bore fruit just as the Bulls produced a championship team, and which the Bulls would undermine.

Free-riding is the diversion of value from a business rival's efforts without payment. [For example, suppose there are two retailers of the same brand of electronic equipment who sell in the same neighborhood. If one provides an attractive showroom and hires salespeople to explain and demonstrate the equipment, the price of the product must build in these ancillary costs. If the other retailer simply sells the equipment off the shelf, without any ancillary services, it can sell at a lower price because it avoids these costs. Consumers can thus obtain all of the ancillary services for free from the first retailer, and then buy the product from the second at the lower price; this means that the second retailer has had a "free ride" on the services of the first. However, this will either force the first retailer to stop providing the services, which is detrimental to consumer welfare, or require the manufacturer of the brand to restrict the second retailer in some fashion, to prevent its free riding.] (brackets in original).

What gives this the name free-riding is the lack of charge. . . . Put the retailers in a contractual relation, however, and they could adjust their accounts so that the person providing a valuable service gets paid. When payment is possible, free-riding is not a problem because the "ride" is not free. Here lies the flaw in the NBA's story. It may (and does) charge members for value delivered. As the NBA itself emphasizes, there are substantial revenue transfers, propping up the weaker clubs in order to promote vigorous competition on the court. Without skipping a beat the NBA may change these payments to charge for the Bulls' ride. If the $40 million of advertising time that NBC will provide during the four years of its current contract also promotes WGN's games, then the league may levy a charge for each game shown on a superstation, or require the club to surrender a portion of its revenues. Major league baseball does exactly this and otherwise allows its teams access to superstations. Avoidance of free-riding therefore does not justify the NBA's 20-game limit.

* * *

Because of the way in which issues have become separated in this litigation, we do not decide whether revenue-sharing from superstation broadcasts is consistent with the antitrust laws. Needless to say, we also do not decide whether any of the cooperative arrangements by which the league hires the services of the players comports with the Sherman Act. (The National Basketball Players Association, concerned that we might do some such thing by accident, has filed a brief urging us to guard our tongues.) It is enough to say that if the league may levy a tax on superstation broadcasts, then there is no free-riding. And if the league may not levy a tax, then a direct limit with the same effect as a tax is unjustifiable. Either way the NBA comes up short, and under *NCAA* the failure of its justifications eliminates the need for the district judge to define a market.

The NCAA argued that restrictions on the number of games telecast spread revenues and exposure among universities, helping to produce balanced competition on the field and hence making the games actually telecast more exciting, to the benefit of fans. Distributing telecasts among schools served, in the NCAA's view, as a substitute for the draft and other controls professional leagues deployed to the same end. The Supreme Court found the argument unpersuasive. It is hard to see how similar balance arguments by professional leagues, which make the most of drafts, trades, and revenue-pooling to foster exciting games, could be more compelling. Unless the Supreme Court is prepared to modify *NCAA*, the district court did not commit clear error in applying the "quick look" version of the Rule of Reason and rejecting the NBA's arguments.

Affirmed.

Having lost this effort to implement its 20-game limit on superstation broadcasts, the NBA tried a different approach. It added a provision to its network contract with Turner Network Television (TNT) that prohibited all NBA teams from having their games televised on a superstation on the same night that another NBA game was being televised on TNT. When the Bulls and WGN challenged this "superstation same night rule," Judge Will had to confront these two important issues affecting the scope of the SBA protection.

First, Judge Will rejected the NBA's effort to fit their revised scheme into the SBA exemption. He noted that neither the Bulls nor WGN had transferred game rights to the league or the league to any other party. As the Seventh Circuit affirmed, "the [SBA] applies only when the league has 'transferred' a right to 'sponsored telecasting.'" Moreover, because each team retains the right to televise on its particular over-the-air or cable outlet the *same games* that are televised by TNT, the league's transfer of rights to TNT cannot be characterized as exclusive." 808 F. Supp. 646, 648–49 (N.D. Ill. 1992).

As to the second issue, Judge Will ruled that the SBA would not apply, because TNT did not appear to be "sponsored telecasting."

> In its status as a cable television programming service, however, it is not clear that TNT constitutes "sponsored telecasting" as that term is used in the SBA. Although it is indeed a hybrid programming service, TNT is perhaps better characterized as subscription television for the following reasons. First, . . . a viewer must pay to receive TNT through the costs of hook-up fees, monthly cable fees and even additional monthly "premium cable" fees charged by some local cable operators for TNT. . . . Second, TNT derives its revenues predominantly from

"subscriptions" [$232 million in 1991] as opposed to advertising revenues from paying "sponsors" [$138 million in 1991]. Third, prior and subsequent legislative history demonstrates that "sponsored telecasting" as used in the SBA is limited to free commercial television as opposed to cable....

... "Sponsored telecasting" is not expressly defined by either the SBA or by any subsequent case law. In its report on the proposed legislation, the House Judiciary Committee noted only that "[t]he bill does not apply to closed circuit or subscription television." While the plain meaning of the term "subscription television" in 1961 might arguably have referred only to a pay-per-view service, it seems equally likely that the term "sponsored telecasting" would not have included such hybrid services as TNT and ESPN. "Sponsored telecasting" in 1961 referred to "free" television—the national network and local over-the-air broadcasting provided at no direct cost to viewers. The NBA's attempt to construe TNT as such "sponsored telecasting" simply because it contains commercial advertisements and is not offered on a pay-per-view basis is unconvincing....

Id. at 649–50.

Because its contracts with TNT and NBC were about to expire after the 1992–93 season, the NBA did not appeal Judge Will's second ruling. Instead, the league tried again to "rearrange" its affairs to achieve the same economic goals, but in a legally-insulated fashion. The NBA first amended its by-laws (with the Bulls and Nets dissenting) to have its teams confer copyright in all game telecasts on the league. Then, in its new television contract with NBC, the league assigned to NBC the exclusive right to televise all 1,100 regular season games. In return, NBC agreed that after selecting its 25 or so favored games, it would authorize the NBA to license Turner Broadcasting to telecast up to 85 games on its TNT cable and WTBS superstation channels. Then, after Turner had picked its games, the NBA could authorize individual teams to telecast the remaining games on local channels—but never on superstations. The new NBA rules also provided that, if its ban on superstation telecasts were to be struck down, a club like the Bulls that chose to use a superstation like WGN would have to pay a fee to the NBA that reflected the difference in the fair market value between local and national markets.

Needless to say, both the Bulls and WGN immediately returned to Judge Will with another antitrust claim against these new arrangements. In a lengthy opinion, Judge Will found that the series of arrangements that resulted in the superstation ban were illegal, because the new regime simply accomplished through different mechanisms the exact same result that he had already held to be illegal. 874 F. Supp. 844 (N.D. Ill.1995). On the SBA issue, although the contract with NBC involved "sponsored telecasting," it ran afoul of § 1292's exception to the exemption by prohibiting the telecasting of games in certain areas, by limiting NBC to 25 games, and by prohibiting the games eventually reassigned to the teams from being broadcast on superstations outside the teams' local areas.

Judge Will then found the superstation ban to be illegal under antitrust law, using a "quick-look" Rule of Reason analysis. He reasoned that the league's arrangement obviously restricted broadcast output, while the league had not proven any significant procompetitive benefit. The judge did endorse the NBA position that charging some fee to the Bulls for superstation telecasts was appropriate in order to offset the free-rider effect. However, the fee could not be set at an unreasonably high level so as effectively to restrict output. *Id.* at 868–69. Judge Will ordered the NBA not to limit the Bulls to fewer than 30 superstation telecasts. He left it for the parties to try to negotiate the appropriate fee for those telecasts. Failing that, future litigation would be needed to determine if any fee the NBA in fact imposed was too high because it cut back on broadcast output; if so, the NBA would still be, *de facto*, in violation of § 1.

The NBA appealed the ruling that its current superstation ban was illegal. Federal taxation as well as internal managerial and political problems blocked the league taking over the role as *licensor* of all its members teams' home broadcasts. Thus, if the league wanted to function just as *regulator* of such local team licensing, it had to do so under the scrutiny of antitrust law.

CHICAGO PROFESSIONAL SPORTS LTD. PARTNERSHIP & WGN V. NBA (BULLS II)
95 F.3d 593 (7th Cir. 1996)

EASTERBROOK, CIRCUIT JUDGE.

In the six years since they filed this antitrust suit, the Chicago Bulls have won four National Basketball Association titles and an equal number of legal victories. Suit and titles are connected. The Bulls want to broadcast more of their games over WGN television, a "superstation" carried on cable systems nationwide. The Bulls' popularity makes WGN attractive to these cable systems; the large audience makes WGN attractive to the Bulls. Since 1991 the Bulls and WGN have been authorized by injunction to broadcast 25 or 30 games per year. 754 F. Supp. 1336 (1991). We affirmed that injunction in 1992, *see* 961 F.2d 667, and the district court proceeded to determine whether WGN could carry even more games—and whether the NBA could impose a "tax" on the games broadcast to a national audience, for which other superstations have paid a pretty penny to the league. After holding a nine-week trial and receiving 512 stipulations of fact, the district court made a 30-game allowance permanent, 874 F. Supp.

844 (1995), and held the NBA's fee excessive, 1995-2 Trade Cas. ¶ 71,253. Both sides appeal. The Bulls want to broadcast 41 games per year over WGN; the NBA contends that the antitrust laws allow it to fix a lower number (15 or 20) and to collect the tax it proposed. With apologies to both sides, we conclude that they must suffer through still more litigation.

[The court first rejected the NBA's effort to fit its league rules within the Sports Broadcasting Act (SBA), through the new technique of transferring all broadcast rights to NBC and TBS/TNT, and having the latter return the vast majority of unused games to the individual teams, subject now to restrictions against selling those games to superstations like WGN. Echoing its earlier observation that the SBA must receive "beady-eyed reading" as a special interest exception to the antitrust laws, Judge Easterbrook asserted that "a league has to jump through every [SBA] hoop: partial compliance doesn't do the trick." The only way that the NBA could avail itself of the SBA was by itself taking over and selling broadcast rights in the games of the Bulls (and other) teams. However,] by signing a contract with NBC that left the Bulls, rather than the league, with the authority to select the TV station that would broadcast the games, the NBA made its position under the SBA untenable. For as soon as the Bulls picked WGN, any effort to control cable system retransmission of the WGN signal tripped over § 2 [of the SBA] which barred such restraints except within the home territory of clubs when they are playing.

[Judge Easterbrook next addressed Judge Will's ruling that, while the NBA did have the right to charge the Bulls a fee for sending its games out on a superstation, it should use as its calculation base the "outer market advertising revenues" that WGN generated from cable, and then split this in half with the Bulls. The upshot was that Judge Will cut the fee imposed by the league on the Bulls from roughly $138,000 to $35,000 a game.]

The district court's opinion concerning the fee reads like the ruling of an agency exercising a power to regulate rates. Yet the antitrust laws do not deputize district judges as one-man regulatory agencies. The core question in antitrust is output. Unless a contract reduces output in some market, to the detriment of consumers, there is no antitrust problem. A high price is not itself a violation of the Sherman Act. *See Broadcast Music, Inc. v. CBS, Inc.*, 441 U.S. 1, 9–10, 19–20, 22 n.40 (1979); *Buffalo Broadcasting Co. v. ASCAP*, 744 F.2d 917 (2d Cir. 1984). WGN and the Bulls argue that the league's fee is excessive, unfair, and the like. But they do not say that it will reduce output. They plan to go on broadcasting 30 games, more if the court will let them, even if they must pay $138,000 per telecast. Although the fee exceeds WGN's outer-market revenues, the station evidently obtains other benefits—for example, (i) the presence of Bulls games may increase the number of cable systems that carry the station, augmenting its revenues 'round the clock;' (ii) WGN slots into Bulls games ads for its other programming; and (iii) many viewers will keep

WGN on after the game and watch whatever comes next. Lack of an effect on output means that the fee does not have antitrust significance. Once antitrust issues are put aside, how much the NBA charges for national telecasts is for the league to resolve under its internal governance procedures. It is no different in principle from the question how much (if any) of the live gate goes to the visiting team, who profits from the sale of cotton candy at the stadium, and how the clubs divide revenues from merchandise bearing their logos and trademarks. Courts must respect a league's disposition of these issues, just as they respect contracts and decisions by a corporation's board of directors. *Charles O. Finley & Co. v. Kuhn,* 569 F.2d 527 (7th Cir. 1978); cf. *Baltimore Orioles, Inc. v. Major League Baseball Players Association,* 805 F.2d 663 (7th Cir. 1986).

[The court's discussion of the single entity issue, and Judge Cudahy's concurrence on that issue, was excerpted above in Chapter 5, Section D. The conclusion was that, at a minimum, the district court judgment required reversal for consideration under a full rule of reason analysis. Thus, rather than proving anticompetitive effect simply by demonstrating that the number of NBA games on television was reduced, the plaintiffs would have to prove that the NBA had significant power in an economically relevant market.]

Substantial market power is an indispensable ingredient of every claim under the full Rule of Reason. . . . During the lengthy trial of this case, the NBA argued that it lacks market power, whether the buyers are understood as the viewers of games (the way the district court characterized things in NCAA) or as advertisers, who use games to attract viewers (the way the Supreme Court characterized a related market in *Times-Picayune Publishing Co. v. United States,* 345 U.S. 594 (1953)). College football may predominate on Saturday afternoons in the fall, but there is no time slot when NBA basketball predominates. The NBA's season lasts from November through June; games are played seven days a week. This season overlaps all of the other professional and college sports, so even sports fanatics have many other options. From advertisers' perspective—likely the right one, because advertisers are the ones who actually pay for telecasts—the market is even more competitive. Advertisers seek viewers of certain demographic characteristics, and homogeneity is highly valued. A homogeneous audience facilitates targeted ads: breakfast cereals and toys for cartoon shows, household appliances and detergents for daytime soap operas, automobiles and beer for sports. If the NBA assembled for advertisers an audience that was uniquely homogeneous, or had especially high willingness-to-buy, then it might have market power even if it represented a small portion of airtime. The parties directed considerable attention to this question at trial, but the district judge declined to make any findings of fact on the subject, deeming market power irrelevant. As we see things, market power is irrelevant only if the

NBA is treated as a single firm under *Copperweld*; and given the difficulty of that issue, it may be superior to approach this as a straight Rule of Reason case, which means starting with an inquiry into market power and, if there is power, proceeding to an evaluation of competitive effects.

* * *

Vacated and remanded.

In December 1996, after six years of litigation on this subject, the NBA, the Bulls, and the Chicago Tribune (WGN) finally decided to compromise and settle their dispute, rather than expend even more legal resources in a full-scale rule of reason trial. The reported terms of the settlement permitted the Bulls to broadcast 35 of their games in the Chicago area over WGN, of which only 15 would go out over national cable as a superstation telecast. The league would share revenues from these national broadcasts through controlling some of the advertising spots, in return for dropping its proposed superstation tax. What do these terms indicate were the two sides' assessment of their relative prospects and benefits in settling rather than continuing to litigate this dispute? What we know for sure is that in the post-*WGN* era, the NBA was able to secure new contracts from NBC and TNT that raised the total of $275 million paid by the two networks in 1997–98 to $660 million for 1998–99 and for each of the following three seasons.

NOTES AND QUESTIONS

1. *Doctrine After* Bulls. With the *Bulls* litigation finally at an end, what is the status of the various issues raised along the way concerning the interpretation of the SBA:

 a. What constitutes "sponsored telecasting?" Does the NFL's contract with ESPN qualify for the SBA? What about a league contract with a superstation like WTBS? With a premium channel like HBO?

 b. Does a league qualify for SBA protection if it incorporates a restriction on an individual team's sale of telecasting rights into a league contract with a network that is SBA-protected?

 c. Can a league avoid the limitations of the SBA by assigning exclusive rights in all games to the network, and then requiring the network to license back rights to games it does not televise to the individual clubs, but with restraints on when and how the clubs can allow their games to be telecast?

d. What about NFL Network? Is it sponsored telecasting protected by the SBA? Is an SBA immunity required for a transfer of rights from the NFL to a wholly-owned entity?

2. *Re-Evaluating the Sports Broadcasting Act.* Almost four decades after its enactment, is the SBA good public policy toward sports broadcasting? What are the benefits secured by affording sports leagues this prerogative in the sale of their television rights? What has been the SBA's effect on franchise values? What are the costs of this policy? What effects has the SBA had on the number and price of games that fans can watch (in the NFL and in the NBA)? Are there other ways to secure the legitimate interests of the clubs while reducing any harmful impact on the fans? Consider the Sherman Act jurisprudence as set forth in the *NCAA* case discussed in Chapter 5.

3. *Fees Versus Output Restraints.* After *Bulls II*, can a league charge a fee to an individual team for utilizing any source of revenue (*e.g.*, selling television rights or various stadium revenues) that arguably exploits the reputation and product of the league, without thereby violating antitrust law? Recall the "relocation fee" charged by the NFL to the Rams when it moved from Los Angeles to St. Louis. Does the same justification apply to such relocation fees? By what standard should a court judge whether a fee is legal or illegal? What does your answer imply for the concept of a league requiring any source of revenue to be shared (outside the express authorization by the SBA)?

4. *More on Market Power Under the Rule of Reason.* Judge Easterbrook's opinions in the *Bulls* litigation illustrate the trend toward antitrust analysis founded on classical microeconomic theory. In his second *Bulls* opinion, Easterbrook held that market power was an essential element for a plaintiff to prove anticompetitive effects in a full-blown Rule of Reason case. Does the NBA have market power when selling the rights to telecast its games? What does market power mean in this context? How would a plaintiff go about proving it? Also consider the observation of Judge Richard Posner, who wrote in *Valley Liquors, Inc. v. Renfield Importers., Ltd.*, 678 F.2d 742, 745 (7th Cir. 1982) that firms without market power are unlikely to disserve consumers, and when they do, "market retribution will be swift." If the NBA were to disserve consumers, would market retribution be swift?

5. *Antitrust Law, False Positives, and False Negatives.* For an illuminating exchange about the virtues and vices of antitrust law generally, see Frank A. Easterbrook, *The Limits of Antitrust*, 63 Texas L. Rev. 1 (1984), and Richard S. Markovits, *The Limits to Simplifying Antitrust: A Reply to Professor Easterbrook*, 63 Texas L. Rev. 41 (1984). The extent to which judges or policymakers believe that it is more important to avoid "false positives" (incorrectly finding that legitimate behavior is anticompetitive) rather than "false negatives" (incorrectly finding that anticompetitive behavior is lawful under the rule of reason) plays an important role in antitrust doctrine and its application.

6. *Sports League Decision-Making and Information Asymmetry.* Judge Will indicated on several occasions that there was no evidence that

superstation telecasts actually injure other NBA teams by siphoning fans away from buying their tickets or watching them on TV. Indeed, he found that superstation telecasts have actually increased general interest in the NBA nationwide and thus enhanced the popularity of all NBA teams. If that judgment is correct, why is the NBA so adamant about abolishing superstation telecasts not controlled by the league? Are the other owners simply not as smart or perceptive as Judge Will, or do they have some ulterior unstated motive, or are they simply risk-adverse about policies that might harm their interests? Is that factual finding relevant to the case? Is a general insight from behavioral economics that people often over-estimate adverse effects of changes relevant to the analysis? If the NBA was correct that superstation telecasts were cutting into the television prices charged and revenues earned by many other teams, would that suffice to legalize its limits on those telecasts under the Sherman Act? If the benefits to the Bulls were greater than the harms to other teams, would the ban be lawful where the clubs could not agree on appropriate terms for compensation?

7. *Broadcast Limits and Partnership Concepts.* The essence of the NBA's position was that efforts to limit or abolish superstation telecasts are legal because it is not unlawful for partners in a joint venture to adopt rules that limit the ways in which they are allowed to compete against one another in selling the very product that they jointly produce. Indeed, in general partnership/joint venture law there is a fiduciary duty on the partners not to compete against the venture or its other partners in the venture's line of business or to expropriate an asset belonging to the venture for the partner's own benefit without the permission of the venture. Is this a persuasive antitrust position?

Not surprisingly, Bulls (and Chicago White Sox) owner Jerry Reinsdorf did not challenge the underlying agreement among club owners to limit their "local" broadcasts to assigned geographic territories. Absent this agreement, of course, the Bulls would have been free to license their broadcasts anywhere. That agreement was later challenged in private class action litigation on behalf of sports fans, in the following case. Although this litigation also was settled, on the eve of trial, key antitrust issues were discussed by the trial judge in denying the defendants' motion to dismiss.

LAUMANN V. NHL
56 F. Supp. 3d 280 (S.D.N.Y. 2014)

SHIRA A. SCHEINDLIN, U.S.D.J.:

I. INTRODUCTION

Plaintiffs bring these putative class actions against the National Hockey League ("NHL") and various individual clubs in the league (the "NHL Defendants"); Major League Baseball ("MLB") and various individual clubs in the league (the "MLB Defendants") (together the "League Defendants"); multiple regional sports networks ("RSNs") that produce and distribute professional baseball and hockey programming;[1] two multichannel video programming distributors ("MVPDs" or "distributors"), Comcast and DIRECTV (together with the RSNs, the "Television Defendants" or "broadcasters"); Madison Square Garden Company and the New York Rangers Hockey Club (the "MSG Defendants"); and New York Yankees Partnership and Yankees Entertainment & Sports Network, LLC ("YES") (together the "Yankee Defendants"). Plaintiffs allege violations under Sections 1 and 2 of the Sherman Antitrust Act (the "Sherman Act").

* * *

The Comcast Defendants, the DIRECTV Defendants, the NHL Defendants, and the MLB Defendants now move for summary judgment on the remaining claims. For the reasons that follow, all four motions are DENIED in full.

II. BACKGROUND

. . . The clubs within each League are competitors—both on the field and in the contest to broaden their fan bases. However, the clubs must also coordinate in various ways in order to produce live sporting events, including agreeing upon the game rules and setting a schedule of games for the season. Both leagues divide their member teams into geographic territories and assign each team a home television territory ("HTT") for broadcasting purposes. Neither the Comcast Defendants nor the DIRECTV Defendants played a role in the initial creation of the Leagues' HTTs.

The structure of the territorial broadcasting system is largely uncontested. By League agreement, each club agrees to license its games for telecast only within its designated HTT. The clubs then contract with RSNs through Rights Agreements. The Rights Agreements generally provide each RSN the exclusive right to produce a club's games and telecast them in the HTT.[13] The Agreements do not permit the RSNs to license telecasts for broadcast outside the HTTs. The Rights Agreements also require the RSNs to provide their telecasts to the Leagues without charge for use in the out-of-market packages ("OOM packages"). The clubs keep

---

[1] Several defendant RSNs are owned and controlled by defendant Comcast, several are owned and controlled by defendant DIRECTV, and two are independent of the MVPDs but share ownership with an individual club.

[13] MLB 56.1 ¶ 93; Comcast 56.1 ¶¶ 6, 14; DIRECTV 56.1 ¶ 6; NHL Mem. at 5. Plaintiffs do not challenge the clubs' right to grant production and distribution rights for their own games to only one RSN (hereinafter "content exclusivity"). Such exclusivity is to be distinguished from the exclusivity established by the territorial rules, which prevent each RSN from televising its programming outside the HTT and protect it from competing with the programming of other teams' games within the HTT (hereinafter "territorial exclusivity").

the revenue from their respective Rights Agreements. There are significant differences in the economic value of the various HTTs.

In order to produce the telecasts of live games, the RSNs invest in equipment, production facilities, and a large staff. They also produce "shoulder" programming such as pre-game and post-game shows. The RSNs then sell their programming to MVPDs like Comcast and DIRECTV through Affiliation Agreements, and the MVPDs televise the programming through standard packages sold to consumers within the HTT. Even when an MVPD agrees to carry a RSN, it does not always distribute that RSN throughout its entire territory. The MVPDs acquire the rights to broadcast the games subject to the territorial restrictions in the RSNs' agreements with the Leagues. The MVPDs black out games in unauthorized territories in accordance with those restrictions.

Fans can watch out-of-market games in one of two ways. *First*, some games are televised nationally through contracts between the Leagues and national broadcasters like ESPN and Fox. The clubs have agreed to allow the Leagues to negotiate national contracts on their behalf. The Leagues' agreements with national broadcasters contain provisions requiring the Leagues to preserve the HTTs. The revenues from national broadcasts are shared equally among the clubs.

Second, the Leagues produce OOM packages in both television and Internet format. The television packages—NHL Center Ice and MLB Extra Innings—are available for purchase through MVPDs, including Comcast and DIRECTV. The Internet packages—NHL GameCenter Live and MLB.tv—are available for purchase directly from the Leagues. The OOM packages are comprised of local RSN programming from each of the clubs. As with the national broadcasts, revenues from the OOM packages are shared equally among the clubs.

Each of the OOM packages requires the purchase of the full slate of out-of-market games, even if a consumer is only interested in viewing the games of one team. The OOMs exclude in-market games to "avoid diverting viewers from local RSNs that produce the live game feeds that form the OOM packages." [Quote is from league pleadings.]

In sum, each RSN is the sole producer of its club's games[30] and the sole distributor of those games within the HTT aside from limited nationally broadcasted games. The OOM packages do not show in-market games to avoid competition with the local RSN. Additionally, the territorial broadcast restrictions allow each RSN to largely avoid competing with out-of-market games produced by other RSNs.

---

[30] One exception is that the teams in each League have agreed to permit the visiting team to produce a separate telecast of away games.

Internet streaming rights are owned by the Leagues and/or the clubs. The RSNs have no right to license their programming for Internet streaming directly. The Internet OOM packages are the primary way for fans to view games on the Internet. Additionally, some MVPDs have negotiated with the Leagues to provide Internet streaming of out-of-market games to subscribers of the OOM television packages. Internet streaming of in-market games remains largely unavailable to consumers.

* * *

V. DISCUSSION

* * *

B. The League Defendants Are Not Entitled to Summary Judgment

While territorial divisions of a market are normally per se violations, the Supreme Court has held that a per se approach is inappropriate in the context of sports broadcasting restrictions due to the necessary interdependence of the teams within a League. On the other hand, the procompetitive benefit of the challenged scheme here is not so obvious that the case can be resolved in favor of defendants in the " 'twinkling of an eye.' " Therefore the rule of reason is the appropriate standard in this case.

Plaintiffs have carried their initial burden of showing an actual impact on competition. The clubs in each League have entered an express agreement to limit competition between the clubs—and their broadcaster affiliates—based on geographic territories. There is also evidence of a negative impact on the output, price, and perhaps even quality of sports programming. Plaintiffs' expert, Dr. Roger G. Noll, attests that consumers pay higher prices for live game telecasts, and have less choice among the telecasts available to them, than they would in the absence of the territorial restrictions. Similarly, Dr. Noll estimates that the price of OOM packages would decrease by about fifty percent in a world without the restrictions. Finally, defendants have not argued in these motions that the Leagues lack market power.[112]

Defendants respond by identifying various procompetitive effects of the territorial broadcast restrictions. They claim that the rules: 1) prevent free riding, 2) preclude competition with joint venture products, 3) incentivize investment in higher quality telecasts, 4) maintain competitive balance, 5) preserve a balance between local loyalty and interest in the sport as a whole, and 6) increase the overall number of games that are

---

[112] See MLB Mem. at 12 n.22 (preserving the MLB Defendants' right to challenge plaintiffs' definition of relevant market and market power although "not addressed in this motion"); NHL Mem. at 3 n.3 ("While the NHL Defendants vigorously contest Plaintiffs' proposed market definition and the assertion that NHL Defendants possess market power in any cognizable market, they are not moving for summary judgment on these issues in this motion.").

telecast. Plaintiffs deny that the territorial rules serve the above interests and also challenge the validity of the interests in light of the territorial rules' overall economic impact on competition.

First, defendants argue that the territorial rules prevent free riding. Although avoiding free riding can be a legitimate procompetitive goal in certain contexts, it is not clear how free riding would pose a threat in this case. Defendants argue that the clubs would "free ride" on the popularity and publicity of the Leagues if they were permitted to license their games nationally. However, the same argument could be made for any revenue-producing activity that an individual team undertakes, including local ticket sales. Defendants also claim that the clubs would "free ride" off the OOM packages by nationally licensing individual club broadcasts, but it is the clubs and RSNs who create the programming in the first place. If anything, the OOM packages benefit from the labor and investment of the clubs and RSNs, not the other way around. Defendants' theory of free riding is unclear and unpersuasive.

Second, defendants argue that the Leagues have an unassailable right to prevent the clubs from competing with the "joint venture." However, no case cited by defendants stands for the proposition that a joint venture may always prevent its members from competing with the venture product regardless of anticompetitive consequences. Rather, in each case, the court concluded based on the facts presented that the restraint in question caused no actual harm to competition. "If the fact that potential competitors shared in profits or losses from a venture meant that the venture was immune from § 1, then any cartel could evade the antitrust law simply by creating a joint venture to serve as the exclusive seller of their competing products."

Third, defendants argue that territorial exclusivity encourages the RSNs to invest in higher-quality telecasts, including high-definition cameras, announcers, audio-visual effects, and related pre-game and post-game programming. However, the incentive for added investment is inflated profit stemming from limited competition. "[T]he Rule of Reason does not support a defense based on the assumption that competition itself is unreasonable." To the extent that the Leagues defend *content* exclusivity rather than territorial exclusivity, Dr. Noll predicts that increased competition would overall improve output and consumer satisfaction, an argument that applies with equal force to the quality of telecasts.

Fourth, defendants argue that the territorial restrictions foster competitive balance between the teams and prevent excessive disparities in team quality. Maintaining competitive balance is a legitimate and important goal for professional sports leagues. However, it is unclear whether the territorial restrictions at issue here really serve that purpose. On the one hand, the restrictions protect less popular clubs from competition with more popular teams in their own HTTs. On the other hand, the system requires small market teams to refrain from broadcasting in larger, more populous markets, while big market teams forego only smaller, less populous markets. It is not immediately clear whether the restrictions help or harm competitive balance overall.[120]

Defendants also claim that the revenue sharing aspects of the OOM packages and national broadcasts foster competitive balance. However, there is support in the economic community for the theory that revenue sharing in fact exacerbates competitive imbalance. Even accepting the premise that revenue sharing is beneficial, defendants have not explained why broadcasting contracts are a better mechanism than more direct, limited forms of revenue sharing.

Fifth, defendants claim that they have a legitimate pro-competitive interest in maintaining "a balance between the promotion of [hockey and baseball] as [ ] national game[s] and the need to incentivize Clubs to build their local fan bases." Aside from the fact that these two goals appear to conflict, defendants have not explained what the ideal balance would be, or how they might quantify it. There is no objective measure the Leagues could aspire to attain. Therefore defendants cannot establish that this particular balance between local and national interests is better for consumers, or for demand, than the balance that would prevail in a free market. Moreover, the Leagues purport to bolster regional interest and team loyalty by consciously depriving consumers of out-of-market games they would prefer, which is generally not a permissible aim under the antitrust laws.

Finally, defendants argue that the number of telecasts created and broadcast is greater under the territorial restrictions than it would be in the plaintiffs' "but-for" world. According to defendants, while almost every game is currently available to consumers in one format or another (national broadcast, local RSN, or OOM package), a system dependent on consumer demand could not guarantee that every game would be available everywhere because less popular teams would struggle to get their games produced or televised on their own. Destroying the HTTs would also destroy content exclusivity because OOMs and both competing teams would be able to sell the same game in the same areas. As a result, RSNs would be loathe to give their telecasts to the Leagues to create OOM packages, depriving consumers of the ability to access any and all out-of-market games as they do now. Similarly, national broadcasters would refuse to enter into national contracts without the assurance of exclusivity. Because plaintiffs do not challenge the legality of the OOM packages or

---

[120] *See* [Economist Roger Noll's declaration, at 117] ("Economic research provides no reason to believe that restrictions in competition for television rights contribute to competitive balance, no matter how balance is defined, and some reason to believe that these restrictions actually make balance worse.").

national broadcasts, defendants argue, the territorial system is also immune from challenge as a matter of law.

These arguments are far from compelling. Just because plaintiffs do not directly challenge the legality of the OOM packages and national broadcasts does not mean that preserving them is sufficient justification for the territorial rules. Even the complete disappearance of OOM packages would not necessarily cause consumer harm if the same content could be distributed in another form (such as by RSNs nationwide). The OOMs are simply one form of delivering the content to consumers—a form made necessary by the territorial rules themselves. Moreover, it is certainly conceivable that the OOMs would continue to exist absent the territorial restrictions, given the low added cost of creating the packages and the convenience of bundling to many consumers.

Defendants' assumption that market demand would be insufficient to ensure access to the same number of games is questionable. Indeed, the Television Defendants insist that the sports rights are so valuable that they would compete for those rights vigorously even in the absence of the territorial rules. Moreover, "[a] restraint that has the effect of reducing the importance of consumer preference in setting price and output is not consistent with th[e] fundamental goal of antitrust law." . . .

Defendants cite *Virgin Atlantic Airways Ltd. v. British Airways PLC*, [257 F.3d 256, 264 (2d Cir. 2001)] for the proposition that plaintiffs must identify a less restrictive alternative for any procompetitive effect defendants can identify, even if the overall effect on the economy is overwhelmingly anticompetitive. Such an interpretation, however, is inconsistent with the Supreme Court's mandate that "the essential inquiry [under the rule of reason] . . . [is] whether or not the challenged restraint enhances competition." Indeed, in *United States v. Visa U.S.A., Inc.*, [344 F.3d 229, 243 (2d Cir. 2003], the Second Circuit balanced the alleged procompetitive and anticompetitive effects of the exclusivity rules before requiring the Government to propose any less restrictive alternatives.

* * *

C. The Television Defendants Are Not Entitled to Summary Judgment

1. Liability for the Vertical Agreements

The Television Defendants argue that downstream distributors who simply implement the restrictions of an upstream conspiracy through vertical agreements, without further involvement, cannot be deemed participants in the conspiracy as a matter of law. . . .

* * *

None of the decisions relied on by the Television Defendants held that a downstream entity must request or enforce a restraint in order to be liable for adopting it through agreement. Nor did they indicate that each party to an allegedly unlawful agreement must have equal or even substantial negotiating power in adopting the agreement's terms. Moreover, a downstream entity need not participate in the initial creation of the restraints in order to be liable for adopting them later. "It is elementary that an unlawful conspiracy may be and often is formed without simultaneous action or agreement on the part of the conspirators."

Indeed, it would defy common sense to require proof that the Television Defendants enforced the territorial restrictions when they knew that the structure would be secured through a series of parallel contracts effectively policed by the Leagues. . . . In 2008, MLB attempted to adjust the territorial lines to serve customers who could not watch local games, which would have required clubs and RSNs to cede some territory to the OOM packages. The Comcast RSNs vehemently opposed the proposal and sent the following letter to MLB:

> If MLB were to adopt any new MLB rule permitting MLB Extra Innings and/or MLB.TV to be distributed in unserved or underserved portions of a club's exclusive home television territory, the scope of the exclusivity purchased by the RSN would be unilaterally changed and the financial impact on the prospects and performance of the Comcast RSNs (and, by implication, on the clubs whose rights they hold) would likely be immediate and significant. Accordingly, the Comcast RSNs are unlikely to consider favorably the release of any portion of a home television territory as to which an RSN currently has exclusive rights. In providing distribution information herewith, the Comcast RSNs specifically reserve all of their respective rights and remedies with respect to any change in MLB's current rules and practices that negatively impacts the clubs' respective home television territories and the breadth of the exclusive rights heretofore granted to their corresponding Comcast RSNs.

* * *

On the eve of trial, Judge Scheindlin approved a settlement of the class action, providing substantial fees to plaintiffs' attorneys and terms that could result in an estimated $200 million savings to consumers: a reduced price for the out-of-market package, a new option to subscribe at a $25 savings for out-of-market games of a single team, and an option to stream in-market games for those who already pay for a MVPD subscription.

A NOTE ON REVENUE SHARING

The continued use of exclusive broadcast territories after the *Laumann* settlement means that leagues (other than the NFL, where all television contracts are sold by the league) continue to struggle with the significant inequality in distribution of local broadcasting revenue. This constitutes a major source of inequality in club earnings. The problem is especially acute in MLB, where the disparity in local broadcast revenues has risen even faster than their absolute amounts, and the luxury tax is a limited restraint on the ability of broadcast-rich clubs to outspend rivals in smaller media markets. Because the clubs could no longer rely on the old reserve system to insulate equality of team playing talent from inequality in team earnings, the felt need for greater revenue sharing in Major League Baseball had become acute among small market teams. Understandably, the large market teams continued to resist the idea. Peter Bavasi, former president of the Toronto Blue Jays and the Cleveland Indians, recalled that when the subject of revenue sharing was brought up in league meetings, one of the owners of a large-market team would stand up, begin his comments with "Comrades!," and after embarrassed laughter the topic would quickly be dropped.

As detailed in John Helyar, *Lords of the Realm: The* Real *History of Baseball* (Villard, 1994), by the mid-1990s there was finally general acceptance among the owners of the value of significantly expanding the degree of revenue sharing. The small market teams secured the acquiescence of large market owners by threatening no longer to allow broadcasts from their home stadiums of games played by visiting teams like the Yankees and Dodgers. The larger market owners agreed to a new revenue-sharing formula in the spring of 1994, but only on condition that the players would accept the hard salary cap that the owners would insist upon in collective bargaining that summer, before and after the strike that eliminated that year's World Series. The players were not only strongly opposed to a hard salary cap (or tax), but were also concerned about the potential salary-constraining impact of a progressive revenue-sharing system. Finally, in December 1996, the owners ratified their agreement with the players for a 35% luxury tax on the amount that each of the five highest payrolls exceeded the sixth highest. The parties also agreed on a somewhat less ambitious increase in the revenue-sharing system among the owners.

Ongoing revisions reflected in successive baseball collective agreements extended the principle of revenue sharing even further with an even more complicated set of arrangements. The complex scheme contained three main elements: (1) significant contributions from all net (deducting ballpark expenses) local revenues to a fund divided equally among all 30 teams, (2) additional payments required by high revenue teams to low revenue teams, and (3) new luxury payroll taxes on payrolls over fixed amounts.

3. VERTICAL INTEGRATION OF MEDIA COMPANIES AND ACCESS TO SPORTS BROADCASTING

When *United States v. NFL* was decided, clubs were licensing television rights to over-the-air networks or individual local over-the-air stations. Essential to the understanding of the antitrust issues and business dynamics in today's world is the new method of distribution from rights holders (clubs or leagues) to programmers (including over-the-air networks like Fox, cable networks like ESPN, and internet programmers like MLB.com) to distributors (DirecTV, cable companies, internet companies). Important issues of broadcast regulation arise as well in the new media, as discussed below.

Antitrust economists have coined the term "serial monopoly" to describe the problems caused when consumers face limited competition at retail to buy products for which there are few close substitutes. Although economists usually focus on a nice geometric explanation of how prices are even higher than if a single monopolist is in charge of making and retailing the good, consumers often suffer even more serious harm from the bargaining costs that occur when the "upstream" and "downstream" monopolists can't agree on how to share the spoils. In the sports world, this has become unfortunately too well known to fans, when valuable sports rights are unavailable because their local cable or satellite dish provider (known as an MVPD or multichannel video programming distributor) is in a dispute with a rights seller.

For an illustration, consider the plight of the Nationals and their fans as baseball returned to our nation's capital city. MLB's efforts to relocate the Montreal Expos to Washington foundered on objections by Baltimore Orioles' owner Peter Angelos. After *Raiders,* these objections only had force because of baseball exemption precedents suggested that they would not subject MLB to antitrust liability. All the same, to obtain Angelos' consent, MLB agreed to create a new entity, the Mid-Atlantic Sports Networks (MASN), to broadcast Nationals' games, with the Orioles initially owning 90 percent and paying the Nationals $20 million a year, and the Nationals' share eventually increasing to 33 percent. However, the dominant local cable provider, Comcast, refused to carry MASN games on its cable system because of the proposed price.

FCC regulations, 47 C.F.R. § 76.1301, prohibit MVPDs like Comcast from engaging "in conduct the effect of which is to unreasonably restrain the ability of an unaffiliated video programming vendor to compete fairly." MASN alleged that Comcast's refusal to carry Nationals and Orioles games constituted discrimination by Comcast against MASN, and in favor of other sports programming owned by Comcast. Under FCC regulations, an administrative law judge would have determined the issue; once the case was assigned, however, the parties reached an agreement for Comcast to carry these games at a price 5% lower than that demanded by MASN.

Several important issues arise from this problem. This regulation only applies to alleged discrimination by an MVPD like Comcast (owned by NBC Universal) that also owns sports programming. Is there a sufficient public interest in uninterrupted sports programming to warrant expansion of the FCC's mandatory commercial arbitration proceedings to cover all sports cases? For a number of years, over 70% of Los Angeles households have not had access to Sportsnet LA, a new regional sports network with rights to carry Dodgers games created by Time Warner Cable, the rights purchaser. Time Warner, and its successor, Charter Communications, insisted that rival MVPDs pay $4 per month for every subscriber, whether or not they watch the Dodgers; to date, other MVPDs have rejected these terms and their subscribers lack access to the Dodgers' RSN. A similar legal issue concerns contractual obligations to consumers when MVPDs like Comcast or DirecTV lose retransmission rights. *See, e.g., In re Cablevision Consumer Litig.*, 864 F. Supp. 2d 258 (S.D.N.Y. 2012) (class action demanding partial refund where Comcast lost rights to NFL football for two-week period).

Many of these issues are complicated by the MVPDs' traditional practice of requiring their customers who wish to purchase any programming other than basic free-to-air networks to acquire a package of 40–100 other programs for a single monthly fee. In turn, programmers then seek to bundle their highly popular and niche channels to compel MVPDs to carry as many as possible on their "basic premium" package. *See, e.g., Cablevision Sys. Corp. v. Viacom Int'l Inc.*, 2014-2 Trade Cas. (CCH) ¶ 78,836 (S.D.N.Y.) (denying Viacom's motion to dismiss claims for illegal bundling of various channels).

Just as contract negotiation problems between battling monopolists directly affect consumers, harm to consumers can ensue when a firm that operates in two different markets is able to use its power in one market to advantage its own products in a second market. This antitrust concern has been incorporated into communication regulation. The Cable Television Consumer Protection and Competition Act of 1992 includes various provisions to curb abuses of cable operator's "bottleneck monopoly power." Pub. L. No. 102–385, 106 Stat. 1460. The issues are set forth in the following case.

COMCAST CABLE COMMUNICATIONS, LLC v. FEDERAL COMMUNICATIONS COMMISSION
717 F.3d 982 (D.C. Cir. 2013)

WILLIAMS, SENIOR CIRCUIT JUDGE:

Regulations of the Federal Communications Commission, adopted under the mandate of § 616 of the Communications Act of 1934 and virtually duplicating its language, bar a multichannel video programming distributor ("MVPD") such as a cable company from discriminating against unaffiliated programming networks in decisions about content distribution. More specifically, the regulations bar such conduct when the effect of the discrimination is to "unreasonably restrain the ability of an unaffiliated video programming vendor to compete fairly." 47 C.F.R. § 76.1301(c); *see also* 47 U.S.C. § 536(a)(3). Tennis Channel, a sports programming network and intervenor in this suit, filed a complaint against petitioner Comcast Cable, an MVPD, alleging that Comcast violated § 616 and the Commission's regulations by refusing to broadcast Tennis as widely (*i.e.*, via the same relatively low-priced "tier") as it did its own affiliated sports programming networks, Golf Channel and Versus. (Versus is now known as NBC Sports Network and was originally called Outdoor Life Network; for consistency with the order under review, we refer to it as "Versus.") An administrative law judge ruled against Comcast, ordering that it provide Tennis carriage equal to what it affords Golf and Versus, and the Commission affirmed. *See Tennis Channel, Inc. v. Comcast Cable Commc'ns, LLC*, 27 FCC Rcd. 8508 (July 24, 2012).

[Judge Williams reversed the FCC, finding that the FCC 'failed to identify adequate evidence of unlawful discrimination."]

Comcast, the largest MVPD in the United States, offers cable television programming to its subscribers in several different distribution "tiers," or packages of programming services, at different prices. Since Versus's and Golf's launches in 1995, Comcast—which originally had a minority interest in the two networks, and now has 100% ownership—has generally carried the networks on its most broadly distributed tiers, Expanded Basic or the digital counterpart Digital Starter.

Tennis Channel, launched in 2003, initially sought distribution of its content on Comcast's less broadly distributed sports tier, a package of 10 to 15 sports networks that Comcast's subscribers can access for an extra $5 to $8 per month. In 2005, Tennis entered a carriage contract that gave the Comcast the "right to carry" Tennis "on any . . . tier of service," subject to exclusions irrelevant here. Comcast in fact placed Tennis on the sports tier.

In 2009, however, Tennis approached Comcast with proposals that Comcast reposition Tennis onto a tier with broader distribution. Tennis's proposed agreement called for Comcast to pay Tennis for distribution on a per-subscriber basis. Tennis provided a detailed analysis—which is sealed in this proceeding—of what Comcast would likely pay for that broader distribution; even with the discounts that Tennis offered, the amounts are substantial. Neither the analysis provided at the time, nor testimony received in this litigation, made (much less substantiated) projections of any resulting increase in revenue for Comcast, let alone revenue sufficient to offset the increased fees.

[Comcast rejected the offer, and this litigation ensued.]

The parties agree that Comcast distributes the content of affiliates Golf and Versus more broadly than it does that of Tennis. The question is whether that difference violates § 616 and the implementing regulations. There is also no dispute that the statute prohibits only discrimination *based on* affiliation. Thus, if the MVPD treats vendors differently based on a reasonable business purpose (obviously excluding any purpose to illegitimately hobble the competition from Tennis), there is no violation. The Commission has so interpreted the statute, *Mid-Atlantic Sports Network v. Time Warner Cable Inc.*, 25 FCC Rcd. 18099, ¶ 22 (2010), and the Commission's attorney conceded as much at oral argument; *see also TCR Sports Broad. Holding L.L.P. v. FCC*, 679 F.3d 269, 274–77 (4th Cir. 2012) (discussing the legitimate, non-discriminatory reasons for an MVPD's differential treatment of a non-affiliated network).

[Judge Williams concluded that the FCC had not refuted Comcast's claims that adding the Tennis Channel to a broader tier, and charging all subscribers on that tier for access, would cost Comcast money. Indeed, when Comcast acquired another MVPD that had distributed Tennis Channel more broadly, and then repositioned Tennis Channel on its sports tier (a "negative repo" in MVPD lingo), making it available only for an additional fee, not a single customer complained.]

[Judge Williams suggested that the FCC could have prevailed with evidence that the licensing fee Tennis Channel sought from Comcast for location on its broader tier was equivalent to the incremental revenue that Comcast would have received in 2009 had it shifted Golf and Versus from a sports tier to its broader tier, but no such evidence was offered.]

Without showing any benefit for Comcast from incurring the additional fees for assigning Tennis a more advantageous tier, the Commission has not provided evidence that Comcast discriminated against Tennis on the basis of affiliation. And while the Commission describes at length the "substantial evidence" that supports a finding that the discrimination is based on affiliation, none of that evidence establishes benefits that Comcast would receive if it distributed Tennis more broadly. On this issue the Commission has pointed to no evidence, and therefore obviously not to substantial evidence. . . .

KAVANAUGH, CIRCUIT JUDGE, concurring.

[Judge Kavanaugh read § 616 more narrowly, to require a determination that a company has market power, and he concluded that Comcast does not have market power "in the national video programming distribution market." He interpreted § 616 as incorporating "traditional antitrust principles," noting that the phrase "unreasonably restrain" is a long-standing antitrust term of art.]

So what does antitrust law tell us? In antitrust law, certain activities are considered per se anticompetitive. Otherwise, however, conduct generally can be considered unreasonable only if a firm, or multiple firms acting in concert, have market power. [citing cases.]

This case involves vertical integration and vertical contracts. Beginning in the 1970s (well before the 1992 Cable Act), the Supreme Court has recognized the legitimacy of vertical integration and vertical contracts by firms without market power. [citing cases]. Vertical integration and vertical contracts become potentially problematic only when a firm has market power in the relevant market. That's because, absent market power, vertical integration and vertical contracts are *procompetitive*. Vertical integration and vertical contracts in a competitive market encourage product innovation, lower costs for businesses, and create efficiencies—and thus reduce prices and lead to better goods and services for consumers. *See* Douglas H. Ginsburg, *Vertical Restraints: De Facto Legality Under the Rule of Reason*, 60 Antitrust L.J. 67, 76 (1991) ("Antitrust law is a bar to the use of vertical restraints only in markets in which there is no apparent interbrand competition to protect consumers from a potentially welfare-decreasing restraint on intrabrand competition."); Dennis L. Weisman & Robert B. Kulick, *Price Discrimination, Two-Sided Markets, and Net Neutrality Regulation*, 13 Tul. J. Tech. & Intell. Prop. 81, 99 (2010) ("[M]onopoly power in one market is a necessary condition for anticompetitive effects in almost all models of anticompetitive vertical integration."); *see also* 3B Phillip E. Areeda & Herbert Hovenkamp, *Antitrust Law* ¶ 756a, at 9 (3d ed. 2008) (vertical integration "is either competitively neutral or affirmatively desirable because it promotes efficiency"); Robert H. Bork, *The Antitrust Paradox* 226 (1978) ("vertical integration is indispensable to the realization of productive efficiencies").

Not surprisingly given its procompetitive characteristics, vertical integration and vertical contracts are common and accepted practices in the American economy: Apple's iPhones contain integrated hardware and software, Dunkin' Donuts sells Dunkin' Donuts coffee, Ford produces radiators for its cars, McDonalds sells Big Macs, Nike stores are stocked with Nike shoes, Netflix owns "House of Cards," and so on. As Professors Areeda and Hovenkamp have explained, vertical integration "is ubiquitous in our economy and virtually never poses a threat to competition when undertaken unilaterally and in competitive markets." 3B Areeda & Hovenkamp, *Antitrust Law* ¶ 755c, at 6.

EDWARDS, CIRCUIT JUDGE, concurring [agreed with Judge Williams' analysis but found that the complaint was not timely filed.]

NOTES AND QUESTIONS

1. *FCC's Different Interpretation of § 616*. The FCC's interpretation of § 616 was significantly different than Judge Kavanagh's, a point of dispute not resolved by the panel majority. The FCC concluded:

> 41. Section 616 would serve no function if it existed simply as a redundant analogue to antitrust law. Nothing in the text of Section 616 indicates an intent to mimic existing antitrust law or the "essential facilities" doctrine. The legislative history, moreover, expressly repudiates such a design. The House Report explains, "This legislation provides new FCC remedies and does not amend, and is not intended to amend, existing antitrust laws. All antitrust and other remedies that can be pursued under current law by video programming vendors are unaffected by this section." In short, Section 616 was intended to operate alongside existing antitrust law, and to read Section 616 to simply echo antitrust law would frustrate Congress's clear purpose to grant the Commission new authority to address concerns specific to MVPDs and affiliated programming.

> 42. Contrary to Comcast's arguments, our reading of the history of Section 616 reveals that it was designed to address specific concerns about vertical integration in the video distribution market. Congress was concerned that "vertical integration gives cable operators the incentive and ability to favor their affiliated programming services," thereby leading to reduced competition and diversity of programming. Congress considered prohibiting vertical integration altogether, noting that such an approach "has appeal," but ultimately decided that "[t]o ensure that cable operators do not favor their affiliated programmers over others," it was appropriate to "bar[ ] cable operators from discriminating against unaffiliated programmers." With this goal of protecting competition at its core, Section 616 is structured to prohibit discrimination on the basis of affiliation when such discrimination has the effect of "unreasonably restrain[ing] the ability of an unaffiliated . . . programming vendor to compete fairly."

2. *Is Comcast More Like Dunkin' Donuts or Sears?* Unlike Dunkin' Donuts, McDonalds, and Nike retail outlets, Comcast distributes a lot of programming produced by others and licensed by Comcast. Perhaps the better analogy would be to Sears, which offers its own blue jeans in addition to those made by Levi's or Lee's. If Sears were the only retailer in town, however, and they only carried their house brand, consumers would be harmed. Likewise, if Sears contracted to sell only Lee's, excluding Levi's, and there were no other local retail outlets, there would likely be an antitrust violation. *Standard Fashion Co. v. Magrane-Houston Co.*, 258 U.S. 346 (1922). However, in reality, Sears could legally exclude Levi's, because consumers who wished to purchase Levi's could easily find them at other retail outlets.

In your view, is Comcast more like the only retailer in town, or like a retailer selling its own goods in competition with those of other retailers?

3. *Basic Premium or Sports Tier?* Most cable access disputes in the sports industry concern stalled negotiations over the cost per subscriber to placing a sports channel on the basic premium network. There are few issues concerning placing a sports channel on a special sports tier, where the MVPD is basically acting as a conduit for a specific monthly fee paid only by those channel's viewers. Why should *any* consumer have to pay for programming—be it Fox Sports 1 or the Disney Channel—that they don't wish to pay for? *See* Warren S. Grimes, *The Distribution of Pay Television in the United States: Let an* Unshackled Marketplace Decide, 5 J. Int'l Media & Ent. L. 1 (2013).

4. *Vertical Issues in Recent Antitrust Jurisprudence.* Consumer advocates' concerns about anticompetitive issues that arise from vertical integration were decisively rejected in the recent challenge to the merger of AT&T (which had previously acquired DirecTV) and Time Warner Cable. In *United States v. AT&T Inc.*, 2018 WL 2930849, No. 17-2511 (RJL) (D.D.C. June 12, 2018), the government alleged that the merger would violate § 7 of the Clayton Act. The Government argued that permitting AT&T to acquire Time Warner is likely to substantially lessen competition in the video programming and distribution market nationwide, by enabling AT&T to use Time Warner's "must have" television content to either raise its rivals' video programming costs or, by way of a "blackout," drive those same rivals' customers to its subsidiary, DirecTV. Thus, according to the Government, consumers nationwide will be harmed by increased prices for access to Turner networks, notwithstanding the Government's concession that this vertical merger would result in hundreds of millions of dollars in annual cost savings to AT&T's customers.

By contrast, the defendants argued that high-speed internet access has facilitated a "veritable explosion" of new, innovative video content and advertising offerings over the past five years. Vertically integrated entities like Netflix, Hulu, and Amazon have achieved remarkable success in creating and providing affordable, on-demand video content directly to viewers over the internet. Meanwhile, web giants Facebook and Google have developed new ways to use data to create effective—and lucrative—digital advertisements tailored to the individual consumer. Both video programmers such as Time Warner and video distributors such as AT&T faced declining video subscriptions and flatlining television advertising revenues, while Facebook's and Google's dominant digital advertising platforms have surpassed television advertising in revenue. Watching vertically integrated, data-informed entities thrive as television subscriptions and advertising revenues declined, AT&T and Time Warner concluded that each had a problem that the other could solve: Time Warner could provide AT&T with the ability to experiment with and develop innovative video content and advertising offerings for AT&T's many video and wireless customers, and AT&T could afford Time Warner access to customer relationships and valuable data about its programming. After trial,

Judge Richard Leon found that the government had not sustained its burden of proof on these critical alternative narratives.

D. GROUP LICENSING OF MERCHANDISE AND RELATED INTELLECTUAL PROPERTY RIGHTS

While league sale of television rights is the most visible and financially significant illustration of the issues relating to a league's legal authority to pool and/or restrict its member clubs' intellectual property rights, essentially the same questions are raised by the sale of sports merchandising rights. All the North American leagues follow the lead of the NFL by largely centralizing trademark licensing for merchandising purposes in a single league office to which every club assigns an exclusive right to market its team names and logos. (This is in marked and interesting contrast to the English Premier League, which maintains virtually no centralized marketing other than a league website that refers customers to each club's local site.) By 2009, the total consumer sales of merchandise bearing these league and team identities ranged from $2.82 billion for the MLB to $750 million for the NHL, with the leagues receiving average royalties of approximately eight percent for licensing the use of the trademark rights.

The background source for this significant revenue is a legal system that gives clubs an exclusive property right to a variety of trademarks and copyrights associated with their teams; this system is the topic of Chapter 8, *infra*. This section focuses on the legal and policy issues concerning the ability of teams to come together to sell a single package of marketing rights to the highest bidder. In addition, because players retain some intellectual property—image rights and publicity rights, also discussed in Chapter 8—antitrust and policy considerations also apply to the collective sales of these rights by players associations.

A skirmish relating to the degree of league control of intellectual property rights continues to be a source of contention between the NFL's marketing arm, NFL Properties, and the owner of the Dallas Cowboys, Jerry Jones. Among other complaints, Jones objected to the NFL's system of dividing licensing fee revenues equally among all teams, while the Cowboys successful efforts to portray themselves as "America's Team" led their merchandise to account for more than 25% of total NFL sales. Jones argued that if he had the right to market the Cowboys' name and logo, he would be able to expand total Cowboys' sales and keep a lot more of the financial returns for himself. Jones was unlikely, however, to persuade three-fourths of his fellow owners to change the NFL rules as he wanted. Such intra-league competition would exacerbate revenue disparities between more popular and less popular teams, and require other clubs to focus more time and attention on aggressively competing for merchandise as well as on-field success. In addition, league officials and other owners believe that overall revenue and economies of scale would likely diminish if the league replaced its centralized operation and marketing expertise with marketing efforts of club officials who may be more locally oriented.

In the summer of 1995, the Cowboys' owner sold to Pepsi, Nike, and American Express the right to use the name of the Cowboys' home, Texas Stadium, even though Coca Cola, Reebok, and Visa had paid NFL Properties large amounts for what was supposed to be the exclusive right to exploit the identity of all NFL teams, including the Cowboys. The league filed a $300 million lawsuit against Jones for allegedly having violated the Cowboys' contractual commitment to assign to NFL Properties the sole right to market the team's name and identity. Besides defending the contract claim on the ground that the identity of Texas Stadium was materially different from that of the Cowboys, Jones countered with a $750 million antitrust suit against his fellow owners, asserting that the agreement of the owners to give that exclusive merchandising authority to NFL Properties constituted an illegal "combination . . . in restraint of trade" under Sherman Act § 1.

By early 1997, both Jones and NFL Commissioner Paul Tagliabue had decided that it was in their respective best interests to settle their dispute on terms that allowed Jones to continue his deals between Texas Stadium and its licensees. Similar suits, threatened litigation, and the risk that owners may not agree to renew the NFL Trust Agreement due to expire in 2004 combined to lead owners to modify sponsorship policies. Under revised rules, the teams and NFL Properties now can non-exclusively license marks and logos in several product categories, while in others the league retains the right to grant exclusive licenses to league sponsors.

A similar controversy arose in baseball in early 1997 when George Steinbrenner and his Yankees signed a $95 million sponsorship contract with Adidas. This deal promised the Yankees a far larger amount than its 1/30th equal share of a $325 million proposal that Nike and Reebok had together offered Major League Baseball Enterprises for sponsorship of the entire League. The Yankees and Adidas carefully worded their contract so as not to appear to infringe upon the league's exclusive authority over national and international merchandising and promotion deals. However, the MLB Executive Council judged that the sale inside Yankee Stadium of T-shirts bearing both the Yankees and Adidas logos did not come within the Yankees autonomy in its "Home Licensing Territory." In addition, the Council insisted that the Yankees-Adidas contract must include a "subservience clause" that would subject it to any future changes in the owners Agency Agreement regarding MLB Enterprise's or Properties' authority, which a three-quarters ownership vote could impose and bind the Yankees. For these and a number of other reasons, the Yankees and Adidas partnership filed a preemptive lawsuit, claiming that the entire

MLB central merchandising system violated both federal and Florida antitrust law. MLB responded by suspending Steinbrenner from its Executive Council and the team from membership on any league committees. After significant pre-trial wrangling, the lawsuit was settled with MLB's exclusive licensees outfitting all on-field Yankee personnel, but Adidas becoming an MLB "marketing partner" for various other commercial opportunities.

The NFL and MLB owners were concerned that individual team exploitation of the merchandising market would increase revenue disparities in favor of the successful and popular teams, and would likely reduce the overall league revenues generated despite a broader use of team names on merchandise. Of course, the latter concern is precisely the goal that an antitrust-preserved competitive market is supposed to deliver to consumers—greater output at lower prices. There is no Sports Marketing Act that gives special antitrust immunity to leagues whose owners pool their team names and logos in a central league office that then licenses the right to outsiders.

In addition to collective marketing by clubs, many of the reported antitrust decisions in this area have involved players associations, all of which have for many years persuaded almost all their player-members to assign to the union the exclusive right to grant licenses to use six or more players' names and images as a group ("group licensing" rights). Thus, any licensee that wants to use six or more players from any major sports league for commercial purposes must acquire the players' publicity rights from the union, whereas merchandisers who want an endorsement from five or fewer players must still deal directly with the individual player(s). The revenues from these group licenses have become an important if not predominant source of revenues for the unions, and thus they vigorously defend these rights. *See, e.g., Gridiron.com, Inc. v. NFLPA,* 106 F. Supp. 2d 1309 (S.D. Fla. 2000) (individual licenses from over 150 players for separate webpages linked to Gridiron.com's home page fell within the group license agreement the players had signed with the NFLPA).

For decades, Topps Chewing Gum had dominated the market for the use of a player's likeness on a baseball trading card. For five dollars apiece, it signed up young players as they entered the minor leagues to a contract that gave Topps the exclusive right to use the player's name and likeness on cards that were sold alone or in combination with chewing gum or candy. This right was triggered when the player reached the major leagues and lasted for five years, at $125 a year. Topps then renewed the contracts for another small payment as they neared their expiration. When the increased popularity and sales of trading cards combined with the commencement of Marvin Miller's services as a professional union executive for MLBPA, Topps' plan was no longer sustainable. It agreed to a significant increase in royalty payments in return for exclusive rights to license cards. That license was upheld against antitrust attacks by Topps' competitors: *see Fleer Corp. v. Topps Chewing Gum*, 658 F.2d 139 (3d Cir. 1981).

To bolster its position in negotiations, the MLBPA subsequently obtained its members' agreement to authorize only the MLBPA to market their publicity rights on a group basis and not to renew any individual licenses inconsistent with this scheme. Topps responded with an antitrust suit, claiming violations of both §§ 1 and 2 of the Sherman Act. Following are the judge's reactions to both sides' motions for summary judgment.

TOPPS CHEWING GUM V. MAJOR LEAGUE BASEBALL PLAYERS ASS'N

641 F. Supp. 1179 (S.D.N.Y. 1986)

CONNER, DISTRICT JUDGE.

[The court initially reviewed the precedents studied in Chapter 5 where courts rejected claims that collective decisions in the sports industry were "group boycotts" that were *per se* illegal under § 1.]

The instant case differs from these classic cases in a number of important respects. First, in most of these cases the parties to the agreement were competitors of each other. This is a critical element. The per se rule is not applicable to boycotts that do not involve agreements among competitors. In this case, Topps does not and could not contend that the parties to the alleged boycott, the MLBPA and the major league baseball players, are in any sense competitors with each other.

Second, as noted above, in a classic group boycott, a group of businesses combine to exclude other competitors or potential competitors from their level of the market. Topps certainly does not compete with major league baseball players for the players' publicity rights. Topps merely purchases the rights from the players.

Topps contends, however, that it competes with the MLBPA for the players' publicity rights, and that the MLBPA has instigated the boycott in order to exclude Topps from the market except on those terms the MLBPA dictates. In light of facts set forth above, there can be little doubt that Topps and MLBPA are indeed engaged in a struggle for control of the players' rights. However, it is far from clear that Topps and the MLBPA compete economically at the same level of the market. Topps purchases the rights from the players and uses them in producing and marketing its products. Thus, it is a consumer of the rights. The MLBPA, on the other hand, does not purchase the rights from the players, and does not manufacture or market any products itself. It acts as an agent for the players in licensing manufacturers or distributors of products to use the rights. Thus, the MLBPA is more analogous to a wholesale distributor of the rights. Accordingly, it does not appear to function at the same level in the market as Topps.

Finally, a classic group boycott involves a type of arrangement that is so clearly and consistently anticompetitive that it is inherently illegal. As the Supreme Court stated recently, "[t]he decision to apply the per se rule turns on 'whether the practice facially appears to be one that would always or almost always tend to restrict competition and decrease output.'" *Northwest Wholesale Stationers,* 472 U.S. at 295 (quoting *Broadcast Music, Inc. v. Columbia Broadcasting Sys.,* 441 U.S. 1, 19–20 (1979)). I am not persuaded that the arrangement between the MLBPA and the players is one that clearly restricts competition. In fact, the MLBPA has made a strong argument that the arrangement will enhance competition for players' publicity rights for use on a group basis.

Because Topps has for many years managed to secure exclusive long-term licenses from nearly all minor and major league baseball players to use their photographs on trading cards sold alone or in combination with gum or candy, other companies have not been able to acquire similar licenses. Topps has by all appearances acquired its licenses by hard work and perseverance, and should not now be punished for having been successful in its competitive efforts. *See, e.g., United States v. Aluminum Co. of Am.,* 148 F.2d 416, 430 (2d Cir. 1945). Nonetheless, Topps' competitors are desirous of an opportunity to acquire the rights Topps holds. Topps contends that its competitors can acquire the rights in the same way Topps does—by soliciting ballplayers when they enter the minor leagues. But Topps' competitors have indicated that they are unwilling to do so since that course "would be too expensive, would take too long, and would have too little chance of success." Thus, there is currently little competition for the rights Topps acquires through its player contracts.

However, under the arrangement created by the players and the MLBPA, the tremendous expense, inefficiency, and risk in acquiring the full bundle of rights necessary to market a complete set of baseball trading cards is eliminated. A company interested in acquiring players' publicity rights would not have to solicit a contract from every individual who becomes a professional baseball player. Instead, Topps and its competitors could purchase the necessary grants from a single agent for all of the major league players. Topps' competitors apparently find this an appealing prospect, and would bid against Topps and each other for the rights Topps now acquires with little serious competition. Topps complains that this may drive up the price of the rights. But that is the natural consequence of increased competition for a limited supply of goods, and is not a ground for concluding that the arrangement between the players and the Players Association is necessarily illegal per se.

In view of the important differences between classic group boycotts and the arrangement at issue here, I conclude that *per se* treatment is inappropriate.

* * *

The first issue in any rule of reason analysis is to define the relevant market in which the competitive impact of the defendant's actions are to be examined. The parties here have devoted little attention to this question, and to the extent they have addressed it, they disagree. The MLBPA appears to claim that the relevant market is that of publicity rights for all athletes and performers, whereas Topps contends that it is the market for the publicity rights of major league baseball players for use on a group basis. Thus, there is a disputed issue of material fact that precludes summary judgment.

Another issue in the rule of reason calculus is the intent underlying the defendant's acts. Here the MLBPA claims that its intent is to increase competition in the bidding for players' publicity rights, whereas Topps contends that the Players Association intends to obtain monopoly power over those rights. Again, this is a disputed issue of fact. Finally, rule of reason analysis looks to the effects of the defendant's acts on the relevant market. The MLBPA claims that its acts are procompetitive, while Topps asserts that it is being improperly foreclosed from competing for players' publicity rights. This is yet another question of fact. Summary judgment is obviously unavailable in these circumstances.

[For essentially the same reasons the judge dismissed the motions for summary judgment on the § 2 "monopolization" charge, and directed trials on both issues.]

Summary judgment denied.

The parties settled the litigation before trial, thus leaving unresolved the key legal issues posed by the case. The settlement produced a major change in the Topps-MLBPA-players relationship. Topps continued to sign individual baseball players to card licensing agreements, but these licenses were non-exclusive and paid the MLBPA directly as its members' agent for collecting and distributing their licensing fees.

NOTES AND QUESTIONS

1. *Applying the Rule of Reason.* Suppose the *Topps* case had gone to trial: how would you have ruled on the antitrust rule of reason issues? Should the MLB Players Association have enjoyed antitrust immunity under either

the *Flood* baseball exemption or the statutory labor exemption considered in Chapters 4 and 6 respectively?

2. *Exclusive Contracts and the Rule of Reason.* Change the fact situation so that the MLBPA had made itself the sole agent for all its player-members' licensing rights (which is in fact the case today in all of the major sports for group licensing rights, except for a few holdouts like Barry Bonds), as recognized in *Gridiron.com v. NFLPA*, 106 F. Supp. 2d 1309 (S.D. Fla. 2000), and that the Association had refused to renew the contract with Topps because another card manufacturer (*e.g.*, Fleers) was offering a large premium for an exclusive baseball cards contract. Would these hypothetical variations on the actual scenario have exposed the Association to a much stronger Rule of Reason challenge?

Another licensing-rights dispute involved NHL owners' efforts to require all clubs to migrate their websites to the league's centralized server. For years, NHL owners agreed to give the exclusive right to control the individual clubs' marks and licensing opportunities to the league for virtually all commercial purposes. Madison Square Garden, L.P., which owns the New York Rangers, objected to this arrangement, seeking to preserve its ability to sell merchandise with Rangers' logos and players' names outside the home arena and on the internet other than via NHL.com. MSG claimed that the scheme precluded the Rangers and other entrepreneurial teams from licensing arrangements with lower-cost or higher-quality licensees and from enhancing consumer options compared to those offered via NHL marketing arrangements. In *Madison Square Garden, L.P. v. NHL*, 270 F. App'x 56; 2008–1 Trade Cas. (CCH) ¶ 76,079 (2d. Cir.), the court of appeals affirmed the denial of the Rangers' request for a preliminary injunction against the NHL's implementation of its new media strategy.

> The district court did not abuse its discretion in denying injunctive relief. First, it correctly determined that MSG failed to establish a likelihood of success or sufficiently serious questions under "quick look" analysis. "Quick look" is essentially an abbreviated form of rule of reason analysis, to be used in cases in which the likelihood of anticompetitive effects is so obvious that "an observer with even a rudimentary understanding of economics could conclude that the arrangements in question would have an anticompetitive effect on customers and markets." *Cal. Dental Ass'n v. FTC*, 526 U.S. 756 (1999). A court must abandon "quick look" and proceed to a full-blown rule of reasons analysis, however, "once the defendant has shown a procompetitive justification for the conduct." *Bogan v. Hodgkins*, 166 F.3d 509, 514 n.6 (2d Cir. 1999).

We agree with the district court that "[i]t is far from obvious that [the NHL's ban on independent websites] has no redeeming value." Rather, the district court correctly cited "several procompetitive effects of the New Media Strategy." These procompetitive benefits preclude application of "quick look" analysis. *See Bogan*, 166 F.3d at 514 n.6 (briefly applying "quick look" but returning to Rule of Reason analysis, because the defendant offered "sound allegations of procompetitive benefit").

The district court also did not abuse its discretion in finding that MSG did not establish a likelihood of success or sufficiently serious questions under rule of reason analysis. Under rule of reason, a court must "determine whether restraints ... are reasonable in light of their actual effect on the market and their pro-competitive justifications." First, a plaintiff "bears the initial burden of showing that the challenged action has had an actual adverse effect on competition as a whole in the relevant market." "If the plaintiff succeeds, the burden shifts to the defendant to establish the pro-competitive redeeming virtues of the action. Should the defendant carry this burden, the plaintiff must then show that the same pro-competitive effect could be achieved through an alternative means that is less restrictive of competition."

MSG did not show that the NHL's website ban has had an actual adverse effect on competition in the relevant market. Nor did MSG demonstrate that the many procompetitive benefits of the NHL's restriction could be achieved through an alternative means that is less restrictive of competition. While there will certainly be substantive issues for the district court to address on the merits— for example, how the antitrust laws apply to the NHL as a sports league, and what the relevant market is in this case—the district court's conclusion that preliminary injunctive relief was unwarranted falls well within the range of permissible decisions, and did not constitute an abuse of discretion.

On remand, the district court granted in part the NHL's motion for summary judgment and dismissed all claims other than those relating to centralized assignment of rights to new media. The court found that MSG had waived its claims in various documents releasing the NHL and fellow owners from liability for NHL operations and activities, and that the waiver was not contrary to public policy.

With regard to new media concerns, the court denied summary judgment in a decision that was not particularly encouraging to the Rangers:

At this early stage of litigation, there is no evidence in the record on the crucial question of market definition, let alone the inquiry into how the NHL actually operates as an economic actor in that market.... Therefore the NHL's arguments in favor of dismissal cannot be resolved at the pleading stage, and the motion is denied.

To be sure, MSG faces a tall order in making its case. This Court has already observed that agreements among parents of a joint venture not to compete in the market in which a joint venture operates have generally been upheld. *MSG I*, 2007 WL 3254421 at *6 n.7; *see also United States v. Addyston Pipe & Steel Co.*, 85 F. 271, 280–81 (6th Cir. 1898) (Taft, J.) (restrictions by parents were "of course, only ancillary to the main end of the union, and were to be encouraged"), *aff'd in part, modified in part on other grounds,* 175 U.S. 211 (1899). The reasonableness of the restraint, however, is evaluated under the rule of reason. See *MSG I*, 2007 WL 3254421 at *6 (observing that such agreements have typically been viewed as reasonable ancillary restraints); *Business Elecs. Corp. v. Sharp Elecs. Corp.*, 485 U.S. 717, 729 n. 3 (1988) (also observing that agreements not to compete are "classic" ancillary restraints).

2008–2 Trade Cas. (CCH) ¶ 76,346 (S.D.N.Y.).

MAJOR LEAGUE BASEBALL PROPERTIES, INC. V. SALVINO, INC.

542 F.3d 290 (2d Cir. 2008)

KEARSE, CIRCUIT JUDGE:

Defendant Salvino, Inc. ("Salvino"), appeals from so much of a final judgment of the United States District Court for the Southern District of New York, Richard Conway Casey, Judge, as dismissed its counterclaims alleging that the organization and activities of plaintiff Major League Baseball Properties, Inc. ("MLBP"), as the exclusive licensing agent for Major League Baseball (or "MLB") clubs' intellectual property, violate § 1 of the Sherman Act, 15 U.S.C. § 1, ... For the reasons that follow, we reject Salvino's contentions and affirm the dismissal of its antitrust claim.

I. BACKGROUND

Viewed in the light most favorable to Salvino, as the party against which summary judgment was granted on the claim at issue on this appeal, the following facts are not in dispute.

[Salvino developed a plush, bean-filled toy bear representing various well-known sports personalities. It obtained licenses to use baseball player names and numbers from the MLB Players Association, but included some club logos without a license from MLBP. The latter, an entity in which each of the 30 current MLB clubs (the "Clubs") owns an equal interest, is, with limited exceptions, the exclusive worldwide agent for licensing the use of all names, logos, trademarks, service marks, trade dress, and other intellectual property owned or controlled by the MLB Clubs, MLB's Office of the Commissioner ("BOC"), and MLBP (collectively "MLB Intellectual Property"), on retail products. MLBP also acts as agent for the Clubs with respect to, inter alia, trademark protection, quality control, design services, royalty accounting, and auditing.]

[In October 1999, MLBP learned that Salvino had sold Bammers to the Arizona Diamondbacks baseball club with the Diamondbacks logo on them; Salvino had not obtained an MLBP license to use that logo. MLBP sent Salvino a cease-and-desist letter; Salvino responded by filing an antitrust claim in California. MLBP commenced the present federal trademark action (with attendant state law claims); the California lawsuit was consolidated with the New York litigation. Eventually, all of the parties' respective claims, except Salvino's counterclaims against MLBP, were either abandoned or settled. In the meantime, to the extent pertinent to this appeal from the district court's dismissal of Salvino's § 1 counterclaim, MLBP moved, following some three years of discovery, for summary judgment dismissing that claim.]

1. Major League Baseball

The Major League Baseball teams together produce an entertainment product—the "MLB Entertainment Product"—that consists of approximately 2,400 interrelated, professional baseball games per year played by the 30 MLB Clubs, leading to separate playoff games for the American and National Leagues and culminating each season with the World Series between the champion Clubs from the two Leagues. This entertainment product can be produced only by the Clubs operating together in the form of a league; it cannot be produced by any one individual Club, or even a few Clubs. While squads of players from a single Club could play each other, the organization of the Clubs into a nationwide league with geographic diversity and a common championship goal, pursued in a structured manner employing uniform rules of play, has created a vastly different and more marketable product than is created by scrimmages between squads of players from a single Club or even by ad hoc "barnstorming" games between Clubs outside of a large league structure.

The MLB Entertainment Product, for which cooperation among the Clubs is essential, affects the value of MLB Intellectual Property. For example, during the baseball players' strike in 1994 and 1995, revenues generated by sales of MLBP-licensed products decreased; after the strike ended and MLB games resumed, those revenues increased.

2. MLBP's Licensing and Policing Activities

MLBP was incorporated in 1966 by the then-existing MLB Clubs (under the name Major League Baseball Promotion Corporation) as a wholly-owned subsidiary of MLBE. Each of the current MLB Clubs owns an equal interest in MLBE and shares equally in its profits. Prior to the formation of MLBP in 1966, there had been no centralized source for the licensing of MLB Intellectual Property . . . [Some evidence suggested that the lack of centralization harmed MLB clubs' ability to participate in certain corporate promotional activities.]

When created in 1966, MLBP was given (a) the exclusive right to market and promote the official name and logo of Major League Baseball, (b) a non-exclusive right to license the names and logos of the National and American Leagues, and (c) the right to submit licensing proposals for Club marks to the Clubs for their approval. . . . In 1984, the Agency Agreement increased MLBP's authority by giving it the exclusive right—subject to limited exceptions—to license Club names and logos for use on retail products for national and international (*i.e.*, not merely local) distribution. In 1987, the Agency Agreement further expanded MLBP's authority, granting it the exclusive right (again with limited exceptions) to license Club names and logos for use on products to be sold at retail within the Clubs' respective local markets. Thus, since 1987, the retail sale of any products bearing an MLB Club's name or logos must be licensed by MLBP, even if the products are sold at a concession stand inside the Club's stadium.

[The court discussed the limited exceptions to MLBP exclusivity for a Club to grant licenses with respect to their own intellectual property: products that it gives away at a home game; intellectual property of the visiting Club in such a game may also be used on the "giveaway" product with the approval of the visiting Club and MLBP, use of its own marks to create home video products about the individual Club, to be sold or given away within the Club's home broadcasting territory (as defined for each Club in the Operating Guidelines), the use of its marks on hot dogs and similar items distributed or sold within its home broadcasting territory, and the right, within its home broadcasting territory, to use and license others to use its marks to advertise and promote the Club's cruises and fantasy, educational, or summer camps.]

3. The Market in Which MLBP Licenses Compete

MLBP asserted the view, which Salvino criticized as "a self-serving view," that other sports leagues such as the NBA, the NFL, the NHL, and the Women's National Basketball Association, as well as non-sports entertainment purveyors such as Nickelodeon and Disney, are among MLBP's competitors in the licensing of intellectual property for use on retail products. For example, Team Beans, a competitor of Salvino that obtained licenses for MLB Intellectual Property from MLBP for use on plush toys, also held licenses to use trademarks from a variety of other licensors, including the Olympics, the NFL, the NHL, the MLB Players' Association, and NASCAR.

A market research study conducted for MLBP, whose goals included increasing game attendance, media audiences, and sales of MLB Intellectual Property, found that baseball does not compete with just one sport, or even only with sports. It found that the competitive arena for baseball is " 'a wide range of leisure and entertainment options that vary with target group and lifestyle.' " Thus, the MLBP 1996 Business Plans' list of MLBP's major competitors for intellectual property licensing included the following: branded apparel manufacturers such as Nike, Reebok, Russell, Champion, Big Dog, and No Fear; other sports entities such as the NBA, the NFL, the NHL, NASCAR, collegiate groups, and the 1996 Summer Olympics; and entities, such as Warner Brothers and Disney, that offered licenses to use intellectual property relating to, *e.g.*, Looney Tunes, Power Rangers, Peanuts, Nickelodeon, Batman, SpaceJam, and Goosebumps.

[The court summarized evidence from plaintiff's witnesses that Salvino competed in a broad market against other producers of plush items as well as other sports collectibles. Wayne Salvino testified at his deposition that one advantage to Salvino of the NFL's centralized licensing structure was that NFL Properties offered a package of certain players and all team logos, allowing that entity to serve as a " 'one-stop shop.' "]

4. The Views of the Parties' Respective Economists

Toward the end of the discovery period, MLBP had taken the deposition of Salvino's expert economist, Louis A. Guth, who had prepared a report in which he opined that MLBP functions as an "economic cartel." The Guth Report stated that "MLBP quite likely exercises sufficient control over pricing licenses for use of club marks for plush toys and similar products so that these constitute a relevant market." In his deposition testimony . . . Guth stated that MLBP limits output and sets prices, and he opined that efficient licensing of MLB Intellectual Property could be accomplished through the use of less restrictive alternatives. He testified that the relevant market could be determined by conducting a "discrete choice survey" of consumers to determine whether changes in the prices of various products would affect the consumers' product preferences; however, Guth had conducted no empirical studies of any kind.

MLBP, in support of its motion for summary judgment, presented the April 11, 2003 report of its expert economist, Professor Franklin M. Fisher ("Fisher Report"), analyzing MLBP's functions and the product market within which MLBP operates, and disputing the views of Guth. Fisher opined, inter alia, that MLBP is not a cartel and should instead be viewed as a joint venture; that the relevant product market consists at the very least of licenses for all sports and entertainment intellectual property, rather than just for MLB Intellectual Property; and that the centralization of MLB Intellectual Property licensing and other functions in MLBP produces procompetitive efficiencies.

Fisher pointed out that "[t]he customers [for] MLB Intellectual Property are prospective licensees that use MLB Intellectual Property to sell products." Although Guth had suggested that the relevant market could be determined by conducting a survey to ascertain whether the product preferences of consumers were responsive to retail price variations, Fisher stated that "it is important to be clear that the relevant customers for MLB Intellectual Property are the prospective licensees of intellectual property and it is their demand and the alternatives that they face that determine the boundaries of the relevant market" "The demand of ultimate consumers for goods such as plush toys . . . that use intellectual property . . . is relevant only because such demand influences the derived demand of direct customers, the licensees."

[Fisher also explained his conclusion that MLBP was a joint venture, and not a cartel, by noting that the value of MLB intellectual property is derived largely from the popularity of MLB, which is jointly created by the clubs. As an example, "no matter how successful the Yankees have been, the Yankees marks would have little value over time if the Yankees no longer competed with other Clubs in Major League Baseball. Indeed, the drop in popularity of former Club names, such as the Washington Senators, the Houston Colt 45s, and the St. Louis Browns, demonstrates this fact."]

[Fischer further observed that if clubs were acting solely as a cartel, they would set separate royalty rates for each club's license, to maximize overall profits. He concluded that "the very fact that MLBP does not do this indicates that it faces competition from other entertainment products and is not a cartel." At the same time, he opined that the Clubs' use of MLBP "achieve[s] numerous efficiencies and procompetitive benefits that would not exist if each Club managed and licensed its intellectual property independently." His testimony focused on "one-stop shopping" that saves transaction costs, on quality control and enforcement, and on how joint selling promoted competitive balance.]

Finally, Fisher also opined that because the value of MLB Intellectual Property is dependent on the popularity of the MLB Entertainment Product, and the popularity of the MLB Entertainment Product depends in turn on the integrated efforts of the Clubs, the absence of centralized licensing could lead to various occurrences of what economists refer to as the "free-rider" problem, *i.e.*, one entity's cashing in on the efforts of another. For example, if the Clubs granted licenses directly, a Club that was popular because of its on-field success could cash in on its popularity even though its victories obviously could not have been achieved without the participation of other Clubs. . . .

* * *

Salvino presented no factual evidence to refute the evidence cited in MLBP's summary judgment motion. . . .

* * *

II. DISCUSSION

* * *

[The court rejected Salvino's claim that the MLB licensing agreement was a "naked" output restriction.] Salvino has pointed to no evidence to support its characterizations. It has not cited to any term of the Agency Agreement or to any other agreement. Nor is a reduction in output implicit in the Agency Agreement. The Clubs' agreement to make MLBP their exclusive licensor does not by its express terms restrict or necessarily reduce the number of licenses to be issued; it merely alters the identity of the licenses' issuer.

[Salvino sought to distinguish *Broadcast Music*, discussed in Chapter 5, on the basis that the challenged blanket license in that case was non-exclusive. The majority found that this distinction "loses significance in the context of the differences between the music and sports industries." In the majority's view, the "interdependent interests" of members of sports league distinguish MLBP from an association of individual music composers. This interdependence forecloses "the imposition of per se or quick-look liability."]

[The majority also distinguished the *NCAA v. Board of Regents* case, discussed in Chapter 5.]

Whereas the Supreme Court noted that the NCAA did not act as a selling agent for those whose product was being sold, precisely the opposite is true of MLBP. A college that wished to have more than six of its games televised within a two-year period was forbidden, rather than helped, to do so by the NCAA. MLBP, in contrast, is the licensing agent for the MLB Clubs; it assists the Clubs in the licensing of their intellectual property.

Further, whereas the NCAA plan "create[d] a limitation on output" by limiting the total number of televised games and the number of times any one college's games could be televised, *NCAA*, 468 U.S. at 99, Salvino has not adduced any evidence of a limitation on the number of Club intellectual property licenses available here. . . .

* * *

Second, Salvino has presented no evidence to suggest that the licensing of MLB Intellectual Property is not entirely responsive to demand. MLBP does not issue licenses that are not requested; there is no evidence that an entity that wishes to obtain a license for particular intellectual property is required to accept or pay for a license that encompasses other intellectual property as well.

* * *

[Third, unlike *NCAA v. Board of Regents,* where the Court rejected the contention that the NCAA's restrictive television plan produced procompetitive efficiencies, here] the record shows that, similarly to the blanket licensing at issue in *Broadcast Music,* centralization of the licensing and protection of MLB Intellectual Property has produced many cost-savings and efficiencies. And, in contrast to the effect of the NCAA plan, . . . since the Clubs made MLBP their exclusive licensing agent for all retail products bearing MLB Intellectual Property, the number of licenses and licensees has multiplied.

Moreover, unlike the record in *NCAA*, the present record contains no facts to support Salvino's hypothesis that if MLBP were not the Clubs' exclusive licensor with respect to retail products, even more licenses would be granted. . . .

. . . unlike the NCAA restrictions on televising games, which were "not even arguably tailored to serve" an interest in competitive balance, 468 U.S. at 119, the Clubs' agreement that MLBP's profits from licensing MLB Intellectual Property will be distributed equally among the 30 Clubs is a precisely tailored attempt to achieve, or at least increase, competitive balance.

* * *

. . . Direct licensing by the Clubs, as recommended by Salvino and Guth, would result in the more popular Clubs granting more licenses and receiving more income for their intellectual property than the less popular Clubs would grant and receive. . . . (*See, e.g.,* Salvino brief on appeal at 30 ("If an organization is successful in . . . competition, then it should be entitled to reap the fruits of its acumen.") . . . [MLB expert Fisher replied that this] inequality in licensing income, however, would "overcompensat[e] the popular team for the joint efforts of all Clubs."

Further, the disproportionate distribution of licensing income would foster a competitive imbalance among the Clubs. The concept of "competitive balance" "reflects the expected equality of opportunity to compete and prevail on the field. Competitive balance also relates to the fans' expectations that each team is a potential champion—*i.e.* that each Club has a reasonable opportunity to win each game and also to compete for a championship."

[Because Salvino proffered no evidence that the centralization of licensing in MLBP caused any actual injury to competition or any evidence that MLBP possessed power in the relevant market, the claim fails under the Rule of Reason.]

SOTOMAYOR, CIRCUIT JUDGE, concurring in the judgment:

I concur fully in the judgment. I write separately because I believe the majority endorses an overly formalistic view of price fixing and in so doing avoids addressing directly the central contention of appellant Salvino, Inc. ("Salvino") that the exclusive arrangement between the Major League Baseball clubs (the "Clubs") and Major League Baseball Properties, Inc. ("MLBP") removes all price competition between the Clubs on the licensing of intellectual property in violation of the Sherman Act, *15 U.S.C. § 1*. Further, while I agree with the ultimate outcome of this appeal, I reach my conclusion using a different framework than the majority, applying the doctrine of ancillary restraints, which I believe more efficiently addresses the issues presented here.

* * *

Furthermore, the majority incorrectly believes that the licensing fees are "entirely responsive" to demand. A simple example displays the majority's fallacy. Take Club C, a Club that has two fans A and B. A is willing to pay $15 for a Club C hat while B is willing to pay $12 for the same hat. Assume that Producer P will sell Club C hats at its marginal cost to produce them of $10 and assume that MLBP charges a 20% license fee. Under this scenario, the price for a licensed hat would be $12.50 (price = $10/(1 − 0.20)), and only A would be willing to buy a Club C hat. However, if Club C was pricing its own licenses, it could drop the license fee to 15%, in which case both A and B would be willing to buy Club C hats for $ 11.76, and licensing revenue for Club C would increase from $2.50 to $3.52. As this example shows, the licensing fees here are not totally responsive to consumer demand. Basic principles of economics teach us that as royalty rates increase, the price for licensed goods will increase, and output will decline as fewer consumers are willing to purchase licensed goods at higher prices. This is Salvino's central contention—that if the Clubs were forced to compete with each other for licensing fees, they would offer licenses at lower rates, thereby resulting in lower prices (and increased output) for licensed goods.

* * *

The present dispute is significantly more complex than two competitors creating a "joint venture" for the sole purpose of fixing prices. Here, the MLBP joint venture offers substantial efficiency-enhancing benefits that the individual Clubs could not offer on their own, including decreased transaction costs on the sale of licenses, lower enforcement and monitoring costs, and the ability to one-stop shop (*i.e.,* to purchases licenses from more than one Club in a central location). These procompetitive benefits, MLBP maintains, could not exist without the exclusivity and profit-sharing agreements, the two provisions challenged by Salvino as price fixing. In other words, MLBP argues that even if the effect of the exclusivity and profit-sharing agreements is to eliminate price competition between the Clubs, the purpose of these agreements is to achieve other significant procompetitive benefits, which outweigh any harm from the price restraint. We must decide then whether the Clubs' agreement not to compete with each other on price, which is price fixing in a literal sense, should nevertheless be reviewed under a rule of reason in light of MLBP's other efficiency-enhancing benefits. . . .

* * *

Joint ventures are typically evaluated as a whole under the rule of reason because the competitive effects of an individual restraint are intertwined with the effects of the remainder of the venture. However, under the doctrine of ancillary restraints, when a challenged restraint is not reasonably necessary to achieve any of the efficiency-enhancing purposes of a joint venture, it will be evaluated apart from the rest of the venture. [citations omitted]. This doctrine seeks to distinguish between those restraints that are intended to promote the efficiencies of a joint venture and those that are simply unrelated... The doctrine recognizes that a restraint that is unnecessary to achieve a joint venture's efficiency-enhancing benefits may not be justified based on those benefits. Accordingly, a challenged restraint must have a reasonable procompetitive justification, related to the efficiency-enhancing purposes of the joint venture, before that restraint will be analyzed as part of the venture. If none exists, the challenged restraint must be evaluated on its own and may be *per se* illegal even if the remainder of the joint venture is entirely lawful. . . .

In this case, the exclusivity and profit-sharing provisions of the MLBP agreement are reasonably necessary to achieve MLBP's efficiency-enhancing purposes because they eliminate several potential externalities that may otherwise distort the incentives of individual Clubs and limit the potential efficiency gains of MLBP. Most notable of these externalities is the so-called free-rider problem. Because of the interdependence of the Clubs within the setting of a sports league, free riding would occur if one of the Clubs is able to benefit disproportionately from the actions of Major League Baseball or other Clubs in the licensing of products. This may lead to inefficiencies because the Clubs' incentive to invest in the promotion and development of their intellectual property and other licensed products may be distorted. Both MLBP and Salvino recognize that without the exclusivity and profit-sharing provisions, these externalities could diminish MLBP's efficiency gains.[9] Indeed, Salvino's own expert, Louis

---

[9] Salvino argues that "there are better ways to address" the externalities than these two challenged provisions. Whether the externalities could be eliminated in a substantially less

Guth, admitted in his deposition, when asked whether there would be more or less licenses without the centralized control of MLBP, that he could not give a straight yes or no answer without empirical analysis because of these potential externalities. In other words, Guth conceded that the challenged provisions could have a procompetitive impact related to the efficiency-enhancing purposes of MLBP. Under such circumstances, the challenged restraints must be viewed as ancillary to the joint venture and reviewed under the rule of reason in the context of the joint venture as a whole. *See Rothery Storage,* 792 F.2d at 228 ("[E]limination of the free ride is an efficiency justification available to horizontal restraints that are ancillary to a contract integration.").

[Sotomayor, J., explained why she believes] the ancillary restraints framework is a superior method for analyzing the challenged restraints here because it effectively isolates when an exclusive arrangement should be reviewed under the rule of reason, as a reasonably necessary part of a joint venture, and when it should be reviewed as a naked restraint. Neither *Broadcast Music* nor *NCAA* offer much direct insight into the treatment of exclusivity agreements, except to emphasize the anticompetitive dangers of exclusive arrangements. . . .

Having concluded that the rule of reason is appropriate in this case, I concur fully with the majority's rule-of-reason analysis and agree that summary judgment was properly awarded to MLBP. . . .

Chapter 5 featured the landmark Supreme Court discussion in *American Needle,* which resolved for doctrinal purposes the question whether sports league rules should be characterized as a policy from a "single entity"—the league—or as an agreement among otherwise competing clubs. The merits of the lawsuit, which was an attack on the NFL's rule that gave an exclusive trademark license to a single clothing manufacturer, were remanded for further proceedings. The district court rejected motions for summary judgment and directed that the case proceed to trial. *American Needle, Inc. v. New Orleans La. Saints,* 2014–1 Trade Cas. (CCH) ¶ 78,729 (N.D. Ill.). First, the court conducted a "quick look" analysis that declined to condemn the exclusive licensing arrangement as obviously anticompetitive:

> defendants contend that the exclusive license arrangement encouraged additional licensee commitment and had numerous procompetitive effects, including improvements in product design, quality, distribution, and coordination of styles with other apparel

---

restrictive manner is an inquiry that should generally be part of a rule-of-reason analysis rather than part of a per se or quick-look approach. *See, e.g., Care Heating & Cooling, Inc. v. Am. Standard, Inc.,* 427 F.2d 1008, 1012 (6th Cir. 2005).

items. These contentions are sufficiently supported by evidence and expert opinion to be facially plausible. The plausibility of the claims of procompetitive effect precludes abbreviated review of American Needle's claim. *California Dental Association [v. F.T.C.,* 526 U.S. 756, 778 (1999)].

Next, the court turned to the defendants' motion for summary judgment, first based on the plaintiff's alleged failure to establish an actual anticompetitive effect in a relevant market, as required under the Rule of Reason.

Defendants assert that they are entitled to summary judgment because American Needle has failed to provide evidence of a proper product market that is sufficient to allow its claim to reach a jury. The court is not persuaded that such evidence is required here.

"Since the purpose of the inquiry into market definition and market power is to determine whether an arrangement has the potential for genuine adverse effects on competition, proof of actual detrimental effects, such as a reduction of output, can obviate the need for an inquiry into market power, which is but a surrogate for detrimental effects." *FTC v. Indiana Federation of Dentists,* 476 U.S. 447, 460–61 (1986) [internal citation and quotation marks omitted]. In the present case, American Needle has presented evidence that shortly following the execution of the exclusive arrangement between Reebok and NFL Properties, wholesale prices of licensed hats rose by a significant degree while output of those items dropped, and that the higher prices and lower output continued for years, never returning to their pre-exclusivity levels. These results are the direct anticompetitive effects that the Sherman Act seeks to prevent. *Law v. National Collegiate Athletic Association,* 134 F.3d 1010, 1019 (10th Cir. 1998), *Valley Liquors, Inc. v. Renfield Importers, Ltd.,* 678 F.2d 742, 745 (7th Cir. 1982).

Defendants contend that direct proof of detrimental effects obviates the need for market definition only in horizontal action cases, and that this is a vertical action case. This contention ignores the Supreme Court's holding that despite the teams' use of NFL Properties as the single agent to implement their marketing decisions, and despite the longevity of the arrangement, the decision of each of the NFL teams to grant exclusive licenses to Reebok was horizontal action. "[D]ecisons by the NFLP regarding the teams separately owned intellectual property constitute concerted action." *American Needle, Inc. v. National Football League,* 560 U.S. 183, 201 (2010). The presence of a vertical element of restraint in the form of the NFL Properties transaction with Reebok does not negate the horizontal element recognized by the Court.

Defendants also argue that American Needle's price increase analysis failed to properly assess various factors such as the quality mix of the products sold, but these arguments can be resolved only by determining which of the parties' competing inferences and experts is more credible. Such determinations are properly made by the trier of fact. The court finds that the evidence presented by American Needle would be sufficient to support a jury finding of a less competitive market following the exclusive licensing arrangement. As a result, the court also finds that American Needle need not make a specific showing of the relevant product market to survive summary judgment.

In addition, to the extent that a relevant product market definition could be considered a necessary element of American Needle's Sherman Act claim, the court is unpersuaded by defendants' contention that the market advocated by plaintiff is improper. . . .

. . .

To distinguish the market for NFL team hats from hats bearing logos of teams from other sports, American Needle has presented sales data showing that NFL hat sales are seasonal, rising with the start of the league's season and with the peak of its playoff season. It has also provided analysis purporting to show a lack of correlation between price increases for NFL hats and sales increases for other leagues' hats. Defendants argue with the validity of the analysis of American Needle's expert, but as indicated earlier, the court views this argument as raising issues not properly resolved on summary judgment.

The court noted that the Supreme Court had found college football games a distinctive market, and distinguished *Salvino,* excerpted above, because the entire case was prosecuted on a "quick look" theory rather than a rule of reason and the plaintiff "agreed with MLB's expansive market definition. 542 F.3d at 299–300."

On the eve of trial, the parties settled on terms they did not disclose. However, the NFL recently signed a new exclusive license with New Era for caps with team logos.

Throughout the 20th Century sports fans regularly experienced the value of new technology to enjoy the games they couldn't attend: from radio, to television, to cable, to VCR's. The computer and the internet has emerged as the predominant technology (so far) in this century. For example, in fall 2000 North American fans regularly used cyberspace to get the results of Olympic events taking place in Sydney, Australia, when it was the middle of the night on this continent. Thus, the International Olympic Committee (IOC) authorities enforced a rule that prohibited athletes from keeping a diary on their computers and releasing it over the Internet.

In 1997, the NBA, which had just settled the *WGN* lawsuit, established a much broader rule. The rule prohibited each team from operating its own website, and required the teams to assign all such functions and rights to the central league office to market and then share resulting revenues among all the teams. In early 2000, MLB and the NFL (though still not the NHL) adopted a similar policy for a single league website. The successful creation of Major League Baseball Advanced Media (MLBAM) is detailed in Andrew Zimbalist, *In the Best Interests of Baseball? The Revolutionary Reign of Bud Selig* (Wiley & Co. 2006). Like the marketing arms of the other leagues, MLBAM is a distinct business entity owned by the major league clubs. However, in a significant departure from the typical governance structure, MLBAM is governed not by the entire ownership but by a Board of Directors selected by the owners (a committee of owners and an appointee of the Commissioner), who have a fiduciary duty to all shareholders to maximize the value of the company. Internet revenues have exploded during the last decade, making these entities even more significant in the future.

Owners of such small market baseball teams as the Kansas City Royals are hoping to experience the same kind of benefit from this new media as the Green Bay Packers, for example, secured in football from television four decades earlier. Indeed, MLB ex-Commissioner Selig even suggested that he might use his new powers (described in Chapter 1) to divide these revenues unequally among all teams, with larger shares for smaller-market teams. This means, though, that we may see essentially the same sports internet litigation that we did over the different league approaches to "pooling" the teams' television rights under general antitrust law. One key difference will be that there is no special Sports Broadcasting Act exemption for any type of collective selling of internet rights. Also, baseball will likely again face the question of whether its *Federal Baseball* antitrust immunity can and should cover this crucial new technology. In short, the entire range of issues noted above in the context of merchandising rights is equally presented in the context of internet rights.

NOTES AND QUESTIONS

1. *Trans-Atlantic Marketing Differences?* Are North American hockey fans so very different than English soccer fans that a virtually complete centralization of licensing is most efficient on one side of the Atlantic Ocean but a virtually complete decentralization is most efficient on the other? Why might club-run leagues select these options even if some mixed approach might be optimal?

2. *Why Is Sports Marketing Bimodal?* Most business that operate with "franchises" have a mixed marketing scheme that attempts to optimally balance incentives for team marketing efforts without cannibalizing the national deals. Is antitrust scrutiny of this balancing effort appropriate? Are there any reasons that league owners would restrict each other's ability to market their club, other than legitimate interests in maximizing overall revenue for their league product?

3. *Club Marketing Versus League Marketing.* Suppose that league owners in baseball or football were to adopt and enforce rules that blocked any loopholes in their merchandising programs that would permit "cherry-picking" of a few big-market and/or big-name teams. These loopholes might sharply reduce the ability of NFL or MLB Properties to negotiate valuable league-wide packages with sports footwear or other product companies that value a sports connection. Should Jerry Jones have been able to win his suit against his fellow NFL owners under antitrust law? Should George Steinbrenner have been able to sue MLB in the face of the special *Flood* baseball exemption from antitrust? Should the Little Leagues (or their uniform manufacturers) be able to sue MLB for insisting on their purchase of a trademark license to use team names?

4. *Agreements Not to File Antitrust Suits.* In rejecting some of the New York Rangers' claims in their marketing dispute with the NHL, the district court applied a very complex body of caselaw that seeks to reconcile a policy in favor of permitting private parties to waive litigation rights and a policy that precludes members of a cartel from shielding their activities from challenge. She observed:

> Whether the enforcement of the release would violate public policy is a more difficult question. On the one hand, because "[a] no suit agreement may be one of the devices for shoring up a cartel," *see Sanjuan v. Am. Bd. of Psychiatry & Neurology, Inc.*, 40 F.3d 247, 250 (7th Cir. 1994), the Supreme Court has indicated that it would condemn as against public policy an agreement that "operated . . . as a prospective waiver of a party's right to pursue statutory remedies for antitrust violations," *Mitsubishi Motors Corp. v. Soler Chrysler-Plymouth, Inc.*, 473 U.S. 614, 637 n.19, 105 S. Ct. 3346, 87 L. Ed. 2d 444 (1985). On the other hand, despite a strong public interest in private antitrust enforcement, "this interest does not prevent the injured party from releasing his claim and foregoing the burden of litigation." *Richard's Lumber & Supply Co. v. U.S. Gypsum Co.*, 545 F.2d 18, 20 (7th Cir. 1976) ("A general release . . . is not ordinarily

contrary to public policy simply because it involves antitrust claims.").

Applying these well-settled principles to this case is complicated by the fact that MSG's challenge is to NHL policies, *i.e.*, restraints that form part of the structure of the joint venture and, indeed, in some cases, are built into the NHL Constitution. The Release is neither purely prospective (for this reason, the Release does not bar MSG's challenge to the New Media policy); nor is it purely retrospective in the sense that the League policies would continue to have effect after the Release's execution.

Madison Square Garden v. NHL, 2008 WL 4547518, at *7 (S.D.N.Y. Oct. 10, 2008); 2008–2 Trade Cas. (CCH) ¶ 76,346 (S.D.N.Y.)

5. *The Economics of Collective Licensing.* Do you agree with Professor Fisher's conclusion in *Salvino* that the fact that MLBP licenses all teams at the same rate, instead of charging more for a Yankees license than an Astros license, demonstrates that MLBP faces competition from non-baseball licensors? Given the strong political/business desires of club owners to split profits equally, can you think of any other reasons why MLBP might not choose to price different logos at different rates?

6. *The Merits of the NFL's Exclusive Licensing.* Consider now the merits of the challenge to the NFL's marketing policies in *American Needle*. A critical question is to identify the relevant market for licensing of intellectual property for merchandising purposes. Do you agree with the NFL's claim that it vigorously competes in a highly competitive marketplace with all other clothing, or all other trademarked clothing? If so, restraining the ability of the Packers and Vikings to compete with each other in the sale of licensed merchandise is unlikely to affect competition. Do you agree with the plaintiff's claim that there is a market for "NFL merchandise," so that fans will switch patronage from one club's logos to another if the price is right? If the number of price-sensitive fans is too small to affect competition, and each club effectively has a monopoly for its own logo for its own avid fans, does this mean that there is no meaningful competition between the Packers and Vikings anyway, so that an agreement between the two of them has no anticompetitive effect?

E. BARGAINING DYNAMICS IN SPORTS LEAGUE DECISION-MAKING ABOUT COMMERCIAL PRACTICES

The formal topic of this chapter is antitrust scrutiny of sports league commercial rules, relating to ownership, the number and location of franchises, broadcasting, and licensing of intellectual property for sports-related merchandise. As with labor markets, studied in Chapter 6, Section D, these materials also provide rich insights into how the rules challenged in the cases studied in this chapter were enacted by the sports club owners who control the major decisions in North American sports leagues.

Two important insights by Ronald Coase are highly relevant to the bargaining dynamics of sports league governance. In "The Nature of the Firm," *Economica* 4 (16): 386–405 (1937), Coase wrote that the goal of reducing bargaining costs led businesses to operate within a single firm. Thus, it is less costly for General Motors Corporation to make and assemble most of the parts to an automobile, rather than have the General Auto Assembly Corporation contract with the General Auto Motors Corporation, the General Auto Chassis Corporation, the General Auto Axle Corporation, etc., for parts. This insight suggests that, if cost saving were the only concern, all sports leagues assets would be owned by a single company. For a variety of reasons (consider what they might be), baseball is not provided by "MLB, Inc." but rather by a joint venture of independently owned clubs. Thus, rules concerning ownership, the number and location of franchises, broadcasting, and licensing of intellectual property for sports-related merchandise must be made by agreement among the owners. Moreover, many of these agreements require predictions of how business decisions will play out in the marketplace, now and in the future. As a result, league decisions involve *imperfect information* and *significant bargaining costs*. In "The Problem of Social Cost," 3 J. L. & Econ. 1 (1960), Coase wrote that where information is imperfect and bargaining costs are significant, efficient practices may not result from the rules that govern behavior.

Sports leagues can minimize the problems caused by imperfect information and bargaining costs in a number of ways. As Coase demonstrated, when the net welfare of affected parties would be better off by a change in practices, those who are made worse off by the change can be compensated by payments from those who are made better off. If sports were run by a single corporation, the company's CEO could arrange payments in a manner designed to optimize efficient business practices of all economic actors within the firm. *See, e.g.,* Armen A. Alchian and Harold Demsetz, *Production, Information Costs, and Economic Organization*, 62 Am. Econ. Rev. 777 (1972). The challenge for sports leagues controlled by club owners is to secure an agreement on these "side payments." The principal way in which today's leagues accomplish this goal is through revenue sharing.

We end this chapter with some exercises in bargaining dynamics. Reread the introductory material on bargaining dynamics in Chapter 6, Section D, to consider how law, strategy, and dynamics would lead you to represent a stakeholder in these disputes more effectively.

First Exercise: Revenue Sharing

1. Is adoption of a rule providing for extensive revenue sharing "fair" to owners of teams in larger markets who purchased those teams before the rule was adopted? Is there a way of dealing with reliance on a property right to local revenues? *See* Louis Kaplow, *An Economic Analysis of Legal Transitions,* 99 Harvard L. Rev. 509 (1986), for a valuable analysis of this general type of problem.

2. Will extensive revenue sharing enlarge the total pie available to a league? Will this depend on which revenues are shared and the extent to which teams need to be given incentives to develop local markets? How could a revenue-sharing scheme be designed to maximize its contribution to revenue expansion?

3. Why would revenue sharing among owners have created concerns among players not only on the large market, but also on the small market teams? How could revenue sharing be designed to minimize any constraining effect on salaries from that source, particularly if the players have agreed to a direct salary cap or tax?

4. Suppose that after considerable thought and effort a new revenue-sharing scheme is devised, it proves attractive to a majority of owners, but it cannot get a necessary three-quarters approval because of opposition from the large-market clubs. Is it likely that a commissioner would step in under authority like the "best interests of baseball" authority studied in Chapter 1 to impose his revenue-sharing views?

Second Exercise: Ownership Policies

The infamous racist recordings of Los Angeles Clippers' owner Donald Sterling's opinions about his mistress' choice of escorts to basketball games led to his exclusion from the game under the broad powers conferred upon NBA Commissioner Adam Silver, discussed in Chapter 1. But consider Sterling's business practices wholly separate from racist behavior. Back in 2000, Sports Illustrated ran a story concluding that the franchise's "helplessness, so practiced and so dependable, is clearly the work of just one man—we're thinking of Donald Sterling here." Richard Hoffer, "The Loss Generation," *Sports Illustrated,* Apr. 17, 2000 at 58. More recently, SI investigative reporter George Dohrmann reviewed Sterling's record when the team was in San Diego, before the NBA settled litigation agreeing to allow Sterling to operate in Los Angeles. Incidents included policies to discourage live attendance (to hold down on security and stadium personnel), relying solely on television revenue; directing employees to disregard league rules; hiring as a de facto chief financial officer a woman he had met at the Playboy Club; failing to contribute to league pension funds; failing to pay players; making numerous player personnel decisions to save money rather than field a competitive team; and slicing scouting expenditures. "Recently banned Donald Sterling has long history of clashing with NBA," *available at* http://www.si.com/nba/2014/05/30/donald-sterling-history (updated June 23, 2014).

1. In *NASL v. NFL,* discussed in Section A, the Second Circuit recognized that new owners must be approved by a majority of other owners because "of the economic interdependence of major league team owners" and the "importance of obtaining the loyalty of partners in promoting a common business venture." Why did Sterling's fellow owners tolerate his mismanagement? If you owned an NBA franchise, would you rather have the Clippers managed by Donald Sterling or Microsoft executive Steve Ballmer?

2. In addition to fans, are there others who would benefit if the Clippers were well run?

3. Prior to the scandal, how might you advise a wealthy Angeleno who wanted to buy the Clippers on ways to persuade the league to force Sterling to sell?

Third Exercise: Franchise Relocation

Recall that when the Phoenix Coyotes were insolvent, there were two offers rejected by the bankruptcy judge: a $212.5 million offer from Canadian cellphone magnate James Balsillie, conditioned on his relocating the team to Hamilton, Ontario, and a $140 million from the NHL to keep the team in Phoenix. The club was later sold to IceArizona for $170 million. Consider the following alternative explanations for this outcome, and develop ideas for how those seeking another result (hockey fans in Hamilton, creditors seeking the highest bid, broadcasters seeking the highest ratings, or others) might have changed the result.

1. Higher locally-generated revenues in Hamilton (live gate, local television and radio, and profits on retail sales operations) are estimated to be worth the extra $42.5 million, but the other NHL owners had personal disdain for Balsillie.

2. Relocation to Hamilton would result in lower locally-generated revenues in Toronto and Buffalo, which were greater than $42.5 million.

3. Relocation to Hamilton would result in lower locally-generated revenues in Toronto and Buffalo, which were less than $42.5 million, but the parties could not agree on the amount to make the Maple Leafs and Sabres whole.

4. NHL Commissioner Gary Bettman believed that the addition of another Canadian team would add little to the league's contracts with the national Canadian broadcasters, but the loss of an American Sunbelt team would harm the NHL's contract with NBC.

Fourth Exercise: New Entry

The actual history of baseball in Milwaukee featured the relocation of the Boston Braves to the Midwest in 1953 and their relocation again to Atlanta in 1966, followed by the acquisition by automobile dealer Allan (Bud) Selig of the bankrupt Seattle Pilots in 1970 and their relocation to Milwaukee as the Brewers. Suppose, however, that Seattle remained a viable MLB city (as it became later when the American League added a second Seattle expansion team, the Mariners, in 1977). If you were Selig's counsel in 1971, how would you advise him to pursue his dream of bringing baseball back to Milwaukee?

1. Owners and fans in Milwaukee would obviously gain from another expansion. Who would be less well off if the American League expanded? Could they be compensated?

2. Are there others who would be better off with an expansion? How might they influence the owners to add another team?

Fifth Exercise: Internet Baseball

Currently, the only way to watch local baseball games is through a full digital subscription to your local cable retailer or DirecTV. In some cases, these games are not available when the regional sports network that owns the rights does not have a retransmission agreement. The only way to watch out-of-market baseball games is through a package of almost all games, either on television through ExtraInnings or via the internet at mlb.com. The MLB Executive Vice President, Business, wants to explore ways to maximize total broadcast revenues and is concerned that the current scheme may be sub-optimal.

1. Would MLB make more money offering every game on pay-per-view to anyone?

2. If a new scheme would indeed generate higher total broadcast revenues, would the owners necessarily vote to adopt the scheme? How would you advise the VP on how to create a scheme that minimized owner opposition?

3. Who else would benefit? Can their benefits be monetized and added to the pot?

Sixth Exercise: Innovative Club Marketing

The Brooklyn Nets are owned by Mikhail Prokhorov, who mastered the post-Soviet transition in Russia to become a multi-billionaire. Suppose that Prokhorov (a graduate of the Moscow Finance Institute) observed the huge marketing successes enjoyed by English Premier League clubs in emerging markets like China, and wants to emulate their efforts by pushing to make the Nets the "Team of Russia." Like the EPL, all NBA international television rights are sold by the league, but, unlike the EPL, merchandise rights are likewise centralized. Prokhorov believes he can significantly improve on the efforts of NBA International in sales to Russia.

1. Assuming Prohkorov is correct, why would his fellow owners object to an exception in the NBA's scheme of centralized marketing for the Nets in Russia?

2. Assuming the Nets guaranteed that the NBA's share of merchandise profits from Russian sales exceeded current figures, who would be worse off by granting him permission for the sale?

3. Who else would be better off were Prokhorov permitted to market the Nets in Russia? Can their interests be monetized?

A Final Note: Overall Restructuring of the League

The three antitrust chapters have focused to a significant degree on the challenges involved when league rules are adopted by club owners who run the league. Recall the insight from the Australian *South Sydney* case characterizing the economic activity of sports league competition as being divided between "competition organizing services" and "team services." In *Governance and Vertical Integration in Team Sports*, 25 Contemp. Econ. Pol. 616 (2007), co-author Stephen F. Ross and economist Stefan Szymanski argue that a system where an independent commercial entity (MLB, Inc., or NHL, LLC) organizes the competition and licenses separate clubs to participate may yield several efficiency benefits:

- The ability to draw up rules and regulations that meet the best interests of the league as a whole (consumers, owners, and players) rather than the interests of any particular group or faction.

- The ability to market products of the league that are truly joint, such as broadcast rights, in such a way as to maximize the return to the league as a whole.

- The ability to facilitate [welfare]-improving entry into the league through the adoption of systems such as promotion and relegation.

Suppose Warren Buffett were to agree with this analysis, and were to seek to acquire the controlling interest in the centralized organizing operation of a sports league.

1. If this analysis were correct, then the value of "MLB, Inc." plus the combined value of the 30 MLB clubs, shed of their power to run the league and split all league revenues between them, would be higher than the current combined value of all MLB clubs. If so, would owners agree to this scheme?

2. What problems would Buffett encounter in getting owners to agree to his proposal?

3. This sort of proposal would likely require a change in the MLB Constitution requiring support from three-fourths of the owners. How might Buffett secure the minimum number of yes votes?

4. What stakeholders might be worse off if MLB were restructured in this manner?

5. Who else might be better off? Can their interests be monetized and used by Buffett to provide further financial incentives?

CHAPTER 8

INTELLECTUAL PROPERTY LAW AND SPORTS*

■ ■ ■

The core business of the sports industry is to sell an intangible product—access to observe an athletic contest that can generate thrill, pride, emotional attachment, and community (as well as their antipodes). In this way the sports industry resembles other branches of the broader entertainment industry, including live theater and music concerts. Through the 19th Century, these entertainment products were accessible only to fans who purchased tickets for live attendance, limiting the potential audience and revenue. With the invention of film, recording, radio, and television, 20th Century sports and entertainment audiences exploded, transforming the organization and economics of the industry. Sports revenue streams proliferated, including the sale of broadcasting rights, licensing of trademarks and team logos, corporate sponsorship deals, and athlete endorsement contracts. Each of these sources of revenue, and others that continue to evolve in the 21st Century (*e.g.*, internet-driven digital media), depend on the definition and enforceability of intellectual property rights, primarily copyright, trademark, and rights of publicity.

To further explain, unlike a manufacturer of a tangible product such as an automobile or a pair of shoes, the sports team owner's principal product—the live athletic competition—takes no permanent material form and is highly perishable. This quality of unscripted, short-lived suspense is also a large part of sports' appeal. Of course, sports team ownership often comes with significant assets, such as player contracts, a venue lease, the right to share in league revenues and vote on league operations, equipment and uniforms, team names, marks, logos, and historical records, and a fan base. Fans attending the game might also spend money on food, beverages, and merchandise in addition to the ticket price. But the ongoing prosperity of professional and many collegiate and amateur sports enterprises

---

* The Casebook Website (http://pennstatelaw.psu.edu/SportsTextWebsite) contains citations to scholarly and other commentary on a variety of topics discussed in this chapter, including: legal and policy issues concerning sports broadcasting; rights to real-time game accounts and game and player scores and statistics; the tension between sports industry intellectual property claims and freedom of speech; the impact of new technology, the internet and social media on intellectual property rights; the appropriate scope of athlete publicity rights; application of publicity rights to ancillary sports entertainment products such as video games and fantasy sports; and the expansion of trademark protection.

depends primarily on reaching the largest possible audience for the live contest through distribution of game audio, video, and digital content, locally, nationally, and even globally.

This verity is substantiated by the history of television contracts in football, baseball, basketball and hockey. In 1962, the NFL's first league-wide television contract (with CBS) paid $4.65 million, or $320,000 for each of the 14 clubs. Major League Baseball's national contract paid $3 million to its 20 teams. By 2018, NFL clubs were earning over $7 billion every year from television rights fees, and over two-thirds of football's total revenues came from broadcasting. Although the other three major leagues earn significantly less from national television, that revenue combined with their local and regional television deals contributes over 50% to baseball's and basketball's bottom lines, and more than 20% to hockey's. Investing in sports programming has paid off for network rights-holders, who can count on it generating the highest television ratings and corresponding advertising rates. Sports programming has also driven the development of subscription distribution channels, at first cable systems and superstations, and later satellite television providers and internet streaming services.

Public interest in sports contests, and in the leagues, teams, and athletes that produce them, has translated into other commercial opportunities. Licensing the use of sports names and logos on merchandise now generates over $25 billion annually in global retail revenue. Sports sponsorship spending in North America exceeded $17 billion in 2018. Players have been among the chief beneficiaries of this marketing phenomenon, in terms of both rising salaries and the earning potential of their celebrity. All players associations now market group licenses to use union member names and likenesses on everything from trading cards to apparel. These initiatives not so incidentally have served as a union war chest for the fierce labor struggles over player mobility and compensation, discussed in Chapters 2, 3, and 4.

Intellectual property law is indispensable in enabling the producers of sports events to generate and capture significant revenues from these intangible assets. However, it does so through legal rules that are somewhat in tension with the antitrust laws studied in earlier chapters. Intellectual property law initially creates an exclusive property right—in a game broadcast, a team logo, or a player's celebrity—that would otherwise reside in the public domain, vulnerable to exploitation by outside entrepreneurs. Where exclusive property rights control products or services for which fans do not have reasonable substitutes, the rights result in market power that can be exploited. In the case of some sports television broadcasts, that market power is further insulated from antitrust scrutiny by special interest legislation, allowing leagues to sell their property rights at a collective premium, and then divide up the proceeds in line with membership votes. Meanwhile, technological advances have enlarged the popular conception of the public domain, pushing back against expansive intellectual property protection in sports.

This chapter addresses the contours of these exclusive property rights, beginning with the right to game accounts and the scope of copyright protection for game broadcasts. Next considered are the rights of individual participants, including athletes and coaches, to control and capitalize on their names, images, and identities. Finally, the chapter turns to how the law of trademark and unfair competition is applied to sports-related trademarks, logos, and other identifying symbols.

A. REAL-TIME GAME ACCOUNTS AND THE RIGHT TO BROADCAST GAMES

The first significant source of sports revenue from off-site audiences was licensed radio broadcasts, particularly of baseball games. Teams overcame initial concerns that radio broadcasts would cannibalize ticket sales when they realized that easy and regular access to games over-the-air enhanced their appeal in the local community. Radio also made it possible for fans across the country to enjoy post-season play-off and championship games. Teams gladly sold radio stations the right to install announcers with microphones inside the ballpark to describe the events of the game to the audience at home.

Keep in mind, however, that unlike seats, which only one person can occupy at the same time, a host of broadcasters can simultaneously transmit game information without physically interfering with each other. A game broadcast is thus a quasi "public good" in the sense that (a) consumption of the good—listening to or viewing the game—does not reduce its availability to others, and (b) providers of the good find it difficult to exclude from consumption those who do not pay for it. But a radio or television station is typically prepared to pay the team a substantial sum for the broadcast rights only if they are *exclusive*. Exclusivity enables the broadcaster to charge higher fees to advertisers to associate their products with the broadcast.

Furthermore, at the advent of sports broadcasting, federal copyright laws did not protect simultaneously recorded broadcasts such as sporting events. Of course, the club could limit access to the ballpark to those stations that had licensed broadcast rights. Even so, in the 1920s and 1930s, unlicensed radio stations broadcast baseball "re-creations" by announcers who lifted game descriptions from telegraph transmissions, and instantaneously relayed their own pitch-by-pitch embellishments. Indeed, in his early career as a radio announcer, former President Ronald Reagan used to re-create Chicago Cubs and White Sox games from Des Moines, Iowa. The telegraph receiving agent would hand him a piece of paper stating "#12, out, 4–3," and young Reagan would tell his listeners about the hard-hit ground ball that the second baseman had fielded and then thrown to first base for the narrow out.

1. COMMON LAW PROPERTY RIGHTS IN LIVE GAME ACCOUNTS

During the early days of sports broadcasting, if teams were going to block free use of game information and assert a property right in the games themselves, this right was going to have to come from general common law doctrine, such as state misappropriation, unfair competition, and contract law. In what might have been a path-breaking decision, *National Exhibition v. Teleflash*, 24 F. Supp. 488 (S.D.N.Y. 1936), a federal district judge refused to enjoin a station from broadcasting a game via telephone from inside a ballpark. The judge noted that the club had failed to include a restriction on such activity on the face of the ticket the announcer had purchased to gain access to the park. The *Teleflash* contract-based analysis was overtaken by other doctrinal approaches in the next crucial ruling.

PITTSBURGH ATHLETIC CO. V. KQV BROADCASTING CO.
24 F. Supp. 490 (W.D. Pa. 1938)

SCHOONMAKER, DISTRICT JUDGE.

[For several decades prior to the construction of Three Rivers Stadium, the Pittsburgh Pirates baseball team played their home games at Forbes Field. Forbes Field was unlike its more modern counterparts in that it was simply enclosed by fences that precluded unauthorized entry, but still permitted the game to be seen from outside vantage points. By the 1930s, though, fans were admitted to the ballpark only on condition that they not give out any news of the game while it was in progress.

The Pittsburgh Athletic Company, which owned the Pirates, licensed to General Mills the exclusive right to broadcast play-by-play descriptions or accounts of Pirates games. General Mills in turn contracted with the National Broadcast Company (NBC) to broadcast the games over two Pittsburgh radio stations, KDKA & WWSW. At the same time, however, a rival radio station, KQV, was also broadcasting Pirates games. By stationing observers at leased vantage points outside Forbes Field, KQV received information about the progress of the games and provided simultaneous broadcasts.

The Pirates' owners sought an injunction to stop these "pirated" descriptions of their games, in which they asserted an underlying property right.]

* * *

It is perfectly clear that the exclusive right to broadcast play-by-play descriptions of the games played by the "Pirates" at their home field rests in the plaintiffs, General Mills, and the Socony-Vacuum Oil Company under the contract with the Pittsburgh Athletic Company. That is a property right of the plaintiffs with which defendant is interfering when it broadcasts the play-by-play description of the ball games obtained by the observers on the outside of the enclosure.

The plaintiffs and the defendant are using baseball news as material for profit. The Athletic Company has, at great expense, acquired and maintains a baseball park, pays the players who participate in the game, and has, as we view it, a legitimate right to capitalize on the news value of their games by selling exclusive broadcasting rights to companies which value them as affording advertising mediums for their merchandise. This right the defendant interferes with when it uses its broadcasting facilities for giving out the identical news obtained by its paid observers stationed at points outside Forbes Field for the purpose of securing information which it cannot otherwise acquire. This, in our judgment, amounts to unfair competition, and is a violation of the property rights of the plaintiffs. For it is our opinion that the Pittsburgh Athletic Company, by reason of its creation of the game, its control of the park, and its restriction of the dissemination of news therefrom, has a property right in such news, and the right to control the use thereof for a reasonable time following the games.

* * *

On the unfair competition feature of the case, we rest our opinion on the case of *International News Service v. Associated Press*, 248 U.S. 215 [1918]. In that case the court enjoined the International News Service from copying news from bulletin boards and early editions of Associated Press newspapers, and selling such news so long as it had commercial value to the Associated Press. The Supreme Court said:

> Regarding the news, therefore, as but the material out of which both parties are seeking to make profits at the same time and in the same field, we hardly can fail to recognize that for this purpose, and as between them, it must be regarded as quasi property, irrespective of the rights of either as against the public. . . .

248 U.S. at 236. And again:

> The right of the purchaser of a single newspaper to spread knowledge of its contents gratuitously, for any legitimate purpose not unreasonably interfering with the complainant's right to make merchandise of it, may be admitted; but to transmit that news for commercial use, in competition with complainant—which is what

defendant has done and seeks to justify—is a very different matter....

248 U.S. at 239–40.

* * *

Defendant contends it is not unfairly competing with any of the plaintiffs because it obtains no compensation from a sponsor or otherwise from its baseball broadcasts. It concedes, however, that KQV seeks by its broadcast of news of baseball games to cultivate the good will of the public for its radio station. The fact that no revenue is obtained directly from the broadcast is not controlling, as these broadcasts are undoubtedly designed to aid in obtaining advertising business.

Defendant seeks to justify its action on the ground that the information it receives from its observers stationed on its own property without trespassing on plaintiffs' property, may be lawfully broadcast by it. We cannot follow defendant's counsel in this contention for the reasons above stated.

* * *

Injunction granted.

NOTES AND QUESTIONS

1. *Common Law Property Right in Game Broadcasts.* What rationale(s) did the *Pittsburgh Athletic* court provide for establishing a common law property right in game broadcasts? Which one do you find most persuasive? Is there something about the venue that justifies creating this property right? That is, does the right depend on the team playing in a privately owned or operated facility? If so, when the City of Hartford leased the public Civic Center to the World Figure Skating Championships, could the event organizer prohibit local telecasts in favor of ABC, the exclusive television rights-holder? *See Post Newsweek v. Travelers*, 510 F. Supp. 81 (D. Conn. 1981). Or is the right dependent on the fact that the event would not exist at all but for the organizer's efforts at staging it? If so, could the Boston Athletic Association sell exclusive rights to one local station to telecast the Boston Marathon that is being run on public streets? *See WCVB-TV v. Boston Athletic Association*, 926 F.2d 42 (1st Cir. 1991).

2. *"Hot News" Doctrine.* The key precedent cited in *Pittsburgh Athletic* was the Supreme Court decision in *International News Service v. Associated Press*, 248 U.S. 215 (1918). The *INS* case originated the "hot news" misappropriation doctrine when it held INS liable for unfair competition for using early East Coast editions of the AP wire to rewrite World War I news stories and distribute that news the same day to its own subscribers in the

western United States. The Court was concerned that allowing INS to take and sell the benefit of AP's investigations and reporting would eventually eliminate AP's incentive to invest in that work and effort. Was *Pittsburgh Athletic* justified in applying *INS* to sports events and establishing a similar property right in game information?

3. *First Amendment.* In *Zacchini v. Scripps-Howard Broadcasting Co.*, 433 U.S. 562 (1977), a decision explored further in Section C of this chapter, a narrow Supreme Court majority cited *Pittsburgh Athletic* approvingly in rejecting a First Amendment defense to liability for violating publicity rights in an athletic performance. The Court held that a television station had no free speech right to telecast the celebrated "Flying" Zacchini's entire 15-second "human cannonball" act on the local news because it would undermine his economic incentives for investing in the act. In rejecting free speech immunity for the newscast, the *Zacchini* Court emphasized that the station had broadcast the performer's entire act, not merely information about or descriptions of the act. In delineating the property right in game broadcasts, what should the relevance be of the amount of information conveyed?

4. *Off-Site Viewability of Game: Redux.* In an interesting unreported 2002 case, the Chicago Cubs sued several bars that were located on rooftops overlooking Wrigley Field and charged a premium for patrons to enter during Cubs games. The bars were not broadcasting the images or information about the games, only allowing their patrons to watch without having to pay the Cubs for a ticket. What, if any, legal theories could the Cubs assert to try to enjoin this practice? Is this case factually similar to *Pittsburgh Athletic*? Should the result be the same? What would an injunction look like—forbid the bars to be open during Cubs games? Forbid the bars to impose a cover charge? Require all patrons in the bar during games to buy a ticket from the Cubs? Would your answers be any different if the bars allowed a local TV station to set up a camera and microphone on their premises and telecast the games?

After settlement discussions between the Cubs and the rooftop bar owners failed, the club sought and received City of Chicago approval to build more seating and erect seven new outfield signs and two Jumbotrons that would largely block the field view from the rooftop bars. The rooftop owners filed a lawsuit against the City and the Cubs claiming that it violated a 20-year revenue-sharing contract between the bars and team. Ultimately the Seventh Circuit Court of Appeals interpreted the contract to reject that claim, and also refused to subject the Cubs' alleged monopolistic behavior to antitrust scrutiny because it was part of the immunized "business of baseball" (see Chapter 4, Section D). Nonetheless, what are your views about whether it is appropriate public policy to allow businesses (or even residents) that fortuitously have a view of the playing field to enjoy and even profit from allowing people to watch the games without compensating the Cubs?

2. CONTRACTUAL SOLUTIONS TO GAME BROADCAST OWNERSHIP

From the 1950s to the 1990s, an increasing reliance on contract sidelined the *Pittsburgh Athletic* approach to ownership of game broadcasts. Language inserted in admission tickets and media credentials restricted commercial use or distribution of live game information and depictions without the team's consent. Enforcement of these provisions was simplified by the location and design of new stadiums and arenas, which made it essentially impossible to produce a game broadcast without access to the facility.

Consider this ticket disclaimer language used by a major league sports team:

> Photographs, videos or other accounts or descriptions (whether data, textual or visual) of all or any part of the football game or of any game-related activities created by the ticket holder may be used only for personal, non-commercial uses. Any transmission or other distribution to any commercial enterprise, and any public performance or display, are strictly prohibited.

As a practical matter in the smartphone era, how can a team and its venue enforce this provision, in particular the prohibition of "any public performance or display" of game descriptions? What legal remedies are available? Does this mean a spectator can't post a photograph or video of the game on social media? Does that depend on the spectator's privacy settings on his Instagram or Twitter account? Ticket disclaimers are contracts of adhesion, non-negotiable by the purchaser. Should this affect their enforceability?

Leagues and teams also resorted to contract to resolve any lingering ambiguity after *Pittsburgh Athletic* as to whether a visiting team, or the league itself, shared with the home team any ownership in the game broadcast. Each league eventually established by rule or joint venture agreement the members' respective rights in this regard. (For an early case in which the NFL had not anticipated this problem, see *Johnson-Kennedy Radio Corp. v. Chicago Bears Football Club*, 97 F.2d 223 (7th Cir. 1938), where the then-Chicago Cardinals sought to block its opponent, the Chicago Bears, from broadcasting a Cardinals home game on the Bears' licensed radio station.) As discussed in Chapter 7, when leagues periodically revisit contractual restraints on member clubs' broadcast property rights, they often must contend with intervening market developments and tensions between large and small markets, and between successful and struggling teams.

3. ADVANCING TECHNOLOGY AND APPROPRIATION OF REAL-TIME GAME ACCOUNTS

With the advance of modern communications tools, the ability to discover and disseminate game facts in new and commercially viable ways has frustrated the ownership claims of sports event producers. Case in point is the NBA's lawsuit against Motorola, Inc., and its partner, Sports Team Analysis and Tracking System, Inc. (STATS). In 1994, these two partners were licensed by Major League Baseball to provide real-time baseball game information on a portable electronic pager device—SportsTrax—that they sold to subscribers. The success of that venture led the partners to approach the NBA to expand their service into basketball. The NBA demurred, hoping to develop its own pager service. Motorola and SportsTrax nonetheless decided to generate and transmit NBA game information by themselves, without a license from the league.

In 1996, SportsTrax began offering subscribers real-time information about NBA game action, updated every two to three minutes. To obtain game information, STATS hired reporters to watch or listen to broadcasts of NBA games and continuously key into their computers the score, ball possession, shots taken and made, fouls, clock updates, and the like. A fan could use a SportsTrax pager to keep track of key elements of every NBA game being played around the country. Additional real-time game information was available on STATS's AOL website, but in the early days of the internet, this was a less user-friendly option.

The NBA responded with a lawsuit alleging federal copyright and trademark infringement, and New York state common law claims of commercial misappropriation of the NBA's property rights in its games. The federal infringement claims failed because neither the underlying NBA games nor the information about those games were copyrightable "original works of authorship" under the Copyright Act. As explained in the decision below, the misappropriation claim failed because of a complex doctrine known as copyright preemption, which foils attempts to seek state law protection for uncopyrightable elements of a work.

NBA v. MOTOROLA
105 F.3d 841 (2d Cir. 1997)

WINTER, CIRCUIT JUDGE.

A. *Summary of Ruling*

The issues before us are ones that have arisen in various forms over the course of this century as technology has steadily increased the speed and quantity of information transmission. . . .

With the advance of technology, radio stations began "live" broadcasts of events such as baseball games and operas, and various entrepreneurs began to use the transmissions of others in one way or another for their own profit. In response, New York courts created a body of misappropriation law, loosely based on *INS*, that sought to apply ethical standards to the use by one party of another's transmissions of events. . . . In 1976, however, Congress passed legislation expressly affording copyright protection to simultaneously-recorded broadcasts of live performances such as sports events. Such protection was not extended to the underlying events.

The 1976 amendments also contained provisions preempting state law claims that enforced rights "equivalent" to exclusive copyright protections when the work to which the state claim was being applied fell within the area of copyright protection. [Although] a "hot-news" *INS*-like claim survives preemption, . . . much of New York misappropriation law after INS goes well beyond "hot-news" claims and is preempted.

B. Copyrights in Events or Broadcasts of Events

In our view, the underlying basketball games do not fall within the subject matter of federal copyright protection because they do not constitute "original works of authorship." . . . Unlike movies, plays, television programs, or operas, athletic events are competitive and have no underlying script. . . . For many of these reasons, Nimmer on Copyright concludes that the "[f]ar more reasonable" position is that athletic events are not copyrightable.

As noted, recorded broadcasts of NBA games—as opposed to the games themselves—are now entitled to copyright protection. . . . Although the broadcasts are protected under copyright law, the district court correctly held that Motorola and STATS did not infringe NBA's copyright because they reproduced only facts from the broadcasts, not the expression or description of the game that constitutes the broadcast.

C. The State-Law Misappropriation Claim

1. *Preemption Under the Copyright Act*

When Congress amended the Copyright Act in 1976, it provided for the preemption of state law claims that are interrelated with copyright claims in certain ways. Under 17 U.S.C. § 301, a state law claim is preempted when: (i) the state law claim seeks to vindicate "legal or equitable rights that are equivalent" to one of the bundle of exclusive rights already protected by copyright law under 17 U.S.C. § 106—styled the "general scope requirement"; and (ii) the particular work to which the state law claim is being applied falls within the type of works protected by the Copyright Act under Sections 102 and 103—styled the "subject matter requirement."

* * *

[The court first concluded that the "subject matter requirement" for preemption had been established.] Although game broadcasts are copyrightable while the underlying games are not, the Copyright Act should not be read to distinguish between the two when analyzing the preemption of a misappropriation claim based on copying or taking from the copyrightable work. We believe that:

> Once a performance is reduced to tangible form, there is no distinction between the performance and the recording of the performance for the purposes of preemption under § 301(a). Thus, if a baseball game were not broadcast or were telecast without being recorded, the Players' performances similarly would not be fixed in tangible form and their rights of publicity would not be subject to preemption. By virtue of being videotaped, however, the Players' performances are fixed in tangible form, and any rights of publicity in their performances that are equivalent to the rights contained in the copyright of the telecast are preempted.

Baltimore Orioles [*v. Major League Baseball Players Ass'n*, 805 F.2d 663, 675 (7th Cir. 1986)](citation omitted).

Copyrightable material often contains uncopyrightable elements within it, but Section 301 preemption bars state law misappropriation claims with respect to uncopyrightable as well as copyrightable elements.

* * *

Under the general scope requirement. Section 301 "preempts only those state law rights that 'may be abridged by an act which, in and of itself, would infringe one of the exclusive rights' provided by federal copyright law." [Citation omitted.] However, certain forms of commercial misappropriation otherwise within the general scope requirement will survive preemption if an "extra-element" test is met. As stated in *Altai*:

> But if an "extra element" is "required instead of or in addition to the acts of reproduction, performance, distribution or display, in order to constitute a state-created cause of action, then the right does not lie 'within the general scope of copyright,' and there is no preemption."

We turn, therefore, to the question of the extent to which a "hot-news" misappropriation claim based on *INS* involves extra elements and is not the equivalent of exclusive rights under a copyright. Courts are generally agreed that some form of such a claim survives preemption.

[The court rejected the district court's reliance on pre-1976 New York misappropriation cases that were based on "amorphous concepts" of "commercial immorality" or society's "ethics."] Such concepts are virtually synonymous for wrongful copying and are in no meaningful fashion distinguishable from infringement of a copyright. The broad misappropriation doctrine relied upon by the district court is, therefore, the equivalent of exclusive rights in copyright law.

* * *

Our conclusion, therefore, is that only a narrow "hot-news" misappropriation claim survives preemption for actions concerning material within the realm of copyright. In our view, the elements central to an *INS* claim are: (i) the plaintiff generates or collects information at some cost or expense; (ii) the value of the information is highly time-sensitive; (iii) the defendant's use of the information constitutes free-riding on the plaintiff's costly efforts to generate or collect it; (iv) the defendant's use of the information is in direct competition with a product or service offered by the plaintiff; (v) the ability of other parties to free-ride on the efforts of the plaintiff would so reduce the incentive to produce the product or service that its existence or quality would be substantially threatened.

INS is not about ethics; it is about the protection of property rights in time-sensitive information so that the information will be made available to the public by profit-seeking entrepreneurs. If services like AP were not assured of property rights in the news they pay to collect, they would cease to collect it. The ability of their competitors to appropriate their product at only nominal cost and thereby to disseminate a competing product at a lower price would destroy the incentive to collect news in the first place. The newspaper-reading public would suffer because no one would have an incentive to collect "hot news."

We therefore find the extra elements—those in addition to the elements of copyright infringement—that allow a "hot news" claim to survive preemption are: (i) the time-sensitive value of factual information, (ii) the free-riding by a defendant, and (iii) the threat to the very existence of the product or service provided by the plaintiff.

2. *The Legality of SportsTrax*

We conclude that Motorola and STATS have not engaged in unlawful misappropriation under the "hot-news" test set out above. To be sure, some of the elements of a "hot-news" *INS*-claim are met . . .

However, there are critical elements missing in the NBA's attempt to assert a "hot-news" *INS*-type claim. As framed by the NBA, their claim compresses and confuses three different informational products. The first product is generating the information by playing the games; the second product is transmitting live, full descriptions of those games; and the third product is collecting and retransmitting strictly factual information about the games. The first and second products are the NBA's primary business: producing basketball games for live attendance and licensing copyrighted broadcasts of those games. The collection and retransmission of strictly factual material about the games is a different product: *e.g.*, box-scores in newspapers, summaries of statistics on television sports news, and real-time facts to be transmitted to pagers. In our view, the NBA has failed to show any competitive effect whatsoever from SportsTrax on the first and second products and a lack of any free-riding by SportsTrax on the third.

With regard to the NBA's primary products—producing basketball games with live attendance and licensing copyrighted broadcasts of those games—there is no evidence that anyone regards SportsTrax or the AOL site as a substitute for attending NBA games or watching them on television. In fact, Motorola markets SportsTrax as being designed "for those times when you cannot be at the arena, watch the game on TV, or listen to the radio. . . ."

The NBA argues that the pager market is also relevant to a "hot-news" *INS*-type claim and that SportsTrax's future competition with Gamestats satisfies any missing element. We agree that there is a separate market for the real-time transmission of factual information to pagers or similar devices, such as STATS's AOL site. However, we disagree that SportsTrax is in any sense free-riding off Gamestats.

An indispensable element of an INS "hot-news" claim is free-riding by a defendant on a plaintiff's product, enabling the defendant to produce a directly competitive product for less money because it has lower costs. SportsTrax is not such a product. The use of pagers to transmit real-time information about NBA games requires: (i) the collecting of facts about the games; (ii) the transmission of these facts on a network; (iii) the assembling of them by the particular service; and (iv) the transmission of them to pagers or an on-line computer site. Appellants are in no way free-riding on Gamestats. Motorola and STATS expend their own resources to collect purely factual information generated in NBA games to transmit to SportsTrax pagers. They have their own network and assemble and transmit data themselves.

To be sure, if appellants in the future were to collect facts from an enhanced Gamestats pager to retransmit them to SportsTrax pagers, that would constitute free-riding and might well cause Gamestats to be unprofitable because it had to bear costs to collect facts that SportsTrax did not. If the appropriation of facts from one pager to another pager service were allowed, transmission of current information on NBA games to pagers or similar devices would be substantially deterred because any potential transmitter would know that the first entrant would quickly encounter a lower cost competitor free-riding on the originator's transmissions.[9]

---

[9] It may well be that the NBA's product, when enhanced, will actually have a competitive edge because its Gamestats system will apparently be used for a number of in-stadium services as well as the pager market, resulting in a certain amount of cost-sharing. Gamestats might also

However, that is not the case in the instant matter. SportsTrax and Gamestats are each bearing their own costs of collecting factual information on NBA games, and, if one produces a product that is cheaper or otherwise superior to the other, that producer will prevail in the marketplace. This is obviously not the situation against which INS was intended to prevent: the potential lack of any such product or service because of the anticipation of free-riding.

For the foregoing reasons, the NBA has not shown any damage to any of its products based on free-riding by Motorola and STATS, and the NBA's misappropriation claim based on New York law is preempted.

Reversed.

NOTES AND QUESTIONS

1. *Scope of Copyright Preemption.* Was the Second Circuit right in holding that federal copyright law preempts the NBA's state law misappropriation claim? If the NBA cannot use state law to protect uncopyrightable elements of its games, should federal law step in to give the NBA exclusive control over live descriptions and sale of game events? Does your answer depend on whether that control is exerted before or after the information is put into the public domain by television or radio broadcasts? Would any such intellectual property conferred on the league improperly intrude upon the First Amendment rights of Motorola and STATS (an issue the Second Circuit did not have to address in this case)?

2. *Preemption Subject Matter Requirement.* The Second Circuit held that the subject matter requirement for preemption was met because the real-time data about NBA games, though not copyrightable, were contained in a copyrighted broadcast. Would the answer be different if the defendants obtained the information they put on their pager system from some means other than watching and/or listening to copyrighted broadcasts (*e.g.*, by stationing someone in the arena with a computer like in the old *Teleflash* case, or by positioning someone at a vantage point outside the facility like in the *Pittsburgh Athletic* case)? What if a game was not broadcast at all?

3. *Future of* Pittsburgh Athletic. Does *Motorola* implicitly overturn *Pittsburgh Athletic* as applied to the latter's facts? Under what circumstances can someone with access to facts about a sports event repurpose them for commercial benefit? How would this logic apply to major boxing matches, which now primarily air on pay-for-view? Consider *Twentieth Century Sporting Club v. Transradio Press Service, Inc.*, 165 Misc. 71, 300 N.Y.S. 159 (1937), which enjoined local television stations from using facts obtained from a Joe

---

have a temporal advantage in collecting and transmitting official statistics. Whether this is so does not affect our disposition of this matter, although it does demonstrate the gulf between this case and *INS*, where the free-riding created the danger of no wire service being viable.

Louis fight broadcast to provide "up to the minute descriptions" in competition with NBC, the promoter's exclusive broadcast rights-holder. After *Motorola*, could a digital news service permissibly arrange for a reporter to watch a fight on pay-for-view television and simultaneously describe to the internet audience the key developments in the fight as they are taking place? Is your answer different if the reporter shared smartphone video of the television screen?

4. *Future of the Hot News Doctrine.* Has the internet made the hot news doctrine obsolete? Information, images, and video are now transmitted via satellite or the internet instantaneously at nominal cost. How does this development affect the calculus of time sensitivity in applying the hot news doctrine? Does a competitor's misappropriation of bare news facts underlying another organization's work continue to pose a significant threat to economic incentives to produce that work?

4. PROPERTY RIGHTS IN INTERNET REPORTING

As internet coverage of sports events proliferated, courts confronted the "novel and compelling question of who has the 'right' to report the news, produced and gathered by others, in an age of near-instantaneous information." *Morris Commc'ns Corp. v. PGA Tour, Inc.*, 235 F. Supp. 2d 1269, 1272 (M.D. Fla. 2002), *aff'd*, 364 F.3d 1288 (11th Cir. 2004). In *Morris*, the PGA Tour successfully defended an antitrust challenge to tournament media regulations it enforced to maintain a commercial advantage for its Real-Time Scoring System (RTSS). The RTSS enabled the PGA Tour to publish "real-time" golf scores on the pgatour.com website and on the website of USA Today, which had paid for the privilege.

To support the RTSS, the PGA Tour had invested significant resources to monitor each golf hole during its tournaments, and collect and relay scoring information to electronic "leaderboards" throughout the golf course and to the PGA Tour's media center and website. In this way, the PGA Tour could provide up-to-date scores to both on-site spectators and television viewers for as many as 200 players on all 18 holes of its 100+ acre golf courses. The PGA Tour prohibited the use of mobile devices by the press or public during tournaments, making the RTSS the sole source of compiled golf scores for the full list of competing golfers. Beginning in 1999, the PGA Tour also conditioned media access to tournaments on agreeing to its On-Line Service Regulations (OLSR). To give pgatour.com and USA Today priority, the OLSR prohibited credentialed media from publishing or selling scoring information until either (1) thirty minutes after a player's shot or (2) pgatour.com published that information. In 2000, the PGA Tour amended the OLSR to allow credentialed media to instantly transmit scores on their own websites, but prohibited them from selling or syndicating scores to third parties without first purchasing a special license from the PGA Tour, as USA Today had.

Morris Communications was a media firm that published traditional print and web-based newspapers, and regularly covered golf events. Morris's golf reporters relied on the PGA Tour's on-site media center to obtain real-time scores, which Morris then transmitted to its own news outlets and sold to third-party subscribers. When the PGA Tour refused to allow Morris to transmit tournament scores to third parties such as the Denver Post and Dallas Morning News without first paying for a license, Morris sued under federal and state antitrust laws, claiming that the PGA Tour was leveraging its exclusive power over the gathering of the scores to suppress competition in the market for the distribution of real-time golf scores over the internet.

MORRIS COMMUNICATIONS CORPORATION V. PGA TOUR
235 F. Supp. 2d 1269 (M.D. Fla. 2002)

SCHLESINGER, DISTRICT JUDGE.

* * *

[T]he PGA Tour itself has acknowledged that the OLSR were implemented in order to maintain a commercial advantage....

Thus, the record seems to clearly indicate that the OLSR have the purpose and effect of giving the PGA Tour a commercial advantage in the syndication market and disadvantaging potential competitors, including Morris. As discussed below, this does not necessarily mean that the PGA Tour has violated any antitrust laws....

* * *

III. Analysis

A. *Antitrust claims*

Morris asserts four antitrust claims: 1) monopolization of the Internet markets, 2) unlawful refusal to deal, 3) monopoly leveraging, and 4) attempted monopolization of the Internet markets.... [T]he Court will first address the PGA Tour's assertions that valid business reasons justify the exclusionary practice found in the OLSR, because valid business reasons are a defense to the antitrust claims....

Free-riding

Morris asks the Court to force the PGA Tour to provide Morris with the compilation of scores, for which the PGA Tour spends considerable money and time creating, at no cost to Morris. While Morris does invest its own cost in re-keying the scores for syndication, Morris free-rides on the PGA Tour's efforts in compiling the scores. As Morris admits in its Memorandum of Law, "Morris cannot duplicate the functions of RTSS, which depends on the efforts of hundreds of volunteers each week." Even if it is the efforts of "volunteers", the PGA Tour has still invested time and money in the organization and technology to make RTSS possible.

[The court distinguishes *Motorola*.] [T]he information that Motorola used to create its product was in the public domain, having been broadcast on television or radio. Specifically, Motorola-paid reporters, who had heard the radio or television broadcast scores, reported the information to a central location and merely relayed what had been known to the world. Golf, unlike basketball, precludes a single person gathering all the information occurring on all 18 holes. So when television and radio cover a basketball game, the score is presented to the public through those media outlets, allowing Motorola to obtain the information and republish it. If Morris were able to gather scores from all 18 holes through a television or radio broadcast, Morris could then republish that information, absent a hot-news exception. However, golf's atypical format prevents any single television or radio broadcast from providing results from all 18 holes live. The PGA Tour does publish the scores in the media center, but the media cannot disseminate that information except as the PGA Tour's press credentials allow them to do. As a result, the scores which, are not protected by copyright, remain outside the public domain and within the PGA Tour's control, because the PGA Tour provides access with certain restrictions.

* * *

Morris additionally argues that even if there is free-riding, it must reach the level that would justify a "hot news" property right. However, the Court finds that to be a business justification free-riding does not have to reach the level that the *Motorola* court held necessary for a hot news exception. The *Motorola* court required the free-riding to be so pervasive that all incentives to undertake an activity would be lost. See *Motorola*, 105 F.3d at 853. However, to be a valid business reason, a much lower level of free riding will justify excluding competitors. See *Areeda*, Antitrust Law, Vol. III, ¶ 658(f) ("once a proffered business purpose has been accepted as asserted in good faith and not as pretense, the defense does not require 'balancing' of social gains against competitive harms . . .").

Property Right in the Scores

. . . For the following reasons, the Court finds that the PGA Tour does have a property right in the scores compiled by the use of RTSS, but that property right vanishes when the scores are in the public domain.

The PGA Tour's property right does not come from copyright law, as copyright law does not protect factual information, like golf scores. However, the PGA Tour controls the right of access to that information and can place restrictions on those attending the private event, giving the PGA Tour a property right that the Court will protect.

* * *

[T]he instant case deals with facts that are not subject to copyright protection. The compiler of the information . . . collects information, which it created, at a cost. Also the events occur on private property to which the general public does not have unfettered access, and the creator of the event can place restrictions upon those who enter the private property. The vastly increased speed that the Internet makes available does not change the calculus or the underlying property right. Accordingly, the PGA Tour, like the exchanges in the ticker cases, has a property right in the compilation of scores, but that property right disappears when the underlying information is in the public domain.

Broadcast Rights on the Internet

Whether the PGA Tour has a separate right to license or sell broadcast rights on the Internet, like sports and entertainment producers currently enjoy in dealing with television and radio, is a novel question. . . .

. . . Both parties would certainly agree that the Internet provides an opportunity to profit from a product by selling advertisement. Television, radio, and print media operate on a similar, if not identical, principle: the selling of advertisement to viewers, listeners, or readers of entertainment, be it sports, entertainment, or news. Therefore, the Court finds that the PGA Tour has a right to sell or license its product, championship golf, and its derivative product, golf scores, on the Internet in the same way the PGA Tour currently sells its rights to television broadcasting stations.[24]

Accordingly, the Court finds that the PGA Tour is justified in its restrictions because (1) Morris free-rides on the PGA Tour's efforts, (2) the PGA Tour has a property right in the scores before they are in the public domain, and (3) the PGA Tour has the right to license or sell broadcasting rights of its products over the Internet.

* * *

Unlawful Refusal to Deal

[I]n this case, Morris is seeking access to the media center and the scoring system at no cost, putting it at a competitive advantage to the PGA Tour. The PGA Tour offers access to the scores through a license as evidenced by its contract with USA Today, and Morris is free to negotiate for the purchase of a license which would put it on a competitive plane with the PGA Tour.

---

[24] With the emergence of "web-casting" and "streaming" video and other rapid advancements in technology, a negative answer to the question of whether the PGA Tour has broadcast rights on the Internet would stymie advancement and reduce incentive to create entertainment and sports programming by foreclosing a lucrative market. To hold otherwise would be similar to a court finding that Major League Baseball could not sell broadcasting rights to television stations in the 1940s with the advent of television.

[The court dismisses all of Morris' antitrust claims.]

NOTES AND QUESTIONS

1. *Nature of the Property Right.* Is it significant that the PGA Tour asserted the property right as a defense to an antitrust claim? Would the *Morris Communications* court have recognized the property right if the PGA Tour had sued because Morris used camera drones above the golf course to obtain access to real-time scores without the need for a PGA Tour press credential? Could the PGA Tour in that case prohibit Morris from publishing the scores on the internet? Does the answer depend on whether state law has articulated the misappropriation tort to require the "extra elements" of a "hot news" situation?

2. *Theorizing the Property Right.* What is the basis for articulating a property right that the PGA Tour might affirmatively assert? Public policy? The moral right that the creator of a sports event has in the information about the event? The extent to which the creator has physical power to control and thus condition the right of access to that information? How does that theory operate in the digital age of instantaneous access to information and casual unauthorized retransmission of that information?

3. *Copyright Preemption.* Under what circumstances would the PGA Tour's state law misappropriation claim be preempted by the Copyright Act? Would this depend on whether the tournament was on television or radio in a copyrighted broadcast? If yes, would that depend on whether the real-time scores were discernible from the broadcast? Does the preemption analysis depend on the nature of the sport and how it is covered on television?

4. *Reconcilable Law?* Are the *Motorola* and *Morris Communications* decisions reconcilable? If so, what are the key distinguishing facts? With the advent of legalized sports gambling in the United States, *see Murphy v. Nat'l Collegiate Athletic Ass'n*, 138 S. Ct. 1461 (2018), leagues and teams will undoubtedly redouble their efforts to obtain—through litigation, legislation, or private ordering—intellectual property protection for game-related statistics and information. Compare sports entities around the world, which have long embraced gambling affiliations. For example, English Premier League football clubs such as Liverpool and Arsenal have contracted with leading U.K. gambling houses to serve as the clubs' "official bookmaker." The gambling house pays the club a royalty in exchange for being allowed to set up betting facilities at the club's stadium and on its internet sites. Other European sports entities have entered into official sponsorships with betting companies and license the use of club intellectual property. Under U.S. law, how successful would leagues be in barring sportsbooks from using game information and other intellectual property? Might this be a potential source of large new revenues for U.S. sports leagues?

B. COPYRIGHT IN THE GAME BROADCASTS

Copyright law finds its roots in the Constitution itself, which authorizes Congress "To promote the Progress of Science and useful Arts, by securing for limited Times to Authors and Inventors the exclusive Right to their respective Writings and Discoveries." Article I, § 8, cl. 8. The operating premise then and now is that granting creators exclusive right to control and license use of their works provides the incentive to invest the time, effort, and resources in production of those works for the benefit of society at large. Congress enacted the first copyright statute in 1789, and has periodically amended the law since to keep pace with technological developments.

The Copyright Act of 1976 was the first iteration to extend federal copyright protection to live sports broadcasts once they are "fixed in any tangible medium of expression," *i.e.*, recorded simultaneously with transmission. 17 U.S.C. § 102(a). Copyright owners currently enjoy six statutorily defined exclusive rights: (1) to reproduce the copyrighted work; (2) to prepare derivative works; (3) to distribute copies; (4) to publicly perform the copyrighted work; (5) to publicly display the copyrighted work; and (6) to digitally transmit the work. 17 U.S.C. § 106. Copyright duration now lasts for the author's life plus 70 years. For a work made for hire, that is, owned by a business, the copyright endures for 95 years.

1. NO COPYRIGHT PROTECTION FOR IDEAS OR FACTS

Two key limitations on a sports event producer's "ownership" of its games nonetheless survive the 1976 Copyright Act. First, copyright protection extends only to "original works of authorship" and not "to any idea, procedure, process, system, method of operation, concept, principle, or discovery. . . ." 17 U.S.C. § 102. As explained in *Motorola*, a live sports performance cannot amount to a "work of authorship":

> Sports events are not "authored" in any common sense of the word. There is, of course, at least at the professional level, considerable preparation for a game. However, the preparation is as much an expression of hope or faith as a determination of what will actually happen. Unlike movies, plays, television programs, or operas, athletic events are competitive and have no underlying script. Preparation may even cause mistakes to succeed, like the broken play in football that gains yardage because the opposition could not expect it. Athletic events may also result in wholly unanticipated occurrences, the most notable recent event being in a championship baseball game in which interference with a fly ball caused an umpire to signal erroneously a home run.

What "authorship" there is in a sports event, moreover, must be open to copying by competitors if fans are to be attracted. If the inventor of the T-formation in football had been able to copyright it, the sport might have to come to an end instead of prospering. Even where athletic preparation most resembles authorship—figure skating, gymnastics, and, some would uncharitably say, professional wrestling—a performer who conceives and executes a particularly graceful and difficult—or, in the case of wrestling, seemingly painful—acrobatic feat cannot copyright it without impairing the underlying competition in the future. A claim of being the only athlete to perform a feat doesn't mean much if no one else is allowed to try.

105 F.3d at 846. Thus, an upstart basketball league is free to stage a basketball game for profit, employing all the same rules, mechanics, and plays as the NBA, without that league's consent. *See Hoopla Sports and Entertainment, Inc. v. Nike, Inc.*, 947 F. Supp. 347 (N.D. Ill. 1996).

Second, even after the broadcast "expression" of a game is "fixed," copyright does not protect facts or create exclusive property rights in the bare events of the game—no more than it does for the events of a war, a crime, or a political convention. *See Feist Publications v. Rural Telephone Service*, 499 U.S. 340 (1991) (telephone directory's compilation of facts—names, addresses, phone numbers—not entitled to copyright); *Miller v. Universal City Studios*, 650 F.2d 1365 (5th Cir. 1981) (docudrama may use facts it learned from book about actual kidnapping). Thus, as long as Ronald Reagan's radio recreations of baseball games comprised his own expression of what was happening, he was not violating the copyrighted expression of another announcer's broadcast a half inning or so earlier. Likewise, today's digital sports journalists do not infringe copyright when they offer real-time unique commentary on sports events, and doing so is itself a copyrightable expression.

2. FAIR USE OF COPYRIGHTED WORKS

Another important doctrine, now embodied in § 107 of the Copyright Act, gives everyone the right to make "fair use" of a copyrighted work. The following case provides an intriguing example of an effort to appeal to fair use in the sports broadcasting context.

NEW BOSTON TELEVISION V. ENTERTAINMENT SPORTS PROGRAMMING NETWORK (ESPN)
215 U.S.P.Q. 755, 1981 WL 1374 (D. Mass. Aug. 3, 1981)

ZOBEL, DISTRICT JUDGE:

[New Boston Television owns and operates WSBK-TV, which licensed the exclusive rights to broadcast Red Sox baseball and Bruins hockey games. The Red Sox retained the copyright in the baseball telecasts, and paid WSBK one-half of all copyright royalties. The Bruins and WSBK jointly owned the copyright in the hockey telecasts.

The recently created ESPN cable channel negotiated with WSBK to rebroadcast excerpts of the Bruins and Red Sox telecasts on its SportsCenter program, but they could not agree on terms. ESPN proceeded to use the WSBK broadcasts, which then filed suit for copyright infringement. ESPN asserted several defenses, principally fair use.]

* * *

The fair use defense is a judicially developed doctrine which is now codified in the Copyright Revision Act of 1976, 17 U.S.C. § 107. It has been defined as "a privilege in others than the owner of the copyright to use the copyrighted material in a reasonable manner without his consent; notwithstanding the monopoly granted to the owner." *Rosemont Enterprises, Inc. v. Random House, Inc.*, 366 F.2d 303, 306 (2d Cir. 1966). The doctrine "offers a means of balancing the exclusive rights of the copyright holder with the public's interest in the dissemination of information affecting areas of universal concern, such as art, science, and industry." *Wainwright Securities, Inc. v. Wall Street Transcript Corp.*, 558 F.2d 91, 94 (2d Cir. 1977).

Fair use is a question which depends on the facts of each particular case, evaluated in light of certain criteria: 1) the purpose and character of the use, including whether such use is of a commercial nature or is for nonprofit educational purposes; 2) the nature of the copyrighted work; 3) the amount and substantiality of the portion used in relation to the copyrighted work as a whole; and 4) the effect of the use upon the potential market for or value of the copyrighted work.

Defendants assert that as to the first of these factors, their use is primarily for "news" purposes and hence should be protected by the fair use doctrine in order to assure the public's right of access to newsworthy information. While protection of the public right of access to such information is a primary justification for the fair use defense, this right is sufficiently protected merely by enabling defendants to report the underlying facts which the plaintiff's videotapes record. It does not however permit defendants to appropriate the plaintiff's expression of that information by copying the plaintiff's films themselves. "The fair use doctrine is not a license for corporate theft, empowering a court to ignore a copyright whenever it determines the underlying work contains material of possible public importance." *Iowa State University v. American Broadcasting Cos.*, 621 F.2d 57, 61 (2d Cir. 1980).

Defendants rely on *Time Incorporated v. Bernard Geis Assoc.*, 293 F. Supp. 130 (S.D.N.Y. 1968), in which the Court determined that the reproduction of frames of the Zapruder film in a book inquiring into the assassination of President Kennedy was fair use. However, the unique and extraordinary nature of that historical event renders that case distinguishable from the case at bar. In addition, while the defendants in *Geis* had no opportunity to record the event themselves, defendants here are under no such impediment. Moreover, defendants are engaged in copying for commercial exploitation. That fact is not dispositive and would not preclude a finding of fair use, but it is a factor which adds to the plaintiffs' case in evaluating likelihood of their success on the merits.

Defendants assert that their use is *de minimis* because it amounts to no more than two minutes out of each videotape owned by plaintiffs. However, it is the quality of the use rather than its quantity which is determinative. The excerpts used by defendants in this case, although of relatively short duration, are the "highlights" of each broadcast and as such their use may be considered substantial.

Defendants contend that plaintiffs have failed to demonstrate that their transmission has had any effect on the present or potential market for plaintiffs' copyright in that plaintiffs have made no attempt to sell excerpts from their programming to any cable networks in the past, and have experienced no diminution in the substantial revenue that they receive from the three major television networks who do pay plaintiffs for the right to broadcast highlights on their respective news shows. Assuming it to be true that plaintiffs have made no attempt to market their broadcasts within the cable field, a fact which has not been established, this does not permit defendants to appropriate plaintiffs' copyrighted material and effectively preclude such efforts in the future. It is for plaintiffs, not defendants, to determine when and in what manner they choose to exploit their copyright. Evidence of plaintiffs' revenues from the three major networks lends further credence to their claim that defendant's use deprives them of substantial additional revenue to which they are entitled as the owners of the copyright to these materials.

* * *

Injunction granted.

NOTES AND QUESTIONS

1. *Nature of Copyrighted Work.* Do you agree with this judicial application of fair use to sports event highlights? As a matter of public policy, wouldn't consumers be better served if television newscasts could use short game clips rather than just the bare scores and statistics? How does that use compare to one television newscast reporting on current events by using clips from another station's newscasts? If intellectual property rights accommodated

ESPN's use, what harm, if any, would be inflicted on WSBK, or the Red Sox and Bruins?

2. *Game Highlights Market.* What do you think was the impact of *New Boston Television* on the marketplace? Would your views on fair use change if the marketplace no longer seemed to function and fans interested in watching highlights were required to switch multiple channels to watch highlights only on those networks that were licensees of the original broadcast? Today the major sports leagues and other sports event producers routinely grant free use of video and audio excerpts from copyrighted broadcasts subject to restrictions that, for example, limit the total number of minutes a program can use and set the usage period to expire within a few days of the game. Is this an implicit acknowledgement that sharing game highlights does not erode the market for the copyrighted broadcast, and thus such use is fair?

3. *Amount and Substantiality of Portion Used.* Shortly after *New Boston Television*, a closely divided Supreme Court ruled that recording television shows for later in-home, personal viewing is non-infringing fair use of a copyrighted broadcast. *See Sony Corp. of America v. Universal City Studios*, 464 U.S. 417 (1984). Significantly, the Supreme Court held the reproduction of an entire broadcast is permissible in this context. Does that logic equally apply to home taping of sports broadcasts? Consider a sports bar that did not want to pay the $1,000 business "pay-per-view" fee for a championship boxing match, and so had a patron pay the $35 residential fee, tape the fight at home, and then relay videotapes to the sports bar every few rounds. *See Cablevision of Michigan v. Sports Palace*, 27 F.3d 566 (6th Cir. 1994). Should these actions be deemed fair or unfair uses under copyright doctrine, whether by the sports bar or by the patron?

4. *Social Media Sharing of Sports Clips.* Fans now routinely share sports highlights via social media, which the leagues tolerate as a way to drive interest and excitement in the game. However, it is by no means clear that the highly fact-intensive fair-use inquiry protects this activity. This troubling uncertainty and its potential impact on internet service providers led to passage of the 1998 Digital Millennium Copyright Act. The DMCA provides a safe harbor from copyright liability to entities that host content if they (i) expeditiously take down potentially infringing content upon receiving notice, (ii) had no actual or constructive knowledge of the infringing behavior, and (iii) derived no financial benefit directly attributable to the infringement. While service providers are not required to self-police for infringing content, immunity is not available to websites that maintain editorial control over the posted content or actively solicit the content. *See Viacom Int'l, Inc. v. YouTube, Inc.*, 676 F.3d 19, 29 (2d Cir. 2012).

In this spirit, in 2016, an English court applying that country's fair use doctrine upheld an infringement claim against Fanatix, a social media app that invited fans to upload eight-second clips of sports broadcasts, which could then be viewed for 24 hours. Users could search for their favorite sport or team and view clips on the app or visit the Fanatix website which separately aggregated and published clips. The court found the clips were sufficiently substantial, despite their short duration, because most contained key moments of contests. Although the court acknowledged that "citizen journalism" can merit fair use protection as a form of protected news reporting, it found that the app's primary purpose was sharing clips with other users rather than reporting on them. *See England and Wales Cricket Board Ltd v Fanatix*, 2016 EWHC 575 (Ch) (March 18, 2016). What standards should U.S. courts use to assess the information sharing rights of citizen journalists?

3. PUBLIC PERFORMANCE OF COPYRIGHTED WORKS

Copyright law has steadily expanded to give authors exclusive control over who can transform their work into derivative versions (via various forms of new technology), and who can publicly perform the work. Sports broadcasting in particular poses the question whether a business that simply turns on the television for its customers has publicly performed a game telecast and thereby infringed a copyright. The Copyright Act of 1976 says yes, broadly defining "public performance" to include performance or transmission of the work to "a place open to the public or at any place where a substantial number of persons outside of a normal circle of a family and its social acquaintances is gathered." 17 U.S.C. § 101. At the same time, though, Congress exempted from liability "communication of a transmission embodying a performance ... of a work by the public reception of the transmission on a single receiving apparatus of a kind commonly used in private homes." 17 U.S.C. § 110(5). This "home use" exemption covers the local candy store that plays an iPod on a speaker box, but not a sports bar that displays NFL games on eight screens on a Sunday afternoon.

The scope and limits of the "home use" exemption have complicated efforts of leagues and teams to enforce "blackout" rules designed to control which games are going into which markets. In *NFL v. McBee & Bruno's, Inc.*, 792 F.2d 726 (8th Cir. 1986), the National Football League sought to enforce blackout rules prohibiting telecasts of home games within the team's "home territory" (*i.e.*, a 75-mile radius) unless the game is sold out 72 hours in advance. St. Louis sports bars were using satellite dish antennae to intercept the raw signal of the local NFL team's game before it reached the broadcast network, and then displayed the blacked-out home game on television screens for customers. The Eighth Circuit held that the raw game feed was sufficiently "fixed" to merit copyright protection, and that displaying it was a public performance. The court rejected the bars' argument that their actions constituted a "home use," ruling that the type of apparatus used to receive the transmission was not "commonly found in private homes" at the time. Consider whether the decision would come out the same way today, when the same satellite apparatus enjoys widespread residential use.

Technological advances have muddied application of the "public performance" doctrine. In *NFL v. PrimeTime 24 Joint Venture,* 211 F.3d 10 (2d Cir. 2000), the Second Circuit upheld a district court's injunction against a satellite carrier that was picking up television signals of NFL games in the U.S. and then transmitting the games to cable companies and subscribers in Canada. PrimeTime held a statutory license to do that for American subscribers who did not have direct over-the-air broadcast reception, but this U.S. license did not apply to Canadian viewers. The court rejected PrimeTime's argument that the unlicensed "public performance" of the NFL's copyrighted material "does not occur until the signal is actually received by the viewing public" in their homes, and was therefore subject to Canadian rather than American copyright law. The Second Circuit ruled instead that "each step in the process by which a protected work wends its way to the audience," is part of the public performance, and that the key early "predicate act" of receiving and transmitting the signals took place south of the U.S.-Canadian border. Would the outcome be the same if a foreign carrier first picked up over-the-air signals from American stations of games in the U.S. by putting a large antenna just over the border in Canada, Mexico, or Cuba, and then transmitted these game signals to subscribers all over the world?

The NFL and NBA filed a similar copyright infringement claim against iCrave TV.com, a Canadian company that was also picking up over-the-air U.S. game signals, but webcast them across the border to Canadian fans. *NFL v. iCraveTV,* 53 U.S.P.Q.2d 1831 (W.D. Pa. Feb. 8, 2000). iCrave argued that Canadian law authorized the webcasts in Canada, and that it took adequate measures to avoid infringing U.S. copyrights by requiring users to enter a Canadian area code to verify their location. That, however, did not stop a significant number of American-based football fans from entering Canadian area codes. The court held that an extra-territorial actor can be held liable for an infringing public performance that occurs within the United States, and enjoined iCrave from transmitting its signal. This effectively barred iCrave's activities worldwide. With the internet enabling global webcasts, how should a court reconcile U.S. law with conflicting intellectual property protections abroad?

Equipment manufacturers and service providers continue their attempts to avoid the public performance doctrine, and corresponding liability for copyright infringement, through technological work-arounds. Aereo, Inc. was one such company, which sold a service that allowed its subscribers to view live and time-shifted streams of over-the-air television on internet-connected devices. It did so by leasing to each user an individual antenna and digital video recorder (DVR) situated in a remote warehouse that they could access over the internet. The existence of an individual antenna for each user distinguished Aereo from other services that retransmit or stream video content, including sports events, because it required subscriber intervention to select and play a program. The Supreme Court sharply divided over whether this distinction made a difference in an infringement lawsuit brought by a consortium of major broadcasters, including those that broadcast all the major U.S. sports.

AMERICAN BROADCASTING COMPANIES, INC. V. AEREO, INC.
134 S. Ct. 2498 (2014)

JUSTICE BREYER delivered the opinion of the Court.

The Copyright Act of 1976 gives a copyright owner the "exclusive righ[t]" to "perform the copyrighted work publicly." 17 U.S.C. § 106(4). The Act's Transmit Clause defines that exclusive right as including the right to

> "transmit or otherwise communicate a performance . . . of the [copyrighted] work . . . to the public, by means of any device or process, whether the members of the public capable of receiving the performance . . . receive it in the same place or in separate places and at the same time or at different times." § 101.

We must decide whether respondent Aereo, Inc., infringes this exclusive right by selling its subscribers a technologically complex service that allows them to watch television programs over the Internet at about the same time as the programs are broadcast over the air. We conclude that it does.

* * *

This case requires us to answer two questions: First, in operating in the manner described above, does Aereo "perform" at all? And second, if so, does Aereo do so "publicly"? We address these distinct questions in turn.

Does Aereo "perform"? . . . Phrased another way, does Aereo "transmit . . . a performance" when a subscriber watches a show using Aereo's system, or is it only the subscriber who transmits? . . .

* * *

[The court traced the judicial and legislative history that led to passage of the 1976 Copyright Act, which aligned cable systems with broadcasters who publicly perform copyrighted work and must pay for the right to do so, in the case of cable systems, through a compulsory licensing and royalty payment scheme.] This history makes clear that Aereo is not simply an equipment provider. Rather, Aereo, and not just its subscribers, "perform[s]" (or "transmit[s]"). Aereo's activities are substantially similar to those of the CATV companies that Congress amended the Act to reach. Aereo sells a service that allows subscribers to watch television programs, many of which are copyrighted, almost as they are being broadcast. In providing this service, Aereo uses its own equipment, housed in a centralized warehouse, outside of its users' homes. By means of its technology (antennas, transcoders, and servers), Aereo's system "receive[s] programs that have been released to the public and carr[ies] them by private channels to additional viewers." *Fortnightly* [*Corp. v. United Artists Television, Inc.*], 392 U.S. [390], 400 [1968]. It "carr[ies] . . . whatever programs [it] receive[s]," and it offers "all the programming" of each over-the-air station it carries. . . .

In other cases involving different kinds of service or technology providers, a user's involvement in the operation of the provider's equipment and selection of the content transmitted may well bear on whether the provider performs within the meaning of the Act. But the many similarities between Aereo and cable companies, considered in light of Congress' basic purposes in amending the Copyright Act, convince us that this difference is not critical here. We conclude that Aereo is not just an equipment supplier and that Aereo "perform[s]."

Next, we must consider whether Aereo performs petitioners' works "publicly," within the meaning of the Transmit Clause. Under the Clause, an entity performs a work publicly when it "transmit[s] . . . a performance . . . of the work . . . to the public." § 101. . . .

As we have said, an Aereo subscriber receives broadcast television signals with an antenna dedicated to him alone. Aereo's system makes from those signals a personal copy of the selected program. It streams the content of the copy to the same subscriber and to no one else. One and only one subscriber has the ability to see and hear each Aereo transmission. The fact that each transmission is to only one subscriber, in Aereo's view, means that it does not transmit a performance "to the public."

In terms of the Act's purposes, these differences do not distinguish Aereo's system from cable systems, which do perform "publicly." Viewed in terms of Congress' regulatory objectives, why should any of these technological differences matter? They concern the behind-the-scenes way in which Aereo delivers television programming to its viewers' screens. They do not render Aereo's commercial objective any different from that of cable companies. Nor do they significantly alter the viewing experience of Aereo's subscribers. Why would a subscriber who wishes to watch a television show care much whether images and sounds are delivered to his screen via a large multisubscriber antenna or one small dedicated antenna, whether they arrive instantaneously or after a few seconds' delay, or whether they are transmitted directly or after a personal copy is made? And why, if Aereo is right, could not modern CATV systems simply continue the same commercial and consumer-oriented activities, free of copyright restrictions, provided they substitute such new technologies for old? Congress would as much have intended to protect a copyright holder from the unlicensed activities of Aereo as from those of cable companies.

* * *

We do not see how the fact that Aereo transmits via personal copies of programs could make a difference. The Act applies to transmissions "by means of any device or process." And retransmitting a television program using user-specific copies is a "process" of transmitting a performance. A "cop[y]" of a work is simply a "material objec[t] . . . in which a work is fixed . . . and from which the work can be perceived, reproduced, or otherwise communicated." So whether Aereo transmits from the same or separate copies, it performs the same work; it shows the same images and makes audible the same sounds. Therefore, when Aereo streams the same television program to multiple subscribers, it "transmit[s] . . . a performance" to all of them.

Moreover, the subscribers to whom Aereo transmits television programs constitute "the public." Aereo communicates the same contemporaneously perceptible images and sounds to a large number of people who are unrelated and unknown to each other. This matters because, although the Act does not define "the public," it specifies that an entity performs publicly when it performs at "any place where a substantial number of persons outside of a normal circle of a family and its social acquaintances is gathered." The Act thereby suggests that "the public" consists of a large group of people outside of a family and friends.

Aereo and many of its supporting amici argue that to apply the Transmit Clause to Aereo's conduct will impose copyright liability on other technologies, including new technologies that Congress could not possibly have wanted to reach. We agree that Congress, while intending the Transmit Clause to apply broadly to cable companies and their equivalents, did not intend to discourage or to control the emergence or use of different kinds of technologies. But we do not believe that our limited holding today will have that effect.

* * *

JUSTICE SCALIA, with whom JUSTICE THOMAS and JUSTICE ALITO join dissenting.

This case is the latest skirmish in the long-running copyright battle over the delivery of television programming.

* * *

. . . Aereo does not provide a prearranged assortment of movies and television shows. Rather, it assigns each subscriber an antenna that—like a library card—can be used to obtain whatever broadcasts are freely available. Some of those broadcasts are copyrighted; others are in the public domain. The key point is that subscribers call all the shots: Aereo's automated system does not relay any program, copyrighted or not, until a subscriber selects the program and tells Aereo to relay it. Aereo's operation of that system is a volitional act and a but-for cause of the resulting performances, but, as in the case of the copy shop, that degree of involvement is not enough for direct liability.

* * *

III. Guilt By Resemblance

The Court's conclusion that Aereo performs boils down to the following syllogism: (1) Congress amended the Act to overrule our decisions holding that cable systems do not perform when they retransmit over-the-air broadcasts; (2) Aereo looks a lot like a cable system; therefore (3) Aereo performs.

* * *

. . . [W]hatever soothing reasoning the Court uses to reach its result ("this looks like cable TV"), the consequence of its holding is that someone who implements this technology "perform[s]" under that provision. That greatly disrupts settled jurisprudence which, before today, applied the straightforward, bright-line test of volitional conduct directed at the copyrighted work. If that test is not outcome determinative in this case, presumably it is not outcome determinative elsewhere as well. And it is not clear what the Court proposes to replace it. Perhaps the Court means to adopt (invent, really) a two-tier version of the Copyright Act, one part of which applies to "cable companies and their equivalents" while the other governs everyone else.

* * *

That leaves as the criterion of cable-TV-resemblance nothing but th'ol' totality-of-the-circumstances test (which is not a test at all but merely assertion of an intent to perform test-free, ad hoc, case-by-case evaluation). It will take years, perhaps decades, to determine which automated systems now in existence are governed by the traditional volitional-conduct test and which get the Aereo treatment. (And automated systems now in contemplation will have to take their chances.) The Court vows that its ruling will not affect cloud-storage providers and cable-television systems, but it cannot deliver on that promise given the imprecision of its result-driven rule. . . .

I share the Court's evident feeling that what Aereo is doing (or enabling to be done) to the Networks' copyrighted programming ought not to be allowed. . . . [W]hat we have before us must be considered a "loophole" in the law. It is not the role of this Court to identify and plug loopholes. It is the role of good lawyers to identify and exploit them, and the role of

Congress to eliminate them if it wishes. Congress can do that, I may add, in a much more targeted, better informed, and less disruptive fashion than the crude "looks-like-cable-TV" solution the Court invents today.

We came within one vote of declaring the VCR contraband 30 years ago in *Sony* [*Corp. of America v. Universal City Studios, Inc.*, 464 U.S. 417 (1984)]. The dissent in that case was driven in part by the plaintiffs' prediction that VCR technology would wreak all manner of havoc in the television and movie industries. . . . The Networks make similarly dire predictions about Aereo. We are told that nothing less than "the very existence of broadcast television as we know it" is at stake. Aereo and its amici dispute those forecasts and make a few of their own, suggesting that a decision in the Networks' favor will stifle technological innovation and imperil billions of dollars of investments in cloud-storage services. We are in no position to judge the validity of those self-interested claims or to foresee the path of future technological development. Hence, the proper course is not to bend and twist the Act's terms in an effort to produce a just outcome, but to apply the law as it stands and leave to Congress the task of deciding whether the Copyright Act needs an upgrade.

NOTES AND QUESTIONS

1. *The Cable System Analogy.* On remand to the district court, Aereo argued that it was entitled to continue its services as long as it complied with regulations governing cable system retransmission of television signals, which resolve infringement claims through a compulsory license-statutory royalty scheme (*see* Section B, Parts 4 and 5 below). The district court rejected this argument as "suffer[ing] from the fallacy that simply because an entity performs copyrighted works in a way similar to cable systems it must then be deemed a cable system for all other purposes of the Copyright Act." *Am. Broad. Companies, Inc. v. Aereo, Inc.*, No. 12-CV-1540, 2014 WL 5393867, at *3 (S.D.N.Y. Oct. 23, 2014). Following this ruling, Aereo ceased operations. Given that the Supreme Court elevated function over form in applying the public performance doctrine to Aereo, should the district court have treated Aereo as a cable system for all purposes of the Copyright Act?

2. *Amending the Copyright Act.* Justice Scalia's dissent disclaims judicial competence to foresee future technological development, instead relying on Congress to "upgrade" the Copyright Act to address advances such as internet retransmission services. How likely is it that Congress will take up this call? What do past Copyright Act amendments tell us about the ability of legislative solutions to keep pace with technology?

3. *Future Technological Innovation.* Has the *Aereo* ruling affected the future of cloud computing and other new technologies? Or is the holding sufficiently limited so that it is unlikely to have wider impact beyond Aereo's

specific methods? How can we tell? How much longer will *Aereo* be relevant considering the "cord-cutting" phenomenon in which sports television viewers are forgoing cable television subscriptions in favor of an alternative internet-based or wireless service?

4. PASSIVE CARRIER EXEMPTION TO PUBLIC PERFORMANCE

As alluded to in *Aereo*, the advent of cable television in the 1960s and 1970s raised issues under copyright law, sharpened by the retransmission of sports broadcasts. To explain, cable systems pay fees, usually per subscriber, to the television stations and networks they carry. Copyright owners of retransmitted shows demanded that cable systems also compensate them for publicly performing works that had been licensed only to the television station or network. When the Supreme Court rejected this claim, *see Fortnightly Corp. v. United Artists Television*, 392 U.S. 390 (1968), Congress stepped in with the 1976 revisions of the Copyright Act to strike a compromise.

First, Congress created a special "passive carrier exemption" for retransmission of broadcast signals by

> any carrier who has no direct or indirect control over the content or selection of the primary transmission or over the particular recipients of the secondary transmission, and whose activities with respect to the secondary transmission consist solely of providing wires, cable, or other communications channels for the use of others.

17 U.S.C. § 111(a)(3). This provision protected cable television systems that do nothing but receive and deliver an unaltered signal to the ultimate viewer, and exercise no control over the programming transmitted. *See NFL v. Insight Telecommunications Corp.*, 158 F. Supp. 2d 124 (D. Mass. 2001) (middleman that merely relayed unaltered signal from Boston television stations to Bell Canada not liable for subsequent transmission over border to Canadian cable subscribers). In effect, the passive carrier exemption amounts to a compulsory license from the owners of copyrighted television programming to the cable systems.

Second, Congress required cable systems to pay statutorily prescribed royalties into a Copyright Royalty Board, which annually distributes them to the copyright owners of sports broadcasts and other television shows. The statutory royalty scheme avoided cable systems needing to enter "unworkable separate negotiations with numerous copyright holders," and advanced the "public interest . . . in a continuing supply of varied programming to viewers." *Eastern Microwave, Inc. v. Doubleday Sports, Inc.*, 691 F.2d 125, 132 (2d Cir. 1982). While the statutory formula for royalty payments generated a total of $12 million in 1978, it produces about $300 million a year today.

Although the statutory royalty scheme simplified business for cable systems, it set copyright holders against each other as they annually petition the Board as to how this money should be divided up among the numerous copyright owners across multiple categories of programming. Sports leagues and teams are adamant that their programming has driven the growth of cable retransmission and subscriber fees, and that royalty payments should correspond to comparative market value and not sheer volume of programming. They have argued for weighing more heavily program ratings and the demographic makeup of the respective audiences, as measured by commercial advertiser preferences. Other categories of program suppliers, including movies and syndicated programs such as soap operas and game shows, prefer allocating funds based on the amount of airtime. Do you agree with the sports leagues' approach for distributing the statutory royalties? How does the "superstation" phenomenon, described below, affect your views?

5. SUPERSTATIONS AND THE COMPULSORY LICENSING-ROYALTY SCHEME

Independent local television stations with nationwide cable carriage have earned the sobriquet "superstation." In the early days of cable, this phenomenon disrupted relationships among sports rights owners and their television partners. Problems arose particularly in baseball and basketball, where most games air on local stations pursuant to copyright licenses from the local clubs. Contrast the NFL where the league centrally controls and manages most game broadcast licensing through national network contracts.

As might be expected, among the first independent local stations to become superstations were those that carried sports broadcasts. In the pre-internet era, superstations were a game-changer, *e.g.*, the White Sox fan who left Chicago to attend college in Boston or to retire to Florida could now follow her favorite team on television from anywhere in the country, rather than relying on newspaper box scores. At the time of the emergence of superstations, existing broadcast contracts with local teams set royalties corresponding to local over-the-air viewership. Most of these contracts had not anticipated cable retransmission and the corresponding windfall in station revenues (through increased advertising income and subscriber fees). In the *Eastern Microwave* case cited above, the New York Mets tried to tap into this windfall by suing a retransmitter of signals from broadcast stations to cable systems, but the court held that the retransmitter qualified as a passive carrier exempt from copyright under the 1976 Act. 691 F.2d at 130–31. While the Mets may have lost that initial legal battle, they ultimately won the economic war. As the contracts with superstations like WOR (or WGN, WPIX and KTVT) expired, the teams involved were able to negotiate new rights fees that reflected the higher economic value derived from their local station's new national market.

Crucial to that effort was Ted Turner, then owner of the most "super" of all superstations, WTBS in Atlanta, as well as Atlanta's baseball Braves and basketball Hawks. Turner developed new technology for transmitting the WTBS signal to cable systems throughout the country, by which he could remove the local advertising incorporated in the original programming in Atlanta, and sell separate commercial time to advertisers in the national market. Local stations in distant markets considered WTBS a threat for at least two reasons. First, they had to compete with WTBS sports broadcasts. Second, despite holding exclusive local licenses for broadcasting syndicated shows (*e.g.*, talk shows, game shows, soap operas), they had to compete with WTBS, which had the Atlanta license for those shows. The owner of television stations in Minneapolis, Albuquerque, and St. Petersburg challenged the compatibility of this new technology and broadcasting venture with the 1976 Copyright Act regime, arguing that WTBS was no longer entitled to the passive carrier exemption and cable stations that carry it cannot qualify for participation in the compulsory license scheme.

The Eight Circuit disagreed in *Hubbard Broadcasting, Inc. v. Southern Satellite Systems and TBS*, 777 F.2d 393 (8th Cir. 1985):

> ... Hubbard argues that Turner, by substituting commercials at the primary transmission stage, accomplishes indirectly what Congress has concluded cable systems cannot do directly. As a result, Hubbard contends that cable systems carrying WTBS cannot qualify for the compulsory license of section 111(c)(1) with respect to the WTBS transmission. We disagree.
>
> In adopting section 111(c)(3), Congress concluded that to allow cable television systems to alter the primary transmission by substituting commercials would significantly alter the basic nature of the cable retransmission service, and make its function similar to that of a broadcaster. Further, the placement of substitute advertising in a program by a cable system on a "local" signal harms the advertiser and, in turn, the copyright owner, whose compensation for the work is directly related to the size of the audience that the advertiser's message is calculated to reach. On a "distant" signal, the placement of substitute advertising harms the local broadcaster in the distant market because the cable system is then competing for local broadcasting dollars without having comparable programming costs. Consequently, Congress "attempted broadly to proscribe the availability of the

compulsory license if a cable system substitutes commercial messages."

Congress, in forbidding commercial substitution by cable systems, sought to ensure the competitive compatibility of the cable system and the local broadcaster. Cable systems, when retransmitting local signals, would retransmit exactly what was received and in so doing would neither undercut the local broadcaster's ability to generate local advertising revenues nor jeopardize the ability of creators of programming to receive a fair return for their product based upon the size of the audience that the advertiser's message was calculated to reach. In other words, the status quo relationship between local broadcasters and copyright holders would be protected and facilitated. With respect to distant signal retransmission, Congress sought to ensure that cable systems were not allowed, while claiming protection of the compulsory license, to compete for local advertising dollars without having to bear comparable programming costs. . . .

[W]e conclude that none of the concerns raised by Congress in adopting section 111(c)(3) are implicated by Turner's practices. WTBS, in placing only national advertising on the microwave signal, seeks to and in fact can economically address only the national advertising market. Turner cannot effectively address the local advertising markets served by Hubbard. Thus, Turner does not compete with Hubbard for local advertising dollars.

Further, to the extent Turner and Hubbard compete for national advertising dollars, that competition will exist regardless of Turner's current practices since even absent the microwave signal, Turner's UHF signal will continue to reach a national market and carry national advertising. And, unlike a cable system that substitutes commercials without bearing programming costs, Turner has the same types of programming costs as Hubbard.

Finally, we also conclude that Turner's development of two separate WTBS signals has no adverse impact on the interests of the copyright holders. These individuals or companies, when contracting with Turner, know that WTBS signals will be available nationwide as well as locally and are entirely free to take those steps necessary to assure that they are compensated accordingly. At bottom, no copyright holder is deceived by the extent of Turner's market or the commercial content of the signals; no advertiser reaches a smaller market than anticipated; and no local broadcaster is forced to compete with Turner on any greater level than would exist absent Turner's transmission of two television signals.

We affirm the district court's dismissal of Hubbard's action.

NOTES AND QUESTIONS

1. *Copyright Legislation and Technological Change.* As technology has advanced, courts have struggled to apply the Copyright Act, which has been criticized as too fact-specific and lacking provisions that articulate more general principles. One principle the *Hubbard* court was able to identify is that compulsory licenses are available only to truly passive carriers, and not to a cable system that substitutes commercial messages. Do you agree with the *Hubbard* court that Turner's commercial substitution in its national WTBS feed did not raise the concerns the Act sought to address? What does this decision tell you about the tension between the Copyright Act's twin goals of stimulating artistic creativity and making such works available to the public?

2. *League Restraints on Superstations.* What about league rules that purport to regulate cable retransmission, which we read about in Chapter 7 in connection with the NBA's attempt to limit Chicago Bulls broadcasts on WGN? Compare Major League Baseball's rules in the early 1980s, which permitted baseball teams in the playoffs to broadcast their games on their local channels, but sold to a network (for a large fee) the exclusive right to national broadcasts. When the Braves made the 1982 National League playoffs, was either MLB or ABC entitled to block WTBS's retransmission of Braves' playoff games across the country? From the point of view of the "best interests" of the league, what do you think should be MLB's policy about whether any games should be telecast on superstations, and if so, how the revenues should be allocated?

3. *Market Solutions.* Given the pace of technology, should we prefer the free market to generate solutions for compensating creators, rather than rely on periodic legislative updates of copyright laws? Are there any practical obstacles in the way of sports teams (or copyright owners of other programs) negotiating agreements for the showing of their events on cable or the internet? Any differences from the *New Boston-ESPN* case we saw earlier about game highlights on the news? Precisely what kinds of economic losses does a team or league suffer by not being able to withhold its consent to internet streaming of its games? Are these the kinds of losses that the law should compensate?

C. ATHLETE PUBLICITY RIGHTS

Public interest in sports has translated into celebrity for athletes, and even coaches and other sports personalities. Companies have turned to elite athletes like LeBron James, Serena Williams, Cristiano Ronaldo, and Tiger Woods, to promote all categories of consumer products and services, from athletic equipment and apparel to car insurance. Celebrity has enabled elite athletes to match or exceed their playing salaries with revenue from endorsement contracts. Athletes who are most successful in selling their name, image, and identity are those who carefully cultivate a public persona and strategically develop multiple brand relationships. Although the vast majority of professional athletes cannot earn substantial sums from licensing publicity rights individually, players associations have proven adept at facilitating collective licensing of publicity rights that permit ordinary players to earn supplementary income in this way.

To protect the commercial value of their image and fame, athletes rely on state law rights of publicity, including the right to: (a) protect their reputation from association with uncongenial goods and services, and (b) exclusively authorize the use of their name and likeness for commercial purposes. Although the nature and scope of publicity rights vary considerably from state to state, they all are limited by First Amendment freedoms of speech and expression. This section will explore the origins and scope of the right of publicity, and the most common defenses to a publicity-right infringement claim.

1. ORIGINS OF THE RIGHT OF PUBLICITY

State right-of-publicity laws have their origins in the tort of defamation and in the common law right to privacy. Defamation law has long created liability for statements about anyone that are false and injurious. But defamation suits are difficult to win, especially for athletes who as public figures face a heavier burden of proof. *See New York Times v. Sullivan,* 376 U.S. 254 (1964). In addition, most commentary on athletic performance comprises opinion, which is not legally actionable even if it harms an athlete's reputation. *See Time, Inc. v. Johnston,* 448 F.2d 378, 380 (4th Cir. 1971) (derogatory description of former professional basketball player's on-court performance not actionable, even though published nine years after he retired, because he remained a public figure who assumed the risk of good or bad publicity about his public performance); *Turner v. Wells,* 879 F.3d 1254, 1271 (11th Cir. 2018) (law firm investigatory report describing conduct of professional football coach is nonactionable opinion because statements are a "subjective assessment of [the coach's] conduct ... not readily capable of being proven true or false"). Another limitation of defamation law is that it does not cover situations where an athlete's name or likeness is merely being associated with a product, without a false statement of endorsement or quantifiable harm.

Accordingly, athletes and other celebrities initially sought to control use of their name and likeness through privacy torts, which fall into one of four categories: (1) intrusion upon seclusion or solitude; (2) public disclosure of embarrassing private facts; (3) publicity which places a person in a false light in the public eye; and (4) appropriation of name or likeness. *See* William Prosser, *Privacy,* 48 Cal. L. Rev. 383, 389 (1960). The first three categories address intrusions into one's private life and affairs, and courts generally recognize that even a celebrity is entitled to some degree of personal privacy. Thus, in *Jason Pierre-Paul v. ESPN*, 2016 WL 4530884 (S.D. Fla. Aug. 29, 2016), the court allowed a professional football player to pursue invasion of privacy claims against a media company and its reporter who disclosed medical information about the player's hand injury from a fireworks mishap. The *Pierre-Paul* court held that even legitimate public interest in a celebrity athlete's medical condition must yield to limits on publication of private facts imposed by "common decency" and "regard to the feelings of the individual." *See also Bollea v. Gawker Media LLC*, 2016 WL 4073660 (Fla. Cir. Ct. June 8, 2016) (online media company required to pay $140 million in damages to former professional wrestler Hulk Hogan for publishing unauthorized sextape); *Erin Andrews v. Marriott International Inc.*, No. 11C-4831 (Tenn. Cir. Ct. Mar. 7, 2016) (jury awarded sports reporter $55 million in damages when hotel peeping Tom posted nude videos of her on the internet); *Spahn v. Julian Messner, Inc.*, 21 N.Y.2d 124, 233 N.E.2d 840 (1967) (unauthorized falsified biography of baseball player violated statutory right to privacy).

As for the fourth privacy tort—misappropriation of name or likeness—early on celebrities who advanced such claims encountered resistance from the courts, which doubted whether protection should extend to athletes who had actively sought fame. Thus, David O'Brien, a legendary college and professional football player who had moral objections to drinking or endorsing beer was unable to stop a brewery from using his photo in its annual football calendar containing game schedules. *See O'Brien v. Pabst Sales*, 124 F.2d 167 (5th Cir. 1941). The court ruled that because O'Brien had freely permitted past publicity uses of his picture, he had no right of privacy to stop Pabst's use which, in the absence of a statement that he endorsed the beer, "could not possibly disgrace or reflect upon or cause him damage." *Id.* at 170–71. Do you agree that Pabst's use of O'Brien's picture could not possibly injure him? What if, as was alleged, O'Brien was a member of a temperance group and the calendar caused him great embarrassment and humiliation?

A decade later, a U.S. court dramatically altered the legal playing field in another sports-related case. In *Haelan Laboratories v. Topps Chewing Gum*, 202 F.2d 866 (2d Cir. 1953), two firms had signed agreements with baseball players authorizing use of their names and pictures on bubblegum trading cards. Haelan, the firm with the first and supposedly "exclusive" license to that effect, sued Topps for inducing breach of its contract. Topps' defense was that both sets of contracts amounted to no more than the players' release from liability for invasion of privacy, and no separate "name and likeness" property right existed. The Second Circuit disagreed, identifying an independent and assignable common law right to the publicity value of one's name and picture:

> [I]t is common knowledge that many prominent persons (especially actors and ball-players), far from having their feelings

bruised through public exposure of their likenesses, would feel sorely deprived if they no longer received money for authorizing advertisements, popularizing their countenances, displayed in newspapers, magazines, busses, trains and subways. This right of publicity would usually yield them no money unless it could be made the subject of an exclusive grant which barred any other advertiser from using their pictures.

202 F.2d at 868.

This new brand of intellectual property heralded the transformation of the Major League Baseball Players Association into a real union. After *Haelen*, the Players Association took over the sale of baseball card licenses and other group marketing efforts by the players, funding a war chest that enabled tough stances at the collective bargaining table, as we saw in the chapters on labor law. Annual group licensing revenue for the major league players associations has swelled, by 2018 reaching over $40 million for the MLBPA, and over $150 million for the NFL Players Association. Indeed, a by-product of this combination of law and economics is that the Internal Revenue Service maintains that the descendible publicity right is a taxable asset in a dead celebrity's estate. *See Estate of Andrews v. United States*, 850 F. Supp. 1279 (E.D. Va.1994). Settling divisions among courts, many states now recognize that the right of publicity is descendible.

In the 65 years since *Haelan*, over 40 states have established—either through judicial pronouncement or legislative enactment—at least a narrow right to recover for misappropriation of celebrity. The Restatement (Third) of Unfair Competition § 46 defines an infringer of the right of publicity as "[o]ne who appropriates the commercial value of a person's identity by using without consent the person's name, likeness, or other indicia of identity for purposes of trade." However, states vary widely in their articulation of the elements of a publicity-right infringement claim.

2. IDENTIFIABILITY OF THE PUBLICITY-RIGHT OWNER

To vindicate a publicity right, the celebrity must show, at a minimum, that she is identifiable in the commercial promotion of a product or service. The question of "identifiability" has been answered broadly to include situations where the public would identify the celebrity even if a name or picture is not used. Consider the *Sports Illustrated* 1994 swimsuit edition, which ran an advertisement for Killian's Red Beer using a drawing of an old-time baseball game with a pitcher in an unusual windup position. Long-retired pitcher Don Newcombe was well known to fans of his era as the only player to use that peculiar style of windup. The Ninth Circuit ruled under California statutory and common law that Newcombe, who was a recovering alcoholic and upset that his identity was used to promote beer, had a triable claim for publicity right infringement. *See Newcombe v. Adolf Coors Co.*, 157 F.3d 686 (9th Cir. 1998). Is this the right result considering that the ad ran 34 years after Newcombe retired from baseball, did not show his jersey number or face, and did not depict any particular team's uniform or stadium?

Other cases address the identifiability issue in connection with:

(i) *Nicknames and Catchphrases.* Playgirl Magazine published a stylized drawing of a nude black male seated with his gloved hands on the ropes in the corner of a boxing ring, accompanied with lascivious verse that referred to the figure as "the Greatest." The court found sufficient facial resemblance to Mohammed Ali, when coupled with use of Ali's well-known appellation, to violate the fighter's publicity rights. *See Ali v. Playgirl*, 447 F. Supp. 723 (S.D.N.Y. 1978). The court also emphasized that the illustration contained no "informational or newsworthy dimension." Should such content change the analysis? *See also Johnny Carson v. Here's Johnny Portable Toilets*, 698 F.2d 831 (6th Cir. 1983) (talk show host Johnny Carson prevailed on claim against portable toilet manufacturer's use of phrases "Here's Johnny" and "The World's Foremost Commodian"); *Hirsch v. S.C. Johnson & Son, Inc.*, 90 Wis. 2d 379, 280 N.W.2d 129 (1979) (football great Elroy "Crazylegs" Hirsch prevailed on claim against "Crazylegs" women's shaving gel).

(ii) *Abandoned Name.* Basketball great Kareem Abdul-Jabbar sued for a violation of his publicity rights when General Motors used his former name, Lew Alcindor, in a car commercial. The court held that Abdul-Jabbar did not abandon the name and that the California statute's reference to "name or likeness" is a "flexible proposition" that includes indicia of identity beyond one's current use. *Abdul-Jabbar v. General Motors Corp.*, 75 F.3d 1391, 1399–1400 (9th Cir. 1996). Should it matter that the car commercial used the name Lew Alcindor in the context of an informational trivia quiz about his legendary college basketball achievements?

(iii) *Distinctive Attributes.* A cigarette commercial showed several racing cars at the track, including one that resembled the car of famed driver Lothar Motschenbacher, with its solid red color and narrow white pinstripe. Although the commercial altered Motschenbacher's car number, the court found a publicity right violation because the "distinctive decorations appearing on the car" were sufficient to cause "persons to think the car in question was plaintiff's and to infer that the person driving the car was the plaintiff." *Motschenbacher v. R.J. Reynolds Tobacco*, 498 F.2d 821, 826–27 (9th Cir. 1974); *see also Midler v. Ford Motor Co.*, 849 F.2d 460, 461 (9th Cir. 1988) (Bette Midler stated viable publicity rights claim against car company's use of "sound-alike" singer in television commercial). Would the court have reached this result if the product were not as controversial as cigarettes? *See White v. Samsung Elec. Am., Inc.*, 971 F.2d

1395 (9th Cir. 1992) (robot dressed and posed like Vanna White next to "Wheel of Fortune" set sufficiently identified her to state publicity rights claim).

3. SCOPE OF THE COMMON LAW RIGHT OF PUBLICITY

To recover on a common law right of publicity claim, the plaintiff typically must show that the defendant's commercial appropriation of plaintiff's identity somehow resulted in injury to plaintiff. Early cases focused on the unauthorized use of a celebrity's image for the purpose of false endorsement of or association with a good or service. The right has expanded over time, however, to protect celebrity status itself. Thus, LeBron James sought to stop a brewery from "benefitting" from his image when it retweeted a viral photo of the great basketball player taken when he jokingly swiped a "Dortmunder Gold" beer bottle from a surprised courtside server during a playoff game. Despite the photo remaining ubiquitous on social media, the brewery agreed to delete its tweet, which had added the caption "G.O.A.T. with G.O.L.D." (The first set of initials stands for "greatest of all time.") Should the law recognize and compensate this type of "injury"? Does it make a difference that the brewery's retweet added a caption? It has been argued that a celebrity's image is a public good that is infinitely consumable without being depleted, and thus James suffered no harm here. Conversely, it has been argued that a celebrity is harmed by over-exposure or low-quality exposure of his identity. Does that argument carry weight in the internet age?

One justification for the right of publicity is that every person is entitled to the fruit of her labors. *See* Melville B. Nimmer, *The Right of Publicity*, 19 Law & Contemp. Probs. 215–16 (1954). Accordingly, a celebrity is entitled to the value of her persona because she has expended considerable time, effort, skill, and resources to develop it. This theory underpins the ruling in *Uhlaender v. Henricksen*, 316 F. Supp. 1277 (D. Minn. 1970). The *Uhlaender* court upheld the MLB Players Association's publicity rights claim against the "Negamco's Major League Baseball" board game, which used the names and statistics of over 500 professional ballplayers, identified by team, uniform number, and playing positions. In a forerunner of today's fantasy sports contests, the game used playing statistics to provide computations of the relative value of players and to determine board game outcomes. In finding that a celebrity has a "legitimate proprietary interest in his public personality," the court noted:

> A celebrity must be considered to have invested his years of practice and competition in a public personality which eventually may reach marketable status. That identity, embodied in his name, likeness, statistics and other personal characteristics, is the fruit of his labors and is a type of property.

Id. at 1282. The court further held that this property interest required enjoining the unauthorized use of players' names and statistics. Must one be a celebrity to be entitled to this property right?

Other courts favoring the right of publicity have emphasized the prevention of unjust enrichment. Thus, in the Bette Midler case cited above, the district court judge described the car company's conduct in using a sound-alike singer as that "of the average thief." 849 F.2d at 462. How can you tell when an unauthorized user of celebrity identity has been enriched in a way that is unjust? Alternatively, courts have enforced publicity rights as necessary to create economic incentives to acquire the skills and talents that generate fame, as in the *Zacchini* case. But, as one commentator suggests:

> Practically any creation of a private property right will increase the incentive of the holder to develop the underlying resource. Nevertheless, in many situations in which development incentives would be strengthened, the courts nonetheless refuse to create a private right. For instance, there might be more new football plays if courts enforced rights over them. Nevertheless, these rights do not exist.

Mark F. Grady, *A Positive Economic Theory of the Right of Publicity*, 1 UCLA Ent. L. Rev. 97, 111 (1994). Critics of the right of publicity argue that "allowing celebrities to control the meanings of their constructed personas deprives us all of the ability to 'recode' or reinterpret these texts for our own personal expression." Roberta Rosenthal Kwall, *Fame*, 73 Ind. L.J. 1, 3 (1997). Professor Kwall further notes that intellectual property regimes are particularly fertile ground for exploration of a "fundamental issue pertinent to all forms of property ownership[:] what should be the appropriate degree of public access to private property." As discussed below, cases presenting conflicts with the First Amendment provide some answers.

4. FIRST AMENDMENT AND THE RIGHT OF PUBLICITY: INTRODUCTION

While the right of publicity has proven a financial bonanza for elite athletes, it raises public policy questions when enforcement of one person's publicity right restrains another's freedom of speech. Copyright law justifies that restraint as necessary to create incentives for more speech. But publicity rights provide no such incentive. To the contrary, restricting the use of celebrity identities impedes the communication of ideas.

The Supreme Court addressed this tension in *Zacchini v. Scripps-Howard Broadcasting*, 433 U.S. 562 (1977). As noted earlier, Hugo "the Flying" Zacchini performed a "human cannonball" act in which he was shot from a cannon in a fenced-in area of the county fair. A local television station sent a reporter to the fair to videotape Zacchini's fifteen-second act, and then showed the entire performance on its newscast. By a narrow 5–4 majority, the Supreme Court held that enforcement of Zacchini's publicity rights under Ohio state law did not abridge the television station's First Amendment rights:

> The broadcast of a film of petitioner's entire act poses a substantial threat to the economic value of that performance.... [T]his act is the product of [Zacchini's] own talents and energy, the end result of much time, effort, and expense. Much of its economic value lies in the "right of exclusive control over the publicity given to his performance": if the public can see the act free on television, it will be less willing to pay to see it at the fair.... [T]he broadcast of petitioner's entire performance, unlike the unauthorized use of another's name for purposes of trade ... goes to the heart of petitioner's ability to earn a living as an entertainer.

433 U.S. at 575–76.

The *Zacchini* case differs in two key respects from *Haelan* and its successors. First, as the dissent emphasized, this case involved a newscast, worthy of far greater constitutional protection than commercial marketing. Second, as the majority accentuated, this broadcast was not simply an "appropriation of an entertainer's reputation to enhance the attractiveness of a commercial product, but the appropriation of the very activity by which the entertainer acquired his reputation in the first place." Like the judge in *Pittsburgh Athletic*, the Court was concerned that the latter form of appropriation would dilute the performer's economic incentives to make the necessary investment in developing the skills and appeal required for an entertainment performance that the public would watch and enjoy. Does *Zacchini* suggest that publicity rights require a balancing of the athlete's economic interests against the public's right to newsworthy information?

Consider these sports cases that explore the First Amendment limits on celebrity publicity rights:

(i) *Parody and the First Amendment.* "Cardtoons" were self-described "parody" trading cards featuring caricatures of major league baseball players who were readily identifiable despite pseudonyms that lampooned their public persona and teams (*e.g.*, Treasury Bonds for Barry Bonds, and Los Angeles Codgers for Dodgers). Language on the cards expressly disclaimed any official endorsement. Relying on the First Amendment, the Tenth Circuit dismissed the MLBPA's publicity right claim, distinguishing this branch of intellectual property as less deserving of protection, especially in the case of celebrity parodies that offer important social commentary. The court rejected the athletes' economic justifications for enforcing their publicity rights because "the commercial value of their identities are merely a by-product of their performance values," and the cards would not displace athletes' commercial opportunities given how unlikely it was that MLBPA would license self-parody. *Cardtoons v. MLB Players Association*, 95 F.3d 959, 972–75 (10th Cir. 1996). Why was Cardtoons allowed to continue operating when, as we read earlier, player publicity-right claims forced the Negamco MLB board game out of business?

(ii) *Use for Purposes of Advertising or Trade.* When is the commercial use of a celebrity athlete's name or identity protected by the First Amendment as sufficiently informational or newsworthy, as opposed to primarily for purposes of trade? See *Titan Sports v. Comics World*, 870 F.2d 85 (2d Cir. 1989) (whether First Amendment protects a magazine's insertion of glossy, oversized posters of professional wrestlers depends on whether magazine used photos for "purposes of trade"). In *Montana v. San Jose Mercury News*, 34 Cal. App. 4th 790, 40 Cal. Rptr. 2d 639 (1995), the San Jose Mercury published a special Souvenir Section of the newspaper to celebrate the San Francisco 49ers' fourth Super Bowl victory. An artistic rendition of quarterback Joe Montana appeared with reportage on the section's front page, which the Mercury later reprinted in poster form and sold for $5. Montana then sued the Mercury, not challenging the original newspaper picture and story, but just the poster reprint featuring his likeness. His claim failed on two grounds: (1) the posters reported newsworthy items of public interest and (2) a newspaper has a constitutional right to promote itself by reproducing its news stories.

Compare *Jordan v. Jewel Food Stores, Inc.*, 743 F.3d 509 (7th Cir. 2014), in which Michael Jordan sued Jewel Food, a Chicago grocery store, over an ad in *Sports Illustrated*'s commemorative issue, congratulating the athlete on his induction into the pro basketball hall of fame. The ad displayed basketball shoes bearing Jordan's number 23, and saluted "a fellow Chicagoan who was just around the corner for so many years," echoing the store's slogan, "good things are just around the corner." In rejecting the First Amendment defense and remanding the claim for trial, the Seventh Circuit ruled the ad "is no less 'commercial' because it promotes brand awareness or loyalty," rather than specifically proposing a commercial transaction. *Id.* at 518. Jewel Food settled with Jordan rather than go to trial, but a similar case against another Chicago grocery chain that had advertised in the commemorative issue resulted in an $8.9 million verdict for Jordan, an amount based in part on his standard endorsement contract value. See *Jordan v. Dominick's Finer Foods*, 2015 WL 5086730 (N.D. Ill. Aug. 25, 2015). Does this amount fairly reflect the injury to Jordan? What factors should determine whether a communication about an athlete's achievements has a sufficient economic motivation to defeat the speaker's First Amendment rights? See *Abdul-Jabbar v. General Motors Corp.*, 75 F.3d 1391, 1299–1400 (9th Cir. 1996) (publicity rights claim can go forward against car advertisement that incorporated trivia quiz about former basketball player's award-winning play).

(iii) *Artistic Expression.* NHL player Tony Twist earned notoriety as a brutal enforcer, inspiring the violent, Mafia-themed comic book *Spawn* to introduce a new character named "Anthony 'Tony Twist' Twistelli" who committed the most heinous crimes. While the only evident resemblance between the comic book character and the real Tony Twist was their name, the creator repeatedly told the media that he borrowed the name from the hockey player. When the real Twist learned of this, he sued claiming violation of his publicity rights through a defamatory misappropriation of his name. In *Doe, a/k/a Tony Twist v. TCI Cablevision*, 110 S.W.3d 363 (Mo. 2003), the Missouri Supreme Court ruled that the First Amendment did not immunize *Spawn*, because it used Twist's identity primarily for commercial benefit, not as a vehicle for artistic expression. The court observed:

> Twist made a submissible case that respondents' use of his name and identity was for a commercial advantage. Nonetheless, there is still an expressive component in the use of his name and identity as a metaphorical reference to tough-guy "enforcers." And yet, respondents agree (perhaps to avoid a defamation claim) that the use was not a parody or other expressive comment or a fictionalized account of the real Twist. As such, the metaphorical reference to Twist, though a literary device, has very little literary value compared to its commercial value. On the record here, the use and identity of Twist's name has become predominantly a ploy to sell comic books and related products rather than an artistic or literary expression, and under these circumstances, free speech must give way to the right of publicity.

Id. at 374.

On remand, the jury awarded $15 million in damages to Twist. An appellate court upheld the verdict based on evidence that the "predominant purpose" for using the "Tony Twist" name was "commercial gain," not "artistic expression," including evidence that *Spawn* specifically marketed its products to hockey fans. 207 S.W.3d 52, 59 (Mo. Ct. App. 2006). What are your views about the right of an author to use any celebrity names for his evil or heroic characters? Do you agree with the court that the proper measures of damages in this right of publicity case should include both emotional as well as financial harm *Spawn* inflicted on Twist?

The Masters golf tournament was the occasion for another court to balance the First Amendment right of free expression against a celebrity's right not to have his or her name or identity exploited for commercial purposes. "Sports artist" Rick Rush created a painting entitled *The Masters of Augusta* that depicted Tiger Woods mid-swing, with six other golf greats, including Jack Nicklaus and Arnold Palmer, looking down on him. Jireh Publishing Company then sold 700 serigraph prints for $700 each, and many more small lithographs for $15 apiece. Woods, who for several years had earned over $70 million from endorsements annually, sued claiming violation of both his trademark and publicity rights in his work and image.

ETW CORP. v. JIREH PUBLISHING, INC.
332 F.3d 915 (6th Cir. 2003)

GRAHAM, DISTRICT JUDGE.

* * *

II. *Trademark Claims Based on the Unauthorized Use of the Registered Trademark "Tiger Woods"*

* * *

ETW claims that Jireh infringed the registered mark "Tiger Woods" by including these words in marketing materials which accompanied the prints of Rush's painting. The words "Tiger Woods" do not appear on the face of the prints, nor are they included in the title of the painting. The words "Tiger Woods" do appear under the flap of the envelopes which contain the prints, and Woods is mentioned twice in the narrative which accompanies the prints.

The Lanham Act provides a defense to an infringement claim where the use of the mark "is a use, otherwise than as a mark, ... which is descriptive of and used fairly and in good faith only to describe the goods ... of such party [.]" 15 U.S.C. § 1115(b)(4). In evaluating a defendant's fair use defense, a court must consider whether defendant has used the mark: (1) in its descriptive sense; and (2) in good faith.

A celebrity's name may be used in the title of an artistic work so long as there is some artistic relevance. The use of Woods's name on the back of the envelope containing the print and in the narrative description of the print are purely descriptive and there is nothing to indicate that they were used other than in good faith. The prints, the envelopes which contain them, and the narrative materials which accompany them clearly identify Rush as the source of the print. Woods is mentioned only to describe the content of the print.

The district court properly granted summary judgment on ETW's claim for violation of its registered mark, "Tiger Woods," on the grounds that the claim was barred by the fair use defense as a matter of law.

III. *Trademark Claims Under 15 U.S.C. § 1125(a) Based on the Unauthorized Use of the Likeness of Tiger Woods*

* * *

Here, ETW claims protection under the Lanham Act for any and all images of Tiger Woods. This is an untenable claim. ETW asks us, in effect, to constitute Woods himself as a walking, talking trademark. Images and likenesses of Woods are not protectable as a trademark because they do not perform the trademark function of designation. They do not distinguish and identify the source of goods. They cannot function as a trademark because there are undoubtedly thousands of images and likenesses of Woods taken by countless photographers, and drawn, sketched, or painted by numerous artists, which have been published in many forms of media, and sold and distributed throughout the world. No reasonable person could believe that merely because these photographs or paintings contain Woods's likeness or image, they all originated with Woods.

We hold that, as a general rule, a person's image or likeness cannot function as a trademark. . . .

Here, ETW does not claim that a particular photograph of Woods has been consistently used on specific goods. Instead, ETW's claim is . . . a sweeping claim to trademark rights in every photograph and image of Woods. Woods, like [Babe] Ruth, is one of the most photographed sports figures of his generation, but this alone does not suffice to create a trademark claim.

The district court properly granted summary judgment on ETW's claim of trademark rights in all images and likenesses of Tiger Woods.

IV. *Ohio Right to Privacy Claims, and the First Amendment Defense*

* * *

B. *First Amendment Defense*

The protection of the First Amendment is not limited to written or spoken words, but includes other mediums of expression, including music, pictures, films, photographs, paintings, drawings, engravings, prints, and sculptures. Speech is protected even though it is carried in a form that is sold for profit. The fact that expressive materials are sold does not diminish the degree of protection to which they are entitled under the First Amendment. Publishers disseminating the work of others who create expressive materials also come wholly within the protective shield of the First Amendment. Even pure commercial speech is entitled to significant First Amendment protection.

Rush's prints are not commercial speech. They do not propose a commercial transaction. Accordingly, they are entitled to the full protection of the First Amendment. Thus, we are called upon to decide whether

Woods's intellectual property rights must yield to Rush's First Amendment rights.

* * *

E. *Application of the Law to the Evidence in this Case*

The evidence in the record reveals that Rush's work consists of much more than a mere literal likeness of Woods. It is a panorama of Woods's victory at the 1997 Masters Tournament, with all of the trappings of that tournament in full view, including the Augusta clubhouse, the leader board, images of Woods's caddy, and his final round partner's caddy. These elements in themselves are sufficient to bring Rush's work within the protection of the First Amendment. The Masters Tournament is probably the world's most famous golf tournament and Woods's victory in the 1997 tournament was a historic event in the world of sports. A piece of art that portrays a historic sporting event communicates and celebrates the value our culture attaches to such events. It would be ironic indeed if the presence of the image of the victorious athlete would deny the work First Amendment protection. Furthermore, Rush's work includes not only images of Woods and the two caddies, but also carefully crafted likenesses of six past winners of the Masters Tournament: Arnold Palmer, Sam Snead, Ben Hogan, Walter Hagen, Bobby Jones, and Jack Nicklaus, a veritable pantheon of golf's greats. Rush's work conveys the message that Woods himself will someday join that revered group.

* * *

In regard to the Ohio law right of publicity claim, we conclude that Ohio would construe its right of publicity as suggested in the Restatement (Third) of Unfair Competition, Chapter 4, Section 47, Comment d., which articulates a rule analogous to the rule of fair use in copyright law. Under this rule, the substantiality and market effect of the use of the celebrity's image is analyzed in light of the informational and creative content of the defendant's use. Applying this rule, we conclude that Rush's work has substantial informational and creative content which outweighs any adverse effect on ETW's market and that Rush's work does not violate Woods's right of publicity.

We further find that Rush's work is expression which is entitled to the full protection of the First Amendment and not the more limited protection afforded to commercial speech. When we balance the magnitude of the speech restriction against the interest in protecting Woods's intellectual property right, we encounter precisely the same considerations weighed by the Tenth Circuit in *Cardtoons* [*L.C. v. Major League Baseball Players Ass'n,* 95 F.3d 959 (10th Cir. 1996)]. These include consideration of the fact that through their pervasive presence in the media, sports and entertainment celebrities have come to symbolize certain ideas and values in our society and have become a valuable means of expression in our culture. As the Tenth Circuit observed "[c]elebrities ... are an important element of the shared communicative resources of our cultural domain." *Cardtoons,* 95 F.3d at 972.

In balancing these interests against Woods's right of publicity, we note that Woods, like most sports and entertainment celebrities with commercially valuable identities, engages in an activity, professional golf, that in itself generates a significant amount of income which is unrelated to his right of publicity. Even in the absence of his right of publicity, he would still be able to reap substantial financial rewards from authorized appearances and endorsements. It is not at all clear that the appearance of Woods's likeness in artwork prints which display one of his major achievements will reduce the commercial value of his likeness.

While the right of publicity allows celebrities like Woods to enjoy the fruits of their labors, here Rush has added a significant creative component of his own to Woods's identity. Permitting Woods's right of publicity to trump Rush's right of freedom of expression would extinguish Rush's right to profit from his creative enterprise.

After balancing the societal and personal interests embodied in the First Amendment against Woods's property rights, we conclude that the effect of limiting Woods's right of publicity in this case is negligible and significantly outweighed by society's interest in freedom of artistic expression.

Finally, applying the transformative effects test adopted by the Supreme Court of California in *Comedy III* [*Productions, Inc. v. Gary Saderup, Inc.,* 25 Cal.4th 387, 21 P.3d 797 (2001)], we find that Rush's work does contain significant transformative elements which make it especially worthy of First Amendment protection and also less likely to interfere with the economic interest protected by Woods' right of publicity. Unlike the unadorned, nearly photographic reproduction of the faces of The Three Stooges in *Comedy III*, Rush's work does not capitalize solely on a literal depiction of Woods. Rather, Rush's work consists of a collage of images in addition to Woods's image which are combined to describe, in artistic form, a historic event in sports history and to convey a message about the significance of Woods's achievement in that event. Because Rush's work has substantial transformative elements, it is entitled to the full protection of the First Amendment. In this case, we find that Woods's right of publicity must yield to the First Amendment.

* * *

Dismissal Affirmed.

NOTES AND QUESTIONS

1. *Judicial Balancing.* The Missouri Supreme Court in the Tony Twist case and the Sixth Circuit in the Tiger Woods case reached exactly opposite conclusions. The first determined that *Spawn's* use of Tony Twist's name was primarily commercial and thus not entitled to First Amendment protection, while the second concluded that Rick Rush's use of Tiger Woods' image in the painting was expressive, non-commercial, and thus protected. Is there something about the use of Woods' image that made it more worthy of constitutional immunity than the use of Twist's name in a comic book, or do the opinions simply reflect different judicial views about the balance between the right of publicity and the First Amendment?

2. *Economic Justification for Publicity Rights.* As in *Cardtoons*, the court in the Tiger Woods case discounts the economic value of publicity rights for an athlete who "engages in an activity, professional golf, that in itself generates a significant amount of income which is unrelated to his right of publicity." Why is the rights owner's wealth or alternative sources of income relevant to the balance between the First Amendment and the right of publicity? Is a wealthy rights owner less entitled to exploit his copyrights, trademarks, or publicity rights than a needier rights owner, or is this factor only relevant in cases involving celebrity rights of publicity?

3. *Consumer Welfare Concerns.* The redistribution of wealth inherent in recognition of the athlete's publicity right has made it correspondingly more expensive for fans to enjoy collecting baseball cards, wearing basketball sneakers, and swinging golf clubs. In this light, what justifies awarding athletes exclusive control over their image in cases like that of Tiger Woods where there is no association of the athlete with another product other than his own persona? Is that control necessary to provide adequate incentives for the development of the players' talents and performance? Should we want to provide additional incentives for the especially talented few to achieve celebrity status? Or does a broad right of publicity suitably recognize athletes' "moral" right to control and exploit their own identities, rather than to enrich others?

4. *Mass-Produced Goods.* Based on the Sixth Circuit's analysis, could a self-proclaimed artist put Tiger Woods' picture on a T-shirt or coffee mug with an inspirational phrase, sell it without Woods' consent, and claim First Amendment protection because the item expresses some piety about achieving greatness? Does attaching a "message" to a mass-produced, profit-generating item immunize the inclusion of a celebrity likeness? Or must the producer be recognized in some formal way as an "artist"? How should a court or jury decide where to draw the line between art and commercial products? Is the distinction a question of fact or law?

What if the mass-produced good is a book on the history of baseball using names and pictures of former ballplayers? In *Gionfriddo v. MLB*, 94 Cal. App. 4th 400, 114 Cal. Rptr. 2d 307 (1st Dist. 2001), the court held that MLB's use of retired players' images and identifying information in its websites, documentaries, and game day programs enjoyed full First Amendment protection accorded to noncommercial speech and were "public affairs" uses exempt from consent under the California right of publicity statute. That statutory exemption is premised on the public's "right to know"—should that right extend to information about topics that concededly do not rise to the level of news? Do you agree with the court that MLB's uses did not harm the players' economic interests, and may have even enhanced their marketability?

5. *Consent to Publicity Use.* The PGA Tour membership contract with players, including Tiger Woods, authorizes the PGA to license member images for use by tournament sponsors. Despite this consent to publicity use, Woods forced the PGA to remove his image and identifying information from the advertisements of tournament sponsor Mercedes Benz. Contrast this outcome with a class action brought by PGA Tour caddies, seeking publicity rights compensation for wearing the required caddie bib that displays sponsor logos. The Ninth Circuit dismissed those claims with prejudice, holding the caddies were bound by their consent in the standard PGA caddie contract to wear the uniforms prescribed by the tournament. *See Hicks v. PGA Tour, Inc.*, 897 F.3d 1109 (9th Cir. 2018). Although the caddies lost on the issue of contract construction, the court granted leave to replead antitrust and unfair competition claims. What do you make of the constraints on less-wealthy caddies in exploiting their publicity rights?

5. FIRST-SALE DOCTRINE

The "first sale" doctrine provides that those who purchase a product that contains copyrighted or trademarked material are free to resell or dispose of the particular material good as they see fit. Otherwise, every time people traded or sold a used book or a team-logo jacket, they would have to obtain a license from the author or team. Courts have extended this doctrine to the right of publicity. In *Allison v. Vintage Sports Plaques*, 136 F.3d 1443 (11th Cir.1998), a company purchased a large group of trading cards, elaborately framed them (sometimes including a small clock), and then resold them as "Limited Edition of Authentic Collectibles" at a much higher price. The Eleventh Circuit dismissed the state-law publicity-right claims brought by the athletes depicted in the trading cards, under the "first sale" doctrine:

> Appellants argue that the right of publicity differs from other forms of intellectual property because the former protects "identity," whereas the latter protect "a particular photograph or product." The first-sale doctrine should not apply, they reason, because a celebrity's identity continues to travel with the tangible property in which it is embodied after the first sale. We find two significant problems with appellants' argument. First, the distinction that appellants draw between what is protected by the right of publicity and what is protected by other forms of intellectual property rights, such as copyright, is not sound.

Copyright law, for example, does not exist merely to protect the tangible items, such as books and paintings, in which the underlying expressive material is embodied; rather, it protects as well the author's or artist's particular expression that is included in the tangible item. . . .

Second, and more important in our view, accepting appellants' argument would have profoundly negative effects on numerous industries and would grant a monopoly to celebrities over their identities that would upset the delicate balance between the interests of the celebrity and those of the public. [citation omitted] Indeed, a decision by this court not to apply the first-sale doctrine to right of publicity actions would render tortious the resale of sports trading cards and memorabilia and thus would have a profound effect on the market for trading cards, which now supports a multi-billion dollar industry. . . . Such a holding presumably also would prevent, for example, framing a magazine advertisement that bears the image of a celebrity and reselling it as a collector's item, reselling an empty cereal box that bears a celebrity's endorsement, or even reselling a used poster promoting a professional sports team. Refusing to apply the first-sale doctrine to the right of publicity also presumably would prevent a child from selling to his friend a baseball card that he had purchased, a consequence that undoubtedly would be contrary to the policies supporting that right.

A holding that the first-sale doctrine does limit the right of publicity, on the other hand, would not eliminate completely a celebrity's control over the use of her name or image; the right of publicity protects against unauthorized use of an image, and a celebrity would continue to enjoy the right to license the use of her image in the first instance—and thus enjoy the power to determine when, or if, her image will be distributed. Appellants in this case, for example, have received sizable royalties from the use of their images on the trading cards at issue, images that could not have been used in the first place without permission.

* * *

The issue before us, then, is whether the district court properly resolved as a matter of law that Vintage's plaques merely are the cards themselves repackaged, rather than products separate and distinct from the trading cards they incorporate. . . .

We conclude that the district court properly determined that, as a matter of law, Vintage merely resells cards that it lawfully obtains. We think it unlikely that anyone would purchase one of Vintage's plaques for any reason other than to obtain a display of the mounted cards themselves. Although we recognize that the plaques that include a clock pose a closer case, we conclude that it is unlikely that anyone would purchase one of the clock plaques simply to obtain a means of telling time, believing the clock to be, for example, a "Hershisher Clock" or an "Allison Clock." Because reselling a product that was lawfully obtained does not give rise to a cause of action for violation of the right of publicity, we hold that the district court correctly entered summary judgment in favor of Vintage on the right of publicity claim.

136 F.3d. at 1448–51.

NOTES AND QUESTIONS

1. *Publicity Rights Versus Copyright.* What do you make of the athletes' argument that publicity rights are entitled to greater protection than copyrights under the circumstances of *Allison*? Does the court strike the right balance here between the public interest in freely disposing of personal property and the athletes' interest in capturing the appreciation in the value of their image? How relevant is it that the athletes had already been paid a royalty for use of the image?

2. *Same Versus New-and-Different Product.* The *Allison* court affirmed "as a matter of law" that the resold product, albeit modified, was functionally the same as the original. Was this a question of law or fact? That is, could no reasonable jury have found otherwise, or could a reasonable jury conclude that some people might buy a plaque embedded with a clock primarily to tell time? If someone took a 3″ x 4″ trading card and blew it up into identical 3′ x 4′ posters for sale, would the posters have the same function as the original trading card or a different function as a wall decoration? Other than the functionality test, how else might you determine if the resold product is the same as the original and protected by the first-sale doctrine?

3. *Group Licensing.* The major professional league player unions administer group licensing schemes whereby players confer exclusive rights to the union to license their images and names to vendors who use them in groups of six or more. *See generally Gridiron.com v. NFLPA*, 106 F. Supp. 2d 1309 (S.D. Fla. 2000) (website linking to six or more separate player web pages violated NFLPA's group licensing rights). If Vintage were to take the trading cards of six or more NFL players and put them on the same plaque, would the NFLPA have a valid claim that it had the exclusive group licensing rights of the players?

6. GAME BROADCASTS AND THE RIGHT OF PUBLICITY

Whatever the intrinsic merits of publicity rights for athlete and other celebrities, these rights require accommodation of other branches of property law. Most crucial is the question whether broadcasting a game or sports events violates athlete publicity rights. That is, just as stations and networks need a license from the club to broadcast the game, do the clubs also need a license from their player-employees to display the players' likeness and performance on the screen?

Like so many other owner-player disputes in sports, this issue simmered in baseball for years before finally surfacing in *Baltimore Orioles v. Major League Baseball Players Ass'n*, 805 F.2d 663 (7th Cir. 1986). In 1982, the MLBPA announced to both clubs and broadcasters that telecasts without the players' consent constituted misappropriation of the players' property right in their performance on the field. In ensuing litigation, the Seventh Circuit disagreed, first holding that the players are employees who play ballgames within the scope of their employment as a "work for hire." Accordingly, the clubs own the game broadcast copyright under the statutory presumption, unrebutted by anything in baseball's labor agreements, that the employer owns the copyright in a work made for hire. Second, the court agreed that the broadcasts infringed players' rights of publicity, but held that the clubs' federal copyright preempted those state law publicity claims. Addressing many of the same issues encountered in *Motorola*, the court rejected the players' reliance on *Zacchini* to assert a publicity right to control telecasts of their performances:

> Because the exercise of the Clubs' right to broadcast telecasts of the games infringes the Players' rights of publicity in their performances, the Players' rights of publicity are equivalent to at least one of the rights encompassed by copyright, *viz.*, the right to perform an audiovisual work. Since the works in which the Players claim rights are fixed in tangible form and come within the subject matter of copyright, the Players' rights of publicity in their performances are preempted.
>
> The Players argue that their rights of publicity in their performances are not equivalent to the rights contained in a copyright because rights of publicity and copyrights serve different interests. In their view, the purpose of federal copyright law is to secure a benefit to the public, but the purpose of state statutory or common law concerning rights of publicity is to protect individual pecuniary interests. We disagree.
>
> The purpose of federal copyright protection is to benefit the public by encouraging works in which it is interested. To induce individuals to undertake the personal sacrifices necessary to

create such works, federal copyright law extends to the authors of such works a limited monopoly to reap the rewards of their endeavors. Contrary to the Players' contention, the interest underlying the recognition of the right of publicity also is the promotion of performances that appeal to the public. The reason that state law protects individual pecuniary interests is to provide an incentive to performers to invest the time and resources required to develop such performances. In *Zacchini v. Scripps-Howard Broadcasting Co.*, 433 U.S. 562 (1977), the principal case on which the Players rely for their assertion that different interests underlie copyright and the right to publicity, the Supreme Court recognized that the interest behind federal copyright protection is the advancement of the public welfare through the encouragement of individual effort by personal gain, action for violation of the right to publicity "is closely analogous to the goals of patent and copyright law." *Id.* at 573. Because the right of publicity does not differ in kind from copyright, the Players' rights of publicity in their performances cannot escape preemption.

In this litigation, the Players have attempted to obtain *ex post* what they did not negotiate *ex ante*. That is to say, they seek a judicial declaration that they possess a right—the right to control the telecasts of major league baseball games—that they could not procure in bargaining with the Clubs. The Players' aim is to share in the increasingly lucrative revenues derived from the sale of television rights for over-the-air broadcasts by local stations and national networks and for distribution by subscription and pay cable services. Contrary to the Players' contention, the effect of this decision is not to grant the Clubs perpetual rights to the Players' performances. The Players remain free to attain their objective by bargaining with the Clubs for a contractual declaration that the Players own a joint or an exclusive interest in the copyright of the telecasts.

NOTES AND QUESTIONS

1. *Derivative Works and Compilations.* Although *Baltimore Orioles* resolved team ownership of the copyright in the initial game broadcast, what about subsequent derivative uses of that footage? May the teams (or leagues) license excerpts from the telecast to filmmakers wanting to produce a docudrama about the exploits of the Manning family of NFL quarterbacks? To an athletic shoe manufacturer wanting to show Stephen Curry in a commercial advertisement? How would you distinguish these uses from what took place in *Baltimore Orioles*? *See Ventura v. Titan Sport, Inc.*, 65 F.3d 725 (8th Cir. 1995)

(professional wrestling color commentator had publicity right to control collateral use of his videotaped performances).

This issue surfaced in *Dryer v. National Football League*, 814 F.3d 938 (8th Cir. 2016), in which a class of retired NFL players claimed that NFL Films violated their publicity rights by including game footage and player interviews in film compilations. The players sought to avoid copyright preemption by arguing that the films represent commercial speech subject to state regulation, and not artistic or informational expression. The court disagreed, finding that although the films promoted the NFL brand, they did not propose a commercial transaction or appear on other media as paid advertisements. Rather the films "tell stories," "exist as products in their own right," and "represent speech of independent value and public interest." *Id.* at 943–44 (also ruling that the players' appearance in the films did not convey a false endorsement of the NFL). Note that NFL collective bargaining agreements post-dating the retirees' playing careers expressly convey to the league non-exclusive player publicity rights for purposes such as historical films. Why do you think the league thought this was necessary given the *Dryer* analysis, as well as the *Baltimore Orioles* case? Why would the players be willing to grant those rights?

2. *Reproduction and Distribution of Copyrighted Works.* Copyright affords rights owners the exclusive right to reproduce or distribute copies of their work. Accordingly, photographers have the right to sell reprints of their photos or authorize others to do so. In *Maloney v. T3Media, Inc.*, 853 F.3d 1004 (9th Cir. 2017), the NCAA did precisely that, licensing its photo library to a website, which then sold digital copies of the photos to the public. The Ninth Circuit ruled that copyright preempted the publicity rights claims of former members of a college basketball team whose images appeared in the photos. The *Maloney* decision distinguished images used in unrelated advertising, or in "merchandise" like a coffee mug, from those incorporated into a copyrighted artistic visual work distributed for "personal use." Because the digital reprints fell in the latter category, the publicity rights claim was preempted. Do you agree with this distinction? If so, what counts as merchandise? What if the website mailed the buyer a poster of the image, rather than transmitted a digital copy? Why should a digital copy of an image be treated differently from a physical copy? Is the website's use of the images to drive sales of reprints a separate act of advertising that violates the athletes' publicity rights?

The *Maloney* decision also has uncertain implications for license negotiations involving athletes. It suggests that, absent a contractual provision to the contrary, when athletes agree to be photographed, they are giving implied consent to the holder of the copyright to use the photograph for related purposes, including distributing the photo as a product and without having to obtain publicity rights. While a professional athlete will be able to negotiate usage rights and compensation at the outset, how does this ruling impact college athletes? Does the NCAA's amateurism principle, discussed in Chapter 11, which precludes the athletes from demanding payment from the NCAA or its photographers during college, affect your thinking about the result in *Maloney*?

3. *Copyright Preemption.* Compare the Supreme Court's *Zacchini* decision, which predates the copyright preemption doctrine. Does *Baltimore Orioles* imply that if a television station asserts a copyright preemption defense rather than a First Amendment right, it could now defeat Zacchini's state publicity law claim? Or is *Baltimore Orioles* distinguishable from *Zacchini* on the grounds of "authorship" of the copyrighted work? Should we treat professional athletes differently depending on whether they are employees of a team like a professional baseball player, independent contractors like a golfer on the PGA Tour, or amateur athletes like a college basketball player in the Final Four?

4. *Amateur Athletes.* What if the athletes asserting a right of publicity in a game broadcast are unpaid college students? Are such claims more viable when the athletic performances are not "works for hire"? In *Marshall v. ESPN Inc.*, 111 F. Supp. 3d 815 (M.D. Tenn. 2015), *aff'd*, 668 F. App'x 155 (6th Cir. 2016), college athletes sued the conferences, networks, and licensors who profit from broadcasting college football and basketball games. With respect to their claims brought under the Tennessee right-of-publicity statute, the court held that inclusion of athlete images in a sports broadcast is a "fair use" and not an unauthorized endorsement, despite the inclusion of advertisements in the broadcast. The court noted the Tennessee statute's "legitimate goal of avoiding unreasonable impediments to the broadcasting of important matters of public interest, including sporting events." Consider whether this public interest is as vital when athletes' performances are featured in ancillary entertainment products, as discussed below.

7. FIRST AMENDMENT DEFENSE AND ANCILLARY ENTERTAINMENT PRODUCTS

In the case of professional sports game broadcasts and derivative uses of that footage that contain the likeness of the athlete-employee performing the services for which he was paid, the right of publicity yields to the contractual employment relationship. In the case of works that convey newsworthy information, artistic expression, or social commentary, such as a reprinted news article, a transformative portrait, or parody trading cards, the right of publicity defers to the First Amendment. What about ancillary entertainment products such as sports video games and fantasy sports contests, which make commercial use of player names, performance statistics, and in some cases pictures and digital representations? A series of publicity rights challenges sought to clarify under what circumstances the producer needs to obtain licenses from players or their unions for these uses, or is entitled to First Amendment immunity. As we read here, context matters, and courts to date have reached opposite conclusions in fantasy sports versus video games.

C.B.C. DISTRIBUTION AND MARKETING, INC. V. MAJOR LEAGUE BASEBALL ADVANCED MEDIA, L.P.
505 F.3d 818 (8th Cir. 2007)

ARNOLD, CIRCUIT JUDGE.

C.B.C. Distribution and Marketing, Inc., brought this action for a declaratory judgment against Major League Baseball Advanced Media, L.P., to establish its right to use, without license, the names of and information about major league baseball players in connection with its fantasy baseball products. Advanced Media counter-claimed, maintaining that CBC's fantasy baseball products violated rights of publicity belonging to major league baseball players and that the players, through their association, had licensed those rights to Advanced Media, the interactive media and Internet company of major league baseball. The Major League Baseball Players Association [PA] intervened in the suit, joining in Advanced Media's claims and further asserting a breach of contract claim against CBC. The district court granted summary judgment to CBC, *see C.B.C. Distrib. and Mktg., Inc. v. Major League Baseball Advanced Media, L.P.*, 443 F. Supp. 2d 1077 (E.D. Mo. 2006), and Advanced Media and the Players Association appealed. We affirm.

I.

CBC sells fantasy sports products via its Internet website, e-mail, mail, and the telephone. Its fantasy baseball products incorporate the names along with performance and biographical data of actual major league baseball players. Before the commencement of the major league baseball season each spring, participants form their fantasy baseball teams by "drafting" players from various major league baseball teams. Participants compete against other fantasy baseball "owners" who have also drafted their own teams. A participant's success, and his or her team's success, depends on the actual performance of the fantasy team's players on their respective actual teams during the course of the major league baseball season. Participants in CBC's fantasy baseball games pay fees to play and additional fees to trade players during the course of the season.

[From 1995–2004, the MLBPA granted CBC a license for "the names, nicknames, likenesses, signatures, pictures, playing records, and/or biographical data of each player" (the "Rights") to be used in association with CBC's fantasy baseball products.]

In 2005, after the 2002 agreement expired, the Players Association licensed to Advanced Media, with some exceptions, the exclusive right to use baseball players' names and performance information "for exploitation via all interactive media." Advanced Media began providing fantasy baseball games on its website, MLB.com, the official website of major league baseball. It offered CBC, in exchange for a commission, a license to promote the MLB.com fantasy baseball games on CBC's website but did not offer CBC a license to continue to offer its own fantasy baseball products. This conduct by Advanced Media prompted CBC to file the present suit, alleging that it had "a reasonable apprehension that it will be sued by Advanced Media if it continues to operate its fantasy baseball games."

* * *

[On appeal from the district court's grant of summary judgment to CBC, the court noted that it applies traditional *de novo* review and must predict how the Missouri Supreme Court would resolve the issue of Missouri state law.]

II.

A.

An action based on the right of publicity is a state-law claim. *See Zacchini v. Scripps-Howard Broad. Co.*, 433 U.S. 562, 566 (1977). In Missouri, "the elements of a right of publicity action include: (1) That defendant used plaintiff's name as a symbol of his identity (2) without consent (3) and with the intent to obtain a commercial advantage." *Doe v. TCI Cablevision*, 110 S.W.3d 363, 369 (Mo. 2003), *cert. denied*, 540 U.S. 1106 (2004). The parties all agree that CBC's continued use of the players' names and playing information after the expiration of the 2002 agreement was without consent. The district court concluded, however, that the evidence was insufficient to make out the other two elements of the claim, and we address each of these in turn.

With respect to the symbol-of-identity element, the Missouri Supreme Court has observed that " 'the name used by the defendant must be understood by the audience as referring to the plaintiff.' " The state court had further held that "[i]n resolving this issue, the fact-finder may consider evidence including 'the nature and extent of the identifying characteristics used by the defendant, the defendant's intent, the fame of the plaintiff, evidence of actual identification made by third persons, and surveys or other evidence indicating the perceptions of the audience.' " *Doe*, 110 S.W.3d at 370 (quoting *Restatement (Third) of Unfair Competition* § 46 cmt. d).

Here, we entertain no doubt that the players' names that CBC used are understood by it and its fantasy baseball subscribers as referring to actual major league baseball players. CBC itself admits that: In responding to the appellants' argument that "this element is met by the mere confirmation that the name used, in fact, refers to the famous person asserting the violation," CBC stated in its brief that "if this is all the element requires, CBC agrees that it is met." We think that by reasoning that "identity," rather than "mere use of a name," "is a critical element of the right of publicity," the district court did not understand that when a name alone is sufficient to establish identity, the defendant's use of that name satisfies the plaintiff's burden to show that a name was used as a symbol of identity.

It is true that with respect to the "commercial advantage" element of a cause of action for violating publicity rights, CBC's use does not fit neatly into the more traditional categories of commercial advantage, namely, using individuals' names for advertising and merchandising purposes in a way that states or intimates that the individuals are endorsing a product. *Cf. Restatement (Third) of Unfair Competition* § 47 cmt. a, b. But the Restatement, which the Missouri Supreme Court has recognized as authority in this kind of case, also says that a name is used for commercial advantage when it is used "in connection with services rendered by the user" and that the plaintiff need not show that "prospective purchasers are likely to believe" that he endorsed the product or service. *Restatement (Third) of Unfair Competition* § 47 & cmt. a. We note, moreover, that in Missouri, "the commercial advantage element of the right of publicity focuses on the defendant's intent or purpose to obtain a commercial benefit from use of the plaintiff's identity." *Doe*, 110 S.W.3d at 370–71. Because we think that it is clear that CBC uses baseball players' identities in its fantasy baseball products for purposes of profit, we believe that their identities are being used for commercial advantage and that the players therefore offered sufficient evidence to make out a cause of action for violation of their rights of publicity under Missouri law.

B.

CBC argues that the First Amendment nonetheless trumps the right-of-publicity action that Missouri law provides. . . .

The Supreme Court has directed that state law rights of publicity must be balanced against First Amendment considerations, *see Zacchini v. Scripps-Howard Broad.*, 433 U.S. 562 (1977), and here we conclude that the former must give way to the latter. First, the information used in CBC's fantasy baseball games is all readily available in the public domain, and it would be strange law that a person would not have a First Amendment right to use information that is available to everyone. It is true that CBC's use of the information is meant to provide entertainment, but "[s]peech that entertains, like speech that informs, is protected by the First Amendment because '[t]he line between the informing and the entertaining is too elusive for the protection of that basic right.'" *Cardtoons, L.C. v. Major League Baseball Players Ass'n*, 95 F.3d 959, 969 (10th Cir. 1996) [citation omitted]; *see also Zacchini*, 433 U.S. at 578. We also find no merit in the argument that CBC's use of players' names and information in its fantasy baseball games is not speech at all. We have held that "the pictures, graphic design, concept art, sounds, music, stories, and narrative present in video games" is speech entitled to First Amendment protection. Similarly, here CBC uses the "names, nicknames, likenesses, signatures, pictures, playing records, and/or biographical data of each player" in an interactive form in connection with its fantasy baseball products.

Courts have also recognized the public value of information about the game of baseball and its players, referring to baseball as "the national pastime." *Cardtoons*, 95 F.3d at 972. A California court, in a case where Major League Baseball was itself defending its use of players' names, likenesses, and information against the players' asserted rights of publicity, observed, "Major league baseball is followed by millions of people across this country on a daily basis. . . . The public has an enduring fascination in the records set by former players and in memorable moments from previous games. . . . The records and statistics remain of interest to the public because they provide context that allows fans to better appreciate (or deprecate) today's performances." *Gionfriddo v. Major League Baseball,* 94 Cal. App. 4th 400, 411, 114 Cal. Rptr. 2d 307 (2001). The Court in *Gionfriddo* concluded that the "recitation and discussion of factual data concerning the athletic performance of [players on Major League Baseball's website] command a substantial public interest, and, therefore, is a form of expression due substantial constitutional protection." *Id.* We find these views persuasive.

In addition, the facts in this case barely, if at all, implicate the interests that states typically intend to vindicate by providing rights of publicity to individuals. Economic interests that states seek to promote include the right of an individual to reap the rewards of his or her endeavors and an individual's right to earn a living. Other motives for creating a publicity right are the desire to provide incentives to encourage a person's productive activities and to protect consumers from misleading advertising. *See Zacchini,* 433 U.S. at 573, 576; *Cardtoons,* 95 F.3d at 973. But major league baseball players are rewarded, and handsomely, too, for their participation in games and can earn additional large sums from endorsements and sponsorship arrangements. Nor is there any danger here that consumers will be misled, because the fantasy baseball games depend on the inclusion of all players and thus cannot create a false impression that some particular player with "star power" is endorsing CBC's products.

Then there are so-called non-monetary interests that publicity rights are sometimes thought to advance. These include protecting natural rights, rewarding celebrity labors, and avoiding emotional harm. *See Cardtoons,* 95 F.3d at 973. We do not see that any of these interests are especially relevant here, where baseball players are rewarded separately for their labors, and where any emotional harm would most likely be caused by a player's actual performance, in which case media coverage would cause the same harm. We also note that some courts have indicated that the right of publicity is intended to promote only economic interests and that non-economic interests are more directly served by so-called rights of privacy. *See, e.g., id.* at 967; *Gionfriddo,* 94 Cal. App. 4th at 409 (2001; *see also Haelan Laboratories v. Topps Chewing Gum,* 202 F.2d 866, 868 (2d Cir. 1953). For instance, although the court in *Cardtoons,* 95 F.3d at 975–76, conducted a separate discussion of non-economic interests when weighing the countervailing rights, it ultimately concluded that the non-economic justifications for the right of publicity were unpersuasive as compared with the interest in freedom of expression. "Publicity rights . . . are meant to protect against the loss of financial gain, not mental anguish." Id. at 976. We see merit in this approach.

Because we hold that CBC's *First Amendment* rights in offering its fantasy baseball products supersede the players' rights of publicity, we need not reach CBC's alternative argument that federal copyright law preempts the players' state law rights of publicity.

* * *

[Affirmed.]

As explained in Chapter 11, in the last 10 years college athletes have launched multifaceted litigation attacking the principles of amateurism by which the National Collegiate Athletic Association (NCAA) has curtailed their opportunities to monetize their talents and celebrity. One lawsuit, initially captioned *Keller v. Electronic Arts,* asserted publicity rights claims against the NCAA and a video game developer for using avatars in college football video games that closely resembled actual former college football players. Defendants moved to strike the complaint as a strategic lawsuit against public participation (SLAPP) under California's anti-SLAPP statute, asserting First Amendment rights to their creative expression as embodied in the video game. In a landmark decision for college sports and for ancillary sports entertainment products, the court sustained the publicity rights claims.

IN RE NCAA STUDENT-ATHLETE NAME & LIKENESS LICENSING LITIGATION
724 F.3d 1268 (9th Cir. 2013)

BYBEE, CIRCUIT JUDGE:

Video games are entitled to the full protections of the First Amendment, because "[l]ike the protected books, plays, and movies that preceded them, video games communicate ideas—and even social messages—through many familiar literary devices (such as characters, dialogue, plot, and music) and through features distinctive to the medium (such as the player's interaction with the virtual world)." *Brown v. Entm't Merchs. Ass'n*, 131 S. Ct. 2729, 2733 (2011). Such rights are not absolute, and states may recognize the right of publicity to a degree consistent with the First Amendment. *Zacchini v. Scripps-Howard Broad. Co.*, 433 U.S. 562, 574–75 (1977). In this case, we must balance the right of publicity of a former college football player against the asserted First Amendment right of a video game developer to use his likeness in its expressive works.

The district court concluded that the game developer, Electronic Arts ("EA"), had no First Amendment defense against the right-of-publicity claims of the football player, Samuel Keller. We affirm. Under the "transformative use" test developed by the California Supreme Court, EA's use does not qualify for First Amendment protection as a matter of law because it literally recreates Keller in the very setting in which he has achieved renown. The other First Amendment defenses asserted by EA do not defeat Keller's claims either.

I

[Keller played quarterback for Arizona State University and then the University of Nebraska.] EA is the producer of the *NCAA Football* series of video games, which allow users to control avatars representing college football players as those avatars participate in simulated games. In *NCAA Football,* EA seeks to replicate each school's entire team as accurately as possible. Every real football player on each team included in the game has a corresponding avatar in the game with the player's actual jersey number and virtually identical height, weight, build, skin tone, hair color, and home state. EA attempts to match any unique, highly identifiable playing behaviors by sending detailed questionnaires to team equipment managers. Additionally, EA creates realistic virtual versions of actual stadiums; populates them with the virtual athletes, coaches, cheerleaders, and fans realistically rendered by EA's graphic artists; and incorporates realistic sounds such as the crunch of the players' pads and the roar of the crowd.

EA's game differs from reality in that EA omits the players' names on their jerseys and assigns each player a home town that is different from the actual player's home town. However, users of the video game may upload rosters of names obtained from third parties so that the names do appear on the jerseys. In such cases, EA allows images from the game containing athletes' real names to be posted on its website by users. . . .

In the 2005 edition of the game, the virtual starting quarterback for Arizona State wears number 9, as did Keller, and has the same height, weight, skin tone, hair color, hair style, handedness, home state, play style (pocket passer), visor preference, facial features, and school year as Keller. In the 2008 edition, the virtual quarterback for Nebraska has these same characteristics, though the jersey number does not match, presumably because Keller changed his number right before the season started.

Objecting to this use of his likeness, Keller filed a putative class-action complaint in the Northern District of California asserting, as relevant on appeal, that EA violated his right of publicity under California Civil Code § 3344 and California common law. . .

A

The California Supreme Court formulated the transformative use defense in *Comedy III Productions, Inc. v. Gary Saderup, Inc.*, 25 Cal. 4th 387 (2001). The defense is "a balancing test between the First Amendment and the right of publicity based on whether the work in question adds significant creative elements so as to be transformed into something more than a mere celebrity likeness or imitation." The California Supreme Court explained that "when a work contains significant transformative elements, it is not only especially worthy of First Amendment protection, but it is also less likely to interfere with the economic interest protected by the right of publicity." The court rejected the wholesale importation of the copyright "fair use" defense into right-of-publicity claims, but recognized that some aspects of that defense are "particularly pertinent."

Comedy III gives us at least five factors to consider in determining whether a work is sufficiently transformative to obtain First Amendment protection. First, if "the celebrity likeness is one of the 'raw materials' from which an original work is synthesized," it is more likely to be transformative than if "the depiction or imitation of the celebrity is the very sum and substance of the work in question." Second, the work is protected if it is "primarily the defendant's own expression"—as long as that expression is "something other than the likeness of the celebrity." This factor requires an examination of whether a likely purchaser's primary motivation is to buy a reproduction of the celebrity, or to buy the expressive work of that artist. Third, to avoid making judgments concerning "the quality of the artistic contribution," a court should conduct an inquiry "more quantitative than qualitative" and ask "whether the literal and imitative or the creative elements predominate in the work." Fourth, the California Supreme Court indicated that "a subsidiary inquiry" would be useful in close cases: whether "the marketability and economic value of the challenged work derive primarily from the fame of the celebrity depicted." Lastly, the court indicated that "when an artist's skill and talent is manifestly subordinated to the overall goal of creating a conventional portrait of a celebrity so as to commercially exploit his or her fame," the work is not transformative.

[The court described four cases where California courts have applied the transformative use test to: (1) disallow T-shirts and lithographs with "literal, conventional depictions of The Three Stooges so as to exploit their fame"; (2) permit comic books that based grotesque and villainous characters on famous rock musicians because the characters "are not just conventional depictions of plaintiffs but contain significant expressive content" and distort the likeness "for purposes of lampoon, parody, or caricature" as part of "a larger story, which is itself quite expressive"; (3) permit a video game character based on a famous singer because it was a "fanciful, creative character" that was "unlike any public depiction" of the singer; (4) disallow the *Band Hero* video game's use of avatars of the rock band No Doubt that were "literal recreations of the band members," doing "the same activity by which the band achieved and maintains its fame."]

* * *

With these cases in mind as guidance, we conclude that EA's use of Keller's likeness does not contain significant transformative elements such that EA is entitled to the defense as a matter of law. The facts of *No Doubt* [*v. Activism Publishing Inc.*, 192 Cal. App. 4th 1018, 122 Cal. Rptr. 3d 397 (2011),] are very similar to those here. EA is alleged to have replicated Keller's physical characteristics in *NCAA Football,* just as the members of No Doubt are realistically portrayed in *Band Hero*. Here, as in *Band Hero,* users manipulate the characters in the performance of the same activity for which they are known in real life—playing football in this case, and performing in a rock band in *Band Hero*. The context in which the activity occurs is also similarly realistic—real venues in *Band Hero* and realistic depictions of actual football stadiums in *NCAA Football*. As the district court found, Keller is represented as "what he was: the starting quarterback for Arizona State" and Nebraska, and "the game's setting is identical to where the public found [Keller] during his collegiate career: on the football field."

* * *

The Third Circuit came to the same conclusion in *Hart v. Electronic Arts, Inc.*, 717 F.3d 141 (3d Cir. 2013). In *Hart*, EA faced a materially identical challenge under New Jersey right-of-publicity law, brought by former Rutgers quarterback Ryan Hart. *See id.* at 163 n. 28 ("*Keller* is simply [*Hart*] incarnated in California."). Though the Third Circuit was tasked with interpreting New Jersey law, the court looked to the transformative use test developed in California. *See id.* at 158 n. 23 (noting that the right-of-publicity laws are "strikingly similar . . . and protect similar interests" in New Jersey and California, and that "consequently [there is] no issue in applying balancing tests developed in California to New Jersey"); *see also id.* at 165 (holding that "the Transformative Use Test is the proper analytical framework to apply to cases such as the one at bar"). Applying the test, the court held that "the *NCAA Football* . . . games at issue . . . do not sufficiently transform [Hart]'s identity to escape the right of publicity claim," reversing the district court's grant of summary judgment to EA. *Id.* at 170.

As we have, the Third Circuit considered the potentially transformative nature of the game as a whole, *id.* at 166, 169, and the user's ability to alter avatar characteristics, *id.* at 166–68. Asserting that "the lack of transformative context is even more pronounced here than in *No Doubt*," *id.* at 166, and that "the ability to modify the avatar counts for little where the appeal of the game lies in users' ability to play as, or alongside [,] their preferred players or team," *id.* at 168 (internal quotation marks omitted), the Third Circuit agreed with us that these changes do not render the *NCAA Football* games sufficiently transformative to defeat a right-of-publicity claim.

Given that *NCAA Football* realistically portrays college football players in the context of college football games, the district court was correct in concluding that EA cannot prevail as a matter of law based on the transformative use defense at the anti-SLAPP stage.

B

[The court considered EA's argument, predicated on *Rogers v. Grimaldi*, 875 F.2d 994 (2d Cir. 1989), that the First Amendment permits use of a celebrity's name in a creative work when doing so is artistically relevant and not misleading as to whether the celebrity endorses the work.]

The right of publicity protects the *celebrity,* not the *consumer.* Keller's publicity claim is not founded on an allegation that consumers are being illegally misled into believing that he is endorsing EA or its products. Indeed, he would be hard-pressed to support such an allegation absent evidence that EA explicitly misled consumers into holding such a belief. . . . Instead, Keller's claim is that EA has appropriated, without permission and without providing compensation, his talent and years of hard work on the football field. The reasoning of the *Rogers* and *Mattel* courts—that artistic and literary works should be protected unless they explicitly mislead consumers—is simply not responsive to Keller's asserted interests here.

* * *

C

[The court weighed EA's defenses asserted under: (a) the California common law principle that the right of publicity does not lie for the "publication of matters in the public interest," *Montana v. San Jose Mercury News, Inc.*, 34 Cal. App. 4th 790 (1995); and (b) the California statute that permits the "use of a name, voice, signature, photograph, or likeness in connection with any news, public affairs, or sports broadcast or account, or any political campaign." Cal. Civ. Code § 3344(d).]

California courts have generally analyzed the common law defense and the statutory defense separately, but it is clear that both defenses protect only the act of publishing or reporting. By its terms, § 3344(d) is limited to a "broadcast or account," and we have confirmed that the common law defense is about a publication or reporting of newsworthy items. However, most of the discussion by California courts pertains to whether the subject matter of the communication is of "public interest" or related to "news" or "public affairs," leaving little guidance as to when the communication constitutes a publication or reporting.

[I]n *Gionfriddo v. Major League Baseball*, retired professional baseball players alleged that Major League Baseball violated their right of publicity by displaying "factual data concerning the players, their performance statistics, and verbal descriptions and video depictions of their play" in game programs and on its website. The court reasoned that "[t]he recitation and discussion of factual data concerning the athletic performance of these plaintiffs command a substantial public interest, and, therefore, is a form of expression due substantial constitutional protection." And in *Montana*, former NFL quarterback Joe Montana brought a right-of-publicity action against a newspaper for selling posters containing previously published pages from the newspaper depicting the many Super Bowl victories by Montana and the San Francisco 49ers. The court found that "[p]osters portraying the 49'ers' [sic] victories are . . . a form of public interest presentation to which protection must be extended." . . .

EA is not publishing or reporting factual data. EA's video game is a means by which users can play their own virtual football games, not a means for obtaining information about real-world football games. Although EA has incorporated certain actual player information into the game (height, weight, etc.), its case is considerably weakened by its decision not to include the athletes' names along with their likenesses and statistical data. EA can hardly be considered to be "reporting" on Keller's career at Arizona State and Nebraska when it is not even using Keller's name in connection with his avatar in the game. Put simply, EA's interactive game is not a publication of facts about college football; it is a game, not a reference source. These state law defenses, therefore, do not apply.

Affirmed.

NOTES AND QUESTIONS

1. *First Amendment Balancing.* What factors did the Eighth Circuit in *C.B.C. Distribution* find determinative in ruling that the First Amendment rights of the fantasy sports provider outweigh the players' image rights? State-law protection of image rights often seeks to create incentives for individuals to make investments in their own success so that their image rights have

commercial value. How would the Eighth Circuit's factors apply to the use of New York Yankee Aaron Judge's name and statistics? Does your answer depend on whether the question came up today or when he was an unknown minor leaguer investing time and effort in his baseball future?

2. *False Endorsement.* After *C.B.C Distribution*, a football fantasy sports website relied on the decision to refuse to continue paying license fees to the NFL Players Association, and then sued for a declaration that the First Amendment superseded the football players' publicity rights. *See CBS Interactive Inc. v. Nat'l Football League Players Ass'n, Inc.*, 259 F.R.D. 398 (D. Minn. 2009). The court rejected the NFLPA's attempts to distinguish football from baseball, including its assertion that the football fantasy site packaged player information in a way that conveyed a false endorsement. Rather, the court concluded the site was "akin to newspapers and magazines" where no one believes the subjects of news reports are endorsing either the publisher or the third-party advertisers in that publication. *Id.* at 419. Does this analogy persuade you?

3. *Transformative Use Test.* Circuit Judge Thomas dissented in *NCAA Student-Athlete*, concluding that "the creative and transformative elements of the games predominate over the commercial use of the likenesses of the athletes within the games." The dissent principally relied on the video game's omission of athlete names and provision of gamer autonomy to change athletes' abilities and appearances and to create entirely new virtual players. These and similar features convinced the dissenter that the "marketability and economic value of the game comes from the creative elements within, not from the pure commercial exploitation of a celebrity image." Did the majority or the dissent correctly apply the transformative use test? After the *NCAA Student-Athlete* ruling, EA stopped producing college athlete video games and cannot resume as long as the NCAA prohibits compensation of college athletes for their likenesses. Does this development affect your view of the proper balance between athlete image rights and public access to informative and creative works?

4. *Incidental Use.* In *Davis v. Elec. Arts Inc.*, 775 F.3d 1172 (9th Cir. 2015), the Ninth Circuit replayed its *NCAA Student-Athlete* analysis to reject EA's First Amendment defenses to similar right-of-publicity claims brought by former professional football players who were depicted in a version of a video game that included "historic teams." In *Davis*, EA offered the additional defense that its use of former player likenesses was protected as "incidental" under a California doctrine that immunizes fleeting or trivial use of celebrity. EA asserted that because its game depicted several thousand players, any individual player's likeness has only a de minimis commercial value. The court rejected this argument, observing that the video games went to great lengths to achieve realism in depicting the former players, and prominently featured them as icons of the game. Recall what *Uhlaender v. Henricksen*, 316 F. Supp. 1277 (D. Minn. 1970), said about how celebrity value derives from investing "years of practice and competition in a public personality which eventually may

reach marketable status." Does the *Davis* case suggest that EA's incidental use theory would prevail if the athletes were lesser known?

5. *Information in the Public Domain.* The majority in *NCAA Student-Athlete* distinguished EA's video games from the fantasy baseball products at issue in *C.B.C. Distribution*, because the latter merely uses publicly available data, but the video games also use the athlete likenesses. The Ninth Circuit majority was not swayed by the argument that EA generated the likenesses from publicly available data. 724 F.3d at 1283 n.12. Does the majority's distinction make sense to you? If so, how are fantasy sports providers able to use player photographs without obtaining group licenses from the players' unions? See the next note for a possible answer.

6. *Public Interest in the Information.* The court in *NCAA Student-Athlete* also addressed California's statutory exemption from liability for unauthorized uses of celebrity that concern a topic of public interest. A similar exemption in the Indiana right-of-publicity statute was at issue in *Daniels v. FanDuel, Inc.*, 884 F.3d 672 (7th Cir.), *certified question accepted*, 94 N.E.3d 696 (Ind. 2018). Daniels and fellow former college football players sued to block the use of their names, pictures, and on-field statistics by fantasy sports providers FanDuel and DraftKings. The district court held that the Indiana statute permitted the use based on the public interest in the athletes' sports performances and statistics. Because no Indiana state judge had yet interpreted the statute's public interest exemption, the Seventh Circuit stayed the appeal and referred to the Indiana Supreme Court the question: "Whether online fantasy-sports operators that condition entry on payment, and distribute cash prizes, need the consent of players whose names, pictures, and statistics are used in the contests, in advertising the contests, or both." At this writing, the Indiana court has yet to rule. How would you rule?

7. *Wearable Technology and the Right to Privacy/Publicity.* Player performance information and statistics increasingly include biometric data generated by wearable (and soon ingestible and implantable) technology. Leagues and players unions will need to negotiate exactly what information may be collected, who owns it, and how it may be shared and used. To the extent such data reveal personal health information, athletes may possess federal privacy rights against disclosure, in addition to state law privacy protections. When the data identify particular athletes, the question will inevitably arise whether players retain a publicity right in the data that requires their consent for use. Will the answer depend on whether the data are already in the public domain, for example, because somehow incorporated in game broadcasts? Or whether the data concern a topic of public interest?

8. *Sports Gambling.* As previously noted in discussion of league and team rights to game accounts and information, legalized sports gambling will further complicate the debate over the appropriate contours of sports industry intellectual property rights. *See Murphy v. Nat'l Collegiate Athletic Ass'n*, 138 S. Ct. 1461 (2018). Given the fantasy sports disputes described here, players and their unions are likely to lodge publicity rights claims against sportsbooks,

in parallel with leagues' and teams' property claims. Meanwhile, leagues have lobbied state legislatures to require sportsbooks to compensate them for "integrity" costs and intellectual property rights as a condition of taking bets on their games. Is this issue more amenable to a legislative solution than to a judicial reckoning?

D. TRADEMARK RIGHTS

A trademark or service mark is a word, symbol, or logo, used to identify a particular product or service, and to distinguish that good from the products or services of another. For example, the trademark "Nike" and the Nike "swoosh" identify the shoes made by Nike and distinguish them from shoes made by other companies (*e.g.*, Puma or Reebok). Similarly, "ESPN" distinguishes the sports programming of one media company from that of another (*e.g.*, Sky Sports). In contrast, Golden State Warriors fans buy merchandise with their team's logo because they want to show their affinity to the Warriors, not because they care whether the Warriors are the source or authorizing agent for the good. Accordingly, for sports franchise owners, trademark rights also offer a means of realizing the celebrity value of their team's (not their players') name and identity. Significant sports industry revenue now comes from merchandising team trademarks, logos, and other identifying insignia. In 2018, Forbes Magazine listed the New York Yankees name and insignia as the single most popular sports team brand in the world, and valued that asset alone (apart from the team itself) at over $700 million.

Unlike copyright or rights of publicity which protect authorship or identity, the property right of trademark is a function of *use* of a name, logo, or design. Trademark law's primary purpose is to protect consumers from confusion in their choice or use of goods, not to protect the mark owner's business interest. Thus, mark owners do not have an absolute right to stop someone else from using their names and symbols. Rather, they can block that action only if it is likely to cause confusion or deception of consumers in the sale of competing goods. Trademarks thereby make it easier for consumers to quickly identify the source of a given good and create incentives for producers to preserve and enhance the attractive qualities of those goods. Brand-name recognition also attracts infringers who attempt to trade on the good will and reputation of the mark owner's product, and can undermine that good will with an inferior version of the product. As long as the mark owner continues to use the mark as a source identifier, it can pursue legal remedies to stop subsequent use by a competing product. *See Nat'l Collegiate Athletic Ass'n v. Kizzang LLC*, 304 F. Supp. 3d 800 (S.D. Ind. 2018) (NCAA entitled to block sports website's use of "Final 3" and "April Madness"). As you read the cases that follow, question to what extent consumers care about the source of team logo apparel, and whether trademark protection in that setting disserves the consumer by raising prices for those goods.

Trademark protections are found in both state and federal law. The main federal statute is the Lanham Act, enacted in 1946 and periodically amended since then. 15 U.S.C. §§ 1051, *et seq*. Although the Lanham Act protects a mark regardless of whether it is federally registered, registration of a mark confers significant benefits, including presumptive nationwide ownership of the mark and exclusive rights to use the mark for the subject goods or services. Registration also enables the mark owner to bring an infringement suit in federal court and potentially recover treble damages, attorneys' fees, and other remedies.

1. SPORTS TEAM NAMES

To serve as a trademark, a name must be distinctive, that is, it must be capable of identifying the source of a particular good. The more distinctive a mark, the greater the legal protection, determined by the relationship between the mark and the underlying product. Courts group marks into four categories, from most to least distinctive: (1) arbitrary or fanciful, (2) suggestive, (3) descriptive, or (4) generic. Sports team names generally fall into one of the two most distinctive categories, earning a high degree of protection. For example, the NHL's Anaheim "Ducks" is an arbitrary name as it bears no logical relationship to the underlying product. The Nashville "Predators" and the Philadelphia "Flyers" are suggestive names, connoting desirable qualities in a hockey team. All those marks therefore receive strong legal protection. *See In Re WNBA Enterprises, LLC*, 70 U.S.P.Q.2d 1153 (T.T.A.B. June 11, 2003) (WNBA team name Orlando "Miracle" is a suggestive, not descriptive, mark). Descriptive marks, such as "National Hockey League" and the city designations in each of the above NHL team names, convey something about the product and merit protection only if they have acquired "secondary meaning" through the user's efforts to associate the mark with a particular business. *See Maryland Stadium Auth. v. Becker*, 806 F. Supp. 1236, 1241 (D. Md. 1992), *aff'd*, 36 F.3d 1093 (4th Cir. 1994) ("promotional efforts and the media coverage given to the new baseball park had conferred a secondary meaning upon the name Camden Yards").

All major U.S. sports leagues strive, though advertising and media coverage, to associate team names with member clubs and thereby acquire secondary meaning for their marks. But unrelated business decisions, such as to relocate a franchise, expand or contract the league, or build a stadium across a state line, can expose vulnerabilities in trademark ownership. For example, when the NFL's Oakland team announced its move to Las Vegas, the league had to contend with multiple earlier-filed opportunistic trademark applications for the name Las Vegas Raiders. *See also Nat'l Football League Properties, Inc. v. New Jersey Giants, Inc.*, 637 F. Supp.

507 (D.N.J. 1986) (enjoining "New Jersey Giants" mark similar to NFL New York Giants, created to take advantage of team's new home stadium location); *Johnny Blastoff, Inc. v. Los Angeles Rams Football Co.*, 188 F.3d 427 (7th Cir. 1999) (holding that someone filing a state registration for "St. Louis Rams" the day after the team announced it was moving from Los Angeles to St. Louis did not have a valid right in the mark). The following sports trademark dispute provides an apt introduction to this branch of the law, as well as flashback to an NFL franchise move encountered in Chapter 7.

INDIANAPOLIS COLTS V. METROPOLITAN BALTIMORE FOOTBALL CLUB
34 F.3d 410 (7th Cir. 1994)

POSNER, CHIEF JUDGE.

[The Baltimore Colts had played in that city for 32 years when, in 1984, the owner, Robert Irsay, moved the team to Indianapolis, literally under cover of darkness. The NFL, worried about the prospects of an antitrust lawsuit, decided not to block the relocation of the team and allowed the team to keep its nickname as the Indianapolis Colts. The sudden and secretive move outraged Baltimore fans, who tried to get the team back through various means. They were somewhat appeased when, in 1993, the Canadian Football League (CFL) granted Baltimore a franchise, which the new owner (and the fans) wanted to name the Colts. When the NFL threatened legal action, the team adopted the name Baltimore CFL Colts. Not satisfied with that variation on the old name, the Indianapolis Colts and the NFL sued to block any use of the word "Colts" in the CFL team name. After the district judge granted a preliminary injunction, the Baltimore team appealed.]

* * *

The Baltimore team wanted to call itself the "Baltimore Colts." To improve its litigating posture (we assume), it has consented to insert "CFL" between "Baltimore" and "Colts." A glance at the merchandise in the record explains why this concession to an outraged NFL has been made so readily. On several of the items "CFL" appears in small or blurred letters. And since the Canadian Football League is not well known in the United States—and "CFL" has none of the instant recognition value of "NFL"—the inclusion of the acronym in the team's name might have little impact on potential buyers even if prominently displayed. Those who know football well know that the new "Baltimore Colts" are a new CFL team wholly unrelated to the old Baltimore Colts; know also that the rules of Canadian football are different from those of American football and that teams don't move from the NFL to the CFL as they might from one conference within the NFL to the other. But those who do not know these things—and we shall come shortly to the question whether there are many of these football illiterate—will not be warned off by the letters "CFL." The acronym is a red herring, and the real issue is whether the new Baltimore team can appropriate the name "Baltimore Colts." The entire thrust of the defendants' argument is that it can.

They make a tremendous to-do over the fact that the district judge found that the Indianapolis Colts abandoned the trademark "Baltimore Colts" when they moved to Indianapolis. Well, of course; they were no longer playing football under the name "Baltimore Colts," so could not have used the name as the team's trademark; they could have used it on merchandise but chose not to, until 1991 (another story—and not one we need tell). When a mark is abandoned, it returns to the public domain, and is appropriable anew—in principle. In practice, because "subsequent use of [an] abandoned mark may well evoke a continuing association with the prior use, those who make subsequent use may be required to take reasonable precautions to prevent confusion." J. Thomas McCarthy, *McCarthy on Trademarks and Intellectual Property* § 17.01 [2] (3d ed. 1994) at p. 17–3. This precept is especially important where, as in this case, the former owner of the abandoned mark continues to market the same product or service under a similar name, though we cannot find any previous cases of this kind. No one questions the validity of "Indianapolis Colts" as the trademark of the NFL team that plays out of Indianapolis and was formerly known as the Baltimore Colts. If "Baltimore CFL Colts" is confusingly similar to "Indianapolis Colts" by virtue of the history of the Indianapolis team and the overlapping product and geographical markets served by it and by the new Baltimore team, the latter's use of the abandoned mark would infringe the Indianapolis Colts' new mark. The Colts' abandonment of a mark confusingly similar to their new mark neither broke the continuity of the team in its different locations—it was the same team, merely having a different home base and therefore a different geographical component in its name—nor entitled a third party to pick it up and use it to confuse Colts fans, and other actual or potential consumers of products and services marketed by the Colts or by other National Football League teams, with regard to the identity, sponsorship, or league affiliation of the third party, that is, the new Baltimore team. . . .

Against this the defendants cite to us with great insistence *Major League Baseball Properties, Inc. v. Sed Non Olet Denarius, Ltd.*, 817 F. Supp. 1103, 1128 (S.D.N.Y. 1993), which, over the objection of the Los Angeles Dodgers, allowed a restaurant in Brooklyn to use the name "Brooklyn Dodger" on the ground that "the 'Brooklyn Dodgers' was a non-transportable cultural institution separate from the 'Los Angeles Dodgers.'" The defendants in our case argue that the sudden and greatly resented departure of the Baltimore Colts for Indianapolis made the name "Baltimore Colts" available to anyone who would continue the "nontransportable cultural institution" constituted by a football team located in the City of Baltimore. We think this argument very weak, and need not even try to distinguish *Sed Non Olet Denarius* since district court decisions are not authoritative in this or any court of appeals. If it were a Supreme Court decision it still would not help the defendants. The "Brooklyn Dodger" was not a baseball team, and there was no risk of confusion. ... The only claim in our court is that a significant number of consumers will think the new Baltimore team the successor to, or alter ego of, or even the same team as the Baltimore Colts and therefore the Indianapolis Colts, which is the real successor. No one would think the Brooklyn Dodgers baseball team reincarnated in a restaurant.

A professional sports team is like Heraclitus's river: always changing, yet always the same. When Mr. Irsay transported his team, the Baltimore Colts, from Baltimore to Indianapolis in one night in 1984, the team remained, for a time anyway, completely intact: same players, same coaches, same front-office personnel. With the passage of time, of course, the team changed. Players retired or were traded, and were replaced. Coaches and other nonplaying personnel came and went. But as far as the record discloses there is as much institutional continuity between the Baltimore Colts of 1984 and the Indianapolis Colts of 1994 as there was between the Baltimore Colts of 1974 and the Baltimore Colts of 1984.... The Colts were Irsay's team, it was moved intact, there is no evidence it has changed more since the move than it had in the years before. There is, in contrast, no continuity, no links contractual or otherwise, nothing but a geographical site in common, between the Baltimore Colts and the Canadian Football League team that would like to use its name. Any suggestion that there is such continuity is false and potentially misleading.

Potentially; for if everyone knows there is no contractual or institutional continuity, no pedigree or line of descent, linking the Baltimore-Indianapolis Colts and the new CFL team that wants to call itself the "Baltimore Colts" (or, grudgingly, the "Baltimore CFL Colts"), then there is no harm, at least no harm for which the Lanham Act provides a remedy, in the new Baltimore team's appropriating the name "Baltimore Colts" to play under and sell merchandise under. If not everyone knows, there is harm. Some people who might otherwise watch the Indianapolis Colts (or some other NFL team, for remember that the NFL, representing all the teams, is a co-plaintiff) on television may watch the Baltimore CFL Colts instead, thinking they are the "real" Baltimore Colts, and the NFL will lose revenue. A few (doubtless very few) people who might otherwise buy tickets to an NFL game may buy tickets to a Baltimore CFL Colts game instead. Some people who might otherwise buy merchandise stamped with the name "Indianapolis Colts" or the name of some other NFL team may buy merchandise stamped "Baltimore CFL Colts," thinking it a kin of the NFL's Baltimore Colts in the glory days of Johnny Unitas rather than a newly formed team that plays Canadian football in a Canadian football league. It would be naive to suppose that no consideration of such possibilities occurred to the owners of the new Baltimore team when they were choosing a name, though there is no evidence that it was the dominant or even a major consideration.

Confusion thus is possible, and may even have been desired; but is it likely? There is great variance in consumer competence, and it would be undesirable to impoverish the lexicon of trade names merely to protect the most gullible fringe of the consuming public. The Lanham Act does not cast the net of protection so wide. The legal standard under the Act has been formulated variously, but the various formulations come down to whether it is likely that the challenged mark if permitted to be used by the defendant would cause the plaintiff to lose a substantial number of consumers. Pertinent to this determination is the similarity of the marks and of the parties' products, the knowledge of the average consumer of the product, the overlap in the parties' geographical markets, and the other factors that the cases consider. The aim is to strike a balance between, on the one hand, the interest of the seller of the new product, and of the consuming public, in an arresting, attractive, and informative name that will enable the new product to compete effectively against existing ones, and, on the other hand, the interest of existing sellers, and again of the consuming public, in consumers' being able to know exactly what they are buying without having to incur substantial costs of investigation or inquiry.

* * *

[The court then compared the market research surveys conducted by the two sides. After criticizing the methodology used by the defendant's expert, Michael Rappeport, the court analyzed the study conducted by the plaintiff's expert.]

* * *

The plaintiffs' study, conducted by Jacob Jacoby, was far more substantial and the district judge found it on the whole credible. The 28-page report with its numerous appendices has all the trappings of social scientific rigor. Interviewers showed several hundred consumers in 24 malls scattered around the country shirts and hats licensed by the defendants for sale to consumers. The shirts and hats have "Baltimore CFL Colts" stamped on them. The consumers were asked whether they were football fans, whether they watched football games on television, and whether they ever bought merchandise with a team name on it. Then they were asked, with reference to the "Baltimore CFL Colts" merchandise that they were shown, such questions as whether they knew what sport the team played, what teams it played against, what league the team was in, and whether the team or league needed someone's permission to use this name, and if so whose.... There were other questions, none however obviously loaded, and a whole other survey, the purpose of which was to control for "noise," in which another group of mallgoers was asked the identical questions about a hypothetical team unappetizingly named the "Baltimore Horses." The idea was by comparing the answers of the two groups to see whether the source of confusion was the name "Baltimore Colts" or just the name "Baltimore," in which event the injunction would do no good since no one suggests that the new Baltimore team should be forbidden to use "Baltimore" in its name, provided the name does not also include "Colts."

* * *

Jacoby's survey of consumers reactions to the "Baltimore CFL Colts" merchandise found rather astonishing levels of confusion not plausibly attributable to the presence of the name "Baltimore" alone, since "Baltimore Horses" engendered much less.... Among self-identified football fans, 64% thought that the "Baltimore CFL Colts" was either the old (NFL) Baltimore Colts or the Indianapolis Colts. But perhaps this result is not so astonishing. Although most American football fans have heard of Canadian football, many probably are unfamiliar with the acronym "CFL," and as we remarked earlier it is not a very conspicuous part of the team logo stamped on the merchandise. Among fans who watch football on television, 59% displayed the same confusion; and even among those who watch football on cable television, which attracts a more educated audience on average and actually carries CFL games, 58% were confused when shown the merchandise. Among the minority not confused about who the "Baltimore CFL Colts" are, a substantial minority, ranging from 21 to 34% depending on the precise sub-sample, thought the team somehow sponsored or authorized by the Indianapolis Colts or the National Football League....

[W]e cannot say that the district judge committed a clear error in crediting the major findings of the Jacoby study and inferring from it and the other evidence in the record that the defendants' use of the name "Baltimore CFL Colts" whether for the team or on merchandise was likely to confuse a substantial number of consumers....

Affirmed.

Coda: Baltimore fans finally saw the return of NFL football in 1996 when the historic Cleveland Browns franchise relocated there. The NFL conditioned the move on renaming the team in order to leave the name "Browns" for Cleveland to use should it ever acquire another NFL franchise (which it did in 1999 with a new expansion franchise). Baltimore's NFL football team is now called the Ravens.

NOTES AND QUESTIONS

1. *Same Name, Different City or Sport.* What was the precise source of the trademark claim in the Colts case? Could an NFL team in a different city, *e.g.*, Green Bay, have objected if Baltimore had chosen its name, *e.g.*, the Packers, for its CFL franchise? Or was the real issue that the two Colts teams were playing the same sport? For example, could the St. Louis baseball Cardinals sue the Arizona football Cardinals (or could they have sued the NFL team back in 1959, when the football Cardinals relocated from Chicago to St. Louis)? What about the overlap between the NHL New York Rangers and the MLB Texas Rangers, or the NFL New York Jets and the NHL Winnipeg Jets? Note that in 1997, a federal district judge refused to grant an injunction to the barnstorming Harlem Wizards basketball team to block the NBA's Washington franchise from changing its name from Bullets to Wizards. *See Harlem Wizards Entertainment Basketball, Inc. v. NBA Properties*, 952 F. Supp. 1084 (D. N.J. 1997).

2. *Team Logos, Insignia, and Colors.* Is the issue merely the use of the same team name? Could the Baltimore CFL team have used a different nickname (*e.g.*, the "Ponies") with the same NFL Colts blue and white horseshoe logo? Courts have recognized that distinctive helmet and uniform designs and colors, and team mascots such as the chicken of the San Diego Padres and Bucky Badger of the University of Wisconsin, also serve to identify particular teams and can function as trademarks. *See Bd. of Supervisors for Louisiana State Univ. Agric. & Mech. Coll. v. Smack Apparel Co.*, 550 F.3d 465 (5th Cir. 2008) (university color schemes have acquired secondary meaning and are protected marks); *Univ. Book Store v. Board of Regents of the Univ. of Wisconsin*, 33 U.S.P.Q.2d 1385 (T.T.A.B. June 22, 1994) (although some consumers buy Bucky Badger apparel only because it's "cute," the symbol is not "merely ornamental" and signifies university sponsorship). What if a color scheme has a functional purpose, as team uniform colors do in helping team members, spectators, and officials differentiate among players on the field? Should the first team to use a particular color scheme be able to prohibit any subsequent uniform use?

3. *Disclaimers.* Should use of team names, logos and other insignia be permitted if the user makes clear that the sports entity is *not* authorizing their venture? What more should the CFL have done to communicate such a disclaimer?

4. *Likelihood of Confusion.* What is the relevant population for determining "likelihood of confusion" for trademark purposes? Should it be people who identify themselves as football fans? People in Indianapolis and/or in Baltimore? People who might actually buy NFL and/or CFL merchandise?

5. *Trademark Infringement Factors.* The *Colts* decision refers to an earlier district court decision in *Major League Baseball Properties v. Sed Non*

Olet Denarius, 817 F. Supp. 1103 (S.D.N.Y.1993). That case was the by-product of an even more notorious sports franchise move—the Dodgers' flight from Brooklyn to Los Angeles in 1958. The relocated baseball club had registered the word "Dodgers," and had licensed merchandisers to use both "Los Angeles Dodgers" and "Brooklyn Dodgers." On this basis, the club warned off a 1966 effort to name a Continental Football League team the Brooklyn Dodgers. However, it never challenged a Brooklyn restaurant named Dodgers Cafe during its operation from 1942 to 1968.

In 1991, though, the Dodgers filed a trademark infringement action against a new Brooklyn restaurant opened by some Dodgers fans—the Brooklyn Dodgers Sports Bar and Restaurant. Though the original team nickname commemorated "dodging" Brooklyn streetcars, the restaurant logo included a depiction of the Artful Dodger, a character from Charles Dickens' *Oliver Twist*. The restaurant did, however, draw heavily upon the illustrious history of the city's baseball team—naming dishes after famous Dodgers players, decorating the restaurant with Dodgers memorabilia, and selling licensed Brooklyn Dodgers merchandise.

The federal judge dismissed the claim after applying the standard trademark litigation factors:

a) Strength of the plaintiff's trademark

b) Similarity between the parties' marks

c) Proximity of their products

d) Likelihood that the plaintiff will "bridge the gap" between the two markets

e) Evidence of actual confusion

f) Presence or absence of good faith on the part of the defendant

g) Quality of defendant's services

h) Sophistication of likely purchasers

What balance would you strike among these and any other relevant factors in a case such as this one? Suppose that some ex-Oakland Raiders football fans had started a restaurant in Oakland bearing that name after the team moved to Las Vegas? How would the judges of the Ninth Circuit—located in San Francisco—respond?

2. OTHER SPORTS PHRASES AND DESIGNATIONS

As noted, trademark in sports extends far beyond team names. Texas A&M University claims ownership of the mark "12th Man"—a phrase that recognizes fan spirit and support of the university's football team. Its vigilance in protecting that mark led to lawsuits against the NFL's Seattle Seahawks and Indianapolis Colts, both of which ultimately settled by licensing use of the phrase. *See also New York Yankees P'ship v. Evil Enterprises, Inc.*, 2013 WL 1305332 (T.T.A.B. Feb. 8, 2013) (sustaining

New York Yankees' opposition to third party's registration of "Baseball's Evil Empire").

Similarly, the NFL's defense of the phrase "Super Bowl" is legendary. It has filed dozens of suits to stop unauthorized use of the phrase, including seeking to block a restaurant from trademarking its registration of "Souper Bowls." When the Philadelphia Eagles last played in the Super Bowl, a hometown sports bar resorted to identifying the annual event as the "Birds Big Game" to avoid NFL censure. In 2003, the NFL filed a trademark infringement suit against the fledgling National Women's Football League (NWFL), not for its use of that name or letters, but for using other marks, like "SupHer Bowl," and team logos that the NFL claimed were confusingly similar to its teams' marks. Although the case settled without a judicial ruling, what is your view about the legal merits of an infringement action against a new women's league that is largely unknown to the public and unlikely to survive (as the NWFL did not)? Why would the NFL bother to bring such a suit? It could not have been worried that consumers might mistakenly purchase NWFL tickets or merchandise when they meant to buy the NFL equivalents. An answer to this question is suggested in a suit involving the name of one of the sports world's most prestigious events— the men's Masters Golf Tournament at the National course in Augusta, Georgia.

Northwestern Mutual Life (NML) sponsored a Ladies Professional Golf Association Tournament, held one week after the Augusta Masters. NML named the tournament the "Ladies Masters at Moss Creek Plantation," in part to promote its new real estate development at that location. Augusta National immediately secured an injunction blocking any use of the word "Masters." *See Augusta National v. Northwestern Mutual Life Insurance*, 193 U.S.P.Q. 210 (S.D. Ga. 1976). As the judge put it:

> [T]he use of the term "Masters" by NML in the name of its planned annual tournament, "Ladies Masters at Moss Creek Plantation," is likely to confuse the public into believing that Augusta National also sponsors the women's tournament. From this factual premise, logic compels the conclusion that if Augusta National's reputation is high, defendant will be "trading" on that reputation and "reaping where it has not sown." If Augusta National's good will is of great value, defendant will be sharing in it without having contributed to its growth. Logic compels, too, the conclusion that if NML "sins," they will be "visited upon" Augusta National. If NML mismanages the tournament, Augusta National will suffer the consequences in loss of good will and reputation; and this without having a hand in it. In sum, there would be a confusion of businesses in which plaintiff would no longer be master of its own destiny.

The case presents a classic example of the reasons for the creation of equity jurisprudence calling for the exercise of the conscience of a long-footed chancellor.

193 U.S.P.Q. at 220.

Athletes have also sought to trademark personal catchphrases, logos, and mannerisms. While athletes cannot trademark an actual physical pose, they can trademark symbols, words, phrases, and designs that attempt to capture that pose. For example, Olympic sprinter Usain Bolt has trademarked an icon of his signature "lightning bolt" stance. Former NFL quarterback Tim Tebow holds the trademark for "Tebowing," a term that refers to the kneeling prayer stance Tebow took before games. New England Patriots tight end Rob Gronkowski has trademarked his silhouette spiking a football. Two cautions about such personal marks: First, the U.S. Patent and Trademark Office refuses to register sports-related slogans and taglines that consist entirely of "merely informational" matter. Thus, they rejected the trademark applications of NFLer Marshawn Lynch for "I'm just here so I won't get fined" and tennis great John McEnroe for "You cannot be serious." *See* USPTO Examination Guide 2–17 (July 2017). Second, unlike publicity rights, to maintain control over a trademark, the athlete must use it on commercial goods or risk forfeiting the mark.

NOTES AND QUESTIONS

1. *Secondary Meaning.* In light of the *Augusta National* decision, how would you decide a case brought by the promoters of the National Invitation Tournament in New York for men's college basketball teams, against the Women's National Invitation Tournament, which held its event for several years in the 1990s in Amarillo, Texas, and invited eight women's college basketball teams that did not qualify for the NCAA tournament? What distinctions, if any, do you see between the two cases? Consider the *Augusta National* finding that "in the public's mind, the word "Masters" in the context of golf and golf tournaments, has come to mean 'a single thing coming from a single source,' that is to say, a golf tournament sponsored by Augusta National."

2. *Reverse Confusion.* "Reverse confusion" occurs when a junior (second) user of a mark is much more famous than the senior (or first) user. The problem is not that consumers will mistakenly believe that the infringer's product is affiliated with or endorsed by the trademark owner, but rather that they will mistakenly believe that the trademark owner's product originates with or is endorsed by the infringer. In *Illinois High Sch. Ass'n v. GTE Vantage, Inc.*, 99 F.3d 244 (7th Cir. 1996), the court found that even though the Illinois high school basketball tournament had used the term "March Madness" long before

its association with the NCAA men's basketball tournament, the NCAA only began using the term after the media's frequent use had firmly linked it with the NCAA tournament in the minds of most consumers. That is, the broadcaster CBS, not the NCAA, caused the confusion. Thus, the court concluded that the IHSA and the NCAA had become joint owners of "March Madness," which led them to form a joint venture, the March Madness Athletic Association, to monitor and license the use of the term. *See March Madness Athletic Ass'n v. Netfire, Inc.*, 162 F. Supp. 2d 560 (N.D. Tex. 2001); *see also Dream Team Collectibles, Inc. v. NBA Properties, Inc.*, 958 F. Supp. 1401 (E.D. Mo. 1997) (factual issue whether NBA or media responsible for public association of "Dream Team" mark with NBA players).

3. MERCHANDISING OF SPORTS TRADEMARKS

The major economic value of a sports name or logo is not to adorn the players uniforms in games and thereby identify teams, but rather to market sports-related merchandise valued at tens of billions of dollars annually. Thus, in the *Colts* case, the NFL's principal motivation for suing was not the likelihood that football fans would be confused about whether they were buying tickets to watch the NFL Colts or the CFL Colts on the field. Rather, NFL Properties wanted to make sure that fans would not buy T-shirts and other paraphernalia licensed by the Baltimore CFL Colts, rather than by the Indianapolis Colts. Sports entities expend large sums of money to invest their symbols and colors with a strong secondary meaning of identification with a team, and argue that because such symbols create and perpetuate the good will of the member clubs, they perform the function of valid service marks. *See Nat'l Football League Properties, Inc. v. Consumer Enterprises, Inc.*, 26 Ill. App. 3d 814, 327 N.E.2d 242 (1975) (observing that trademarks "indicate sponsorship or origin in addition to their ornamental value").

Use of trademark law to secure such protection poses an analytical problem. Recall that the nature and objective of trademark law is to encourage producers like Nike and Augusta National to develop distinctive names and symbols to identify their products, by barring other producers from attaching the same names and symbols to other products and thence misleading consumers looking to enjoy (and pay for) their favorite running shoes or golf tournament. Producers do not, however, receive a copyright-like monopoly in their name and symbol that blocks others from using it for non-confusing purposes. Pepsi, for example, can use the words "Coca Cola" in an advertisement that tries to draw an unfavorable comparison with its own product. So also could the CFL refer to the NFL's Super Bowl in advertising how closely-contested are CFL championship Grey Cup games.

In the case of sports merchandising, though, leagues and teams are selling names and symbols in and of themselves, thus allowing fans wearing a T-shirt to identify with their favorite teams and sports. If the T-shirt carried the name and likeness of a celebrated athlete, the publicity right we encountered earlier gives the individual the exclusive legal authority to license or bar use of his name and likeness for that purpose. Teams or leagues, by contrast, are business organizations, and thus cannot use this legal outgrowth of the right of personal privacy. Some other justification had to be found for granting the "right" to control merchandise that includes a team or university name. It was offered in a 1975 judicial ruling that greatly expanded trademark doctrine to protect sports merchandise and promotional goods.

BOSTON PROFESSIONAL HOCKEY ASSOCIATION V. DALLAS CAP AND EMBLEM MFG., INC.
510 F.2d 1004 (5th Cir. 1975)

RONEY, CIRCUIT JUDGE.

[Prior to this case, NHL hockey teams had organized National Hockey League Services (NHLS) to serve as their exclusive licensing agent. NHLS licensed numerous manufacturers to use the team names and symbols in various merchandise, including an exclusive license with Lion Brothers Company to manufacture embroidered emblems depicting the team logos. Between 1968 and 1971, Dallas Cap & Emblem sought to obtain a similar license. Unable to do so, the company then proceeded to manufacture the emblems for sale to sporting goods stores in various states.

When the NHL teams ultimately sued for trademark infringement, their complaint alleged that Dallas Cap's manufacture and sale of the team symbols constituted (1) an infringement of the plaintiffs' registered marks in violation of 15 U.S.C.A. § 1114; (2) false designation of origin in violation of 15 U.S.C.A. § 1125; and (3) common law unfair competition. The district court held that a disclaimer informing consumers that the products were not officially authorized by the NHL was a sufficient remedy. The NHL teams appealed.]

* * *

Nearly everyone is familiar with the artistic symbols which designate the individual teams in various professional sports. The question in this case of first impression is whether the unauthorized, intentional duplication of a professional hockey team's symbol on an embroidered emblem, to be sold to the public as a patch for attachment to clothing, violates any legal right of the team to the exclusive use of that symbol. Contrary to the decision of the district court, we hold that the team has an interest in its own individualized symbol entitled to legal protection against such unauthorized duplication.

* * *

The Case

The difficulty with this case stems from the fact that a reproduction of the trademark itself is being sold, unattached to any other goods or services. The statutory and case law of trademarks is oriented toward the use of such marks to sell something other than the mark itself. The district court thought that to give plaintiffs protection in this case would be tantamount to the creation of a copyright monopoly for designs that were not copyrighted. The copyright laws are based on an entirely different concept than the trademark laws, and contemplate that the copyrighted material, like patented ideas, will eventually pass into the public domain. The trademark laws are based on the needed protection of the public and business interests and there is no reason why trademarks should ever pass into the public domain by the mere passage of time.

Although our decision here may slightly tilt the trademark laws from the purpose of protecting the public to the protection of the business interests of plaintiffs, we think that the two become so intermeshed when viewed against the backdrop of the common law of unfair competition that both the public and plaintiffs are better served by granting the relief sought by plaintiffs.

Underlying our decision are three persuasive points. First, the major commercial value of the emblems is derived from the efforts of plaintiffs. Second, defendant sought and ostensibly would have asserted, if obtained, an exclusive right to make and sell the emblems. Third, the sale of a reproduction of the trademark itself on an emblem is an accepted use of such team symbols in connection with the type of activity in which the business of professional sports is engaged. We need not deal here with the concept of whether every artistic reproduction of the symbol would infringe upon plaintiffs' rights. We restrict ourselves to the emblems sold principally through sporting goods stores for informal use by the public in connection with sports activities and to show public allegiance to or identification with the teams themselves.

* * *

[The court turned directly to the question whether the plaintiffs had proven elements (4) and (5) of a § 1114 violation, *i.e.*, whether the symbols were used in connection with the sale of goods and whether such use was likely to cause confusion, mistake, or deception.]

* * *

The fourth requisite of a § 1114 cause of action is that the infringing use of the registered mark must be in connection with the sale, offering for sale, distribution or advertising of any goods. Although the district court did not expressly find that plaintiffs had failed to establish element four, such a finding was implicit in the court's statement that "in the instant case, the registered trade mark is, in effect, the product itself."

Defendant is in the business of manufacturing and marketing emblems for wearing apparel. These emblems are the products, or goods, which defendant sells. When defendant causes plaintiffs' marks to be embroidered upon emblems which it later markets, defendant uses those marks in connection with the sale of goods as surely as if defendant had embroidered the marks upon knit caps. *See Boston Professional Hockey Association, Inc. v. Reliable Knitting Works,* 178 U.S.P.Q. (BNA) 274 (E.D. Wis. 1973). The fact that the symbol covers the entire face of defendant's product does not alter the fact that the trademark symbol is used in connection with the sale of the product. The sports fan in his local sporting goods store purchases defendant's fabric and thread emblems because they are embroidered with the symbols of ice hockey teams. Were defendant to embroider the same fabric with the same thread in other designs, the resulting products would still be emblems for wearing apparel but they would not give trademark identification to the customer. The conclusion is inescapable that, without plaintiffs' marks, defendant would not have a market for his particular product among ice hockey fans desiring to purchase emblems embroidered with the symbols of their favorite teams. It becomes clear that defendant's use of plaintiffs' marks is in connection with the sale, offering for sale, distribution, or advertising of goods and that plaintiffs have established the fourth element of a § 1114 cause of action.

The fifth element of a cause of action for mark infringement under 15 U.S.C.A. § 1114 is that the infringing use is likely to cause confusion, or to cause mistake or to deceive. The district court decided that there was no likelihood of confusion because the usual purchaser, a sports fan in his local sporting goods store, would not be likely to think that defendant's emblems were manufactured by or had some connection with plaintiffs. . . . In this case, however, the district court overlooked the fact that the Act was amended to eliminate the source of origin as being the only focal point of confusion. The confusion question here is conceptually difficult. It can be said that the public buyer knew that the emblems portrayed the teams' symbols. Thus, it can be argued, the buyer is not confused or deceived. This argument misplaces the purpose of the confusion requirement. The confusion or deceit requirement is met by the fact that the defendant duplicated the protected trademarks and sold them to the public knowing that the public would identify them as being the teams' trademarks. The certain knowledge of the buyer that the source and origin of the trademark symbols were in plaintiffs satisfies the requirement of the Act. The argument that confusion must be as to the source of the manufacture of the emblem itself is unpersuasive, where the trademark, originated by the team, is the triggering mechanism for the sale of the emblem.

* * *

Additional Defenses to Relief

Defendant makes two arguments against an extension of Lanham Act protection to plaintiffs which need consideration. Adopting the district court's rationale, defendant asserts first, that plaintiffs' marks when embroidered on emblems for wearing apparel are functional and thus serve no trademark purpose and, second, that there is some overriding concept of free competition which, under the instant facts, would remove plaintiffs from the protective ambits of the Lanham Act.

The short answer to defendant's arguments is that the emblems sold because they bore the identifiable trademarks of plaintiffs. This fact clearly distinguishes the case from *Pagliero v. Wallace China Co.*, 198 F.2d 339 (9th Cir. 1952), relied upon by the district court. *Pagliero* involved designs on chinaware which were neither trademarked, patented nor copyrighted. The court found no unfair competition on the ground that the designs were functional, that is, they connoted other than a trademark purpose. "The attractiveness and eye-appeal of the design sells the china," 198 F.2d at 343–344, not the trademark character of the designs. In the case at bar, the embroidered symbols are sold not because of any such aesthetic characteristic but because they are the trademarks of the hockey teams. Those cases which involved utilitarian articles such as pole lamps, *Sears, Roebuck & Co. v. Stiffel Co.*, 376 U.S. 225 (1964), fluorescent lighting fixtures, *Compco Corp. v. Day-Brite Lighting, Inc.*, 376 U.S. 234 (1964), and toggle clamps, *West Point Mfg. Co. v. Detroit Stamping Co.*, 222 F.2d 581, 105 U.S.P.Q. (BNA) 200 (6th Cir. 1955), all involved products which had a consumer demand regardless of their source or origin. The principles involved in those cases are not applicable to a trademark symbol case where the design or symbol has no demonstrated value other than its significance as the trademark of a hockey team.

The argument that the symbols could be protected only if copyrighted likewise misses the thrust of trademark protection. A trademark is a property right which is acquired by use. *Trade-Mark Cases*, 100 U.S. 82 (1879). It differs substantially from a copyright, in both its legal genesis and its scope of federal protection. The legal cornerstone for the protection of copyrights is Article I, section 8, clause 8 of the Constitution. In the case of a copyright, an individual creates a unique design and, because the Constitutional fathers saw fit to encourage creativity, he can secure a copyright for his.... After the expiration of the copyright, his creation becomes part of the public domain. In the case of a trademark, however, the process is reversed. An individual selects a word or design that might otherwise be in the public domain to represent his business or product. If that word or design comes to symbolize his product or business in the public mind, the individual acquires a property right in the mark. The acquisition of such a right through use represents the passage of a word or design out of the public domain into the protective ambits of trademark law. Under the provisions of the Lanham Act, the owner of a mark acquires a protectable property interest in his mark through registration and use.

The time limit on copyright protection not being sufficient for plaintiffs' purposes, they acquainted the public with their marks and thereby created a demand for those marks. Through extensive use, plaintiffs have acquired a property right in their marks which extends to the reproduction and sale of those marks as embroidered patches for wearing apparel. What plaintiffs have acquired by use, the substantive law of trademarks as it is embodied in the Lanham Act will protect against infringement. There is no overriding policy of free competition which would remove plaintiffs, under the facts of this case, from the protective ambits of the Lanham Act.

* * *

Reversed and remanded.

NOTES AND QUESTIONS

1. *Expansion of Trademark.* Boston Hockey produced a major and controversial expansion in the scope of trademark law, still being debated today. Trademark law scholars have contested the misappropriation and "free-riding" theories underlying that decision, asserting the result has been to reduce market competition, chill free expression, and transfer revenue from fans to teams and their licensees. *See* Mark A. Lemley & Mark P. McKenna, *Owning Mark(et)s*, 109 Mich. L. Rev. 137, 168 (2010). Nonetheless, decisions in the sports context since *Boston Hockey* acknowledge that trademark law protects against confusion not just as to source, but also as to sponsorship. For example, in *Univ. of Georgia Athletic Ass'n v. Laite*, 756 F.2d 1535, 1546 (11th Cir. 1985), a brewery sold "Battlin' Bulldog Beer" with a logo that portrayed an English bulldog like the University of Georgia mascot. The court found "irrelevant" that no one believed the university had gone into the brewing business: " '[C]onfusion' need not relate to the origin of the challenged product. Rather, 'confusion' may relate to the public's knowledge that the trademark, which is 'the triggering mechanism' for the sale of the product, originates with the plaintiff." *Id.* at 1547. Do you agree that it is irrelevant whether anyone believed the university brewed the beer? If a mark owner can preclude uses even in markets it does not now and never intends to serve, what is the cost/benefit to the consumer?

2. *Lanham Act Amendment.* In 1988, Congress amended the Lanham Act to expressly protect sponsorship confusion, as opposed to source confusion. The new language defined infringement to include deception as to "association . . . or as to the origin, sponsorship, or approval" of goods, services, or commercial activities. 15 U.S.C. § 1124(a). While this amendment was not necessarily intended to codify *Boston Hockey* (consumers were not confused

that the NHL team sponsored the emblem manufacturer), it did expand recognition of merchandising rights. Why do you think Congress believed this amendment to be necessary?

With the 1988 amendment, the Act prohibited as infringing a third party's unauthorized use of a trademark as long as consumers would likely, and erroneously, mentally associate the mark's owner with that use. Some believe that this expansion of trademark has reinforced the presumption that merchandised products are sponsored by trademark owners, thus in a circular fashion increasing the likelihood of consumer confusion. Would it be preferable to allow unauthorized users to avoid liability through disclaimers of any affiliation with mark owners? How do you think this prohibition has affected competition and consumer prices? Consider whether this prohibition facilitates commerce or creates scarcity of critical commercial resources, *i.e.*, aesthetically functional product features such as colors and designs, as well as the language to describe one's products.

3. *Copyright Versus Trademark.* The *Boston Hockey* court observed that copyright would not provide adequate protections for mark owners because of its finite duration, as opposed to trademark rights, which last indefinitely while the owner continues to use the mark. In addition, copyright damages in this case would likely be far less than trademark damages because copyright entitles the holder to recoup profits only to the extent attributable to the item's design. But no one was buying the emblems because of their appearance; they were buying them because of their association with a team. Thus, in *Bouchat v. Baltimore Ravens Football Club, Inc.*, 346 F.3d 514, 520 (4th Cir. 2003), a court affirmed the award of zero copyright damages to the creator of the "Flying B" logo that the NFL Ravens had copied without consent, based on the finding that the team's profits from the logo were not attributable to the copyright infringement but to its own value-creating activities. How would you go about demonstrating that fan interest in a team logo derived from associational value, and not an aesthetically appealing design? Is this always the case?

Consider also the Supreme Court's decision in *Star Athletica, LLC v. Varsity Brands, Inc.*, 137 S. Ct. 1002 (2017), which upheld a copyright in cheerleader uniforms that gave exclusive rights to one company to use the chevrons, zigzags, and stripes that characterize those uniforms. The Court held that because copyright protection extends to "pictorial, graphic, or sculptural" works, it must also cover "industrial" designs that incorporate these features. Reaction to the decision was highly critical, pointing out that when such features have a functional purpose, the copyright monopoly is inappropriate. That said, what is your advice to sports trademark owners regarding uniform colors, designs, and other insignia? Would it be now wise to double-down and register a copyright as well?

4. *Delay or Laches.* As noted earlier, mark owners must remain vigilant in protecting trademark rights that they hope to monetize, and they closely monitor all markets and environments where unauthorized use might occur.

Thus, in *University of Pittsburgh v. Champion Products Inc.*, 686 F.2d 1040 (3d Cir.), *cert. denied*, 495 U.S. 1087 (1982), the court held that a university could not recover damages for trademark infringement that occurred during a 36-year delay in objecting to the unauthorized sale of promotional items bearing its name and mascot. However, the court issued an injunction against future unauthorized use. When should delay in enforcing a trademark be deemed abandonment of that mark, or otherwise defer to a junior user's reliance interest in developing a business based on the mark?

4. FAIR USE OF A TRADEMARK

A pair of infringement suits involving the Boston Marathon invite examination of when an unauthorized user may assert a fair use defense to trademark infringement. Since 1897, the Boston Marathon has been run annually on Patriots Day, under the auspices of the non-profit Boston Athletic Association (BAA). But it was only since the 1980s that the BAA sought to assert intellectual property rights in the event. In the first case, *BAA v. Sullivan*, 867 F.2d 22 (1st Cir. 1989), the BAA sued a clothing manufacturer that sold T-shirts depicting the event, including its name and pictures of runners. Although the First Circuit acknowledged "that a trademark, unlike a copyright or patent, is not a 'right in gross' that enables a holder to enjoin all reproduction," the court concluded that "when a manufacturer intentionally uses another's mark as a means of establishing a link in consumers' minds with the other's enterprise, and directly profits from that link, there is an unmistakable aura of deception." It further observed:

> [g]iven the undisputed facts that (1) defendants intentionally referred to the Boston Marathon on its shirts, and (2) purchasers were likely to buy the shirts precisely because of that reference, we think it fair to presume that purchasers are likely to be confused about the shirt's source or sponsorship. We presume that, at the least, a sufficient number of purchasers would be likely to assume—mistakenly—that defendant's shirts had some connection with the official sponsors of the Boston Marathon. In the absence of any evidence that effectively rebuts this presumption of a "likelihood of confusion," we hold that plaintiffs are entitled to enjoin the manufacture and sale of defendant's shirts.

867 F.2d at 34.

That decision laid the groundwork for the second case, arising out of the BAA's grant of an exclusive license to WBZ-TV, the local Channel 4 station, to telecast the race. Nevertheless, WCVB-TV, Channel 5 in Boston, continued to televise the race with cameras in helicopters and along the marathon route, and regularly used the phrase Boston Marathon before, during, and after its unauthorized telecast. The BAA went back to court, relying not on the *Pittsburgh Athletic* case, but on trademark law as interpreted in *Sullivan*. The unlicensed station, WCVB-TV argued that it was entitled to make fair use of the name Boston Marathon in reporting on the event, and the First Circuit agreed.

WCVB-TV v. Boston Athletic Ass'n
926 F.2d 42 (1st Cir. 1991)

Breyer, Chief Judge.

* * *

[The Court initially noted the "likelihood of confusion" standard for trademark infringement cases.]

* * *

Obviously, we do not have before us the common, garden variety type of "confusion" that might arise with typical trademark infringement. This is not a heartland trademark case, where, for example, plaintiff uses the words "Big Tom" to mark his apple juice, defendant (perhaps a big man called Tom) uses the same words (or perhaps similar words, *e.g.*, "Large Tommy") on his own apple juice label, and plaintiff says customers will confuse defendant's apple juice with his own. *See, e.g., Beer Nuts, Inc. v. Clover Club Foods Co.*, 805 F.2d 920 (10th Cir. 1986) ("Beer Nuts" and "Brew Nuts" confusingly similar); 2 J. McCarthy § 23.3 at 56 ("Cases where a defendant uses an identical mark on competitive goods hardly ever find their way into the appellate reports . . . [and] are 'open and shut'. . . ."). No one here says that Channel 5 is running its own marathon on Patriot's Day, which a viewer might confuse with the BAA's famous Boston Marathon.

Rather, BAA argues that the confusion here involved is somewhat special. It points to cases where a defendant uses a plaintiff's trademark in connection with a different type of good or service and a plaintiff claims that the public will wrongly, and confusedly, think that the defendant's product somehow has the plaintiff's official "O.K." or imprimatur. The Eleventh Circuit, for example, found trademark law violated when the defendant, without authorization, used the plaintiff's football team mark, a bulldog, not in connection with a different football team, but, rather, on his beer mugs. *See University of Georgia Athletic Ass'n v. Laite*, 756 F.2d 1535 (11th Cir. 1985). This circuit has found trademark law violated, when the defendant, without authorization, used this very appellant's foot race mark, "Boston Marathon," on his t-shirts, sold during the event, permitting the customer to wrongly or confusedly think that his t-shirts were somehow "official." *See Boston Athletic Ass'n v. Sullivan*, 867 F.2d 22 (1st Cir. 1989). BAA goes on to say that Channel 5's use of those words will lead viewers, wrongly, and confusedly, to believe that Channel 5 (like the t-shirt seller) has a BAA license or permission or authorization to use the words, *i.e.*, that it broadcasts with the BAA's official imprimatur. It also notes that this court, in *Sullivan*, listed circumstances that create a "rebuttable presumption" of confusion. And, it quotes language from *Sullivan*, in which this court, citing *International News Service v. Associated Press*, 248 U.S. 215 (1918), said that the defendant's t-shirts were "clearly designed to take advantage of the Boston Marathon and to benefit from the good will associated with its promotion by plaintiffs," and that defendants obtained a "free ride" at the plaintiffs' expense; they "reap where [they have] not sown." *Sullivan*, 867 F.2d at 33. Appellants say that Channel 5 is doing the same here.

In our view, the cases BAA cites, and *Sullivan* in particular, do not govern the outcome of this case. Nor can we find a likelihood of any relevant confusion here. First, the *Sullivan* opinion, taken as a whole, makes clear that the court, in using the language appellants cite, referring to a "free ride," and taking "advantage" of another's good will, did not intend to depart from ordinary principles of federal trademark law that make a finding of a "likelihood of confusion" essential to a conclusion of "violation." As a general matter, the law sometimes protects investors from the "free riding" of others; and sometimes it does not. The law, for example, gives inventors a "property right" in certain inventions for a limited period of time; *see* 35 U.S.C. 101 *et seq.*; it provides copyright protection for authors; *see* 17 U.S.C. 101 *et seq.*; it offers certain protections to trade secrets. *See generally* 2 J. McCarthy § 29.16. But, the man who clears a swamp, the developer of a neighborhood, the academic scientist, the school teacher, and millions of others, each day create "value" (over and above what they are paid) that the law permits others to receive without charge. Just how, when and where the law should protect investments in "intangible" benefits or goods is a matter that legislators typically debate, embodying the results in specific statutes, or that common law courts, carefully weighing relevant competing interests, gradually work out over time. The trademark statute does not give the appellants any "property right" in their mark except "the right to prevent confusion." And, nothing in *Sullivan* suggests the contrary.

Second, the "rebuttable presumption" of confusion that this court set forth in *Sullivan* does not apply here. We concede that the *Sullivan* court said that "there is a rebuttable presumption" of confusion "about the shirts' source or sponsorship" arising from the fact that the defendants used the words "Boston Marathon" on the shirts, which use made customers more likely to buy the shirts. The court wrote that when a manufacturer intentionally uses another's mark as a means of establishing a link in consumers' minds with the other's enterprise, and directly profits from that link, there is an unmistakable aura of deception. *Sullivan*, 867 F.2d at 35. As we read these words, they mean that the *Sullivan* record indicated that the defendant wanted to give the impression that his t-shirt was an "official" t-shirt, a fact that, in the sports world, might give a shirt, in the eyes of sports fans, a special "cachet." It makes sense to presume confusion about a relevant matter (namely, official sponsorship) from such an intent, at least in the absence of contrary evidence.

Here, however, there is no persuasive evidence of any intent to use the words "Boston Marathon" to suggest official sponsorship of Channel 5's broadcasts. To the contrary, Channel 5 offered to "broadcast whatever disclaimers" the BAA might want—"every thirty seconds, every two minutes, every ten minutes"—to make certain no one thought the channel had any special broadcasting status. Nor is there any evidence that Channel 5 might somehow profit from viewers' wrongly thinking that the BAA had authorized its broadcasts. Indeed, one would ordinarily believe that television viewers (unlike sports fans who might want to buy an official t-shirt with the name of a favorite event, team or player) wish to see the event and do not particularly care about the relation of station to event-promoter.

Third, and perhaps most importantly, the record provides us with an excellent reason for thinking that Channel 5's use of the words "Boston Marathon" would not confuse the typical Channel 5 viewer. That reason consists of the fact that those words do more than call attention to Channel 5's program; they also describe the event that Channel 5 will broadcast. Common sense suggests (consistent with the record here) that a viewer who sees those words flash upon the screen will believe simply that Channel 5 will show, or is showing, or has shown, the marathon, not that Channel 5 has some special approval from the BAA to do so. In technical trademark jargon, the use of words for descriptive purposes is called a "fair use," and the law usually permits it even if the words themselves also constitute a trademark. If, for example, a t-shirt maker placed the words "Pure Cotton" (instead of the words "Boston Marathon") on his t-shirts merely to describe the material from which the shirts were made, not even a shirt maker who had a registered trademark called "Pure Cotton" could likely enjoin their sale. As Justice Holmes pointed out many years ago, "when the mark is used in a way that does not deceive the public we see no such sanctity in the word as to prevent its being used to tell the truth." *Prestonettes Inc. v. Coty*, 264 U.S. 359, 368.

This is not a case where it is difficult to decide whether a defendant is using particular words primarily as a mark, i.e., as an "attention getting symbol," or primarily as a description. Here there is little in the record before us to suggest the former (only the large size of the words on the screen); while there is much to show the latter (timing, meaning, context, intent, and surrounding circumstances). Consequently, the appellants have shown no real likelihood of relevant confusion.

We also note that the only federal court which has decided a case nearly identical to the one before us, a case in which a station planning to televise a public parade was sued by the parade's promoter who had granted "exclusive" rights to another station, reached a conclusion similar to the one we draw here. *See Production Contractors, Inc. v. WGN Continental Broadcasting Co.*, 622 F. Supp. 1500, 1504 (N.D. Ill.1985). Reviewing the promoter's Lanham Act claim that the "unauthorized" broadcast would create a "false impression" of sponsorship, the court concluded that it fell "far short of establishing likelihood of confusion" among viewers that the defendant station was the "official" or "authorized" broadcaster of the parade. Similarly, we do not see how Channel 5's broadcast could likely confuse viewers that it bore the imprimatur of the BAA.

* * *

Affirmed.

———

Fair use was interposed by the NFL Players Association in defense of an NFL lawsuit challenging a $1.6 million sponsorship agreement between the union's licensing subsidiary Players Inc. and Coors to designate it the "Official Beer of the NFL Players." *NFL v. Coors Brewing Co.*, 205 F.3d 1324 (2d Cir. 1999). In this case, however, the NFL secured a preliminary injunction barring the use. While the NFL owners said their primary concern was reputational harm from their players endorsing alcoholic beverages, they were also worried that this use of the "NFL" trademark would devalue their own deals worth millions of dollars with Miller Brewing and Anheuser-Busch. The court rejected Players Inc.'s argument that its use of "NFL" was merely descriptive, because "the record is transparent that Coors wanted to capitalize on the good will inherent in the NFL trademark." *Id.* at 1324. Was this the right decision? Would the union's licensing Coors as the "Official Beer of the NFLPA" produce the same result? What about the "Official Beer of Professional Football Players"? Would the Players Association be able to reap essentially the same return by using these alternative endorsements?

The question of whether a team name is merely descriptive has come up in other contexts. When celebrity players (or their unions) license their publicity rights to merchandisers, can those merchandisers identify the players as being "an NFL player" or a "Yankee," or must the merchandiser also obtain a trademark license from the league and/or team? In *NBA Properties and NFL Properties v. Dahlonega*, 41 F. Supp. 2d 1341 (N.D. Ga. 1998), the court granted summary judgment to the plaintiff sports leagues on the claim that trading card companies violated their trademark rights by selling cards in which players wore the full team uniform. The trading card companies had licensed player image rights, but not team trademarks. The court, however, referred to a jury whether removal of team names and logos, leaving just the uniform color and design, caused the necessary consumer "confusion" about the role of the team in this card product.

Contrast *Major League Baseball Properties v. Pacific Trading Cards*, 48 U.S.P.Q.2d 1944 (S.D.N.Y. 1998), where the court refused to restrain baseball cards displaying players in their uniforms, cards that had been licensed by the Players Association but not by MLB or its teams. As the judge explained:

> ... the reason a child may have to trade two cards of a player of lesser quality for one Cal Ripken Jr. card is found in the differences in the players' records and has nothing to do with differences in the quality of the teams' uniforms or the distinctiveness of their logos.

Id. at *2.

Which of these results seems correct? More reasonable? As a practical matter, most merchandisers today now obtain both publicity rights licenses from the players and trademark licenses from the league or team before employing these marketing approaches.

Golf has also contributed to the evolution of this area of trademark law. In *Resorts of Pinehurst v. Pinehurst National Corporation*, 148 F.3d 417 (4th Cir. 1998), the historic Pinehurst Resort and Country Club won a lawsuit against another golf course near the Village of Pinehurst barring it from using that town's name in its title, because the name had acquired a secondary trademark meaning, at least in the minds of golfers. Should that same reasoning apply to allow the resort to block a merchant from opening up a business in the town under the name Pinehurst Sporting Goods, or Pinehurst Hardware Store? What about a business in some other town in North Carolina using those trade names? On the other hand, in *Pebble Beach v. Tour 18 I Ltd.*, 155 F.3d 526 (5th Cir. 1998), the Fifth Circuit held that it was lawful for the defendant to market (with a disclaimer) a new golf course in the town of Humble, Texas, that was labeled "America's Greatest 18 Holes" with each hole designed to resemble famous holes from Pinehurst, Pebble Beach, Sea Pines, and other great courses in America.

NOTES AND QUESTIONS

1. *Effectiveness of Disclaimers.* Are there differences in the doctrinal approaches used by the First Circuit panels in the two *Boston Marathon* cases? Between the First Circuit and the Fifth Circuit's decision in *Boston Hockey*? As a tangible test, what would have been the First Circuit's response if Sullivan had followed the suggestion of the district court in *Boston Hockey* and added to its T-shirt label the notation "*Not* sponsored or authorized by the BAA?"

2. *Descriptive Fair Use.* A junior user, even a direct competitor, may fairly use another party's descriptive trademark to describe its product. Thus, in *SportFuel, Inc. v. Pepsico, Inc. & The Gatorade Co.*, 2018 WL 2984830 (N.D. Ill. June 14, 2018), a court upheld Gatorade's fair use of the phrase "sport fuel," despite it serving as the trademark of a competing sports drink, because it is descriptive of Gatorade's products and services, and the company used the phrase in good faith. Similarly, in *Oaklawn Jockey Club, Inc. v. Kentucky Downs, LLC*, 184 F. Supp. 3d 572, 577 (W.D. Ky. 2016), *aff'd*, 687 F. App'x 429 (6th Cir. 2017), the court upheld as fair use a gambling service's display of names such as Churchill Downs in identifying the geographic origin of the racetracks where races were held. What do these decisions tell you about the importance of adopting distinctive, rather than merely descriptive, trademarks as source identifiers?

3. *Nominative Fair Use/Parody.* Use of another's trademark for the purpose of comparative advertising, social commentary, or parody can also be a non-infringing fair use. Recall the *Cardtoons* case in which the court rejected athlete publicity-right claims against parody trading cards. The court similarly rejected trademark claims because the cards did not create consumer confusion regarding their source. The court observed that "as with all successful parodies, the effect of the cards is to amuse, rather than confuse." *Cardtoons, L.C. v. Major League Baseball Players Ass'n*, 95 F.3d 959, 967 (10th Cir. 1996).

How should courts draw the line between amusement and confusion in future cases, especially given the rapid speed of internet memes that parody sports? Does it depend on the purported social value of the commentary being offered? The golf equipment company Titleist sued a parody company I Made Bogey over gear that uses Titleist's distinct font, but swaps in the word "Titties." Does the offensiveness of the parody bolster an infringement claim? *See also Corp. of Gonzaga Univ. v. Pendleton Enterprises, LLC*, 55 F. Supp. 3d 1319 (E.D. Wash. 2014) (court blocked a radio station and bar from using university symbols where concerned fans were outraged at supposed university affiliation with scatological and sexist humor); *Dallas Cowboys Cheerleaders, Inc. v. Pussycat Cinema, Ltd.*, 604 F.2d 200 (2d Cir. 1979) (enjoining "sexually depraved film" *Debbie Does Dallas*, whose star wore uniform similar to Dallas Cowboy cheerleader).

4. *Consumer Perception.* Given creative lawyering, litigation-related surveys of consumer confusion are likely to elicit it to some degree. The reality is that, because of the current blend of legal action and industry reaction, a large part of the consuming public probably does believe that the products they are buying with merchandising names and symbols carry the authorization of the parties that created those names and symbols. On the other hand, if the law were to make it clear that any manufacturer could sell clothing with the Dallas Cowboys or Chicago Bulls name and logo on it, as long as the item carried a specific disclaimer, customers would not assume that any such product carried the *imprimatur* of the Cowboys, the Bulls, and their respective leagues. What is your view of how the law should seek to shape consumer perceptions?

5. TRADEMARK DILUTION

The Federal Trademark Dilution Act of 1995 amended the existing Lanham Act to grant the "owner of a *famous mark*" injunctive relief and potentially damages if others used its mark in ways that "cause *dilution* of the distinctive quality of the mark." Notably, the new cause of action does not require proof that an unauthorized use creates a likelihood of confusion or actual economic harm. As revised in 2006, the Act requires the dilution claimant to first show that the mark is "widely recognized by the general consuming public of the United States as a designation of source of the goods or services of the mark's owner." 15 U.S.C. § 1125(c)(2)(A). Famous sports trademarks include those of all major professional leagues and teams, national sports governing bodies such as the NCAA or the United States Olympic Committee, Division I university football and basketball teams, and signature sporting events such as the Masters golf tournament, the Kentucky Derby, major sports all-star games, and the NCAA's March Madness basketball tournament.

Dilution of a famous mark can occur either by "blurring" that "impairs the distinctiveness of the famous mark" or by "tarnishment" that "harms the reputation of the famous mark." To determine whether dilution has occurred, courts will consider the following factors:

1. the degree of similarity between the subject mark and the famous mark;
2. the degree of inherent or acquired distinctiveness of the famous mark;
3. the extent to which the owner of the famous mark is exclusively using the mark;
4. the degree of the mark's recognition;
5. whether the use of the mark was intended to create an association with the famous mark; and
6. any actual association between the mark and the famous mark.

In sports world cases decided under the revised Dilution Act, courts have emphasized the harm to the mark owner arising from association with the unauthorized user's inferior goods and services. *See Dallas Cowboys Football Club, Ltd. v. America's Team Properties*, 616 F. Supp. 2d 622 (N.D. Tex. 2009) (tarnishing of "America's Team" mark demonstrated by defendant's distribution of shoddy wristbands that misspelled the word "basketball"); *New York City Triathlon LLC v. NYC Triathlon Club Inc.*, 95 U.S.P.Q.2d 1451 (S.D.N.Y. 2010) (athletic club's name diluted by defendant's "pattern of sub-par business practices and poor customer support").

Consider also whether "fair use" can serve as a defense to a trademark dilution claim. In *New York Yankees Partnership v. IET Products and Services, Inc.*, No. 91189692 (T.T.A.B. May 8, 2015), the Yankees successfully opposed trademark registration for marks including "House That Juice Built" because they diluted its famous mark "House That Ruth Built." The Trademark Trial and Appeal Board firmly stated that the fair use defense in trademark dilution cases cannot succeed at the registration phase if the defendant's use is commercial. Recall that registration is not required to use and claim ownership of a trademark. So, the parody business can proceed to operate and assert the defense in court if necessary. Should a business have to take this risk? Should we be concerned that this approach to trademark registration risks chilling free expression?

Another piece of federal legislation further extended trademark protection to the internet. The Anticybersquatting Consumer Protection Act of 1999 established a cause of action for registering, trafficking in, or using a domain name confusingly similar to, or dilutive of, a trademark or personal name. 15 U.S.C. § 1125(d). In the sports industry, teams and athletes have availed themselves of the Act's protections to combat opportunists who use a domain name with the bad faith intent to profit from the goodwill of their trademarks and celebrity. Cybersquatters typically offer to sell a domain to a person or company who owns a trademark contained within the name at an inflated price, a tactic the Act can be used to defeat. But difficulties can arise when the domain owner can show it legitimately uses its domain name, as the Brooklyn Nets learned when they attempted to retrieve Nets.com from a first-user telecommunications and internet company. With the proliferation of top-level domains (*e.g.*, .com, .biz, .net), owners of famous marks will need to be ever more vigilant to protect them on the internet.

NOTES AND QUESTIONS

1. *Dilution and* Boston Hockey. The trademark dilution amendment does not necessarily endorse the broad protection of logos granted by *Boston Hockey*, because not all unauthorized uses of a mark tarnish or blur. Thus, it has been argued that the dilution provision should not provide relief in merchandising cases. Yet, in *Texas Tech Univ. v. Spiegelberg*, 461 F. Supp. 2d 510, 524 (N.D. Tex. 2006), a court held that defendant's unauthorized use of Texas Tech's famous "Double T" and "Raider Red" logos diluted those marks, even though used on precisely the same type of merchandise sold by official licensees. The court nonetheless found that defendant's products "will likely blur the uniqueness [and] result in diminished individuality of the officially licensed products." Why did Texas Tech lodge dilution claims in addition to its fairly open-and-shut case for trademark infringement? Were the Texas Tech marks sufficiently famous to merit protection under the dilution provision?

How will this interpretation of the dilution provision affect the risk tolerance of third parties who might have a legitimate fair use defense in trademark?

2. *Reputational Harm.* For many years, the NFL and other sports leagues expressed displeasure about gambling on their games, given the potential for point-shaving and game-throwing. In 1976, when the Delaware State Lottery hosted a sports lottery based on weekly results of NFL games, the League filed suit, deploring this "forced association with gambling." The League argued that Delaware's use of its game scores, listed solely by team city, misappropriated its reputation and popularity and violated its trademarks, despite the absence of any NFL team names or insignia in lottery materials. In a decision that may inform current debate over league property rights in connection with legalized sports gambling, the court permitted Delaware's usage subject to a disclaimer that the lottery had no affiliation with the NFL. *See NFL v. Governor of the State of Delaware*, 435 F. Supp. 1372 (D. Del. 1977).

How does this result square with *Pittsburgh Athletic*? This case predates the Trademark Dilution Act—would the NFL have a stronger case today under that statute? Which branch of intellectual property provides the leagues with the strongest basis to assert control over use of their assets (game information, trademarks, identifying insignia) in the context of sports betting?

3. *Interests of Businesses Versus Individuals.* In appraising the desirability for sports of the expansion of trademark to protect against dilution, consider first the situation of teams and leagues. Should they be entitled to the same exclusive property rights in their names and symbols as are now given to athletes by the law of publicity rights? Even a disclaimer of endorsement will not immunize unauthorized use of an athlete's name and likeness. Are there tangible distinctions between the interests of athletes as persons and teams as business entities that warrant any difference in legal treatment?

4. *Interests of Sports Fans.* Consider now the interests of sports fans. Suppose that there are a large number of consumers in the sports market who would like to wear a shirt or cap with their favorite team's logo on it, but do not much care whether this is an "official" product—at least do not care enough to want to add the team's five to ten percent licensing fee to the purchase price of the merchandise. Should the law deny fans this informed choice in a competitive marketplace in order to ensure that hundreds of millions of dollars a year in licensing fees continue to be channeled to sports leagues? What affirmative social values are served by such a legal regime?

6. AMBUSH MARKETING

Ambush marketing is a strategy to obtain commercial benefit by creating an association with a sports event that the marketer does not officially sponsor. An ambush advertisement "may only remind customers of the event, or it may go further to create the misleading impression that the company is an official sponsor regarding these goods or services or is affiliated with the event." Ambush advertising, 5 *McCarthy on Trademarks and Unfair Competition* § 27:66 (5th ed.). If an ambush marketing campaign creates a misleading impression, it potentially triggers a dilution claim under Lanham Act § 43(a). However, if the business does not engage in counterfeiting or illegal use of trademarks, but simply develops a creative advertising campaign around the event, it can free ride on the event's popularity and minimize legal consequences.

Famous examples of successful ambush marketing tactics include at the 2009 Wimbledon tennis tournament, when Pringles potato chips distributed to fans waiting outside specially marked tubes of its product that mirrored the packaging of tennis ball cans, with the words, "These are not tennis balls." At the 2010 South Africa World Cup, Dutch brewer Bavaria hired three dozen women to attend a soccer game clad in its signature orange color, to the dismay of the official beer sponsor Budweiser. Although FIFA, the World Cup's organizer, won civil remedies against Bavaria under the South African Merchandise Marks Act, Bavaria's website was one of the most visited worldwide in the days after the stunt. Event organizers, especially those that need sponsorship money to fund production costs, have grown increasingly wary of ambush and its potential to erode the value of official sponsorships.

A prime target of ambush marketing has been the Olympic Games, which in Winter 1992 were the setting for one of the earliest known examples. Visa, the official credit card sponsor launched an ad campaign boasting how the "Olympics don't take American Express," technically true because spectators could purchase tickets to the games only with Visa credit cards. American Express shot back during the Summer 1992 Olympics in Barcelona with a series of television spots featuring the slogan, "When you go to Spain, you'll need a passport—but you don't need a Visa." As recently as the 2018 PyeongChang Winter Olympics, Budweiser—not a sponsor—achieved ambush marketing notoriety with a television commercial featuring ice hockey legends cheering at a hockey game designed to evoke powerful memories of the legendary Olympic victory of the 1980 U.S. hockey team. Perpetually at risk of ambush, the International Olympic Committee (IOC) now insists that any nation seeking to host an Olympic Games must enact anti-ambush marketing legislation, and it has imposed ironclad regulations of athlete social media use and product endorsements leading up to and during the games, at risk of expulsion from competition.

Consistent with this approach, Congress in the Amateur Sports Act of 1978 (as amended by the Ted Stevens Olympic & Amateur Sports Act of 1998), 36 U.S.C. § 371 *et seq.*, gave the U.S. Olympic Committee an explicit statutory right to prohibit commercial and promotional uses of the USOC's name and emblem, the five interlocking rings symbolic of the Olympic Games, and the words Olympic or Olympiad, as well as the names and symbols of the Paralympics and Pan American Games. This right prevails irrespective of consumer confusion about use of the marks. *See San Francisco Arts & Athletics v. USOC*, 483 U.S. 522 (1987) (upholding constitutionality of Act as applied to block use of "Gay Olympic Games"). The Amateur Sports Act is addressed in greater detail in Chapter 13, Section B.

The Amateur Sports Act has also provided occasion for addressing what constitutes ambush marketing. In *United States Olympic Comm. v. American Media, Inc.*, 156 F. Supp. 2d 1200 (D. Colo. 2001), the USOC contended that the defendant violated the Act when it published a magazine that used the Olympic name and symbol in describing Olympic events and schedules. Offering a succinct recital of the harms from ambush marketing, the USOC claimed that this unauthorized use will "likely impair the USOC's relationships with its existing and prospective sponsors, suppliers, and other licensees and undermine their willingness to pay . . . royalties" for their association with the Olympics. *Id.* at 1204 (citation omitted). The court, however, strictly construed the Act's special trademark rights to bar only uses for the purposes of trade or to induce a sale of some good or service, and permitted the magazine unless the USOC could prove likelihood of confusion under the regular provisions of the Lanham Act.

Likelihood of confusion remains the standard for adjudicating most ambush marketing claims. In *Fed'n Internationale De Football Ass'n v. Nike, Inc.*, 285 F. Supp. 2d 64, 66 (D.D.C. 2003), Nike was permitted to continue using "USA 03" in connection with its sponsorship of the U.S. Women's National Soccer Team, over the objections of FIFA, which sought to use a similar mark—"USA 2003"—for the 2003 Women's World Cup soccer tournament taking place across the U.S. FIFA was unable to prove the requisite consumer confusion because its mark was not inherently distinctive and FIFA had not invested much in associating those words specifically with that year's World Cup. On the issue of Nike's good faith, the court acknowledged that Nike had opportunistically established precedence in the "USA 03" mark:

> Nike's careful use of a mark that might be affiliated with both [the U.S. team and the World Cup event] is not necessarily an indication of bad faith, but instead of savvy marketing. Whenever that team plays in this country, it is to be expected that the sponsors of both the team and the event would want to use trademarks that reflect the United States and that emphasize this year's date. Nike's doing so here thus may not indicate a deliberate attempt to deceive the buying public.

Id. at 74. *See National Hockey League v. Pepsi-Cola Canada Ltd.*, 1992 WL 1326159, 92 D.L.R. 4th 349 (Brit. Columbia Sp. Ct. 1992), *aff'd*, 1995 WL 1728674, 59 C.P.R. (3d) 216 (1995) (dismissing NHL's suit in Canada against Pepsi for running a "home team" contest promotion during the Stanley Cup playoffs because Pepsi's advertising campaign, which included a disclaimer, did not give a false impression of official sponsorship); *Mastercard Intern. Inc. v. Sprint Communications Co. L.P.*, 30 U.S.P.Q.2d 1963, 1994 WL 97097 (S.D.N.Y. 1994), *aff'd*, 23 F.3d 397 (2d Cir. 1994) (enjoining as deceptive Sprint's use of World Cup marks to convey official sanctioning of its telephone calling cards, which rights belonged to Mastercard).

NOTES AND QUESTIONS

1. *Good Faith and Savvy Marketing.* In the FIFA case discussed above, do you agree that Nike was merely "savvy" in this situation, and did not act in bad faith? How would you advise FIFA going forward to protect event sponsorship rights and revenues?

2. *Free Speech Concerns.* Given that sporting event producers have limited legal recourse in the case of ambush marketing, many have resorted to counter-tactics such as negotiating with broadcasters and venues to decline advertising from competitors of official sponsors. The NFL for the Super Bowl and the USOC for the Olympic Games both demand that local governments enact ordinances that establish "clean zones" around stadia where unauthorized advertising is prohibited. Consider whether these curbs on non-sponsor activity conflict with U.S. constitutional values. Although courts have historically offered less protection to commercial speech than to noncommercial speech, such restrictions still must serve legitimate governmental interests. What interest does the government have in prohibiting nonmisleading, non-safety-threatening commercial advertisements? Indeed, is the right to grant "official sponsorships" a property interest worth protecting at all from competitive advertising?

7. FIRST AMENDMENT CONSIDERATIONS IN TRADEMARK

The discussion above leads to the question: to what extent does the First Amendment's free speech protections supersede the Lanham Act's trademark rights and restrictions? This chapter earlier discussed how the First Amendment protected artist Rick Rush from publicity-rights liability to Tiger Woods when he created and sold prints of his *Masters of Augusta* painting of Woods along with other golfing greats after the 1997 Masters Tournament. A similar case arose with respect to a series of paintings produced by artist and long-time University of Alabama football fan Daniel Moore, which he collectively called *"Great Moments in Crimson Tide Football History."* These artworks depicted scenes from Alabama football games that in various places displayed Crimson Tide logos or other trademarks on the players' uniforms, as well as the colors and design of the

Crimson Tide uniforms, without a license from the University. When the University demanded Moore pay royalties, he refused, believing he did not need the University's permission to paint historical events as long as he did not use the University's marks outside the "image area" of the paintings. Furthermore, Moore gave a copyright license to a company that used reproductions of his Crimson Tide paintings on merchandise such as coffee mugs and calendars.

The University sued Moore for trademark infringement. In a split decision, the district court upheld Moore's right to use the University's marks in his paintings or prints because they were legitimate works of art entitled to First Amendment protection (as well as a fair use under the Lanham Act), but banned the use of Moore's artwork on functional merchandise. On appeal, the Eleventh Circuit affirmed the finding that the First Amendment protected Moore's paintings and prints, as well as calendars containing prints of the artwork. *University of Alabama Bd. of Trustees v. New Life Art, Inc.*, 683 F.3d 1266 (11th Cir. 2012). It adopted the Second Circuit's test for balancing the interests, articulated in *Rogers v. Grimaldi*, 875 F.2d 994 (2d Cir. 1989):

> We believe that in general the Act should be construed to apply to artistic works only where the public interest in avoiding consumer confusion outweighs the public interest in free expression. In the context of allegedly misleading titles using a celebrity's name, that balance will normally not support application of the Act unless the title has no artistic relevance to the underlying work whatsoever, or if it has some artistic relevance, unless the title explicitly misleads as to the source of the work.

* * *

> In this case, we readily conclude that Moore's paintings, prints, and calendars are protected under the *Rogers* test. The depiction of the University's uniforms in the content of these items is artistically relevant to the expressive underlying works because the uniforms' colors and designs are needed for a realistic portrayal of famous scenes from Alabama football history. Also there is no evidence that Moore ever marketed an unlicensed item as "endorsed" or "sponsored" by the University, or otherwise explicitly stated that such items were affiliated with the University. Moore's paintings, prints, and calendars very clearly are embodiments of artistic expression, and are entitled to full First Amendment protection. The extent of his use of the University's trademarks is their mere inclusion (their necessary inclusion) in the body of the image which Moore creates to memorialize and enhance a particular play or event in the University's football history. Even if "some members of the public

would draw the incorrect inference that [the University] had some involvement with [Moore's paintings, prints, and calendars,] . . . that risk of misunderstanding, not engendered by any overt [or in this case even implicit] claim, . . . is so outweighed by the interest in artistic expression as to preclude" any violation of the Lanham Act.

683 F.3d at 1278–79. The Eleventh Circuit reversed the district court's judgment for the University on the placement of Moore's artwork on coffee mugs and other merchandise, but only because Moore had previously obtained a license from the University. On remand, the district court found that Moore had not violated the terms of the licensing agreement. But the issue of whether the First Amendment or fair use doctrine would protect such use in the absence of a licensing agreement was not addressed.

NOTES AND QUESTIONS

1. *Balancing First Amendment Interests.* Should the test for balancing the plaintiff's interests against the First Amendment interests be the same in trademark cases where the plaintiff's right is established by federal statute as it is in cases where the plaintiff has a right of publicity under state law? The Eleventh Circuit in *University of Alabama* avoided this question by noting that the publicity rights cases it cited as precedent, like *Rogers*, also involved claims of false endorsement under the Lanham Act, but the implication was that the analysis of when First Amendment rights apply would be the same in all cases. Do you agree?

2. *Types of Artwork.* Should the Eleventh Circuit holding apply to all forms of artwork? This case involved a painting of scenes of Alabama football players playing in a game, which was then made into prints and sold. Would the result be different if the painting were simply a posed portrait of the star quarterback wearing his Alabama uniform? Would your answer as to whether the University's trademarks were infringed depend on whether the player had consented to the portrait (i.e., licensed his publicity rights)? What if the artworks being sold were reprints of photographs taken of famous scenes in Alabama football history rather than paintings? Are photographs any less valued works of art for purposes of the balancing test?

3. *Functional Merchandise.* How would you come out in applying the balancing test to the use of otherwise protected artwork on coffee mugs or other functional merchandise like T-shirts? If the First Amendment protects an artist's use of a celebrity's image or a team's trademark in a painting or print that can be hung on a wall, should it also protect the use of that art image when placed and then sold on a coffee mug, T-shirt, place mat, or any other type of product? If no, what would the difference in the balancing analysis be in a case involving artwork placed on a canvas whose function is to decorate a

wall and a case involving artwork placed on a coffee mug whose function is to hold a beverage?

The First Amendment again intersects with the Lanham Act in challenges to sports teams that use racially stereotyped mascots, including the Washington Redskins. *See Pro-Football, Inc. v. Blackhorse*, 112 F. Supp. 3d 439 (E.D. Va. 2015), *vacated*, 709 F. App'x 182 (4th Cir. 2018). The *Blackhorse* litigation arose out of Lanham Act § 2(a), known as the "disparagement" clause. This provision authorized the federal Trademark Trial and Appeal Board (TTAB) to refuse to register a trademark, or to cancel an existing registration, if the mark:

> Consists of or comprises immoral, deceptive, or scandalous matter; or matter which may disparage or falsely suggest a connection with persons, living or dead, institutions, beliefs, or national symbols, or bring them into contempt, or disrepute. . . .

15 U.S.C. § 1152(a). On this basis, over the course of 25 years, Native Americans petitioned to cancel six trademark registrations held by Pro-Football, Inc., the owner of the Washington Redskins. In 2014, the Board deregistered the Redskins mark as disparaging to Native Americans. That ruling was affirmed in a district court decision that rejected the team's arguments that the trademarks were intended as a tribute and that cancellation of the registrations violated the team's free speech rights.

While the *Blackhorse* case was on appeal, a separate case involving the music industry made its way to the Supreme Court, raising an identical issue. *Matal v. Tam*, 137 S. Ct. 1744 (2017), concerned a rock band named The Slants, comprised of Asian-American musicians who adopted that name as a commentary on cultural and political discussions about race and society. The TTAB denied the band's trademark registration under § 2(a), finding the name to be disparaging of Asians. In a landmark 8–0 decision, the Supreme Court invalidated the Lanham Act's disparagement clause, a decision which led to the eventual reinstatement of the Redskins trademarks as well.

MATAL V. TAM
137 S. Ct. 1744 (2017)

JUSTICE ALITO, delivered the opinion of the Court.

This case concerns a dance-rock band's application for federal trademark registration of the band's name, "The Slants." "Slants" is a derogatory term for persons of Asian descent, and members of the band are Asian-Americans. But the band members believe that by taking that slur as the name of their group, they will help to "reclaim" the term and drain its denigrating force.

The Patent and Trademark Office (PTO) denied the application based on a provision of federal law prohibiting the registration of trademarks that may "disparage . . . or bring . . . into contemp[t] or disrepute" any "persons, living or dead." 15 U.S.C. § 1052(a). We now hold that this provision violates the Free Speech Clause of the First Amendment. It offends a bedrock First Amendment principle: Speech may not be banned on the ground that it expresses ideas that offend.

I

A

"The principle underlying trademark protection is that distinctive marks—words, names, symbols, and the like—can help distinguish a particular artisan's goods from those of others." . . . A trademark "designate[s] the goods as the product of a particular trader" and "protect[s] his good will against the sale of another's product as his." . . . It helps consumers identify goods and services that they wish to purchase, as well as those they want to avoid.

"[F]ederal law does not create trademarks." . . . Trademarks and their precursors have ancient origins, and trademarks were protected at common law and in equity at the time of the founding of our country. . . . The foundation of current federal trademark law is the Lanham Act, enacted in 1946. . . .

Under the Lanham Act, trademarks that are "used in commerce" may be placed on the "principal register," that is, they may be federally registered. . . . There are now more than two million marks that have active federal certificates of registration. . . . This system of federal registration helps to ensure that trademarks are fully protected and supports the free flow of commerce.

* * *

B

Without federal registration, a valid trademark may still be used in commerce. . . . And an unregistered trademark can be enforced against would-be infringers in several ways. Most important, even if a trademark is not federally registered, it may still be enforceable under § 43(a) of the Lanham Act, which creates a federal cause of action for trademark infringement. . . . Unregistered trademarks may also be entitled to protection under other federal statutes, such as the Anticybersquatting Consumer Protection Act. . . .

Federal registration, however, "confers important legal rights and benefits on trademark owners who register their marks." . . . Registration on the principal register (1) "serves as 'constructive notice of the registrant's claim of ownership' of the mark"; (2) "is 'prima facie evidence of the validity of the registered mark and of the registration of the mark, of the owner's ownership of the mark, and of the owner's exclusive right to use the registered mark in commerce on or in connection with the goods or services specified in the certificate' "; and (3) can make a mark " 'incontestable' " once a mark has been registered for five years." . . . Registration also enables the trademark holder "to stop the importation into the United States of articles bearing an infringing mark." . . .

C

The Lanham Act contains provisions that bar certain trademarks from the principal register. . . . At issue in this case is one such provision, which we will call "the disparagement clause." This provision prohibits the registration of a trademark "which may disparage . . . persons, living or dead, institutions, beliefs, or national symbols, or bring them into contempt, or disrepute." § 1052(a). This clause appeared in the original Lanham Act and has remained the same to this day. . . .

When deciding whether a trademark is disparaging, an examiner at the PTO generally applies a "two-part test." The examiner first considers "the likely meaning of the matter in question, taking into account not only dictionary definitions, but also the relationship of the matter to the other elements in the mark, the nature of the goods or services, and the manner in which the mark is used in the marketplace in connection with the goods or services." . . . "If that meaning is found to refer to identifiable persons, institutions, beliefs or national symbols," the examiner moves to the second step, asking "whether that meaning may be disparaging to a substantial composite of the referenced group." If the examiner finds that a "substantial composite, although not necessarily a majority, of the referenced group would find the proposed mark . . . to be disparaging in the context of contemporary attitudes," a prima facie case of disparagement is made out, and the burden shifts to the applicant to prove that the trademark is not disparaging. What is more, the PTO has specified that "[t]he fact that an applicant may be a member of that group or has good intentions underlying its use of a term does not obviate the fact that a substantial composite of the referenced group would find the term objectionable."

D

Simon Tam is the lead singer of "The Slants." He chose this moniker in order to "reclaim" and "take ownership" of stereotypes about people of Asian ethnicity. . . . The group "draws inspiration for its lyrics from childhood slurs and mocking nursery rhymes" and has given its albums names such as "The Yellow Album" and "Slanted Eyes, Slanted Hearts."

Tam sought federal registration of "THE SLANTS," on the principal register, but an examining attorney at the PTO rejected the request, applying the PTO's two-part framework and finding that "there is . . . a substantial composite of persons who find the term in the applied-for mark offensive." The examining attorney relied in part on the fact that "numerous dictionaries define 'slants' or 'slant-eyes' as a derogatory or offensive term." The examining attorney also relied on a finding that "the band's name has been found offensive numerous times"—citing a performance that was canceled because of the band's moniker and the fact that "several bloggers and commenters to articles on the band have indicated that they find the term and the applied-for mark offensive."

Tam contested the denial of registration . . . to no avail. [The court describes the proceedings in the TTAB and lower federal courts.] The Government filed a petition for certiorari, which we granted in order to decide whether the disparagement clause "is facially invalid under the Free Speech Clause of the First Amendment."

* * *

III

Because the disparagement clause applies to marks that disparage the members of a racial or ethnic group, we must decide whether the clause violates the Free Speech Clause of the First Amendment. And at the outset, we must consider three arguments that would either eliminate any First Amendment protection or result in highly permissive rational-basis review. Specifically, the Government contends . . . that trademarks are government speech, not private speech. . . .

A

The First Amendment prohibits Congress and other government entities and actors from "abridging the freedom of speech"; the First Amendment does not say that Congress and other government entities must abridge their own ability to speak freely. And our cases recognize that "[t]he Free Speech Clause . . . does not regulate government speech." . . .

As we have said, "it is not easy to imagine how government could function" if it were subject to the restrictions that the First Amendment imposes on private speech. " '[T]he First Amendment forbids the government to regulate speech in ways that favor some viewpoints or ideas at the expense of others,' " but imposing a requirement of viewpoint-neutrality on government speech would be paralyzing. When a government entity embarks on a course of action, it necessarily takes a particular viewpoint and rejects others. The Free Speech Clause does not require government to maintain viewpoint neutrality when its officers and employees speak about that venture.

Here is a simple example. During the Second World War, the Federal Government produced and distributed millions of posters to promote the war effort. There were posters urging enlistment, the purchase of war bonds, and the conservation of scarce resources. These posters expressed a viewpoint, but the First Amendment did not demand that the Government balance the message of these posters by producing and distributing posters encouraging Americans to refrain from engaging in these activities.

But while the government-speech doctrine is important—indeed, essential—it is a doctrine that is susceptible to dangerous misuse. If private speech could be passed off as government speech by simply affixing a government seal of approval, government could silence or muffle the expression of disfavored viewpoints. For this reason, we must exercise great caution before extending our government-speech precedents.

At issue here is the content of trademarks that are registered by the PTO, an arm of the Federal Government. The Federal Government does not dream up these marks, and it does not edit marks submitted for registration. Except as required by the statute involved here, an examiner may not reject a mark based on the viewpoint that it appears to express. Thus, unless that section is thought to apply, an examiner does not inquire whether any viewpoint conveyed by a mark is consistent with Government policy or whether any such viewpoint is consistent with that expressed by other marks already on the principal register. Instead, if the mark meets the Lanham Act's viewpoint-neutral requirements, registration is mandatory. . . .

In light of all this, it is far-fetched to suggest that the content of a registered mark is government speech. If the federal registration of a trademark makes the mark government speech, the Federal Government is babbling prodigiously and incoherently. It is saying many unseemly things. It is unashamedly endorsing a vast array of commercial products and services. And it is providing Delphic advice to the consuming public. . . .

*   *   *

Holding that the registration of a trademark converts the mark into government speech would constitute a huge and dangerous extension of the government-speech doctrine. For if the registration of trademarks constituted government speech, other systems of government registration could easily be characterized in the same way.

Perhaps the most worrisome implication of the Government's argument concerns the system of copyright registration. If federal registration makes a trademark government speech and thus eliminates all First Amendment protection, would the registration of the copyright for a book produce a similar transformation?

The Government attempts to distinguish copyright on the ground that it is "'the engine of free expression,'" but as this case illustrates, trademarks often have an expressive content. Companies spend huge amounts to create and publicize trademarks that convey a message. It is true that the necessary brevity of trademarks limits what they can say. But powerful messages can sometimes be conveyed in just a few words.

Trademarks are private, not government, speech.

* * *

IV

Having concluded that the disparagement clause cannot be sustained under our government-speech or subsidy cases or under the Government's proposed "government-program" doctrine, we must confront a dispute between the parties on the question whether trademarks are commercial speech and are thus subject to the relaxed scrutiny. . . . We need not resolve this debate between the parties because the disparagement clause cannot withstand even *Central Hudson* review. Under *Central Hudson*, a restriction of speech must serve "a substantial interest," and it must be "narrowly drawn." . . .

It is claimed that the disparagement clause serves two interests. First, the Government asserts an interest in preventing "'underrepresented groups'" from being "'bombarded with demeaning messages in commercial advertising.'" . . . But no matter how the point is phrased, its unmistakable thrust is this: The Government has an interest in preventing speech expressing ideas that offend. And, as we have explained, that idea strikes at the heart of the First Amendment. Speech that demeans on the basis of race, ethnicity, gender, religion, age, disability, or any other similar ground is hateful; but the proudest boast of our free speech jurisprudence is that we protect the freedom to express "the thought that we hate."

The second interest asserted is protecting the orderly flow of commerce. Commerce, we are told, is disrupted by trademarks that "involv[e] disparagement of race, gender, ethnicity, national origin, religion, sexual orientation, and similar demographic classification." Such trademarks are analogized to discriminatory conduct, which has been recognized to have an adverse effect on commerce.

A simple answer to this argument is that the disparagement clause is not "narrowly drawn" to drive out trademarks that support invidious discrimination. The clause reaches any trademark that disparages *any person, group, or institution*. It applies to trademarks like the following: "Down with racists," "Down with sexists," "Down with homophobes." It is not an anti-discrimination clause; it is a happy-talk clause. In this way, it goes much further than is necessary to serve the interest asserted.

The clause is far too broad in other ways as well. The clause protects every person living or dead as well as every institution. Is it conceivable that commerce would be disrupted by a trademark saying: "James Buchanan was a disastrous president" or "Slavery is an evil institution"?

There is also a deeper problem with the argument that commercial speech may be cleansed of any expression likely to cause offense. The commercial market is well stocked with merchandise that disparages prominent figures and groups, and the line between commercial and non-commercial speech is not always clear, as this case illustrates. If affixing the commercial label permits the suppression of any speech that may lead to political or social "volatility," free speech would be endangered.

For these reasons, we hold that the disparagement clause violates the Free Speech Clause of the First Amendment. The judgment of the Federal Circuit is affirmed.

JUSTICE KENNEDY, with whom JUSTICE GINSBURG, JUSTICE SOTOMAYOR, and JUSTICE KAGAN join, concurring in part and concurring in the judgment. (omitted)

JUSTICE THOMAS, concurring in part and concurring in the judgment. (omitted)

NOTES AND QUESTIONS

1. *Commercial Versus Noncommercial Speech.* How would you answer the question that the Supreme Court avoided in *Matal*: are trademarks commercial speech accorded only relaxed scrutiny as free expression? Do you agree that limiting any speech on the basis it leads to political or social "volatility" endangers all free speech? In a decision following shortly after *Matal*, the Federal Circuit ruled that Lanham Act § 2(a)'s bar on registering immoral or scandalous marks is also an unconstitutional restriction of free speech. *In re Brunetti*, 877 F.3d 1330 (Fed. Cir. 2017). Notably, the court applied strict scrutiny to that Lanham Act provision because it "regulates the expressive components of speech, not the commercial components of speech." *Id.* at 1349.

2. *Justice Kennedy's Concurrence.* In his concurrence, Justice Kennedy offered a different take on the issues in *Matal*, focusing on the government's argument that the law is viewpoint neutral. He rejected this assertion because "[t]o prohibit all sides from criticizing their opponents makes a law more viewpoint based, not less so," and noted that "[t]he Government may not insulate a law from charges of viewpoint discrimination by tying censorship to the reaction of the speaker's audience." 137 S. Ct. at 1766. Does this approach mean that any trademark, no matter how outrageous or offensive, should be entitled to registration? Should we be concerned about such an outcome, or can we rely on the marketplace and consumer reaction to ameliorate the risk?

3. *Native American Mascots in Sports.* The original petition to cancel the Redskins' trademark registration was filed in 1992. In the years since then, hundreds of colleges and high schools have discontinued the use of Native American mascots. By 2005, the NCAA had adopted a policy that prohibits NCAA institutions from displaying "hostile and abusive" Native American names, mascots, or images. Some institutions were able to satisfy the NCAA that their references to Native Americans were inoffensive, but not the University of North Dakota Fighting Sioux, despite a lawsuit by members of the Sioux tribe seeking to *retain* the nickname. *See Spirit Lake Tribe of Indians ex rel. Comm. of Understanding & Respect v. Nat'l Collegiate Athletic Ass'n,* 715 F.3d 1089 (8th Cir. 2013) (dismissing claim that NCAA unlawfully discriminated against the tribe in banning UND's use of the name). Ultimately, a statewide referendum led North Dakota to retire the name. How can trademark owners mitigate the risk that their naming choices will be overtaken by new and different perspectives on our history and culture? Consider the approach of the NBA Washington Wizards, formerly the Bullets, which in 1997 changed the club's nickname to avoid association with gun violence, and did so through a marketing campaign that included a naming contest for fans and a corporate social responsibility component. Despite the post-*Matal* reinstatement of its trademarks, should the Washington Redskins take a preemptive approach and voluntarily change its name?

CHAPTER 9

AGENT REPRESENTATION OF THE ATHLETE*

■ ■ ■

For most of the history of professional team sports, from the founding of the first professional baseball league in 1876 through the 1960s, the vast majority of athletes represented themselves in negotiating their player contracts. This was largely the byproduct of the industry norm that a club "owned" any player it had introduced to the major leagues and then controlled his career from that point forward. Because using a negotiating agent would not have improved the player's lot in any meaningful way, there was little incentive to retain and pay such an agent. Indeed, many teams refused to deal directly with sports agents in salary negotiations.

By the 1970s, four dramatic developments in professional sports gave agents a foothold. First, free agency allowed veteran players to sell their services on the open market. Second, upstart leagues in football, hockey, and basketball created competition for player services, driving up salaries. Both of these first two developments led players to seek assistance in navigating among competing offers for their services. Third, player unions came into their own, extracting significant concessions from ownership, while formally delegating the role of salary negotiator to sports agents. Fourth, television revenues and endorsement deals were booming, placing even more money on the table for players.

Professional athletes came to value negotiating and money management expertise to exploit opportunity and maximize wealth creation during their usually short and always unpredictable careers. An agent with talent and experience is better equipped to deal with the seasoned general managers who bargain on behalf of the team owners. Added to this financial value is the agent's role as an emotional buffer—insulating the player's ego and relationship with the team from frank discussion about his abilities, performance, and where he fits within the club's salary scale. While negotiating the player contract remains an agent's core service, many agents now also handle endorsement deals and

---

* The Casebook Website (http://pennstatelaw.psu.edu/SportsTextWebsite) contains citations to scholarly and other commentary on a variety of topics discussed in this chapter, including: the business of sports agents; sports agents and corruption in college sports, the agent-client relationship; sports agent ethics; the financial management role of agents; the agent's role in unionized sports; sports agent fee arrangements; sports agent conflicts of interest; the attorney-agent; government and union regulation of sports agents; criminal prosecutions of sports agents.

offer a menu of management services relating to tax and estate planning, investing and financial management, budgeting and bill paying, intellectual property protection, athletic training and health, real estate, charitable giving, and domestic arrangements. In non-team sports such as golf and tennis, where athletes' earnings from their sport depend on how they fare in tournaments and not on a negotiated employment contract, the agent's role increasingly focuses on generating revenue opportunities for their clients outside the sport.

Meanwhile, rising player salaries and the commissions to be earned from negotiating those salaries and other revenue deals made the career of sports agent more appealing. By the early 2000s, the aggregate number of sports agents registered in the four major sports leagues—MLB, NBA, NFL, and NHL—amounted to almost one agent for every two players on their combined rosters. Recruiting practices became increasingly cutthroat as agencies needed to sign prominent clients to attract others. To offer the full range of now-expected services, those firms also required a deep bench of agents with knowledge of the sport, its collective bargaining agreement and player policies, applicable agent and financial advisor regulations, negotiation skills, industry norms, and revenue streams. These demands led to consolidation and corporatization of the business as smaller firms and independent agents lacked the resources to lure and keep clients. That same consolidation now means that it is more likely than ever that a sports agency represents multiple athletes in the same sport, even playing the same position or on the same team. With other participants in the industry attaining celebrity status—including coaches, managers, and owners—a sports agency also might find itself representing both athletes and management.

As the sports agent business has become more competitive and multiplex, it has also been associated with dubious competence and ethics. Among the ills that have plagued the business are conflicts of interest, fraud, self-dealing, negligence, ineptitude, client poaching, and illegal recruiting tactics that sabotage college athlete eligibility and prospects. Despite the agent's purported role as protector of athletes' interests in relation to team owners, the need arose to protect athletes' interests in relation to agents, resulting in extensive regulation of agents, first by players associations, and later by Congress and state legislatures. This chapter first sets forth basic agency law principles that underlie the athlete-agent relationship and the distinct vulnerabilities of that relationship. It next explores the role of agents in a unionized workplace, and the corresponding players association regulation of sports agents. Government regulation of sports agents is examined, as well as the additional ethical constraints on agents who are also attorneys.

A. LEGAL RELATIONSHIP BETWEEN SPORTS AGENTS AND ATHLETE-CLIENTS

1. AGENCY LAW BASICS

The sports agent-athlete relationship is subject to common law agency principles, modified in part by some of the unique structures of the sports industry. In broad terms, sports agency is a consensual, usually contractual relationship where the athlete as principal grants authority to the agent to act on behalf of and under the control of the athlete in dealing with third parties and pursuing the athlete's interests. In the case of the major professional sports leagues, the express contract creates and governs the relationship, because the players associations mandate the use of standard representation agreements and/or compliance with agent regulations. Consistent with agency law, all the players unions expressly impose on the agent the fiduciary duties of loyalty, honesty, and competence towards the athlete.

The Restatement of Agency apportions an agent's fiduciary duties into two distinct buckets. The "duty of loyalty" primarily requires an agent to avoid conflicts of interest and self-dealing, to preserve confidentiality, and to follow the principal's instructions. Restatement (Third) of Agency §§ 8.02–8.06 (2006). The agent's "duty of performance" requires care, competence, and diligence, as well as acting only within the scope of actual authority granted by the principal, complying with the law, accounting for all of the principal's funds, and keeping the principal apprised of all matters that may affect his interests. Restatement (Third) of Agency §§ 8.07–8.12 (2006).

Two aspects of the duty of loyalty merit closer examination in view of the economic model for today's sports agencies. First, most sports agents are paid through commissions on the athlete's earnings. This practice can risk running afoul of the agent's duty not to engage in self-dealing or acquire material benefit from a third party in connection with business conducted on behalf of the principal. Restatement (Third) of Agency § 8.02. Second, many sports agencies represent multiple clients whose interests may conflict. In such situations, the agent is duty-bound to fully disclose and obtain the athlete's informed consent to the conflict, and thereafter to deal in good faith with each principal. Restatement (Third) of Agency § 8.06.

In *Burleson v. Earnest*, 153 S.W.2d 869 (Tex. Civ. App. 1941), the court in a real estate dispute alleging agent self-dealing and conflict of interest summarized the relevant common law rules that apply equally to sports agents:

> The law is well established in this state, as well as every other jurisdiction in this country, that in all cases where the

relationship of principal and agent is shown, the principal is entitled to the best efforts and unbiased judgment of his agent. For reasons founded in public policy the law denies the right of an agent to assume any relationship that is antagonistic to his duty to his principal, and it has many times been held that the agent cannot be both buyer and seller at the same time nor connect his own interests with property involved in his dealings as an agent for another.

The rule is founded on the danger of imposition and the presumption of the existence of fraud, inaccessible to the eye of the Court. The policy of the rule is to shut the door against temptation, and which, in the cases in which such a relationship exists, is deemed to be, of itself, sufficient to create the disqualification. This principle, like most others, may be subject to some qualification in its application to particular cases, but, as a general rule, it appears to be well settled in the English and in our American Jurisprudence. [citation omitted]

The courts have, throughout the entire history of our jurisprudence, shown a jealous attitude toward an agent who becomes involved in the property of his principal and have held him to strict account for his dealings . . . . Even where the parties bargain for themselves, once the agency is established, the principal is entitled to the skill, knowledge and advice of his agent and to communicate with him without the slightest fear of betrayal. . . . The question, therefore, does not relate to the mala fides of the agent nor to whether or not a greater sum might have been procured for the property, nor even to whether or not the vendor received full value therefor. The self-interest of the agent is considered a vice which renders the transaction voidable at the election of the principal without looking into the matter further than to ascertain that the interest of the agent exists.

Id. at 874. While it may seem that in sports agency, an agent's interest is naturally aligned with the principal because they both benefit from maximizing the athlete's earnings, can you anticipate when this might not be the case?

2. STANDARDS FOR AGENT PERFORMANCE

Although the duty of loyalty is most often implicated in sports agent-athlete disputes, we turn briefly first to the agent's duty of performance. Consider what standard the law should establish for the level of agent competence and quality of representation owed by agents to their athlete-clients. The one appellate case that has explored this issue involved an agent for professional football players.

ZINN V. PARRISH
644 F.2d 360 (7th Cir. 1981)

BARTELS, SENIOR DISTRICT JUDGE.

This is an appeal in a diversity action by Leo Zinn from a judgment of the District Court for the Northern District of Illinois, Eastern Division, wherein he sought to recover agent fees due him under a personal management contract between him and the defendant Lemar Parrish. . . .

[The court recounted the facts of the dispute. Zinn had been managing professional athletes for two decades when he agreed to serve as agent for Parrish, who was selected by the Cincinnati Bengals in the 1970 NFL draft. Under their Professional Management Contract, Zinn received a 10% commission in return for agreeing to use his "reasonable efforts" on Parrish's behalf in "negotiating job contracts, furnishing advice on business investments, securing professional tax advice at no additional costs, and obtaining endorsement contracts." Zinn was also supposed to try to secure "gainful off-season employment" for Parrish if he so requested, from which Zinn would receive a commission only if the work was "in the line of endorsements, marketing, and the like." The agency contract automatically renewed every year, unless one side gave 30 days written notice of termination.

For Parrish's first four years with the Bengals, Zinn negotiated base salaries for his client of $16,500, $18,500, $27,000, and $35,000. By the end of the 1973 season, Parrish had become a Pro Bowl cornerback and the rival World Football League (WFL) had appeared on the scene. In the spring of 1974, Zinn had some preliminary conversations with the WFL's Jacksonville Sharks, but decided not to pursue this option, a sound decision because the WFL folded midway through the 1975 season. Instead, Zinn negotiated four new one-year contracts with the Bengals that paid $250,000 over 1974–1977, plus a $30,000 signing bonus. After signing the Bengals contracts, Parrish told Zinn by phone and letter that he "no longer needed his services." Parrish refused to pay Zinn any commission on those new contracts, and Zinn sued.

Other services Zinn performed for Parrish included arranging for tax return preparation, screening and forwarding stock market recommendations, assisting in the purchase and management of a four-unit apartment building, and procuring one endorsement contract. However, Zinn had not been able to obtain any off-season work for Parrish. Instead, he had advised his client to return to college in the off-season to secure a degree to prepare himself for life when his NFL career had ended.]

In summing up Zinn's performance under the contract, Parrish testified as follows:

Q: Did you ever ask Zinn to do anything for you, to your knowledge, that he didn't try to do?

A: I shall say not, no.

Discussion

[The court first held that the contract between Zinn and Parish was not void under federal securities law that prohibits Zinn from giving investment advice without being a registered adviser. The court said that isolated transactions with a client incident to the main purpose of a management contract to negotiate football contracts did not constitute engaging in the business of advising others on investment securities.]

We consider next the district court's judgment that Zinn failed to perform the terms and conditions of his contract. . . .

Employment Procurement

Zinn's obligation under the 1971 Management Contract to procure employment for Parrish as a pro football player was limited to the use of "reasonable efforts." At the time the contract was signed, Parrish was already under contract with the Cincinnati Bengals for the 1970–1971 season, with a one-year option clause for the 1971–1972 season exercisable by the Bengals. Parrish could not, without being in breach of his Bengals contract, enter into negotiations with other teams for the 1971–72 season. The NFL's own rules prevented one team from negotiating with another team's player who had not yet attained the status of a "free agent." At no time relevant to this litigation did Parrish become a free agent. Thus, unless he decided to contract for future services for the year following the term of the option clause with the Canadian or World Football League, Parrish's only sensible course of action throughout the time Zinn managed him was to negotiate with the Bengals.

Parrish had no objection to Zinn's performance under the professional management contract for the first three years up to 1973, during which time Zinn negotiated football contracts for Parrish. A drastic change, however, took place in 1974 when a four-season contract was negotiated with the Bengals for a total of $250,000 plus a substantial signing bonus. At that time, the new World Football League came into existence and its teams, as well as the teams of the Canadian Football League, were offering good terms to professional football players as an inducement to jump over to their leagues from the NFL. In order to persuade Parrish to remain with the team, the Bengals club itself first initiated the renegotiation of Parrish's contract with an offer of substantially increased compensation. This was not surprising.

Parrish claims, however, that Zinn should have obtained offers from the World Football League that would have placed him in a stronger negotiating position with the Bengals. This is a rather late claim. It was not mentioned in Parrish's letter of termination, and is entirely speculative. Given what Zinn accurately perceived as the unreliability of any offers he might have obtained from the WFL, his representation of Parrish during this period was more than reasonable.

* * *

Other Obligations

We focus next on the other obligations, all incidental to the main purpose of the contract. The first of these refers to "[n]egotiating employment contracts with professional athletic organizations and others." . . . [T]he evidence clearly shows that Zinn performed substantial services in negotiating with the Bengals by letter, telephone, and in person when he and Parrish were flown at the Bengals' expense to Cincinnati for the final stage of negotiations on the 1974–1977 series of contracts.

Zinn was further obligated to act in Parrish's professional interest by providing advice on tax and business matters, by "seek[ing] . . . endorsement contracts," and by making "efforts" to obtain for Parrish gainful off-season employment. Each of these obligations was subject to an implied promise to make "good faith" efforts to obtain what he sought. Under Illinois law, such efforts constitute full performance of the obligations. Until Parrish terminated the contract, the evidence was clear that Zinn made consistent, good faith efforts to obtain off-season employment and endorsement contracts. Indeed the district court found that Zinn at all times acted in good faith, with a willingness "to provide assistance within his ability." The district court confused success with good faith efforts in concluding that Zinn's failure to obtain in many cases jobs or contracts for Parrish was a failure to perform. Moreover, Zinn did give business advice to Parrish on his real estate purchases, and he did secure tax advice for him.

Parrish fully accepted Zinn's performance for the years 1970, 1971, 1972, and 1973 by remitting the 10% due Zinn under the contract. Parrish was at all times free to discharge Zinn as his agent before a new season began. Instead, he waited until Zinn had negotiated a series of contracts worth a quarter of a million dollars for him before letting Zinn know over the phone that his services were no longer required. That call, coupled with Parrish's failure to make the 10% commission payments as they came due, was a breach of the 1971 contract. . . . Therefore Zinn has a right to recover a 10% commission on all amounts earned by Parrish under the 1974, 1975, 1976, and 1977 Bengals contracts.

We must disagree with the district court's interpretation of the terms of the contract, and Zinn's obligations thereunder, and also with its findings and conclusions concerning Zinn's performance. Insofar as the district court made any findings of fact which are inconsistent with the foregoing, we find them to be clearly erroneous. [Appeal granted.]

NOTES AND QUESTIONS

1. *Standard of Performance.* How does the court formulate the standard of performance expected of a sports agent? How does this standard compare with the "duty of fair representation" imposed by labor law on the players association (*see* Chapter 2, Section H)? With the standard of care required of a lawyer who represents a player in any transaction? Is the standard used in *Zinn* appropriate for the sports agent business?

2. *Principal's Duty to the Agent.* A principal also owes a duty to the agent to deal with the agent fairly and in good faith. *See* Restatement (Third) of Agency § 8.15 (2006). This duty requires the athlete to provide the sports agent with information about risks of physical harm or pecuniary loss that the athlete knows or should know are present in the agent's work but are unknown to the agent. *See* Chris Deubert, *What's A "Clean" Agent to Do? The Case for A Cause of Action Against A Player's Association*, 18 Vill. Sports & Ent. L.J. 1, 34 (2011).

How would such a duty have applied in *Bias v. Advantage International, Inc.*, 905 F.2d 1558 (D.C. Cir. 1990), where the estate of college basketball star Len Bias sued his agent, Lee Fentress, for negligent performance of agent duties. Bias died from cocaine use only two days after the Boston Celtics selected him second in the 1986 NBA draft. His survivors faulted Fentress for failing to finalize a million-dollar insurance policy and an endorsement contract with Reebok prior to Bias's death. The suit was summarily dismissed on the grounds that (a) no life insurer would have issued the policy to a drug user, and (b) the agent could not reasonably have been expected to finalize an endorsement contract in only two days. Assuming Fentress was unaware of Bias's drug use, what would Bias's duty have been to deal fairly with his agent? To what degree should an agent's duty be dependent on the principal's cooperation?

3. *Agent Malpractice in Negotiating the Playing Contract.* How can an athlete identify and protect against agent malpractice in the routine aspects of the role—*e.g.*, negligently negotiating a below-market salary, failing to seek various contract guarantees or injury protection, or giving bad advice about what salary to "hold out" for? Consider the case of NFL linebacker LaVar Arrington, who signed a Redskins playing contract negotiated by his agent Carl Poston, without either of them realizing that the team had failed to include a $6.5 million bonus the parties had allegedly agreed upon. Arrington ultimately settled with the Redskins to receive half the bonus amount, but he did not pursue any recourse against his agent. To the contrary, he testified on Poston's behalf in disciplinary proceedings brought against the agent by the

NFL Players Association. What explains player loyalty to the agent in this setting?

4. *Agent Obligations After Execution of the Playing Contract.* Once the playing contract is signed, what is the agent's role in explaining contract details to the athlete-client and ensuring compliance with contract obligations? Take the case of NFL cornerback Tarell Brown, who in 2013 forfeited a $2 million roster bonus because he was unaware of a contract clause that required him to participate in voluntary team workouts to earn the bonus. Brown fired his agent Brian Overstreet for not alerting him to this contract obligation, but did not bring a lawsuit. In 2004, wide receiver Dennis Northcutt lost out on potentially millions of dollars when his agent Jerome Stanley missed a deadline to void the last three years of his contract and make him a free agent eligible to renegotiate his contract. The NFLPA took disciplinary measures against Stanley, but the player brought a grievance against the team, not his agent. Consider also that most players unions, including the NFLPA, now require agents to maintain professional liability insurance, whether or not an agent is an attorney. Yet neither NFL player pursued that remedy. Why do you think players don't bring agent malpractice claims, although suits for medical and legal malpractice have become quite common?

B. BREAKDOWNS IN THE AGENT-ATHLETE RELATIONSHIP

Stories are legion of sports agent misconduct and ethical compromises. In one of the most egregious cases, William "Tank" Black, a leading football agent of the late 1990s, was sentenced to five years in prison after a federal jury convicted him of defrauding over two dozen athlete-clients of $12 million through multiple investment schemes. This sentence was imposed on top of a prior sentence of nearly seven years for Black's role in laundering over $1 million for a drug ring in Detroit. In addition, his shady practices in recruiting student athletes led to investigations by the state of Florida and the NFLPA, both of which eventually decertified him. *See generally Hilliard v. Black*, 125 F. Supp. 2d 1071 (N.D. Fla. 2000) (agent liable to athletes for investment scam). This section examines breakdowns in the relationship between an agent and the athlete-client, providing a glimpse of the working life of an agent and the degree to which many elite athletes have ceded financial autonomy to advisors.

1. AGENT BREACH OF FIDUCIARY DUTIES TO ATHLETE-CLIENT

Sports agent dereliction of fiduciary duties to athlete-clients has arisen in diverse contexts. Particularly susceptible are athletes making the transition from high school or collegiate sports to the professional level, when their youth and naiveté lead them to rely heavily on the agent's care and skill in performing on their behalf. *See Jones v. Childers*, 18 F.3d 899

(11th Cir. 1994) (football player's "lack of sophistication in investment matters" cited in holding agent liable for fraud and racketeering).

To hold sports agents accountable for misconduct, athletes traditionally have relied on civil lawsuits for breach of contract, breach of fiduciary duty, and fraudulent misrepresentation. *See Terrell v. Childers*, 920 F. Supp. 854 (N.D. Ill. 1996) (professional basketball player sued agent for fraud and mismanagement of his finances and investments). Another avenue for policing agents is through reporting misdeeds to players unions and professional associations, discussed in more detail in subsequent sections of this chapter. In addition, criminal and administrative law enforcement agencies are empowered to pursue sports agents who offend laws of general applicability or specialized agent regulations. *See United States v. Gatto*, 295 F. Supp. 3d 336 (S.D.N.Y. 2018) (sustaining indictment charging, inter alia, that sports agent conspired with marketing executives and college basketball coaches to defraud universities by bribing high school players to commit to attending specific schools and then retain agent's services); *People v. Sorkin*, 64 A.D.2d 680, 407 N.Y.S.2d 772 (1978) (upholding substantial jail term for agent who misappropriated over $1 million of client hockey players' funds).

Most player agents, however, do not rob, cheat, or steal from their clients. They are not destructive, devious, or inept. Although the practice of sports agency is not always polite and well-mannered, it is not generally sullied by criminal misconduct. The more important question posed by cases of agent misconduct is whether they manifest merely the occasional abuse that occurs in any type of commercial undertaking, or instead are symptomatic of a deeper imbalance in the player-agent relationship. Can we trust the marketplace to drive out most of the bad agents in favor of the good, relying on general criminal or civil law to deal with the few "bad apples" that remain? Or should we devise a systematic regulatory program targeted at sports agents? If the latter, who should devise and enforce the program, and with what objectives? A case of outright fraud against a young professional basketball player provoked a federal judge who had formerly served as general counsel to the Securities and Exchange Commission to recommend (in a footnote) an interesting solution to the problem.

WILLIAMS V. CWI, INC.
777 F. Supp. 1006 (D.D.C. 1991)

SPORKIN, DISTRICT JUDGE.

This claim was brought by a young professional basketball player and his wife—Reginald and Kathy Williams—against a financial advisor and his associated companies to recover $50,000 that the Williams had entrusted to the defendant, Waymon Hunt through one of his affiliated companies. Plaintiffs also seek to recover certain costs and expenses that they incurred as a result of Mr. Hunt's actions. Plaintiffs have also prayed for punitive damages.

* * *

I. Findings of Fact

The facts clearly show that Reginald Williams, a gifted young professional basketball player, and his wife, Kathy, were unsophisticated in matters of finance and business. In the late 1980's, upon his graduation from Georgetown University where he had a distinguished career as a star basketball player, Mr. Williams signed a million-dollar-a-year contract with the Los Angeles Clippers, a National Basketball Association team. As a result of this lucrative contract, Mr. Williams and his wife were looking for opportunities to invest part of Mr. Williams substantial earnings.[1] He was directed to Waymon Hunt, a financial planner, and his company, CWI, Inc., by his wife's parents. . . .

The Williams first met Mr. Hunt in June of 1988. At that time, they agreed that Mr. Hunt would provide the Williams with financial and tax advice, including preparation of the Williams' tax returns. At approximately that time, Mr. Hunt brought to the Williams' attention an opportunity for investment involving the purchase of a product styled atmospheric reverse refrigeration heating units (hereinafter referred to as "units"). Because of how these units were supposed to perform, they were represented as being capable of producing an investment return and tax benefits.

The Williams agreed to buy $1 million worth of these units through a Hunt affiliated company, Success Through Association ("STA"). [The court described how Hunt failed to disclose that he operated and controlled STA and that, as of September 1988, that company had only $301.50 in its bank account. Hunt convinced the Williams to buy $1 million worth of STA units in a deal that would be financed by the Williams paying a $50,000 deposit and borrowing $950,000 through an STA-arranged loan. The deal further

---

[1] Like many young professional athletes, Mr. Williams was earning a considerable salary but had no experience in making investments or managing his money. He needed reliable expert advice and did not find any readily available. Because Mr. Williams' predicament appears to be a recurring problem for basketball players and other athletes who suddenly receive large disposable incomes, it seems that it would be appropriate for either the NBA, or the player's team, or the players' organization to develop a three-pronged program to assist these young people. First, they could offer at least some rudimentary education in business and finance. Second, they could assemble a package of low risk blue-chip investments for young players that will provide for their futures as well as a system for referring them to wise and ethical professionals who can advise them on managing money. Third, they might offer a financial incentive for players to place a portion of their funds in a deferred investment program. Perhaps the League and the players' association could even establish their own high-grade, low-risk investment fund. In this way, young athletes would be protected from highly speculative ventures like the one involved in this case.

stipulated that if the purchase could not be made, STA would return the Williams' deposit in full by December 16, 1988.]

Waymon Hunt agreed to arrange for the $950,000 in financing. The Williams signed a purchase agreement and forwarded $50,000 to STA, but no money was ever remitted to the purported manufacturer and seller of the units. Immediately upon STA's receipt of the $50,000, Hunt appropriated the money for his own use. Hunt did not obtain the $950,000 of financing.

Around the time of this transaction, there was an internal battle among the owners of the company that manufactured and sold the units, and the company was placed in receivership. While it later turned out that Mr. Hunt was able to contact a second seller and manufacturer, no purchase of the units ever came to pass. The parties have stipulated that the $50,000 sent to Mr. Hunt's company, STA, was never used to purchase reverse refrigeration units from any entity.

Mr. Hunt has attempted to deviate from the agreement he provided to the Williams, an agreement he drafted, by stating that he was entitled to the $50,000 as a finder's fee for locating financing for the project. He has produced two cashier's checks to show that he spent $68,000 on a fee he paid to a Georgia company, Aslanien Ltd., to obtain financing. He claims he did this on the Williams' behalf, but his testimony is not credible. While this Court cannot deny that Mr. Hunt may have discussed some financing for the purchase of the so-called reverse refrigeration units, it was clear he did not have the Williams in mind when he sent the first check for $34,000 to Aslanien, Ltd. since he wrote that check before the Williams ever signed a contract or purchase order for the units. It is not even clear that they knew about the investment opportunity before Hunt sent the check to Aslanien. Hunt admitted that the second check for $34,000 sent in November of 1988 was sent on behalf of other clients and not the Williams. It is clear that the $50,000 sent to STA by the Williams was to be a down payment on the units. It was not a finder's fee or any other kind of advance fee. Indeed Mr. Hunt conceded in his testimony before the Court that he owes the Williams the $50,000 they sent to him. Although he testified that he does not have the funds to pay the Williams now, he clearly acknowledges that under his agreement with them, he owes them the money.

The Williams are entitled to a judgment against Mr. Hunt on both contract and fraud theories. The contract provided that the money be repaid "if for any reason [STA] cannot fulfill [the Williams] request...." It is also clear that Mr. Hunt's actions with respect to the Williams prove that Mr. Hunt defrauded the Williams. Hunt flat out misappropriated the money given to him. He dissembled when the Williams periodically asked about their investment and its status. He said "things were going fine" when they were not. He never told them that the $50,000 had not been sent to the manufacturer, nor did he inform them that he had not obtained financing. Hunt misrepresented the status of the arrangement when he prepared the Williams' tax returns on which Hunt took certain deductions and credits that could only be taken if a transaction had in fact been consummated. The Williams incurred significant expenses because of Mr. Hunt's violation of the contract and fraudulent conduct.

[The court awarded $87,500 to the Williams in recovery of their $50,000 down payment, attorneys fees and litigation costs, and amounts related to rectifying their unwitting misrepresentations on their tax returns, including tax preparer fees and penalties and interest owed to the IRS and California state tax authorities.] The Williams may not collect tax savings they claim they might have enjoyed had they received legitimate financial advice. It would be too speculative to assume post hoc what investments they might have chosen and what savings they might have received.

* * *

Finally, plaintiffs seek punitive damages. The Court finds that they are warranted in this case. Mr. Hunt's egregious behavior was utterly unworthy of someone who calls himself a professional. His fraudulent conduct put the plaintiffs at risk of committing tax fraud. In recognition of these facts, the Court will award $50,000 in punitive damages, an amount that reflects the $50,000 down payment that was misappropriated and that was the basis for the grievous errors made on the Williams tax returns and caused them to incur substantial costs and expenses. . . .

NOTES AND QUESTIONS

1. *Athlete Vulnerability.* A recurring theme in civil cases involving young athletes is their relative unsophistication, as demonstrated in the *Williams* case above and the *Shaw* case discussed in Chapter 4, Section A. Do you agree that these clients more than others are vulnerable to corrupt agents and advisors, and merit additional protection from the courts?

2. *Private Efforts to Protect Athletes.* In the footnote to the *Williams* decision, the court exhorted the NBA to develop assistance programs that offer players business and finance education, low-risk investment advice, advisor referrals, and proprietary investment opportunities. The major sports leagues all now offer their players some wealth management education, life skills training, and career transition services. The players associations have also stepped up to varying degrees. In 2002, the NFLPA specifically responded to the problem of professional athletes falling victim to poor financial advice and even outright fraud by offering its members a service to vet financial advisers. As part of that service, the NFLPA performs "[b]ackground checks and due

diligence . . . to ensure that financial advisors meet our eligibility standards." NFLPA Regulations and Code of Conduct Governing Registered Player Financial Advisors 2 (2017). Financial advisors have the incentive to participate in this voluntary program because once screened, their names are included on a non-public list provided to players.

In 2006, some current and former NFL players who relied on the NFLPA's registered financial advisor list sued the NFLPA claiming it negligently performed background checks on a financial advisor who perpetrated an investment scam in which the players collectively lost over $20 million. The suit also named the NFL, alleging that its background check on the financial advisor was also inadequate. The players pursued these claims despite liability disclaimers in both the financial advisor regulations and the collective bargaining agreement that players are solely responsible for their personal finances. Ultimately, the Eleventh Circuit dismissed the players' claims because they were preempted under § 301 of the National Labor Relations Act (*see* Chapter 3, Section D), and must be brought under the CBA's private dispute resolution procedures. *See Atwater v. Nat'l Football League Players Ass'n*, 626 F.3d 1170 (11th Cir. 2010). Although victorious in court, the NFLPA briefly suspended its financial advisor program and strengthen its requirements. Later iterations of both the NFLPA financial advisor regulations and the labor agreement toughened the disclaimer language to further block potential liability to players for the acts of dishonest financial advisors. What role do you think the leagues and players unions should play in protecting athletes from financial harms?

3. *Public Efforts to Protect Athletes.* Aside from agent-specific federal legislation, federal law has played an important, albeit sporadic, role in regulating athletes. Tank Black, mentioned above, was prosecuted under federal wire act and money laundering statutes. Sports agents including Fairron Newton, Myron Piggie, and Vinnie Porter have been prosecuted variously under federal mail fraud, money laundering, and tax statutes. *See, e.g., United States v. Piggie*, 303 F.3d 923, 924 (8th Cir. 2002) (agent compensated elite high school basketball players in violation of NCAA rules).

The Securities and Exchange Commission has vigorously enforced its regulations in filing civil and criminal actions against agents, including accusing Donald Lukens of defrauding his numerous athlete-clients out of millions of dollars during the 1990s. Other SEC actions in the sports industry include fraud and theft charges against financial advisor Howard Golub, who was sentenced to 10 to 12 years in prison and ordered to pay restitution to athlete-clients. A 2018 report calculated that from 2004 to 2016, professional athletes suffered almost $500 million in fraud-related loss. *See* Spiegelhalter and Silvertown, *Athletes Targeted by Fraud* 2 (2018 Ernst & Young). The report identified risk factors for athletes such as shortage of time to manage their own finances, reliance on nonqualified or inexperienced people, misplaced trust, under-supervised advisors, and exploitation by family and friends. Is it possible to develop private industry standards or legislative solutions to address these risks? What would those look like?

2. DUTY TO ACT LOYALLY FOR PRINCIPAL'S BENEFIT: FEE DISPUTES

The fiduciary standard prohibits the sports agent from pursuing self-interest as a motivating force in actions taken on the athlete's behalf. One of the first major sports agents, Bob Woolf, was the target of the first major lawsuit claiming that an agent breached that duty by maximizing his own compensation at the expense of his client. Woolf represented Andrew Brown of the NHL Pittsburgh Penguins, and in that capacity fielded competing offers for the player from the Penguins and from the Indianapolis Racers of the upstart World Hockey Association. Woolf convinced Brown to accept the Racers much richer offer, perhaps because it would generate a larger agent commission. When the Racers soon after encountered financial problems, and ultimately filed for bankruptcy, Brown lost much of his promised salary, while Woolf was paid his commission in full, a disparity that led to this lawsuit.

BROWN V. WOOLF
554 F. Supp. 1206 (S.D. Ind. 1983)

STECKLER, DISTRICT JUDGE.

[Andrew Brown played hockey for the Pittsburgh Penguins during the 1973–74 season under a contract negotiated by his agent Bob Woolf. In July 1974, the Penguins offered Brown a non-guaranteed two-year contract at $80,000 a year. Woolf advised Brown to reject that offer and to sign instead with the Indianapolis Racers of the World Hockey Association, a new team in a new league. The Racers deal was a five-year guaranteed contract, at $160,000 per season.]

On July 31, 1974, plaintiff signed a five-year contract with the Racers. Thereafter, it is alleged the Racers began having financial difficulties. Plaintiff avers that Woolf continued to represent plaintiff and negotiated two reductions in plaintiff's compensation including the loss of a retirement fund at the same time defendant was attempting to get his own fee payment from the Racers. Ultimately the Racers' assets were seized and the organizers defaulted on their obligations to plaintiff. He avers that he received only $185,000.00 of the total $800,000.00 compensation under the Racer contract but that defendant received his full $40,000.00 fee (5% of the contract) from the Racers.

Plaintiff alleges that defendant made numerous material misrepresentations upon which he relied both during the negotiation of the Racer contract and at the time of the subsequent modifications. Plaintiff further avers that defendant breached his fiduciary duty to plaintiff by failing to conduct any investigation into the financial stability of the Racers, failing to investigate possible consequences of the deferred compensation package in the Racers' contract, failing to obtain guarantees or collateral, and by negotiating reductions in plaintiff's compensation from the Racers while insisting on receiving all of his own. Plaintiff theorizes that such conduct amounts to a prima facie case of constructive fraud for which he should receive compensatory and punitive damages and have a trust impressed on the $40,000.00 fee defendant received from the Racers.

* * *

Indiana cases contain several formulizations of the tort of constructive fraud. Generally it is characterized as acts or a course of conduct from which an unconscionable advantage is or may be derived, or a breach of confidence coupled with an unjust enrichment which shocks the conscience, or a breach of duty, including mistake, duress or undue influence, which the law declares fraudulent because of a tendency to deceive, injure the public interest or violate the public or private confidence. Another formulization found in the cases involves the making of a false statement, by the dominant party in a confidential or fiduciary relationship or by one who holds himself out as an expert, upon which the plaintiff reasonably relies to his detriment. The defendant need not know the statement is false nor make the false statement with fraudulent intent.

The Court believes that both formulizations are rife with questions of fact, inter alia, the existence or nonexistence of a confidential or fiduciary relationship, and the question of reliance on false representations, as well as questions of credibility.

Defendant argues that despite the customary existence of such fact questions in a constructive fraud case, judgment is appropriate in this instance because plaintiff has produced nothing to demonstrate the existence of fact questions. He makes a similar argument in the motion for partial summary judgment on the punitive damages issue.

In this case, defendant has offered affidavits, excerpts of depositions, and photocopies of various documents to support his motions. He contends that such materials demonstrate that reasonable minds could not conclude that defendant did the acts with which the complaint charges him. In response, plaintiff rather belatedly offered portions of plaintiff's depositions as well as arguing that issues such as those raised by a complaint based on constructive fraud are inherently unsuited to resolution on a motion for summary judgment.

Having carefully considered the motions and briefs and having examined the evidentiary materials submitted, the Court concludes that summary judgment would not be appropriate in this action. The Court is not persuaded that there are no fact questions remaining unresolved in this controversy such that defendant is entitled to judgment as a matter of law.

Summary dismissal refused.

NOTES AND QUESTIONS

1. *Incentives and Conflicts in Fee Structures.* What was the true source of Brown's dispute with Woolf—the agent's fee or that the agent's self-interest sabotaged the player's career? To the extent the fee is at issue, what caused the problem—the amount of the fee, how it was calculated, or when it was paid? Does a straight-commission compensation system inevitably create a conflict of interest between the agent's and the athlete's self-interests? How would you structure an agent fee system to provide the best incentives for agents to act loyally for the principal's benefit?

2. *Constructive Fraud Theory.* The *Brown* court endorsed a theory of constructive fraud, which posits that even if the agent did not intend to deceive, the law should impose liability where the agent's actions gave him an unfair advantage over the athlete. The theory is premised on the idea that the fiduciary relationship induced the athlete to place his trust and confidence in the agent and relax the care and vigilance he would ordinarily exercise in the circumstances. Should application of this theory depend on the athlete's individual circumstances, for example his level of education and experience?

3. *Players Union Fee Regulation.* The problem of excessive agent fees has been ameliorated by union regulation of agents. For example, the NFLPA caps the agent fee for negotiating a playing contract at three percent, with a default fee of 1.5 percent unless the agent convinces the player he's worth more. The NBPA caps such fees at four percent. These unions further lower the fee cap when the player's salary is predetermined by collective bargaining agreement pay scales or established market values, such as rookies, players earning the league minimum, and players tagged as franchise or transition players. Presumably, the idea here is that the agent's fee should be tied to the time, difficulty, and skill of the work involved. Contrast the players associations in the NHL and MLB, which set no fee caps and allow the market to dictate the fees charged by agents, typically between four and ten percent. Which of these approaches make the most sense to you? Are there differences among these sports that justify different approaches to regulating agent fees?

4. *Demographics of Agents in Team Sports.* The demographics of agents differ noticeably between the NBA and NFL on the one hand, and the NHL and MLB on the other. In the latter leagues, the vast majority of players are represented either by agents with many clients or by attorneys with whom they or their families had pre-existing relationships. By contrast, many more NBA and NFL players retain agents who represent a few clients and who solicited them. This difference is likely because NBA/NFL players typically come directly from college programs and choose agents under the NCAA's tight regulation of amateur status, while MLB/NHL players make those decisions during their multi-year minor league professional careers. Consider whether

this disparity explains the different approach to agent fee regulation described in the previous note, and why.

5. *State Regulation of Boxer Agreements.* State regulations governing boxing require promoters to file a boxer's contract with the appropriate state commission. When boxing promoter Don King failed to do so for certain one-sided and exploitative agreements with heavyweight champion Mike Tyson, a court invalidated those agreements to comply with state regulations that protect boxers from "improvident arrangements." *Tyson v. King*, 2000 WL 35572295 (S.D.N.Y. 2000). The *Tyson* court observed that the agreements, which gave King more money from Tyson's fights than the boxer received, violated the "strong public policy" that prohibits a promoter from having a pecuniary interest in a boxer. Why do you think team sports are not subject to a similar public policy and regulatory regime?

6. *Arbitration of Fee Disputes.* Arbitrators often resolve agent fee disputes pursuant to dispute resolution clauses in the union-mandated standard representation agreements. The NFLPA's arbitration clause is typical:

> Any and all disputes between Player and Contract Advisor involving the meaning, interpretation, application, or enforcement of this Agreement of the obligations of the parties under this Agreement shall be resolved exclusively through the arbitration procedures set forth in Section 5 of the NFLPA Regulations Governing Contract Advisors.

See Wichard v. Suggs, 95 F. Supp. 3d 935 (E.D. Va. 2015) (confirming arbitration award to football player's agent as consistent with "the essence" of the standard representation agreement). As stressed in Chapter 3, courts afford great deference to arbitration awards. *See Wasserman Media Grp., LLC v. Bender*, 2011 WL 1886460 (S.D.N.Y. May 16, 2011) (confirming award to basketball player's agent under Federal Arbitration Act); *Octagon, Inc. v. Richards*, 2010 WL 3932272 (E.D. Va. Oct. 5, 2010) (upholding fee award to track athlete's agent, despite evidence that agent violated state law regarding student athletes).

3. AGENT CONFLICTS OF INTEREST

A more fundamental ethical, as well as legal, issue arising in the comparatively closed sports world is agent representation of actual and potential conflicting interests. Consolidation and diversification in the industry has exacerbated this issue, with mega-agencies like Creative Artists Agency, Excel Sports Management, and Wasserman dominating the business. CAA represents more than 800 athletes in baseball, football, hockey, basketball, soccer, tennis, and golf, in addition to Olympians, coaches, broadcasters, and other sports personalities.

Consider the story of SFX Sports Group, which in the late 1990s acquired 21 smaller sports agencies. As a result, SFX Sports for a time represented approximately 16 percent of all MLB players, and significant numbers of basketball and football players. SFX Sports' parent company was then acquired by Clear Channel Entertainment (now iHeartMedia), raising the further complication that two of Clear Channel's major shareholders were owners of major league teams. In other words, the same company—Clear Channel—could be sitting on both sides of a player-team transaction. Thus, the players unions at the time insisted that Clear Channel create a separate and autonomous corporate wing to negotiate player contracts with any teams. Should the clients be satisfied that this structure adequately ameliorates any conflicts? The legal (as opposed to the ethical) reason why Clear Channel had to take that special action in sports is displayed vividly by the following case.

DETROIT LIONS AND BILLY SIMS V. JERRY ARGOVITZ
580 F. Supp. 542 (E.D. Mich. 1984)

DEMASCIO, DISTRICT JUDGE.

The plot for this Saturday afternoon serial began when Billy Sims, having signed a contract with the Houston Gamblers on July 1, 1983, signed a second contract with the Detroit Lions on December 16, 1983. On December 18, 1983, the Detroit Lions, Inc. (Lions) and Billy R. Sims filed a complaint in the Oakland County Circuit Court seeking a judicial determination that the July 1, 1983, contract between Sims and the Houston Gamblers, Inc. (Gamblers) is invalid because the defendant Jerry Argovitz (Argovitz) breached his fiduciary duty when negotiating the Gamblers' contract and because the contract was otherwise tainted by fraud and misrepresentation. Defendants promptly removed the action to this court based on our diversity of citizenship jurisdiction.

For the reasons that follow, we have concluded that Argovitz's breach of his fiduciary duty during negotiations for the Gamblers' contract was so pronounced, so egregious, that to deny rescission would be unconscionable.

Sometime in February or March 1983, Argovitz told Sims that he had applied for a Houston franchise in the newly formed United States Football League (USFL). In May 1983, Sims attended a press conference in Houston at which Argovitz announced that his application for a franchise had been approved. The evidence persuades us that Sims did not know the extent of Argovitz's interest in the Gamblers. He did not know the amount of Argovitz's original investment, or that Argovitz was obligated for 29 percent of a $1.5 million letter of credit, or that Argovitz was the president of the Gamblers' Corporation at an annual salary of $275,000 and 5 percent the yearly cash flow. The defendants could not justifiably expect Sims to comprehend the ramifications of Argovitz's interest in the Gamblers or the manner in which that interest would create an untenable conflict of interest, a conflict that would inevitably breach Argovitz's fiduciary duty to Sims. Argovitz knew, or should have known, that he could not act as Sims' agent under any circumstances when dealing with the Gamblers. Even the USFL Constitution itself prohibits a holder of any interest in a member club from acting "as the contracting agent or representative for any player."

Pending the approval of his application for a USFL franchise in Houston, Argovitz continued his negotiations with the Lions on behalf of Sims. [The court described the offers and counter-offers that began on April 5, 1983: Argovitz (and his associate Burrough) initially asked the Lions for $6 million over four years, and the Lions responded with $1.5 million over five years. As the court remarked, "[t]he negotiating process was working. The Lions were trying to determine what Argovitz really believed the market value for Sims really was." But after confirmation of his Gamblers franchise, Argovitz reduced his demands on behalf of Sims to half of what he originally asked. The court found that, on June 1, "Argovitz and the Lions were only $500,000 apart," and on June 22, "the Lions and Argovitz were very close to reaching an agreement on the value of Sims' services."]

Apparently, in the midst of his negotiations with the Lions and with his Gamblers franchise in hand, Argovitz decided that he would seek an offer from the Gamblers. Mr. Bernard Lerner, one of Argovitz's partners in the Gamblers, agreed to negotiate a contract with Sims. Since Lerner admitted that he had no knowledge whatsoever about football, we must infer that Argovitz at the very least told Lerner the amount of money required to sign Sims and further pressed upon Lerner the Gamblers' absolute need to obtain Sims' services. In the Gamblers' organization, only Argovitz knew the value of Sims' services and how critical it was for the Gamblers to obtain Sims. In Argovitz's words, Sims would make the Gamblers' franchise.

On June 29, 1983, at Lerner's behest, Sims and his wife went to Houston to negotiate with a team that was partially owned by his own agent. When Sims arrived in Houston, he believed that the Lions organization was not negotiating in good faith; that it was not really interested in his services. His ego was bruised and his emotional outlook toward the Lions was visible to Burrough and Argovitz. Clearly, virtually all the information that Sims had up to that date came from Argovitz. Sims and the Gamblers did not discuss a future contract on the night of June 29th. The negotiations began on the morning of June 30, 1983, and ended that afternoon. At the morning meeting, Lerner offered Sims a $3.5 million five-year contract, which included three years of skill and injury guarantees. The offer included a $500,000 loan at an interest rate of one percent over prime. It was from this loan that Argovitz planned to receive the $100,000 balance of his fee for acting as an agent in negotiating a contract with his own team. Burrough testified that Sims would have accepted that offer on the spot because he was finally receiving the guarantee that he had been requesting from the Lions, guarantees that Argovitz dropped without too much quarrel. Argovitz and Burrough took Sims and his wife into another room to discuss the offer. Argovitz did tell Sims that he thought the Lions would match the Gamblers financial package and asked Sims whether he (Argovitz) should telephone the Lions. But, it is clear from the evidence that neither Sims nor Burrough believed that the Lions would match the offer. We find that Sims told Argovitz not to call the Lions for purely emotional reasons. As we have noted, Sims believed that the Lions' organization was not that interested in him and his pride was wounded. Burrough clearly admitted that he was aware of the emotional basis for Sims' decision not to have Argovitz phone the Lions, and we must conclude from the extremely close relationship between Argovitz and Sims that Argovitz knew it as well. When Sims went back to Lerner's office, he agreed to become a Gambler on the terms offered. At that moment, Argovitz irreparably breached his fiduciary duty. As agent for Sims he had the duty to telephone the Lions, receive its final offer, and present the terms of both offers to Sims. Then and only then could it be said that Sims made an intelligent and knowing decision to accept the Gamblers' offer.

During these negotiations at the Gamblers' office, Mr. Nash of the Lions telephoned Argovitz, but even though Argovitz was at his office, he declined to accept the telephone call. Argovitz tried to return Nash's call after Sims had accepted the Gamblers' offer, but it was after 5 p.m. and Nash had left for the July 4th weekend. When he declined to accept Mr. Nash's call, Argovitz's breach of his fiduciary duty became even more pronounced. Following Nash's example, Argovitz left for his weekend trip, leaving his principal to sign the contracts with the Gamblers the next day, July 1, 1983. The defendants, in their supplemental trial brief, assert that neither Argovitz nor Burrough can be held responsible for following Sims' instruction not to contact the Lions on June 30, 1983. Although it is generally true that an agent is not liable for losses occurring as a result of following his principal's instructions, this rule of law is not applicable when the agent has placed himself in a position adverse to that of his principal.

During the evening of June 30, 1983, Burrough struggled with the fact that they had not presented the Gamblers' offer to the Lions. He knew, as does the court, that Argovitz now had the wedge that he needed to bring finality to the Lions' negotiations. [The court "view[ed] with disdain" how during the crucial 24 hours in which Sims made the decision to sign with the Gamblers, Argovitz was absent and did not use the wedge of the Gamblers' offer to further negotiate with the Lions.] . . . The evidence here convinces us that Argovitz's negotiations with the Lions were ongoing and it had not made its final offer. Argovitz did not follow the common practice described by both expert witnesses. He did not do this because he knew that the Lions would not leave Sims without a contract and he further knew that if he made that type of call Sims would be lost to the Gamblers, a team he owned.

On November 12, 1983, when Sims was in Houston for the Lions game with the Houston Oilers, Argovitz asked Sims to come to his home and sign certain papers. He represented to Sims that certain papers of his contract had been mistakenly overlooked and now needed to be signed. Included among those papers he asked Sims to sign was a waiver of any claim that Sims might have against Argovitz for his blatant breach of his fiduciary duty brought on by his glaring conflict of interest. Sims did not receive independent advice with regard to the wisdom of signing such a waiver. Despite having sold his agency business in September, Argovitz did not even tell Sims' new agent of his intention to have Sims sign a waiver. Nevertheless, Sims, an unsophisticated young man, signed the waiver. This is another example of the questionable conduct on the part of Argovitz who still had business management obligations to Sims. In spite of his fiduciary relationship he had Sims sign a waiver without advising him to obtain independent counseling.

Argovitz's negotiations with Lustig, Jim Kelly's agent, illustrates the difficulties that develop when an agent negotiates a contract where his personal interests conflict with those of his principal. Lustig, an independent agent, ignored Argovitz's admonishment not to "shop" the Gamblers' offer to Kelly. Lustig called the NFL team that he had been negotiating with because it was the "prudent" thing to do. The Gamblers agreed to pay Kelly, an untested rookie quarterback, $3.2 million for five years. His compensation was $60,000 less than Sims', a former Heisman Trophy winner and a proven star in the NFL. Lustig also obtained a number of favorable clauses from Argovitz; the most impressive one being that Kelly was assured of being one of the three top paid quarterbacks in the USFL if he performed as well as expected. If Argovitz had been free from conflicting interests he would have demanded similar benefits for Sims. Argovitz claimed that the nondisclosure clause in Kelly's contract prevented him from mentioning the Kelly contract to Sims. We view this contention as frivolous. Requesting these benefits for Sims did not require disclosure of Kelly's contract. Moreover, Argovitz's failure to obtain personal guarantees for Sims without adequately warning Sims about the risks and uncertainties of a new league constituted a clear breach of his fiduciary duty.

* * *

We are mindful that Sims was less than forthright when testifying before the court. However, we agree with plaintiff's counsel that the facts as presented through the testimony of other witnesses are so unappealing that we can disregard Sims' testimony entirely. We remain persuaded that on balance, Argovitz's breach of his fiduciary duty was so egregious that a court of equity cannot permit him to benefit by his own wrongful breach. We conclude that Argovitz's conduct in negotiating Sims' contract with the Gamblers rendered it invalid.

* * *

Rescission granted.

NOTES AND QUESTIONS

1. *Duty of Loyalty.* Identify each act (or omission) by Argovitz that breached his duty of loyalty to Sims. Would you consider any such act standing alone to be de minimis, or should any one of them justify voiding Sims's contract with the Gamblers?

2. *Informed Consent to Conflicts of Interest.* Upon full disclosure by the agent, an athlete can consent to a conflict of interest and continue the representation, or refuse to do so and seek new representation. This assumes that athlete-clients have the sophistication and business acumen to comprehend the circumstances and nature of the conflict presented. *See Hernandez v. Childers*, 806 F. Supp. 1368 (N.D.Ill.1992) (agent's detailed disclosures regarding personal involvement in investment not sufficient to defeat baseball player's conflict of interest claim). Do you believe Sims could have made such an informed determination? Why wasn't disclosure to Sims of Argovitz's ownership of the Gamblers franchise sufficient to waive the conflict? If a player upon full disclosure effectively consents to a conflict, should that immunize the agent from the player's claims that the agent negligently performed due to the conflict? How should a court weigh the equities when the player intentionally selects a conflicted agent in the belief that the conflict helps the player, *i.e.*, that the agent is likely to exploit the conflict for the player's benefit?

3. *Conflict Situations.* Contrast *Argovitz* with the following situations:

   a. Jerry Kapstein, one of the most prominent baseball agents for two decades, married the daughter of Joan Kroc, then owner of the San Diego Padres, and regularly advised his mother-in-law about her ownership interests. Should that relationship have barred Kapstein from representing players on the Padres? On the Dodgers? On the NFL Los Angeles Rams?

   b. Larry Fleisher and Alan Eagleson were the founders and long-time leaders of the NBA and NHL Players Associations, respectively. They were also sports agents who had full rosters of individual clients among their association members. Was this appropriate? *See Major Indoor Soccer League & Professional Soccer Players Ass'n (PROSPA)*, NLRB Ruling, Nov. 15, 1983.

c. Because successful agents represent a number of players, conflicts are almost inevitable and sometimes are compounded by the impact of a salary cap. If a sports agent represents two pitching aces who are both free agents, how should he negotiate with a team trying to sign both? What if an agent represents two players on the same team with upcoming contract renegotiations? What if the agent represents a Division I college basketball coach who advises his stars to use the agent as their representative when they leave college for the professional ranks?

d. Multifaceted firms, such as International Management Group (IMG), not only represent many tennis players but they also promote, manage, and even sponsored tournaments on the tennis tour. Is this dual representation legitimate? Should the body responsible for the tour be able to impose limitations on such inter-relationships? *See Volvo North America Corp. v. Men's International Professional Tennis Council (MIPTC)*, 857 F.2d 55 (2d Cir. 1988).

4. *Athlete Self-Management.* Some premier athletes have succeeded in avoiding the risk of conflicts of interest by founding their own management agencies to negotiate contracts and make endorsement deals for themselves. LeBron James's marketing company offers an example of this new financial model, handling all aspects of his business ventures. Similarly, golfer Rory McIlroy and tennis players Roger Federer, Andy Murray, and Rafael Nadal each left high profile companies and, taking their previous agents with them, set up their own agencies. Does this approach work only for superstar players with tremendous marketing capabilities? Or is there a version of self-management that would be equally effective for the average player? *See* Jodi S. Balsam, *"Free My Agent": Legal Implications of Professional Athletes' Self-Representation*, 16 Wake Forest J. Bus. & Intell. Prop. L. 510 (2016).

4. DISPUTES BETWEEN SPORTS AGENTS

As a result of the intense competition for clients, athletes regularly move from one agency to another, enabled by standard representation agreements that permit either party to terminate by providing short written notice (*e.g.*, five days for NFL player agents). Agents also regularly switch agencies, especially during the recent era of conglomeration of the agency business. These moves can trigger litigation about contract terms and agent fees owed, and courts have considered when aggressive business tactics cross ethical and legal boundaries.

SPEAKERS OF SPORT, INC. V. PROSERV, INC.
178 F.3d 862 (7th Cir. 1999)

POSNER, CHIEF JUDGE.

The plaintiff, Speakers of Sport, appeals from the grant of summary judgment to the defendant, ProServ, in a diversity suit in which one sports agency has charged another with tortious interference with a business relationship and related violations of Illinois law. The essential facts, construed as favorably to the plaintiff as the record will permit, are as follows. Ivan Rodriguez, a highly successful catcher with the Texas Rangers baseball team, in 1991 signed the first of several one-year contracts making Speakers his agent. ProServ wanted to expand its representation of baseball players and to this end invited Rodriguez to its office in Washington and there promised that it would get him between $2 and $4 million in endorsements if he signed with ProServ—which he did, terminating his contract (which was terminable at will) with Speakers. This was in 1995. ProServ failed to obtain significant endorsement for Rodriguez and after just one year he switched to another agent who the following year landed him a five-year $42 million contract with the Rangers. Speakers brought this suit a few months later, charging that the promise of endorsements that ProServ had made to Rodriguez was fraudulent and had induced him to terminate his contract with Speakers.

The parties agree that the substantive issues in this diversity suit are governed by Illinois law, and we do not look behind such agreements so long as they are reasonable, as this one is. . . .

Speakers could not sue Rodriguez for breach of contract, because he had not broken their contract, which was, as we said, terminable at will. Nor, therefore, could it accuse ProServ of inducing a breach of contract. . . . But Speakers did have a contract with Rodriguez, and inducing the termination of a contract, even when the termination is not a breach because the contract is terminable at will, can still be actionable under the tort law of Illinois, either as an interference with prospective economic advantage or as an interference with the contract at will itself. Nothing turns on the difference in characterization.

There is in general nothing wrong with one sports agent trying to take a client from another if this can be done without precipitating a breach of contract. That is the process known as competition, which though painful, fierce, frequently ruthless, sometimes Darwinian in its pitilessness, is the cornerstone of our highly successful economic system. Competition is not a tort, but on the contrary provides a defense (the "competitor's privilege") to the tort of improper interference. It does not privilege inducing a breach of contract—conduct usefully regarded as a separate tort from interfering with a business relationship without precipitating an actual breach of contract—but it does privilege inducing the lawful termination of a contract that is terminable at will. Sellers (including agents, who are sellers of services) do not "own" their customers, at least not without a contract with them that is not terminable at will.

There would be few more effective inhibitors of the competitive process than making it a tort for an agent to promise the client of another agent to do better by him—which is pretty much what this case comes down to. It is true that Speakers argues only that the competitor may not make a promise that he knows he cannot fulfill, may not, that is, compete by fraud. Because the competitor's privilege does not include a right to get business from a competitor by means of fraud, it is hard to quarrel with this position in the abstract, but the practicalities are different. If the argument were accepted and the new agent made a promise that was not fulfilled, the old agent would have a shot at convincing a jury that the new agent had known from the start that he couldn't deliver on the promise. Once a case gets to the jury, all bets are off. The practical consequence of Speakers' approach, therefore, would be that a sports agent who lured away the client of another agent with a promise to do better by him would be running a grave legal risk.

This threat to the competitive process is blocked by the principle of Illinois law that promissory fraud is not actionable unless it is part of a scheme to defraud, that is, unless it is one element of a pattern of fraudulent acts. By requiring that the plaintiff show a pattern, by thus not letting him rest on proving a single promise, the law reduces the likelihood of a spurious suit; for a series of unfulfilled promises is better (though of course not conclusive) evidence of fraud than a single unfulfilled promise.

Criticized for vagueness, and rejected in most states, the Illinois rule yet makes sense in a case like this, if only as a filter against efforts to use the legal process to stifle competition. Consider in this connection the characterization by Speakers' own chairman of ProServ's promise to Rodriguez as "pure fantasy and gross exaggeration"—in other words, as puffing. Puffing in the usual sense signifies meaningless superlatives that no reasonable person would take seriously, and so it is not actionable as fraud. Rodriguez thus could not have sued ProServ (and has not attempted to) in respect of the promise of $2–$4 million in endorsements. If Rodriguez thus was not wronged, we do not understand on what theory Speakers can complain that ProServ competed with it unfairly.

The promise of endorsements was puffing not in the most common sense of a cascade of extravagant adjectives but in the equally valid sense of a sales pitch that is intended, and that a reasonable person in the position of the "promisee" would understand, to be aspirational rather than enforceable—an expression of hope rather than a commitment. It is not as if ProServ proposed to employ Rodriguez and pay him $2 million a year. That would be the kind of promise that could found an enforceable obligation. ProServ proposed merely to get him endorsements of at least that amount. They would of course be paid by the companies whose products Rodriguez endorsed, rather than by ProServ. ProServ could not force them to pay Rodriguez, and it is not contended that he understood ProServ to be warranting a minimum level of endorsements in the sense that if they were not forthcoming ProServ would be legally obligated to make up the difference to him.

It is possible to make a binding promise of something over which one has no control; such a promise is called a warranty. But it is not plausible that this is what ProServ was doing—that it was guaranteeing Rodriguez a minimum of $2 million a year in outside earnings if he signed with it. The only reasonable meaning to attach to ProServ's so-called promise is that ProServ would try to get as many endorsements as possible for Rodriguez and that it was optimistic that it could get him at least $2 million worth of them. So understood, the "promise" was not a promise at all. But even if it was a promise (or a warranty), it cannot be the basis for a finding of fraud because it was not part of a scheme to defraud evidenced by more than the allegedly fraudulent promise itself.

It can be argued, however, that competition can be tortious even if it does not involve an actionable fraud (which in Illinois would not include a fraudulent promise) or other independently tortious act, such as defamation, or trademark or patent infringement, or a theft of a trade secret; that competitors should not be allowed to use "unfair" tactics; and that a promise known by the promisor when made to be unfulfillable is such a tactic, especially when used on a relatively unsophisticated, albeit very well to do, baseball player.... The doctrine's conception of wrongful competition is vague—"wrongful by reason of ... an established standard of a trade or profession," or "a violation of recognized ethical rules or established customs or practices in the business community," or "improper because they [the challenged competitive tactics] violate an established standard of a trade or profession, or involve unethical conduct, ... sharp dealing[, or] overreaching." [citations omitted] Worse, the established standards of a trade or profession in regard to competition, and its ideas of unethical competitive conduct, are likely to reflect a desire to limit competition for reasons related to the self-interest of the trade or profession rather than to the welfare of its customers or clients. [T]he tort of interference with business relationships should be confined to cases in which the defendant employed unlawful means to stiff a competitor, and ... the case law is generally consistent with this position as a matter of outcomes as distinct from articulation.

Invoking the concept of "wrongful by reason of ... an established standard of a trade or profession," Speakers points to a rule of major league baseball forbidding players' agents to compete by means of misrepresentations. The rule is designed to protect the players, rather than their agents, so that even if it established a norm enforceable by law Speakers would not be entitled to invoke it; it is not a rule designed for Speakers' protection. In any event its violation would not be the kind of "wrongful" conduct that should trigger the tort of intentional interference; it would not be a violation of law.

[The court evaluated Speakers' claim that ProServ violated the Illinois Consumer Fraud and Deceptive Business Practices Act, rejecting it largely because Speakers is not a consumer.]

* * *

We add that even if Speakers could establish liability under either the common law of torts or the deceptive practices act, its suit would fail because it cannot possibly establish, as it seeks to do, a damages entitlement (the only relief it seeks) to the agent's fee on Rodriguez's $42 million contract. That contract was negotiated years after he left Speakers, and by another agent. Since Rodriguez had only a year-to-year contract with Speakers—terminable at will, moreover—and since obviously he was dissatisfied with Speakers at least to the extent of switching to ProServ and then when he became disillusioned with ProServ of not returning to Speakers' fold, the likelihood that Speakers would have retained him had ProServ not lured him away is too slight to ground an award of such damages. Such an award would be the best example yet of puffing in the pie-in the-sky sense.

Affirmed.

NOTES AND QUESTIONS

1. *The Competitor's Privilege.* The *Speakers* court considers fierce competition to be the cornerstone of our economic system, and refuses to condemn shady conduct by sports agents in poaching clients. What limits does the court impose, if any, on the "competitor's privilege"? How do those limits circumscribe the conduct of an agent towards a prospective client? Towards a competing agent? *See Wright v. Bonds*, 117 F.3d 1427 (9th Cir. 1997) (agent did not wrongfully interfere with contract by contacting baseball player represented by another agent, and then lying about it); *Bauer v. The Interpublic Group of Companies, Inc.*, 255 F. Supp. 2d 1086 (N.D. Cal. 2003) (agent unable to establish that competitor who lured away his client was responsible for anonymous letters disparaging the agent).

2. *Players Association Regulation of Sports Agents.* At least one court has held that the existence of players association regulation of sports agents is reason not to hold an agent liable under state statutory prohibitions of deceptive business practices. In *Champion Pro Consulting Grp., Inc. v. Impact Sports Football, LLC*, 845 F.3d 104 (4th Cir. 2016), a sports agency alleged that

a competitor recruited college football players by using "runners," cash inducements, and other practices reviled under NFLPA regulation of agents. In view of the "well-established internal systems of governance already in place," the court declined to intervene to avoid creating overlapping and possibly conflicting mechanisms for supervision of agents. *Id.* at 110. Do you agree that courts in these situations should defer to private regulation of sports agents? The *Champion* court further observed that the allegations of agent misconduct were "indicative of the industry in which these parties operate and [therefore] outside the scope of business activities" the state statute is designed to address. *Id.* Should the standard for deceptive business practices vary with the cutthroat nature of the industry?

3. *Non-Compete Clauses.* With sports agents frequently switching agencies, non-compete clauses have become standard practice to prevent them from stealing away their old firm's clients when they move to a new firm. State law governs non-compete clauses, and most states require them to be reasonable and to permit the departing employee to earn a living. *See Steinberg Moorad & Dunn Inc. v. Dunn*, 136 F. App'x 6 (9th Cir. 2005) (vacating $44 million judgment in favor of agent's former firm because non-competition clause was invalid to extent it prevented agent from "pursuing his trade"). Furthermore, when a non-compete clause restricts a sports agent's ability to ply his trade, it affects both athletes' rights to select the agent of their choice and players unions' federal authority to regulate agents' conduct. How would you weigh these interests against protecting an agency's investment in training an agent and supporting the agent in recruiting clients?

4. *Athlete's Best Interests.* What are the risks to the athlete who bounces from agent to agent with little regard to loyalty or scruples? Are athletes always motivated purely by economic interests, or are there competing, highly personal considerations that can motivate their contractual decision-making? *See* Michael A. McCann, *It's Not About the Money: The Role of Preferences, Cognitive Biases, and Heuristics Among Professional Athletes*, 71 Brook. L. Rev. 1459, 1482 (2006). Consider whether there is value to professional athletes in developing long-term relationships with their advisors.

C. AGENT REPRESENTATION OF UNIONIZED ATHLETES

As explained in Chapter 2, once a workforce unionizes, the certified union has the exclusive authority to negotiate all terms and conditions of employment for all members in the bargaining unit. Like their counterparts in the entertainment industry, though, players associations have traditionally exercised this statutory authority only to the extent of negotiating minimum salaries, benefits, and job protections—a level of basic rights that is guaranteed to every player, whether a rookie or superstar. The collective bargaining agreement in each team sport allows every player to try to negotiate more advantageous terms—in particular, high guaranteed salaries. This approach is premised on the variability of player-employee talent and market value in sports, as opposed to the ordinary employment setting.

In addition, players associations delegate to player representatives—sports agents—a portion of the exclusive bargaining authority they have been granted under the Labor Act to represent all the players in their respective leagues. These representatives, however, must submit to a union certification process that can include meeting minimal education requirements, attending seminars, and passing a written examination. The first union to regulate sports agents was the NFLPA in 1983, followed by the NBPA (1985), the MLBPA (1987), and the NHLPA (1995). All four associations have adopted comprehensive regulatory schemes that address agent competence, ethics, and fair competition for athletes-clients.

Consensus has emerged over time that players associations are best equipped to regulate agents, and possess the incentives and the resources to develop the regulatory competence needed to improve the quality of agent representation. Further, once an agent has learned and complied with a union's requirements, he or she can represent any player and deal with any team in that sport.

1. UNION AUTHORITY TO REGULATE AGENTS

Labor law, specifically the union's exclusive bargaining authority, provides the source of an association's authority to impose binding regulations on agents. But while unions can, and do, delegate their exclusive authority to the individual athletes and their agents, a union may delegate its statutory prerogatives conditionally, and only in favor of agents of whom the union approves. When players associations adopt the latter posture, both the collective bargaining agreement and the labor laws preclude a club from negotiating individual contracts with agents who are not certified for that purpose by the association. In effect, the clubs become the enforcers of the association's regulatory program, because they must refuse to deal with any agent who has not secured and retained the association's stamp of approval.

While its bargaining relationship with the league may give the players association the leverage to impose its certification program on agents, this power secured under labor law does not necessarily insulate the regime from challenge under other laws—in particular, antitrust law. In effect, the players are agreeing to a standard set of terms upon which they will purchase the services of player agents—one term being the maximum agency fee—and the players collectively require agents to subscribe to these terms as a condition of doing business in this sport. Should such restraints on the agent market be considered an illegal restraint of trade under the Sherman Act? As one might suspect, players associations answer this question in the negative—asserting the same labor exemption from antitrust that leagues have relied on to protect their limitations on player mobility and salary based on the terms of the collective bargaining agreements negotiated with the unions.

In the following case, the NBPA attempted to ward off the first legal challenge to association regulation of agents. It arose out of accusations by basketball great Kareem Abdul-Jabbar that his agent Thomas Collins engaged in a variety of breaches of fiduciary duty and financial improprieties that cost the player close to $1 million. Although Abdul-Jabbar and Collins eventually settled these claims, Collins during the dispute had allowed his NBPA certification to lapse. When he sought recertification, the NBPA investigated the Abdul-Jabbar allegations and decided not to recertify Collins. Collins was entitled to appeal the denial to a union arbitrator, but instead brought this suit.

COLLINS v. NBPA & GRANTHAM
850 F. Supp. 1468 (D. Col. 1991), *affirmed per curiam*, 976 F.2d 740 (10th Cir. 1992)

MATSCH, DISTRICT JUDGE.

[Collins brought an antitrust challenge against the NBPA-NBA collective bargaining agreement which forbids NBA teams from negotiating with agents who are not certified by the NBPA.]

* * *

Like other sports and entertainment unions, the NBPA believes that the collective good of the entire represented group is maximized when individualized salary negotiations occur within a framework that permits players to exert leverage based on their unique skills and personal contributions. The NBPA therefore has authorized the players or their individually selected agents to negotiate individual compensation packages. This delegation of representational authority to individual players and their agents has always been limited solely to the authority to negotiate individual compensation packages, and to enforce them through the grievance-arbitration procedure established by the NBPA-NBA Agreement.

Player agents were unregulated by the NBPA before 1986. By the mid-1980s, a substantial number of players had complained to the officers of the NBPA about agent abuses. Specifically, players complained that the agents imposed high and non-uniform fees for negotiation services, insisted on the execution of open-ended powers of attorney giving the agents broad powers over players' professional and financial decisions, failed to keep players apprised of the status of negotiations with NBA teams, failed to submit itemized bills for fees and services, and, in some cases, had conflicts of interest arising out of representing coaches and/or general managers of NBA teams as well as players. Many players believed they were bound by contract not to dismiss their agents regardless of dissatisfaction with their services and fees, because the agents had insisted on the execution of long-term agreements. Some agents offered money and other inducements to players, their families and coaches to obtain player clients.

In response to these abuses, the NBPA established the Regulations, a comprehensive system of agent certification and regulation, to insure that players would receive agent services that meet minimum standards of quality at uniform rates. First, the Regulations provide that a player agent may not conduct individual contract negotiations unless he signs the "Standard Player Agent Contract" promulgated by the Committee. The "Standard Player Agent Contract" limits player agent fees by prohibiting any fee or commission on any contract which entitles the player to the minimum salary and by limiting agent fees on all contracts. Second, the Regulations contain a "code of conduct" which specifically prohibits an agent from providing or offering money or anything of value to a player, a member of a player's family or a player's high school or college coach for the purpose of inducing the player to use that agent's services. The code also prohibits agents from engaging in conduct that constitutes an actual or apparent conflict of interest (such as serving as an agent for a player while also representing an NBA team, general manager or head coach), engaging in any unlawful conduct involving dishonesty, fraud, deceit, misrepresentation, or engaging in any other conduct that reflects adversely on his fitness to serve in a fiduciary capacity as a player agent or jeopardizes the effective representation of NBA players.

Third, the Regulations restrict the representation of players to individuals who are certified player agents, and set up a program for the certification of agents who are then bound by the Regulations' fee restrictions and code of conduct. [The court listed the grounds for denying certification, including making false or misleading statements in the application for certification, misappropriated funds, engaged in fraud or other conduct that "significantly impacts adversely on his credibility, integrity or competence to serve in a fiduciary capacity on behalf of players," or is unwilling to swear to comply with agent regulations. Agents denied certification may demand final and binding arbitration.]

After unilaterally promulgating the Regulations, the NBPA obtained, in arms length collective bargaining, the NBA's agreement to prohibit all member teams from negotiating individual player salary contracts with any agent who was not certified by the NBPA.

[The court described Collins' misconduct with respect to Abdul-Jabbar as determined by an NBPA investigation, and the resulting decision to deny recertification. Collins responded with an antitrust complaint that characterized the NBPA's actions as a "group boycott" and per se violation of the Sherman Act in restraining him from representing individual basketball players in salary negotiations with their teams. The court concluded that the NBPA's actions were immune from antitrust scrutiny under the statutory and non-statutory labor exemptions.]

* * *

Both the Regulations and Article XXXI [of the CBA] are within the statutory exemption from antitrust regulation. When promulgating the Regulations and when negotiating Article XXXI, the NBPA acted in its own interest, independently of any employers and without denying access to rival employers. The number and identity of the employers remains unchanged regardless of the Regulations or Article XXXI. A union's actions are in its "self-interest" if they bear a reasonable relationship to a legitimate union interest. The NBPA regulatory program fulfills legitimate union purposes and was the result of legitimate concerns: it protects the player wage scale by eliminating percentage fees where the agent does not achieve a result better than the collectively bargained minimum; it keeps agent fees generally to a reasonable and uniform level, prevents unlawful kickbacks, bribes, and fiduciary violations and protects the NBPA's interest in assuring that its role in representing professional basketball players is properly carried out. Although Collins claims any benefit is in the *player's* self-interest, not the union's, it is impossible to separate the two—the union is composed of its members and exists solely to serve the players. When the players benefit, the union benefits as well.

The second prong of the [labor exemption] test is also met.... The NBPA did not combine with a non-labor group or a non-party to a labor dispute when promulgating the Regulations or negotiating Article XXXI. The NBPA unilaterally developed its Regulations in response to agent abuses and to benefit its members. It did not develop them in collusion with the employer group or to assist the employer group effort to restrain competition or control the employer group's product market.

* * *

Even if Article XXXI of the Agreement were not entitled to the statutory exemption, it would be immune from antitrust review under the nonstatutory exemption to the antitrust laws. The Supreme Court has determined that when a union-employer agreement falls within the protection of the national labor policy, a proper accommodation between the policy favoring collective bargaining under the NLRA and the congressional policy favoring free competition in business markets requires that some agreements be accorded a limited nonstatutory labor exemption from antitrust sanctions. Unlike the statutory exemption which immunizes activities that are expressly described in the Clayton and Norris LaGuardia Acts, the nonstatutory exemption immunizes labor arrangements that are the ordinary implication of activities contemplated by the federal labor laws. When the agreement is reached through bona fide, arms-length bargaining between the union and the employers, and the terms of the agreement are not the product of an initiative by the employer group but were sought by the union in an effort to serve the legitimate interests of its members, it is free from antitrust scrutiny.

* * *

The nonstatutory exemption similarly immunizes the Regulations from Sherman Act scrutiny. The Regulations were unilaterally developed in response to player complaints and to further NBPA labor policies. The NBPA-NBA Agreement, including Article XXXI, was agreed to in arms-length collective bargaining. The provision was not sought "at the behest of or in combination with" any employer or other non-labor group as forbidden by *Jewel Tea*. There is no economic benefit to the NBPA or the NBA member teams as a result of this provision and there is no effect on the employer's product or service market as a result of the provision.

Summary dismissal granted.

NOTES AND QUESTIONS

1. *Appeal to Tenth Circuit.* On appeal, a non-precedential decision of the Tenth Circuit affirmed the district court's conclusion that "the statutory labor exemption from the Sherman Act permits the NBPA to establish a certification procedure for player agents." *Collins v. Nat'l Basketball Players Ass'n*, 976 F.2d 740 (10th Cir. 1992); *see also Players1st Sports Management Group v. National Football League*, 2018 WL 4623061 (D. Mass. Sept. 26, 2018) (holding nonstatutory labor exemption shields union and league from antitrust challenge to agent regulation).

The Tenth Circuit also addressed Collins' claim that the NBPA did not have authority to discipline him for conduct unrelated to negotiating player contracts with his clients' professional teams:

> On appeal, Collins now acknowledges that the NBPA has the statutory authority to establish player agent regulations. But he maintains his attack on the Committee's decision to deny his certification because it was based in part on its finding that he had breached his fiduciary duty as an investment agent and money manager. He argues that his conduct outside of negotiations between players and their teams is not a legitimate interest of the union because it has no bearing on the union's interest in the wage scale and working conditions of its members.
>
> The district court properly rejected this argument. The NBPA established the Regulations to deal with agent abuses, including agents' violations of their fiduciary duties as labor negotiators. It was entirely fair for the Committee to conclude that a man who had

neglected his fiduciary duties as an investment agent and money manager could not be trusted to fulfill his fiduciary duties as a negotiator. The integrity of a prospective negotiating agent is well within the NBPA's legitimate interest in maintaining the wage scale and working conditions of its members.

Id. at 740. Should unions be allowed to regulate agents for misconduct or incompetence other than as a contract negotiator? What if union members wanted Collins to represent them in that capacity, despite his improprieties in other settings? Should certification be denied to an agent because, for example, he is convicted of drug use? Because he publicly disagrees with the union's bargaining strategy? On the other hand, what is an appropriate standard of incompetence in contract negotiations? Could certification be denied because an agent negotiated a contract the union believed was far below market value?

2. *Agents Bound by Collective Bargaining Agreement.* In *White v. Nat'l Football League*, 92 F. Supp. 2d 918 (D. Minn. 2000), the court held that NFL player agents are bound by the league's collective bargaining agreement even though they were not signatories. The court cited to *Collins* in finding implied consent based on agents' awareness that they are permitted to negotiate player contracts only because the players association has delegated a portion of its exclusive representational authority to them. The *White* court also relied on the fact that player agents reap significant economic benefits from their relationship with the NFLPA, and expressly agree to be bound by NFLPA agent regulations.

The labor agreement's dominion over agents was also noted in *Black v. NFLPA*, 87 F. Supp. 2d 1 (D.D.C. 2000). There, the court summarily dismissed Tank Black's tort suit against the NFLPA, in which he alleged that a three-year suspension for paying college athletes to become his clients interfered with his contractual relationships with current clients. The court ruled that any such tort claim was so "inextricably intertwined with consideration of the terms of the labor contract" that it was preempted by § 301 of the federal Labor Management Relations Act. *See generally* Chapter 3, Section D. *Cf. Indep. Sports & Entm't, LLC v. Fegan*, 2017 WL 2598550 (C.D. Cal. May 30, 2017) (in dispute between sports agency and agent who allegedly violated non-compete clause, § 301 does not preempt state contract action where no issue as to union's authority to regulate or discipline agents).

A 1993 case involving baseball agent Barry Rona produced even more challenges for association regulation and arbitral scrutiny of agent behavior. Before becoming an agent, Rona worked for the league's Player Relations Committee (PRC), the counterpart to the Players Association in collective bargaining. He was the PRC's general counsel from 1974 to 1986, and its Executive Director from 1986 to 1990. During that period, Rona had gained an enormous amount of experience and understanding of player relations in baseball, but also was present for the baseball owners' mid-

1980s conspiracy to eliminate bidding for free agents and to hold down player salaries. After leaving MLB, he began to represent football and basketball players, and then filed an application for certification as a baseball player agent was filed with the MLBPA. The MLBPA refused to certify him, based on § 2(C) of its Regulations, which barred certification of anyone whose conduct "may adversely affect his credibility [or] integrity . . . to serve in a representative and/or fiduciary capacity on behalf of players." In its rejection letter to Rona, the Players Association stated:

> In the Association's judgment, your conduct during the conspiracy cannot be explained away or excused as simply a matter of typical adversarial behavior. For the fact is that you were, if not the architect, then at least a master builder of a devastating, profound, and prolonged violation of Players' rights, the extent of which cannot be overestimated. Over an extended period of time, the Clubs undertook a scheme intended to deprive all declared free agents of the market for their services, a market that was established through the Association's good faith, arm's length negotiations with the Clubs—and you. . . .
>
> In sum, it is the Association's conclusion that because you engaged in the above-described conduct and, indeed, had principal responsibility for it, you are unfit to be certified to represent players. Indeed, in the circumstances, we think it is extreme ill grace that, for your own economic interests, you now seek to align yourself with the interests of the very players you helped victimize.

Rona challenged the decision in the following arbitration.

BARRY RONA AND MAJOR LEAGUE BASEBALL PLAYERS ASSOCIATION
(Arbitration, 1993)

COLLINS, ARBITRATOR.

[The sole question for the arbitrator was whether the Association's factual findings were supported by "substantial evidence on the record as a whole," and whether its legal conclusions were "arbitrary and capricious." In his analysis, the arbitrator quoted extensively from the New York Code of Professional Responsibility which spelled out both the client's right to "zealous legal representation" and the lawyer's obligation "not to assist clients to engage in wrongful acts."]

* * *

It is clear to this Arbitrator that any institutional policy which by its terms or application would penalize a lawyer for providing, or would create a disincentive for a lawyer not to provide, zealous representation within the limits of the code, would transgress the public policy on which the Code rests. A corollary to this is that lawyers acting as such can only be judged, in terms of the ethics of their behavior, by the standards set forth in the Code. In addition there would seem to be serious questions whether determinations as to whether or not a lawyer has acted ethically can be made by other than the courts and whether or not such determinations can be based on anything less than a preponderance of the evidence.

The evidence in this proceeding establishes that the PRC [Major League Baseball Player Relations Committee] is a New York corporation domiciled in New York, that from 1974 or 1975 until late 1985, sometime before January 1, 1986, Rona served the PRC only in a legal capacity, first as Counsel and later General Counsel, and that from late 1985 until his termination in December 1989 he also was the PRC's Executive Director, a post to which he was formally named in August 1986. Thus the collusion that . . . existed in the 1985 free agent market must have been devised and implemented when Rona was acting solely in a legal capacity for the PRC. While he thereafter assumed an additional leading role in the PRC, the evidence establishes only that his subsequent relationship to the collusion in the 1985 and 1986 free agent markets was only in his capacity as a lawyer—evaluating his clients' cases, advising them, questioning them, speaking publicly on their behalf, and serving on the [arbitration panels that resolved the collusion disputes]. In fact neither [panel] mentioned Rona in their opinions dealing respectively with the 1985 and 1986 free agent markets. As to 1987, there is evidence that Rona was a knowing participant in activities that related directly to the collusion that the [panel] found existed in that year's free agent market. However, all such activities by Rona, whatever their propriety, were conducted by Rona in his capacity as the principal inside lawyer for the PRC, working in conjunction with PRC outside counsel. . . . While the Players Association asserts that Rona bore some other responsibility for the collusion because of his role as PRC Executive Director, that is purely speculative. Since Rona's relationship to the collusion was only that of lawyer representing clients, the significance of Rona's actions for his credibility and integrity, in this Arbitrator's opinion, had to be judged solely in terms of the applicable New York law—the New York Code of Professional Responsibility.

It is mystifying why the Players Association failed to measure Rona's actions against the standards in the Code or even to acknowledge that such standards existed. . . . The Arbitrator is strongly inclined to view the Players Association's evaluation of Rona's credibility and integrity without any reference to the applicable official standards as itself constituting arbitrary and capricious action within the meaning of the Regulations. In any event, even when the evidence is measured by the Code's standards, the Arbitrator finds that the Players Association acted arbitrarily and capriciously in rejecting Rona's application.

The Players Association's conclusion that Rona was part of the collusion in the 1985 and 1986 free agent markets because he was a leading figure in the PRC is fundamentally at odds with the Code's very clear position that lawyers do not act unethically merely because they represent individuals or institutions that are found to have engaged in wrongful activities. And there is no evidence, nor any finding ... that it was or should have been obvious to Rona that his clients were acting "merely for the purpose of harassing or maliciously injuring any person" within the meaning of DR2–110 or DR7–102. On the contrary, he expressed his "concerns" to his clients, asked them directly whether they were involved in collusion to destroy the free agent markets in 1985 and 1986 and, when they replied negatively, allowed them to so testify under oath.... Rona acted entirely properly within the meaning of EC7–5—his allowing his clients to have their day in court to attempt under oath to refute the circumstantial evidence that they were engaged in collusion can hardly be termed taking a "frivolous legal position" in contravention of EC7–5. This Arbitrator believes that these are not even close questions. For the foregoing reasons the Arbitrator concludes that the Players Association's rejection of Rona's application because of his alleged involvement in the 1985 and 1986 collusion was arbitrary and capricious.

* * *

Under the Regulations the Arbitrator has no jurisdiction to judge the merits of Rona's argument; he only has jurisdiction to review, on a substantial evidence, arbitrary-capricious basis the Association's response to Rona's argument. However, Rona's argument is not [in] the Arbitrator's opinion frivolous—he was entitled to have the Association consider the merits of his argument. That the Association never considered the argument, and could not have considered it, is clear to the Arbitrator. The Association's denial letter makes no effort to treat Rona's activities in 1987 separate and apart from his alleged participation in the 1985 and 1986 collusion. On the contrary, it refers to 1987 as a "graphic illustration of [his] central role ... in the conspiracy." And, even more importantly, the Association never considered the possibility that Rona could be viewed as not bearing any responsibility for the 1985 and 1986 collusion. On the contrary, in its rejection letter, in its statements to this Arbitrator, and in the testimony in this proceeding of its representatives, it has heaped extraordinary opprobrium on Rona, much of which ... is referable only to the events in 1985 and 1986, and not 1987, or is explainable only in terms of Rona's alleged involvement in the collusion in all three years. Having failed to consider, in fact having been incapable of fairly considering the arguments Rona advanced in support of his application, the Association acted, in this Arbitrator's opinion, arbitrarily and capriciously.

Agent certification ordered.

NOTES AND QUESTIONS

1. *Analysis of Rona.* The MLBPA objected to the arbitrator's ruling in *Rona* on the ground that he had exceeded his arbitral authority by focusing on external law, rather than on the standards the union established in the Player Agent Regulations. Do you agree with that objection? What are the odds that the union would win a challenge in court, given the standards for judicial review of arbitration awards?

2. *Players as Agents.* During his playing career, Jose Canseco, then with the Boston Red Sox (and before he admitted steroid use), tried to create a new sports management firm targeted especially at Latin American players. Canseco proposed to hire a certified agent to represent players in their direct negotiations with clubs. The plan foundered, though, when the MLBPA deemed it to be an unacceptable conflict of interest for one player's firm to be representing other players. Do you agree with that judgment, at least from the point of view of the Players Association (as distinct from the league)?

3. *Agents and Player Work Stoppages.* During the 1994 season-ending player strike, the owners briefly considered staging baseball replacement games. In response, the MLBPA reportedly considered a ban against any of its certified agents representing replacement players. Would such a ban have violated the union's duty of fair representation, as explained in Chapter 2, Section H? If so, would the labor exemption, explained in Chapter 6, Section D, insulate the players association rule from antitrust challenge?

4. *Agent Loyalty to the Union.* A lengthy 1998–99 labor battle between NBA owners and NBPA player-members also generated another union-agent conflict and arbitration ruling, *In re NBPA Committee on Agent Regulation and Stephen M. Woods* (1999). Agent Woods had been a fervent and publicly outspoken dissenter from the negotiating strategy of NBPA President Patrick Ewing and Executive Director Billy Hunter. Indeed, on behalf of his basketball clients, he even filed some unfair labor practice charges with the NLRB alleging unfair NBPA representation of its members, although these charges were all eventually withdrawn. An NBPA arbitrator upheld the NBPA's decision to decertify Woods as an agent, on the premise that a certified player agent owed a fiduciary duty of loyalty to the players union as well as to his player clients. Woods had apparently violated this duty not just by filing the unfair labor practice charges, but also by making public statements that attacked the union's bargaining positions, were derogatory of the union leaders, and often contained false as well as confidential information. How does the decertification in the *Woods* case compare with the *Rona* ruling we have just read? Does Woods have a viable antitrust claim that this union action is an unreasonable restraint of player agent free trade?

2. EXAMPLES AND IMPACT OF PLAYER ASSOCIATION AGENT REGULATION

Despite the agent litigation described above, players association regulation has evoked remarkably little complaint from established practitioners in this field, many of whom have served as advisers to the unions in the development and administration of these programs. Most of the regulatory schemes comprise four essential elements:

(i) Application form and approval process;

(ii) Standards of conduct including duty of loyalty and fiduciary duties;

(iii) Continuing duty to disclose information to the union; and

(iv) Dispute resolution process.

In designing these elements of agent regulation, the unions must grapple with the tension between the goal of "consumer protection" of their athlete members and the desire to allow each member to select an agent of his choosing.

The NFLPA offers a model of agent regulation, periodically reexamining and amending its regulations as needed to address persistent and emerging problems with agent competence and ethics. Over the years these amendments have included, for example, requiring agents to have negotiated at least one contract during a three-year period in order to retain certification; imposing heightened educational requirements including a postgraduate degree or demonstrated negotiation experience; prohibiting recruitment of clients while an agent is suspended; requiring written disclosure to clients of representation of any college or professional coaches; imposing a continuing duty to inform the union of criminal offenses and civil complaints; and passing a re-certification test of CBA knowledge every two years. As you review the regulation excerpts below, consider the design choices made by the NFLPA and what motivated them.

NFLPA REGULATIONS GOVERNING CONTRACT ADVISORS
(as amended through August 2016)

Section 1: Scope of Regulations

A. Persons Subject to Regulations

No person (other than a player representing himself) shall be permitted to conduct individual contract negotiations on behalf of a player* and/or assist in or advise with respect to such negotiations with NFL Clubs after the effective date of these Regulations unless he/she is (1) currently certified as a Contract Advisor pursuant to these Regulations; (2) signs a Standard Representation Agreement with the player (See Section 4;

Appendix D); and (3) files a fully executed copy of the Standard Representation Agreement with the NFLPA, along with any contract(s) between the player and the Contract Advisor for other services to be provided.

B. Activities Covered

The activities of Contract Advisors which are governed by these Regulations include: the providing of advice, counsel, information or assistance to players with respect to negotiating their individual contracts with Clubs and/or thereafter in enforcing those contracts; the conduct of individual compensation negotiations with the Clubs on behalf of players; and any other activity or conduct which directly bears upon the Contract Advisor's integrity, competence or ability to properly represent individual NFL players and the NFLPA in individual contract negotiations, including the handling of player funds, providing tax counseling and preparation services, and providing financial advice and investment services to individual players.

Section 2: Certification

After the effective date of these Regulations, any person who wishes to perform the functions of a Contract Advisor as described in Section 1 above must be certified by the NFLPA...

C. Grounds for Denial of Certification

Grounds for denial of Certification shall include, but not be limited to, the following:

- The applicant has made false or misleading statements of a material nature in his/her application;
- The applicant has misappropriated funds, or engaged in other specific acts such as embezzlement, theft or fraud, which would render him/her unfit to serve in a fiduciary capacity on behalf of players;
- The applicant has engaged in any other conduct that significantly impacts adversely on his/her credibility, integrity or competence to serve in a fiduciary capacity on behalf of players;
- The applicant is unwilling to swear or affirm that he/she will comply with these Regulations and any amendments hereto and/or that he/she will abide by the fee structure contained in the Standard Representation Agreement incorporated into these Regulations;
- The applicant has been denied certification by another professional sports players association;

- The applicant directly or indirectly solicited a player for representation as a Contract Advisor during the period of time between the filing of his/her Application for Certification and Certification by the NFLPA;
- The applicant has not received a degree from an accredited four-year college/university and a post-graduate degree from an accredited college/university....

Section 3: Standard of Conduct for Contract Advisors

A. General Requirements

A Contract Advisor shall be required to:

(1) Disclose on his/her Application, and thereafter upon request of the NFLPA, all information relevant to his/her qualifications to serve as a Contract Advisor, including, but not limited to, background, special training, experience in negotiations, past representation of professional athletes, and relevant business associations or memberships in professional organizations;

(2) Pay an application fee pursuant to Section 2 above unless waived;

(3) Pay the annual fee and provide proof of any required insurance documents in a timely manner;

(4) Attend an NFLPA seminar on individual contract negotiations each year;

(5) Comply with the maximum fee schedule and all other provisions of these Regulations and any amendments thereto;

(6) Execute and abide by the printed Standard Representation Agreement with all players represented, and file with the NFLPA a copy of that fully executed agreement along with any other agreement(s) for additional services that the Contract Advisor has executed with the player...

(9) Provide on or before May 1 each year, to every player who he/she represents, with a copy to the NFLPA, an itemized statement covering the period beginning March 1 of the prior year through February 28 or 29 of that year, which separately sets forth both the fee charged to the player for, and any expenses incurred in connection with, the performance of the following services:

(a) individual player salary negotiations,

(b) management of the player's assets,

Sec. C Agent Representation of Unionized Athletes 691

(c) financial, investment, legal, tax and/or other advice to the player, and

(d) any other miscellaneous services;

(10) Permit a person or firm authorized by a former or current player-client to conduct an audit of all relevant books and records pertaining to any services provided to that player;

(11) Complete a notarized updated Application for Certification on or before an annual date to be determined by the NFLPA. Such annual update shall include, without limitation, disclosure of the names of any financial advisors the Contract Advisor is recommending or has recommended to players within the past year. A failure to comply with this Section 3(A)(11) shall result in immediate suspension of the Contract Advisor's Certification.

(13) Provide the NFLPA with all materials that the NFLPA deems relevant with respect to any investigation conducted pursuant to these Regulations and in all other respects cooperate fully with the NFLPA;

(14) Fully comply with applicable state and federal laws;

(15) Become and remain sufficiently educated with regard to NFL structure and economics, applicable Collective Bargaining Agreements and other governing documents, basic negotiating techniques, and developments in sports law and related subjects. To ascertain whether the Contract Advisor is sufficiently educated with regard to the above-related subjects, the NFLPA may require a Contract Advisor to pass a Contract Advisor examination. A failure to pass an examination administered pursuant to this Section 3(A)(15) shall result in immediate suspension of the Contract Advisor's Certification. . . .

(16) Disclose in an addendum (in the form attached as Appendix G) attached to the Standard Representation Agreement between the Contract Advisor and player, the names and current positions of any NFL management personnel, NFL Coaches, other professional league coaches or college coaches whom Contract Advisor represents or has represented in matters pertaining to their employment by or association with any NFL club, other professional league club or college;

(17) Act at all times in a fiduciary capacity on behalf of players;

(18) Comply with and abide by all of the stated policies of the NFLPA;

(19) In connection with payments for assistance in recruiting any player: [prepare disclosure forms identifying other contract advisors who helped recruit the player, and provide the form to the player and have him sign it]

B. Prohibited Conduct

Contract Advisors are prohibited from:

(1) Representing any player in individual contract negotiations with any Club unless he/she (i) is an NFLPA Certified Contract Advisor; (ii) has signed the Standard Representation Agreement with such player; and (iii) has filed a copy of the Standard Representation Agreement with the NFLPA along with any other contract(s) or agreement(s) between the player and the Contract Advisor;

(2) Providing or offering money or any other thing of value to any player or prospective player to induce or encourage that player to utilize his/her services;

(3) Providing or offering money or any other thing of value to a member of the player's or prospective player's family or any other person for the purpose of inducing or encouraging that person to recommend the services of the Contract Advisor;

(4) Providing materially false or misleading information to any player or prospective player in the context of recruiting the player as a client or in the course of representing that player as his Contract Advisor;

(5) Representing or suggesting to any player or prospective player that his/her NFLPA Certification is an endorsement or recommendation by the NFLPA of the Contract Advisor or the Contract Advisor's qualifications or services;

(6) Directly or indirectly borrowing money from any player (whether or not the player is a client), either by receiving the funds directly from the player or by the player providing collateral for or agreeing to guarantee a loan to the Contract Advisor by another party;

(7) Holding or seeking to hold, either directly or indirectly, a financial interest in any professional football club or in any other business entity when such investment could create an actual conflict of interest or the appearance of a conflict of interest in the representation of NFL players;

(8) Engaging in any other activity which creates an actual or potential conflict of interest with the effective representation of NFL players;

Sec. C   Agent Representation of Unionized Athletes   693

(9) Soliciting or accepting money or anything of value from any NFL Club in a way that would create an actual or apparent conflict with the interests of any player that the Contract Advisor represents;

(10) Negotiating and/or agreeing to any provision in a player contract which deprives or purports to deprive that player of any benefit contained in any collectively bargained agreement between the NFL and the NFLPA or any other provision of any applicable documents which protect the working conditions of NFL players;

(11) Negotiating and/or agreeing to any provision in any agreement involving a player which directly or indirectly violates any stated policies or rules established by the NFLPA;

(12) Concealing material facts from any player whom the Contract Advisor is representing which relate to the subject of the player's individual contract negotiation;

(13) Failing to advise the player and to report to the NFLPA any known violations by an NFL Club of a player's individual contract;

(14) Engaging in unlawful conduct and/or conduct involving dishonesty, fraud, deceit, misrepresentation, or other activity which reflects adversely on his/her fitness as a Contract Advisor or jeopardizes his/her effective representation of NFL players;

(15) Failure to comply with the maximum fee provisions contained in Section 4 of these Regulations;

(16) Circumventing the maximum fee provisions contained in Section 4 of these Regulations by knowingly and intentionally increasing the fees that Contract Advisor charges or otherwise would have charged the player for other services including, but not limited to, financial consultation, money management, and/or negotiating player endorsement agreements; . . .

(18) Filing any lawsuit or other proceeding against a player for any matter which is subject to the exclusive arbitration provisions contained in Section 5 of these Regulations; . . .

(21) (a) Initiating any communication, directly or indirectly, with a player who has entered into a Standard Representation Agreement with another Contract Advisor and such Standard Representation Agreement is on file with the NFLPA if the

communication concerns a matter relating to [that player's current contract advisor, SRA, status with an NFL club, or services to be provided under an SRA or otherwise. However, the ban doesn't apply when: the player initiates such communications, the player has less than 60 days remaining on his current NFL Player Contract and has not yet signed a new SRA, and when the agent is sending general advertising directed at players in general.] . . .

(26) Directly or indirectly soliciting a prospective rookie player for representation as a Contract Advisor (a "rookie" shall be defined as a person who has never signed an NFL Player Contract) if that player has signed a Standard Representation Agreement prior to a date which is thirty (30) days before the NFL Draft and if thirty (30 days have not elapsed since the Agreement was signed and filed with the NFLPA.

A Contract Advisor who engages in any prohibited conduct as defined above shall be subject to discipline [including fines, suspension of certification, and decertification].

As the NFLPA excerpt illustrates, in designing an agent regulatory program, key issues include:

a. *Coverage.* Who is an "agent" for purposes of such regulation? Union authority to regulate extends only to people who represent players in connection with their employment contracts with teams. Who serves as such a representative? What about the "runners" who assist in recruiting clients? How should such regulation resolve conflicts with state bar codes governing agents who are also lawyers licensed to practice in the relevant jurisdiction? Should unions defer to state regulations that govern dealings between agents and college players or graduates who are not yet on a professional roster?

b. *Eligibility.* What qualifications should be demanded of someone seeking certification as an approved agent? A law degree? Participation in a training program? A passing score on a test of knowledge of the relevant material in this area of practice? (Should such a test be a one-time entrance exam or one that has to be taken and passed periodically?) A probationary term until successful negotiation of a certain number of player contracts?

c. *Financial Responsibility.* Should the agent have to demonstrate financial responsibility to practice in this field? Through posting a surety bond? For how large an amount? Just for money managers or also for contract negotiators?

d. *Solicitation of Business.* Should any active solicitation of players by agents be permitted? Should the agent be permitted to provide something of value to a player as an inducement to sign the agency contract? Should the agent be able to pay third parties for referrals of players? Most important of all, should agents be restricted from even contacting college players whose eligibility has not yet expired?

e. *Fees.* Within the players associations, the driving force behind regulatory efforts tends to be player concerns about the size of agent fees. An important issue is whether any ceiling at all should be imposed on agent fees, especially a ceiling devised by the players association. If there is to be such a fee scale, should it be based on an hourly rate or a percentage figure? If a percentage, should it be a single rate or one that rises and falls depending on the size of the underlying contract? What is the appropriate percentage figure? Should the base exclude the minimum salary amounts mandated by the collective agreement or amounts paid as incentive bonuses? What about non-guaranteed contract amounts, especially those contained in long-term deals?

Is the same fee percentage appropriate for the negotiation of a player's contract with the team as for the negotiation of an endorsement contract with a product manufacturer or a promotional contract with an outside business? (Players associations do not have authority to regulate these fees, and they generally run in the 10–20% range.) How will the association's answer to these issues likely influence the agent's incentives in negotiations (*e.g.*, to pursue incentive bonuses and long-term deals)?

NOTES AND QUESTIONS

1. *NFLPA Discipline of Agents.* Among the disciplinary measures the NFLPA can impose under its agent regulations are suspension and decertification, during which time the agent may not represent an NFL player or engage in "recruiting activities." At the prospect of losing one's livelihood, most agents appeal such discipline, but rarely gain relief. *See Kivisto v. Nat'l Football League Players Assoc.*, 435 F. App'x 811 (11th Cir. 2011) (dismissing agent's complaint seeking to avoid arbitration of his decertification). In recent years, the NFLPA has cracked down on agents who violate its rules, including the following disciplinary actions:

- Brian Brundage's 2017 indefinite suspension based on a federal indictment for fraud and tax evasion;
- Ben Dogra's 2016 six-month suspension and fine for unspecified rules violations;
- Vinnie Porter's 2015 suspension following his financial fraud arrest (reinstated when the charges were dropped);

- Marc Lillibridge's 2015 suspension for undisclosed "extraordinary circumstances";
- Marty Magid's 2013 six-month suspension and fine for failing to submit required paperwork for his clients' restructured playing contracts;
- John Rickert's 2013 suspension and fine for failing to pay fees owed to another contract advisor;
- 2013 fines against Ethan Lock, Eric Metz, and Vance Malinovic of LLM Sports Managements for failing to disclose interests in a company that provided services to athletes; and
- Gary Wichard's 2010 nine-month suspension for his role in a recruiting scandal involving the University of North Carolina.

What do you think is driving this crackdown—the union, the players, the honest agents? How do you think the NFLPA's tough regulatory stance has affected its relationship with the agency industry?

2. *Other Player Union Discipline.* The NBPA has also toughened its agent regulation, most recently in 2016 when it reinforced its ban on an agent representing both an NBA player and a coach or general manager. The 2016 amendments to NBPA agent regulations also require: decertifying agents who haven't represented a player in a five-year period, disclosure of the use of paid recruiters, and disclosure when an agent refers players to financial advisers. In addition, new agents will now need to pass a written examination to become certified, as in the NFL. Whether these revisions will bring greater vigor to NBPA disciplinary activity has yet to be seen. The NBPA has rarely suspended an agent, a recent notable exception being its 2008 year-long suspension of Calvin Andrews for illegal recruiting tactics and payments involving the University of Southern California basketball star O.J. Mayo.

The MLBPA has also periodically updated its agent regulations, with 2010 additions that primarily address fair competition for clients, a 2013 prohibition against agents lending money to players without the union's approval, and the introduction in 2015 of a written exam and background check for agent applications. In a bizarre 2018 case, the MLBPA suspended agent Jason Wood for allegedly filming his clients with a hidden camera.

3. *Which Regulations Matter Most?* Note that players association activity in enforcing agent regulations seems to tilt towards disciplining agent misconduct in representing a player in contract negotiations or managing a client's finances. When it comes to consumer protection in the recruiting of athletes, unions seem more reluctant to suspend an agent. What explains or justifies this imbalance?

3. AGENT AS CONTRACT NEGOTIATOR IN UNIONIZED SPORTS: DEALING WITH THE CBA CONSTRAINTS

In negotiating the modern playing contract, agents need to be experts in that league's economic structures, and particularly the constraints of salary cap/tax systems. With every successive CBA's tweak to a league's system, athletes, their agents, and individual team executives have strong market incentives to find loopholes in the labor agreement that permit the team to show the player enough money to entice him to sign. A game of cat-and-mouse ensues as individual player contracts require commissioner approval, and possibly also union or arbitrator vetting of whether the contract satisfies the existing rules. Even if a borderline contract gains approval, the parties may well agree to modify the rules to block off such loopholes for the future.

An example in football is the Cowboys' 1995 contract with Deion Sanders, which offered $35 million over seven years, and a $13 million signing bonus, straining the club's salary cap. The NFL's collectively bargained rules required prorating signing bonuses across the length of the player contract for purposes of salary cap calculations. This meant that Sanders' $13 million bonus, while paid immediately, was attributed at $1.87 million to each of the seven years of his contract. The Cowboys then agreed to pay Sanders only $178,000 a year in base salary for the first three years, leaping to $5 or $6 million for each of the remaining years (plus the prorated bonus). This move meant that the team could void the contract in 1998, thereby causing four-sevenths of the signing bonus (the still unamortized amount) to be "counted" in 1999, the year in which the salary cap expired under the labor agreement. Even if the Cowboys did not void the contract, the bulk of the money paid under it would be pushed into the uncapped "out years" (in their hope, then, that the labor agreement and thus the cap would not be extended past 1998). The NFL Commissioner disallowed the contract as violating the spirit, if not the explicit terms, of the League's salary cap system. Following a grievance filed by the Players Association on behalf of Sanders, the parties eventually worked out a settlement that increased by $400,000 the amount attributed from Sanders' bonus to the Cowboys salary cap figures in each of the first three years.

After the Sanders dispute, NFL and NFLPA officials revised their collective bargaining agreement for the future to require that if the amount of signing bonuses attributable to uncapped years exceeds total base salaries in capped years, 50% of that amount must be reallocated back into the capped years. Also, no base salary could increase by more than 30% over the prior year's base salary amount. In return for that concession to the League, the players union extracted an increase in the minimum salary from $178,000 to $250,000 (and adjusted annually thereafter). Thus, Deion Sanders not only helped return the 1995 Super Bowl to Dallas, but his agent's contract device actually produced a pay hike for a large number of minimum-salaried players in the League.

Baseball agents have also exercised their creativity in avoiding CBA strictures, notably through personal-service deals and special "milestone" bonus clauses. Typical personal-service contracts for ballplayers pay for post-retirement promotional appearances and ceremonial roles. Milestone bonus clauses reward player achievements such as the 3,000th hit or breaking a home-run record. In the late 1990s and early 2000s, baseball agents negotiated such agreements worth tens of millions of dollars for star players like Albert Pujols, Ryan Zimmerman, and Alex Rodriguez, enabling clubs to avoid paying luxury taxes on their payrolls. As a result, the MLB and the union agreed to no longer approve such deals because they violated CBA prohibitions against both contract incentives based on statistical achievements and agreements that cover obligations beyond the athlete's playing career.

Finally, basketball agent Eric Fleisher notoriously attempted to circumvent NBA salary cap rules when he represented Joe Smith in 1999 as a free agent negotiating to join the Minnesota Timberwolves. However, Fleisher and the team executives went beyond merely exploiting a loophole. The Wolves were already over the salary cap at the time, and so Fleisher and Smith agreed to negotiate three small one-year contracts in exchange for an under-the-table deal guaranteeing Smith a mega-contract for year four. They were motivated by the NBA's Larry Bird rule that permits teams to exceed the salary cap to re-sign their own players. When the scheme was uncovered, Smith's deal was voided, the Wolves were fined $3.5 million and forfeited their first-round draft picks for four years, Wolves executives were suspended, and Fleisher made NBA history by becoming the first agent ever fined by the league ($57,000).

NOTES AND QUESTIONS

1. *Player Association Reaction to Creative Contracting.* What should the players association's position be when agents bring their creativity to bear on player contracts, exploiting loopholes in the CBA? Why is it in the interest of the union and its members, as illustrated above, to close those loopholes?

2. *Player Association Contract Assistance to Its Members.* Players associations collect and archive information about every player contract, most of which follow the standard form contract. The associations have the capability to make these data available and reasonably comprehensible to players in the sport, ideally on a comparative basis. Given the digitizing of this information and the advances in analytics, what remains of an agent's value-

proposition in the context of negotiating the player contract? The NFLPA, for example, makes available to its players free advice, contract review, and statistical comparisons of contracts to ensure the player is getting fair market value. One of the 2016 amendments to the NFLPA agent regulations requires agents to consult with the union before finalizing certain veteran contracts, apparently out of concern that agents were agreeing to language that placed players' guaranteed money at risk. What risks are associated with the union having access to ongoing confidential contract negotiations among multiple players and teams?

D. AGENT RECRUITING OF COLLEGE ATHLETES

The single feature of the sports agent business that contributes most to its characterization as sleazy is the way some agents recruit clients from college. Rather than the athlete paying the agent above the table for his services, the agent pays the athlete below the table to induce the athlete to sign a representation agreement, a practice that violates NCAA regulations requiring students to compete as amateurs. Agents often deliver these illicit payments through an intermediary (their "runner"), who is typically around the same age as the athletes. The runner befriends an athlete, picks up the bills for his entertainment, and then delivers the athlete as a client to the agent when the athlete is about to relinquish his college eligibility and turn professional. If these payments are ever disclosed (even after the fact), negative consequences ensue for the agent, the player, and the school, which can incur significant penalties for having played in NCAA-regulated events using athletes who were no longer amateurs. Chapter 11 examines the legal and policy issues generated by compulsory amateurism of student-athletes, especially in commercialized college sports like football and men's basketball. This section examines questions of agent integrity in the context of college athletics.

1. AGENT RECRUITING TACTICS AND ENFORCEABILITY OF REPRESENTATION AGREEMENTS

Predating enactment of government regulation of agents discussed later in this chapter, a 1980s case of agent corruption of college athletes produced notoriety and multiple lawsuits. Norby Walters was a successful representative of musicians and entertainers. With Lloyd Bloom, a young acquaintance, Walters expanded into representing athletes, especially football players. Acting as Walters' "runner," Bloom approached college players and offered a cash sum and subsequent monthly payments, in return for the player signing an agency contract post-dated to January 2nd of the player's senior year (after the player's final football season). All agreed to keep the whole arrangement confidential so that the player would not lose his collegiate eligibility, something that would diminish his professional marketability.

Walters and Bloom quickly enjoyed remarkable success. In 1985, they signed ten college players, two of whom were 1986 first-round NFL draft picks. In 1986, they signed 35 players, eight of whom were 1987 first round draft picks. All in all, Walters and Bloom invested roughly $800,000 in recruiting some 60 college players, most in football and a handful of basketball players. However, this economic venture unraveled and spawned numerous legal proceedings for reasons explained in the next case.

NORBY WALTERS AND LLOYD BLOOM V. BRENT FULLWOOD
675 F. Supp. 155 (S.D.N.Y. 1987)

BRIEANT, CHIEF JUDGE.

[In the summer of 1986, Norby Walters and Lloyd Bloom induced Brent Fullwood, star running back for Auburn University, to sign a post-dated representation agreement in return for an immediate payment of $4,000 (secured by a promissory note) and another $4,000 during the fall football season. That spring, the Green Bay Packers selected Fullwood as the fourth pick in the 1987 NFL draft. By that time, however, Fullwood had defected to another agent and repudiated his deal with Walters and Bloom. Thus, Walters and Bloom sued Fullwood, seeking not only to recover the $8,000 they had already paid him, but also to collect the promised 5% commission on Fullwood's multi-million-dollar contract. The key issue posed to the federal judge was whether the secret arrangement between the agents and Fullwood, which had put the player in violation of NCAA regulations, was an enforceable contract under New York law.]

* * *

> "We are living in a time when college athletics are honeycombed with falsehood, and when the professions of amateurism are usually hypocrisy. No college team ever meets another today with actual faith in the other's eligibility."

—President William Faunce of Brown University, in a speech before the National Education Association, 1904.

The N.C.A.A. was organized in 1906 largely to combat such evils. Its constitution provides in relevant part that:

> Any individual who contracts or who has ever contracted orally or in writing to be represented by an agent in the marketing of the individual's athletic ability or reputation in a sport no longer shall be eligible for intercollegiate athletics in that sport.

N.C.A.A. Constitution, sec. 3–1–(c). Section 3–1–(a) prohibits any player from accepting pay in any form for participation in his college sport, with an exception for a player seeking, directly without the assistance of a third party, a loan from an accredited commercial lending institution against future earnings potential solely in order to purchase insurance against disabling injury.

This Court concludes that the August 1986 loan security agreement and the W.S. & E. agency agreement between Fullwood and the plaintiffs violated Secs. 3–1–(a) and 3–1–(c) of the N.C.A.A. Constitution, the observance of which is in the public interest of the citizens of New York State, and that the parties to those agreements knowingly betrayed an important, if perhaps naive, public trust. Viewing the parties as *in pari delicto*, we decline to serve as "paymaster of the wages of crime, or referee between thieves." We consider both defendant Fullwood's arbitration rights under the N.F.L.P.A. Agents' Regulations, and plaintiffs' rights on their contract and promissory note with Fullwood, unenforceable as contrary to the public policy of New York. "The law 'will not extend its aid to either of the parties' or 'listen to their complaints against each other, but will leave them where their own acts have placed them.'"

Absent these overriding policy concerns, the parties would be subject to the arbitration provisions set forth in section seven of the N.F.L.P.A. Agents' Regulations, and plaintiffs' rights under the contract and promissory note with Fullwood also would be arbitrable. However, under the "public policy" exception to the duty to enforce otherwise-valid agreements, we should and do leave the parties where we find them.

It is well settled that a court should not enforce rights that arise under an illegal contract.

* * *

An agreement may be unenforceable in New York as contrary to public policy even in the absence of a direct violation of a criminal statute, if the sovereign has expressed a concern for the values underlying the policy implicated. In *In re Estate of Walker*, 476 N.E.2d 298, 301 (1985), the Court of Appeals refused to enforce a bequest of adoption decrees to the testator's adopted daughters, concluding that such a bequest, though not criminal, was contrary to public policy. The court concluded, " '[W]hen we speak of the public policy of the state, we mean the law of the state, whether found in the Constitution, the statutes or judicial records.' Those sources express the public will and give definition to the term. A legacy is contrary to public policy, not only if it directly violates a statutory prohibition . . . but also if it is contrary to the social judgment on the subject implemented by the statute."

* * *

The New York State legislature has spoken on the public policies involved in this case, by expressing a concern for the integrity of sporting events in general, and a particular concern for the status of amateur athletics. *See, e.g.*, New York Tax Law sec. 1116(a)(4) (McKinney's supp. 1987) (granting tax exemption to any organization "organized and operating exclusively . . . to foster national or international amateur sports competition"); New York Penal Law Secs. 180.35, 180.40 (McKinney's supp. 1987) (establishing criminal sanctions for sports bribery).

Even were we not convinced of the legislative concern for the values underlying sec. 3–1–(c) of the N.C.A.A. Constitution, New York case law prevents judicial enforcement of contracts the performance of which would provoke conduct established as wrongful by independent commitments undertaken by either party. Not all contracts inducing breaches of other agreements fall within this rule, but those requiring fraudulent conduct are unenforceable as contrary to the public policy of New York.

* * *

In the case before us, no party retains enforceable rights. To the extent plaintiffs seek to recover on the contract or promissory note signed by Fullwood, their wrongful conduct prevents recovery; to the extent Fullwood seeks to compel arbitration, as provided for in the N.F.L.P.A. Agents' Regulations, his own wrongs preclude resort to this Court.

All parties to this action should recognize that they are the beneficiaries of a system built on the trust of millions of people who, with stubborn innocence, adhere to the Olympic ideal, viewing amateur sports as a commitment to competition for its own sake. Historically, amateur athletes have been perceived as pursuing excellence and perfection of their sport as a form of self-realization, indeed, originally, as a form of religious worship, with the ancient games presented as offerings to the gods. By demanding the most from themselves, athletes were believed to approach the divine essence. Through athletic success, the Greeks believed man could experience a kind of immortality.

There also is a modern, secular purpose served by Secs. 3–1–(a) and 3–1–(c) of the N.C.A.A. Constitution. Since the advent of intercollegiate sports in the late 19th century, American colleges have struggled, with varying degrees of vigor, to protect the integrity of higher education from sports-related evils such as gambling, recruitment violations, and the employment of mercenaries whose presence in college athletic programs will tend to preclude the participation of legitimate scholar-athletes.

Sections 3–1–(a) and 3–1–(c) of the N.C.A.A. Constitution were instituted to prevent college athletes from signing professional contracts while they are still playing for their schools. The provisions are rationally related to the commendable objective of protecting the academic integrity of N.C.A.A. member institutions. A college student already receiving payments from his agent, or with a large professional contract signed and ready to take effect upon his graduation, might well be less inclined to observe his academic obligations than a student, athlete or not, with uncertainties about his future career. Indeed, he might not play at his college sport with the same vigor and devotion.

The agreement reached by the parties here, whether or not unusual, represented not only a betrayal of the high ideals that sustain amateur athletic competition as a part of our national educational commitment; it also constituted a calculated fraud on the entire spectator public. Every honest amateur player who took the field with or against Fullwood during the 1986 college football season was cheated by being thrown in with a player who had lost his amateur standing.

In August 1986, Brent Fullwood was one of that select group of college athletes virtually assured of a lucrative professional sports contract immediately upon graduation, absent serious injury during his senior year. The fruits of the system by which amateur players become highly paid professionals, whatever its flaws, were soon to be his. That is precisely why plaintiffs sought him out. Both sides of the transaction knew exactly what they were doing, and they knew it was fraudulent and wrong. This Court and the public need not suffer such willful conduct to taint a college amateur sports program.

[Suit dismissed.]

NOTES AND QUESTIONS

1. *Public Policy Analysis.* The *Fullwood* decision rests heavily on a perceived New York public policy to protect the integrity of amateur athletics. Do you agree that such a state policy existed at the time? Does one exist today, and if so, where is it manifested? Why is violation of this policy so abhorrent that it justifies nullification of a contract?

2. *Arbitration Requirement.* As an NFLPA-certified agent, Walters was subject to agent regulations that require arbitration of disputes with a player. Accordingly, Fullwood sought to defend Walters's suit in arbitration, a request the federal court denied, holding "[t]he principles requiring non-enforcement of contracts on public policy grounds apply equally to arbitration agreements." Was this a decision the court was entitled to make? How should we reconcile the court's approach with the favoring of arbitration required by federal labor law, as highlighted in Chapter 3?

A state court judge disagreed with the *Fullwood* decision on the arbitration issue, sending to an NLFPA arbitrator claims involving yet another player recruited by Walters through illicit payments and a post-dated representation contract. *See Walters v. Harmon*, 135 Misc.2d 905, 416 N.Y.S.2d 874 (1987). The arbitrator voided the representation agreement between Walters and Ron Harmon, but on totally different grounds. Although the arbitrator acknowledged that the contract violated NCAA rules, he did not take those rules into consideration. Nor did he regard Harmon as an innocent victim of fraud or unequal bargaining power. Instead, he held that the agency agreement was null and void under NFLPA regulations, which if not enforced could lead to "unfettered bribery" and "bidding wars between contract advisors for the rights to represent athletes." The arbitrator did find that Walters had provided valuable services to Harmon, who was required to pay for them in *quantum meruit*, along with reimbursement of Walters's out-of-pocket representation expenses.

3. *Agent Redress in Case of Unenforceable Representation Agreement*. As in *Harmon*, the court in *Total Economic Athletic Management of America v. Pickens*, 898 S.W.2d 98 (Mo. 1995), agreed that an agent is owed something, even if the representation agreement is not enforceable. There, agent Howard Misle sued college football star Bruce Pickens for repudiating an agency contract that Misle had induced with gifts of cash and a luxury car, in violation of both NCAA and NFLPA regulations. Misle sought contract damages of the specified agent fee of four percent of the value of the multi-million-dollar contract Pickens ultimately signed with the Atlanta Falcons. A jury declined to enforce the contract as written, but awarded $20,000 in damages. Affirming the award on appeal, the court held:

> In the context of professional sports, the player's breach of an agency agreement does not necessarily entitle the agent to commission. Technically, the agent is only entitled to damages for breach of contract, *i.e.*, the value of the promised performance reduced by any expenses saved. In addition, the agent is entitled to his commission only if he can show that, had he been permitted to continue performance, he would have been able to consummate the contracts upon which he claims commission.

Id. at 108.

These and similar cases involving soured relationships between college players and agents pose the question whether rogue agents should be awarded any compensation or reimbursement for their efforts? Or should they receive no redress as a punitive deterrent against such behavior? To what extent should your answer depend on the degree of "innocence" of the college player involved? What about similar advance payments to athletes who never had or have now exhausted college eligibility (*e.g.*, minor league baseball players)? Current union regulations of agents typically bar such payments as well. Why do you suppose they do so?

4. *Ethics of Illicit Payments to College-Athletes*. Walters and Bloom were not unique in paying college players money to sign post-dated agency contracts. Even aside from its deceptive nature, this practice raises significant ethical and legal questions. Why would Walters and Bloom believe it was financially

worthwhile to pay clients to sign with them? If a player takes a "signing bonus" from an agent, shouldn't that obligate the player to honor the contract later on? How does that situation differ from a player contract with a team that pays a signing bonus? Even when the agent offers no money, is it ever proper for an agent to pursue college athletes as potential clients? Should it matter whether the athlete's college eligibility has expired?

2. ENFORCING NCAA AMATEURISM RULES AGAINST AGENT MISCONDUCT

Rulings in both the *Fullwood* and *Harmon* cases demonstrate that an agent who pays off student-athletes risks only losing that money and being unable to enforce the agency contract. This risk has proven to have little deterrent value against such agent misconduct. Furthermore, while judge-made contract law and player association regulations attempt to protect the interests of the athlete in this situation, they do not address the interests of the college, which is not a party to the agency relationship.

Because agent payments to athletes constitute violations of the NCAA amateurism principles, they also subject the college to a considerable risk of tangible loss. For example, Walters and Bloom secretly signed Alabama's star basketball forward, Derrick McKey, to an agency contract, after which the unknowing school used McKey in the next NCAA tournament. When the NCAA discovered this fact, it required Alabama to forfeit two games it had won and repay the $250,000 the university had received from the tournament. Even if the university learns of an agency contract in time to declare the player ineligible, the university loses one of its best players and thus the chance for a successful season, both athletically and financially. Of course, the risk of loss of eligibility will deter some student-athletes from violating NCAA agent rules, and university compliance efforts often include educating students to these risks.

Yet, the question arises how to put legal teeth behind the NCAA eligibility rules that ban receiving benefits from agents. As a private association, the NCAA lacks the authority to directly regulate the agent industry or sanction agents who impair a college athlete's eligibility, and its eligibility rules are not directly enforceable in court. Many agents candidly treat the NCAA rules as optional. Norby Walters stated that he believed that ignoring the NCAA code was "no different than bending the Knights of Columbus rules." However, federal law enforcement authorities took interest in Walters's sports practice when they learned that members of a New York organized crime family were his partners and investors, and they helped enforce player contracts with physical threats and violence. This connection came to light in March 1987, when a masked man beat the wife of a former Notre Dame quarterback because she was an associate of a Chicago-based sports agent that had attracted a client away from Walters and Bloom. The Chicago U.S. Attorney's office and FBI opened an investigation and ultimately brought criminal charges against Walters.

To establish its jurisdiction in the *Walters* case, the government developed the theory that it was criminal fraud for the player and his agent to hide their relationship in order to maintain the player's scholarship and his NCAA eligibility. This constituted federal mail fraud by virtue of the school mailing the player's annual signed eligibility form to the NCAA head office. Repeated use of this practice further constituted a violation of the Racketeer Influenced and Corrupt Organizations Act (RICO). Under that theory, any time an agent signed a contract with a player who continued to play college ball, both the player and the agent were committing a federal crime, irrespective of whether any money was changing hands. After a long and complex journey through the criminal justice system, the Seventh Circuit was finally required to appraise the legal validity of that theory.

UNITED STATES V. NORBY WALTERS
997 F.2d 1219 (7th Cir. 1993)

EASTERBROOK, CIRCUIT JUDGE.

* * *

"Whoever, having devised . . . any scheme or artifice to defraud, or for obtaining money or property by means of false or fraudulent pretenses, representations, or promises . . . places in any post office or authorized depository for mail matter, any matter or thing whatever to be sent or delivered by the Postal Service . . . or knowingly causes [such matter or thing] to be delivered by mail" commits the crime of mail fraud. Norby Walters did not mail anything or cause anyone else to do so (the universities were going to collect and mail the forms no matter what Walters did), but the Supreme Court has expanded the statute beyond its literal terms, holding that a mailing by a third party suffices if it is "incident to an essential part of the scheme," *Pereira v. United States*, 347 U.S. 1, 8 (1954). While stating that such mailings can turn ordinary fraud into mail fraud, the Court has cautioned that the statute "does not purport to reach all frauds, but only those limited instances in which the use of the mails is a part of the execution of the fraud." *Kann v. United States*, 323 U.S. 88, 95 (1944). Everything thus turns on matters of degree. Did the schemers foresee that the mails would be used? Did the mailing advance the success of the scheme? Which parts of a scheme are "essential?" Such questions lack obviously right answers, so it is no surprise that each side to this case can cite several of our decisions in support. . . .

"The relevant question . . . is whether the mailing is part of the execution of the scheme as conceived by the perpetrator at the time." *Schmuck v. United States*, 489 U.S. 705, 715 (1989). Did the evidence establish that Walters conceived a scheme in which mailings played a role? We think not—indeed, that no reasonable juror could give an affirmative answer to this question. Walters hatched a scheme to make money by taking a percentage of athletes' pro contracts. To get clients he signed students while college eligibility remained, thus avoiding competition from ethical agents. To obtain big pro contracts for these clients he needed to keep the deals secret so the athletes could finish their collegiate careers. Thus deceit was an ingredient of the plan. We may assume that Walters knew that the universities would ask athletes to verify that they were eligible to compete as amateurs. But what role do the mails play? The plan succeeds so long as the athletes conceal their contracts from their schools (and remain loyal to Walters). Forms verifying eligibility do not help the plan succeed; instead they create a risk that it will be discovered if a student should tell the truth. And it is the forms, not their mailing to the Big Ten, that pose the risk. For all Walters cared, the forms could sit forever in cartons. Movement to someplace else was irrelevant. In *Schmuck*, where the fraud was selling cars with rolled-back odometers, the mailing was essential to obtain a new and apparently "clean" certificate of title; no certificates of title, no marketable cars, no hope for success. Even so, the Court divided five to four on the question whether the mailing was sufficiently integral to the scheme. A college's mailing to its conference has less to do with the plot's success than the mailings that transferred title in *Schmuck*.

* * *

No evidence demonstrates that Walters actually knew that the colleges would mail the athletes' forms. The record is barely sufficient to establish that Walters knew of the forms' existence; it is silent about Walters' knowledge of the forms' disposition. The only evidence implying that Walters knew that the colleges had students fill out forms is an ambiguous reference to "these forms" in the testimony of [one of the student-athletes]. . . . Recall that Walters was trying to break into the sports business. Counsel specializing in sports law told him that his plan would not violate any statute. These lawyers were unaware of the forms (or, if they knew about the forms, were unaware that they would be mailed). The prosecutor contends that Walters neglected to tell his lawyers about the eligibility forms, spoiling their opinion; yet why would Walters have to brief an expert in sports law if mailings were foreseeable even to a novice?

* * *

There is a deeper problem with the theory of this prosecution. The United States tells us that the universities lost their scholarship money. Money is property; this aspect of the prosecution does not encounter a problem under *McNally v. United States*, 483 U.S. 350 (1987). Walters emphasizes that the universities put his 58 athletes on scholarship long before he met them and did not pay a penny more than they planned to do. But a jury could conclude that had Walters' clients told the truth, the colleges would have stopped their scholarships, thus saving money. So we must assume that the universities lost property by reason of Walters' deeds. Still, they were not out of pocket to Walters; he planned to profit by taking a percentage of the players' professional incomes, not of their scholarships. Section 1341 condemns "any scheme or artifice to defraud, or for obtaining money or property" (emphasis added). If the universities were the victims, how did he "obtain" their property? Walters asks.

* * *

In this case the mail fraud statute has been invoked to shore up the rules of an influential private association [the NCAA]. [The court compares the NCAA to a cartel whose rules are designed to deter "cheaters" who undermine the profitability of participating universities.] . . . Fanciful? Not at all. Many scholars understand the NCAA as a cartel, having power in the market for athletes. The NCAA depresses athletes' income—restricting payments to the value of tuition, room, and board, while receiving services of substantially greater worth. The NCAA treats this as desirable preservation of amateur sports; a more jaundiced eye would see it as the use of monopsony power to obtain athletes' services for less than the competitive market price. Walters then is cast in the role of a cheater, increasing the payments to the student athletes. Like other cheaters, Walters found it convenient to hide his activities. If, as the prosecutor believes, his repertory included extortion, he has used methods that the law denies to persons fighting cartels, but for the moment we are concerned only with the deceit that caused the universities to pay stipends to "professional" athletes. For current purposes it matters not whether the NCAA actually monopsonizes the market for players; the point of this discussion is that the prosecutor's theory makes criminals of those who consciously cheat on the rules of a private organization, even if that organization is a cartel. We pursue this point because any theory that makes criminals of cheaters raises a red flag.

Cheaters are not self-conscious champions of the public weal. They are in it for profit, as rapacious and mendacious as those who hope to collect monopoly rents. Maybe more; often members of cartels believe that monopoly serves the public interest, and they take their stand on the platform of business ethics, while cheaters' glasses have been washed with cynical acid. Only Adam Smith's invisible hand turns their self-seeking activities to public benefit. It is cause for regret if prosecutors, assuming that persons with low regard for honesty must be villains, use the criminal laws to suppress the competitive process that undermines cartels. Of course federal laws have been used to enforce cartels before. . . . But what is it about [the mail fraud statue] that labels as a crime all deceit that inflicts any loss on anyone? Firms often try to fool their competitors, surprising them with new products that enrich their treasuries at their rivals' expense. Is this mail fraud because large organizations inevitably use the mail? "Any scheme or artifice to defraud, or for obtaining money or property by means of false or fraudulent pretenses, representations, or promises" reads like a description of schemes to get money or property by fraud rather than methods of doing business that incidentally cause losses.

* * *

Reversed.

NOTES AND QUESTIONS

1. *Future of Criminal Prosecution for NCAA Violations.* The *Walters* decision suggests that federal prosecution of agent misbehavior under federal law is not a viable option. *See also Abernathy v. State*, 545 So.2d 185 (Ala. Crim. App. 1988) (unsuccessful prosecution of agent for "tampering with a sporting contest" by paying Auburn football star). Yet, in 2017 the Manhattan U.S. Attorney's office revived the theory underlying the *Walters* prosecution, criminalizing NCAA violations and indicting college basketball coaches, shoe company marketing executives, and sports agents for bribery, honest services wire fraud, and travel act conspiracy. In one alleged scheme, the coaches took cash bribes from financial advisers, business managers and others, and facilitated bribes directly to student-athletes in exchange for pressuring those athletes to retain the services of these advisers once they entered the NBA. In a second alleged scheme, a top Adidas executive worked in connection with the advisers to funnel bribes to high-school players and their families to induce them to attend universities sponsored by Adidas, and to choose Adidas as their sponsor when they turned pro. A third alleged scheme involved bribes to assistant coaches and youth basketball coaches to steer athletes to particular schools. *See United States v. Gatto*, 295 F. Supp. 3d 336 (S.D.N.Y. 2018) (sustaining indictment). Is it appropriate to use criminal law in this sphere?

2. *Honest Services Fraud Theory.* In *Skilling v. United States*, 561 U.S. 358 (2010), the Supreme Court scaled back the prosecution theory that the mail fraud statute covers schemes to defraud a private-sector employer where the "loss" sustained is not monetary, but rather an intangible right to "honest services." The Court allowed honest service fraud prosecutions of offenders who, in violation of a fiduciary duty, participated in bribery or kickback schemes, but excluded more "amorphous" cases involving conflicts of interest and undisclosed self-dealing. In which category would you place the schemes alleged in the NCAA basketball indictment described in the previous note?

3. *NCAA Student Antitrust Litigation.* The *Walters* decision observes that "a more jaundiced eye would see [the NCAA rules] as the use of monopsony power to obtain athletes' services for less than the competitive market price."

This statement anticipates by over 20 years recent student-athlete antitrust challenges to NCAA eligibility rules. *See Jenkins v. National Collegiate Athletic Association*, 4:14-cv-02758 (N.D. Cal. 2014). One rule being challenged is the NCAA ban on using an agent, supposedly to maintain a clear line of demarcation between collegiate and professional sports. Yet, the ban affects athletes at a time they are most in need of experienced counsel in navigating a path to the pros. The NCAA has relaxed aspects of the "no-agent" rule since *Walters*, including recently opening the door for elite college basketball players to hire agents while in college without losing eligibility. Do you think permitting college-athletes to sign with agents will promote or discourage ethical behavior by agents?

E. GOVERNMENT REGULATION OF AGENTS

The substantive issues and cases presented in the prior sections raise a broader systemic question: what role should government play—at both the federal and state levels—in directly regulating agents to secure high quality and ethical representation of athletes? As it turns out, that role has been largely confined to protecting universities from the single problem exemplified by the *Walters* case—agent recruiting of college athletes whose eligibility has not yet expired. The states entered the field first.

1. STATE LEGISLATION

The representation of athletes is an occupation that can be subjected to the kinds of legal controls that now govern activities ranging from medicine to hairdressing. While some agents have argued that such regulatory and licensing schemes violate the federal Constitution's "dormant" commerce clause by imposing an unreasonable burden on interstate commerce, this argument seems unlikely to prevail under current constitutional standards. *See South Dakota v. Wayfair, Inc.*, 138 S. Ct. 2080 (2018) (internet seller's physical presence in taxing state is not necessary for state to require seller to collect and remit its sales tax). Labor law preemption, however, poses a less surmountable barrier to state regulation of agents' representation of *unionized* athletes. Because NLRB-certified unions are the exclusive bargaining representatives of employees, and they delegate some of this authority to their certified agents, state regulation of any of these agents' representation of union members would interfere with the exercise of protected concerted activity.

The pioneer in regulating sports agents was the California legislature, which in 1982 enacted the Athlete Agents Act that required agents engaging in activities in the state to register with the Secretary of State and to follow the rules set forth in the statute. Numerous states adopted similar laws, resulting in a patchwork of agent regulation with varying definitions of covered student-athletes, registration procedures and renewals, disclosure requirements, educational prerequisites, exemptions (*e.g.*, for attorneys), procedures for notifying educational institutions of agency contracts with college-athletes, and enforcement methods. By the 1990s, 28 states were in the business of regulating sports agents, most of which were home to one or more colleges that are traditional powers in either football or basketball. However, this regulation was largely ineffective, with few agents bothering to register and few states dedicating resources to law enforcement.

In 2000, a commission on uniform state laws promulgated the Uniform Athlete Agent Act (UAAA), a version of which has been adopted in 43 states as of 2018. The UAAA is periodically revised, most recently in 2015 when it was restyled the Revised Uniform Athlete Agent Act (RUAAA). The prefatory note to the RUAAA reads:

> With the immense amount of money at stake for a wide variety of professional athletes and those who represent them, the commercial marketplace in which athlete agents operate is extremely competitive. While seeking to best position one's clients and to maximize their potential income is both legal and good business practice, the recruitment of a student athlete while he or she is still enrolled in an educational institution can and will cause substantial eligibility problems for both the student and the institution, which can in turn lead to severe economic sanctions and loss of scholarships. The problem is more acute where an unscrupulous agent misleads a student, especially where the athlete is not aware of the implications of signing the agency agreement or where an agency contract is entered without notice to the institution. In response to these issues, the Uniform Athlete Agents Act (UAAA) was promulgated by the Uniform Law Commission (ULC) in 2000. . . .
>
> [S]everal states have amended the act to, among other things, deal with a perceived lack of enforcement, broaden the coverage of the act to individuals who do not necessarily recruit or solicit a student athlete to enter into an agency contract, and require notice to educational institutions prior to contact. It became evident that the variations from state to state put uniformity at risk and may have discouraged reputable agents from complying with the act. To deal with these issues, the Uniform Law Commission adopted the Revised Uniform Athlete Agents Act (RUAAA) in July of 2015.

The RUAAA, like its predecessors and like agent regulation in non-adopter states, focuses on the harm done to amateur athletes and their universities when athletes sign with agents before their eligibility has expired. To protect against this harm, the RUAAA regulates agent interactions with amateur athletes in several ways, including:

1. Agents must register with the state and disclose training, experience, education, criminal convictions, civil determinations of false or deceptive representations, and any disciplinary action against the agent. Agents may not contact a student-athlete without first being registered. To encourage compliance with the Act, registration in one state entitles the agent to reciprocity in other RUAAA states.

2. All representation agreements must be in writing, signed by both parties, with clear provisions specifying agent compensation and a statement as to the athlete agent's registration status.

3. All representation agreements must contain an explicit bold warning, signed by the student-athlete, that by entering into the agreement, the athlete may be forfeiting any further NCAA eligibility. The athlete is then given a 14-day "cooling off" period within which to change his mind and cancel the agreement.

4. Agents are prohibited from offering "anything of value to any person to induce a student athlete" to enter into a representation agreement.

5. The agent and/or the athlete must notify the educational institution within 72 hours that a representation agreement has been signed.

The RUAAA's restrictions on agent dealings with college athletes are enforced by a variety of sanctions, including criminal prosecution with the possibility of imprisonment or fines, and a right conferred on the institution and the student-athlete to sue the agent for damages suffered as the result of the agent's conduct. A university's damages can include financial losses associated with NCAA discipline. Finally, there is an administrative penalty of up to $50,000 for violation of the statute.

At least three states, including California, continue to regulate agents under non-UAAA laws. California has periodically reformed its agent legislation, now known as the Miller-Ayala Act, to enlarge substantive requirements and impose stiffer penalties for violations than does the UAAA. The Miller-Ayala Act includes a cause of action against agents; it empowers not just institutions and athletes, but any "adversely affected" party to file a state court suit for actual and punitive damages arising out of an agent's violation, specifying a minimum award of $50,000. In addition, if a court finds that an agent violated the Miller-Ayala Act, it *must* revoke that agent's privileges to do business in the state for at least one year and order the agent to disgorge fees. The University of Southern California availed itself of these remedies in the 1990s, suing sports agent Robert Caron after learning that he had given three USC football players benefits that rendered them ineligible to play. USC settled out of court, receiving $50,000 in damages from the agent.

The appropriate scope and practical effects of such state regulation raise serious questions. For example, given the national cast to professional sports, should the reach of the state regulation turn on the agent's home base, or the player's home base, or the location of the college from which the player is coming, or the location of the team to which he is going, or all of the above? With nearly every state insisting on agent registration, each requiring its own registration fees, surety bonds, and administrative paperwork, the cumulative cost of such regulation inevitably reduces either the number of agents who are competing to work on behalf of athletes or the number of active agents who are complying with the licensing requirements.

Further, despite legislative consensus on the need for agent regulation, it has neither served as a significant deterrent to agent misconduct nor resulted in significant enforcement. On the criminal side, only a handful of UAAA prosecutions have been brought, including:

- 2017 North Carolina prosecution of Terry Watson for providing thousands of dollars in improper benefits to three former UNC players to induce them to sign with him.
- 2008 Alabama prosecution of Raymond Savage, a Virginia-based agent, for failing to register under Alabama's UAAA and initiating contact with a student athlete. Savage's runner, Jason Goggins, was also indicted for the same violations.
- 2006 Louisiana prosecution of Charles Taplin for violating the Act's registration and notification provisions by texting to Louisiana State University football players on behalf of an agent, and of former LSU strength coach Travelle Gaines for inviting players to his home to meet an agent.

A 2010 Associated Press study found that more than half of the then-42 states that had enacted a version of the UAAA had yet to revoke or suspend any agent registrations, or impose any sort of penalty on agent misconduct. According to the AP study, Texas was a lone outlier, with 31 agents receiving civil discipline and paying fines totaling $17,500. Why aren't states doing more to enforce the UAAA? How should state-level investigators and prosecutors prioritize these cases against high-level felonies and violent crime?

2. FEDERAL LEGISLATION

In 2004, Congress entered the agent regulation field by enacting the Sports Agent and Responsibility Trust Act (SPARTA). 15 U.S.C. §§ 7801 *et seq.* This Act brought sports agent activity under the regulatory jurisdiction of the Federal Trade Commission and imposed disclosure and conduct duties on agents that can be enforced by state attorneys general or the FTC. As a federal enactment, SPARTA is not vulnerable to the possible constitutional and labor law impediments facing state regulation.

SPARTA emulates much of the original UAAA and forbids sports agents from: (1) giving false or misleading information to a student-athlete; (2) making false or misleading promises or misrepresentations to a student-athlete; (3) providing anything of value to the student or any individual associated with the student, including friends and family; (4) failing to disclose in writing that the student may lose eligibility to compete as a student-athlete if he or she signs an agency contract; and (5) predating or postdating contracts. The act also requires the agent and athlete to notify the athletic director at the student's school within 72 hours of signing a contract. Violations can be enforced under the Federal Trade Commission Act as unfair or deceptive acts or practices punishable by fines of up to $11,000 per incident, to be paid by the sports agent. The Act expressly supplements current state agent regulation laws; it does not replace or preempt these laws since nothing in it is inconsistent with any state requirements.

Although SPARTA appears to provide a national, uniform standard and framework for deterring unethical agent conduct, the FTC to date has not taken any action against an agent under SPARTA. Does this suggest to you important differences in the competence and concern of the respective government sources of regulation? What explains the federal government's total lack of enforcement of SPARTA?

3. ETHICS RULES GOVERNING ATTORNEY-AGENTS

Many sports agents are also attorneys who must also comply with rules of professional conduct. These ethical obligations are potentially a competitive disadvantage insofar as non-attorney agents are not equally bound. While some attorney-agents have argued that they should not be subject to professional codes with respect to non-legal work for athletes, that theory largely has been rejected. *See, e.g., Matter of Frederick J. Henley*, 478 S.E.2d 134 (Ga. 1996); *Cuyahoga County Bar Assoc. v. Glenn*, 649 N.E.2d 1213 (Ohio 1995); Illinois State Bar Assoc., Op. No. 700 (Nov. 4, 1980) (attorneys who act as sports agents are subject to bar rules). In any event, it is incumbent on attorney-agents to make clear that athletes who hire them gain an advantage by retaining an agent who is held to a higher standard in terms of both ethics and competence. Consider some of the attorney rules most relevant in this context, from the American Bar Association's Model Rules of Professional Conduct (2016):

Rule 1.1 Competence

A lawyer shall provide competent representation to a client. Competent representation requires the legal knowledge, skill, thoroughness and preparation reasonably necessary for the representation.

Rule 1.5 Fees

(a) A lawyer shall not make an agreement for, charge, or collect an unreasonable fee or an unreasonable amount for expenses. The factors to be considered in determining the reasonableness of a fee include the following:

(1) the time and labor required, the novelty and difficulty of the questions involved, and the skill requisite to perform the legal service properly; . . .

(3) the fee customarily charged in the locality for similar legal services; . . .

(6) the nature and length of the professional relationship with the client;

(7) the experience, reputation, and ability of the lawyer or lawyers performing the services; . . . .

Rule 1.7 Conflict of Interest: Current Clients

(a) Except as provided in paragraph (b), a lawyer shall not represent a client if the representation involves a concurrent conflict of interest. A concurrent conflict of interest exists if:

(1) the representation of one client will be directly adverse to another client; or

(2) there is a significant risk that the representation of one or more clients will be materially limited by the lawyer's responsibilities to another client, a former client or a third person or by a personal interest of the lawyer.

(b) Notwithstanding the existence of a concurrent conflict of interest under paragraph (a), a lawyer may represent a client if:

(1) the lawyer reasonably believes that the lawyer will be able to provide competent and diligent representation to each affected client;

(2) the representation is not prohibited by law;

(3) the representation does not involve the assertion of a claim by one client against another client represented by the lawyer in the same litigation or other proceeding before a tribunal; and

(4) each affected client gives informed consent, confirmed in writing.

Rule 1.8 Conflict Of Interest: Current Clients: Specific Rules

(a) A lawyer shall not enter into a business transaction with a client or knowingly acquire an ownership, possessory, security or other pecuniary interest adverse to a client unless:

(1) the transaction and terms on which the lawyer acquires the interest are fair and reasonable to the client and are fully disclosed and transmitted in writing in a manner that can be reasonably understood by the client;

(2) the client is advised in writing of the desirability of seeking and is given a reasonable opportunity to seek the advice of independent legal counsel on the transaction; and

(3) the client gives informed consent, in a writing signed by the client, to the essential terms of the transaction and the lawyer's role in the transaction, including whether the lawyer is representing the client in the transaction.

(b) A lawyer shall not use information relating to representation of a client to the disadvantage of the client unless the client gives informed consent, except as permitted or required by these Rules.

(c) A lawyer shall not solicit any substantial gift from a client, including a testamentary gift, or prepare on behalf of a client an instrument giving the lawyer or a person related to the lawyer any substantial gift unless the lawyer or other recipient of the gift is related to the client. . . .

Rule 5.5 Unauthorized Practice Of Law; Multijurisdictional Practice Of Law

(a) A lawyer shall not practice law in a jurisdiction in violation of the regulation of the legal profession in that jurisdiction, or assist another in doing so.

(b) A lawyer who is not admitted to practice in this jurisdiction shall not:

(1) except as authorized by these Rules or other law, establish an office or other systematic and continuous presence in this jurisdiction for the practice of law; or

(2) hold out to the public or otherwise represent that the lawyer is admitted to practice law in this jurisdiction.

Rule 7.3 Solicitation of Clients

. . .

(b) A lawyer shall not by in-person, live telephone or real-time electronic contact solicit professional employment from a prospective client when a significant motive for the lawyer's doing so is the lawyer's pecuniary gain, unless the person contacted is a:

(1) lawyer;

(2) a person who has a family, close personal, or prior professional relationship with the lawyer or law firm; or

(3) person who routinely uses for business purposes the type of legal services offered by the lawyer.

(c) A lawyer shall not solicit professional employment even when not otherwise prohibited by paragraph (b), if:

(1) the target of the solicitation has made known to the lawyer a desire not to be solicited by the lawyer; or

(2) the solicitation involves coercion, duress or harassment. . . .

NOTES AND QUESTIONS

1. *Competence.* A non-lawyer has no formal competency requirement such as those contained in the Model Rules. However, under common law, an agent is under the legal duty to represent an athlete with competence on par with that displayed by others who represent athletes. As discussed above, athletes can bring malpractice claims against negligent non-attorney agents. Why might this remedy be less effective than a similar claim against an attorney-agent? What other ways can athletes hold accountable attorneys who have not adequately served their interests?

2. *Fees.* Although agent fees for player contract negotiation services are fixed by some leagues, other leagues leave that up to the player and agent to negotiate. And fees for management services and negotiating other revenue deals are similarly unregulated for non-attorney agents. An attorney, however, may charge only a "reasonable" fee. How do you think that affects, in practice, the way attorneys structure revenue deals for their clients?

3. *Conflicts of Interest.* An attorney-agent is ostensibly more sensitive to the potential for conflicts of interest in representing different athletes and other sports industry participants. Thus, an attorney-agent arguably will not give one athlete-client precedence over another in negotiating a deal based on their relative star quality. In negotiating an endorsement deal, an attorney-agent will avoid recommending a deal in order to collect a fee, and must consider the athlete's long-term interests. In obtaining informed consent from an athlete-client to a potential or actual conflict of interest, an attorney-agent is more likely to provide the necessary disclosures and ensure the client's consent is fully knowledgeable. Do you agree that attorney-agents will in reality conduct themselves and their athlete-clients' business more ethically and loyally?

4. *Solicitation.* Identify the ways that the Model Rules ban on attorney solicitation is more restrictive and less restrictive than UAAA and SPARTA regulation of recruitment of college athletes. In what ways do you think the professional rules compel attorney-agents to vary their recruitment practices from non-attorneys? While there is no guarantee that attorney-agents will avoid aggressive recruitment practices, consider how much more the lawyer has to lose if caught.

5. *Unauthorized Practice of Law.* Attorney-agents with active sports practices will unavoidably serve athlete-clients in multiple jurisdictions as players move from college to the pros and from team to team. How can an attorney in this situation comply with the requirement to be licensed as a lawyer everywhere she actually practices? Implicit in the competitive tension between non-attorney agents and attorney agents is that non-attorney agents themselves are engaging in unauthorized practice of law. However, few jurisdictions actively enforce their UPL restrictions, and have little incentive to do so against sports agents increasingly subject to parallel—if similarly rarely enforced—ethical regulations. To what extent has this regulatory failure allowed non-attorney agents to exploit their "operational" freedom vis-à-vis attorney agents to dominate the business and possibly its reputation?

CHAPTER 10

INTERCOLLEGIATE SPORTS: THE NCAA AND ITS MEMBER INSTITUTIONS*

■ ■ ■

A. BACKGROUND

Before exploring the law of intercollegiate sports, it is essential to understand what the National Collegiate Athletic Association ("NCAA") is, and how it functions. The NCAA is an organization comprised of 1,117 member institutions—colleges and universities—in 100 athletics conferences allocated over three Divisions. While the 500 employees of the NCAA interpret and support member legislation, run championships, and manage programs that benefit student-athletes, the college and university presidents work through a committee structure to create the rules and regulations that govern athletic competition and eligibility requirements. This is a large operation, annually involving almost 500,000 athletes on 19,500 teams, with 90 championships in 24 sports.

At its core, then, the NCAA follows the parameters set out collectively by college and university presidents, under the current leadership of a former university president, Mark Emmert. The funding for the NCAA and its 500 employees comes almost entirely from the NCAA Division I basketball tournament, March Madness, which generates over $1 billion annually, mostly through television contracts.

Those who describe the NCAA tell two competing narratives. The NCAA's narrative centers on the concept of the student-athlete, one who engages in sport for the love of the game, and as part of one's education and collegiate experience. Article II of the NCAA's constitution explains:

> Student-athletes shall be amateurs in an intercollegiate sport, and their participation should be motivated primarily by education and by the physical, mental and social benefits to be derived. Student participation in intercollegiate athletics is an avocation, and student-athletes should be protected from exploitation by professional and commercial enterprises.

---

* The Casebook Website (http://pennstatelaw.psu.edu/SportsTextWebsite) contains citations to scholarly and other commentary on a variety of topics discussed in this chapter, including college sports and the NCAA, the *Tarkanian* case, the *Board of Regents* case, coaching contracts, NCAA infractions, and the Penn State scandal.

NCAA Constitution and By-Laws § 2.9 (2017–18).

This amateurism principle emphasizes education—amateur athletes come to the university campus to receive an education, with athletics merely being part of that education. Indeed, the NCAA's advertisements have often noted that most of its athletes are "going pro" in vocations other than sports.

As stated, the NCAA model also endeavors to "protect" student-athletes from exploitation by professional and commercial enterprises. As explained in this chapter and the next, the NCAA takes its amateurism principle seriously, banning from competition any individuals who receive significant financial benefits outside of tuition, room, board, books, and a most recently approved cost of attendance. Because the approved financial benefits all relate to education, they do not, from the NCAA's perspective, compromise the amateur status of the athletes. The NCAA's byzantine rulebook prohibits even de minimis benefits, such as giving an athlete a ride or buying him a cup of coffee, all in the name of protecting amateurism.

The NCAA penalizes the institutions where such benefits are conferred, even where the benefits come from third party boosters and fans. The university is responsible, under NCAA rules, for the actions of all of its boosters with respect to its student-athletes. This responsibility extends also to the self-reporting of violations. The NCAA Infractions Committee mitigates sanctions in some cases where an institution reports its violations. As explored below, institutions often sanction themselves prior to Infractions decisions.

The second narrative stresses the significant amount of money that the revenue sports—college football and college basketball—generate, with both being $1 billion industries. These soaring financial figures have caused many to claim that commercialization jeopardizes the principles that supposedly make intercollegiate sports unique, including amateurism. While few doubt that the NCAA's stated purpose is genuine and being met for the hundreds of thousands of student-athletes participating in non-revenue sports, serious questions arise as to whether the mass public appeal and commercial opportunities in big-time college sports, particularly in Division I-A football and Division I men's basketball, is in fundamental tension with the NCAA's stated purpose of conducting intercollegiate sports "in a manner designed to protect and enhance the physical and educational welfare of student-athletes" (Article 2.2).

Despite six-figure live attendance at some Division I-A football games and lucrative television contracts, the NCAA and its member institutions still claim that all student-athletes should remain "amateurs" whose participation is "motivated primarily by education and by the physical, mental, and social benefits" of athletics, and who are to "be protected from exploitation by professional and commercial enterprises" (Article 2.6).

Many of those who repeat this second narrative find these claims dubious, and instead characterize college athletics as a big business with the luxury of largely free labor, or at the very least, labor with a restricted salary cap of tuition, room, board, books, and cost of attendance. They stress that many athletes come to the university to enhance their ability to become a professional athlete, despite the slim odds of realizing that dream. These critics claim that the NCAA and its member institutions exploit the revenue sport athletes by denying them a share in the profits they generate. For some the solution is paying the athletes; for others it is reducing the commercial pressure on the current model to develop a better version of the status quo.

The second narrative further questions the educational opportunities offered to revenue sport athletes, who often spend sixty or more hours per week on athletics during the season. Even with tutors, the time demands of sports participation—particularly the revenue sports—can make academic performance very challenging, especially where the student involved struggled to qualify academically in the first place. Certainly, universities have incentive to compromise academic integrity, especially where an athlete's eligibility is at stake.

Those repeating the first narrative, however, can tell success stories that occur at the intersection of academics and athletics. The NCAA and its member institutions point out that athletes graduate at a higher rate than non-athletes, though in many cases, it is the success of the non-revenue sport athletes that makes the difference. In addition, it is clear that the overall academic profile of many institutions has risen because athletics attracts strong non-athlete students to attend, as the proverbial "front porch" of the university.

Nonetheless, athletics can sometimes pose a problem for the academic pursuits of strong students, where the demands of the athletic team make taking certain classes or enrolling in certain majors virtually impossible. The recent phenomenon of clustering, where many members of one athletic team all major in the same discipline and/or take the same series of pre-approved classes, bears this out. Even where academic advisors, students, tutors, and faculty are all working together to ensure athletes have a legitimate and robust academic experience, the pressure generated by intercollegiate athletics raises serious questions about the NCAA's narrative at certain institutions.

Finally, it is no secret that some athletes have little or no interest in academics and attend universities as a required stepping stone to a professional career. With the NBA requiring one year and the NFL three years, elite athletes in football and basketball choose NCAA athletics largely because there is no other established option to become a high draft pick. Not surprisingly, the use of college athletics exclusively as a professional stepping stone creates tension with the education and amateurism ideals advanced by the NCAA.

NOTES AND QUESTIONS

1. *Student-Athlete or Exploited Laborer?* Of the two narratives above, which do you find to be the most persuasive? Would allowing athletes a share of the money generated change your answer? Why or why not? Might the two narratives both describe the same underlying reality? Are there other narratives you find more persuasive?

2. *Academic Reform?* NCAA rules require athletes to enroll in 9 credit hours a semester to remain eligible. Would you consider waiving this requirement? What if athletes had the option of not attending class during the semester of their athletics season, and went to school full-time, with no athletics practices or games, in the other semester? This would require making basketball a one-semester sport, and eliminating spring football practice, but do you think that would alleviate some of the pressure on academics? Students could complete two years of school over a four year athletic career, and then have two years as a regular student after realizing that professional sports was not an option. The cost to the university would be an additional two years of room and board. Is this a feasible proposal? Why or why not? For a more in-depth investigation into this type of approach, *see* William W. Berry III, *Educating Athletes,* 81 Tenn. L. Rev. 795 (2014).

3. *Amateurism.* As we explore the application of the NCAA's amateurism rules below, as well as the past and present legal challenges to those rules, keep in mind that other options may exist. One approach that many have suggested is the Olympic model, where athletes do not receive compensation for athletic performance, but can earn revenue from off-campus activities that exploit their athletic talents. These could include endorsements, autograph signing, promotional events, non-scholastic athletics exhibitions, teaching and coaching their sport, and employment by sports-industry firms. Consider the off-campus earning opportunities of scholarship students in other disciplines, such as music or computer science. Why should student-athletes alone risk losing their scholarships and eligibility when they exploit the talents that earned them that scholarship in the first place?

B. PROCEDURAL DUE PROCESS

The NCAA's oversight of college athletics has been the subject of a number of legal challenges. One of the most important of these challenges came in the late 1970s when Jerry Tarkanian, the basketball coach of the University of Nevada at Las Vegas (UNLV) challenged a suspension resulting from alleged rules violations. At the end of the 1977 season, UNLV announced that, pursuant to an NCAA directive, the school was suspending Tarkanian for two years based on his alleged major violations of NCAA rules. The two main charges against Tarkanian were that he had arranged for payment of a flight home for one of his players, and that he had arranged for an instructor to give another player a passing grade in a course the player did not attend.

The NCAA's Committee on Infractions found that the violations had occurred. The Committee put UNLV's basketball program on probation for two years and required the university to suspend Tarkanian as coach for those two years or face further penalties. Both federal constitutional and state statutory law required UNLV, a state university, to give Tarkanian, its tenured coach, a due process hearing before suspending him. Although the hearing officer did not believe that any violations had occurred, he concluded that UNLV had no choice but to suspend Tarkanian if the school wanted to remain part of the NCAA.

In response, Tarkanian sued both UNLV and the NCAA. The Nevada courts found that the NCAA proceedings had denied Tarkanian procedural "due process" guaranteed by the Fourteenth Amendment. Operating on the assumption that the NCAA was a "state actor" governed by the federal constitution, the trial court issued injunctions barring UNLV's suspension of Tarkanian and NCAA retaliation against UNLV. The Nevada Supreme Court affirmed. The case finally reached the United States Supreme Court in 1988; by then Tarkanian had amassed one of the highest winning percentages of all active coaches in college basketball.

NCAA v. TARKANIAN
488 U.S. 179 (1988)

JUSTICE STEVENS for the Court.

* * *

II

Embedded in our Fourteenth Amendment jurisprudence is a dichotomy between state action, which is subject to scrutiny under the Amendment's Due Process Clause, and private conduct, against which the Amendment affords no shield, no matter how unfair that conduct may be. As a general matter the protections of the Fourteenth Amendment do not extend to "private conduct abridging individual rights." *Burton v. Wilmington Parking Authority*, 365 U.S. 715, 722 (1961).

"Careful adherence to the 'state action' requirement preserves an area of individual freedom by limiting the reach of federal law" and avoids the imposition of responsibility on a State for conduct it could not control. When Congress enacted § 1983 as the statutory remedy for violations of the Constitution, it specified that the conduct at issue must have occurred "under color of" state law; thus, liability attaches only to those wrongdoers "who carry a badge of authority of a State and represent it in some capacity, whether they act in accordance with their authority or misuse it." *Monroe v. Pape*, 365 U.S. 167, 172 (1961). As we stated in *United States v. Classic*, 313 U.S. 299, 326 (1941):

> Misuse of power, possessed by virtue of state law and made possible only because the wrongdoer is clothed with the authority of state law, is action taken "under color of" state law.

In this case Tarkanian argues that the NCAA was a state actor because it misused power that it possessed by virtue of state law. He claims specifically that UNLV delegated its own functions to the NCAA, clothing the Association with authority both to adopt rules governing UNLV's athletic programs and to enforce those rules on behalf of UNLV. Similarly, the Nevada Supreme Court held that UNLV had delegated its authority over personnel decisions to the NCAA. Therefore, the court reasoned, the two entities acted jointly to deprive Tarkanian of liberty and property interests, making the NCAA as well as UNLV a state actor.

These contentions fundamentally misconstrue the facts of this case. In the typical case raising a state action issue, a private party has taken the decisive step that caused the harm to the plaintiff, and the question is whether the State was sufficiently involved to treat that decisive conduct as state action. This may occur if the State creates the legal framework governing the conduct; if it delegates its authority to the private actor; or sometimes if it knowingly accepts the benefits derived from unconstitutional behavior. Thus, in the usual case we ask whether the State provided a mantle of authority that enhanced the power of the harm-causing individual actor.

This case uniquely mirrors the traditional state action case. Here the final act challenged by Tarkanian—his suspension—was committed by UNLV. A state university without question is a state actor. When it decides to impose a serious disciplinary sanction upon one of its tenured employees, it must comply with the terms of the Due Process Clause of the Fourteenth Amendment to the Federal Constitution. Thus when UNLV notified Tarkanian that he was being separated from all relations with the University's basketball program, it acted under color of state law within the meaning of 42 U.S.C. § 1983.

The mirror image presented in this case requires us to step through an analytical looking glass to resolve it. Clearly UNLV's conduct was influenced by the rules and recommendations of the NCAA, the private party. But it was UNLV, the state entity, that actually suspended Tarkanian. Thus the question is not whether UNLV participated to a critical extent in the NCAA's activities, but whether UNLV's actions in compliance with the NCAA rules and recommendations turned the NCAA's conduct into state action.

We examine first the relationship between UNLV and the NCAA regarding the NCAA's rulemaking. UNLV is among the NCAA's members and participated in promulgating the Association's rules; it must be assumed, therefore, that Nevada had some impact on the NCAA's policy determinations. Yet the NCAA's several hundred other public and private member institutions each similarly affected those policies. Those institutions, the vast majority of which were located in States other than Nevada, did not act under color of Nevada law. It necessarily follows that the source of the legislation adopted by the NCAA is not Nevada but the collective membership, speaking through an organization that is independent of any particular State.

State action nonetheless might lie if UNLV, by embracing the NCAA's rules, transformed them into state rules and the NCAA into a state actor. UNLV engaged in state action when it adopted the NCAA's rules to govern its own behavior, but that would be true even if UNLV had taken no part in the promulgation of those rules. In *Bates v. State Bar of Arizona*, 433 U.S. 350 (1977), we established that the State Supreme Court's enforcement of disciplinary rules transgressed by members of its own bar was state action. Those rules had been adopted in toto from the American Bar Association Code of Professional Responsibility. It does not follow, however, that the ABA's formulation of those disciplinary rules was state action. The State Supreme Court retained plenary power to reexamine those standards and, if necessary, to reject them and promulgate its own. So here, UNLV retained the authority to withdraw from the NCAA and establish its own standards. The University alternatively could have stayed in the Association and worked through the Association's legislative process to amend rules or standards it deemed harsh, unfair, or unwieldy.[15] Neither UNLV's decision to adopt the NCAA's standards nor its minor role in their formulation is a sufficient reason for concluding that the NCAA was acting under color of Nevada law when it promulgated standards governing athlete recruitment, eligibility, and academic performance.

Tarkanian further asserts that the NCAA's investigation, enforcement proceedings, and consequent recommendations constituted state action because they resulted from a delegation of power by UNLV. UNLV, as an NCAA member, subscribed to the statement in the Association's bylaws that NCAA "enforcement procedures are an essential part of the intercollegiate athletic program of each member institution." It is, of course, true that a state may delegate authority to a private party and

---

[15] Furthermore, the NCAA's bylaws permit review of penalties, even after they are imposed, "upon a showing of newly discovered evidence which is directly related to the findings in the case, or that there was a prejudicial error in the procedure which was followed in the processing of the case by the Committee." UNLV could have sought such a review, perhaps on the theory that the NCAA's investigator was biased against Tarkanian, as the Nevada trial court found in 1984. The NCAA Committee on Infractions was authorized to "reduce or eliminate any penalty" if the University had prevailed.

thereby make that party a state actor. Thus, we recently held that a private physician who had contracted with a state prison to attend to the inmates' medical needs was a state actor. But UNLV delegated no power to the NCAA to take specific action against any University employee. The commitment by UNLV to adhere to NCAA enforcement procedures was enforceable only by sanctions that the NCAA might impose on UNLV itself.

Indeed, the notion that UNLV's promise to cooperate in the NCAA enforcement proceedings was tantamount to a partnership agreement or the transfer of certain University powers to the NCAA is belied by the history of this case. It is quite obvious that UNLV used its best efforts to retain its winning coach—a goal diametrically opposed to the NCAA's interest in ascertaining the truth of its investigators' reports. During the several years that the NCAA investigated the alleged violations, the NCAA and UNLV acted much more like adversaries than like partners engaged in a dispassionate search for the truth. The NCAA cannot be regarded as an agent of UNLV for purposes of that proceeding. It is more correctly characterized as an agent of its remaining members which, as competitors of UNLV, had an interest in the effective and evenhanded enforcement of NCAA's recruitment standards. Just as a state-compensated public defender acts in a private capacity when she represents a private client in a conflict against the State, the NCAA is properly viewed as a private actor at odds with the State when it represents the interests of its entire membership in an investigation of one public university.

The NCAA enjoyed no governmental powers to facilitate its investigation. It had no power to subpoena witnesses, to impose contempt sanctions, or to assert sovereign authority over any individual. Its greatest authority was to threaten sanctions against UNLV, with the ultimate sanction being expulsion of the University from membership. Contrary to the premise of the Nevada Supreme Court's opinion, the NCAA did not—indeed, could not—directly discipline Tarkanian or any other state university employee.[18] The express terms of the Confidential Report did

---

[18] Tarkanian urges us to hold, as did the Nevada Supreme Court, that the NCAA by its rules and enforcement procedures has usurped a traditional, essential state function. Quite properly, he does not point to the NCAA's overriding function of fostering amateur athletics at the college level. For while we have described that function as "critical," *NCAA v. Board of Regents of the University of Oklahoma*, 468 U.S. 85, 120 (1984), by no means is it a traditional, let alone an exclusive, state function. Cf. *San Francisco Arts & Athletics, Inc. v. United States Olympic Committee*, 483 U.S. 522, 545 (1987) ("Neither the conduct nor the coordination of amateur sports has been a traditional government function."). Tarkanian argues instead that the NCAA has assumed the state's traditional and exclusive power to discipline its employees. "[A]s to state employees connected with intercollegiate athletics, the NCAA requires that its standards, procedures and determinations become the State's standards, procedures and determinations for disciplining state employees," he contends. "The State is obligated to impose NCAA standards, procedures and determinations making the NCAA a joint participant in the State's suspension of Tarkanian." This argument overlooks the fact that the NCAA's own legislation prohibits it from taking any direct action against Tarkanian. Moreover, suspension of Tarkanian is one of many recommendations in the Confidential Report. Those recommendations as a whole were intended to bring UNLV's basketball

not demand the suspension unconditionally; rather, it requested "the University . . . to show cause" why the NCAA should not impose additional penalties if UNLV declines to suspend Tarkanian. Even the University's vice president acknowledged that the Report gave the University options other than suspension: UNLV could have retained Tarkanian and risked additional sanctions, perhaps even expulsion from the NCAA, or it could have withdrawn voluntarily from the Association.

Finally, Tarkanian argues that the power of the NCAA is so great that the UNLV had no practical alternative to compliance with its demands. We are not at all sure this is true,[19] but even if we assume that a private monopolist can impose its will on a state agency by a threatened refusal to deal with it, it does not follow that such a private party is therefore acting under color of state law.

In final analysis the question is whether "the conduct allegedly causing the deprivation of a federal right [can] be fairly attributable to the State." It would be ironic indeed to conclude that the NCAA's imposition of sanctions against UNLV—sanctions that UNLV and its counsel, including the Attorney General of Nevada, steadfastly opposed during protracted adversary proceedings—is fairly attributable to the State of Nevada. It would be more appropriate to conclude that UNLV has conducted its athletic program under color of the policies adopted by the NCAA, rather than that those policies were developed and enforced under color of Nevada law.

Reversed.

JUSTICE WHITE dissented and filed an opinion in which JUSTICES BRENNAN, MARSHALL and O'CONNOR joined.

All agree that UNLV, a public university, is a state actor, and that the suspension of Jerry Tarkanian, a public employee, was state action. The question here is whether the NCAA acted jointly with UNLV in suspending Tarkanian and thereby also became a state actor. I would hold that it did.

I agree with the majority that this case is different on its facts from many of our prior state action cases. As the majority notes, in our "typical case raising a state action issue, a private party has taken the decisive step that caused the harm to the plaintiff." In this case, however, which in the majority's view "uniquely mirrors the traditional state action case," the final act that caused the harm to Tarkanian was committed, not by a private party, but by a party conceded to be a state actor. Because of this

---

program into compliance with NCAA rules. Suspension of Tarkanian was but one means toward achieving that goal.

[19] The University's desire to remain a powerhouse among the nation's college basketball teams is understandable, and nonmembership in the NCAA obviously would thwart that goal. But that UNLV's options were unpalatable does not mean that they were nonexistent.

difference, the majority finds it necessary to "step through an analytical looking glass" to evaluate whether the NCAA was a state actor.

* * *

On the facts of the present case, the NCAA acted jointly with UNLV in suspending Tarkanian. First, Tarkanian was suspended for violations of NCAA rules, which UNLV embraced in its agreement with the NCAA. As the Nevada Supreme Court found in its first opinion in this case, "[a]s a member of the NCAA, UNLV contractually agrees to administer its athletic program in accordance with NCAA legislation." Indeed, NCAA rules provide that NCAA "enforcement procedures are an essential part of the intercollegiate athletic program of each member institution."

Second, the NCAA and UNLV also agreed that the NCAA would conduct the hearings concerning violations of its rules. Although UNLV conducted its own investigation into the recruiting violations alleged by the NCAA, the NCAA procedures provide that it is the NCAA Committee on Infractions that "determine[s] facts related to alleged violations," subject to an appeal to the NCAA Council. As a result of this agreement, the NCAA conducted the very hearings the Nevada Supreme Court held to have violated Tarkanian's right to procedural due process.

Third, the NCAA and UNLV agreed that the findings of fact made by the NCAA at the hearings it conducted would be binding on UNLV. By becoming a member of the NCAA, UNLV did more than merely "promise to cooperate in the NCAA enforcement proceedings." It agreed, as the University Hearing Officer appointed to rule on Tarkanian's suspension expressly found, to accept the NCAA's "findings of fact as in some way superior to [its] own." By the terms of UNLV's membership in the NCAA, the NCAA's findings were final and not subject to further review by any other body, and it was for that reason that UNLV suspended Tarkanian, despite concluding that many of those findings were wrong.

In short, it was the NCAA's findings that Tarkanian had violated NCAA rules, made at NCAA-conducted hearings, all of which were agreed to by UNLV in its membership agreement with the NCAA, that resulted in Tarkanian's suspension by UNLV. On these facts, the NCAA was "jointly engaged with [UNLV] officials in the challenged action," and therefore was a state actor.

* * *

The majority states in conclusion that "[i]t would be ironic indeed to conclude that the NCAA's imposition of sanctions against UNLV—sanctions that UNLV and its counsel, including the Attorney General of Nevada, steadfastly opposed during protracted adversary proceedings—Is fairly attributable to the State of Nevada." I agree. Had UNLV refused to suspend Tarkanian, and the NCAA responded by imposing sanctions against UNLV, it would be hard indeed to find any state action that harmed Tarkanian. But that is not this case. Here, UNLV did suspend Tarkanian, and it did so because it embraced the NCAA rules governing conduct of its athletic program and adopted the results of the hearings conducted by the NCAA concerning Tarkanian, as it had agreed that it would. Under these facts, I would find that the NCAA acted jointly with UNLV and therefore is a state actor.

NOTES AND QUESTIONS

1. *Aftermath.* While the NCAA won this major legal victory over Tarkanian, it was not able to remove him immediately from the college basketball court. Further litigation in the lower courts kept Tarkanian in place through the 1989–90 season, which UNLV capped with its first national championship.

2. *On the Merits.* In appraising the merits of the *Tarkanian* ruling, consider the following issues:

    a.   What claims could be made by Jerry Tarkanian, had the NCAA been found to be a state actor, that cannot be made by him with the NCAA found to be a private association? (The latter treatment is considered below.)

    b.   Should NCAA action toward a student-athlete at a private school such as Duke or Notre Dame constitute state action, or is it indistinguishable from a baseball commissioner's action toward a Pete Rose or a George Steinbrenner? In other words, is there anything special about the function of regulating sports in educational institutions? Are there any material legal differences in the structures of the NCAA and of a professional sports league and in the manner in which the respective members conduct their athletic businesses?

    c.   When the NCAA takes action against a state university such as UNLV or UCLA, is there a stronger case for judicial scrutiny than when the NCAA imposes sanctions on its private members? How much choice did UNLV have to defy the NCAA and respect Tarkanian's due process rights? On the other hand, could the NCAA afford to have different procedural rules for disciplining state and private schools and their personnel? Are there legal instruments more appropriate than the Constitution for challenging NCAA restraints on institutional or personal choices?

3. *When Do State Actors Bind Themselves to Private Decision-Making?* The constitutional doctrine concerning when state involvement with private parties constitutes "state action" is a difficult one, more fully explored in courses in constitutional law. *Tarkanian* holds that state actors are free to bind

themselves to decisions of a private actor, the NCAA. Suppose the NCAA adopted a rule requiring racial discrimination in athletics? Of course member schools couldn't adhere to such a rule under numerous civil rights and education statutes, but if these statutes did not exist, do you think the Supreme Court would follow *Tarkanian* and hold that public universities were free to impose such a rule at the behest of a private party?

In several works, Professor John Nowak (himself a former member of the NCAA Infractions Committee) has offered a way to reconcile and make sense of these cases. These cases always involve an irreconcilable conflict between the plaintiff's asserted right (to receive all procedural rights required by the Due Process Clause) and the private defendant's conduct (to take adverse action against the plaintiff without giving him these rights). The issue is whether the Constitution requires the state to prefer one private party's rights over another. Thus, in cases of racial discrimination, the Court is more likely to find "state action" than in procedural cases. As Nowak observes, this question "has nothing to do with finding a minimum quantum of state activity." *See* Robert Glennon & John Nowak, *A Functional Analysis of the Fourteenth Amendment "State Action" Requirement*, 1976 Sup. Ct. Rev. 221; John Nowak & Ronald Rotunda, *American Constitutional Law* § 12.5. *Tarkanian* thus reflects the Court's judgment that the Constitution does not require a finding that Tarkanian's private interest in a fairer hearing trumps the NCAA's private interest in informal hearings.

The Supreme Court in *Brentwood Academy v. Tennessee Secondary Schools Athletic Ass'n*, 531 U.S. 288 (2001), added another layer to the law of whether the Constitution (and 42 U.S.C. § 1983) applies to sports governing organizations as "state actors," this time involving an association that governs high school sports. At the time, the Tennessee Secondary Schools Athletic Association ("TSSAA") consisted of about 350 public and private high schools in the state of Tennessee, with 84 percent of its members being public and the other 16 percent being private schools. One of the latter, Brentwood Academy, was an affluent Christian school just outside Nashville, and a long-time football powerhouse in the state.

The TSSAA charged the Brentwood football coach, Carlton Flatt, with violating several rules in 1996. One alleged violation involved an invitation sent to 13 notable eighth-grade student players to come to a spring training practice. Another involved giving some students free tickets to the Brentwood games. After it found Brentwood guilty of these violations, the TSSAA stripped the school of its 1996 state football championship, fined it $3,000, and placed it on probation for four years. Brentwood then went to federal court to challenge the legality of the TSSAA action on several grounds, including under the federal Constitution's due process and free speech protections.

The district court, at 13 F. Supp. 2d 670 (M.D. Tenn. 1998), found the TSSAA to be a "state actor," and that a ban on recruiting potential high school students on the basis of athletics (rather than academics and the like) violated the school's First Amendment right to free speech. The Sixth Circuit, at 180 F.3d 758 (6th Cir. 1999), reversed on the ground that the TSSAA was just as much a private actor as the NCAA (whose member colleges are also largely public, although by a much smaller majority) and thus not subject to any constitutional restraints. The Supreme Court took the case for review of that issue.

In February 2001, the Court issued a 5–4 decision, this time holding that the TSSAA was indeed a state actor. Justice Stevens was the only justice that switched his vote from the *Tarkanian* case, amidst several court retirements and appointments. Justice Souter explained the Court's decision as follows:

> To be sure, it is not the strict holding in *Tarkanian* that points to our view of this case, for we found no state action on the part of the NCAA. We could see, on the one hand, that the university had some part in setting the NCAA's rules, and the Supreme Court of Nevada had gone so far as to hold that the NCAA had been delegated the university's traditionally exclusive public authority over personnel. But on the other side, the NCAA's policies were shaped not by the University of Nevada alone, but by several hundred member institutions, most of them having no connection with Nevada, and exhibiting no color of Nevada law. Since it was difficult to see the NCAA, not as a collective membership, but as surrogate for the one State, we held the organization's connection with Nevada too insubstantial to ground a state action claim.
>
> But dictum in *Tarkanian* pointed to a contrary result on facts like ours, with an organization whose member public schools are all within a single State. "The situation would, of course, be different if the [Association's] membership consisted entirely of institutions located within the same State, many of them public institutions created by the same sovereign." . . .
>
> B
>
> Just as we foresaw in *Tarkanian*, the "necessarily fact-bound inquiry," leads to the conclusion of state action here. The nominally private character of the Association is overborne by the pervasive entwinement of public institutions and public officials in its composition and workings, and there is no substantial reason to claim unfairness in applying constitutional standards to it.
>
> The Association is not an organization of natural persons acting on their own, but of schools, and of public schools to the

extent of 84% of the total. Under the Association's bylaws, each member school is represented by its principal or a faculty member, who has a vote in selecting members of the governing legislative council and board of control from eligible principals, assistant principals and superintendents.

Although the findings and prior opinions in this case include no express conclusion of law that public school officials act within the scope of their duties when they represent their institutions, no other view would be rational, the official nature of their involvement being shown in any number of ways. Interscholastic athletics obviously play an integral part in the public education of Tennessee, where nearly every public high school spends money on competitions among schools. Since a pickup system of interscholastic games would not do, these public teams need some mechanism to produce rules and regulate competition. The mechanism is an organization overwhelmingly composed of public school officials who select representatives (all of them public officials at the time in question here), who in turn adopt and enforce the rules that make the system work. Thus, by giving these jobs to the Association, the 290 public schools of Tennessee belonging to it can sensibly be seen as exercising their own authority to meet their own responsibilities. Unsurprisingly, then, the record indicates that half the council or board meetings documented here were held during official school hours, and that public schools have largely provided for the Association's financial support. . . .

In sum, to the extent of 84% of its membership, the Association is an organization of public schools represented by their officials acting in their official capacity to provide an integral element of secondary public schooling. There would be no recognizable Association, legal or tangible, without the public school officials, who do not merely control but overwhelmingly perform all but the purely ministerial acts by which the Association exists and functions in practical terms. Only the 16% minority of private school memberships prevents this entwinement of the Association and the public school system from being total and their identities totally indistinguishable.

To complement the entwinement of public school officials with the Association from the bottom up, the State of Tennessee has provided for entwinement from top down. State Board members are assigned ex officio to serve as members of the board of control and legislative council, and the Association's ministerial employees are treated as state employees to the extent of being eligible for membership in the state retirement system.

* * *

> The entwinement down from the State Board is therefore unmistakable, just as the entwinement up from the member public schools is overwhelming. Entwinement will support a conclusion that an ostensibly private organization ought to be charged with a public character and judged by constitutional standards; entwinement to the degree shown here requires it.

531 U.S. at 297–302 (2001). Justice Thomas, writing for Justices Rehnquist, Scalia, and Kennedy, dissented, arguing that

> [w]e have never found state action based upon mere 'entwinement.' Until today, we have found a private organization's acts to constitute state action only when the organization performed a public function; was created, coerced, or encouraged by the government; or acted in a symbiotic relationship with the government. [This decision] not only extends state-action doctrine beyond its permissible limits but also encroaches upon the realm of individual freedom that the doctrine was meant to protect.

NOTES AND QUESTIONS

1. *NCAA Versus TSSAA.* What are the distinctions between the TSSAA and the NCAA that led the Court to different results? Are those distinctions persuasive? Is there any merit to Justice Thomas' warning, 531 U.S. at 314 n.7, that "it is not difficult to imagine that application of the majority's entwinement test could change the result reached in [*Tarkanian*], so that the National Collegiate Athletic Association's actions could be found to be state action given its large number of public institution members that virtually control the organization"? For a further limitation, see the not-for-citation "unpublished" opinion in *Cohane v. NCAA*, 215 F. App'x 13 (2d Cir. 2007), allowing a complaint to proceed based on allegations that, unlike UNLV, Cohane's employer (Buffalo, a New York public university) did not contest charges adversely to the NCAA, but rather colluded with the NCAA and fired Cohane in an attempt to placate the Infractions Committee, in addition to compelling witnesses to testify and suborning perjury. The Second Circuit concluded, "at this point in the litigation, it was error for the District Court to interpret Tarkanian as holding categorically that the NCAA can never be a state actor when it conducts an investigation of a state school."

2. *Scope of Brentwood Academy.* How broadly does *Brentwood Academy* sweep? Does it now render all state high school athletic governing associations state actors subject to the Constitution, or is it narrowly limited to its specific facts? Again, Justice Thomas' dissent offers a view: "Because the majority never defines 'entwinement,' the scope of its holding is unclear. If we are

fortunate, the majority's fact-specific analysis will have little bearing beyond this case." 513 U.S. at 314. How might a state association structure itself and operate in such a way to avoid the conclusion reached in *Brentwood Academy*?

3. *Aftermath*. The Supreme Court revisited this controversy six years later. *Tennessee Secondary Sch. Ath. Ass'n v. Brentwood Academy*, 551 U.S. 291 (2007). The Court held that the TSSAA's procedures were consistent with constitutional requirements of due process and that the substance of the anti-recruiting rule did not violate the First Amendment.

C. ANTITRUST LIMITS ON THE NCAA'S INSTITUTIONAL OVERSIGHT

While the Constitution does not restrict the actions of the NCAA (assuming *Tarkanian* was correct in holding it is not a state actor), antitrust law does place limits on its power and authority. Antitrust law can restrict the manner in which the NCAA governs its member institutions. This chapter examines how antitrust law limits the NCAA's ability to restrict its member institutions in the private marketplace, as well as the salaries of university-employed coaches. Chapter 11 explores how the NCAA's regulations on student-athletes, including its amateurism rules, might also contravene the Sherman Act.

NCAA v. BOARD OF REGENTS OF THE UNIV. OF OKLAHOMA & UNIV. OF GEORGIA ATHLETIC ASS'N
468 U.S. 85 (1984)

[*See supra* Chapter 5, Section C for text of case.]

NOTES AND QUESTIONS

1. *Effect of Television on Attendance*. Part of the NCAA's antitrust defense rested on its claim that televising the games would harm the product on the field by decreasing attendance at football games. Over thirty years later, what do you think about this argument, in light of the widespread television coverage of almost all NCAA football games, at least in Big-5 conference schools?

2. *Effect of Amateurism on Attendance*. In *O'Bannon v. NCAA*, 802 F.3d 1049 (9th Cir. 2015), *see infra* Chapter 11, Section C, the NCAA relied heavily on the following language from *Board of Regents* in arguing that compensating intercollegiate athletics would destroy the product of college football:

> Moreover, the NCAA seeks to market a particular brand of football—college football. The identification of this "product" with an academic tradition differentiates college football from and makes it more popular than professional sports to which it might otherwise be

comparable, such as, for example, minor league baseball. In order to preserve the character and quality of the "product," athletes must not be paid, must be required to attend class, and the like. And the integrity of the "product" cannot be preserved except by mutual agreement; if an institution adopted such restrictions unilaterally, its effectiveness as a competitor on the playing field might soon be destroyed. Thus, the NCAA plays a vital role in enabling college football to preserve its character, and as a result enables a product to be marketed which might otherwise be unavailable. In performing this role, its actions widen consumer choice—not only the choices available to sports fans but also those available to athletes—and hence can be viewed as procompetitive.

NCAA v. Bd. of Regents, 468 U.S. at 101–02. While the district court in *O'Bannon* did not view this language as dispositive, 7 F. Supp. 955, 999 (N.D. Cal. 2014), do you think the amateur character of intercollegiate athletics (at least as the NCAA defines it) is quintessential to the product on the field? If universities started paying their athletes, would that affect attendance? This argument is part of the *O'Bannon* case, and currently being litigated in the *Jenkins* case, discussed *infra* in Chapter 11, Section C. Is this argument different than the one with respect to television that the Court rejected in *Board of Regents*? Why or why not?

3. *Economic Competition, Academic Competition, or Athletic Competition?* If an NCAA rule fixing the level of output of the NCAA members' athletic programs is anticompetitive on its face, as Justice Stevens opines, and thus can be declared in violation of section 1 under a "quick look" rule of reason, how would the NCAA rules that fix the maximum number of contests every school's teams in each sport can play survive a challenge by a member school that wanted its football team to play 15 games every year, or its baseball team to play 75 games every year? What procompetitive arguments could the NCAA make in defense of these output limiting rules? Would such arguments be any more persuasive than those rejected by the Court in *Board of Regents*? How do rules about athletic competition or academic competition differ from rules about economic competition under antitrust law?

4. *The NCAA After* Board of Regents. The practical effect of *Board of Regents* is that the NCAA lost the opportunity to receive revenue from college football, which currently is an industry worth over $1 billion annually. It learned from its mistakes quickly, though, and has been able to leverage the NCAA March Madness basketball tournament into a corporate blockbuster, alone worth over $1 billion annually. Ironically, in light of *Board of Regents*, it is the television ratings that drive this economic windfall. Most of the money is sent to the member institutions, but the NCAA retains enough to cover its entire annual operating budget.

In late 1989, the NCAA created a Cost Reduction Committee to address what many of its members felt was a "catastrophic cost spiral" affecting their athletic programs. Individual institutions felt pressure to spend more money to recruit high quality coaches and players in order to stay athletically competitive with their rivals (in the words of the NCAA, "to keep up with Joneses"). This was so, even though financial reports were indicating that many schools were losing significant amounts of money from this effort. The Cost Reduction Committee made a number of recommendations at the 1992 NCAA Convention to address this cost problem. The Convention adopted the Committee's proposed "Restricted Earnings Coach Rule." This new Rule 11.02.03 required that institutions designate one of the limited number of coaches allowed each school in each sport (with the exception of football) as a "restricted earnings coach." The NCAA set a salary limit of $12,000 during the academic year and $4,000 during the summer months—which was said to be roughly equivalent to the average amounts that schools had previously paid to those designated as "graduate assistant coaches." The NCAA Rule figure did not vary with earnings and living costs in different communities and contained no provision for annual adjustment to inflation.

In basketball, the Rule limited each team to one head coach, two assistants, and one restricted earnings coach. A number of coaches designated as RECs had previously been earning $60,000 to $70,000 a year. Early on, the new rule produced the following strange spectacle: when Duke's head coach Mike Krzyzewski (whose total annual earnings were then around $1 million) became sick during the 1994–95 season, long-time, but suddenly part-time, restricted earnings coach Pete Gaudet replaced him, earning a salary of only $12,000 (down dramatically from the $71,000 he had earned in the previous year). Gaudet could and did have another part-time job teaching physical education. Nonetheless, that job was also subject to close NCAA scrutiny: Gaudet had to be demonstrably qualified for that teaching function; his physical education rate of pay had to be the same as was paid to his counterparts in that role; and the actual portion of the physical education salary that he received had to be proportionate to the ratio of time spent on that function compared to the time spent coaching the Blue Devils.

Gaudet, along with other restricted earnings coaches in basketball, became plaintiffs in a class action antitrust suit. Two decades earlier, there had been an unsuccessful suit against another NCAA rule that had imposed limits on the size of coaching staffs, a ceiling that had required especially sizeable football programs to dismiss a number of their assistants. *See Hennessey v. NCAA*, 564 F.2d 1136 (5th Cir. 1977). Since then, though, the Supreme Court had made it clear in *Board of Regents* that many NCAA regulations might be found to violate antitrust law. In

LAW v. NCAA
134 F.3d 1010 (10th Cir. 1998)

EBEL, CIRCUIT JUDGE.

[After retracing the history and rationale offered by the NCAA for its "restricted earnings coach" rule, and the background antitrust principles and precedents epitomized by *NCAA v. Board of Regents* decision excerpted above, the circuit panel then began analyzing the substantive specifics of this case. The first issue was whether plaintiffs had to prove that this NCAA rule made a tangible difference in the market for their services, given that this particular category of coach made up just 8% of the overall number of basketball coaching positions after adding in Division II and III, high schools, and professional teams.]

The NCAA misapprehends the purpose in antitrust law of market definition, which is not an end unto itself but rather exists to illuminate a practice's effect on competition. In *Board of Regents*, the Court rejected an early identical argument from the NCAA that a plan to sell television rights could not be condemned under the antitrust laws absent proof that the NCAA had power in the market for television programming. "As a matter of law, the absence of proof of market power does not justify a naked restriction on price or output. To the contrary, when there is an agreement not to compete in terms of price or output, 'no elaborate industry analysis is required to demonstrate the anticompetitive character of such an agreement.'" No "proof of market power" is required where the very purpose and effect of a horizontal agreement is to fix prices so as to make them unresponsive to a competitive marketplace. Thus, where a practice has obvious anticompetitive effects—as does price-fixing—there is no need to prove that the defendant possesses market power. Rather, the court is justified in proceeding directly to the question of whether the procompetitive justifications advanced for the restraint outweigh the anticompetitive effects under a "quick look" rule of reason.

We find it appropriate to adopt such a quick look rule of reason in this case. Under a quick look rule of reason analysis, anticompetitive effect is established, even without a determination of the relevant market, where the plaintiff shows that a horizontal agreement to fix prices exists, that the agreement is effective, and that the price set by such an agreement is more favorable to the defendant than otherwise would have resulted from the operation of market forces. *See* Gary R. Roberts, *The NCAA, Antitrust, and Consumer Welfare*, 70 Tul. L. Rev. 2631, 2636–39 (1996) (citing *Board of Regents*, 468 U.S. at 109–10). Under this standard, the undisputed evidence supports a finding of anticompetitive effect. The NCAA adopted the REC Rule to reduce the high cost of part-time coaches' salaries, over $60,000 annually in some cases, by limiting compensation to entry-level coaches to $16,000 per year. The NCAA does not dispute that the cost-reduction has effectively reduced restricted-earnings coaches' salaries. Because the REC Rule was successful in artificially lowering the price of coaching services, no further evidence or analysis is required to find market power to set prices. Thus, in the case at bar, the district court did not need to resolve issues of fact pertaining to the definition of the relevant market in order to support its decision on summary judgment that the REC Rule is a naked price restraint.

The NCAA contends that the district court misapplied *Board of Regents*, a case in which the Court had before it detailed factual findings that resulted from a trial. The NCAA is right about the procedural posture of *Board of Regents*, but wrong about its significance. In *Board of Regents* the Supreme Court relied on the district court's findings that the television plan in fact resulted in horizontal price restraints. Because the REC Rule is a horizontal price restraint on its face, similar factual findings are not required in this case. Further, although in *Board of Regents* the Court found that the parties had proven factually that the NCAA had market power in the defined market of college football, the Court said that as a matter of law it did not need to analyze market power because horizontal price restraints are so obviously anticompetitive.

Finally, the NCAA cites *Hennessey v. NCAA*, 564 F.2d 1136 (5th Cir. 1977) (per curiam). In Hennessey, assistant football and basketball coaches challenged a NCAA bylaw limiting the number of assistant coaches member institutions could employ at any one time. The Fifth Circuit upheld the rule, concluding that the plaintiff failed to show that the rule was an unreasonable restraint of trade after weighing the anticompetitive effects with the procompetitive benefits of the restriction.

Hennessey is not controlling for a variety of reasons. First, the REC Rule is distinguishable from the agreement at issue in *Hennessey*. *Hennessey* addresses a restriction on the number of assistant coaches that a Division I school could employ whereas the REC Rule limits salary of a certain category of coaches. Therefore, the analysis of the reasonableness of the restraint in *Hennessey*, which did not involve a naked restriction on price, will not control the analysis of the reasonableness of the REC Rule.

Second, the *Hennessey* court placed the burden of showing the unreasonableness of the coaching restriction in that case on the plaintiff and then found that the plaintiff could not make such a showing because the rule had only recently been implemented. In our analysis, the plaintiff only has the burden of establishing the anticompetitive effect of the restraint at issue. Once the plaintiff meets that burden, which the coaches have done in this case by showing the naked and effective price-fixing character of the agreement, the burden shifts to the defendant to justify the restraint as a "reasonable" one. It is on this step that the defendant NCAA stumbles. Thus, we disagree with the Fifth Circuit's allocation of the burden of proof in *Hennessey*, and we note that this shift in the burden of proof could explain the difference in outcome between our case and *Hennessey*.

B. Procompetitive Rationales

Under a rule of reason analysis, an agreement to restrain trade may still survive scrutiny under Section 1 if the procompetitive benefits of the restraint justify the anticompetitive effects. Justifications offered under the rule of reason may be considered only to the extent that they tend to show that, on balance, "the challenged restraint enhances competition." *Board of Regents*, 468 U.S. at 104.

In *Board of Regents* the Supreme Court recognized that certain horizontal restraints, such as the conditions of the contest and the eligibility of participants, are justifiable under the antitrust laws because they are necessary to create the product of competitive college sports. Thus, the only legitimate rationales that we will recognize in support of the REC Rule are those necessary to produce competitive intercollegiate sports. The NCAA advanced three justifications for the salary limits: retaining entry-level coaching positions; reducing costs; and maintaining competitive equity. We address each of them in turn.

1. Retention of Entry-Level Positions

The NCAA argues that the plan serves the procompetitive goal of retaining an entry-level coaching position. The NCAA asserts that the plan will allow younger, less experienced coaches entry into Division I coaching positions. While opening up coaching positions for younger people may have social value apart from its effect on competition, we may not consider such values unless they impact upon competition. *See Superior Court Trial Lawyers*, 493 U.S. at 423–24 (rejecting argument by trial lawyers that boycott of court-appointed work was justified to promote the social value of increasing the quality of representation); *FTC v. Indiana Fed'n of Dentists*, 476 U.S. 447, 462–64 (1986) (refusing to consider ethical policy of insuring proper dental care as a valid procompetitive end); *Board of Regents*, 468 U.S. at 117 (rejecting justifications offered to support a challenged restraint that do not promote competition as "inconsistent with the basic policy of the Sherman Act"); *National Soc'y of Prof'l Engineers*, 435 U.S. at 695–96 (holding that policy goals such as protecting public safety and promoting ethical behavior do not qualify as legitimate procompetitive objectives unless they serve to "regulate and promote" competition).

The NCAA also contends that limiting one of the four available coaching positions on a Division I basketball team to an entry level position will create more balanced competition by barring some teams from hiring four experienced coaches instead of three. However, the REC Rule contained no restrictions other than salary designed to insure that the position would be filled by entry-level applicants; it could be filled with experienced applicants. In addition, under the REC Rule, schools can still pay restricted-earnings coaches more than $16,000 per year by hiring them for physical education or other teaching positions. In fact, the evidence in the record tends to demonstrate that at least some schools designated persons with many years of experience as the restricted-earnings coach. The NCAA did not present any evidence showing that restricted-earnings positions have been filled by entry-level applicants or that the rules will be effective over time in accomplishing this goal. Nothing in the record suggests that the salary limits for restricted-earnings coaches will be effective at creating entry-level positions. Thus, the NCAA failed to present a triable issue of fact as to whether preserving entry-level positions served a legitimate procompetitive end of balancing competition.

2. Cost Reduction

The NCAA next advances the justification that the plan will cut costs. However, cost-cutting by itself is not a valid procompetitive justification. If it were, any group of competing buyers could agree on maximum prices. Lower prices cannot justify a cartel's control of prices charged by suppliers, because the cartel ultimately robs the suppliers of the normal fruits of their enterprises. Further, setting maximum prices reduces the incentive among suppliers to improve their products. Likewise, in our case, coaches have less incentive to improve their performance if their salaries are capped. As the Supreme Court reiterated in *Superior Court Trial Lawyers*, 493 U.S. at 423, "the Sherman Act reflects a legislative judgment that ultimately competition will produce not only lower prices, but also better goods and services ... This judgment recognizes that all elements of a bargain—quality, service, safety, and durability—and not just the immediate cost, are favorably affected by the free opportunity to select among alternative offers."

The NCAA adopted the REC Rule because without it competition would lead to higher prices. The REC Rule was proposed as a way to prevent Division I schools from engaging in behavior the association termed "keeping up with the Joneses," *i.e.*, competing. However, the NCAA cannot argue that competition for coaches is an evil because the Sherman Act "precludes inquiry into the question whether competition is good or bad." *National Soc'y of Prof'l Engineers*, 435 U.S. at 695.

While increasing output, creating operating efficiencies, making a new product available, enhancing product or service quality, and widening consumer choice have been accepted by courts as justifications for otherwise anticompetitive agreements, mere profitability or cost savings have not qualified as a defense under the antitrust laws. The NCAA's cost containment justification is illegitimate because the NCAA

> ... improperly assumes that antitrust law should not apply to condemn the creation of market power in an input market. The exercise of market power by a group of buyers virtually always results in lower costs to the buyers—a consequence which arguably is beneficial to the members of the industry and ultimately their consumers. If holding down costs by the exercise of market power over suppliers, rather than just by increased efficiency, is a procompetitive effect justifying joint conduct, then section 1 can never apply to input markets or buyer cartels. That is not and cannot be the law.

Roberts, 70 Tul. L. Rev. at 2643. Reducing costs for member institutions, without more, does not justify the anticompetitive effects of the REC Rule.

The NCAA argues that reducing costs can be considered a procompetitive justification because doing so is necessary to maintain the existence of competitive intercollegiate sports. Emphasizing the deficits many college sports programs faced prior to the adoption of the REC Rule, the NCAA quotes with approval language from the opinion in *Hennessey* to support its claim that reducing costs serves as a procompetitive benefit:

> Colleges with more successful programs, both competitively and economically, were seen as taking advantage of their success by expanding their programs, to the ultimate detriment of the whole system of intercollegiate athletics. Financial pressures upon many members, not merely to "catch up", but to "keep up," were beginning to threaten both the competitive, and the amateur, nature of the programs, leading quite possibly to abandonment by many. "Minor" and "minority" sports were viewed as imperiled by concentration upon the "money makers," such as varsity football and basketball.
>
> Bylaw 12–1 [the rule at issue in *Hennessey*] was, with other rules adopted at the same time, intended to be an "economy measure". In this sense it was both in design and effect one having commercial impact. But the fundamental objective in mind was to preserve and foster competition in intercollegiate athletics-by curtailing, as it were, potentially monopolistic practices by the more powerful, and to reorient the programs into their traditional role as amateur sports operating as part of the educational process.

564 F.2d at 1153.

We are dubious that the goal of cost reductions can serve as a legally sufficient justification for a buyers' agreement to fix prices even if such cost reductions are necessary to save inefficient or unsuccessful competitors from failure. Nevertheless, we need not consider whether cost reductions may have been required to "save" intercollegiate athletics and whether such an objective served as a legitimate procompetitive end because the NCAA presents no evidence that limits on restricted-earning coaches' salaries would be successful in reducing deficits, let alone that such reductions were necessary to save college basketball. Moreover, the REC Rule does not equalize the overall amount of money Division I schools are permitted to spend on their basketball programs. There is no reason to think that the money saved by a school on the salary of a restricted-earnings coach will not be put into another aspect of the school's basketball program, such as equipment or even another coach's salary, thereby increasing inequity in that area.

3. Maintaining Competitiveness

We note that the NCAA must be able to ensure some competitive equity between member institutions in order to produce a marketable product: a "team must try to establish itself as a winner, but it must not win so often and so convincingly that the outcome will never be in doubt, or else there will be no marketable 'competition.'" Michael Jay Kaplan, *Annotation, Application of Federal Antitrust Laws to Professional Sports*, 18 A.L.R. Fed. 489 § 2(a) (1974). The NCAA asserts that the REC Rule will help to maintain competitive equity by preventing wealthier schools from placing a more experienced, higher-priced coach in the position of restricted-earnings coach. The NCAA again cites *Hennessey* to support its position, and again we find *Hennessey* to be unpersuasive for the reasons previously articulated.

While the REC Rule will equalize the salaries paid to entry-level coaches in Division I schools, it is not clear that the REC Rule will equalize the experience level of such coaches.[15] Nowhere does the NCAA prove that the salary restrictions enhance competition, level an uneven playing field, or reduce coaching inequities. Rather, the NCAA only presented evidence that the cost reductions would be achieved in such a way so as to maintain without "significantly altering," "adversely affecting," or "disturbing" the existing competitive balance. The undisputed record reveals that the REC Rule is nothing more than a cost-cutting measure and shows that the only consideration the NCAA gave to competitive balance was simply to structure the rule so as not to exacerbate competitive imbalance. Thus, on its face, the REC Rule is not directed towards competitive balance nor is the nexus between the rule and a compelling need to maintain competitive

---

[15] For example, some more-experienced coaches may take restricted-earnings coach positions with programs such as those at Duke or North Carolina, despite the lower salary, because of the national prominence of those programs. In fact, absent the REC Rule, the market might produce greater equity in coaching talent, because a school with a less-prominent basketball program might be able to entice a more-experienced coach away from a prominent program by offering a higher salary.

balance sufficiently clear on this record to withstand a motion for summary judgment.

Affirmed.

NOTES AND QUESTIONS

1. *Aftermath.* After the Tenth Circuit rejected the NCAA's appeal of the liability verdict in this case, the district court held a trial on damages. This 1996 jury verdict awarded $22.3 million in actual damages, which was automatically trebled to $66.9 million by the Clayton Antitrust Act, with legal fees also added. The NCAA then filed an appeal of the damage calculation, but the parties settled the case in the spring of 1999 with the NCAA agreeing to pay a total of $54.5 million to the plaintiffs and their lawyers. It took another year for the groups on both sides (both the coaches and the schools) to decide how to divide up this settlement and its costs.

2. *Implications for Student-Athletes?* District Court Judge Vratil had earlier rejected for lack of factual support the NCAA's defense of its coaching salary cap on only the last and least paid coach on each team as necessary to preserve the fiscal solvency of colleges. She also rejected the argument on the legal ground that an anticompetitive restraint on the labor market could not be supported by procompetitive justifications in the product market for college sports. Is this legal position compatible with the host of antitrust cases we have read from professional sports or the Supreme Court's dictum in *Board of Regents*? Would it permit the NCAA to justify academic and amateurism regulations on student-athlete eligibility? Most importantly, would it permit strict limits on athletic scholarships and other compensation? If applied literally, would this in effect recreate a new rule of per se illegality?

3. *What's Really Going on Here?* The Cost Reduction Commission found that many schools were spending money on coaches' salaries that were not being recouped by revenues from big-time sports. Why do universities spend more on money-losing programs?

D. CONTRACTS

Two kinds of sports contracts are unique in intercollegiate athletics. The first is the coach contract, which is extraordinary in its economic impact on the institution (and state in many cases). Head football and basketball coaches are typically among the highest paid state employees, serve term contracts, and often have large buyout provisions for early termination. In short, the economic impact of these contracts on the university makes them worthy of serious attention.

Second, in recent years, conferences have sought to stem the tide of schools moving out of their conference. As a result, the conferences create by-laws and contractual arrangements that require institutions leaving a conference to pay an exit fee, usually amounting to tens of millions of dollars. In addition, conferences require departing institutions to wait a certain time period before moving their athletic teams to the new conference. These contracts remain important because their limits, and the ability of schools to circumvent those limits, can impact a number of institutions and conferences in significant economic ways.

1. COACHING CONTRACTS

With the removal of any restrictions on coach salaries, the free agent market for coaches has exploded in recent years. The top college football coaches now make upwards of $7 million per year, and the growth in salaries has also extended to assistant football coaches, some of whom make over $1 million per year. Critics have decried this increase in pay, but after *Law v. NCAA*, antitrust law seems to prohibit any sort of salary cap or limit on coach pay. As such, contract law has become increasingly important. Unfortunately for universities, the bargaining power lies with the coaches in large part because of external pressure on university presidents to have competitive athletic programs, particularly in football and/or basketball.

Besides salary and duration, another important provision of coaching contracts addresses termination. When institutions terminate coaches, they often must pay out the remainder of the salary due under the contract, unless the coach has behaved in a way that results in him being fired for cause. Having an unsuccessful team on the field typically does not constitute "cause" for termination under most contracts. The institution, though, has the second worry of the coach leaving to coach a higher paying or more athletically prominent institution. The next case examines one university's attempt to address that issue.

VANDERBILT UNIVERSITY V. DINARDO
174 F.3d 751 (6th Cir. 1999)

GIBSON, CIRCUIT JUDGE.

Gerry DiNardo resigned as Vanderbilt's head football coach to become the head football coach for Louisiana State University. As a result, Vanderbilt University brought this breach of contract action. The district court entered summary judgment for Vanderbilt, awarding $281,886.43 pursuant to a damage provision in DiNardo's employment contract with Vanderbilt. DiNardo appeals, arguing that the district court erred in concluding: (1) that the contract provision was an enforceable liquidated damage provision and not an unlawful penalty under Tennessee law; (2) that Vanderbilt did not waive its right to liquidated damages; (3) that the Addendum to the contract was enforceable; and (4) that the Addendum applied to the damage provision of the original contract. DiNardo also argues that there are disputed issues of material fact precluding summary judgment. We affirm the district court's ruling that the employment contract contained an enforceable liquidated damage provision and the award of liquidated damages under the original contract. We conclude, however, that there are genuine issues of material fact as to whether the Addendum was enforceable. We therefore reverse the judgment awarding liquidated damages under the Addendum and remand the case to the district court.

On December 3, 1990, Vanderbilt and DiNardo executed an employment contract hiring DiNardo to be Vanderbilt's head football coach. Section one of the contract provided:

> The University hereby agrees to hire Mr. DiNardo for a period of five (5) years from the date hereof with Mr. DiNardo's assurance that he will serve the entire term of this Contract, a long-term commitment by Mr. DiNardo being important to the University's desire for a stable intercollegiate football program. . . .

The contract also contained reciprocal liquidated damage provisions.

Vanderbilt agreed to pay DiNardo his remaining salary should Vanderbilt replace him as football coach, and DiNardo agreed to reimburse Vanderbilt should he leave before his contract expired. Section eight of the contract stated:

> Mr. DiNardo recognizes that his promise to work for the University for the entire term of this 5-year Contract is of the essence of this Contract to the University. Mr. DiNardo also recognizes that the University is making a highly valuable investment in his continued employment by entering into this Contract and its investment would be lost were he to resign or otherwise terminate his employment as Head Football Coach with the University prior to the expiration of this Contract. Accordingly, Mr. DiNardo agrees that in the event he resigns or otherwise terminates his employment as Head Football Coach (as opposed to his resignation or termination from another position at the University to which he may have been reassigned), prior to the expiration of this Contract, and is employed or performing services for a person or institution other than the University, he will pay to the University as liquidated damages an amount equal to his Base Salary, less amounts that would otherwise be deducted or withheld from his Base Salary for income and social security tax purposes, multiplied by the number of years (or portion(s) thereof) remaining on the Contract.

During contract negotiations, section eight was modified at DiNardo's request so that damages would be calculated based on net, rather than gross, salary. Vanderbilt initially set DiNardo's salary at $100,000 per year. DiNardo received salary increases in 1992, 1993, and 1994.

On August 14, 1994, Paul Hoolahan, Vanderbilt's Athletic Director, went to Bell Buckle, Tennessee, where the football team was practicing, to talk to DiNardo about a contract extension. (DiNardo's original contract would expire on January 5, 1996). Hoolahan offered DiNardo a two-year contract extension. DiNardo told Hoolahan that he wanted to extend his contract, but that he also wanted to discuss the extension with Larry DiNardo, his brother and attorney.

Hoolahan telephoned John Callison, Deputy General Counsel for Vanderbilt, and asked him to prepare a contract extension. Callison drafted an addendum to the original employment contract which provided for a two-year extension of the original contract, specifying a termination date of January 5, 1998. Vanderbilt's Chancellor, Joe B. Wyatt, and Hoolahan signed the Addendum.

On August 17, Hoolahan returned to Bell Buckle with the Addendum. He took it to DiNardo at the practice field where they met in Hoolahan's car. DiNardo stated that Hoolahan did not present him with the complete two-page addendum, but only the second page, which was the signature page. DiNardo asked, "what am I signing?" Hoolahan explained to DiNardo, "[i]t means that your contract as it presently exists will be extended for two years with everything else remaining exactly the same as it existed in the present contract." Before DiNardo signed the Addendum, he told Hoolahan, "Larry needs to see a copy before this thing is finalized." Hoolahan agreed, and DiNardo signed the document. DiNardo explained that he agreed to sign the document because he thought the extension was the "best thing" for the football program and that he "knew ultimately, Larry would look at it, and before it would become finalized he would approve it." Hoolahan took the signed document without giving DiNardo a copy.

On August 16, Larry DiNardo had a telephone conversation with Callison. They briefly talked about the contract extension, discussing a salary increase. Larry DiNardo testified that as of that date he did not know that Gerry DiNardo had signed the Addendum, or even that one yet existed.

DiNardo stated publicly that he was "excited" about the extension of his contract, and there was an article in the August 20, 1994, newspaper, *The Tennessean*, reporting that DiNardo's contract had been extended by two years.

On August 25, 1994, Callison faxed to Larry DiNardo "a copy of the draft Addendum to Gerry's contract." Callison wrote on the fax transmittal sheet: "[l]et me know if you have any questions." The copy sent was unsigned. Callison and Larry DiNardo had several telephone conversations in late August and September, primarily discussing the television and radio contract. Callison testified that he did not recall discussing the Addendum, explaining: "[t]he hot issue . . . was the radio and television contract." On September 27, Callison sent a fax to Larry DiNardo concerning the television and radio contract, and also added: "I would like your comments on the contract extension." Larry DiNardo testified that he neither participated in the drafting nor suggested any changes to the Addendum.

In November 1994, Louisiana State University contacted Vanderbilt in hopes of speaking with DiNardo about becoming the head football coach for L.S.U. Hoolahan gave DiNardo permission to speak to L.S.U. about the position. On December 12, 1994, DiNardo announced that he was accepting the L.S.U. position.

Vanderbilt sent a demand letter to DiNardo seeking payment of liquidated damages under section eight of the contract. Vanderbilt believed that DiNardo was liable for three years of his net salary: one year under the original contract and two years under the Addendum. DiNardo did not respond to Vanderbilt's demand for payment.

Vanderbilt brought this action against DiNardo for breach of contract. DiNardo removed the action to federal court, and both parties filed motions for summary judgment. The district court held that section eight was an enforceable liquidated damages provision, not an unlawful penalty, and that the damages provided under section eight were reasonable. *Vanderbilt University v. DiNardo,* 974 F. Supp. 638, 643 (M.D. Tenn. 1997). The court held that Vanderbilt did not waive its contractual rights under section eight when it granted DiNardo permission to talk to L.S.U. and that the Addendum was enforceable and extended the contract for two years. *Id.* at 643–45. The court entered judgment against DiNardo for $281,886.43. *Id.* at 645. DiNardo appeals.

I.

DiNardo first claims that section eight of the contract is an unenforceable penalty under Tennessee law. DiNardo argues that the provision is not a liquidated damage provision but a "thinly disguised, overly broad non-compete provision," unenforceable under Tennessee law.

* * *

Contracting parties may agree to the payment of liquidated damages in the event of a breach. *See Beasley v. Horrell,* 864 S.W.2d 45, 48 (Tenn.Ct.App.1993). The term "liquidated damages" refers to an amount determined by the parties to be just compensation for damages should a breach occur. *See id.* Courts will not enforce such a provision, however, if the stipulated amount constitutes a penalty. *See id.* A penalty is designed to coerce performance by punishing default. *See id.* In Tennessee, a provision will be considered one for liquidated damages, rather than a penalty, if it is reasonable in relation to the anticipated damages for breach, measured prospectively at the time the contract was entered into, and not grossly disproportionate to the actual damages. *See Beasley,* 864 S.W.2d at 48; *Kimbrough & Co. v. Schmitt,* 939 S.W.2d 105, 108 (Tenn.Ct.App.1996). When these conditions are met, particularly the first, the parties probably intended the provision to be for liquidated damages. However, any doubt as to the character of the contract provision will be resolved in favor of finding it a penalty. *See Beasley,* 864 S.W.2d at 48.

The district court held that the use of a formula based on DiNardo's salary to calculate liquidated damages was reasonable "given the nature of the unquantifiable damages in the case." 974 F. Supp. at 642. The court held that parties to a contract may include consequential damages and even damages not usually awarded by law in a liquidated damage provision provided that they were contemplated by the parties. *Id.* at 643. The court explained:

> The potential damage to [Vanderbilt] extends far beyond the cost of merely hiring a new head football coach. It is this uncertain potentiality that the parties sought to address by providing for a sum certain to apply towards anticipated expenses and losses. It is impossible to estimate how the loss of a head football coach will affect alumni relations, public support, football ticket sales, contributions, etc.... As such, to require a precise formula for calculating damages resulting from the breach of contract by a college head football coach would be tantamount to barring the parties from stipulating to liquidated damages evidence in advance.

Id. at 642.

DiNardo contends that there is no evidence that the parties contemplated that the potential damage from DiNardo's resignation would go beyond the cost of hiring a replacement coach. He argues that his salary has no relationship to Vanderbilt's damages and that the liquidated damage amount is unreasonable and shows that the parties did not intend the provision to be for liquidated damages.

DiNardo's theory of the parties' intent, however, does not square with the record. The contract language establishes that Vanderbilt wanted the five-year contract because "a long-term commitment" by DiNardo was "important to the University's desire for a stable intercollegiate football program," and that this commitment was of "essence" to the contract. Vanderbilt offered the two-year contract extension to DiNardo well over a year before his original contract expired. Both parties understood that the extension was to provide stability to the program, which helped in recruiting players and retaining assistant coaches. Thus, undisputed evidence, and reasonable inferences therefrom, establish that both parties understood and agreed that DiNardo's resignation would result in Vanderbilt suffering damage beyond the cost of hiring a replacement coach.

This evidence also refutes DiNardo's argument that the district court erred in presuming that DiNardo's resignation would necessarily cause damage to the University. That the University may actually benefit from a coaching change (as DiNardo suggests) matters little, as we measure the reasonableness of the liquidated damage provision at the time the parties entered the contract, not when the breach occurred, *Kimbrough & Co.*, 939 S.W.2d at 108, and we hardly think the parties entered the contract anticipating that DiNardo's resignation would benefit Vanderbilt.

The stipulated damage amount is reasonable in relation to the amount of damages that could be expected to result from the breach. As we stated, the parties understood that Vanderbilt would suffer damage should DiNardo prematurely terminate his contract, and that these actual damages would be difficult to measure. *See Kimbrough & Co.*, 939 S.W.2d at 108.

Our conclusion is consistent with a decision by the Tennessee Court of Appeals in *Smith v. American General Corporation,* No 87-79-II, 1987 WL 15144 (Tenn. Ct. App. Aug.5, 1987). In that case, an individual sued his former employer for breach of an employment contract. *Id.* at *1. The employee had a three-year contract, and the contract provided for a single lump sum payment of all remaining compensation in the event of a breach by the employer. *Id.* at *1–2. When the employer reduced the employee's duties, he quit, and sued seeking to enforce the liquidated damage provision. The employer argued the provision was a penalty, and that the employee should only be able to recover his total salary under the contract reduced by the employee's earnings in his new job. The Tennessee court rejected these arguments, concluding that even though the usual measure of damage is the difference between an employee's old and new salaries, here, the parties reasonably contemplated "special damage," including the intangible damage to the employee's prestige and career. *Id.* at *6. The court found that the parties expressly recognized the importance to the employee of the continuation of his employment, and it was "clearly within the contemplation of the parties that, if [the employee] should not be retained in his position . . . he would suffer unliquidated damages which would be difficult of proof." *Id.* at *7.

Our reasoning follows that of *Smith.* Vanderbilt hired DiNardo for a unique and specialized position, and the parties understood that the amount of damages could not be easily ascertained should a breach occur. Contrary to DiNardo's suggestion, Vanderbilt did not need to undertake an analysis to determine actual damages, and using the number of years left on the contract multiplied by the salary per year was a reasonable way to calculate damages considering the difficulty of ascertaining damages with certainty. *See Kimbrough & Co.*, 939 S.W.2d at 108. The fact that liquidated damages declined each year DiNardo remained under contract, is directly tied to the parties' express understanding of the importance of a long-term commitment from DiNardo. Furthermore, the liquidated damages provision was reciprocal and the result of negotiations between two parties, each of whom was represented by counsel.

We also reject DiNardo's argument that a question of fact remains as to whether the parties intended section eight to be a "reasonable estimate" of damages. The liquidated damages are in line with Vanderbilt's estimate of its actual damages. *See Kimbrough & Co.*, 939 S.W.2d at 108–09. Vanderbilt presented evidence that it incurred expenses associated with recruiting a new head coach of $27,000.00; moving expenses for the new coaching staff of $86,840; and a compensation difference between the coaching staffs of $184,311. The stipulated damages clause is reasonable under the circumstances, and we affirm the district court's conclusion that the liquidated damages clause is enforceable under Tennessee law.

* * *

[The Court rejected DiNardo's argument that Vanderbilt waived its right to liquidated damages when it granted DiNardo permission to discuss the coaching position with L.S.U. The Court, by contrast accepted DiNardo's argument that there was a factual dispute with respect to the enforceability of an addendum to the contract, and remanded that part of the case to the district court for trial. The parties settled subsequent to the Sixth Circuit's decision.]

* * *

We affirm in part, reverse in part, and remand the case to the district court for further proceedings consistent with this opinion.

DAVID A. NELSON, CIRCUIT JUDGE, concurring in part and dissenting in part.

If section eight of the contract was designed primarily to quantify, in an objectively reasonable way, damages that the university could be expected to suffer in the event of a breach, such damages being difficult to measure in the absence of an agreed formula, the provision is enforceable as a legitimate liquidated damages clause. If section eight was designed primarily to punish Coach DiNardo for taking a job elsewhere, however, the provision is a penalty unenforceable under Tennessee law. My colleagues on the panel and I are in agreement, I believe, on both of these propositions. We disagree, however, as to section eight's primary function.

It seems to me that the provision was designed to function as a penalty, not as a liquidation of the university's damages. Insofar as the court holds otherwise, I am constrained to dissent. In all other respects, I concur in Judge Gibson's opinion and in the judgment entered pursuant to it.

My principal reasons for viewing section eight as a penalty are these: (1) although the damages flowing from a premature resignation would normally be the same whether or not Coach DiNardo took a job elsewhere, section eight does not purport to impose liability for liquidated damages unless the coach accepts another job; (2) the section eight formula incorporates other variables that bear little or no relation to any reasonable approximation of anticipated damages; and (3) there is no evidence that the parties were attempting, in section eight, to come up with a reasonable estimate of the university's probable loss if the coach left. I shall offer a few words of explanation on each of these points.

Section eight does not make Coach DiNardo liable for any liquidated damages at all, interestingly enough, unless, during the unexpired term of his contract, he "is employed or performing services for a person or institution other than the University. . . ." But how the coach spends his post-resignation time could not reasonably be expected to affect the university's damages; should the coach choose to quit in order to lie on a beach somewhere, the university would presumably suffer the same damages that it would suffer if he quit to coach for another school. The logical inference, therefore, would seem to be that section eight was intended to penalize the coach for taking another job, and was not intended to make the university whole by liquidating any damages suffered as a result of being left in the lurch.

This inference is strengthened, as I see it, by a couple of other anomalies in the stipulated damages formula. First, I am aware of no reason to believe that damages arising from the need to replace a prematurely departing coach could reasonably be expected to vary in direct proportion to the number of years left on the coach's contract. Section eight, however, provides that for every additional year remaining on the contract, the stipulated damages will go up by the full amount of the annual take-home pay contemplated under the contract. Like the "other employment" proviso, this makes the formula look more like a penalty than anything else.

Second, the use of a "take-home pay" measuring stick suggests that the function of the stick was to rap the coach's knuckles and not to measure the university's loss. Such factors as the number of tax exemptions claimed by the coach, or the percentage of his pay that he might elect to shelter in a 401(k) plan, would obviously bear no relation at all to the university's anticipated damages.

Finally, the record before us contains no evidence that the contracting parties gave any serious thought to attempting to measure the actual effect that a premature departure could be expected to have on the university's bottom line. On the contrary, the record affirmatively shows that the university did not attempt to determine whether the section eight formula would yield a result reasonably approximating anticipated damages. The record shows that the university could not explain how its anticipated damages might be affected by the coach's obtaining employment elsewhere, this being a subject that the draftsman of the contract testified he had never thought about. And the record shows that the question of why the number of years remaining on the contract would have any bearing on the amount of the university's damages was never analyzed either.

In truth and in fact, in my opinion, any correspondence between the result produced by the section eight formula and a reasonable approximation of anticipated damages would be purely coincidental. What section eight prescribes is a penalty, pure and simple, and a penalty may not be enforced under Tennessee law. On remand, therefore, in addition to instructing the district court to try the factual questions identified in Judge Gibson's opinion, I would instruct the court to determine the extent of any actual damages suffered by the university as a result of Coach DiNardo's breach of his contract. Whether more than the section eight figure or less, I believe, the university's actual damages should be the measure of its recovery.

NOTES AND QUESTIONS

1. *Aftermath.* DiNardo's tenure at LSU was mixed. He had a promising start, reversing six straight LSU losing seasons with two Independence Bowl wins and a Peach Bowl win. This was enough to convince LSU boosters to pay Vanderbilt his damages after he lost the lawsuit. After two consecutive losing seasons, though, LSU fired DiNardo and replaced him with Nick Saban, who won a national championship at LSU.

2. *Enforceable Liquidated Damages?* The court held that the contractual provision was an enforceable liquidated damages provision because the damages that DiNardo owed were in reasonable relation to the damages actually suffered. Do you agree with the court's reading of the facts? On the field, one can make a case that DiNardo's performance (19 wins in 4 years) was significantly better than the coaches immediately before (10 wins in 5 years) or after (9 wins in 4 years), but as the court indicated, the damages issue goes beyond wins and losses. Nonetheless, Vanderbilt did not have a winning season or go to a bowl game until 2008, almost 15 years after DiNardo left. In light of *DiNardo*, how should universities draft contract provisions covering coaches leaving? Is the model Vanderbilt used one you would follow?

3. *Effect of Athletics on Contract Interpretation.* To what degree did the nature of DiNardo's job as a football coach shape the outcome of this case? Does the speculative nature of the true cost of replacing a football coach inform the

liquidated damages determination? If a university put a similar provision in an academic dean's contract, would a court view it the same way?

4. *Property Interests.* Do coaches have constitutional property interests in their positions arising out of their contracts? It depends upon the language used by the parties in drafting the contract. If a university cannot fire a coach without cause, then the coach retains a property interest in the salary due to him under the contract. On the other hand, if the coach has a contract that is "not continuing in nature" or "may be terminated at the pleasure of the board," then no property interest exists. *See Kish v. Iowa Central Community College*, 142 F. Supp. 2d 1084, 1097 (N.D. Iowa 2001) (citing *Board of Regents v. Roth*, 408 U.S. 564 (1972) ("To succeed on a procedural due process claim, [a public employee] must establish that he had a constitutionally protected property interest, that is, a 'legitimate claim of entitlement' to continued employment by the [public entity].").

5. *Contract Perquisites.* In addition to salary, college football and basketball coaches often receive a package of benefits, some through the university, some through third parties. These can include radio and television shows, automobiles, and country club memberships. The contractual language that delineates these benefits is important, particularly when the university terminates the coach. Georgia Tech fired its head football coach, Franklin "Pepper" Rodgers in 1979. Rodgers' contract, however, continued through 1981, and his contract was with the athletic association.

Rodgers sued to retain the perquisites listed in his contract until its end date, even though he was no longer the head football coach. In *Rodgers v. Georgia Tech Athletic Association*, 303 S.E.2d 467 (1983), the Georgia Court of Appeals held that Rodgers was not entitled to any perquisites related to the performance of the job as head coach, such as a secretary and funds to attend football conferences, but reversed summary judgment with respect to items that did not relate directly to the job of coaching the team, such as tickets to professional sporting events and use of an automobile.

6. *Sovereign Immunity.* Mike Leach was the successful coach of the Texas Tech football team from 2000–09. In 2009, however, Texas Tech fired Leach for cause following an incident involving one of his players, Adam James. James accused Leach of forcing him to stand in an equipment room for the duration of practice when James refused to practice while suffering from a concussion. Texas Tech subsequently fired Leach, calling his refusal to apologize to James "an act of insubordination."

Leach sued Texas Tech for wrongful termination, alleging that his firing related to acrimonious contract negotiations, not the James incident. Unfortunately for Leach, the Texas Court of Appeals held that the common law doctrine of sovereign immunity, based on language in the Texas Constitution, barred Leach's suit against Texas Tech. *See Leach v. Texas Tech University*, 335 S.W.3d 386 (2011). Specifically, the court held that the university did not waive its sovereign immunity with respect to breach of contract claims. If certain state universities are immune from breach of contract suits, how does the negotiation of a contract between a coach and a university change?

2. CONFERENCE REALIGNMENT

In addition to coach contracts, conferences have, in recent years, engaged in more robust contractual arrangements with their member institutions. The first wave of conference realignment occurred in 1991, with Arkansas and South Carolina moving to the Southeastern Conference (SEC), expanding it to 12 teams and allowing for a lucrative conference championship game in football. Soon after, Florida State joined the Atlantic Coast Conference (ACC) and Penn State joined the Big Ten. In 1996, the Big 8 Conference and the Southwest Conference joined to form the Big 12.

In 2003–04, Boston College, Miami, and Virginia Tech all left the Big East to join the ACC. The ACC paid $5 million to settle a lawsuit filed by the Big East over the defections. Conferences began to restructure their contracts with member institutions, imposing economic penalties for leaving and instituting waiting periods.

As television money increased, however, further shifts became inevitable. The rise of the Big Ten network, and the University of Texas' own network opened the door to more lucrative arrangements that depended on having access to major media markets. The SEC, ACC, and Pac-12 have all followed suit, establishing their own television networks.

The next major shift of schools came during this growth, beginning in 2011, with the SEC expanding to add Missouri and Texas A&M; the Big Ten expanding to include Rutgers, Nebraska, and Maryland; the ACC again raiding the Big East in welcoming Louisville, Pittsburgh, Syracuse, and Notre Dame (in basketball only).

As growing leagues sought to get a foothold in major television markets, leagues left behind sought to receive some compensation for their economic loss, particularly in light of the contractual provisions penalizing leaving. The attempt to enforce such contracts demonstrates the slippery nature of conference-university relationships in major college sports. The next case is one such lawsuit.

ACC v. UNIVERSITY OF MARYLAND
230 N.C. App. 429, 751 S.E.2d 612 (2013)

HUNTER, J.

[In 2012, the University of Maryland decided to end their long-standing affiliation with the Atlantic Coast Conference to join the Big Ten Conference. The ACC filed a lawsuit in North Carolina state court seeking a declaration that the substantial financial penalties for withdrawing from the conference provided for in Conference policies were legally valid. Maryland contested the court's jurisdiction, and this appeal followed.]

* * *

The ACC is a North Carolina unincorporated nonprofit association with its principal place of business in Greensboro, North Carolina. When the complaint in this action was filed, the ACC's membership consisted of twelve colleges and universities located along the eastern seaboard. In addition to the University of Maryland, the ACC's membership included Boston College, Clemson University, Duke University, Florida State University, the Georgia Institute of Technology, the University of Miami, the University of North Carolina, North Carolina State University, the University of Virginia, Virginia Polytechnic Institute and State University, and Wake Forest University.

On 13 September 2011, in response to a growing concern that a member institution's withdrawal from the ACC could cause financial damage to the conference, the Council unanimously voted to amend the ACC Constitution to establish a mandatory withdrawal payment at one and one-quarter times the total operating budget of the ACC. Defendants' representative on the Council proposed the factor used in the calculation and voted for the amendment.

The ACC alleges that after the September 2011 vote, the potential financial damage that would result from a member institution's withdrawal substantially increased. In response, the Council voted in September 2012 to change the formula used to calculate the withdrawal payment from one and one-quarter to three times the total operating budget of the ACC. Defendants' representative on the Council voted against this measure.

Not long after the Council voted to increase the withdrawal payment, Defendants informed the ACC on 19 November 2012 of their decision to withdraw from the ACC. On the same day, Defendants held a press conference publicly announcing their decision to withdraw from the ACC and to join the Big Ten Conference.

The ACC alleges that the University of Maryland's withdrawal from the ACC subjects them to a mandatory withdrawal payment in the amount of $52,266,342. [Maryland objected on grounds of lack of personal jurisdiction and "based upon the sovereign immunity of the State of Maryland."]

* * *

[The Court found that it had jurisdiction to hear the interlocutory appeal, and should review the question of law de novo.]

IV. Analysis

Having determined that this Court has jurisdiction to hear Defendants' appeal and the appropriate standard of review, we now address whether the trial court erred in denying Defendants' motion to dismiss on the grounds of sovereign immunity. Defendants contend that the extension of comity in this case would not violate public policy and that they are entitled to sovereign immunity under the laws of Maryland. We disagree and affirm the trial court's order.

As previously stated, under the rule of comity in North Carolina, rights acquired under the laws or judgments of a sister state will be given force and effect in North Carolina if not against public policy. *See, e.g., Cox v. Roach*, 723 S.E.2d 340, 346 (N.C. App. 2012). Moreover,

> [t]o render foreign law unenforceable as contrary to public policy, it must violate some prevalent conception of good morals or fundamental principle of natural justice or involve injustice to the people of the forum state. This public policy exception has generally been applied in cases such as those involving prohibited marriages, wagers, lotteries, racing, gaming, and the sale of liquor.

Id. (quoting *Boudreau v. Baughman*, 368 S.E.2d 849, 857–58 (N.C. 1988) (quotation marks omitted).

In the context of the sovereign immunity doctrine, our Supreme Court has used public policy to effectively waive the State's sovereign immunity in causes of action grounded in contract. *Smith v. State*, 222 S.E.2d 412, 423–24 (1976). In making this decision, the *Smith* Court was moved by the following public policy considerations:

> (1) To deny the party who has performed his obligation under a contract the right to sue the state when it defaults is to take his property without compensation and thus to deny him due process; (2) To hold that the state may arbitrarily avoid its obligation under a contract after having induced the other party to change his position or to expend time and money in the performance of his obligations, or in preparing to perform them, would be judicial sanction of the highest type of governmental tyranny; (3) To attribute to the General Assembly the intent to retain to the state the right, should expedience seem to make it desirable, to breach its obligation at the expense of its citizens imputes to that body "bad faith and shoddiness" foreign to a democratic government; (4) A citizen's petition to the legislature for relief from the state's breach of contract is an unsatisfactory and frequently a totally inadequate remedy for an injured party; and (5) The courts are a proper forum in which claims against the state may be presented and decided upon known principles.

Id. at 423–24. Accordingly, public policy is violated in North Carolina when the State is allowed to assert sovereign immunity as a defense to causes of action based on contract. It would seem plain, then, that because the ACC is seeking a declaration as to the parties' rights and obligations under the terms of the ACC Constitution, it would violate public policy to extend comity to Defendants' claim of sovereign immunity. To this line of reasoning, Defendants raise three objections that we address in turn.

First, Defendants contend that *Boudreau* limits the public policy exception to matters of marriages, family, and morals. *See Boudreau*, 322 N.C. at 342, 368 S.E.2d at 858 ("This public policy exception has generally been applied in cases such as those involving prohibited marriages, wagers, lotteries, racing, gaming, and the sale of liquor."). However, as the language of *Boudreau* makes clear, the examples provided therein are nonexclusive and merely represent what has qualified under the exception as a general matter. Moreover, other language in *Boudreau* is consistent with the policy considerations at issue in *Smith*. Compare *id.* at 342, 368 S.E.2d 849, 368 S.E.2d at 857–58 ("To render foreign law unenforceable as contrary to public policy, it must violate some prevalent conception of good morals or fundamental principle of natural justice or involve injustice to the people of the forum state." (emphasis added)), with *Smith*, 289 N.C. at 320, 222 S.E.2d at 423 ("To hold that the state may arbitrarily avoid its obligation under a contract . . . would be judicial sanction of the highest type of governmental tyranny."). Thus, the language of *Boudreau* explicitly provides that any injustice to the people of the forum state implicates the public policy exception, not merely matters of marriages, family, and morals. Here, Defendants' are attempting to immunize themselves from a determination of their responsibilities under an alleged contract with the ACC—a North Carolina entity. Under the rationale of *Smith*, such an action violates public policy.

Second, Defendants contend that Cox stands for the proposition that "North Carolina courts extend sovereign immunity to and are to dismiss an action brought by North Carolina residents in North Carolina Courts against the educational institutions of sister states which enjoy sovereign immunity in the courts of those states." In Cox, this Court extended comity to the University of Virginia's claim of sovereign immunity and affirmed the trial court's decision to grant the University's motion to dismiss. *Cox*, 723 S.E.2d at 346–47.

However, it does not follow that because we decided to extend comity to the University of Virginia in *Cox* we must, ipso facto, extend sovereign immunity to all the educational institutions of our sister states irrespective of the attendant circumstances. *Cox* is distinguishable from the present case because it dealt with tort claims being asserted against the University of Virginia, not a cause of action on a contract. *See id.* at 342; *see also Kawai*, 567 S.E.2d at 217 (" 'Suits against the State, its agencies and its officers for alleged tortious acts can be maintained only to the extent authorized by the Tort Claims Act, and that Act authorizes recovery only for negligent torts. Intentional torts committed by agents and officers of the State are not compensable under the Tort Claims Act.'" (quoting *Wojsko v. State*, 47 N.C. App. 605, 610, 267 S.E.2d 708, 711 (1980)). Thus, at least with respect to torts not covered by the Torts Claims Act, the state is entitled to defend tort suits by claiming sovereign immunity. Such a defense does not contravene public policy in North Carolina. Thus, this Court properly extended comity to the University of Virginia in *Cox*. Here, however, extending comity to Defendants in a cause of action based on an alleged contract would violate the clear public policy articulated in *Smith*. For these reasons, the same principles that we applied in *Cox* lead us to the opposite conclusion here—comity will not be extended to allow Defendants to escape a determination as to their rights and obligations under an alleged contract.

Third, Defendants contend that the holding in *Smith*—that the State has no sovereign immunity defense in causes of action based on contract—is limited to actions claiming a breach of contract. Accordingly, Defendants contend that because the ACC seeks declaratory relief, the waiver found in *Smith* does not apply and Defendants are entitled to sovereign immunity.

As an initial matter, we note that even though the underlying claim in Smith was for breach of contract, our Supreme Court did not limit its holding to such actions:

> We hold, therefore, that whenever the State of North Carolina, through its authorized officers and agencies, enters into a valid contract, the State implicitly consents to be sued for damages on the contract in the event it breaches the contract. Thus, in this case and in causes of action on contract arising after the filing date of this opinion, ... the doctrine of sovereign immunity will not be a defense to the State. The State will occupy the same position as any other litigant.

* * *

Furthermore, even though the underlying claim in *Smith* was for breach of contract, the public policy considerations underlying the Court's rationale are equally persuasive here. Specifically, we are moved by the consideration in *Smith* that

> [t]o hold that the state may arbitrarily avoid its obligation under a contract after having induced the other party to change his position or to expend time and money in the performance of his obligations, or in preparing to perform them, would be judicial sanction of the highest type of governmental tyranny.

Smith, 289 N.C. at 320, 222 S.E.2d at 423. The Court's holding in *Smith* explicitly waived the State's sovereign immunity in "causes of action on contract" and we can discern no sound reason to limit that language to breach of contract claims when the Court's stated rationale is equally persuasive with respect to declaratory relief actions seeking to ascertain the rights and obligations owed under an alleged contract. *See Ferrell v. Dep't of Transp.*, 334 N.C. 650, 654–55, 435 S.E.2d 309, 312–13 (1993) (relying on the public policy considerations articulated in *Smith* to find a waiver of the State's sovereign immunity in a declaratory judgment action). Such declaratory relief actions are a "cause of action on contract" sufficient to waive the State's sovereign immunity.

Accordingly, because the public policy of this state does not allow the State of North Carolina to avoid its obligations in contract, we cannot extend comity to Defendants' claim of sovereign immunity. Furthermore, because we find that the extension of comity in this case would violate public policy, we decline to consider—as would be required if we had reached the opposite conclusion—whether Defendants would be entitled to sovereign immunity as a matter of Maryland law.

V. Conclusion

For the foregoing reasons, we affirm the order of the trial court denying Defendants' motion to dismiss and terminate the stay entered by this Court on 18 April 2013.

Affirmed.

NOTES AND QUESTIONS

1. *Aftermath.* Soon after the court's decision, Maryland and the ACC settled their case, with Maryland paying a $31.3 million exit fee to the ACC.

2. *Sovereign Immunity in Interstate Contracts.* Here, the Court denied Maryland's claim for sovereign immunity. Unlike Texas (*see Leach* case in notes above), North Carolina does not allow the state to claim immunity in breach of contract cases. Might a difference here be the interstate (instead of intrastate) nature of the contract? If a school was leaving the Big 12 instead of the ACC, and the case was brought in Texas, same result? What if the ACC was headquartered in Maryland instead of North Carolina? Same result?

3. *Changed Circumstances as Non-Performance?* The Maryland-ACC case was not the only litigation that emerged from conference realignment. In 2011, West Virginia left the Big East for the Big 12. When the Big East attempted to enforce its contractual relationship with West Virginia to delay its move and force it to pay an exit fee, West Virginia filed suit challenging the contract itself. Arguing that the Big East was "no longer a viable and competitive football conference," West Virginia argued that the court should

set aside its agreement because the Big East's implosion amounted to a breach of contract. West Virginia also argued that the contract violated antitrust law as an unreasonable restraint of trade, even though it had willingly agreed to the bylaws. The case, however, soon settled, with the Big 12 schools contributing $20 million of the $31 million exit fee paid by West Virginia in exchange for immediate release from its contract with the Big East.

4. *Past Conduct as Estoppel?* Not long after West Virginia left the Big East, Rutgers left as well, joining the Big 10. Recognizing the bylaw requirements of a $10 million exit fee and a 27-month waiting period. Rutgers immediately filed suit against the Big East, seeking release from the contract. Part of their complaint argued that the Big East was estopped from enforcing the contract based on the prior exits of Pittsburgh, Syracuse, and West Virginia, none of which waited the full 27 months before leaving. Rutgers also argued that the Big East failed to collect the full amount of exit fees from other institutions, such that its exit bylaws were "void and of no effect as between the parties."

The parties eventually settled the lawsuit, with Rutgers paying an $11.5 million exit fee, and being able to participate the next season in the Big 10. Rutgers officials estimated that the move to the Big 10 would result in it making an additional $200 million over the next 12 years. The Big East subsequently reorganized, dropping football completely and moving forward as a basketball league largely made up of Catholic institutions.

E. NCAA INFRACTIONS

One of the NCAA's primary roles is to monitor rules infractions and punish institutions that transgress its rules. This section looks at the range of available sanctions, and the scope of that power. Chapter 11 explores how the recruiting rules work in practice.

The worst penalty that the NCAA can give is the "death penalty"—a requirement that an institution cease playing a particular sport for a year or more. The "death penalty" rule (in NCAA By-law Art. 19.6.2.3.2(a)) allows the NCAA to terminate for up to two years a school's program in a sport in which a major rules violation is committed within five years of another major rules violation in any sport. In the cases below, pay attention to whether the NCAA chose to impose the death penalty, and assess whether its decision was proper.

Second, this section examines situations where the conduct of the university falls outside the typical provision of economic benefits to students and instead involves some other shortcoming. In these cases, which involve the intersection of athletics with criminal conduct, the core question is whether the NCAA ought to police such behavior, and if so, under what kind of standard or approach it should use.

1. THE DEATH PENALTY

SOUTHERN METHODIST UNIVERSITY INFRACTIONS REPORT
NCAA Committee on Infractions, February 25, 1987

I. Origin of the Case.

On October 21, 1986, an NCAA enforcement representative interviewed a former football team member from the university (and the young man's mother) who reported possible major violations of NCAA legislation. On October 27, a television sportscaster and film crew interviewed the university's former director of athletics, former head football coach and the former administrative assistant to the director of athletics concerning possible payments of cash to the young man.

* * *

II. Findings of Violations as Stipulated by Southern Methodist University and the NCAA Enforcement Staff.

Violations of the principles governing amateurism and extra benefits to student-athletes [NCAA Constitution 3-1-(a)-(1), 3-1-(a)-(3) and 3-1-(g)-(5)]--During the period September 1985 through December 1986, monthly payments ranging from $50 to $725 were made to numerous student-athletes in the sport of football from funds provided by an outside representative of the university's athletics interests.

Specifically, subsequent to the conclusion of an NCAA infractions case in August 1985, certain key athletics department staff members agreed that promises made to student-athletes prior to the 1984–85 academic year during the young men's recruitment should continue to be fulfilled. Previous cash payments to the student-athletes had gone undetected by the NCAA, and the involved staff members agreed to continue the payments and to distribute them to the young men. It was understood that such payments would not be made to new student-athletes. An outside athletics representative who had been disassociated from the university's athletics program for involvement in the NCAA infractions case provided the funds for these payments.

As a result of these arrangements, 13 football team members received payments during the 1985–86 academic year that totaled approximately $47,000, and eight student-athletes continued to receive payments from September through December 1986 that totaled approximately $14,000. Payments were not continued subsequent to December 1, 1986, and reportedly, all but three of the student-athletes have exhausted their eligibility.

III. Factors Considered in Judgment of Case.

A. At the June 1985 NCAA special Convention, the NCAA membership enacted a series of mandatory penalties applicable to member institutions found guilty of repeat major violations. A "repeat major violation" is a second major violation found at an institution within a five-year period following the starting date of a major penalty.

At the February 13, 1987, hearing before the Committee on Infractions, the university agreed that repeat major violations had been committed by key members of both the football coaching staff and the athletics administrative staff, and another person for whose actions Southern Methodist University is responsible. A statement of the violations that the university agrees took place is set forth in Part II of this Infractions Report.

The issue, therefore, that the Committee on Infractions has confronted is whether to impose the mandatory penalties, the so-called "death penalty," or to exercise its discretion to impose less serious penalties because of unique circumstances in the case.

B. The present infractions case does present some unique circumstances that arguably call for the committee to exercise its discretion to impose less than the mandatory penalties. The efforts of the university in this investigation are commendable, and the dedicated work of the university's faculty athletics representative, Lonnie Kliever, went far beyond what could fairly be expected of a single faculty athletics representative. So impressed was the NCAA enforcement staff with the efforts of Mr. Kliever that the staff joined in the university's request that the committee impose penalties that were substantially less severe than those prescribed by the membership for a repeat major violation. Specifically, the staff joined with the university in urging that no football season be canceled. The university recommended a cancellation of two nonconference games for two seasons, while the enforcement staff recommended that all nonconference games be canceled for two years. Otherwise, the university and enforcement staff were in agreement with regard to coaching staff, grant-in-aid and recruiting reductions. The penalties recommended by the university are attached as Appendix A.

C. The committee gave serious and prolonged consideration to the recommendations of both the university and the enforcement staff, but declined to accept either recommendation. Factors that the committee believes call for more substantial penalties than those recommended include the following:

1. As a committee of the Association, the Committee on Infractions is bound by the judgment of the membership. That judgment was made absolutely clear in the recently adopted legislation and provides that

serious repeat violators are to receive heavy penalties. That legislation was passed by an overwhelming majority of the membership.

2. Not only is Southern Methodist University a repeat major violator, but its past record of violations is nothing short of abysmal. Both the current infractions case and the university's 1985 infractions case involved major violations that occurred at times when the university was on NCAA probation for previous serious violations. These violations and additional past infractions cases demonstrate that numerous individuals associated with the university's athletics program, including key staff members and outside representatives, have been committed to achieving athletics success through deliberate and flagrant violations of fundamental NCAA rules that were designed to maintain equal and fair competition.

3. Past efforts at the university to design a program to gain a competitive advantage over the university's competitors by cheating did achieve its apparent goal—a winning record and national prominence for its football program.

4. As recently as September 1986, the university requested the committee to grant relief from an earlier penalty. This request was made at a time when some key athletics department staff members knew full well the cheating that caused the penalty to be imposed was continuing, and those individuals deliberately failed to disclose this fact.

5. Three unidentified enrolled student-athletes with eligibility remaining who have received improper payments refuse to identify themselves despite efforts by the university to persuade them to do so and despite the fact that they were offered limited immunity by the Committee on Infractions.

6. Although institutional personnel who were responsible for the football program have been separated from the university, the terms of their separation are unknown, and there has been no acknowledgment of the identity of those staff members who are most responsible for the flagrant, continuing violations found in this case.

7. There was no explanation in this case from the former director of athletics or the former head football coach regarding the reasons violations continued to occur after the appearance of the university's representatives before the committee in April 1985. During that appearance, assurances were given to the committee that all known violations had been disclosed and that every effort would be made to avoid violations in the future. Both assurances turned out to be false.

8. The continuing source of the funds for the violations found in this case was a university booster who the institution assured the committee in 1985 had been disassociated from the athletics program. The fact of this disassociation was stressed by the university as evidence of institutional

remedial action at the time of its April 1985 hearing. Yet, when it subsequently became apparent in August 1985 that payments to football team members had not stopped, this booster was requested by key athletics department staff members to continue to fund the payments that were distributed through the athletics department. This arrangement was concealed by certain institutional staff members.

D. The penalties that the committee determined to be appropriate in this case are severe, but they differ in some respects from the prescribed repeat major violator penalties set forth in Section 7-(d) of the NCAA enforcement procedures. The committee accepted the view that there are uniquenesses in this case, but concluded that the university should be permitted to rebuild a football program only under carefully controlled conditions. The committee is satisfied that the university went to extraordinary efforts to uncover wrongdoing in its program in this case, and the committee is encouraged that there is evidence of actions by the university to obtain full compliance with NCAA regulations. Therefore, although the committee's penalties are intended to eliminate a program that was built on a legacy of wrongdoing, deceit and rule violations, the penalties also are intended to permit a new beginning for football at the university under a timetable that provides some relief from the recovery period required by the prescribed penalty structure. In addition, it should be noted that one of the prescribed penalties would have prohibited the university's membership on NCAA committees and denied institutional voting privileges for four years. These penalties were not imposed, in part because the institution's actions in this case demonstrate that it should be permitted to participate in the consideration of significant issues facing NCAA athletics programs.

IV. Committee on Infractions Penalties.

A. _Probation_. The university shall be placed on probation until September 1, 1990, it being understood that should any of the penalties in this case be set aside for any reason other than by appropriate action of the Association, the penalties shall be reconsidered by the Committee on Infractions; further, the university shall conduct annual audits of the expenses and income of its football team members during the probationary period (_i.e._, by September 1, 1988, 1989 and 1990) to ensure that these student-athletes can meet their financial obligations without improper financial assistance, and the university shall report the results of these audits in writing to the NCAA enforcement staff, and finally, the NCAA shall conduct a review of the university's athletics policies and procedures prior to the expiration of this probationary period, which shall include an in-person visit to the university.

B. _Football Games_. The university shall be prohibited from participating in any football game or scrimmage with outside competition in 1987. During the 1988 football season, the university shall be limited to no more than seven games or scrimmages against outside competition, none of which shall be a "home" game; further, the university shall not be permitted to participate in "live" television appearances in the 1988 season or in postseason competition following that season.

    C. <u>Practice</u>. During the 1987 calendar year, practice in the sport of football at the university shall be limited to conditioning programs [Page 6] only, and no football equipment may be used other than helmets and shoes. Teaching of football fundamentals or techniques shall be prohibited; no instruction, including walking through plays or watching films, shall be permitted. The university shall be permitted to resume normal practice activities in the spring of 1988.

    D. <u>Coaches</u>. The university shall be limited to the use of no more than one head football coach and five full-time assistant football coaches until August 1, 1989.

    E. <u>Grants-in-Aid</u>. No student-athlete in the sport of football shall receive initial, athletically related financial aid (as set forth in O.I. 600) that would be countable in the 1987–88 academic year at the university; further, no more than 15 student-athletes shall be recipients of initial, athletically related financial aid that would be countable in the 1988–89 academic year, and finally, no student-athlete who receives countable financial aid for the 1988–89 academic year shall be permitted to receive such aid until at least the beginning of that academic year at the university.

    F. <u>Recruiting</u>. No member of the university's football coaching staff shall be permitted to participate in any off-campus recruiting activities (except the evaluation of prospects during football evaluation periods only) until August 1, 1988. Further, no prospective student-athlete in the sport of football shall be provided an expense-paid recruiting visit to the university until the beginning of the 1988–89 academic year, and no more than 45 such visits shall be permitted during that academic year.

    G. <u>Disassociation</u>. The university shall show cause within 15 days of receipt of this report why additional institutional penalties should not be imposed upon the university if it fails to take further corrective action in regard to the nine outside representatives who were disassociated for varying periods of time in the university's 1985 infractions case. In the committee's view, such action should permanently prohibit these individuals from providing the university's athletics program with any financial contributions or other support services for any purpose. These individuals should not be permitted to retain membership in the university's booster organizations and should not be permitted to receive any special athletics benefits from the university other than those available to the general public. . . .

The committee's penalties in this case are severe, and they are designed to compensate for the great competitive advantage that Southern Methodist University has gained through long-term abuses and a pattern of purposeful violations of NCAA regulations. The penalties also have deterrent value for others who might be tempted to follow the example set by Southern Methodist University; however, the penalties also are intended to achieve a long-term rehabilitative objective. The present administration of the university has expressed its hope for a new beginning in athletics, and canceling the football season in 1987 will afford an opportunity for the university to start a new football program based on integrity and fair play rather than on wrongdoing and deception.

NOTES AND QUESTIONS

1. *Aftermath.* The SMU case was unprecedented at the time, and has never been replicated. The decision destroyed the SMU football program for a generation, with its next bowl game coming in 2009.

2. *The Death Penalty.* Given the crippling effect of the death penalty, should the NCAA ever impose it? If so, did SMU deserve it? Why or why not?

3. *NCAA Appellate Model.* The NCAA's current process has 2 levels: the Committee on Infractions (COI) and the NCAA Infractions Appeals Committee (IAC). As is typical with lower courts, the COI performs all of the fact finding in the case, while the IAC reviews the sanctions to determine if they are appropriate. After a COI decision, the institution and any penalized individuals have the ability to appeal to the IAC. The IAC reviews the COI decision using a clear error deferential standard as to the findings of the COI.

The NCAA created the IAC in 1992 in the aftermath of the Tarkanian litigation. SMU thus could not have appealed the COI decision above. If it could have appealed, do you think the outcome would have been the same?

UNIVERSITY OF ALABAMA, TUSCALOOSA
PUBLIC INFRACTIONS APPEALS COMMITTEE REPORT
NCAA Infractions Appeals Committee, September 17, 2002

[The COI accused Alabama of violating NCAA bylaws on recruiting, honesty standards, salary control, and extra benefits. Specifically, three athletics department representatives paid a football recruit $20,000 as well as additional benefits. There were numerous other examples of benefits being provided to football recruits.

Further, an athletics department representative paid a high school football coach a significant amount of money to induce a star lineman to attend Alabama. Finally, strippers entertained recruits in university housing during their official visit.

Prior to the case, the university took a number of corrective actions, including self-imposing penalties. These included a reduction in scholarships and recruiting limitations.

The COI imposed a 2-year post-season ban and a 5-year probation term.]

* * *

We have addressed violations by athletics representatives in a number of prior cases. The issue in the University of Nevada, Las Vegas, case was whether it was appropriate to impose a ban on postseason competition against an institution whose athletics representatives had made cash payments to a prospective student-athlete and an enrolled student-athlete. We held that such a penalty was appropriate as a deterrent to future violations by bringing the "violations to the attention of the institution's boosters as well as the institution." (UNLV Public Infractions Appeals Committee Report, page 11, February 16, 2001) In that case, we discussed the application of Bylaw 19.6.2.1–(f). We found it unnecessary to decide there whether one of the three conditions of the bylaw must be satisfied as a condition to imposing a postseason ban because the case was subject to the repeat violator Bylaw 19.6.2.3.

In this case, we have a similar situation because the institution is subject to the repeat violator bylaw. The Committee on Infractions has discretion to ban postseason competition under this bylaw if such a penalty is not excessive or inappropriate. We have already concluded that such a ban is not inappropriate in a case involving violations by athletics representatives.

A ban on postseason competition is one of the most serious penalties that can be imposed on an institution. It deprives the institution and its student-athletes of the opportunity to achieve the highest level of success in their sport. It also prevents the fans and other supporters of the program from enjoying the full success of a season of competition. Because the violations in this case were numerous and particularly egregious, we conclude that the imposition of such a penalty is appropriate under the facts of the case.

The institution contended that, although it is responsible for the conduct of its athletics representatives, it was not, and was not found to be, at fault with respect to their actions. Without institutional fault, the institution argued that it is inappropriate to impose penalties on it for violations committed by its athletics representatives. This argument is based on the fact that the Committee on Infractions did not make a finding of lack of institutional control. As discussed above, we upheld the institutional sanction of a postseason ban in the UNLV case based on athletics representative violations for a repeat violator where there were no findings of lack of institutional control. Moreover, the Committee on Infractions noted in this case that the athletics representatives were "not the typical representatives" due to their "favored access and 'insider status'." (Committee on Infractions report page 3) The Committee found this status:

> ". . . not only gives credence to their claims of authority within a program but also, and however unintended, serves to reward them for the illicit activities in which they engage. Moreover, special access and insider status likely ease the way for illicit conduct by rogue representatives both by identifying prospects for them and by fostering (or contributing to) the belief of prospects and their parents that the representative's conduct is sanctioned by the university and in its best interest as well as that of the prospect." (Committee on Infractions report page 3).

The Committee concluded that this favored access and insider status created "greater university responsibility for any misconduct in which they engage." (Committee on Infractions report page 3) We agree.

The remaining question is whether the penalty is excessive. The two-year postseason ban imposed here is one of the longest imposed by the Committee on Infractions. However, in its report, the Committee on Infractions indicated that it seriously considered imposing the repeat violator penalty set forth in Bylaw 19.6.2.3.2–(a) and prohibiting outside competition in football (the "death penalty"). Its articulated bases for considering this penalty were the institution's status as a "two-time repeat violator" (1995 and 1999), the very serious nature of the recruiting violations and its view that the institution "bears some responsibility for the special status . . . within the athletics department" enjoyed by two of the athletics representatives. (Committee on Infractions report page 29)

Although finding this a "very close question," the Committee on Infractions declined to impose the death penalty due to "the particular circumstances of this case and of the university's infractions history." (Committee on Infractions report page 29) Although the Committee did not elaborate in the report on what it meant by the "particular circumstances" of the institution's infractions history, it appears that the Committee considered cooperation of the institution in reporting the 1999 violation as a mitigating factor. This is consistent with the view the Committee took in its 1999 report on this matter. In that report, the Committee recognized that the institution had made great strides after the 1995 violation by creating "an environment of compliance" and stated: "Rather than impose institutional penalties, the Committee commends the university for its effective institutional control and proactive compliance . . . ." (Public Infractions Report for the University of Alabama, Tuscaloosa, page 3, February 9, 1999). The Infractions Appeals Committee agrees with this assessment of the 1999 report. However, even if the nature of the 1999 case mitigates the institution's status as a two-time repeat violator, the institution remains a repeat violator as a result of the 1995 report.

In further explaining why it did not impose the death penalty, the Committee on Infractions contrasted this case with the prior case (Southern Methodist University, February 25, 1987) in which this penalty was imposed. In that case, the Committee noted that there was "a demonstrated blatant disregard for NCAA rules that permeated throughout the entire university and its governance structure." (Committee on Infractions report page 29) The Committee found the circumstances of this case in sharp contrast. Here "university officials cooperated fully with the enforcement staff, often at great personal criticism, in a diligent effort to develop complete information regarding the violations." (Committee on Infractions report page 29) The Committee concluded "[h]ad this candor and cooperation been lacking, the death penalty (as well as substantial penalties in addition to those imposed in this case) would have been imposed." (Committee on Infractions report pages 29–30)

In the recent Howard University case, we encouraged the Committee on Infractions "to include in its report in future cases a fuller explanation of the basis of the penalties imposed and the extent of the consideration given to any degree of institutional cooperation sufficient to be a mitigating factor." (Howard Public Infractions Appeals committee Report, page 31, July 16, 2002). The Infractions Appeals Committee commends the Committee on Infractions for its explanation of the rationale for the penalties it imposed and the extent to which the institution's cooperation operated to mitigate those penalties. It is clear from the Committee's report that it did properly consider institutional cooperation as a "significant factor" and accorded it "substantial weight in determining and imposing" penalties here. (Mississippi page 19)

Finally, the institution argued that the two-year postseason ban and five-year probation are excessive compared to the penalties imposed in other cases involving repeat violators. Consistency in penalties so that comparable cases receive comparable penalties is a factor to consider in determining whether a penalty is excessive or inappropriate. We recognize that it is difficult to meaningfully compare cases because there are so many disparate variables in the cases. We also recognize that the Committee on Infractions must have latitude in tailoring remedies to the particular circumstances involved in each case and that the universe of relevant cases is not static, but evolving. In this case, the Committee on Infractions carefully considered the nature, number and seriousness of the violations, the conduct and motives of those involved in the violations, the corrective actions taken by the institution, the institution's exemplary cooperation and its repeat violator status.

The Committee on Infractions compared this case with the only case in which the death penalty was imposed and appropriately distinguished this case from that one. In the hearing on appeal, it adequately demonstrated the consistency of the result in this case with other recent cases.

* * *

For all of the foregoing reasons, we conclude that the two-year postseason ban and five-year period of probation imposed in this case are not excessive or inappropriate, and affirm Penalties III-B-3 and III-B-2.

NOTES AND QUESTIONS

1. *Aftermath.* Unlike SMU's program, Alabama's football program recovered quickly. After missing 2 years of bowls, it returned to a bowl game in 2004. It hired Nick Saban in 2007, and won 5 national championships in the next 10 years.

2. *When to Impose the Death Penalty.* Do you think the COI and IAC were correct here in choosing not to impose the death penalty? Note the factual similarities between the SMU and the Alabama cases: repeat offenders, paying recruits, multiple new violations. What in the NCAA COI's eyes was different here? Do you find that distinction persuasive?

3. *Cooperation as Mitigation.* One of the distinctions that the COI found between SMU and Alabama (and the IAC found persuasive) was the full cooperation by University of Alabama officials who provided complete information to the NCAA enforcement staff. Indeed, the COI intimated that absent this cooperation, Alabama might have received the death penalty. The NCAA COI often rewards university compliance departments for self-reporting violations, and imposes more serious punishments (as with SMU) where universities do not disclose violations. Should the degree to which a university is forthcoming about violations and/or cooperates with NCAA enforcement staff factor into the sanction for violations? Why or why not?

4. *Due Process and Subpoena Power.* One reason that the NCAA COI rewards self-reporting is its lack of subpoena power. The COI cannot force anyone not associated with a university to testify, provide information, or otherwise cooperate with investigators. As a result, obtaining evidence is often a problem in compliance cases, particularly when the athlete that received improper benefits has completed his or her eligibility and is no longer a student.

Further, the NCAA procedures do not provide many of the evidentiary protections that civil or criminal lawsuits do, including the ability to cross-examination all witnesses interviewed by the enforcement staff. As we have learned, though, the NCAA is not a state actor, and its procedures thus do not have to meet constitutional due process requirements. On the other hand, the NCAA does not have the subpoena power of a public authority. In your view, are such limitations significant enough to undermine the legitimacy of the process? Why or why not?

5. *Lack of Institutional Control.* A second core principle, the requirement of institutional control, has emerged in part from the lack of subpoena power and the resulting dependence of the NCAA on institutional self-reporting of violations. The NCAA constitution provides,

> The control and responsibility for the conduct of intercollegiate athletics shall be exercised by the institution itself and by the conference(s), if any, of which it is a member. Administrative control or faculty control, or a combination of the two, shall constitute institutional control (NCAA Const. sec. 6.01).

Thus, where a university does not put in place adequate safeguards to monitor possible violations, it is guilty of exercising a lack of institutional control. In such cases, universities face additional sanctions, beyond the sanctions for the violations themselves.

The idea is that an institution's carelessness or failure to monitor adequately fosters an environment where violations are more likely to occur and more likely to go undetected. As you read the excerpt from the Miami case below, pay attention to the discussion concerning the lack of institutional control. Should institutions face a second punishment for failing to prevent and/or monitor violations? Keep in mind such violations can be as simple as improper phone calls, text messages, or de minimis benefits provided to recruits and/or student-athletes.

UNIVERSITY OF MIAMI PUBLIC INFRACTIONS REPORT
NCAA Committee on Infractions, October 22, 2013

[The COI accused Miami of 18 allegations that primarily involved widespread and significant recruiting inducements and extra benefits. Many of the allegations centered around a known representative of the institution's athletics interests ("the booster") freely entertaining numerous prospects and student-athletes at his home, on his yacht and in various public settings. The booster paid for entertainment, food and various gifts. This booster also was a significant donor of the football and men's basketball programs and had a visible presence around the programs.]

* * *

The committee concludes that former assistant football coaches B and C were involved in unethical conduct by providing impermissible benefits or inducements and providing false or misleading information to the enforcement staff and the institution. The former head men's basketball coach's violations were the result of his failure to promote an atmosphere for compliance. The committee also concludes that former assistant men's basketball coaches A and B were involved in recruiting violations by providing impermissible benefits or inducements and in some instances using the booster to facilitate the provision of those benefits or inducements. Former assistant men's basketball coach B committed unethical conduct in connection with those recruiting violations. The institution demonstrated a failure to monitor its programs and the booster's activities. The institution also failed to have the proper policies and procedures in place during the relevant time period, which led to the committee concluding that there was a lack of institutional control.

The committee acknowledges and accepts the extensive and significant self-imposed penalties by the institution, and prescribes the following principal penalties: three years of probation, a reduction in the maximum number of athletics awards in football and men's basketball, restrictions on unofficial visits, a five-game suspension for the former head men's basketball coach, and two-year show-cause orders for former assistant football coaches B and C and former assistant men's basketball coach B.

III. FINDINGS OF FACT

The committee divides the institution's major infractions case into four distinct areas. The first and second areas involve major infractions in connection with two of the institution's highly visible sports programs, football (Part A) and men's basketball (Part B). Many of the violations in the football and men's basketball program are separate and distinct violations with one common link. That common link is the booster who, over a series of interviews, reported nearly a decade's worth of violations. The violations came to light primarily as a result of the reporting provided by the booster.

A third area involves major infractions investigated and initially submitted to the NCAA by way of the summary disposition process. These violations are largely the result of telephone and text-messaging violations in nearly all sport programs and included an admission on the part of the institution that it failed to monitor its programs. The violations were contained within the unprocessed June 2011 Summary Disposition Report and later incorporated in the enforcement staff's notice of allegations as allegations 15, 16 and 17. *See* Section C.

The fourth area concerns the institution's administration and overall control of its intercollegiate athletics program and commitment to rules education, monitoring and compliance.

* * *

IV. ANALYSIS

The violations in this case fall largely into the following areas: recruiting violations and the provision of impermissible benefits to student-athletes and prospects by representatives of the institution's athletics interests and prospective sports agents; the provision of impermissible supplemental income to assistant coaches; recruiting violations and the provision of impermissible benefits by assistant coaches; unethical conduct by former assistant football coaches and an assistant men's basketball coach; the former head men's basketball coach's failure to promote an atmosphere for compliance; telephone and text-messaging violation; and a lack of institutional control.

* * *

L. LACK OF INSTITUTIONAL CONTROL. [NCAA Constitution 2.8.1, 6.01.1.]

From 2002 through 2010, the institution failed to exercise institutional control and failed to monitor the administration of football and the men's basketball programs. The institution also failed to exercise control and failed to monitor the conduct of the highly recruited prospects, enrolled student-athletes, and coaching staffs in those high-profile programs. The institution did very little to control or to monitor the conduct of the booster. In fact, it was the institution that encouraged the booster to become connected to those sport programs, but provided no oversight to identify any potential concerns or violations. Additionally, the institution failed to monitor football and all of its other sports programs to ensure compliance with telephone and text-messaging legislation. None of the eight coaches or the approximately 30 student-athletes involved in the numerous major violations in this case took any meaningful steps to report the events. The failures of the coaches and student-athletes were either the result of a lack of understanding of the rules, or an attitude of indifference towards compliance. The failings of the institution enabled a culture of noncompliance to exist within the institution. The committee concludes that the facts found and the violations set forth in the Analysis sections above constitute a lack of institutional control.

* * *

The NCAA Constitution requires that each member institution comply with all applicable rules and regulations of the NCAA. It also requires that each institution monitor its programs to ensure compliance and to identify and report to the NCAA any instances where compliance has not been achieved. *See* NCAA Constitution 2.8.1. Further, the Constitution mandates that the institution's administration or faculty "or a combination of the two," exercise control and responsibility for the conduct of intercollegiate athletics. NCAA Constitution 6.01.1

The committee, however, does not base its conclusion that the institution failed to exercise institutional control solely on the booster's status or failing to monitor him. In assessing whether a member lacks institutional control, the committee considers whether adequate compliance measures exist; whether those compliance measures were appropriately conveyed to those who need to be aware of them; whether the compliance measures are monitored to ensure they are followed; and whether upon learning that a violation may have occurred, the institution takes timely and appropriate action.

The committee is concerned that former assistant football coach C reported being told to discuss violations or potential violations with the recruiting coordinator, a colleague on the coaching staff, and not a compliance officer. An institution should have policies and procedures for staff members to seek guidance on compliance related issues and report potential violations confidentially. As demonstrated by the majority of the widespread unreported violations identified in this case, the institution did not have adequate policies and procedures in place for staff members to report potential violations without fear of consequence.

The failure to implement proper policies, procedures and an internal monitoring system is one measure the committee has identified as an indicator that an institution lacks control over its intercollegiate athletics program. In this case, policies that the institution did have in place were disregarded or unevenly applied.

Policies and procedures that effectively deter and detect violations are essential to an internal monitoring system. As provided in allegations 15, 16 and 17, the institution also lacked the personnel, policies, and monitoring systems to ever detect text messages or to regularly detect improper or ill-timed recruiting telephone calls.

Further, the former associate director of athletics/compliance took the position that the compliance staff monitored sidelines, stands, suite areas, and bus-loading zones at home and away football games. However, these efforts failed to detect and deter a number of violations that occurred during football contests, including but not limited to prospects access to suite areas, interactions between the booster and prospects and the receipt of extra benefits and inducements.

The institution did not routinely compare telephone logs and telephone bills to ensure that the coaching staff was properly recording or logging telephone contacts and also that those contacts were consistent with NCAA legislative requirements. The committee has consistently concluded that rules education alone is not enough. The institution did not fully meet its responsibility to monitor its programs to ensure compliance and to identify and report those instances where "compliance has not been achieved." *See* NCAA Constitution 2.8.1. Because the institution lacked an adequate monitoring system and had policies that were disregarded or not communicated, it failed to establish a proper internal monitoring system.

Aside from the texting and telephone violations, the reports of secondary violations during the relevant time period, the institution did not identify a single instance of the booster's impermissible benefits or recruiting activity, separate from the enforcement staff's investigation and as identified in this report. According to the institution, the booster's access through the student-athlete scholarship program did not contribute to the violations. The committee concludes to the contrary because for years, the booster was able to meet and develop relationships with student-athletes. Some of these relationships enabled the booster to provide impermissible benefits to numerous student-athletes resulting in violations of NCAA bylaws.

Without monitoring systems or other internal controls, the chain of introductions that began between the booster and the student-athlete scholarship program were permitted to grow over time. While the institution contends that the booster operated "in the shadows" in places "that institutional eyes don't often frequent," the committee concludes otherwise. The booster visibly entertained small and large groups of student-athletes and operated in the public view of the institution and the nearby city of Miami.

The committee notes also that the staff infrequently consulted the institution's policy on occasional meals each year and there is no documentation to support or authorize the booster's activity. Because the institutional staff did not consult or follow institutional policies regarding occasional meals, the institution did not adequately make occasional meal policies available to the individuals involved.

The former assistant football coaches reported inconsistent practices when documenting unofficial visits and there may have been confusion as to staff responsibility for that task. The committee concludes that the institution, prospects and enrolled student-athletes, coaches, staff, and boosters committed extensive recruiting and impermissible benefits/inducements violations because the institutional staff members lacked the basic knowledge of NCAA rules applicable to recruiting operations.

Additionally, due to the lack of documentation there was no way to track and monitor the distribution of institutional gear. As a result, the impermissible distribution of institutional gear to student-athletes went unnoticed.

The institution's documentation program did not adequately monitor the athletics department's activities. As a result, numerous violations went undetected.

During the hearing, the officials from the institution described the institution's compliance program as "extensive" and, in the response to the notice of allegations, the institution stated that it "went to great lengths to exert institutional control and to foster a culture of compliance" through rules education. However, the committee concludes that the institution's rules education was inadequate and that the institution failed to monitor its programs to ensure compliance.

While the committee agrees that many, if not all, of those interviewed reported receiving rules education at team meetings, the committee questions the effectiveness and consistency of that rules education given the number of student-athletes, coaches and other athletics staff members involved in violations. Five coaches in football and three coaches in men's basketball either had a poor understanding of the rules or felt comfortable breaking them. Additionally, more than 30 student-athletes were involved with the booster, many of whom accepted extra benefits.

For nearly a decade, the booster provided, and student-athletes received a range of impermissible benefits. For nearly a decade, those benefits were completely undetected. It does not appear that the institution conducted an assessment of the effectiveness of its compliance program, particularly in its high-profile sports to determine whether there was any concern for potential violations. Had the institution routinely examined its sports programs, it may have been alerted to the potential for NCAA violations and amended its policies and procedures to combat those identified risks.

Either way, the institution is responsible for the conduct of its intercollegiate athletics program. The scope of that responsibility covers the actions of staff and individuals representing the institution's athletics interests.

In this case it is apparent that individuals within and outside of the program were involved with, and aware of numerous violations. It is also apparent that the former head men's basketball coach failed to promote an atmosphere of compliance. There is nothing to suggest, however, that the institution failed to take timely and appropriate action when it became clear that these violations had occurred. Notwithstanding that, however, an institution is required to put adequate systems in place to prevent and detect violations, as well as take action when they occur.

The committee finds that the institution is responsible for the conduct of individuals in their sports programs, if adequate compliance measures are not in place; they are not effectively communicated to the individuals, or, they are not monitored to ensure that such measures are being followed. The committee concludes that adequate compliance measures did not exist to prevent or effectively deter the violations from occurring in this case.

Institutional Control and Representatives of an Institution's Athletics Interests

As the committee has stated in previous infractions cases, institutions have a greater responsibility to monitor athletics representatives with "insider" or favored status. *See University of Alabama*, Case No. M173 (February 1, 2002), *University of Arkansas*, Case No. M183 (April 17, 2003), *University of Michigan*, Case No. M191 (May 8, 2003), *University of Central Florida*, Case No. M361 (July 31, 2012). In some of those cases, the committee specified that a failure to monitor and control these athletics representatives is demonstrative of either an institutional failure to monitor (*Arkansas*) or a lack of institutional control (*Central Florida*). With regard to the issue of institutional responsibility pertaining to "insider boosters," the committee wrote the following in the *Alabama* decision:

> But those athletics representatives provided favored access and "insider" status, frequently in exchange for financial support, are not the typical representative. Their favored access and insider status creates both a greater university obligation to monitor and direct their conduct and a greater university responsibility for any misconduct in which they engage.
>
> This case is apt illustration of the unequivocal obligation to monitor closely those athletics representatives whose financial contributions provide a level of visibility, insider status, and favored access within athletics programs. Their insider status not only gives credence to their claims of authority within a program but also, and however unintended, serves to reward them for the illicit activities in which they engage. [*Alabama* at p. 3]

In *Alabama*, although the committee did not conclude that there was a lack of institutional control, it warned the membership of the obligation to closely monitor "insider boosters" and the greater responsibility institutions bear for the impermissible activity in which these boosters engage. In a later case, *Arkansas*, a failure to monitor was concluded by the committee in large part because of the NCAA violations in which an "insider booster" was implicated. By the time the committee considered Central Florida, it concluded a lack of institutional control was appropriate, primarily because of the institution's failure to scrutinize and control the illicit activity of "insider boosters." In its *Central Florida* decision, the committee wrote the following:

> Through its decisions in several cases adjudicated in the past decade, the committee has warned the membership of a greater obligation to monitor those individuals, like representative 1, who have insider status, and when violations occur, there is an enhanced responsibility for any violations they may commit. In the introduction of this report, the committee cited the 2003 Michigan decision which was illustrative in the context of this case. [*Central Florida* at p. 53]

* * *

The booster at the center of this case was extremely "visible," as reflected in the above activities. By granting him special access and celebrating him with the naming of a student lounge, it is clear that the institution embraced him. He certainly did not "fly under the radar," as the institution asserts but rather was a major supporter of their athletics programs, which creates a greater responsibility to monitor.

Moreover, the record establishes that a former associate director of athletics/compliance had general concerns about donors being provided "way too much access" to the student-athletes, and he voiced those concerns to the athletics administration in place at the time. In November 2007, the former associate director of athletics/compliance actually had an altercation with the booster and again raised those concerns with senior athletics administrators. There is nothing in the record that suggests institutional steps were taken to address the concerns raised by the former associate director of athletics.

The institution failed to exercise control over its football and men's basketball programs. The institution lacked sufficient institutional policies and procedures, as well as lacked adequate monitoring efforts, both of which contributed to their lack of control. The facts as found demonstrate that a number of the indicia of institutional control were absent at the institution. Finally, the committee looked to past cases to analyze the booster's activities. Considering the facts as found and past cases as guidance, the committee concludes that the institution lacked institutional control. The committee concludes that the facts as found constitute violations of NCAA Constitution 2.8.1 and Bylaw 6.01.1.

* * *

V. PENALTIES.

The committee considered the institution's cooperation in the processing of all parts of this case. Cooperation during the infractions process is addressed in NCAA Bylaw 19.01.3 - Responsibility to Cooperate and NCAA Bylaw 32.1.4 – Cooperative Principle (2011–12 Division I NCAA Manual). The committee finds that the cooperation exhibited by the institution was consistent with its obligation under Bylaws 19.01.3.3 and 32.1.4.

In addition to its cooperation, the committee notes that the institution understood the nature and the scope of the allegations that were pending. It is clear that the institution substantially agreed with a majority of the violations. It is also clear that the institution, even before the committee conducted the June 2013 hearing, took responsibility for violations, particularly in the football program. For two seasons, the institution limited its football program to regular season competition only, eliminating any postseason competition opportunities, including the 2012 Atlantic Coast Conference Championship game.

Finally, in full consideration of the institution's presentation at the hearing, submissions into the record and conduct to date, the committee prescribes the following sanctions.

Those self-imposed by the institution are so noted:

1. Public reprimand and censure.

2. Three years of probation from October 22, 2013, through October 21, 2016.

Football Program

3. Reduction in Athletics Awards. The total number of athletically related financial aid awards in football shall be reduced by a combined total of nine during the 2014–15, 2015–16 and 2016–17 academic years. The institution shall reduce the total number of athletics awards during each academic year. The institution has the option of assigning the reductions during those years.

4. During the 2014–15 and 2015–16 academic years, the institution shall be limited when providing complimentary admissions to prospects on unofficial visits. The institution may provide a prospect with complimentary admissions for a maximum of one home athletics event. All other restrictions for unofficial visits, not addressed in the committee's decision, may be found in the applicable bylaws, including NCAA Bylaw 13.7.

5. The institution imposed bans on the football team's participation in postseason bowl games following both the 2011 and 2012 seasons, and withheld the football team from participating in the 2012 ACC Championship game.

6. The institution reduced official paid visits for 2012–13 by 20 percent. The reduction resulted in a total of 36 visits. The institution shall certify that this penalty has been fulfilled in its first annual compliance report.

7. The institution reduced fall evaluations in 2012–13. The institution therefore used 36 of the permissible 42. The institution shall certify that this penalty has been fulfilled in its first annual compliance report.

8. The institution limited coaches during the 2012–13 contact period. The institution reduced available contact days by 20 percent. The institution shall certify that this penalty has been fulfilled in its first annual compliance report.

* * *

[Miami self-imposed a series of penalties and show cause bans on its former assistant football coaches involved in the violations]

Men's Basketball Program

12. Reduction in Athletics Awards. The total number of athletically related financial aid awards in men's basketball shall be reduced by a combined total of three during the 2014–15, 2015–16 and 2016–17 academic years. The institution shall reduce the total number of athletics awards by one during each academic year.

* * *

[Miami self-imposed a series of penalties and show cause bans on its former head men's basketball coach and the assistant basketball coach involved in the violations. In addition, the Report provided a long list of minor penalties related the sports listed above as well as a series of institutional penalties.]

NOTES AND QUESTIONS

1. *Aftermath.* Miami's athletic programs did not suffer as much as SMU's football team did, but they were not able to bounce back as quickly as Alabama's football team did. In 2017–18, however, its football team returned to national prominence, and its basketball team made the NCAA tournament for the third year in a row.

2. *When to Impose the Death Penalty, Part II.* How do you compare the violations at Miami with the violations at SMU and Alabama? The extensive and flagrant nature of Miami's violations would seem to make the death penalty at least a possibility, but the NCAA did not think so. How did they distinguish this case? Are these cases all similar? Or are there important differences?

3. *NCAA Subpoena Power Issues.* As a private association, the NCAA lacks subpoena power to assist its investigations. The NCAA has no leverage to compel an individual no longer employed by a university or no longer an athlete to participate in its investigation, much less testify. This makes the enforcement process much more difficult, particularly when the case involves third parties and occurs over a number of years.

In the Miami case, the investigators on the COI went too far and broke the NCAA's own rules in investigating the case. The NCAA admitted that its investigators "improperly" obtained information by working too closely with a criminal defense attorney for Nevin Shapiro. In addition, the NCAA paid Miami attorney Maria Elena Perez for taking two depositions in a bankruptcy case involving one of Shapiro's companies and sharing information from that case. Do you think that the NCAA's malfeasance affected the outcome in the Miami case? On a broader note, to what extent does the lack of subpoena power affect the legitimacy of the NCAA process? Are there alternatives to the current system that would be better?

4. *Lack of Institutional Control.* The lack of institutional control found here had as much to do with the lack of safeguards within the athletic department, as with the rampant disregard for the rules displayed by the booster in question and other members of the athletic department and coaching staffs. Should the focus here be more on the quantity and frequency of the benefits? Or on the lack of a system to monitor phone calls? To what extent do the proof problems present in compliance cases make the presence or absence of monitoring systems an easy target by which to assess compliance?

Around the time of the Miami case, an unprecedented number of major infractions cases occurred at high profile programs, including Ohio State, Tennessee, Auburn, Southern California, Georgia Tech, West Virginia, and Syracuse. In response, the NCAA implemented a new punishment structure in 2013.

The new structure separated infractions into four tiers: (1) Level I: Severe Breach of Conduct; (2) Level II: Significant Breach of Conduct; (3) Level III: Breach of Conduct; and (4) Level IV: Incidental Issues, with Level I being the most serious.

Level I violations (Severe Breach of Conduct) are those that:

"... seriously undermine or threaten the integrity of the NCAA collegiate model as set forth in the Constitution and bylaws, including any violation that provides or is intended to provide a substantial or extensive recruiting, competitive or other advantage, or a substantial or extensive impermissible benefit."

Examples of Level I violations include: lack of institutional control, academic fraud, failure to cooperate in an enforcement investigation, unethical or dishonest conduct, and head coach responsibility for a Level I violation by a member of his staff.

Level II violations (Significant Breach of Conduct) are those that:

"Violations that provide or are intended to provide more than a minimal but less than a substantial or extensive recruiting, competitive or other advantage; includes more than a minimal but less than a substantial or extensive impermissible benefit; or involves conduct that may compromise the integrity of the NCAA collegiate model as set forth in the Constitution and bylaws."

Examples of Level II violations include: failure to monitor, systemic violations not rising to the level of lack of institutional control, multiple recruiting violations, and collective Level III violations. Level III violations (Breach of Conduct) are those that:

"are isolated or limited in nature; provide no more than a minimal recruiting, competitive or other advantage; and do not include more than a minimal impermissible benefit. Multiple Level IV violations may collectively be considered a breach of conduct."

Finally, Level IV violations (Breach of Conduct) are those that:

"are inadvertent and isolated, technical in nature and result in a negligible, if any, competitive advantage. Level IV infractions generally will not affect eligibility for intercollegiate athletics."

The goal of this new structure is to add legitimacy to the infractions system by creating a more uniform way of categorizing behavior and promoting consistency in sanctioning. In the words of the NCAA, the COI is seeking to provide "credible accountability." In addition, this revised system has placed more responsibility on head coaches for infractions that occur in their programs. New penalties have included suspension of coaches for multiple games during the season, as in the case of basketball coaches Jim Boeheim of Syracuse and Rick Pitino of Louisville (before he was fired). The core sanctions remain—postseason bans, scholarship reductions, and financial sanctions—with the stated goal of deterring misconduct and preventing advantages stemming from providing improper benefits to athletes.

2. SANCTIONING CRIMINAL CONDUCT

Beyond serious infractions cases and the challenge of finding appropriate sanctions, the NCAA has faced a different kind of issue in recent years where criminal conduct has been connected to athletic programs. The Penn State scandal in particular provided a very serious challenge to the NCAA. In 2011, the NCAA (and the general public) learned that a former Penn State assistant football coach, Jerry Sandusky, had sexually molested young boys in various locations, including locker rooms in Penn State athletic facilities. These incidents spanned a decade, and some Penn State employees at least suspected that these criminal acts were occurring.

Sandusky was eventually convicted of multiple counts of unlawful contact with minors, corruption of minors, and endangering the welfare of children, and sentenced to 30 to 60 years in prison. In addition, Penn State's athletic director Tim Curley and vice president Gary Schultz pled guilty to child endangerment, and president Graham Spanier was convicted on that charge (after an acquittal on more serious conspiracy allegations). All three began serving prison sentences of between 4 months and 2 years in 2018.

Penn State's legendary football coach Joe Paterno could possibly have faced similar scrutiny, but he died in January 2012, three months after the scandal broke. Shortly after the scandal erupted, the Penn State Board of Trustees commissioned an investigation of the entire episode by former FBI director Richard Freeh, who issued a lengthy report. It concluded that the Penn State officials noted above had failed to disclose information they knew concerning Sandusky's sexual abuse.

Relying primarily on the Freeh Report, President Mark Emmert announced on July 23, 2012 that the NCAA's Executive Committee was levying several sanctions against Penn State for fostering an unhealthy culture that allowed the Sandusky crimes to happen and go unreported. The sanctions included: (a) a fine of $60 million; (b) banning the football team from post-season play for five seasons (through the 2016 season); (c) reducing the number of football scholarships Penn State could give from 2012 through 2015 to 15 a year and a total of no more than 65 (the normal maximum for a Division I-A school is 85); and (d) requiring Penn State retroactively to forfeit 112 wins earned from 1998 through 2011 (the years that Sandusky was committing his crimes), which caused Coach Paterno to lose his status as the winningest Division I-A football coach of all time. Emmert stated at the same time as he announced the sanctions that the Penn State Board of Trustees had agreed to sign a consent form accepting the penalties and agreeing not to contest them.

Later, the media reported that the threat of the death penalty (shutting the football program down entirely) factored into Penn State's decision to accept the sanctions. In 2014, the NCAA began restoring some of the football scholarships so that Penn State was able to give 20 in 2014 (for a total of 75), and 25 (a full complement) thereafter so it would have a full allotment of 85 by the 2016 season. The stated reason for reducing this penalty was that the University had made strong good-faith efforts to change its culture by adopting many of the 119 recommendations the Freeh Report had made. In September 2014, the NCAA lifted the ban on post-season play two years earlier than originally imposed, allowing the Penn State football team to play and defeat Boston College by one point in overtime in the New Era Pinstripe Bowl in Yankee Stadium two days after Christmas in 2014.

The legal fallout from all these events was extensive. Many victims of Sandusky's crimes filed lawsuits against Penn State, with the university settling those claims for damages in over 30 cases. Pennsylvania Governor Tom Corbett filed an antitrust suit against the NCAA in January 2013 claiming that its sanctions against Penn State constituted an illegal restraint of trade. The district court granted the NCAA's motion to dismiss on the ground that none of the sanctions had any plausible anticompetitive effect in any relevant market. *Pennsylvania v. NCAA*, 948 F. Supp. 2d 416 (M.D. Pa. 2013).

In February 2013, a report commissioned by Joe Paterno's family found that the Freeh Report was in many respects factually wrong, speculative, and fundamentally flawed. Based on this Report, Coach Paterno's wife and children, his estate, and five members of the Penn State Board filed a lawsuit in Pennsylvania state court claiming that by rushing to judgment and falsely publicly accusing Joe Paterno of covering up Sandusky's criminal behavior, the NCAA and President Emmert had committed various torts and interfered with the NCAA's contract with the University. The plaintiffs in that case sought an injunction setting aside the consent agreement between the NCAA and the Penn State trustees (that it claimed was coerced) and several of the sanctions, including the one that vacated 112 of Coach Paterno's victories.

That same month, the Pennsylvania legislature passed Senate Bill 187, called the Endowment Act, requiring that any fines assessed against Penn State by the NCAA be put into a special trust fund and distributed to the Pennsylvania Commission on Crime and Delinquency to be thereafter paid out to Pennsylvania organizations that fight or treat child abuse.

State Senator Jake Corman and Treasurer Rob McCord then filed suit against the NCAA in state court in Harrisburg seeking to require the NCAA to spend the $60 million in fines collected from Penn State exclusively in Pennsylvania, not only because of the Endowment Act, but also because the monies are state funds legally under the oversight of the Senate Appropriations Committee that Corman chairs. The NCAA then filed a separate suit in federal district court in Harrisburg claiming that the Endowment Act violates the U.S. Constitution because it interferes with a private contract.

In January 2015, the NCAA settled these lawsuits by agreeing to restore the 112 wins it had previously struck from the records (thereby once again making Joe Paterno the winningest Division I-A football coach in history) and to spend the $60 million fine on child abuse prevention and treatment programs in Pennsylvania. Thus, by 2015, the NCAA had either lifted, substantially reduced, or modified all the sanctions imposed against Penn State.

In 2018, another sex abuse scandal followed this sordid saga, and involved Larry Nassar, a Michigan State physician. Nassar, a team doctor for USA Gymnastics, molested hundreds of mostly female young athletes, as part of his "medical care." Nassar pleaded guilty to seven counts of criminal sexual conduct, admitting to sexually assaulting and abusing young girls under the guise of providing medical treatment. As part of his plea deal, 144 victims gave victim impact statements. In all, Nassar will be serving three prison sentences, two of 40–125 years for molestation and abuse, and another 60-year sentence for child pornography.

Nassar had been an associate professor at Michigan State since 1997. Questions immediately arose, as with the Penn State scandal, concerning whether the university knew about Nassar's criminal behavior. In the wake of the revelations about Nassar, both the Michigan State president and athletic director resigned. Michigan State also agreed to pay over $500 million in total to 332 victims of Nassar.

The NCAA sent a letter in January 2018 asking for more information concerning the scandal. Unlike Penn State, it did not commission a law firm to prepare an outside report. In May 2018, Michigan State reported that it did not find any NCAA rules violations in relation to the Larry Nassar case, and in August 2018, the NCAA's enforcement unit confirmed that conclusion.

NOTES AND QUESTIONS

1. *Role of the NCAA.* Should the NCAA regulate and punish universities for the criminal activity that occurs in their athletic departments or with their athletes? Or should the punishments merely be what the criminal justice system elects to impose? In the Penn State case, for instance, the criminal law was able to reach the alleged malfeasance of the administrators, not just Sandusky. Does this make the NCAA's punitive actions not only inappropriate, but also unnecessary? Or should the NCAA intervene as the governing body for intercollegiate sports?

2. *Appropriate Sanctions.* If the NCAA should regulate the criminal conduct of members of university athletic departments, how should it punish any malfeasance? There is a strong case that current athletes should not suffer for the sins of others in the athletic department, but perhaps there should be some sanction, particularly where university officials engage in wrongful or criminal behavior. Do you agree with the NCAA's actions in punishing Penn State? Do you agree with the NCAA's ultimate decision to mitigate Penn State's punishment?

3. *Penn State Versus Michigan State.* What facts might differentiate these cases? What facts might make them similar? Do the NCAA's actions in the *Penn State* case constitute a binding precedent requiring some response?

4. *Role of Infractions.* One of the criticisms of the Penn State decision was that it was made outside of the NCAA's normal infractions process. Was this a wise approach? Why do you think the NCAA did not follow a similar approach with Michigan State?

5. *Oversight.* While the NCAA has clearly distinguished criminal cases from recruiting violation cases, both types of cases assume university responsibility for oversight of third party behavior. Nevin Shapiro, for instance, was engaged in rules violations for which the university was responsible, because he paid athletes in violation of the amateurism rules.

With respect to Sandusky, and perhaps with respect to Nassar, the basis for NCAA sanctions will be the failure of the university to intervene and stop the behavior at issue. Is holding the university liable for the criminal acts of its employees under NCAA rules the same as holding the university liable for amateurism violations by boosters? What if the acts of the boosters (as in Shapiro's case) involve some kind of criminal activity?

CHAPTER 11

INTERCOLLEGIATE SPORTS: THE ATHLETE-UNIVERSITY RELATIONSHIP*

■ ■ ■

The previous chapter examined the NCAA and its member institutions. This chapter turns to the relationship between the athlete and the university, under the overlay of NCAA regulations. After examining the recruiting process and how athletes make it into the university, the chapter explores the student-athlete relationship, and the legal challenges to that relationship.

A. RECRUITING AND SCHOLARSHIPS

1. ADMISSIONS STANDARDS

NCAA rules specify the academic credentials required of athletes who graduate from high school and want to play in intercollegiate athletics. In order to facilitate this process, the NCAA runs a clearinghouse of information to help high school students through the process of obtaining eligibility. As explored below, the NCAA has adopted a sliding scale through which a student must receive a minimum combination of high school grades and test scores. In addition, the students must achieve a minimum grade point average in a number of required high school courses.

For years, university admissions departments have struggled with the weight and value ascribed to standardized admissions tests. With athletes, these conflicts can become more pronounced as some athletes in revenue sports have test scores that fall below some institution's requirements. Much of the controversy in placing too much weight on standardized tests stems from empirical data showing that test outcomes are disparate based on race, and have built-in biases.

(a) Race Discrimination

In its early days, the NCAA followed a policy of college "home rule" in allowing schools to make the judgment about whether or not to admit

---

* The Casebook Website (http://pennstatelaw.psu.edu/SportsTextWebsite) contains citations to scholarly and other commentary on a variety of topics discussed in this chapter, including admissions standards, academic standards, the university-athlete agreement, amateurism, and challenges to the student-athlete model.

athletes into their classes. At its 1964 Convention, though, the membership adopted a "1.6 Predictor Rule" that conditioned eligibility for participating in intercollegiate sports upon the student-athlete's academic prospects for meeting a minimum 1.6 predicted grade point average (GPA) in college. This prediction was based on the student's high school GPA and class ranking, combined with their Scholastic Aptitude Test (SAT) or American College Test (ACT) scores, as assessed through expectancy tables that incorporated statistics for over 40,000 students at more than 80 colleges.

The debate about the impact of this rule surfaced in the federal courts in a case involving Centenary College's effort to play a center who had not met this 1.6 Predictor standard—future NBA Hall of Famer Robert Parish, who would later help lead the Boston Celtics to three NBA championships in the 1980s. Keep in mind as you read this decision that it precedes *Tarkanian*, so the court is holding the NCAA and a private university to the requirements of the Equal Protection Clause. The substantive analysis remains valid today only as applied to public universities.

PARISH V. NCAA
361 F. Supp. 1220 (W.D. La. 1973)

DAWKINS, CHIEF JUDGE.

* * *

Parish, 7' 1" in height, denominated a "super-athlete," was recognized during his last high school year by national magazines, newspapers, and sports columnists as probably the number one or number two leading basketball prospect in the United States, in the manner of Wilt Chamberlain and Lew Alcindor. He was named to several All-American high school teams and chosen by the Basketball News as the number one high school graduate basketball player in the country. Of course, he was recruited, even courted, by almost every major college in the nation.

In order to fulfill the requirements of NCAA's 1.600 Rule, Parish took the ACT twice, his score being an 8. Regrettably, before achieving such prominence, he had been somewhat deprived, both educationally and economically; and probably began to aspire ambitiously toward a full higher education only after "the baskets began to swish." With this score, most colleges "backed off" because they felt Parish could not meet the 1.600 requirement.

* * *

[Centenary, however, did sign Parish up to the then-standard four-year athletic scholarship after converting his ACT test scores to SAT scores (which he still did not meet). Though he did have significantly higher college grades than the NCAA minimum, the Association suspended him and several of his teammates from playing basketball, and so they went off to court. As the judge put it, he was facing] a "Hobson's choice," which we do not relish at all, considering the empathy we hold for all of these competing interests: 1) the careers of these young athletes; 2) their present and future prospects; 3) the outstanding degree of culture contributed by the institution known as Centenary College, locally, regionally, and nationally, since well before the War Between the States; and finally, 4) the nationwide elevation of scholastic and athletic standards developed by NCAA for so many years.

* * *

Addressing the merits, even if [education] is a right or privilege protected by the Constitution, we hold that the 1.600 Rule withstands the denial of equal protection attack because it has a rational relationship to legitimate State (or national) purposes. Obviously, the challenged action by NCAA is not subject to strict judicial scrutiny. Therefore, we turn to the traditional standard of review which requires only that the NCAA's system be shown to bear some rational relationship to legitimate purposes. NCAA adopted the 1.600 Rule as a means of insuring that the athlete be an integral part of the student body and to maintain intercollegiate athletics as an integral part of the education program. Mr. Byers, of NCAA, summarized the need for these rules, as establishing a minimum standard which would prevent exploitation of athletes by the college or university, that is, setting up and agreeing to the prediction process by NCAA's members in order to prevent recruitment for athletic purposes alone of young men who had relatively poor chances of obtaining academic degrees; to encourage institutions with lower standards to elevate those standards to be more compatible with other institutions; and to discourage the unsound academic and economic practices of the past which had allowed indiscriminate granting of scholarships, resulting in too many athletes dropping out after their freshman or sophomore years. This rule was adopted to prevent abuses and at the time it was thought that this rule would solve the problem.

Notwithstanding, NCAA now has determined (since its action involving Centenary, Parish, and his teammates) that the rule was inadequate. This is based upon the fact that the 1.600 Rule was repealed and the 2.00 Rule was enacted in its stead. In *Associated Students v. NCAA* (May 25, 1973, Civil No. S-2754, E.D. Cal.), Judge McBride stated:

> Without deciding the question, it appears that this classification is reasonably related to the purposes of the 1.600 Rule.

However, he concluded that the 1.600 Rule, as interpreted by Official Interpretation 418 (O.I. 418) did not meet muster as to equal protection constitutional requirements. We agree that the 1.600 Rule's classification is reasonable, not arbitrary, and rests upon a ground having a fair and substantial relation to NCAA's object in enacting the legislation, so that all persons similarly circumstanced shall be treated alike, *i.e.*, the Rule bears a rational relationship to the legitimate purposes for which it was enacted. Although application of the Rule may produce seemingly unreasonable results in certain situations, this is not unusual, for use of generalized rules frequently produces irrational results in isolated circumstances. Such results do not condemn those rules under traditional equal protection scrutiny. Here, NCAA has advanced one step at a time, addressing itself to the phase of the problem which then seems most acute to it.

Plaintiffs also presented evidence to show that the SAT and ACT tests discriminated against all of them in some form. One (Parish) came from a minority group, one from a rural school, etc. This type of evidence was rejected as having no weight in *Murray v. West Baton Rouge Parish School Board*, 472 F.2d 438 (5th Cir. 1973):

> Plaintiffs have made a broad-based attack on the use of psychological testing at Port Allen Elementary School. The focus of the attack appears to be that the tests are being used to discriminate against the black students. There is absolutely no evidence that the testing is being used to foster segregation in the class rooms, . . . and despite conclusionary allegations to the contrary, there is no evidence whatsoever that the tests are being administered in a discriminatory manner. If, as plaintiffs claim, there are a few black students whose educational progress has been wrongly retarded because of this testing, it is most unfortunate. But as a federal court we cannot intervene absent some well-defined constitutional deprivation. There is no factual showing that the tests are culturally biased, discriminatorily conceived, or even that they had a discriminatory effect. That the tests might not be an educationally valid one for a few individual children does not, in and of itself, give rise to constitutional deprivation. On the record before us, we can find no constitutional fault with the testing in the Port Allen Elementary School.

We take judicial notice of the fact that, at the time in question, the particular tests involved here under NCAA's Rule 1.600 were administered throughout the nation; almost every college in the United States required a score from one test or the other for admission purposes. We, therefore, must reject plaintiffs' claim as to this issue. We also note that members of the black race have been perhaps the greatest beneficiaries of numerically disproportionate participation in intercollegiate athletics; and they have done so under the aegis of the 1.600 Rule.

In *Associated Students*, supra, the Court stated:

* * *

Bearing in mind that the central purpose of the 1.600 Rule is to insure that the individual who participates in intercollegiate athletics is capable of succeeding academically at the college level, this new classification is over-inclusive and not rationally related to the objective of the rule insofar as it declares ineligible not only those student athletes who fail to predict a minimum 1.600 grade point average and who have not yet completed their first year in college, and not only those student athletes who fail to achieve a minimum 1.600 grade point average for the first year in college, but additionally those student athletes who demonstrated by the conclusion of the first year that they have the ability to achieve academic success by actually earning at least a 1.600 grade point average. Once a student has an earned grade point average achieved over a reasonable period of time, then it is unreasonable, in light of the purposes of the rule, to impose sanctions against the student based on the fact that he failed to predict a certain grade point average. Instead, any sanctions imposed should be predicated on the actual grade point average attained by the student.

* * *

With this conclusion, we respectfully but regretfully disagree. It is our considered view that the Court in the just quoted decision overlooked the fact that one of the purposes of the official interpretation of the 1.600 Rule is to prevent schools from granting scholarships to those students who, after taking part in testing procedures, do not show a possibility of attaining a degree before entering college.

Under that decision, all member schools could recruit all those athletes whose entrance examinations did not predict successful graduation and then, if they did obtain a higher grade-point average than 1.600 after the first year in school, they would be entitled to participate in NCAA sponsored athletic events thenceforth. The Court's decision there effectively would prevent enforcement of the 1.600 Rule, which the Court already had determined to be rational in order to achieve NCAA's stated objective.

We cannot fathom how the official interpretation creates a classification which is in nonconformance with equal protection standards. In order to meet that objective, determination of eligibility must be made at the time of application and certification; to make it at a later date simply destroys the classification which the Court already had conceded to be reasonable. This decision in effect would allow colleges to recruit ineligible athletes and hope they will meet graduation prediction standards after their first year grades are in, thus becoming eligible for their entire collegiate athletic life. As stated, it is our considered opinion that NCAA's official interpretation of its 1.600 Rule does not create a classification which violates the equal protection requirements of the Constitution.

Case dismissed.

NOTES AND QUESTIONS

1. *Aftermath.* Although the Fifth Circuit upheld the lower court's decision in favor of the NCAA on appeal, *see Parish v. NCAA*, 506 F.2d 1028 (5th Cir. 1975), the NCAA repealed the 1.600 Rule in the early 1970s. Instead, the NCAA required scholarship athletes to have only a minimum 2.0 GPA from high school. Why do you think the NCAA changed its rules after *Parish*? Is "home rule" a good approach or is it problematic?

2. *Development of the Rule.* In 1983, the NCAA adopted Proposition 48, which required that the mandatory 2.00 high school GPA had to come from core academic courses in English, mathematics, science, history, and other subjects reviewed and approved by the NCAA. Most significantly, student-athletes also had to score a minimum of 700 on the SAT or 15 on the ACT. Unlike the 1.6 Predictor Rule in the *Parish* case, the original version of Proposition 48 did not make the SAT (or GPA) minimum an absolute barrier to college sports. A student-athlete who met either of, though not both, the SAT and GPA criteria received "partial qualifier" status and could still enroll in college on an athletic scholarship. Partial qualifiers, though, were not eligible to play (though they could practice) in their freshman year, during which they had to demonstrate satisfactory progress in the college's academic program.

In 1992, the NCAA further tightened athlete eligibility standards by adopting Proposition 16. For Division I colleges, the minimum high school GPA standard was raised from 2.00 to 2.5 in 13, not just 11, core academic courses. Athletes who had higher than minimum test scores could have a somewhat lower GPA (and vice versa): *e.g.*, the minimum GPA was 2.00 for an athlete who scored 900 on the SAT. In 1995, the NCAA adopted a sliding scale requiring minima in both areas.

3. *Effect of* Tarkanian *on Proposition 48/16 challenges*. With the *Tarkanian* case effectively foreclosing a constitutional attack on these NCAA rules, public interest lawyers seeking to challenge NCAA initial eligibility standards focused on Title VI of the federal Civil Rights Act of 1964, which provides that "no person shall, on the grounds of race, color, or national origin, be excluded from participation in, be denied the benefit of, or be subjected to discrimination under any program receiving any federal financial assistance."

Under this federal *statutory* law, it is sufficient for a finding of illegal discrimination that use of SAT scores has had a disparate *impact* on African-

Americans, regardless of whether they were adopted for the purpose of discriminating against (*i.e.*, disparate *treatment* of) African-Americans, providing the defendant cannot justify the policy. *See Griggs v. Duke Power Co.*, 401 U.S. 424 (1971) (so interpreting Title VII, the employment part of the Civil Rights Act), and *Groves v. Alabama State Board of Education*, 776 F. Supp. 1518 (M.D. Ala. 1991) (applying Title VII jurisprudence to a Title VI attack on minimum SAT scores for admission to a state teachers' college). *See also Sharif by Salahuddin v. New York State Educ. Dept.*, 709 F. Supp. 345 (S.D.N.Y.1989) (finding that New York State violated Title IX of the federal Education Amendments of 1972 when it used SAT scores alone, rather than a combination of high school GPA and SAT, to award college scholarships based on academic achievement in high school, because the SAT (though not the GPA) scores of female students had been consistently lower than those of male students).

4. *Home Rule.* Under the home rule approach, each institution applies its own academic standards. If a critical NCAA principle is the appropriate integration of athletics and academics, then why isn't the appropriate regulation one that requires athletes' academic record to resemble those of other students at the university? To answer this question, it is worth considering the competing values of amateurism and education on the one hand versus competitive equity on the other hand.

CURETON V. NCAA

37 F. Supp. 2d 687 (E.D. Pa., 1999), *rev'd on other grounds*, 198 F.3d 107 (3d Cir. 1999)

BUCKWALTER, J.

The primary question presented by the parties' cross-motions for summary judgment is whether Title VI of the Civil Rights Act of 1964 ("Title VI"), 42 U.S.C. § 2000d et seq., and certain implementing regulations promulgated thereunder, prohibit colleges and universities, through the auspices of the National Collegiate Athletic Association ("NCAA"), from requiring students to achieve a minimum score on either of two standardized tests as a condition of eligibility to participate in intercollegiate athletics and/or receive athletically related financial aid during their freshman year.

* * *

I. BACKGROUND

[The two named plaintiffs, Leatrice Shaw and Tai Kwan Cureton, had graduated with honors from their Philadelphia high school in June 1996, ranking 5th and 27th respectively in their senior year class of 305 students. Both Shaw and Cureton were also topflight track and field runners who had been actively recruited by Division I colleges around the country. However, they failed to achieve the minimum SAT or ACT required to qualify for participation in NCAA athletics. Shaw still secured an athletic scholarship as a "partial qualifier" with Miami University's Division I track and field team, although she was not able to compete in her 1996–97 freshman year. Cureton's athletic ineligibility as a freshman rendered him unattractive to Division I schools, and thus he ended up at Division III Wheaton College, which does not offer any athletic scholarships.]

II. DISCUSSION

* * *

B. IS THE NCAA SUBJECT TO TITLE VI?

[The district court answered this question in the affirmative. It was this holding that was reversed by the court of appeals, and is discussed below after this excerpt on the merits of the Title VI analysis.]

C. DOES PROPOSITION 16 HAVE AN UNJUSTIFIED DISPARATE IMPACT?

In *Griggs v. Duke Power Co.*, 401 U.S. 424 (1971), the Supreme Court introduced the theory of disparate impact discrimination by holding that a plaintiff need not necessarily prove intentional discrimination in order to establish that an employer has violated Title VII of the Civil Rights Act of 1964, 42 U.S.C. § 2000e et seq. Since then, "facially neutral employment practices that have significant adverse effects on protected groups have been held to violate the Act without proof that the employer adopted those practices with a discriminatory intent." *Watson v. Fort Worth Bank and Trust*, 487 U.S. 977, 986–87 (1988) (O'Connor, J., plurality opinion).

The disparate impact theory is premised upon the notion that "some employment practices, adopted without a deliberately discriminatory motive, may in operation be functionally equivalent to intentional discrimination." *Id.* at 987. That is, it does not purport to strive for equal results at the institution, but to ensure that individuals are not the victims of unintentional discrimination and thus, treated unequally. See *The Supreme Court 1988 Term Leading Cases, Title VII—Evidentiary Requirements in Disparate-Impact Cases*, 103 Harv. L. Rev. 350, 356–57 (1989) (arguing that the Supreme Court reshaped disparate impact law in accordance with a theory of "equal treatment," which "seeks to guarantee fair process," rather than a "theory of equal achievement, which strives for fair results—racial parity after years of discrimination"). Moreover, "the evidence in these 'disparate impact' cases usually focuses on statistical disparities, rather than specific incidents, and on competing explanations for those disparities." *Watson*, 487 U.S. at 987.

Although the disparate impact theory was originally developed in cases involving employment discrimination, courts have subsequently applied the theory to claims brought pursuant to the regulations implementing Title VI. *See, e.g., NAACP v. Medical Ctr., Inc.*, 657 F.2d 1322, 1331 (3d Cir. 1981); *New York Urban League, Inc. v. New York*, 71

F.3d 1031, f1036 (2d Cir. 1995); *Quarles v. Oxford Mun. Separate Sch. Dist.*, 868 F.2d 750, 754 n.3 (5th Cir. 1989); *Larry P. v. Riles*, 793 F.2d 969, 982 nn.9–10 (9th Cir. 1984); *Elston v. Talladega County Bd. of Educ.*, 997 F.2d 1394, 1407 & n. 14 (11th Cir. 1993).

In order to establish a prima facie case of disparate impact discrimination, a plaintiff must initially demonstrate that the application of a specific facially neutral selection practice has caused an adverse disproportionate effect, to wit, excluding the plaintiff and similarly situated applicants from an educational opportunity. *See Wards Cove Packing Co. v. Atonio*, 490 U.S. 642, 656–57 (1989) (superseded in part by statute). Where such a showing has been made, the burden of rebuttal shifts to the defendant, who must demonstrate that the selection practice causing the disproportionate effect is nonetheless justified by an "educational necessity," which is analogous to the "business necessity" justification applied under Title VI. *See Board of Educ. of the City Sch. Dist. of New York v. Harris*, 444 U.S. 130, 151 (1979). The defendant bears only a burden of producing evidence to sustain its educational necessity. *See Wards Cove*, 490 U.S. at 659–60. But cf. 42 U.S.C. §§ 2000e(m), 2000e–2k(1)(A) (requiring the defendant under Title VII to bear both a burden of production and persuasion on its business necessity justification).

Finally, even where a defendant meets that burden, a plaintiff may ultimately prevail by discrediting the asserted educational justification, or by proffering an equally effective alternative practice that results in less racial disproportionality while still serving the articulated educational necessity. *See Watson*, 487 U.S. at 998. The ultimate burden of proving that the selection practice caused a discriminatory effect against a protected group always remains with the disparate-impact plaintiff. *See Wards Cove*, 490 U.S. at 659–60.

1. Whether Proposition 16 Causes a Racially Disproportionate Effect

[The court took note of an NCAA memorandum that found]:

African-American and low-income student-athletes have been disproportionately impacted by Proposition 16 standards. Of those African-American student-athletes appearing on a Division I Institution Request List submitted to the NCAA Initial Eligibility Clearinghouse, 26.6 percent did not meet Proposition 16 standards in 1996 and 21.4 percent did not qualify in 1997 (compared to 6.4 percent of white student-athletes in 1996 and 4.2 percent in 1997). This disproportionate impact also is seen (to a lesser degree) for other ethnic-minority groups. . . .

* * *

NCAA Division I Academics/Eligibility/Compliance Cabinet Subcommittee on Initial-Eligibility Issues Mem., July 27, 1998, at 7 (Exhibit C to Pls.' Opening).

* * *

Plaintiffs also point to a July 29, 1994 memorandum issued just prior to the adoption of Proposition 16, which states in the Executive Summary: "The Association's own research ... provides dramatic evidence of the disparate impact on both the current rules and those scheduled to go into effect in 1995 [Proposition 16] on minority student athletes." Report of the Special NCAA Comm. to Review Initial-Eligibility Standards Mem., July 29, 1994, at 2. Finally, Plaintiffs look to a report prepared by the United States Department of Education, which cites that only 46.4% of the African-American college-bound high school seniors met Proposition 16's requirements, as compared to approximately 67% of white college-bound high school seniors. *See* Pls.' Ans. (Exhibit 3 thereto). The report also indicates that the Proposition 16 cutoff score was the factor that caused the greatest degree of disparate impact because only 67.4% of African-American college-bound student-athletes cleared the test score hurdle, as compared to 91.1% of white college-bound student-athletes. *See id.* According to Plaintiffs, the essence of the disparate impact is that Proposition 16's cutoff score affects people of all races differently in that white student-athletes apply to Division I schools in greater numbers and are excluded less, while African-American student-athletes apply to Division I schools in smaller numbers and are excluded more.

* * *

The NCAA further argues that the ultimate goal of Proposition 16 is to raise the African-American student-athlete graduation rate. That is, the standards project that the black graduation rate will increase to 59.2%, which would be 94.8% of the projected white graduation rate of 62.5%. *See* Petr. Aff. P 4 (Exhibit C to Def.'s Response). The NCAA maintains that Plaintiffs have not disputed that African-Americans are graduating at higher rates; that the gap between African-Americans and white graduation rates has declined since the adoption of stricter initial eligibility rules; or that more African-American student-athletes are graduating since the adoption of the test score requirement.

The NCAA also contends that the increased number of African-Americans receiving athletic scholarships relative to their composition in the general student body is further proof of how college athletics has, in fact, benefited this group. According to the NCAA, although the initial eligibility rules have reduced the number of incoming African-American student-athletes, they have concomitantly resulted in creating more opportunities to graduate for those athletes that meet the eligibility standards. Thus, if graduation, and not freshman-year athletics, is the opportunity at stake here, the NCAA maintains that Plaintiffs have failed to demonstrate the requisite disproportionate effect.

Notwithstanding its attempt to reframe the lawsuit, the NCAA never disputes the veracity of the statements made in their own documents. These admissions and the bare statistics themselves plainly evince that African-Americans are being selected by Proposition 16 at a rate disproportionately lower than whites sufficient to infer causation.

* * *

Moreover, the Court finds unpersuasive the NCAA's argument that a selection practice having a disproportionate "beneficial" impact on the protected group can compensate for any disproportionate adverse impact on that same group. That singular fact misdirects the Court's inquiry. The alleged beneficial impact (increased graduation rates) redounds at the "back-end" while the adverse impact occurs up-front.

> Irrespective of the form taken by the discriminatory practice, an [institution's] treatment of other members of the plaintiffs' group can be "of little comfort to the victims of . . . discrimination." Title [VI] does not permit the victim of a facially discriminatory policy to be told that he has not been wronged because other persons of his or her race or sex [benefited]. That answer is no more satisfactory when it is given to victims of a policy that is facially neutral but practically discriminatory.

Connecticut v. Teal, 457 U.S. 440, 455 (1982) (quoting *International Bhd. of Teamsters v. United States*, 431 U.S. 324, 342 (1977)).

Accordingly, the Court concludes that Plaintiffs have established a prima facie showing of a racially disproportionate effect sufficient to shift the burden of rebuttal to the NCAA.

2. Whether Proposition 16 Is Justified by an Educational Necessity

Under the educational necessity prong of the analysis, "the dispositive issue is whether a challenged practice serves, in a significant way, the legitimate [educational] goals of the [institution]." *Wards Cove*, 490 U.S. at 659. That is, the practice in question must bear a demonstrable "manifest relationship" to a legitimate goal. *See Connecticut v. Teal*, 457 U.S. 440, 446 (1982) (quoting *Griggs*, 401 U.S. at 432). "The touchstone of this inquiry is a reasoned review of the [institution's] justification for [its] use of the challenged practice. . . . There is no requirement that the challenged practice be 'essential' or 'indispensable' " to the institution. *Wards Cove*, 490 U.S. at 659. Rather, the defendant's burden of production at this stage is met only when the institution is able to offer some proof that the device serves identified legitimate and substantive [educational] goals. That is, the defendant's burden [is] to identify the particular [educational] goal and to present evidence of how the [challenged practice] "serves in a significant way" the identified goal. Merely being abstractly rational, as opposed to arbitrary, would not suffice. The defendant, therefore, has some burden of presenting objective evidence . . . factually showing a nexus between the selection device and a particular [educational] goal. Without evidence of such a relationship it cannot be said that the defendant has presented any evidence that the "challenged" practice serves, in a significant way, the legitimate [educational] goals of the [institution]. *Newark Branch, NAACP v. Town of Harrison, New Jersey*, 940 F.2d 792, 804 (3d Cir. 1991) (quoting Mack A. Player, *Is Griggs Dead? Reflecting (Fearfully) on* Wards Cove Packing Co. v. Atonio, 17 Fla. St. U. L. Rev. 1, 32 (1989)).

The NCAA has proffered the following two goals as underlying the promulgation of Proposition 16: (1) raising student-athlete graduation rates, and (2) closing the gap between black and white student-athlete graduation rates. The Court will address the legitimacy of these goals before continuing to discuss whether a manifest relationship exists between Proposition 16 and those goals.

a. Are these legitimate goals of the NCAA?

* * *

With respect to the NCAA's first proffered objective of raising student-athlete graduation rates, this Court concludes that it is a legitimate educational goal. An educational institution's primary mission is to educate and graduate as many students as possible who meet the level of academic proficiency deemed sufficient by the institution. Thus, raising graduation rates is directly in line with that mission. Here, as the surrogate of the colleges and universities in Division I, the NCAA is properly setting academic standards for student-athletes in hopes of improving the rate at which they graduate.

* * *

The same conclusion cannot be reached for the NCAA's second proffered objective of closing the gap between black and white student-athlete graduation rates. Not only is there no support for an educational institution (let alone its surrogate) to engage in such a goal, but the proffered goal was unequivocally not the purpose behind the adoption of the initial eligibility rules. Absolutely nothing in the record—transcripts of convention proceedings, research results, or memoranda—even suggest that this was a goal that motivated the promulgation of Proposition 16 or 48. Indeed, the Court finds it difficult to reconcile the NCAA's current articulation of such a goal with their own documents plainly evincing that only two goals motivated the adoption of Proposition 16 and 48: "(1) raising of graduation rates, and (2) allowing more individuals access to the finite number of athletics opportunities available." NCAA Division I Academics/ Eligibility/Compliance Cabinet Subcommittee on Initial-Eligibility Issues

Mem., July 27, 1998, at 4 (Exhibit 2 to Pls.' Ans.). The NCAA does not even make the (unpersuasive) argument that its concern over "access to the finite number of athletic opportunities" is somehow equivalent to decreasing the graduation gap—the educational opportunity on which the NCAA would prefer this Court to focus. In fact, the NCAA's counsel opened oral argument before this Court by stating that the legitimate goal of the organization was to improve the academic performance of student-athletes, the best measure of which was graduation rates. No mention was made that a second objective of closing the black-white graduation gap existed.

* * *

The Court agrees that closing the black-white graduation rate gap is, as the NCAA states, "a subject of longstanding concern in the educational and civil rights communities." Def.'s Response at 15. However, that desirable outcome of Proposition 16, actual or projected, is simply a collateral benefit of promulgating a rule that sets heightened academic standards. Actually proffering such a "back-end" balancing between graduation rates as an express objective underlying Proposition 16 is in direct violation of the Supreme Court's prohibition against using a "bottom-line" defense to disparate impact cases involving pass/fail selection practices. *See Connecticut v. Teal*, 457 U.S. 440, 452–56 (1982) (achieving an appropriate racial balance after utilizing employer's entire promotional process did not preclude plaintiffs from establishing a prima facie case of disparate impact resulting from an examination administered to determine initially the employees eligible for promotion; moreover, such a "bottom-line" justification is an impermissible defense to employer liability).

Moreover, this explicitly race-based goal stands in stark contrast to the characterization of Proposition 16 as a facially neutral selection rule. The NCAA's continued contention that this goal underlies the promulgation of Proposition 16 raises serious questions concerning whether Proposition 16 is functioning simply as a proxy for a racial quota. This is especially so in light of the NCAA's research finding that "these group differences can be accounted for by taking into account the other high-school academic variables. This means that the prediction equation does not function differently for different racial groups." Report of the Special NCAA Comm. to Review Initial-Eligibility Standards, July 29, 1994, at 4, NCAA 15642 (Exhibit 19 to Pls.' Ans.).

Accordingly, the Court concludes that raising student-athlete graduation rates is a legitimate goal of the NCAA, but closing the gap between black and white student-athlete graduation rates is not.

b. Is there a manifest relationship?

* * *

Initially, the Court notes that the NCAA has not validated the use of the SAT, or any particular cutoff score of the SAT, as a predictor of student-athlete graduation rates.

* * *

Aside from the validity of using the SAT as an accurate predictor of student-athlete graduation rates, the record makes abundantly clear that, prior to adopting Proposition 16, the NCAA devoted substantial discussion towards the anticipated effects (raising graduation rates) and desired outcomes (increasing access to opportunities) of requiring additional high school course work, using core GPA and SAT cutoff scores, and allowing for the index or sliding scale. Specifically, the 820 cutoff score being challenged in this action is roughly one standard deviation below the SAT national mean, suggesting that the NCAA referred to an independent objective standard in identifying this particular cutoff score. What is special about a cutoff one standard deviation from the mean is that "for any test, regardless of how carefully it was prepared, statistical analysis, based on the normal distribution curve, shows that there is 68% probability that successive scores would fall within a range of one standard deviation from an actual score." *Guardians*, 630 F.2d at 102. Thus, the Court cannot conclude that the 820 cutoff score was arbitrarily selected in the sense that the particular cutoff in question was randomly chosen from the possible values of 400 through 1600.

But these facts only demonstrate that the NCAA was being abstractly rational. "Under *Wards Cove* the defendant's burden of production involves something beyond mere articulation of a rational basis for the challenged practice." *Harrison*, 940 F.2d at 802. It is apparent that, because the NCAA has relied exclusively on the predictive ability of the SAT on graduation rates of student-athletes in justifying the cutoff score, it has failed to analyze the issue in terms of what factors affect the graduation rate in addition to Proposition 16, thereby concomitantly failing to control for those variables. By simply pointing to the end result of graduation rates, the NCAA can all too obviously point to some relationship between choosing a particular cutoff score and increased graduation rates. However, it cannot possibly know with any degree of certainty whether the predicted increases in graduation rates are attributable to numerous factors other than the 820 cutoff score.

* * *

A review of the entire record indicates that it is notable more for what it does not present than for what it does. The Court appreciates the NCAA's intent that "the eligibility standards limit freshman participation in intercollegiate competition to those students who have demonstrated a minimum level of readiness for college academic work." Spanier Aff. P 7 (Exhibit B to Def.'s Response). However, the NCAA has failed to justify either (1) that its choice of a 820 cutoff score is reasonable and consistent with normal expectations of the acceptable proficiency of student-athletes towards attaining a college degree; (2) that its choice of a 820 cutoff score is the logical "break-point" in the distribution of SAT scores relevant to meeting its goal of raising student-athlete graduation rates (and increasing access to opportunities); or (3) that its choice of a 820 cutoff score is a valid measure of the minimal ability necessary to raise the graduation rates of student-athletes above those achieved prior to Proposition 16, let alone prior to Proposition 48. Indeed, the NCAA has not even articulated what it would consider normal expectations of the acceptable proficiency of student-athletes towards attaining a college degree or what it would consider the minimal ability necessary to graduate. It relies, instead, on vague, unsupported notions such as the presumption "that students earning a [820] SAT have serious reading problems." 1995 NCAA Convention Proceedings, at 258 (statement of Freeman Hrabowski).

* * *

The lack of justification behind the choice of the 820 cutoff is circumstantially revealed, for example, by the student-athletes in the partial qualifier region, whom the NCAA admits "look very similar in performance to several groups of student-athletes who are full qualifiers with lower GPAs.... The data indicate that partial qualifiers are performing at a slightly higher level than low-GPA full qualifiers. Taken as a whole, it is difficult to distinguish the academic performance of the partial qualifier from the performance of some qualifiers." NCAA Division I Academics/Eligibility/Compliance Cabinet Subcommittee on Initial-Eligibility Issues Mem., July 27, 1998, at 4. The fact is that the difference in graduation rates of partial qualifiers and certain full qualifiers is not statistically significant.

* * *

Accordingly, the Court concludes that the NCAA has not produced any evidence demonstrating that the cutoff score used in Proposition 16 serves, in a significant way, the goal of raising student-athlete graduation rates. Even if the NCAA had offered evidence sufficient to shift the inquiry back to Plaintiffs to show that they have carried their burden of persuasion, the Court concludes, as already shown above, that Plaintiffs have more than amply carried this burden by demonstrating that the racially adverse impact caused by the SAT cutoff score is not justified by any legitimate educational necessity.

In reaching this result, the Court stresses that this case does not preclude the use the SAT, or any particular cutoff score of the SAT, in the

NCAA's adoption of an initial eligibility rule. It may be "that no strong statistical basis exists for the use of any particular single minimum test score," but that is for the NCAA to determine more definitively after undertaking an appropriate analysis justifying an independent basis for choosing a cutoff score.

* * *

3. Whether There are Equally Effective Alternative Practices to Proposition 16

Notwithstanding the Court's conclusion above, Plaintiffs would ultimately prevail as they have carried their burden of persuasion to proffer an equally effective alternative practice that results in less racial disproportionality while still serving the goal of raising student-athlete graduation rates. Under Title VI, "equally effective" means equivalent, comparable, or commensurate, rather than identical. *See, e.g., Alexander v. Choate*, 469 U.S. 287, 294 (1985). The Third Circuit has even held that Plaintiffs may prevail "where they are able to suggest a viable alternative to the challenged practice which has the effect of reducing disparate impact and the employer refuses to adopt the alternative." *Newark Branch, NAACP v. Town of Harrison*, New Jersey, 940 F.2d 792, 798 (3d Cir. 1991) (emphasis added).

[The court found that alternative models in the NCAA's own memorandum were equally effective at achieving educational goals. These involved allowing partial qualifiers to become full qualifiers based on a sliding scale and lowering the minimum SAT score to 600, which is about two standard deviations below the national mean. The court examined statistics showing that while Proposition 16 would result in somewhat higher graduation rates, the small percentage increase was not sufficient to justify using a standard that had a disproportionate adverse impact.]

NOTES AND QUESTIONS

1. *Aftermath.* On appeal, the Third Circuit reversed this decision, but for jurisdictional, not substantive reasons. *Cureton v. NCAA*, 198 F.3d 107 (3d Cir. 1999). The plaintiffs filed the suit only against the NCAA, and not the Division I member schools where Shaw and Cureton sought and were denied athletic eligibility. Thus, the plaintiffs had to prove that the NCAA itself is subject to the requirements of Title VI of the Civil Rights Act as a "recipient of federal funds" (The schools where the plaintiffs sought to enroll were clearly subject to the statute). That same year, the Supreme Court held in a related statutory case that the NCAA was not subject to Title VI or Title IX because it was not a recipient of federal funds despite acting as a conduit for some federal appropriations transmitted to member schools. *NCAA v. Smith*, 525 U.S. 459 (1999).

2. *Private Enforcement of Title VI Foreclosed.* Another decision of the Supreme Court, *Alexander v. Sandoval*, 532 U.S. 275 (2001), also made it unlikely that student-athletes will be able to successfully sue specific Division I schools where they would have been eligible to attend but for the NCAA's rules. In *Sandoval*, a narrowly divided Court held that Title VI, unlike Title VII, does not afford a private right of action based on disparate impact. Only the federal government can challenge the NCAA rules based on their disparate impact. Student-athletes have to prove intentional discrimination.

3. *Disparate Impact.* Should the NCAA cease using standardized tests to determine eligibility for intercollegiate athletics, given the known racial disparities in test outcomes? Do you agree with the district court's decision in *Cureton*?

4. *Impact on Minorities.* Does NCAA regulation of academic eligibility on balance hinder or assist minorities in higher education? Consider the purposes of the regulation and whether the regulation actually results in fewer minorities participating in college sports. Even if the regulation on balance assists minorities in the aggregate, should we be concerned about a negative impact on a portion of the minority student population?

(b) Sliding Scale and APR

For purposes of initial freshman eligibility, the NCAA made some important revisions to Propositions 48 and 16 after the *Cureton* decision. First, the core curriculum requirement in high school has been raised again to 16 academic courses (4 years of English, 3 years of Math, 2 years of Science, 1 additional course in either English, Math, or Science, 2 years of social science, and four years of "additional academic coursework.") Second, in these core courses, while students may have a sliding scale of grades relative to their SAT or ACT scores, they have to secure at least a 2.00 cumulative grade point average. The NCAA has a pure sliding scale on the SAT or ACT side, one that requires a student who receives no more than a 400 SAT for just signing his name to have at least a 3.55 GPA in his 16 core high school courses.

In January 2005, the NCAA adopted another landmark reform with regard to academic progress. Each university team had to satisfy an official Academic Progress Rate (APR) or have its permitted scholarships reduced. This APR consists roughly of a 50 percent graduation rate over a five-year period and involves complex calculations and penalty determinations. If a school's average falls below a minimum APR, and a player becomes academically ineligible and then leaves the school, the school cannot replace him for at least one year. There is a 10 percent ceiling on the total number of team scholarships that can be lost; *i.e.*, 9 of football's 85 scholarship ceiling and 2 of basketball's 12.

In addition, if the deficiency continues, there are further penalties that can come into play, including a reduction in the amount of time a team can practice each week (with the time spent instead on academic activities), a reduction in number of competitions in which the team can participate, and a variety of other penalties, including coaching suspensions and restricted NCAA membership privileges.

And starting with the 2008–09 season, the additional penalty of a ban on post-season play was added for a team that did not achieve a 900 APR four-year average or above a 930 APR average in the previous two years. This penalty has been assessed most notably against the men's team at the University of Connecticut in 2012–13, two years after it won the NCAA Division I men's championship and the year before it won that title again. Finally, the ultimate possible penalty is a one-year suspension for a school's entire athletic program from NCAA membership.

NOTES AND QUESTIONS

1. *Purpose of Regulation.* What are the purposes of the NCAA's eligibility regulations for both the admission and academic progress of college athletes? Could they be better served by some type of federal government legislation and regulation?

2. *Sliding Scale.* If the NCAA does need to regulate the admission of college athletes, must it consider standardized tests as well as high school grades and courses? Is the NCAA now striking an appropriate balance by allowing sufficiently high grades in core courses to compensate for any standardized test score?

3. *Home Rule Revisited.* Should the NCAA instead consider the variant admission standards of its member schools so that each would have to limit how much it could depart from the high school records it demands of its average admits? Why should the same standards be imposed on, say, Stanford and Memphis? Is the same preparation required for academic progress at each institution?

4. *Eligibility Versus Academic Progress.* Should the NCAA be concerned only with the academic progress of the athletes its member schools choose to admit rather than with the pre-college academic records and potential of these athletes? Why does it need to regulate the latter as well as the former? Is regulation of the former more difficult and demanding of more administrative resources? Are the NCAA's current academic progress standards and incentives adequate and appropriate?

(c) Disability Law

The other long-time key feature of Proposition 48–16 is its insistence upon a minimum GPA in a host of "core courses" in high school to permit a student to compete in college sports in his or her freshman year. This initially much less controversial provision has already generated extensive litigation under a different branch of antidiscrimination law, the one designed to protect the disabled.

As mentioned above, the NCAA now requires students to have passed 16 core courses. Excluded from this *academic* standard are not only courses that are for vocational or personal service purposes, but also those that are "remedial, special education, or compensatory courses" designed for high school students with special learning problems. But the federal Rehabilitation Act of 1973 has long applied to all institutions that receive financial assistance from the government (*de facto*, encompassing all private as well as public colleges with students, not just professors, who receive any federal funding). The Americans with Disabilities Act of 1990 (ADA) expanded this federal antidiscrimination policy to cover a large array of purely private institutions that operate a place of "public accommodation" (including perhaps the NCAA). These laws protect not just those with physical disability, but also those with certain forms of learning disability (*e.g.*, dyslexia or attention deficit disorder). Chapter 14 explores some applications of the ADA to professional sports.

It took some time for the NCAA to focus its attention on the implications of Proposition 48–16 for the disabled. By the mid-1990s, though, the Association had not only recognized that those student-athletes would often have to take the SAT or ACT in a non-standard format, but they also might need a specially designed high school curriculum. The NCAA established a Special Subcommittee on Initial-Eligibility Waivers to conduct case-by-case reviews of the administrative exclusion of certain high school courses that did not seem to meet the academic core course standard. The Subcommittee decided that in order to accommodate the learning disabled, a "remedial" course could be treated as "core" if the course was designed to help the student proceed in a different format at a slower pace, but was aimed at the same intellectual content as the basic course at that school. The following judicial opinion addressed the question whether this somewhat more flexible NCAA regime had sufficiently accommodated the needs of this legally protected minority group.

GANDEN V. NCAA
1996 WL 680000 (N.D. Ill. 1996)

MANNING, DISTRICT JUDGE.

[Chad Ganden graduated at the age of 18 from Naperville North High School in June 1996, and was recruited by Michigan State as one of the fastest young swimmers in the United States. Even so, Ganden's learning disability—a "decoding" problem that primarily affects reading and writing skills—had seriously impeded Ganden's success in his suburban Chicago classroom. From his freshman through junior years, Ganden's cumulative

GPA was just 2.09. That learning condition was diagnosed at the end of his junior year, and the high school devised an Individualized Education Plan (IEP) for Ganden. This plan consisted of books on tape, a special resources study hall, and five courses to address his weaknesses—courses in Basic Communications Skills, Basic Composition Skills, Basic World Culture, LRC Typing, and LRC Computer. With the help of these additional resources, Ganden's GPA reached 3.0 in his senior year. Ganden took the ACT three times under special testing standards for his disability, and achieved a "compiled" score of 76. Under the NCAA bylaws, this ACT score required a GPA of 2.275 in 13 core courses. Unfortunately, only 11 of Ganden's high school courses met the general NCAA standard, and his cumulative GPA in these was just 2.136. Ganden could neither receive an athletic scholarship nor compete in intercollegiate sports.

Michigan State applied for a waiver for Ganden under the NCAA procedures for addressing the situation of disabled student-athletes who did not qualify under its rules. The Department of Justice, which had been discussing with the NCAA leadership the compatibility of these academic requirements with the ADA, specifically requested a waiver for Ganden. The NCAA Subcommittee was prepared to count Ganden's Basic Composition, Writing, and World History courses as "core courses," because they were an *academic* "accommodation to his learning disability." Adding these courses to Ganden's record satisfied the 13-core course requirement, but left his GPA at 2.153, below the 2.275 required for someone with his 76 ACT. That meant that Ganden was a "partial qualifier" who was able to receive a Michigan State scholarship and practice with its swimming team, but was not permitted to compete during his freshman year.

Ganden had asked the Subcommittee to include the LRC Typing and Computing courses in his core academic component. The Subcommittee did so to the extent of adding them to the calculation of the cumulative GPA (now 2.21), but would not let them replace other courses as part of the top 13 academic courses, which would move Ganden's cumulative GPA to above the 2.275 minimum required of someone at his ACT score level. Ganden thus filed suit under the ADA, seeking an injunction that would permit him to compete in his freshman year as a full qualifier under NCAA rules that were made compatible with his learning disability, his improved academic record after this disability had been diagnosed, and other external factors indicating he would succeed in college.

The district judge concluded that if Ganden were likely to succeed on the merits, he should be entitled to interim injunctive relief, because "an elite level swimmer only has a competitive life span of a few years, peaking between the ages of nineteen and twenty-one." If Ganden had to wait for trial, he would "lose an entire year of competitive competition . . . that was likely to inhibit his development as a swimmer during a critical point in his career." The judge also concluded that the NCAA was governed by the

ADA, as a private body that *"operates . . . a place of public accommodation."* The NCAA's certification rules function as a "ticket" for effective student-athlete use of Michigan State's physical facilities, because the rules determine whether the university can give them financial support, coaching, practice time, and competitive performance in athletic events taking place in those facilities.

The judge then turned to the crucial substantive issue whether the NCAA bylaws and procedures had the effect of "screening" Ganden out of college sports because of his learning disability, and if so, whether the NCAA had refused to take reasonable steps to accommodate its standards to Ganden's disability.]

1. Discrimination on the Basis of Disability.

The court rejects the NCAA's contention that Ganden cannot establish a causal link between its denial of Ganden's waiver application and his learning disability. The NCAA asserts that it denied Ganden's waiver application because he failed to meet the minimum eligibility requirements through his combined GPA and ACT scores. In support, the NCAA cites to *Sandison v. Michigan High School Athletic Ass'n*, 64 F.3d 1026 (6th Cir. 1995), in which two learning disabled students argued that a high school athletic association's age limitation excluded them from competition on the basis of their disabilities. Dismissing their claims under the ADA and the Rehabilitation Act of 1973, *Sandison* explained that "the plaintiffs' respective learning disability does not prevent the two students from meeting the age requirements, the passage of time does . . ." *Id.* at 1033 & 1036; *Johannesen v. NCAA*, No. 96 C 197 PHX ROS, p. 7 (D.C.Ariz.1996).

The court respectfully disagrees with this analysis. In implementing civil rights legislation for the disabled, Congress recognized that discrimination on the basis of a disability is "most often the product, not of invidious animus, but rather of thoughtlessness and indifference—of benign neglect." *Alexander v. Choate*, 469 U.S. 287, 297 & n. 12 (1985). Accordingly, the ADA and Rehabilitation Act focus on whether the defendant has provided a reasonable accommodation to an individual on the basis of a known disability.[10] In the instant case, the evidence strongly suggests that Ganden failed to take the requisite "core courses" or satisfy the remaining eligibility criteria because of his disability.[11] When they

---

[10] In respect to Ganden's claim under section 12182(b)(2)(A)(i), the provision expressly prohibits eligibility criteria that "screen out or tend to screen out" persons on the basis of their disability. Because the NCAA's definition of "core course" explicitly excludes special education, compensatory and remedial courses, this definition provides at least a prima facie case of a disparate impact on learning disabled students. Although the NCAA considered some of his remedial courses as "core," it did not consider all of his remedial courses as "core." If the NCAA had considered these two remaining remedial courses as "core," he would have satisfied the GPA standard.

[11] Each of Ganden's counselors testified that Ganden's disability required him to take remedial courses in order to succeed at college preparatory courses. These witnesses also explained that summer school courses were not an option for Ganden. In addition, Ganden has presented

reviewed his waiver application, the NCAA Subcommittee was aware of this condition and how it affected his ability to meet their eligibility requirements. Consequently, Ganden has presented a strong prima facie case that there is a causal link between the NCAA refusal to certify Ganden a "qualifier" and his learning disability.

2. Reasonable Modifications.

The court next addresses whether Ganden's requested modifications are reasonable or would "fundamentally alter" the nature of the privilege or accommodation to which he has been denied access. In determining whether reasonable accommodations have been provided under Title III, precedent interpreting the Rehabilitation Act and Title II of the ADA are instructive. *Vande Zande v. Wisc. Dept. of Admin.*, 44 F.3d 538, 542 (7th Cir. 1995); *see Allison v. Dept. of Corrections*, 94 F.3d 494, 497 (8th Cir. 1996). In particular, the Title III analysis is identical to the analysis determining whether a disabled plaintiff is "otherwise qualified" to participate in a program under the other statutes. *See Johnson v. Florida High School Activities Ass'n, Inc.*, 899 F. Supp. 579, 583 n. 5 (M.D. Fl. 1995). Under each provision, a modification is unreasonable if it imposes an "undue financial and administrative burden" or requires a "fundamental alteration" in the nature of the privilege or program. *Id.*; *see Pottgen v. Missouri State High School Activities Ass'n*, 40 F.3d 926, 930 (8th Cir. 1994).

This analysis requires that the court examine the particular eligibility criteria and the nature of the privilege that it monitors. The criteria at issue are the minimum GPA requirements and the "core course" definition that is instrumental in computing a student's GPA. The privilege at issue is the NCAA's intercollegiate athletic program. Ganden narrowly characterizes this privilege as swimming competitions. However, this cramped view ignores the broader nature and role of NCAA intercollegiate athletics. The NCAA is not merely a swimming group, but an integral part of the college community. The NCAA was created to promote the concept of the student-athlete through both athletic excellence and academic development. It offers its competitors more than an opportunity to swim, but also to represent the NCAA's member institutions. Towards this general purpose of the privilege, the eligibility requirements (1) insure that student-athletes are representative of the college community and not recruited solely for athletics; (2) insure that a student-athlete is academically prepared to succeed at college; and (3) preserve amateurism in intercollegiate sports.

---

evidence of the severity of his decoding disability and its effect on his academic performance. The record also indicates that assistance tailored toward his disability has permitted him to significantly improve his academic performance.

As an initial matter, the court does not believe that any alteration to the NCAA's eligibility requirements would "fundamentally alter" the nature of the privilege offered. In support of this position, the NCAA cites to two recent decisions holding that any waiver to an age cap for high school sports leagues would "fundamentally alter" the high school programs. *See Sandison*, 64 F.3d 1026 (Title II); *Pottgen*, 40 F.3d 926 (Title II). First, those cases found that requiring an individual assessment of each overage student would constitute an undue burden for the defendant. *Sandison*, 64 F.3d at 1034; *see also Pottgen*, 40 F.3d at 931 (refusing to assess eligibility criteria in light of plaintiffs' circumstances because it would [require] exhaustive evidentiary investigation by defendant for each disabled student). In contrast, the NCAA already has instituted an individual assessment process particularly intended to review student-athletes academic records and abilities. More importantly, the court believes that these decisions failed to adequately analyze the purposes of the act in light of the specific claims for modifications; *i.e.*, the circumstances of the plaintiff and learning disabled students. *Johnson*, 899 F. Supp. at 584. Rather, these courts simply asked whether the eligibility requirement served any important interests of the program. Like most rationally created procedural requirements, the court found that the age requirement did, and concluded that any alteration to those rules would fundamentally alter the program. *Pottgen*, 40 F.3d at 930 ("Waiving an essential eligibility standard would constitute a fundamental alteration in the nature of the [athletic] program."); *see Sandison*, 64 F.3d at 1035.

This analysis ignores the central issue under the ADA: Are reasonable accommodations possible in light of the disability. *See Johnson*, 899 F. Supp. at 584. Reasonable accommodation is a fact-bound inquiry, *see Sandison*, 64 F.3d at 1034, looking to whether the modification required for the plaintiff would "do violence to the admittedly salutary purposes underlying the [ ] rule." *Pottgen*, 40 F.3d at 932 (dissent). Therefore, a court must look to the underlying purposes of an eligibility requirement to determine if the modification would undermine those purposes in the circumstances of the plaintiff. Otherwise, any modification of a rule rationally tailored to the denied privilege would be unreasonable.

Although the court does not believe that any modification to the NCAA's eligibility requirements would "fundamentally alter" the nature of its accommodation, the court finds that Ganden does not have a reasonable likelihood of demonstrating that his requested modification would not "fundamentally alter" that accommodation. There is little doubt that the GPA and "core course" requirements generally serve important interests of the NCAA athletics. Because of its dual mission, the NCAA has an important interest in insuring that its student-athletes are prepared to succeed at college. Whatever criticism one may level at GPA and the national standardized tests, these provide significant objective predictors of a student's ability to succeed at college. The "core course" criteria further serves the dual interest of insuring the integrity of that GPA and independently insuring that the student has covered the minimum subject matter required for college.

However, in the case of learning disabled students, the NCAA may be able to serve these purposes and insure that a student has the necessary academic capabilities through consideration of additional factors. In fact, through its waiver application process, the NCAA provides such individualized consideration. In the case of learning disabled students, a generally improving academic record may indicate that prior remedial courses adequately substituted for earlier "core courses," even if not qualitatively and quantitatively identical to other "core courses." In such circumstances, some remedial courses may have served the same role as approved "core courses" to other students. Therefore, the record indicates that Title III requires the NCAA to consider a students' progress in his or her IEP courses and overall high school career.

Ganden could only satisfy the required GPA if the Subcommittee actually counted his two LRC courses as "core:" if the Subcommittee replaced other "core course" grades with the grades from the LRC courses. However, in contrast to Ganden's other remedial courses, neither of the LRC courses appear remotely similar to the subject areas of "core courses." While Title III may require the NCAA to count courses as "core" even if they are not substantively identical to approved "core courses," it does not require the NCAA to count courses with little substantive similarity. Whatever skills such a course may provide to the student, they cannot be said to substitute for earlier "core courses." Similarly, the grades from such courses do not provide valid indications of the student's academic potential. Based upon the current record, the court finds that this modification would "fundamentally alter" the privilege of participation in intercollegiate swimming.

The court also finds that lowering the minimum GPA for Ganden would "fundamentally alter" the nature of the privilege. Unlike a modification to the "core course" definition, lowering the GPA minimum directly removes the NCAA's primary objective tool to determine a student's academic capabilities. While circumstances may exist where such a modification are necessary, the court finds that it is generally unreasonable to require the NCAA to lower this basic standard. Instead, Title III would focus on less drastic modifications affecting the computation of the GPA, such as modifications to the "core course" requirement.

As Ganden argues, Title III requires the NCAA to individually assess his request for modifications. However, the NCAA provided such an assessment. The Subcommittee reviewed Ganden's case for over one hour. It received an application prepared by a member institution with a strong interest in procuring a waiver on his behalf. This package included his academic record, a psychological report focusing on his disability as well as his efforts and successes in overcoming it, and arguments on his behalf from MSU. In addition, the record indicates that the Subcommittee was aware of the Department of Justice's efforts and arguments on his behalf. After this review, the Subcommittee accommodated Ganden through granting him "partial qualifier" status.

While there is some doubt whether the NCAA actually counted Ganden's three "Basic" courses as "core" in consideration of his disability or MSU's reliance argument, the record reveals that the Subcommittee did consider Ganden's disability, his efforts to overcome it, and his impressive academic gains during his final two years of high school. Even though he did not meet the minimum GPA, it still granted Ganden "partial qualifier" status. Title III does not require the NCAA to simply abandon its eligibility requirements, but only to make reasonable modifications to them. The record reveals that the NCAA did precisely that.

* * *

4. Conclusion.

Although Ganden has demonstrated some likelihood of success on the merits with respect to questions of subject matter jurisdiction, the court finds that he has not shown a reasonable likelihood of success on the critical allegation that the NCAA's denial of his waiver application constituted "discrimination" under § 12182(b)(2) of Title III . . .

Injunction denied.

NOTES AND QUESTIONS

1. *Aftermath.* In the fall of 1997, just before Ganden was to begin varsity swimming for Michigan State in his sophomore year, the Department of Justice announced that its Civil Rights Division had concluded that the NCAA's eligibility rules and procedures did not adequately accommodate the situation and needs of Ganden and other learning-disabled athletes. The remedies proposed by the Department for this alleged ADA violation were to restore a fourth year of eligibility for Ganden and 33 other learning-disabled athletes who had lost their freshman athletic year, plus financial compensation for Ganden and four others who had filed complaints under this federal law. When the NCAA did not immediately accept this proposal, the Clinton Justice Department filed its own lawsuit under the ADA, forcing the NCAA to agree to settle all these cases in May 1998. While not admitting that it was a "place of public accommodation" subject to the ADA, the NCAA not only paid some money to each of these disabled plaintiffs, but it also altered its rules to accommodate their successors.

2. *A Different View of the NCAA and the ADA.* In *Butler v. NCAA*, 1996 WL 1058233 (W.D.Wash.1996), a federal district judge reached a contrary conclusion to that of *Ganden*. This unpublished opinion granted the plaintiff's motion for a preliminary injunction, finding that the NCAA was subject to the ADA because it "operated" a facility of "public accommodation."

3. *Current Approach.* Since *Ganden*, the NCAA now deems certain special education high school courses to be core academic, but only for documented learning-disabled student-athletes. And even if the latter cannot become eligible as college freshmen, they are given a fourth year of athletic eligibility if they have completed a substantial part of their college degree by the time they have reached their fifth year. Since the NCAA modified its policies for when learning disabled students can seek and receive waivers from the NCAA's initial eligibility requirements, there have been no new lawsuits filed against the NCAA raising this type of ADA or Rehabilitation Act claim. Under the current practice, the NCAA typically grants most waiver requests from learning disabled students for an initial eligibility waiver.

4. *Impact on Disabled.* Assuming the NCAA is governed by Title III of the Americans with Disabilities Act as an operator of a "place of public accommodation," what responsibilities does it have toward students with learning disabilities to provide reasonable accommodation to their disabilities when applying its regulations on admission standards, including those defining requisite "core" high school courses? Must it give individualized consideration to each applicant with learning disabilities rather than apply strictly its standards? If so, should the critical question be whether the learning disabled student's record is as predictive of academic success in college as the minimum required of the non-disabled? Or does the reasonable accommodation requirement demand taking greater risk with the disabled? Does the NCAA now provide adequate accommodation to the learning disabled?

2. THE UNIVERSITY-ATHLETE AGREEMENT

Assuming the athlete meets the eligibility requirements, the athlete can enter into an agreement with the University that operates much like a unilateral contract. This agreement has three separate parts: the national letter of intent, the financial aid agreement, and the university's rules and regulations.

Generally speaking, the university agrees to provide the athlete with tuition, room, board, books, and in some cases, cost of attendance. In exchange, the athlete agrees to attend the university, meet the university's academic requirements, and participate in intercollegiate athletics. Historically, these agreements had a one-year term, renewable annually for up to four years of eligibility. Now, universities can provide a legally-enforceable guarantee that athletes abiding by university rules will receive promised financial aid for four years.

The National Letter of Intent (NLI) is the initial agreement that the athlete enters into during high school. The primary functions of the letter are to bar other schools from recruiting the athlete and secure a scholarship for the athlete. If the athlete decides not to honor the letter of intent, the athlete must sit out a year unless the athletic director releases him or her from that agreement. A number of rules govern the execution of the national letter of intent. First and foremost, each sport has one or two "signing periods" when athletes can sign the letter. If the athlete is a minor, the parent must also sign the letter. Also, coaches cannot be present at the signing of the letter.

The NCAA has made it clear that the athlete remains bound to the letter even if the coach decides to leave the university, though schools presumably could release an athlete in such a case. From the perspective of the NCAA, the NLI is an agreement between the athlete and the university, even though the coach may be the central reason the athlete signs the NLI. Beyond the NLI, the athlete-university relationship is an agreement that governs the interaction between the athlete and the institution during his or her time as a student. The next case explores the scope of this relationship.

TAYLOR V. WAKE FOREST
191 S.E.2d 379 (N.C. Ct. App. 1972)

CAMPBELL, JUDGE.

[Gregg Taylor was recruited by and signed a letter of intent to play football for Wake Forest University. The grant—in—aid, or athletic scholarship, provided as follows:

> This Grant, if awarded, will be for 4 years provided I conduct myself in accordance with the rules of the Conference, the NCAA, and the Institution. I agree to maintain eligibility for intercollegiate athletics under both Conference and Institutional rules. Training rules for intercollegiate athletics are considered rules of the Institution, and I agree to abide by them. If injured while participating in athletics supervised by a member of the coaching staff, the Grant or Scholarship will be honored; and the medical expenses will be paid by the Athletic Department. This grant, when approved, is awarded for academic and athletic achievement and is not to be interpreted as employment in any manner whatsoever.

Taylor played for Wake Forest's football team in his freshman year. During the fall semester he compiled a grade point average of 1.0 (out of 4.0), far below the 1.35 the school required all students to have at the end of the freshman year. Taylor did not attend the spring football practices, and his GPA for the spring semester rose to 1.9. He then decided not to play football in the fall of his sophomore year; his GPA rose again, to 2.4.

Because of his refusal to play football, Wake Forest's Scholarship Committee, on the recommendation of the Faculty Athletic Committee, revoked his scholarship as of the end of his sophomore year. Taylor nevertheless remained at Wake Forest and graduated on time. He sued to recover $5,500 in expenses incurred during his last two years because he had lost his scholarship. Faced with Wake Forest's motion for summary dismissal, Taylor contended that under the relevant contract doctrines there was a genuine issue for a jury to determine—whether or not he had "acted reasonably and in good faith in refusing to participate in the football program at Wake Forest when such participation interfered with reasonable academic progress."]

* * *

The plaintiffs' position depends upon a construction of the contractual agreement between plaintiffs and Wake Forest. As stated in the affidavit of George J. Taylor, the position of the plaintiffs is that it was orally agreed between plaintiffs and the representative of Wake Forest that:

> [I]n the event of any conflict between educational achievement and athletic involvement, participation in athletic activities could be limited or eliminated to the extent necessary to assure reasonable academic progress.

And plaintiffs were to be the judge as to what "reasonable academic progress" constituted.

We do not agree with the position taken by plaintiffs. The scholarship application filed by Gregg Taylor provided:

> I agree to maintain eligibility for intercollegiate athletics under both Conference and Institutional rules. Training rules for intercollegiate athletics are considered rules of the Institution, and I agree to abide by them.

Both Gregg Taylor and his father knew that the application was for "Football Grant-In-Aid Or A Scholarship," and that the scholarship was "awarded for academic and athletic achievement." It would be a strained construction of the contract that would enable the plaintiffs to determine the "reasonable academic progress" of Gregg Taylor. Gregg Taylor, in consideration of the scholarship award, agreed to maintain his athletic eligibility and this meant both physically and scholastically. As long as his grade average equaled or exceeded the requirements of Wake Forest, he was maintaining his scholastic eligibility for athletics. Participation in and attendance at practice were required to maintain his physical eligibility. When he refused to do so in the absence of any injury or excuse other than to devote more time to studies, he was not complying with his contractual obligations.

Summary judgment granted.

NOTES AND QUESTIONS

1. *The Move to Multi-Year Scholarships.* Sometime after *Taylor* (and after a similar verdict in *Begley v. Mercer University*, 367 F. Supp. 908 (E.D. Tenn.1973)), the NCAA amended its Division I rules to provide that "where a student's athletic ability is taken into consideration in any degree in awarding financial aid, such aid shall not be awarded in excess of one academic year." Article 15.3.3.1. While high school athletes could learn that the practice of the athletic department is to recommend renewal of financial aid, this rule explicitly forbade any assurance that renewal is automatic (even for an athlete who suffers a career-ending injury). Why would the NCAA impose these constraints on its own members' freedom of action? Could the NCAA justify these constraints if challenged in an antitrust suit?

In 2012, the NCAA amended its rule to allow (but not require) member institutions in Division I to give multi-year scholarships not to exceed five years and to provide continued financial aid to student-athletes who had exhausted their playing eligibility but needed more time to graduate. By 2015, all of the Power-5 conference schools (as well as Notre Dame) had agreed to offer multi-year athletic scholarships.

2. *The Question of Renewal.* Under what circumstances is it ethically and legally appropriate for a school not to renew a scholarship (or to cancel a multi-year scholarship) for a student who has neither exhausted eligibility nor graduated? Because he or she was a poor player? Injured? Academically ineligible? Missed practice once a week in order to attend chemistry lab? If the school refuses to renew the scholarship for an inappropriate reason, does the student-athlete have any legal remedy against the school? At its annual convention in January 2015, the NCAA's newly autonomous subdivision of the Big Five conferences voted to prohibit its schools from rescinding a scholarship for athletic reasons.

3. *Leaving Early.* As explored below, there are a growing number of players who are leaving college early to play professional sports. NCAA rules have (not very successfully) sought to reduce those numbers by taking away the college eligibility of anyone who opts into the draft (football) or anyone who is actually selected in the draft (basketball). Suppose a college was to add a condition to its standard scholarship terms that required student-athletes who accept a scholarship in their first year to complete their full four years of play at the school, or perhaps have to pay over a certain proportion of their professional earnings during the years they still "owed" the school. The college athletic director might say that he is asking for no more than the standard renewable options that musicians, for example, must give their record

companies as part of the contract for their first recording. Should such a contract term be enforceable against student athletes (or student musicians or actors with college scholarships)? Should one's judgment depend on whether the decision is made by individual universities like Ohio State and Georgetown, or the NCAA membership as a whole?

4. *Grounds for Alleging Breach of Promise and Tortious Conduct by Universities.* A similar case, *Jackson v. Drake University*, 778 F. Supp. 1490 (S.D. Iowa 1991), involved contract and tort claims by Terrell Jackson in a dispute with Drake University. Jackson claimed that when Drake recruited him, basketball coach Tom Abatemarco promised him both the right to play basketball and an environment conducive to high academic achievement. When Jackson got to Drake, the coaches allegedly pressured him to take easy courses and submit plagiarized papers, and denied him adequate study time. When Jackson complained about the situation, Abatemarco was said to have harassed him at practice, called him foul names, and made him run extra drills and do extra exercises. In the middle of his sophomore year, Jackson quit the team. He filed suit against the school alleging breach of contract, educational malpractice, negligent misrepresentation in recruiting, and fraud. The court dismissed the contract claim because the entitlements upon which it was based, especially the right to play basketball, were not expressly contained in Jackson's scholarship documents. Citing Ross, *see infra* Section B.2., the court dismissed the educational malpractice claim, finding it was not a viable tort in Iowa. The court did, however, order a trial of the negligent misrepresentation and fraud claims, according to the following legal specifications:

> To properly state a claim of negligent misrepresentation, Jackson must allege that the defendant, in the course of its business or profession or employment, supplied false information for the guidance of others in their business transactions, that the information was justifiably relied on by the plaintiff, and the defendant failed to exercise reasonable care or competence in communicating the information. To state a claim for fraud, Jackson must allege a material misrepresentation, made knowingly, with the intent to induce Jackson to act, upon which he justifiably relied, with damages.

Id. at 1494.

3. NCAA RECRUITING REGULATIONS

The NCAA's constitution and bylaws contain extensive regulations concerning the recruiting of student-athletes and limits on benefits available to recruits. Arguably a core principle comes from § 1.3.1, which provides,

> The competitive athletics programs of member institutions are designed to be a vital part of the educational system. A basic purpose of this Association is to maintain intercollegiate athletics

as an integral part of the educational program and the athlete as an integral part of the student body and, by so doing, retain a clear line of demarcation between intercollegiate athletics and professional sports.

NCAA Article § 1.3.1.

In the eyes of the NCAA, providing non-educational benefits to recruits has the effect of making them professionals, and compromising their amateur status. The principle of amateurism, discussed *supra* in Chapter 10, sets forth the idea of amateur "student-athletes," who are "motivated primarily by education and by the physical, mental and social benefits to be derived." NCAA Article § 2.9. The NCAA's rules thus serve to protect the amateur "from exploitation by professional and commercial enterprises." NCAA Article § 2.9. The principle governing recruiting underscores these ideas, explaining,

> The recruiting process involves a balancing of the interests of prospective student-athletes, their educational institutions and the Association's member institutions. Recruiting regulations shall be designed to promote equity among member institutions in their recruiting of prospective student-athletes and to shield them from undue pressures that may interfere with the scholastic or athletics interests of the prospective student-athletes or their educational institutions.

NCAA Article § 2.11.

The competing purposes, then, of NCAA recruiting rules are to protect the amateur status of its athletes and to promote equity in recruiting and fair competition. Interestingly, these echo the two narratives concerning the NCAA we raised at the beginning of Chapter 10. On the one hand, making sure athletes remain amateurs, at least as the NCAA defines the concept (tuition, room, board, books, and sometimes cost of attendance), is a paramount concern connected strongly to the concept of education. On the other hand, limiting recruiting methods by some schools that other schools may not be able to match, policing improper conduct, and eliminating cheating in recruiting promotes the fair competition that many coaches and athletic directors demand.

To be sure, the byzantine rulebook goes to great lengths to heavily regulate all aspects of recruiting, and prevent even de minimis benefits to prospective student-athletes. Specifically, these rules regulate contacts between coaches and recruits, evaluation of recruits, offers and inducements that universities can make to recruits, the recruiting materials universities can provide, the transportation a university can provide, official paid visits to campus, unofficial non-paid visits, entertainment, reimbursement, and employment of individuals associated with the recruit, sports camps, high school all-star games, precollege expenses, recruiting calendars, and so forth. From the NCAA's perspective, *every* improper benefit matters.

Consider the purpose of these detailed rules. Are they designed primarily to further the academic mission of the university? To preclude exploitation of athletes in the recruiting process? To maintain the strong, lucrative commercial product that college sports has become? If the rules were relaxed, would Alabama and USC gain a significant additional recruiting advantage over Mississippi State and Cal?

Under this regime, student athletes bear a significant degree of responsibility for preserving their amateur status. The general bylaw principle explains:

> The recruitment of a student-athlete by a member institution or any representative of its athletics interests in violation of the Association's legislation, as acknowledged by the institution or established through the Association's infractions process, shall result in the student athlete becoming ineligible to represent that institution in intercollegiate athletics... A student is responsible for his or her involvement in a violation of NCAA regulations during the student's recruitment, and involvement in a Level I or Level II violation may cause the student to become permanently ineligible for intercollegiate athletics competition at that institution.

NCAA Article 13.01.1. Athletes accepting benefits thus might not only lose the ability to play for a particular school, but also can lose the ability to compete altogether. Under NCAA rules, once an athlete accepts benefits, his or her amateur status can be lost forever.

Recruiting rules likewise cast a wide net around institutions by making them responsible for third party actions. As the NCAA constitution states,

> An institution's "responsibility" for the conduct of its intercollegiate athletics program shall include responsibility for the acts of an independent agency, corporate entity (*e.g.*, apparel or equipment manufacturer) or other organization when a member of the institution's executive or athletics administration, or an athletics department staff member, has knowledge that such agency, corporate entity or other organization is promoting the institution's intercollegiate athletics program.

NCAA Article § 6.4.1. This same proviso applies to individuals as well (§ 6.4.2), meaning that a university is responsible for every third party interaction with a prospective recruit—a heavy administrative burden. Universities regularly report their violations to the NCAA. Compliance offices create monitoring systems to track phone calls, contacts, expenditures, and all of the recruiting activities of their coaches.

The enforcement arm of the Committee on Infractions (COI) decides whether to investigate a program, and if a case is necessary. The judicial arm of the COI then conducts a hearing, determines what violations exist, and what the appropriate sanction should be. The next case is a recent example of a serious recruiting violation.

UNIVERSITY OF LOUISVILLE
PUBLIC INFRACTIONS APPEALS COMMITTEE REPORT
NCAA Infractions Appeals Committee, February 20, 2018

* * *

VI. PENALTIES IMPOSED BY THE COMMITTEE ON INFRACTIONS. * * *

Financial penalties (VI-3): The institution shall pay a financial penalty of $5,000 (institution imposed). The former operations director knew that his actions violated NCAA legislation. The student-athletes who participated in the striptease dances, prostitution and "tipping" of the strippers became ineligible for competition. They knew or should have known that their actions were contrary to NCAA legislation. Therefore, consistent with former Bylaw 19.5.2–(i) and Bylaw 31.2.2.4, the IAC's [Infractions Appeals Committee] report in *Purdue University* (2000), IAC Report No. 306 in *University of Memphis* (2010) and IAC Report No. 414 in *Syracuse University* (2015), the institution shall return to the NCAA all of the monies it has received to date through conference revenue sharing for its appearances in the 2012, 2013, 2014 and 2015 NCAA Men's Basketball Tournaments. Future revenue distributions that are scheduled to be provided to the institution from those tournaments shall be withheld by the conference and forfeited to the NCAA. A complete accounting of this financial penalty shall be included in the institution's annual compliance reports and, after the conclusion of the probationary period, in correspondence from the conference to the Office of the Committees on Infractions.

Vacation of records (VI-12): The COI has not previously dealt with a case like this. A team staff member arranged striptease dances and acts of prostitution for enrolled student-athletes and prospects who eventually enrolled at the institution. Some of the prospects were minors. By his actions, the former operations director rendered those student-athletes and prospects ineligible for competition. The violations were serious, intentional, numerous and occurred over multiple years. Therefore, pursuant to former Bylaw 19.5.2–(h) and Bylaw 31.2.2.3, and consistent with IAC Report No. 306 in *University of Memphis* (2010) and IAC Report

414 in *Syracuse University* (2015), the institution shall vacate all regular season and conference tournament wins in which ineligible student-athletes competed from the time they became ineligible through the time they were reinstated as eligible for competition through either the student-athlete reinstatement process or through a grant of limited immunity. Further, if any of the student-athletes competed in the NCAA Division I Men's Basketball Championships at any time they were ineligible, the institution's participation in the championships shall be vacated. The individual records of the ineligible student-athletes shall also be vacated. Further, the institution's records regarding men's basketball, as well as the record of the head coach, will reflect the vacated records and will be recorded in all publications in which men's basketball records are reported, including, but not limited to, institutional media guides, recruiting material, electronic and digital media plus institutional, conference and NCAA archives. Any institution which may subsequently hire the head coach shall similarly reflect the vacated wins in his career records documented in media guides and other publications cited above. Head coaches with vacated wins on their records may not count the vacated wins to attain specific honors or victory "milestones" such as 100th, 200th or 500th career victories. Any public reference to these vacated contests shall be removed from athletics department stationery, banners displayed in public areas and any other forum in which they may appear. Any trophies or other team awards attributable to the vacated contests shall be returned to the Association.

To ensure that all institutional and student-athlete vacations, statistics and records are accurately reflected in official NCAA publication and archives, the sports information director (or other designee as assigned by the director of athletics) must contact the NCAA media coordination and statistics staff and appropriate conference officials to identify the specific student-athletes and contests impacted by the penalties. In addition, the institution must provide the NCAA media coordination and statistics staff a written report detailing those discussions. This document will be maintained in the permanent files of the NCAA media coordination and statistics department. This written report must be delivered to the NCAA media coordination and statistics staff no later than 45 days following the initial infractions decision release or, if the vacation penalty is appealed, at the conclusion of the appeals process. A copy of the written report shall also be delivered to the Office of the Committees on Infractions (OCOI) at the same time.

VII. ISSUES RAISED ON APPEAL. In its written appeal, Louisville asserted that the Committee on Infractions abused its discretion when prescribing penalties VI-3 and VI-12.

IX. INFRACTIONS APPEALS COMMITTEE'S RESOLUTION OF THE ISSUES RAISED ON APPEAL. In reviewing this case, a penalty prescribed by the hearing panel, including determinations regarding the existence and weighing of any aggravating or mitigating factors, shall not be set aside on appeal except on a showing by the appealing party that the hearing panel abused its discretion. The hearing panel determines the credibility of the evidence. [The standard on review is abuse of discretion].

As we stated in the *Alabama State University* case:

". . .we conclude that an abuse of discretion in the imposition of a penalty occurs if the penalty: (1) was not based on a correct legal standard or was based on a misapprehension of the underlying substantive legal principles; (2) was based on a clearly erroneous factual finding; (3) failed to consider and weigh material factors; (4) was based on a clear error of judgment, such that the imposition was arbitrary, capricious, or irrational; or (5) was based in significant part on one or more irrelevant or improper factors." [*Alabama State University, Infractions Appeals Committee Public Report*, June 30, 2009, Page No. 23].

Louisville challenged the vacation of records from the 2011–12, 2012–13, 2013–14 and 2014–15 academic years, as well as having to return the revenue earned from its appearances in the 2012, 2013, 2014 and 2015 NCAA Men's Basketball Tournaments.

* * *

In its review of the case, the committee agreed with the Committee on Infractions that the involved student-athletes knew or should have known they were receiving improper benefits in violation of NCAA legislation. In fact, the institution conceded the student athletes received improper benefits during the oral argument. [Infractions Appeals Committee Oral Argument Transcript, Page Nos. 8, 19–23]. Because the student-athletes received improper benefits, it follows they competed while ineligible, which in turn supports the vacation of records and financial penalties imposed by the Committee on Infractions. In response to the institution's argument that one of the involved student athletes who competed while ineligible would have been reinstated, it is the committee's position there is no guarantee regarding the reinstatement process. [*Georgia Institute of Technology Infractions Appeals Committee Public Report* March 9, 2012, Page No. 14]. The institution is not free from punishment now based on an assumption regarding the reinstatement process with respect to other student-athletes at different institutions.

Pursuant to Bylaw 19.9.7–(g), a vacation of records penalty is appropriate when there are ineligible student-athletes involved in competition. The Committee on Infractions has significant discretion to fashion appropriate penalties for the overall infractions at issue in a case. [*St. Mary's College of California Infractions Appeals Committee Public*

Report October 14, 2013, Page No. 6]. While the Committee on Infractions retains discretion to apply (or not apply) the vacation penalty under any circumstances it believes appropriate, this committee has indicated the likelihood of such a penalty is significantly increased when any of the following aggravating factors are present:

1. Academic fraud;

2. Serious intentional violations;

3. Direct involvement of a coach or high-ranking school administrator;

4. A large number of violations;

5. Competition while academically ineligible;

6. Ineligible competition in a case that includes a finding of failure to monitor or a lack of institutional control; or

7. When vacation of a similar penalty would be imposed if the underlying violations were secondary.

[*Georgia Tech Infractions Appeals Committee Public Report* Page No. 14].

This committee recognizes the factors involved in vacation of records cases continue to evolve and expand. Because this case involved serious and intentional violations, which Louisville agreed were reprehensible and inexcusable [Infractions Appeals Committee Oral Argument Transcript, Page No. 9], direct involvement of an institutional staff member, and a large number of violations, the Committee on Infractions was within its legislated authority to impose the vacation of records penalty. Given the reprehensible nature of the violations, which resulted in ineligible student-athletes competing over a four-year time period, the Committee on Infractions was also within its authority to impose the financial penalties assessed in this case. For this reason, the committee did not find an abuse of discretion in the imposition of the penalties in this case.

Notwithstanding this committee's outcome in this case, we are concerned the Committee on Infractions did not sufficiently articulate how it balanced the mitigating factors, including the institution's self-imposed penalties, with the aggravating factors. A thorough articulation of mitigating and aggravating factors helps the institution appearing before the Committee on Infractions to understand the reasons underlying the penalties imposed as an element of fundamental fairness; it informs the NCAA membership for general deterrence and educational purposes; and helps this committee better evaluate on appeal whether the Committee on Infractions has appropriately weighed all the factors relevant to setting penalties in order to determine whether a penalty imposed is excessive and an abuse of discretion. We consider this component of the Committee on Infractions' decision-making process and the Committee on Infractions' written decision of critical importance. [*Florida State University Infractions Appeals Committee Public Report* January 5, 2010, Page Nos. 11–12].

X. CONCLUSION. The penalties are affirmed.

NCAA Infractions Appeals Committee

NOTES AND QUESTIONS

1. *Aftermath.* Louisville fired its head basketball coach, Rick Pitino, soon after the decision came down. The reason for his termination, though, was the discovery of a new set of violations related to the recruitment of an athlete allegedly compensated with $100,000. These allegations emerged as part of a federal probe that so far has involved the arrest of 10 individuals for corruption and bribery.

2. *Louisville Recruiting Violations.* While the presence of violations is clear here (and in most cases), the real question is whether the sanction is appropriate. Do you agree with the decision of the IAC? Why or why not?

3. *Bag Man? University of Mississippi Infractions Case.* Also in 2018, the NCAA COI held that recruiting violations by the University of Mississippi warranted a two-year post-season ban in football. At the heart of the case was the allegation that an assistant coach had helped arrange for a booster to pay a recruit $10,000. The recruit, who incidentally enrolled at archrival Mississippi State, was granted immunity for his testimony. Ole Miss has appealed the COI decision, and its appeal before the IAC is pending. The case raised the issue of "bag men," wealthy donors who provide money to recruits and their families as an inducement to attend their university. Many believe that this practice is widespread, particularly in the SEC, and that Ole Miss was the unfortunate institution to be caught. An incident from months earlier made an investigation more likely. Laremy Tunsil was interviewed on the night of the NFL draft. He had dropped multiple spots in the draft after an anonymous hacker released a photo on social media of him smoking marijuana. He admitted during the ensuing press conference that he had received money from Ole Miss assistant coaches, but the NCAA was unable to prove that to be true, even with text messages that hinted as much.

4. *Recruiting Barbeques?* The University of Tennessee basketball infractions case from a few years prior sheds additional insight into the restrictions of the NCAA recruiting rules. Coach Bruce Pearl hosted a barbeque at his house for prospective players and their families in violation of NCAA rules. Pearl lied about the party to investigators, who ultimately found pictures on social media of the party. Pearl received a show cause order and was unable to coach for several years.

5. *Excessive Phone Calls?* In 2008, Indiana basketball coach Kelvin Sampson was responsible for five major NCAA violations for misusing phone

calls and text messages in violation of NCAA rules. The rules impose very specific limits on the kind and timing of contact coaches can make with potential recruits. Sampson abused those rules, which resulted in serious sanctions for him as a coach and for the Indiana basketball program.

6. *Fair Play or Paternalism?* The NCAA recruiting rules discussed above exist to promote fair play in recruiting in light of the amateurism rules. Are such rules appropriate or paternalistic? Are the rules too restrictive, applying so broadly as to limit basic human contact? Should athletes be prevented from receiving any valuable benefits during recruitment in light of the millions of dollars that coaches earn annually? Or does the amount of money on the line for coaches require the NCAA's regulation?

7. *Can Lines Be Drawn Between Recruitment Benefits?* If the NCAA allowed barbecues at coaches' houses, could they effectively distinguish dinners at fancy restaurants or parties with prostitutes? How would you draw lines in recruitment rules?

B. THE STUDENT-ATHLETE

After the foregoing discussion of the limitations on athletes receiving benefits as recruits, this next section explores the impact of NCAA and university rules on other aspects of student-athlete experience. We first explore the expectation that the university provide academic opportunity, and then examine the rules on transferring institutions, before moving to the limits imposed by the principle of amateurism, including NCAA rules concerning becoming a professional, entering drafts, and employing agents.

1. ACADEMIC OPPORTUNITY

(a) Access to Education

As discussed above, the student-athlete has a claim to a legitimate opportunity to an education. The university, as an institution of higher learning, bears significant responsibility in affording such opportunities to intercollegiate athletes, while also ensuring that athletes do not engage in academic fraud. Some fear that the university's real interest may lie in athletic performance, not academic competence, despite the rhetoric of the NCAA and its member institutions. The next case explores a challenge to a university's failure to provide academic opportunity followed by an example of widespread academic fraud.

ROSS V. CREIGHTON UNIV.
740 F. Supp. 1319 (N.D. Ill. 1990)

NORDBERG, DISTRICT JUDGE.

One day in July 1987, Kevin Ross, a former college basketball player, barricaded himself in a high-rise hotel room in downtown Chicago and threw assorted pieces of furniture out the window. As Ross currently recalls it, the defenestrated furniture "symbolized" the employees of Creighton University, whose alleged misdeeds he blames for the onset of this "major depressive episode." Ross now sues the university in contract and tort. The gist of Ross's Amended Complaint is that Creighton caused this episode and otherwise injured him by recruiting him to attend the school on a basketball scholarship while knowing that Ross, who scored nine points out of a possible 36 on the American College Test, was pitifully unprepared to attend Creighton, which is a private school whose average student in the year Ross matriculated, 1978, scored 23.2 points on the ACT.

COMPLAINT

Ross, who is six feet and nine inches tall, was a high school basketball star in Kansas City, Kansas, when Creighton recruited him. Creighton knew that Ross could not handle college-level studies, but kept him eligible for the basketball team by recommending that he enroll in "bonehead" (Ross's description) courses, such as ceramics, marksmanship, and the respective theories of basketball, track and field, and football. Under its rules, the university would not have accepted the pursuit of this esoteric curriculum by a non-athlete. After four years, when his basketball eligibility expired, Ross had earned only 96 of the 128 credits required to graduate, maintaining a "D" average. His reading skills were those of a seventh-grader; his overall language skills, those of a fourth-grader.

In order to get Ross remedial education, representatives of Creighton made arrangements for Ross to attend Chicago's Westside Preparatory School, an elementary and high school whose founder, Marva Collins, has drawn national attention for her abilities as an educator. As its name suggests, Westside Prep is a school for children, not for adults. Ross says that Creighton representatives made four trips to Chicago to discuss Ross's enrollment. The agreement to enroll Ross is spelled out in a letter dated July 29, 1982, from Collins to Creighton's athletic director. The letter, countersigned by a Creighton official and returned to Collins, obligated Creighton to pay for Ross's tuition, special tutoring, books and living expenses. Ross attended Westside in 1982 and 1983. He later attended Roosevelt University, also located in Chicago, but dropped out after 1985 for want of money. Ross's furniture-throwing outburst took place on July 23, 1987. He was arrested and ordered to make restitution in the amount of $7,500.

* * *

ROSS'S TORT CLAIM

... Ross says [his tort] claim is a hybrid of "negligent infliction of emotional distress" and "educational malpractice." These strands of tort law "intertwine" to form the novel tort of "negligence in recruiting and repeatedly re-enrolling an athlete utterly incapable—without substantial tutoring and other support—of performing the academic work required to make educational progress," exacerbated by the enrollment of plaintiff in a school with children half his age and size. Before considering the merits of this tort, the Court must unravel its separate threads.

Educational malpractice is a tort theory beloved of commentators, but not of courts. While often proposed as a remedy for those who think themselves wronged by educators (*see, e.g.,* J. Elson, *A Common Law Remedy for the Educational Harms Caused by Incompetent or Careless Teaching,* 73 Nw. U. L. Rev. 641 (1978)), educational malpractice has been repeatedly rejected by the American courts.

* * *

Whether to create a cause of action for educational malpractice is, of course, a question for the Court, which determines as a matter of law whether a duty runs from defendant to plaintiff. It is a matter of considering sound social policy, guided by looking to " '[t]he likelihood of injury, the magnitude of the burden of guarding against it and the consequences of placing that burden upon defendant.' "

* * *

This Court believes the same general concerns would lead the Illinois courts to reject the tort of educational malpractice. Admittedly, the term "educational malpractice" has a seductive ring to it; after all, if doctors, lawyers, accountants and other professionals can be held liable for failing to exercise due care, why can't teachers? The answer is that the nature of education radically differs from other professions. Education is an intensely collaborative process, requiring the interaction of student with teacher. A good student can learn from a poor teacher; a poor student can close his mind to a good teacher. Without effort by a student, he cannot be educated. Good teaching methods may vary with the needs of the individual student. In other professions, by contrast, client cooperation is far less important; given a modicum of cooperation, a competent professional in other fields can control the results obtained. But in education, the ultimate responsibility for success remains always with the student. Both the process and the result are subjective, and proof or disproof extremely difficult.

* * *

It also must be remembered that education is a service rendered on an immensely greater scale than other professional services. If every failed student could seek tort damages against any teacher, administrator and school he feels may have shortchanged him at some point in his education, the courts could be deluged and schools shut down. The Court believes that Illinois courts would avert the flood and the educational loss. This is not to say that the mere worry that litigation will increase justifies a court's refusal to remedy a wrong; it is to say that the real danger of an unrestrained multiplication of lawsuits shows the disutility of the proposed remedy. If poor education (or student laziness) is to be corrected, a common law action for negligence is not a practical means of going about it.

* * *

[Having rejected both the general tort of educational malpractice and Ross' claim for negligent infliction of emotional distress, the court then asked whether Ross nonetheless has a cause] of action that is *sui generis*? Ross argues that he does, contending that "the present case is so unique and egregious that, despite the lack of precedent, a cause of action should be found to exist." Ross basically argues that a special tort be created for the benefit of student athletes, or more precisely, for the benefit of student athletes whose academic performance would not have qualified them to be students had they not been athletes. In Ross's view, "The present case does not question classroom methodology or the competence of instruction. Rather the issue is whether Plaintiff should ever have been admitted to Creighton and whether, once admitted, Creighton had a duty to truly educate Plaintiff and not simply to maintain his eligibility for basketball. . . ."

Ross's inability to plead a cause of action under existing law strongly counsels against creating a new cause of action in his favor. Rules serve little purpose if they are not reasonably predictable and if they do not apply across the board, for one cannot conform behavior to the unknowable. *See* A. Scalia, *The Rule of Law as a Law of Rules*, 56 U. Chicago L. Rev. 1175, 1178–79 (1989). Even a new rule declared through the evolutionary process of the common law ought fairly be deduced from existing doctrine—something that cannot be said for Ross's claim. The policy reasons considered by the Illinois courts further counsel against recognition of this new duty. Schools would be forced to undertake the delphic science of diagnosing the mental condition of potential recruits. And why should the cause of action be limited to student athletes? Shouldn't all students who actually pay tuition also have an equal right to recover if they are negligently admitted, and once negligently admitted, have a right to recover if the school negligently counsels and educates them? To allow Ross to recover might redress a wrong (assuming, for sake of argument, that he was in fact exploited), but it would also endanger the admissions prospects of thousands of marginal students, as schools scrambled to factor into their admissions calculations whether a potentially "negligent admission" now could cost unforeseeable tort damages later. The Court should not and will not craft a new tort for Ross.

On appeal, the Seventh Circuit Court of Appeals upheld the summary dismissal of Ross' tort theory of educational malpractice, but took a somewhat different view of Ross' contract claim.

ROSS V. CREIGHTON UNIV.
957 F.2d 410 (7th Cir. 1992)

RIPPLE, CIRCUIT JUDGE.

* * *

It is held generally in the United States that the "basic legal relation between a student and a private university or college is contractual in nature. The catalogues, bulletins, circulars, and regulations of the institution made available to the matriculant become a part of the contract." Indeed, there seems to be "no dissent" from this proposition. As the district court correctly noted, Illinois recognizes that the relationship between a student and an educational institution is, in some of its aspects, contractual. It is quite clear, however, that Illinois would not recognize all aspects of a university-student relationship as subject to remedy through a contract action. "A contract between a private institution and a student confers duties upon both parties which cannot be arbitrarily disregarded and may be judicially enforced." However, "a decision of the school authorities relating to the academic qualification of the students will not be reviewed.... Courts are not qualified to pass an opinion as to the attainments of a student . . . and . . . courts will not review a decision of the school authorities relating to academic qualifications of the students."

There is no question, we believe, that Illinois would adhere to the great weight of authority and bar any attempt to repackage an educational malpractice claim as a contract claim. As several courts have noted, the policy concerns that preclude a cause of action for educational malpractice apply with equal force to bar a breach of contract claim attacking the general quality of an education. "Where the essence of the complaint is that the school breached its agreement by failing to provide an effective education, the court is again asked to evaluate the course of instruction . . . [and] is similarly called upon to review the soundness of the method of teaching that has been adopted by an educational institution."

To state a claim for breach of contract, the plaintiff must do more than simply allege that the education was not good enough. Instead, he must point to an identifiable contractual promise that the defendant failed to honor. Thus, . . . if the defendant took tuition money and then provided no education, or alternately, promised a set number of hours of instruction and then failed to deliver, a breach of contract action may be available. *See Zumbrun v. University of Southern California*, 101 Cal. Rptr. 499 (1972) (breach of contract action allowed against university when professor declined to give lectures and final exam, and all students received a grade of "B"). Similarly, a breach of contract action might exist if a student enrolled in a course explicitly promising instruction that would qualify him as a journeyman, but in which the fundamentals necessary to attain that skill were not even presented. In these cases, the essence of the plaintiff's complaint would not be that the institution failed to perform adequately a promised educational service, but rather that it failed to perform that service at all. Ruling on this issue would not require an inquiry into the nuances of educational processes and theories, but rather an objective assessment of whether the institution made a good faith effort to perform on its promise.

We read Mr. Ross' complaint to allege more than a failure of the University to provide him with an education of a certain quality. Rather, he alleges that the University knew that he was not qualified academically to participate in its curriculum. Nevertheless, it made a specific promise that he would be able to participate in a meaningful way in that program because it would provide certain specific services to him. Finally, he alleges that the University breached its promise by reneging on its commitment to provide those services and, consequently, effectively cutting him off from any participation in and benefit from the University's academic program. To adjudicate such a claim, the court would not be required to determine whether Creighton had breached its contract with Mr. Ross by providing deficient academic services. Rather, its inquiry would be limited to whether the University had provided any real access to its academic curriculum at all.

Accordingly, we must disagree respectfully with our colleague in the district court as to whether the contract counts of the complaint can be dismissed at the pleadings stage. In our view, the allegations of the complaint are sufficient to warrant further proceedings. We emphasize, however, the narrow ground of our disagreement. We agree—indeed we emphasize—that courts should not "take on the job of supervising the relationship between colleges and student-athletes or creating in effect a new relationship between them." We also recognize a formal university-student contract is rarely employed and, consequently, "the general nature and terms of the agreement are usually implied, with specific terms to be found in the university bulletin and other publications; custom and usages can also become specific terms by implication." Nevertheless, we believe that the district court can adjudicate Mr. Ross' specific and narrow claim that he was barred from any participation in and benefit from the University's academic program without second-guessing the professional judgment of the University faculty on academic matters.

Affirmed in part, remanded in part.

NOTES AND QUESTIONS

1. *Aftermath.* Despite Creighton's failure to educate him, Mr. Ross returned to grade school and after learning to read, received his college degree. His case also created change within the NCAA, which responded by establishing the Eligibility Center to ensure that college-bound student-athletes understand the requirements to participate in NCAA athletics.

2. *Still a Problem?* In 2014, CNN released a study that estimated that between 7% and 18% of revenue athletes read at an elementary school level. *See* https://www.cnn.com/2014/01/07/us/ncaa-athletes-reading-scores/index.html. Are the NCAA and its member institutions taking adequate safeguards to ensure that the education of all student-athletes is legitimate?

3. *Pressure to Win.* To what extent does the pressure to win undermine the athlete's pursuit of an education? When athletes spend 60 hours a week on athletics, is education possible? Do you think the increased commercialism of college sports adds to such pressure?

4. *Tutoring.* Most Power-5 universities have extensive academic tutoring programs to help student-athletes. To what extent does this approach create a great educational value for student-athletes and help make their educational experience robust? Alternatively, does such an approach encourage institutions to cut corners academically? The next case is an example of an institution cutting corners, or at the very least, allowing corners to be cut.

UNIVERSITY OF NORTH CAROLINA AT CHAPEL HILL PUBLIC INFRACTIONS DECISION

NCAA Committee on Infractions, 2017

* * *

III. FINDINGS OF FACT

Generally, the facts of this case are not in dispute. They involve courses offered and administered in what was formerly known as the Department of African and Afro-American (AFRI/AFAM) studies. The trouble with the courses centered around the department chair and the secretary. In the background, but integrally involved in the conduct at issue, was UNC's Academic Support Services for Student-Athletes (ASPSA) personnel. ASPSA received funding from athletics and interacted with athletics staff, coaches and student-athletes on a daily basis. ASPSA, however, was organized and housed under the College of Arts and Sciences. While clear on paper, the mixed reporting lines perpetuated the continued and unchallenged use of the courses. To a lesser extent, the facts also surround the academic conduct of a long-time UNC staff member (instructor/counselor).

Various internal and external reviews have dubbed the courses different names. Most simply, they have become known as "paper courses." In short, the courses involved no class attendance; limited, if any, faculty oversight; and liberal grading. The paper courses included both independent studies and courses listed as standard lectures but taught as independent studies. From 1989 to 2011, more than 6,000 students, including student-athletes, enrolled in courses that may have been administered as paper courses. Although the exact number of paper courses is unknown, the Cadwalader report [the independent investigation of UNC's classes by the Cadwalader law firm] conservatively estimated 3,100 students took a paper course involving irregular instruction. The record in this case includes only estimates on the number of courses and student-athletes involved. Although voluminous, the record is limited in specificity related to individual courses and student-athletes.

Nature and Administration of the Paper Courses

With respect to paper courses, there is little dispute. The classes did not meet. They rarely, if at all, directly involved a faculty member. They required the submission of a paper, occasionally two shorter papers. The papers were often graded by the secretary, who admitted she did not read every word and occasionally did not read every page. The papers consistently received high grades. At the hearing, UNC stood by its paper courses. UNC indicated that the work was assigned, completed, turned in and graded under the professor's guidelines. UNC also asserted that the grades are recorded on the students' transcripts and continue to count.

Generally, the AFRI/AFAM department offered paper courses in one of two ways: (1) independent studies; or (2) lecture courses structured as independent studies. Today, those courses appear on students' and student-athletes' transcripts as valid independent studies or lecture courses and were accepted to fulfill UNC's graduation requirements. UNC listed the courses in that manner in course bulletins. Neither the transcripts nor the course bulletins identify how the courses were administered or taught.

While independent studies and lecture courses are regular experiences for students on college campuses, the paper courses were, as UNC defined them, "irregular." UNC's chancellor elaborated on that characterization at the infractions hearing, succinctly describing them as having "inconsistent professorial involvement in teaching and grading." She and others further explained that the courses failed to meet UNC's high standards and expectations. Although the courses failed to meet UNC's own expectations, UNC repeatedly stressed at the infractions hearing that nothing about the courses themselves, the way they were administered or the way they were graded, violated then-existing policies. UNC admitted the courses would violate its current policies.

Enrollment in the courses literally began, continued and ended with the secretary. Generally, she controlled the administration of department offerings, administration of courses and, eventually, grading of many of the submitted papers. In both her written response and at the infractions hearing, she identified that the courses were meant to assist all UNC students who had difficult circumstances. If any student had extenuating circumstances, the secretary would accommodate them with a paper course. For students, those circumstances included schedule and work conflicts, campus obligations and, on occasion, difficult personal circumstances. For student athletes, those circumstances included athletic obligations (*i.e.*, practice, meetings, games and other athletically related activity). These arrangements started with a case-by-case approach, but as word spread and popularity soared, the secretary had to adjust her approach to handle the demand. To facilitate that demand, the secretary relied on academic counselors (both academic counselors for students and ASPSA counselors) to identify extenuating circumstances. Eventually the secretary began requesting that ASPSA counselors consolidate their student-athlete class requests into a list and submit it to her rather than individually sending over each of the student-athletes. She did not request lists from other academic counselors. On occasion, ASPSA personnel would email the secretary, asking what paper courses AFRI/AFAM (or the secretary) would be offering and requesting that she offer others.

Once enrolled in the courses, student-athletes or ASPSA staff usually received the assigned topic from the secretary. During her interview, she acknowledged that she would provide paper topics but indicated that all paper topics were faculty approved. ASPSA records indicate that while student-athletes may not have met with faculty members, they did work with ASPSA staff on writing and structuring research papers. Further, sometimes ASPSA staff turned in student athletes' completed papers. As it relates to the quality of the work, at least some interviewees suggested that the courses required little academic work and substance.

Most ASPSA counselors knew that papers would likely receive an A or a B. Others knew, or had suspicions, that the secretary actually graded the papers. * * * As far as her grading method, the secretary admitted that she did not read every word of every paper submitted. But in following the department chair's instructions, if the paper met his stated requirements, she gave it an A or a B.

ASPSA personnel recognized the positive impact the paper courses had on student-athletes' grade-point averages (GPAs). Around the time of the secretary's retirement, a former ASPSA associate director met with the football staff regarding promoting academic responsibility among its student-athletes. In that presentation, she included a slide that indicated the paper courses were part of the "solution in the past" but no longer existed. The slide specifically indicated four characteristics of the courses where student-athletes were not required to: (1) go to class; (2) take notes or stay awake; (3) meet with professors; and (4) pay attention or necessarily engage with the material. The presentation also included comparisons of student-athletes' GPAs with and without paper courses. Of the eight examples, all had AFAM GPAs of 3.2 or higher and other GPAs lower than 2.036, with six of the eight student-athletes' other GPAs falling below 2.0.

* * *

[The report discussed the violations by the University officials that failed to report the academic fraud. The panel then considered the other allegations.]

The case involved three other allegations: (1) unethical conduct and extra benefits related to student-athletes' access to and assistance in the paper courses; (2) unethical conduct by the instructor/counselor for providing impermissible academic assistance to student-athletes; and (3) a failure to monitor and lack of institutional control.

* * *

The enforcement staff identified six actions that taken alone or in combination purportedly constituted active management of the courses and extra benefit violations. In part, UNC claimed that there were no extra benefit violations because its actions were required and/or permitted under Bylaw 16.3.1.1. [This Bylaw mandates "academic counseling and tutoring services" and permits "other academic and support services that the institution, at its discretion, determines to be appropriate and necessary for the academic success of its student-athletes."] UNC mischaracterized the bylaw and its obligations. Bylaw 16.3.1.1 is not without limits. And it is not intended to be used as a shield for an academic program gone awry. It is intended to support, not replace, student-athletes' academic efforts. Supplanting student-athletes' academic efforts, responsibilities and educational experiences can violate NCAA legislation. Regardless, the panel cannot conclude that ASPSA's or athletics personnel's actions taken alone, in combination or in totality resulted in extra benefits. The record covers nearly two decades of information. It touches broad concepts but fails to establish specific or systemic activities limited to student-athletes. While student-athletes certainly benefited from the courses and ASPSA assistance, the record indicates that similar assistance was generally available to all students. Therefore, the panel cannot conclude that violations occurred.

* * *

[The Cadwalader report concluded that systematic academic fraud had occurred at UNC. The University initially affirmed these findings, but later attempted to recharacterize what happened on its campus as academically honest. Even so, the panel concluded] that it is more likely than not that student-athletes received fraudulent credit by the common understanding of what that term means. It is also more likely than not that UNC personnel used the courses to purposely obtain and maintain student-athletes' eligibility. These strong possibilities, however, are not the operative or controlling starting points to the membership's academic fraud analysis. What ultimately matters is what UNC says about the courses. In addition to rejecting its early admissions and distancing itself from the Cadwalader report in the infractions process, UNC took the firm position that the courses were permissible and UNC will continue to honor the grades. Despite the fact that the courses failed to meet, involved little, if any, faculty engagement, and were often graded by the secretary, UNC argued the courses violated no UNC policy. UNC further claimed that work was assigned, completed and graded, and the grades counted towards a UNC degree.

* * *

The COI, however, has not confirmed allegations on such a broad and convoluted set of facts or on academic allegations where the institution repeatedly affirms during the infractions process that the conduct did not violate its policies in place at the relevant time.

UNC has offered two diametrically opposed characterizations of the courses, seemingly dependent on the venue. Even if the panel were to assign more credibility to UNC's initial admissions to SACS [the Southern Association of Colleges and Schools which accredits the University of North Carolina], the case record does not support overriding UNC's recent positions. The record was voluminous. It also included information spanning nearly two decades and interviews where subjects had difficulty recalling circumstances and events. This lack of specificity inhibited the panel's ability to test and probe certain theories. Therefore, the panel cannot confirm the allegations and conclude that academic fraud occurred. Further, the record's limitations did not establish a firm basis for the panel issuing new allegations.

* * *

As the panel previously noted, the NCAA's role in academic violations is limited. While the NCAA defers academic fraud determinations to member institutions, there is no such deference requirement for impermissible academic assistance. But there are circumstances where the question whether impermissible academic assistance occurred itself requires academic judgments. In those circumstances, the COI must tread carefully. A violation must be clear on its face. Here, there are gaps in the record in the nature of the assistance the instructor/counselor provided. The record includes partial email chains, iterations of draft papers and lacks complete and final work. The record required the panel to assess the edits and suggestions down to the line-by-line and word basis. The panel was not in a position to make these academic judgements. The facts are further complicated by the many roles in which the instructor/counselor served during her tenure at the institution. At the hearing, she maintained that whether she was the director of the ethics center, an instructor, ASPSA counselor for women's basketball student-athletes or an advisor for non-athletes, she approached each student in the same manner and provided each with the same amount of assistance. Mainly, that included providing her students and student-athletes with reference materials, outlines, model papers and exercises involving reconstructing arguments.

Considering the record and the instructor/counselor's credible statements at the hearing, the panel cannot conclude that she committed unethical conduct. Similarly, because she thoroughly explained her approach to all students and student-athletes she encountered, which is not refuted by the record material, the panel cannot conclude that she provided women's basketball student-athletes with extra benefits. It is not clear on the face of the record that the conduct supported impermissible academic assistance. The dual role as instructor and academic counselor is a significant issue, one that member institutions must approach with caution. Proper policies and procedures regarding appropriate behaviors are essential to ensure individuals have a clear understanding of what is appropriate and what is not.

* * *

The record, however, does not establish specific, intentional or systemic efforts tied to athletics motives. The record was full of email chains, missing academic work and interviews conducted, in some circumstances, more than five years after the classes ceased. Those materials required the panel to, at best, infer motives based on the large number of student-athletes who took the courses and received high marks. While student-athletes and athletics programs likely benefitted from utilizing the courses for eligibility purposes, regular students likely benefitted from them as well. Without the proper athletics touchpoints, however, the COI cannot conclude free-standing failure to monitor or lack of institutional control violations occurred based solely on deficient administrative structures. Here, absent the attenuated fact that potentially around two thousand student-athletes took these courses, the record does not demonstrate that those failures had an athletics motive. Based on the posture of the record and in light of the secretary's statements at the hearing related to the nature of the courses, the conduct did not involve those athletics touchpoints.

In a more limited inquiry, the enforcement staff also alleged UNC failed to monitor and lacked control with respect to the instructor/ counselor's conduct. The panel acknowledges that her multiple positions complicated her reporting lines and roles within UNC. The panel recognizes UNC employed questionable oversight with regard to her various activities. However, based on the record that required the panel to parse isolated sentences and potential suggested changes to draft papers within partial email chains, the instructor/counselor's testimony that she treated all students equally and the panel's not substituting its judgment on pure academic matters, the panel could not conclude the instructor/counselor committed violations. As such, the panel cannot conclude UNC failed monitor the instructor/counselor or that it lacked control.

Although the panel could not conclude academic, failure to monitor or lack of institutional control violations occurred, UNC originally adopted SACS' characterization of the conduct as academic fraud. UNC also admitted that the courses did not meet its standards and it let its students down. Bylaw 19.9.10 permits panels to recommend that the NCAA president forward a copy of the public infractions decision to accrediting bodies when the panel determines academic violations or questionable academic conduct occurred. Those circumstances are present here. Therefore, the panel will recommend that the NCAA president forward a copy of the public infractions decision to SACS.

NOTES AND QUESTIONS

1. *Lack of Consequences?* Which university's academic malfeasance was worse? To what extent do such attempts to cut corners undermine the NCAA's narrative of education and student-athlete? In order to protect that narrative, do they require the imposition of stiff penalties, including the "death penalty" described in the last chapter? Is it troubling that neither Creighton nor North Carolina suffered any major athletic consequences for their academic fraud?

2. *Adequacy of Self-Policing?* Should the NCAA's role be to hold universities accountable? Or is the better model to defer to the university's policing of itself? Universities have strong motivations to conduct their academic programs with honesty. On the other hand, the pressure to win is non-ceasing. Did North Carolina adequately self-police before being prodded by the NCAA?

3. *Pressure of Athletics on Academics.* As discussed below, athletes at Northwestern seeking union representation questioned the balance between academics and athletics, particularly in big-time revenue sports. Do the demands of college athletics make academic fraud likely or even inevitable? Could the NCAA create rules that might reduce the pressure on athletes in this context? How would you frame such rules?

4. *Role of the NCAA.* Do you agree with the COI's characterization of its role in the North Carolina case? Or should it take a more active role in regulating academic fraud? Also, do you buy the COI's reasoning that making

an opportunity available to non-athletes somehow removes it from NCAA scrutiny because it is not a "benefit" given just to athletes?

5. *Athlete Versus Non-Athlete Benefits.* Part of the COI's reasoning related to the neutrality of the benefit offered, *i.e.*, it was provided to athletes and non-athletes alike. Why should it matter that non-athletes enjoyed the same benefits? Could a booster avoid scrutiny under recruiting rules by buying a car for a recruit and another car for the recruit's non-athlete friend?

(b) Transfer Rules

The NCAA has adopted a number of different rules respecting the ability of student-athletes to transfer to its member institutions from other academic institutions. Articles 14.5–14.7. Among other things, these rules concern the eligibility of transfer students to participate in intercollegiate athletics at their new institution. Article 14.5.5.1.

The NCAA transfer rules serve to restrict the ability of athletes to play sports immediately for their new school in certain situations. The "residency rule" allows transfers to participate in the practices and workouts of the team, but forbids participation in athletic competitions for one year (two semesters or three quarters) after the transfer. Article 14.5.5.1. For undergraduate students at four-year universities, the residency rule applies to almost all transfers.

The general rule provides:

> A student who transfers (see Bylaw 14.5.2) to a member institution from any collegiate institution is required to complete one full academic year of residence (see Bylaw 14.02.14) at the certifying institution before being eligible to compete for or to receive travel expenses from the member institution (see Bylaw 16.8.1), unless the student satisfies the applicable transfer requirements or qualifies for an exception as set forth in this bylaw

Article 14.5.5.1. The central exception to this presumption is in the "One-Time Transfer Exception" rule found in Bylaw 14.5.5.2.10. This exception allows for transfers to begin play immediately when transferring from one four-year institution to another. Generally, this exception is not available for athletes in the following sports: baseball, basketball, bowl subdivision football or men's ice hockey. Article 14.5.5.2.10(a). In addition, the student must be (1) transferring for the first time, (2) be academically eligible if he or she had remained at their current institution, and (3) have approval in writing from their current institution. Article 14.5.5.2.10(b)–(d). Where the institution refuses to grant approval to transfer, the student-athlete has the right to a hearing outside the athletic department at their home institution. Article 14.5.5.2.10.1.

The graduate transfer rule addresses when a student-athlete may be eligible to play intercollegiate athletics at a second institution once the student-athlete has graduated from the first institution. Under the rules, athletes have five years to complete four years of eligibility. The process of redshirting student-athletes, particularly in football, has created an increase in the number of student-athletes who, in theory, could be eligible to transfer under these circumstances. Historically, most student-athletes would just enroll in a graduate program at their home institution to complete their eligibility. In recent years, though, student-athletes have sought both academic and athletic opportunities by transferring at this stage of their eligibility.

The current rule allows graduate students in baseball, basketball, men's ice hockey, and bowl subdivision football to transfer under certain conditions:

> A graduate student who is enrolled in a graduate or professional school of an institution other than the institution from which he or she previously received a baccalaureate degree may participate in intercollegiate athletics if the student fulfills the conditions of the one-time transfer exception set forth in Bylaw 14.5.5.2.10 and has eligibility remaining per Bylaw 12.8. A graduate student who does not meet the one-time transfer exception due to the restrictions of Bylaw 14.5.5.2.10–(a) shall qualify for this exception, provided:
>
> (a) The student fulfills the remaining conditions of Bylaw 14.5.5.2.10.
>
> (b) The student has at least one season of competition remaining; and
>
> (c) The student's previous institution did not renew his or her athletically related financial aid for the following academic year.

Article 14.6.1.

The NCAA review process considers hundreds of transfer applications each year, and grants some waivers. The review process, however, is not a transparent one, partially because of privacy concerns related to the student-athletes applying for transfer. The five-person appellate committee weighs a number of individualized considerations in deciding on the eligibility of the student-athlete that wants to transfer.

The NCAA or the athletic departments of its member institutions cannot restrict a student from transferring from one institution. The rules simply can restrict a student-athlete from participating in intercollegiate athletics at the new institution. The consequence, though, is not just preventing a student to participate in athletics; the more significant consequence can be the loss of a scholarship, which makes attending the graduate program at the new institution more financially difficult.

In 2017–18, the NCAA convened a working group to study the transfer rules in light of the growing number of graduate transfers. The NCAA Division I Council adopted the new proposal, which contains two significant changes. Students no longer have to request permission to transfer and get a release from their current athletic department; instead students simply notify athletics of their intent to transfer. Students still must sit out a year unless they fall under an exception as discussed above. Second, institutions can terminate a student's financial aid at the end of the semester that the student provides notice of their intent to transfer. This rule places the risk on the student, not the institution. In addition, conferences can still place restrictions on transfers as well.

Even with the proposed reforms, the transfer rules place significant limits on the ability to move schools and maintain immediate eligibility. The next case is a student's antitrust challenge to the residence requirement.

DEPPE V. NCAA
893 F.3d 498 (7th Cir. 2018)

SYKES, CIRCUIT JUDGE.

This case raises an antitrust challenge to the NCAA's "year in residence" rule, which requires student-athletes who transfer to a Division I college to wait one full academic year before they can play for their new school. A Division I football player filed a class-action lawsuit alleging that the rule is an unlawful restraint of trade in violation of § 1 of the Sherman Act. The district court dismissed the suit on the pleadings.

We affirm. The year-in-residence requirement is an eligibility rule clearly meant to preserve the amateur character of college athletics and is therefore presumptively procompetitive under *NCAA v. Board of Regents of University of Oklahoma*, 468 U.S. 85 (1984), and *Agnew v. NCAA*, 683 F.3d 328 (7th Cir. 2012).

I. Background

The case comes to us from a dismissal on the pleadings, *see* FED. R. CIV. P. 12(b)(6), so we take the following factual account from the complaint, accepting the allegations as true. Peter Deppe was a star punter in high school, and several schools recruited him to play college football. He chose Northern Illinois University ("NIU"), a Division I school, and enrolled in June 2014 as a preferred walk-on. In other words, NIU invited him to join the football team but did not offer him an athletic scholarship. Deppe decided to "red shirt" his first year; this meant that he practiced with the team during the 2014 season but did not compete, and the clock did not run on his four years of NCAA athletic eligibility.

Shortly after Deppe enrolled, an NIU football coach told him that he would start receiving an athletic scholarship in January 2015. That coach soon left NIU, however, and the head football coach later informed Deppe that he would not receive the scholarship after all. Sometime in 2015 NIU signed another punter, reducing Deppe's chances of getting playing time or receiving an athletic scholarship, so in the fall of 2015 he started shopping around for a new football program.

The University of Iowa, another Division I school, was interested. Coaches at Iowa told Deppe they wanted him to join the team if he would be eligible to compete during the 2016–2017 season. Deppe's parents asked the NCAA about their son's eligibility to play. The NCAA responded that under its year-in-residence rule, Deppe would be ineligible to compete for one year following his transfer.

The year-in-residence bylaw appears in the eligibility section of the *NCAA Division I Manual*. It provides:

> 14.5.5.1 General Rule. A transfer student from a four-year institution shall not be eligible for intercollegiate competition at a member institution until the student has fulfilled a residence requirement of one full academic year (two full semesters or three full quarters) at the certifying institution.

NCAA Division I Manual, 183, http://www.ncaapublications.com/product downloads/D118.pdf.

The NCAA permits a one-time transfer with immediate athletic eligibility in certain limited circumstances. The so-called one-time transfer exception is available to a Division I football player only if he transfers from a school in the Football Bowl Subdivision to a school in the Football Championship Subdivision with two or more seasons of athletic eligibility remaining, or if he transfers from a Football Championship school that offers athletic scholarships to a Football Championship school that does not. *Id.*, 184–85, § 14.5.5.2.10. The exception was unavailable to Deppe because he intended to transfer from one Football Bowl school to another.

In addition, a player who transfers due to difficult personal or family circumstances or other extenuating circumstances may apply for a waiver of the NCAA's requirement that a student-athlete's four years of playing time be completed in five calendar years. *Id.*, 79, § 12.8.1; *Id.*, 81, § 12.8.1.7; *Id.*, 88–89, § 12.8.6. The NCAA informed Deppe that if he wanted to try to obtain a waiver, the school to which he planned to transfer would have to initiate the process on his behalf. In November 2015 the University of Iowa granted Deppe academic admission. But a few days later, Iowa football staff notified him that the team had decided to pursue another punter who had immediate eligibility and the school would not initiate the waiver process for him.

Deppe sued the NCAA on behalf of himself and a proposed class alleging that two of the Association's bylaws violate § 1 of the Sherman Act: the year-in-residence requirement, and a rule capping the number of athletic scholarships a school can grant each year. He dropped his challenge to the scholarship cap; only the year-in-residence rule remains at issue. Deppe argued that the bylaw is an unlawful restraint of trade and that student-athletes would receive more generous athletic scholarships if they could transfer more freely.

The NCAA moved to dismiss the complaint under Rule 12(b)(6), arguing that the year-in-residence bylaw is an eligibility rule and thus is presumptively procompetitive under *Board of Regents* and *Agnew* and need not be tested for anticompetitive effect under a full rule-of-reason analysis. The district judge agreed and dismissed the case.

II. Discussion

* * *

Section 1 of the Sherman Act declares illegal "[e]very contract, combination in the form of trust or otherwise, or conspiracy, in restraint of trade or commerce." 15 U.S.C. § 1. To prevail in a suit alleging a violation of § 1, the plaintiff must prove three elements: "(1) a contract, combination, or conspiracy; (2) a resultant unreasonable restraint of trade in [a] relevant market; and (3) an accompanying injury." *Agnew*, 683 F.3d at 335 (quoting *Denny's Marina, Inc. v. Renfro Prods., Inc.*, 8 F.3d 1217, 1220 (7th Cir. 1993)). This case centers on the second element—specifically, whether the NCAA's year-in-residence bylaw is an unreasonable restraint of trade.

The Supreme Court considered the antitrust implications of NCAA regulations in *Board of Regents*. The case raised a Sherman Act challenge to the Association's restrictions on televising college football games. 468 U.S. at 91–92. The details are not important here; for our purposes, it's enough to note that the Court found the restrictions unlawful under § 1 of the Act. *Id.* at 120. Along the way to that holding, the Court had this to say about antitrust challenges to the NCAA's bylaws more generally:

> It is reasonable to assume that most of the regulatory controls of the NCAA are justifiable means of fostering competition among amateur athletic teams and therefore procompetitive because they enhance public interest in intercollegiate athletics. The specific restraints on football telecasts that are challenged in this case do not, however, fit into the same mold as do rules defining the conditions of the contest, the eligibility of participants, or the manner in which members of a joint enterprise shall share the responsibilities and the benefits of the total venture.

Id. at 117. The Court closed its decision by observing that "[t]he NCAA plays a crucial role in the maintenance of a revered tradition of amateurism in college sports" and "needs ample latitude" to play that role, and that "the preservation of the student-athlete in higher education adds richness and diversity to intercollegiate athletics and is entirely consistent with the goals of the Sherman Act." *Id.* at 120.

In *Agnew* we read this language from *Board of Regents* to mean that although the Sherman Act applies to the NCAA, "most [of the Association's] regulations will be a 'justifiable means of fostering competition among amateur athletic teams[ ]' and are therefore procompetitive." 683 F.3d at 341 (quoting *Bd. of Regents*, 468 U.S. at 117). We also understood these passages as "a license to find certain NCAA bylaws that 'fit into the same mold' as those discussed in *Board of Regents* to be procompetitive . . . at the motion-to-dismiss stage" without the need for analysis under the rule-of-reason framework. *Id.* (internal citation omitted) (quoting *Bd. of Regents*, 468 U.S. at 117, 110 n.39). Accordingly, we held that "the first—and possibly only—question to be answered when NCAA bylaws are challenged is whether the NCAA regulations at issue are of the type that have been blessed by the Supreme Court, making them presumptively procompetitive." *Id.*

Agnew involved a challenge to the NCAA's scholarship cap and its prohibition of multiyear scholarships. *Id.* at 332. Extrapolating from *Board of Regents*, we distilled the following legal standard for determining whether a § 1 challenge in this context may go forward or should be dismissed on the pleadings: an NCAA bylaw is presumptively procompetitive when it is "clearly meant to help maintain the 'revered tradition of amateurism in college sports' or the 'preservation of the student-athlete in higher education.' " *Id.* at 342–43 (quoting *Bd. of Regents*, 468 U.S. at 120). On the other hand, "if a regulation is not, on its face, helping to 'preserve a tradition that might otherwise die,' " no such presumption is warranted. *Id.* at 343 (quoting *Bd. of Regents*, 468 U.S. at 120).

Importantly here, we also explained that "[m]ost—if not all—eligibility rules . . . fall within the presumption of procompetitiveness" established in *Board of Regents*. *Id.* After all, "the Supreme Court explicitly mentioned eligibility rules as a type that 'fit[s] into the same mold' as other procompetitive rules." *Id.* (alteration in original). And because eligibility rules "define what it means to be an amateur or a student-athlete," they are "essential to the very existence of the product of college football." *Id.*

The rules challenged in *Agnew* did not govern athletic eligibility or otherwise "fit into the same mold" of the presumptively procompetitive regulations mentioned in *Board of Regents*. *Id.* at 344–45. But the absence of a procompetitive presumption did "not equal a finding that [the rules] are anticompetitive;" rather, it simply meant that they could not be presumed procompetitive at the pleadings stage. *Id.* at 345. So we moved to the next step in the § 1 analysis and determined that the complaint failed to identify a relevant cognizable market and affirmed the dismissal of the suit on that basis. *Id.* at 345–47.

Unlike the bylaws at issue in *Agnew*, the year-in-residence requirement is plainly an eligibility rule. It appears in the eligibility section of the NCAA Division I Manual. On its face, it governs a transfer student's eligibility for intercollegiate athletic competition. In particular, the bylaw suspends a transfer student's athletic eligibility until the student has spent one full academic year at his new college.

Deppe insists that the year-in-residence rule does not "fit within the contours of a traditional eligibility bylaw." On the contrary, the rule falls neatly in line with other rules courts have characterized as eligibility rules. In *Agnew* we gave the example of a class-attendance requirement to explain why eligibility rules are entitled to a procompetitive presumption. We said: "There may not be such a thing as a student athlete, for instance, if it was not for the NCAA rules requiring class attendance, and thus no detailed analysis would be necessary to deem such rules procompetitive." *Id.* at 343 (internal quotation marks and citation omitted). Bylaws that have been classified as eligibility rules include: a bylaw revoking a student-athlete's eligibility to compete if he enters the professional draft or hires a professional agent, *Banks v. NCAA*, 977 F.2d 1081, 1082–83 (7th Cir. 1992); a rule allowing the suspension of a college football program for illicitly compensating players beyond scholarships, *McCormack v. NCAA*, 845 F.2d 1338, 1343 (5th Cir. 1988); and a bylaw making student-athletes ineligible to compete at a graduate school different from their undergraduate institution, *Smith v. NCAA*, 139 F.3d 180, 186 (3d Cir. 1998), *vacated on other grounds by NCAA v. Smith*, 525 U.S. 459 (1999). We have no difficulty concluding that the year-in-residence bylaw is an eligibility rule.

As we've noted, most NCAA eligibility rules are entitled to the procompetitive presumption announced in *Board of Regents* because they define what it means to be a student-athlete and thus preserve the tradition and amateur character of college athletics. *Agnew*, 683 F.3d at 343. Deppe has not persuaded us that the year-in-residence requirement is the rare exception to this general principle. Indeed, the complaint alleges that Division I football student-athletes would transfer more often if not for the year-in-residence rule. Without it student-athletes could be "traded" from year to year like professional athletes. A college player could begin the season playing for one school and end the season playing for its rival. Uninhibited transfers with immediate eligibility to play would risk severing the athletic and academic aspects of college sports, threatening the character of intercollegiate athletics. The year-in-residence rule guards against that risk and thus is "clearly meant to help maintain the 'revered tradition of amateurism in college sports.'" *Id.* at 342 (quoting *Bd. of Regents*, 468 U.S. at 120).

Deppe points to the exceptions and the possibility of a waiver of the Association's five-year rule, arguing that if these forms of relief are available, then the year-in-residence requirement is actually unnecessary to the survival of college football. This argument is a nonstarter. To begin, the test under *Agnew* is not whether college athletics could survive without this bylaw, but rather whether the rule is clearly meant to help preserve the amateurism of college sports. And scrutinizing the NCAA's bylaws as Deppe suggests conflicts with the Supreme Court's admonition in *Board of Regents* that the NCAA needs "ample latitude" to preserve the product of college sports. 468 U.S. at 120. That the NCAA allows some avenues for relief does not suggest that the year-in-residence requirement is aimed at an objective other than the maintenance of the amateur character of the college game. Instead it suggests that the NCAA is willing to allow players certain flexibility where doing so will not damage the product of college football.

Next, Deppe argues that the NCAA enforces the year-in-residence requirement for economic reasons and not to preserve the product of college football. He asks us to infer an economic motive from the fact that the one-time transfer exception is unavailable to most Division I football, basketball, and ice-hockey players—the highest-revenue sports programs in the NCAA. This argument ignores the innocent explanation that these are precisely the athletes who are most vulnerable to poaching. Without transfer restrictions, the players in these high-revenue sports could be traded like professional athletes.

Deppe also argues that because the year-in-residence requirement impedes transfers, it lowers the administrative costs associated with player movement, including recruiting and retention expenditures. That is, schools are saving money they would otherwise need to spend on more generous scholarships to tempt their student-athletes to stay, as well as money necessary to recruit and train new players to replace those who leave. But the fact that colleges may save money as a consequence of the year-in-residence requirement does not mean that the bylaw is fundamentally aimed at containing costs rather than preserving the amateur character of college football.

Last, Deppe argues that at bottom, the year-in-residence rule serves economic interests because it "preserves the hegemony of the top 'Power 5' conferences"—the most powerful group of schools in the NCAA. He asserts that these schools recruit the most talented high-school athletes and that the year-in-residence rule prevents those student athletes from transferring to less powerful schools. But the rule impedes transfers in both directions. Without it, the "Power 5" schools could poach rising stars from smaller schools, which would risk eroding the amateur character of the college game.

In sum, the year-in-residence rule is, on its face, a presumptively procompetitive eligibility rule under *Agnew* and *Board of Regents*. Accordingly, a full rule-of-reason analysis is unnecessary. Deppe's Sherman Act challenge to the NCAA's year-in-residence bylaw fails on the pleadings. AFFIRMED.

Notes and Questions

1. *Tracking* Board of Regents. As mentioned in Chapter 10, and in the *O'Bannon* opinion below, the court in *Deppe* relied on dicta from *Board of Regents* to support its understanding of amateurism. Does giving the Court's dicta significant weight ignore the economic realities of the transfer situation?

2. *Extending Prior Precedent*. The court in *Deppe* also distinguished its 2012 decision in *Agnew v. NCAA*, 683 F.3d 328 (7th Cir. 2012), where it reached the same result but not at the 12(b)(6) stage of the pleadings. In *Agnew*, athletes challenged the then-prohibition against multiyear scholarships and the cap on the number of scholarships as antitrust violations under the Sherman Act. The court found that these were not eligibility rules, like in *Deppe*, but still upheld the rules as procompetitive. The *Agnew* court relied on language from *Board of Regents*, explaining that NCAA rules have a procompetitive purpose when they manifest the " 'revered tradition of amateurism in college sports' or the 'preservation of the student-athlete in higher education.' " *Agnew*, 683 F.3d at 342–43.

3. *Eligibility Rules (Athletic Competition) Versus Economic Rules (Economic Competition)*. The court in *Deppe* held that eligibility rules do not even require analysis under the Sherman Act because they are procompetitive in nature. By contrast, economic rules, like the one in *Board of Regents* face more intense antitrust scrutiny. Why?

4. *Transfer Rules*. The NCAA's transfer rule requires student-athletes in certain sports (football, basketball, baseball, and hockey) to sit out a year if they transfer from one institution to another, barring a release from the athletic director. Under the rule, athletes can practice with their new team, but cannot play for a year. Do you think the rule is fair, or excessively paternalistic? Should athletic directors have this much control over athletes?

5. *Hardship Waivers*. The NCAA has a committee that considers hardship waivers, and in some cases will allow immediate eligibility. If the move by the athlete is for family reasons, the NCAA might grant a waiver. Similarly, if a program violates NCAA rules and goes on probation, the NCAA may grant a release to the athletes not involved in the infractions case. The

NCAA does not, however, typically grant waivers simply because the coach decides to leave.

2. THE PRINCIPLE OF AMATEURISM AND THE SCOPE OF JUDICIAL REVIEW

As indicated in the previous section on recruiting and in Chapter 10, the principle of amateurism lies at the heart of the NCAA's core mission. What amateurism has meant, over time, has not been static. Originally, in its English origins, amateurs received no compensation for participation in athletics. Over time, the NCAA expanded its definition to permit compensation when expressly authorized by its own rules, largely including the costs of education—tuition, room, board, and books. More recently, and in light of *O'Bannon v. NCAA*, see Section C *infra*, universities are providing the cost of attendance—external costs necessary to attend the university—to scholarship athletes.

(a) Pre-College Sports and Amateurism

The next two cases explore the consequence, with respect to one's amateur status, of receiving compensation connected to athletic participation prior to participating in intercollegiate sports. Jeremy Bloom's case also explores the possibility of receiving compensation for endorsements, a topic also covered in the *O'Bannon* case. *Bloom* is also an important precedent establishing the ability of student-athletes to challenge interpretations of NCAA bylaws under a contract law theory.

BLOOM V. NCAA
93 P.3d 621 (Colo. Ct. App. 2004)

Opinion by JUDGE DAILEY.

In this dispute concerning eligibility to play college football, plaintiff, Jeremy Bloom, appeals the trial court's order denying his request for a preliminary injunction against defendants, the National Collegiate Athletic Association (NCAA) and the University of Colorado (CU). We affirm.

[Bloom, a world-class skier and a very gifted football player, had failed in his attempt to comply with NCAA rules that permit student-athletes to maintain their amateur eligibility in one sport while turning professional in another sport. Although Stanford Quarterback John Elway was permitted to receive a huge bonus check to play minor league baseball for a New York Yankees farm team, and Bloom was allowed to receive prize money for skiing, NCAA rules barred him from earning endorsement income from ski-related products, which is a principal source of income for professional skiers.]

IV. Standing

We reject the NCAA's assertion that Bloom lacked standing to pursue claims for breach of contract or arbitrary and capricious action on the part of the NCAA.

* * *

A person not a party to an express contract may bring an action on the contract if the parties to the agreement intended to benefit the nonparty, provided that the benefit claimed is a direct and not merely incidental benefit of the contract. While the intent to benefit the nonparty need not be expressly recited in the contract, the intent must be apparent from the terms of the agreement, the surrounding circumstances, or both. *Parrish Chiropractic Ctrs., P.C. v. Progressive Cas. Ins. Co.*, 874 P.2d 1049, 1056 (Colo. 1994).

Here, the trial court found, and we agree, that the NCAA's constitution, bylaws, and regulations evidence a clear intent to benefit student-athletes. And because each student-athlete's eligibility to compete is determined by the NCAA, we conclude that Bloom had standing in a preliminary injunction hearing to contest the meaning or applicability of NCAA eligibility restrictions. *See Hall v. NCAA*, 985 F. Supp. 782, 796–97 (N.D. Ill. 1997) (given importance of NCAA's function to benefit student-athletes, and NCAA's role in determining eligibility of student-athletes, court assumed student-athlete was likely to succeed in proving third-party beneficiary standing vis-a-vis the contract between the NCAA and its members); *see also NCAA v. Brinkworth*, 680 So. 2d 1081, 1083 (Fla. Dist. Ct. App. 1996).

* * *

... [T]o the extent Bloom's claim of arbitrary and capricious action asserts a violation of the duty of good faith and fair dealing that is implied in the contractual relationship between the NCAA and its members, his position as a third-party beneficiary of that contractual relationship affords him standing to pursue this claim....

V. Probability of Success

Bloom contends that the trial court erred in assessing the probability of success on his contract claims. We disagree....

A. Interpretation of NCAA Bylaws

* * *

Bloom relies on NCAA Bylaw 12.1.2, which states that "[a] professional athlete in one sport may represent a member institution in a different sport." He asserts that, because a professional is one who "gets paid" for a sport, a student-athlete is entitled to earn whatever income is customary for his or her professional sport, which, in the case of professional skiers, primarily comes from endorsements and paid media opportunities.

We recognize that, like many others involved in individual professional sports such as golf, tennis, and boxing, professional skiers obtain much of their income from sponsors. We note, however, that none of the NCAA's bylaws mentions, much less explicitly establishes, a right to receive "customary income" for a sport.

To the contrary, the NCAA bylaws prohibit every student-athlete from receiving money for advertisements and endorsements.... Additionally, while NCAA Bylaw 12.5.1.3 permits a student-athlete to continue to receive remuneration for activity initiated prior to enrollment in which his or her name or picture is used, this remuneration is only allowed, if, as pertinent here, "the individual became involved in such activities for reasons independent of athletics ability; ... no reference is made in these activities to the individual's name or involvement in intercollegiate athletics; [and] ... the individual does not endorse the commercial product."

* * *

In our view, when read together, the NCAA bylaws express a clear and unambiguous intent to prohibit student-athletes from engaging in endorsements and paid media appearances, without regard to: (1) when the opportunity for such activities originated; (2) whether the opportunity arose or exists for reasons unrelated to participation in an amateur sport; and (3) whether income derived from the opportunity is customary for any particular professional sport.

The clear import of the bylaws is that, although student-athletes have the right to be professional athletes, they do not have the right to simultaneously engage in endorsement or paid media activity and maintain their eligibility to participate in amateur competition. And we may not disregard the clear meaning of the bylaws simply because they may disproportionately affect those who participate in individual professional sports.

Further, the record contains ample evidence supporting the trial court's conclusion that this interpretation is consistent with both the NCAA's and its member institutions' construction of the bylaws.... Thus, even if the bylaws were viewed as ambiguous, the record supports the trial court's conclusion that the bylaws would ultimately be interpreted in accordance with the NCAA's and its member institutions' construction of those bylaws.

B. Application of Bylaws to Bloom

The United States Supreme Court has recognized the NCAA as "the guardian of an important American tradition," namely, amateurism in intercollegiate athletics. *See NCAA v. Bd. of Regents,* 468 U.S. 85, 101 (1984).

[The court found that the NCAA seeks to keep student participation in intercollegiate athletics as an "avocation" and pursued the "legitimate purpose of retaining the 'clear line of demarcation between intercollegiate athletics and professional sports.' "]

The trial court noted that salaries and bonuses are an acceptable means for attaining income from professional sports, but endorsement income is not acceptable if a student-athlete wishes to preserve amateur eligibility. According to NCAA officials: (1) endorsements invoke concerns about "the commercial exploitation of student-athletes and the promotion of commercial products"; and (2) it is not possible to distinguish the precise capacity in which endorsements are made. A CU official related that generally, the endorsement rule prevents students from becoming billboards for commercialism, and in Bloom's case, there would "be no way to tell whether he is receiving pay commensurate with his . . . football ability or skiing ability."

* * *

In this case, Bloom presented evidence that some of his acting opportunities arose not as a result of his athletic ability but because of his good looks and on-camera presence. However, the record contains evidence that Bloom's agent and the Tommy Hilfiger company marketed Bloom as a talented multi-sport athlete, and a representative from a talent agency intimated that Bloom's reputation as an athlete would be advantageous in obtaining auditions for various entertainment opportunities. Further, the NCAA indicated, when asked to interpret its rules, that it was unable, due to insufficient information, to determine which of Bloom's requested media activities were, in fact, unrelated to his athletic ability or prestige.

Under these circumstances, we perceive no abuse of the trial court's discretion in failing to fault the NCAA for refusing to waive its rules, as requested by CU, to permit Bloom "to pursue any television and film opportunities while he is a student-athlete at CU." *See Cole v. NCAA,* 120 F. Supp. 2d 1060, 1071–72 (N.D.Ga.2000) (NCAA decisions regarding "challenges of student-athletes are entitled to considerable deference," and courts are reluctant to replace the NCAA as the "decision-maker on private waiver applications"); *see also NCAA v. Lasege, supra,* 53 S.W.3d at 83 (voluntary athletic associations "should be allowed to 'paddle their own canoe' without unwarranted interference from the courts").

Bloom also asserts that the NCAA is arbitrary in its application of the endorsement and media bylaws. He notes that, while the NCAA would bar him from accepting commercial endorsements, it will allow colleges to commercially endorse athletic equipment by having students wear the equipment, with identifying logos and insignias, while engaged in intercollegiate competition. But the trial court determined, and we agree, that this application of the bylaws has a rational basis in economic necessity: financial benefits inure not to any single student-athlete but to member schools and thus to all student-athletes, including those who participate in programs that generate no revenue.

* * *

The record thus supports the trial court's findings that the NCAA's administrative review process is reasonable in general and that it was reasonably applied in this case. As such, these findings, as well as those with respect to the NCAA's application of its bylaws, are not manifestly arbitrary, unreasonable, or unfair. *See Bd. of County Comm'rs v. Fixed Base Operators, Inc., supra,* 939 P.2d at 467.

For these reasons, we agree with the trial court that Bloom failed to demonstrate a reasonable probability of success on the merits.

* * *

NOTES AND QUESTIONS

1. *Aftermath.* Following this decision, Bloom decided not to appeal any further. He had success playing football, but was unable to sustain a pro career, and also failed in his later attempt at Olympic skiing. Should the NCAA have previously granted the University of Colorado's petition for a waiver of its rule, given Bloom's unique situation? On what basis could the NCAA grant the petition without creating a precedent that would effectively undermine the rule? Is the NCAA rule sensible?

2. *Amateurism and Use of Name, Image, Likeness.* Do you agree that Bloom receiving endorsements would compromise his amateur status in such a way that the NCAA is right to prohibit it? What about compensation for modeling? Is it a fair characterization of the situation that the NCAA rule serves to protect Bloom from exploitation by third parties? Do you find the rule justifiable or paternalistically unreasonable? Explain. What makes a university's use of (and accompanying financial profit from) its athletes' likenesses acceptable, but an athlete's use of their own likeness to make money unacceptable, at least in terms of the principle of amateurism?

3. *Limits of Injunctive Relief.* Even if counsel for a student-athlete or a member school develops a persuasive legal theory to empower a court to grant injunctive relief and allow the athlete to participate in athletic competition

following a determination of ineligibility, they face another hurdle. The NCAA and a number of state high school athletic associations have a rule that requires member schools to forfeit any victories and repay any revenues earned from games in which the athlete plays, if the challenged NCAA or high school association ruling is later upheld by the courts. This rule discourages schools from seeking judicial review.

NCAA v. LASEGE
53 S.W.3d 77 (Ky. 2001)

I. INTRODUCTION

The National Collegiate Athletic Association ("NCAA") moves this Court for interlocutory relief under [Court Rule] 65.09 and asks us to vacate the Jefferson Circuit Court's temporary injunction which (1) declares Respondent Lasege eligible to participate in NCAA intercollegiate basketball and (2) prohibits the NCAA from imposing future sanctions against Lasege or Respondent University of Louisville ("U of L") pursuant to its NCAA Bylaw 19.8 restitutionary powers. We find that the NCAA has demonstrated "extraordinary cause" justifying CR 65.09 relief and we vacate the temporary injunction in its entirety.

* * *

[Lasege, a citizen of Nigeria, a country in West Africa, enrolled at the University of Louisville during the 1999–2000 academic year with the intention of playing for its intercollegiate men's basketball team. In March 2000, U of L declared Lasege ineligible to play intercollegiate basketball because he had previously entered into professional basketball contracts and had received preferential benefits that compromised his amateur status. The NCAA declined to reinstate Lasege].

The NCAA described the factual basis for its findings as follows:

> Prior to enrollment, SA [Student Athlete] asserts he left his home in Nigeria to go to Russia in order to obtain a visa to come to the U.S. so that SA could go to school. SA was provided with an airline ticket ($800) to Russia from Nigeria by the Russian Sports Agency, New Sport. While in Russia, SA signed a contract with New Sport in Russia to represent SA regarding playing basketball for the professional club system in Moscow. As a result of the New Sport three-year contract, SA was to receive a salary of $9,000 a year with additional monetary incentives based on athletic performance. SA asserts he did not receive a salary but did receive living accommodations and meals for approximately 18 months valued at $1,170. SA was provided a driver, a cook, a visa to Russia ($70), clothing ($75) and a round-trip ticket from Moscow to Nigeria ($798). SA signed a second contract with a professional

basketball team, which was to provide SA with a salary, furnished apartment, utilities but no telephone, two round-trip airline tickets to return to Nigeria and a car for personal needs if SA should obtain a Russian driver's license. SA asserts he did not receive a salary from the second contract. SA competed with two junior teams in 13 contests. One of the teams was a junior team of the professional team SA signed the second contract with, and both junior teams were financially supported by professional teams. SA practiced with two professional teams but did not compete. SA was provided an airline ticket ($750) and visa ($50) to Canada from Moscow by an individual in Canada who knew of SA due to his athletics ability, which constituted a violation of 12.1.1.6. This individual provided SA with lodging and meals ($2,000) for approximately eight months. Individual also provided SA with automobile transportation to and lodging while at institution for an unofficial visit ($342.50), airline tickets, meals and lodging at another collegiate institution for an unofficial visit ($538) and a one-way airline ticket to institution for initial college enrollment ($101.50) for the 1999–00 academic year.

* * *

On November 27, 2000, Lasege filed a Motion and Complaint in Jefferson Circuit Court seeking a temporary injunction requiring the NCAA to reverse its decision as to U of L's request and to immediately reinstate his eligibility to play basketball at U of L. After conducting an evidentiary hearing, the trial court found that the complaint presented a substantial question as to whether the NCAA's ruling was arbitrary and capricious. Specifically, the trial court: (1) suggested that the NCAA had ignored what it described as "overwhelming and mitigating circumstances," including economic and cultural disadvantages, a complete ignorance of NCAA regulations, and elements of coercion associated with execution of the contracts; (2) believed the NCAA's determination to conflict with the NCAA's own amateurism guidelines and past eligibility determinations regarding athletes who had engaged in similar violations; (3) expressed its doubts about whether the first contract signed by Lasege was legally enforceable as an agency contract both because of Lasege's minority at the time he executed it and because the trial court disputed that the contract created an agency relationship; and (4) opined that a clear weight of evidence suggested Lasege committed these violations not in order to become a professional athlete, but only to obtain a visa which would allow him to become a student-athlete in the United States.

The trial court found that Lasege would suffer substantial collateral consequences from an erroneous and adverse eligibility determination, balanced the equities in favor of Lasege, and ordered "the NCAA and its members . . . to immediately restore the intercollegiate eligibility of

Muhammed Lasege so as to allow him to participate in all NCAA basketball contests." The trial court also addressed U of L's concern that the NCAA could impose sanctions under NCAA Bylaw 19.8 if the injunction was subsequently vacated. NCAA Bylaw 19.8 allows the NCAA to seek restitution from member institutions who permit student-athletes found ineligible by the NCAA to compete for their athletic teams pursuant to court orders which are later vacated. The trial court therefore "declare[d] that NCAA Bylaw 19.8 is invalid because it prevents parties from availing themselves of the protections of the courts" and ordered:

> ... that the University of Louisville shall abide by this injunction and shall not prohibit Muhammed Lasege from engaging in intercollegiate basketball;
>
> IT IS FURTHER ORDERED AND ADJUDGED that the NCAA and its members are hereby ordered to take no action to prevent or interfere with the University of Louisville's ability to abide by this Order by attempting to enforce NCAA Bylaw 19.8.

After the trial court entered the temporary injunction, Lasege played basketball for U of L during the 2000–2001 season.

While Lasege played, the NCAA sought interlocutory relief under CR 65.07, but the Court of Appeals found the trial court's findings supported by substantial evidence and denied the NCAA's motion....

The NCAA thus seeks interlocutory relief from this Court.

III. DISCUSSION

III(A)—STANDARD OF REVIEW

Cases involving challenges to eligibility decisions made by voluntary athletic associations such as the Kentucky High School Athletic Association ("KHSAA") or, as in this case, the NCAA, pose special difficulties for our circuit courts. Such cases are invariably time-sensitive as they are typically filed in the midst of an athletic season, often on the cusp of postseason competition. Because athletic seasons are usually completed before either a final decision on the merits by the trial court or appellate review, a circuit court's ruling granting or denying a temporary injunction will typically, as a practical matter, decide the issue of whether a student-athlete competes. In *KHSAA v. Hopkins County Board of Education,* [552 S.W.2d 685, 690 (Ky. App. 1977)], the Court of Appeals recognized the inherent limitations courts face in such determinations:

> This case demonstrates that courts are a very poor place in which to conduct interscholastic athletic events, especially since this type of litigation is most likely to arise at playoff or tournament time. If an injunction or restraining order is granted

erroneously, it will be practically impossible to unscramble the tournament results to reflect the ultimate outcome of the case.

Since, by definition, temporary injunctions attempt to place the parties in a position most likely to minimize harm before the court can finally decide the issues raised in a complaint, trial courts are asked to make significant decisions with less-than-complete information. As such, these determinations differ from most decisions reached by trial courts. There are no "drive-through windows" on courthouses for a good reason—judicial decision making demands thought and deliberation of all relevant evidence. The problem is further magnified by the fact that challenges to a voluntary athletic association's eligibility decision typically present issues which require considerable reflection. In general, the members of such associations should be allowed to "paddle their own canoe" without unwarranted interference from the courts. Nonetheless, relief from our judicial system should be available if voluntary athletic associations act arbitrarily and capriciously toward student-athletes. Thus, cases involving challenges to a voluntary athletic association's eligibility decisions involve difficult assessments of a plaintiff's probability of succeeding on his or her claim and complex balancing of competing interests. Because the values a trial court assigns to these competing interests will depend, in part, upon the trial court's assessment of the probability that the athletic association's determination was correct, a circuit court's ruling as to temporary injunctive relief largely hinges upon its preliminary determination of the merits of the plaintiff's claim. Claimants will generally demonstrate potential injuries which justify injunctive relief only when they can show a substantial probability that the athletic association's ruling was arbitrary and capricious. "Longshot" claims which have little hope of prevailing when the buzzer sounds will not justify injunctive relief.

* * *

In this case, we find that the trial court abused its discretion by: (1) substituting its judgment for that of the NCAA on the question of Lasege's intent to professionalize; (2) finding that the NCAA has no interest in this case which weighs against injunctive relief; and (3) declaring NCAA Bylaw 19.8 invalid. This combination of clearly erroneous conclusions constitutes extraordinary cause warranting CR 65.09 [interlocutory] relief.

III(B)—REINSTATEMENT OF LASEGE'S ELIGIBILITY

... The trial court made a preliminary determination/n that "the arbitrary nature of the enforcement of its by-laws by the members of the NCAA and its committees raises a substantial issue concerning the merits of their rules." The trial court further found that "Mr. Lasege faces irreparable harm because without reinstatement, he will not be able to continue in classes, and may be deported back to Nigeria." Although we agree with the trial court's assessment of the magnitude of the harm from an erroneous NCAA eligibility decision, we find that Lasege's chances of prevailing on the merits of his claim are too remote to justify injunctive relief. We believe the trial court clearly erred when assessing the merits of Lasege's claim.

In our opinion, the trial court wrongfully substituted its judgment for that of the NCAA after it analyzed the evidence and reached a different conclusion as to Lasege's intent to professionalize. The mere fact that a trial court considering mitigating evidence might disagree with the NCAA's factual conclusions does not render the NCAA's decision arbitrary or capricious. We have held that a ruling is arbitrary and capricious only where it is "clearly erroneous, and by 'clearly erroneous' we mean unsupported by substantial evidence." Here, the NCAA's ruling has strong evidentiary support—Lasege unquestionably signed contracts to play professional basketball and unquestionably accepted benefits. Contrary to the trial court's allegations of disparate treatment, the NCAA submits that no individual has ever had his or her eligibility reinstated after committing a combination of rules violations akin to those compiled by Lasege. The NCAA's eligibility determinations are entitled to a presumption of correctness—particularly when they stem from conceded violations of NCAA regulations. Although we recognize that Lasege's mitigation evidence is relevant to a review of the NCAA's determination, we believe the trial court simply disagreed with the NCAA as to the weight which should be assigned to this evidence. Accordingly, we believe the trial court abused its discretion when it found that Lasege had a high probability of success on the merits of his claim.

We also find "extraordinary cause" warranting CR 65.09 relief in the trial court's balancing of the equities. The trial court's order contrasts Lasege's risk of irreparable injury with the NCAA's interest and states that "the NCAA, on the other hand, will not suffer any potential harm by this court's order." We find this conclusion clearly erroneous, and accordingly believe the trial court's subsequent balancing of the equities suffers from an inherent computational error.

The NCAA unquestionably has an interest in enforcing its regulations and preserving the amateur nature of intercollegiate athletics. As the trial court entered a *temporary* injunction on the basis of its *preliminary* findings, the trial court could eventually determine that the NCAA properly denied the reinstatement request. If that is the case, the trial court's order would have erroneously allowed an ineligible player to participate in intercollegiate athletics. While the NCAA has no identifiable interest in the arbitrary application of its regulations to the detriment of a student-athlete, it certainly has an interest in the proper application of those regulations to ensure competitive equity.

* * *

III(C)—PROHIBITION OF NCAA BYLAW 19.8 RESTITUTION

[The trial court's order with respect to the NCAA's Restitution Rule states:] The Court also understands that U of L fears that Bylaw 19.8 could be enforced against it. That bylaw permits sanctions to be imposed by the NCAA against member schools if the Court order should be set aside or reversed in some manner. This Court has never seen such an agreement between members of an association that allows sanctions for turning to the courts for assistance when a perceived wrongdoing exists. *See Kentucky High School Athletic Ass'n v. Hopkins Co. Bd. of Educ., Ky. App.*, 552 S.W.2d 685 (1977); *Crocker v. Tennessee Secondary School Athletic Ass'n*, 908 F.2d 972 (6th Cir. 1990). The judicial power of this Commonwealth cannot be thwarted by members of an association such as the NCAA. *Craft v. Commonwealth, Ky.*, 343 S.W.2d 150 (1961). Consequently, this court declares that the NCAA Bylaw 19.8 is invalid because it prevents parties from availing themselves of the protections of the courts.

In context, therefore, the trial court's order "that the NCAA and its members are hereby ordered to take no action to prevent or interfere with the University of Louisville's ability to abide by this Order by attempting to enforce NCAA Bylaw 19.8" declares an NCAA Bylaw invalid within the Commonwealth of Kentucky and insulates U of L from restitutionary sanctions for allowing Lasege to participate as a member of its intercollegiate men's basketball team.

At the outset, we observe that the trial court's order gives no indication that it engaged in a CR 65.04 analysis before enjoining the NCAA in this regard, and that reason standing alone would require us to vacate this portion of the injunction. It appears that the trial court included this prophylactic measure, at U of L's urging, simply to facilitate its other order by permitting U of L the "risk-free" right to allow Lasege to play basketball. In any event, we can find no interest which would justify such injunctive relief. Accordingly, we find that the trial court abused its discretion when it prohibited the NCAA from seeking NCAA Bylaw 19.8 restitution.

By becoming a member of the NCAA, a voluntary athletic association, U of L agreed to abide by its rules and regulations. NCAA Bylaw 19.8 is one of those regulations, and it specifically provides that the NCAA can attempt to restore competitive equity by redistributing wins and losses and imposing sanctions upon a member institution which allows an ineligible player to participate under a subsequently-vacated court order, even if that order requires the institution to allow the player to participate. As the Indiana Supreme Court recently noted when addressing an identical issue concerning the Indiana High School Athletic Association ("IHSAA")'s restitution rule, such contractual risk allocation is no stranger to the courts:

> Contracts frequently allocate risks of unfavorable litigation results. For example, contracting parties agree that should a judgment, order or settlement prohibit a party from enjoying the benefits of the agreement, that party shall have no further obligations with respect to the contract. Doctors and attorneys purchase insurance so as to protect themselves from the consequences of lawsuits. Couples may sign prenuptial agreements dictating what is to occur should a trial judge determine that the prenuptial agreement is unenforceable. Such agreements show no disrespect to the courts.
>
> We presume that the judgments of our trial courts are correct and valid—but sometimes they are wrong. If a school wants to enjoy the benefits of membership in the IHSAA, the school agrees to be subject to a rule that permits the IHSAA to require the school to forfeit victories, trophies, titles and earnings if a trial court improperly grants an injunction or restraining order prohibiting enforcement of IHSAA eligibility rules. Such an agreement shows no disrespect to the institution of the judiciary.
>
> Member schools voluntarily contract to abide by the rules of the organization in exchange for membership in the association. One of those rules is the Restitution Rule. Undeniably, the Restitution Rule imposes hardship on a school that, in compliance with an order of a court which is later vacated, fields an ineligible player. On the other hand, use of an ineligible player imposes a hardship on other teams that must compete against the teams fielding ineligible players. While schools will contend that is unfair when they have to forfeit victories earned with an ineligible player on the field because they complied with a court order, competing schools will reply that it is unfair when they have to compete against a team with an ineligible student athlete because a local trial judge prohibited the school or the IHSAA from following the eligibility rules. The Restitution Rule represents the agreement of IHSAA members on how to balance those two competing interests. The Restitution Rule may not be the best method to deal with such situations. However, it is the method which the member schools have adopted. And in any event, its enforcement by the IHSAA does not impinge upon the judiciary's function.[18]

---

[18] *IHSAA v. Reyes,* 694 N.E.2d 249, 257–8 (Ind. 1997). See also *Cardinal Mooney High School v. Michigan High School,* 437 Mich. 75, 467 N.W.2d 21 (Mich. 1991). * * *

In fact, contrary to the belief of the trial court the concept of "risk-free" injunctive relief is unheard of—CR 65.05 requires the party in whose favor the injunction is granted to post a bond and wrongfully enjoined parties may recover compensatory damages. Here, U of L and the other NCAA members reached an agreement as to how competitive equity should be restored in the event of an erroneous court determination regarding a player's eligibility, and the trial court simply released U of L from that obligation.

The trial court's belief that the NCAA's Restitution Rule "thwarts the judicial power" is simply without foundation. NCAA Bylaw 19.8, like the Restitution Rules enforced by many state high school athletic associations "does not purport to authorize interference with any court order during the time it remains in effect, but only authorizes restitutive penalties when a temporary restraining order is ultimately dissolved and the challenged eligibility rule remains undisturbed in force." The authority of the courts is thus in no way compromised, and NCAA Bylaw 19.8 merely allows for post-hoc equalization when a trial court's erroneously granted temporary injunction upsets competitive balance. If the trial court's preliminary conclusions carry the day, and a student-athlete's eligibility is confirmed by final determination, no restitutionary remedy is warranted or appropriate, and NCAA Bylaw 19.8 provides for none.

* * *

[Dissenting opinion by JOHNSTONE, J., omitted].

NOTES AND QUESTIONS

1. *Aftermath.* The decision of the Kentucky Supreme Court effectively ended Lasege's college basketball career. He did not make it to the NBA. An excellent student, Lasege later received an MBA from the Wharton school.

2. *Pre-NCAA Remuneration.* Should receiving money for athletics prior to coming to college disqualify an athlete from NCAA participation? Do you agree with the NCAA that Lasege's prior experiences should remove his amateur status? Or should past experience be irrelevant to the amateurism determination?

3. *Benefit?* Did the benefit received by Lasege somehow create an unfair playing field with respect to other amateur athletes? Was the pre-Louisville benefit to Lasege really just the experience itself or the actual compensation?

4. *An Alternative Solution?* By-law 19.08 responds to concerns that a "home court" local judge would distort intercollegiate competition by injunctive relief that permitted ineligible players to participate, but does so at the expense of any meaningful review of NCAA eligibility decisions. Would a preferable alternative be an NCAA rule that required all prospective athletes

and schools to agree to arbitrate any legal claims regarding eligibility, and then create an impartial tribunal that could render a quick and final judgment?

(b) Pro Contracts and Amateurism

As with pre-college remuneration, engaging in off-the-field acts furthering one's professional career, such as hiring an agent or entering a draft prior to the completion of one's eligibility, violates NCAA rules. Thus, an athlete loses amateur status not only for receiving pay or a promise of pay for current athletic competition, but also for "sign[ing] a contract or commitment of any kind to play professional athletics" in the future (Article 12.1.1(c)). The next case illustrates this rule in operation.

SHELTON V. NCAA
539 F.2d 1197 (9th Cir. 1976)

WRIGHT, CIRCUIT JUDGE.

The principal issue in this appeal is whether the NCAA rule declaring ineligible for intercollegiate athletics in a particular sport any student who has ever signed a contract to play that professional sport violates the Equal Protection Clause of the constitution.

* * *

Appellee Shelton does not deny that he signed a professional contract with an American Basketball Association team which resulted in his being declared ineligible by Oregon State University. Indeed, he contends that the contract is unenforceable because he was induced to sign it by fraud and undue influence. The legal enforceability of the contract is the subject of a separate action brought by Shelton against the professional team which is now pending before the district court. Shelton urges that the NCAA rule making him ineligible despite the alleged defects in the contract creates an impermissible classification in violation of the Equal Protection Clause. He wants the rule suspended while his litigation and the college basketball season continue.

Our review on such questions is limited. None of the parties contends that the NCAA rule infringes upon a fundamental right which would necessitate strict judicial scrutiny. Instead, we must examine the rule to determine whether it rationally furthers some legitimate purpose. If it does, then our review is complete.

The rule purports to promote and protect amateurism in intercollegiate athletics. None of the parties seriously contends that this goal is illegitimate. Instead they dispute the means chosen by the NCAA to achieve it.

Shelton believes that it is unreasonable to treat as a professional one who alleges that the contract which he signed is unenforceable. In effect, he contends that the NCAA rule is overinclusive because if he is successful in his other action and the contract is declared unenforceable he is not nor would he ever have been a professional.

In a similar case two years ago, *Associated Students, Inc. v. NCAA*, 493 F.2d 1251 (9th Cir. 1974), this court reviewed another NCAA eligibility rule which was challenged on equal protection grounds. We recognized that the application of such rules may produce unreasonable results in certain situations. Nonetheless, we found that the rule did not violate the equal protection clause. Moreover, we did so although we recognized that the rule and its enforcement provisions might not be the best means for achieving the desired goal. It is not judicial business to tell a voluntary athletic association how best to formulate or enforce its rules.

We believe that the present appeal is controlled by *Associated Students*. The general rule under which Shelton was declared ineligible may from time to time produce unfortunate results. If an individual were subsequently successful in gaining a legal declaration that a professional contract was in fact void from its inception, a ruling that he was ineligible in the interim between his signing and the court's judgment might cause hardship. But the potential hardship does not make the rule irrational or unrelated to its goal. Moreover, hardship could be avoided by not signing a pro-contract. Reliance on a signed contract as an indication that a student's amateur status has been compromised is rationally related to the goal of preserving amateurism in intercollegiate athletics.

While our function is to determine only if the NCAA has selected a method of protecting amateurism which is reasonably related to that goal, an examination of the alternatives suggested by Shelton supports the conclusion that the rule in question withstands an equal protection challenge. Shelton argues that the rule should allow for cases such as his own where alleged defects in formation of the contract render it a nullity. The NCAA and its member institutions cannot simply take an athlete's word that his signed contract is void. An eligibility rule limited to contracts that would withstand a court test would be no rule at all. One could sign a contract, then allege that it was unenforceable and participate at will in college athletics while maintaining an option to enter the professional ranks at any time. Clearly, this would obliterate any remaining distinctions between amateur and professional athletes.

The alternative would be extremely burdensome. In the context of this appeal, for instance, the NCAA and its member institutions would be placed in the position of having to predict the outcome of Shelton's action against the professional basketball team. In order to do so they would likely have to undertake extensive investigations of the facts and time consuming hearings involving the parties. Even then, they would have no assurance that their decision would be compatible with the ultimate determination of the courts.

We hold that an effort to avoid this tangled set of affairs through the use of an easily applied and generally reliable criterion is rationally related to a legitimate purpose and does not, therefore, violate the equal protection clause.

Case dismissed.

NOTES AND QUESTIONS

1. *Aftermath*. After *Shelton*, the NCAA amended the rule to make clear that merely *signing* a professional contract will cost the student-athlete his amateur status, "regardless of [the contract's] legal enforceability or any consideration received." Article 12.1.3.

2. *Constitutional Challenge?* If *Tarkanian* had not foreclosed a constitutional challenge, would this rule be rationally related to a legitimate objective? What is the objective? Are there circumstances under which the application of this rule would not further the objective? Should the NCAA be required to create exceptions for every conceivable irrational application of a rule that is generally reasonable?

(c) Drafts and Amateurism

Whatever the merits of this NCAA policy, it is now clear that any player who reaches an agreement with a professional team thereby gives up his amateur status and eligibility to play for a college in that sport.

Player drafts pose a problem of the interplay of professional and college sports, one that can be and has been handled in different fashions. The earliest a player can now be drafted in hockey is when he reaches the age of 18; in baseball when he graduates from high school; in basketball one year after high school; and in football three years after he graduates from high school.

Under MLB and NHL rules, any team can draft a player who satisfies that league's eligibility conditions, irrespective of whether the player opts into the draft. If the player chooses to go on to college instead of playing professionally (usually in the minor leagues for a period), he is entitled to do so, and the team drafting him loses its rights to that draft pick after a certain point. (This fact gives some players considerably greater leverage in extracting a more generous signing bonus offer from the drafting team.)

In football and basketball, though, it has always been assumed that college teams will provide the training and development of future professional athletes: that is why players in the past became automatically eligible for the NFL and NBA drafts only after they had used up their four years of eligibility in college play. Spurred by Spencer Haywood's antitrust challenges in the 1970s, the NBA did allow players to opt into the draft earlier. Then, after experiencing threatened litigation by Craig Heyward in 1988 and Barry Sanders in 1989 (both of whom were exempted from the existing rule), the NFL followed suit, though still limiting that option to players who have been out of high school for three years. This revised NFL rule was upheld by the Second Circuit in the *Clarett v. NFL* case covered in Chapter 6.

Prior to 1994, making themselves subject to a professional league draft immediately cost basketball and football players their college eligibility under NCAA Article 12.2.4.2, which labeled a player "professional" if he "asks to be placed on the draft list . . . of a professional league in that sport." This rule risked considerable hardship to college players not picked as high as they expected, or perhaps not drafted at all.

After evolving through several iterations, the most recent version of the draft rules adopted in August 2018 will allow certain basketball players to return to college with their eligibility intact if they enter the NBA draft but are undrafted. To date, the new rules do not extend to college football players and the NFL draft.

NOTES AND QUESTIONS

1. *Loss of Amateur Status.* Should participation in a draft make an athlete lose amateur status? Why is this true for football, but not basketball, hockey, and baseball? Is there a legitimate distinction between the two outside of the difference in revenue generated in intercollegiate competitions?

2. *Drafts.* Do the parity and fair competition values of a draft outweigh the economic restriction such an approach places on college athletes? Would a free market system be preferable?

(d) Agents and Amateurism

Another key component of this NCAA "professionalism" doctrine is that it declares a player ineligible if he or she has "ever agreed (orally or in writing) to be represented by an agent for the purpose of marketing his or her athletic ability or reputation in that sport." Article 12.3.1. Chapter 9 explores the sports law problems posed by agents such as Norby Walters, who paid players money while they were still in college and covered up that tangible professional status of their clients. Under NCAA rules, though, it is equally disqualifying for a player to hire (and agree to pay) the best-qualified and most ethical of agents in order to discover their true professional athletic value (and some states have even made it criminal for the agent to reach a secret agreement with players who have not given up their college eligibility). To help fill that gap, not just the schools, but also the NBA and NFL have now set up advisory committees to give interested players a prediction (though not a guarantee) of where they would likely be drafted that year. Even so, to receive independent advice while still not forfeiting his future college eligibility—not only before the draft, but even afterwards in baseball when contract offers are being made—the player must hire someone who is billed as the "family advisor," and who is not authorized to "negotiate" on behalf of the athlete with the drafting team. These rules were the subject of a rare successful challenge in Ohio state courts.

OLIVER V. NCAA
155 Ohio Misc. 2d 17, 920 N.E.2d 203 (2009)

TONE, JUDGE.

* * *

FACTS

The plaintiff, Andrew Oliver, is a resident of Vermilion, Erie County, Ohio. In 2006, the plaintiff graduated from Vermilion High School, where he was the primary pitcher for its baseball team. The plaintiff is currently in his junior year of college at Oklahoma State University ("OSU"). Since August 2006, the plaintiff has pitched for the baseball team at OSU.

The defendant, the National Collegiate Athletic Association ("NCAA"), is an unincorporated business association having its principal place of business in Marion County, Indiana; it has member institutions not only in Oklahoma but also in Ohio. . . .

The plaintiff, in February 2006, retained the services of Robert M. Baratta, Tim Baratta, and Icon Sports Group, d.b.a. Icon Law Group, as his sports advisors and attorneys. In June of the same year, the Minnesota Twins of Major League Baseball drafted the plaintiff in the 17th round of the draft. At the end of the summer, the Minnesota Twins met with the plaintiff and his father at the Oliver family home in Vermilion before the plaintiff left for his freshman year of college. Tim Baratta also attended the meeting, at his own request, at the Oliver home. During the meeting the Minnesota Twins offered the plaintiff $390,000 to join their organization. After heeding the advice of his father, the plaintiff rejected the offer and chose to attend OSU in the fall on a full scholarship for which he had already signed a letter of intent in the fall of 2005.

As a result of deciding to go to OSU and accepting amateur status, the plaintiff would not be eligible for the draft again until his junior year of college in June 2009. The plaintiff played his freshman and sophomore years for OSU, and during that period he never received any invoices requesting payment for any services rendered by his advisors. In fact, the plaintiff avers that the advisors provided nothing of value to him.

In March 2008, plaintiff decided to terminate the Barattas and Icon Sports and retain the Boras Corporation. The plaintiff communicated his intentions of termination to Robert Baratta. At that time, Robert Baratta attempted to reconnect with the plaintiff and his father, but to no avail. In April 2008, the plaintiff received a letter and an invoice from the Barattas for $113,750 for legal services.... The plaintiff has argued that the contract is fictitious and the assistance stated in it was in fact never performed.

On May 19, 2008, the previous attorneys mailed, faxed, and e-mailed a letter to the defendant complaining about the plaintiff and reporting alleged violations by the plaintiff, *i.e.* the meeting at the Olivers' home that Tim Baratta had attended. As a result of the allegations, OSU and the defendant investigated the alleged violations in relationship to the plaintiff's amateur status. In May 2008, the plaintiff was indefinitely suspended from playing baseball and was informed by OSU staff that he had violated NCAA Bylaw 12.3.1 by (1) allowing his previous attorneys to contact the Minnesota Twins by telephone and (2) by allowing Tim Baratta to be present in his home when a representative from the Minnesota Twins tendered an offer to him.

On August 18, 2008, the plaintiff was reinstated as a result of a temporary restraining order issued by this court. However, in October 2008, OSU filed for reinstatement of the plaintiff with the NCAA even though the temporary restraining order had reinstated the plaintiff. Subsequently, in December 2008, the plaintiff was suspended for one year and charged a year of eligibility by the defendant. The penalty was subsequently reduced to 70 percent of the original suspension and no loss of eligibility for the plaintiff.

* * *

To the extent that the plaintiff's claim of arbitrary and capricious action asserts a violation of the duty of good faith and fair dealing that is implied in the contractual relationship between the NCAA and its members, his position as a third-party beneficiary of that contractual relationship affords him standing to pursue his claims.

* * *

III. GOOD FAITH AND FAIR DEALING

Even though the obligation of good faith exists in a contractual relationship, this is not an invitation for this court to rewrite the benefit bestowed on the parties. The court agrees with the defendant that this is not a case about whether the court agrees or disagrees with the bylaws in question. * * * Therefore, the defendant, and for that matter OSU, was required to deal honestly and reasonably with the plaintiff as a third-party beneficiary regarding their contractual relationship. Surely each party is entitled to the benefit of its bargain. With that stated, if this court determines that Bylaw 12.3.2.1 is void because it is against the public policy of Ohio or because it is arbitrary and capricious, and Bylaw 19.7 interferes with the delegation of judicial power to the courts of this state, then the defendant has not dealt with the plaintiff honestly or reasonably and the defendant has breached the contract.

The court continues this analysis by examining the plaintiff's argument that he retained lawyers to represent him and that those lawyers are subject to the exclusive regulation of the Ohio Supreme Court. Thus the defendant, according to the plaintiff, had no authority to promulgate Bylaw 12.3.2.1. The plaintiff asserts that the bylaw promulgated by the defendant prevented his lawyers from competently representing him. Therefore the plaintiff argues, the bylaw is void because it is against public policy. Bylaw 12.3.2.1 states:

> A lawyer may not be present during discussions of a contract offer with a professional organization or have any direct contact (in person, by telephone or by mail) with a professional sports organization on behalf of the individual. A lawyer's presence during such discussions is considered representation by an agent.

In contrast, the defendant argues that Bylaw 12.3.2.1 helps to retain a clear line of demarcation between collegiate and professional sports that is a fundamental goal of the member institutions. Furthermore, according to the defendant, it preserves an amateur model of collegiate athletics, and the defendant contends that this court should not intervene since the bylaw is the will of the NCAA membership.

It is important to fully understand the fact pattern of what transpired and what caused the plaintiff to be pronounced ineligible. At the end of the summer of 2006, representatives from the Minnesota Twins met with the plaintiff and his father at the Oliver home. According to the plaintiff's testimony, the plaintiff's father contacted the Barattas to inform them of the meeting. Tim Baratta told the plaintiff's father that he thought he should be there. While all the parties were at the Oliver home, the Twins offered the plaintiff a $390,000 contract, which he rejected after seeking the advice of his father. However, Tim Baratta's presence at the Oliver home, even though no testimony ever portrayed that Mr. Baratta was involved in any of the conversations between the plaintiff and the Twin's representative, just Baratta's presence (the presence of an attorney/advisor who advised the plaintiff that he would keep his amateurism status safe) in that room, violated Bylaw 12.3.2.1 and stripped the plaintiff of his eligibility to play baseball through the entire season.

Let us also remember that the rules and testimony are clear that amateurism is the bedrock and founding principle of the NCAA. And so, the court has listened to and read much about Bylaw Article 12, set forth in the NCAA division manual, which is entitled "Amateurism" and sets forth the rules governing the protection of a student-athlete's amateur status that must be maintained in order for an athlete to participate in an intercollegiate sports program.

* * *

[T]he crux of this case falls under Bylaw 12.3.2, which carves out an exception to the no agent rule by allowing a student-athlete to retain a lawyer (not even the defendant can circumvent an individual's right to counsel). Yet, the exception to the rule, *i.e.*, NCAA Bylaw 12.3.2 which allows legal counsel for student-athletes attempts to limit an attorney's role as to that representation and, in effect, such as in the case here, puts the onus on the student-athlete.

The status of the no-agent rule, as firmly pointed out in the direct testimony of Kevin Hennon, vice president of membership services, is a prohibition against agents, not lawyers. Therein lies the problem.

It is impossible to allow student-athletes to hire lawyers and attempt to control what that lawyer does for his client by Bylaws 12.3.2 or 12.3.2.1. These rules attempt to say to the student-athlete that he or she can consult with an attorney but that the attorney cannot negotiate a contract with a professional sport's team. This surely does not retain a clear line of demarcation between amateurism and professionalism. The student-athlete will never know what his attorney is doing for him or her, and quite frankly neither will the defendant. The evidence is very clear that this rule is impossible to enforce and as a result is being enforced selectively. Further, as in this case, it allows for exploitation of the student-athlete "by professional and commercial enterprises," in contravention of the positive intentions of the defendant.

Was Baratta's presence in that room a clear indication that the plaintiff, a teenager who had admitted at trial that he was in no position to negotiate a professional contract and whose father testified to the same, was a professional? According to Bylaw 12.3.2.1, the no-agent rule, he was. As such the following issues must be resolved: Is the no-agent rule against the public policy of Ohio? Is it arbitrary? Is it capricious?

The plaintiff testified that he hired the Barattas in part because they were attorneys and they promised that they would protect his amateur status. From the testimony given at trial, the court is aware that the defendant permits student-athletes and their parents to negotiate contracts while in the presence of a sports representative but to have an attorney present in the room would in some way smear the line of demarcation between what is amateurism and what is professionalism. An attorney's duty, in Ohio, in Oklahoma, in all 50 states, is to represent his client competently. . . .

For a student-athlete to be permitted to have an attorney and then to tell that student-athlete that his attorney cannot be present during the discussion of an offer from a professional organization is akin to a patient hiring a doctor, but the doctor is told by the hospital board and the insurance company that he cannot be present when the patient meets with a surgeon because the conference may improve his patient's decision-making power. Bylaw 12.3.2.1 is unreliable (capricious) and illogical (arbitrary) and indeed stifles what attorneys are trained and retained to do.

The process advanced by the NCAA hinders representation by legal counsel, creating an atmosphere fraught with ethical dilemmas and pitfalls that an attorney consulting a student-athlete must encounter. Will the attorney be able to advance what is best for the client or will a neutral party, the NCAA, tie his hands? What harm could possibly befall the student-athlete if such a rule were not found? What occurs if the parents of a student are attorneys or for that matter sport agents? What would have happened if Tim Baratta had been in the kitchen or outside or on the patio instead of in the same room as His client when the offer from the Minnesota Twins was made to the plaintiff?

This court appreciates that a fundamental goal of the member institutions and the defendant is to preserve the clear line of demarcation between amateurism and professionalism. However, to suggest that Bylaw 12.3.2.1 accomplishes that purpose by instructing a student-athlete that his attorney cannot do what he or she was hired to do is simply illogical. . . . [N]o entity, other than that one designated by the state, can dictate to an attorney where, what, how, or when he should represent his client. With all due respect, surely that decision should not be determined by the NCAA and its member institutions, no matter what the defendant claims is the purpose of the rule. If the defendant intends to deal with this athlete or any athlete in good faith, the student-athlete should have the opportunity to have the tools present (in this case an attorney) that would allow him to make a wise decision without automatically being deemed a professional, especially when such contractual negotiations can be overwhelming even to those who are skilled in their implementation.

* * *

After this court has engaged in a balancing process that was designed to weigh the equities between the parties, the court determines by clear and convincing evidence that the plaintiff would suffer immediate and irreparable injury, loss, or damage if injunctive relief is not granted. If an injunction is not granted, the plaintiff would suffer loss of his college baseball experience, impairment or loss of his future baseball professional career, loss in being available for the upcoming draft because he is less likely to be seen, and ongoing damage to the plaintiff's reputation and baseball career.

In comparison, the defendant's witnesses stated that if relief were granted, it would be confusing as to which institutions would have to follow this court's ruling. Would it be Ohio members, Oklahoma members, all institutions? However, since this court has personam jurisdiction, this argument is not as persuasive as the plaintiff's and the scales of justice have tilted in the plaintiff's favor.

Judgment accordingly.

NOTES AND QUESTIONS

1. *Loss of Amateur Status, Part II.* Should hiring an agent make an athlete lose amateur status? What is the justification for this rule? Do you find it persuasive?

2. *The Line Between Amateur and Professional.* The NCAA's strict definition of "amateur" status is supposed to "maintain a clear line of demarcation between college athletics and professional sports." In that regard, is there a defensible reason for the very different treatment afforded to baseball players who are drafted without their permission by a MLB team after three years in college (which by itself does not cost them their college eligibility), basketball players who elect into the NBA draft (who can now retrieve their eligibility only if no team picks them), and football players (who give up any college football future when they opt into the NFL draft)?

3. *The Need for an Agent.* With respect to any or all of the leagues, should a player be free to hire a real "agent" to determine his true market value in professional sports before deciding whether to enter or return to college sports? Indeed, suppose a player is picked low in the draft, is offered and signs a contract to play with that team eventually (but with no money paid now), and wants to return to college to finish both his athletic and academic careers there. Is it vital for the NCAA to bar any such contract for *future* professional services in order to maintain its "clear line of demarcation" from professional leagues? What exactly is the demarcation line between an NCAA football venture such as Ohio State (which Orlando Pace left in 1997), and the NFL's St. Louis Rams (which Pace joined as the league's number one draft pick that year)? Certainly, there is a great deal of movement of highly-paid coaches (such as Rick Pitino and Nick Saban) between these two settings, with the college programs often outbidding the professional teams for highly-valued coaches' services. The broader issue that runs through all of these questions and cases in this chapter is whether, given the financial stakes now riding on big-time

college sports, courts should defer to NCAA efforts to maintain the *amateur* status of its players (as opposed to the *academic* status discussed above).

BANKS V. NCAA
977 F.2d 1081 (7th Cir. 1992)

COFFEY, CIRCUIT JUDGE.

[Braxston Banks entered Notre Dame in 1986 as a highly rated football prospect. By the end of his freshman year he was the starting fullback on the varsity team. But Banks injured his knee early in his sophomore year and started only a handful of games during that season and the next one. Banks decided to sit out his entire senior year (1989) to give his knee a chance to recover fully. By that time, Banks' classmate, Anthony Johnson, had become Notre Dame's starting fullback and the top-rated NFL prospect at that position.

In the winter of 1990, Banks debated whether to turn professional with Johnson or to return to Notre Dame for a fifth year, for which he was eligible under NCAA rules and for which Notre Dame was ready to give him another year's full scholarship. After extensive discussions with NFL scouts and a player-agent known to his family, Banks decided in March 1990 to enter the NFL draft and to sign a representation agreement with the agent. To make himself eligible for the draft, the NFL required Banks to sign a form whereby he "irrevocably renounced any and all remaining college eligibility." As far as the NCAA was concerned, its own By-laws 12.2.4 and 12.3 dictated that either of Banks' actions—entering the draft or signing an agent representation contract—would cost Banks his future college eligibility.

Unfortunately, the condition of Banks' knee hampered his performance at the NFL tryout camp in Indianapolis in early April. Thus no team selected Banks in any of the twelve rounds of the late April draft, and no team was willing to sign him to a free-agent contract. Though Banks returned to Notre Dame in the summer of 1990 to finish his degree, the NCAA would not give him a waiver from its rules to permit Banks to play for Notre Dame that fall. As a result, Banks launched this antitrust suit against the NCAA, not claiming any right to be paid while playing for the very popular and profitable Notre Dame team, but just the necessary freedom to learn what were his professional prospects if he chose to leave college. The judge granted the NCAA's motion under Rule 12(b)(6) for summary dismissal because of Banks' failure to state a valid antitrust claim.]

* * *

IV. Rule 12(b)(6) Dismissal of a Rule—of—Reason Case

Banks' primary contention on appeal is that because the record is not thoroughly developed, it was inappropriate for the district court to decide that the NCAA no-draft and no-agent rules were pro-competitive in ruling on a Rule 12(b)(6) motion to dismiss. . . . The district court decided the case not on the basis of the relative anti-competitive effect of the rules versus the pro-competitive impact, but on the ground of Banks' absolute failure to allege an anti-competitive effect. . . . Since the district judge's decision was based on Banks' failure to allege an anti-competitive effect on an identifiable market, the argument that the court improperly determined that the rules were reasonable on a motion to dismiss is without merit.

V. The Validity of the Antitrust Claim

* * *

[Plaintiff's] allegations identify two markets: (1) NCAA football players who enter the draft and/or employ an agent and (2) college institutions that are members of the NCAA. Another reading of the complaint might even have deduced a third market, the NFL player recruitment market. But regardless of how charitably the complaint is read, it has failed to define an anti-competitive effect of the alleged restraints on the markets.

The dissent reasons that Banks has alleged that the NCAA no-draft rule has an anti-competitive effect in the market for college football players. The dissent claims this anti-competitive effect is the no-draft rule "foreclosing players 'from choosing a major college football team based on the willingness of the institution to waive or change [the no-draft] rule.'" This allegation can at best be described as inaccurate and further fails to allege an anti-competitive impact. First, as Banks states in his amended complaint, the NCAA has adopted the no-draft, no-agent, and other substantive rules to which all NCAA member institutions "have agreed, and do in fact, adhere." Contrary to Banks' erroneous allegation, an NCAA member institution may not waive or change the no-draft rule at its discretion, for it is rather obvious that only the National Collegiate Athletic Association can waive or change one of its substantive rules. Any school that sought to waive or change the rules would forfeit its ability to participate in NCAA sanctioned events.

Second, as the district court held, the complaint has failed to allege an anti-competitive impact. The failure results from Banks' inability to explain how the no-draft rule restrains trade in the college football labor market. The NCAA Rules seek to promote fair competition, encourage the educational pursuits of student-athletes and prevent commercialism. . . .

As the Supreme Court in *Board of Regents* stated: "most of the regulatory controls of the NCAA [are] a justifiable means of fostering competition among the amateur athletic teams and therefore are procompetitive because they enhance public interest in intercollegiate athletics." The Court further explained:

> The NCAA seeks to market a particular brand of football—college football. The identification of this "product" with an academic tradition differentiates college football from and makes it more popular than professional sports to which it might otherwise be comparable, such as, for example, minor league baseball. In order to preserve the character and quality of the "product," athletes must not be paid, must be required to attend class, and the like. And the integrity of the "product" cannot be preserved except by mutual agreement; if an institution adopted such restrictions unilaterally (restrictions on eligibility rules), its effectiveness as a competitor on the playing field might soon be destroyed. Thus, the NCAA plays a vital role in enabling college football to preserve its character, and as a result enables a product to be marketed which might otherwise be unavailable. In performing this role, its actions widen consumer choice—not only the choices available to sports fans but also those available to athletes—and hence can be viewed as procompetitive.

468 U.S. at 102.

The no-draft rule has no more impact on the market for college football players than other NCAA eligibility requirements such as grades, semester hours carried, or requiring a high school diploma. They all constitute eligibility requirements essential to participation in NCAA sponsored amateur athletic competition. Banks might just as well have alleged that only permitting a student five calendar years in which to participate in four seasons of intercollegiate athletics restrains trade. Banks' allegation that the no-draft rule restrains trade is absurd. None of the NCAA rules affecting college football eligibility restrain trade in the market for college players because the NCAA does not exist as a minor league training ground for future NFL players but rather to provide an opportunity for competition among amateur students pursuing a collegiate education.[12] Because the no-draft rule represents a desirable and legitimate attempt "to keep university athletics from becoming professionalized to the extent that profit making objectives would overshadow educational objectives," the no-draft rule and other like NCAA regulations preserve the bright line of demarcation between college and "play for pay" football. We consider college football players as student-athletes simultaneously pursuing

---

[12] This conclusion is buttressed by the fact that a very small number of college athletes go on to participate in professional athletics. Of the over 12,000 Division I-A college football players, less than 300 go on to the NFL each year. In fact, it has been calculated that of the elite 336 players drafted each year, only 49 percent make NFL teams and after 5 years only 35 percent are still with an NFL team.

academic degrees that will prepare them to enter the employment market in non-athletic occupations, and hold that the regulations of the NCAA are designed to preserve the honesty and integrity of intercollegiate athletics and foster fair competition among the participating amateur college students.

In order for the NCAA Rules to be considered a restraint of trade in violation of § 1 of the Sherman Act, Banks must allege that the no-draft and no-agent rules are terms of employment that diminish competition in the employment market (*i.e.*, college football).

The dissent refers to NCAA member colleges as "purchasers of labor" in the college football player market and the players as "suppliers" in this market.[13] After likening colleges to "purchasers of labor," the dissent extends the analogy to conclude that colleges offer material terms of employment to their college players and that the no-draft rule is a "material term of employment" that harms competition in the college football labor market.

In contrast to professional football, NCAA student-athletes are required to attend class, maintain a minimum grade point average, and enroll and complete a required number of courses to obtain a degree. The no-draft rule is evidence of the academic priority of the NCAA because it forecloses a student-athlete from hiring an agent or entering the NFL draft and after failing to meet the professional standards, returning to play college football to improve his football skills in hopes of entering an upcoming draft. In denying a college football player the right to play professional football (entering the NFL draft) and then return to college football, the no-draft rule merely serves as an NCAA eligibility requirement and precludes the existence of a college football labor market for athletes who are ineligible by NCAA standards.

Secondly, we disagree with the dissent's allegation that NCAA member schools are "purchasers of labor," as the operation of the NCAA eligibility and recruiting requirements prohibits member colleges from engaging in price competition for players. We fail to understand how the dissent can allege that NCAA colleges purchase labor through the grant-in-aid athletic scholarships offered to college players when the value of the scholarship is based upon the school's tuition and room and board, not by

---

[13] We disagree with Banks' allegation in paragraph 22(c) of his Amended Complaint that the NCAA no-draft and no-agent Rules give the college player only one realistic chance of being drafted in the NFL, because the college player (1) can enter the draft any time during his college career (Tommy Maddox of UCLA was just drafted by Denver although he had two more years of eligibility); (2) enter the draft, then play for another league like the CFL, WFL, or ARENA LEAGUE, or even sit out for a year and then reenter the draft (Bo Jackson was a first round draft choice of Tampa Bay, but he chose to play baseball instead, the next year he was drafted by the Los Angeles Raiders with whom he signed); or (3) complete his eligibility before entering the draft.

Recently 97 of the 107 NCAA Division I-A football programs imposed strict guidelines on NFL scouts to prevent plucking student-athletes from colleges.

the supply and demand for players. Elimination of the no-draft and no-agent rules would fly in the face of the NCAA's amateurism requirements. Member schools might very well be exposed to agents offering the services of their football playing clients to the highest bidder. In representing their "pro athlete" clients, the agents would in all probability attempt to bargain with the NCAA school and might very well expect the school to offer their client an attractive contract, possibly involving automobiles, condominiums, and cash as compensation in contravention of the NCAA amateurism rules. Such arrangements might involve cash compensation payable only in the future after the player has completed his college eligibility and continues with an NFL club. The involvement of professional sports agents in NCAA football would turn amateur intercollegiate athletics into a sham because the focus of college football would shift from educating the student-athlete to creating a "minor-league" farm system out of college football that would operate solely to improve players' skills for professional football in the NFL. We should not permit the entry of professional athletes and their agents into NCAA sports because the cold commercial nature of professional sports would not only destroy the amateur status of college athletics but more importantly would interfere with the athletes' proper focus on their educational pursuits and direct their attention to the quick buck in pro sports.

The no-agent and no-draft rules are vital and must work in conjunction with other eligibility requirements to preserve the amateur status of college athletics, and prevent the sports agents from further intruding into the collegiate educational system.

* * *

The dissent takes a surprisingly cynical view of college athletics and contends that "colleges squeeze out of their players one or two more years of service" because the no-draft rule forces the player to choose between continued collegiate eligibility and entering the draft. This description of players "selling their services" to NCAA colleges stands in stark contrast to the academic and amateurism requirements of the vast majority of college athletic programs that, in compliance with the NCAA rules and regulations, are foreclosed from offering cash compensation or "non-permissible awards, extra benefits, or excessive or improper expenses not authorized by NCAA legislation. . . ." The fact that a minority of schools (such as the University of Houston)[17] "use" athletes rather than encourage and foster their students' academic pursuits, does not negate the fact that

---

[17] Recently, the NCAA released the graduation rates of Division I NCAA member schools. These statistics reveal that only 14 percent of scholarship athletes in football graduated from the University of Houston within six years of their matriculation in 1983–84 or 1984–85. In addition, the NCAA reported that zero percent of black football athletes at the University of Houston graduated within six years of their enrollment in 1983–84 or 1984–85, whereas 33 percent of white football players at Houston graduated within six years of their enrollment in 1983–84 or 1984–85.

all NCAA member colleges encourage and require their student-athletes to carry a minimum number of semester credits and maintain a minimum grade point average equivalent to the academic program the university's non-athletic students follow.

* * *

We agree with the district court's finding that the plaintiff has failed to allege an anti-competitive effect on a relevant market; at best Banks has merely attempted to frame his complaint in antitrust language. While Banks alleges a restraint on the market of college football players, college institutions who are members of the NCAA, and perhaps an NFL player recruitment market, the complaint fails to explain how these alleged restraints diminish competition in or among the markets. In our review of Banks' arguments in his appellate briefs as well as our review of the oral argument, we have been unable to discern a cogent argument articulated even on appeal that the alleged restraints impose an anti-competitive effect on the alleged markets. The appellant merely claims that there is an anti-competitive effect, but he fails to explain what it is. While Banks might possibly have been able to allege an anti-competitive impact on a relevant market through a more carefully drafted complaint or an amendment to his complaint, he failed to do so. It is not for us, as appellate judges, to restructure his complaint for him.

Affirmed.

FLAUM, CIRCUIT JUDGE, concurring in part and dissenting in part.

* * *

As the NCAA concedes, Banks defined two markets in his complaint, only one of which it is necessary to address here: the nationwide labor market for college football players. NCAA member colleges are the purchasers of labor in this market, and the players are the suppliers. The players agree to compete in football games sponsored by the colleges, games that typically garner the colleges a profit, in exchange for tuition, room, board and other benefits.

It is hardly a revelation that colleges fiercely compete for the most promising high school football players—the players who, incidentally, are most likely to feel constrained by the challenged rules two or three years down the line. If the no-draft rule were scuttled, colleges that promised their athletes the opportunity to test the waters in the NFL draft before their eligibility expired, and return if things didn't work out, would be more attractive to athletes than colleges that declined to offer the same opportunity. The no-draft rule eliminates this potential element of competition among colleges, the purchasers of labor in the college football labor market. It categorically rules out a term of employment that players, the suppliers of labor in that market, would find advantageous.

* * *

It should come as no surprise that the no-draft rule operates to the detriment of the players, and that colleges benefit from the fact that their athletes feel tied to the institution for four years. Consider, for example, athletes who are known in the vernacular as "bubble" players. These athletes are excellent competitors at the collegiate level, but for various reasons are considered less than certain NFL prospects. Bubble players who wish to market their wares in the professional market after their sophomore or junior year will forego entry into the NFL draft because, if they are not selected (or fail to join a team after being selected), the rule will prevent them from returning to college to hone their skills and try again in subsequent years. *See* Note, *Sherman Act Invalidation of the NCAA Amateurism Rules*, 105 Harv. L. Rev. 1299, 1311 (1992). The rule permits colleges to squeeze out of their players one or two more years of service, years the colleges might have lost had the ability to enter the draft without consequence to eligibility been the subject of bargaining between athletes and colleges. The rule thereby distorts the "price" of labor in the college football labor market to the detriment of players.

The NCAA disputes this characterization, maintaining that the no-draft rule is not "anticompetitive" as the term is employed under the Sherman Act. At the heart of its argument is the contention that "there is no price competition as such among colleges for players because the 'price,' the value of grant-in-aid, is determined by the school's tuition, room, and board, not by the supply of and demand for players." This analysis of the college football labor market is partially correct; in that market, players exchange their labor for in-kind benefits, not cash. At least ideally. *But see* Johnson, *Defense Against the NCAA*, U.S. News & World Rep., Jan. 13, 1992, at 25 (improper cash payments made to football players at Auburn University); Johnson, *Playing for Pay in Texas*, Newsweek, Mar. 16, 1987, at 32 (same at Southern Methodist University).

It is unrealistic, however, to suggest that the value of those in-kind benefits is limited solely to tuition, room and board. If this were true, the best football players would attend the most expensive private universities that would admit them, for these universities would offer, under the NCAA's analysis, the most "valuable" compensation for their services. Assuming some regional loyalties, private colleges such as Syracuse University, the University of Southern California, and Notre Dame would consistently outrecruit public colleges such as Penn State, UCLA and the University of Michigan. As anyone familiar with college football well knows, this is not the case. The reason is simple. Athletes look to more than tuition, room and board when determining which college has offered them the most attractive package of in-kind benefits. Some athletes look primarily to the reputation of a particular program or coach as a "feeder" into the NFL; others believe that the quality of a university's academic program and the commitment of the coaching staff to scholarly pursuits is more important. Some athletes look to whether a college will offer them a cushy, high-paying job during the summer or school year; others might be attracted by state-of-the-art training facilities. And some athletes, if given the chance, would look to whether a college would allow them to enter the NFL draft and return if they did not join a professional team.

All of these things—with the exception of the last item—are "terms of employment" that currently sweeten the pot for athletes choosing among college football programs. They provide, apart from tuition, room and board, the means by which colleges, as purchasers of labor, attract and compensate their players, the suppliers of labor. That the medium of exchange is non-monetary does not alter the fact that these benefits constitute the "price" of labor in the college football market, or that the categorical elimination of one of those benefits harms competition in that market. The NCAA's protestations notwithstanding, there can be no doubt that Banks has alleged an anticompetitive effect in a relevant market.

* * *

Banks easily clears the threshold ["of connecting the injury claimed to the purposes of the antitrust laws"]. The no-draft rule, as noted, is anticompetitive because it constitutes an agreement among colleges to eliminate an element of competition in the college football labor market. The purposes of the antitrust laws are served when employers are prevented from tampering with the employment market in this precise way. "Just as antitrust law seeks to preserve the free market opportunities of buyers and sellers of goods, so also it seeks to do the same for buyers and sellers of employment services...." Banks' injury—namely, the revocation of his eligibility and consequent loss of his athletic scholarship during his final year at Notre Dame—"flows from" the precise anticompetitive aspects of the NCAA rules that he set out in his complaint.

The NCAA also raises the issue of harm to consumers; it contends that Banks' complaint is deficient because it does not "reasonably support the inference that consumers are harmed by the operation of the no-draft and no-agent rules." Whether harm to consumers is the sine qua non of antitrust injury is an issue over which there is currently a split in this circuit. Some of our cases hold that a plaintiff, to satisfy the antitrust injury requirement, must demonstrate that the challenged practice causing him harm also harms consumers by reducing output or raising prices. *Stamatakis Indus., Inc. v. King*, 965 F.2d 469, 471 (7th Cir. 1992); *Chicago Professional Sports Ltd. Partnership v. National Basketball Ass'n.*, 961 F.2d 667, 670 (7th Cir. 1992). Others hold that application of the antitrust laws "does not depend in each particular case upon the ultimate demonstrable consumer effect." *Fishman v. Estate of Wirtz*, 807 F.2d 520,

536 (7th Cir. 1986); *see also Chicago Professional Sports*, 961 F.2d at 677 (Cudahy, J., concurring).

One can dispense with the NCAA's contention without choosing sides in this dispute. To see why, it is important first to identify the consumers and the market at issue in this case. By "consumers," the NCAA apparently means people who watch college football. These individuals certainly are consumers in the college football product market, but the market at issue here is the college football labor market, and the NCAA member colleges are consumers in that market. It would be counterintuitive to require Banks to demonstrate that the no-draft and no-agent rules harm the colleges, the very entities that established those rules. I doubt very strongly that the rule laid out in *Chicago Professional Sports*, to the extent it is valid elsewhere, was intended to apply in this context. Concerted action among consumers that lowers prices harms competition as much as concerted action among producers that raises prices. The distinction should be irrelevant to any discussion of antitrust injury. Professors Areeda and Turner, when discussing the right of laborers to challenge antitrust violations in the labor market, put things nicely:

> It would be perverse ... to hold that the very object of the law's solicitude and the persons most directly concerned—perhaps the only persons concerned—could not challenge the restraint.... The standing of such plaintiffs is undoubted and seldom challenged.

Banks has alleged that the NCAA rules harm competition to the detriment of producers in the college football labor market, and that his injuries are directly related to that harm. This is sufficient to establish "antitrust injury" in this context.

I add here a caveat to avert any potential misunderstandings. My point is only that Banks has properly alleged an anticompetitive effect in a relevant market and has demonstrated antitrust injury, and hence that his damages action should survive the NCAA's motion to dismiss. But this is, of course, only the first step. To ultimately prevail, Banks also must demonstrate, under the rule of reason, that the no-agent and no-draft rules, despite their anticompetitive effects, are not "justifiable means of fostering competition among amateur athletic teams and therefore procompetitive" on the whole. It may very well be that the no-draft and no-agent rules are essential to the survival of college football as a distinct and viable product, in which case Banks would lose. A lively debate has arisen among those who have already considered this matter. I opt not to join the fray here, for I think it unwise to weigh pro-and anticompetitive effects under the rule of reason on a motion to dismiss.

Today's decision, by holding that Banks has not alleged that the rules are anticompetitive in the first instance, deprives him of the opportunity to join this issue on remand. As I have discussed, it is difficult to reconcile this holding with a sound reading of Banks' complaint. On a broader level, I am also concerned that today's decision—unintentionally, to be sure, for it suggests that a "more artfully drafted complaint" could have alleged an anticompetitive effect in this market—will provide comfort to the NCAA's incredulous assertion that its eligibility rules are "noncommercial." The NCAA would have us believe that intercollegiate athletic contests are about spirit, competition, camaraderie, sportsmanship, hard work (which they certainly are) . . . and nothing else. Players play for the fun of it, colleges get a kick out of entertaining the student body and alumni, but the relationship between players and colleges is positively noncommercial. It is consoling to buy into these myths, for they remind us of a more innocent era—an era where recruiting scandals were virtually unknown, where amateurism was more a reality than an ideal, and where post-season bowl games were named for commodities, not corporations. On the flip side, it is disquieting to think of college football as a business, of colleges as the purchasers of labor, and of athletes as the suppliers.

The NCAA continues to purvey, even in this case, an outmoded image of intercollegiate sports that no longer jibes with reality. The times have changed. College football is a terrific American institution that generates abundant nonpecuniary benefits for players and fans, but it is also a vast commercial venture that yields substantial profits for colleges. The games provide fans with entertaining contests to watch, and athletes with an opportunity to display and develop their strength, skills and character, but they are saleable products nonetheless. An athlete's participation offers all of the rewards that attend vigorous competition in organized sport, but it is also labor, labor for which the athlete is recompensed. The no-draft and no-agent rules may, ultimately, pass muster under the rule of reason. But, putting the adequacy of Banks' complaint to the side, contending that they have no commercial effect on competition in the college football labor market, or that there is no market of that type at all, is chimerical:

> The true stake is this decades-long gentleman's agreement between the NFL and the college powers-that-be that has kept all but a handful of football playing collegians from turning pro before their four-year use to their schools is exhausted. The pros get a free farm system that supplies them with well-trained, much publicized employees. The colleges get to keep their players the equivalent of barefoot and pregnant.

Klein, *College Football: Keeping 'em Barefoot*, Wall St. J., Sept. 4, 1987, at 15.

When confronted with the clash between soothing nostalgia and distressing reality, it is oftentimes difficult to resist the call of tennis champion Andre Agassi, who when hawking cameras off the court tells us that "image is everything." But we must remember that Agassi's domain, at least in this instance, is television. What may be true there is decidedly not under the lens of the antitrust laws. Having found that Banks has cleared the threshold of alleging an anticompetitive effect in a relevant market, I would reverse the district court's dismissal of his damages action and remand for further proceedings.

NOTES AND QUESTIONS

1. *Basis for Decision.* Was the holding in *Banks* based upon a deficiency in pleadings, or upon the court's view that the nature of college sports makes it impossible for a student-athlete to formulate an antitrust claim against the NCAA's amateurism and academic eligibility rules? If the former, how should Banks have crafted his complaint to satisfy the court? If the latter, do you agree with that substantive position?

2. *Consequences of Antitrust Liability.* The *Banks* majority argued that if the NCAA's "no draft" and "no agent" rules were held illegal under § 1, the same fate must befall all other NCAA eligibility requirements. If a court found unreasonable the NCAA's bar against Banks' returning for his senior year, must the same antitrust verdict follow for the NCAA rules that limit Notre Dame's (and other colleges') financial expenditures for athletes to reimbursement of standard educational expenses? Or can these two features of NCAA "amateurism" be distinguished under the antitrust Rule of Reason?

3. *Employee-Athletes.* The majority opinion in Banks states: "In order for the NCAA Rules to be considered a restraint of trade in violation of § 1 of the Sherman Act, Banks must allege that the no-draft and no-agent rules are terms of employment that diminish competition in the employment market (*i.e.*, college football)." Do you agree that antitrust laws can only apply if the student-athletes are ruled to be employees and the NCAA restraints to be terms of employment? These issues are considered in more detail in the next section.

4. *Gaines v. NCAA.* The Middle District of Tennessee rejected a challenge similar to Banks' in *Gaines v. NCAA,* 738 F. Supp. 738 (1990). Brad Gaines, a former Vanderbilt player, sought to regain his eligibility after entering the draft and failing to get a contract. The court found that the no-draft rule did not violate the Sherman Act.

5. *NCAA Basketball Reforms.* At the time that this book was going to press, the NCAA announced a series of reforms related to college basketball. These included giving elite high school and college basketball players the right to hire agents and the ability to return to school and retain eligibility if they went into the draft and did not agree to a contract. In addition, the NBA, USA basketball, and the NCAA were in discussions to change the one and done rule and allow high school athletes to again go directly to the NBA. Are these positive reforms? Or do they undermine amateurism? Also, is there a

qualitative difference between football and basketball players that makes these changes more appropriate for basketball than for football?

C. CHALLENGING THE STUDENT-ATHLETE MODEL

As the two NCAA narratives of amateurism and commercialism increasingly conflict, athletes have challenged and continue to challenge the student-athlete model on both labor and antitrust grounds. As we will see, antitrust provides a more plausible path to challenge the current model.

1. LABOR CHALLENGES

One underlying theory of these challenges has centered on the argument that athletes should be treated as university employees, not mere student-athletes. In *Waldrep v. Texas Employers Insurance Ass'n*, 21 S.W.3d 692 (2000), for instance, an athlete attempted to claim employee status in order to receive workers compensation benefits for a football injury. The Texas Court of Appeals rejected the claim, finding the athlete to be only a student. *See also Rensing v. Indiana State Univ.*, 444 N.E.2d 1170 (Ind. 1983) (holding that an injured college football player was not entitled to workers compensation because he was not an employee of the university). More recently, athletes at Northwestern had greater initial success making a similar claim that they were university employees.

In March 2014, the NLRB's regional director in Chicago ruled that the scholarship recipient members of the Northwestern football team were employees of the University and thus were eligible to hold a representation election to determine if a majority of the employees wanted to be represented for purposes of collective bargaining by a union (CAPA) that would serve as their exclusive bargaining representative. Although the full Board ultimately overturned this decision, the opinion matters for its rhetoric, which informs the antitrust question explored in *O'Bannon*. The regional director's rhetoric, contrary to *Deppe* and *Banks*, suggests that the ideal of the student-athlete does not exist for Northwestern football players. He opines that they are simply athletes, not students.

The essence of the decision was that the scholarship football players met the criteria for being classified as employees in light of the following: (1) they provide a valuable service to the university (as demonstrated by the substantial revenue and public relations benefits the university receives), (2) they are compensated (with scholarships that include tuition, fees, books, room and board), (3) they are required to perform services for the university as a condition of receiving that compensation, and (4) their "work" is controlled by supervisors employed by the university (their coaches).

The regional director also stressed: (a) the players spend huge amounts of time on their football duties, sometimes as much as 40 to 50 hours a week, which is far more than they spend on their studies; (b) the work for which the players are compensated, playing football, has no relationship to their degree-seeking academic work and they receive no academic credit for it; (c) the university employees who supervise the players are not faculty, but rather non-academic coaches; and (d) the compensation the players receive is not financial aid for academic purposes.

One month after the regional director's decision was announced, a representation election was held by secret ballot. During that month, Northwestern football coach Pat Fitzgerald and other university officials tried to persuade the players to vote against recognizing the union by telling them that a union would not be able to obtain anything more for them than they already received and that unionization of college athletes would destroy college athletics. Similarly, football coaches, athletics directors, and university presidents, as well as several politicians, publicly derided the decision, some going so far as to suggest that their schools might shut down their scholarship athletic programs rather than face collective bargaining with a players union. The NLRB then announced the day before the election that the ballots would be impounded and no results announced pending the decision by the full Board on appeal.

Two years later, the NLRB vacated the regional director's decision and the election, deciding that whether or not the athletes were university employees, a bargaining unit including only them and not players for the other universities in the Big Ten would not be appropriate. The Board noted these other universities are all public institutions over which the Board has no jurisdiction. The Board offered no opinion on whether athletes were employees for purposes of the NLRA.

NOTES AND QUESTIONS

1. *A Northwestern Bargaining Unit?* If the NLRB had ruled that the Northwestern football players were employees for purposes of the NLRA, and the union had won the certification election, what would the practical effect have been on the Northwestern football program? About what could the players have bargained with the university? Presumably they could not bargain effectively about being compensated beyond NCAA rules. Could they have bargained to lighten practice schedules without putting their team at a competitive disadvantage against their Big Ten rivals? Would any ruling in favor of the union also have meant that other Northwestern teams could organize unions? That teams at other private universities could do so?

2. *Limited to Private Institutions.* Because the NLRA governs only private employers, the legal impact of the decision could have potentially applied only to private colleges and universities. The athletes at the public universities that make up a majority of all NCAA divisions would be governed by the public sector labor laws of their various states. How likely do you think it is that the agencies and courts in the various states would apply their public employee labor laws consistently in the same way as the NLRB applied the federal law? If some or all states took a different view and found student-athletes not to be employees of their universities, what would the system look like, and with what consequences, with athletes at private schools eligible to unionize under federal law but those in many state universities barred from doing so?

3. *Non-Revenue Sport Employees?* To what degree should the reasoning that led the Regional Director NLRB to find the Northwestern football players to be employees apply equally to athletes on the other Northwestern athletic teams who receive scholarships? Should student-athletes on the men's and women's basketball teams, which are so-called "head count" sports where every scholarship recipient receives a full grant-in-aid like football players, also be eligible to organize a union? What about the student-athletes on the so-called "equivalency" sport teams like tennis and golf that receive only partial, often very small, tuition waivers? What about the players on any of these teams who are "walk-ons" and receive no athletic scholarships but do receive some other types of benefits like special academic tutoring and individualized weight training, or who receive academic scholarships not tied directly to their athletic performance? Might your answer to all of these questions turn on whether the athletes on any particular team are providing a valuable service for the university, one of the criteria relied on by the NLRB regional director?

4. *Title IX Implications.* If some or all of the student-athletes at a particular university are deemed to be employees, how does that impact the application of Title IX requirements to that school? Title IX prohibits gender discrimination in "educational programs." Are athletes deemed to be employees then not considered to be in educational programs so that they would not be counted in any Title IX analyses? Would your answer depend on whether or not the "employee" athletes elected to form a union?

5. *Effect on Antitrust.* Perhaps most significantly, how would the NLRB's classification of student-athletes as employees for labor law purposes affect whether NCAA rules that limit how and how much student-athletes can be compensated are found to violate § 1 of the Sherman Act? Remember Judge Coffey's comment in *Banks* that in order to find the NCAA rule stripping eligibility from athletes who declare for a professional draft to be an antitrust violation the court would have to find that the players are employees. Would Judge Coffey have decided *Banks* differently had the NLRB earlier treated them as employees? For a proposal concerning how the NCAA could use labor law as a shield against antitrust claims, see William W. Berry III, *How Labor Law Could Save the NCAA*, Slate.com, March 31, 2014.

6. *Loss of Eligibility Concerns.* Finally, if the student-athletes at some private universities elect to be represented by a union, would any NCAA or conference restraints on how much they can be compensated or when they forfeit their eligibility be immune from antitrust challenge because of the labor exemption that applies to unionized professional athletes, as explained in Chapter 6? If any such restraints were otherwise found to be antitrust violations, how would any remedy be structured if the violation applied to student-athletes at public universities who were not recognized as employees but not to employee student-athletes at private universities where the labor exemption protected the rule?

BERGER V. NCAA
843 F.3d 285 (7th Cir. 2016)

KANNE, CIRCUIT JUDGE.

Former student athletes at the University of Pennsylvania ("Penn") sued Penn, the National Collegiate Athletic Association ("NCAA"), and more than 120 other NCAA Division I universities and colleges alleging that student athletes are employees who are entitled to a minimum wage under the Fair Labor Standards Act ("FLSA"). The district court disagreed. We agree with the district court and hold that student athletes are not employees and are not covered by the FLSA.

I. BACKGROUND

Gillian Berger and Taylor Hennig ("Appellants") are former students at Penn who participated on Penn's women's track and field team. Like many collegiate athletic teams across the country, Penn's women's track and field team is regulated by the NCAA. The NCAA is a member-driven, unincorporated association of 1121 colleges and universities. It is divided into three divisions—Divisions I, II, and III—based roughly on the size of the schools and their athletic programs. Penn's women's track and field team competes in Division I, which includes the largest colleges and universities in the country.

Appellants sued Penn, the NCAA, and more than 120 other NCAA Division I member schools ("Appellees"), alleging that student athletes are "employees" within the meaning of the FLSA, 29 U.S.C. § 201. Accordingly, Appellants contend that the NCAA and its member schools violated the FLSA by not paying their athletes a minimum wage. Appellees moved to dismiss under Federal Rules of Civil Procedure 12(b)(1) and 12(b)(6).

The district court granted Appellees' motions, holding that (1) Appellants lacked standing to sue any of the Appellees other than Penn, and (2) Appellants failed to state a claim against Penn because student athletes are not employees under the FLSA. This appeal followed.

II. ANALYSIS

[The court affirmed the district court's dismissal of claims against parties other than Penn for lack of standing.]

* * *

We now turn to the merits with regard to Penn, over which no one disputes that we have jurisdiction. The district court dismissed Appellants' suit against Penn for failure to state a claim. [The court summarized judicial interpetations of this standard, construing the complaint in the light most favorable to the non-moving party and accepting well-pleaded facts as true.]

* * *

The FLSA requires "[e]very employer" to pay "his employees" a minimum wage of $7.25 per hour. 29 U.S.C. § 206(a)(1)(c). Section 203(e)(1) defines "employee" in an unhelpful and circular fashion as "any individual employed by an employer." 29 U.S.C. § 203(e)(1). Section 203(g) broadly defines "employ" as "to suffer or permit to work." 29 U.S.C. § 203(g). Thus, to qualify as an employee for purposes of the FLSA, one must perform "work" for an "employer." "Work" is not defined by the Act.

Under the FLSA, the plaintiff bears the burden of establishing that he or she performed work for an employer and is therefore entitled to compensation. *Melton v. Tippecanoe Cty.*, 838 F.3d 814, 818 (7th Cir. 2016). Here, to survive the motions to dismiss, Appellants had to allege facts, which taken as true, establish that they were employees and performed work for Penn.

Although "[t]he Supreme Court has instructed the courts to construe the terms 'employee' and 'employer' expansively under the FLSA," *Vanskike v. Peters*, 974 F.2d 806, 807 (7th Cir. 1992) (citing *Nationwide Mut. Ins. Co. v. Darden*, 503 U.S. 318, 326 (1992)), the Court has also held that the definition of "employee" "does have its limits." *Tony & Susan Alamo Found. v. Sec'y of Labor*, 471 U.S. 290, 295 (1985). "Because status as an 'employee' for purposes of the FLSA depends on the totality of circumstances rather than on any technical label, courts must examine the 'economic reality' of the working relationship" between the alleged employee and the alleged employer to decide whether Congress intended the FLSA to apply to that particular relationship. *Vanskike*, 974 F.2d at 808.

To guide this inquiry, courts have developed a variety of multifactor tests. For example, we have applied a seven-factor test to determine whether migrant laborers are employees for purposes of the FLSA. *Sec'y of Labor v. Lauritzen*, 835 F.2d 1529, 1535–538 (7th Cir. 1987). Similarly, the Second Circuit created a "non-exhaustive set of [seven] considerations" to help determine when an intern is an employee under the FLSA. *Glatt v.*

Fox Searchlight Pictures, Inc., 811 F.3d 528, 536–37 (2d Cir. 2015). Appellants liken student athletes to interns and contend that we should use the Second Circuit's test set forth in *Glatt* to determine whether student athletes are employees under the FLSA. We disagree.

It is true, as Appellants note, that the district court cited the Second Circuit's test favorably. But the district court also declined to follow that test here. Instead, the court concluded correctly that our approach "to determining who is an employee under the FLSA is . . . a flexible one." (R. 238 at 15.) The court then discussed our decision in *Vanskike*, in which we rejected the strict application of a similar multifactor test in favor of a more flexible standard. 974 F.2d at 809.

We have declined to apply multifactor tests in the employment setting when they "fail to capture the true nature of the relationship" between the alleged employee and the alleged employer. *Id.* In *Vanskike*, we considered whether an inmate at a state prison was an employee under the FLSA. *Id.* at 806. Like Appellants here, the inmate in *Vanskike* urged us to apply a multifactor test to determine whether an employment relationship existed. We rejected the application of that test because it was "not the most helpful guide in the situation presented." *Id.* at 809. Rather than follow a specific test, we examined the economic reality of the alleged employment relationship and concluded that the prisoner was not an employee. *Id.* at 809–10.

The district court followed the reasoning of *Vanskike* and held that the "factors used in the trainee and private-sector intern context fail to capture the nature of the relationship between the Plaintiffs, as student athletes, and Penn." (R. 238 at 15). We agree with the district court and decline to apply the test set forth in *Glatt* here.

As the Supreme Court has noted, there exists "a revered tradition of amateurism in college sports." *Nat'l Collegiate Athletic Ass'n v. Bd. of Regents of Univ. of Okla.*, 468 U.S. 85, 120 (1984). That long-standing tradition defines the economic reality of the relationship between student athletes and their schools. To maintain this tradition of amateurism, the NCAA and its member universities and colleges have created an elaborate system of eligibility rules. *See O'Bannon v. Nat'l Collegiate Athletic Ass'n*, 802 F.3d 1049, 1054–55 (9th Cir. 2015)(outlining the development of these rules). We have held that these rules "define what it means to be an amateur or a student-athlete, and are therefore essential to the very existence of" collegiate athletics. *Agnew v. Nat'l Collegiate Athletic Ass'n*, 683 F.3d 328, 343 (7th Cir. 2012). The multifactor test proposed by Appellants here simply does not take into account this tradition of amateurism or the reality of the student-athlete experience. In short, it "fail[s] to capture the true nature of the relationship" between student athletes and their schools and is not a "helpful guide." *Vanskike*, 974 F.2d at 809.

* * *

[The court reviewed prior decisional law interpreting workers' compensation statutes, and concluded that student athletes are not employees in that context.]

The Department of Labor, through its Field Operations Handbook ("FOH"), has also indicated that student athletes are not employees under the FLSA. The FOH "is an operations manual that provides Wage and Hour Division . . . investigators and staff with interpretations of statutory provisions, procedures for conducting investigations, and general administrative guidance." . . . We agree with Appellants that the provisions in this handbook are not dispositive, but they certainly are persuasive. . . .

Chapter ten of the FOH "contains interpretations regarding the employment relationship required for the [FLSA] to apply." *Field Operations Handbook (FOH)*, § 10a00. Section 10b24 specifically addresses the employment status of university or college students. This section is broken into two subsections—subsection (a) and subsection (b).

Subsection (a) discusses situations when university or college students are not treated as employees under the FLSA. Under this subsection, "University or college students who participate in activities generally recognized as *extracurricular* are generally not considered to be employees within the meaning of the [FLSA]." § 10b24(a) (emphasis added). This subsection then cross-references another section, § 10b03(e), which states the following:

> As part of their overall educational program, public or private schools . . . may permit or require students to engage in activities in connection with dramatics, student publications, glee clubs, bands, choirs, debating teams, radio stations, intramural and *interscholastic athletics* and other similar endeavors. Activities of students in such programs, conducted primarily for the benefit of the participants as a part of the educational opportunities provided to the students by the school or institution, are not work of the kind contemplated by [the FLSA] and do not result in an employer-employee relationship between the student and the school. . . ." (emphasis added).

Subsection (b), "[o]n the other hand" discusses situations in which "an employment relationship will generally exist with regard to students. . . ." § 10b24(b). Under this subsection, students who participate in a work-study program and, for example, "work at food service counters or sell programs or usher at athletic events, or who wait on tables or wash dishes in dormitories in anticipation of some compensation" are "generally considered employees under the [FLSA]." *Id.*

Appellants compare NCAA-regulated athletes to the work-study participants of § 10b24(b) and argue that these athletes should be deemed employees under the FLSA. In so doing, Appellants contend that § 10b24(a)'s reference to "extracurricular" activities and § 10b03(e)'s reference to "interscholastic athletics" refer only to "student-run, interscholastic club sports," and not to NCAA-regulated sports. (Appellants' Br. at 18).

To support this argument, Appellants point to the many differences between club sports and NCAA-regulated sports—the most obvious of which being that club sports are largely student-run, whereas NCAA-regulated sports are heavily supervised by university-employed staff. We agree that NCAA-regulated sports are very different from club sports, but we disagree that this warrants different treatment under the clear language of the FOH.

Section 10b24(a) categorically states that students who participate in "extracurricular" activities are generally not considered employees. Section 10b03(e) includes "interscholastic athletics" in a list of activities that do not constitute "work." These references are not limited to activities that are entirely student run. In fact, most of the activities included in § 10b03(e)'s list are not student run. Appellants have not presented any persuasive argument to suggest that the Department of Labor intended to limit this language to student-run activities. We therefore reject Appellants' linguistic limitation.

Because NCAA-regulated sports are "extracurricular," "interscholastic athletic" activities, we do not believe that the Department of Labor intended the FLSA to apply to student athletes. We find the FOH's interpretation of the student-athlete experience to be persuasive.

Appellants in this case have not, and quite frankly cannot, allege that the activities they pursued as student athletes qualify as "work" sufficient to trigger the minimum wage requirements of the FLSA. Student participation in collegiate athletics is entirely voluntary. Moreover, the long tradition of amateurism in college sports, by definition, shows that student athletes—like all amateur athletes—participate in their sports for reasons wholly unrelated to immediate compensation. Although we do not doubt that student athletes spend a tremendous amount of time playing for their respective schools, they do so—and have done so for over a hundred years under the NCAA—without any real expectation of earning an income. Simply put, student-athletic "play" is not "work," at least as the term is used in the FLSA. We therefore hold, as a matter of law, that student athletes are not employees and are not entitled to a minimum wage under the FLSA. . . .

III. CONCLUSION

For the foregoing reasons, we AFFIRM the district court's grant of Appellees' motions to dismiss.

HAMILTON, CIRCUIT JUDGE, concurring.

I join Judge Kanne's opinion for the court but wish to add a note of caution. The plaintiffs in this case were students who participated in track and field at the University of Pennsylvania. Like other Ivy League schools, Penn does not offer athletic scholarships. Also, as far as I know, track and field is not a "revenue" sport at Penn or any other school. In this case, therefore, the economic reality and the sometimes frayed tradition of amateurism both point toward dismissal of these plaintiffs' claims. *See generally, e.g., O'Bannon v. National Collegiate Athletic Ass'n*, 802 F.3d 1049, 1054–55 (9th Cir. 2015) (holding that NCAA compensation rules for Division I men's basketball players and Football Bowl Subdivision football players violated federal antitrust laws).

Because the plaintiffs in this case did not receive athletic scholarships and participated in a non-revenue sport, they pursued a broad theory. The logic of their claim would have included not only any college athlete in any sport and any NCAA division, but also college musicians, actors, journalists, and debaters. That broad theory is mistaken, as Judge Kanne's opinion explains. I am less confident, however, that our reasoning should extend to students who receive athletic scholarships to participate in so-called revenue sports like Division I men's basketball and FBS football. In those sports, economic reality and the tradition of amateurism may not point in the same direction. Those sports involve billions of dollars of revenue for colleges and universities. Athletic scholarships are limited to the cost of attending school. With economic reality as our guide, as I believe it should be, there may be room for further debate, perhaps with a developed factual record rather than bare pleadings, for cases addressing employment status for a variety of purposes.

NOTES AND QUESTIONS

1. *Employee-Athletes?* Do you agree with the Seventh Circuit's conclusion that college athletes are not employees? Does the NLRB regional director's analysis of the Northwestern football program provide a more persuasive counter view?

2. *Revenue Versus Non-Revenue.* To what extent is the employee-athlete argument limited to revenue sport athletes? The concurrence in *Berger* suggests that the outcome might be different in the case of revenue sport athletes. Do you agree? How could revenue-producing athletes be

distinguished for purposes of the FLSA, which does not contain any applicable exemption?

3. *Effect of Applying the FLSA to College Athletes?* What would be the likely effect on college athletic programs if they were forced to compensate all participants? Would it be likely that teams would be eliminated by many universities and colleges, most of which must subsidize their athletic department?

2. ANTITRUST CHALLENGES

In 2008, Ed O'Bannon saw his likeness in an EA Sports video game, with the avatar mimicking his basketball moves and mannerisms. O'Bannon sued EA Sports and the NCAA, who had sold his likeness to EA Sports. The suit grew, with the case becoming a class action. EA Sports settled, leaving the case as an antitrust challenge against the NCAA and its rules proscribing payments for use of the plaintiff athletes' names, images, or likenesses.

The district court held that the NCAA's amateurism rule violated antitrust law, but concluded that $5,000 per year, held until students finished school, would remedy the antitrust issue. The Ninth Circuit weighed in next.

O'BANNON v. NCAA
802 F.3d 1049 (9th Cir. 2015)

BYBEE, CIRCUIT JUDGE.

Section 1 of the Sherman Antitrust Act of 1890, 15 U.S.C. § 1, prohibits "[e]very contract, combination . . ., or conspiracy, in restraint of trade or commerce." For more than a century, the National Collegiate Athletic Association (NCAA) has prescribed rules governing the eligibility of athletes at its more than 1,000 member colleges and universities. Those rules prohibit student-athletes from being paid for the use of their names, images, and likenesses (NILs). The question presented in this momentous case is whether the NCAA's rules are subject to the antitrust laws and, if so, whether they are an unlawful restraint of trade.

After a bench trial and in a thorough opinion, the district court concluded that the NCAA's compensation rules were an unlawful restraint of trade. It then enjoined the NCAA from prohibiting its member schools from giving student-athletes scholarships up to the full cost of attendance at their respective schools and up to $5,000 per year in deferred compensation, to be held in trust for student-athletes until after they leave college. As far as we are aware, the district court's decision is the first by any federal court to hold that any aspect of the NCAA's amateurism rules violate the antitrust laws, let alone to mandate by injunction that the NCAA change its practices.

We conclude that the district court's decision was largely correct. Although we agree with the Supreme Court and our sister circuits that many of the NCAA's amateurism rules are likely to be procompetitive, we hold that those rules are not exempt from antitrust scrutiny; rather, they must be analyzed under the Rule of Reason. Applying the Rule of Reason, we conclude that the district court correctly identified one proper alternative to the current NCAA compensation rules—*i.e.*, allowing NCAA members to give scholarships up to the full cost of attendance—but that the district court's other remedy, allowing students to be paid cash compensation of up to $5,000 per year, was erroneous. We therefore affirm in part and reverse in part.

* * *

In August 2014, the NCAA announced it would allow athletic conferences to authorize their member schools to increase scholarships up to the full cost of attendance. The 80 member schools of the five largest athletic conferences in the country voted in January 2015 to take that step, and the scholarship cap at those schools is now at the full cost of attendance. Marc Tracy, *Top Conferences to Allow Aid for Athletes' Full Bills,* N.Y. Times, Jan. 18, 2015, at SP8.

In addition to its financial aid rules, the NCAA has adopted numerous other amateurism rules that limit student-athletes' compensation and their interactions with professional sports leagues. An athlete can lose his amateur status, for example, if he signs a contract with a professional team, enters a professional league's player draft, or hires an agent. And, most importantly, an athlete is prohibited—with few exceptions—from receiving *any* "pay" based on his athletic ability, whether from boosters, companies seeking endorsements, or would-be licensors of the athlete's name, image, and likeness (NIL).

C.   The O'Bannon *and* Keller *Litigation*

[The court reviewed the facts underlying the publicity rights claims brought by Ed O'Bannon and Sam Keller, which were consolidated in the Northern District of California and which were discussed in Chapter 8. Judge Bybee, author of this decision, also authored the 2013 Ninth Circuit decision allowing those claims to proceed. After remand, the district court granted certification of a class of current and former student-athletes to pursue injunctive and declaratory relief for unauthorized use of their names, images, and likenesses in videogames.]

* * *After class certification was granted, the plaintiffs voluntarily dismissed their damages claims with prejudice. The plaintiffs also settled their claims against EA and CLC, and the district court preliminarily approved the settlement. *O'Bannon* and *Keller* were deconsolidated, and in June 2014, the antitrust claims against the NCAA at issue in *O'Bannon* went to a bench trial before the district court.

* * *

The court held that the plaintiffs had identified two legitimate, less restrictive alternatives to the current NCAA rules: (1) allowing schools to award stipends to student-athletes up to the full cost of attendance, thereby making up for any "shortfall" in their grants-in-aid, and (2) permitting schools to hold a portion of their licensing revenues in trust, to be distributed to student-athletes in equal shares after they leave college. *Id.* at 1005–06. The court determined that neither of these alternatives to the total ban on NIL compensation would undermine the NCAA's procompetitive purposes. The court also held that it would be permissible for the NCAA to prohibit schools from funding these stipends or trusts with anything other than revenue derived from the use of players' NILs. *Id.* at 1005.

After entering judgment for the plaintiffs on their antitrust claims, the district court permanently enjoined the NCAA from prohibiting its member schools from (1) compensating FBS football and Division I men's basketball players for the use of their NILs by awarding them grants-in-aid up to the full cost of attendance at their respective schools, or (2) paying up to $5,000 per year in deferred compensation to FBS football and Division I men's basketball players for the use of their NILs, through trust funds distributable after they leave school. The NCAA timely appealed, and we have jurisdiction under 28 U.S.C. § 1291.

* * *

III

On appeal, the NCAA contends that the plaintiffs' Sherman Act claim fails on the merits, but it also argues that we are precluded altogether from reaching the merits, for three independent reasons: (1) The Supreme Court held in *NCAA v. Board of Regents of the University of Oklahoma,* 468 U.S. 85 (1984), that the NCAA's amateurism rules are "valid as a matter of law"; (2) the compensation rules at issue here are not covered by the Sherman Act at all because they do not regulate commercial activity; and (3) the plaintiffs have no standing to sue under the Sherman Act because they have not suffered "antitrust injury." We find none of these three arguments persuasive.

A. Board of Regents *Did Not Declare the NCAA's Amateurism Rules "Valid as a Matter of Law"*

* * *

Applying the Rule of Reason, the Court struck down the television rules on the ground that they did not serve any legitimate procompetitive purpose. *Id.* at 113–20. It then concluded its opinion by stating:

> The NCAA plays a critical role in the maintenance of a revered tradition of amateurism in college sports. There can be no question but that it needs ample latitude to play that role, *or that the preservation of the student-athlete in higher education adds richness and diversity to intercollegiate athletics and is entirely consistent with the goals of the Sherman Act.* But consistent with the Sherman Act, the role of the NCAA must be to preserve a tradition that might otherwise die; rules that restrict output are hardly consistent with this role. Today we hold only that the record supports the District Court's conclusion that by curtailing output and blunting the ability of member institutions to respond to consumer preference, the NCAA has restricted rather than enhanced the place of intercollegiate athletics in the Nation's life.

Id. at 120 (emphasis added).

Quoting heavily from the language in *Board of Regents* that we have emphasized, the NCAA contends that any Section 1 challenge to its amateurism rules must fail as a matter of law because the *Board of Regents* Court held that those rules are presumptively valid. We disagree.

The *Board of Regents* Court certainly discussed the NCAA's amateurism rules at great length, but it did not do so in order to pass upon the rules' merits, given that they were not before the Court. Rather, the Court discussed the amateurism rules for a different and particular purpose: to explain why NCAA rules should be analyzed under the Rule of Reason, rather than held to be illegal per se. The point was a significant one. Naked horizontal agreements among competitors to fix the price of a good or service, or to restrict their output, are usually condemned as per se unlawful.

* * *

Board of Regents, in other words, did not approve the NCAA's amateurism rules as categorically consistent with the Sherman Act. Rather, it held that, because many NCAA rules (among them, the amateurism rules) are part of the "character and quality of the [NCAA's] 'product,'" *Id.* at 102, no NCAA rule should be invalidated without a Rule of Reason analysis. The Court's long encomium to amateurism, though impressive-sounding, was therefore dicta.

* * *

What is more, even if the language in *Board of Regents* addressing amateurism were *not* dicta, it would not support the tremendous weight that the NCAA seeks to place upon it. The Court's opinion supports the proposition that the preservation of amateurism is a legitimate procompetitive purpose for the NCAA to pursue, but the NCAA is not asking us to find merely that its amateurism rules are procompetitive; rather, it asks us to hold that those rules are essentially exempt from antitrust scrutiny. Nothing in *Board of Regents* supports such an exemption. To say that the NCAA's amateurism rules are procompetitive, as *Board of Regents* did, is not to say that they are automatically lawful; a restraint that serves a procompetitive purpose can still be invalid under the Rule of Reason if a substantially less restrictive rule would further the same objectives equally well. *See Bd. of Regents,* 468 U.S. at 101 n. 23 ("While as the guardian of an important American tradition, the NCAA's motives must be accorded a respectful presumption of validity, it is nevertheless well settled that good motives will not validate an otherwise anticompetitive practice.").

* * *

In sum, we accept *Board of Regents'* guidance as informative with respect to the procompetitive purposes served by the NCAA's amateurism rules, but we will go no further than that. The amateurism rules' validity must be proved, not presumed.

B. *The Compensation Rules Regulate "Commercial Activity"*

The NCAA next argues that we cannot reach the merits of the plaintiffs' Sherman Act claim because the compensation rules are not subject to the Sherman Act at all. The NCAA points out that Section 1 of the Sherman Act applies only to "restraint[s] of trade or commerce," 15 U.S.C. § 1, and claims that its compensation rules are mere "eligibility rules" that do not regulate any "commercial activity."

This argument is not credible. Although restraints that have no effect on commerce are indeed exempt from Section 1, the modern legal understanding of "commerce" is broad, "including almost every activity from which the actor anticipates economic gain." Phillip Areeda & Herbert Hovenkamp, *Antitrust Law: An Analysis of Antitrust Principles and Their Application,* ¶ 260b (4th ed.2013). That definition surely encompasses the transaction in which an athletic recruit exchanges his labor and NIL rights for a scholarship at a Division I school because it is undeniable that both parties to that exchange anticipate economic gain from it. * * *

It is no answer to these observations to say, as the NCAA does in its briefs, that the compensation rules are "eligibility rules" rather than direct restraints on the terms of agreements between schools and recruits. True enough, the compensation rules are written in the form of eligibility rules; they provide that an athlete who receives compensation other than the scholarships specifically permitted by the NCAA loses his eligibility for collegiate sports. The mere fact that a rule can be characterized as an "eligibility rule," however, does not mean the rule is not a restraint of trade; were the law otherwise, the NCAA could insulate its member schools' relationships with student-athletes from antitrust scrutiny by renaming every rule governing student-athletes an "eligibility rule." The antitrust laws are not to be avoided by such "clever manipulation of words." *Simpson v. Union Oil Co. of Cal.,* 377 U.S. 13, 21–22 (1964).

In other words, the substance of the compensation rules matters far more than how they are styled. And in substance, the rules clearly regulate the terms of commercial transactions between athletic recruits and their chosen schools: a school may not give a recruit compensation beyond a grant-in-aid, and the recruit may not accept compensation beyond that limit, lest the recruit be disqualified and the transaction vitiated. The NCAA's argument that its compensation rules are "eligibility" restrictions, rather than substantive restrictions on the price terms of recruiting agreements, is but a sleight of hand. There is real money at issue here.

* * *

By contrast, the rules here—which regulate what compensation NCAA schools may give student-athletes, and how much—*do* relate to the NCAA's business activities: the labor of student-athletes is an integral and essential component of the NCAA's "product," and a rule setting the price of that labor goes to the heart of the NCAA's business. Thus, the rules at issue here are more like rules affecting the NCAA's dealings with its coaches or with corporate business partners—which courts have held to be commercial—than they are like the Bylaw challenged in *Smith. See Bd. of Regents,* 468 U.S. at 104–13 (applying Sherman Act to rules governing NCAA members' contracts with television networks); *Law v. NCAA,* 134 F.3d 1010, 1024 (10th Cir. 1998) (applying Sherman Act to NCAA rules limiting compensation of basketball coaches).

* * *

Because the plaintiffs have shown that, absent the NCAA's compensation rules, video game makers would likely pay them for the right to use their NILs in college sports video games, the plaintiffs have satisfied the requirement of injury in fact and, by extension, the requirement of antitrust injury.

IV

Having rejected all of the NCAA's preliminary legal arguments, we proceed to review the plaintiffs' Section 1 claim on the merits. * * *

Like the district court, we follow the three-step framework of the Rule of Reason: "[1] The plaintiff bears the initial burden of showing that the restraint produces significant anticompetitive effects within a relevant market. [2] If the plaintiff meets this burden, the defendant must come forward with evidence of the restraint's procompetitive effects. [3] The plaintiff must then show that any legitimate objectives can be achieved in a substantially less restrictive manner." *Tanaka v. Univ. of S. Cal.*, 252 F.3d 1059, 1063 (9th Cir. 2001) (citations and internal quotation marks omitted).

A. *Significant Anticompetitive Effects Within a Relevant Market*

As we have recounted, the district court made the following factual findings: (1) that a cognizable "college education market" exists, wherein colleges compete for the services of athletic recruits by offering them scholarships and various amenities, such as coaching and facilities; (2) that if the NCAA's compensation rules did not exist, member schools would compete to offer recruits compensation for their NILs; and (3) that the compensation rules therefore have a significant anticompetitive effect on the college education market, in that they fix an aspect of the "price" that recruits pay to attend college (or, alternatively, an aspect of the price that schools pay to secure recruits' services). These findings have substantial support in the record.

* * *

... the NCAA makes three modest arguments about why the compensation rules do not have a significant anticompetitive effect. First, it argues that because the plaintiffs never showed that the rules reduce output in the college education market, the plaintiffs did not meet their burden of showing a significant anticompetitive effect. Second, it argues that the rules have no anticompetitive effect because schools would not pay student-athletes anything for their NIL rights in any event, given that those rights are worth nothing. And finally, the NCAA argues that even if the district court was right that schools would pay student-athletes for their NIL rights, any such payments would be small, which means that the compensation rules' anticompetitive effects cannot be considered significant.

We can dispose of the first two arguments quickly. First, the NCAA's contention that the plaintiffs' claim fails because they did not show a decrease in output in the college education market is simply incorrect. * * * But this argument misses the mark. Although output reductions are one common kind of anticompetitive effect in antitrust cases, a "reduction in output is not the *only* measure of anticompetitive effect." Areeda & Hovenkamp ¶ 1503b(1) (emphasis added).

* * *

Second, the NCAA's argument that student-athletes' NILs are, in fact, worth nothing is simply a repackaged version of its arguments about injury in fact, which we have rejected.

Finally, we reject the NCAA's contention that any NIL compensation that student-athletes might receive in the absence of its compensation rules would be de minimis and that the rules therefore do not significantly affect competition in the college education market. This "too small to matter" argument is incompatible with the Supreme Court's holding in *Catalano, Inc. v. Target Sales, Inc.*, 446 U.S. 643 (1980) (per curiam). * * * The Court was not concerned with whether the agreement affected the market adversely: "It is no excuse that the prices fixed are themselves reasonable." *Id.* at 647.

* * *

Because we agree with the district court that the compensation rules have a significant anticompetitive effect on the college education market, we proceed to consider the procompetitive justifications the NCAA proffers for those rules.

B. *Procompetitive Effects*

As discussed above, the NCAA offered the district court four procompetitive justifications for the compensation rules: (1) promoting amateurism, (2) promoting competitive balance among NCAA schools, (3) integrating student-athletes with their schools' academic community, and (4) increasing output in the college education market. The district court accepted the first and third and rejected the other two.

* * *

... the NCAA focuses its arguments to this court entirely on the first proffered justification—the promotion of amateurism....

The district court acknowledged that the NCAA's current rules promote amateurism, which in turn plays a role in increasing consumer demand for college sports. *O'Bannon,* 7 F. Supp. 3d at 978. The NCAA ... argues to us that the district court gave the amateurism justification short shrift, in two respects. First, it claims that the district court erred by focusing solely on the question of whether amateurism increases consumers' (*i.e.,* fans') demand for college sports and ignoring the fact that amateurism also increases choice for student-athletes by giving them "the only opportunity [they will] have to obtain a college education while playing competitive sports *as students.*" Second, it faults the district court for being inappropriately skeptical of the NCAA's historical commitment to amateurism....

The NCAA is correct that a restraint that broadens choices can be procompetitive. The Court in *Board of Regents* observed that the difference between college and professional sports "widen[s]" the choices "available to athletes." *Bd. of Regents,* 468 U.S. at 102. But we fail to see how the restraint at issue in this particular case—*i.e.,* the NCAA's limits on student-athlete compensation—makes college sports more attractive to recruits, or widens recruits' spectrum of choices in the sense that *Board of Regents* suggested.

* * *

The NCAA's second point has more force—the district court probably underestimated the NCAA's commitment to amateurism. *See Bd. of Regents,* 468 U.S. at 120 (referring to the NCAA's "revered tradition of amateurism in college sports"). But the point is ultimately irrelevant.

* * *

We thus turn to the final inquiry—whether there are reasonable alternatives to the NCAA's current compensation restrictions.

C. *Substantially Less Restrictive Alternatives*

The third step in the Rule of Reason analysis is whether there are substantially less restrictive alternatives to the NCAA's current rules. We bear in mind that—to be viable under the Rule of Reason—an alternative must be "virtually as effective" in serving the procompetitive purposes of the NCAA's current rules, and "without significantly increased cost." *Cnty. of Tuolumne v. Sonora Cmty. Hosp.,* 236 F.3d 1148, 1159 (9th Cir. 2001) (internal quotation marks omitted). We think that plaintiffs must make a strong evidentiary showing that its alternatives are viable here. Not only do plaintiffs bear the burden at this step, but the Supreme Court has admonished that we must generally afford the NCAA "ample latitude" to superintend college athletics. . . .

The district court identified two substantially less restrictive alternatives: (1) allowing NCAA member schools to give student-athletes grants-in-aid that cover the full cost of attendance; and (2) allowing member schools to pay student-athletes small amounts of deferred cash compensation for use of their NILs. *O'Bannon,* 7 F. Supp. 3d at 1005–07. We hold that the district court did not clearly err in finding that raising the grant-in-aid cap would be a substantially less restrictive alternative, but that it clearly erred when it found that allowing students to be paid compensation for their NILs is virtually as effective as the NCAA's current amateur-status rule.

1. Capping the permissible amount of scholarships at the cost of attendance

The district court did not clearly err in finding that allowing NCAA member schools to award grants-in-aid up to their full cost of attendance would be a substantially less restrictive alternative to the current compensation rules. All of the evidence before the district court indicated that raising the grant-in-aid cap to the cost of attendance would have virtually no impact on amateurism: Dr. Mark Emmert, the president of the NCAA, testified at trial that giving student-athletes scholarships up to their full costs of attendance would not violate the NCAA's principles of amateurism because all the money given to students would be going to cover their "legitimate costs" to attend school. Other NCAA witnesses agreed with that assessment. *Id.* at 983. Nothing in the record, moreover, suggested that consumers of college sports would become less interested in those sports if athletes' scholarships covered their full cost of attendance, or that an increase in the grant-in-aid cap would impede the integration of student-athletes into their academic communities. *Id.*

The NCAA, along with fifteen scholars of antitrust law appearing as *amici curiae,* warns us that if we affirm even this more modest of the two less restrictive alternative restraints identified by the district court, we will open the floodgates to new lawsuits demanding all manner of incremental changes in the NCAA's and other organizations' rules. The NCAA and these *amici* admonish us that as long as a restraint (such as a price cap) is "reasonably necessary to a valid business purpose," it should be upheld; it is not an antitrust court's function to tweak every market restraint that the court believes could be improved.

We agree with the NCAA and the *amici* that, as a general matter, courts should not use antitrust law to make marginal adjustments to broadly reasonable market restraints. *See, e.g., Bruce Drug, Inc. v. Hollister, Inc.,* 688 F.2d 853, 860 (1st Cir. 1982) (noting that defendants are "not required to adopt the least restrictive" alternative); *Am. Motor Inns, Inc. v. Holiday Inns, Inc.,* 521 F.2d 1230, 1249 (3d Cir. 1975) (denying that "the availability of an alternative means of achieving the asserted business purpose renders the existing arrangement unlawful if that alternative would be less restrictive of competition no matter to how small a degree"). The particular restraint at issue here, however—the grant-in-aid cap that the NCAA set below the cost of attendance—is not such a restraint. To the contrary, the evidence at trial showed that the grant-in-aid cap has no relation whatsoever to the procompetitive purposes of the NCAA: by the NCAA's own standards, student-athletes remain amateurs as long as any money paid to them goes to cover legitimate educational expenses.

Thus, in holding that setting the grant-in-aid cap at student-athletes' full cost of attendance is a substantially less restrictive alternative under the Rule of Reason, we are not declaring that courts are free to micromanage organizational rules or to strike down largely beneficial market restraints with impunity. Rather, our affirmance of this aspect of the district court's decision should be taken to establish only that where, as here, a restraint is *patently and inexplicably* stricter than is necessary to accomplish all of its procompetitive objectives, an antitrust court can and should invalidate it and order it replaced with a less restrictive alternative.

A compensation cap set at student-athletes' full cost of attendance is a substantially less restrictive alternative means of accomplishing the NCAA's legitimate procompetitive purposes. And there is no evidence that this cap will significantly increase costs; indeed, the NCAA already permits schools to fund student-athletes' full cost of attendance. The district court's determination that the existing compensation rules violate Section 1 of the Sherman Act was correct and its injunction requiring the NCAA to permit schools to provide compensation up to the full cost of attendance was proper.

2. Allowing students to receive cash compensation for their NILs

In our judgment, however, the district court clearly erred in finding it a viable alternative to allow students to receive NIL cash payments untethered to their education expenses. Again, the district court identified two procompetitive purposes served by the NCAA's current rules: "preserving the popularity of the NCAA's product by promoting its current understanding of amateurism" and "integrating academics and athletics." *O'Bannon,* 7 F. Supp. 3d at 1005; *see also Board of Regents,* 468 U.S. at 117 ("It is reasonable to assume that most of the regulatory controls of the NCAA are justifiable means of fostering competition among amateur athletic teams and therefore procompetitive because they enhance public interest in intercollegiate athletics."). The question is whether the alternative of allowing students to be paid NIL compensation unrelated to their education expenses, is "virtually as effective" in preserving amateurism as *not* allowing compensation. *Cnty. of Tuolumne,* 236 F.3d at 1159 (internal quotation marks omitted).

We cannot agree that a rule permitting schools to pay students pure cash compensation and a rule forbidding them from paying NIL compensation are both *equally* effective in promoting amateurism and preserving consumer demand. Both we and the district court agree that the NCAA's amateurism rule has procompetitive benefits. But in finding that paying students cash compensation would promote amateurism as effectively as not paying them, the district court ignored that not paying student-athletes is *precisely what makes them amateurs.*

Having found that amateurism is integral to the NCAA's market, the district court cannot plausibly conclude that being a poorly-paid professional collegiate athlete is "virtually as effective" for that market as being as amateur. Or, to borrow the Supreme Court's analogy, the market for college football is distinct from other sports markets and must be "differentiate[d]" from professional sports lest it become "minor league [football]." *Bd. of Regents,* 468 U.S. at 102.

Aside from the self-evident fact that paying students for their NIL rights will vitiate their amateur status as collegiate athletes, the court relied on threadbare evidence in finding that small payments of cash compensation will preserve amateurism as well the NCAA's rule forbidding such payments. Most of the evidence elicited merely indicates that paying students large compensation payments would harm consumer demand more than smaller payments would—not that small cash payments will preserve amateurism. Thus, the evidence was addressed to the wrong question. Instead of asking whether making small payments to student-athletes served the same procompetitive purposes as making no payments, the evidence before the district court went to a different question: Would the collegiate sports market be better off if the NCAA made small payments or big payments? For example, the district court noted that a witness called by the NCAA, Bernard Muir, the athletic director at Stanford University, testified that paying student-athletes modest sums raises less concern than paying them large sums. The district court also relied on Dr. Dennis's opinion survey, which the court read to indicate that in the absence of the NCAA's compensation rules, "the popularity of college sports would likely depend on the size of payments awarded to student-athletes." *O'Bannon,* 7 F. Supp. 3d at 983. Dr. Dennis had found that payments of $200,000 per year to each athlete would alienate the public more than would payments of $20,000 per year. *Id.* at 975–76, 983. At best, these pieces of evidence indicate that small payments to players will impact consumer demand less than larger payments. But there is a stark difference between finding that small payments are less harmful to the market than large payments—and finding that paying students small sums is virtually as effective in promoting amateurism as not paying them.

The other evidence cited by the district court is even less probative of whether paying these student-athletes will preserve amateurism and consumer demand. The district court adverted to testimony from a sports management expert, Daniel Rascher, who explained that although opinion surveys had shown the public was opposed to rising baseball salaries during the 1970s, and to the decision of the International Olympic Committee to allow professional athletes to compete in the Olympics, the public had continued to watch baseball and the Olympics at the same rate after those changes. *Id.* at 976–77. But professional baseball and the Olympics are not fit analogues to college sports. The Olympics have not been nearly as transformed by the introduction of professionalism as college sports would be.

Finally, the district court, and the dissent, place particular weight on a brief interchange during plaintiffs' cross-examination of one of the NCAA's witnesses, Neal Pilson, a television sports consultant formerly employed at CBS. Pilson testified that "if you're paid for your performance, you're not an amateur," and explained at length why paying students would harm the student-athlete market. Plaintiffs then asked Pilson whether his opinions about amateurism "depend on the level of the money" paid to players, and he acknowledged that his opinion was "impacted by the level." When asked whether there was a line that "should not be crossed" in paying players, Pilson responded "that's a difficult question. I haven't thought about the line. And I haven't been asked to render an opinion on that." When pressed to come up with a figure, Pilson repeated that he was "not sure." He eventually commented that "I tell you that a million dollars would trouble me and $5,000 wouldn't, but that's a pretty good range." When asked whether deferred compensation to students would concern him, Pilson said that while he would not be as concerned by deferred payments, he would still be "troubled by it."

So far as we can determine, Pilson's offhand comment under cross-examination is the sole support for the district court's $5,000 figure. But even taking Pilson's comments at face value, as the dissent urges, his testimony cannot support the finding that paying student-athletes small sums will be virtually as effective in preserving amateurism as not paying them. Pilson made clear that he was not prepared to opine on whether pure cash compensation, of any amount, would affect amateurism. Indeed, he was never asked about the impact of giving student-athletes small cash payments; instead, like other witnesses, he was asked only whether big payments would be worse than small payments. Pilson's casual comment—"[I] haven't been asked to render an opinion on that. It's not in my report"—that he would not be troubled by $5,000 payments is simply not enough to support the district court's far-reaching conclusion that paying students $5,000 per year will be as effective in preserving amateurism as the NCAA's current policy.

The difference between offering student-athletes education-related compensation and offering them cash sums untethered to educational expenses is not minor; it is a quantum leap. Once that line is crossed, we see no basis for returning to a rule of amateurism and no defined stopping point; we have little doubt that plaintiffs will continue to challenge the arbitrary limit imposed by the district court until they have captured the full value of their NIL. At that point the NCAA will have surrendered its amateurism principles entirely and transitioned from its "particular brand of football" to minor league status. *Bd. of Regents,* 468 U.S. at 101–02. In light of that, the meager evidence in the record, and the Supreme Court's admonition that we must afford the NCAA "ample latitude" to superintend college athletics, *Bd. of Regents,* 468 U.S. at 120, we think it is clear the district court erred in concluding that small payments in deferred compensation are a substantially less restrictive alternative restraint. We thus vacate that portion of the district court's decision and the portion of its injunction requiring the NCAA to allow its member schools to pay this deferred compensation.

V

By way of summation, we wish to emphasize the limited scope of the decision we have reached and the remedy we have approved. Today, we reaffirm that NCAA regulations are subject to antitrust scrutiny and must be tested in the crucible of the Rule of Reason. When those regulations truly serve procompetitive purposes, courts should not hesitate to uphold them. But the NCAA is not above the antitrust laws, and courts cannot and must not shy away from requiring the NCAA to play by the Sherman Act's rules. In this case, the NCAA's rules have been more restrictive than necessary to maintain its tradition of amateurism in support of the college sports market. The Rule of Reason requires that the NCAA permit its schools to provide up to the cost of attendance to their student athletes. It does not require more.

We vacate the district court's judgment and permanent injunction insofar as they require the NCAA to allow its member schools to pay student-athletes up to $5,000 per year in deferred compensation. We otherwise affirm. The parties shall bear their own costs on appeal.

AFFIRMED IN PART and VACATED IN PART.

THOMAS, CHIEF JUDGE, concurring in part and dissenting in part:

I largely agree with all but one of the majority's conclusions. I respectfully disagree with the majority's conclusion that the district court clearly erred in ordering the NCAA to permit up to $5,000 in deferred compensation above student-athletes' full cost of attendance.

* * *

There was sufficient evidence in the record to support the award. The district court's conclusion that the proposed alternative restraint satisfied the Rule of Reason was based on testimony from at least four experts-including three experts presented by the NCAA-that providing student-athletes with small amounts of compensation above their cost of attendance most likely would not have a significant impact on consumer interest in college sports. *O'Bannon,* 7 F. Supp. 3d at 976–77, 983–84, 1000–01. It was also based on the fact that FBS football players are currently permitted to accept Pell grants in excess of their cost of attendance, and the fact that Division I tennis recruits are permitted to earn up to $10,000 per year in prize money from athletic events before they enroll in college. *Id.* at 974, 1000. The majority characterizes the weight of this evidence as "threadbare." Op. at 1077. I respectfully disagree.

* * *

II

The disagreement between my view and the majority view largely boils down to a difference in opinion as to the procompetitive interests at stake. The majority characterizes our task at step three of the Rule of Reason as determining "whether the alternative of allowing students to be paid NIL compensation unrelated to their education expenses is 'virtually as effective' in preserving *amateurism* as not allowing compensation." Op. at 1076 (emphasis added). This conclusion misstates our inquiry. Rather, we must determine whether allowing student-athletes to be compensated for their NILs is 'virtually as effective' in preserving *popular demand for college sports* as not allowing compensation. In terms of antitrust analysis, the concept of amateurism is relevant only insofar as it relates to consumer interest.

* * *

Plaintiffs are not required, as the majority suggests, to show that the proposed alternatives are "virtually as effective" at preserving the concept of amateurism as the NCAA chooses to define it. Indeed, this would be a difficult task, given that "amateurism" has proven a nebulous concept prone to ever-changing definition. *See O'Bannon,* 7 F. Supp. 3d at 973–75 (describing the ways that the NCAA's definition of amateurism has changed over time). Even today, the NCAA's conception of amateurism does not fall easily into a bright line rule between paying student-athletes and not paying them. Tennis players are permitted to receive payment of up to $10,000 per year for playing their sport. A tennis player who begins competing at a young age could presumably earn upwards of $50,000 for playing his sport and still be considered an amateur athlete by the NCAA.

The NCAA insists that consumers will flee if student-athletes are paid even a small sum of money for colleges' use of their NILs. This assertion is contradicted by the district court record and by the NCAA's own rules regarding amateurism. The district court was well within its right to reject it. Division I schools have spent $5 billion on athletic facilities over the past 15 years. The NCAA sold the television rights to broadcast the NCAA men's basketball championship tournament for 12 years to CBS for $10.8 billion dollars. The NCAA insists that this multi-billion dollar industry would be lost if the teenagers and young adults who play for these college teams earn one dollar above their cost of school attendance. That is a difficult argument to swallow. Given the trial evidence, the district court was well within its rights to reject it.

III

The national debate about amateurism in college sports is important. But our task as appellate judges is not to resolve it. Nor could we. Our task is simply to review the district court judgment through the appropriate lens of antitrust law and under the appropriate standard of review. In the end, my disagreement with the majority is founded on the appropriate standard of review. After an extensive bench trial, the district court made a factual finding that payment of $5,000 in deferred compensation would not significantly reduce consumer demand for college sports. This finding was supported by extensive testimony from at least four expert witnesses. There was no evidence to the contrary. Therefore, on this record, I cannot agree with the majority that the district court clearly erred when it determined that paying student-athletes up to $5,000 per year would be "virtually as effective" at preserving the pro-competitive benefits of the current rule. Therefore, I would affirm the district court in all respects.

For these reasons, I concur in part and dissent in part.

NOTES AND QUESTIONS

1. *Aftermath.* The practical effect of *O'Bannon* is that institutions now may provide the cost of attendance to student-athletes, an amount between $1,500 and $6,000 per year, depending on locale. In 2017, the NCAA settled another class action lawsuit, *Alston v. NCAA* (including the *White v. NCAA* plaintiffs) for $208 million. This compensation provided for cost of attendance (in the amount of $5,000 to $7,500) for all men's and women's basketball players, and FBS football players from the 2008–09 season until the 2016–17 season.

2. *Effect of O'Bannon.* The *O'Bannon* case is particularly significant because it holds that the NCAA's amateurism rules violated antitrust law, but that providing cost of attendance to athletes is sufficient to remedy that violation. It is clear that the NCAA rules are anti-competitive, but the case turns on the extent of the pro-competitive justification. Do you agree with the court's conclusion that paying athletes could affect the product of intercollegiate athletics? Do you think many people would stop attending or watching games if universities paid athletes? Could payment lead to many universities not being able to compete financially? Might this all depend on how much the athletes were paid and under what system?

3. *District Court Opinion.* The Ninth Circuit opinion does not address a couple of important holdings of the district court. First, the district court held that the NCAA restrictions on athletes' own use of name, image, & likeness do not violate the Sherman Act. The Ninth Circuit opinion only addresses the potential share of licensure revenue. Second, the district court opinion makes clear that it is not a valid antitrust defense to restrain trade in order to

reallocate revenue from one sport in order to pay for another. The Court of Appeals did not contest the district court's rejection of this justification.

4. *Slippery Slope.* Judge Bybee's opinion characterizes the district court's decision to allow $5,000 per year as a payment as opening a Pandora's box and sliding down a slippery slope to professionalism in college sports. Do you agree with Bybee's characterization?

5. *Relation to Education.* Judge Bybee found that the NCAA's amateurism principle did not justify denying athletes the full cost of attendance. The reason for this is that such expenses are related to the student's education. In other words, the pro-competitive justification of amateurism does not apply to educational expenses. Is Bybee correct on this issue? If he is, what other remuneration or benefits could college athletes receive as part of their "education?" Automobiles? Computers? Graduate school tuition?

6. *Bypassing the Olympic Model.* As noted above, an important part of the *O'Bannon* opinion at the district court level included the determination that NCAA restrictions on athlete endorsements do not violate antitrust law. While the NCAA is free to adopt the Olympic model of amateurism, *O'Bannon* clearly holds that antitrust law does not mandate it. Is there nonetheless a good case for adopting this model, which would enable prominent college athletes to be compensated, without imposing costs on universities that would detract from their educational mission?

IN RE: NCAA ATHLETIC GRANT-IN-AID CAP ANTITRUST LITIGATION
2018 WL 1524005 (N.D. Cal. 2018)

WILKEN, J.

In this multidistrict litigation, student-athlete Plaintiffs allege that Defendants National Collegiate Athletic Association (NCAA) and eleven of its member conferences fixed prices for the payments and benefits that the students may receive in return for their elite athletic services. Now pending are cross-motions for summary judgment. For the reasons set forth below, the cross-motions for summary judgment are granted in part and denied in part.

* * *

Plaintiffs initiated these actions in 2014 and 2015, attacking the NCAA's cap on their grant-in-aid itself, rather than merely the association's restrictions on sharing NIL revenue.

* * *

Therefore, only claims for injunctive relief remain pending.

[The court held that res judicata and collateral estoppel did not bar plaintiffs' claims.]

[Because there was no dispute between the parties, the court granted summary judgment on the applicable market definition, and the presence of anticompetitive restraints, adopting the same findings as in *O'Bannon*.]

* * *

B. Procompetitive Benefits of the Restraints

Next, Plaintiffs identify the NCAA rule changes discussed above, which have generally increased but continue to fix various benefits related to athletic participation that a member school may provide for its student-athletes or permit them to receive from outside sources. *See* Section I above. They also identify new concessions by Defendants that benefits and gifts that are related to athletic participation but are above the cost of attendance are connected neither to education nor to their understanding of amateurism. . . . Plaintiffs contend that because Defendants permit student-athletes to be paid money that does not go "to cover legitimate educational expenses," they are not amateurs. *O'Bannon*, 802 F.3d at 1075. Plaintiffs also identify a number of expenses that they contend are tethered to education but are still disallowed.

While the restraints challenged in this case overlap with those in O'Bannon, the specific rules at issue are not the same. Challenges to the NCAA's rules must be assessed on a case-by-case basis under the rule of reason, and O'Bannon's holding that there were procompetitive justifications for the rules challenged in that case would not necessarily require the Court to find that different rules, challenged in this case, also have the same procompetitive effects. 802 F.3d at 1063 (citing *NCAA v. Bd. of Regents of the Univ. of Okla.*, 468 U.S. 85 (1984)) ("we are not bound by *Board of Regents* to conclude that every NCAA rule that somehow relates to amateurism is automatically valid"). The Court rejects Defendants' contention that merely because all of the then-existing NCAA Bylaws were part of the record in O'Bannon, the Court necessarily adjudicated in Defendants' favor all possible challenges to any of those rules. The reasoning of *O'Bannon* will be very relevant in assessing whether the rules in this case have procompetitive effects. However, like the NIL rules in *O'Bannon*, the validity of the specific rules challenged in this case "must be proved, not presumed." *Id.* at 1064.

Defendants also present evidence that paying student-athletes would detract from the integration of academics and athletics in the campus community.

* * *

Accordingly, the Court will deny the parties' cross-motions for summary adjudication of the question of whether the challenged NCAA rules serve Defendants' asserted procompetitive purposes of integrating academics with athletics and preserving the popularity of the NCAA's product by promoting its current understanding of amateurism.

C. Less Restrictive Alternatives

The final step in the rule-of-reason analysis is whether Plaintiffs can "make a strong evidentiary showing" that any legitimate objectives can be achieved in a substantially less restrictive manner. *O'Bannon*, 802 F.3d at 1074. Plaintiffs do not move for summary judgment on this issue, but seek to prove at trial their contention that the NCAA's rules are "*patently and inexplicably* stricter than is necessary to accomplish" the NCAA's procompetitive objectives. *O'Bannon*, 802 F.3d at 1075. Defendants, on the other hand, move for summary judgment that all less restrictive alternatives proposed in this case are foreclosed by *O'Bannon*. The Court finds that because Plaintiffs challenge different rules and propose different alternatives from those considered in *O'Bannon*, the Court is not precluded from considering this factor.

* * *

As discussed, Plaintiffs in this case do not challenge restrictions on distribution of licensing revenue derived from NILs, as was the case in *O'Bannon*. Rather, they challenge NCAA rules relating to the benefits that schools may offer student-athletes to compete for their recruitment. The less restrictive alternatives that they propose in this case are different from those reviewed in *O'Bannon*. As the Ninth Circuit explained, to "say that the NCAA's amateurism rules are procompetitive, as *Board of Regents* did, is not to say that they are automatically lawful; a restraint that serves a procompetitive purpose can still be invalid under the Rule of Reason if a substantially less restrictive rule would further the same objectives equally well." *O'Bannon*, 802 F.3d at 1063–64 (citing *Bd. of Regents*, 468 U.S. at 101 n.23); *see also id.* at 1063 ("we are not bound by *Board of Regents* to conclude that every NCAA rule that somehow relates to amateurism is automatically valid").

The first less restrictive alternative that Plaintiffs propose is allowing the Division I conferences, rather than the NCAA, to set the rules regulating education and athletic participation expenses that the member institutions may provide. Plaintiffs argue that this alternative would be substantially less restrictive because it would allow conferences to compete to implement rules that attract student-athletes while still maintaining the popularity of college sports and balancing the integration of academics and athletics. They contend that none of the conferences has market power and, thus, their rule-making would not be subject to an antitrust challenge.

Plaintiffs contend that their proposed conference-autonomy system is based on actual experience in a closely analogous context. It could "operate like the college athletic system during the first half of the 20th Century, when each conference had its own compensation rules." Roger Noll Rep. at 30. To support their argument that such autonomy is viable as a less restrictive alternative to NCAA regulations, Plaintiffs have identified new NCAA Bylaws, adopted on August 7, 2014 (after the *O'Bannon* trial), that grant the Power Five Conferences autonomy to adopt or amend rules on a variety of topics. *See* Defs. Ex. 1 at 27–28 (Bylaw 5.3.2.1). The Bylaws now grant autonomy to the Power Five Conferences to legislate, for example, regarding "a student-athlete's individual limit on athletically related financial aid, terms and conditions of awarding institutional financial aid, and the eligibility of former student-athletes to receive undergraduate financial aid"; pre-enrollment expenses and support; student-athletes securing loans to purchase loss-of-value and disability insurance; and awards, benefits and expenses for student-athletes and their family and friends. *Id.*; *see also* Daniel A. Rascher Rep. at 12–13 & n.21, 172–182 (discussing proposed less restrictive alternatives). The existence of these exceptions for the Power Five Conferences constitutes evidence sufficient to raise a factual question that allowing relevant areas of autonomy for all Division I conferences would be a less restrictive alternative to current NCAA rules.

* * *

Plaintiffs propose a second less restrictive alternative, requesting that the Court enjoin all national rules that prohibit or limit any payments or non-cash benefits that are tethered to educational expenses, or any payments or benefits that are incidental to athletic participation. *See* Rascher Rep. at 173–177. Their position is that because Defendants already permit some payments and benefits in these two categories above the cost of attendance, it would be virtually as effective in serving the NCAA's procompetitive purposes to require the NCAA to allow all benefits in either category. Plaintiffs contend that this alternative could be applied with or without conference autonomy because abolishing the NCAA restraints would be a less restrictive alternative to the current system regardless of whether conference rules were permitted as a replacement.

In support of this contention, Plaintiffs first identify evidence that Defendants already allow schools to offer some benefits above the cost of attendance that are related to athletic participation but not tethered to education. *See, e.g.*, Noll Rep. at 17–18 (discussing categories of benefits); NCAA (Lennon) Depo. at 58:20–59:16 (same). For example, schools can pay the expenses for an athlete's spouse and children to attend a playoff game, because such expenses are incidental to athletic participation, but not the expenses of parents, grandparents, or siblings. NCAA (Lennon) Depo. at 186:1–16; *see also id.* at 86:17–87:13 (schools may reimburse students' national championship, Olympic trials and national team tryout costs).

* * *

To be clear, if Defendants prevail in demonstrating the same procompetitive justifications that the Court found in *O'Bannon*, the NCAA will still be able to prohibit its member schools from paying their student-athletes cash sums unrelated to educational expenses or athletic participation. *O'Bannon*, 802 F.3d at 1078–79. Under such circumstances, the Court will not consider any proposed less restrictive alternative by which Plaintiffs seek payment untethered to one of these two categories.

Plaintiffs have proffered evidence supporting two possible less restrictive alternatives not previously presented for decision or ruled upon, raising a genuine issue of material fact as to whether they can meet their evidentiary burden to show that such alternatives would be virtually as effective as the challenged restraints in advancing Defendants' procompetitive objectives. They do not seek summary judgment in their favor on this factor. Defendants have failed to show that these proposed less restrictive alternatives are foreclosed by *O'Bannon*. Accordingly, the Court will deny summary judgment on the question of less restrictive alternatives.

NOTES AND QUESTIONS

1. *Challenging the NCAA Model Directly.* Currently pending before the same California district court that tried *O'Bannon* is a new case, *In re: NCAA Athletic Grant-in-Aid Cap Antitrust* (formerly *Alston v. NCAA* and *Jenkins v. NCAA*), that engages in a broader challenge to the NCAA model itself. The plaintiffs are seeking an injunction against the NCAA's enforcement of grant-in-aid amateurism rules on the ground that such rules violate antitrust law. The district court has held that, at the very least, the plaintiffs can pursue arguments for less restrictive alternatives, but are limited by the Ninth Circuit's *O'Bannon* decision. The case was being tried at the time this book went to press.

2. *Less Restrictive Alternative #1.* The plaintiffs argue for two new possible less restrictive alternatives to the grant-in-aid rules in light of the defendant's procompetitive justification for the restraint. First, allowing the Division I conferences, rather than the NCAA, to set the rules regulating education and athletic participation expenses that the member institutions may provide. The conferences would possess less market power, and pose lesser restraints on the plaintiffs. Do you agree? Or would the conferences essentially regulate grant-in-aids the same way that the NCAA does? For a proposal concerning a conference-centric model, see William W. Berry III, *Amending Amateurism*, 68 Ala. L. Rev. 551 (2016).

3. *Less Restrictive Alternative #2.* Plaintiffs propose a second less restrictive alternative, requesting that the Court enjoin all national rules that

prohibit or limit any payments or non-cash benefits that are tethered to educational expenses, or any payments or benefits that are incidental to athletic participation. Their position is that because Defendants already permit some payments and benefits in these two categories above the cost of attendance, it would be virtually as effective in serving the NCAA's procompetitive purposes to require the NCAA to allow all benefits in either category. Do you find this argument persuasive?

In their brief, plaintiffs listed

> "Specific athletic participation benefits that currently are permitted—*in addition* to a full COA grant-in-aid—include: "gift suite" participation awards, such as televisions, iPods, and designer watches and sunglasses; loss-of-value insurance in the event that a college injury harms an athlete's earning prospects as a *professional*; apparel, equipment, and supplies; the costs of transportation and lodging for *certain family* members to attend championship contests; the costs of transportation and lodging for *spouses and children* to attend athletics contests; contest entry fees and costs of facility usage; expenses for the athletes associated with national championships, Olympic trials, and national team tryouts; and a *per diem* paid to athletes for away games that the membership could decide to increase without "violating the principle of amateurism, because that is not related to the principle of amateurism, but an incidental expense." The gift suites, for example, can collectively total thousands of dollars of compensation to athletes in excess of COA."

Plaintiffs thus argue:

> Critically, Defendants concede that providing these participation benefits exceeding COA has hurt neither the "collegiate model" nor consumer demand. Rather, Defendants' survey expert testified that providing, *e.g.*, gift suites and transportation benefits may actually "*foster*" demand because consumers may feel positively about colleges doing more for students. Defendants' provision of ever-increasing participation benefits in excess of COA that are "*not related to the principle of amateurism*"—without any harm to consumer demand—factually eviscerates their amateurism justification.

Again, do you find this persuasive? Or are these merely incidental items that have no real bearing on the amateur status of the employee?

4. *The Weight of O'Bannon.* Even so, the district court must follow the Ninth Circuit's decision in *O'Bannon*. Judge Wilken's opinion warns:

> To be clear, if Defendants prevail in demonstrating the same procompetitive justifications that the Court found in *O'Bannon*, the NCAA will still be able to prohibit its member schools from paying their student-athletes cash sums unrelated to educational expenses

or athletic participation. *O'Bannon*, 802 F.3d at 1078–79. Under such circumstances, the Court will not consider any proposed less restrictive alternative by which Plaintiffs seek payment untethered to one of these two categories.

Thus, the less restrictive alternatives would either have to be tethered to educational expenses or athletic participation.

CHAPTER 12

GENDER EQUITY IN SPORTS*

■ ■ ■

Enactment of Title IX in the 1970s has led to a much-needed surge in athletic opportunities and resources for female student-athletes over the last fifty years. In the early 1970s, only a small percentage of student-athletes were women, and women's sports received just two percent of the athletics funding. Women's sports in college did not even come within the purview of the NCAA. Instead, there was a separate and severely under-funded Association of Intercollegiate Athletic Women (AIAW).

Then, in 1972, the Congress adopted Title IX to prohibit discrimination in federally funded educational programs based on sex:

> No person ... shall, on the basis of sex, be excluded from participation in, be denied the benefit of, or be subjected to discrimination under any education program or activity receiving federal financial assistance.

When the Senate considered the statute again in 1974, Sen. John Tower (R-Texas) offered an amendment (that NCAA leadership supported) that would have excluded revenue-generating college sports from the purview of Title IX's coverage of "education program or activity." Title IX's original sponsor, Sen. Birch Bayh (D-Indiana), strongly opposed the amendment, arguing that Title IX should be comprehensive in scope and not exclude sports. 118 Cong. Rec. 5804 (1972). The Senate rejected the Tower Amendment. Instead, it adopted an amendment by Sen. Jacob Javits (R-NY) that required the Department of Health, Education and Welfare (whose relevant duties were later assigned to the Department of Education) to issue regulations to include "reasonable provisions considering the nature of particular sports." P.L. 93–380, Title VIII, Part D, § 844, 88 Stat. 612 (1974). In the late 1970s, President Carter's administration issued Regulations and Policy Interpretations designed to flesh out Title IX's implications for sports in college and high school.

In the early 1980s, the Supreme Court secured for sports essentially the same result that Senator Tower sought. In *Grove City College v. Bell*, 465 U.S. 555 (1984), the Court read Title IX as governing only the specific

---

* The Casebook Website (http://pennstatelaw.psu.edu/SportsTextWebsite) contains citations to scholarly and other commentary on a variety of topics discussed in this chapter, including Title IX and its regulation of the use of resources and administration of athletics departments under its rules.

college programs that received federal financial assistance, which did not include athletic departments. The Civil Rights Restoration Act of 1987 (20 U.S.C.A. § 1681, et seq. (1988)), however, explicitly extended Title IX's coverage to *all* the programs of an educational institution that receive *any* federal aid (including grants or loans to its students), bringing Title IX fully into play for college sports. Then, in the early 1990s, the Supreme Court sharply raised the legal stakes in these disputes by permitting private suits for damages and attorney fees by any woman asserting that she had been personally harmed by the school's violation of Title IX. *See Franklin v. Gwinnett County Public Schools*, 503 U.S. 60 (1992) (involving a high school student's claim of sexual harassment by a teacher). This set off a wave of Title IX suits in the mid-1990s, with the plaintiffs winning almost all of the judicial rulings.

Almost five decades after Title IX was first enacted, athletic departments are closer than ever to achieving gender equity. The addition of 803 women's teams since 1988 is a clear sign of progress. In 2017–18, almost 44% of college athletes were women, receiving around a third of overall athletic expenditures. At schools without football, spending is virtually equal between the genders. (Football schools spend an average of 60% of their budget on that one sport, and thus skew comparisons.)

A. ADMINISTRATIVE DEVELOPMENT OF TITLE IX

Title IX states a very general statutory prohibition of sex-based exclusion from participation, denial of benefits, or discrimination under educational programs. There was very little congressional material (*e.g.*, no Committee Report) about what was envisaged for the bill as a whole, and only two mentions of college sports in the entire congressional deliberations. The Act did go on to state that Title IX was not to

> ... be interpreted to require any educational institution to grant preferential or disparate treatment to the members of one sex on account of an imbalance which may exist with respect to the total number or percentage of persons of that sex participating in or receiving the benefits of any federally supported program or activity, in comparison with the total number or percentage of persons of that sex in any community, state, section, or other area: Provided, that this subsection shall not be construed to prevent the consideration in any hearing or proceeding under this chapter of statistical evidence tending to show that such an imbalance exists with respect to the participation in, or receipt of the benefits of, any such program or activity by the members of one sex.

Even the latter provision did no more than reject pure statistical disparities as themselves a violation of the statute; such statistical material can be and is regularly used (along with other factors) to find "discrimination."

In 1975, pursuant to a Congressional directive, the Health, Education and Welfare Department (HEW) promulgated regulations that further spelled out the implications of Title IX, including its application to athletic programs. Over the next three years, HEW received more than one hundred complaints under the Act. In response to this onslaught, HEW's Office of Civil Rights (OCR) issued a Policy Interpretation in 1979, which elaborated in much greater detail the meaning of equal educational opportunity, including in college and high school sports programs. That same year, Congress split HEW into a Department of Health and Human Services (HHS) and a Department of Education (DED). The latter department, through its OCR, took principal responsibility for the administration of Title IX.

As in the statute itself, the Title IX Regulations begin by stating that the statutory requirement of "equality" is not necessarily violated by "unequal aggregate expenditures for members of each sex or unequal expenditures for male and female teams." 51 Fed. Reg. 20,524 (1986). Instead, the test for compliance is a comparison of the

> ... availability, quality and kinds of benefits, opportunities and treatment afforded members of both sexes. Institutions will be in compliance if the compared program components are equivalent, that is, equal or equal in effect. Under this standard, identical benefits, opportunities or treatment are not required, provided the overall effect of any differences is negligible.

44 Fed. Reg. 71,415 (1979). For purposes of judging whether there actually is "equal athletic opportunity," the federal regulations direct that the amounts spent on athletic scholarships be on a "substantially proportional basis to the number of male and female participants in the institution's athletic programs," 44 Fed. Reg. 71,414 (1979). In addition, the following program factors must be taken into account:

1. Whether the selection of sports and levels of competition effectively accommodate the interests and abilities of members of both sexes;

2. Provision of equipment and supplies;

3. Scheduling of games and practice time;

4. Travel and per diem allowance;

5. Opportunity to receive coaching and academic tutoring;

6. Assignment and compensation of coaches and tutors;

7. Provision of locker rooms, practice and competitive facilities;

8. Provision of medical training services;

9. Provision of housing and dining facilities and services;

10. Publicity.

34 C.F.R. § 106.41(c) (1990).

Three different general categories of Title IX complaints have surfaced alleging sex discrimination in educational athletic programs. One involves the claim that there has been an unequal allocation of *resources*, and therefore of opportunities for women to play on women's-only teams—with gender segregated teams being the standard practice in college sports. The second involves unequal treatment in the *administration* of such women's programs—in particular, disparity in pay and benefits offered to the (often-male) coaches of the women's teams. The third category involves denial of *access* by female (or occasionally male) athletes to the only team in a sport that the school has chosen to confine to one gender.

The bulk of the cases and controversies have arisen in the first category, particularly focused on the number of women allowed to participate in athletics rather than the number of dollars spent on the operation of the women's teams. On this question, an oft-cited three-pronged test set forth in the 1979 OCR Policy Interpretation applies. The test is that a school is in compliance with Title IX with respect to participation opportunities if any of the following questions can be answered affirmatively:

(1) Whether intercollegiate level participation opportunities for male and female students are provided in numbers substantially proportionate to their respective enrollments; or

(2) Where the members of one sex have been and are underrepresented among intercollegiate athletes, whether the institution can show a history and continuing practice of program expansion which is demonstrably responsive to the developing interest and abilities of the members of that sex; or

(3) Where the members of one sex are underrepresented among intercollegiate athletes, and the institution cannot show a continuing practice of program expansion such as that cited above, whether it can be demonstrated that the interests and abilities of the members of that sex have been fully and effectively accommodated by the present program.

B. RESOURCES

The dispute that produced the most academic writing about Title IX involved Brown University. The Ivy League, of which Brown is a member, is the setting where college sports first began in the 1850s, and where American-style football evolved in the 1870s. Not until the late 1960s and early 1970s did all Ivy League universities finally integrate their undergraduate colleges by accepting women into their academic as well as athletic programs. By that time, the Ivy League was no longer part of the NCAA's highly commercialized Division IA, and it did not provide athletic scholarships as such to its students.

Ironically, though, by the 1990s, Ivy League schools offered more varsity athletic opportunities to both their female and male students than schools in any other college conference. Under the 1995 Equity in Athletics Disclosure Act, schools must provide both the OCR and the public with relevant data about participation in and financing of their male and female athletic programs. The first such report, for the 1995–96 academic year, disclosed that while at Washington State University women were both 47% of the student-athletes and of undergraduate students, there were eight female and five male teams. Harvard University, by contrast, had a slight disparity in those two ratios, 40% to 44%, but it provided a total of 41 intercollegiate teams to its students (20 female and 21 male teams). Princeton had almost as many teams as Harvard and offered varsity athletic positions to 24% of all women students.

In 1971, Brown University merged with Pembroke College, a women's-only school. One of the early steps in that joint venture was to increase substantially the athletic opportunities for its new female students; by 1977, Brown had created 14 women's varsity teams. Over the next decade, however, just a single women's team was added, such that by 1991–92 Brown had 15 women's teams and 16 men's teams. Even so, Brown did not have equity, as the total number of participants on all teams was 328 women (37%) and 566 men (63%), however, largely because of the size of the football team.

At the time, though, the NCAA and most of its members were engaged in a cost reduction program (the effort that generated the "restricted earnings coach" rule and the *Law* litigation we read about in Chapter 10. Like a number of schools, the Brown administration announced that it was going to reduce its athletic budget by cutting four varsity sports—two women's teams in volleyball and gymnastics (which would generate savings of approximately $37,000 and $24,000) and two men's teams in water polo and golf (which would save $9,000 and $7,000 respectively). While significantly more dollars were cut from the women's than the men's programs, the relative number of team posidtions remained essentially the same, at 37%–63%; however, women made up approximately 48% of

Brown's student body. The university told the team members that they could continue playing in those sports as "intercollegiate clubs," but without financial assistance or support services from the school, and likely with sharply reduced opportunities to compete against varsity teams at other schools. The members of the women's teams (led by gymnast Amy Cohen) chose, instead, to file suit under Title IX, and they won a preliminary injunction against Brown's elimination of the women's varsity teams. Brown appealed that decision, and received the first circuit court opinion about how Title IX applied to intercollegiate athletics.

COHEN V. BROWN UNIVERSITY
991 F.2d 888 (1st Cir. 1993)

SELYA, CIRCUIT JUDGE.

* * *

III. Title IX and Collegiate Athletics

* * *

A. Scope of Title IX.

At its inception, the broad proscriptive language of Title IX caused considerable consternation in the academic world. The academy's anxiety chiefly centered around identifying which individual programs, particularly in terms of athletics, might come within the scope of the discrimination provision, and, relatedly, how the government would determine compliance. The gridiron fueled these concerns: for many schools, the men's football budget far exceeded that of any other sport, and men's athletics as a whole received the lion's share of dedicated resources—a share that, typically, was vastly disproportionate to the percentage of men in the student body.

[The judge then described the evolution of the Title IX legislation and its administrative interpretation. After quoting the key passage from the OCR Policy Interpretation set out above, the court continued.]

... The first benchmark furnishes a safe harbor for those institutions that have distributed athletic opportunities in numbers "substantially proportionate" to the gender composition of their student bodies. Thus, a university which does not wish to engage in extensive compliance analysis may stay on the sunny side of Title IX simply by maintaining gender parity between its student body and its athletic lineup.

The second and third parts of the accommodation test recognize that there are circumstances under which, as a practical matter, something short of this proportionality is a satisfactory proxy for gender balance. For example, so long as a university is continually expanding athletic opportunities in an ongoing effort to meet the needs of the underrepresented gender, and persists in this approach as interest and ability levels in its student body and secondary feeder schools rise, benchmark two is satisfied and Title IX does not require that the university leap to complete gender parity in a single bound. Or, if a school has a student body in which one sex is demonstrably less interested in athletics, Title IX does not require that the school create teams for, or rain money upon, otherwise disinterested students; rather, the third benchmark is satisfied if the underrepresented sex's discernible interests are fully and effectively accommodated.[13]

It seems unlikely, even in this day and age, that the athletic establishments of many coeducational universities reflect the gender balance of their student bodies. Similarly, the recent boom in Title IX suits suggests that, in an era of fiscal austerity, few universities are prone to expand athletic opportunities. It is not surprising, then, that schools more often than not attempt to manage the rigors of Title IX by satisfying the interests and abilities of the underrepresented gender, that is, by meeting the third benchmark of the accommodation test. Yet, this benchmark sets a high standard: it demands not merely some accommodation, but full and effective accommodation. If there is sufficient interest and ability among members of the statistically underrepresented gender, not slaked by existing programs, an institution necessarily fails this prong of the test.

Although the full-and-effective-accommodation standard is high, it is not absolute. Even when male athletic opportunities outnumber female athletic opportunities, and the university has not met the first benchmark (substantial statistical proportionality) or the second benchmark (continuing program expansion) of the accommodation test, the mere fact that there are some female students interested in a sport does not ipso facto require the school to provide a varsity team in order to comply with the third benchmark. Rather, the institution can satisfy the third benchmark by ensuring participatory opportunities at the intercollegiate level when, and to the extent that, there is "sufficient interest and ability among the members of the excluded sex to sustain a viable team and a reasonable expectation of intercollegiate competition for that team. . . ." Staying on top of the problem is not sport for the short-winded: the institution must remain vigilant, "upgrading the competitive opportunities available to the historically disadvantaged sex as warranted by developing abilities among

---

[13] OCR also lists a series of illustrative justifications for the disparate treatment of men's and women's athletic teams, including (1) sports that require more resources because of the nature of the game (e.g., contact sports generally require more equipment), (2) special circumstances, such as an influx of first-year players, that may require an extraordinary infusion of resources, (3) special operational expenses (e.g., crowd control at a basketball tournament), as long as special operational expense needs are met for both genders and (4) affirmative measures to remedy past limitations on athletic opportunities for one gender.

the athletes of that sex," until the opportunities for, and levels of, competition are equivalent by gender.[15]

Brown argues that DED's Policy Interpretation, construed as we have just outlined, goes so far afield that it countervails the enabling legislation. Brown suggests that, to the extent students' interests in athletics are disproportionate by gender, colleges should be allowed to meet those interests incompletely as long as the school's response is in direct proportion to the comparative levels of interest. Put bluntly, Brown reads the "full" out of the duty to accommodate "fully and effectively." It argues instead that an institution satisfactorily accommodates female athletes if it allocates athletic opportunities to women in accordance with the ratio of interested and able women to interested and able men, regardless of the number of unserved women or the percentage of the student body that they comprise.

Because this is mountainous terrain, an example may serve to clarify the distinction between Brown's proposal and our understanding of the law. Suppose a university (Oooh U.) has a student body consisting of 1,000 men and 1,000 women, a one to one ratio. If 500 men and 250 women are able and interested athletes, the ratio of interested men to interested women is two to one. Brown takes the position that both the actual gender composition of the student body and whether there is unmet interest among the underrepresented gender are irrelevant; in order to satisfy the third benchmark, Oooh U. must only provide athletic opportunities in line with the two to one interested athlete ratio, say, 100 slots for men and 50 slots for women. Under this view, the interest of 200 women would be unmet—but there would be no Title IX violation.

We think that Brown's perception of the Title IX universe is myopic. The fact that the overrepresented gender is less than fully accommodated will not, in and of itself, excuse a shortfall in the provision of opportunities for the underrepresented gender. Rather, the law requires that, in the absence of continuing program expansion (benchmark two), schools either meet benchmark one by providing athletic opportunities in proportion to the gender composition of the student body (in Oooh U.'s case, a roughly equal number of slots for men and women, as the student body is equally divided), or meet benchmark three by fully accommodating interested athletes among the underrepresented sex (providing, at Oooh U., 250 slots for women).

---

[15] If in the course of adding and upgrading teams, a university attains gender parity between its athletic program and its student body, it meets the first benchmark of the accommodation test. But, Title IX does not require that a school pour ever-increasing sums into its athletic establishment. If a university prefers to take another route, it can also bring itself into compliance with the first benchmark of the accommodation test by subtraction and downgrading, that is, by reducing opportunities for the overrepresented gender while keeping opportunities stable for the underrepresented gender (or reducing them to a much lesser extent).

In the final analysis, Brown's view is wrong . . . as a matter of law, for DED's Policy Interpretation, which requires full accommodation of the underrepresented gender, draws its essence from the statute. Whether Brown's concept might be thought more attractive, or whether we, if writing on a pristine page, would craft the regulation in a manner different than the agency, are not very important considerations. Because the agency's rendition stands upon a plausible, if not inevitable, reading of Title IX, we are obligated to enforce the regulation according to its tenor.

* * *

The record reveals that the court below . . . properly recognized that even balanced use of the budget-paring knife runs afoul of Title IX where, as here, the fruits of a university's athletic program remain ill-distributed after the trimming takes place. Because the district court understood this principle, and because its findings of fact as to the case's probable outcome are based on substantial evidence, the court's determination that plaintiffs are likely to succeed on the merits is inexpugnable.

Injunction affirmed.

NOTES AND QUESTIONS

1. *Aftermath.* This First Circuit opinion opened the door to continued litigation against Brown to establish gender equity. The class action case that ensued is below.

2. *Colorado State.* Two months after the *Brown* decision, the Tenth Circuit rendered a similar judgment in a suit involving Colorado State University (CSU): *Roberts v. Colorado State Bd. of Agriculture*, 998 F.2d 824 (10th Cir.1993). In 1992, CSU announced that it was eliminating both the men's varsity baseball program (with its fifty-five players) and the women's varsity softball team (with its eighteen players). These cutbacks left in place the ten-percentage point differential between the female share of student enrollment and of varsity athletes. The women's softball team secured an injunction under Title IX against Colorado's State Board of Agriculture (the government entity in charge of the state university), prohibiting this cutback in the women's side of the school's athletic program.

3. *Other Settlements.* The lawsuits against Brown and Colorado State (as well as one against Indiana U. of Penn.) all involved challenges to university decisions to eliminate certain women's varsity sports as part of broader cutbacks in the schools' athletic programs. In 1993, settlements were reached in two pending class action suits (against California State University and the University of Texas) that had asserted a right under Title IX to have new women's sports added to the athletic programs. In both cases, the schools settled the litigation by promising that within the next several years, their respective ratios of female and male athletes would be brought to within five

percentage points of the female-male ratios in their student bodies. To some extent this goal would be accomplished by adding more women's sports, paid for by increasing the athletic budgets (for example, through increased student fees). They planned to eliminate the remaining disparity by reducing the number of male varsity athletes (partly by cutting back on the number of non-scholarship "walk-on" members of male teams, such as football).

Male athletes also began to file lawsuits challenging what they perceived to be a gender-related disparity in cutbacks of athletic programs by universities that were worried about litigation by female athletes. Among the suits initiated in 1993 was one case brought by the male swimmers at the University of Illinois. Faced with a $600,000 budgetary deficit in its athletic program, the University decided to cut four varsity teams—men's and women's diving, men's fencing, and men's swimming. The selection criteria included such factors as team costs, competitive success, and student and spectator interest in the sports. It was conceded, though, that a major reason why women's swimming was not cut along with the men's program was the administration's concern about Title IX liability. While the University's student body was 44% women, its female varsity athletes comprised only 23% of the total. Members of the men's swimming team then filed suit, contending that they were the victims of reverse discrimination that violated both Title IX and the Equal Protection provisions of the Constitution. After losing in the district court, the men's team appealed to the Seventh Circuit, which rendered the first appellate ruling on this variation on the equal sporting rights theme.

KELLEY V. UNIVERSITY OF ILLINOIS
35 F.3d 265 (7th Cir. 1994)

CUMMINGS, CIRCUIT JUDGE.

* * *

III.

The University's decision not to terminate the woman's swimming program was—given the requirements of Title IX and the applicable regulation and policy interpretation—extremely prudent. The percentage of women involved in intercollegiate athletics at the University of Illinois is substantially lower than the percentage of women enrolled at the school. If the University had terminated the women's swimming program, it would have been vulnerable to a finding that it was in violation of Title IX. Female participation would have continued to be substantially disproportionate to female enrollment, and women with a demonstrated interest in an intercollegiate athletic activity and demonstrated ability to compete at the intercollegiate level would be left without an opportunity to participate in their sport. The University could, however, eliminate the men's swimming program without violating Title IX since even after eliminating the program, men's participation in athletics would continue to be more than substantially proportionate to their presence in the University's student body. And as the caselaw makes clear, if the percentage of student-athletes of a particular sex is substantially proportionate to the percentage of students of that sex in the general student population, the athletic interests of that sex are presumed to have been accommodated. The University's decision to retain the women's swimming program—even though budget constraints required that the men's program be terminated—was a reasonable response to the requirements of the applicable regulation and policy interpretation.

Plaintiffs contend, however, that the applicable regulation and policy interpretation pervert Title IX. Title IX, plaintiffs contend, "ha[s] through some alchemy of bureaucratic regulation been transformed from a statute which prohibits discrimination on the basis of sex into a statute that mandates discrimination against males . . ." Or, as plaintiffs put it later: "If a university is required by Title IX to eliminate men from varsity athletic competition . . . , then the same Title IX [sh]ould require the university to eliminate women from the academic departments where they are over[-]represented. Such a result would be ridiculous."

We agree that such a result would be ridiculous. But Congress itself recognized that addressing discrimination in athletics presented a unique set of problems not raised in areas such as employment and academics. Congress therefore specifically directed the agency in charge of administering Title IX to issue, with respect to "intercollegiate athletic activities," regulations containing "reasonable provisions considering the nature of particular sports." Pub. L. No. 93–380, 88 Stat. 484, 612. And where Congress has specifically delegated to an agency the responsibility to articulate standards governing a particular area, we must accord the ensuing regulation considerable deference. *Chevron U.S.A. v. Natural Resources Defense Council, Inc.*, 467 U.S. 837, 844 (1984) (Where Congress has expressly delegated to an agency the power to "elucidate a specific provision of a statute by regulation," the resulting regulations should be given "controlling weight unless they are arbitrary, capricious, or manifestly contrary to the statute.")

The regulation at issue here is neither "arbitrary . . . [n]or manifestly contrary to the statute." The regulation provides that notwithstanding Title IX's requirement that "[n]o person . . . shall, on the basis of sex, be excluded from participation in any . . . activity," a school may "sponsor separate teams for members of each sex where selection for such teams is based upon competitive skill or the activity involved is a contact sport." Such a provision is not at odds with the purpose of Title IX and we do not understand plaintiffs to argue that it is. And since [the regulation] is not manifestly contrary to the objectives of Title IX, this court must accord it deference. Plaintiffs, while they concede the validity of [the regulation], argue that the substantial proportionality test contained in the agency's policy interpretation of that regulation establishes a gender-based quota system, a scheme they allege is contrary to the mandates of Title IX. But the policy interpretation does not, as plaintiffs suggest, mandate statistical balancing. Rather the policy interpretation merely creates a presumption that a school is in compliance with Title IX and the applicable regulation when it achieves such a statistical balance. Even if substantial proportionality has not been achieved, a school may establish that it is in compliance by demonstrating either that it has a continuing practice of increasing the athletic opportunities of the under-represented sex or that its existing programs effectively accommodate the interests of that sex.

Moreover, once it is agreed Title IX does not require that all teams be co-ed—a point the plaintiffs concede—and that 34 C.F.R. § 106.41 is therefore a valid regulation, schools must be provided some means of establishing that despite offering single-sex teams, they have provided "equal athletic opportunit[ies] . . . for both sexes." Undoubtedly the agency responsible for enforcement of the statute could have required schools to sponsor a women's program for every men's program offered and vice versa. Requiring parallel teams would certainly have been the simplest method of ensuring equality of opportunity—and plaintiffs would doubtless have preferred this approach since, had it been adopted, the men's swimming program would likely have been saved. It was not unreasonable, however, for the agency to reject this course of action. Requiring parallel teams is a rigid approach that denies schools the flexibility to respond to the differing athletic interests of men and women.[8] It was perfectly acceptable, therefore, for the agency to chart a different course and adopt an enforcement scheme that measures compliance by analyzing how a school has allocated its various athletic resources.

This Court must defer to an agency's interpretation of its regulations if the interpretation is reasonable, a standard the policy interpretation at issue here meets. Measuring compliance through an evaluation of a school's allocation of its athletic resources allows schools flexibility in meeting the athletic interests of their students and increases the chance that the actual interests of those students will be met. And if compliance with Title IX is to be measured through this sort of analysis, it is only practical that schools be given some clear way to establish that they have satisfied the requirements of the statute. The substantial proportionality contained in Benchmark 1 merely establishes such a safe harbor.

---

[8] Requiring parallel teams would, for example, require the University either to terminate the football program or to begin a women's team, even if female students had little interest in that sport but had great interest in other sports.

Since the policy interpretation maps out a reasonable approach to measuring compliance with Title IX, this Court does not have the authority to condemn it. Plaintiffs' claim that the University of Illinois violated Title IX when it terminated the men's swimming program is, therefore, rejected. The University's actions were consistent with the statute and the applicable regulation and policy interpretation. And despite plaintiffs' assertions to the contrary, neither the regulation nor the policy interpretation run afoul of the dictates of Title IX.

IV.

Plaintiffs' final argument is that the defendants' decision to eliminate the men's swimming program while retaining the women's program denied them equal protection of law as guaranteed by the Fourteenth Amendment. While the effect of Title IX and the relevant regulation and policy interpretation is that institutions will sometimes consider gender when decreasing their athletic offerings, this limited consideration of sex does not violate the Constitution. Congress has broad powers under the Due Process Clause of the Fifth Amendment to remedy past discrimination. *Metro Broadcasting, Inc. v. Federal Communications Comm'n*, 497 U.S. 547, 565–566 (1990). Even absent a specific finding that discrimination has occurred, remedial measures mandated by Congress are "constitutionally permissible to the extent that they serve important governmental objectives . . . and are substantially related to achievement of those ends." *Id.* at 565; *see also Mississippi University for Women v. Hogan*, 458 U.S. 718, 728 (1982). There is no doubt but that removing the legacy of sexual discrimination—including discrimination in the provision of extra-curricular offerings such as athletics—from our nation's educational institutions is an important governmental objective. We do not understand plaintiffs to argue otherwise.

Plaintiffs' complaint appears, instead, to be that the remedial measures required by Title IX and the applicable regulation and policy interpretation are not substantially related to their purported goal. Plaintiffs contend that the applicable rules allow "the University to . . . improve its statistics without adding any opportunities for women . . . ," an outcome they suggest is unconstitutional. But to survive constitutional scrutiny, Title IX need not require—as plaintiffs would have us believe—that the opportunities for the under-represented group be continually expanded. Title IX's stated objective is not to ensure that the athletic opportunities available to women increase. Rather its avowed purpose is to prohibit educational institutions from discriminating on the basis of sex. And the remedial scheme established by Title IX and the applicable regulation and policy interpretation are clearly substantially related to this end. Allowing a school to consider gender when determining which athletic programs to terminate ensures that in instances where overall athletic opportunities decrease, the actual opportunities available to the underrepresented gender do not. And since the remedial scheme here at issue directly protects the interest of the disproportionately burdened gender, it passes constitutional muster.

* * *

Affirmed.

NOTES AND QUESTIONS

1. *Consequences of Title IX.* One consequence of Title IX has been the elimination of non-revenue male sports teams. The claim that this violates Title IX, as made in *Kelley*, does not pass muster. In order to create gender equity, where the number of male athletic scholarships is disproportionate to female athletic scholarships (in light of the gender breakdown of the student body), an institution must either increase the number of female scholarships or decrease the number of male scholarships. The budget issues at the time of *Kelley* resulted in Illinois choosing the second option. As the *Kelley* court pointed out, if eliminating male teams violated the statute (or the Constitution for that matter), it would be difficult to achieve gender equity.

2. *Gender Neutral.* As the *Kelley* court intimates, Title IX mandates equality of opportunity for the underrepresented group. If a university needed to eliminate a women's athletic team in order to increase the percentage of male athletes, it could do so if it were necessary to achieve equity in the number of scholarships in light of the composition of the student body.

This first wave of decisions under Title IX involved requests for preliminary injunctions and/or summary judgments from one side or the other. Brown University's athletic program was also the subject of the first full-scale trial of a Title IX case. By this time, Amy Cohen and her gymnastic and volleyball classmates had long since graduated from Brown. Instead, the lawsuit had become a class action on behalf of all present and future Brown women students who might want to participate in intercollegiate sports. While the percentage of women among Brown's varsity athletes had increased slightly from 37% in 1990–91 to 38% in 1993–94, the percentage of women in Brown's classes had increased from 48% to 51% in that same period. Thus, while Brown had 16 varsity *teams* both for men and for women students-athletes, there was a 13-point gap between the percentage of women team *members* and students.

Brown now pressed an argument that had been alluded to in earlier cases—that the latter gap actually reflected a disparity in male and female student *interests* in varsity sports, and that Brown's programs provided more than "equal accommodation" to the female interests. The trial judge rejected this argument: in his view, not only was measurement of such true student interests inherently difficult, but it was legally irrelevant under the OCR standard. Since Brown had stopped expanding women's sports, while still leaving this statistical disparity between its female athlete and student ratios, the university had to meet *all* existing women student interests and abilities in any particular varsity sport (which clearly existed at Brown in volleyball and gymnastics).

The reaction of Brown President Vartan Gregorian to the trial verdict was that this reading of Title IX was "tantamount to quotas." (Gregorian was also upset that anyone but the University's president could tell "his" University what to do.) In filing its appeal, Brown's counsel also placed some hope in two major Equal Protection decisions rendered by the Supreme Court since the First Circuit's initial *Cohen* decision. In *Adarand Constructors, Inc. v. Pena*, 515 U.S. 200 (1995), the Court had overruled *Metro Broadcasting v. FCC*, 497 U.S. 547 (1990) (a case that had been relied on by the First Circuit in *Cohen*); the Court there required that even benign federal affirmative action programs in favor of previously discriminated-against groups—there a racial group—have to pass the same "strict scrutiny" standard that is applied to negative state discrimination. A year later came *United States v. Virginia*, 518 U.S. 515 (1996), which dealt with the state of Virginia's effort to preserve its all-male Virginia Military Institute (VMI), and to offer women with military aspirations a female-only program instead. In this case, the Supreme Court did not utilize the traditional "intermediate scrutiny" to judge whether gender-based classifications were "substantially related to an important government objective." Instead, the Court majority subjected Virginia's actions to "skeptical scrutiny of official action denying rights or opportunities based on sex" (518 U.S. at 531), and eventually concluded that the state did not provide the "exceedingly persuasive justification" needed for its exclusion of female applicants from VMI.

While Justice Scalia in *Virginia* accused the Court majority of having "drastically revised our established standards for reviewing sex-based classifications" (*id*. at 2291), Brown University asserted that *Virginia* and *Adarand* required the First Circuit to take a second look at the application of Title IX to its case. The following opinion (by a new circuit panel) produced the first Title IX division within an appeals court.

COHEN V. BROWN UNIVERSITY
101 F.3d 155 (1st Cir. 1996)

BOWNES, CIRCUIT JUDGE.

* * *

IV.

* * *

A.

Title IX is not an affirmative action statute; it is an anti-discrimination statute, modeled explicitly after another anti-discrimination statute, Title VI. No aspect of the Title IX regime at issue in this case—inclusive of the statute, the relevant regulation, and the pertinent agency documents—mandates gender-based preferences or quotas, or specific timetables for implementing numerical goals.

Like other anti-discrimination statutory schemes, the Title IX regime permits affirmative action. In addition, Title IX, like other anti-discrimination schemes, permits an inference that a significant gender-based statistical disparity may indicate the existence of discrimination. Consistent with the school desegregation cases, the question of substantial proportionality under the Policy Interpretation's three-part test is merely the starting point for analysis, rather than the conclusion; a rebuttable presumption, rather than an inflexible requirement. *See, e.g., Swann v. Charlotte-Mecklenburg Bd. of Educ.*, 402 U.S. 1, 25 (1971). In short, the substantial proportionality test is but one aspect of the inquiry into whether an institution's athletics program complies with Title IX.

* * *

[The court then retraced and reaffirmed the earlier *Cohen* panel's treatment of the Title IX regulatory issues. In particular, the majority here specifically rejected Brown's principal argument—that the existing demands of its women students for varsity athletic opportunities were being accommodated as much if not more than were the demands of its male students. This position, the Court said, did not satisfy the third prong of the Policy Interpretation that required "full and effective" accommodation of all the athletic demands of the currently under-represented female student. The court dismissed Brown's effort to use the Title VII equal employment opportunity analogy to try to paint the Policy Interpretation as creating an illegitimate quota system in the athletic sphere.]

* * *

E.

* * *

It is imperative to recognize that athletics presents a distinctly different situation from admissions and employment and requires a different analysis in order to determine the existence vel non of discrimination. While the Title IX regime permits institutions to maintain gender-segregated teams, the law does not require that student-athletes attending institutions receiving federal funds must compete on gender-segregated teams; nor does the law require that institutions provide completely gender-integrated athletics programs. To the extent that Title IX allows institutions to maintain single-sex teams and gender-segregated athletics programs, men and women do not compete against each other for places on team rosters. Accordingly, and notwithstanding Brown's protestations to the contrary, the Title VII concept of the "qualified pool" has no place in a Title IX analysis of equal athletics opportunities for male and female athletes because women are not "qualified" to compete for positions on men's teams, and vice-versa. In addition, the concept of "preference" does not have the same meaning, or raise the same equality concerns, as it does in the employment and admissions contexts.

Brown's approach fails to recognize that, because gender-segregated teams are the norm in intercollegiate athletics programs, athletics differs from admissions and employment in analytically material ways. In providing for gender-segregated teams, intercollegiate athletics programs necessarily allocate opportunities separately for male and female students, and, thus, any inquiry into a claim of gender discrimination must compare the athletics participation opportunities provided for men with those provided for women. For this reason, and because recruitment of interested athletes is at the discretion of the institution, there is a risk that the institution will recruit only enough women to fill positions in a program that already underrepresents women, and that the smaller size of the women's program will have the effect of discouraging women's participation.

In this unique context, Title IX operates to ensure that the gender-segregated allocation of athletics opportunities does not disadvantage either gender. Rather than create a quota or preference, this unavoidably gender-conscious comparison merely provides for the allocation of athletics resources and participation opportunities between the sexes in a non-discriminatory manner. . . .

* * *

F.

Brown has contended throughout this litigation that the significant disparity in athletics opportunities for men and women at Brown is the result of a gender-based differential in the level of interest in sports and that the district court's application of the three-part test requires universities to provide athletics opportunities for women to an extent that exceeds their relative interests and abilities in sports. Thus, at the heart of this litigation is the question whether Title IX permits Brown to deny its female students equal opportunity to participate in sports, based upon its unproven assertion that the district court's finding of a significant disparity in athletics opportunities for male and female students reflects, not discrimination in Brown's intercollegiate athletics program, but a lack of interest on the part of its female students that is unrelated to a lack of opportunities.

We view Brown's argument that women are less interested than men in participating in intercollegiate athletics, as well as its conclusion that institutions should be required to accommodate the interests and abilities of its female students only to the extent that it accommodates the interests and abilities of its male students, with great suspicion. To assert that Title IX permits institutions to provide fewer athletics participation opportunities for women than for men, based upon the premise that women are less interested in sports than are men, is (among other things) to ignore the fact that Title IX was enacted in order to remedy discrimination that results from stereotyped notions of women's interests and abilities.

Interest and ability rarely develop in a vacuum; they evolve as a function of opportunity and experience. The Policy Interpretation recognizes that women's lower rate of participation in athletics reflects women's historical lack of opportunities to participate in sports. *See* 44 Fed. Reg. at 71,419 ("Participation in intercollegiate sports has historically been emphasized for men but not women. Partially as a consequence of this, participation rates of women are far below those of men"). . . .

Thus, there exists the danger that, rather than providing a true measure of women's interest in sports, statistical evidence purporting to reflect women's interest instead provides only a measure of the very discrimination that is and has been the basis for women's lack of opportunity to participate in sports. Prong three requires some kind of evidence of interest in athletics, and the Title IX framework permits the use of statistical evidence in assessing the level of interest in sports.[15]

---

[15] Under the Policy Interpretation, institutions may determine the athletic interests and abilities of students by nondiscriminatory methods of their choosing provided:
   a. The processes take into account the nationally increasing levels of women's interests and abilities;
   b. The methods of determining interest and ability do not disadvantage the members of an underrepresented sex;
   c. The methods of determining ability take into account team performance records; and
   d. The methods are responsive to the expressed interests of students capable of intercollegiate competition who are members of an underrepresented sex.
44 Fed. Reg. at 71,417.

Nevertheless, to allow a numbers-based lack-of-interest defense to become the instrument of further discrimination against the underrepresented gender would pervert the remedial purpose of Title IX. We conclude that, even if it can be empirically demonstrated that, at a particular time, women have less interest in sports than do men, such evidence, standing alone, cannot justify providing fewer athletics opportunities for women than for men. Furthermore, such evidence is completely irrelevant where, as here, viable and successful women's varsity teams have been demoted or eliminated. We emphasize that, on the facts of this case, Brown's lack-of-interest arguments are of no consequence. As the prior panel recognized, while the question of full and effective accommodation of athletics interests and abilities is potentially a complicated issue where plaintiffs seek to create a new team or to elevate to varsity status a team that has never competed in varsity competition, no such difficulty is presented here, where plaintiffs seek to reinstate what were successful university-funded teams right up until the moment the teams were demoted. . . .[16]

On these facts, Brown's failure to accommodate fully and effectively the interests and abilities of the underrepresented gender is clearly established. . . . Under these circumstances, the district court's finding that there are interested women able to compete at the university-funded varsity level is clearly correct. Finally, the tremendous growth in women's participation in sports since Title IX was enacted disproves Brown's argument that women are less interested in sports for reasons unrelated to lack of opportunity. *See, e.g.*, Mike Tharp et al., *Sports crazy! Ready, set, go. Why we love our games*, U.S. News & World Report, July 15, 1996, at 33–34 (attributing to Title IX the explosive growth of women's participation in sports and the debunking of "the traditional myth that women aren't interested in sports"). [Note that in a portion of *Brown I* not included in the

---

The 1990 version of the Title IX Athletics Investigator's Manual, an internal agency document, instructs investigating officials to consider, inter alia, the following: (i) any institutional surveys or assessments of students' athletics interests and abilities, see Valerie M. Bonnette & Lamar Daniel, *Department of Education, Title IX Athletics Investigator's Manual* at 22 (1990); (ii) the "expressed interests" of the underrepresented gender, id. at 25; (iii) other programs indicative of interests and abilities, such as club and intramural sports, sports programs at "feeder" schools, community and regional sports programs, and physical education classes, id.

As the district court noted, however, the agency characterizes surveys as a "simple way to identify which additional sports might appropriately be created to achieve compliance. . . . Thus, a survey of interests would follow a determination that an institution does not satisfy prong three; it would not be utilized to make that determination in the first instance." *Cohen III*, 897 F. Supp. at 210 n.51; see 1990 *Investigator's Manual* at 27 (explaining that a survey or assessment of interests and abilities is not required by the Title IX regulation or the Policy Interpretation but may be required as part of a remedy when OCR has concluded that an institution's current program does not equally effectively accommodate the interests and abilities of students).

[16] The district court found that the women's gymnastics team had won the Ivy League championship in 1989–90 and was a "thriving university-funded varsity team prior to the 1991 demotion;" that the donor-funded women's fencing team had been successful for many years and that its request to be upgraded to varsity status had been supported by the athletics director at the time; that the donor-funded women's ski team had been consistently competitive despite a meager budget; and that the club-status women's water polo team had demonstrated the interest and ability to compete at full varsity status. *Cohen III*, 879 F. Supp. at 190.

prior excerpt, the First Circuit had observed, in this regard, that Brown University had introduced no "evidence in the record that men are any more likely to engage in athletics than women, absent socialization and disparate opportunities." 991 F.2d at 900.]

Brown's relative interests approach is not a reasonable interpretation of the three-part test. This approach contravenes the purpose of the statute and the regulation because it does not permit an institution or a district court to remedy a gender-based disparity in athletics participation opportunities. Instead, this approach freezes that disparity by law, thereby disadvantaging further the underrepresented gender. Had Congress intended to entrench, rather than change, the status quo—with its historical emphasis on men's participation opportunities to the detriment of women's opportunities—it need not have gone to all the trouble of enacting Title IX.

* * *

Of course, a remedy that requires an institution to cut, add, or elevate the status of athletes or entire teams may impact the genders differently, but this will be so only if there is a gender-based disparity with respect to athletics opportunities to begin with, which is the only circumstance in which prong three comes into play. Here, however, it has not been shown that Brown's men students will be disadvantaged by the full and effective accommodation of the athletics interests and abilities of its women students.

VII.

[While the circuit court majority upheld the district court's ruling that Brown's athletic program was in violation of Title IX, the panel refused to endorse the remedial order that required Brown to upgrade its existing women's gymnastics, fencing, skiing, and water polo teams to university-funded varsity status. The Court said that Brown should have the option to cut back, instead, on its men's varsity slots in order to put itself in compliance with the law.]

* * *

There can be no doubt that Title IX has changed the face of women's sports as well as our society's interest in and attitude toward women athletes and women's sports. In addition, there is ample evidence that increased athletics participation opportunities for women and young girls, available as a result of Title IX enforcement, have had salutary effects in other areas of societal concern.

One need look no further than the impressive performances of our country's women athletes in the 1996 Olympic Summer Games to see that Title IX has had a dramatic and positive impact on the capabilities of our women athletes, particularly in team sports. These Olympians represent the first full generation of women to grow up under the aegis of Title IX. The unprecedented success of these athletes is due, in no small measure, to Title IX's beneficent effects on women's sports, as the athletes themselves have acknowledged time and again. What stimulated this remarkable change in the quality of women's athletic competition was not a sudden, anomalous upsurge in women's interest in sports, but the enforcement of Title IX's mandate of gender equity in sports.

Affirmed in part, reversed in part, and remanded for further proceedings. No costs on appeal to either party.

TORRUELLA, CHIEF JUDGE (Dissenting).

Because I am not persuaded that the majority's view represents the state of the law today, I respectfully dissent.

* * *

II. Brown's Equal Protection Challenge

* * *

A. The District Court's Construction of the Three-Prong Test

1. *Prong One*

A central issue in this case is the manner in which athletic "participation opportunities" are counted. During the 1990–91 academic year, Brown fielded 16 men's and 15 women's varsity teams on which 566 men and 328 women participated. By the 1993–94 year, there were 12 university-funded men's teams and 13 university funded women's teams. These teams included 479 men and 312 women. Based on an analysis of membership in varsity teams, the district court concluded that there existed a disparity between female participation in intercollegiate athletics and female student enrollment.

Even assuming that membership numbers in varsity sports is a reasonable proxy for participation opportunities—a view with which I do not concur—contact sports should be eliminated from the calculus. The regulation at 34 C.F.R. § 106.41 (1995)(b) provides that an academic institution may operate separate teams for members of each sex "where selection of such teams is based upon competitive skill or the activity involved is a contact sport." 34 C.F.R. § 106.41(b). . . . The regulation, therefore, allows schools to operate single-sex teams in contact sports. In counting participation opportunities, therefore, it does not make sense to include in the calculus athletes participating in contact sports that include only men's teams. For example, if a university chooses to sponsor a football team, it is permitted to sponsor only a men's team. Not all sports are the same and the university should be given the flexibility to determine which activities are most beneficial to its student body. By including in its accounting a contact sport that requires very large numbers of participants, *e.g.*, football, the district court skews the number of athletic participants—making it impossible for the university to provide both men's and women's teams in other sports.

If the athletes competing in sports for which the university is permitted to field single-sex teams are excluded from the calculation of participation rates, the proportion of women participants would increase dramatically and prong one might be satisfied. If so, the inquiry ends and Brown should be judged to be in compliance.

2. Prong Two

The district court concluded, and the majority appears to agree, that Brown failed to satisfy prong two because "merely reducing program offerings to the overrepresented gender does not constitute program expansion for the underrepresented gender." This is a curious result because the entire three-prong test is based on relative participation rates. Prong one, for example, requires that participation opportunities be provided proportionately to enrollment, but does not mandate any absolute number of such opportunities. The district court's conclusion with respect to prong two, however, implies that a school must not only demonstrate that the proportion of women in their program is growing over time, it must also show that the absolute number of women participating is increasing.[26]

Under the district court's interpretation, a school facing budgetary constraints must, in order to comply with prong two, increase the opportunities available to the underrepresented gender, even if it cannot afford to do so.... I see no possible justification for this interpretation—the regulation is intended to protect against discrimination, not to promote athletics on college campuses. A school is not required to sponsor an athletic program of any particular size. It is not for the courts, or the legislature, for that matter, to mandate programs of a given size. The most that can be demanded is that athletics be provided in a non-discriminatory manner.

* * *

3. Prong Three

Prong three of the three-prong test states that, where an institution does not comply with prongs one or two, compliance will be assessed on the basis of

> whether it can be demonstrated that the interests and abilities of the members of the [proportionately underrepresented] sex have been fully and effectively accommodated by the present program.

---

[26] This requirement presents a dilemma for a school in which women are less interested in athletics, as Brown contends is the case. Under such conditions, a school may be unable to succeed under the second prong because there may not be enough interested female students to achieve a continuing increase in the number of female participants.

44 Fed. Reg. 71,413, 71,418 (December 11, 1979).

According to the district court, Brown's athletics program violates prong three because members of the proportionately underrepresented sex have demonstrated interest sufficient for a university-funded varsity team that is not in fact being funded. The district court asserts that this is not a quota. Brown, on the other hand, argues that prong three is satisfied when (1) the interests and abilities of members of the proportionately underrepresented gender (2) are accommodated to the same degree as the proportionately overrepresented gender.

The district court's narrow, literal interpretation should be rejected because prong three cannot be read in isolation. First, as Brown points out, the Regulation that includes prong three provides that, in assessing compliance under the regulation, "the governing principle in this area is that the athletic interests and abilities of male and female students be equally effectively accommodated." *Policy Interpretation*, 44 Fed. Reg. 71,413, 71,414. Thus, Brown contends, to meet "fully"—in an absolute sense—the interests and abilities of an underrepresented gender, while unmet interest among the overrepresented gender continues, would contravene the governing principle of "equally effective accommodation" of the interests and abilities of students of both genders.

It is also worthwhile to note that to "fully" accommodate the interests and abilities of the underrepresented sex is an extraordinarily high— perhaps impossibly so—requirement. How could an academic institution with a large and diverse student body ever "fully" accommodate the athletic interests of its students? Under even the largest athletic program, it would be surprising to find that there is not a single student who would prefer to participate in athletics but does not do so because the school does not offer a program in the particular sport that interests the student. To read fully in an absolute sense would make the third prong virtually impossible to satisfy and, therefore, an irrelevant addition to the test....

In light of the above, Brown argues that prong three is in fact ambiguous with respect to whether "fully" means (1) an institution must meet 100% of the underrepresented gender's unmet reasonable interest and ability, or (2) an institution must meet the underrepresented gender's unmet reasonable interest and ability as fully as it meets those of the overrepresented gender. I agree with Brown that, in the context of OCR's Policy Interpretation, prong three is susceptible to at least these two plausible interpretations.

Additionally, § 1681(a), a provision enacted by Congress as part of Title IX itself, casts doubt on the district court's reading of prong three. 20 U.S.C. § 1681(a) (1988). As Brown points out, Title IX, of which the Policy Interpretation is an administrative interpretation, contains language that prohibits the ordering of preferential treatment on the basis of gender due to a failure of a program to substantially mirror the gender ratio of an institution. Specifically, with respect to Title IX's guarantee that no person shall be excluded on the basis of sex from "participation in, denied the benefits of or subjected to discrimination under any education program or activity receiving Federal financial assistance," 20 U.S.C. § 1681(a),

> nothing contained [therein] shall be interpreted to require any educational institution to grant preferential or disparate treatment to the members of one sex on account of an imbalance which may exist with respect to the total number or percentage of persons of the sex participating in or receiving the benefits of any federally supported program or activity, in comparison with the total number or percentage of persons of that sex in any community.

Id. § 1681(b). Section 1681(b) provides yet another reason why the district court's reading of prong three is troublesome and why Brown's reading is a reasonable alternative.

* * *

B. The District Court's Interpretation and the Resulting Equal Protection Problem

The district court's interpretation of prongs one and three creates an Equal Protection problem, which I analyze in two steps. First, the district court's interpretation creates a quota scheme. Second, even assuming such a quota scheme is otherwise constitutional, appellees have not pointed to an "exceedingly persuasive justification," *see Virginia*, 116 S. Ct. at 2274, for this particular quota scheme.

1. The Quota

I believe that the three prong test, as the district court interprets it, is a quota. I am in square disagreement with the majority, who believe that "no aspect of the Title IX regime at issue in this case . . . mandates gender-based preferences or quotas." Put another way, I agree that "Title IX is not an affirmative action statute," but I believe that is exactly what the district court has made of it. As interpreted by the district court, the test constitutes an affirmative action, quota-based scheme.

* * *

The majority claims that "neither the Policy Interpretation nor the district court's interpretation of it, mandates statistical balancing." The logic of this position escapes me. A school can satisfy the test in three ways. The first prong is met if the school provides participation opportunities for male and female students in numbers substantially proportionate to their enrollments. This prong surely requires statistical balancing. The second prong is satisfied if an institution that cannot meet prong one can show a "continuing practice of program expansion which is demonstrably responsive to the developing interest and abilities of the members of the underrepresented sex." 44 Fed. Reg. at 71,418. It can hardly be denied that this prong requires statistical balancing as it is essentially a test that requires the school to show that it is moving in the direction of satisfying the first prong. Establishing that a school is moving inexorably closer to satisfying a requirement that demands statistical balancing can only be done by demonstrating an improvement in the statistical balance. In other words, the second prong also requires balancing. Finally, the third prong, interpreted as the majority advocates, dispenses with statistical balancing only because it chooses to accord zero weight to one side of the balance. Even a single person with a reasonable unmet interest defeats compliance. This standard, in fact, goes farther than the straightforward quota test of prong one. According to the district court, the unmet interests of the underrepresented sex must be completely accommodated before any of the interest of the overrepresented gender can be accommodated.[28]

A pragmatic overview of the effect of the three-prong test leads me to reject the majority's claim that the three-prong test does not amount to a quota because it involves multiple prongs. In my view it is the result of the test, and not the number of steps involved, that should determine if a quota system exists. Regardless of how many steps are involved, the fact remains that the test requires proportionate participation opportunities for both sexes (prong one) unless one sex is simply not interested in participating (prong three). It seems to me that a quota with an exception for situations in which there are insufficient interested students to allow the school to meet it remains a quota. All of the negative effects of a quota remain,[29] and the school can escape the quota under prong three only by offering preferential treatment to the group that has demonstrated less interest in athletics.

2. *"Extremely Persuasive Justification" Test*

In view of the quota scheme adopted by the district court, and Congress' specific disavowal of any intent to require quotas as part of Title IX, appellees have not met their burden of showing an "exceedingly

---

[28] The problem with the majority's argument can be illustrated with a hypothetical college admissions policy that would require proportionality between the gender ratio of the local student aged population and that of admitted students. This policy is comparable to prong one of the three prong test and is, without a doubt, a quota. It is no less a quota if an exception exists for schools whose gender ratio differs from that of the local population but which admit every applicant of the underrepresented gender. It remains a quota because the school is forced to admit every female applicant until it reaches the requisite proportion. Similarly, the district court's interpretation requires the school to accommodate the interests of every female student until proportionality is reached.

[29] Nor does the second prong of the test change the analysis. That prong merely recognizes that a school may not be able to meet the quotas of the first or third prong immediately, and therefore deems it sufficient to show program expansion that is responsive to the interests of the underrepresented sex.

persuasive justification" for this gender-conscious exercise of government authority. As recently set forth in *Virginia*, "parties who seek to defend gender-based government action must demonstrate an 'exceedingly persuasive justification' for that action." *Virginia*, 116 S. Ct. at 2274. . . .

I believe that the district court's interpretation of the Policy Interpretation's three-prong test poses serious constitutional difficulties. "Where an otherwise acceptable construction of a statute would raise serious constitutional problems, [we] construe the statute to avoid such problems unless such construction is plainly contrary to the intent of Congress." *Edward J. DeBartolo Corp. v. Florida Gulf Coast Bldg. & Constr. Trades Council*, 485 U.S. 568 (1988); *see NLRB v. Catholic Bishop of Chicago*, 440 U.S. 490, 507 (1979). To the extent that Congress expressed a specific intent germane to the district court's interpretation, Congress, if anything, expressed an aversion to quotas as a method to enforce Title IX. As a result, I opt for Brown's construction of prong three, which, as we have discussed, infra, is also a reasonable reading.

III. Evidentiary Issues

In disputes over the representation of women in athletic programs, it is inevitable that statistical evidence will be relevant. There is simply no other way to assess participation rates, interest levels, and abilities. . . . [H]owever, when the level of interest among women at Brown is at issue, the court adopts a [very] critical attitude towards statistical evidence: "There exists the danger that, rather than providing a true measure of women's interest in sports, statistical evidence purporting to reflect women's interest instead provides only a measure of the very discrimination that is and has been the basis for women's lack of opportunity." In other words, evidence of differential levels of interest is not to be credited because it may simply reflect the result of past discrimination.

The refusal to accept surveys of interest levels as evidence of interest raises the question of what indicators might be used. The majority offers no guidance to a school seeking to assess the levels of interest of its students. Although the three-prong test, even as interpreted by the district court, appears to allow the school the opportunity to show a lack of interest, the majority rejects the best—and perhaps the only—mechanism for making such a showing.

Brown claims that the district court erred in excluding evidence pertaining to the relative athletic interests of men and women at the university. Brown sought to introduce the NCAA Gender Equity Study and the results of an undergraduate poll on student interest in athletics, but was not permitted to do so. The majority is unsympathetic to Brown's claim that the disparity between athletic opportunities for men and women reflect a gender-based difference in interest levels. Indeed, despite Brown's attempt to present evidence in support of its claim, the majority characterizes Brown's argument as an "unproven assertion."[30]

* * *

In addition, the majority has put the power to control athletics and the provision of athletic resources in the hands of the underrepresented gender. Virtually every other aspect of college life is entrusted to the institution, but athletics has now been carved out as an exception and the university is no longer in full control of its program. Unless the two genders participate equally in athletics, members of the underrepresented sex would have the ability to demand a varsity level team at any time if they can show sufficient interest. Apparently no weight is given to the sustainability of the interest, the cost of the sport, the university's view on the desirability of the sport, and so on.

* * *

Accordingly, I would reverse and remand for further proceedings.

Notes and Questions

1. *Aftermath.* The court's decision clearly establishes Title IX as requiring equity in athletic opportunities for women. The decision gave support to the OCR, which continues to enforce Title IX under its three-prong test.

2. *Anti-Discrimination Versus Affirmative Action.* The majority opinion makes clear that Title IX is an anti-discrimination statute, not an affirmative action statute. What is the difference? Why is this difference significant?

3. *Torruella Dissent.* What is the basis for the dissenter's view? Do you find his argument persuasive? Why or why not?

The role of Executive Branch administrators in setting Title IX enforcement policy continued with further clarifications concerning the three-prong approach reflected in Department of Education Guidelines. In

---

[30] Among the evidence submitted by Brown are: (i) admissions data showing greater athletic interest among male applicants than female applicants; (ii) college board data showing greater athletic interest and prior participation rates by prospective male applicants than female applicants; (iii) data from the Cooperative Institutional Research Program at UCLA indicating greater athletic interest among men than women; (iv) an independent telephone survey of 500 randomly selected Brown undergraduates that reveals that Brown offers women participation opportunities in excess of their representation in the pool of interested, qualified students; (v) intramural and club participation rates that demonstrate higher participation rates among men than women; (vi) walk-on and try-out numbers that reflect a greater interest among men than women; (vii) high school participation rates that show a much lower rate of participation among females than among males; (viii) the NCAA Gender Equity Committee data showing that women across the country participate in athletics at a lower rate than men.

2005, a Bush Administration official in the Department's Office of Civil Rights issued an additional clarification. The clarification provided:

> Under the third compliance option, an educational institution is in compliance with Title IX's mandate to provide equal athletic participation opportunities if, despite the underrepresentation of one sex in the intercollegiate athletics program, the institution is fully and effectively accommodating the athletic interests and abilities of its students who are underrepresented in its current varsity athletic program offerings. An institution will be found in compliance with part three unless there exists a sport (s) for the underrepresented sex for which all three of the following conditions are met: (1) unmet interest sufficient to sustain a varsity team in the sport(s); (2) sufficient ability to sustain an intercollegiate team in the sport(s); and (3) reasonable expectation of intercollegiate competition for a team in the sport(s) within the school's normal competitive region. Thus, schools are not required to accommodate the interests and abilities of all their students or fulfill every request for the addition or elevation of particular sports, unless all three conditions are present. In this analysis, the burden of proof is on OCR (in the case of an OCR investigation or compliance review), or on students (in the case of a complaint filed with the institution under its Title IX grievance procedures), to show by a preponderance of the evidence that the institution is not in compliance with part three.

Moreover, the letter indicated that a properly devised survey can demonstrate

> insufficient interest to support an additional varsity team for the underrepresented sex will create a presumption of compliance with part three of the three-part test and the Title IX regulatory requirement to provide nondiscriminatory athletic participation opportunities. The presumption of compliance can only be overcome if OCR finds direct and very persuasive evidence of unmet interest sufficient to sustain a varsity team, such as the recent elimination of a viable team for the underrepresented sex or a recent, broad-based petition from an existing club team for elevation to varsity status.

In 2010, the Obama Administration's Assistant Secretary of Education for Civil Rights announced that this letter had been withdrawn. The policy change reflected in the letter seems to be that email or internet surveys can no longer be the principle basis for demonstrating the absence of unmet need under Prong Three. The letter, however, reaffirmed standing policy that OCR would find a violation if (1) there was unmet interest in a particular sport, (2) there is sufficient ability to sustain a team in the sport, and (3) there was reasonable expectation of competition for the team.

This dispute plays out most clearly at schools where those likely to participate in a new varsity sport are current students. How does the policy work at Division I schools where almost all beneficiaries of an institution's decision to add a new sport will be newly recruited athletes, who would otherwise be student-athletes at other institutions?

Around the same time that Brown implemented the court's decision and added new women's teams, a Louisiana district court judge rejected the major legal premise to the *Cohen* opinion, though she ultimately reached the same verdict on the specific facts of her case. *See Pederson v. Louisiana State University*, 912 F. Supp. 892 (M.D. La.1996). Louisiana State had first created a football team in 1893, a baseball team in 1908, and several other men's varsity sports after that. Not until 1977, though, did LSU create its first women's varsity teams: volleyball, gymnastics, basketball, tennis, and swimming, with golf added in 1979 and track and field in 1981. Women's fast-pitch softball was also made a varsity sport in 1979 but then dropped in 1982 for no expressed reasons. By the 1990s, LSU's student body was 49% female, but its varsity athletes were just 29% female. In 1993, pursuant to a Southeastern Conference mandate (which LSU had initially opposed), the school announced that it would create women's varsity soccer and softball. Play in soccer had begun in 1995 on a limited basis, and softball, with a coach hired, was planned to start in the spring of 1997. Even so, this lawsuit was filed in 1994 by female student-athletes in those sports who wanted quicker and stronger action from the school.

In the course of her lengthy opinion, Judge Rebecca Doherty disagreed with the circuit court decisions in *Cohen I* and *Roberts* that had endorsed the OCR's Title IX Policy Interpretation, with its proportionality standard between female athletes and female students. In the judge's opinion, it was a mistake to assume that "the same percentage of [the school's] male population as its female population has the ability to participate and the interest or desire to participate in sports at the same competitive level" (p. 913). Nonetheless, because LSU had produced no "credible evidence to establish what the interests and abilities of its student population are" (p. 915), the school was found liable based on the combination of overall statistical disparity, demonstrated interest and ability in these particular sports among at least some of its current students, and the lack of ongoing expansion of athletic opportunities for its female students as a whole. While Judge Doherty was prepared to issue injunctive relief for the future, she rejected this first-ever request by student-athletes for monetary damages under Title IX. On the assumption that Title IX authorized damages only for *intentional* violations, the Judge said that while this question is "a very close one," LSU's violations were not intentional. "Rather, they are a result of arrogant ignorance, confusion regarding the practical requirements of the law, and a remarkably outdated view of women and athletics which created the byproduct of resistance to change" (p. 918).

On appeal, the Fifth Circuit reversed only this damages part of the district court's judgment. *See* 201 F.3d 388 (5th Cir. 2000). The appeals court not only confirmed the conclusion that LSU's 49% to 29% gap between the female share of all undergraduate students and of athletes constituted a violation of Title IX, but also decided that this was "intentional discrimination," rather than just "arrogant ignorance" based on "archaic and antiquated" views about what women really wanted. The Court relied in particular on the comments and conduct of LSU's Athletic Director, Joe Dean, who had called one of the plaintiffs "honey," "cutie," and "sweetie," said he preferred women's soccer over other sports because the players looked "cute in their shorts," and had disbanded women's softball back in 1982 because of what he judged to be "immoral" sexual preferences by many of its players.

If LSU provided the quintessential example of what not to do in responding to the requirements of Title IX, Syracuse University provides a counter-example of how schools can comply with Title IX even when they are unable to achieve proportionality. The Second Circuit case below assesses a challenge to the response of the Syracuse athletic department to Title IX.

BOUCHER V. SYRACUSE UNIVERSITY
164 F.3d 113 (2d Cir. 1999)

CALABRESI, CIRCUIT JUDGE.

Former female club athletes at Syracuse University ("Syracuse" or "the University") appeal from an April 3, 1998 judgment of the United States District Court for the Northern District of New York (Frederick J. Scullin, Jr., J.) granting summary judgment to Syracuse on a Title IX accommodation claim. Plaintiffs also appeal two orders of June 12, 1996. The first such order dismissed their Title IX equal treatment claims, and the second conditionally certified a class.

We affirm in part, dismiss the appeal in part, and vacate and remand in part.

FACTS AND PROCEDURAL HISTORY

Plaintiff students "individually and on behalf of all others similarly situated" filed suit in May of 1995 against Syracuse University, alleging numerous violations of Title IX of the Education Amendments of 1972, 20

U.S.C. §§ 1681–1688, and its governing regulations. Seven of the eight named plaintiffs were at that time members of Syracuse's club lacrosse team and the eighth was a member of the University's club softball team. All plaintiffs have since graduated from the University.

The plaintiffs argued that Syracuse discriminated against female athletes in its allocation of participation opportunities (which includes decisions regarding which varsity teams to field as well as how many opportunities for participation by female varsity athletes are thereby created as a result of those decisions). Plaintiffs also alleged that Syracuse provided unequal benefits to varsity female athletes as compared to varsity male athletes, and provided unequal scholarship funding to varsity female athletes as compared to varsity male athletes.

Plaintiffs sought class certification in view of the fact that college students are a fluid group and that without such certification, mootness issues would likely arise. *See, e.g., Cook v. Colgate Univ.*, 992 F.2d 17, 19–20 (2d Cir. 1993) (holding a Title IX appeal moot, once plaintiffs, seeking injunctive relief, had graduated). In their equal treatment claims, plaintiffs asked for declaratory and injunctive relief ordering the University to provide equal benefits and scholarships to varsity male and female athletes. In their accommodation claim, plaintiffs sought the establishment of varsity lacrosse and softball teams for women.

Just over 50% of the Syracuse's student population is female, yet, when this complaint was filed, women made up only 32.4% of its athletes. In its 1993–94 National Collegiate Athletic Association submission, Syracuse stated that of its 681 varsity student-athletes, 217 were women, while 464 were men. These numbers reflected a 19% disparity between the percentage of varsity athletes who were female and the percentage of the University's students who were female.

At the time that this suit was begun in May of 1995, the University funded eleven men's varsity teams and nine women's varsity teams. Just prior to the filing of the complaint, Syracuse announced a plan to add two new varsity women's teams to its athletic program-women's varsity soccer and women's varsity lacrosse. These teams began to play, respectively, in the 1996–97 and the 1997–98 academic years, thus bringing the number of varsity teams funded by the school to eleven men's and eleven women's.

The University established five of its nine women's varsity teams in 1971 when it first funded women's varsity sports. It dropped one of these sports (fencing) in 1972, and replaced it with field hockey. Crew was added as a women's varsity team in 1977. Three additional women's sports were added to the varsity roster in 1981. After 1981, no new women's varsity team was created by the University until the addition of the varsity soccer team in 1997. Thus, until the filing of this complaint in 1995, fourteen years passed by without the University creating any new women's varsity teams. In the course of this litigation, Syracuse announced plans to institute a varsity women's softball team which, according to the University's representations at oral argument, will begin play in the 1999–2000 academic year.

* * *

On June 12, 1996, the district court granted summary judgment to the University on plaintiffs' equal treatment claims-those that challenged the alleged unequal allocation of benefits and scholarships between varsity men's and women's teams (brought under 34 C.F.R. § 106.41(c)(2)–(8), (10) and 34 C.F.R. § 106.37). The court held that since none of the named plaintiffs were varsity athletes, they did not have standing to assert the equal treatment claims. Its ruling on this issue was proper and we affirm the dismissal of plaintiffs' equal treatment claims substantially for the reasons the district court gave. *See Boucher v. Syracuse Univ.*, No. 95-CV-620, 1996 WL 328444 (N.D.N.Y. June 12, 1996). At the same time, the court ruled that plaintiffs could go forward with their accommodation claim and additionally deemed that the plaintiffs could pursue an equal treatment claim challenging the allocation of funds between male and female club teams-an action that the plaintiffs had not brought and never litigated. *See id.* at *4.

In a separate order issued the same day, the district court held that the plaintiffs' proposed class included members with conflicting interests. *See Boucher v. Syracuse Univ.*, No. 95-CV620, 1996 WL 328441, at *2 & n. 2 (N.D.N.Y. June 12, 1996). Finding that "the factual allegations [of plaintiffs' complaint] only address the need for women's varsity lacrosse and women's varsity softball," the court defined two possible classes: present and future lacrosse players who desire to play varsity lacrosse, and present and future softball players who want to play varsity softball. *Id.* at *2.

The district court reached its conclusion as to appropriate classes by analyzing whether lacrosse and softball players could exist together as one class under Rule 23. That rule requires that: (1) questions of law or fact are common to the class; (2) claims or defenses of the representative parties are typical of those of the class; (3) class representatives are members of the class who possess the same interests and suffered the same injuries as class members; and (4) members of the class are so numerous that joinder would be impracticable. *See* Fed. R. Civ. P. 23(a). Although it found that commonality and typicality existed, the court determined that the two classes were in conflict because " 'in an era of static enrollment and increasing financial demands on institutions of higher learning, the resources available for intercollegiate athletic programs are finite' " and hence that compliance might well be achieved by the elevation of one sport and not the other. *Boucher*, 1996 WL 328441, at *4 (quoting *Bryant v.*

Colgate Univ., 93-CV-1029, 1996 WL 328446, at *15 (N.D.N.Y. June 11, 1996)).

Since the majority of plaintiffs were lacrosse players, the court decided to certify only the current and future "would be" varsity lacrosse players. This certification was made conditional on a demonstration by plaintiffs that joinder of all relevant members of the class would be impractical. *See id.* at *5. The district court did not certify a class of women, current and future, who wished to play varsity softball "because of the potential conflict of interest discussed above." *Id.* at *4 n. 4.

* * *

DISCUSSION

A. Lacrosse.

Syracuse argues that this appeal is moot because it has already implemented a varsity women's lacrosse team and that there is, therefore, nothing left for the certified class to pursue. The plaintiffs counter that the appeal is not moot for two reasons. First, they state that they sought to amend their complaint in the district court to add a claim for damages and that the court improperly denied their motion. Second, they argue that their suit did not merely seek class certification of current and future students interested in playing varsity lacrosse, but that they also sought class certification of current and numerous future students interested in playing varsity softball, itself not yet a varsity sport.

It may well be that mootness would have been avoided had plaintiffs originally requested damages in their complaint. *See Cook*, 992 F.2d at 19–20 (noting that "a viable claim for damages generally avoids mootness of the action," but finding a Title IX appeal moot where plaintiffs had graduated, had sought relief solely on their own behalf, and had not appealed the district court's denial of their request for damages); *see also id.* at 19 (holding that an interest in preserving an award of attorneys' fees "is insufficient, standing alone, to sustain jurisdiction"). A request for damages, however, will not avoid mootness if it was "inserted after the complaint was filed in an attempt to breathe life into a moribund dispute." *McCabe v. Nassau County Med. Ctr.*, 453 F.2d 698, 702 (2d Cir.1971).

In the case before us, plaintiffs did not seek to amend their complaint to add a damages claim until three months after the University filed its motion for summary judgment and six months after the district court granted the University leave to file that motion. Moreover, in their papers in opposition to the University's motion, plaintiffs' counsel represented that if the district court were to enter an order binding the University to its promise to establish varsity women's lacrosse and softball teams, then "plaintiffs shall submit an application for attorney's fees as there is no longer a controversy between the parties" (emphasis added). And on appeal, plaintiffs' counsel, despite being asked numerous times at oral argument to specify precisely what relief plaintiffs sought, failed ever to mention damages. *See Perrucci v. Gaffey*, 450 F.2d 356, 358 (2d Cir. 1971) (dismissing appeal as moot where pro se plaintiff indicated at oral argument that he was not concerned with damages allegations). Under the circumstances, we are satisfied that the district court did not err in denying plaintiffs leave to amend their complaint to add a damages claim.

We, therefore, hold that insofar as plaintiffs' complaint sought a varsity lacrosse team, the claim is now moot, given that the team has been created and is already participating in intercollegiate play. *See County of Los Angeles v. Davis*, 440 U.S. 625, 631–32 (1979) (finding case moot where there was no reasonable expectation that the alleged violation would recur). Accordingly, we take no position on whether the safe harbor defense made by Syracuse and granted by the district court was valid.

B. Softball.

Plaintiffs also contest the district court's failure to certify a sub-class of current and future women interested in playing varsity softball. They argue that this issue is not moot because such a team has not yet begun play. We agree with both contentions.

District judges have broad discretion over class definition. But under Rule 23(c)(1), courts are "required to reassess their class rulings as the case develops." *Barnes v. The American Tobacco Co.*, 161 F.3d 127, 140 (3d Cir. 1998) (citing *Kuehner v. Heckler*, 778 F.2d 152, 163 (3d Cir. 1985)); *see also Marisol A. v. Giuliani*, 126 F.3d 372, 378–79 (2d Cir. 1997) (affirming class certification but ordering a district court to divide the certified class into subclasses); *Richardson v. Byrd*, 709 F.2d 1016, 1019 (5th Cir. 1983) ("Under Rule 23 . . . [t]he district judge must define, redefine, subclass, and decertify as appropriate in response to the progression of the case from assertion to facts."). And we agree with the Fifth Circuit that "[o]rdinarily, if a court discerns a conflict . . . the proper solution is to create subclasses of persons whose interests are in accord." *Payne v. Travenol Labs, Inc.*, 673 F.2d 798, 812 (5th Cir.1982). We conclude that although the district court correctly found potential conflicts between members of a class that included both women interested in playing varsity lacrosse and women who wished to play varsity softball, it should have certified two sub-classes-one for each sport-rather than certifying only one class and excluding from that class members of the second.

That being said, the University represented both to the district court and to this Court that a varsity women's softball team is in the process of being established, and that the team will begin play during the 1999–2000 academic year. Because full implementation of a varsity women's softball team would render the remaining live aspect of this case moot, we again choose not to reach the merits of the University's safe harbor defense, and prefer instead to remand the case to the district court with instructions to dismiss the case if the University completes its plan to institute a varsity women's softball team by the date indicated. Should the University not live up to its representations, the district court is ordered to certify a class of current and future women students interested in playing varsity softball and to revisit the merits of the case at that time.

C. Club Athletes.

Although nowhere in their complaint did plaintiffs challenge the allocation of funding between female and male club sports at Syracuse, the district court certified a class of female club athletes to prosecute such a claim. The plaintiffs did not pursue discovery or take any action on this claim-which was essentially created by the district court. Nonetheless, the court granted summary judgment to Syracuse. This was error. A court cannot create a cause of action that a party did not raise (and has no intention of pursuing) and then decide the issue against that party. Beyond the fact that the court is without the power to do so, any ruling on such unargued claims makes law and may bind parties on issues not adequately presented. Such results are to be rigorously avoided. We therefore vacate the district court's ruling on this claim.

D. A Broader Claim.

From time to time, appellants have suggested that their real claim in this suit is to represent all women, present and future, who wish to be varsity athletes at Syracuse-regardless of sport. And in this respect they suggest that "[i]nterest and ability rarely develop in a vacuum; they evolve as a function of opportunity and experience." *Cohen v. Brown Univ.*, 101 F.3d 155, 179 (1st Cir.1996) ("Cohen II"), *cert. denied*, 520 U.S. 1186 (1997). They add that it was to ensure such opportunities that Congress passed Title IX. For this reason, they further contend that the importance of Title IX cannot be overstated.

We are inclined to agree. But just as the district court cannot establish a claim for equal treatment for club athletes when that is not presented, so also we cannot create a class of those women who are interested in varsity athletics at Syracuse generally when that issue was never clearly presented in the complaint nor during the prosecution of this case. Too often, both in their briefs, and at oral argument, plaintiffs in this case have made clear that their interests are more specific: equal treatment among varsity athletes, and varsity status for women's lacrosse and softball. Accordingly, we take no position on the merits of such a broader suit. Cf. *Cohen II*, 101 F.3d 155 (upholding suit brought by a similar class against Brown University); *Cohen I*, 991 F.2d 888. It, and the applicability or not of the safe harbor provisions of Title IX as defenses to it, are simply not before us.

* * *

We affirm the district court's dismissal of the plaintiffs' equal treatment claims with respect to varsity athletes for lack of standing. We dismiss the plaintiffs' appeal as to varsity lacrosse as moot. We vacate the district court's class certification order and its order granting summary judgment to the defendant University on plaintiffs' equal treatment claim with respect to club athletes. We remand the case to the district court for further proceedings consistent with this opinion with respect to the plaintiffs' claim as to varsity softball.

AFFIRMED in part, DISMISSED in part, VACATED and REMANDED in part.

NOTES AND QUESTIONS

1. *Syracuse Versus LSU and Brown.* What distinguishes the approach adopted toward Title IX of Syracuse as compared to LSU and Brown? What can athletic directors learn from these opinions?

2. *Safe Harbors.* Of the three safe harbors—proportionality, continued practice of expansion, and satisfaction of the interests of female students in adding another sport—which do you think is the easiest to satisfy? Which is the most difficult?

3. *Challenges of Compliance.* When attempting to comply with Title IX, what tensions does the athletic director face? On the one hand, adding a new sport can generate excitement and opportunity, but also can be a really expensive endeavor, particularly when new facilities are needed, in addition to hiring coaches, buying uniforms and equipment, and subsidizing travel. On the other hand, shutting down a sport to save money can help the budget, but can draw anger and resentment from alumni and fans. Successful fundraising is often a key ingredient underpinning many of these kinds of decisions.

Two lines of inquiry remain in considering this vital issue in both sports and higher education. One is strictly legal in character: what *must* colleges now do in their varsity athletic programs? The other is about the underlying policy question: what *should* colleges do, either the same or more or less than what the circuit courts have endorsed in *Cohen* and the other cases?

Kelley was not the last attempt by male athletes to challenge the disbanding of a men's athletic team. Five years after *Kelley*, two circuit courts rendered decisions about the appropriate treatment of such university action under Title IX. The cases involved claims made by male students that decisions by Illinois State and California State Universities to eliminate male teams to establish a close proportion between the male-female student body and varsity athletes amounted to reverse discrimination in violation of the statute. In both cases, *Boulahanis v. Board of Regents of Illinois State Univ.*, 198 F.3d 633 (7th Cir.1999), and *Neal v. Board of Trustees of California State Universities*, 198 F.3d 763 (9th Cir.1999), the circuit courts followed the lead of the Seventh Circuit five years earlier in its *Kelley* decision, rejected these claims, and accepted the 1979 Policy Interpretation of the Department of Health, Education and Welfare.

In the *Neal* case, in particular, while female students outnumbered the males by 64 percent to 36 percent in 1996, the male students had taken 61 percent of varsity roster spots and 68 percent of athletic scholarship funds. This prompted a lawsuit by the California chapter of the National Organization for Women (NOW) and a consent decree to move the proportion of female athletes to within 5 percent of the proportion of female undergraduates. As partial implementation of that decree, the California State University at Bakersfield (CSUB) decided to reduce all its male team rosters rather than eliminate any of them. Even though the CSUB men's wrestling team was reduced to 27 (then to 25) members, it continued to win the Pac-10 Conference title (although a Division II school in every other sport) and be near the top in the national championship. When the wrestling team filed a lawsuit in the name of Stephen Neal who was not only NCAA, but also world, champion in heavyweight wrestling, the California district court found that "capping the size of the men's team . . . to meet the gender proportionality required in the consent decree" violated the federal Title IX law. On appeal, the Ninth Circuit reached the opposite conclusion.

NEAL V. BOARD OF TRUSTEES OF CALIFORNIA STATE UNIVERSITIES
198 F.3d 763 (9th Cir. 1999)

HALL, CIRCUIT JUDGE.

[After reviewing the facts and the history of both Title IX and the regulations drafted by the Department of Education's Office for Civil Rights (OCR), the circuit court stated as follows.]

> . . . The drafters of these regulations recognized a situation that Congress well understood: male athletes had been given an enormous head start in the race against their female counterparts for athletic resources, and Title IX would prompt universities to level the proverbial playing field.

Appellees recognize that, given this backdrop, it would be imprudent to argue that Title IX prohibits the use of all gender-conscious remedies. Appellees therefore suggest that gender-conscious remedies are appropriate only when necessary to ensure that schools provide opportunities to males and females in proportion to their relative levels of interest in sports participation. By contrast, Appellants contend that schools may make gender-conscious decisions about sports-funding levels to correct for an imbalance between the composition of the undergraduate student body and the composition of the undergraduate student athletic participants pool. This disagreement has real significance: Men's expressed interest in participating in varsity sports is apparently higher than women's at the present time—although the "interest gap" continues to narrow—so permitting gender-conscious remedies until the proportions of students and athletes are roughly proportional gives universities more remedial freedom than permitting remedies only until expressed interest and varsity roster spots correspond.

[After reviewing the reading of Title IX by the First Circuit in *Cohen v. Brown University*, 991 F. 2d 888 (1st Cir.1993) and 101 F. 3d 155 (1st Cir.1996), the *Neal* court continued . . .]

The reason for *Cohen I*'s rejection of Brown's/Appellees' "interest" test was clear enough: "Given that the survey of interests and abilities would begin under circumstances where men's athletic teams have a considerable head start, such a rule would almost certainly blunt the exhortation that schools should 'take into account the nationally increasing levels of women's interests and abilities' and avoid 'disadvantaging members of an under-represented sex. . . .'" 991 F.2d at 900. In other words, Appellees' interpretation of Title IX would have allowed universities to do little or nothing to equalize men's and women's opportunities if they could point to data showing that women were less interested in sports. But a central aspect of Title IX's purpose was to encourage women to participate in sports: the increased number of roster spots and scholarships reserved for women would gradually increase demand among women for those roster spots and scholarships.[4]

* * *

[As the courts in *Cohen* and other Title IX cases have emphasized]

. . . women's interest in sports appeared to be lower than men's, but the genders' interests were slowly but surely converging, which was precisely the reason why requiring only that each gender's expressed interest in participating be accommodated equally would freeze the inequality of the status quo.

Title IX is a dynamic statute, not a static one. It envisions continuing progress toward the goal of equal opportunity for all athletes and

---

[4] That is, the creation of additional athletic spots for women would prompt universities to recruit more female athletes, in the long run shifting women's demand curve for sports participation. As more women participated, social norms discouraging women's participation in sports presumably would be further eroded, prompting additional increases in women's participation levels.

recognizes that, where society has conditioned women to expect less than their fair share of the athletic opportunities, women's interest in participating in sports will not rise to a par with men's overnight. The percentage of college athletes who are women rose from 15% in 1972 to 37% in 1998, and Title IX is at least partially responsible for this trend of increased participation by women. Title IX has altered women's preferences, making them more interested in sports, and more likely to become student athletes. *See* Note, *Cheering on Women and Girls in Sports: Using Title IX to Fight Gender Role Oppression*, 110 Harv. L. Rev. 1627, 1640–41 (1997). Adopting Appellees' interest-based test for Title IX compliance would hinder, and quite possibly reverse, the steady increases in women's participation and interest in sports that have followed Title IX's enactment.[8]

We REVERSE, and VACATE the preliminary injunction.

NOTES AND QUESTIONS

1. *Same Failing Argument.* The *Neal* plaintiffs made the same argument as in *Kelley* and other cases—that disbanding the wrestling team discriminated against the male athletes. Remedying discrimination cannot be, in itself, discriminatory, at least in the context of Title IX. *But see Ricci v. DeStefano*, 557 U.S. 557 (2009) (finding remedying disparate impact can constitute disparate treatment under Title VII).

2. *The Context of Revenue: Blame Game?* Within the context of many athletic departments, the money generated by the revenue sports supports the non-revenue sports like wrestling. While the wrestlers might blame gender equity and Title IX for their loss of scholarships, the bigger picture is often that the athletic department cannot financially support their team. Should the wrestlers really be blaming the revenue sport athletes for not earning enough money to support them? Or the coaches of other sports for taking too much of the athletic budget and not leaving enough money for them? Should they blame themselves for not generating enough revenue?

---

[8] The amicus brief filed by USA Wrestling and a number of other organizations repeatedly invokes the *Adarand* line of cases and Title VII precedents to suggest that the scope of remedial action to correct for disparities among groups is quite limited. Those precedents are not relevant in the context of collegiate athletics. Unlike most employment settings, athletic teams are gender-segregated, and universities must decide beforehand how many athletic opportunities they will allocate to each sex. As a result, determining whether discrimination exists in athletic programs requires gender-conscious, group-wide comparisons. Because men are not "qualified" for women's teams (and vice versa), athletics require a gender-conscious allocation of opportunities in the first instance. The paradigm that has motivated the Supreme Court's more recent reverse-discrimination jurisprudence simply does not fit the case at bar.

Shortly after the Supreme Court refused to address the Title IX issues posed by the *Cohen* case, the National Women's Law Center (NWLC) raised a new issue about the application of Title IX to college sports. The NWLC charged 25 universities with having failed to provide their female athletes with a proportionate share of athletic scholarship funding. The Title IX standard appealed to here would require women athletes to receive within one percentage point the same proportion of their college's expenditures on athletic scholarships as the female share of all the school's athletes (not of the whole student body). The NWLC asserted that the gap meant that the average woman athlete there receives $25,000 less in scholarship assistance over a four-year college career than does her male counterpart.

The problem stems to some extent from the interplay of Title IX and NCAA rules, not just from individual school policies. The NCAA distinguishes between two different kinds of sports: one labeled "head count," which requires full scholarships for any athlete receiving one, and the other "equivalency," which permits partial scholarships that divide up the available maximum numbers among a large roster of players. Football, with its 85 permitted full scholarships, is the major "head count" sport, with basketball (at 13 scholarships) being the only other men's sport in this category. The four women's head count sports—basketball (15), volleyball (12), gymnastics (12), and tennis (8)—together comprise 47 positions. If these were the only sports involved, the award of 98 full-time scholarships (68%) to male athletes and 47 (or 32%) to female, might, it could be argued, satisfy the Title IX proportionality test on this score since every athlete, male and female, would be receiving a full grant-in-aid.

What has been happening historically is that colleges have both reduced the number of positions they have offered on the men's "equivalency" teams (as well as reducing the number of "walk-on" football players without scholarships), and also significantly increased the number of equivalency positions offered on women's teams—in order to place themselves closer to compliance with the *Cohen* standard of female student *participation* in intercollegiate sports. This tactic has, however, exacerbated the gap between the female share of scholarship dollars as compared to the female percentage of all athletes. One possible solution, of course, is to raise the number of equivalency scholarships permitted for female sports, but this has raised a concern among Division I schools that do not play lucrative Division I-A football because they will be at a competitive disadvantage to their Division I-A competitors in non-revenue-producing women's sports on which they cannot afford to spend more dollars.

To date, however, litigation over the number of sports offered to each gender has been largely limited to barring schools from cutting women's sports or upholding voluntary decisions to eliminate men's sports. What would happen if a typical Division I school were sued to challenge the *status quo*? For example, if Penn State were sued because it continues to fail to achieve proportionality, are there many female students in Happy Valley with the interest and ability to compete at the Big Ten level in any sport not currently offered on the varsity level? If not, has Penn State satisfied Prong Three? How would you determine both interest and ability?

NOTES AND QUESTIONS

1. *Can Policy Interpretation Be Improved?* Having read the leading appellate decisions on Title IX challenges to university athletic policies, what is your assessment of the 1979 OCR Policy Interpretation? Setting aside any constitutional questions, do you think that the Policy Interpretation establishes desirable social policy? If not, how would you modify the standards that its sets? Should proportionality be based instead on the athletic interests of the men and women in a school's student body or perhaps on the interests of those in its applicant or potential applicant pool? If so, how should those interests be determined? Will any test be circular because opportunities generate interests?

2. *Addressing the Loss of Men's Teams?* Is the elimination of many collegiate teams a problem that Title IX policy can and should address? Does Title IX provide the Department of Education authority to require schools to achieve gender equity by the expansion of women's programs rather than the contraction of viable men's programs? Does Title IX provide authority to require the NCAA to restrict the size of football teams? Alternatively, can the Department of Education exclude football, or perhaps all revenue producing sports, from the calculation of athletic opportunities? Should it do so? Or should universities and colleges have to decide between allocating a substantial proportion of men's athletic opportunities to football or instead having a greater variety of men's teams?

3. *Constitutionality of the Policy Interpretation.* Should the standards set by the Policy Interpretation be treated as requiring "quotas?" Regardless, inasmuch as the standards are based on gender, must they be subjected to some form of heightened scrutiny under any constitutional equal protection challenge? If so, should they be able to survive such scrutiny? What exactly is the compelling justification for the standards? Is it the avoidance of future or the remedying of past discrimination by the school? What other justification might be compelling in this context?

In recent years, there has been little path breaking litigation involving Title IX. A handful of individuals have brought claims that their universities have violated their rights under Title IX under very specific circumstances, but most of these suits have ended in settlements and none have added significantly to the body of legal doctrine. The primary impetus for change in the way universities try to comply with the law has come from two sources, (1) the NCAA itself through its certification process that every Division I athletic program must go through once every ten years and that essentially requires schools to be in compliance with the same standards as those set by Title IX, and (2) the Department of Education's Office of Civil Rights, which monitors universities' compliance and responds to specific complaints of possible violations with Title IX audits and demands for reforms as a condition of continuing eligibility for receiving federal funds.

One activity, though, poses a new question to consider under Title IX—do members of cheerleading and dance squads count for Title IX purposes? The Second Circuit was the first appellate court to explore that question.

BIEDIGER V. QUINNIPIAC UNIVERSITY
691 F.3d 85 (2d Cir. 2012)

RAGGI, CIRCUIT JUDGE.

Quinnipiac University appeals pursuant to 28 U.S.C. § 1292(a)(1) from a permanent injunction ordered on July 22, 2010, by the United States District Court for the District of Connecticut (Stefan R. Underhill, *Judge*), after a bench trial at which Quinnipiac was found to have violated Title IX of the Education Amendments of 1972 ("Title IX") by failing to afford equal participation opportunities in varsity sports to female students. *See Biediger v. Quinnipiac Univ.*, 728 F. Supp. 2d 62 (D. Conn. 2010). Quinnipiac argues that the injunction, which prohibits any such future discrimination, should be vacated because it is based on a Title IX ruling infected by errors in counting the varsity athletic participation opportunities afforded Quinnipiac's female students in the 2009—10 school year.

Specifically, Quinnipiac faults the district court for excluding from its count of the total athletic participation opportunities afforded female students: (1) 11 roster positions on the women's indoor and outdoor track and field teams, held by members of Quinnipiac's women's cross-country team who were required to join the track teams even though they were unable to compete in 2009—10 because they were injured or "red-shirted"; and (2) all 30 roster positions on Quinnipiac's nascent women's competitive cheerleading team, based on a finding that the team did not afford the athletic participation opportunities of a varsity sport. Quinnipiac further contends that, even if these 41 roster positions should not count as varsity athletic participation opportunities for women, the district court erred in concluding that (3) the resulting 3.62% disparity between the percentage of all participation opportunities in varsity sports afforded female students (58.25%) and the percentage of enrolled female undergraduates (61.87%) established a Title IX violation warranting the challenged injunctive relief.

We identify no merit in these arguments, and we affirm the challenged injunction substantially for the reasons stated by the district court in its comprehensive and well reasoned opinion.

I. *Background*

A. *Quinnipiac's Decision To Eliminate Women's Volleyball Prompts This Title IX Action*

This lawsuit has its origins in Quinnipiac's March 2009 announcement that in the 2009—10 academic year, it would eliminate its varsity sports teams for women's volleyball, men's golf, and men's outdoor track and field, while simultaneously creating a new varsity sports team for women's competitive cheerleading. Plaintiffs, five Quinnipiac women's volleyball players and their coach, Robin Sparks, filed this action in April 2009, charging the university with violating Title IX by denying women equal varsity athletic participation opportunities, and seeking an injunction that, among other things, prevented Quinnipiac from eliminating its women's volleyball team. After a hearing, the district court preliminarily enjoined Quinnipiac from withdrawing support from its volleyball team, finding that Quinnipiac systematically and artificially increased women's teams' rosters and decreased men's teams' rosters to achieve the appearance of Title IX compliance. *See Biediger v. Quinnipiac Univ.*, 616 F. Supp. 2d 277 (D.Conn.2009). The district court subsequently certified a plaintiff class of all present and future female Quinnipiac students who had been or would be harmed by the alleged Title IX discrimination and sought injunctive relief. *See Biediger v. Quinnipiac Univ.*, No. 3:09-cv-621 (SRU), 2010 WL 2017773 (D. Conn. May 20, 2010). In June 2010, the district court conducted a bench trial on plaintiffs' claim of disproportionate allocation of athletic participation opportunities and, finding in their favor, granted permanent injunctive relief.

* * *

[The Court recounted the basic provisions of Title IX.]

In a 2008 letter, OCR explained that a genuine athletic participation opportunity must take place in the context of a "sport." Letter from Stephanie Monroe, Assistant Sec'y for Civil Rights, OCR, U.S. DOE, to Colleagues, at 1–2 (Sept. 17, 2008) ("2008 OCR Letter"). If a school is a member of a recognized intercollegiate athletic organization, such as the National Collegiate Athletic Association ("NCAA"), that subjects the activity at issue to its organizational requirements, OCR will "presume" that the activity is a sport and that participation can be counted under Title IX. *Id.* at 1–2. But if that presumption does not apply or has been rebutted, OCR will determine whether the activity qualifies as a sport by reference to several factors relating to "program structure and administration" and "team preparation and competition." *Id.* at 1–4.

Eight years earlier, in 2000, OCR had issued two letters stating that cheerleading, whether of the sideline or competitive variety, was presumptively not a sport, and that team members could not be counted as athletes under Title IX. While the letters indicated OCR's willingness to review particular cheerleading programs on a case-by-case basis, the parties stipulated in the district court that, since 2000, OCR has never recognized an intercollegiate varsity cheerleading program to be a sport for Title IX purposes. *See Biediger v. Quinnipiac Univ.*, 728 F. Supp. 2d at 92. Nor has Quinnipiac ever sought OCR recognition of its competitive cheerleading program as a sports activity. *See id.* at 85.

* * *

[The court reviewed the district court opinion, which held that Quinnipiac had improperly double counted track athletes and members of the cheerleading squad. It also explained that it deferred to the OCR's interpretation of its own guidelines.]

Here, Quinnipiac elected to defend against plaintiffs' discrimination claim *only* by reference to the first safe harbor created by the three-part test, arguing that its athletics program provided "substantially proportionate" athletic participation opportunities to women. For reasons we discuss *infra* at 99–108, the district court reasonably found to the contrary, thus simultaneously rejecting Quinnipiac's defense and finding for plaintiffs on the first element of their disparate treatment claim. To the extent that plaintiffs further offered evidence that Quinnipiac's disproportionate provision of athletic participation opportunities failed fully and effectively to accommodate the athletic interests and abilities of its female undergraduates insofar as it eliminated the women's volleyball team, Quinnipiac did not dispute the point. Nor did it attempt to argue that the school has a history of expanding women's athletic participation opportunities.

In sum, as a matter of Quinnipiac's litigation strategy, resolution of this case effectively turned on whether Quinnipiac's sex based treatment of varsity athletes provided its female students with genuine athletic participation opportunities substantially proportionate to their enrollment. Because the district court found that it did not, plaintiffs carried their burden to prove unlawful disparate treatment. In these circumstances, *amicus curiae's* challenge to the judicial deference accorded the agency's 1979 Policy Interpretation generally, or its articulated three-part test specifically, is unpersuasive.

* * *

[The Court rejected Quinnipiac's method of counting track athletes.]

D. *Athletic Participation Opportunities for Women in Competitive Cheerleading: The Determination That the Activity Does Not Yet Qualify as a "Sport"*

Competitive cheerleading, which Quinnipiac decided to create as a new women's varsity sport team for 2009—10, is a late twentieth-century outgrowth of traditional sideline cheerleading. Whereas sideline cheerleaders generally strive to entertain audiences or solicit crowd reaction at sport or school functions, a competitive cheerleading team seeks to pit its skills against other teams for the purpose of winning. *See Biediger v. Quinnipiac Univ.*, 728 F. Supp. 2d at 78. Thus, to distinguish the two activities, competitive cheerleaders

> do not attempt to elicit crowd response; generally do not use pom-poms, megaphones, signs, or other props associated with [sideline] cheerleading teams; . . . wear uniforms consisting of shorts and jerseys, much like what women's volleyball players don; and emphasize the more gymnastic elements of sideline cheerleading, such as aerial maneuvers, floor tumbling, and balancing exercises, to the exclusion of those activities intended to rally the watching audience.

Id. (observing that competitive cheerleading is an "athletic endeavor" that might be described as "group floor gymnastics" (internal quotation marks omitted)).

The district court nevertheless concluded that the 30 roster positions that Quinnipiac assigned competitive cheerleading for 2009—10 could not be counted under Title IX because the activity did not yet afford the participation opportunities of a varsity "sport." *See id.* at 101.

Preliminary to reaching this conclusion, the district court observed that competitive cheerleading is not yet recognized as a "sport," or even an "emerging sport," by the NCAA action that would have triggered a presumption in favor of counting its participants under Title IX. *See id.* at 93–94 (citing 2008 OCR Letter). Nor has DOE recognized competitive cheerleading as a sport; to the contrary, in two letters in 2000, OCR indicated competitive cheerleading is presumptively not a sport, while leaving open the possibility for a different conclusion with respect to a particular cheerleading program. *See* April 2000 OCR Letter at 3; May 2000 OCR Letter at 1. There is, however, no record evidence of any competitive cheerleading program being recognized by DOE as a sport. *See Biediger v. Quinnipiac Univ.*, 728 F. Supp. 2d at 92.

Mindful of these circumstances, the district court proceeded carefully to review the structure, administration, team preparation, and competition of Quinnipiac's competitive cheerleading program to determine whether it nevertheless qualified as a sport whose athletic participation opportunities should be counted for purposes of Title IX. *See* 2008 OCR Letter at 2–4 (listing factors relevant to identifying activity as sport). Again, we only briefly summarize the district court's detailed findings, which find ample support in the record evidence. The district court found that in terms of the team's operating budget, benefits, services, and coaching staff, competitive cheerleading was generally structured and administered by Quinnipiac's athletics department in a manner consistent with the school's other varsity teams. *See Biediger v. Quinnipiac Univ.*, 728 F. Supp. 2d at 95. The district court noted two "minor" exceptions to this conclusion: Quinnipiac did not afford its competitive cheerleading team locker space; and because the NCAA did not recognize competitive cheerleading as a sport, the team did not receive NCAA catastrophic injury insurance and had to obtain it from a separate provider. *Id.* at 99; *see id.* at 95. With respect to factors relating to the team's preparation and competition, the district court found that the competitive cheerleading team's practice time, regimen, and venue were consistent with other varsity sports. *See id.* at 96. Further, as with other varsity sports, the length of the competitive cheerleading season and the minimum number of competitions in which a team would participate were pre-determined by a governing athletic organization, the recently formed National Competitive Stunt and Tumbling Association, of which Quinnipiac was a founding member. *See id.* at 82–83, 96–97. Finally, the purpose of the team—to compete athletically at the intercollegiate varsity level—was akin to that of other varsity sports. *See id.* at 99.

At the same time, however, the district court identified a number of circumstances that sufficiently distinguished Quinnipiac's competitive cheerleading program from traditional varsity sports as to "compel[ ] the decision that, for the 2009—10 season," the program could not "be counted as a varsity sport for purposes of Title IX." *Id.* First, Quinnipiac did not—and, in 2009—10, could not—conduct any off-campus recruitment for its competitive cheerleading team, in marked contrast not only to the school's other varsity sports teams but also to a typical NCAA Division I sports program. *See id.* at 95–96, 99. The district court explained the significance of this circumstance: "Although the women on the Quinnipiac competitive cheer team were athletically able, they would have been all the more talented had [Coach] Powers been able to seek out the best competitive cheerleaders around the country, as any other varsity coach would have been able to do." *Id.* at 99.

More important, no uniform set of rules applied to competitive cheerleading competition throughout the 2009—10 season. Indeed, in the ten competitions in which the Quinnipiac team participated during the regular season, it was judged according to five different scoring systems. *See id.* at 97. Further, in these competitions, Quinnipiac did not face only varsity intercollegiate competitive cheerleading teams. Rather, it was challenged by "a motley assortment of competitors," *id.* at 98, including collegiate club opponents who did not receive varsity benefits, collegiate sideline cheerleading teams, and all-star opponents unaffiliated with a particular academic institution, some of whom may still have been high-school age, *see id.* at 97–98. As the district court observed, "application of a uniform set of rules for competition and the restriction of competition to contests against other varsity opponents" are the "touchstones" of a varsity sports program. *Id.* at 99–100. "Those features ensure that play is fair in each game, that teams' performances can be compared across a season, and that teams can be distinguished in terms of quality." *Id.* at 100.

The concerns raised by these irregularities in season competition were only aggravated by aspects of post-season play. Notably, competitive cheerleading offered no progressive playoff system leading to a championship game. *See id.* at 98. Rather, it provided an open invitational, which neither excluded any team on the basis of its regular season performance nor ranked or seeded participating teams on that basis. *See id.* Instead, all entrants competed in a single championship round in which the team with the highest score won. *See id.* That round, moreover, was subject to a new rule of competition that had not applied to Quinnipiac in any of its regular season competitions: a mandatory 45–60 second "spirit" segment in which a team was judged by the intensity of the response it elicited from the crowd and the number of the sponsoring brand's props that it employed, features that Quinnipiac's coach confirmed were more characteristic of sideline rather than competitive cheerleading. *See id.* at 98–99. Viewing the totality of these circumstances, the district court concluded that the competitive cheerleading team's post-season competition did not conform to expectations for a varsity sport.

Most other varsity sports would have used some system to separate teams and competitors in terms of quality, and would have ranked, seeded, or excluded teams on the basis of their performances during the regular season. Moreover, any other varsity sport would not have imposed new rules of competition in the post-season that teams did not follow during the regular season. *Id.* at 100.

Based on these findings, as well as those pertaining to regular season play, the district court concluded that Quinnipiac's competitive cheerleading team did not compete in circumstances indicative of varsity sports. Thus, it ruled that Quinnipiac's 30 roster positions for competitive cheerleading could not be counted for Title IX purposes because the activity did not yet afford women genuine participation opportunities in a varsity sport. *See id.* at 100–01.

In challenging this conclusion, Quinnipiac questions the weight the district court assigned the various factors it identified as supporting or undermining recognition of competitive cheerleading as a genuine varsity sport. Quinnipiac argues that this court should decide the question *de novo*. We generally accord considerable discretion to a factfinder in deciding what weight to assign competing evidence pointing toward different conclusions. *See Diesel Props. S.r.l. v. Greystone Bus. Credit II LLC*, 631 F.3d at 52 (" 'Where there are two permissible views of the evidence, the factfinder's choice between them cannot be clearly erroneous.' ") (quoting *Anderson v. Bessemer City*, 470 U.S. 564, 574 (1985)). But the point merits little discussion here because, even assuming that *de novo* review were warranted, we conclude for the same reasons stated in detail by the district court and summarized in this opinion that, although there are facts on both sides of the argument, in the end, the balance tips decidedly against finding competitive cheerleading presently to be a "sport" whose participation opportunities should be counted for purposes of Title IX. Like the district court, we acknowledge record evidence showing that competitive cheerleading can be physically challenging, requiring competitors to possess "strength, agility, and grace." *Biediger v. Quinnipiac Univ.*, 728 F. Supp. 2d at 101. Similarly, we do not foreclose the possibility that the activity, with better organization and defined rules, might some day warrant recognition as a varsity sport. But, like the district court, we conclude that the record evidence shows that "that time has not yet arrived." *Id.*

Accordingly, we conclude that the district court was correct not to count the 30 roster positions assigned to competitive cheerleading in determining the number of genuine varsity athletic participation opportunities that Quinnipiac afforded female students.

[The Court concluded by finding that a 3.62% disparity was enough to find a Title IX violation where under the proportionality requirement (the safe harbor Quinnipiac claimed)].

III. Conclusion

To summarize, we conclude as follows:

1. For purposes of determining the number of genuine varsity athletic participation opportunities that Quinnipiac afforded women students, the district court correctly declined to count:

a. five roster positions on the women's indoor track team and six roster positions on the women's outdoor track team because these were held by cross-country runners who (i) were required to join the indoor and outdoor track teams even though they could not compete on those teams because they were injured or red-shirted and (ii) did not receive any additional benefits from membership on the track teams beyond those received as injured or red-shirted off-season members of the cross-country team;

b. any of the 30 roster positions for women's competitive cheerleading because that activity was not yet sufficiently organized or its rules sufficiently defined to afford women genuine participation opportunities in a varsity sport.

2. Where the 3.62% disparity between the percentage of women students enrolled at Quinnipiac and the percentage of women listed on varsity sports teams was largely caused by Quinnipiac's voluntary decisions with respect to its athletics programs and reasonably remedied by the addition of more athletic opportunities for women, the district court correctly concluded that the disparity demonstrated a failure to provide substantially proportionate athletic participation opportunities as required by Title IX.

Accordingly, the district court's order enjoining Quinnipiac from continuing to discriminate against female students by failing to provide them with equal athletic participation opportunities is AFFIRMED.

NOTES AND QUESTIONS

1. *Biediger.* Do you agree with the OCR and the *Biediger* court? Should cheerleaders count for Title IX purposes? Is there a distinction to be drawn between sideline cheerleaders and competitive dance teams?

2. *Effects of Counting Cheerleaders.* What is the cost of counting cheerleaders as athletes under Title IX? As *Biediger* demonstrates, other women's sports may be eliminated as a consequence. On the other hand, large dance teams, some with as many as 30 members, might provide some counterweight to football. This is not an easy question, when one considers the kind of opportunity competitive cheerleading and dance offers female students, and the degree to which that opportunity might be similar to (or different than) the opportunity to participate in more traditional sports.

3. *Do Olympics Change Title IX Analysis?* As cheer and dance teams grow in popularity and competitiveness, they start to look more like athletic teams and less like simply units that are ancillary to another competition. Indeed, it is possible that competitive cheer will be an Olympic sport in the near future. In light of the *Biedinger* opinion, what facts might tip the balance in favor of counting cheer and dance squad members under Title IX? Are any of these facts insurmountable? Do you see this determination changing over time?

4. *Reframing the Discussion?* Are there other ways to frame the Title IX discussion? Consider the novel argument by Northwestern Professor Kimberly Yuracko, in her article *One For You and One For Me: Is Title IX's Sex-Based Proportionality Requirement for College Varsity Athletic Positions Defensible*, 97 Nw. U.L. Rev. 731 (2003). Yuracko argues that

> The proportionality requirement may be best understood and explained as an attempt to promote certain widely shared values

about the kinds of skills and attributes that girls and boys should be encouraged to develop. It may be, in other words, that the strongest and the most honest justification for proportionality is that it encourages girls to develop a sense of their own bodily agency and to develop a conception of themselves as agents in their social and physical world.

Id. at 791. Title IX accomplishes this, Yuracko suggests, by creating athletic role models for girls, and

> proportionality may be one part of a social reconstruction project aimed at changing the cultural tags associated, not only with competitive athletics, but also with physical agency more generally. Proportionality may encourage girls to think of themselves and their bodies in a different way by tagging competitive physical activity as in equal part female, rather than exclusively male. Proportionality may, therefore, be part of a larger project to change the social meaning attached to femaleness from passive beauty or sex object to strong physical agent.

Id. at 796. Do you find Yuracko's argument persuasive? How might it apply to the dance team member question?

5. *Other Competitive Activities?* What ultimately makes athletics distinct from other extracurricular pursuits? Is it simply the challenges and discipline of intercollegiate competition? If marching bands or glee clubs engage in such competitions, should they be covered? How about debate or other speech teams? Chess or mathematics teams?

C. ATHLETIC PROGRAM ADMINISTRATION

Whatever one's judgment about the current legal and policy debates in this area, Title IX undoubtedly has been a great success in affording dramatically greater opportunities for female athletes and their fans. In 1971–72, just before Title IX was enacted, there were 300,000 female athletes in high school and 30,000 in college. Over forty years later, in 2017–18, there were over three million females playing in high school and over 200,000 playing for college varsity teams.

Ironically, though, while Title IX ushered in this huge expansion in female *participation* in college (and high school) sports, that same era witnessed a marked decline in women's share of the *administration* of these athletic programs. The source of this trend is easy to trace. In the early 1970s, the "separate but unequal" women's athletic programs formed their own body, the Association of Intercollegiate Athletics for Women (AIAW), to play a role analogous in the governance of women's sports to that of the NCAA in men's sports. In the late 1970s, though, the NCAA, having failed in its effort to roll back Title IX's coverage of college sports, decided to take control of the now-burgeoning women's sports programs.

As a result of its greater financial resources and television exposure, the NCAA was successful in its quest. After failing in an antitrust suit, see *AIAW v. NCAA*, 558 F. Supp. 487 (D.D.C. 1983), aff'd, 735 F.2d 577 (D.C. Cir.1984), the AIAW folded in 1982.

The more immediate financial and legal concerns relate to the substantial disparity in pay between the coaches of male and female teams. Unlike participation rates, accurate compensation data is difficult to obtain, in large part because many coaches receive significant portions of their overall compensation from outside sources that are not reported by their universities. Even so, it is widely known that the coaches of men's teams in Division I receive compensation packages that are substantially greater than the packages received by the coaches of the women's teams (whether or not those coaches are men or women).

Both Title IX and the federal Equal Pay Act provide possible sources of legal challenges to this apparent discrepancy in cases where the coach of the women's team is also a woman. The next case explores that question.

STANLEY V. UNIVERSITY OF SOUTHERN CALIFORNIA
13 F.3d 1313 (9th Cir. 1994)

ALARCON, CIRCUIT JUDGE.

* * * Coach Stanley has not offered proof to contradict the evidence proffered by USC that demonstrates the differences in the responsibilities of the persons who serve as head coaches of the women's and men's basketball teams. Coach Raveling's responsibilities as head coach of the men's basketball team require substantial public relations and promotional activities to generate revenue for USC. These efforts resulted in revenue that is 90 times greater than the revenue generated by the women's basketball team. Coach Raveling was required to conduct twelve outside speaking engagements per year, to be accessible to the media for interviews, and to participate in certain activities designed to produce donations and endorsements for the USC Athletic Department in general. Coach Stanley's position as head coach did not require her to engage in the same intense level of promotional and revenue-raising activities. This quantitative dissimilarity in responsibilities justifies a different level of pay for the head coach of the women's basketball team. See *Horner v. Mary Inst.*, 613 F.2d 706, 713–14 (8th Cir.1980) (evidence that male physical education teacher had a different job from a female physical education teacher because he was responsible for curriculum precluded finding that jobs were substantially similar; court may consider whether job requires more experience, training, and ability to determine whether jobs require substantially equal skill under EPA).

The evidence presented by USC also showed that Coach Raveling had substantially different qualifications and experience related to his public relations and revenue-generation skills than Coach Stanley. Coach Raveling received educational training in marketing, and worked in that field for nine years. Coach Raveling has been employed by USC three years longer than Coach Stanley. He has been a college basketball coach for 31 years, while Coach Stanley has had 17 years' experience as a basketball coach. Coach Raveling had served as a member of the NCAA Subcommittee on Recruiting. Coach Raveling also is the respected author of two bestselling novels. He has performed as an actor in a feature movie, and has appeared on national television to discuss recruiting of student athletes. Coach Stanley does not have the same degree of experience in these varied activities. Employers may reward professional experience and education without violating the EPA.

Coach Raveling's national television appearances and motion picture presence, as well as his reputation as an author, make him a desirable public relations representative for USC. An employer may consider the marketplace value of the skills of a particular individual when determining his or her salary. *Horner*, 613 F.2d at 714. Unequal wages that reflect market conditions of supply and demand are not prohibited by the EPA. *EEOC v. Madison Community Unit Sch. Dist. No. 12*, 818 F.2d 577, 580 (7th Cir.1987).

The record also demonstrates that the USC men's basketball team generated greater attendance, more media interest, larger donations, and produced substantially more revenue than the women's basketball team.[1] As a result, USC placed greater pressure on Coach Raveling to promote his team and to win. The responsibility to produce a large amount of revenue is evidence of a substantial difference in responsibility. *See Jacobs v. College of William and Mary*, 517 F. Supp. 791, 797 (E.D. Va.1980) (duty to produce revenue demonstrates that coaching jobs are not substantially equal), aff'd without opinion, 661 F.2d 922 (4th Cir.), *cert. denied*, 454 U.S. 1033 (1981).

---

[1] The total average attendance per women's team game during Coach Stanley's tenure was 751 as compared to 4,035 for the men's team during the same period. The average sales of season ticket passes to faculty and staff for women's games were 13, while the average sales for men's games were 130. Alumni and other fans, on average, purchased 71 passes for women's home games as compared to over 1,200 season passes for men's home games during the same period. A season pass to the men's home games was more than double the price of a season pass to women's home games.

The same disparity exists with respect to media interest in the men's and women's basketball teams. Television and radio stations paid USC to broadcast the men's basketball games; all of the home games and many games off campus were broadcast on network or cable stations. All of the games were broadcast on commercial radio. Approximately three of the women's basketball games were broadcast on cable stations as part of a contract package that also covered several other sports.

Donations and endowments were likewise greater for the men's basketball team, totaling $66,916 during the time period of Coach Stanley's contract, as compared to $4,288 for the women's basketball team. The same was true for revenue production. While the women's basketball team produced a total revenue of $50,262 during Coach Stanley's four years, the men's team generated $4,725,784 during the same time period.

Coach Stanley did not offer evidence to rebut USC's justification for paying Coach Raveling a higher salary. Instead, she alleged that the women's team generates revenue, and that she is under a great deal of pressure to win.[2]

We agree with the district court in *Jacobs* that revenue generation is an important factor that may be considered in justifying greater pay. We are also of the view that the relative amount of revenue generated should be considered in determining whether responsibilities and working conditions are substantially equal. The fact that the men's basketball team at USC generates 90 times the revenue than that produced by the women's team adequately demonstrates that Coach Raveling was under greater pressure to win and to promote his team than Coach Stanley was subject to as head coach of the women's team.

Coach Stanley's reliance on *Burkey v. Marshall County Board of Education*, 513 F. Supp. 1084 (N.D. W. Va.1981), and *EEOC v. Madison Community Unit School District No. 12*, 818 F.2d 577 (7th Cir.1987), to support her claim of sex discrimination is misplaced. In *Burkey*, the women coaches were "uniformly paid one-half (1/2) of the salary which male coaches of comparable or identical boys' junior high school sports were paid." Here, however, Coach Stanley has not shown that her responsibilities were identical.

Coach Stanley argues that *Jacobs* is distinguishable because, in that matter, the head basketball coach of the women's team was not required to produce any revenue. Coach Stanley appears to suggest that a difference in the amount of revenue generated by the men's and women's teams should be ignored by the court in comparing the respective coaching positions. We disagree.

In *Madison*, the Seventh Circuit held that the plaintiff established a prima facie EPA claim because "male and female coaches alike testified that the skill, effort, and responsibility required were the same and the working conditions [were] also the same—not merely similar—which is all the Act requires." In the instant matter, the uncontradicted evidence shows that Coach Raveling's responsibilities, as head coach of the men's basketball team, differed substantially from the duties imposed upon Coach Stanley.

Coach Stanley contends that the failure to allocate funds in the promotion of women's basketball team demonstrated gender discrimination. She appears to argue that USC's failure to pay her a salary

---

[2] Coach Stanley also alleged that, as head coach, she had won four national women's basketball championships, but that Coach Raveling had won none. In addition, while head coach at USC, Coach Stanley was named PAC-10 Coach-of-the-Year in 1993 and the women's basketball team played in the last three NCAA Tournaments and advanced to the NCAA Sweet Sixteen in 1993 and the NCAA Elite Eight in 1992. She also described numerous speaking engagements in which she had participated.

equal to that of Coach Raveling was the result of USC's "failure to market and promote the women's basketball team." The only evidence Coach Stanley presented in support of this argument is that USC failed to provide the women's team with a poster containing the schedule of games, but had done so for the men's team. This single bit of evidence does not demonstrate that Coach Stanley was denied equal pay for equal work. Instead, it demonstrates, at best, a business decision to allocate USC resources to the team that generates the most revenue.

The district court also was "unconvinced" by Coach Stanley's claim that USC's disparate promotion of men's and women's basketball teams had "caused the enormous differences in spectator interest and revenue production." The court rejected Coach Stanley's assertion that the differences were due to societal discrimination and that this was evidence of a prima facie case under the EPA. The court reasoned that societal discrimination in preferring to witness men's sports in greater numbers cannot be attributed to USC. We agree.

At this preliminary stage of these proceedings, the record does not support a finding that gender was the reason that USC paid a higher salary to Coach Raveling as head coach of the men's basketball team than it offered Coach Stanley as head coach of the women's basketball team. Garrett's affidavit supports the district court's conclusion that the head coach position of the men's team was not substantially equal to the head coach position of the women's team. The record shows that there were significant differences between Coach Stanley's and Coach Raveling's public relations skills, credentials, experience, and qualifications; there also were substantial differences between their responsibilities and working conditions. The district court's finding that the head coach positions were not substantially equal is not a "clear error of judgment."

* * *

Affirmed.

NOTES AND QUESTIONS

1. *Aftermath.* After failing to obtain immediate injunctive relief, Stanley filled in during the 1995–96 season at Stanford, temporarily replacing its women's basketball coach who had taken a year's leave of absence to coach the women's team at the 1996 Atlanta Olympics. Stanley was then hired to coach the University of California team, beginning in the 1996–97 season. Eventually her quest for damages from USC was summarily dismissed, a judgment that was affirmed 2–1 in *Stanley v. University of Southern California*, 178 F.3d 1069 (9th Cir. 1999). There, the court explained,

> Both sides agreed that "the men's and women's coaching jobs share a common core of tasks ... recruiting athletes and administering the basketball programs. USC's basic defense, though, was that Raveling had 'greater revenue generating responsibilities, that he is under greater media and spectator pressure to produce a winning program, and that he actually generates more revenue for the University.' Relying on an October 1997 Notice issued by President Clinton's Equal Employment Opportunity Commission (EEOC) as interpretation guidelines for 'sex discrimination in the compensation of sports coaches in educational institutions,' Stanley claimed that these differences between the two jobs resulted from the University's historically disparate treatment of male and female teams; namely, its decision to invest in and promote the men's program more than the women's program." USC's response was that this disparity in coaching responsibilities and team revenues was because even now "there simply is not a sufficient spectator or media market for women's basketball games."
>
> Because that essentially factual issue could not be decided on a motion for summary dismissal, the majority instead based its decision on another "factor other than sex." The salary differential between the female and male coaches could instead be explained by the fact that Raveling had coached for 14 more years than Stanley, had twice been named national coach of the year, had once coached the men's Olympic team, had authored several books on basketball, and had many years more experience in marketing and promotion.
>
> Coaches with substantially more experience and significantly superior qualifications may of course be paid more than their less experienced and qualified counterparts, even when it is the male coach who has the greater level of experience and qualifications.

Id. at 1079–80. Judge Pregerson expressed a strong but brief dissent on that score.

> By focusing on the difference between Stanley's and Raveling's qualifications, the majority skips over the many ways in which gender discrimination insidiously affected the University's treatment of the women's basketball program and Stanley as its Head Coach. The University's half-hearted promotion of the women's basketball program, its intensive marketing of the men's basketball program, and the formidable obstacles Stanley faced as a woman athlete in a male-dominated profession contributed to this disparate treatment.
>
> It is hard for me to square these realities with the majority's ruling denying Stanley relief without a trial.

Id. at 1080.

    2. *Equal Pay Act Litigation.* The Equal Pay Act requires plaintiffs to demonstrate that they are paid less than members of the other sex are paid

"on jobs the performance of which requires equal skill, effort, and responsibility, and which are performed under similar working conditions." The Act also provides employers four affirmative defenses, including demonstrating that any difference is "based on any other factor than sex." Did the court in *Stanley* deny injunctive relief because it did not think Stanley could establish her prima facie case, or because it thought USC could demonstrate a "factor other than sex" affirmative defense? Title VII of the 1964 Civil Rights Act also prohibits gender-based pay discrimination, but incorporates the Equal Pay Act affirmative defenses. What kinds of differences in responsibilities and qualifications between the women's and men's teams' coaching jobs should suffice to block future Stanleys from winning pay discrimination claims? Is paying a wage set by an external labor market, either through another offer or a prior salary not a "factor other than sex"? Are female coaches of women's teams ever likely to be successful challenging a compensation disparity with a coach of a revenue-producing men's sport?

3. *Title IX as a Remedy?* Title IX bars discrimination against female student-athletes, whereas the Equal Pay Act and Title VII proscribe discrimination in pay against female employees. Had the coach of USC's women's basketball team been a man, he would have had no claim under the Equal Pay Act regardless of how little he was paid because he could not claim that he was discriminated against on the basis of his gender, rather than on basis of the gender of the players he coaches. Might a disparity between the compensation for the coaches of the men's and women's teams constitute evidence of a violation of Title IX, however, because it violates the school's obligation to offer equal opportunity to its female and male *athletes*? How would the plaintiff coach of the women's basketball team argue that his/her players were discriminated against or injured because he/she was paid less than the men's team's coach? Because he/she didn't work as hard as if he/she had been paid more? Because the school could have hired a better coach than him/her had the salary been higher?

4. *Can Colleges Assign Coaches Based on the Gender of the Players?* Both the EPA and Title VII are symmetrical; they prohibit discrimination against males as well as against females. Thus, a male coach can claim unlawful discrimination under the EPA if he can prove that a female coach with the same qualifications performing essentially the same duties was paid more than he was paid. Title VII does provide employers a narrow "bona fide qualification" defense to sex discrimination in hiring. The Supreme Court, however, has held that this defense is only available for jobs that "all or substantially" members of the excluded defense cannot perform. Should being a female be a bona fide qualification for coaching a women's team? Although not under the EPA, could a male applicant to coach a female team claim unlawful discrimination if a less qualified female is hired for the job? In this regard, *see Medcalf v. Trustees of the Univ. of Pennsylvania*, 71 F. App'x 924 (3d Cir. 2003) (affirming a jury verdict that the University of Pennsylvania violated Title VII when it discriminated against Andrew Medcalf, an assistant

coach of the women's crew team, by hiring a clearly less qualified woman as the head coach without even granting him an interview.)

5. *Viability of Title VII Actions?* The coverage of sex discrimination by Title VII does not ensure its eradication in college sports coaching. If Pat Summitt, the now deceased legendary head coach of Tennessee's frequent national champion women's basketball team, had applied to be the head coach of a men's team at a Division I school, she would have had a legal claim if a less qualified male were hired (as is quite likely). What do you think her prospects of prevailing on that claim would have been, however? What would be the likely prospects for a suit by a woman who has been denied a position as a football coach, when the woman, though never having played football, had a successful coaching record in a variety of sports? *See Oates v. District of Columbia*, 647 F. Supp. 1079 (D.D.C. 1986), *aff'd*, 824 F.2d 87 (D.C. Cir. 1987). Or by a woman who sought a job as athletic director of a school's program whose main popular attractions were football and men's basketball? *See Wynn v. Columbus Municipal Separate School Dist.*, 692 F. Supp. 672 (N.D. Miss.1988).

6. *Jackson v. Birmingham Bd. of Educ.* The Supreme Court in 2005 addressed an important issue about the reach of Title IX and who has standing to raise a claim under the statute. *Jackson v. Birmingham Bd. of Educ.* 544 U.S. 167 (2005). The male coach of a public high school girls' basketball team complained to school authorities when he discovered that his team was not receiving equal funding and equal access to athletic equipment and facilities. He then received negative work evaluations and ultimately was removed as the girls' coach. He brought suit alleging that the school board had retaliated against him. The Supreme Court, by a 5–4 majority, in an opinion by Justice O'Connor, ruled that retaliation against a person, male or female, because he or she complains of sex discrimination constitutes intentional "discrimination" "on the basis of sex," in violation of Title IX. The decision, however, does not fully settle whether a coach would have standing under Title IX to bring an action complaining not of retaliation against him, but rather of unequal treatment of female athletes. The Court could hold that the coach was not within the protected zone of interests.

D. ACCESS

An even more fundamental question lurks beneath the surface of the legal and policy issues we have addressed on gender equity in college sports. All of the prior cases assumed that there could be a women's and a men's team in basketball and most other college sports (with football a conspicuous exception). Such segregation of black and white athletes would never be suggested as an appropriate solution to the issues of racial disparity raised by Proposition 48 and other NCAA policies considered in the previous two chapters. It is intriguing, then, that there has been little discussion or debate about gender segregation in college sports. For an extended critique, *see* Karen L. Tokarz, *Separate but Unequal Educational*

Sports Programs: The Need for a New Theory of Equality, 1 Berkeley Women's L.J. 201 (1985).

The tacit assumption of both the administrative and judicial reading of Title IX is that colleges will establish *separate* teams for their female and male students, and that the institution must then provide *equal* positions and support for their women's and men's teams. The federal regulations adopted under Title IX in 1975 were quite frank on this point.

> (b) *Separate teams.* Notwithstanding the requirements of paragraph (a) of this section, a recipient may operate or sponsor separate teams for members of each sex where selection for such teams is based upon competitive skill or the activity involved is a contact sport. However, where a recipient operates or sponsors a team in a particular sport for members of one sex but operates or sponsors no such team for members of the other sex, and athletic opportunities for members of that sex have previously been limited, members of the excluded sex must be allowed to try-out for the team offered unless the sport involved is a contact sport. For the purposes of this part, contact sports include boxing, wrestling, rugby, ice hockey, football, basketball and other sports the purpose or major activity of which involves bodily contact.

After having been named as one of the 25 schools in the scholarship disparity complaint filed by NWLC in June 1997, Duke University found itself the target of yet another Title IX suit in September 1997—this one filed by a woman who claimed that she had not been given a fair opportunity to make the Duke football team.

Heather Mercer had been the place-kicker for her Yorktown Heights high school team that won the New York State Class B championship in 1993, with Mercer named as the third-team All-State place-kicker. After enrolling at Duke in the fall of 1994, Mercer sought to make the Blue Devils football squad. At the end of Duke's 1995 spring training session, Mercer was the first place-kicker selected by the "rising seniors" to play in the Blue-White game, and her last-minute, 28-yard field goal won the game for the Blues. While Blue Devils coach Fred Goldsmith apparently said after that game that Mercer had made the team (for the first time in Division I college football history), she was not invited to the team's summer football camp, nor permitted that fall to wear a football uniform and sit on the sidelines even during home games (an opportunity given to all male walkons, including place-kickers). When that situation continued into her 1997 senior year, Mercer sued Duke under Title IX, seeking monetary damages that Mercer said she would use to create a scholarship fund for future female place-kickers.

Duke's basic legal defense to this claim was that while the HEW Regulations said that if a school did not offer a separate team for each sex, it must then allow members of the "excluded sex" whose "athletic opportunities . . . have previously been limited" to try out for the other sex's team, this rule did not apply to a "contact sport," which certainly included football. In *Mercer v. Duke University*, 190 F.3d 643 (4th Cir.1999), the Fourth Circuit rejected that position even for what Duke had characterized as the "traditionally all-male bastion of college football." *Id.* at 648. The reason is that

> [o]nce an institution has allowed a member of one sex to try out for a team operated by the institution for the other sex in a contact sport, subsection (b) is no longer applicable, and the institution is subject to the general antidiscrimination provision of sub-section (a).

Id.

This still left open the question of whether Duke had actually been discriminating against Mercer because of her gender. The case went to trial in October 2000 and it took the North Carolina jury just two hours to find Duke liable. Goldsmith, who had been dismissed in 1998 for coaching a losing team, admitted in his testimony that he had been embarrassed by the teasing from rival coaches for having to have a woman on his squad. Apparently Mercer had been told by the coach to sit in the stands rather than on the sidelines where she was a "distraction" to the players, and was invited to give up this "little boys' sport" in favor of girls' beauty pageants and the like. Thus the jury rejected Duke's claim that Mercer had simply been released from the team (as were several other male place kickers) because of her lack of relative skills.

Nonetheless, Mercer was able to secure only $1 in compensatory damages for her actual financial losses. The jury did find that Duke had engaged in intentional and malicious discrimination against Mercer and awarded her $2 million in punitive damages. While Mercer immediately said she would donate that award to create a new college scholarship program for female high school place kickers, the University appealed this damages judgment to the Fourth Circuit. In *Mercer v. Duke University*, 50 F. App'x 643 (2002), the Circuit panel rendered a brief *per curiam* opinion on the damages issue, holding that because the Supreme Court had just ruled in *Barnes v. Gorman*, 536 U.S. 181 (2002), that punitive damages were not available to private plaintiffs under Title VI of the Civil Rights Act (and also the Americans With Disabilities Act), they cannot be awarded under Title IX either. After a brief career on Wall Street, Mercer returned to the sports field as a world-class poker player.

NOTES AND QUESTIONS

1. *Can Equality of Access Substitute for Equality of Opportunity?* Could a college meet its Title IX obligations by allowing female students to compete for positions on enough male teams to give them potential access to a proportionate number of athletic positions?

2. *Justifications for Blocking Access?* Should schools, including secondary schools, be permitted to prevent a girl from trying out for any sport in which she is able to compete, even sports with some degree of physical contact? Should it matter whether the school offers competition in that same sport in an all-female team? At what age level, or competition level, the school participates?

3. *Single Sport Considerations.* The Department of Education's Title IX Regulations at 34 C.F.R. § 106.41 allow a school to maintain a single sport only for one sex without allowing members of the opposite sex to try out only if it is a "contact sport" and "athletic opportunities for members of [the excluded] sex have previously been limited." If a school does not offer a male team in a non-contact sport, such as volleyball or crew, should a court require it to allow boys to try out for spots on a female team? Even if the school offers males an equal number of other athletic opportunities?

While these issues of gender integration of sports are untested in college athletics, it is a different matter in high school and elementary school sports. Indeed, female student athletes at this level have on occasion filed suit under Title IX to require their schools to integrate the teams in certain sports. The following decision illustrates one judicial response.

HOOVER V. MEIKLEJOHN
430 F. Supp. 164 (D. Col. 1977)

MATSCH, DISTRICT JUDGE.

[The plaintiff, a 16-year-old eleventh grade student, was barred from playing for her public high school's junior varsity soccer team. She challenged a rule adopted by the Colorado High School Activities Association that limited soccer (but not baseball or cross country running) to males. The Association had relied on advice from its medical committee that girls playing soccer on mixed-sex teams risked their health and safety.]

* * *

Primarily, the committee was concerned with risks attendant upon collisions in the course of play. While the rules of soccer prohibit body contact (except for a brush-type shoulder block when moving toward the ball), there are frequent instances when players collide in their endeavors to "head" the ball. In those instances, contact is generally in the upper body area.

There is agreement that after puberty the female body has a higher ratio of adipose tissue to lean body weight as compared with the male, and females have less bone density than males. It is also true that, when matured, the male skeletal construct provides a natural advantage over females in the mechanics of running. Accordingly, applying the formula of force equals mass times acceleration, a collision between a male and a female of equal weights, running at full speed, would tend to be to the disadvantage of the female. It is also true that while males as a class tend to have an advantage in strength and speed over females as a class, the range of differences among individuals in both sexes is greater than the average differences between the sexes. The association has not established any eligibility criteria for participation in interscholastic soccer, excepting for sex. Accordingly, any male of any size and weight has the opportunity to be on an interscholastic team and no female is allowed to play, regardless of her size, weight, condition or skill.

* * *

The defendants on the board of education and the professional educators in control of the activities association have concluded that the game of soccer is among those which serve an educational purpose and governmental funds have been provided for it. It is a matter of common knowledge that athletics are a recognized aspect of the educational program offered at American colleges and universities and that many of them offer scholarships to males and females for their agreement to participate in intercollegiate sports competition. Such offers result from organized recruiting programs directed toward those who have demonstrated their abilities on high school teams. Accordingly, the chance to play in athletic games may have an importance to the individual far greater than the obvious momentary pleasure of the game.

Accordingly, the claim of the plaintiff class in this case is properly characterized as a denial of an equal educational opportunity.

* * *

Brown v. Board of Education, 347 U.S. 483 (1954), held that blacks were denied a constitutionally protected equality when they were forced to attend schools established only for those of the same race. As suggested by Justice Brennan in *Frontiero v. Richardson*, 411 U.S. 677, 686 (1973), a classification according to sex is comparable to race in that it is "an immutable characteristic determined solely by the accident of birth."

* * *

The Supreme Court has exhibited an obvious reluctance to label sex as a "suspect" classification because the consequences of the application of the many "invidious" discrimination precedents to all separations by sex could lead to some absurd results. For example, would the Constitution preclude separate public toilets?

* * *

In a very recent Supreme Court opinion, *Craig v. Boren*, 429 U.S. 190 (1976), Mr. Justice Brennan, writing for the Court, attempted to define a new standard of review, saying:

> To withstand constitutional challenge, previous cases establish that classifications by gender must serve important governmental objectives and must be substantially related to achievement of those objectives.

That language may be considered a "middle-tier approach," requiring something between "legitimate" and "compelling," viz., "important," and something more than a "rational" relationship but less perhaps than "strict scrutiny," viz., "substantially" related.

* * *

... Because of its flexibility and sensitivity to the notion of equality itself, [the following three-pronged] method of analysis is particularly appropriate to the present case.

1. The Importance of the Opportunity Being Unequally Burdened or Denied

The opportunity not merely burdened but completely denied to the plaintiff and the class she represents is the chance to compete in soccer as a part of a high school educational experience. Whether such games should be made available at public expense is not an issue. The content of an educational program is completely within the majoritarian control through the representatives on the school board. But, whether it is algebra or athletics, that which is provided must be open to all. The Court in *Brown* expressed a constitutional concern for equality in educational opportunity and this controversy is squarely within that area of concern. Accordingly, without reference to any label that would place this opportunity on one of two or more "tiers," it must be given a great importance to Donna Hoover and every other individual within her class. Surely it is of greater significance than the buying of beer, considered in *Craig*, supra.

2. The Strength of the State Interest Served in Denying It

The defendants in this case have sought to support the exclusionary rule by asserting the state interest in the protection of females from injury in this sport. While the evidence in this case has shown that males as a class tend to have an advantage in strength and speed over females as a class and that a collision between a male and a female would tend to be to the disadvantage of the female, the evidence also shows that the range of differences among individuals in both sexes is greater than the average differences between the sexes. The failure to establish any physical criteria to protect small or weak males from the injurious effects of competition with larger or stronger males destroys the credibility of the reasoning urged in support of the sex classification. Accordingly, to the extent that governmental concern for the health and safety of anyone who knowingly and voluntarily exposes himself or herself to possible injury can ever be an acceptable area of intrusion on individual liberty, there is no rationality in limiting this patronizing protection to females who want to play soccer.

3. The Character of the Group Whose Opportunities Are Denied

Women and girls constitute a majority of the people in this country. To be effective citizens, they must be permitted full participation in the educational programs designed for that purpose. To deny females equal access to athletics supported by public funds is to permit manipulation of governmental power for a masculine advantage.

Egalitarianism is the philosophical foundation of our political process and the principle which energizes the equal protection clause of the Fourteenth Amendment. The emergence of female interest in an active involvement in all aspects of our society requires abandonment of many historical stereotypes. Any notion that young women are so inherently weak, delicate or physically inadequate that the state must protect them from the folly of participation in vigorous athletics is a cultural anachronism unrelated to reality. The Constitution does not permit the use of governmental power to control or limit cultural changes or to prescribe masculine and feminine roles.

It is an inescapable conclusion that the complete denial of any opportunity to play interscholastic soccer is a violation of the plaintiff's right to equal protection of the law under the Fourteenth Amendment. This same conclusion would be required under even the minimal "rational relationship" standard of review applied to classifications which are not suspect and do not involve fundamental rights. The governmental purpose in fielding a soccer team is to enhance the secondary school educational experience. The exclusion of girls to protect them from injury cannot be considered to be in furtherance of that educational objective. If the purpose of the exclusionary rule is the protection of health, safety and welfare of the students, it is arbitrary to consider only the general physiological differences between males and females as classes without any regard for the wide range of individual variants within each class.

While Rule XXI is invalid under either method of analysis, there is a difference between them which is revealed in considering both the remedy required here and the possible ramifications of this case for future controversies.

There is no contention in this case that the Constitution compels soccer competition with teams composed of the best players, regardless of sex. Donna Hoover sought a chance to play on the boys' team only because there is no girls' team. The parties here agree that the effective equalization of athletic opportunities for members of both sexes would be better served by comparable teams for members of each sex and that under current circumstances mixed-sex teams would probably be dominated by males. Accordingly, it is conceded that "separate but equal" teams would satisfy the equality of opportunity required by the Constitution. The "separate but equal" doctrine was articulated in *Plessy v. Ferguson*, 163 U.S. 537 (1896), approving racial separation in transportation facilities. The doctrine was rejected for education in *Brown*, supra, upon the conclusion that racial separation was inherently unequal because it involved a stigmatizing inferiority for the minority race. No such effect is conceivable for a separation of athletic teams by sex.

* * *

Given the lack of athletic opportunity for females in past years, the encouragement of female involvement in sports is a legitimate objective and separation of teams may promote that purpose. It may also justify the sanction of some sports only for females, of which volleyball may be an example.

Separate soccer teams for males and females would meet the constitutional requirement of equal opportunity if the teams were given substantially equal support and if they had substantially comparable programs. There may be differences depending upon the effects of such neutral factors as the level of student interest and geographic locations. Accordingly, the standard should be one of comparability, not absolute equality.

In arriving at the conclusion that the defendants are in violation of the Fourteenth Amendment by providing interscholastic soccer only for male high school students, I am aware that there will be many concerned about the ramifications of this ruling. Football, ice hockey and wrestling are also made available only for males in Colorado, and volleyball is provided only for females. While there is now no reason to rule beyond the specific controversy presented by the evidence, it would seem appropriate to make some general observations about constitutional concerns in athletic programs supported by public funds.

The applicability of so fundamental a constitutional principle as equal educational opportunity should not depend upon anything so mutable as customs, usages, protective equipment and rules of play. The courts do not have competence to determine what games are appropriate for the schools or which, if any, teams should be separated by sex. What the courts can and must do is to insure that those who do make those decisions act with an awareness of what the Constitution does and does not require of them. Accordingly, it must be made clear that there is no constitutional requirement for the schools to provide any athletic program, as it is clear that there is no constitutional requirement to provide any public education. What is required is that whatever opportunity is made available be open to all on equal terms. It must also be made clear that the mandate of equality of opportunity does not dictate a disregard of differences in talents and abilities among individuals. There is no right to a position on an athletic team. There is a right to compete for it on equal terms.

* * *

Order granted.

NOTES AND QUESTIONS

1. *Effect on Colorado High Schools.* What actions does this ruling allow Colorado high schools to take? Consider each of the following scenarios: (1) a school allows girls to try out for the school's only soccer team, but over a period of several years few girls try out and none make the team; (2) a school requires half the players on the school's only soccer team to be girls; (3) a school has both boys' and girls' soccer teams, but disbands the girls' team when only three girls come out for the team, and then refuses to let the three girls try out for the boys' team; (4) a school has a boys-only soccer team and a girls-only field hockey team (each team has the same number of players).

2. *Risk of Injury in Mixed Sports?* In the present, unlike the 1970s, few would argue that mixed soccer poses a serious risk of injury to young girls. But what about football or ice hockey? Should either of these sports be mixed-sex or just single sex? How should the court rule in a case involving a sixteen-year-old girl who wants to try out for the men's wrestling team when the school has no girl's wrestling program? *See Saint v. Nebraska School Activities Ass'n*, 684 F. Supp. 626 (D. Neb.1988) (granting a temporary order requiring the state association to allow a girl to compete on the high school wrestling team because there was no showing that the ban promoted the stated goal of protecting the health and safety of girls). How about a case in which a young woman sues to be permitted to compete in the regional Golden Gloves boxing competition? *See Lafler v. Athletic Board of Control*, 536 F. Supp. 104 (W.D. Mich. 1982) (dissolving a temporary order that would have allowed a girl to compete in a Golden Gloves Boxing tournament after finding no violation of equal protection because (a) there was no state action, and (b) the different body make-up of males and females make it appropriate to have different rules and thus different competitions in boxing for the two genders).

3. *Males in Female Sports?* The opposite question arises if a boy wishes to participate in a sport for which his school offers only a girls' team—for example, in field hockey or volleyball. Should courts allow boys to try out for spots on a "girls'" team if there is no boys' team in that sport? What would likely happen if that were the rule? Should it matter whether the sport is a "contact sport?" *Compare Kleczek v. Rhode Island Interscholastic League,* 612 A.2d 734 (R.I. 1992) (holding that boys do not have any right to play on the girls' field hockey team), *with Williams v. School District of Bethlehem,* 799 F. Supp. 513 (E.D. Pa.1992), *rev'd,* 998 F.2d 168 (3d Cir.1993) (holding that it is a factual question whether field hockey is a "contact sport" that would justify a girl's-only team under Title IX or the Pennsylvania Constitution).

4. *Contact Sport Exception.* The Dept. of Education's Title IX Regulations at 34 C.F.R. § 106.41 expressly allow a school to maintain a single sport for one gender only without allowing members of the opposite gender to try out if it is a "contact sport." This regulation further states that "contact sports include boxing, wrestling, rugby, ice hockey, football, basketball, and other sports the purpose or major activity of which involves bodily contact." What is the policy justification for allowing schools to exclude any female from trying out for the school's only team in a "contact sport" even if she is big enough, fast enough, and strong enough to hold her own against the males? Whatever the rationale, does it justify including basketball in the list of such sports? Ice hockey, but not field hockey?

5. *Horner v. KHSAA.* The Kentucky High School Athletic Association (KHSAA) serves as the agent of the Kentucky State Board for Elementary and Secondary Education, for regulation of interscholastic sports in Kentucky. The KHSAA grants official "sanction" to a sport for purposes of creating a state tournament only when the sport has secured interest in participation among at least 25% of member schools (though such sanction, once granted, is preserved as long as at least 15% of members maintain their participation). The KHSAA had sanctioned ten sports for boys, including baseball, and eight for girls, including slow-pitch softball. The latter sport was first approved in 1982, after a school survey found that 44% of Association members wanted to play it. A 1988 survey found just nine percent membership interest in girl's fast-pitch softball, which had risen to 17% (or 50 schools around the state) by 1992. Because the minimum 25% figure had not been met, the KHSAA refused to grant "sanction" to the sport. Member schools did retain the freedom to compete among themselves in such a non-sanctioned sport, and girls had the freedom to play on a boy's baseball team if their member schools did not offer girl's fast-pitch softball.

Lori Ann Horner and eleven other female student athletes in Kentucky filed suit against both the KHSAA and its parent Board, alleging that the failure to sanction girl's fast-pitch softball violated both their Equal Protection and Title IX rights. The tangible concern was that in college sports, both the NCAA and the NAIA had sanctioned girl's fast-pitch, but not slow-pitch, softball. This meant that Kentucky girls who were playing softball were at a disadvantage relative to their classmates in other sanctioned sports (boys' or girls') in securing athletic scholarships when they went to college. Should the KHSAA's "25 percent" rule be found in violation of the constitutional right to equal protection? Or of the Title IX jurisprudence we have seen in OCR Regulations and *Cohen* and other circuit court opinions? *See Horner v. Kentucky High School Athletic Ass'n*, 43 F.3d 265 (6th Cir.1994).

6. *Michigan HSAA*. The Michigan High School Athletic Association serves the same role in its state as the KHSAA. For years, it had scheduled the girls' season in basketball, volleyball, soccer, golf, swimming, and tennis to be played during a time of the year normally not associated with the sport, primarily so as to allow schools to offer girls' sports without having to duplicate facilities that the boys utilized during their more traditional seasons. The mothers of several girls filed a class action lawsuit on behalf of their daughters claiming that requiring them to play during nontraditional and less advantageous seasons disadvantaged them in a variety of ways. The district court held that such off-season scheduling of girls' sports, while boys' sports were always played during the traditional seasons, violated Title IX, the Equal Protection clause of the 14th Amendment, and the Michigan Civil Rights Act. *See Communities for Equity v. Michigan High School Athletic Ass'n*, 178 F. Supp. 2d 805 (W.D. Mich. 2001). What would the MHSAA and its member schools have to do to correct this violation? Must it schedule both boys' and girls' sports in the traditional seasons, even if many schools lack the facilities adequately to accommodate both at the same time? Would it be sufficient if some boys' sports were switched to nontraditional seasons so the girls in those sports could play during the traditional seasons? What if the boys' sports switched were golf, swimming, and tennis, while the girls still played nontraditional seasons in basketball, soccer, and volleyball?

7. *Clark v. Arizona Interscholastic Ass'n*. In *Clark v. Arizona Interscholastic Ass'n.*, 695 F.2d 1126 (9th Cir.1982), a group of boys sued when they were barred by Arizona rules from playing on their school's volleyball team, which was limited to girls. In dismissing the suit, the court asserted:

> As discussed above, the governmental interest claimed is redressing past discrimination against women in athletics and promoting equality of athletic opportunity between the sexes. There is no question that this is a legitimate and important governmental interest.
>
> The only question that remains, then, is whether the exclusion of boys is substantially related to this interest. The question really asks whether any real differences exist between boys and girls which justify the exclusion; *i.e.*, are there differences which would prevent realization of the goal if the exclusion were not allowed.
>
> The record makes clear that due to average physiological differences, males would displace females to a substantial extent if they were allowed to compete for positions on the volleyball team. Thus, athletic opportunities for women would be diminished. As discussed above, there is no question that the Supreme Court allows

for these average real differences between the sexes to be recognized or that they allow gender to be used as a proxy in this sense if it is an accurate proxy. This is not a situation where the classification rests on "'archaic and overbroad' generalizations" or "the baggage of sexual stereotypes." Nor is this a situation involving invidious discrimination against women, or stigmatization of women. The [Arizona Interscholastic Association] is simply recognizing the physiological fact that males would have an undue advantage competing against women for positions on the volleyball team. The situation here is one where there is clearly a substantial relationship between the exclusion of males from the team and the goal of redressing past discrimination and providing equal opportunities for women.

We recognize that specific athletic opportunities could be equalized more fully in a number of ways. For example, participation could be limited on the basis of specific physical characteristics other than sex, a separate boys' team could be provided, a junior varsity squad might be added, or boys' participation could be allowed but only in limited numbers. The existence of these alternatives shows only that the exclusion of boys is not necessary to achieve the desired goal. It does not mean that the required substantial relationship does not exist. . . .

In this case, the alternative chosen may not maximize equality, and may represent trade-offs between equality and practicality. But since absolute necessity is not the standard, and absolute equality of opportunity in every sport is not the mandate, even the existence of wiser alternatives than the one chosen does not serve to invalidate the policy here since it is substantially related to the goal. That is all the standard demands. While equality in specific sports is a worthwhile ideal, it should not be purchased at the expense of ultimate equality of opportunity to participate in sports. As common sense would advise against this, neither does the Constitution demand it.

695 F.2d, at 1131. Do you agree with the court's reasoning? When, if ever, should sports teams be integrated by gender (as they clearly must be by race)? Does your answer differ depending on whether the level of play is elementary school, high school, college, or professional? (Recall that private sports activities are covered by the Civil Rights Act.) Is there a stigma of female athletic inferiority created by "separate but equal" teams? If teams were integrated by gender and selected on the basis of ability alone, would this enhance or reduce equality of athletic opportunity? How much of the current differential between female and male athletic performance is due to physiology, and how much is due to resources and socialization? Is integration the ideal way for aspiring female athletes to overcome the latter obstacles?

CHAPTER 13

INTERNATIONAL AND OLYMPIC SPORTS*

■ ■ ■

In most areas of international law, it is difficult to create a set of principles that all countries will agree to in writing, much less actually enforce. Sport is perhaps unique in this sense. For the most part, all of the countries that participate in Olympic sports agree to and abide by (at least presently) the authority of the Court of Arbitration of Sport (CAS) as a decisionmaking body with respect to disputes in international and Olympic sports. Created by the International Olympic Committee (IOC) and operated by the International Council of Arbitration for Sport (ICAS) in Lausanne, Switzerland, CAS conducts arbitrations of international disputes related to sport. Countries have increasingly deferred to its arbitral decisions, as explored in *Pechstein* later in the chapter. CAS has in many ways relieved the inherent tension between the external legal regulation and the internal governance of sport.

As we will see, having a centralized adjudicatory tribunal is essential in light of the extraordinarily complex structure that governs International and Olympic sports. At the apex of the Olympic structure is the IOC, headquartered in Lausanne, Switzerland, which owns and controls the Olympic Games. The IOC in turn entrusts the various national Olympic committees (NOCs) to oversee the process of determining which athletes will compete for their respective countries in the Olympics. In the United States, this governing body is the United States Olympic Committee (USOC). Under the Amateur Sports Act of 1978 (as amended by the Ted Stevens Olympic & Amateur Sports Act of 1998), 36 U.S.C. § 371 *et seq.*, the USOC oversees all matters relating to U.S. participation in the Olympic, Pan American, and Paralympic Games, as well as with performing several other specific functions related to the promotion of "amateur athletic activity" in the United States.

In addition to the NOCs, each sport has its own governing body, both on the international (international sports federations or ISFs) and national levels (national governing bodies or NGBs). There are almost one hundred different international sports federations (ISFs), running the spectrum from the most widely known and highly commercialized sports like soccer,

---

* The Casebook Website (http://pennstatelaw.psu.edu/SportsTextWebsite) contains citations to scholarly and other commentary on a variety of topics discussed in this chapter or in prior editions, including the history of the Olympics, critiques of Olympic governance, and the cases in the chapter.

gymnastics, track and field, and ice skating to the most obscure like fistball, muaythai, wushu, and flying disc. The IOC recognizes 41 of these ISFs as governing Olympic sports eligible to participate in the Olympic Games, 34 in the Summer Olympics and 7 in the Winter Olympics.

Each of the ISFs conducts its own world championships and sanctions other independently operated contests. The ISFs also determine and enforce eligibility standards for participation in those contests. With respect to the Olympics, the ISFs also determine eligibility for participation by individual athletes in the Olympic Games within the context of the broader rules established by the IOC. The ISFs thus play a significant role in determining who can participate in their sport in the Olympics and other international competitions.

In addition to the ISFs, most sports have national federations, often called "national governing bodies" (NGBs) that operate under the umbrella of the international federation (the ISF). The NGB exercises many of the eligibility and promotional functions of the international body. The NGB in each sport in each country holds the qualifying events that determine which athletes are to represent the country in the Olympic Games (and in many sports, the world championships sponsored by the international federation). As with the IOC, governments (at least in theory) do not control the NGBs, which are private entities. In some countries, the NGBs control power and money through their role in overseeing commercialized professional sport (as is the case with European soccer), in some cases using a portion of professional revenues to organize and support youth and recreational sport in their country (as is the case with New Zealand rugby). By contrast, American NGBs function independently of major professional sports leagues.

As explained below, the burden of regulating performance-enhancing drugs has become increasingly difficult, and so the IOC established the World Anti-Doping Agency (WADA) in 1999 to help address this issue. An independent non-profit like CAS, WADA establishes the doping rules for international sports and the Olympics, while also participating in the policing of doping violations. As with the IOC-NOCs and the ISF-NGBs, there are national anti-doping agencies that report to WADA and help implement its rules and guidelines. In the United States, the anti-doping agency is the United States Anti-Doping Agency (USADA).

Having provided an overview of the constellation of national and international organizations involved in regulating the Olympics and many international competitions, we now take a brief look at the ways in which two of these entities work in practice before exploring some consequences of their decision-making processes later in the chapter.

A. ROLE OF INTERNATIONAL ORGANIZATIONS

The nature of international competitions necessitates a governing body that can adopt and implement eligibility rules while avoiding review by courts or administrative agencies in individual countries. As with other areas of international law, finding a way in which to establish legitimacy and authority to which others would submit was a central concern. Specifically, there was a need for an institution to standardize the venue and the procedures used to resolved sports disputes without leaving individual disputes to the inconsistencies and biases of national courts in countries that had a vested interest in the outcome of the cases. Further, there was a need to set standardized substantive doping rules rather than leave the burden of adopting and enforcing such rules to the individual sport federations that often lacked the resources or the expertise to be effective and that occasionally even failed to recognize basic principles of fairness and due process.

In light of this challenge, the IOC created CAS and WADA. As explained, the role of CAS is to adjudicate the disputes; the role of WADA is to develop the doping rules.

1. THE COURT OF ARBITRATION FOR SPORT (CAS)

Established by the IOC in Delhi, India in 1984, CAS initially consisted of around 60 selected arbitrator members, almost all of whom were European. In 1994, the IOC created the International Council of Arbitration for Sport (ICAS) to oversee CAS. Governed by its own self-perpetuating, 20-person board of highly respected jurists, ICAS was a new, independent organization under Swiss law, and gave CAS new legitimacy and separation from the IOC.

The success of the CAS in becoming the forum of choice for almost all sports disputes depended on the willingness of various sports federations to amend their rules to require that CAS adjudicate the disputes within their respective sports. While few had done so under the old structure when CAS was simply a division of the IOC, the IOC now began to pressure and influence federations to do so. One by one, the international federations amended their rules, and required national federations, event organizers, and individual athletes to sign contracts agreeing to submit any disputes they have with one another to the CAS. By the end of the 20th Century, most federations had recognized the jurisdiction of CAS to settle disputes internal to their sports, even long-time hold outs IAAF (track & field) and FIFA (soccer). Even if a federation does not submit to CAS directly, CAS may hear the disputes it has involving doping if it is a signatory to the WADA Code.

Some of the salient procedural aspects of CAS are as follows:

- The official languages of CAS are English and French, and CAS conducts its proceedings in one of these two languages.

- The Code of Sports-Related Arbitration (The CAS Code) governs CAS's structure, operation, and procedure. As is typical for an arbitral tribunal, there are no fixed rules of evidence, with each three-arbitrator panel able to consider or exclude what it believes appropriate under the circumstances.

- The CAS Code distinguishes between an Ordinary Division and an Appeals Division. Both sets of proceedings are closed.
  - The Ordinary Division hears cases in the first instance that typically relate to a contractual relationship between the parties such as those involving television or sponsorship rights, athlete-agent contracts, or disputes between a national and international federation.
  - The Appeals Division hears appeals from the decisions of arbitral tribunals established either in a country or within a sports federation. Most typically these involve challenges brought by athletes to sanctions imposed on them by their sport's NGB or their national anti-doping authority.

- Although the CAS Code distinguishes between these two internal divisions, as a practical matter the procedures followed are nearly identical for both, and even cases heard on appeal from an earlier arbitration panel are heard by the CAS panel de novo without giving any deference to the earlier factual or legal findings.

- CAS also has what it calls "consultation procedures" that create a method for parties to seek an advisory opinion about a sports legal issue, and more recently it has established a Mediation Division where parties can seek the assistance of CAS appointed mediators to help resolve disputes without formal litigation.

- Beginning with the Atlanta Olympics in 1996, CAS has sent a group of CAS arbitrators to the site of the Games to be available to hear and resolve on an expedited basis (within 24 hours) any emergency disputes. CAS Ad Hoc Division panels also have heard disputes at other international sporting events.

- Cases heard by the Ad Hoc Division generally fall into two categories—appeals by athletes who have been denied access to compete in the Games for any of a variety of reasons and appeals to the outcome of an event for such reasons as failure by judges to adhere to the rules, equipment failure, discovery corrupt judging, or cheating.

The "law" that the CAS generally interprets and enforces derives from the private rules established by the various organizations that make up the world sports movement, including the Olympic Charter, the constitutions and rules of the IOC and international federations, the World Anti-Doping Agency Code, and the rules of national sports and anti-doping agencies. In interpreting and applying the relevant rules in a given case, CAS arbitrators look to the CAS Code for procedural guidance, but employ general principles of substantive law, and if there is no generally accepted principle then the arbitrators must look to the law of the country most directly involved in the case.

Because they are arbitration awards, CAS decisions technically are not binding precedent. Even so, CAS publishes and indexes digests of all Appeals Division and Ad Hoc Division awards, which parties often cite in subsequent CAS cases. CAS arbitrators typically attempt to make their awards consistent with previous decisions. As such, the growing body of published CAS awards has created a *lex sportiva*—a coherent body of international sports law that is "anational" in that it transcends national laws and applies uniformly throughout the world.

All CAS awards are appealable to the Swiss Federal Tribunal (SFT), and parties cannot waive that right. *See Canas v. ATP Tour* (Swiss Federal Tribunal 2007). Nonetheless, the grounds for a successful appeal are very narrow. The SFT has held that under Swiss law the only grounds upon which it may grant an appeal are: (1) the appealing party was effectively denied the right to be heard before the arbitral tribunal; (2) the arbitral panel was constituted irregularly; (3) the panel lacked impartiality; (4) the panel erred in finding that it had jurisdiction over the matter decided; (5) the panel's award exceeded its authority as submitted to it; and (6) the panel's award contravened public policy as defined under Swiss law (which the Court has defined very narrowly because "it must be understood as a universal rather than a national concept, intended to penalize incompatibility with the fundamental legal or moral principles acknowledged in all civilized states"). *N.J.Y.W. v. Fédération Internationale de Natation (FINA)*, 5P.83/1999/Translation (Switz.), 31 March 1999, in DIGEST OF CAS AWARDS II: 1998–2000 at 775, 779 (Matthieu Reeb ed., 2002). The SFT's recognition of the CAS as a legitimate independent arbitral body whose decisions receive the full recognition under Swiss law has served as an international certification of CAS's authority. *See, e.g. Lazutina* and *Danilova v. IOC* cases, [Swiss Federal

Tribunal 2003], (explaining that in a case appealing an IOC decision, CAS is a legitimate and independent arbitral body whose decisions must "be considered true awards, equivalent to the judgments of State courts.").

Litigants have appealed less than five percent of CAS determinations, with less than one percent of those appeals being successful. In short, CAS decisions are, for all practical purposes, final decisions.

2. THE WORLD ANTI-DOPING AGENCY (WADA)

As with CAS, countries have generally accepted the authority of WADA, albeit with the IOC's insistence. Headquartered in Montreal, Canada, WADA's importance lies in its ability to establish and develop a set of uniform and transparent rules to address the issue of doping. The mission of the WADA includes research, education, development of anti-doping capacities, and monitoring and enforcing the World Anti-Doping Code (WADA Code).

As mentioned above, most countries have a national anti-doping organization that reports to WADA. The national anti-doping organizations are often responsible for testing athletes and imposing sanctions with the NGB, as well as investigating potential WADA violations. The USADA's investigation of Lance Armstrong, for instance, exposed his doping that had previously avoided detection.

WADA has an extensive set of complex rules. The most basic rule is that its scheme is a strict liability one. If athletes test positive for a banned substance, they have violated the Code, irrespective of their intent. Even if one ingests a substance unknowingly or accidentally, they have violated WADA. Mitigation, to the extent any exists, comes with respect to the sanction, not the guilt determination.

The original WADA Code underwent a substantial revision that became effective as of January 1, 2015. The new document governs all aspects of the effort to combat the use of banned substances in sport throughout the world, except the professional unionized sports leagues in the United States that have collectively bargained rules dealing with drugs and drug testing. The 2015 WADA Code sets forth detailed rules that:

- list all of the substances that are banned from being artificially put into an athlete's body,
- establish the procedures for determining when and under what conditions athletes are to be tested for banned substances,
- provide for the procedures and methods by which selected laboratories will scientifically evaluate urine or blood samples for banned substances,

- establish the scientific thresholds that define a violation for each substance, and
- set forth the penalties for violations.

Some other general principles include:

- Article 2 of the WADA Code requires athletes randomly selected for testing to report their location at all times during the window between selection and testing.
- Testing can consist of urine or blood samples, or both. WADA immediately divides the sample into 2 containers, the A sample and the B sample. For a positive test, both samples must be positive.
- Article 3 of the Code establishes evidentiary burdens and the standards of proof. All burdens of proof must meet the standard of "comfortable satisfaction," which WADA officials regard as the functional equivalent of "clear and convincing evidence" in the United States—something between a preponderance of the evidence and beyond a reasonable doubt.
- To the extent that an athlete wants to mitigate his or her sanction, the athlete must likewise prove any underlying facts or evidence by "comfortable satisfaction."
- Article 4 of the Code establishes the criteria and procedures by which WADA determines which substances to include on the "prohibited list," as well as any acceptable uses of such substances.
- Article 5 of the Code covers all of the testing rules, Articles 6 and 7 address the technical aspects of testing and the handling of results, and Article 8 addresses the appellate procedure
- Article 10 provides the sanctions for violations. The presence of a banned substance during a qualification results in immediate disqualification. A first out-of-competition violation of the Code by an athlete triggers an automatic four-year suspension from the sport. The automatic suspension may be reduced by half if the athlete can establish with comfortable satisfaction that the presence of the banned substance in the body was not intentional, and it may be eliminated entirely if the athlete can establish with comfortable satisfaction that he/she bears no fault or negligence whatsoever for the banned substance being in the

body. The penalties for repeat violations increase sharply, with a third intentional violation resulting in a lifetime ban.

One final consideration is worth noting with respect to WADA and drug testing generally. It is not a black and white question of whether a substance is present; instead it is a question of whether the amount of a substance exceeds a certain threshold. This is because many of the banned substances increase the amounts of hormones that already exist naturally in the body.

NOTES AND QUESTIONS

1. *Centralized Tribunal.* What are the advantages of having a centralized international tribunal in CAS? Are there disadvantages? Would national courts be preferable?

2. *Arbitration Versus Judicial Proceeding.* In a CAS arbitration, three arbitrators are chosen from an approved list of over 300 neutrals. The decision of the three individuals is essentially not appealable, and does not require use of the rules of evidence. Is this approach preferable to a judicial proceeding? Preferable to case decided by a jury? If some kind of judicial proceeding is preferable, which court?

3. *Double Jeopardy?* In cases where an athlete wins an appeal from a positive drug test in neutral arbitration proceedings in her home country or within her sports federation, WADA can force relitigation of that case *de novo* in an appeal to CAS. Does this constitute double jeopardy? Or is the determination of a national arbitration proceeding different than a criminal jury finding of not guilty? This scenario played itself out in cases involving U.S. distance runner Mary Decker Slaney (for excessive testosterone levels), Scotland's 200-meter European champion Doug Walker (for nandrolone), and British 100-meter champion Linford Christie (for nandrolone). Should national courts refuse to recognize the international panel's decision as being fundamentally unfair because of its double-jeopardy nature? Or should national courts defer to the judgment of the international tribunal because national arbitrators may be biased in favor of their country's athletes and potentially inconsistent results may also result from different national standards? Does this perhaps explain why the CAS requires that appeals from national or federation arbitration decisions be heard *de novo*?

4. *Considering WADA's List of Banned Substances.* Another set of questions arises out of WADA's now standardized list of banned substances for all sports. For one, is it appropriate to have the same substances banned in every sport, even though it is generally recognized that some substances only give a competitive advantage in some, but not all, sports? In addition, some drugs on the list, like cocaine and marijuana, may not provide a competitive

advantage but WADA proscribes them nonetheless. Is this necessary? Why or why not?

B. THE UNITED STATES IN INTERNATIONAL SPORTS

The federal statute that governs Olympic sports in the United States is the Amateur Sports Act of 1978. The legislation expanded the USOC's power to coordinate all amateur athletic activity in the United States. It also gave the USOC the power to recognize (or to withdraw recognition from) an amateur sports organization as the NGB in each sport. Under the statute, there exists an arbitration remedy for dispute resolution among members as well as those "relating to the opportunity of any amateur athlete, coach, trainer, or other person to participate in certain protected competitions."

Further, the Act empowers these governing bodies to perform various functions related to their sports:

- to conduct "amateur athletic competition" in the United States; to sanction other such competitions inside and outside the United States;
- to determine eligibility standards for participation in such competitions;
- to select the athletes to represent the United States in the Olympic, Paralympic, and Pan American Games;
- to represent or to select a representative for the United States in the international federations; and
- generally to govern and promote all "amateur athletic activities" in their respective sports in the United States.

In 1998, Congress passed sweeping amendments to the Amateur Sports Act (ASA) affecting a number of significant matters. In addition to renaming it the Ted Stevens Olympic and Amateur Sports Act (ASA), the amendments:

- formalized the rights and procedures available to athletes in challenging eligibility decisions;
- expanded the list of protected trademarks that the USOC controls (whether or not an alleged infringement creates any consumer confusion);
- brought the Paralympic Games and issues relating to disabled athletes within the scope of the Act;
- formalized the involvement of athletes and national sports governing bodies in the USOC's governing process;

- gave federal courts exclusive jurisdiction over ASA cases, but banned the issuance of injunctions within 21 days of the start of an Olympic event;
- codified extensive prior case law that the ASA does not create a private right of action; and
- created the office of an ombudsman to provide independent advice and counsel to athletes about applicable laws and procedures.

1. JUDICIAL REVIEW OF SPORTS GOVERNING BODIES

A crucial legal issue is when, under what legal theories, and under what standard of review, an American court should overturn a decision by one of these governing bodies. The following highly publicized case depicts some of the key legal arguments that have been made about this issue.

DEFRANTZ V. UNITED STATES OLYMPIC COMMITTEE
492 F. Supp. 1181 (D.D.C.), *aff'd*, 701 F.2d 221 (D.C. Cir. 1980)

PRATT, JUDGE.

Plaintiffs, 25 athletes and one member of the Executive Board of defendant United States Olympic Committee (USOC), have moved for an injunction barring defendant USOC from carrying out a resolution, adopted by the USOC House of Delegates on April 12, 1980, not to send an American team to participate in the Games of the XXII Olympiad to be held in Moscow in the summer of 1980. Plaintiffs allege that in preventing American athletes from competing in the Summer Olympics, defendant has exceeded its statutory powers and has abridged plaintiffs' constitutional rights.

* * *

According to its Rules and By-laws, the International Olympic Committee (IOC) governs the Olympic movement and owns the rights of the Olympic games. IOC Rules provide that National Olympic Committees (NOC) may be established "as the sole authorities responsible for the representation of the respective countries at the Olympic Games," so long as the NOC's rules and regulations are approved by the IOC. The USOC is one such National Olympic Committee.

The USOC is a corporation created and granted a federal charter by Congress in 1950. This charter was revised by the Amateur Sports Act of 1978. Under this statute, defendant USOC has "exclusive jurisdiction" and authority over participation and representation of the United States in the Olympic Games.

* * *

On December 27, 1979, the Soviet Union launched an invasion of its neighbor, Afghanistan. That country's ruler was deposed and killed and a new government was installed. . . .

President Carter termed the invasion a threat to the security of the Persian Gulf area as well as a threat to world peace and stability, and he moved to take direct sanctions against the Soviet Union. These sanctions included a curtailment of agricultural and high technology exports to the Soviet Union, and restrictions on commerce with the Soviets. The Administration also turned its attention to a boycott of the summer Olympic Games [in Moscow] as a further sanction against the Soviet Union.

* * *

[The President put great pressure on the USOC not to send a team to the 1980 Games, even to the point of threatening to withhold federal funding from the USOC, to revoke its tax exemptions, and to invoke the International Emergency Economic Powers Act to forbid any athletes from traveling to the Soviet Union during the games. In addition, the House of Representatives passed a resolution, by a vote of 386 to 12, opposing U.S. participation in the Games.]

* * *

[On April 12, 1980], [a]fter what USOC President Kane describes in his affidavit as "full, open, complete and orderly debate by advocates of each motion," the House of Delegates, on a secret ballot passed, by a vote of 1,604 to 798, a resolution [declaring that the USOC would not send a team to Moscow unless international conditions changed dramatically.]

* * *

1. The Amateur Sports Act of 1978

Plaintiffs allege in their complaint that by its decision not to send an American team to compete in the summer Olympic Games in Moscow, defendant USOC has violated the Amateur Sports Act of 1978. . . . Reduced to their essentials, these allegations are that the Act does not give, and that Congress intended to deny, the USOC the authority to decide not to enter an American team in the Olympics, except perhaps for sports-related reasons, and that the Act guarantees to certain athletes [a right to compete in the Olympic Games.] . . .

* * *

The principal substantive powers of the USOC are found in § 375(a) of the Act.[12] In determining whether the USOC's authority under the Act

---

[12] They are to: "(1) serve as the coordinating body for amateur athletic activity in the United States directly relating to international amateur athletic competition; (2) represent the United

encompasses the right to decide not to participate in an Olympic contest, we must read these provisions in the context in which they were written. In writing this legislation, Congress did not create a new relationship between the USOC and the IOC. Rather, it recognized an already longexisting relationship between the two and statutorily legitimized that relationship with a federal charter and federal incorporation.[13] The legislative history demonstrates Congressional awareness that the USOC and its predecessors, as the National Olympic Committee for the United States, have had a continuing relationship with the IOC since 1896. Congress was necessarily aware that a National Olympic Committee is a creation and a creature of the International Olympic Committee, to whose rules and regulations it must conform. The NOC gets its power and its authority from the IOC, the sole proprietor and owner of the Olympic Games.

In view of Congress' obvious awareness of these facts, we would expect that if Congress intended to limit or deny to the USOC powers it already enjoyed as a National Olympic Committee, such limitation or denial would be clear and explicit. No such language appears in the statute. Indeed, far from precluding this authority, the language of the statute appears to embrace it. For example, the "objects and purposes" section of the Act speaks in broad terms, stating that the USOC shall exercise "exclusive jurisdiction" over ". . . all matters pertaining to the participation of the United States in the Olympic Games. . . ." We read this broadly stated purpose in conjunction with the specific power conferred on the USOC by the Act to "represent the United States as its national Olympic committee in relations with the International Olympic Committee," and in conjunction with the IOC Rules and By-laws, which provide that "representation" includes the decision to participate. In doing so, we find a compatibility and not a conflict between the Act and the IOC Rules on the issue of the authority of the USOC to decide whether or not to accept an invitation to field an American team at the Olympics. The language of the statute is broad enough to confer this authority, and we find that Congress must have intended that the USOC exercise that authority in this area, which it already enjoyed because of its long-standing relationship with the

---

States as its national Olympic committee in relations with the International Olympic Committee . . . ; (3) organize, finance, and control the representation of the United States in the competitions and events of the Olympic Games . . . and obtain, either directly or by delegation to the appropriation national governing body, amateur representation for summer games." 36 U.S.C. § 375(a)(1), (2), (3). The "objects and purposes" section of the Act includes the provision, also found in the 1950 Act, that the USOC shall "exercise exclusive jurisdiction . . . over all matters pertaining to the participation of the United States in the Olympic Games . . . including the representation of the United States in such games." *Id.* § 374(3).

[13] To the extent the USOC was granted extended power by the 1978 Act, the legislative history makes clear, and the plaintiffs do not dispute the fact, that these powers were primarily designed to give the USOC supervisory authority over United States amateur athletic groups in order to eliminate the numerous and frequent jurisdictional squabbles among schools, athletic groups and various national sports governing bodies.

IOC. We accordingly conclude that the USOC has the authority to decide not to send an American team to the Olympics.

Plaintiffs next argue that if the USOC does have the authority to decide not to accept an invitation to send an American team to the Moscow Olympics, that decision must be based on "sports-related considerations." In support of their argument, plaintiffs point to §§ 392(a)(5) and (b) of the Act, which plaintiffs acknowledge "are not in terms applicable to the USOC," but rather concern situations in which national governing bodies of various sports, which are subordinate to the USOC, are asked to sanction the holding of international competitions below the level of the Olympic or Pan American Games in the United States or the participation of the United States athletes in such competition abroad. These sections provide that a national governing body may withhold its sanctions only upon clear and convincing evidence that holding or participating in the competition "would be detrimental to the best interests of the sport." Plaintiffs argue by analogy that a similar "sports-related" limitation must attach to any authority the USOC might have to decide not to participate in an Olympic competition. We cannot agree.

The provision on which plaintiffs place reliance by analogy is specifically concerned with eliminating the feuding between various amateur athletic organizations and national governing bodies which for so long characterized amateur athletics. As all parties recognize, this friction, such as the well-publicized power struggles between the NCAA and the AAU, was a major reason for passage of the Act, and the provisions plaintiffs cite, among others, are aimed at eliminating this senseless strife, which the Senate and House Committee reports indicate had dramatically harmed the ability of the United States to compete effectively in international competition. In order to eliminate this internecine squabbling, the Act elevated the USOC to a supervisory role over the various amateur athletic organizations, and provided that the USOC establish procedures for the swift and equitable settlement of these disputes. As indicated above, it also directed that the national governing bodies of the various sports could only withhold their approvals of international competition for sports-related reasons. Previously, many of these bodies had withheld their sanction of certain athletic competitions in order to further their own interests at the expense of other groups and to the detriment of athletes wishing to participate.

In brief, this sports-related limitation is intimately tied to the specific purpose of curbing the arbitrary and unrestrained power of various athletic organizations subordinate to the USOC not to allow athletes to compete in international competition below the level of the Olympic Games and the Pan American Games. This purpose has nothing to do with a decision by the USOC to exercise authority granted by the IOC to decide not to participate in an Olympic competition.

* * *

We therefore conclude that the USOC not only had the authority to decide not to send an American team to the summer Olympics, but also that it could do so for reasons not directly related to sports considerations.

(b) *Athletes' Statutory Right to Compete in the Olympics*

* * *

Plaintiffs argue that the Report of the President's Commission on Olympic Sports, which was the starting point for the legislation proposed, and the legislative history support their argument that the statute confers an enforceable right on plaintiffs to compete in Olympic competition. Again, we are compelled to disagree with plaintiffs.

The legislative history and the statute are clear that the "right to compete," which plaintiffs refer to, is in the context of the numerous jurisdictional disputes between various athletic bodies, such as the NCAA and the AAU, which we have just discussed, and which was a major impetus for the Amateur Sports Act of 1978. Plaintiffs recognize that a major purpose of the Act was to eliminate such disputes. However, they go on to argue that the Report which highlighted the need for strengthening the USOC in order to eliminate this feuding, made a finding that there is little difference between an athlete denied the right to compete because of a boycott and an athlete denied the right to compete because of jurisdictional bickering.

The short answer is that although the Congress may have borrowed heavily from the Report of the President's Commission, it did not enact the Report. Instead, it enacted a statute and that statute relates a "right to compete" to the elimination of jurisdictional disputes between amateur athletic groups, which for petty and groundless reasons have often deprived athletes of the opportunity to enter a particular competition. . . .

The Senate Report makes clear that the language relied on by plaintiffs is not designed to provide any substantive guarantees, let alone a Bill of Rights. Further, to the extent that any guarantees of a right to compete are included in the USOC Constitution as a result of this provision, they do not include a right that amateur athletes may compete in the Olympic Games despite a decision by the USOC House of Delegates not to accept an invitation to enter an American team in the competition. This provision simply was not designed to extend so far. Rather, it was designed to remedy the jurisdictional disputes among amateur athletic bodies, not disputes between athletes and the USOC itself over the exercise of the USOC's discretion not to participate in the Olympics.

* * *

Because we conclude that the rights plaintiffs seek to enforce do not exist in the Act, and because the legislative history of the Act nowhere allows the implication of a private right of action, we find that plaintiffs have no implied private right of action under the Amateur Sports Act of 1978 to maintain this suit.

2. Constitutional Claims

Plaintiffs have alleged that the decision of the USOC not to enter an American team in the summer Olympics has violated certain rights guaranteed to plaintiffs under the First, Fifth and Ninth Amendments to the United States Constitution. . . .

(a) State Action

Although federally chartered, defendant is a private organization. Because the Due Process Clause of the Fifth Amendment, on which plaintiffs place great reliance, applies only to actions by the federal government, plaintiffs must show that the USOC vote is a "governmental act," *i.e.*, state action. In defining state action, the courts have fashioned two guidelines. The first involves an inquiry into whether the state

> . . . has so far insinuated itself into a position of interdependence with (the private entity) that it must be recognized as a joint participant in the challenged activity.

Here, there is no such intermingling, and there is no factual justification for finding that the federal government and the USOC enjoyed the "symbiotic relationship" which courts have required to find state action. The USOC has received no federal funding[25] and it exists and operates independently of the federal government. Its chartering statute gives it "exclusive jurisdiction" over "all matters pertaining to the participation of the United States in the Olympic Games. . . ." 36 U.S.C. § 374(3). To be sure, the Act does link the USOC and the federal government to the extent it requires the USOC to submit an annual report to the President and the Congress. But this hardly converts such an independent relationship to a "joint participation."

The second guideline fashioned by the courts involves an inquiry of whether:

> . . . there is a sufficiently close nexus between the state and the challenged action of the regulated entity so that the action of the latter may be fairly treated as that of the state itself.

---

[25] Federal funds were authorized under the Amateur Sports Act of 1978 but have never been appropriated. But the mere receipt of federal funds by a private entity, without more, is not enough to convert that entity's activity into state action. *Spark v. Catholic University of America*, 510 F.2d 1277 (D.C. Cir. 1975).

... In the instant case, there was no requirement that any federal government body approve actions by the USOC before they become effective.

Plaintiffs argue that by the actions of certain federal officials, the federal government initiated, encouraged, and approved of the result reached (i.e., the vote of the USOC not to send an American team to the summer Olympics). Plaintiffs advance a novel theory. Essentially, their argument is that the campaign of governmental persuasion, personally led by President Carter, crossed the line from "governmental recommendation," which plaintiffs find acceptable and presumably necessary to the operation of our form of government, into the area of "affirmative pressure that effectively places the government's prestige behind the challenged action," and thus, results in state action. We cannot agree.

* * *

Here there is no [requisite governmental] control. The USOC is an independent body, and nothing in its chartering statute gives the federal government the right to control that body or its officers. Furthermore, the facts here do not indicate that the federal government was able to exercise any type of "de facto" control over the USOC. The USOC decided by a secret ballot of its House of Delegates. The federal government may have had the power to prevent the athletes from participating in the Olympics even if the USOC had voted to allow them to participate, but it did not have the power to make them vote in a certain way. All it had was the power of persuasion. We cannot equate this with control. To do so in cases of this type would be to open the door and usher the courts into what we believe is a largely nonjusticiable realm, where they would find themselves in the untenable position of determining whether a certain level, intensity, or type of "Presidential" or "Administration" or "political" pressure amounts to sufficient control over a private entity so as to invoke federal jurisdiction.

We accordingly find that the decision of the USOC not to send an American team to the summer Olympics was not state action, and therefore, does not give rise to an actionable claim for the infringements of the constitutional rights alleged.

(b) Constitutionally Protected Rights

... Were we to find state action in this case, we would conclude that defendant USOC has violated no constitutionally protected right of plaintiffs.

We note that other courts have considered the right to compete in amateur athletics and have found no deprivation of constitutionally protected rights. As the Government has pointed out in *Parish v. National Collegiate Athletic Association*, 506 F.2d 1028 (5th Cir. 1975), basketball players sought an injunction to prevent the NCAA from enforcing its ruling declaring certain athletes ineligible to compete in tournaments and televised games. The court stated that:

> the privilege of participation in interscholastic activities must be deemed to fall . . . outside the protection of due process.

Plaintiffs have been unable to draw our attention to any court decision which finds that the rights allegedly violated here enjoy constitutional protection, and we can find none. Plaintiffs would expand the constitutionally-protected scope of liberty and self-expression to include the denial of an amateur athlete's right to compete in an Olympic contest when that denial was the result of a decision by a supervisory athletic organization acting well within the limits of its authority. Defendant has not denied plaintiffs the right to engage in every amateur athletic competition. Defendant has not denied plaintiffs the right to engage in their chosen occupation. Defendant has not even denied plaintiffs the right to travel, only the right to travel for one specific purpose. We can find no justification and no authority for the expansive reading of the Constitution which plaintiffs urge. To find as plaintiffs recommend would be to open the floodgates to a torrent of lawsuits. The courts have correctly recognized that many of life's disappointments, even major ones, do not enjoy constitutional protection. This is one such instance.

Case dismissed.

NOTES AND QUESTIONS

1. *State Action?* Should the federal government be able to enact a law delegating what in many countries is a governmental function to a private group, then exert enormous political pressure on that group to make a certain decision, and still argue that there is insufficient government involvement to trigger constitutional protections for those adversely affected by that decision? The courts have uniformly refused to recognize as state action the decisions of any of the national or international athletic governing bodies. *See, e.g., Behagen v. Amateur Basketball Ass'n of the United States*, 884 F.2d 524 (10th Cir. 1989); *International Olympic Comm. v. San Francisco Arts & Athletics*, 781 F.2d 733 (9th Cir. 1986), *aff'd*, 483 U.S. 522 (1987). Thus, like the NCAA after the *Tarkanian* decision in Chapter 10, these organizations do not have to provide constitutional due process or equal protection to those affected by their decisions. Does this mean that these bodies can do whatever they want? Could the USOC decide not to send a team to the Olympics in retaliation for an IOC decision not to award the 2016 Games to Chicago, or because the IOC refused to enter a licensing agreement with an American company? If constitutional arguments are unavailable, what other legal claims are available to disappointed athletes?

2. *Constitutional Violation?* Even if the court had found that the USOC was a state actor, would the plaintiffs have prevailed on their constitutional claims? What constitutional rights, if any, did the USOC arguably violate?

3. *Antitrust Law?* One question stemming from the Amateur Sports Act is the extent to which the USOC, a national sports governing body, or its international counterparts, are subject to American antitrust law, especially since the courts have found such bodies to be private, non-governmental actors. The American courts have not really addressed the issue, with the exception of *Cady v. TAC*, No. C 89-1737 (N.D. Cal. May 25, 1989), an unpublished opinion holding that The Athletics Congress (TAC) was exempt from antitrust law because of the power Congress vested in it. Was this the proper result?

In Europe, by contrast, there is a rich jurisprudence on this topic where courts have drawn a distinction between "purely sporting" rules that are not subject to competition law and commercial rules that are subject to competition law. Should antitrust law apply here? Is the USOC fundamentally similar to or different than the NCAA?

2. ATHLETE ELIGIBILITY STANDARDS

Some of the most controversial decisions by sports federations involve athlete eligibility—either establishing eligibility standards or applying the standards in individual cases. Prior to the widespread agreement to submit to CAS, conflicts arose between the decisions of international governing bodies and interpretation of the same evidence by national courts.

REYNOLDS V. INTERNATIONAL AMATEUR ATHLETIC FEDERATION
841 F. Supp. 1444 (S.D. Ohio 1992)

KINNEARY, DISTRICT JUDGE.

[Harold "Butch" Reynolds was the world track and field record holder at 400 meters who had won the silver medal at the 1988 Olympic Games in Seoul, South Korea. Following the "Herculis Meet" event in Monte Carlo, Monaco, on August 12, 1990, Reynolds was randomly selected to provide a urine sample. In October 1990, Reynolds was informed that he had tested positively for the anabolic steroid nandrolone, and was suspended by the IAAF for two years, which would have cost him a spot in the 1992 Olympic Games in Barcelona, Spain.

Reynolds brought suit in federal court in his home state of Ohio, arguing that the test results were erroneous—based in part on the fact that a urine sample from an August 19 track meet in Berlin one week after the Monte Carlo meet had tested negative. The district judge dismissed this initial suit on the ground that Reynolds first had to use the athletic system's administrative process. Reynolds thus sought an arbitration hearing pursuant to the Amateur Sports Act of 1978 and the constitution of the U.S. Olympic Committee (USOC). Following a hearing in June 1991, the arbitrator issued an opinion that exonerated Reynolds.

> The arbitrator finds that the Respondent's suspension of Mr. Reynolds was improper; that there is clear and convincing evidence that the "A" sample and the "B" sample did not emanate from the same person and the "B" sample did not confirm the "A" sample; that there is substantial evidence that neither the "A" sample or the "B" sample emanated from the Claimant; and that Claimant should be declared eligible to compete in the qualifying rounds for the World Game Championships on June 12, 1991.

Both TAC and the IAAF refused to accept this ruling because it had not complied with the adjudicative procedures under IAAF Rule 59, which were initially administered by the domestic track and field body (in the U.S., this was TAC). Reynolds thus asked TAC to conduct a hearing, which took place that September. After 12 hours of testimony and arguments and two weeks of deliberation, the three person TAC panel also exonerated Reynolds. They wrote:

> The panel, after hearing the matters before it, the testimony of witnesses and expert witnesses from both sides, documents and exhibits, hereby finds that Mr. Harry "Butch" Reynolds has cast substantial doubt on the validity of the drug test attributed to him. The panel finds that the "B" sample positive result reported by the Lafarge Laboratory has been impeached by clear and convincing evidence.

This time, the IAAF refused to accept the TAC verdict and, under its Rule 20, ordered yet another arbitration of this dispute. In a two-day hearing in London, England, on May 11–12, 1992, counsel for TAC and the IAAF presented their respective positions; after just two hours of deliberations, the three-member panel issued a seven-page decision that found "no doubt" about Reynolds' guilt.

With the Olympic trials to select members of the U.S. track and field team for the Games in Barcelona scheduled just two weeks later, Reynolds went back to court in Ohio, suing the IAAF for breach of contract, defamation, tortious interference with a business relationship, and denial of contractual due process. The IAAF refused to participate in these proceedings, contending that an American court had no jurisdiction over its international regime. This time, the district judge found that Reynolds' claim satisfied Ohio's "long-arm" statutory jurisdiction, which covered nonresident defendants who "transact any business in the state," or who "cause tortious injury" to someone in the state even by out-of-state actions, as long as the defendant regularly engages in business in the state. This finding raised the more fundamental question of whether such a state jurisdictional rule complied with the Due Process standard in the U.S.

Constitution, one that requires out-of-state defendants to have sufficient minimum contact with the state such "that the maintenance of the suit does not offend 'traditional notions of fair play and substantial justice.'" *International Shoe Co. v. Washington*, 326 U.S. 310, 316 (1945).]

* * *

I. Personal Jurisdiction of This Court Over the IAAF

The Court believes that it may constitutionally exercise personal jurisdiction over the IAAF. Initially, the Court must sharply reject the IAAF and TAC's position that the IAAF is not subject to the jurisdiction of *any* court *anywhere* in the world. At the hearing, TAC's counsel expressed the view that the IAAF is "infallible" and its decisions must not be reviewable by this Court—or any other. Indeed, IAAF vice president Arne Ljungqvist has been quoted as stating:

> Civil courts create a lot of problems for our anti-doping work, but we have said we don't care in the least what they say. We have our rules, and they are supreme. . . .

. . . It is simply an unacceptable position that the courts of this country cannot protect the individual rights of United States citizens where those rights are threatened by an association which has significant contacts with this country, which exercises significant control over both athletes and athletic events in this country, which acts through an agent organization in this country,[6] and which gains significant revenue from its contracts with United States companies.

Regarding the inquiry which this Court must make . . . , it is manifest that the IAAF has purposefully availed itself of the privilege of acting in Ohio, and has caused direct consequences to the Plaintiff in Ohio. This Court has previously listed in detail the facts supporting this conclusion and they will not be recounted here. Suffice it to say, as a general matter, Ohio athletes are subject to the Rules of the IAAF, the IAAF gains substantial revenue from the activities of these athletes, and the IAAF has recognized a track and field event to be held in Ohio. With respect to Mr. Reynolds specifically, the IAAF has contributed expense money so that Mr. Reynolds could compete in two events recognized by the IAAF, has published arguably defamatory statements which were circulated in Ohio publications, and has committed acts which may be found to have

---

[6] The Court finds untenable what is apparently the tactic of the IAAF to insulate itself from the jurisdiction of any court: despite the incredible power and influence which it directly wields over track and field athletics in the United States and throughout the world, the IAAF continually maintains that it has no direct contact with any country or athlete, and that it only acts or has any outside contact through its member organizations, such as TAC. While that may be true, it must then be conceded that TAC is an agent of the IAAF and personal jurisdiction may be found to exist through TAC's contacts with this forum.

tortiously interfered with Mr. Reynolds' business relationships with both United States and Ohio companies.

Furthermore, this Court believes that as the IAAF acts through its member organizations, it is reasonable to subject the IAAF to jurisdiction anywhere its member organizations may be subject to suit. The evidence before the Court establishes that the IAAF distributes money to athletes through its member organizations, notifies athletes of positive drug test results through its member organizations, and provides adjudication of disputed drug test results in the first instance through its member organizations. Essentially, the IAAF refuses to have any contact with individual athletes, instead forcing such athletes to approach the IAAF through the national organizations. Thus, this Court holds, as the Tenth Circuit held in *Behagen v. Amateur Basketball Ass'n*, [744 F.2d 731 (10th Cir. 1984)], that an international organization which acts through its members may be subject to the jurisdiction of a particular court based upon a member's contacts with, and activity in, the forum. Where, as here, the member organization has intervened as a Defendant in the action, the exercise of personal jurisdiction is beyond question.

* * *

In accordance with all of the foregoing . . . , this Court holds that the IAAF's failure to enter a timely objection to personal jurisdiction, which failure resulted in the inability of the Plaintiff to obtain the necessary discovery to establish the facts upon which he asserts the jurisdiction of this Court rests, results in the waiver of the IAAF's right to contest the personal jurisdiction of this Court. . . .

II. The Preliminary Injunction

* * *

The issue of greatest import to this Court, to the parties, and to *amicus*, is the threat of the IAAF to "contaminate," or in other words, suspend any athlete who competes against Mr. Reynolds knowing that he is currently deemed ineligible to participate in IAAF track and field events. The Court not only finds the threat unconvincing, it finds it to be an inappropriate consideration to weigh against the harm which will befall Mr. Reynolds if he is wrongfully prevented from participating in track and field competitions due to his IAAF Ineligibility status.

The IAAF's threat is unconvincing for several reasons. First, it is not at all clear that IAAF's contamination rule is mandatory in nature. Indeed, documents and testimony adduced at the preliminary injunction hearing cast considerable doubt upon this proposition, and lead this Court to conclude that it is not always strictly enforced. Furthermore, it is equally unclear that the IAAF would attempt to prevent United States track and field athletes uninvolved in this litigation from participating in the

Olympics on the basis of Rule 53(ii) alone. The loss of some of the event's top competitors, the resulting public outcry, and the possible loss of substantial revenue to the IAAF, all lead this Court to conclude that widespread "contamination" of American athletes by the IAAF is unlikely.

Even if, however, this Court considered such contamination to be the likely result if an injunction were to issue, the Court finds such a threat *by the Defendant IAAF* to be an entirely inappropriate consideration. It is, of course, axiomatic that in considering the merits of a preliminary injunction, the Court must consider whether the injunction will harm others. However, it is the impassioned conviction of the Court that such harm to others does not, and indeed, should not, include harm to others *caused by the voluntary and intentional acts of the Defendant*. To hold otherwise would be to allow the IAAF to hold the entire American Olympic team against an unfavorable decision from this Court. . . .

This Court also believes that Reynolds has established a likelihood of success on the merits of his claims. With respect to the validity of the drug test performed at the Lafarge Laboratory on the urine sample provided by Reynolds in Monte Carlo, this Court believes—as did the American Arbitration Association arbitrator and the TAC hearing panel—that Reynolds has created a substantial doubt as to the accuracy of the reported results. Not only did Reynolds' expert testify as to numerous deficiencies in the Lafarge Laboratories' testing procedure,[9] he also testified as to several inconsistencies with the actual test results which make it highly unlikely that both samples actually originated with Mr. Reynolds.[10] Finally, and perhaps most egregious of all, Plaintiff's expert testified that nandrolone is known to remain in an individual's body for a considerable period of time, and the fact that Reynolds' urine allegedly tested positive for two metabolites of nandrolone on August 12, 1990, and tested negative for nandrolone one week later on August 19, 1990, casts considerable doubt on the validity of the August 12 test.

With respect to the claims in Reynolds Complaint, the Court finds it likely that they are meritorious. First, it appears likely that a contractual relationship exists between the Plaintiff and both the IAAF and TAC, and it further appears that the IAAF breached this contract when it departed from its own guidelines and regulations regarding appropriate drug testing procedures. Second, it appears likely that the IAAF—with disregard for its own policy of confidentiality—maliciously released to the world media information that Reynolds had tested positive for the steroid nandrolone

---

[9] For instance, Plaintiff's expert testified that the laboratory failed to attach proper chain of custody documentation to the urine samples provided by Reynolds, failed to use an "internal standard" to assist it in interpreting the results, and failed to use a positive quality control.

[10] Plaintiff's expert testified that the "picture" of naturally occurring steroids should be relatively the same for both samples of urine if, as alleged, they were both supplied by Reynolds. He concluded, however, that because the naturally occurring steroids in the two samples created extremely different "pictures," the two could not have originated with the same individual.

before Reynolds was accorded a hearing before TAC as prescribed by IAAF rules. It is reasonable to infer that the IAAF knew that such information would cause third parties to void existing endorsement contracts and prevent others from entering into such contracts. As such, Reynolds is likely to succeed on his claim of defamation and tortious interference with a business relationship.

* * *

Injunction granted.

NOTES AND QUESTIONS

1. *Aftermath.* The court in *Reynolds* enjoined the IAAF and TAC "from interfering, impeding, threatening to impede or interfere in any way [with] the Plaintiff's ability to compete in all international and national amateur track and field competitions. . ." TAC allowed Reynolds to run in the 400-meter race at the Olympic trials in New Orleans, at which Reynolds qualified only as an alternate on the 4x400 meter relay team. But the USOC refused to grant Reynolds credentials to travel with the U.S. Olympic team to Barcelona, based on the IAAF's refusal to allow him to compete. After the Olympics, the IAAF announced that because of Reynolds' legal challenge, it was extending his suspension from August 1992 through the end of that year. In December 1992, Judge Kinneary, finding that the IAAF had "purposefully avoided the truth," entered a default damages award of $27.3 million (approximately $7 million in compensatory damages and $20 million in punitive damages), and made his earlier injunction permanent.

2. *Enforcement of $27 Million Judgment.* Reynolds had the practical problem of how to enforce his $27 million judgment. He began garnishment proceedings against four American corporations (including Coca-Cola) that owed the IAAF money for sponsorship deals. The IAAF argued that the Ohio federal courts lacked personal jurisdiction. In finding for the IAAF on appeal, the Sixth Circuit explained:

> In short, the IAAF is based in England, owns no property and transacts no business in Ohio, and does not supervise U.S. athletes in Ohio or elsewhere. Its contacts with Reynolds in Ohio are superficial, and are insufficient to create the requisite minimum contacts for personal jurisdiction.

Reynolds v. IAAF, 23 F.3d 1110 (6th Cir. 1994).

3. *Minimum Contacts?* The Sixth Circuit did not hold that an international governing federation would never be subject to the personal jurisdiction of any American court; it held only that, on the facts of this case, the IAAF was not subject to the jurisdiction of the Ohio courts. Under what

circumstances would an international governing body be subject to a state's jurisdiction in cases like *Reynolds*? Consider the following scenarios:

    a. Reynolds sues the IAAF in Georgia, where the IAAF, the USOC, and other federations were engaged in extensive preparation for the 1996 Atlanta Olympics.

    b. Reynolds sues the IAAF in Indiana, where TAC's (now USAT&F's) headquarters and offices are located.

    c. Reynolds sues the IAAF in New York, where several corporations that sponsor IAAF events, and TV networks that purchase television rights to IAAF events, are headquartered? Would it matter if the contracts with these entities were negotiated or signed in New York?

    d. Reynolds sues the IAAF in California, where the IAAF has sanctioned track meets and held its own World Track & Field Championships in the recent past.

    e. Reynolds sues the IAAF in Ohio, but the meet at which he was alleged to have tested positive occurred in Texas, and the laboratory at which the sample was tested was located in Louisiana. What if the meet or the laboratory were in Ohio?

4 *Nationalism Versus Deference to International Institutions.* Should courts in the United States—or in any country—review and overturn the decisions of an international sports governing body? If so, under what standard of review and on what grounds? The IAAF contends that if the courts of every nation could overturn its decisions, the Federation could not govern effectively because national political interests would influence many courts to overturn any IAAF decision contrary to the interests of their country's athletes. Therefore, the IAAF does not recognize the jurisdiction of any court, anywhere.

LINDLAND V. UNITED STATES WRESTLING ASSOCIATION
227 F.3d 1000 (7th Cir. 2000)

EASTERBROOK, CIRCUIT JUDGE.

Readers of our prior opinions (or the sports pages) know that Keith Sieracki and Matt Lindland both believe that they are entitled to be the U.S. entrant in the 76 kilogram weight class of Greco-Roman wrestling at the 2000 Olympic Games. They have met twice in championship bouts where the Olympic spot was the victor's reward: Sieracki won the first by a score of 2–1; Lindland won the second by a score of 8–0. Each claims that his victory entitles him to the slot in Sydney. Lindland protested the result of the first match through the hierarchy of USA Wrestling, the national governing body for amateur wrestling. After USA Wrestling rejected his protests, Lindland commenced arbitration, which was his right under the Ted Stevens Olympic and Amateur Sports Act. *See* 36 U.S.C. § 220529(a).

Arbitrator Burns ordered the rematch, which Lindland won. USA Wrestling was unwilling to accept this outcome; instead of sending Lindland's name to the United States Olympic Committee (USOC) as its nominee for the Games, it told the USOC to send Sieracki and listed Lindland only as a person eligible to compete in the event of injury. Lindland then sought confirmation of the Burns Award under § 9 of the Federal Arbitration Act, 9 U.S.C. § 9, and in an opinion issued on August 24 we held that Lindland is entitled to that relief-which, we pointedly added, means that he is entitled to be USA Wrestling's nominee to the USOC. *Lindland v. USA Wrestling Association, Inc.*, 230 F.3d 1036 (7th Cir. 2000).

Later that day, USA Wrestling informed the USOC that Sieracki remained its nominee. Its explanation for this defiance was that a second arbitrator, in a proceeding initiated by Sieracki, had disagreed with Arbitrator Burns and directed USA Wrestling to make Sieracki its nominee on the basis of his victory in the first match. USA Wrestling had no excuse for following Arbitrator Campbell's unreviewed award rather than a decision of a federal court confirming Arbitrator Burns's award, and on August 25 we issued a writ of mandamus requiring the district court to ensure that USA Wrestling implemented the Burns Award "immediately and unconditionally." *Lindland v. US Wrestling Association, Inc.*, 228 F.3d 782 at 783 (7th Cir. 2000), On August 26 USA Wrestling finally complied, but the USOC then refused to accept Lindland as a member of the team, asserting that USA Wrestling's nomination of Lindland was untimely because Sieracki's name already had been sent to the International Olympic Committee (IOC) in Lausanne, Switzerland.

Lindland then returned to the district court, asking it to compel the USOC to send his name to the IOC. Sieracki fought back by asking a different district court (in Denver, Colorado) to confirm the Campbell Award. The district judge in Denver sensibly transferred that request to the Northern District of Illinois under 28 U.S.C. § 1404, consolidating all proceedings arising out of the dispute. The Northern District ordered the USOC to request the IOC to substitute Lindland for Sieracki. The USOC has done so, and the IOC has made the substitution. The Northern District also denied Sieracki's petition to confirm the Campbell Award. Two appeals ensued. We expedited the briefing and affirmed both decisions on September 1, promising that this opinion would follow with an explanation.

Although Lindland now is a member of the U.S. team, and the IOC's deadline for making changes has expired, the dispute is not moot. The Games begin at 4 A.M. on September 15 (Chicago time), and the 76 kilogram classification in Greco-Roman Wrestling does not get underway until September 24. The IOC accepted a substitution of Lindland for Sieracki after its deadline, remarking that it was willing to make the change because the USOC acted under judicial order. This implies that if we now confirmed the Campbell Award (including its provision annulling the Burns Award) and directed the USOC to substitute Sieracki for Lindland, the IOC would accept that change as well. We therefore address the merits-starting with what is logically the first issue, whether to confirm the Campbell Award.

Lindland had argued to Arbitrator Burns that USA Wrestling's grievance proceedings were flawed. Arbitrator Burns agreed and ordered the rematch as a remedy in lieu of directing USA Wrestling to reconsider Lindland's protest to the judging of his match with Sieracki. Arbitrator Campbell went over the same ground, disagreed with Arbitrator Burns about the adequacy of USA Wrestling's processes and adding that in his view the result of the first match (which everyone calls "Bout #244") had not been affected by any errors in applying the scoring rules for Greco-Roman Wrestling. It is not a surprising view for Arbitrator Campbell to have taken, because the proceedings began amicably. Sieracki initiated the arbitration to defend his initial victory, and USA Wrestling, the respondent, likewise defended both the scoring of the match and the conduct of its internal appeals. (Lindland intervened to defend the Burns Award, but, having already won the rematch, was more interested in preserving that victory than in litigating from scratch.) What is surprising was that Arbitrator Campbell not only approved the result of the original Bout #244 and the adequacy of USA Wrestling's grievance procedures but also directed it to ignore the result of the rematch-that is, Arbitrator Campbell directed USA Wrestling not to implement the Burns Award.

Sieracki argues that the Campbell Award is no less confirmable under the standards of the Federal Arbitration Act than was the Burns Award, *see* 9 U.S.C. § 10, and if he is entitled to confirmation of the Campbell Award then we should set aside the confirmation of the Burns Award (because relief from the Burns Award is part of the Campbell Award). Certainly there is no evidence that the Campbell Award is the result of "corruption," "fraud," "evident partiality," or any similar bar to confirmation. The district court refused to enforce the Campbell Award because the Burns Award had been enforced already, and it read *Consolidation Coal Co. v. United Mine Workers*, 213 F.3d 404 (7th Cir. 2000), as precluding enforcement of incompatible awards. Only one of these athletes can be on the Olympic Team, and the district judge thought that federal courts should not order the USOC to send both. Sieracki replies that arbitrators need not follow judicial notions of preclusion-a good point about arbitrators, *see Brotherhood of Maintenance of Way Employees v. Burlington Northern R.R.*, 24 F.3d 937 (7th Cir. 1994), but not about judges. Once the Burns Award was confirmed, it was no longer simply the view of a fellow arbitrator with which Campbell could disagree. But this may not be a complete answer. If the Campbell Award is understood to vacate the Burns Award, then confirmation of the Campbell Award logically entails vacating the prior confirmation of the Burns Award. That step would not leave USA Wrestling under conflicting judicial instructions. (Nor is it clear that conflict is an irremediable evil. Injunctions create property rights, which may be altered by private agreements. Bargaining among Sieracki, Lindland, and USA Wrestling could lead to a settlement that would relieve USA Wrestling of any incompatible obligations. *See* Guido Calabresi & A. Douglas Melamed, Property Rules, Liability Rules, and Inalienability: One View of the Cathedral, 85 Harv. L.Rev. 1088 (1972).)

Definitive resolution of the right way to handle conflicting awards, after one has been confirmed, may await another day. The Campbell Award could not be confirmed even if it were the sole award. It is doubly flawed: first, the entire proceeding appears to have been ultra vires; second, the award violates the Commercial Rules of the American Arbitration Association, under which the proceeding was conducted. 36 U.S.C. § 220529(b)(2). Because Arbitrator Campbell exceeded his powers, his award cannot be confirmed. 9 U.S.C. § 10(a)(4).

Sieracki initiated an arbitration not to contest a final decision by USA Wrestling but to protest the Burns Award. Sieracki filed his demand for arbitration on August 11, two days after the Burns Award and three days before his rematch with Lindland (and thus before any issues associated with that bout could have arisen). The Stevens Act does not authorize arbitration about the propriety of another arbitrator's decision. Section 220529(a) provides:

> A party aggrieved by a determination of the corporation under section 220527 or 220528 of this title may obtain review by any regional office of the American Arbitration Association.

What is arbitrable is "a determination of the corporation under section 220527 or 220528 of this title". Arbitrator Burns is not "the corporation" (a term defined in § 220501 as the USOC, though some of its powers have been delegated to national governing bodies such as USA Wrestling); what is more, neither he nor USA Wrestling (in implementing the Burns Award to the extent of scheduling the rematch) rendered "a determination under section 220527 or 220528 of this title". Section 220528 deals with applications to replace national governing bodies. Section 220527 specifies remedies that athletes have within national governing bodies such as USA Wrestling. Lindland exhausted his remedies within USA Wrestling and obtained "a determination of the corporation under section 220527 of this title", and thus was entitled to arbitrate his grievance. Sieracki, by contrast, did not initiate any proceedings within the scope of § 220527. Although § 220527(b)(1) allows athletes to forego exhaustion when time is too short to allow decision, it does not allow bypass of a claim under §

220527—that is, a contention that a national governing body has failed "to comply with sections 220522, 220524, and 220525 of this title". 36 U.S.C. § 220527(a). Sieracki did not have such a claim and therefore was not entitled to arbitration under the Stevens Act even if it was proper to pretermit administrative remedies. No other provision of which we are aware supports arbitration whose sole subject is the decision of a prior arbitrator. The Stevens Act would be self-destructive if it authorized such proceedings, which would lead to enduring turmoil (as happened here) and defeat the statute's function of facilitating final resolution of disputes, *see* § 220529(d).

Even if the second arbitration had been authorized, however, the outcome would have been forbidden by the rules under which it was conducted. Rule 48 of the AAA's Commercial Rules provides that an "arbitrator is not empowered to redetermine the merits of any claim already decided." Sieracki stresses, as our opinion of August 24 acknowledged, that judicial ideas about issue and claim preclusion need not apply in arbitration. But arbitrators assuredly are bound by the contracts and other rules that give them power to act. An arbitrator who throws aside those rules and implements his "own brand of industrial justice" oversteps his powers, and the resulting award must be set aside. *Steelworkers v. Enterprise Wheel & Car Corp.*, 363 U.S. 593, 597 (1960); *Paperworkers v. Misco, Inc.*, 484 U.S. 29, 36 (1987). What the Steelworkers Trilogy declared about "industrial justice" is equally true of commercial or athletic justice. Arbitrators are not ombudsmen; they are authorized to resolve disputes under contracts and rules, not to declare how the world should work in the large. Arbitrator Campbell did not misinterpret Rule 48; he decided to ignore it utterly. The whole point of the Campbell proceeding was to redecide the issues that had been before Arbitrator Burns, and the Campbell Award directs USA Wrestling to disregard the Burns Award. Campbell observed, correctly, that Sieracki was not a party to the Burns proceedings, but the other participants in the proceedings before Arbitrator Campbell were parties to the Burns proceedings. By the time Campbell acted, the Burns Award had "already decided" that the nomination to the Olympic team would depend on a rematch between Sieracki and Lindland. Whatever powers Campbell possessed vis-à-vis Sieracki, he lacked the power to order USA Wrestling to nominate anyone other than the winner of the rematch. The Campbell Award therefore is not entitled to confirmation.

This conclusion makes it unnecessary to decide whether, by participating in the Campbell proceedings, Lindland waived or forfeited his entitlement to the benefits of the Burns Award. The Campbell Award is invalid, so it does not bind Lindland or anyone else. But we shall not conceal our doubt about this argument. The "waiver" to which Sieracki and USA Wrestling point is simply Lindland's assent to the terms of participation in the Olympic Games, one of which is submitting to final and binding arbitration of disputes. How such a document can surrender the final and binding effect of the Burns Award is a mystery. When Sieracki and USA Wrestling entered into their friendly arbitration in an effort to escape from the unwelcome Burns Award, Lindland was in a tough spot. It would not be sensible to say that he waived the benefits of an award already in hand by trying to persuade Arbitrator Campbell to follow his duties under AAA Rule 48 or by attempting to persuade Campbell that Burns acted wisely (and thus to avert the problems that have ensued from Campbell's contrary decision). Nor is it sensible to say, as Sieracki does, that Lindland won a race to the courthouse. The Campbell Award is invalid, so timing is immaterial. Lindland is entitled to USA Wrestling's nomination because (a) Arbitrator Burns ordered USA Wrestling to hold a rematch, and (b) Lindland won that rematch. If Sieracki had prevailed in the rematch, he would be on the Olympic Team today. Athletic disputes should be settled on the playing field-as the Burns Award provided.

* * *

Lindland and USA Wrestling were the only parties to the Burns proceedings. All the Burns Award (coupled with Lindland's victory in the rematch of Bout #244) requires is that USA Wrestling send Lindland's name to the USOC as USA Wrestling's nominee for the team. By the time USA Wrestling finally complied with the Burns Award—11 days after Lindland won the rematch, and 2 days after we enforced the Burns Award-the deadline for making nominations had passed, and the USOC declared that it would send Sieracki to Sydney. The district court's injunction, the IOC's acceptance of Lindland, and the USOC's appeal followed.

Most of the USOC's submission on appeal misunderstands the basis of the injunction. Consider, for example, the USOC's lengthy argument, based on *Michels v. United States Olympic Committee*, 741 F.2d 155 (7th Cir. 1984) (which interpreted the predecessor to § 220527), that there is no private right of action to enforce the Stevens Act. That may or may not be so under the current version of the statute; we need not decide, because Lindland did not file suit to enforce the Stevens Act. He sued to enforce the Burns Award, and the Federal Arbitration Act provides the necessary private right of action. The dispositive question is whether the order (and eventually the injunction) entered against USA Wrestling binds the USOC too. This depends on Fed.R.Civ.P. 65(d):

> Every order granting an injunction and every restraining order . . . is binding only upon the parties to the action, their officers, agents, servants, employees, and attorneys, and upon those persons in active concert or participation with them who receive actual notice of the order by personal service or otherwise.

The USOC, as a party to the proceedings to enforce the Burns Award, received actual notice of our decision on August 24 requiring USA Wrestling to nominate Lindland forthwith. USA Wrestling tarried, but the USOC knew what USA Wrestling was required to do and easily could have taken our decision as equivalent to a formal nomination by USA Wrestling on August 24—when it would have been timely under the USOC's rules. The district court's injunction requires the USOC to do what it should and would have done had USA Wrestling timely complied with the decision of August 24. This order is proper if the USOC is a person "in active concert or participation with" USA Wrestling.

Briefing the "active concert or participation" issue at our instructions, the USOC contends that it is an independent organization, entitled to make the final decision. No one doubts this, but the "active concert or participation" clause supposes legal distinctiveness; if USA Wrestling and the USOC were the same party, the order would be binding directly. The "active concert or participation" clause is designed to prevent what may well have happened here: the addressee of an injunction, eager to avoid its obligations, persuades a friendly third party to take steps that frustrate the injunction's effectiveness. *See Reich v. Sea Sprite Boat Co.*, 50 F.3d 413 (7th Cir. 1995). The USOC has given every indication of willingness to lend a hand. For example, it responded to the initiation of the Campbell proceedings by promising to respect their outcome-which entails a promise to ignore the outcome of the Burns proceedings. The events of August 24 also imply that USA Wrestling and the USOC acted in concert. On the evening of August 24 USA Wrestling sent the USOC one document "notifying" it of this court's decision and a second document nominating Sieracki. The USOC decided to accept the nomination of Sieracki, knowing full well that this nomination violated a decision of this court. The inference that USA Wrestling and the USOC undertook a joint effort to defeat the Burns Award (and our decision) is very strong.

That inference could be overcome by a demonstration that the USOC had an independent ground of decision. No one doubts that the USOC may adopt its own criteria and make its own selections. 36 U.S.C. § 220505(c). Thus if, for example, Lindland failed a drug test, or if his behavior at past international competitions had brought shame on the team (as the U.S. Olympic hockey team did en masse in 1998), then the USOC could have sent Sieracki to the Games. Similarly, if the USOC regularly made its own judgments about athletic prowess, then a determination that Sieracki is the wrestler most likely to succeed in Sydney would be respected by the federal judiciary. Yet in response to a question posed by this court (and a similar one posed by the district court), the USOC failed to identify even a single instance in which it has not forwarded to the IOC the nomination of a national governing body such as USA Wrestling. Its promise to send whichever athlete Arbitrator Campbell selected abjures any independent role; indeed, that promise is the best evidence that USA Wrestling and the USOC have acted jointly to implement the Campbell Award despite judicial enforcement of the Burns Award.

When on August 15 it originally sent to the IOC the full list of USA Wrestling's nominees (a list that included Sieracki despite Lindland's victory on August 14), the USOC did not make an independent decision about their athletic skills; instead the certification says that the list (and the USOC's approval) is "based on the selection criteria devised and previously approved by the USOC" and in particular that "[t]he selection of the NGB athlete nominations were [sic] conducted in our estimation according to the policies and procedures approved by the USOC for the 2000 Olympic Summer Games." In other words, the USOC investigated only to ensure that USA Wrestling followed the rules for selecting its nominees. One of these rules (quoted in our August 24 opinion) specifies that the winner of Bout #244 would be USA Wrestling's nominee in the 76 kilogram classification. Lindland is the winner of Bout #244 and the recipient of USA Wrestling's (belated) nomination. Under the USOC's own rules, therefore, Lindland is entitled to the position on the Olympic Team. This makes it very hard to understand the USOC's position as anything other than a continuation of the view disparaged in our August 24 opinion: a belief by the USOC that athletes who pursue their rights under the Stevens Act should be penalized. The district court was entitled to prevent the USOC from carrying out that view under the pretext that USA Wrestling's nomination of Lindland arrived too late.

Nonetheless, the USOC insists, it is entitled to do as it pleases-defying injunctions to its heart's content-if it manages to stall until only three weeks remain before the Games. For this proposition it relies on another part of the Stevens Act, 36 U.S.C. § 220509(a):

> The corporation shall establish and maintain provisions in its constitution and bylaws for the swift and equitable resolution of disputes involving any of its members and relating to the opportunity of an amateur athlete, coach, trainer, manager, administrator, or official to participate in the Olympic Games, the Paralympic Games, the Pan-American Games, world championship competition, or other protected competition as defined in the constitution and bylaws of the corporation. In any lawsuit relating to the resolution of a dispute involving the opportunity of an amateur athlete to participate in the Olympic Games, the Paralympic Games, or the Pan-American Games, a court shall not grant injunctive relief against the corporation within 21 days before the beginning of such games if the corporation, after consultation with the chair of the Athletes' Advisory Council, has provided a sworn statement in writing executed by an officer of the corporation to such court that its

constitution and bylaws cannot provide for the resolution of such dispute prior to the beginning of such games.

Saturday, August 26, was the 21st day before the "beginning" of the Sydney Olympics. The USOC filed in the district court an affidavit parroting the statutory terms and insists that, as a result, the district court was powerless to enforce the Burns Award.

Section 220509(a) is designed to prevent a court from usurping the USOC's powers when time is too short for its own dispute-resolution machinery to do its work. The premise of the USOC's argument is that the dispute among Lindland, Sieracki, and USA Wrestling is one to be resolved by the USOC's internal processes, which can't be done at this late date. This is just another variation of the USOC's misunderstanding about the genesis of the district court's order. Lindland has not asserted a private right of action to enforce the Stevens Act, nor has he attempted to initiate a new dispute-resolution process before the USOC. His claim depends on the Burns Award, which was issued on August 9, well outside the 21-day window, and the decision of this court, also issued before the 21st day. The only question on the table is whether USA Wrestling and the USOC will comply with obligations that had been established before that three-week period. The USOC's liability stems from its obligation as an entity "in active concert or participation with" USA Wrestling to avoid frustrating the order enforcing the Burns Award.

We do not for one second believe that Congress set out to reward intransigence, so that the USOC can protect scofflaws among the national governing bodies, or itself defy judicial orders if, on the 21st day before the Olympic torch enters the stadium, the President of the USOC is not already in prison for contempt. There is no dispute for the USOC to resolve, so its inability under its constitution and bylaws to act on short notice is not important. All the USOC had to do was implement this court's decision of August 24 (enforcing the Burns Award of August 9); all we hold is that delay in compliance with an obligation judicially articulated before the 21st day does not entitle the USOC to escape that obligation. To put this in the statutory language, the prohibition applies only if "such dispute"-that is, a dispute to be handled under the USOC's procedures-can't be resolved in the time remaining before the games. When no "such dispute" survives into the three-week period (because it had been resolved earlier), § 220509(a) does not preclude enforcement of the outstanding decision.

Senator Stevens himself may have a different view about the effect of § 220509(a). At the behest of the USOC, he wrote a letter asking the district judge to vacate its order. Our reading of the letter implies that the USOC misinformed the Senator about the nature of the controversy and the reason the district judge had ordered the USOC to send Lindland's name to the IOC, but no matter. Legislative history is a chancy subject;

subsequent legislative history is weaker still, *Pierce v. Underwood*, 487 U.S. 552, 566–68 (1988); *Weinberger v. Rossi*, 456 U.S. 25, 35 (1982); *Regional Rail Reorganization Act Cases*, 419 U.S. 102, 132 (1974), indeed is an oxymoron, *see Continental Can Co. v. Chicago Truck Drivers Pension Fund*, 916 F.2d 1154, 1157 (7th Cir. 1990), and a letter or affidavit written as a form of constituent service is the bottom of the pecking order. *See Bread Political Action Committee v. FEC*, 455 U.S. 577, 582 n. 3 (1982). Letters written after a statute's enactment were not presented in the course of debate and so are not the sort of views that may be credible because other members of the legislature rely on them and may impose penalties on those who misrepresent, or misunderstand, the text. Compare William N. Eskridge, Jr., Dynamic Statutory Interpretation 210–38 (1994), and McNollgast, Positive Canons: The Role of Legislative Bargains in Statutory Interpretation, 80 Geo. L.J. 705 (1992), with John F. Manning, Textualism as a Nondelegation Doctrine, 97 Colum.L.Rev. 673 (1997).

A letter from a Member of Congress telling a judge how to decide a pending case reflects a misunderstanding of the difference between legislative and judicial functions. Senator Stevens played a leading role in the creation of § 220509, but he has no role in adjudication. Giving weight to such a letter would only invite other litigants to pester Members of Congress for expressions of support-or Members of Congress to pester the courts with their latest views about how laws should be implemented and cases decided. It is best, we think, for each institution to hew to its constitutional function. *See Bread PAC*; *Abbott v. Virginia Beach*, 879 F.2d 132, 136 (4th Cir. 1989); *Environmental Defense Fund, Inc. v. Wheelabrator Technologies, Inc.*, 725 F. Supp. 758, 769–70 (S.D.N.Y. 1989); Stephen F. Williams, Legislative History and the Problem of Age, 66 Geo. Wash. L. Rev. 1366, 1369 & n.12 (1998).

Affirmed.

NOTES AND QUESTIONS

1. *Aftermath.* Lindland won the silver medal at the summer 2000 Olympics in Sydney, and followed it up with a silver medal in the 2001 World Championships. Nicknamed "The Law," Lindland became the coach of the U.S. Olympic Greco-Roman Wrestling team in 2014.

2. *Which Award?* Was the court correct in adopting the Burns report and rejecting the Campbell report? Does it matter that Sieracki was not present at the Burns hearing? Why or why not?

3. *Lindland or Sieracki.* If you were choosing which wrestler should represent the U.S. team, which one would you pick? Why?

C. RECENT CASES IN INTERNATIONAL SPORT

Having looked at CAS, it is now instructive to examine some of the most important cases from the past five years. We consider three major cases from three different areas:

- nationalism—the review of CAS decisions within one's own national courts in *Pechstein*;
- systematic doping—the Russian doping scandal
- hyperandrogenism—the *Chand* case

1. NATIONALISM

As with other areas of international law, international sports law can create enforcement issues. CAS provides a tribunal under which enforcement is possible. But is international enforcement preferable? Or should national courts have a say? The next case explores these questions.

PECHSTEIN V. INTERNATIONAL SKATING UNION
Federal Court of Justice, Germany, 2016
Case KZR 6/15 [2016], SchiedsVZ [2016] p 218–26

Decision:

In reply to the Second Defendant's writ of certiorari (*Revision*), the partial final and the partial interim judgement of the anti-trust division of the Higher Regional Court of Munich of 15 January 2015 is hereby set aside insofar as the Court of Appeal has found against the Second Defendant in the said judgement.

The Plaintiff's appeal against the judgement of the Regional Court of Munich I of 26 February 2014 is dismissed in its entirety.

The costs of the appeal proceedings shall be borne by the Plaintiff.

The facts of the case:

1 The Plaintiff is an internationally successful speed skater. The First Defendant—which is not involved in the appeal proceedings—is the German National Association for speed skating, which has its registered offices in Munich. The Second Defendant is the International Skating Union (hereinafter referred to as ISU); the ISU has its registered offices in Switzerland. Both federations are organised in accordance with the "one place principle", *i.e.*, there is only one German and one international federation that organise speed skating competitions on the national and international level.

2 On 2 January 2009, during the period before the speed skating world championships in Hamar (Norway) on 7 and 8 February 2009, the Plaintiff signed a registration form provided by the Second Defendant. If

the Plaintiff had not signed this registration form, she would not have been permitted to compete. By signing the form, the Plaintiff undertook, inter alia, to comply with the Second Defendant's anti-doping regulations. Furthermore, she also signed an arbitration agreement that provided that any disputes should be brought before the Court of Arbitration for Sport (hereinafter referred to as CAS) in Lausanne and that the jurisdiction of the ordinary courts of law should be excluded.

3   During the World Championships in Hamar, blood samples were taken from the Plaintiff; these samples showed elevated reticulocyte counts. The Second Defendant considered this to be evidence of doping. Its disciplinary commission decided on 1 July 2009 to ban the Plaintiff from competition with retroactive effect as of 7 February 2009 for two years on the ground of illegal blood doping, to annul the results obtained by the Plaintiff during the competitions on 7 February 2009 and to strip her of the points, awards and medals that she had won. In a letter dated 19 July 2009, the First Defendant informed the Plaintiff that she was also excluded from training as a result of this ban and that her status as a member of the team for the Olympic Winter Games 2010 had been suspended.

4   The Plaintiff and the First Defendant appealed to the CAS against the decision of the disciplinary commission. On 29 September 2009, the CAS submitted its Rules of Procedure for these proceedings, in which, inter alia, it determined its own jurisdiction. These Rules of Procedure were signed by the parties. In an award dated 25 November 2009, the CAS dismissed the appeals almost without exception . . . .

5   The Plaintiff appealed against this award to the Swiss Federal Tribunal; . . . . [this appeal was dismissed].

6   By the present action, the Plaintiff requests a declaratory judgement stating that her ban due to doping was unlawful, and a decision ordering the Defendants to pay compensation for the material damage suffered by her, as well as compensation for her pain and suffering. . .

Statement of reasons:

7   A.   The Court of Appeal based its decision essentially on the following reasons:

* * *

[The Court of Appeal had held that (1) German courts have jurisdiction over Pechstein's case, (2) the arbitration agreement is invalid under German law as it violates German antitrust law. Specifically, the lower court determined that the lack of justification for CAS and its market power created a presumption of abuse under antitrust law.]

22   II.   However, the complaint is inadmissible due to the Second Defendant pleading the arbitration agreement.

23   1.   By signing the registration for the competition at the Second Defendant's request, the Plaintiff and the Defendants entered into an arbitration agreement pursuant to sections 1025 et seq. of the Code of Civil Procedure. The CAS is a "true" court of arbitration within the meaning of the Code of Civil Procedure and not merely an association tribunal or any other dispute resolution body.

24   a)   The general outlines of the position of the judiciary power within the governmental structure and its relationship with the citizens have been established as fundamental principles of the German legal system. A judge must observe a proper distance and neutrality; the nature of a judge's work excludes any possibility that it could be done by uninvolved third parties. As regards arbitration, the function and effect of which constitutes substantive jurisprudence, no exception to this principle is made. Consequently, a "true" court of arbitration by which access to the court of law can be effectively excluded can only exist in cases where the arbitration court called upon to decide the particular case represents an independent and neutral instance.

25   b)   The CAS represents such an independent and neutral instance. Unlike a federation or association tribunal, it is not incorporated into any particular federation or association. As an institution, it is independent of the sports federations and Olympic Committees that support it; it is intended to ensure uniform jurisdiction across all federations.

26   c)   The procedure of drawing up the list of arbitrators of the CAS indicates no structural imbalance impairing the independence and neutrality of the CAS to such an extent that its position as a "true" court of arbitration could be called into question. [The Court continued to explain all of the ways in which the CAS process sets up a neutral and independent arbtration system.]

* * *

40   2.   The arbitration agreement between the parties of 2 January 2009 covers the claims for damages raised by the Plaintiff.

41   When the Plaintiff signed the registration form of 2 January 2009, she submitted to the articles of association of the Second Defendant. The registration form expressly refers to art. 26 of the articles of association, as well as to the right of decision of the CAS with regard to final and absolute arbitral awards binding upon the Second Defendant, its members and all participants in events organised by the Second Defendant, to the total exclusion of the jurisdiction of all ordinary courts. Art. 26 of the Second Defendant's articles of association in force at the time set out the responsibilities of the CAS. According to this, claims for damages and other claims against the Second Defendant, which could otherwise have been

brought before a civil court, were to be subject to the exclusive jurisdiction of the CAS.

42   3.   The arbitration agreement between the parties is valid.

* * *

46   c)   The arbitration agreement entered into by the parties is valid. It does not infringe the prohibition of abuse under anti-trust law pursuant to section 19 of the Act against Restraints of Competition in the version applicable to this dispute, in force until 29 June 2013 (hereinafter referred to as the "old version"), which would render it invalid pursuant to sec. 134 of the German Civil Code.

* * *

50   The fact that the fight against doping is of paramount importance worldwide has never been denied by either party and is undisputed. Against this background, a uniform system of arbitration is intended to implement the anti-doping rules of the WADC in an effective manner and in accordance with uniform case law. If this task were left to the courts in the individual states, the goal of international sporting arbitration would be jeopardised. No one has succeeded as yet in drawing up a system of rules capable of maintaining international sports arbitration, while, at the same time, completely avoiding the deficiencies in connection with the appointment of independent arbitrators and the proceedings in general that results from the significant influence exercised by the international sports federations and the Olympic Committees. The CAS procedure has been criticised in the past—inter alia due to the case law of the Swiss Federal Tribunal—, which has already led to modifications of these procedural rules. The statutes of the CAS, as they currently stand, contain procedural rules for the appointment of arbitrators which can be considered as acceptable.

* * *

52   The right of access to justice, which is derived from the rule-of-law principle in conjunction with the fundamental rights, particularly with Art. 2 para. 1 of the German Constitution, guarantees access to courts governed by the state and staffed with independent judges However, it is possible to waive this right to access to the state courts and to agree on arbitration instead, as long as the parties have submitted voluntarily to the arbitration agreement and the resulting waiver of a decision by state judicial authority.

* * *

59   (2)   On the other hand, the imposition of arbitration proceedings constitutes a procedural safeguard of the Second Defendant's autonomy as an association, which is equally guaranteed as a fundamental right (Art. 9

para. 1 of the German Constitution). Sports federations such as the Second Defendant promote sports in general and particularly their own sport by creating the prerequisites for organised sport. To achieve the relevant goals, it is of fundamental importance to ensure that the rules apply to all athletes and are implemented everywhere in accordance with uniform standards. It is therefore generally recognised, particularly in the area of international sport, that arbitration agreements determining the jurisdiction of a particular court of arbitration are required to ensure a uniform procedure with regard to the implementation of the rules of sports law. Particularly in the area of doping, uniform application of the anti-doping rules of the federations and of the WADC is indispensable to ensure fair international sporting competitions for all athletes. Furthermore, a uniform court of arbitration for sport can contribute to the development of international sports law. Further advantages of an international sports arbitration, as compared to state courts, include the specialist knowledge of the arbitrators, the speed of the decision-making process, which is of paramount importance for the athlete involved in such proceedings, and the international recognition and execution of arbitral awards.

60 Concerning the Second Defendant, it must further be remembered that it is, in turn, obliged by Art. 13.2.1 in conjunction with Art. 23.2.2 WADC to insist on arbitration agreements designating the CAS as the court of arbitration. Due to the ratification of the International Convention against Doping in Sport of 19 October 2005 by the Federal Republic of Germany, the principles of the WADC represent contractual law which is binding under international law. Furthermore, the International Olympic Committee, in compliance with its obligation under Art. 20.1.2 WADC, makes its recognition of international sport federations dependent on their compliance with the rules laid down in the WADC.

61 (3) The result of the balancing of these rights and interests leads to the conclusion that the Second Defendant, with its requirement that the arbitration agreement proposed by it, be signed, has not abused its dominant market position in the meaning of sec. 19 of the Act against Restraints of Competition, old version

62 This result is due, on the one hand, to the fact that not only the federations but also, and more particularly, the athletes benefit from the aforementioned advantages of sports arbitration, since these depend on fair conditions during competition to be able to exercise their sport (professionally, if applicable). This includes, but is not limited to, uniform application of the anti-doping rules, which, at present, can only be guaranteed by the CAS as a globally recognised court of sports arbitration. However, to ensure, on the other hand, that the Plaintiff's fundamental rights to access to justice and free exercise of her profession are protected to the greatest possible extent, the standards applied to the independence and neutrality of the CAS must not be too low. As already stated above, the

list of CAS arbitrators basically contains a sufficient number of independent and neutral persons; furthermore, in particular the Second Defendant, as the opposing party in these proceedings, does not have institutional supremacy in connection with the drawing up of the list of arbitrators and the composition of the court of arbitration. Moreover, the Plaintiff was not without legal remedies if she had factual misgivings concerning the impartiality and neutrality of the arbitral tribunal. Rather, the statutes and the Procedural Rules of the CAS contain suitable regulations in case of conflict of interest. Moreover there is also the option—exercised by the Plaintiff—of having the arbitral awards of the CAS reviewed by the federal courts of Switzerland to a certain extent. According to the case law of the Swiss Federal Tribunal, this legal remedy, which resembles the German proceedings pursuant to sec. 1059 of the Code of Civil Procedure regarding reversal of an arbitral award, cannot be excluded in the arbitration agreement. There is no further reaching right for a decision particularly by a German state court. Rather, the German legal system recognises both foreign judgements and foreign arbitral awards if the relevant requirements have been fulfilled (sec. 328 of the Code of Civil Procedure and/or Art. V of the New York Convention on the Recognition and Enforcement of Foreign Arbitral Awards of 10 June 1958 (New York Convention)).

* * *

64 cc) An arbitration agreement naming the CAS as the relevant court of arbitration does not violate the rights of the Plaintiff in the light of Art. 6 ECHR, either.

* * *

67 ee) Finally, an invalidity of the arbitration agreement cannot be based on Swiss law, either.

NOTES AND QUESTIONS

1. *CAS as a Legitimate Tribunal.* The German Federal Court of Justice, the highest court in Germany, rejected Pechstein's claim that requiring her to sign the CAS arbitration agreement in order to compete violated both her rights to a judicial remedy and also German antitrust law. In particular, the court was satisfied by the neutral, independent, decentralized approach of CAS with arbitrators drawn from a large pool to hear Pechstein's appeal. Do you share the same confidence as the Federal Court of Justice in the legitimacy of CAS as a decision-making body?

2. *Consequences of Nationalism.* If the German court had upheld the lower court's determination that German law took precedence over the arbitration agreement, what would the consequence be for the ISF? How could

different sport governing bodies regulate the use of performance enhancing drugs if they were subject to the jurisdiction of each participating nation's courts?

3. *Cf.* Reynolds. Compare *Pechstein* with *Reynolds*, above, a pre-CAS case. Does the adequacy of the system rest on the correctness of the arbitral outcome? In other words, arbitral systems seem to work well if the arbitrators make good decisions, but where they err, is there a risk in concentrating such power in the hands of three individuals? How does this compare to the state and federal courts as institutions assigned to decide cases? Which system is more prone to injustice? Why?

4. *CAS as the Final Authority*. For now, all countries participating in the Olympics have agreed to abide by the CAS arbitral system. As we will see, avoiding national courts can be particularly important where doping involves a co-ordinated effort of many athletes and trainers in a single country. Why do you think countries are so willing to relinquish control over their athletes when they are often unwilling to enter into international treaties, and often unwilling to abide by the treaties they ratify? Are sports somehow fundamentally different? Certainly, as the *Defrantz* case above shows, Olympic sports are not immune to political intervention.

5. *Overbroad Arbitration Clauses*. In September 2018, the Court of Appeal of Brussels agreed to hear Belgian football club RFC Seraing United's challenge to FIFA's ban on third-party ownership of football clubs. Seraing had entered into a deal with Doyen, a third party investor, to fund its football operations. Seraing and Doyen argued that FIFA's ban violates EU law. CAS and the Swiss Federal Tribual had both ruled against Seraing in this case already. The Court of Appeal of Brussels, however, held that the arbitration decision and subsequent appeal were invalid. Unlike the lower court ruling *Pechstein*, however, the court did not find that national courts supersede CAS. Rather, the court held that the FIFA arbitration agreement was overly broad and vague, and thus did not constitute an agreement to arbitrate the third-party ownership issue.

2. SYSTEMATIC DOPING

While individual doping cases are the standard fare for the Court of Arbitration of Sport, the Russian doping scandal of the 2010s is unprecedented. The next case provides an example of CAS attempting to assess the IOC's attempt to address this problem.

ZUBKOV V. INTERNATIONAL OLYMPIC COMMITTEE
Court of Arbitration for Sport, 2018
CAS 2017/A/5422

PROF. DR. CHRISTOPH VEDDER, PANEL PRESIDENT.

I. PARTIES

1. Mr. Aleksandr Zubkov (the "Athlete" or "Appellant") is a Russian bobsleigh athlete who participated in four Olympic Winter Games (Nagano 1998 (luge), Torino 2006, Vancouver 2010, and Sochi 2014). At the VXII Olympic Winter Games which took place in Sochi, Russia in 2014 (the "Sochi Games"), the Athlete finished first in both the 2-Man and 4-Man Bobsleigh competitions.

2. The International Olympic Committee (the "IOC" or "Respondent") is the world governing body of Olympic sport having its registered offices in Lausanne, Switzerland. The IOC is incorporated as an association pursuant to articles 60 et seq. of the Swiss Civil Code.

II. FACTUAL BACKGROUND

* * *

A. Background Facts

1. Facts Common to the Sochi Appeals

4. As explained below, the Athlete's appeal has been heard before the Court of Arbitration for Sport (the "CAS") jointly with the appeals of 38 other Russian athletes who were found by the IOC Disciplinary Commission to have committed anti-doping rule violations ("ADRVs") at the Sochi Games. For ease of reference, in this Award the joint appeal proceedings are referred to as the "Sochi Appeals", while the Athlete and the 38 other athletes are referred to collectively as the "Sochi Appellants".

5. In addition to the facts specific to the Athlete's appeal, there are various factual circumstances that are common to all of the Sochi Appeals. Those common facts are summarised in this section of the Award.

a. The Sochi Games and the emergence of allegations of systematic doping and evasion of doping controls by Russian athletes

6. The Sochi Games took place between 7 and 23 February 2014. The Russian national team enjoyed significant success at the Sochi Games: Russian athletes ended up first in the overall medal table and won a total of 33 medals including 13 gold medals. This represented a very significant improvement from the national team's performance in the previous Olympic Winter Games in Vancouver in 2010, where Russia finished eleventh in the medal table.

7. Each of the Sochi Appellants competed at the Sochi Games and provided urine samples as part of mandatory doping controls carried out during the Games. None of those samples tested positive for the presence of any prohibited substances.

8. Later that year, on 3 December 2014, a German television channel broadcast a documentary concerning the alleged existence of an extensive secret, an institutional doping programme within the All-Russia Athletics Federation.

b. The WADA Independent Commission

9. On 16 December 2014, following the broadcast of those allegations, the World AntiDoping Agency ("WADA") announced the appointment of an independent commission (the "Independent Commission") to investigate the allegations as a matter of urgency.

The formal terms of reference, which were published on 16 January 2015, required the Independent Commission to:

> "conduct an independent investigation into doping practices; corrupt practices around sample collection and results management; and, other ineffective administration of anti-doping processes that implicate Russia, the International Association of Athletics Federations (IAAF), athletes, coaches, trainers, doctors and other members of athletes' entourages; as well as, the accredited laboratory based in Moscow and the Russian Anti-Doping Agency (RUSADA)."

10. The three members of the Independent Commission appointed by WADA were Mr. Richard W. Pound QC, former President of WADA, Prof. Richard H. McLaren, an experienced CAS arbitrator and Professor of Law at Western University in Ontario, Canada, and Mr. Günter Younger, Head of the Cybercrime Department at Bavarian Landeskriminalamt in Munich, Germany.

11. On 9 November 2015, the Independent Commission delivered its final report (the "IC Report"). The IC Report contained a detailed account of the Independent Commission's findings concerning the:

> "systemic failures within the IAAF and Russia that prevent or diminish the possibility of an effective anti-doping program, to the extent that neither ARAF, RUSADA, nor the Russian Federation can be considered Code-compliant".

12. The IC Report explained that the Independent Commission's investigation had "confirmed the existence of widespread cheating through the use of doping substances and methods to ensure, or enhance the likelihood of, victory for athletes and teams" in Russia. The cheating was carried out "by the athletes' entourages, officials and the athletes

themselves". The IC Report went on to explain that the investigation had established the existence of:

- "A Deeply Rooted Culture of Cheating" which included "widespread" and "long standing" acceptance of cheating "at all levels". The Independent Commission had identified the existence of a "fundamentally flawed mindset that is deeply ingrained in all levels of Russian athletics".

- "Exploitation of Athletes", including the deployment of "coercive activities" to compel athletes to participate in doping activities.

- "Confirmed Athletes Cheating", in particular the "consistent and systematic use of performance enhancing drugs by many Russian athletes". In addition, a significant percentage of athletes "were unwilling to participate" in the Independent Commission's investigation.

- "Confirmed Involvement by Doctors, Coaches and Laboratory Personnel" who "acted as enablers for systematic cheating along with athletics coaches".

13. The IC Report went on to make an extensive number of detailed findings regarding the existence, scope, mechanics and consequences of that doping scheme.

c. The WADA Independent Person Reports (the McLaren Reports)

14. On 19 May 2016, WADA announced that it had appointed Prof. Richard McLaren to conduct an independent investigation into the allegations made by Dr. Grigory Rodchenkov. Dr. Rodchenkov was the former director of the formerly WADA accredited laboratory in Moscow (the "Moscow Laboratory") and the official on-site anti-doping laboratory in Sochi (the "Sochi Laboratory"). After leaving Russia in 2015, Dr. Rodchenkov made a series of widely publicised allegations concerning the existence of a sophisticated doping scheme before, during, and after the Sochi Games.

15. The terms of reference set by WADA directed Prof. McLaren:

"To establish whether:

1. There has been manipulation of the doping control process during the Sochi Games, including but not limited to, acts of tampering with the samples within the Sochi Laboratory.

2. To identify the modus operandi and those involved in such manipulation.

3. To identify any athlete that might have benefited from those alleged manipulations to conceal positive doping test[s].

4. To identify if this modus operandi was also happening within the Moscow Laboratory outside the period of the Sochi Games.

5. There is any other evidence or information held by Grigory Rodchenkov."

16. On 16 July 2016, Prof. McLaren submitted his first report (the "First McLaren Report") to WADA. The report was published shortly before the 2016 Summer Olympic Games in Rio de Janeiro, Brazil. The First McLaren Report provided the following summary of Prof. McLaren's "Key Findings":

"1. The Moscow Laboratory operated, for the protection of doped Russian athletes, within a State-dictated failsafe system, described in the report as the Disappearing Positive Methodology.

2. The Sochi Laboratory operated a unique sample swapping methodology to enable doped Russian athletes to compete at the Games.

3. The Ministry of Sport directed, controlled and oversaw the manipulation of athlete's [sic] analytical results or sample swapping, with the active participation of the FSB, CSP, and both Moscow and Sochi Laboratories."

17. On 9 December 2016—exactly one year after the publication of the IC Report—Prof. McLaren delivered his second report (the "Second McLaren Report"). Chapter 6 of the Second McLaren Report contained detailed findings concerning the existence of a far-reaching doping programme at the Sochi Games. Prof. McLaren concluded that there had been:

"a carefully orchestrated conspiracy, which included the complicity of Russian sports officials within the MofS, CSP, Moscow based Sochi Laboratory personnel, RUSADA, the Russian Olympic Organising Committee, athletes, and the FSB".

He explained that while "it will never be possible to establish the exact number of individuals involved or their specific roles", the overall effect of the programme deprived other competitors of a level playing field at the Sochi Games.

18. In the Second McLaren Report, Prof. McLaren explained that the Russian Ministry of Sport had developed a list of favoured athletes who would be provided with a "cocktail" of performance-enhancing drugs to aid their performance at the Sochi Games.

According to Prof. McLaren, the athletes on that list "were considered protected and their samples would be automatically swapped during the games" pursuant to the scheme; he therefore referred to those athletes as "protected athletes".

19. Prof. McLaren went on to explain that a key aspect of the programme to facilitate and conceal this doping was the creation of "a catalogued bank of clean urine from the protected athletes". That repository of clean urine would be "maintained on site to facilitate the swapping" of dirty samples for clean, i.e. drug-free samples. In summary:

- Prior to the Sochi Games, protected athletes provided clean samples of their own urine in plastic beverage bottles.
- Those samples were delivered to the Moscow Laboratory where they were tested to ensure they were, in fact, clean.
- Once that had been verified, the clean samples were provided to the Centre of Sports Preparation of National Teams of Russia ("CSP") and catalogued under each athlete's name in preparation for future delivery to the Federal Security Services ("FSB").
- In the period before the Sochi Games, a "clean urine bank" was established at the FSB Command Centre, which was situated immediately adjacent to the Sochi Laboratory. Inside that building a dedicated room containing several large freezers was set up for the purpose of storing the clean urine samples.

20. The Second McLaren Report went on to describe how, having established a bank of clean urine samples in the building next door to the Sochi Laboratory, sophisticated arrangements were implemented to facilitate the covert swapping of urine samples provided by protected athletes at doping control tests during the Sochi Games. The arrangements involved the surreptitious removal of the athletes' B sample bottles, which were provided to an FSB officer who had devised a technique for removing and replacing the plastic caps on the bottles without detection. Prof. McLaren explained that, in order to facilitate this process, athletes who underwent doping control tests would secretly send images of their doping control forms ("DCF") to particular persons who would then transmit this information to the Sochi Laboratory, thereby enabling the laboratory to identify which of the anonymised sample bottles needed to have their contents substituted with clean urine belonging to the relevant athletes.

21. According to Prof. McLaren's summary of the evidence provided by Dr. Rodchenkov, a key aspect of the doping scheme was the creation and use of a so-called "Sochi Duchess List". This list contained the names of 37 Russian athletes "whose samples were to be automatically swapped for

their own clean urine stored in the FSB Command Center at Sochi". Those athletes' samples needed to be swapped because the athletes "had been authorised to use the cocktail of oxandrolone, methenolone and trenbolone during the Games".

22. According to Prof. McLaren, while the narrative summarised above "seems like fiction", the conclusions of his reports were based on "immutable facts" established by forensic testing including analysis of scratch marks on sample bottles, analysis of salt concentration in urine samples from the Sochi Games and a comparative DNA analysis of various samples from athletes identified as protected athletes.

* * *

e. The IOC Disciplinary Commission

25. In December 2016, the IOC appointed a Disciplinary Commission chaired by Prof. Denis Oswald and also comprising Mr. Juan Antonio Samaranch and Mr. Patrick Baumann (the "IOC DC"). The IOC DC was responsible for investigating potential ADRVs committed by individual Russian athletes at the Sochi Games. In late 2016 and in 2017, the IOC DC initiated formal disciplinary proceedings against a number of Russian athletes, alleging that those athletes knowingly and actively engaged in an elaborate State-orchestrated doping and cover-up scheme at the Sochi Games.

26. In November and December 2017, the IOC DC delivered its final decisions containing findings that the Sochi Appellants and several other Russian athletes committed ADRVs through their participation in such a scheme. The IOC DC retrospectively disqualified each of those athletes from the relevant events they had participated in at the Sochi Games and declared each athlete ineligible to participate in any future editions of the Games of the Olympiad or the Olympic Winter Games.

* * *

62. The Athlete's request for relief was drafted as follows: "(1) that the Decision of the IOC Disciplinary Commission in the matter of Aleksandr Zubkov... dated 6 December 2017 be annulled; (2) that the Panel find that the Appellant's due process rights were violated by the IOC Disciplinary Commission; (3) that the IOC be ordered to pay the costs of the arbitration (if any) and the Appellant's legal fees and expenses."

* * *

IX. MERITS

* * *

1. Definition of ADRVs

659. Pursuant to Article 2 of the IOC ADR, "Article 2 of the Code (*i.e.* the WADC) applies to determine anti-doping rule violations."

* * *

B. Commission of ADRVs by the Athlete

688. In the decision under appeal, the IOC DC found that a wide-ranging and orchestrated scheme of doping and concealment of positive doping tests was conducted during the Sochi Games. On the basis of that finding, it then went on to conclude that the Athlete had personally committed various ADRVs, namely:

- violations of Article 2.2 of the WADC in the form of using a prohibited substance, *i.e.* the Duchess Cocktail, and using a prohibited method, *i.e.* urine substitution;
- a violation of Article 2.5 of the WADC, viz. tampering with any part of the doping control; and
- a violation of Article 2.8 of the WADC, viz. cover-up of and complicity in the commission of an ADRV.

* * *

(c) Conclusion on ADRV under Article 2.2 of the WADC

815. In conclusion, for the reasons set out above, the Panel finds that the IOC has discharged its burden of establishing to the comfortable satisfaction of the Panel that the Athlete used both a prohibited substance and a prohibited method and, thus, committed ADRVs pursuant to Article 2.2 of the WADC.

* * *

3. Tampering, Art. 2.5 of the WADC

816. Article 2.5 of the WADC provides that "tampering or attempted tampering with any part of doping control" constitutes an ADRV. No further definitional elements are provided for in that provision.

817. The Comment to Article 2.5 of the WADC explains: "This Article prohibits conduct which subverts the Doping Control process but which would not otherwise be included in the definition of Prohibited Methods."

* * *

821. The Panel considers that urine substitution which is a prohibited method pursuant to the Prohibited List falls exclusively under Article 2.2

of the WADC and, therefore, Article 2.5 of the WADC does not apply. However, the Athlete committed the ADRV under Article 2.2 of the WADC by providing clean urine rather than by swapping his urine himself.

822. In this situation the question arises whether the actions allegedly taken by the Athlete which are arguably indispensable parts of urine substitution, *i.e.* the provision of clean urine in advance of the Sochi Games, incomplete closing of his sample bottles, and transmitting images of his DCF to third persons are equally covered by Article 2.2 of the WADC and thus exempt from the application of Article 2.5 of the WADC or could, considered as such and independent of a link to the sample-swapping, constitute acts of tampering under Article 2.5 of the WADC. Undoubtedly, examined in isolation, those acts are irregular and would violate the applicable WADA rules on doping control and constitute tampering or attempted tampering.

823. However, the Panel does not have to make such determination since, in the context of Article 2.2 of the WADC, the Panel is not satisfied that the Athlete deliberately did not fully close the bottles or transmitted pictures of his DCFs to third persons. The provision of clean urine by the Athlete took place well in advance of the Sochi Games and, therefore, falls outside the scope of application in time of Article 2.5 of the WADC as determined by the term "doping control" which, in turn, is defined in Appendix 1 to the WADC as "from the test distribution planning through to ultimate disposition of any appeal. . . ."

824. The IOC DC did not even examine whether or not there existed any act required for the commission of tampering under Article 2.5 of the WADC. Instead, the IOC DC, in its appealed decision, without any further explanation ruled that:

> "subsidiarily, the same circumstances shall in any event be deemed as constitutive of a violation of art. 2.5 of the 2009 WADC".

825. In general terms, for the Panel, it is a misconception of the relationship between Article 2.2 of the WADC and Article 2.5 of the WADC to conclude that, if the requirements of Article 2.2 of the WADC are met, the requirements of Article 2.5 of the WADC automatically are met too. To the contrary, if the elements of Article 2.2 concerning a prohibited method are fulfilled, as the Comment to Article 2.5 of the WADC clarifies, recourse to Article 2.5 of the WADC is excluded.

826. Accordingly, the Panel does not find that the Athlete committed an ADRV of tampering under Article 2.5 of the WADC.

4. Cover-up, Complicity, Art. 2.8 of the WADC

827. Article 2.8 of the WADC provides that the following conduct shall constitute an ADRV:

"Administration or Attempted administration to any Athlete In-Competition of any

Prohibited Method or Prohibited Substance, or administration or Attempted administration to any Athlete Out-of-Competition of any Prohibited Method or any Prohibited Substance that is prohibited Out-of-Competition, or assisting, encouraging, aiding, abetting, covering up or any other type of complicity involving an anti-doping rule violation or any Attempted anti-doping rule violation."

* * *

848. The Athlete's use of a prohibited method, *i.e.* the provision of clean urine in advance of the Sochi Games which facilitated the urine substitution, and the Athlete's use of a prohibited substance, *i.e.* the Duchess Cocktail, do not constitute acts by which the Athlete encouraged, assisted, or covered up either physically or psychologically, fellow athletes to commit ADRVs. Nor did the IOC submit that the Athlete engaged in any other actions that might have assisted other athletes to commit ADRVs. The evidence does not establish that the Athlete provided assistance or encouragement "horizontally"—*i.e.* directly in relation to other athletes— nor did he provide assistance or encouragement "vertically", *i.e.* through coaches or support personnel. Instead, it is apparent that the Athlete acted on his own behalf and in his own interest, rather than in the interests of his fellow athletes. Unlike in the Torino case, there is no evidence of cooperation between the Athlete and other athletes engaged in committing ADRVs.

849. For the reasons set out above, the Panel is not comfortably satisfied that the Athlete committed any act or omission that knowingly assisted, encouraged or covered up the commission of an ADRV under Article 2.2 to Article 2.7 of the WADC by any other athlete. Accordingly, the Panel does not find that the Athlete committed an ADRV under Article 2.8 of the WADC.

* * *

C. Sanctions

[The Panel upheld the sanction of disqualification of results from the 2014 Olympics.]

* * *

d. Length of the Olympic Ineligibility, Article 7.3 of the IOC ADR

880. Article 7.3 of the IOC ADR grants discretion to the IOC to declare an athlete ineligible to participate in Olympic Games "temporarily or permanently", *i.e.* for one, several or any subsequent editions of the Games.

881. The Panel is comfortably satisfied that the Appellant committed an individual ADRV in the form of the use of a prohibited method, according to Article 2.2 of the WADC by providing clean urine for the purpose of having his samples substituted at the Sochi Games which actually happened with his sample collected after the 4-man bobsleigh competition on 23 February 2014 and an individual ADRV in the form of the use of a prohibited substance, also in violation of Article 2.2 of the WADC.

882. The Panel, however, was not required to, and did not, examine whether the ADRV committed by the Appellant was part of a cover-up scheme orchestrated during the Sochi Games with the aim of allowing Russian athletes to take the Duchess Cocktail before or during the Sochi Games and to be protected against positive findings in their samples. Therefore, the Panel is unable to base any sanction on the Athlete on the alleged scheme and the alleged involvement of the Appellant in such scheme.

883. In its appealed decision, the IOC DC based the determination of a lifetime ineligibility mainly if not exclusively on the fact that, according to its findings, the Athlete participated in the alleged sample-swapping scheme. The IOC DC relied not so much on the fact "that specific violations of the IOC ADR were committed" but much more on the fact that the individual ADRVs "were part of a conspiracy, which infected and subverted the Olympic Games in the worst possible manner".

884. In contrast to the IOC DC's conclusions, the Panel was only able to find to its comfortable satisfaction that the Athlete committed individual ADRVs in the form of the use of a prohibited method and of a prohibited substance under Article 2.2 of the WADC, but no ADRV of tampering under Article 2.5 of the WADC and, in particular, no individual ADRV of covering-up or complicity in violation of Article 2.8 of the WADC. Consequently, the Panel is unable to find a lifetime ineligibility an appropriate sanction.

885. Furthermore, when considering the length of the Olympic ineligibility to be imposed on the Appellant, the Panel takes into account that the IOC, by its decision of 5 December 2017, suspended the Russian National Olympic Committee for its involvement in the scheme only for one edition of the Olympic Winter Games. The IOC opted to sanction those who are the true instigators of the alleged scheme with a minimal ban of one edition of the Olympic Games while the IOC DC sanctioned the athletes who only benefitted from the scheme with a lifetime ban.

886. Therefore, the Panel rules that the Appellant is ineligible to compete in one edition of the Olympic Winer Games subsequent to the Sochi Games, *i.e.* the Olympic Winter Games 2018 in PyeongChang.

* * *

X. CONCLUSIONS

889. Having thoroughly considered the submissions of the Parties, the written evidence as well as the oral evidence and testimonies provided at the six-day hearing, the Panel, for the reasons set out above, finds that the Athlete committed ADRVs in the form of the use of a prohibited method, *i.e.* urine substitution, pursuant to Article 2.2 of the WADC in connection with M2.1 of the 2014 WADA Prohibited List, and in the form of use of a prohibited substance under Article 2.2 of the WADC. The Panel was unable to find the commission of either an ADRV in the form of tampering with doping control in accordance with Article 2.5 of the WADC or an ADRV in the form of cover-up of or complicity in an ADRV under Article 2.8 of the WADC.

890. In reaching these conclusions, the Panel wishes to underscore what it has not decided in this appeal. The Panel has not made a ruling on whether and to what extent the alleged doping scheme during the Sochi Games existed and how it operated even though it recognizes that there is significant evidence that it was in place and worked. Moreover, the Panel did not consider it possible to conclude that the mere existence of a general doping and cover-up scheme, even if established, would inexorably lead to a conclusion that the Athlete committed the ADRVs alleged by the IOC.

891. What the Panel, in the appeal of an individual Athlete against the findings of various ADRVs by inference from the alleged doping and cover-up scheme, did decide is simply that for all of the reasons set out in this award, the evidence presented before the Panel only justified the conclusion to the comfortable satisfaction of the Panel that the Athlete individually committed ADRVs in violation of Article 2.2 of the WADC.

892. Based on the finding of two individual ADRVs committed by the Athlete, the Panel concludes that the imposition of a lifetime ineligibility to participate in whatever capacity in Olympic Winter Games as well as in Games of the Olympiad is not appropriate in relation to the seriousness of the individual ADRVs and, therefore, declares the Athlete ineligible to participate in any capacity for the next edition of the Olympic Winter Games, *i.e.* the Winter Games in PyeongChang 2018.

893. Accordingly, the Panel concludes that the Athlete's appeal against the operative-part only decision of the IOC DC rendered on 24 November 2017 and the reasoned decision of 6 December 2017 is partially upheld, and the appealed decision partially set aside and modified accordingly.

NOTES AND QUESTIONS

1. *Reverse Lifetime Ban?* Zubkov's case was one of 39 decided just prior to the 2018 Winter Olympics in PyeongChang. The same panel heard all of the cases. It reversed 28 of the cases in their entirety, finding no doping violation and upholding the results from the Sochi Olympics. The other 11 cases, including Zubkov, resulted in an upholding of the finding of doping and the disqualification of the Sochi results, but a reversal of the lifetime ban, reducing the ban to just the 2018 Olympics. Do you agree with the panel's decision to reverse the IOC's lifetime ban on the Russian athletes? Why or why not?

2. *Proper Sanction?* As indicated in the opinion, the size and scope of the systematic Russian doping was unprecedented in the history of the Olympics, and resulted in Russian athletes participating under the Olympic flag in PyeongChang. As such, it is difficult and complicated to determine how to sanction both Russia and its athletes in light of this far-reaching scheme. Do you think the Court of Arbitration for Sport is the appropriate institution to have the final word on the punishment? Is arbitration a good method by which to make decisions such as the one in this case?

3. HYPERANDROGENISM

In recent years, female intersex athletes have drawn increasing scrutiny, in part because of their success in women's sports. Born with female sexual organs, these athletes naturally have a higher amount of testosterone than others with such organs. The additional testosterone contributes in some way to their success.

The International Association of Athletics Federations (IAAF) has attempted to regulate the participation of such athletes, restricting participation when endogenous testosterone levels (as opposed to exogenous testosterone levels resulting from doping) exceed a certain level. The next case is a recent challenge to the IAAF's regulations.

CHAND V. INTERNATIONAL ASS'N OF ATHLETICS FEDERATIONS
Court of Arbitration for Sport, 2017
CAS 2014/A/3759

THE HON. JUSTICE ANNABELLE CLAIRE BENNETT, PANEL PRESIDENT.

I. PARTIES

1. Dutee Chand (the "Athlete") is a 19 year-old female athlete of Indian nationality. During her career to date she has won a number of national junior athletics events in India. In addition, she won gold medals in the women's 200 metres sprint and the women's 4 x 400 metre sprint relay at the Asian Junior Track and Field Championships in Taipei in May 2014.

2. The Athletics Federation of India (the "AFI") is the national governing body for the sport of athletics in India.

3. The International Association of Athletics Federations (the "IAAF") is the international governing body of the sport of athletics, recognised as such by the International Olympic Committee. It has its seat and headquarters in Monaco. The IAAF recognises the AFI as its member federation for India.

II. OVERVIEW OF THE CASE

4. This case concerns a challenge to the validity of the IAAF Regulations Governing Eligibility of Females with Hyperandrogenism to Compete in Women's Competition (the "Hyperandrogenism Regulations"). The Hyperandrogenism Regulations place restrictions on the eligibility of female athletes with high levels of naturally occurring testosterone to participate in competitive athletics. In particular, the Athlete challenges the Hyperandrogenism Regulations on the basis that: (a) they discriminate unlawfully against female athletes and against athletes who possess a particular natural physical characteristic; (b) they are based on flawed factual assumptions about the relationship between testosterone and athletic performance; (c) they are disproportionate to any legitimate objective; and (d) they are an unauthorised form of doping control. The IAAF rejects each of those arguments.

5. The case raises complex legal, scientific, factual and ethical issues. The parties' submissions draw upon a diverse range of expert scientific evidence, factual accounts of the evolution of the Hyperandrogenism Regulations and the experiences of female athletes who were subjected to their "gender testing" and "sex verification" predecessors, and philosophical arguments about the meaning of fairness in sport. The length of this Award is a reflection of the complexity of those issues, and the exceptional care and detail in which they were presented to the Panel by the parties' representatives.

III. FACTUAL BACKGROUND

* * *

9. In 2013, the Ministry promulgated a Standard Operative Procedure to identify circumstances (female Hyperandrogenism) in which a particular sports person will not be eligible to participate in competitions in the female category (the "Standard Operative Procedure"). The Standard Operative Procedure created rules and procedures governing the investigation, diagnosis and eligibility to compete of hyperandrogenic female athletes in India. The document is binding on the SAI.

* * *

11. According to the Athlete, Mr Dogra asked her to undergo a "routine doping test". The following day, on 27 June 2014, the Athlete met the Chairperson of the AFI Medical Commission, Dr Arun Mendiratta, in Delhi. The Athlete claims Dr Mendiratta told her that the AFI was creating a "high performance profile" for her and they therefore needed to conduct a routine medical examination to check if she had any diseases. The Athlete claims she was told that, because no nurses were available to conduct a blood test, she would need to undergo an ultrasound examination instead. The Athlete says that she was confused by the examination and did not understand why an ultrasound scan was conducted in place of a blood test.

12. According to the AFI, the Athlete and another athlete underwent ultrasound examinations in Delhi after they had both complained of chronic abdominal pains. Dr Mendiratta said that in June 2014 several participants at the National Inter State Athletics Championships had expressed concerns to the AFI about the Athlete's appearance and questioned whether she should be permitted to compete in female athletics events. However he denied that the medical examination in Delhi had anything to do with investigating the Athlete's sex or gender or testing for possible hyperandrogenism.

* * *

15. It is common ground that following the medical examination in Delhi, the Athlete travelled on to an SAI training camp in Bangalore and was subjected to further medical examinations by the SAI. The Athlete stated that those tests included blood tests, clinical tests by a gynaecologist, karyotyping, an MRI examination and a further ultrasound examination.

16. According to the Athlete, on 13 July 2014 Dr Sarala of the SAI notified her that she would not be permitted to compete in the forthcoming World Junior Championships and would not be eligible for selection for the Commonwealth Games because her "male hormone" levels were too high.

* * *

27. On 31 August 2014, the AFI delivered a letter to the Athlete (which was dated 29 August 2014) informing her that she was provisionally suspended from participating in any athletics events with immediate effect (the "Decision Letter"). The Decision Letter stated:

> Based on your medical reports received from Sports Authority of India and a copy of the same has already been handed over to you by SAI in person, you are hereby provisionally stopped from participation in any Competition in athletics with immediate effect. To be eligible for participation, you are further advised to follow the annexed IAAF guidelines.

The Decision Letter did not contain any further information about the basis of the Athlete's suspension, the content of the medical reports referred to in the first sentence of the letter, or the Athlete's rights of appeal. According to the Athlete, the letter incorrectly enclosed the IAAF Sex Reassignment Regulations rather than the Hyperandrogenism Regulations.

* * *

29. On 18 September 2014, the Athlete sent a letter to the Secretary General of the AFI asking the AFI to reconsider the decision to revoke her eligibility to participate in all international or national athletics competitions. The letter stated, inter alia, that:

> The high androgen level produced by my body is natural. I have not doped or cheated. If I follow the IAAF guidelines you have attached, I will have to undergo medical intervention in order to reduce my naturally-produced androgen level. Experts tell me that the basis for this policy is unscientific and that these interventions are invasive often irreversible and will harm my health now and into my future. I feel perfectly healthy and I have no health complaints so I do not want to undergo these procedures because the experts also tell me they are likely to have serious side effects. I also understand that these interventions will most likely decrease my performance level because of the serious side effects and because they will interfere with the way my body has worked my whole life. Also, I am unable to understand why I am asked to fix my body in a certain way simply for participation as a woman. I was born a woman, reared up as a woman, I identify as a woman and I believe I should be allowed to compete with other women, many of whom are either taller than me or come from more privileged backgrounds, things that most certainly give them an edge over me. I request that you allow me to compete again in national events without having to undergo medical intervention. I also request you to allow me to be a part of the Indian team in international competitions. The IAAF policy has a provision that says you can make me provisionally eligible while I contest my case. I understand that IAAF may have asked you for my medical reports and records, but I request you not to share my private and confidential medical reports and information with the IAAF or any other organization without my consent. I have spent nearly half of my life working hard to excel in athletics and to make my country proud. I hope I am allowed to continue to do so without feeling coerced to undergo medical intervention for participation as a woman. Please allow me to run competitively. If you feel that you are compelled by the IAAF to go ahead with

the suspension, I request you to support my appeal to the Court of Arbitration for Sport.

* * *

B. The Issues

32. The issues that arise for determination by the CAS Panel in this appeal may be summarised as follows: (a) Do the Hyperandrogenism Regulations discriminate impermissibly against certain female athletes on the basis of: (i) a natural physical characteristic; and/or (ii) sex? (b) Should the Hyperandrogenism Regulations be declared invalid on the basis that there is insufficient scientific evidence: (i) that endogenous testosterone improves athletic performance in female athletes; and/or (ii) that 10 nmol/L is the scientifically correct threshold at which female athletes are in the "male range" of endogenous testosterone and therefore enjoy the benefits of male levels of androgens? (c) Are the Hyperandrogenism Regulations disproportionate in the context of: (i) the fact they discriminate on the basis of a natural physical characteristic and/or sex; and/or (ii) the harm they cause to female athletes? (d) Are the Hyperandrogenism Regulations invalid because they are a form of unauthorised anti-doping sanction in violation of Articles 4.3.3, 10 and 23.2.2 of the World Anti-Doping Agency Code?

* * *

42. The Hyperandrogenism Regulations are of "mandatory application" to all female athletes who compete or seek to compete in international athletics competitions. In addition, they are also "recommended as a guide to National Federations" for the management of cases that arise at national level (Regulation 1.2).

* * *

58. The Regulation goes on to specify the lower limit of "the normal range": Androgen levels for the purposes of paragraph 6.5 are measured by the levels of Total Testosterone in serum. Normal male range Total Testosterone Levels - $\geq$ 10 nmol/L.

59. Regulation 6.6 places a hyperandrogenic athlete under a burden of proving (where applicable) that her body is resistant to androgens and therefore her naturally elevated testosterone levels do not confer any competitive advantage: The burden of proof shall be on the athlete to establish, where applicable, that she has an androgen resistance such that she derives no competitive advantage from androgen levels in the normal male range and the standard of proof in such a case shall be by a balance of probabilities. 60. Regulation 6.7 provides that when the Expert Medical Panel is making its recommendation in accordance with the criteria in

Regulation 6.5, the applicable standard of proof "shall be to the comfortable satisfaction of the Panel".

* * *

62. Under Regulation 7.1, the IAAF Medical Manager is responsible for making a final decision on the athlete's eligibility to compete, taking into account the recommendation made by the Expert Medical Panel.

* * *

67. The Hyperandrogenism Regulations are accompanied by Explanatory Notes. The Notes provide the following explanation of the rationale underpinning the Regulations: The IAAF's role as the international governing body for the sport of Athletics is first and foremost to guarantee the fairness and integrity of the competitions that are organised under its Rules. Men typically achieve better performances in sport because they benefit from higher levels of androgens than women and this is predominantly why, for reasons of fairness, competition in Athletics is divided into separate men's and women's classifications. By extension, since it is known today that there are rare cases of females with [hyperandrogenism] competing in women's competitions, in order to be able to guarantee the fairness of such competitions for all female competitors, the new Regulations stipulate that no female with [hyperandrogenism] shall be eligible to compete in a women's competition if she has functional androgen levels [testosterone] that are in the male range. Moreover, from the athlete's health perspective, there is scientific consensus as regards the importance of determining the presence (and source) of high levels of androgens in females. The early diagnosis of [hyperandrogenism] is considered critical to an effective therapeutic strategy.

* * *

IAAF Competition Rules 2014–2015

* * *

70. Rule 141 provides:

Sex categories

3. Competition under these Rules is divided into men's and women's classifications. When a Mixed Competition is organised outside the stadium or in one of the limited cases set out in Rule 147, separate men's and women's classification results should be declared or otherwise indicated.

4. An athlete shall be eligible to compete in men's competition if he is recognised as a male in law and is eligible to compete under the Rules and Regulations.

5. An athlete shall be eligible to compete in women's competition if she is recognised as a female in law and is eligible to compete under the Rules and Regulations.

6. The Council shall approve Regulations to determine the eligibility for women's competition of (a) females who have undergone male to female sex reassignment; and (b) females with hyperandrogenism. An athlete who fails or refuses to comply with the applicable Regulations shall not be eligible to compete.

* * *

IV. PROCEEDINGS BEFORE THE COURT OF ARBITRATION FOR SPORT

* * *

82. On 25 November 2014, the Athlete filed a request for provisional relief with the CAS Court Office. The Athlete sought an order permitting her to compete in athletics events until a decision was rendered in her appeal. The request stated that the Athlete was "under significant pressure to undergo medical intervention from her major sponsor". It explained that after several months of being suspended from competing, the Athlete was giving serious consideration to undergoing medical treatment instead of pursuing her appeal. In these circumstances, provisional measures were said to be necessary in order to protect the Athlete from irreparable harm.

* * *

IX. MERITS

* * *

B. Issue 1: Discrimination

448. The Hyperandrogenism Regulations only apply to female athletes. It is not in dispute that it is prima facie discriminatory to require female athletes to undergo testing for levels of endogenous testosterone when male athletes do not. In addition, it is not in dispute that the Hyperandrogenism Regulations place restrictions on the eligibility of certain female athletes to compete on the basis of a natural physical characteristic (namely the amount of testosterone that their bodies produce naturally) and are therefore prima facie discriminatory on that basis too.

449. The Athlete contended, and the IAAF did not submit to the contrary, that the IOC Charter, the IAAF Constitution and the laws of Monaco all provide that there shall not be discrimination and that these provisions are higher-ranking rules that prevail. Accordingly, unless the Hyperandrogenism Regulations are necessary, reasonable and proportionate, they will be invalid as inconsistent with the IOC Charter, the IAAF Constitution and the laws of Monaco.

450. The Panel concludes that, on their face, the Hyperandrogenism Regulations are discriminatory. It follows that the onus shifts to the IAAF to establish that the Hyperandrogenism Regulations are necessary, reasonable and proportionate for the purposes of establishing a level playing field for female athletes. Such an approach is consistent with the countervailing requirements for sport and is recognised in a wide range of domestic and international laws, including laws directed to the prohibition of discrimination generally. The Panel will address the question of justification below under Issue 3: Proportionality.

C. Issue 2: Scientific basis for the Hyperandrogenism Regulations

* * *

510. First, the parties agree that it is reasonable and proportionate to divide athletes into male and female categories. Secondly, there should be an objective criterion or criteria to police this divide. Thirdly, gender testing is not an appropriate criterion. Fourthly, athletes may be female while still possessing high levels of testosterone, and thereby increased LBM, which creates a competitive advantage. Fifthly, whether a person is a female is a matter of law. Sixthly, there is no evidence before the Panel that legal recognition as a female varies in most countries other than reference by the parties to the fact that there are a small number of countries where a person's status as a male or female is determined exclusively by a process of self-identification. Seventhly, the level of endogenous testosterone and sensitivity to testosterone may provide an appropriate criterion to divide normal male and female populations. However, eighthly, there are females such as those with DSDs who have high levels of endogenous testosterone relative to other females and are sensitive to testosterone and remain females. There is no separate category in which those athletes may compete (for example, an "intersex" category). Ninthly, the Hyperandrogenism Regulations only apply to females. Tenthly, if the Regulations apply to a female to preclude her competing as a female, she may not compete as a male. That is, the Regulations do not police the male/female divide but establish a female/female divide within the female category. Eleventhly, the criteria of a level of endogenous testosterone of 10 nmol/L with a degree of virilisation as an indicator of 'masculine traits', are based on the best available science concerning the typical ranges of testosterone in males and females and physical indications of androgen sensitivity. Justification for a rule that excludes some females from competing in the female category on the basis of a natural physical characteristic.

511. The distinction between male and female is a matter of legal recognition. Nevertheless, as explained above, the Panel is of the view that levels of endogenous testosterone are a key biological indicator of the

difference between males and females. However, that is not the use to which endogenous testosterone is being put under the Hyperandrogenism Regulations. It is not being used to determine whether an athlete should compete either as a male or as a female. Instead, it is being used to introduce a new category of ineligible female athletes within the female category. The necessity and proportionality of that restriction therefore requires particularly careful analysis.

512. As noted above, there are only two categories of competition: male and female. These categories are together intended to cover all athletes who wish to participate in competitive athletics. Female athletes who exhibit high levels of endogenous testosterone may include females with intersex characteristics. As an intersex population exists, and is represented in female athletics, it must be accepted that these athletes may exhibit characteristics across a range, from those within the normal female range to those within the normal male range. Where an athlete is female, and thereby only eligible to compete as a female, is it reasonable and proportionate to impose a test that excludes her from the female athlete category for the purposes of competition, when she exhibits, naturally, the characteristic most closely associated with male competitive advantage? The Panel need to be satisfied on a balance of probabilities that it is.

513. The Panel considers that every athlete must in principle be afforded the opportunity to compete in one of the two categories and should not be prevented from competing in any category as a consequence of the natural and unaltered state of their body. A rule that prevents some women from competing at all as a result of the natural and unmodified state of their body is antithetical to the fundamental principle of Olympism that "Every individual must have the possibility of practising sport, without discrimination of any kind". So too is a rule that permits an athlete to compete on condition that they undergo a performance-inhibiting medical intervention that negates or reduces the effect of a particular naturally occurring genetic feature. Excluding athletes from competing at all on the basis of a natural genetic advantage, or conditioning their right to compete on undergoing medical intervention which reduces their athletic performance, imposes a significant detriment on the athletes concerned, and is therefore only valid if it is clearly established to be a necessary and proportionate means of achieving fair competition.

* * *

517. The premise underpinning the Hyperandrogenism Regulations is therefore that some members of the female class have a competitive advantage over other members of the female class that is similar to the performance advantage enjoyed by male athletes. In other words, the Hyperandrogenism Regulations are based on an implicit assumption that hyperandrogenic females enjoy a significant performance advantage over

their nonhyperandrogenic peers, which outranks the influence of any other single genetic or biological factor, and which is of comparable significance (if not identical magnitude) to the performance advantage that males typically enjoy over females. That is, it is the degree of competitive advantage that is said to make for unfair competition and absence of a level playing field.

* * *

519. Once an athlete is legally recognised as female, the Panel considers that an athlete must be permitted to compete in the female category unless her naturally high androgen levels confer a significant performance advantage over other female competitors, comparable to the performance advantage that male athletes enjoy over female athletes. Has the IAAF established that women with levels of endogenous testosterone of at least 10 nmol/L and who are androgen-sensitive have a sufficiently clear and significant competitive advantage over other females such that there may be a fairness-based reason why they should be precluded from competing as females, or at all?

520. This raises the question whether the IAAF can demonstrate a correlation between this level of testosterone in females and a real competitive advantage that interferes with fair competition within the female category. This question cannot simply be answered by noting that male athletes have a particular advantage over female athletes. This is because the Hyperandrogenism Regulations are not concerned with upholding a male/female divide and because other factors besides testosterone that may also contribute to the significant male athletic advantage over females have not been evaluated and discounted.

521. There is a class of female athletes who, by reason of DSDs, have high levels of endogenous testosterone. These athletes are female but have a medical or genetic condition that is believed to give them an athletic advantage. On the evidence, this advantage does not arise directly from the level of endogenous testosterone but rather arises from the effect of testosterone on the body, specifically an increase in LBM. However, importantly, there is no evidence before the Panel—and it is understood that there is presently no available evidence—as to the quantitative effect on female athletic performance of levels of endogenous testosterone above 10 nmol/L.

522. In other words, there is presently insufficient evidence about the degree of the advantage that androgen-sensitive hyperandrogenic females enjoy over non-hyperandrogenic females. In the Panel's opinion this is significant. It is not self-evident that a female athlete with a level of testosterone above 10 nmol/L would enjoy the competitive advantage of a male athlete, which performance advantage would be, on the IAAF's evidence, in the order of 10–12% (the approximate difference, on the

evidence of the IAAF, between men and women and, therefore, an unfair advantage), rather than, say, 1% (a relatively marginal advantage, having regard to the many other variables that contribute to athletic performance).

* * *

525. During the course of his oral evidence before the Panel, Dr Bermon noted the significant over-representation of DSD individuals in the population of elite female athletes. Dr Bermon suggested that a female athlete with functioning androgen receptors and 15 nmol/L endogenous testosterone would experience a performance advantage of approximately 3% over a female athlete with 1.5 nmol/L endogenous testosterone.

* * *

526. The Panel notes, in this regard, that the performance advantage of approximately 3% suggested by Dr Bermon is significantly smaller than the 10%–12% difference between elite male and elite female athletic performance referred to by the IAAF in its appeal brief, the 10% difference in male/female performance referred to by Professor Ritzen and Professor Hirschberg in their joint expert report, and the 12.64% difference in male/female performance referred to in Dr Bermon's report. The Panel does not place great weight on the 3% figure referred to by Dr Bermon; however, it does demonstrate that the IAAF recognises that the performance advantage that hyperandrogenic females enjoy over normal females may be of a different order to the performance advantage that males enjoy over females.

527. The Panel considers the lack of evidence regarding the quantitative relationship between enhanced levels of endogenous testosterone and enhanced athletic performance to be an important issue. While a 10% difference in athletic performance certainly justifies having separate male and female categories, a 1% difference may not justify a separation between athletes in the female category, given the many other relevant variables that also legitimately affect athletic performance. The numbers therefore matter.

528. The Panel accepts that exogenous testosterone improves athletic performance in male and female athletes. The Panel has also concluded that the Athlete has failed to establish on the balance of probabilities that exogenous and endogenous testosterone have different effects on the body. However, in order to justify excluding an individual from competing in a particular category on the basis of a naturally occurring characteristic such as endogenous testosterone, it is not enough simply to establish that the characteristic has some performance enhancing effect. Instead, the IAAF needs to establish that the characteristic in question confers such a significant performance advantage over other members of the category that

allowing individuals with that characteristic to compete would subvert the very basis for having the separate category and thereby prevent a level playing field. The degree or magnitude of the advantage is therefore critical.

* * *

530. The determinative factor adopted by the IAAF in the Hyperandrogenism Regulations is not only a high level of testosterone in the male range but also a medical examination intended to give an assessment of the likely effect of the testosterone on the athlete's body. However, the examination involves what may be termed a qualitative assessment about the extent of the athletic performance advantage that the athlete derives from their high androgen levels. In light of the paucity of data concerning the magnitude of the performance advantage that hyperandrogenic females typically derive from enhanced androgen levels, the IAAF has not established that the medical examination does enable a reliable conclusion to be reached as to the degree of competitive advantage that results from a level of endogenous testosterone over 10nmol/L in an athlete. In this regard, the Panel agrees with Dr Bermon, Professor Hirschberg and Professor Ritzen that "[t]he lack of definitive research linking female hyperandrogenism and sporting performance is problematic".

531. It follows that the Panel is unable to conclude that the Hyperandrogenism Regulations fulfil their stated purpose. This may be because available data are not yet available. The evidence is that there are inadequate data to establish or refute hypotheses in this area. In the context of this issue, the onus lies on the IAAF. The IAAF has not established, on the balance of probabilities that the Hyperandrogenism Regulations apply only to exclude female athletes that are shown to have a competitive advantage of the same order as that of a male athlete.

532. On the basis of the evidence currently before the Panel, the Panel is unable to conclude on the balance of probabilities that androgen-sensitive hyperandrogenic female athletes enjoy such a substantial performance advantage over non-hyperandrogenic female athletes that excluding them from competing in the female category, and thereby excluding them from competing at all unless they take medication or undergo treatment, is a necessary and proportionate means of preserving fairness in athletics competition and/or policing the binary male/female classification. In particular, while the evidence indicates that higher levels of naturally occurring testosterone may increase athletic performance, the Panel is not satisfied that the degree of that advantage is more significant than the advantage derived from the numerous other variables which the parties acknowledge also affect female athletic performance: for example, nutrition, access to specialist training facilities and coaching, and other

genetic and biological variations. Further evidence as to the quantitative relationship between androgen levels in hyperandrogenic females and increased athletic performance is therefore required before the IAAF can discharge its onus of establishing that the Hyperandrogenism Regulations are a necessary and proportionate means of achieving the IAAF's stated objective.

Conclusion

533. The Panel has accepted that testosterone is a key causative factor in the increased LBM in males. The Panel accepts that increased LBM confers a competitive advantage. The Panel accepts the evidence that male athletes have a competitive advantage over female athletes of the order of 10–12%; that LBM is of key importance in conferring this advantage; and that separation between male and female athletes is therefore justifiable in the interests of fair competition. There is, however, an assumption involved in the Hyperandrogenism Regulations as a proportionate justification for discriminating between females. The assumption is that an endogenous testosterone level within the male range + virilisation (indicating sensitivity to the high level of testosterone) = a degree of competitive advantage over non-hyperandrogenic females of commensurate significance to the competitive advantage that male athletes enjoy over female athletes.

534. This assumption may well be proved valid but, on the present evidence, the Panel cannot be satisfied on the balance of probabilities that this is so. The Panel has accepted that testosterone is the best indicator of performance difference between male and female athletes. However, the evidence does not go so far as to equate, or correlate, the level of testosterone in females with a percentage increase in competitive advantage. The evidence does not, for example, establish an advantage of the order of 12% rather than, say 1% or 3%. Once the degree of competitive advantage is established, the IAAF would then need to consider, if the degree of advantage were well below 12%, whether that justified excluding women with that advantage from the female category.

535. . . . The onus is on the IAAF to establish that the degree of competitive advantage conferred by a testosterone level above 10 nmol/L accords with the degree of competitive advantage that justifies the male/female divide such that it is reasonable and proportionate to render females with, and sensitive to, that level of testosterone ineligible to compete as female athletes. The evidence before the Panel has not enabled the IAAF to fulfil that onus.

536. For these reasons, the Panel finds that the IAAF has not discharged its burden of establishing that the criteria in the Hyperandrogenism Regulations are necessary and proportionate to pursue

the legitimate objective of regulating eligibility to compete in female athletics to ensure fairness in athletic competition.

537. In reaching this conclusion, the Panel wishes to reiterate that its conclusion does not reflect any bad faith or incompetence on the part of the IAAF. On the contrary, the IAAF has acted with conspicuous diligence and good faith throughout the process of consulting, drafting and implementing the Hyperandrogenism Regulations. The Panel accepts that the IAAF, which represents the interests of athletes, including female athletes, has decided that it is in the interest of fair competition in the female category to exclude athletes who, naturally, have characteristics that give them a similar competitive advantage to that enjoyed by male athletes. The evidence before the Panel was that the IAAF considers this to be necessary and proportionate. For the reasons explained above, the Panel has reached a different conclusion. The Panel's view is that the evidence has not established that competition against hyperandrogenic females to whom the existing Regulations apply is unfair due to superior sport performance caused by high levels of testosterone.

538. It may be that evolving scientific evidence or the compilation of existing evidence and data will reach a sufficient level of proof of unacceptable competitive advantage to enable a specific standard to be reached, either by reference to testosterone or by reference to, for example, LBM or otherwise . . .

* * *

543. By contrast, anti-doping sanctions seek to punish and deter certain prohibited conduct, namely the deliberate or inadvertent ingestion of performance enhancing substances. In particular, anti-doping rules are concerned with limiting the distorting effect of external substances that give athletes advantages over other competitors who have not received the same extrinsic performance aid. The concept of "endogenous doping" is therefore a contradiction in terms.

544. The Hyperandrogenism Regulations are an eligibility rule. They are not framed in terms of prohibited conduct and sanctions for corresponding "violations". They do not impose penalties on athletes who have particular levels of naturally occurring testosterone. Nor do they involve any reprimand or censure (indeed, the Regulations stress the importance of keeping the outcomes of examinations confidential). While female athletes who have endogenous testosterone above 10 nmol/L and who are not androgen resistant will be prevented from competing, those individuals can immediately resume competing as soon they meet the eligibility criteria (for example, by taking pharmacological steps to reduce their testosterone levels beyond 10 nmol/L). All of these factors indicate that the Hyperandrogenism Regulations are not a form of anti-doping control.

* * *

546. For all these reasons, the Panel rejects the Athlete's fourth ground of challenge.

F. Conclusion and next steps

547. For the reasons explained above, the Panel concludes that the IAAF has not discharged its onus of establishing that the Hyperandrogenism Regulations are necessary and proportionate to pursue the legitimate objective of organising competitive female athletics to ensure fairness in athletic competition. Specifically, the IAAF has not provided sufficient scientific evidence about the quantitative relationship between enhanced testosterone levels and improved athletic performance in hyperandrogenic athletes. In the absence of such evidence, the Panel is unable to conclude that hyperandrogenic female athletes may enjoy such a significant performance advantage that it is necessary to exclude them from competing in the female category.

548. In these circumstances, the Panel is unable to uphold the validity of the Regulations. The Panel therefore suspends the Hyperandrogenism Regulations for a period of two years, subject to the following provisos. At any time during that two-year period, the IAAF may submit further written evidence to the CAS concerning the magnitude of the performance advantage that hyperandrogenic females enjoy over other females as a result of their abnormally high androgen levels. In the event that the IAAF submits such evidence, the Panel will issue further directions enabling the Athlete to respond to that evidence and listing the matter for a further hearing for the Panel to consider whether that evidence is sufficient to establish the validity of the Regulations. In the event that the IAAF does not file any evidence within that two-year window (or if it notifies the CAS in writing that it does not intend to file such evidence) then the Hyperandrogenism Regulations shall be declared void.

* * *

NOTES AND QUESTIONS

1. *Aftermath.* Chand has remained eligible and continues to improve as a sprinter. In June 2018, Chand broke the 100m national record for India with a time of 11.29 seconds.

2. *Testosterone the Answer?* Do you agree with the panel that the IAAF's procedure of basing eligibility on testosterone levels is inadequate? Why or why not? Is allowing Chand to compete more unfair to other competitors than it would be to her to prevent her from competing?

3. *Unfair to Competitors?* How is any claim of unfairness against Chand from other competitors different from claims of unfairness by basketball players against extraordinarily tall competitors? Or are they the same? Should extraordinarily tall women have to compete in men's basketball?

4. *Regulate Males?* If some males are advantaged in certain competitions because they have extraordinarily high testosterone levels, even for males, should the IAAF also ban their participation in such events? If not, what is the basis for banning competitors like Chand? Is it a sufficient distinction that Chand could compete as a male?

5. *Defining Gender Categories.* The IAAF accepts Chand's self-classification as a female. Would their regulation be on stronger grounds had they not done so, but instead used testosterone levels as a basis for gender classification, and simply treated her as a male for purposes of competition? Should IAAF have to accept all self-classifications, perhaps out of respect for the dignity of competitors? What about a person born with male sexual organs who undergoes surgery to become female, but does not suppress testosterone levels?

6. *New Guidelines.* The IAAF issued new guidelines in April 2018. The IAAF classifies female athletes who are "androgen-sensitive" and have circulating testosterone levels above five (5) nmol/L (nanomole/litre) as "DSD", which stands for "Difference of Sexual Development". Athletes who fall in this category will be deemed eligible to participate in Restricted Events in an International Competition (or set a World Record in a Restricted event at a competition that is not an International Competition) only if they meet the following conditions:

(a) she must be recognised by law either as female or as intersex (or equivalent);

(b) she must reduce her blood testosterone level to below five (5) nmol/L for a continuous period of at least six months (*e.g.*, by use of hormonal contraceptives); and

(c) thereafter she must maintain her blood testosterone level below five (5) nmol/L continuously (ie: whether she is in competition or out of competition) for so long as she wishes to remain eligible.

It is widely believed that the new rules have been formulated specifically to target South African athlete Caster Semenya, the current 800m Olympic champion. Caster has been subjected to scrutiny ever since 2009, when she dominated the track and field events for that distance and won by more than 2 seconds. Ms. Semenya filed a case with CAS in 2018 to challenge the new rules. Are the new rules in an improvement over the ones challenged in *Chand*? Will they protect fair competition? Or allow for discrimination?

7. *Why Limit Regulation to Certain Events?* The new IAAF regulations apply only to athletes who participate in women's running events between 400m and 1 mile like Ms. Semenya. These regulations make Ms. Chand's CAS case moot, as she is a sprinter. The IAAF restricted application of its

hyperandrogeny rules to races longer than 400m because it found that high testosterone had the more identifiable competitive impact on such races. Is that limitation a justifiable one? Why or why not?

Chapter 14

Health and Safety Issues in Sports[*]

■ ■ ■

Participation in sports can be risky. Sports-related injuries—to athletes, spectators, and other participants in sports—are ubiquitous. In other contexts, a person who suffers an injury might have a tort action alleging negligence or intentional harm. Conduct that amounts to battery or assault can lead to criminal charges. But in athletic competition, injuries that result from otherwise tortious physical contact are generally not actionable if they fall within the inherent risks of the sport. In other words, the duties of care owed in the context of sport accommodate the special characteristics of athletic competition and the public policy favoring it.

This chapter first examines the application of tort and criminal law principles to injury-causing conduct during athletic competition, and how courts have modified those principles in this distinctive setting. It next addresses health and safety off the field as it relates to the unique concerns of professional athletes. Also covered is disability in sport, and the extent to which a sport must modify its rules to accommodate disabled athletes or may limit their participation to avoid health risks to themselves and others.

A. INJURIES FROM PLAYING THE GAME

1. INJURY TO ATHLETES—TORT LIABILITY

The special problems that sports pose to tort litigation occur most vividly in cases in which an injured athlete files suit against another athlete whose actions during the game allegedly caused the injury. The aim of a sporting event is to produce spirited athletic competition on the field, the ice, or the floor. In sports such as boxing, football, and ice hockey, a central feature of the contest is the infliction of violent contact on the opponent. This is not the anticipated outcome of ordinary interactions in society. In other sports, such as basketball and baseball, violent contact is

---

[*] The Casebook Website (http://pennstatelaw.psu.edu/SportsTextWebsite) contains citations to scholarly and other commentary on a variety of topics discussed in this chapter, including: general overview of athletic injury litigation; a comparative analysis of the law of torts and sports in Canada; the ethics of bodily contact sports; participant liability for coparticipant sports injuries; legal response to career-ending and life-threatening injuries; criminal prosecution and other forms of regulation of sports violence; sports medicine and medical malpractice; sports product liability and hazardous facilities; and athletes and disability.

1049

an expected risk, if not a desired outcome, of intense competition. The question arises—when does such contact fall so far outside the rules of the game that the injury-inflicting player is liable for damages or criminal penalties for his conduct?

HACKBART V. CINCINNATI BENGALS, INC. (HACKBART I)
435 F. Supp. 352 (D. Col. 1977)

MATSCH, DISTRICT JUDGE.

This case arises as a result of an incident which occurred in the course of a professional football game played between the Denver Broncos and the Cincinnati Bengals, in Denver, Colorado, on September 16, 1973.

* * *

[The court describes a play in the second quarter of the game, with Denver in the lead, 21–3. Cincinnati had the ball on offense and during a forward pass play to Charles "Booby" Clark, Denver intercepted the ball and ran it back to midfield. The injury to Denver defensive player Dale Hackbart arose in the aftermath of the interception. Once in possession of the ball, Denver was on offense, and so Hackbart attempted to legally block Clark to take him out of the play. Hackbart fell down, and as both he and Clark watched the play unfold upfield, Clark "acting out of anger and frustration, but without a specific intent to injure," struck Hackbart so hard in the back of his head that both players fell to the ground.] Both players arose and, without comment, went to their respective teams along the sidelines. They both returned to play during the second half of the game.

Because no official observed it, no foul was called on the disputed play and Dale Hackbart made no report of this incident to his coaches or to anyone else during the game. Mr. Hackbart experienced pain and soreness to the extent that he was unable to play golf as he had planned on the day after the game, he did not seek any medical attention and, although he continued to feel pain, he played on specialty team assignments for [two more games]. The Denver Broncos then released Mr. Hackbart on waivers and he was not claimed by any other team. After losing his employment, Mr. Hackbart sought medical assistance, at which time it was discovered that he had a neck injury. When that information was given to the Denver Broncos Football Club, Mr. Hackbart received his full payment for the 1973 season pursuant to an injury clause in his contract.

* * *

The claim of the plaintiff in this case must be considered in the context of football as a commercial enterprise. . . . Football is a recognized game which is widely played as a sport. . . . The basic design of the game is the same at the high school, college and professional levels. The differences are largely reflective of the fact that at each level the players have increased physical abilities, improved skills and differing motivations.

Football is a contest for territory. . . . The most obvious characteristic of the game is that all of the players engage in violent physical behavior.

The rules of play which govern the method and style by which the NFL teams compete include limitations on the manner in which players may strike or otherwise physically contact opposing players. During 1973, the rules were enforced by six officials on the playing field. The primary sanction for a violation was territorial, with the amounts of yardage lost being dependent upon the particular infraction. Players were also subject to expulsion from the game and to monetary penalties imposed by the league commissioner. . . .

Many violations of the rules do occur during each game. . . . Disabling injuries are also common occurrences in each contest. Hospitalization and surgery are frequently required for repairs. Protective clothing is worn by all players, but it is often inadequate to prevent bodily damage. . . .

The violence of professional football is carefully orchestrated. Both offensive and defensive players must be extremely aggressive in their actions and they must play with a reckless abandonment of self-protective instincts. The coaches make studied and deliberate efforts to build the emotional levels of their players to what some call a "controlled rage." . . .

The large and noisy crowds in attendance at the games contribute to the emotional levels of the players. Quick changes in the fortunes of the teams, the shock of violent collisions and the intensity of the competition make behavioral control extremely difficult, and it is not uncommon for players to "flare up" and begin fighting. The record made at this trial indicates that such incidents as that which gave rise to this action are not so unusual as to be unexpected in any NFL game.

The end product of all of the organization and effort involved in the professional football industry is an exhibition of highly developed individual skills in coordinated team competition for the benefit of large numbers of paying spectators, together with radio and television audiences. It is appropriate to infer that while some of those persons are attracted by the individual skills and precision performances of the teams, the appeal to others is the spectacle of savagery.

Plaintiff's Theories of Liability

[T]he plaintiff contends that Charles Clark's foul was so far outside of the rules of play and accepted practices of professional football that it should be characterized as reckless misconduct . . . .

Alternatively, the plaintiff claims that his injury was at least the result of a negligent act by the defendant. The difference in these contentions is but a difference in degree. Both theories are dependent upon a definition of a duty to the plaintiff and an objective standard of conduct based upon the hypothetical reasonably prudent person. Thus, the question is what would a reasonably prudent professional football player be expected to do under the circumstances confronting Charles Clark in this incident?

* * *

It is wholly incongruous to talk about a professional football player's duty of care for the safety of opposing players when he has been trained and motivated to be heedless of injury to himself. The character of NFL competition negates any notion that the playing conduct can be circumscribed by any standard of reasonableness.

Both theories of liability are also subject to the recognized defenses of consent and assumption of the risk. Here the question is what would a professional football player in the plaintiff's circumstances reasonably expect to encounter in a professional contest?

All of the witnesses with playing or coaching experience in the NFL agreed that players are urged to avoid penalties. The emphasis, however, is on the unfavorable effects of the loss of yardage, not the safety of the players. It is undisputed that no game is without penalties and that players frequently lose control in surges of emotion.

The conflict in the testimony is the difference in the witnesses' opinions as to whether Mr. Clark's act of striking the plaintiff on the back of the head in reaction to anger and frustration can be considered as "a part of the game." Several former players denounced this incident and said that Mr. Clark's conduct could not be considered customary or acceptable.

It is noteworthy that while this incident was clearly shown on the Denver Broncos' defensive game films, which were routinely reviewed by the defensive players and coaching staff, none of them made it a matter of special attention or concern.

Upon all of the evidence, my finding is that the level of violence and the frequency of emotional outbursts in NFL football games are such that Dale Hackbart must have recognized and accepted the risk that he would be injured by such an act as that committed by the defendant Clark on September 16, 1973. Accordingly, the plaintiff must be held to have assumed the risk of such an occurrence. Therefore, even if the defendant breached a duty which he owed to the plaintiff, there can be no recovery because of assumption of the risk.

* * *

The Application of Tort Principles to Professional Football. A Question of Social Policy

While the foregoing findings of fact and conclusions of law are determinative of the claim made by Dale Hackbart against Charles Clark and his employer, this case raises the larger question of whether playing field action in the business of professional football should become a subject for the business of the courts. . .

To this time professional football has been a self-regulated industry. The only protection which NFL contract players have beyond self-defense and real or threatened retaliation is that which is provided by the league rules and sanctions. It may well be true that what has been provided is inadequate and that these young athletes have been exploited and subjected to risks which should be unacceptable in our social order. In this respect, it is interesting to compare football with boxing. Because of the essential brutality of the contest, prize fighting has been held to be unlawful unless conducted under the sanction and authority of a governmental commission.

Football has been presumed to be lawful and, indeed, professional football has received the implicit approval of government because these contests take place in arenas owned by local governments and the revenues are subject to taxation. Like coal mining and railroading, professional football is hazardous to the health and welfare of those who are employed as players.

What is the interest of the larger community in limiting the violence of professional football? That question concerns not only the protection of the participants, but also the effects of such violence on those who observe it. Can the courts answer this question? I think not. An ordinary citizen is entitled to protection according to the usages of the society in which he lives, and in the context of common community standards there can be no question but that Mr. Clark's blow here would generate civil liability. It would involve a criminal sanction if the requisite intent were present. The difference here is that this blow was delivered on the field of play during the course of action in a regularly scheduled professional football game. . . .

There is no discernible code of conduct for NFL players. The dictionary definition of a sportsman is one who abides by the rules of a contest and accepts victory or defeat graciously. That is not the prevalent attitude in professional football. There are no Athenian virtues in this form of athletics. The NFL has substituted the morality of the battlefield for that of the playing field, and the "restraints of civilization" have been left on the sidelines.

Mr. Justice Holmes' simple statement of the function of tort law and the evidentiary record now before me clearly reveal the density of the thicket in which the courts would become entangled if they undertook the task of allocation of fault in professional football games. The NFL rules of play are so legalistic in their statement and so difficult of application because of the speed and violence of the play that the differences between violations which could fairly be called deliberate, reckless or outrageous and those which are "fair play" would be so small and subjective as to be incapable of articulation. The question of causation would be extremely difficult in view of the frequency of forceful collisions. The volume of such litigation would be enormous and it is reasonable to expect that the court systems of the many states in which NFL games are played would develop differing and conflicting principles of law. It is highly unlikely that the NFL could continue to produce anything like the present games under such multiple systems of overview by judges and juries. If there is to be any governmental involvement in this industry, it is a matter which can be best considered by the legislative branch.

My conclusion that the civil courts cannot be expected to control the violence in professional football is limited by the facts of the case before me. I have considered only a claim for an injury resulting from a blow, without weaponry, delivered emotionally without a specific intent to injure, in the course of regular play in a league-approved game involving adult, contract players. Football as a commercial enterprise is something quite different from athletics as an extension of the academic experience and what I have said here may have no applicability in other areas of physical competition.

Judgment for defendants.

HACKBART V. CINCINNATI BENGALS, INC. (HACKBART II)
601 F.2d 516 (10th Cir. 1979)

DOYLE, CIRCUIT JUDGE.

The question in this case is whether in a regular season professional football game an injury which is inflicted by one professional football player on an opposing player can give rise to liability in tort where the injury was inflicted by the intentional striking of a blow during the game.

* * *

The evidence at the trial uniformly supported the proposition that the intentional striking of a player in the head from the rear is not an accepted part of either the playing rules or the general customs of the game of professional football. . . .

[T]he district court's assumption was that Clark had inflicted an intentional blow which would ordinarily generate civil liability and which might bring about a criminal sanction as well, but that since it had occurred in the course of a football game, it should not be subject to the restraints of the law; that if it were it would place unreasonable impediments and restraints on the activity. The judge also pointed out that courts are ill-suited to decide the different social questions and to administer conflicts on what is much like a battlefield where the restraints of civilization have been left on the sidelines. . . .

III.
WHETHER INTENTIONAL INJURY IS ALLOWED BY EITHER WRITTEN RULE OR CUSTOM

Plaintiff . . . maintains that tort law applicable to the injury in this case applies on the football field as well as in other places. On the other hand, plaintiff does not rely on the theory of negligence being applicable. This is in recognition of the fact that subjecting another to unreasonable risk of harm, the essence of negligence, is inherent in the game of football, for admittedly it is violent. . . .

Contrary to the position of the court then, there are no principles of law which allow a court to rule out certain tortious conduct by reason of general roughness of the game or difficulty of administering it.

Indeed, the evidence shows that there are rules of the game which prohibit the intentional striking of blows. Thus, Article 1, Item 1, Subsection C, provides that:

> All players are prohibited from striking on the head, face or neck with the heel, back or side of the hand, wrist, forearm, elbow or clasped hands.

Thus the very conduct which was present here is expressly prohibited by the rule which is quoted above.

The general customs of football do not approve the intentional punching or striking of others. That this is prohibited was supported by the testimony of all of the witnesses. They testified that the intentional striking of a player in the face or from the rear is prohibited by the playing rules as well as the general customs of the game. Punching or hitting with the arms is prohibited. Undoubtedly these restraints are intended to establish reasonable boundaries so that one football player cannot intentionally inflict a serious injury on another. Therefore, the notion is not correct that all reason has been abandoned, whereby the only possible remedy for the person who has been the victim of an unlawful blow is retaliation.

* * *

V.

IS THE STANDARD OF RECKLESS DISREGARD OF THE RIGHTS OF OTHERS APPLICABLE TO THE PRESENT SITUATION?

The Restatement of Torts Second, § 500, distinguishes between reckless and negligent misconduct. Reckless misconduct differs from negligence, according to the authors, in that negligence consists of mere inadvertence, lack of skillfulness or failure to take precautions; reckless misconduct, on the other hand, involves a choice or adoption of a course of action either with knowledge of the danger or with knowledge of facts which would disclose this danger to a reasonable man. Recklessness also differs in that it consists of intentionally doing an act with knowledge not only that it contains a risk of harm to others as does negligence, but that it actually involves a risk substantially greater in magnitude than is necessary in the case of negligence. The authors explain the difference, therefore, in the degree of risk by saying that the difference is so significant as to amount to a difference in kind.

Subsection (f) also distinguishes between reckless misconduct and intentional wrongdoing. To be reckless the *act* must have been intended by the actor. At the same time, the actor does not intend to cause the harm which results from it. It is enough that he realized, or from the facts should have realized, that there was a strong probability that harm would result even though he may hope or expect that this conduct will prove harmless. Nevertheless, existence of probability is different from substantial certainty which is an ingredient of intent to cause the harm which results from the act.

Therefore, recklessness exists where a person knows that the act is harmful but fails to realize that it will produce the extreme harm which it did produce. It is in this respect that recklessness and intentional conduct differ in degree.

In the case at bar the defendant Clark admittedly acted impulsively and in the heat of anger, and even though it could be said from the admitted facts that he intended the act, it could also be said that he did not intend to inflict serious injury which resulted from the blow which he struck.

In ruling that recklessness is the appropriate standard and that assault and battery is not the exclusive one, we are saying that these two liability concepts are not necessarily opposed one to the other. Rather, recklessness under § 500 of the Restatement might be regarded, for the purpose of analysis at least, a lesser included act.

Assault and battery, having originated in a common law writ, is narrower than recklessness in its scope. In essence, two definitions enter into it. The assault is an attempt coupled with the present ability to commit a violent harm against another. Battery is the unprivileged or unlawful touching of another. Assault and battery then call for an intent, as does recklessness. But in recklessness the intent is to do the act, but without an intent to cause the particular harm. It is enough if the actor knows that there is a strong probability that harm will result. Thus, the definition fits perfectly the fact situation here. Surely, then, no reason exists to compel appellant to employ the assault and battery standard which does not comfortably apply fully in preference to the standard which meets this fact situation. . . .

* * *

The cause is reversed and remanded for a new trial. . . .

NOTES AND QUESTIONS

1. *Football as a "Commercial Enterprise."* The court in *Hackbart I* was reluctant to apply tort doctrine to professional football because it is a commercial enterprise built on abandoning the "restraints of civilization." The court also worried that judges, who may not be football fans, would not be able to determine whether a rules violation has occurred. Instead, the court deferred to the NFL's internal disciplinary mechanisms, including on-field penalties and league suspensions and fines, to "carefully orchestrate" the violence. Should a particular judge's familiarity with the game make a difference in the outcome of the litigation?

2. *League Self-Policing.* Do you agree that leagues such as the NFL are capable of self-policing for excessive violence so that participants should be excused from civil tort liability? Should tort liability turn on the quality of the league's self-policing? Does it inform your thinking that some leagues, including the NFL, review all game footage after-the-fact, in part for the purpose of identifying and penalizing foul play, whether or not it was flagged during the game?

3. *Conduct Not "Part of the Game."* An issue both *Hackbart I* and *II* confronted is how to distinguish between aggressive conduct that is "part of the game," and reckless conduct that is not. Note that in concluding that Clark was reckless, the *Hackbart II* court relied on the fact that Clark's conduct "is expressly prohibited by the rule [against striking with a forearm]." Note also that no official saw or penalized the conduct during the game. Even with instant replay review, experienced game officials struggle with applying the playing rules. Furthermore, every off-season, the NFL tweaks its playing rules for a variety of reasons, including to control the violence of the game. Given the uncertainty about rules interpretation this produces, are courts competent to assess whether a player's conduct violates a game rule?

Furthermore, is it possible to draw a line between permitted aggressiveness and prohibited recklessness in football? The *Hackbart II* court concluded that Clark's conduct fit the definition of recklessness because he intended the act and should have known "there was a strong probability that harm would result." Given the emotional content of the game—stirred up by coaches, teammates, and the crowd—is it fair to infer in the moment of contact that a player has constructive knowledge of probable harm? If not, what sort of evidence would be necessary to infer that knowledge? Consider *Green v. Pro Football, Inc.*, 31 F. Supp. 3d 714 (D. Md. 2014), where the court allowed an injured professional football player to pursue his intentional tort claim against an opposing team and its coach for instituting a bounty program wherein that team's players were given financial rewards for deliberately injuring opposing players. In that case, a by-product of the 2012 revelations of the New Orleans Saints bounty scandal discussed in Chapter 1, Section D, substantial evidence of specific intent to injure existed. What should an injured player's recourse be shy of such evidence?

4. *Compensating the Injured Athlete.* After the *Hackbart II* court remanded the case for trial, Hackbart settled his claim for $200,000. How would you allocate this payment between the joint tortfeasors, Clark and the Bengals? *See Tomjanovich v. California Sports, Inc.*, 1979 WL 210977 (S.D. Tex. Oct. 10, 1979) (Los Angeles Lakers liable to pay $3 million damage award when its player punched opposing player during on-court fight, resulting in career-ending injuries); *Averill v. Luttrell*, 44 Tenn. App. 56, 311 S.W.2d 812 (1957) (team vicariously liable for catcher's conduct when he slugged a batter who threw his bat at pitcher in response to several "brush-back" pitches); *Nathans v. Offerman*, 922 F. Supp. 2d 271 (D. Conn., 2013) (club might be held vicariously liable when its batter charges the mound, bat in hand, after being hit by a pitch). Should this type of liability be addressed and compensated through other mechanisms, such as the league's labor agreement and medical and pension benefits, or state workers' compensation benefits? Why shouldn't a coparticipant shoulder liability for on-field conduct that would get him arrested if he did it in the parking lot?

5. *Standard of Liability for Professional Athletes.* In post-*Hackbart* cases, courts have been reluctant to impose tort liability on professional athletes for playing field injuries in the absence of intentional or reckless conduct beyond a mere rules violation. *See, e.g., McKichan v. St. Louis Hockey Club, L.P.*, 967 S.W.2d 209 (Mo. Ct. App. 1998) (hockey goaltender could not recover for injuries from severe body check after referee's whistle had blown because "rough play is commonplace in professional hockey"). The logic underpinning this standard was explained in *Turcotte v. Fell*, 68 N.Y.2d 432, 502 N.E.2d 964 (1986). There, the court absolved a professional jockey who crossed lanes during a race, in violation of the "foul riding" rules governing the sport, and severely injured another jockey. The court held that professional athletes consent to the risk of injury even from conduct that violates the rules:

> Manifestly, a professional athlete is more aware of the dangers of the activity, and presumably more willing to accept them in exchange for a salary, than is an amateur. . . . The rules of the sport, however, do not necessarily limit the scope of the professional's consent. Although the foul riding rule is a safety measure, it is not by

its terms absolute for it establishes a spectrum of conduct and penalties, depending on whether the violation is careless or willful and whether the contact was the result of mutual fault. As the rule recognizes, bumping and jostling are normal incidents of the sport.... Plaintiff does not claim that Fell intentionally or recklessly bumped him, he claims only that as a result of carelessness, Fell failed to control his mount as the horses raced for the lead and a preferred position on the track. While a participant's "consent" to join in a sporting activity is not a waiver of all rules infractions, nonetheless a professional clearly understands the usual incidents of competition resulting from carelessness, particularly those which result from the customarily accepted method of playing the sport, and accepts them. They are within the known, apparent and foreseeable dangers of the sport and not actionable and thus plaintiffs' complaint against defendant Fell was properly dismissed.

Id. at 441. What differentiates this case from the facts in *Hackbart*?

6. *Recreational Athletes.* Recreational sports similarly raise the issue of the appropriate standard for coparticipant liability for on-field injury. In *Knight v. Jewett*, 3 Cal. 4th 296, 834 P.2d 696 (1992), the California Supreme Court denied the claim of a coparticipant who lost a finger as a result of a collision in a touch football game, holding that she assumed the risk of injury from "normal energetic conduct [that] often includes accidentally careless behavior":

[L]iability properly may be imposed on a participant only when he or she intentionally injures another player or engages in reckless conduct that is totally outside the range of the ordinary activity involved in the sport.... The courts have concluded that vigorous participation in such sporting events likely would be chilled if legal liability were to be imposed on a participant on the basis of his or her ordinary careless conduct.... [E]ven when a participant's conduct violates a rule of the game and may subject the violator to internal sanctions prescribed by the sport itself, imposition of *legal liability* for such conduct might well alter fundamentally the nature of the sport by deterring participants from vigorously engaging in activity that falls close to, but on the permissible side of, a prescribed rule.

Id. at 318; *see also Gauvin v. Clark*, 404 Mass. 450, 537 N.E.2d 94 (1989) (applying reckless disregard standard in denying recover to hockey player against opponent who struck him in the abdomen in violation of rules).

Contrast *Nabozny v. Barnhill*, 31 Ill. App. 3d 212, 334 N.E.2d 258 (1975), in which an Illinois court allowed a claim arising out an amateur soccer match where one player, in clear violation of safety rules, kicked the other team's goaltender in the head:

This court believes that the law should not place unreasonable burdens on the free and vigorous participation in sports by our youth.

However, we also believe that organized, athletic competition does not exist in a vacuum. Rather, some of the restraints of civilization must accompany every athlete onto the playing field. One of the educational benefits of organized athletic competition to our youth is the development of discipline and self-control.... A reckless disregard for the safety of other players cannot be excused. To engage in such conduct is to create an intolerable and unreasonable risk of serious injury to other participants. We have carefully drawn the rule announced herein in order to control a new field of personal injury litigation.

Id. at 260; *see also Bourque v. Duplechin*, 331 So. 2d 40 (La. Ct. App. 1976) (softball second baseman could recover for injuries caused by baserunner who ran out of his way to cause the collision). How would you strike the right balance between encouraging participation in sports and deterring reckless play? Which sports rules violations should trigger tort liability—only those related to player safety?

7. *Non-Contact Sports.* Courts have also examined whether the assumption of the risk doctrine absolves negligence in non-contact sports, largely concluding it does. In *Shin v. Ahn*, 42 Cal. 4th 482, 165 P.3d 581 (2007), the California Supreme Court extended the logic of the *Knight* case noted above to the sport of golf, rejecting the argument that liability should be imposed because the defendant failed to observe golf's rules of etiquette in hitting his tee shot without first ascertaining plaintiff's whereabouts. *See also Anand v. Kapoor*, 15 N.Y.3d 946, 942 N.E.2d 295 (2010) ("The manner in which Anand was injured—being hit without warning by a 'shanked' shot while one searches for one's own ball—reflects a commonly appreciated risk of golf."); *Bowman v. McNary*, 853 N.E.2d 984 (Ind. App. 2006) (denying recovery to a member of a high school girls' golf team, blinded when her teammate unintentionally struck her in the head with a golf club during a driving-range practice).

Violent acts that are clearly beyond the pale of the game and the law have taken place in the sports arena. A notable example occurred in 1965 when Juan Marichal of the San Francisco Giants, upset at having been grazed by Los Angeles Dodgers' catcher John Roseboro's throw back to the mound, turned and struck Roseboro in the head with his bat. MLB suspended Marichal for eight days (one start) in the middle of the pennant race and fined the miscreant $1,750. Roseboro sued Marichal and collected $7,500 out of court. Did the Commissioner and the judiciary treat this wisely? What is the appropriate legal treatment of the following "closer calls?"

(i) A pitcher throws a ball far inside the plate and strikes the batter who has come up to the plate after the previous batter had hit a three-run home run.

(ii) A runner from first base slides, with spikes up, into the second baseman some distance away from the base, to break up a double play in a close late-inning game.

(iii) A hard-hitting football free safety "blind sides" a wide receiver running a post pattern across the middle of the field, just after the ball has passed over both their heads.

2. INJURY TO ATHLETES—CRIMINAL LIABILITY

When an athlete sustains an injury not during the ordinary course of play but from contact that the rules directly prohibit or that occurred during stoppages from play, criminal liability might be considered. Ice hockey has attracted the most attention from law enforcement, given the accepted practice of in-game fights. When those fights involve prohibited stick slashes, criminal prosecutions have ensued.

Regina v. Green and *Regina v. Maki* were two such prosecutions that arose from a single incident during a 1969 preseason game between the Boston Bruins and the St. Louis Blues in Ottawa, Canada. A routine fight got out of hand when the Bruins' Ted Green and the Blues' Wayne Maki both slashed each other with their sticks, conduct specifically prohibited by the rules. So violent was the exchange that Green sustained a skull fracture. Canadian law enforcement filed criminal charges against both Maki and Green for conduct that exceeded the contact permitted by the rules and to which the players ostensibly consented. In separate decisions, the provincial court judges who tried the cases acquitted both players. In *Regina v. Green*, 16 D.L.R.3d 137 (Can. Ont. Prov. Ct. 1970), the judge addressed the "consent" defense as follows:

> There is no doubt that the players who enter the hockey arena consent to a great number of assaults on their person, because the game of hockey as it is played in the National Hockey League, which is the league I am dealing with, could not possibly be played at the speed at which it is played and with the force and vigour with which it is played, and with the competition that enters into it, unless there were a great number of what would in normal circumstances be called assaults, but which are not heard of. No hockey player enters onto the ice of the National Hockey League without consenting to and without knowledge of the possibility that he is going to be hit in one of many ways once he is on that ice.
>
> I think it is notable that Mr. Maki in his evidence, when he was questioned about the fact that he was struck in the face by Mr. Green's glove, said this had happened to him hundreds of times. I think within our experience we can come to the conclusion that this is an extremely ordinary happening in a hockey game

and the players really think nothing of it. If you go in behind the net with a defenseman, particularly one who is trying to defend his zone, and you are struck in the face by that player's glove, a penalty might be called against him, but you do not really think anything of it; it is one of the types of risk one assumes.

One now gets the most difficult problem of all, in my opinion: since it is assumed and understood that there are numerous what would normally be called assaults in the course of a hockey game, but which are really not assaults because of the consent of the players in the type of game being played, where do you draw the line? It is very difficult in my opinion for a player who is playing hockey with all the force, vigour and strength at his command, who is engaged in the rough and tumble of the game, very often in a rough situation in the corner of the rink, suddenly to stop and say, "I must not do that. I must not follow up on this because maybe it is an assault; maybe I am committing an assault." I do not think that any of the actions that would normally be considered assaults in ordinary walks of life can possibly be, within the context that I am considering, considered assaults at all.

See also Regina v. Maloney, 28 C.C.C.2d 323 (Can. Ont. 1976) (players are presumed to consent to conduct "inherent in and reasonably incidental to the normal laying of the game").

In *Regina v. Maki*, 14 D.L.R.3d 164 (Can. Ont. Prov. Ct. 1970), the judge expressed a different view, concluding that a hockey fight could amount to criminal assault, but acquitting Maki on the grounds of self-defense:

If the fact situation in this case had been such that no doubt was raised in my mind regarding self defense, I would not have hesitate[d] to convict the accused. The defense of consent would in my opinion have failed. Although no criminal charges have been laid in the past pertaining to athletic events in this country, I can see no reason why they could not be in the future where the circumstances warrant and the relevant authorities deem it advisable to do so. No sports league, no matter how well organized or self policed it may be, should thereby render the players in that league immune from criminal prosecution. . . .

Thus all players, when they step onto a playing field or ice surface, assume certain risks and hazards of the sport, and in most cases the defense of consent as set out in 230 of the Criminal Code would be applicable. But as stated above there is a question of degree involved, and no athlete should be presumed to accept malicious, unprovoked or overly violent attack.

But a little reflection will establish that some limit must be placed on a player's immunity from liability. Each case must be decided on its own facts so it is difficult, if not impossible, to decide how the line is to be drawn in every circumstance. But injuries inflicted in circumstances which show a definite resolve to cause serious injury to another, even when there is provocation and in the heat of the game, should not fall within the scope of the implied consent. [citation omitted]

The adoption of such principles in the future, would, I feel certain, be a benefit to the players, of course, to the general public peace and, in particular, to young aspiring athletes who look to the professionals for guidance and example.

Consider the implications of the two defenses offered in these cases: consent and self-defense. One could read the *Green* decision as implying that we are not always expected to control ourselves—so long as we are playing sports. Relying on the defense of consent in sports violence cases is in tension with societal interest in controlling violence, on and off the ice. A promoter who wants to attract "full-blooded" fans can make the sport really violent and no crimes would be committed since all the participants "consented." By this reasoning self-defense might be a better approach to avoiding criminal liability for sports violence. But then, did the acquittal of Maki on self-defense grounds mean that Green did assault Maki? Or vice versa?

Although the Ontario courts acquitted Green and Maki, a British Columbia judge took Canadian law in a different direction reviewing the actions of Boston Bruin Marty McSorley in a fight against Vancouver Canucks Donald Brashear. McSorley had lost an earlier fight against Brashear, who later taunted McSorley on the bench when his Bruins were losing the game. Just seconds before the end of the contest with the Canucks three goals ahead, the Bruins' coach sent McSorley back onto the ice to instigate another confrontation. To get Brashear's attention and provoke the fight, McSorley swung his stick and hit him on the head, giving Brashear a concussion that left him unable to play for several weeks. This time in addition to the standard five minutes penalty for fighting—which both players had received earlier in the game—NHL Commissioner Gary Bettman suspended McSorley for the remainder of the season. There was no right to appeal the Commissioner's discipline to an arbitrator under hockey's collective bargaining agreement.

Despite what the NHL called unusually "harsh and decisive" action against the player, the British Columbia Crown Prosecutor's office charged McSorley with "criminal assault with a weapon." At the criminal trial, the critical issue was whether McSorley had intended to hit Brashear on the shoulder or on the head (and helmet) with his stick.

REGINA v. MCSORLEY
2000 British Columbia Prov. Ct. 116 (Criminal Div. 2000)

KITCHEN, JUDGE.

This is my decision on the charge against Marty McSorley that he assaulted Donald Brashear with his hockey stick during a hockey game on February 21, 2000. . . .

Some may view the matter as a trial of the game of hockey itself. If that is the expectation, my decision will be a disappointment. My only concern is whether Marty McSorley is guilty of the specific charge alleged against him. That is not to say that the McSorley/Brashear incident should not prompt a healthy discussion of hockey and the role of violence in the sport. . . .

A related issue includes the question of whether the criminal law process should be preempted where discipline procedures have been taken by the hockey authorities. Again, I must emphasize that this is not an issue related to a determination of whether Mr. McSorley has committed a crime.

There are many groups that claim authority to discipline their members. Some are statutory, such as law societies and judicial councils, and some exist by virtue of private contractual arrangements such as in the case of the National Hockey League. . . . In my view, there should be a heavy onus on those purporting to preempt the normal criminal process, particularly where it is a private organization such as a group of hockey owners. Statutory bodies must act in the public interest; businessmen have no such obligation. . . .

[T]he object of the game of hockey is to put the puck in the net—the opposing net. Many of the written rules of the game deal with the legitimate means by which that may be done. Many other written rules deal with the consequences that will follow if the rules are not obeyed. . . . But those written rules are only part of the picture. There is also an unwritten code of conduct, agreed to by the players and officials, that is superimposed on the written rules. This code of conduct deals mainly with situations where the written rules are breached, and the code then comes into play. For example, the written rules prohibit slashing with the stick, but the unwritten code says that slashing is permissible as long as it is during play, and not to the head. Of course, when a slash is employed, and it is observed by the referee, there are consequences; a penalty is called. . . .

There is a further complication. The referees and linesmen exercise considerable discretion in assessing penalties. This exercise of discretion is seen by them as setting guidelines for the players so that the players will know what tolerance there will be for breaches of the written rules. Presumably the players are then expected to govern themselves accordingly. This requires the players to have a thorough knowledge of the written rules, a familiarity with the unwritten code, and an understanding of the guidelines the referee is signaling to the players during the game through his assessment and non-assessment of penalties. . . . It is within this somewhat indefinite framework that players must play the game.

It is the position of the Crown that this body of evidence permits only two possibilities—that McSorley deliberately struck Brashear to the head without Brashear's consent, or that he recklessly struck him to the head, not necessarily aiming for the head directly. Recklessness in this case may be likened to wilful blindness—ignoring a known risk. . . . If the blow to the head was intentional, it is common ground that it was an assault. Brashear himself said in evidence that he did not consent to being struck in that manner. The other witnesses agreed that stick blows to the head were not permitted in either the written rules, or the unwritten code. [E]vidence [established] that players in the NHL would not accept a blow such as that as part of the game

If the slash was intended for the shoulder, delivered with the intention of starting a fight, my conclusion would be that it was within the common practices and norms of the game.

I conclude that the following occurred. McSorley had fought Brashear and he had been briefly hurt. He was nevertheless prepared to fight him again, but Brashear frustrated his attempts to do so. Brashear taunted the Boston players and was seen to be responsible for taking the Boston goalie out of the game. This was all fairly routine for McSorley. He was credible when he said he was prepared to let things wind down at the end of the game.

Then [the Bruins coach] effectively directed him to get Brashear with about twenty seconds left. This was really too little time to fight but he felt himself pressured to do something. He found himself gliding in from centre ice toward Brashear, sizing him up for possible ways to confront him. Brashear crossed directly in front of him, presenting an easy target. Brashear was the focus of all of McSorley's and Boston's frustrations. McSorley had to do something; he might still be able to start a fight. . . . He had an impulse to strike him in the head. His mindset, always tuned to aggression, permitted that. He slashed for the head. A child, swinging as at a Tee ball, would not miss. A housekeeper swinging a carpetbeater would not miss. An NHL player would never, ever miss. Brashear was struck as intended.

Mr. McSorley, I must find you guilty as charged.

The judge in *McSorley* declined to impose a fine or jail sentence, instead agreeing to a "conditional discharge"—a probationary term that required 18 months of good behavior. The judge based this gentle penalty on his belief that McSorley's "act was unpremeditated. It was impulsive, committed when McSorley was caught in a squeeze—attempting to follow an order [from his coach] to fight with Brashear when there was too little time to do so." When is leniency in criminal sentencing justified by the convict's claim that he was "just following orders"?

NOTES AND QUESTIONS

1. *Application of Criminal Law to Competition Violence.* Clearly the typical punching and shoving that occurs during a hockey fight would not produce criminal liability, while a hockey player pulling out a gun and shooting a competitor to death undoubtedly would. But at what point does on ice violence cross the line to where it is appropriate to use the criminal courts to punish or deter it? Does your answer turn on the nature of the act or on the motives of the perpetrator—or both? Should the standard be different from sport to sport: *i.e.*, should violence by a hockey player against a competitor be viewed differently than violence by a basketball or baseball player? Or a golfer or tennis player?

2. *Home Versus Away Team.* It is exceedingly rare for a prosecutor to bring criminal charges against a home-team player for in-competition violence. Consider whether this is because the psychology of sport creates a disproportionate tendency to use excessive force when playing on the road or before a neutral audience. Or does this imbalance result, in the United States at least, from the fact that most local prosecutors are elected? The one case of home-team criminal prosecution occurred in Canada where career government attorneys customarily make prosecutorial decisions. In *Regina v. Bertuzzi*, 2004 BCPC 472 (Can. B.C. Prov. Ct. 2004), British Columbia authorities charged the Vancouver Canucks' Todd Bertuzzi with criminal assault for his vicious attack on the Colorado Avalanche's Steve Moore, which ended Moore's career. Bertuzzi pled guilty and received a conditional discharge and one year's probation. In addition, the NHL suspended Bertuzzi indefinitely and fined his club $250,000 for "failure to prevent the atmosphere that may have led to" the incident.

Compare this outcome to the New Orleans Saints bounty scandal where for three seasons, Saints coaches allegedly established a bonus pool to pay team members for injuring opposing star players. *See* Chapter 1, Section D. Although the NFL Commissioner imposed harsh punishments on the players and other team personnel involved, no local prosecutor—either home or away—brought any criminal charges.

3. *Tort Versus Criminal Liability.* In the Bertuzzi case described above, Moore, the injured player, also brought a civil suit seeking $38 million in pecuniary and punitive damages against Bertuzzi, the Canucks coach, and the team, which they ultimately settled confidentially. Consider the differences between the elements and burdens of proof for tort and criminal liability. As

noted in *McSorley*, and in the tort cases we read, coparticipant sports violence that results in injury is not culpable if it is "within the common practices and norms of the game." Criminal law provides for the defense of consent just as tort law provides for the defense of assumption of the risk. In a criminal prosecution, however, any reasonable doubt as to any element of the offense will result in acquittal. Does this alone explain why so few prosecutors pursue incidents of sports violence?

4. *Consent to Physical Contact Outside the Rules.* While consent is a defense in prosecutions of sports violence, courts have held that in some circumstances, coparticipants could not legally consent to overly violent contact. In an early prosecution of a professional boxer for a blow that killed his opponent, the jury was instructed that "the public has an interest in the personal safety of its citizens" and that citizens "cannot lawfully engage in" a sport so dangerous that it is likely to cause death. *People v. Fitzsimmons*, 34 N.Y.S. 1102, 1109 (1895); *see People v. Freer*, 381 N.Y.S.2d 976 (1976) ("[T]here is a limit to the magnitude and dangerousness of a blow to which another is deemed to consent."); *State v. Shelley*, 85 Wash. App. 24, 33, 929 P.2d 489 (1997) ("There is nothing in the game of basketball, or even rugby or hockey, that would permit consent as a defense to such conduct."). The difficulty is in drawing the boundaries of that consent in accordance with the "reasonably foreseeable hazards of joint participation in a lawful, athletic contest." *Id.* at 26. Given this difficulty, how should we apply criminal law's rule of lenity that requires a court to apply any unclear or ambiguous law in the manner most favorable to the defendant?

5. *Recreational Sports.* Would you expect prosecutions of sports violence to be more or less frequent in the recreational sports setting? In *People v. Schacker*, 670 N.Y.S.2d 308 (1998), the court dismissed criminal charges against a recreational hockey player who struck an opponent in a game, after the play was over and the whistle had blown, causing minor injuries. Expressing concern that the prosecution would undermine public policy "intended to facilitate free and vigorous participation in athletic activity," the court observed:

> [A]thletic competition includes intentional conduct that has the appearance of criminal acts. . . . Thus, in order to allege a criminal act which occurred in a hockey game, the factual portion of the information must allege acts that show that the intent was to inflict physical injury which was unrelated to the athletic competition. Although play may have terminated, the information herein does not show that the physical contact had no connection with the competition. Furthermore, the injuries must be so severe as to be unacceptable in normal competition, requiring a change in the nature of the game. That type of injury is not present in this case.

Id. at 309–10. Contrast *People v. Hall*, 999 P.2d 207 (Col. 2000), in which a court reinstated a reckless manslaughter charge against a skier who was moving so fast and out of control that he collided with and killed another skier.

The court found probable cause to believe that the defendant, a former ski racer, consciously disregarded the substantial and unjustifiable risk of injury to others. What explains the different outcomes in these two cases? The degree of injury inflicted? The level of the athlete's skill? Using the language of *Schacker*, does the prosecution of the skier in *Hall* require a change in the nature of the sport?

6. *Legislative Solutions.* The policy question posed by these cases has periodically interested the U.S. Congress in legislating against sports violence. One 1980 bill, the Sports Violence Act, would have created a new federal criminal offense of "excessive violence during professional sporting events," defined as force that "has no reasonable relationship to the competitive goals of the sport; is unreasonably violent; and could not be reasonably foreseen, or was not consented to, by the injured person, as a normal hazard to such person's involvement in such sports events." All major sports league commissioners opposed the bill, which died in committee and was never revived. If the bill had passed, would it be easier to resolve the factual issues, such as consent, raised by these incidents? Would a Sports Violence Act serve as a criminal court test run, at taxpayers' expense, for potential tort claims by injured athletes? Why did the major sports commissioners oppose the Sports Violence Act? Does this imply that federal intervention to deal with sports violence is not in the best interests of the game?

3. INJURY TO SPECTATORS

Cases involving injuries to spectators at sports events also take a distinctive approach to tort law. Spectator injuries typically involve a flying object that has entered the stands. Because this happens so frequently in baseball, courts refer to the legal doctrine as the "baseball rule."

JANE COSTA V. THE BOSTON RED SOX BASEBALL CLUB
61 Mass. App. Ct. 299, 809 N.E.2d 1090 (2004)

COHEN, J.

On a September evening in 1998, the plaintiff and three companions attended a Boston Red Sox baseball game at Fenway Park. They arrived late, at the top of the fifth inning. The plaintiff took her seat in an unscreened area in the upper box section on the first base line, more or less behind the Red Sox dugout. Several players from the visiting team, the Detroit Tigers, batted before their side was retired. In the bottom of the fifth, the first batter for the Red Sox was Darren Lewis. On a count of one ball and two strikes, Lewis hit a line drive foul ball into the stands along the first base line. The ball struck the plaintiff in the face, causing severe, permanent injuries. She had been in the ballpark no more than ten minutes when she was hurt.

It is not disputed that, while passively watching the game, the plaintiff's life was forever changed by this tragic event. What is disputed is whether the defendant Boston Red Sox Baseball Club may be compelled to compensate the plaintiff for her injuries. A judge of the Superior Court granted the defendant's motion for summary judgment. We agree that, as matter of law, the plaintiff may not recover on the only theory she advances—negligent failure to warn of the danger of being hit by a foul ball—and, accordingly, we affirm.

We view the summary judgment record, as we are required to do, in the light most favorable to the plaintiff. In addition to the facts outlined above, the record reveals the following.

Foul ball injuries occur with some regularity at Fenway Park. A spreadsheet produced by the defendant, summarizing five years of data during the 1990's, showed that the annual number of injuries sustained by patrons from foul balls ranged from thirty-six to fifty-three, with a substantial number requiring medical attention. While some of these incidents were listed as involving patrons who were injured while attempting to catch the ball, many others were not. Moreover, avoiding injury from a ball hit into the stands sometimes may be close to impossible. According to a professor of engineering retained by the plaintiff, the plaintiff had virtually no time to react to the ball that came her way. He determined, with the help of a range finder, that the distance from the plaintiff's seat to home plate was forty-seven yards, or 141 feet. By analyzing a videotape of the game, he also determined that the minimum speed of the baseball at the time it struck the plaintiff was ninety miles per hour, or 132 feet per second. Thus, he concluded, the plaintiff had no more than 1.07 seconds from the time Lewis hit the ball to take evasive action.

At her deposition, the plaintiff professed marked ignorance of the sport of baseball. Except for one occasion when she sat in the bleachers with her father when she was eight years old, she had never attended a baseball game prior to the night of the accident. She had not seen baseball on television except while changing channels, and did not watch sports reports or read about sports in the newspaper. Before the evening of her injury, she understood a foul ball to be one that simply rolled off to the side after being hit. As atypical as this may seem in "Red Sox Nation," we accept for present purposes (as we must) that the plaintiff had no subjective understanding of the risks posed by an errant foul ball.

There is an area behind home plate where netting protects approximately 2,511 seats; however, the plaintiff does not contend that the netting should have extended to the area where she was seated, or otherwise question the design of the ballpark. She claims only that she was entitled to an adequate warning of the dangers of sitting in an unprotected location so that she could have made an informed choice whether to remain there. She acknowledges the existence of a disclaimer printed on her admission ticket but maintains that she did not look at the ticket and that, in any event, the disclaimer was not adequate to discharge the defendant's duty to warn, particularly since the print was extremely small. She notes that, after the date of her injury, signage was installed along the first base line reading "BE ALERT. FOUL BALLS AND BATS HURT." Such signage, according to the plaintiff, was feasible and necessary before her accident. She claims that had she been adequately informed of the danger, she would not have exposed herself to the risk of injury presented by the location of her seat.

We turn now to the relevant law. It has been more than fifty years since a case like the plaintiff's has been considered on appeal in Massachusetts. In *Shaw v. Boston Am. League Baseball Co.*, 325 Mass. 419, 90 N.E.2d 840 (1950), the Supreme Judicial Court held, as matter of law, that a baseball club was not liable to a spectator who was injured by a foul ball. Shaw rested on the doctrine of assumption of risk and therefore turned on the plaintiff's subjective knowledge and appreciation of the danger. The plaintiff in Shaw was an admitted "fan" who had attended many baseball games and who knew that fast-moving foul balls often landed in the stands. On those facts, the court had little difficulty concluding that the defendant was shielded from liability because the "plaintiff's position [was] that of a spectator familiar with the game who was injured by an ordinary risk of the game which she had voluntarily assumed."

The present case stands on a different footing from Shaw, both legally and factually. As to claims arising on or after January 1, 1974, assumption of risk was abolished as an affirmative defense, . . . and here the plaintiff must be taken as ignorant of the danger of being hit by a foul ball. In spite of these distinctions, however, we conclude that the plaintiff still cannot recover . . . "Before liability for negligence can be imposed, there must first be a legal duty owed by the defendant to the plaintiff, and a breach of that duty proximately resulting in the injury." Here, the asserted duty is the duty to warn of the dangers of foul balls. Although an owner or possessor of land owes to all persons lawfully on the premises a common law duty of reasonable care to maintain the property in a reasonably safe condition and "to warn visitors of any unreasonable dangers of which the landowner is aware or reasonably should be aware," the duty to warn does not extend to dangers that would be obvious to persons of average intelligence. "Where a danger would be obvious to a person of ordinary perception and judgment, a landowner may reasonably assume that a visitor has knowledge of it and, therefore, 'any further warning would be an empty form' that would not reduce the likelihood of resulting harm."

This principle exists independently of the doctrine of assumption of risk. . . . As the Supreme Judicial Court explained, the abolition of assumption of risk as an affirmative defense did "not alter the plaintiff's burden in a negligence action to prove that the defendant owed him a duty of care in the circumstances, and thus [left] intact the open and obvious danger rule, which operates to negate the existence of a duty of care," at least insofar as a duty to warn is concerned.

Viewing the present case through the lens of the defendant's duty, we are persuaded that the potential for a foul ball to enter the stands and injure a spectator who is seated in an unscreened area is, as matter of law, sufficiently obvious that the defendant reasonably could conclude that a person of ordinary intelligence would perceive the risk and need no additional warning. Even someone of limited personal experience with the sport of baseball reasonably may be assumed to know that a central feature of the game is that batters will forcefully hit balls that may go astray from their intended direction. We therefore hold that the defendant had no duty to warn the plaintiff of the obvious danger of a foul ball being hit into the stands.

The result we reach is consistent with the vast majority of reported decisions involving injuries to spectators at baseball games. Although cases in other jurisdictions have turned on a variety of tort doctrines, they reflect a consensus that baseball stadium owners should not be held responsible for injuries to spectators that result from balls leaving the field during play—at least if adequate safety screening has been provided to protect areas of the stadium in the vicinity of home plate, where the danger is thought to be most acute. As a consequence, injured fans like the plaintiff are left to bear the costs of their injuries, even though they played no role in causing them except by choosing to attend the game.

In its amicus brief, the office of the commissioner of baseball, paraphrasing Justice Cardozo, justifies this result with the cavalier observation that "the timorous may always choose to stay at home." Perhaps a more gracious approach would be for major league baseball to elect to internalize the costs of unavoidable injuries sustained by fans through no fault of their own. On the theory the plaintiff has asserted, however, we do not so require.

Judgment affirmed.

NOTES AND QUESTIONS

1. *Open and Obvious Danger.* In declining to impose a duty to warn on the baseball club, the *Costa* court held that the risk of foul balls is open and obvious to anyone attending a baseball game. Should it matter whether a spectator is sufficiently knowledgeable about the game? Should it matter where the spectator is sitting or how early in the game the injury occurred?

Should it matter that errant baseballs are not just a common, expected danger of baseball, but actually one of the reasons why fans come to games? *See Rudnick v. Golden West Broadcasters*, 156 Cal. App. 3d 793, 202 Cal. Rptr. 900 (Ct. App. 1984) ("the chance to apprehend a misdirected baseball is as much a part of the game as the seventh inning stretch or peanuts and Cracker Jack").

2. *Enterprise Liability.* What do you think about the *Costa* dictum that MLB should "elect to internalize the costs of unavoidable injuries?" In other industries, when a risk is characteristic of an enterprise, courts have been willing to hold the enterprise strictly liable for resulting injury. That is, nonnegligent accident costs are imposed on the activity, not on the random victim. Why not in sports? What more could baseball stadiums do to protect fans from stray balls, and would those measures appreciably detract from spectator enjoyment of the game? *See Benejam v. Detroit Tigers, Inc.*, 246 Mich. App. 645, 651, 635 N.W.2d 219 (2001) (rejecting liability for injury from flying shard of a broken bat and noting the "inherent value in having most seats unprotected by a screen because baseball patrons generally want to be involved with the game in an intimate way"); *Payne v. Office of the Comm'r of Baseball*, 2016 WL 6778673 (N.D. Cal. Nov. 16, 2016), *aff'd*, 705 F. App'x 654 (9th Cir. 2017) (dismissing class action suit seeking to compel MLB to increase protective netting in its ballparks). Why have the courts preferred a policy favoring spectator enjoyment over risk avoidance?

3. *Ticket Disclaimer.* Costa's game ticket included a disclaimer that read in relevant part: "The holder assumes all risk and danger incidental to the game of baseball including specifically (but not exclusively) the danger of being injured by thrown bats and thrown or batted balls and agrees that the participating clubs, their agents and players are not liable for injuries resulting from such causes." Does this language have any legal import? If not, why bother putting it on the ticket? Should courts permit a facility operator to contractually modify its duty of care?

4. *Recreational Sports.* Should the *Costa* reasoning apply to a backyard pick-up softball game? *Judge v. Carrai*, 77 Mass. App. Ct. 803, 934 N.E.2d 276 (2010) (both organizer of the game and hosts, as owners of the softball equipment, owed guest a duty of care).

5. *Facility Amenities and Spectator Distractions.* Courts are willing to deviate from the Baseball Rule's quasi-immunity when facility amenities increase the dangers associated with game attendance. The Idaho Supreme Court, in a case of first impression, declined to adopt the Baseball Rule where a foul ball flew into a "multi-purpose" club area and hit a spectator, causing him to lose an eye. *Bud Rountree v. Boise Baseball*, 154 Idaho 167, 296 P.3d 373 (2013). *See also Maisonave v. Newark Bears Professional Baseball Club, Inc.*, 185 N.J. 70, 881 A.2d 700 (2005) (spectator did not assume the risk of being hit by a foul ball when he was at a concession stand in the concourse and not at his seat); *Jones v. Three Rivers Mgmt. Corp.*, 483 Pa. 75, 394 A.2d 546 (1978) (fan struck when standing in concourse allowed to sue because architectural features of stadium impaired sightlines to field).

The New Mexico Supreme Court took a middle road in rejecting the Baseball Rule in a case where a child sitting in a picnic area was struck by a baseball:

> [A]n owner/occupant of a commercial baseball stadium owes a duty that is symmetrical to the duty of the spectator. Spectators must exercise ordinary care to protect themselves from the inherent risk of being hit by a projectile that leaves the field of play and the owner/occupant must exercise ordinary care not to increase that inherent risk.

Edward C. v. City of Albuquerque, 148 N.M. 646, 658–59, 241 P.3d 1086 (2010). Contrast *Turner v. Mandalay Sports Entertainment, LLC*, 124 Nev. 213, 180 P.3d 1172 (2008), in which the Nevada Supreme Court narrowly reaffirmed the Baseball Rule to immunize stadium operators for foul-ball injuries to fans struck at any location inside the stadium, not just when sitting in their seats. The court held that a fan assumed the risk of being hit by a ball even while eating at a picnic area with restricted views of the field. The dissent in *Turner* would have followed *Maisonave*, the New Jersey case cited above. Which is the best approach for determining the duty of a baseball club towards spectators?

Courts are split as to whether other game-time distractions—such as a mascot's antics—limit the scope of the Baseball Rule. *Compare Lowe v. California League of Prof. Baseball*, 56 Cal. App. 4th 112, 65 Cal. Rptr. 2d 105 (1997) (fan struck by flying ball when distracted by team mascot permitted to sue because mascot's presence was not necessary to the game), *with Harting v. Dayton Dragons Prof'l Baseball Club, L.L.C.*, 171 Ohio App. 3d 319, 870 N.E.2d 766 (2007) (given prevalence of team mascots at sporting events, mascot's antics did not excuse fan from paying attention to action on the field).

6. *Other Sports Projectiles.* The Baseball Rule has been applied to hockey pucks, even when a spectator was hit during pre-game warmups when crowds of fans obstructed her view. *See Nemarnik v. Los Angeles Kings Hockey Club, L.P.*, 103 Cal. App. 4th 631, 638, 127 Cal. Rptr. 2d 10 (2002) ("it is undisputed that ice hockey spectators face a known risk of being hit by a flying puck"). However, in *Allred v. Capital Area Soccer League, Inc.*, 194 N.C. App. 280, 669 S.E.2d 777 (2008), the court held that a spectator at a soccer game injured by a struck ball was entitled to pursue her claim based on lack of knowledge of the risk of injury. At the time of this ruling, soccer was still emerging as a spectator sport in the U.S. Do you think that was outcome determinative? *See also Coomer v. Kansas City Royals*, 437 S.W.3d 184 (Mo. 2014) (rejecting application of the Baseball Rule when a fan was hit by a flying hotdog thrown by team mascot).

7. *Spectator Conduct.* Occasionally spectator conduct causes injury to others, especially in cases where spectators scramble to claim a ball that goes into the stands. *See Hayden v. University of Notre Dame*, 716 N.E.2d 603 (Ind. App. 1999) (university has duty to protect spectators from that foreseeable risk). Entirely unforeseeable was the violent and unprecedented altercation that occurred among players and fans at a 2004 Detroit Pistons home game

against the Indiana Pacers. After two players engaged in a shoving match, a home-team fan threw a beverage at Pacers forward Ron Artest. Artest responded by entering the stands and attacking one spectator. Other players and spectators joined the fray, resulting in NBA suspensions for all the players and injuries for some of the fans. *See* Chapter 3, Section B. In one of the resulting spectator tort suits, *Haddad v. O'Neal*, 2006 WL 3532686 (E.D. Mich. Oct. 19, 2006), a federal jury found the player and team were not liable for the spectator's injuries because the player was acting in defense of teammates. To what extent do spectators assume the risk of rowdy fan behavior?

8. *Premises Liability in General.* Beyond a sport's known projectile hazards, facility operators are subject to standard premises liability principles in force in their jurisdiction. Generally, facility operators have a duty to maintain a reasonably safe environment for invitees. This includes using reasonable care to regulate crowd control and invitee conduct during sporting events. *See Brisbin v. Washington Sports & Entm't, Ltd.*, 422 F. Supp. 2d 9, 13 (D.D.C. 2006) (spectator injured when another spectator fell on her could pursue her negligence claim only if supported by expert testimony on "the appropriate standard of care Washington Sports should have met based on the Center's physical layout").

B. HEALTH AND SAFETY OFF THE FIELD

Injuries and medical conditions from playing sports can be precipitated or exacerbated by the off-field decisions and practices of leagues, teams, and their personnel. Leagues closely monitor their game presentations and periodically adjust their playing rules to enhance both entertainment value and player safety. Leagues hire and train game officials to enforce those playing rules and keep the game safe. Teams hire health care professionals, including physicians, physical therapists, and athletic trainers, to provide for the physical well-being of their athletes. Playing surfaces and equipment are inspected and upgraded to promote safety as well as to improve athletic performance. The discharge of these duties and many other functions of sports leagues and teams is subject to the standard of reasonable care to avoid foreseeable harm to the athletes.

1. MEDICAL MALPRACTICE

Sports teams usually employ physicians and other health care professionals to provide athletes with a range of services, including prevention, diagnosis, treatment, and rehabilitation of injuries and medical conditions. Regardless of who pays their salary, team physicians are first and foremost bound by their professional code and legal duty to prioritize the patient-athlete's health. Even so, the singular relationship among a team, its players, and the team doctor is susceptible to conflicts of interest arising out of the need for the athlete to heal quickly and help the team win. Team medical staff face undeniable pressure to subordinate the athlete's well-being to the team's and often the athlete's own strong desire that he or she return to play. Athletes may pursue malpractice claims when the team physician's judgment appears compromised by the team's need for the player's services. Recovery for malpractice against team medical professionals, however, is complicated in team sports by (1) league collective bargaining agreements and standard playing contracts, and (2) state workers' compensation rules.

First, in unionized sports, the labor agreement typically provides contractual injury protection guarantees and disability benefits to athletes for playing injuries. *See Giles v. Bert Bell/Pete Rozelle NFL Player Ret. Plan*, 2013 WL 6909200 (D. Md. Dec. 31, 2013) (interpreting NFL players' disability benefits plan). As discussed in Chapter 3, Section D, players who dispute the team's assessment of their rights under those agreements must submit their claims to binding arbitration under federal labor law that preempts tort suits. *See Smith v. Houston Oilers, Inc.*, 87 F.3d 717 (5th Cir. 1996) (requiring arbitration of claims arising out of allegedly abusive rehabilitation program); *Boogaard v. Nat'l Hockey League*, 126 F. Supp. 3d 1010 (N.D. Ill. 2015) (requiring arbitration of claims arising out of hockey players' substance abuse); *Sherwin v. Indianapolis Colts, Inc.*, 752 F. Supp. 1172 (N.D.N.Y. 1990) (requiring arbitration of claims of inadequate medical care and intentionally withholding information about player's injury). A tort claim is available only if the player's allegations do not implicate the collective bargaining agreement. *See Bentley v. Cleveland Browns Football Co.*, 194 Ohio App. 3d 826, 958 N.E.2d 585 (2011) (claims for fraud and negligent misrepresentation in treating players' staph infection do not implicate the CBA); *Brown v. Nat'l Football League*, 219 F. Supp. 2d 372 (S.D.N.Y. 2002) (allowing player's tort claim for career-ending eye injury caused when referee struck him with penalty flag because based on state law duty independent of CBA).

Second, in most states, businesses that employ workers must purchase workers' compensation insurance. Where an employer team pays for this coverage and provides the benefits to an injured player, those benefits become the player's exclusive remedy. Injured players are statutorily barred from bringing tort suits against the team and co-employees. Thus, in *Stringer v. Minnesota Vikings Football Club, LLC*, 705 N.W.2d 746 (Minn. 2005), the Minnesota Supreme Court held that when a Vikings team member died of heat stroke during training camp, his survivors could not recover in a tort action against the team medical staff who treated him. *See also DePiano v. Montreal Baseball Club, Ltd.*, 663 F. Supp. 116 (W.D. Pa. 1987), *aff'd*, 838 F.2d 1205 (3d Cir. 1988) (workers' compensation was exclusive remedy for team doctor's negligent medical treatment of minor league baseball player).

An injured athlete may be able to recover in tort against team medical personnel who are independent contractors, rather than co-employees. In

Bryant v. Fox & Chicago Bears, 162 Ill. App. 3d 46, 515 N.E.2d 775 (1987), the court held that two Bears players were not limited to statutory remedies, and reinstated their medical malpractice claims against the team physician because the team treated the doctor as an independent contractor, paying him fees for services provided, without issuing a W-2 or making Social Security deductions. In addition, some states have been willing to carve out exceptions from workers' compensation exclusivity for claims that an employer intentionally inflicted physical injury.

KRUEGER V. SAN FRANCISCO FORTY NINERS
189 Cal. App. 3d 823, 234 Cal. Rptr. 579 (Ct. App. 1987)

NEWSOM, ASSOCIATE JUSTICE.

Appellant began playing professional football with the San Francisco 49'ers (hereafter respondent or the 49'ers) in 1958. He was a defensive lineman for the 49'ers until retiring in 1973, missing only parts of two seasons due to injuries. During his career, however, appellant played despite suffering numerous injuries. . . .

The injuries and damages to appellant's left knee are the focus of the present suit. While in college in 1955, appellant had surgery on his left knee to repair a torn meniscus. Then, in October of 1963, he ruptured the medial collateral ligament in his left knee. Dr. Lloyd Taylor, a physician who treated 49'ers' players, performed an operation on the knee which, appellant was told, effectuated a "good repair." Thereafter, appellant engaged in rehabilitative therapy with the team trainer and was given a knee brace which he later wore while playing until he removed it in 1967.

Dr. Taylor noted in his report of the operation that the anterior cruciate ligament—the function of which is to prevent the tibia from shifting forward on the femur—"appeared to be absent" from appellant's left knee. Such an injury can produce instability in the knee, particularly if combined with other injuries. According to appellant, he was not told that his left knee evidently lacked the anterior cruciate ligament.

In the spring of 1964, appellant began experiencing pain and considerable swelling in his left knee. He again received treatment from physicians retained by the 49'ers, specifically Dr. Taylor and Dr. Lloyd Milburn, which consisted of aspiration of bloody fluid from the knee by means of a syringe and contemporaneous injection of novocain and cortisone, a steroid compound. Appellant testified that he received approximately 50 such "Kepplemann" treatments during 1964, and an average of 14 to 20 per year from 1964 to 1973. Dr. Milburn could not recall administering Kepplemann treatments with such frequency, and testified that his records indicated only seven such treatments. Appellant also testified that he was never advised by the 49'ers medical staff of the dangers associated with steroid injections in the knee, such as possible rupturing of tendons, weakening of joints and cartilage, and destruction of capillaries and blood vessels. He also offered expert medical testimony that the adverse effects of steroids were known at that time. The same medical expert also testified that the number of steroid injections appellant claimed to have undergone would have been inappropriate and quite "unusual."

Appellant's left knee continued to plague him during his football career, and in 1971 he underwent another operation performed by Dr. Taylor to remove "loose bodies" in the knee resulting from chronic chondromalacia patella—thinning and loss of cartilage on the undersurface of the kneecap, a condition fully consistent with known adverse reaction to prolonged steroid use. X-rays taken between 1964 and 1971 revealed "degenerative post-traumatic changes" in appellant's left knee joint. Appellant testified—without contradiction—that he was not told of either of these afflictions by the 49'ers medical staff.

Krueger also testified that he suffered a "hit" on the outside of the knee during a game in 1970. He felt a piece of the knee break off. Notwithstanding the obvious severity of the injury, appellant was given Empirin codeine and directed to return to the game. For the remainder of the season, he could feel a "considerable piece of substance" dislodged on the outside of his left knee joint; nevertheless, he played the remaining five games of the season. At no time did the team doctors ever advise him that he risked permanent injury by continuing to play without surgery. Krueger testified unequivocally that, had he been advised not to play, he would have followed that advice. . . .

Appellant retired from football following the 1973 season. . . . Not until 1978 was appellant treated again for his injured knee. At that time, he received a Kepplemann treatment from Dr. Milburn, and x-rays were taken of both legs. According to appellant it was not until this visit to Dr. Milburn in 1978 that he was shown x-rays of his knees and advised for the first time that he suffered from chronic and permanent disability in the knee.

Defendant was referred to Dr. Taylor, who subsequently performed on him a tibial osteotomy, which is a shaving of planes from the leg bone followed by regrafting of the tendons and ligaments to the bone. The operation did nothing to alleviate appellant's severe discomfort, and in fact, he thereafter developed calcification in the knee and suffered greater pain than had been the case before the surgery. He presently suffers from traumatic arthritis and a crippling degenerative process in the left knee. He cannot stand up for prolonged periods, and cannot run. He is also unable to walk on stairs without severe pain. His condition is degenerative and irreversible.

Appellant's action was for fraud or deceit. . . . "Deceit may be negative as well as affirmative; it may consist in suppression of that which it is one's duty to disclose, as well as in the declaration of that which is false." [citation omitted] [T]he intentional concealment of a material fact is actionable fraud only if there is a fiduciary relationship giving rise to a duty to disclose it. The relationship between physician and patient is fiduciary in nature and creates a duty to disclose. . . .

As to the crucial issue of full disclosure, . . . we find the evidence uncontradicted; as will appear, the requisite disclosure was never made. That the team physicians *withheld* no material information from Krueger is not, in our view, the proper focus of inquiry. The critical question is whether full *disclosure* of his medical condition was ever made to Krueger. . . .

The physician must disclose to the patient all information necessary to make a knowledgeable decision about proposed treatment. The duty to disclose is imposed so that patients might meaningfully exercise their right to make decisions affecting their own bodies. Hence, even if the patient rejects a recommended procedure, the duty to disclose is nonetheless recognized.

* * *

In our opinion, the duty of full disclosure within the context of a doctor-patient relationship defines the test for concealment or suppression of facts under Civil Code section 1710, subdivision (3). The failure to make such disclosure constitutes not only negligence, but—where the requisite intent is shown—fraud or concealment as well. A physician cannot avoid responsibility for failure to make full disclosure by simply claiming that information was not withheld.

The testimony that, following his knee surgery in 1963, Krueger was not advised of the adverse effects of steroid injections, or of the risks associated with the continued pursuit of his profession, was uncontradicted. That is, while respondent produced testimony that the physicians treating appellant told him of the general nature of his injury, and did not conceal certain information from him, there is no evidence that appellant was ever informed of the continuing risks associated with his injuries. Hence, the requisite disclosure was never made. . . .

[W]e think the record unequivocally demonstrates that, in its desire to keep appellant on the playing field, respondent consciously failed to make full, meaningful disclosure to him respecting the magnitude of the risk he took in continuing to play a violent contact sport with a profoundly damaged left knee. . . . [I]t is in this palpable failure to disclose, viewed in the light of the 49'ers compelling obvious interest in prolonging appellant's career, that we find the intent requisite for a finding of fraudulent concealment. . . . [Krueger] was entitled . . . to rely upon respondent's physicians for medical treatment and advice without consulting outside sources or undertaking independent investigation.

Turning to the issues of proximate cause and damages, we note the trial court's finding that appellant's desire to continue playing was so intense that he would have continued even had he been informed of the magnitude of the risk involved. This finding seems to us mere conjecture. Appellant demonstrated throughout his football career a courageous—some might say foolhardy—willingness to endure pain and injuries for the sake of his team and employer, but no credible evidence suggests that he ever assessed and accepted the prospect of permanent disability. On the contrary, he testified that he would have retired had respondent's physicians recommended that course of action, and no contrary evidence was offered by respondent.

Motion for dismissal denied.

The 49ers paid Krueger more than $1 million to settle the litigation. Numerous other notable athletes have successfully sued their team doctors for medical malpractice in the treatment (or non-treatment) of their injuries:

1. Dick Butkus, the Chicago Bears linebacker, collected a $600,000 settlement in 1974 for harm caused by cortisone injections into his injured knee.

2. Bill Walton, the Portland Trail Blazers center, collected a substantial amount from the team doctor (not from the Blazers) for the use of painkillers that aggravated his injured foot in 1977 and severely limited his subsequent career.

3. Kenny Easley, the Seattle Seahawks' All-Pro safety, sued and collected from both the team doctor and the drug manufacturer after the Advil drug he took for an injured ankle caused severe kidney damage and cut short his career in 1987.

4. Mike Robitaille, a defenseman for the Vancouver Canucks, won a substantial court award because the team and its doctor dismissed his complaints about an injury as purely mental, and subsequent play had permanently damaged his spinal cord. *Robitaille v. Vancouver Hockey Club*, 3 W.W.R. 481 (Can. B.C.C.A. 1981).

5. In *Classen v. Izquierdo*, 137 Misc.2d 489, 520 N.Y.S.2d 999 (Sup. Ct. 1987), the court denied summary dismissal (based on assumption of risk) in a suit brought by the widow of a boxer who died in the tenth round of a 1979 boxing match at Madison Square Garden, after the ringside physician (appointed by the State Athletic Commission, not the Garden) examined the fighter at the end of the ninth round and let the match continue.

6. Marty Barrett, the former Red Sox second baseman, was awarded $1.7 million against the Red Sox and team physician and limited partner, Arthur Pappas, in 1995. The jury determined that in the midst of a Red Sox pennant race, Pappas removed part of Barrett's anterior crucial ligament (generally requiring a year of rehabilitation), but told Barrett and the press that he had only removed cartilage so that Barrett could continue to play on his injured knee.

7. In 2000, Merril Hoge, the former Chicago Bears running back, was awarded $1.6 million against John Munsell, the Bears' team physician, after being improperly cleared to play after suffering a concussion. Hoge claimed Munsell failed to warn him of the danger of returning to play prior to recovering completely. When Hoge returned to play, he suffered a career ending concussion with permanent brain function injury.

8. Philadelphia Flyer Dave Babych won a $1.37 million jury award against the team physician, Dr. Arthur Bartoluzzi, for allegedly having "made him play with a broken foot" in the 1998 NHL playoffs. Thus, Dr. Bartoluzzi felt compelled to give up that medical role with both the Flyers and the NFL Philadelphia Eagles because his malpractice insurer informed him that it would no longer cover his sports practice.

9. In 2002, Jeff Novak, an offensive lineman for the Jacksonville Jaguars, won a $5.3 million jury award against his NFL team's physician, Dr. Stephen Lucie, who cleared him to play a 1998 pre-season game that severely aggravated an earlier leg injury and ended his career. While the trial judge overturned that jury verdict for lacking a "reasonable basis," Novak immediately appealed and forced Lucie and his insurer to settle the lawsuit by paying him $2.2 million.

Cases like these have led several malpractice insurers to stop covering doctors who provide medical care to professional athletes, or to require team physicians to sign explicit employment agreements with their teams. In *Daniels v. Seattle Seahawks*, 92 Wash. App. 576, 968 P.2d 883 (1998), a player who was misdiagnosed, and whose subsequent injury prematurely ended his career, sued the Seahawks' team physician for malpractice. The court found that the physician's detailed employment contract with the Seahawks controlled the physician's conduct while performing his contractual duties, and as a result, the player could bring only workers' compensation claims against the team. Even though team physicians under employment contracts retain sole responsibility for medical decisions, the courts have continued to find that the teams maintain the requisite control over the team physicians to qualify them as employees.

Collective bargaining agreements increasingly articulate and expand upon players' rights with respect to medical care. The NFL's 2011–2020 Collective Bargaining Agreement entitles players to seek second medical opinions from independent providers at the team's expense. It further spells out the relationship between team doctor and athlete-patient:

Doctor/Patient Relationship. The cost of medical services rendered by Club physicians will be the responsibility of the respective Clubs, but each Club physician's primary duty in providing player medical care shall be not to the Club but instead to the player-patient. This duty shall include traditional physician/patient confidentiality requirements. In addition, all Club physicians and medical personnel shall comply with all federal, state, and local requirements, including all ethical rules and standards established by any applicable government and/or other authority that regulates or governs the medical profession in the Club's city. All Club physicians are required to disclose to a player any and all information about the player's physical condition that the physician may from time to time provide to a coach or other Club representative, whether or not such information affects the player's performance or health. If a Club physician advises a coach or other Club representative of a player's serious injury or career threatening physical condition which significantly affects the player's performance or health, the physician will also advise the player in writing. The player, after being advised of such serious injury or career-threatening physical condition, may request a copy of the Club physician's record from the examination in which such physical condition was diagnosed and/or a written explanation from the Club physician of the physical condition.

NOTES AND QUESTIONS

1. *Physician-Patient Relationship.* The *Krueger* court described the physician-patient relationship as a fiduciary one, imposing a duty of full disclosure and informed consent for medical treatment. Liability, however, depended on Krueger showing that the physician's breach of the duty *caused* his injury, that is, he would have made other treatment decisions or quit playing the sport if he were fully informed. Should an athlete be permitted to continue playing against medical advice, at a risk of permanent disability? What is the team's responsibility here? In competitive sports cultures, some athletes may dissemble about symptoms or pain they are experiencing to hasten return to play. And for a variety of reasons, some athletes simply fail to follow treatment instructions. Such conduct may amount to contributory negligence that bars or limits recovery.

2. *Standard of Care for Malpractice Suits.* Medical negligence is measured by the standard of care that applies in the specific treatment setting. Different states impose different tests for physician conduct, which can depend on the field of medicine and whether the doctor's skill and care is measured against national or local standards. Sports medicine is increasingly recognized as a distinct specialization subject to national standards. *See Zimbauer v. Milwaukee Orthopaedic Grp., Ltd.*, 920 F. Supp. 959 (E.D. Wis. 1996) (requiring baseball pitcher to submit expert testimony on standard of care physician owed for sports medical treatment).

3. *Sports Medicine Malpractice Reform.* What more can sports leagues do to assure appropriate medical care beyond spelling out players' rights and team physician duties in the labor agreement? Options for sports malpractice reform include having the leagues hire doctors as part-time employees, not just independent contractors, to eliminate negligence suits while insulating physicians from team pressure to return athletes to play quickly. Alternatively, players unions could hire the physicians, eliminating the co-employee immunity under workers' compensation and giving players a chance to receive adequate compensation for the premature ending of their careers. This proposal would require some level of league or union financial support for malpractice insurance, in order to give physicians the incentives and protection necessary to continue treating professional athletes.

2. LEAGUE AND TEAM POLICIES AND PRACTICES THAT AFFECT PLAYER HEALTH AND SAFETY

League and team policies and practices also have serious repercussions on player well-being. While injuries are inevitable in sports, especially those like football and hockey that mandate physical collisions, the way that leagues and teams manage player injuries and return-to-play can determine long-term health outcomes. Accusations that injury management practices prioritize team interests over player health and safety have surfaced in a range of lawsuits involving prescription drug medication and concussions.

(a) Prescription Drug Abuse Litigation

In 2014, former NFL players brought a putative class action against the league alleging a policy and practice of encouraging abuse of painkillers to keep players on the field at all costs. *See Dent v. Nat'l Football League*, 902 F.3d 1109 (9th Cir. 2018). The lawsuit alleges both negligent and intentional tortious conduct and violations of federal regulation of prescription drugs:

> [Plaintiffs] alleged that since 1969, the NFL has distributed controlled substances and prescription drugs to its players in violation of both state and federal laws, and that the manner in

which these drugs were administered left the players with permanent injuries and chronic medical conditions.

... [D]uring their years in the NFL, they received copious amounts of opioids, non-steroidal anti-inflammatory medications, and local anesthetics. The complaint claims the NFL encouraged players to take these pain-masking medications to keep players on the field and revenues high, even as the football season got longer and the time between games got shorter, increasing their chances of injury. According to the players, they "rarely, if ever, received written prescriptions ... for the medications they were receiving." Instead, they say they were handed pills in "small manila envelopes that often had no directions or labeling" and were told to take whatever was in the envelopes. During their years of consuming these powerful medications, it is further alleged that no one from the NFL warned them about potential side effects, long-term risks, interactions with other drugs, or the likelihood of addiction. The plaintiffs claim that as a result of their use (and overuse) of these drugs, retired players suffer from permanent orthopedic injuries, drug addictions, heart problems, nerve damage, and renal failure.

2018 WL 4224431, at *2.

Although it falls upon individual teams to hire doctors and trainers to attend to players' medical needs, the *Dent* complaint alleges that the NFL itself directly provided medical care and supplied drugs to players:

- The NFL supplied players with and encouraged players to use opioids to manage pain before, during and after games in a manner the NFL knew constituted a misuse of the medications and violated federal drug laws.

- The NFL directly and indirectly administered and supplied opioids and other controlled substances to injured players to mask their pain on game day, and encouraged players to rely on these drugs to manage pain without regard to the players' medical history or long-term health consequences.

- The NFL supplied players with local anesthetic medications to mask pain and other symptoms stemming from musculoskeletal injury when the NFL knew that doing so constituted a dangerous misuse of such medications.

- NFL doctors and trainers gave players medications without telling them what they were taking or the possible side effects and without proper recordkeeping.

- The NFL made knowing and intentional misrepresentations, including deliberate omissions, about the use and distribution of these medications.

See id. at *2–*3

The Ninth Circuit denied the NFL's motion to dismiss the *Dent* claims as preempted under § 301 of the LMRA. *Id.* The court relied on the *Williams* decision discussed in Chapter 3, Section D, in concluding that the allegations about the NFL providing players with prescription drugs described conduct that was "completely outside the scope of the CBAs" and assailable under federal regulation of controlled substances and state law regarding negligent hiring and retention of medical personnel, misrepresentation, and fraud. *Id.* at *12. At publication time, the *Dent* case was headed back to the district court for pre-trial discovery and further motion practice.

Former players also pursued virtually identical painkiller abuse claims against individual NFL clubs. *See Evans v. Arizona Cardinals Football Club LLC*, 2016 WL 3566945 (N.D. Cal. July 1, 2016) (holding that players' claims against teams were not preempted by § 301, and denying teams' motion to dismiss). Discovery had sufficiently advanced in that suit to permit the district court to grant summary judgment to the defendant clubs, dismissing all claims. *See* 252 F. Supp. 3d 855 (N.D. Cal. 2017) (dismissing fraudulent concealment claims); 262 F. Supp. 3d 935 (N.D. Cal. 2017) (dismissing remaining claims primarily because players did not establish intentional misconduct sufficient to fall within exceptions to workers' compensation exclusivity).

Notably, these lawsuits got the attention of the federal Drug Enforcement Agency, which conducted a few surprise inspections of NFL locker rooms to investigate the misuse of prescription drugs. In addition, the NFLPA filed a grievance alleging the overprescription of painkillers violates the CBA, including the "Doctor/Patient Relationship" provision excerpted above.

Consider what is the best forum to redress the former players' torts claims as well as systemic issues regarding player healthcare—the courts or the collectively bargained arbitral tribunal? Consider also how the NFL collective agreement might address the incentives to over-medicate players.

(b) Concussion Litigation

Systemic threats to player health and safety are also the subject of concussion litigation mounted by both professional and amateur athletes against multiple sports entities. Lawsuits were filed in the wake of scientific advances that suggest that repeated traumatic brain injuries can have latent consequences, including a host of cognitive impairments, degenerative diseases, mental illness, and a condition known as chronic traumatic encephalopathy (CTE).

Starting in 2011, retired NFL players filed lawsuits claiming that the NFL had a duty to address the risks of brain injuries to protect players. Hundreds of similar suits followed, including some styled as class actions. In June 2012, they were consolidated in the Eastern District of Pennsylvania and captioned *In re National Football League Players' Concussion Injury Litigation*. 842 F. Supp. 2d 1378 (U.S. Jud. Pan. Mult. Lit. 2012). The master complaint sought to impose liability on the NFL and its member clubs for negligence, fraud, and misrepresentation in connection with warning players about the risk of head injuries, conducting and disseminating relevant scientific research, developing playing rules and equipment designed to protect players from concussion-related health risks, and developing policies and procedures for dealing with player head injuries and return-to-play. Claims were also lodged against Riddell, the NFL's helmet manufacturer, accusing it of designing a defective product and failing to adequately warn players about its inherent deficiencies.

While motions were pending to dismiss the litigation as to the NFL parties based on § 301 labor preemption, the judge ordered mediation and a settlement resulted. *In re Nat. Football League Players' Concussion Injury Litig.*, 307 F.R.D. 351, 363 (E.D. Pa. 2015), *aff'd*, 821 F.3d 410 (3d Cir. 2016). In its final iteration, the settlement offered over 20,000 former NFL players both medical monitoring and compensation for cognitive injuries. Money was also set aside for medical research. The player compensation fund is uncapped, and as an actuarial matter, the NFL anticipates ultimately paying out over $1 billion to affected players, with awards varying according to years in the league, age at the time of onset of symptoms, and severity of impairment. No player may recover more than $5 million. Approximately 150 former players opted out of the settlement, although that number has since shrunk. Those cases are pending as of this writing, and if pursued, will likely ensure court decisions on issues such as labor preemption and causation.

Both sides in the NFL concussion litigation were highly motivated to reach a settlement. The former players faced debilitating neurological problems that needed immediate attention; pursuing a remedy through litigation might have taken years of discovery, a trial, and inevitable appeals, with a favorable outcome far from certain. By reaching the settlement, the NFL hoped to avoid opening its files to pre-trial discovery and continuing to experience bad public relations for the League and the sport.

The merits of the case suggest that the NFL had a good chance of ultimately prevailing. The NFL argued that the players knew the risks of playing the game at the highest level, and were aware of the effect of repeated impacts to their heads. As an evidentiary matter, retirees who continued to pursue litigation would have had to establish actual causation—*e.g.*, that their conditions resulted from concussions received while playing the NFL as opposed to in high school or college. And finally, labor preemption of most claims was likely, given collective bargaining agreements that specifically addressed player health and safety. Consider then the strategic value of the concussion litigation, aimed not necessarily at obtaining a court judgment but at putting the defendant in a public relations situation where it concludes it must do the "right thing" even if not legally compelled to do so.

With the denial of certiorari review of the NFL concussion settlement in December 2016, the former players began submitting claims. Since that time, the claims process has been plagued with allegations of fraud perpetrated by and against players. The independently administered fund has mechanisms in place to detect fraudulent claims, and hundreds of submissions have been flagged as suspicious. In addition, unscrupulous lenders and lawyers have induced hundreds of retired players to sign dubious contracts for settlement advances and claims services that charge exorbitant fees. Given these complications and delays, consider whether the players would have been better served by pursuing relief in the first instance through their collectively bargained grievance procedures. Notably, the NFL 2011–2020 CBA specifically provides for a "neuro-cognitive disability benefit," a feature designed both to compensate deserving players and firmly preempt future litigation.

Concussion lawsuits are also pending against the NHL and the NCAA. Former NHL players are claiming that the league did not do enough to protect them from the dangers of head trauma, especially in sending them out to fight and expecting them to shake off resulting injuries. The NHL cases have also been consolidated, but by contrast to the NFL, the court has issued multiple substantive rulings, reflecting the NHL's very different litigation strategy of fighting the claims on all fronts. The most recent court decision as of this writing denied class certification to the plaintiffs on their medical monitoring claims, saying state legal standards vary too widely to satisfy the class action requirement that common questions of law predomoniate. *In re: Nat'l Hockey League Players' Concussion Injury Litig.*, 2018 WL 3421343 (D. Minn. July 13, 2018). *See also* 189 F. Supp. 3d 856 (D. Minn. 2016) (denying labor preemption motion pending additional discovery); 2015 WL 1334027 (D. Minn. Mar. 25, 2015) (denying motion to dismiss). Also unlike the NFL litigation, the NHL parties have taken extensive document and deposition discovery of league executives, team owners, and players, most of which has thus far been kept confidential.

College-athletes also filed concussion suits against the NCAA, which were consolidated in 2013 into *In re Nat'l Collegiate Athletic Ass'n Student-Athlete Concussion Injury Litigation*. The athletes' claims track those of

NFL and NHL players, alleging that the NCAA failed in its duty to protect them from the risks of traumatic brain injury. The parties reached a settlement agreement that received preliminary approval in 2016. 2016 WL 3854603 (N.D. Ill. July 15, 2016). A final fairness hearing is scheduled for shortly after this edition goes to print. The settlement provides $75 million for medical monitoring and research and requires member schools to institute return-to-play guidelines under concussion management policies. Although the settlement did not include damages for the plaintiffs, individual athletes are free to pursue compensatory damages in separate personal injury lawsuits.

Finally, concern about sports-related brain injury has now spread to soccer (internationally known as football), primarily because of the risk of subconcussive trauma from repetitive heading of the ball. In the United States, youth soccer players brought a putative class action against FIFA, the sport's international governing body, and other soccer entities, alleging that they failed to adopt and enforce rules that would reduce the risk of preventable injuries resulting from concussions and heading the ball. The court declined to impute "a legal duty to reduce the risks inherent in the sport of soccer" in the absence of facts showing that any defendant took any action that increased those risks. *Mehr v. Fédération Internationale de Football Ass'n*, 115 F. Supp. 3d 1035 (N.D. Cal. 2015) (dismissing suit for lack of personal jurisdiction, lack of subject matter jurisdiction, and failure to state a claim). Nonetheless, the United States Soccer Federation responded with a series of safety initiatives that set strict limits on youth players heading balls.

NOTES AND QUESTIONS

1. *Existential Threat to Contact Sports.* The concussion litigation poses a fundamentally different and possibly existential challenge to contact sports. Most civil and criminal suits involving sports spring from prohibited conduct, both on and off the field. Liability can be avoided when the athlete has given informed consent to the risk. By contrast, the concussion class actions arise from injuries sustained while playing the sport according to its rules and within the participants' reasonable expectations. Avoiding those injuries requires more than simply enforcing existing rules of the game. Furthermore, it may not be possible to obtain informed consent to head injuries where the medical science is still emerging or where society is not willing to tolerate the risk. Should public policy demand radically changing the rules of the game—or even banning the sport—to avoid head injury risk? Consider that game rules inevitably affect amateur and youth participants as well as professionals.

2. *Game Rules Changes.* Since 2002, the NFL has made 50 rules changes intended to eliminate potentially dangerous tactics and reduce the risk of injuries. These changes include prohibiting use of the helmet as a

weapon against defenseless players, banning "horse-collar" tackles when a defender grabs a player's jersey from the back of the neck, and moving the touchback forward to attempt to discourage the kickoff return. Other sports have also tinkered with rules to improve player safety. Beginning with the 2014 season, Major League Baseball outlawed collisions at home plate: a baserunner may not barrel through the catcher and catchers may not block the plate without holding the ball. As of the 2016 season, MLB banned rolling block slides at second base to break up potential double plays. Both rules changes stemmed from game incidents in which players suffered serious orthopedic injuries. Were any of these revised rules fundamental to the game? As professional athletes grow bigger and stronger, with improved nutrition and training, should leagues be anticipating injury risks and proactively adjusting their rules? Should leagues face tort liability for creating rules that put athletes at an undue risk, or should juries stay out of the business of second-guessing competition rules?

3. *Game-Day and Medical Protocols.* In addition to rules changes, the NFL has instituted protocols to monitor and safeguard player health. Game-day staffing rules now mandate an unaffiliated neurotrauma consultant and athletic trainers to assist team medical staffs in identifying concussions and other potential player injuries. When traveling across state lines, every visiting team must retain a local licensed emergency physician affiliated with a nearby trauma center. Dedicated video monitors are provided for injury review. Concussion diagnosis and return-to-participation protocols, including mandatory sit-time, are strictly enforced. What more should the NFL be doing?

Consider the analysis offered by a football players' health study: "Protecting and Promoting the Health of NFL Players" (Harvard Univ. 2016). Among its recommendations are: a ban on adversarial collective bargaining over player health issues; flexible roster caps to encourage players with concussions to sit without penalty to teams; guaranteeing more of player compensation; and fining teams and team doctors for violating rules that protect player health. In addition, every state has enacted some form of legislation requiring monitoring and protection against concussions in youth sports. *See* National Conference of State Legislatures, *Traumatic Brain Injury Legislation,* http://www.ncsl.org/research/health/traumatic-brain-injury-legislation.aspx.

4. *Players Association Exposure.* Some NFL ex-players also sued the NFLPA for complicity in concealing the risk of concussions. A court ruled those claims preempted by federal labor law requiring the players to pursue relief through an unfair representation charge before the NLRB. *See Ballard v. Nat'l Football League Players Ass'n,* 123 F. Supp. 3d 1161 (E.D. Mo. 2015).

5. *Concussion Suits Against Helmet Manufacturers.* The NFL settlement did not resolve the other pending cases against the helmet manufacturers. Product liability claims against helmet manufacturers over the years have been largely unsuccessful. No recent case has found a helmet manufacturer liable for defective design, meaning no reasonable alternative

design exists that could diminish risks of concussions. However, in 2000, Riddell introduced "The Revolution," a helmet it promoted as reducing concussions by 31 percent, despite awareness of studies disputing the claim. Each Riddell helmet contained a warning label indicating that "NO HELMET CAN PREVENT SERIOUS HEAD OR NECK INJURIES . . . contact in football may result in CONCUSSION BRAIN INJURY which no helmet can prevent." (Schutt, a rival manufacturer, went even further with its warning: "To avoid these risks, do not engage in the sport of football.") A few helmet cases involving amateur football players have produced divergent jury results on the adequacy of such warnings.

Against this backdrop, the NFL ex-players' claims against Riddell have proceeded. While a settlement is possible, the manufacturer has less incentive to resolve the matter because of its potential extensive exposure to litigation, currently pending as well as future, brought on behalf of high school and college athletes who use Riddell helmets. In the meanwhile, all helmet manufacturers are researching ways to diminish the risks to athletes by better designing their equipment, which provides an apt segue into our next topic.

3. DEFECTIVE PRODUCTS AND HAZARDOUS FACILITIES

Another attractive third-party target for a tort suit by an injured athlete is the manufacturer of a product used in the game. Sports law was certain to gain a share of expanding product liability litigation. Technological developments, for example in the design and manufacture of aluminum bats, has enhanced the risk of injuries.

SANCHEZ V. HILLERICH & BRADSBY CO.
104 Cal. App. 4th 703, 128 Cal. Rptr. 2d 529 (Ct. App. 2002)

HASTINGS, J.

[Andrew Sanchez, a pitcher, was seriously injured when struck by a line drive hit by an aluminum bat, the "Air Attack 2." He filed suit against the bat manufacturer and others alleging that the design and use of this particular bat significantly increased the inherent risk in baseball that a pitcher would be hit by a line drive. The trial court granted summary judgment concluding that Sanchez would be unable to prove that his injuries resulted from the alleged increased risk the particular bat posed to pitchers. Sanchez appealed.]

The bat used by Correa was a newly designed hollow aluminum alloy bat with a pressurized air bladder which, according to its designer, substantially increases the speed at which the ball leaves the surface of the bat. . . . Prior to the commencement of the 1999 baseball season, appellant had signed a disclaimer form acknowledging that his participation on the team carried a risk of injury, specifically including brain damage, and consenting to assume the risk of such injury. . . .

Jack Mackay, the designer of the Air Attack 2, declared that he had been a designer and tester of bats for nine years and was a paid consultant for H&B's Louisville Slugger division. Mackay was present when time studies were performed on the bat at a Louisville Slugger testing center. He stated that the invention allowed a batter to hit a ball at speeds in excess of that which would have given a pitcher time to avoid being hit. As a result, he opined that the Air Attack 2 *substantially* increased the risk of a pitcher being hit by what he termed a "come backer." Mackay complained to his employers at the Louisville Slugger division of H&B about the increased risks of injuries, but the complaints were ignored and Marty Archer, president of the division, warned Mackay that he should not publicly discuss issues of safety. . . .

Appellant also submitted the declaration of James G. Kent, who had a Ph.D. in kinesiology. Based on his training and review of the evidence, he opined that the ball which struck appellant's head was traveling between 101 and 107.8 miles an hour, probably closer to the latter speed than the former. This would have left appellant a reaction time of .32 to .37 seconds to avoid the ball. This was below the minimum reaction time accepted by the NCAA and other organizations of .39 seconds. As a result, he concluded that appellant's head injury resulted from the increased danger posed by this particular bat. . . .

Discussion

* * *

1. *Assumption of the Risk*

. . . .The essence of a baseball game is the contest between the defense, the pitcher and other players in the field, and the batter, for mastery over what happens to the pitched ball. The batter wants to hit the ball safely, usually away from the defense, so that the batter can advance on the bases. The defense wants to get the batter out, either by striking the batter out, or by causing the batter to hit the ball to a spot where one of the defensive players can make a play on it. Inherent in this mix is the risk that the pitcher, or any infielder, may have to catch, or avoid being hit with, a sharply batted ball. Appellant acknowledged he was aware of this risk. Thus, given the foundational facts of this case, a prima facie showing of assumption of the risk has been established. But appellant argued that use of the Air Attack 2 increased the risk above that inherent in the sport, and presented evidence on the issue. We now review that evidence.

At the time of the accident, the NCAA allowed the use of metal bats, and the bat in use was *apparently* in compliance with NCAA standards. It is undisputed that the Air Attack 2 was designed to cause the ball to come off the bat at a higher launch speed than with wooden bats and older metal bats. It is also undisputed that the inventor of the Air Attack 2 believed the Air Attack 2 *substantially* increased the risk of a pitcher being hit by what he termed a "come backer" and that he complained to his employers at H&B about these increased risks.

Additionally, the evidence submitted by appellant establishes that the Pac-10 and NCAA each believed that new generations of aluminum bats created a significant issue of safety. Before the incident at issue, the NCAA adopted new rules to regulate the exit speed of such bats, but postponed implementation of the rules until a date after this incident.... The NCAA not only believed that the newer aluminum bats created an increased risk of harm to players, it also believed that use of these bats changed the nature of the sport of college baseball.

This case is similar to *Branco v. Kearny Moto Park, Inc.*, 37 Cal. App. 4th 184 (1995). There, participants on bicycles raced around a motocross (BMX) course which contained "jumps" as part of the course. The plaintiff was injured when he crashed and struck the side wall of the landing area of what is described as "an expert caliber jump." He filed suit and the defendants asserted primary assumption of the risk. The trial court granted summary judgment for defendants but the Court of Appeal reversed. "It is not unreasonable to expect a BMX course to refrain from utilizing jumps which by design create an extreme risk of injury. Certainly the jumps, and falls, are inherent to the sport, and under the doctrine of primary assumption of risk, there is no duty to eliminate the jumps entirely, and no duty to protect from injury arising from reasonably designed jumps. However, the sport does not inherently require jumps which are designed in such a way as to create an extreme risk of injury. Accordingly, premised on the duty not to utilize dangerously designed jumps, this case falls under the secondary assumption of risk category, and issues pertaining to [the plaintiff's] comparative fault are for the trier of fact to decide. [The plaintiff's] expert's opinions regarding the design of the jump create a triable issue of material fact whether the million dollar jump was designed in such a way as to create an extreme risk of injury."

Here, appellant's evidence raises a triable issue of material fact whether the design and use of the Air Attack 2 substantially increased the inherent risk appellant faced. The evidence also raises at least a triable issue whether defendants knew of and appreciated the nature of the increased risk....

2. *Causation*

Respondents contended, and the trial court agreed, that because the speed of the ball leaving the bat was never established, no causation attributed to the increased risk of use of the Air Attack 2, if any, could be established.... It is undisputed that Correa, using an Air Attack 2 manufactured by H&B, provided by USC, and approved by the NCAA, hit the ball that fractured appellant's skull. It is also undisputed that the Air Attack 2 was designed to and did increase the speed at which the baseball leaves the bat compared to other metal and wood bats. Thus, absent other factors (none are suggested) it follows that the ball must have reached appellant sooner than if Correa had used a bat other than the Air Attack 2. . . .

* * *

Dr. Kent also relied upon literature from the NCAA regarding reaction times. The letter from the NCAA dated December 4, 1998, quoted above, also has a passage regarding reaction times:

> "Most of the experts providing information to the Baseball Rules Committee believe that a collegiate pitcher needs approximately .4 seconds to react and move to avoid being struck. . . . Most baseball experts believe that a pitcher is between 51 and 52 feet away from the point of impact between the bat and ball at the time of impact, usually in an off-balance position with his glove down and back, and his weight moving forward. At 94 mph the ball will travel 52 feet in approximately .371 seconds. Game conditions using high powered aluminum bats often result in speeds well in excess of 100 mph. At 100 mph, the ball will travel 52 feet in .354 seconds; at 110 mph, a ball will travel 52 feet in .321 seconds. The NCAA Baseball Rules Committee is aware that there is some risk even with wood bats, but believes that the increased risk of injury resulting from the use of high powered aluminum bats is clear. To ignore this risk would, in our opinion, be irresponsible."

This provides independent corroboration for some of the facts relied upon by Dr. Kent and provides further facts relevant to the issue of causation.

We conclude the evidence presented by appellant is sufficient to create a triable issue of fact regarding causation.

* * *

The judgment is reversed and the matter is remanded to the trial court.

NOTES AND QUESTIONS

1. *Standards of the Industry.* Why was the fact that the bat satisfied applicable safety specifications not sufficient to defeat plaintiff's claim in *Sanchez*? Despite the NCAA's approval of the aluminum bat, the court effectively placed a duty on conferences, schools, and coaches to refrain from using permitted equipment. How should such parties determine what

equipment is safe? Consider their incentives in selecting equipment when performance-enhancing gear poses a risk of injury only to the other team.

2. *Player Safety Versus Performance.* Decisions like *Sanchez* put baseball bat manufacturers on notice that they should prioritize player safety, rather than bat performance. Several teams, leagues, and athletic conferences now ban aluminum bats, and they are not permitted in Major League Baseball. Instead, MLB dictates bats that are "a smooth, round stick . . . [made of] one piece of solid wood." Ironically, wooden bats also can be treacherous given their propensity to shatter and send flying shards of wood into the stands. How would you resolve the tension between imposing rigid equipment standards across the sport and allowing athletes some autonomy in selecting gear? What explains the fact that so many amateur and minor leagues continue to permit aluminum bats?

Like any employee, professional athletes who perform their job at an employer-furnished workplace are entitled to protection from hazards that might foreseeably cause injury. For professional athletes, their workplaces are the facilities where they train, practice, and play in games. When those facilities are not properly designed or maintained, resulting in injury to the athlete, there is potential for tort recovery. San Francisco 49ers running back Reggie Bush brought a premises liability case in Missouri state court against the St. Louis Rams and their facility when he suffered a season-ending knee injury during a road game. After surgery, he attempted a comeback, but retired a year later.

The gravamen of Bush's complaint alleged:

36. The Rams owed a duty to the general public and specifically those invited on the field, including, but not limited to, players, coaches, trainers, media, youth football players, cheerleaders, fans, and referees to remove or warn of dangerous conditions in the Dome and to maintain the Dome, including the playing surface and surrounding areas, in a reasonably safe condition.

37. In violation of this duty, the Rams negligently permitted and maintained a dangerous condition to exist at the Dome, creating an unreasonable risk of injury to those invited on the field and surrounding surfaces, including Mr. Bush. Specifically, the turf playing field was surrounded by a slippery concrete surface. This abrupt change in surface was not reasonably safe.

38. As described above, Mr. Bush slipped and fell on the slippery concrete surface, injuring his left knee.

* * *

47. The Rams breached the duty owed to Mr. Bush by one or more of the following negligent acts or omissions:

a. Designing, constructing, and/or setting up the playing field such that it was surrounded by a slippery concrete surface;

b. Failing to cover the slippery concrete surface with padding;

c. Failing to provide warnings related to the concrete surface. . . .

Bush v. St. Louis Rams, LLC., 2016 WL 11295572 (Mo. Cir. Ct. 2016). The Rams responded to the suit by removing it to federal court on the grounds that the collective bargaining agreement governs the terms and conditions of Bush's employment, and as such his state law tort claims would be preempted under § 301 of the Labor Management Relations Act. Bush moved to remand to state court.

BUSH V. ST. LOUIS RAMS
2016 WL 3125869 (E.D. Mo. June 3, 2016)

HAMILTON, JUDGE

At all times relevant to this action, Plaintiff Reginald Bush was a professional football player employed by the San Francisco 49ers. On November 1, 2015, Plaintiff played as a running back for the 49ers in a game against the St. Louis Rams that took place at the Edward Jones Dome in St. Louis, MO. According to Plaintiff, while trying to slow down out-of-bounds after a play had concluded in the first quarter, Plaintiff slipped on a concrete surface surrounding the turf playing field at the Dome. Plaintiff maintains the resultant injury to his left knee ended his football season.

* * *

[T]he Court begins its section 301 preemption analysis with the claim itself, negligence. . . . Plaintiff's negligence claims are premised on the common law duty of care that sports teams owe to their invitees. According to Plaintiff, this duty required the Rams "to remove or warn of dangerous conditions in the Dome and to maintain the Dome, including the playing surface and surrounding areas, in a reasonably safe condition." . . . [T]he Court now must evaluate whether the CBA is the source of Plaintiff's claims, or whether the claims are substantially dependent upon an interpretation of the CBA.

[The court quoted extensively from CBA provisions on: (i) players' rights to medical care and treatment, including club payment of healthcare costs and adherence to the recommendations of the Accountability and Care Committee; (ii) workers' compensation; (iii) injury grievances; and (iv) the joint NFL-NFLPA Committee on Player Safety and Welfare.]

Upon consideration, the Court finds an interpretation of the above provisions is not essential to Plaintiff's case. For example, with respect to Article 39, Sections 1 and 3, the Court finds that neither the cost of medical services rendered by Club physicians (to be paid for by the Club, *i.e.*, the 49ers), nor the provision of preventive, medical, surgical, or rehabilitative care for players by clubs is at issue in Plaintiff's suit. In other words, Plaintiff does not claim he failed to receive contractually mandated care; instead, he claims he was not warned of a dangerous condition existing at the stadium. The same holds true for any responsibilities imposed on the Accountability and Care Committee; in other words, the Court finds the Rams' duty to warn exists independently of the Committee's responsibility to develop a standardized preseason and postseason physical examination, and to develop an educational protocol to inform players of the primary risks associated with playing professional football.

With respect to Articles 41 and 44 of the CBA, and section 9 of the NFL Player Contract, the Court finds those provisions speak to the player's ability to perform under his contract, or otherwise to recover from, his own NFL team. Plaintiff is not a player with the Rams, and so the provisions do not apply.

The strongest argument put forth by the Rams involves Article 50, Section 1. As noted above, that provision requires the establishment of a Joint Committee for the purpose of discussing, among other things, the player safety and welfare aspects of playing equipment, playing surfaces, and stadium facilities. The Joint Committee does not have the power to commit or bind any of the signatories to the CBA, however, nor does the CBA establish a contractually agreed upon standard of care applicable to Plaintiff's claims. . . .

Thus, the Court agrees with Plaintiff that the duties at issue here arise out of the common law duty of care sports teams owe to their invitees, and not out of any particular terms in the CBA. A substantial dependence upon an analysis of the CBA thus cannot serve as a basis for removal, and so Plaintiff's Motion to Remand must be granted.

Reggie Bush tried his claims in front of a St. Louis state court jury in the spring of 2018, a year after the Rams had decamped to Los Angeles. During the trial, the Rams argued that Bush failed to prove the fall caused his injury because he had a long history of knee problems. Missouri law, however, rejects the "eggshell" plaintiff theory, and dictates that a negligent defendant is responsible for all of the harm it causes even when the plaintiff is more susceptible to a worse injury than the average person. The jury found the Rams liable, awarding Bush a total of $12.5 million in compensatory and punitive damages. An appeal is pending as of this writing.

NOTES AND QUESTIONS

1. *Athlete Suits Involving Hazardous Playing Surfaces.* Professional athletes who suffer serious injuries while playing games typically have limited recourse to the courts. Either they have assumed the risk or must resolve their claims through collectively bargained grievance procedures. But hazardous facilities claims offer a loophole. Philadelphia Eagles linebacker DeMeco Ryans sued the Houston Texans and the NFL for a 2014 torn Achilles tendon he says was caused by the patchy grass field at the Houston's NRG Stadium. *Ryans v. Houston NFL Holdings, L.P.*, 2017 WL 1905774 (S.D. Tex. May 9, 2017) (remanding suit, as in *Bush*, because claims do not require interpretation of the CBA and are not subject to labor preemption). The notoriously uneven Houston field generated three lawsuits before the team replaced the playing surface. New York Yankee Dustin Fowler sued the Chicago White Sox and its facility for a 2017 season-ending injury suffered when, as he chased a foul ball, he ran into an unpadded metal electrical box protruding onto the field. What justifies the different treatment of game injuries caused by contact with other players and those caused by contact with playing surfaces?

2. *Other Workplace Facilities.* Given the earning potential and asset value of professional athletes, you would think that their workplaces would be maintained in pristine condition. Yet, Tampa Bay Buccaneers players Lawrence Tynes and Carl Nicks each received multi-million-dollar settlements from the team after a 2013 staph infection outbreak in the team's facilities resulted in career-ending disabilities. The lawsuits claimed that the Bucs actively concealed ongoing incidents of the infection among other individuals who used and visited the team's facilities, and failed to employ necessary sterile techniques. *See Tynes v. Buccaneers Ltd. P'ship*, 134 F. Supp. 3d 1351 (M.D. Fla. 2015) (holding that player's premises liability claims did not arise from CBA).

At the 2015 United States Tennis Open, Canadian player Eugenie Bouchard slipped on a cleaning substance that had been applied to the floor of the trainer's room and sustained a concussion that stalled her career for over two years. As an independent contractor playing an individual, not team, sport, Boucher faced no statutory obstacles to her claims, and a liability-only trial was conducted in early 2018. The jury found the tournament organizer, the United States Tennis Association, 75% liable for negligence, and Bouchard 25% liable because she broke the rules when she entered the trainer's room unaccompanied. The parties reached a confidential settlement prior to the damages phase.

C. DISABILITY AND THE RIGHT TO PLAY

Up to now we have examined the legal remedies available to injured players. Besides providing compensation after the fact, the law also seeks to provide incentives for the adoption of measures that will avoid injury before the fact. Suppose a league screens out players with conditions that might make the player more susceptible to injury. Conversely, suppose a league screens out players whose conditions might endanger other participants. Does the customary freedom of U.S. sports to self-regulate entitle sports organizing bodies to enforce such eligibility standards? Can excluded players obtain legal relief?

While the U.S. Constitution does not confer a right to participate in sports, *City of Cleburne, Tex. v. Cleburne Living Ctr.*, 473 U.S. 432 (1985), athletes with disabilities are protected from discrimination under two federal statutes: the Rehabilitation Act of 1973 (Rehabilitation Act) and the Americans with Disabilities Act of 1990 (ADA). In addition, state human rights laws may provide impaired athletes with legal rights to participate in sports. The main difference between the two federal statutes is that the Rehabilitation Act covers only programs of entities that receive federal financial assistance, such as the sports programs of colleges and universities, while the ADA covers most private entities and employers, such as the major sports leagues.

The requirements for a claim under both Acts are otherwise similar—the plaintiff must show he or she: (a) is an individual with a "disability"; (b) is "otherwise qualified" to participate, with or without reasonable accommodations; and (c) was excluded from participation because of that disability. Before 2009, the statutes defined a disabled person to include someone who has "a physical or mental impairment that substantially limits one or more major life activities," someone who had a record of such an impairment, or someone who was regarded as having such an impairment. However, in response to judicial decisions that had narrowed its coverage, Congress amended the ADA in 2008.

The 2008 amendments retained the basic definition of "disability" but broadened that term's coverage by expanding the statute's nonexclusive list of major life activities to include "caring for oneself, performing manual tasks, seeing, hearing, eating, sleeping, walking, standing, lifting, bending, speaking, breathing, learning, reading, concentrating, thinking, communicating and working," as well as "[m]ajor bodily functions." Major bodily functions include "functions of the immune system, normal cell growth, digestive, bowel, bladder, neurological, brain, respiratory, circulatory, endocrine, and reproductive functions." 42 U.S.C. § 12102. Reasonable accommodations must be provided to anyone who has an impairment that is not transitory or minor.

1. INCREASED RISK TO THE IMPAIRED ATHLETE

This chapter has addressed the situation when, through the tortious conduct of others, injured athletes are unaware of the risks of further sports participation. What if an athlete with a physical impairment is fully informed of the risks and nonetheless wants to participate in a sport? Is the sports contest organizer required to let him or her play? This issue arose in the 1990 case of Mark Seay, a wide receiver for the Long Beach State College football team, who was struck by a stray bullet meant for a street gang member. Seay lost a kidney, and the bullet remained lodged near his heart. The school refused to allow Seay to return to the football team because of the risk of aggravating his injury. Seay sued, and on the eve of trial in March 1990, the school relented and allowed him to play football again—but only in return for a signed waiver of liability that the school hoped the California courts would recognize as valid.

Because college sports are sponsored by institutions that receive federal aid, they are governed by the Rehabilitation Act, which offered the legal basis for the next case.

KNAPP V. NORTHWESTERN UNIVERSITY

101 F.3d 473 (7th Cir. 1996)

EVANS, CIRCUIT JUDGE.

Nicholas Knapp wants to play NCAA basketball for Northwestern University—so badly that he is willing to face an increased risk of death to do so. Knapp is a competent, intelligent adult capable of assessing whether playing intercollegiate basketball is worth the risk to his heart and possible death, and to him the risk is acceptable. Usually, competent, intelligent adults are allowed to make such decisions. This is especially true when, as here, the individual's family approves of the decision and the individual and his parents are willing to sign liability waivers regarding the worst-case scenario should it occur.

Northwestern, however, refuses to allow Knapp to play on or even practice with its men's basketball team. Knapp, currently a sophomore at Northwestern, has the basketball skills to play at the intercollegiate level, but he has never taken the court for his team. Although Northwestern does not restrict him from playing pick-up basketball games, using recreational facilities on campus, or exerting himself physically on his own, the university disqualified Knapp from playing on its intercollegiate basketball team. The issue in this case boils down to whether the school—because of § 504 of the Rehabilitation Act of 1973, as amended, 29 U.S.C. § 794—will be forced to let Knapp don a purple uniform and take the floor as a member of Northwestern's basketball team.

Prior to his senior year of high school Knapp was rated among the best basketball players in Illinois. He was recruited by numerous universities, including Northwestern. At the end of Knapp's junior year at Peoria's Woodruff High School, Northwestern orally offered him an athletic scholarship to play basketball. Knapp orally accepted the offer.

A few weeks into his senior year, Knapp suffered sudden cardiac death—meaning his heart stopped—during a pick-up basketball game. Paramedics used cardiopulmonary resuscitation, defibrillation (*i.e.*, electric shocks), and injections of drugs to bring Knapp back to life. A few weeks later, doctors implanted an internal cardioverter-defibrillator in Knapp's abdomen. The device detects heart arrhythmia and delivers a shock to convert the abnormal heart rhythm back to normal. In other words, if Knapp's heart stops again the device is supposed to restart it.

On the day following his sudden cardiac death, Northwestern informed Knapp and his family that whatever the ultimate medical decision, Northwestern would honor its commitment for a scholarship. Seven weeks after his collapse Knapp signed a national letter of intent to attend Northwestern.

Knapp did not play basketball during his senior year in high school, but he was always a superb student, and in June 1995 he graduated as the valedictorian of his class. In September 1995 he enrolled as a Northwestern student.

On November 7, 1995, Dr. Howard Sweeney, Northwestern's head team physician, declared Knapp ineligible to participate on Northwestern's men's basketball team for the 1995–96 school year. Dr. Sweeney based his decision on Knapp's medical records in which several treating physicians recommended that Knapp not play competitive basketball, the report of team physician Dr. Mark Gardner following a physical examination of Knapp, published guidelines and recommendations following two national medical conferences known as the Bethesda Conferences regarding eligibility of athletes with cardiovascular abnormalities, and recommendations of physicians with whom Dr. Gardner and Dr. Sweeney consulted. After the basketball season ended, Northwestern and the Big Ten declared Knapp permanently medically ineligible to play basketball. Northwestern's athletic director, Rick Taylor, later confirmed that Northwestern will never voluntarily let Knapp play intercollegiate basketball as a Wildcat.

As a result, Knapp has never practiced with the Northwestern team nor played in a college game. His scholarship nevertheless continues and he attends practices (though he is not allowed to do anything but watch, apparently). He also receives other benefits afforded to athletes (such as tutoring, counseling, and training table), in addition to the full range of academic and nonacademic offerings the university provides to all students.

[On the day he was declared ineligible, Knapp filed a federal lawsuit and secured an injunction that barred Northwestern from excluding him from its basketball team for any reason related to his cardiac condition. Northwestern immediately appealed this order to the Seventh Circuit. The circuit court noted that the Rehabilitation Act was the sole basis for Knapp's claim and required him to prove that he has a physical impairment which substantially limits one or more of his major life activities, is otherwise qualified to play basketball, and has been excluded from doing so solely because of his disability. The circuit court also noted that the Act defines "major life activities" to include basic functions "such as caring for one's self, performing manual tasks, walking, seeing, hearing, speaking, breathing, learning, and working," and that they are "those basic activities that the average person in the general population can perform with little or no difficulty."]

* * *

This case is difficult because it does not fit neatly under the Rehabilitation Act. The "disability" Knapp claims is the basis for discrimination against him is not a continuing one like blindness or deafness. At any given moment in time when Knapp's heart is functioning properly his disability does not affect him. He is truly disabled only when his heart stops, which may or may not happen to him again. The disability regarding which Northwestern allegedly discriminates, therefore, actually is the greater risk of harm for Knapp than the risk faced by other male college basketball players. In addition, other impairments usually do not have as severe a result as is possible in this case. A person who is deaf, for instance, will not suddenly die on the basketball court because of that disability. Here, Knapp's disability is all or nothing. Finally, because Knapp's disability affects one of the most central organs of the body, his disability to some extent affects all major life activities—if his heart stops, he will not breathe, see, speak, walk, learn, or work. Once again it is all or nothing—either his heart is functioning and no major life activities are limited at that moment, or it has stopped and the most major life activity of all—living—has been affected.

In any event, the parties here have framed their arguments as involving solely the major life activity of learning. Knapp contends that playing an intercollegiate sport is an integral part of his major life activity of learning and that his education will be substantially limited if he cannot play on the team. He states that he does not believe he can obtain confidence, dedication, leadership, perseverance, discipline, and teamwork in any better way. The district court agreed with him, determining that for Knapp, playing on the Northwestern basketball team was part of the major life activity of learning and that he was substantially limited from such learning by the university....

We do not think that the definition of "major life activity" can be as particularized as Knapp wants it to be. Playing intercollegiate basketball obviously is not in and of itself a major life activity, as it is not a basic function of life on the same level as walking, breathing, and speaking. Not everyone gets to go to college, let alone play intercollegiate sports. We acknowledge that intercollegiate sports can be an important part of the college learning experience for both athletes and many cheering students—especially at a Big Ten school. Knapp has indicated that such is the case for him. But not every student thinks so. Numerous college students graduate each year having neither participated in nor attended an intercollegiate sporting event. Their sheepskins are no less valuable because of the lack of intercollegiate sports in their lives. Not playing intercollegiate sports does not mean they have not learned. Playing or enjoying intercollegiate sports therefore cannot be held out as a necessary part of learning for *all* students.

* * *

We decline to define the major life activity of learning in such a way that the Act applies whenever someone wants to play intercollegiate athletics. A "major life activity," as defined in the regulations, is a basic function of life "such as caring for one's self, performing manual tasks, walking, seeing, hearing, speaking, breathing, learning, and working." These are basic functions, not more specific ones such as being an astronaut, working as a firefighter, driving a race car, or learning by playing Big Ten basketball. . . .

[A]ny narrowing of what constitutes learning for a particular individual occurs within reasonable limits—coverage of the Rehabilitation Act is not open-ended or based on every dream or desire that a person may have. Not every impairment that affects an individual's major life activities is a substantially limiting impairment. The key obviously is the extent to which the impairment restricts the major life activity. . . . An impairment that interferes with an individual's ability to perform a particular function, but does not significantly decrease that individual's ability to obtain a satisfactory education otherwise, does not substantially limit the major life activity of learning.

Because learning through playing intercollegiate basketball is only one part of the education available to Knapp at Northwestern, even under a subjective standard, Knapp's ability to learn is not substantially limited. Knapp's scholarship continues, allowing him access to all academic and—except for intercollegiate basketball—all nonacademic services and activities available to other Northwestern students, in addition to all other services available to scholarship athletes. Although perhaps not as great a learning experience as actually playing, it is even possible that Knapp may "learn" through the basketball team in a role other than as a player. Knapp is an intelligent student and athlete, and the inability to play intercollegiate basketball at Northwestern forecloses only a small portion of his collegiate opportunities. . . . Knapp has not shown that his education and training limit him to do nothing but play basketball. The fact that

Knapp's goal of playing intercollegiate basketball is frustrated does not substantially limit his education. The Rehabilitation Act does not guarantee an individual the exact educational experience that he may desire, just a fair one. Consequently, we hold that Knapp as a matter of law is not disabled within the meaning of the Rehabilitation Act.

Even if we were inclined to find Knapp disabled under the Rehabilitation Act, he would still come up short because we also hold as a matter of law that he is not, under the statute, "otherwise qualified" to play intercollegiate basketball at Northwestern. . . .

Section 794 does not compel educational institutions to disregard the disabilities of disabled persons. It requires only that an "otherwise qualified" disabled person not be excluded from participation in a federally funded program solely because of the disability. In other words, although a disability is not a permissible ground for assuming an inability to function in a particular context, the disability is not thrown out when considering if the person is qualified for the position sought. "An otherwise qualified person is one who is able to meet all of a program's requirements in spite of his handicap" with reasonable accommodation.

Legitimate physical qualifications may in fact be essential to participation in particular programs. . . .

A significant risk of personal physical injury can disqualify a person from a position if the risk cannot be eliminated. But more than merely an elevated risk of injury is required before disqualification is appropriate. Any physical qualification based on risk of future injury must be examined with special care if the Rehabilitation Act is not to be circumvented, since almost all disabled individuals are at a greater risk of injury. . . .

In this case, the severity of the potential injury is as high as it could be—death. [The court summarized the expert testimony that playing intercollegiate basketball would expose Knapp to a risk of death between or one in 34 and one in 100.] These estimates took into account Knapp's internal defibrillator, apparently the only "accommodation" possible for Knapp's condition. Although the doctors indicated that these numbers were merely estimates, all agreed that the risk to Knapp is higher than to the average male collegiate basketball player. Knapp's experts believed it was an acceptable level of risk. Northwestern's experts agreed with the school's team doctors that Knapp's participation in competitive Big Ten basketball presented an unacceptable level of risk. . . .

The district court judge in this case believed that in the face of conflicting opinion evidence regarding risk, and the fact that no scientific data existed to quantify that risk, the decision on whether Knapp should play falls in the lap of the court. . . .

We disagree with the district court's legal determination that such decisions are to be made by the courts and believe instead that medical determinations of this sort are best left to team doctors and universities as long as they are made with reason and rationality and with full regard to possible and reasonable accommodations. In cases such as ours, where Northwestern has examined both Knapp and his medical records, has considered his medical history and the relation between his prior sudden cardiac death and the possibility of future occurrences, has considered the severity of the potential injury, and has rationally and reasonably reviewed consensus medical opinions or recommendations in the pertinent field—regardless whether conflicting medical opinions exist—the university has the right to determine that an individual is not otherwise medically qualified to play without violating the Rehabilitation Act. The place of the court in such cases is to make sure that the decision-maker has reasonably considered and relied upon sufficient evidence specific to the individual and the potential injury, not to determine on its own which evidence it believes is more persuasive.

* * *

We do not believe that, in cases where medical experts disagree in their assessment of the extent of a real risk of serious harm or death, Congress intended that the courts—neutral arbiters but generally less skilled in medicine than the experts involved—should make the final medical decision. Instead, in the midst of conflicting expert testimony regarding the degree of serious risk of harm or death, the court's place is to ensure that the exclusion or disqualification of an individual was individualized, reasonably made, and based upon competent medical evidence. So long as these factors exist, it will be the rare case regarding participation in athletics where a court may substitute its judgment for that of the school's team physicians.

* * *

In closing, we wish to make clear that we are not saying Northwestern's decision necessarily is the right decision. We say only that it is not an illegal one under the Rehabilitation Act. On the same facts, another team physician at another university, reviewing the same medical history, physical evaluation, and medical recommendations, might reasonably decide that Knapp met the physical qualifications for playing on an intercollegiate basketball team. Simply put, all universities need not evaluate risk the same way. What we say in this case is that if substantial evidence supports the decision-maker—here Northwestern—that decision must be respected.

Section 794 prohibits authorities from deciding without significant medical support that certain activities are too risky for a disabled person. Decisions of this sort cannot rest on paternalistic concerns. Knapp, who is an adult, is not in need of paternalistic decisions regarding his health, and his parents—more entitled to be paternalistic toward him than Northwestern—approve of his decision. In regard to cases involving risk of future injury, a school's perception of the threat of such injury cannot be based on unfounded fears or stereotypes; it must be based on objective evidence. But here, where Northwestern acted rationally and reasonably rather than paternalistically, no Rehabilitation Act violation has occurred. The Rehabilitation Act "is carefully structured to replace . . . reflexive actions to actual or perceived handicaps with actions based on reasoned and medically sound judgments. . . ." *Arline*, 480 U.S. at 284–85.

Reversed.

Having lost in the courts, Knapp rejected Northwestern's offer of a free education without basketball, and instead accepted a scholarship from Northeastern Illinois where he began playing (as well as studying) in the 1997–98 season.

NOTES AND QUESTIONS

1. *"Major Life Activity."* The district judge had earlier ruled that college sports was a "major life activity" for someone like Knapp, rejecting Northwestern's argument that it was sufficient for Knapp's life that he would still attend college on scholarship, and could participate in other extracurricular activities like golf or the orchestra. "Because competitive basketball is an important and integral part of Knapp's education and learning experience, I find that intercollegiate basketball is a major life activity for him." As noted above, the ADA, and by cross reference, the Rehabilitation Act was amended in 2008 to more expansively define "major life activities."

Applying the language of the current statute, do you think playing intercollegiate basketball should be treated as a major life activity? If not, was Knapp substantially limited in another major life activity or major bodily function covered by the current statute? Would Knapp, in any event, have to claim a substantially limited major life activity under the current statutory regime? Did he simply contest his exclusion from the team or was he asking for some special accommodation?

2. *"Otherwise Qualified" and Health Risks.* Both district and circuit courts agreed that Knapp could not satisfy the statutory condition that he was "otherwise qualified" to play basketball if there was a "genuine and substantial risk of injury" from this activity. They disagreed as to whether Northwestern's admittedly reasonable assessment of the risk was sufficient, or whether the college had to persuade the court that its appraisal was more reasonable than Knapp's medical experts. Which of these positions is most compatible with the

legislative policy? Should it be dispositive that a judge believed that Knapp's assessment of medical risk was reasonable, even if the college physician's views seemed somewhat more likely?

In *Bragdon v. Abbott*, 524 U.S. 624 (1998), the Court interpreted a "direct threat to . . . health or safety" defense in the ADA. The Court adopted a reasonableness standard, holding that the existence of the risk "must be determined from the standpoint of the person who refuses the treatment or accommodation, and the risk assessment must be based on medical or other objective evidence." *Id.* at 649.

3. *Liability Waivers.* The Seay case suggests that one solution to the policy dilemma here is to require impaired students to sign liability waivers. Why are schools reluctant to take that route? Are they concerned that such waivers may be deemed unenforceable in the event of a tort suit? Or are they concerned that by agreeing to the liability waiver, schools open the door for other athletes with serious medical conditions to sign similar waivers and compete against the advice of their doctors?

4. *Reasonable Accommodation Requirement for Those with Substantially Limited Life Activities.* Both the ADA and the Rehabilitation Act require covered entities to make reasonable accommodations or modifications to participation requirements to enable disabled athletes to play sports. *Alexander v. Choate*, 469 U.S. 287, 300 (1985) ("while a [school] need not be required to make 'fundamental' or 'substantial' modifications to accommodate the handicapped, it may be required to make 'reasonable' ones"); *Grube v. Bethlehem Area Sch. Dist.*, 550 F. Supp. 418, 424 (E.D. Pa. 1982) (requiring high school to reasonably accommodate student with one kidney to play football if he wore a protective flak jacket).

5. *Blanket Eligibility Rules.* Greg Neeld, a star in Canadian Junior A hockey, encountered difficulty transitioning to the pros because he had sight in only one eye. Professional league bylaws imposed blanket prohibitions on playing an athlete with only one eye. Neeld succeeded in obtaining a preliminary injunction against the American Hockey League's enforcement of that rule, relying on New York Human Rights Law. *Neeld v. Am. Hockey League*, 439 F. Supp. 459 (W.D.N.Y. 1977). However, he lost a separate suit against the NHL based on antitrust law. *Neeld v. NHL*, 594 F.2d 1297 (9th Cir. 1979) (bylaw's purpose in promoting safety outweighed anticompetitive effect on excluded athletes). A decade later, Neeld could have sued under the ADA.

Why would the NHL or the NFL bar from the sport a player who lost the use of one eye? Is it the League's concern that a hockey or football collision could cost the player his other eye and thus produce total blindness? How does this situation compare with the one in *Knapp*? Can the league sustain such a policy under the ADA or Rehabilitation Act based on there being a "direct threat" to "health or safety"? *See Wright v. Columbia University*, 520 F. Supp. 789 (E.D. Pa. 1981) (upholding Columbia's decision not to allow student with sight in only one eye to play football "contrary to the express wishes of his parents who, together with their son, have reached a rational decision concerning the risk involved").

2. INCREASED RISK TO OTHER PARTICIPANTS

A disabled athlete may endanger other participants beyond the risks inherent in a given sport. For example, some athletes have expressed concern about perceived health risk from playing sports with an athlete diagnosed as HIV-positive, the virus that causes AIDS (acquired immunodeficiency syndrome). This became a major sports issue in 1991 when Earvin "Magic" Johnson announced that he was retiring from the L.A. Lakers because he had just been diagnosed as HIV-positive. Several months later, Johnson returned to the basketball court for the 1992 NBA All-Star game, and then to the "Dream Team" in the Summer Olympics in Barcelona. Johnson again dropped out of the game in the fall of 1993 when a number of other NBA players (most prominently the Utah Jazz's Karl Malone) raised concerns about the risks of playing against an HIV-infected opponent.

Such concerns arose again in 1995 when Greg Louganis, Olympic gold medalist in diving, announced that he had learned he was HIV-positive sometime before he competed in the 1988 Seoul Games. At the Seoul Olympics, Louganis hit his head on a diving board during a preliminary event, and he bled profusely into the pool, as well as on the hands of the team physician who was treating him. By 1995, it was known that a host of other athletes had died of AIDS (most, though not all, contracted after their retirement): tennis star Arthur Ashe, NFL tight end Jerry Smith, NHL forward Bill Goldsworthy, and NASCAR driver Tim Richmond.

HIV anxiety surfaced again in the winter of 1996, when former WBC heavyweight champion Tommy Morrison was scheduled for a comeback fight in Las Vegas. However, the blood test required by Nevada's state boxing commission disclosed that Morrison was HIV-positive: Nevada revoked Morrison's license to fight in that state, a decision that was honored in all other states. Commissioners in New Jersey, New York, and most other states quickly instituted the same mandatory testing and HIV-positive bans. When Morrison decided to return to boxing in the fall of 1996, he had to fly to Japan to fight before a modest crowd in the morning so that his 98-second knockout of his opponent could be seen on pay-per-view television that night in the United States. It was his last professional fight until a brief comeback in 2007–08.

The following case considers the legality of excluding an athlete known to be HIV positive from participation in a contact sport.

MONTALVO V. RADCLIFFE
167 F.3d 873 (4th Cir. 1996)

NIEMEYER, CIRCUIT JUDGE.

Michael Montalvo, a 12-year old boy with AIDS, was denied admission to a traditional Japanese style martial arts school because of his HIV-positive status. In this action, brought under Title III of the Americans with Disabilities Act (prohibiting discrimination on the basis of disability by places of public accommodation), the district court denied Montalvo relief because his condition posed a significant risk to the health or safety of other students and no reasonable modification could sufficiently reduce this risk without fundamentally altering the nature of the program. We affirm.

I

Southside Virginia Police Karate Association, Inc. operates a karate school in Colonial Heights, Virginia, known as U.S.A. Bushidokan, which is owned by James P. Radcliffe, II. The school teaches exclusively traditional Japanese, combat-oriented martial arts rather than the more prevalent, family-oriented fitness programs offered by most martial arts schools. Within the first three weeks of lessons at U.S.A. Bushidokan, students learn techniques that involve substantial body contact, and within the first few months they apply these techniques to spar in actual combat situations. Radcliffe testified at trial that the sparring often results in injuries which, while minor, are bloody. . . .

He explained that to progress "through the belt," a level of achievement, a student must "engage in combat activity fighting. You have to do the self-defense. It involves contact, that's what we do." Radcliffe noted that inherent in this form of karate are "consistently scratched skin, scratches, gouges, bloody lips, bloody noses, things of that nature."

In May 1997, Luciano and Judith Montalvo applied to enter their 12-year old son, Michael, into group karate classes at U.S.A. Bushidokan because Michael wanted to learn karate with some friends who had already begun lessons there. Luciano Montalvo signed a "Membership Application and Agreement" form in which he warranted that Michael was "in good health and that [he] suffer[ed] from no illness or condition . . . which would possibly be infectious to others" and that the Montalvos understood that "no member [would] use the facilities with any open cuts, abrasions, open sores, infections, [or] maladies with the potential of harm to others." In fact, however, Michael had AIDS. The Montalvos did not disclose that fact to U.S.A. Bushidokan because they were afraid that U.S.A. Bushidokan would not enroll Michael if it knew of his HIV-positive status.

[The court explained that USA Bushidokan learned about Michael's HIV status from an "anonymous source." Radcliffe informed that

Montalvos that Michael would not be allowed to participate in group karate classes, but offered private lessons.]

* * *

II

Title III of the Americans with Disabilities Act ("ADA") was enacted to facilitate disabled individuals' access to places of public accommodation. Consistent with this goal, the Act states broadly:

> No individual shall be discriminated against on the basis of disability in the full and equal enjoyment of the goods, services, facilities, privileges, advantages, or accommodations of any place of public accommodation by any person who owns, leases (or leases to), or operates a place of public accommodation.

42 U.S.C. § 12182(a). The ADA defines "denial of participation" in a program offered by a place of public accommodation to be an act of discrimination. 42 U.S.C. § 12182(b)(1)(A)(i).

Recognizing that the need to protect public health may at times outweigh the rights of disabled individuals, Congress created a narrow exception to this broad prohibition against discrimination based on disability in places of public accommodation. Thus, a place of public accommodation is entitled to exclude a disabled individual from participating in its program "where such individual poses a direct threat to the health or safety of others." 42 U.S.C. § 12182(b)(3) (emphasis added). The Act defines "direct threat" as "a significant risk to the health or safety of others that cannot be eliminated by a modification of policies, practices, or procedures or by the provision of auxiliary aids or services." Id.

When determining whether an individual poses a "direct threat," a place of public accommodation must not base its calculus on stereotypes or generalizations about the effects of a disability but rather must make "an individualized assessment, based on reasonable judgment that relies on current medical knowledge or on the best available *877 objective evidence." 28 C.F.R. § 36.208(c). The relevant factors which the place of public accommodation must weigh and balance are "the nature, duration, and severity of the risk [and] the probability that the potential injury will actually occur."

If the place of public accommodation determines that the individual would pose a significant risk to the health and safety of others, it must then ascertain "whether reasonable modifications of policies, practices, or procedures will mitigate the risk," 28 C.F.R. § 36.208(c), to the point of "eliminat[ing]" it as a "significant risk," 42 U.S.C.§ 12182(b)(3). Under the ADA, a failure to make a reasonable modification is itself an act of discrimination unless the place of public accommodation can demonstrate that implementing the modification would fundamentally alter the nature of the program. See 42 U.S.C. § 12182(b)(2)(A)(ii).

In this case, U.S.A. Bushidokan concedes that its karate school is a place of public accommodation subject to the requirements of Title III and that Michael Montalvo is disabled for purposes of the ADA by virtue of being HIV-positive or having AIDS. Bushidokan also concedes that it denied Michael participation in group karate classes on the basis of his HIV-positive status, the condition that concededly constitutes his disability. But U.S.A. Bushidokan contends that its exclusion of Michael was legally justified because Michael posed a "direct threat" to other members of the karate class. This contention presents two issues: (1) whether Michael's condition posed a significant risk to the health or safety of others and (2) whether reasonable modifications of policies, practices, or procedures were available to eliminate the risk as a significant one. See 42 U.S.C. § 12182(b)(3).

A

While the question of whether Michael's HIV-positive status posed a significant risk to the health or safety of others is a "fact intensive determination," *Rizzo v. Children's World Learning Centers, Inc.*, 84 F.3d 758, 764 (5th Cir. 1996), the evidence in the record before us is ample to support the district court's conclusion that Michael posed such a risk.

First, both the Montalvos' and U.S.A. Bushidokan's medical experts testified that blood-to-blood contact is a means of HIV transmission, and both experts agreed that AIDS is inevitably fatal. In addition, U.S.A. Bushidokan's expert testified without challenge that it was possible to become infected with the virus from blood splashing into the eyes or onto seemingly intact skin.

Second, the type of activity offered at U.S.A. Bushidokan emphasized sparring, attack drills, and continuous body interaction with the result that the participants frequently sustained bloody injuries, such as nose bleeds, cuts inside the mouth, and external abrasions. Radcliffe testified that blood from those injuries is "extremely likely" to come in contact with other students' skin. Even though U.S.A. Bushidokan had a policy of constantly monitoring for bloody injuries and removing for treatment participants with those injuries, the fast-paced, continuous combat exercises hampered U.S.A. Bushidokan's efforts to eliminate contact when such injury occurred. . . .

The nature, duration, and severity of the risk and probability of transmission—factors outlined by *Arline* and the ADA regulations—indicate that a significant risk to the health and safety of others would exist if Michael were allowed to participate in the group karate classes. The nature of the risk, which *Arline* defines as the mode of transmission of the disease, is blood-to-blood or blood-to-eye contact, according to the testimony of both sides' experts. The duration of the risk, which *Arline* defines as how long the carrier is infectious, *see id.*, is for the length of Michael's life. The severity of the risk is extreme because there is no known cure for AIDS, and, as the Montalvos concede, AIDS is inevitably fatal. And although the exact mathematical probability of transmission is unknown, the mode of transmission is one which is likely to occur in U.S.A. Bushidokan's combat-oriented group karate classes because of the frequency of bloody injuries and body contact. Thus, the nature of the risk, combined with its severity, creates a significant risk to the health and safety of hard-style karate class members.

When balancing the *Arline* factors to determine whether a risk is significant, one need not conclude that each factor is significant on its own. Rather, the gravity of one factor might well compensate for the relative slightness of another. Thus, when the disease at risk of transmission is, like AIDS, severe and inevitably fatal, even a low probability of transmission could still create a significant risk. In this case, therefore, we agree with the district court that Michael's condition posed a significant risk to the health and safety of others. . . .

* * *

The experts in this case agreed that HIV can be transmitted through blood-to-blood contact, and the evidence showed that this type of contact occurred frequently in the karate classes at U.S.A. Bushidokan. Thus, the district court's finding that Michael Montalvo posed a significant risk to the health or safety of others is amply supported by the evidence.

B

Even though Michael Montalvo's condition posed a significant risk to the health or safety of others, U.S.A. Bushidokan would still be required to admit him to group karate classes if a reasonable modification could have eliminated the risk as a significant one. The only modification which was both effective in reducing risk to an insignificant level and in maintaining the fundamental essence of U.S.A. Bushidokan's program was its offer of private karate classes to Michael.

In considering other modifications, U.S.A. Bushidokan was entitled to reject the modification that would soften the teaching style of its program. U.S.A. Bushidokan's unique niche in the martial arts market was its adherence to traditional, "hard-style" Japanese karate, and the contact between participants, which causes the bloody injuries and creates the risk of HIV transmission, was an integral aspect of such a program. To require U.S.A. Bushidokan to make its program a less combat-oriented, interactive, contact intensive version of karate would constitute a fundamental alteration of the nature of its program. The ADA does not require U.S.A. Bushidokan to abandon its essential mission and to offer a fundamentally different program of instruction. *See* 42 U.S.C. § 12182(b)(2)(A)(ii).

Similarly, U.S.A. Bushidokan was not required to implement further "universal precautions" such as using eye coverings and wearing gloves. The district court found as a fact that these modifications would not accomplish their goal of eliminating or reducing the otherwise significant risk Michael would pose to his classmates. As Radcliffe testified on behalf of U.S.A. Bushidokan, the suddenness of injuries, the tendency of some wounds to splatter blood, the continuing movement and contact, and the inability to detect injuries immediately all would undermine the effectiveness of these precautions, particularly for places not protected by eye coverings, gloves, or other similar coverings. . . .

U.S.A. Bushidokan did propose the effective modification of giving Michael private karate lessons, and the district court found this modification reasonable. But the Montalvos rejected this proposal. While an ADA plaintiff is under no obligation to accept a proffered, otherwise reasonable modification, *see* 28 C.F.R. § 36.203(c)(1) ("Nothing in this part shall be construed to require an individual with a disability to accept an accommodation . . . under this part that such individual chooses not to accept"), such rejection does not impose liability on U.S.A. Bushidokan for failure to modify its program.

Accordingly, we conclude that U.S.A. Bushidokan, in excluding Michael Montalvo from participating in its combat-oriented group karate classes, did not violate Title III of the ADA because Michael posed a significant risk to the health and safety of others that could not be eliminated by a reasonable modification.

The judgment of the district court is AFFIRMED.

NOTES AND QUESTIONS

1. *Medical Evidence of Risk.* What should be the legal standard for excluding an athlete with an infectious disease from participation in a sport? Was the *Montalvo* medical evidence sufficient to satisfy this standard? *See Bragdon v. Abbott*, 524 U.S. 624, 626–27 (1998) (assessment of risk of HIV transmission "is based on the medical or other objective, scientific evidence available . . . not simply on . . . good-faith belief that a significant risk existed"). Consider *Doe v. Woodford County Board of Education*, 213 F.3d 921 (6th Cir. 2000), where the court ruled that a high school did not violate the Rehabilitation Act or the ADA when it placed a hepatitis-infected member of its basketball team on "hold" pending receipt of medical clearance from his doctor. The court stated:

It is entirely reasonable for defendants to be concerned and arguably were obligated to be concerned with limiting risk of exposure of any contagion to others as well as limiting any injury that John may suffer.... [D]efendants faced potential liability from other students and parents if they allowed John to play on the team and another student accidentally became exposed to John's contagious condition.

Id. at 296. As was intimated in the Lawrence Tynes/Tampa Bay Buccaneers case, athletic event sponsors have a legal duty to use reasonable care to prevent the transmission of contagious diseases. *See Joseph E.G. v. E. Irondequoit Cent. Sch. Dist.*, 708 N.Y.S.2d 537 (N.Y. App. Div. 2000) (allowing claim to go forward against school district based on allegations that it failed to clean wrestling mats properly after wrestler suffered bloody nose).

2. *HIV/AIDS and Major Sports Leagues.* Over time, increased consciousness of the scope and limits of the risk of transmission of HIV/AIDS, led various leagues to announce they would not mandate testing of players for HIV and, in any event, the condition would not bar their playing. There has never been a documented case of HIV transmission during a sporting event, while research indicates the odds of this happening are roughly one of every 400 incidents of unprotected sex with a person of the opposite gender. Do you agree this is a reasonable risk for the major leagues to take? Does this risk vary from sport to sport? What level of risk would require a sport governing body to ban the athlete or to alter the rules of the sport to avoid the risk? How feasible might it be for a sport to offer a "reasonable accommodation?"

3. MODIFYING THE FUNDAMENTAL CHARACTER OF THE GAME

The fundamental character of sports competition depends on all participants playing by the same rules and subject to the same eligibility requirements. This essential feature can create tension with federal disability discrimination laws that mandate reasonable accommodation to enable an impaired athlete to play. The cases above to some extent addressed when reasonable accommodation requires modification to eligibility rules. The next case focuses on to what extent a sport must adjust its playing rules to accommodate a disabled athlete.

Professional golfer Casey Martin suffers from the Klippel-Trenaunay-Weber syndrome, a congenital malformation of his veins that curtails blood circulation in his legs and thus gradually atrophied the calf muscles and tibia bones in his right leg. Notwithstanding this condition and the resulting pain, Martin excelled at playing golf, a sport that typically permits the amateur golfer to ride a cart rather than require walking from shot to shot. During his college career, Martin was permitted to use a cart when he was experiencing severe pain. When he turned pro after college, he had to comply with PGA Tour rules for elite golfers that prohibited riding in carts.

Martin sought to qualify for the PGA Tour in 1997, attending "Q School" where early rounds of play permitted, and sometimes required, riding in a cart. In the final rounds of play, Tour rules required walking and barred Martin from using a cart. However, Martin's lawyer secured a preliminary injunction against enforcement of this rule. *Martin v. PGA Tour, Inc.*, 984 F. Supp. 1320 (D. Ore. 1998). Using a cart, Martin nonetheless narrowly missed making the regular Tour, but he did qualify for a lower-tier tour that allowed carts and where he had some success in 1998. Then Martin and his lawyers went back to court to try to obtain a permanent ruling on whether the ADA mandated a rules change to permit Martin to use a cart.

The relevant terms of the ADA cover athletes in two contexts. Title I requires employers to reasonably accommodate their employees with disabilities. However, in professional golf, players are not employees of the PGA Tour, but rather independent contractors. Thus, Martin sued under Title III, which prohibits disability discrimination in places of "public accommodation." The PGA Tour argued that tournament golf courses are public accommodations only with respect to the space made available to spectators behind the ropes, and not to eligible players out on the course. Martin argued that he was also a "customer" of the PGA, because he paid $3,000 to compete in Q School. The district court agreed with Martin.

As Martin undeniably suffered from a severe physical disability, the next legal question was whether the ADA required the PGA Tour to allow Martin to use a cart as a "reasonable accommodation," or whether cart use would substantially alter the game by giving Martin a competitive advantage over his fellow Tour members who had to walk rather than ride from shot to shot. A number of major golfing figures, led by Arnold Palmer, Jack Nicklaus, and Ken Venturi, testified in favor of the PGA rule as one designed to preserve golf as "a game of stamina." The district court disagreed, rejecting the PGA's argument that full adherence by everyone to its "walking rule" was necessary to fairly "inject the element of fatigue into the skill of shotmaking." Martin won a permanent order allowing him the cart accommodation on the Tour. *Martin v. PGA Tour, Inc.*, 994 F. Supp. 1242 (D. Ore. 1998).

When the Ninth Circuit affirmed the judgment, *Martin v. PGA Tour, Inc.*, 204 F.3d 994 (9th Cir. 2000), and the Seventh Circuit reached the exact opposite conclusion in a similar case, *Olinger v. United States Golf Association*, 205 F.3d 1001 (7th Cir. 2000), the Supreme Court granted certiorari.

PGA TOUR, INC. v. MARTIN
532 U.S. 661 (2001)

MR. JUSTICE STEVENS, delivered the opinion of the Court.

[After describing the Americans With Disabilities Act, the professional golf tours, and the treatment of the *Olinger* and the *Martin* cases by the lower courts, the majority opinion continued.]

* * *

It seems apparent, from both the general rule and the comprehensive definition of "public accommodation," that petitioner's golf tours and their qualifying rounds fit comfortably within the coverage of Title III, and Martin within its protection. The events occur on "golf course[s]," a type of place specifically identified by the Act as a public accommodation. § 12181(7)(L). In addition, at all relevant times, petitioner "leases" and "operates" golf courses to conduct its Q-School and tours. § 12182(a). As a lessor and operator of golf courses, then, petitioner must not discriminate against any "individual" in the "full and equal enjoyment of the goods, services, facilities, privileges, advantages, or accommodations" of those courses. Certainly, among the "privileges" offered by petitioner on the courses are those of competing in the Q-School and playing in the tours; indeed, the former is a privilege for which thousands of individuals from the general public pay, and the latter is one for which they vie. Martin, of course, is one of those individuals. It would therefore appear that Title III of the ADA, by its plain terms, prohibits petitioner from denying Martin equal access to its tours on the basis of his disability. . . .

According to petitioner, Title III is concerned with discrimination [only] against "clients and customers" seeking to obtain "goods and services" at places of public accommodation, whereas it is Title I that protects persons who work at such places. . . . Martin therefore cannot bring a claim under Title III because he is not one of the " 'clients or customers of the covered public accommodation.' " Rather, Martin's claim of discrimination is "job-related" and could only be brought under Title I—but that Title does not apply because he is an independent contractor (as the District Court found) rather than an employee.

* * *

We need not decide whether petitioner's construction of the statute is correct, because petitioner's argument falters even on its own terms. If Title III's protected class were limited to "clients or customers," it would be entirely appropriate to classify the golfers who pay petitioner $3,000 for the chance to compete in the Q-School and, if successful, in the subsequent tour events, as petitioner's clients or customers. In our view, petitioner's tournaments (whether situated at a "golf course" or at a "place of exhibition or entertainment") simultaneously offer at least two "privileges" to the

SEC. C   DISABILITY AND THE RIGHT TO PLAY   1115

public—that of watching the golf competition and that of competing in it. . . . That petitioner identifies one set of clients or customers that it serves (spectators at tournaments) does not preclude it from having another set (players in tournaments) against whom it may not discriminate.

* * *

. . . Petitioner does not contest that a golf cart is a reasonable modification that is necessary if Martin is to play in its tournaments. . . . In this case [ ] the narrow dispute is whether allowing Martin to use a golf cart, despite the walking requirement . . . is a modification that would "fundamentally alter the nature" of those events.

In theory, a modification of petitioner's golf tournaments might constitute a fundamental alteration in two different ways. It might alter such an essential aspect of the game of golf that it would be unacceptable even if it affected all competitors equally; changing the diameter of the hole from three to six inches might be such a modification. Alternatively, a less significant change that has only a peripheral impact on the game itself might nevertheless give a disabled player, in addition to access to the competition as required by Title III, an advantage over others and, for that reason, fundamentally alter the character of the competition. We are not persuaded that a waiver of the walking rule for Martin would work a fundamental alteration in either sense.

As an initial matter, we observe that the use of carts is not itself inconsistent with the fundamental character of the game of golf. From early on, the essence of the game has been shot-making—using clubs to cause a ball to progress from the teeing ground to a hole some distance away with as few strokes as possible. . . . Over the years, there have been many changes in the players' equipment, in golf course design, in the Rules of Golf, and in the method of transporting clubs from hole to hole. . . . Golf carts started appearing with increasing regularity on American golf courses in the 1950's. Today they are everywhere. And they are encouraged. For one thing, they often speed up play, and for another, they are great revenue producers. There is nothing in the Rules of Golf that either forbids the use of carts, or penalizes a player for using a cart. That set of rules, as we have observed, is widely accepted in both the amateur and professional golf world as the rules of the game. The walking rule that is contained in petitioner's hard cards, based on an optional condition buried in an appendix to the Rules of Golf, is not an essential attribute of the game itself.

Indeed, the walking rule is not an indispensable feature of tournament golf either. As already mentioned, petitioner permits golf carts to be used in the SENIOR PGA TOUR, the open qualifying events for petitioner's tournaments, the first two stages of the Q-School, and, until 1997, the third stage of the Q-School as well. Moreover, petitioner allows the use of carts during certain tournament rounds in both the PGA TOUR and the NIKE TOUR. In addition, although the USGA enforces a walking rule in most of the tournaments that it sponsors, it permits carts in the Senior Amateur and the Senior Women's Amateur championships.

Petitioner, however, distinguishes the game of golf as it is generally played from the game that it sponsors call golf at the "highest level." According to petitioner, "[t]he goal of the highest-level competitive athletics is to assess and compare the performance of different competitors, a task that is meaningful only if the competitors are subject to identical substantive rules." The waiver of any possibly "outcome-affecting" rule for a contestant would violate this principle and therefore, in petitioner's view, fundamentally alter the nature of the highest level athletic event. The walking rule is one such rule, petitioner submits, because its purpose is "to inject the element of fatigue into the skill of shot-making," and thus its effect may be the critical loss of a stroke. As a consequence, the reasonable modification Martin seeks would fundamentally alter the nature of petitioner's highest level tournaments even if he were the only person in the world who has both the talent to compete in those elite events and a disability sufficiently serious that he cannot do so without using a cart.

The force of petitioner's argument is, first of all, mitigated by the fact that golf is a game in which it is impossible to guarantee that all competitors will play under exactly the same conditions or that an individual's ability will be the sole determinant of the outcome. For example, changes in the weather may produce harder greens and more head winds for the tournament leader than for his closest pursuers. A lucky bounce may save a shot or two. Whether such happenstance events are more or less probable than the likelihood that a golfer afflicted with Klippel-Trenaunay-Weber Syndrome would one day qualify for the NIKE TOUR and PGA TOUR, they at least demonstrate that pure chance may have a greater impact on the outcome of elite golf tournaments than the fatigue resulting from the enforcement of the walking rule.

Further, the factual basis of petitioner's argument is undermined by the District Court's finding that the fatigue from walking during one of petitioner's 4-day tournaments cannot be deemed significant. . . .

Even if we accept the factual predicate for petitioner's argument—that the walking rule is "outcome affecting" because fatigue may adversely affect performance—its legal position is fatally flawed. Petitioner's refusal to consider Martin's personal circumstances in deciding whether to accommodate his disability runs counter to the clear language and purpose of the ADA. As previously stated, the ADA was enacted to eliminate discrimination against "individuals" with disabilities, and to that end Title III of the Act requires without exception that any "policies, practices, or procedures" of a public accommodation be reasonably modified for disabled "individuals" as necessary to afford access unless doing so would fundamentally alter what is offered. To comply with this command, an individualized inquiry must be made to determine whether a specific modification for a particular person's disability would be reasonable under the circumstances as well as necessary for that person, and yet at the same time not work a fundamental alteration.

To be sure, the waiver of an essential rule of competition for anyone would fundamentally alter the nature of petitioner's tournaments. As we have demonstrated, however, the walking rule is at best peripheral to the nature of petitioner's athletic events, and thus it might be waived in individual cases without working a fundamental alteration. Therefore, petitioner's claim that all the substantive rules for its "highest-level" competitions are sacrosanct and cannot be modified under any circumstances is effectively a contention that it is exempt from Title III's reasonable modification requirement. But that provision carves out no exemption for elite athletes. . . .

Under the ADA's basic requirement that the need of a disabled person be evaluated on an individual basis, we have no doubt that allowing Martin to use a golf cart would not fundamentally alter the nature of petitioner's tournaments. As we have discussed, the purpose of the walking rule is to subject players to fatigue, which in turn may influence the outcome of tournaments. Even if the rule does serve that purpose, it is an uncontested finding of the District Court that Martin "easily endures greater fatigue even with a cart than his able-bodied competitors do by walking." The purpose of the walking rule is therefore not compromised in the slightest by allowing Martin to use a cart. A modification that provides an exception to a peripheral tournament rule without impairing its purpose cannot be said to "fundamentally alter" the tournament. What it can be said to do, on the other hand, is to allow Martin the chance to qualify for and compete in the athletic events petitioner offers to those members of the public who have the skill and desire to enter. That is exactly what the ADA requires. As a result, Martin's request for a waiver of the walking rule should have been granted.

* * *

The judgment of the Court of Appeals is affirmed.

JUSTICE SCALIA, with whom JUSTICE THOMAS joins, dissenting.

In my view today's opinion exercises a benevolent compassion that the law does not place it within our power to impose. The judgment distorts the text of Title III, the structure of the ADA, and common sense. I respectfully dissent.

I

* * *

For many reasons, Title III will not bear such an interpretation. The provision of Title III at issue here (§ 12182, its principal provision) is a public-accommodation law, and it is the traditional understanding of public-accommodation laws that they provide rights for customers.... Surely this has nothing to do with employees and independent contractors.

If there were any doubt left that § 12182 covers only clients and customers of places of public accommodation, it is eliminated by the fact that a contrary interpretation would make a muddle of the ADA as a whole.... Congress expressly excluded employers of fewer than 15 employees from Title I. The mom-and-pop grocery store or laundromat need not worry about altering the nonpublic areas of its place of business to accommodate handicapped employees—or about the litigation that failure to do so will invite. Similarly, since independent contractors are not covered by Title I, the small business (or the large one, for that matter) need not worry about making special accommodations for the painters, electricians, and other independent workers whose services are contracted for from time to time. It is an entirely unreasonable interpretation of the statute to say that these exemptions so carefully crafted in Title I are entirely eliminated by Title III (for the many businesses that are places of public accommodation) because employees and independent contractors "enjoy" the employment and contracting that such places provide. The only distinctive feature of places of public accommodation is that they accommodate the public, and Congress could have no conceivable reason for according the employees and independent contractors of such businesses protections that employees and independent contractors of other businesses do not enjoy.

* * *

[The dissent then addressed the majority's point that Martin was...] a "customer" of the PGA TOUR or of the golf courses on which it is played. That seems to me quite incredible. The PGA TOUR is a professional sporting event, staged for the entertainment of a live and TV audience, the receipts from whom (the TV audience's admission price is paid by advertisers) pay the expenses of the tour, including the cash prizes for the winning golfers. The professional golfers on the tour are no more "enjoying" (the statutory term) the entertainment that the tour provides, or the facilities of the golf courses on which it is held, than professional baseball players "enjoy" the baseball games in which they play or the facilities of Yankee Stadium. To be sure, professional ballplayers participate in the games, and use the ballfields, but no one in his right mind would think that they are customers of the American League or of Yankee Stadium. They are themselves the entertainment that the customers pay to watch. And professional golfers are no different.... Respondent did not seek to "exercise" or "recreate" at the PGA TOUR events; he sought to make money (which is why he is called a professional golfer). He was not a customer buying recreation or entertainment; he was a professional athlete selling it....

The Court relies heavily upon the Q-School. It says that petitioner offers the golfing public the "privilege" of "competing in the Q-School and playing in the tours...." But the Q-School is no more a "privilege" offered for the general public's "enjoyment" than is the California Bar Exam. It is a competition for entry into the PGA TOUR—an open tryout, no different in principle from open casting for a movie or stage production, or walk-on tryouts for other professional sports, such as baseball.... By the Court's reasoning, a business exists not only to sell goods and services to the public, but to provide the "privilege" of employment to the public; wherefore it follows, like night the day, that everyone who seeks a job is a customer.

II

* * *

[E]ven if respondent here is a consumer of the "privilege" of the PGA TOUR competition, I see no basis for considering whether the rules of that competition must be altered. It is as irrelevant to the PGA TOUR's compliance with the statute whether walking is essential to the game of golf as it is to the shoe store's compliance whether "pairness" is essential to the nature of shoes. If a shoe store wishes to sell shoes only in pairs it may; and if a golf tour (or a golf course) wishes to provide only walk-around golf, it may. The PGA TOUR cannot deny respondent access to that game because of his disability, but it need not provide him a game different (whether in its essentials or in its details) from that offered to everyone else....

[As for the Court's conclusion that allowing Martin to use a cart would not "fundamentally alter the nature" of the PGA Tour game], it is worth pointing out that the assumption which underlies that question is false. Nowhere is it writ that PGA TOUR golf must be classic "essential" golf. Why cannot the PGA TOUR, if it wishes, promote a new game, with distinctive rules (much as the American League promotes a game of baseball in which the pitcher's turn at the plate can be taken by a "designated hitter")? If members of the public do not like the new rules—if they feel that these rules do not truly test the individual's skill at "real golf" (or the team's skill at "real baseball") they can withdraw their patronage. But the rules are the rules. They are (as in all games) entirely arbitrary, and there is no basis on which anyone—not even the Supreme Court of the United States—can pronounce one or another of them to be "nonessential" if the rulemaker (here the PGA TOUR) deems it to be essential.

If one assumes, however, that the PGA TOUR has some legal obligation to play classic, Platonic golf—and if one assumes the correctness of all the other wrong turns the Court has made to get to this point—then we Justices must confront what is indeed an awesome responsibility. It has been rendered the solemn duty of the Supreme Court of the United States . . . to decide What Is Golf. I am sure that the Framers of the Constitution, aware of the 1457 edict of King James II of Scotland prohibiting golf because it interfered with the practice of archery, fully expected that sooner or later the paths of golf and government, the law and the links, would once again cross, and that the judges of this august Court would some day have to wrestle with that age-old jurisprudential question, for which their years of study in the law have so well prepared them: Is someone riding around a golf course from shot to shot really a golfer? The answer, we learn, is yes. The Court ultimately concludes, and it will henceforth be the Law of the Land, that walking is not a "fundamental" aspect of golf.

Either out of humility or out of self-respect (one or the other) the Court should decline to answer this incredibly difficult and incredibly silly question. To say that something is "essential" is ordinarily to say that it is necessary to the achievement of a certain object. But since it is the very nature of a game to have no object except amusement (that is what distinguishes games from productive activity), it is quite impossible to say that any of a game's arbitrary rules is "essential." Eighteen-hole golf courses, 10-foot-high basketball hoops, 90-foot baselines, 100-yard football fields—all are arbitrary and none is essential. The only support for any of them is tradition and (in more modern times) insistence by what has come to be regarded as the ruling body of the sport—both of which factors support the PGA TOUR's position in the present case. . . .

Having concluded that dispensing with the walking rule would not violate federal-Platonic "golf" (and, implicitly, that it is federal-Platonic golf, and no other, that the PGA TOUR can insist upon) the Court moves on to [determine] the competitive effects of waiving this nonessential rule. In this part of its analysis, the Court first finds that the effects of the change are "mitigated" by the fact that in the game of golf weather, a "lucky bounce," and "pure chance" provide different conditions for each competitor and individual ability may not "be the sole determinant of the outcome." . . . The Court's empiricism is unpersuasive. "Pure chance" is randomly distributed among the players, but allowing respondent to use a cart gives him a "lucky" break every time he plays. Pure chance also only matters at the margin—a stroke here or there; the cart substantially improves this respondent's competitive prospects beyond a couple of strokes. But even granting that there are significant nonhuman variables affecting competition, that fact does not justify adding another variable that always favors one player.

In an apparent effort to make its opinion as narrow as possible, the Court relies upon the District Court's finding that even with a cart, respondent will be at least as fatigued as everyone else. This, the Court says, *proves* that competition will not be affected.... In ... determining whether waiver of the "nonessential" rule will have an impermissible "competitive effect" by measuring the athletic capacity of the requesting individual, and asking whether the special dispensation would do no more than place him on a par (so to speak) with other competitors, the Court guarantees that future cases of this sort will have to be decided on the basis of individualized factual findings. Which means that future cases of this sort will be numerous, and a rich source of lucrative litigation. One can envision the parents of a Little League player with attention deficit disorder trying to convince a judge that their son's disability makes it at least 25% more difficult to hit a pitched ball. (If they are successful, the only thing that could prevent a court order giving the kid four strikes would be a judicial determination that, in baseball, three strikes are metaphysically necessary, which is quite absurd.)

The statute, of course, provides no basis for this individualized analysis that is the Court's last step on a long and misguided journey. The statute seeks to assure that a disabled person's disability will not deny him equal access to (among other things) competitive sporting events—not that his disability will not deny him an equal chance to win competitive sporting events. The latter is quite impossible, since the very nature of competitive sport is the measurement, by uniform rules, of unevenly distributed excellence. This unequal distribution is precisely what determines the winners and losers—and artificially to "even out" that distribution, by giving one or another player exemption from a rule that emphasizes his particular weakness, is to destroy the game.... In the Court's world, there is one set of rules that is "fair with respect to the able-bodied" but "individualized" rules, mandated by the ADA, for "talented but disabled athletes." The ADA mandates no such ridiculous thing. Agility, strength, speed, balance, quickness of mind, steadiness of nerves, intensity of concentration—these talents are not evenly distributed. No wild-eyed dreamer has ever suggested that the managing bodies of the competitive sports that test precisely these qualities should try to take account of the uneven distribution of God-given gifts when writing and enforcing the rules of competition. And I have no doubt Congress did not authorize misty-eyed judicial supervision of such a revolution.

* * *

And it should not be assumed that today's decent, tolerant, and progressive judgment will, in the long run, accrue to the benefit of sports competitors with disabilities. Now that it is clear courts will review the rules of sports for "fundamentalness," organizations that value their autonomy have every incentive to defend vigorously the necessity of every regulation. They may still be second-guessed in the end as to the Platonic requirements of the sport, but they will assuredly lose if they have at all wavered in their enforcement. The lesson the PGA TOUR and other sports organizations should take from this case is to make sure that the same written rules are set forth for all levels of play, and never voluntarily to grant any modifications. The second lesson is to end open tryouts. I doubt that, in the long run, even disabled athletes will be well served by these incentives that the Court has created.

* * *

NOTES AND QUESTIONS

1. *Fundamental Rules of the Game.* By what standards or criteria are courts now to determine what rules of a governing body are "fundamental" to the sporting product it produces or regulates? Did the Supreme Court majority articulate or implicitly adopt any principles future courts can use to make this judgment, or is this, like obscenity, something that cannot be defined but a court will know it when it sees it?

2. *Standard for Reasonableness of the Accommodation.* Should courts determine whether a requested accommodation fundamentally alters the sporting competition on an individualized basis—*i.e.*, whether accommodating a particular disabled athlete actually gives him an unfair advantage? The majority implicitly endorses this test in finding that Casey Martin would still suffer more fatigue than the other golfers even if he were allowed to use a cart. Or should the reasonableness of the accommodation also depend on a generalized inquiry—*i.e.*, whether the rule in question defines a key aspect of the game so that giving any waiver would by definition fundamentally alter the nature of the game? Does your answer depend on which rule the plaintiff is seeking to waive (*e.g.*, the "no cart" rule vs. a rule requiring that the ball be struck by a club and not propelled by some other device)?

3. *Hypothetical Situations.* Whatever your answer to questions 1 and 2 above, how would you analyze and resolve the following:

   a. A professional golfer weakened by a disease causing muscular degeneration in his arms claims that he can play golf as well as anyone but lacks 25% of the strength of non-disabled golfers. He asks that he be allowed to tee off 25% closer to the green than the other golfers.

   b. A professional baseball player is weakened by the same muscular disease as in a. He asks that he be allowed to use an aluminum or corked bat that has 25% greater exit velocity than the required wood bats.

c. A professional tennis player suffers from a moderately crippling disease that limits his ability to move about on his feet quickly. He argues that he can hit the ball as effectively as anyone but has 25% less mobility than his average non-disabled competitors. He asks that the sidelines on his side of the court be moved in 25% during his matches.

d. A professional golfer has permanent shoulder problems preventing him from swinging his arms with a full rotation. He is able to putt and chip and take half swings as well as anyone, but he cannot drive or take a full swing. He asks that for distances of over 75 yards he be allowed to use a large slingshot that he has devised that would enable him to propel the ball up to a maximum of 300 yards.

e. A basketball player with a severe and sensitive skin condition on his arms and legs asks that he able to play with his limbs completely covered with a nonabrasive fabric, contrary to league game dress rules.

4. *Arbitrariness of Game Rules.* Justice Scalia's dissent argues that by definition every rule of any sport is arbitrary and thus "silly," making it absurd to ask which of them are fundamental. He argues that what is fundamental to any game is not what the rules are but rather that all of them be applied to every competitor equally. How did Justice Stevens respond to this? Is Justice Scalia's argument really with Congress' use of the "fundamentally alter" standard in the statute rather than with the majority's attempt to apply the standard in this case?

5. *Place of Public Accommodation.* The dissent also contends that the ADA's "place of public accommodation" requirement in Title III covers ony businesses that offer to sell or lease goods or services to the public—*i.e.*, the obligation not to discriminate on the basis of disability extends only to a business's "clients or customers." The majority does not disagree with this, but rather argues that Casey Martin is a "client or customer" of the PGA Tour because he had to pay $3,000 in order to sign up for Qualifying School. Is this persuasive? Would the outcome then be different for a sporting tour or governing body that did not require a fee of any kind from those seeking to qualify for a spot on the tour? If the PGA Tour dropped the $3,000 Q-School registration fee, could it again apply its "no cart" policy against Casey Martin?

6. *Floodgates Argument.* Do you share Justice Scalia's concern that the *Martin* ruling will lead to a flood of claims by disabled athletes asking for all sorts of modifications to rules? As of this writing, only a handful of such claims have been litigated to a published decision. In *Kuketz v. Petronelli*, 443 Mass. 355, 821 N.E.2d 473 (2005), the court dismissed a wheelchair user's ADA claim against a private racquetball league that refused to allow him two bounces of the ball while his able-bodied opponents received one bounce, because that accommodation would fundamentally alter the nature of the game. Contrast *Brown v. Elk Grove Unified Sch. Dist.*, 2018 WL 953162 (E.D. Cal. Feb. 20,

2018), in which a high school basketball player's ADA claim was allowed to proceed. The student-athlete did not ask for an accommodation, but alleged that the basketball coach discriminated against him based on his "emotional disturbance disability," denying him a spot on the varsity team. The court held that whether the coach justifiably cut the player for lacking temperamental requirements of a varsity player was not justiciable at the pleading stage.

7. *Legitimacy of the Record Books.* What if it was Tiger Woods who developed a walking disability after winning 14 major tournaments, and needed to use a cart to be able to win five more so he could eclipse Jack Nicklaus' record of 18 major victories? If Tiger then went on to win those five additional majors using a cart, should his record be qualified with an asterisk in the record books?

8. *Competition Between Able-Bodied and Disabled Athletes.* South African Oscar Pistorius was born with congenital absence of the fibula bone in both legs and had them both amputated before he was a year old. Using prosthetic legs, he became an elite runner, taking the gold in Paralympic competitions. He sought to compete against able-bodied athletes, and in 2008, the Court of Arbitration for Sport (CAS) ruled that he could do so, over the objections of the International Association of Athletics Federation, which considered the prosthetics to offer a competitive advantage. Pistorius qualified for the 2012 London Olympics and represented South Africa in both individual and relay races. How should the CAS have judged whether the prosthetic legs provided Pistorius an unfair competitive advantage?

Would it violate U.S. disability laws to refuse to allow a disabled competitor to race in track events against able-bodied runners? Does the *Martin* case provide a framework for analysis? *See McFadden v. Grasmick*, 485 F. Supp. 2d 642 (D. Md. 2007) (granting elite wheelchair racer right to compete alongside footed athletes in high school track meets, but denying preliminary injunction to require state athletic association to count her points in separate wheelchair racing events in determining team track and field state champion); *Badgett v. Alabama High School Athletic Assn.*, 2007 WL 2461928 (N.D. Ala. May 3, 2007) (denying preliminary injunction to enable wheelchair athlete to compete against able-bodied runners in state tournament because doing so would raise legitimate competitive fairness and safety concerns).

9. *Coda.* Recall in Chapter 1, Section D, in the discussion of the origins of organized sports, how it has evolved from private amusement "to a part of society about which the public had a vital interest." *Supra* at 68. In light of the opinions in the *Martin* case, consider how sports law is shaped by the recognition of the immense social, economic, cultural, and geopolitical impact of sports.

INDEX

References are to Pages

ADMISSION OF FRANCHISES
Antitrust, this index

ADMISSIONS STANDARDS
Athlete-University Relationship, this index

AGENT REPRESENTATION
    Generally, 649–718
    Arbitration of disputes, 666, 703, 704
    Attorney-agents, ethics rules governing, 714–718
    Basics of agency law, 651, 652
    Best interests of athlete, 677
    Boxer agreements, state regulation, 666
    Breakdowns in relationship, 657–677
    Collective bargaining agreements
        Agents bound by, 683
        Dealing with CBA constraints in contract negotiations, 697–699
    College athlete recruiting
        Generally, 699–710
        Agents and amateurism, 705–710, 862–880
        Enforceability of representation agreements, 699–705
        Ethics of illicit payments to athletes, 704, 705
        Honest services fraud theory, 709
        NCAA student antitrust litigation, 709, 710
        Recruiting tactics, 699–705
        Redress in case of unenforceable agreement, 704
    Common law principles, 651
    Conflicts of interest
        Generally, 666–672
        Attorney-agents, 715–717
        Examples, 671, 672
        Informed consent, 671
        Self-management, 672
    Constructive fraud, 665
    Demographics of agents, 665
    Discipline of agents, 695, 696
    Disputes between agents, 672–677
    Duty of loyalty, 651, 652, 663–666
    Eligibility for certification, 694
    Ethics
        Attorney-agents, rules governing, 714–718
        Illicit payments to athletes, 704, 705
    Fees and fee disputes
        Generally, 663–666, 695
        Attorney-agents, 715, 717
    Fiduciary duties
        Generally, 651
        Breach of duties, 657–663
    Financial responsibility, 694
    Government regulation of agents, 710–718
    Incentives and conflicts in fee structures, 665
    Informed consent to conflicts of interest, 671
    Legal relationship between agents and clients, 651–657
    Loyalty
        Agent's loyalty to union, 687
        Duty of loyalty, above
    Malpractice in negotiating contract, 656
    Non-compete clauses, 677
    Obligations after execution of contract, 657
    Player association
        Contract assistance to members, 698, 699
        Regulation of agents, 676, 677, 688–696
    Players as agents, 687
    Players union fee regulation, 665
    Poaching clients, 676
    Principal's duty to agent, 656
    Private and public efforts to protect athletes, 661, 662
    Recruiting. College athlete recruiting, above
    Regulation of agents
        Discipline, 695, 696
        Eligibility for certification, 694
        Ethics rules governing attorney-agents, 714–718
        Federal legislation, 713, 714
        Financial responsibility, 694
        Government regulation, 710–718
        Player association regulation, 676, 677, 688–696
        Solicitation of business, 695
        State legislation, 710–713
        Union authority, 678–687
        Who is agent, 694
    Self-management, 672
    Solicitation of business
        Generally, 695
        Attorney-agents, 716–718
    Sports Agent and Responsibility Trust Act (SPARTA), 713, 714
    Standards for agent performance, 652–657

State legislation regulating agents, 710–713
Uniform Athlete Agent Act (UAAA) and revised act, 711–713
Unionized athletes, representation of, 677–699
Unionized sports, agent as contract negotiator, 697–699
Vulnerability of athletes, 661
Who is agent, 694
Work stoppages, 687

AMATEURISM
Athlete-University Relationship, this index
National Collegiate Athletic Association (NCAA), this index

ANTI-DOPING
World Anti-Doping Agency. International and Olympic Sports, this index

ANTITRUST
Generally, 249–329, 331–417, 419–538
Admission and relocation of franchises
Generally, 439–469
Alternative non-antitrust approaches to stakeholder interests in franchise movement, 463–469
Ancillary restraints doctrine, 455
Antitrust claims from contraction, 462
Balancing competitive effects, 454, 455
Bankrupt clubs, relocation of, 456, 457
Bargaining dynamics, franchise relocation and new entry, 535, 536
Comparing relocation dynamics in NFL and MLB, 457
Contraction or entry, league controls, 457–462
Counseling leagues, 457
Direct state legislation, 466, 467
Effect of relocation on league, 440, 441
Eminent domain, attempted use by city to purchase club, 466
Entry or contraction, league controls, 457–462
Environmental laws, blocking undesired relocation based on, 463
Federal legislative reform, 467, 468
Fees for relocation and jury deference to league judgments, 455
Franchise free agency, 440
Intra-metropolitan relocations, 469
Lease terms protecting against relocation, 464–466
Less restrictive alternatives and due process, 455
Lost profits, award of, 450, 451
Monopoly leagues, admission to, 461
Offset of windfall benefit against damages awarded, 451
Promotion and relegation, 462
Refusal of league to permit relocation, 441–457
Rejected entry, evaluating for antitrust claims, 462
State and local law, blocking undesired relocation based on, 463, 466, 467
Alternative league structures, 294–298
Ancillary restraints doctrine, 439, 455
Applicable § 1 standard, 252–256
Balancing competitive effects, 439, 454
Bankrupt clubs, relocation of, 456, 457
Bargaining dynamics in sports league decision-making about commercial practices, 532–538
Baseball exemption. Major League Baseball, this index
Business dynamics of regulating sports labor markets
Generally, 413–417
Constructing labor market rules, 414
Foundational concepts, 413
Individual rights vs. general welfare, 416
Maneuvering to advantage in future, 417
Negotiating rules with union, 415
Business strategy and antitrust scrutiny of internal league regulation, 539 et seq.
Clayton Act, generally, 250
College athletes. Athlete-University Relationship, this index
Commercial practices, bargaining dynamics in sports league decision-making, 532–538
Concerns warranting § 1 scrutiny of sports league decisions, 286
Conduct, monopolizing, 310–316
Contraction of league, 457–462
Economic analysis of restraints in players market
Generally, 332–341
Alternatives to player restraints, 338
Competitive balance, 336, 340, 341, 353
Debt limits, 333
Economic effects of player restraints, 333, 334
Irrational club behavior and need for player restraints, 339, 340
Justifications for player restraints, 334–338
Lowering payroll, restraints as pretext, 340
Pro-competitive objectives, achieving, 339
Revenue sharing, 338
Rookie draft, below

Roster limits, 333
Salary caps, 332, 333
Small market clubs, 335, 353, 354
Types of player restraints, 332, 333
Waiver rules, 333
Essential facilities doctrine, 317, 318, 327
Exclusionary practices, 310
Exclusive lease arrangements, 327
Expansion, monopoly power and, 307–310, 326
Franchise admission. Admission and relocation of franchises, above
Franchise ownership rules
    Generally, 420–439
    Ancillary restraints doctrine and rule of reason, 439
    Anti-competitive theories for rejecting prospective owner, 426
    Balancing procompetitive effects in one market against harm in another, 439
    Business strategy in ownership policy, 426
    Consumer interest in stock purchases, 438
    Cross-ownership restrictions, 422 et seq.
    Current and prospective owners, distinguishing between restrictions on, 426
    Minor leagues, 425, 426
    Public ownership restrictions, 426 et seq.
Free agency, 355 et seq.
Governance structure of league, relevance, 293
Historical background, 250–256
Horizontal and vertical restraints, 255
Intellectual property
    League property, 285, 286
    Merchandise and related IP rights, group licensing, below
Intra-metropolitan relocations, 469
Irrational club behavior and need for player restraints, 339, 340
Judicial recognition of single entity sports defendants, 294
Justifications for player restraints, 334–338
Labor exemption
    Generally, 367–413
    Disclaimer or decertification as option, 412, 413
    Eligibility to play in unionized professional sports post-Brown, 391–399
    Historical background, 367–372
    Initial development of doctrine, 373 et seq.
    Non-statutory exemption
        generally, 369–372
        judicial options, 372, 373
    Supreme Court decision, 377–389
    Outer limits of exemption, 373, 374
    Restraints agreed to by union but sought by management, application to, 374–377
    Statutory exemption, 368, 369
    Supreme Court decision, 377–389
    Union responses post-Brown, 399–413
Legislative support for sports leagues avoidance of rule of reason, 289, 290
Leveraging monopoly power, 323–329
Licensing. Merchandise and related IP rights, group licensing, below
Market definition, 273, 326, 438
Market power under different statutory provisions, 366
Merchandise and related intellectual property rights, group licensing
    Generally, 510–532, 591
    Antitrust suits, agreements not to file, 531, 532
    Club marketing vs. league marketing, 531
    Degree of league control, 510–512
    Economics of collective licensing, 532
    Internet sales and websites, 516–518, 530
    Merits of NFL's exclusive licensing, 532
    Players' publicity rights, 512
    Royalty payments for trading cards, 512, 513
    Rule of reason, 515, 516
Merger of leagues, challenging, 327
Monopoly in professional sports
    Generally, 299–329
    Admission to monopoly leagues, 461
    Antitrust law and monopoly power, 302–307
    Conduct, monopolizing, 310–316
    Elements of monopolization charge, 302, 303
    Essential facilities doctrine, 317, 327
    Exclusionary practices, 310
    Exclusive lease arrangements, 327
    Expansion, monopoly power and, 307–310, 326
    Leveraging monopoly power, 323–329
    Merchandising, 324
    Merger of leagues, challenging, 327
    Predatory spending, 310, 311, 326, 327
    Serial monopoly, 503
    Single league in each sport, consequence of, 329
    Sports marketplace, 302 et seq.
    Stadium monopolization, 316–320, 328
    Supply of players, monopolizing, 310–316
    Television contracts, 320–323

Nature of sports league
    Generally, 274–299
    Alternative league structures, 294–298
    Concerns warranting § 1 scrutiny of sports league decisions, 286
    Governance structure, relevance, 293
    Intellectual property of league, 285, 286
    Non-antitrust contexts, 298, 299
    Owner decisions as analogous to corporate board of directors, 290–293
    Rival clubs as economic and sporting competitors, 287–289, 326
    Rule of reason, 289, 290
    Single entity defense, 274–294
NCAA. National Collegiate Athletic Association, this index
Owner decisions as analogous to corporate board of directors, 290–293
Ownership policies, bargaining dynamics, 534, 535
Ownership rules. Franchise ownership rules, above
Per se or rule of reason, 252–256
Player restraints, types of, 332, 333
Predatory spending, 310, 311, 326, 327
Pro-competitive objectives of player restraints, achieving, 339
Purposes of antitrust laws, 251, 252
Relocation. Admission and relocation of franchises, above
Revenue sharing
    Alternatives to player restraints, 338
    Bargaining dynamics, 534
    Relevance to single entity question, 290
    Television broadcasting, 480
    Television contracts, 502
Rival clubs as economic and sporting competitors, 287–289, 326
Rookie draft, antitrust analysis
    Generally, 341–355
    Competitive balance, enhancing, 353
    Continuation in exchange for veteran free agency, 362
    Exploitation of draftees, 354
    Less restrictive alternatives, 354, 355
    Small market clubs, helping, 353
Rozelle Rule, 257, 355 et seq.
Rule of reason
    Generally, 252–256
    Ancillary restraints doctrine and rule of reason, 439
    Cable TV contracts, 479
    Conference television contracts, 272, 273
    Exclusive contracts, 516
    Full review, 272
    Market definition, 273
    Market power, 493
    Quick look review, 272
    Royalty payments for trading cards, 515, 516
    Rozelle Rule, 257, 355 et seq.
    Sports leagues, 256–273, 289, 290
    When to apply after American Needle, 294
Sherman Act, generally, 250
Single entity defense, 274–294
Single league in each sport, consequence of, 329
Sports governing bodies and international counterparts, applicability of antitrust law, 998
Stadium monopolization, 316–320, 328
Superstation broadcasts
    Generally, 480 et seq.
    Compulsory licensing-royalty scheme, 571–574
Supply of players, monopolizing, 310–316
Television contracts
    Generally, 469–510
    Antitrust immunity, 475, 476
    Basic premium or sports tier, 509
    Broadcast limits and partnership concepts, 494
    Cable networks, 479
    Conference contracts, 272, 273
    FCC blackout rules, 476
    Fees vs. output restraints, 493
    Gate protection vs. radio rights protection, 474
    League decision-making and information asymmetry, 493, 494
    Live gate, harm to, 474
    Monopoly in professional sports, 320–323
    Multichannel video programming distributors, 503 et seq.
    Playoff games, 480
    Pooled rights, collective selling, 475–480
    Revenue sharing, 480, 502
    Sale of television rights by individual clubs, league restrictions, 480–502
    Satellite broadcasting, antitrust challenge, 476 et seq.
    Sports Broadcasting Act of 1961, 475 et seq.
    Superstation broadcasts, 480 et seq., 571–574
    Territorial exclusivity, threat to, 469
    Vertical integration of media companies and access to sports broadcasting, 503–510
    Vertical issues in recent antitrust jurisdiction, 509

ARBITRATION
    Generally, 121–184
Agent-player disputes, 703, 704
Arbitrator selection strategy, 225

Burden of proof, drug usage discipline, 147
Contract interpretation through
    arbitration, 123–127
Court of Arbitration for Sport.
    International and Olympic Sports,
        this index
Deflate-gate, 183, 184
Disciplinary disputes
        Generally, 127–141
        Comparative punishments, 138
        Drug usage discipline, 141–148
        Evidence, arbitrator's authority to
            weigh, 138
        Judicial review, 138, 139
        Just cause, 138
        League rules, 139–141
        Suspension and fine following nolo
            contendere plea, 171 et seq.
Drug usage discipline, 141–148
Evidence, arbitrator's authority to weigh,
    138
Evident partiality, 183, 184
Exclusivity of remedy (§ 301 preemption),
    148–155
Extension of collective bargaining process,
    139
Federal Arbitration Act, 183
Fee disputes, 666
Historical background, 121–123
International and Olympic Sports, this
    index
Judicial review
        Generally, 165–184
        Deflate-gate, 183, 184
        Disciplinary disputes, 138, 139
        Evident partiality, 183, 184
        Fundamental fairness, 184
        Own brand of industrial justice, 165,
            166, 170
        Supreme Court guidance, 165, 166
        Unilaterally appointed arbitrators,
            184
        Vacatur of award, 171, 183
Just cause for discipline, 138
Nolo contendere plea, suspension and fine
    following, 171 et seq.
Performance-enhancing substances, 141–
    148
Reserve system. Mobility Restraints, this
    index
Salary arbitration
        Generally, 156–165
        Criteria, 164, 165
        Hockey and baseball models, 155 et
            seq.
        Last best offer, 156, 157
State regulation and federal preemption,
    154
Suspension and fine following nolo
    contendere plea, 171 et seq.
Unilaterally appointed arbitrators, 184
Vacatur of award, 171, 183

ATHLETE-UNIVERSITY
RELATIONSHIP
    Generally, 787–911
Access to education, 824–837
Admissions standards
        Generally, 787–812
        Disability law, 804–812
        Disparate impact challenge, 792 et
            seq.
        Eligibility vs. academic progress, 804
        High school curriculum
            requirements, 803
        Home rule, 787, 793, 804
        Learning disabled students, 804–812
        Predictor rule, 788, 793
        Propositions 48 and 16, 793, 803
        Race discrimination, 787–803
        Sliding scale and Academic Progress
            Rate (APR), 803, 804
        Title VI challenge, 792 et seq.
Agents and amateurism, 862–880
Amateurism and scope of judicial review
        Generally, 846–880
        Agents and amateurism, 862–880
        Drafts and amateurism, 861, 862
        Line between amateur and
            professional, 868
        Pre-college sports and amateurism
            generally, 846–859
                name, image or likeness, use of,
                    850
        Pro contracts and amateurism, 859–
            861
Antitrust challenges to student athlete
    model
        Generally, 889–911
        Grant-in-aid caps, 905–911
        Less restrictive alternatives, 909, 910
Benefits
        Athlete vs. non-athlete benefits, 837
        Non-educational benefits, 817
Breach of promise, grounds for alleging,
    816
Cost of attendance, providing to student-
    athletes, 904
Drafts and amateurism, 861, 862
Employee status. Labor challenges, below
Gender Equity, this index
Hardship waivers, 845
Judicial review. Amateurism and scope of
    judicial review, above
Labor challenges to student athlete model
        Generally, 880–889
        Antitrust, effect on, 882
        Employee status and union
            representation, 880 et seq.
        FLSA, effect of applying to college
            athletes, 889
        Loss of eligibility concerns, 883
        Revenue vs. non-revenue sports, 882,
            888
        Title IX implications, 882
Learning disabled students, 804–812

Multi-year scholarships, 815
National Letter of Intent (NLI), 813
NCAA recruiting regulations, 816–824
Non-educational benefits, providing, 817
Nonrenewal of scholarship, 815
Players leaving early to play professional sports, 815
Pre-college sports and amateurism, 846–859
Pro contracts and amateurism, 859–861
Race discrimination in admissions, 787–803
Recruiting and scholarships
    Generally, 787–824
    Admissions standards, above
    Multi-year scholarships, 815
    National Letter of Intent (NLI), 813
    NCAA recruiting regulations, 816–824
    Non-educational benefits, providing, 817
    Nonrenewal of scholarship, 815
    University-athlete agreement, 812–816
Sliding scale and Academic Progress Rate (APR), 803, 804
Student-athlete
    Generally, 787 et seq.
    Access to education, above
    Amateurism and scope of judicial review, above
    Antitrust challenges to student athlete model, above
    Labor challenges to student athlete model, above
    Transfer rules, below
Title IX. Gender Equity, this index
Tortious conduct by university, grounds for alleging, 816
Transfer rules
    Generally, 837–846
    Graduate transfer rule, 838
    Hardship waivers, 845
Tutoring programs, 830
University-athlete agreement, 812–816

ATTORNEY-AGENTS
Ethics rules governing, 714–718
Unauthorized practice of law, 716, 718

BANKRUPTCY
Relocation of bankrupt clubs, 456, 457

BARGAINING DYNAMICS
Sports league decision-making about commercial practices, 532–538

BARGAINING UNITS
Labor Law and Collective Bargaining, this index

BASEBALL
Antitrust, this index
Major League Baseball, this index

BROADCASTING
Intellectual Property, this index
Television contracts. Antitrust, this index

BURDEN OF PROOF
Drug usage discipline, 147

BUSINESS DYNAMICS OF REGULATING SPORTS LABOR MARKETS
Antitrust, this index

COACHES
Assignment of coaches based on gender of players, 968
National Collegiate Athletic Association, this index
Pay disparity between male and female coaches, 963 et seq.

COLLECTIVE BARGAINING
Labor Law and Collective Bargaining, this index

COLLEGE ATHLETES
Agent Representation, this index
Athlete-University Relationship, this index
Bargaining units, 90, 91
NCAA. National Collegiate Athletic Association, this index

COMMERCE CLAUSE
Interstate Commerce, this index

COMMERCIAL PRACTICES
Bargaining dynamics in sports league decision-making, 532–538

COMMISSIONERS
Professional Sports Leagues, this index

CONCUSSION LITIGATION
    Generally, 1084–1089
Claims process, 1086
College athletes, 1086, 1087
Existential threat to contact sports, 1087
Game day and medical protocols, 1088
Game rules changes, 1087, 1088
Helmet manufacturer liability, 1088, 1089
Player compensation fund, 1085
Players association exposure, 1088

CONFLICTS OF INTEREST
Agent Representation, this index

CONSENT
Criminal liability for injuries, consent defense, 1063
Informed consent to agent conflicts of interest, 671
Physical contact outside rule, consent to, 1067
Publicity use, consent to, 589

CONTRACTS
Coaching contracts. National Collegiate Athletic Association, this index

Interpretation through arbitration, 123–127
Mobility Restraints, this index

COPYRIGHT
Intellectual Property, this index

CRIMINAL SANCTIONS
Injuries to Athletes, this index
National Collegiate Athletic Association, this index

DEATH PENALTY
National Collegiate Athletic Association, this index

DEFECTIVE PRODUCTS AND HAZARDOUS FACILITIES
Generally, 1089–1096
Aluminum bats, 1089–1093
Industry standards, 1092
Player safety *vs.* performance, 1093
Playing surfaces, hazardous, 1096
Staph infection outbreak, 1096

DISABILITY AND RIGHT TO PLAY
Generally, 1096–1124
Able-bodied and disabled athletes, competition between, 1124
Americans with Disabilities Act, generally, 1097
Arbitrariness of game rules, 1123
Blanket eligibility rules, 1105
Disability, defined, 1097
Floodgates argument, 1123, 1124
Fundamental character of game, modifying, 1112–1124
HIV/AIDS and major sports leagues, 1112
Increased risk to impaired athlete, 1097–1106
Increased risk to other participants, 1106–1112
Liability waivers, 1105
Major life activity, what constitutes, 1104
Medical evidence of risk to others, 1111, 1112
Otherwise qualified and health risks, 1104, 1105
Place of public accommodation, 1123
Reasonable accommodation requirement, 1105, 1122
Record books, legitimacy of, 1124
Rehabilitation Act, generally, 1097
Statutory claims, requirements for, 1097

DISCIPLINARY DISPUTES
Arbitration, this index

DOPING
International and Olympic Sports, this index

DRAFTS
Amateurism, drafts and, 861, 862
Rookie draft. Antitrust, this index

DRUGS AND DRUG USE
Arbitration proceedings, 141–148
Doping. International and Olympic Sports, this index
MLB negotiated drug policy, 37
Performance-enhancing substances, arbitration proceedings, 141–148
Prescription drug abuse litigation, 1082–1084

DUE PROCESS
NCAA infractions, 770
Sports governing organizations and state action requirement, 723–734

DUTY OF FAIR REPRESENTATION
Labor Law and Collective Bargaining, this index

DUTY TO BARGAIN IN GOOD FAITH
Labor Law and Collective Bargaining, this index

EMINENT DOMAIN
Attempted use by city to purchase club, 466

ENVIRONMENTAL LAWS
Blocking undesired relocation based on, 463

FEES AND FEE DISPUTES
Agent Representation, this index

FIDUCIARY DUTIES
Agent Representation, this index
Professional sports leagues, 7–9

FIRST AMENDMENT
Ambush marketing, free speech concerns, 638
Ancillary entertainment products, First Amendment defense, 595–608
Commercial *vs.* noncommercial speech, 647
Parody, 581, 582
Publicity rights of athletes, 580–589
Racially stereotyped mascots, 641 et seq.
Real-time game accounts and right to broadcast games, 545
Trademark, First Amendment considerations, 638–648

FOOTBALL
Antitrust, this index
Concussion Litigation, this index
Injuries to Athletes, this index
National Football League (NFL), this index
World Football League, 193 et seq.

FRANCHISE ADMISSION AND RELOCATION
Antitrust, this index

FRANCHISE OWNERSHIP RULES
Antitrust, this index

GAMBLING
Generally, 54–65
Australian example, 64, 65
Best interests of sport, 64
Legalized gambling, move toward, 56–60
Legislative issues regarding legalized sports gambling, 60–65
Pete Rose, 10–14
Professional and Amateur Sports Protection Act (PASPA), 57–59
Traditional aversion, 54–56

GENDER EQUITY
Generally, 913–980
Access
    Generally, 969–980
    Equality of access *vs.* equality of opportunity, 972
    High school sports, 972–980
    Justifications for blocking access, 972
    Single sport considerations, 972
Athletic program administration, 962–969
Cheerleading and dance squads, 954–962
Coaches
    Assignment of coaches based on gender of players, 968
    Pay disparity between male and female coaches, 963 et seq.
    Title VII remedies, 969
Contact sport exception, 978
Elimination of varsity teams, 918–922
Equal athletic opportunity, 915
Equal Pay Act litigation, 967, 968
High school sports, 972–980
Males in female sports, 978–980
Non-revenue male teams, elimination of, 926
Pay disparity between male and female coaches, 963 et seq.
Resources, 917 et seq.
Reverse discrimination suits by men, 922, 948 et seq.
Risk of injury in mixed sports, 977
Safe harbors, 948
Separate teams for male and female students, 970–972
Single sport considerations, 972
Standing to raise claim, 969
Three-prong test, 939–941
Title IX
    Generally, 913, 914
    Access, above
    Administrative development, 914–916
    Categories of complaints, 916
    Cheerleading and dance squads, 954–962
    Elimination of varsity teams, 918–922
    Equal athletic opportunity, 915
    Interplay with NCAA rules, 952
    Private enforcement actions, 914
    Regulations, 915, 916

Reverse discrimination suits by men, 922, 948 et seq.
Safe harbors, 948
Standing to raise claim, 969
Three-prong test, 939–941

GOOD FAITH
Duty to bargain in good faith. Labor Law and Collective Bargaining, this index

HAZARDOUS FACILITIES
Defective Products and Hazardous Facilities, this index

HEALTH AND SAFETY ISSUES
Generally, 1049–1124
Concussion Litigation, this index
Defective Products, this index
Injuries to Athletes, this index
Injuries to Spectators, this index
Medical Malpractice, this index
Prescription drug abuse litigation, 1082–1084

HIV/AIDS
Risks to game participants, 1112

HOCKEY
Salary arbitration, 155, 156

HYPERANDROGENISM
Generally, 1032–1048

INJURIES TO ATHLETES
Generally, 1049–1061
Compensating injured athlete, 1058
Conduct not part of game, 1057, 1058
Criminal liability
    Generally, 1061–1068
    Competition violence, 1066
    Defenses, 1063
    Home *vs.* away game, 1066
    Legislative solutions, 1068
    Physical contact outside rule, consent to, 1067
    Recreational sports, 1067, 1068
    Tort *vs.* criminal liability, 1066, 1067
Football as commercial enterprise, 1057
Gender equity, risk of injury in mixed sports, 977
Home *vs.* away game, 1066
League self-policing, 1057
Legislative solutions, 1068
Non-contact sports, 1060
Physical contact outside rule, consent to, 1067
Recreational athletes, 1059, 1060, 1067, 1068
Standard of liability for professional athletes, 1058, 1059
Targeting players for on-field injury, 38–49
Tort *vs.* criminal liability, 1066, 1067
Violent acts, 1060, 1061, 1066

INJURIES TO SPECTATORS
Generally, 1068–1074
Contact by spectator, 1073, 1074
Enterprise liability, 1072
Facility amenities and spectator distractions, 1072, 1073
Open and obvious danger, 1071, 1072
Premises liability, 1074
Projectiles, 1073
Recreational sports, 1072
Ticket disclaimer, 1072

INTELLECTUAL PROPERTY
Generally, 539–648
Advancing technology and appropriation of real-time game accounts, 547–553
Advertising or trade, commercial use of athlete's name or identity, 582
Ambush marketing, 635–638
Amount and substantiality of portion used, 562
Ancillary entertainment products, First Amendment defense, 595–608
Anticybersquatting Consumer Protection Act, 634
Antitrust and intellectual property of league, 285, 286
Artistic expression, 583
Artwork, types of, 640
Balancing of interests, 588, 640
Broadcasts
    Copyright in game broadcasts, below
    Real-time game accounts and right to broadcast games, below
    Right of publicity and game broadcasts, 592–595
Business interests *vs.* individual interests, 635
Clips, social media sharing, 562, 563
Commercial *vs.* noncommercial speech, 647
Common law property rights in live game accounts, 542–545
Contractual solutions to game broadcast ownership, 546
Copyright in game broadcasts
    Generally, 558–574
    Fair use of copyrighted works, 559–563
    Game highlights market, 562
    Home use exemption, 563
    Ideas or facts, no copyright protection for, 558, 559
    Nature of copyrighted work, 561
    Passive carrier exemption to public performance, 570, 571
    Portion used, amount and substantiality, 562
    Preemption, 552, 557, 595
    Public performance of copyrighted works, 563–570
    Social media sharing of sports clips, 562, 563
    Superstations and compulsory licensing-royalty scheme, 571–574
    Technological change and copyright legislation, 574
Derivative works and compilations, 593, 594
Descriptive fair use, 632
Dilution of trademark, 633–635
Fair use of copyrighted works, 559–563
Fair use of trademark, 626–632
False endorsements, 606
Fans, interests of, 635
Fantasy sports providers, 605
First Amendment
    Ancillary entertainment products, First Amendment defense, 595–608
    Publicity rights of athletes, 580–589
    Trademark, First Amendment considerations, 638–648
First sale doctrine, 589–592
Functional merchandise, 640
Gambling, 607, 608
Game highlights market, 562
Group licensing, 591
Highlights market, 562
Home use exemption, 563
Hot news doctrine, 544, 545, 553
Ideas or facts, no copyright protection for, 558, 559
Incidental use, 606
Information in public domain, 607
Internet reporting, property rights in, 553–557
Logos, insignia and colors, 615
Nominative fair use, 632
Off-site viewability of game, 545
Parody, 581, 582, 632
Passive carrier exemption to public performance, 570, 571
Phrases and designations, trademark rights, 616–619
Preemption, 552, 557
Privacy torts, 575, 576
Public interest in information, 607
Public performance of copyrighted works
    Generally, 563–570
    Passive carrier exemption to public performance, 570, 571
Publicity rights of athletes
    Generally, 574–608
    Abandoned names, 578
    Advertising or trade, use for, 582
    Amateur athletes, 595
    Ancillary entertainment products, First Amendment defense, 595–608
    Artistic expression, 583
    Catch phrases, 578
    College football video games, 600 et seq.
    Consent to publicity use, 589

Consumer welfare concerns, 588
Copyright vs. publicity rights, 591
Derivative works and compilations, 593, 594
Distinctive attributes, 578
Economic justification, 588
First Amendment, 580–589
First sale doctrine, 589–592
Game broadcasts and right of publicity, 592–595
Identifiability of owner of publicity right, 577–579
Incidental use, 606
Information in public domain, 607
Judicial balancing, 588
Mass produced goods, 588, 589
Misappropriation of celebrity, 577
Nicknames, 578
Origins of right of publicity, 575–577
Parody, 581, 582
Privacy torts, 575, 576
Public interest in information, 607
Reproduction and distribution of copyrighted works, 594
Scope of common law right, 579
Transformative use test, 606
Wearable technology, 607
Racially stereotyped mascots, 641 et seq.
Real-time game accounts and right to broadcast games
    Generally, 541–557
    Advancing technology and appropriation of real-time game accounts, 547–553
    Common law property rights in live game accounts, 542–545
    Contractual solutions to game broadcast ownership, 546
    First Amendment, 545
    Hot news doctrine, 544, 545, 553
    Internet reporting, property rights in, 553–557
    Off-site viewability of game, 545
Reproduction and distribution of copyrighted works, 594
Reputational harm, 635
Reverse confusion, 618, 619
Same name, different city or sport, 615
Same vs. new and different product, 591
Secondary meaning, 609, 618
Social media sharing of sports clips, 562, 563
Sports fans, interests of, 635
Sports gambling, 607, 608
Superstations and compulsory licensing-royalty scheme, 571–574
Team names, trademark rights, 609–616
Technological change and copyright legislation, 574
Trademark rights
    Generally, 608–648
    Anticybersquatting Consumer Protection Act, 634
    Blurring, 633
    Business interests *vs.* individual interests, 635
    Consumer perception, 632
    Descriptive fair use, 632
    Dilution of trademark, 633–635
    Disclaimers, 615, 631
    Distinctiveness of mark, 609
    Fair use of trademark, 626–632
    First Amendment considerations, 638–648
    Infringement factors, 615, 616
    Logos, insignia and colors, 615
    Nominative fair use, 632
    Phrases and designations, 616–619
    Reputational harm, 635
    Reverse confusion, 618, 619
    Same name, different city or sport, 615
    Secondary meaning, 609, 618
    Sports fans, interests of, 635
    Tarnishment, 633
    Team names, 609–616
Transformative use test, 606
Wearable technology, 607

INTERCOLLEGIATE SPORTS
Athlete-University Relationship, this index
NCAA. National Collegiate Athletic Association, this index

INTERNATIONAL AND OLYMPIC SPORTS
Generally, 981–1048
Anti-doping. World Anti-Doping Agency (WADA), below
Arbitration
    Court of Arbitration for Sport (CAS), below
    Double jeopardy, 988
    Vs. judicial proceeding, 988
Athlete eligibility standards, 998–1013
Court of Arbitration for Sport (CAS)
    Generally, 981, 983–986
    Appealability of awards, 985, 986
    As final authority, 1020
    Double jeopardy, 986
    Legitimacy as tribunal, 1019
    Lex sportiva, 985
    Overbroad arbitration clauses, 1020
    Procedural aspects, 984, 985
Doping
    Systematic doping, 1020–1032
    World Anti-Doping Agency (WADA), below
Female intersex athletes, 1032–1048
Gender categories, defining, 1047
Hyperandrogenism
    Generally, 1032–1048
    Gender categories, defining, 1047
    New guidelines, 1047
International Olympic Committee, 981

International sports federations (ISFs), 981, 982
Judicial review of sports governing bodies
    Generally, 990–998
    Antitrust law, applicability, 998
    State action, 997
Jurisdiction over international bodies, 1003, 1004
Lex sportiva, 985
National Olympic committees, 981
Nationalism
    Generally, 1014–1020
    Deference to international institutions, nationalism *vs.*, 1004
Overbroad arbitration clauses, 1020
Systematic doping, 1020–1032
U.S. in international sports
    Generally, 989 et seq.
    Judicial review of sports governing bodies, above
World Anti-Doping Agency (WADA)
    Generally, 986–989
    Banned substances, 988
    Revised Code, 986–988
    Strict liability rule, 986

INTERNET
Anticybersquatting Consumer Protection Act, 634
Baseball, viewing on internet, 536
Merchandise and related intellectual property rights, group licensing, 516–518
Property rights in internet reporting, 553–557

INTERSTATE COMMERCE
Generally, 77–79

JUDICIAL REVIEW
Arbitration, this index
Sports governing bodies. International and Olympic Sports, this index

LABOR LAW AND COLLECTIVE BARGAINING
Generally, 71–120
Antitrust, labor exemption. Antitrust, this index
Arbitration, this index
Bargaining units
    Generally, 85–91
    College athletes, 90, 91
    Community of interest, 85, 86
    Exclusive bargaining authority.
        Union's exclusive bargaining authority, below
    League-wide units, 90
    Multiemployer units, 86, 390
Baseball strike (1994–95), 99 et seq.
Delay in securing final remedy, 85
Discriminatory motive, difficulty of proving, 84

Dissident owners, league reprisals, 114
Duty of fair representation
    Generally, 115–120
    Ministerial *vs.* discretionary actions, 120
    Union's dual constituency, 120
Duty to bargain in good faith
    Generally, 96–106
    Mandatory and permissive topics, 98, 99
    Standards of behavior in bargaining process, 97
    Surface bargaining *vs.* hard bargaining, 96
    Terms and conditions of employment, 97, 98
Economic conflict in sports labor relations, 106–115
Equitable nature of remedies under NLRA, 85
Exclusions from Labor Act, 78, 79
Exclusive bargaining authority. Union's exclusive bargaining authority, below
Exercise of managerial judgment, 80
Fair representation. Duty of fair representation, above
Good faith. Duty to bargain in good faith, above
Historical background, 71–74
Impasse in bargaining, 100, 101
Injured reserve players, 111, 112
Labor Act
    Generally, 74–79
    Employee rights, 79 et seq.
Managerial exclusion, 79
Mandatory and permissive topics, 98, 99
Multiemployer units
    Generally, 86, 390
    League reprisals against dissident owners, 114
NLRB jurisdiction, 77–79
Preemption of state law affecting employer's right to use replacements, 114, 115
Replacement workers, 107, 114, 115
Retaliation. Union activity and employer retaliation, below
Self-regulation of labor disputes, 77
Service time *vs.* pay during strike, 112
Standards of behavior in bargaining process, 97
Surface bargaining *vs.* hard bargaining, 96
Terms and conditions of employment, 97, 98
Third party contracts and obligations of teams using replacements, 115
Union activity and employer retaliation
    Generally, 79–86
    Alternative remedy through arbitration, 85
    Delay in securing final remedy, 85
    Discriminatory motive, difficulty of proving, 84

Equitable nature of remedies under
    NLRA, 85
Exercise of managerial judgment, 80
Union's exclusive bargaining authority
    Generally, 91–96
    Duty of fair representation, above
    Duty to bargain in good faith, above
    Fixed salary scale, 94, 95
    Free market orientation, 94
    Individual bargaining, 93 et seq.
Work stoppage strategy in sports, 112

LEAGUES
Major League Baseball, this index
National Football League, this index
Nature of sports league. Antitrust, this index
Professional Sports Leagues, this index

LEASES
Relocation, stadium lease terms protecting against, 464–466
Stadium leases *vs.* other commercial leases, 469

LGBTQ COMMUNITY
Changing society attitudes, 53, 54

LICENSING
Merchandise and related intellectual property rights, group licensing. Antitrust, this index
Superstations and compulsory licensing-royalty scheme, 571–574

MAJOR LEAGUE BASEBALL
Antitrust exemption
    Generally, 231–247
    Breadth of exemption, 245, 246
    Curt Flood Act, 244–246
    Minors, MLB control over, 246
    Stare decisis, 242, 243
    State antitrust law, immunity from, 246, 247
Blue Ribbon Report, 337, 338
Canadian labor law, 113
Commissioner. Professional Sports Leagues, this index
Constitution, 4, 5
Free agency, 225, 226
Internet baseball, 536
Minors, MLB control over, 246
Reserve system and its demise, 205–228
Salary arbitration, 156, 157, 164, 165
Salary Caps and Taxes, this index
Strike of 1994–95, 99 et seq.

MAJOR LEAGUE SOCCER
Players market, 363 et seq.

MARKETING
Ambush marketing, 635–638
Club marketing *vs.* league marketing, 531

MASCOTS
Racially stereotyped mascots, 641 et seq.

MEDICAL MALPRACTICE
Generally, 1074–1082
Collective bargaining agreements, effect of, 1075
Physician-patient relationship, 1081
Sports medicine malpractice reform, 1082
Standard of care, 1082
Workers' compensation, effect of, 1075, 1076

MERCHANDISE
Functional merchandise, 640
Group licensing of merchandise and related intellectual property rights. Antitrust, this index
Sports trademarks, merchandising, 619–626

MISCONDUCT
Player misconduct, commissioner's authority, 38–49

MOBILITY RESTRAINTS
Generally, 185–247
Assignment clause, 199, 204
Contractual restraints, standards for enforcement
    Generally, 185–205
    Adequate mutuality, 190
    Assignment clause, 199, 204
    Damages *vs.* injunctive relief, 199
    Futures contracts, 197
    International player contract dispute, 199 et seq.
    Intra-league anti-tampering policies, 198
    Multiple contracts, 197
    Negative injunctions, 186 et seq.
    No trade clause, 204, 205
    Personal promise *vs.* economic instrument, 198
    Unclean hands, 192, 193
    Uniqueness of player, 190
Damages *vs.* injunctive relief, 199
Free agency
    Baseball, 225, 226
    Football, 226–228
Futures contracts, 197
Historical background, 186 et seq.
International player contract dispute, 199 et seq.
Intra-league anti-tampering policies, 198
Multiple contracts, 197
Negative injunctions, 186 et seq.
No trade clause, 204, 205
Reserve system
    Generally, 205–228
    Arbitrator selection strategy, 225
    Bargaining catalyst, arbitrator as, 219
    Creation, 186

Demise of, 211 et seq.
Evaluation *vs.* interpretation of system by arbitrator, 219
Past practice, effect of, 219
Salary Caps and Taxes, this index
Trading players, team rights, 199, 204
Unclean hands, 192, 193
World Football League (WFL), 193 et seq.

MONOPOLY
Antitrust, this index

NATIONAL BASKETBALL ASSOCIATION
Salary Caps and Taxes, this index

NATIONAL COLLEGIATE ATHLETIC ASSOCIATION (NCAA)
Generally, 719–786
Academic performance, 721, 722
Admissions standards. Athlete-University Relationship, this index
Agent misconduct, enforcing NCAA amateurism rules, 705–710
Amateurism principle
    Generally, 720, 722
    Athlete-University Relationship, this index
Antitrust limits on institutional oversight
    Generally, 734–743
    Amateurism, effect on attendance, 734, 735
    Quick look rule of reason, 735
    Restricted earnings coaches, 736 et seq.
    Student antitrust litigation, 709, 710
    Television, effect on attendance, 734
Appellate model, 766
Athlete-University Relationship, this index
Coaching contracts
    Generally, 744–754
    Benefits packages, 753
    Changed circumstances as non-performance, 759, 760
    Free agent market, 744
    Liquidated damages provision, 752
    Past conduct as estoppel, 760
    Property interest arising out of contract, 753
    Sovereign immunity defense, 753, 759
    Termination of contract, 744 et seq.
Conference realignment, 754–760
Cost Reduction Committee, 736
Criminal conduct, sanctioning
    Generally, 782–786
    Appropriate sanctions, 785
    Role of NCAA, 785
    University oversight, 785, 786
Criminal prosecutions for NCAA violations, future of, 709
Death penalty
    Generally, 761–782
    Appellate model, 766
    Cooperation as mitigation, 770
    When to impose, 770, 780
Infractions
    Generally, 760–786
    Criminal conduct, sanctioning, above
    Death penalty, above
    Due process, 770
    Infractions Appeals Committee (IAC), 766 et seq.
    Institutional control, lack of, 771 et seq.
    Level I to Level IV violations, 781, 782
    Subpoena power, lack of, 770, 780
Institutional control, lack of, 771 et seq.
Level I to Level IV violations, 781, 782
Procedural due process, 722–734
Recruiting and scholarships. Athlete-University Relationship, this index
Restricted earnings coaches, antitrust challenge, 736 et seq.
Revenue-generating sports, 720, 721
State actor status, 723–734
State involvement with private parties, 729, 730
Student antitrust litigation, 709, 710
Subpoena power, lack of, 770, 780

NATIONAL FOOTBALL LEAGUE
Commercial war between NFL and AFL, 193
Concussion Litigation, this index
Deflate-gate, 183
Free agency, 226–228, 355 et seq.
Injuries to Athletes, this index
Plan B alternative to Rozelle Rule, 359–362
Rozelle Rule, 257, 355 et seq.
Salary Caps and Taxes, this index
Suspension and fine following nolo contendere plea, 171 et seq.
Television contracts. Antitrust, this index

NATIVE AMERICANS
Mascots in sports, 648

OLYMPICS
International and Olympic Sports, this index

OWNERS AND OWNERSHIP
Franchise ownership rules. Antitrust, this index
Offensive personal behavior and changing social attitudes, 49–52

PERFORMANCE-ENHANCING SUBSTANCES
Arbitration proceedings, 141–148

PREEMPTION
Arbitration, exclusivity of remedy (§ 301 preemption), 148–155
Copyright preemption, 552, 557, 595
State law affecting employer's right to use replacements, 114, 115

PREMISES LIABILITY
Defective Products and Hazardous Facilities, this index
Injuries to spectators, 1074

PRESCRIPTION DRUG ABUSE LITIGATION
Generally, 1082–1084

PRODUCTS LIABILITY
Defective Products, this index

PROFESSIONAL SPORTS LEAGUES
Generally, 1 et seq.
Best interests of sport, 31 et seq., 36, 37
Breach of trust, 66–68
Commissioner
    Best interests of sport, 31 et seq.
    Conduct detrimental to general welfare of game, authority over, 14 et seq.
    Disciplinary action against player, 52
    Exceeding scope of authority, 29–31
    History and legal authority, 9 et seq.
    Nullifying club transactions, 27
    Offensive personal behavior and changing social attitudes, 49–54
    Player misconduct, commissioner's authority, 38–49
    Realignment of divisions, 31–33
    Reputation of league, commissioner's function in protecting, 36 et seq.
    Restructuring Committee, 33
Comparative perspectives, 5, 6
Constitutions, 4, 5
Disciplinary action against player, 52
Economic analysis of league structure, 6, 7
External social policies, 68, 69
Fiduciary duties, 7–9
Gambling, this index
Governance, 7–9
Historical background, 3, 4
Joint ventures of club owners, leagues as, 5
Legal status, 3–9
Nature of sports league. Antitrust, this index
Offensive personal behavior and changing social attitudes, 49–54
Player misconduct, commissioner's authority, 38–49
Private association law, 35
Realignment of divisions, 31–33
Reputation of league, commissioner's function in protecting, 36 et seq.

PUBLICITY RIGHTS
Intellectual Property, this index

RECRUITING
Agent Representation, this index
Athlete-University Relationship, this index

RELOCATION
Admission and relocation of franchises. Antitrust, this index
Non-antitrust approaches to stakeholder interests in franchise movement, 463–469

RESERVE SYSTEM
Mobility Restraints, this index

REVENUE SHARING
Antitrust, this index

RIGHT TO PLAY
Disability and Right to Play, this index

ROOKIE DRAFT
Antitrust analysis. Antitrust, this index

RULE OF REASON
Antitrust, this index

SALARY ARBITRATION
Arbitration, this index

SALARY CAPS AND TAXES
Generally, 228–231, 332
Assigning percentage to players, 231
Club caps, 332
Defining revenue, 231
Penalties for exceeding threshold, 230
Soft and hard caps, 229, 230
Specific caps or revenue sharing formula, 230, 231

SEXUAL ASSAULT CHARGES
Discipline by commissioner, 52

SOCIAL MEDIA
Sharing of sports clips, 562, 563

SPECTATORS
Injuries to Spectators, this index

STADIUMS
Lease terms protecting against relocation, 464–466
Monopolization, 316–320

STANDING
Title IX claims, 969

STATE ACTION
Sports governing bodies, 723–734, 997

STATE AND LOCAL LAW
Blocking undesired relocation, 463, 466, 467

STUDENT ATHLETES
Athlete-University Relationship, this index

SUPERSTATIONS
Generally, 480 et seq.
League restraints, 574

TAXES
Salary Caps and Taxes, this index

TELEVISION CONTRACTS
Antitrust, this index

TITLE IX
Gender Equity, this index

TORT LIABILITY
Injuries to Athletes, this index
Injuries to Spectators, this index
Medical Malpractice, this index

TRADEMARK RIGHTS
Intellectual Property, this index

TRADING PLAYERS
Mobility restraints, 199 et seq.

UNIONS
Labor Law and Collective Bargaining, this index
Representation of unionized athletes.
    Agent Representation, this index

UNIVERSITIES
Athlete-University Relationship, this index
NCAA. National Collegiate Athletic Association, this index